DICTIONARY OF
MODERN
COLLOQUIAL
French

DICTIONARY OF
MODERN
COLLOQUIAL
French

RENÉ JAMES HÉRAIL,
L.-ès-L., D.E.S., F.I.L.
Lecturer in French, University of Leeds

EDWIN A. LOVATT
M.A., F.I.L.
Lecturer in French, University of Leeds

 Routledge
Taylor & Francis Group

LONDON AND NEW YORK

First published in 1984
by Routledge
11 New Fetter Lane, London EC4P 4EE

Published in the USA
by Routledge
29 West 35th Street, New York NY 10001

First published as a paperback 1987

Reprinted 2002

Transferred to Digital Printing 2003

Routledge is an imprint of the Taylor & Francis Group

Set in 9pt Bembo
by The University of Leeds Printing Service
and printed in Great Britain
by Selwood Printing Ltd,
Burgess Hill, West Sussex

Library of Congress Cataloging in Publication Data

Hérail, René James, 1939–
Dictionary of modern colloquial French.
1. French language—Dictionaries—English.   2. French
language—Spoken French—Dictionaries.   3. French
language—Slang—Dictionaries.   I. Lovatt, Edwin A.,
1944–   .   II. Title.
PC2640.H47   1984   443'.21   84-8231

British Library CIP data also available

ISBN 0-415-05893-7

To the memory of
ERIC PARTRIDGE
whose work inspired us

CONTENTS

PREFACE

It is a notorious fact that prefaces in dictionaries are seldom read. To those, not-so-few we hope, who will have braved tradition and actually turned to these pages rather than plunge headlong into the 8000 or so headwords we strive to lexicalize, here are a few thoughts and perhaps also a *mode d'emploi*.

Because this bilingual dictionary is intended to assist both French and English speakers, this preface is followed by a *préface*; both introductions attempt to define how each native speaker can best make use of this volume.

Where English speakers are concerned, this dictionary was conceived in order to bridge the gap between the kind of standard French taught in schools, colleges and universities and the less formal language that visitors to France are likely to be confronted with in everyday life.

Since the 1930s, French literature has undergone a radical transformation and the once-clear distinction between written and spoken language has been blurred. The natural consequence of this movement has been that many hitherto shunned, taboo or outlandish words and expressions are now the common currency of every medium of communication. With the whirlwind growth of transcontinental television through cables and satellites, the English speaker is more and more frequently confronted with a bewildering range of 'new French' – the kind of 'off-the-shelf' language that many trad francophones could be forgiven for ignoring. The movement from spoken to written is swifter than ever and this book is offered as a deciphering agent for those avid listeners, viewers and readers who have hitherto felt excluded from that humorous and secret language that contributed so much to making them feel 'foreign'.

Our initial aim in this reference work is to enable the non-native speaker to 'get the drift' of what has been written or said in French and, equally important, to 'tune into' the foreign language wavelength. It is certainly necessary in language comprehension that the listener/reader, before attempting to become a speaker, should be able to weigh up the colloquiality of a word or expression through its contextualizations in both languages. Efforts at becoming a 'slangophone' should nearly always be discouraged, but in this instance, such advice is more pertinent when directed at our French readership. In any case, indiscriminate use of colloquiality can prove to be as perilous as juggling with a Doulton china tea-service. When caught out, the unwary novice can only blush and admit failure – perhaps easier to get over in the circus ring than in a tight social situation! Our aim is to encourage understanding, but to discourage adventurous sorties into unknown territory.

The general approach to dictionaries is that they should offer instant solutions. In the field of colloquial lexicography, this is even harder to achieve than within standard language; whereas 'tried and tested' words, all part of the established lexis, need only be situated as to their specific usage and meanings often without the need of contextualization, colloquial language is by its very nature practically meaningless without the support of back-up phrases that help situate the degree of colloquiality. Rather than arbitrarily grade words as 'vulgar, obscene', etc. or resort to a 'star-rating system', we have endeavoured to place words within standard expressions in both languages, enabling the readers to make up their minds as to the true meaning of a particular linguistic stumbling-block.

Throughout the ten years it has taken us to compile this work, we have had to come to terms with the fact that most 'natives' from either culture have a surprising number of blank spots in the realm of colloquial language. 'I didn't know you could say that' has probably been the most uttered reply we received when we were double-checking public response to what we thought were perfectly comprehensible words and expressions. Working knee-deep in colloquiality, it would have been easy to take it for granted that to the francophone colloquial French is everyday meat, and that to the English speaker English slang is a very frequented area of communication. Having accepted the fact that only a limited number of individuals hold a comprehensive range of 'fringe' words and expressions in their language bank, we resorted to what may at first seem rather condescending, namely to give lexicalized words, wherever possible, three definitions in English – the first register-keyed to the French, the second less colloquial, the third in what could be termed 'standard English' or phrased to explain the hitherto untranslatable. In a way, we see this as a dictionary within a dictionary. How many of us could possibly be expected to know the meaning of 'cottage' – a word with which only male homosexuals are likely to be familiar?

PREFACE

It is not our intention here to embark upon a lengthy explanation of how the dictionary should be used. The method is entirely logical and, we hope, transparent. Each headword is assigned a grammatical category and an alternative spelling if one exists. When the word has several meanings these are given in a numerical sequence with 'straight' (i.e. literal) meanings first, followed by metaphorical extensions; any more figurative usages involving other verbs or nouns come next. Many headwords or sub-headings have added comments, anecdotes or historical information which should be of interest to the reader.

Throughout our formative years at school and university, and even at the time of writing these lines, our biggest gripe where dictionaries are concerned is the near-insolent manner in which some major works treat their readership. Our most abhorred word has always been 'See:', referring the word-searcher to another entry which itself in turn seems quite willing to 'pass the parcel' onto another totally unexpected headword. This is, to us, a rather unethical practice that can only result in well-thumbed volumes and despondency where language students are concerned. Our own experience as teachers of French in British universities is that young people often see dictionaries as a greater source of error than their own fallible memory. At the risk of seeming repetitive and increasing the sheer bulk of this volume, we have chosen to overlap as much as is decently acceptable, particularly where expressions can be located under several keywords.

Beyond being two dictionaries in one, this work attempts to introduce the kind of anecdotic information that gives a totally new dimension to hitherto untraceable words. In some instances, we rely on standard etymological sources, in others we accept the fact that popular etymology 'rules O.K.'. Wherever possible we have not hesitated to introduce *la petite histoire* to explain the birth or survival of words or expressions.

When asked what problems confronted us while compiling a dictionary of modern colloquial French, we have often resorted to the image of a person firing a shot from a moving train onto a target travelling on another train in motion. French and English are *langues vivantes* constantly acquiring new words and discarding redundant ones and nowhere is this more evident than in the realm of speech. In the introduction to *The Synonym Finder* (Rodale Press) Laurence Urdang says 'there is no such thing as a true synonym.' Paraphrasing this great linguist, we could say 'there is no such thing as a perfect translation.' Frequency, distribution and connotation are never really truly matching. Our efforts at offering register-keyed equivalents should therefore be seen as learned attempts rather than dogmatic assertions.

Because it is so difficult to dissociate colloquial speech from standard language, we have as often as necessary resorted to inverted commas to indicate that an English word or expression is colloquial.

To many a 'purist' it would have been wise to cite only literary or 'confirmed' sources for our material, but being basically impure we readily proclaim that *'les mots dans le vent'*, often merely overheard, are worthy of recording for their intrinsic linguistic value. We are providing a rich description of the language – let he who draws up a prescription from it beware! The sheer volume of work needed to ensure documented accuracy of the colloquial language would render a dictionary such as this impossible to complete – even a computer is only as willing as those who feed it are diligent.

In an age of memory banks, word processors and fifth-generation computer technology, our dictionary compiled over these ten years on 6″ × 4″ cards smacks more of 'cottage industry' than the kind of team lexicography with massive back-up and secretarial support that other projects have enjoyed. This *'manuel'* was truly manually produced and only in the ultimate typesetting stage were we able to rely on twentieth-century technology through the University of Leeds Printing Service.

Lexicographers, it has to be said, must rely heavily on fellow lexicographers and existing works. It would indeed be most misleading to intimate that we set about compiling this work without referring to past and present dictionaries. If for no other reason than the constant reassurance that we were not missing any word, our 6′ working table was always laden with as many as two dozen reference works and we depended on the availability of hundreds of books, magazines, tapes, etc. from which to draw substantiation through examples. Access to thousands of hours of sound material from the radio archives of several French-speaking radio stations was also a great asset. Our greatest debt of gratitude is owed to those many students of Leeds University French Department who kept us informed of noteworthy and stable linguistic arrivals. Without the newspaper cuttings, *bandes dessinées*, and sound recordings they collected for us during their 'Year Abroad', we would, indeed, have been starved of up-to-date material.

Whenever a lexicalized word was only previously to be found in a single dictionary, we have felt the need to acknowledge this 'borrowing', but not without first checking that the word was indeed known to French speakers.

PREFACE

The greatest problem facing lexicographers of the colloquial language relates to what to exclude and what to include. On the level of exclusion we have knowingly avoided only half a dozen extremely obscene words, the kind of terms that are both so indecent and far-fetched as to warrant a blue pencil in any manuscript. Where sexism, racialism or anti-semitism raises its ugly little head in language, we have followed Bernard Levin's precept as voiced in an article entitled 'By definition, a word to the unwise' (*The Times*, 29 January 1980) and included that mass of words that reflect society's prejudices. Mr Shloimovitz is certainly right in condemning the use of slanderous terms; to ignore them as a lexicographer is 'a sin against linguistic integrity'. In each case we have endeavoured to indicate how derogatory such appellations were and clearly dissociated standard usage from verbal abuse.

Whereas exclusion was a reasonably easy task, our great problem over the years concerned what to include. If we had followed all the advice we were given and taken each and every hint, our dictionary would have more than a fair sprinkling of regionalisms and hosts of minority-interest words. To treat a dictionary like a refuge for homeless words is, in our opinion, to abuse the good-natured credulity of the readership. Giving a fleetingly overheard expletive or a contrived neologism pride of place in a small reference work is to claim usage by a fair proportion of French-speaking society. Our aim has always been to 'let the dust settle' and only really offer lexicalization to newcomers when they have, so to speak, proven themselves. In a work spanning over fifty years, we have, wherever relevant, given some idea as to when the word or expression enjoyed its greatest vogue. To exclude words because they are no longer in current usage is, in a way, to deny the reader of contemporary literature the full comprehension he seeks. On the other hand, to preserve artificially in formaldehyde a defunct language is a practice to be avoided. We have tried carefully to strike a happy medium by relying heavily on the advice of different generations and we generally applied market research techniques to our language quest.

Inevitably, readers in either language will find gaps in this *Dictionary of Modern Colloquial French* – our request, nay our plea, to them is that they should express their reservations, voice their criticism and contact us through our publishers with their comments and suggestions. From the day this manuscript is in the hands of the printers, we will be preparing material for an 'augmented' edition. Contributions are not merely welcome, they are eagerly awaited and a standard form will be available to all budding co-lexicographers who feel they can assist us in any way.

PREFACE

It is our sincere hope that all who dip into these pages will feel the urge to go beyond mere consultation and enjoy a casual browse, so coming to realize, as we did, that colloquial language be it French, English or Swahili is fun and endlessly fascinating.

January 1984   R.J.H.   E.A.L.

PRÉFACE

Il nous semble plutôt futile d'offrir à nos lexicomanes d'expression française une simple traduction de notre *preface*. Un dictionnaire tel que celui-ci s'adresse de toute évidence à deux 'clientèles' tout à fait différentes qui se serviront de cet ouvrage pour explorer la langue étrangère parlée dans des contextes linguistiques non comparables.

Pour nos amis anglais, ce *Dictionary of Modern Colloquial French* est un outil de compréhension leur permettant de se mettre au diapason du français parlé tel qu'il apparaît de plus en plus dans la langue écrite. Ce 'français sauvage' dont les puristes se détournent avec une moue désabusée est, que nous le voulions ou non, le moyen d'expression qui fait tache d'huile à la radio, à la télévision après avoir imprégné notre vocabulaire courant. Comme le dit fort pertinemment Jacques Cellard dans *La Vie du langage*, 'l'usage engendre la règle, non l'inverse' – reconnaître l'existence du *modern colloquial French*, ce n'est pas l'accepter inconditionellement comme correct, mais se rendre à l'évidence qu'une langue vivante telle que le français ne se censure pas, même au niveau du dictionnaire.

Un des problèmes fondamentaux qu'il nous a fallu affronter dès le début de nos travaux a été celui de savoir ce que nous pouvions inclure et ce qu'il fallait exclure d'un ouvrage qui se veut sérieux, sans se prendre au sérieux. Un des dangers qui guettent le lexicographe explorateur de la langue parlée est celui de se laisser happer inconsciemment par la vulgarité de la langue qu'il manie. Lorsque l'on côtoie une langue qui n'a pas de préjugés, il n'est que trop facile de se laisser aller à des écarts de langage et de plaider le besoin de contextualiser un mot pour mieux l'expliquer.

Comme nous l'avons déjà dit dans notre *preface*, il n'appartient pas au lexicographe de s'ériger en censeur. Nous avons dû souvent, comme bon nombre de nos prédécesseurs, réfléchir au bien-fondé d'inclure un mot dont l'obscénité ou le racisme en garantirait l'exclusion, même dans les ouvrages les plus libéraux. Si l'on veut parler de crise de conscience au niveau du dictionnaire, nous ne la voyons pas sur le plan de la grossièreté mais plutôt sur celui de l'ostracisation de certains groupes minoritaires. Quoi qu'en disent certains esprits bien-pensants, l'exclusion d'un mot dans un dictionnaire ne garantit pas sa mort, loin de là. Le lexicographe, s'il veut préserver sa crédibilité, doit être impartial; reconnaître l'existence d'un mot, d'une expression, ce n'est pas endosser les responsabilités d'un locuteur bourré de préjugés mais plutôt mettre à l'index au moyen d'une parenthèse ceux qui s'abaissent à utiliser un tel langage.

S'il est inconcevable pour un lexicographe d'exclure un mot parce qu'il ne lui plaît pas, la véritable difficulté pour nous tout au long des dix dernières années a été de nous censurer nous-mêmes et de lutter contre le désir d'inclure une foule de 'mots dans le vent'. Vouloir être *'in the swing of things'* sur le plan linguistique, c'est prendre des risques inutiles dans le contexte d'un dictionnaire qui tente de couvrir un demi-siècle de français et d'anglais parlé. Aux dépens d'exemples pétillant d'humour, nous avons souvent dû nous contenter de contextualisations moins 'à la page' mais qui avaient l'avantage par contre de ne pas 'faire date'.

Dans le domaine des dictionnaires de la langue parlée, deux écueils semblent se dresser. Le lexicographe se voit dans l'obligation de choisir entre un glossaire riche en définitions mais pauvre en exemples et un ouvrage où l'illustration sélective de certains mots et expressions se fait aux frais des véritables objectifs d'un dictionnaire. Dans un ouvrage monolingue, il est possible de justifier la présence de nombreux mots en se référant à la littérature, qu'elle soit polissonne ou non. Au niveau des dictionnaires bilingues du langage parlé, il est pratiquement impossible de trouver un dénominateur commun. Dans celui-ci, nous avons tenté de couper la poire en deux en offrant un maximum de vocabulaire, illustré par des exemples en français comme en anglais 'de notre cru'; ces exemples reflètent un usage qui est presque règle, tout en évitant de se complaire dans la vulgarité, même lorsque le besoin s'en faisait sentir.

Si pour nos lecteurs anglais ce dictionnaire de *Modern Colloquial French* est un outil de compréhension, nous imaginons que du point de vue du francophone il faut le considérer comme la preuve vivante que l'humour français est traduisible, que la vulgarité ne connaît pas de frontière, que les jeux de mots douteux et les 'plaisanteries de garçons de bains' sont aussi fréquentes de part et d'autre de la Manche et de l'Atlantique.

Plutôt que Préface, nous aurions pu nous servir du terme moins courant 'Avertissement'; car nous nous devons de rappeler à nos lecteurs qu'il est toujours dangereux de vouloir s'exprimer argotiquement dans une langue où même le vocabulaire courant a ses difficultés.

Afin d'éviter de tomber dans le piège de l'évaluation arbitraire en utilisant des termes tels que 'vulgaire', 'obscène', etc., nous avons eu recours à des exemples contextuels dans les deux langues pour mieux 'situer' le mot ou l'expression en question. Ce qui est vulgaire aujourd'hui ne le sera peut-être pas demain, ce qui l'était hier ne l'est presque plus aujourd'hui.

Les Anglais disent *'There's method in my madness'* – il serait peut-être bon d'expliquer la méthodologie qui fut la nôtre tout au long de la rédaction de cet ouvrage. Lorsque le texte anglais est 'entre guillemets', cela veut dire qu'il s'agit d'expressions ou de mots non-courants qu'il faut éviter de prendre au pied de la lettre. La logique que nous avons tenté de suivre est celle de traductions 'decrescendo' où nous mettons en premier le mot le plus apte (et souvent le plus vulgaire), suivi d'un terme argotique mais moins virulent, et finalement une explication en *standard English* donnant la signification 'pure' du mot français. La conséquence directe de cette structuration des équivalences porte à penser que cet ouvrage est, en fait, un double dictionnaire traduisant d'une part la langue verte en *'slang'* et offrant aussi à ceux qui ignorent l'anglais gouailleur, un point de repère sans ambiguïté. Dans les deux cultures nous avons souvent été surpris par l'ignorance sélective qui affecte la connaissance de la langue maternelle. Il n'est pas rare de rencontrer des francophones qui éprouvent des difficultés, sinon à lire des auteurs comme Simonin, Le Breton ou San-Antonio, du moins à comprendre et à apprécier pleinement la langue qu'ils emploient. De même il n'est pas surprenant d'apprendre qu'il y a une multitude d'anglophones qui pourront toujours se passer du *'rhyming slang'*. Notre but aura été d'écarter le voile qui sépare pudiquement ces indécences parallèles, et de prouver une fois pour toutes que la culture anglo-saxonne sait aussi, quand il le faut, se débarrasser du 'faux-col à manger de la tarte'.

Avant de nous promouvoir lexicographes, nous avons longtemps été et à vrai dire le sommes encore, consommateurs de dictionnaires. Depuis notre plus tendre enfance, ces volumes ont toujours joué un rôle dans notre vie; tels des pavés dans nos cartables, ils ont souvent eu le don de nous irriter profondément.

L'écolier, le linguiste qu'il soit latiniste, germaniste, ou tout simplement ignorant de l'orthographe, de la signification d'un mot dans sa propre langue, a souvent maudit l'ouvrage qui lui refusait la réponse qu'il cherchait. De

PRÉFACE

tous les défauts du dictionnaire, celui qui irrite le plus est le jeu de cache-cache dans lequel le lecteur curieux est renvoyé à d'autres entrées qui souvent, elles aussi, se dérobent judicieusement et renvoient le potache à son point de départ. Ayant souffert de ces va-et-vient qui font rapidement d'un ouvrage neuf un livre d'occasion, nous avons préféré, quitte à enfler ce volume, rappeler deux, parfois trois fois, la signification d'une expression dans son verbe et ses compléments.

Reprenant et amplifiant la citation d'un des plus grands lexicographes de tous les temps qu'un 'dictionnaire sans exemples est un squelette', nous avons ressenti le besoin d'élargir le débat vis-à-vis de nos lecteurs anglais en leur offrant soit l'étymologie populaire soit l'origine historique de certains mots, de certaines expressions. Inévitablement, le lecteur francophone risque de trouver ces 'points sur les i' quelque peu superflus mais si, comme nous l'avons dit, la langue parlée maternelle a ses mystères, qu'il nous soit pardonné d'avoir essayé de la démystifier.

Avant de conclure, nous aimerions faire appel à nos lecteurs et leur demander de bien vouloir nous signaler les mots, les expressions – il y en a certainement beaucoup – que nous avons omis. Nous nous ferons un devoir lors de la prochaine édition de cet ouvrage de considérer chaque cas sur ses mérites et de faire figurer ces absents qui, comme le dit le proverbe, ont toujours tort! Vous pourrez, par l'intermédiaire de notre éditeur, rectifier ce qui vous paraît inexact, inclure des néologismes en voie d'expansion, bref, nous aider à compléter une tâche qui, par sa nature même, ne peut jamais être complète.

janvier 1984   R.J.H.   E.A.L.

ACKNOWLEDGEMENTS

Our thanks for their assistance during the preparation of this volume are due to the French Department of Leeds University who helped with travel and overseas contacts, and the University of Leeds Research Fund Committee who funded much of the early research and preparation.

Special thanks are due to the British Academy who not only supported the project over a number of years through their financial generosity, but also made possible the final typesetting of the manuscript in the form of a machine-readable version.

We are deeply indebted to Mr Gwilym O. Rees of Leeds University and Miss Wendy Lee for their meticulous proofing of the manuscript.

January 1984   R.J.H.   E.A.L.

ABBREVIATIONS

abbr.	abbreviation
adj.	adjective
adv.	adverb
conj.	conjunction
corr.	corruption
dem.	demonstrative
dim.	diminutive
etym.	etymology
exp.	expression
f.	feminine
fig.	figurative
imp.	impersonal
indef.	indefinite
interj.	interjection
interr.	interrogative
intrans.	intransitive
inv.	invariable
iron.	ironical
joc.	jocular
lit.	literal
m.	masculine
mil.	military
n.	noun
num.	numerical
ord.	ordinal
past part.	past participle
pej.	pejorative
pers.	personal
pl.	plural
pol.	police
poss.	possessive
prep.	preposition
pron.	pronoun
pronom.	pronominal
reflex.	reflexive
rel.	relative
sch.	schools and universities
sing.	singular
syn.	synonym
th.	theatre
trans.	transitive
v.	verb
WW I	World War I
WW II	World War II

A

a *n.m.* **1** *Prouver par a + b*: To prove by logical reasoning, with mathematical precision. **2** *C'est l'abc du métier*: It's one of the first things you learn. **3** *De A jusqu'à Z*: Through and through, thoroughly. (This expression is sometimes used in a jocular and ironic way describing a lax approach to a demanding task; it is worth noting that on a French typewriter *A* and *Z* are adjacent on the keyboard.)

à *prep.* **1** Indicates urgency. *A table!* Grub's up! – Come and get it! – Dinner is ready! **2** Substituted for *de* in popular language to mark possession. *Le manteau à ma mère*: My mum's coat.

abalober *v.trans.* To 'flabbergast', to astound. *Alors là, j'en ai été abalobé!* You could have knocked me down with a feather!

abasourdi *past part.* 'Bowled over', astounded. *T'aurais dû voir cette gueule abasourdie!* You should have seen his face!

abat-faim *n.m.* Stodge, near-indigestible food (also: *étouffe-chrétien*).

abat-jour *n.m.* (*joc.*): Topee, colonial helmet.

abattage *n.m.* (also: *abatage*): **1** Talking-to, scolding. *J'ai pris un vache abattage du prof*: Teacher gave me one hell of a slating. **2** (of actor): 'Dash', brio, verve. *Il ne manque pas d'abattage, lui!* He certainly comes over well! **3** *De l'abattage* (also: *du travail d'abattage*): Artistic work of little merit (book, painting etc.) executed purely for the purpose of bringing in money. *Ce n'est pas de l'art, c'est de l'abattage!* These are just pot-boilers! **4** Winning throw at *passe-anglaise*, a popular dice-game with the underworld. **5** (Street-hawkers' and market-traders' slang): Stall-goods, merchandise displayed on an open-air stand. **6** *Maison d'abattage*: 'Cat-house', brothel.

abattis *n.m.pl.* (also: *abatis*): 'Fins and kickers', hands and feet. *Fais gaffe à tes abattis!* Watch out, I'm going to make mince-meat of you! (also: *tu peux numéroter tes abattis!*).

abattre *v.trans.* **1** *Ne pas se laisser abattre*: To 'keep one's pecker up', to remain cheerful against all odds. *A le voir jaffer, on sent bien qu'il ne se laisse pas abattre!* The way he downs his grub, you'd think he hadn't a care in the world! **2** *En abattre*: To get through a pile of work.

abbaye *n.f.* *L'abbaye de Monte-à-regret*: The guillotine.

abbesse *n.f.* 'Madam', brothel-keeper.

abéquer *v.trans.* To feed. *Et qui va nous abéquer?* And who's going to make our grub?

abîmer *v.trans.* To 'pull to pieces', to criticize severely. *Un peu qu'il aime abîmer!* He just loves cutting projects to pieces!

ablette *n.f.* *Taquiner l'ablette* (*joc.*): To do a spot of angling, to go fishing for relaxation.

abloquer *v.intrans.* To 'hand over the readies', to pay up. *Allez, abloque!* Come on, let's have your money!

abondance *n.f.* 'Watered-down plonk', red wine with a lot of water.

abord *D'abord. D'abord et d'une* (*adv.exp.*): First and foremost. *D'abord et d'une, essuie tes targettes!* For a start you can wipe your feet!

abordable *adj.* **1** (of person): Amenable, easy to approach. **2** (of prices): 'Within one's pocket', within reach. *Les fraises maintenant sont très abordables*: Strawberries are now down to a sensible price.

abouler *v.trans.* To give, to hand over. *Aboule tes fafs!* Hand over your (identity) papers!

abouler *v.pronom.* To 'roll up', to 'blow in', to come along. *Alors, tu t'aboules?!* Come on, let's be having you!

aboyeur *n.m.* **1** 'Barker', fairground or night-club tout. **2** 'Rod', 'shooter', handgun.

abracadabrant *adj.* Amazing, startling. *Une histoire abracadabrante*: A cock-and-bull story. (This is a would-be grammatical extension of the hocus-pocus abracadabra incantation.)

abraquer *v.trans.* To obtain by force or deception. *Il m'a abraqué tout mon fric!* He did me out of all my money!

abreuvoir *n.m.* *(joc.)*: 'Watering-hole', 'local', pub. (To judges, barristers, clerks of the court, etc. *l'Abreuvoir* is also the nickname of the bar in the *Palais de Justice* in Paris.)

abricot *n.m.* 'Fanny', 'pussy', vagina.

abruti *n.m.* 'Dumbo', 'chump', fool.

abus *n.m.* *(Il) y a de l'abus!* That's a bit thick! – That's going it a bit far!

acabit *n.m.* Sort, kind. *C'est un gars d'un bon acabit*: He's a good-natured bloke. *Tous! Tous je te dis! Ils sont tous du même acabit, des truands!* They're all tarred with the same brush, crooks the lot of them!

acagnarder *v.pronom.* (also: *accagnarder*): To 'lie low', to hide.

accareuse *n.f.* Chest of drawers.

accolade *n.f.* *Aimer donner l'accolade à la bouteille (joc.)*: To be fond of one's tipple.

accommoder *v.trans.* 1 (of person): To 'duff up', to bash about, to beat up. 2 (verbal violence): To 'play merry hell with someone', to give someone a sharp telling-off. 3 *Accommoder à toutes les sauces*: To put someone or something to a variety of uses. *Ici on m'accommode à toutes les sauces!* I work here under a variety of hats!

accord *n.m.* *D'accord!* O.K.! – You're on! – Agreed! (also: *dac!*).

accordéon *n.m.* 1 *Pantalon en accordéon*: Creased and crumpled trousers. 2 *(pol.)*: Extensive 'form', string of past convictions.

accorder *v.trans.* *Accorder ses violons*: To agree on a course of action. *Si on veut discuter d'égal à égal avec eux, va falloir qu'on accorde nos violons*: To be credible in our negotiations, we're going to have to think in tune.

accordeur *n.m.* *Accordeur de flûtes (joc.)*: J.P., Justice of the Peace.

accoucher *v.intrans.* 1 To speak up, to express one's views (after much stalling). *Alors, tu accouches?!* Well! Out with it! 2 To 'come clean', to confess. *Il a accouché mais il a fallu des forceps*: It took some 'leaning' to get him to own up.

accoutrer *v.trans.reflex.* To 'tog up', to dress with little care.

accroc *n.m.* 'Hitch', snag. *Pour une fois on n'a pas eu d'accrocs*: We were lucky, for once, things went smoothly.

accrochage *n.m.* 1 (of cars): 'Prang', scrape. 2 (Boxing): Clinch. 3 *(mil.)*: Skirmish, brief engagement. 4 *(fig.)*: Set-to, argument.

accroché *past part.* 1 'Hooked', infatuated. *Je crois que cette fois-ci il est vraiment accroché!* I think he's fallen for her in a big way! 2 (Drugs): Hooked, addicted. 3 In debt (with little prospect of clearing one's account).

4 *Avoir le cœur bien accroché*: **a** To be gutsy, to be brave. **b** To be anything but squeamish.

accroche-cœur *n.m.* Kiss-curl.

accroche-pipe *n.m.* 'Kisser', gob, mouth.

accrocher *v.trans.* 1 To 'buttonhole' someone, to hold a person in conversation against his will. 2 To 'nick', to 'collar', to arrest. 3 (of motor vehicle): To 'prang', to have a collision with a stationary object or another vehicle. 4 To 'hock', to pawn. 5 *Accrocher les wagons*: To 'puke', to 'throw up', to vomit. (*Accrochez les wagons!* is the kind of *phrase-excuse* one utters with familiar jocularity when unable to repress a belch.) 6 *Accrocher un paletot*: To fib, to tell a lie.

accrocher *v.intrans.* 1 To 'catch on', to be successful. 2 (of studies): To 'latch on', to 'cotton on', to understand and assimilate. *En math il a du mal à accrocher!* Maths are still quite a stumbling-block with him!

accrocher *v.pronom.* 1 (Cycling slang): To stick to a fellow-competitor, to hang on leech-like at all costs. 2 *S'accrocher (à quelqu'un)*: To buttonhole someone and pester him until he gives in. 3 *Se l'accrocher*: To have to do without, to miss out on something. *Alors là, mon vieux, tu peux te l'accrocher!* I'll tell you for one, you can whistle for it!

accrocher *v.trans.reflex.* 1 To 'have a barney', to have a row with someone. *On est toujours à s'accrocher pour un rien (du tout)*: We're always at each other's throat over trifles. 2 *S'accrocher avec quelqu'un*: To have a set-to, to have a fight with someone.

accrocheur *n.m.* 1 Tenacious bore. 2 'Hanger-on', parasite.

accus *n.m.pl.* *(abbr. accumulateurs)*: 1 Car battery. *Mes accus sont à plat*: I've got a flat battery. 2 *Recharger ses accus (fig.)*: To take a well-deserved rest (literally to recharge one's batteries). 3 *Rechargez les accus!* (of glasses): Fill 'em up, let's have another round! (of drinks).

accuser *v.trans.* *Accuser le coup*: To flinch, to show an emotional reaction. *Et comment qu'il a accusé le coup!* You could see he was upset!

achar *D'achar (adv.exp.)*: Non-stop, relentlessly. *V'là quarante-huit heures qu'il bosse d'achar*: He's been grafting like mad these last two days.

acheter *v.trans.* 1 To 'make a mug of', to make a fool of. *Tu vois pas qu'il t'achète?!* You must have noticed he's taking the mickey out of you! 2 *Acheter à la foire d'empoigne (joc.)*: To 'nick', to 'pinch', to steal. 3 *S'acheter une conduite*: To 'turn over a new leaf', to become a reformed character.

acide *n.m.* (Drugs): Lysergic acid diethylamide (better known to those who indulge in it as L.S.D.).

acompte *n.m. Prendre un acompte (joc.)*: To have pre-marital sex (literally to take some 'nookie' on account).

à-côtés *n.m.pl.* 'Perks', extras. *Dans ton job 'y a toujours de vaches à-côtés!* You've got great perks where you work!

acré *interj.* Watch out! – Look out! *Acré, v'là les cognes!* Watch out! Here come the fuzz! (also: *gaffe!*).

acrobate *n.m.* **1** Cat-burglar. **2** *(fig.)*: Character who always lands on his feet. *Lui faire faillite?! N'y comptez pas, c'est une drôle d'acrobate!* He'll never be in Queer Street, he treads the tightrope of high finance like a real trouper!

acte *n.m.* **1** *Faire acte de présence*: To 'show up', to put in an appearance. **2** *(joc.)*: *Avaler son acte de naissance*: To 'snuff' it, to 'croak', to die (also: *avaler son extrait de naissance*).

acteuse *n.f. (pej.)*: Second-rate actress.

actif *n.m. Avoir à son actif*: To have to one's credit. *A peine quinze berges et il a déjà une vingtaine de pépées à son actif*: He's only fifteen and has already chalked up twenty birds.

activer *v.intrans.* (Imperative only) *Active!* Put your skates on! – Get moving! – Hurry up!

Adam *Proper name. Etre en costume d'Adam*: To be 'in one's birthday suit', to be 'starkers', to be completely naked.

addition *n.f. Payer l'addition (fig.)*: To pay for one's mistakes and sometimes other people's. *Comme de bien entendu, j'ai dû payer l'addition pour vos conneries!* At the end of the day it was muggins who had to pay for the cock-ups!

adieu *n.m.* **1** *Dire adieu à quelque chose (iron.)*: To 'kiss something goodbye'. *Ton fric tu peux lui dire adieu!* That's the last you'll see of your money! **2** *Ça a été adieu Berthe!* It was curtains! – That was it! – All was lost!

adjas *n.m.pl. Mettre les adjas*: To 'scarper', to 'skedaddle', to run off (also: *mettre les bouts*).

adji *n.m. J'ai pas pu le lâcher, il est tout le temps à mes adjis!* I couldn't shake him off, he's always on my tail!

adjupète *n.m. (corr. adjudant)*: Warrant-officer in the armed forces.

Adonis *Proper name. Il se prend pour un Adonis*: He thinks he's the answer to every maiden's prayer!

adresse *n.f. Vous vous trompez d'adresse!* Who the hell do you think I am?! – You've come to the wrong person!

adroper *v.intrans.* To 'put one's skates on', to hurry up. *Allez ouste, adrope!* Get a move on!

affaire *n.f.* **1** Case (usually a criminal one), scandal. *L'affaire des pots de vin a coulé pas mal de mecs!* The slush-fund story sank a few prominent figures, I can tell you! **2** *Avoir son*

affaire *(iron.)*: To get one's 'just deserts', to suffer appropriate punishment. **3** *Ce n'est pas une affaire!* (also: *en voilà une affaire!*): What a lot of fuss about nothing! – It's of no consequence! **4** *La belle affaire! (iron.)*: Is that all?! – Well that's nothing to worry about! **5** *Tirer quelqu'un d'affaire*: To get someone out of trouble. *Il a la paluche secourante, il m'a plus d'une fois tiré d'affaire*: He's the helping kind, more than once he got me out of stuck. **6** *Faire son affaire à quelqu'un*: To 'bump off', to kill someone.

affaires *n.f.pl.* **1** Business, financial affairs. *Comment vont les affaires?* How's trade? **2** Business, personal matters (sometimes in the singular). *Mêle-toi de tes affaires!* Mind your own business! **3** 'Traps', personal belongings. *Prends tes affaires et fous le camp!* Take your things and get lost! **4** Period, menses. *Avoir ses affaires*: To have the decorators in. **5** *Faire ses affaires*: To 'crap', to 'shit', to defecate.

affaler *v.pronom.* To 'sing', to confess. *Au plus petit passage à tabac, le v'là qui s'affale comme une gonzesse!* It didn't take much 'convincing' to get him to spill the beans!

affection *n.f. Etre en retard d'affection (joc.)*: To have 'gone short', to be sex-starved.

affiche *n.f.* **1** 'Fairy', 'pansy', homosexual (the kind who through his mannerisms makes his 'gay status' obvious to all). **2** *Tenir l'affiche* (of play): To have a long run.

affiché *past part. C'est affiché!* It's a dead cert! – It's a certainty!

afficher *v.trans.reflex.* To flaunt oneself, to make oneself conspicuous. *C'est une pute qu'aime bien s'afficher au bras d'un mec qu'a du flouze!* She's the kind of hooker who likes to be seen with wealthy blokes!

affilée *D'affilée (adv.exp.)*: 'At a go', 'at a stretch', continuously. *Travailler comme ça huit heures d'affilée, 'y a vraiment de quoi devenir cinoque!* Working eight hours on the trot is enough to drive you bonkers!

affligé *n.m.* Cripple, disabled person.

afflure *n.f.* Gain, profit.

afflurer *v.trans.* To get, to gain, to receive. (Often with ironic undertones.) *A force de faire le zigoto, tout ce qu'il a affluré c'est cinq ans de taule!* All he got by his tomfoolery was five years' porridge!

affoler *v.trans.reflex.* To 'get in a tizz', to 'be at sixes and sevens', to get flustered. *T'affole pas, ma chatte!* Keep cool, my pet!

affranchi *n.m.* (Underworld slang): One who is part of the *milieu*, or deemed within that group to be trustworthy. *Dédé c'est pas un* *cave, c'est un mec bien, un affranchi!* Andy's no mug. He's a great guy, one of the lads!

affranchi *adj.* 'In the know' and trustworthy (well up where the rules and ethics of the *milieu* are concerned).

affranchir *v.trans.* **1** To 'give someone the low-down' on, to 'put someone in the picture', to familiarize someone with something. **2** To initiate in sexual matters. *Etre affranchie de la cicatrice*: To have been deflowered, to have lost one's virginity.

affréter *v.trans. Affréter un bahut*: To book a cab, to call a taxi.

affreux *n.m.* **1** Ugly and rather musclebound character. **2** Mercenary, professional soldier hired to fight for a foreign army. (When the Belgian Congo was torn by internal strife, the *affreux* were a regular feature of press reports.)

affure *n.f.* 'Jammy' deal, profitable enterprise.

affurer *v.trans.* **1** To make a good profit, to earn a lot of money (usually through business dealings). *Il a affuré le gros paquet*: He hit the big times. **2** To win, to get something pleasant. *Vise un peu la nana qu'il a affurée!* Feast your eyes on that new bird of his! **3** (of age): To reach, to attain. *Il-va bientôt affurer ses soixante berges*: He's knocking on sixty!

affûter *v.trans.* **1** (Underworld slang): To lure, to entice. **2** To 'take for a ride', to 'con', to swindle. **3** *Affûter la forme*: To 'get into shape', to train hard for sporting purposes.

affûtiau *n.m.* **1** 'Thingummy', small object of little value. **2** *(pl.)*: Trinkets, cheap jewellery. (Except when used with jocular intentions, this word belongs to the register of the country bumpkin.)

afnaf *adv.* (also: *afanaf; corr. abbr.* English half-and-half): Fifty-fifty. *Marcher afnaf*: To go halves.

agace-cul *n.m.* 'Joystick', 'cock', penis.

agace-machin *n.m.* **1** Itch, tingling, tickly feeling. **2** 'Joystick', 'cock', penis.

agacer *v.trans.* **1** To 'aggravate', to irritate. **2** To titillate, to taunt sexually. **3** *Agacer le sous-préfet* *(joc.)*: To 'pull one's wire', to 'wank', to masturbate.

agates *n.f.pl.* 'Oglers', 'peepers', eyes. (Originally marbles were made from this semi-precious stone, hence the colloquial meaning.)

âge *n.m. Ne pas porter son âge*: To look young, to look younger than one really is.

agent *n.m. (abbr. agent de police)*: Policeman.

agglo *n.m. (abbr. aggloméré)*: Chipboard, thick board made of wood chips and resin.

agiter *v.trans.* **1** *Les agiter*: To 'skedaddle', to 'make tracks', to scarper. **2** *Se l'agiter*: To 'pull one's wire', to 'wank', to masturbate.

agobilles *n.f.pl.* **1** (Underworld slang): 'Tools of the trade', instruments for breaking and entering. **2** *(joc.)*: 'Bollocks', 'balls', testicles.

agoniser *v.trans. Se faire agoniser*: To be called all sorts of names. (*Agonir de sottises* is the correct form in standard French. *Agoniser* is the popular departure from the norm.)

agoua *n.f.* 'Adam's ale', 'corporation pop', water.

agrafer *v.trans.* **1** To 'nab', to 'collar', to arrest. *Les cognes l'ont agrafé au saut du lit*: The fuzz grabbed him at the crack of dawn. **2** To 'buttonhole', to detain someone in conversation against his/her will. **3** To 'nick', to 'pinch', to steal. *Mais où c'est que t'as agrafé ça?* Where the hell did you get that? **4** To 'tear a strip off someone', to scold. *Et comment qu'il m'a agrafé!* He gave me a right roasting!

agrafes *n.f.pl.* 'Mitts', 'paws', hands.

agreg *n.f. (abbr. agrégation)*: Highest State qualification for teaching in lycées and universities. *Décrocher l'agreg*: To succeed in that exam.

agrément *n.m. Je vous souhaite bien de l'agrément!* (*iron.*): The best of British! (I wish you the best of luck because you'll need it!)

agricher *v.trans.* **1** To 'collar', to grab. *Il m'a agriché par le paletot!* He grabbed me by the coat! **2** To 'nab', to 'collar', to arrest (also: *agriffer*).

agrinche *n.m.* 'Yob', yobbo, loud-mouthed lout.

agrincheur *n.m.* 'Tea-leaf', crook, thief.

agripper *v.trans.reflex.* To have a tussle, to come to blows.

aguicher *v.trans.* To 'give the glad eye', to make eyes at. *De sa guitoune où elle vendait des billets de loterie, elle aimait aussi aguicher des michetons*: From the street booth where she sold lottery tickets, she also liked to attract customers for her 'other trade'.

aguicheuse *n.f.* 'Prick-teaser', girl who leads men on.

aidé *adj. Ne pas être aidé* (*iron.*): To have got a poor helping when Mother Nature dished 'it' out ('it' being looks, brains, etc.). *Ça on peut dire qu'elle n'est vraiment pas aidée!* There's no denying she's as ugly as sin! *Le gosse à mon frangin, il n'est vraiment pas aidé!* That nephew of mine isn't exactly bursting with O-levels!

aigle *n.m.* (*iron.*): Genius. *Ce n'est vraiment pas un aigle, il n'a pas inventé l'eau chaude!* I don't think he's got much up top! (The word is always encountered in a negative clause.)

aigre *n.m. Tourner à l'aigre* (of a conversation): To become acrimonious (also: *tourner au vinaigre*).

aigrefin *n.m.* **1** Con-man. **2** Crook.

aigrette *n.f. Avoir son aigrette:* To be a little drunk, to be slightly tipsy. *Elle s'est enfilé une demi-douzaine d'apéros, et la v'là qu'a son aigrette!* She's had six drinks and is already quite tipsy!

aiguille *n.f.* 'Pickler', key. (Always in a context of dishonest use.)

ail *n.m.* (Most expressions involving the word *ail:* garlic deal with lesbianism.) *Aimer l'ail, se taper de l'ail, bouffer de l'ail:* To be a lesbian. *C'est une drôle de gonzesse, j'ai l'impression qu'elle donne dans le gigot à l'ail!* She's a funny woman, I think she's a bit of a dike!

aile *n.f.* 1 'Fin', arm. 2 *Avoir un coup dans l'aile:* To be tipsy, to be slightly drunk. 3 *Avoir du plomb dans l'aile (fig.):* To have been 'winged', to have suffered a serious set-back. 4 *Croquer de l'aile* (Racing cyclists' slang): To hang on to a car to avoid having to pedal.

aileron *n.m.* 1 'Fin', arm. 2 *En avoir un coup dans les ailerons:* To be tipsy, to be slightly drunk.

ailleurs *adv. Va te faire voir ailleurs!* Get knotted! – Get lost! – Go away!

aimable *adj. Aimable comme une porte de prison (iron.):* Gruff, abrupt.

aimer *v.trans. & intrans.* 1 *J'aime mieux pas!* I'd rather not! 2 *J'aime, j'aime, j'aime! (joc.):* I like it, I like it! 3 *Va te faire aimer!* Get lost! – Go to hell! – Go away!

aïoli *n.m. Donner dans l'aïoli:* To have lesbian tendencies. (See **ail**. This Provence regional dish is strongly flavoured with garlic.)

air *n.m.* 1 *De l'air!* Get lost! – Go away! (literally: Give me breathing space!) 2 *Mettre en l'air:* To 'bump off', to 'do in', to kill. 3 *S'envoyer en l'air:* **a** To 'have it off', to have intercourse. **b** To get high on drugs. 4 *Foutre en l'air:* To dump, to chuck out, to throw away. 5 *Se foutre en l'air:* To 'do oneself in', to commit suicide. 6 *Ne pas manquer d'air:* **a** To be gutsy, to be brave. **b** To be as cheeky as they come. 7 *Pomper l'air à quelqu'un:* To 'get on someone's wick', to be a darned nuisance. *Ecoute, mon vieux, tu me pompes l'air!* I've just about had as much as I can take from you! 8 *Parler en l'air:* To talk without thinking. 9 *Se déguiser en courant d'air:* To make oneself scarce, to disappear in a flash. (The expression 'to vanish into thin air' does not convey the connotation of urgency that the French has.) 10 *Jouer la fille de l'air:* To escape from custody. (In a humorous context, the expression can mean 'to make a lucky escape' from a 'captive' situation, e.g. a boring committee meeting.)

ajète *v.trans.* (Second person singular, imperative only: popular mispronunciation of *achète*.) *Ajète-moi un vélo!* Go on, buy me a bike!

ajisme *n.m. L'ajisme:* The Youth Hostel movement (from *Auberges de la Jeunesse*). *Faire de l'ajisme:* To go youth hostelling.

ajiste *n.m. & f.* A person who belongs to the Youth Hostel Association.

alambic *n.m. Avoir l'alambic qui se désagrège:* To have a stomach ulcer.

alarmiste *n.m. (joc.):* Guard-dog.

albache *n.m.* 'Handle', name.

alboche *n.m. & adj.* 'Jerry', 'Kraut', German.

albroques *n.f.pl.* 'Scratchies', matches (also: *alloufs*).

album *n.m. Album de famille (pol.):* Set of 'mug shots', photographic records of known criminals.

alcotest *n.m.* (also: *alcootest*): 'Breathalyser', device for testing the alcohol level on a motorist's breath.

alevin *n.m.* Young pimp. *Duduche, c'est un alevin, le pain de fesse, il y fait tout juste son apprentissage!* He's just a beginner as a pimp, learning the ropes!

alfa *n.f.* 1 Hair. *N'avoir plus d'alfa sur les hauts plateaux (iron.):* To be as bald as a coot. 2 *(abbr. Alfa-Romeo):* Motor car of that make.

Alfort Proper name *(abbr. Maisons-Alfort) Il fait ses études à Alfort:* He is studying to be a vet. (One of the principal veterinary surgeon training schools is at Maisons-Alfort near Paris.)

Alfred Proper name. *Avoir le bonjour d'Alfred (iron.):* To be left in the lurch (when someone else has scarpered).

algarade *n.f.* 'Barney', quarrel. *Avoir une algarade avec quelqu'un:* To have a ding-dong row with someone.

aligner *v.trans. Aligner le pèze* (also: *les aligner*): To pay up. *D'entrée on lui a dit qu's'il voulait avoir ses faux fafs pronto, faudrait qu'il les aligne!* He was told straight that if he wanted phoney I.D.s quick, he'd have to cough up!

aligner *v.trans.reflex.* 1 *Tu peux toujours t'aligner! (iron.):* You don't stand a chance! 2 *S'aligner avec:* To 'have a barney with', to quarrel violently with someone.

allant *n.m. Avoir de l'allant:* To have plenty of drive. *Dans son job, douze heures d'affilée derrière le zinc, 'faut avoir de la santé et vachement de l'allant:* Serving drinks twelve hours at a stretch, he's got to be in good health and full of zest.

aller *v.intrans.* 1 *Se laisser aller:* **a** To take things easy and relax a little. *En vacances on se laisse un peu aller, ça fait du bien!* In the hols, we try and ease up a bit! **b** To become increasingly lax (in a variety of areas). *Depuis qu'elle est marida, elle se laisse aller!* Since she got hitched, she doesn't seem to give a damn about her appearance!

2 *Aller à*: **a** *(lit.)*: To suit, to fit. *Son costar lui va comme un gant*: That suit of his fits him a treat. **b** *(fig.*, often *iron.)*: To be 'fitting', in keeping with. *Ça lui va bien de parler d'honnêteté!* He's got a nerve, talking about being honest! **3** *Aller sur* (of age): To be 'getting on'. *Il va sur ses quarante berges*: He's knocking on forty. **4** *Y aller de sa réputation*: To stake one's good name. **5** *Comme vous y allez!* That's a bit steep! – That's a bit much! **6** *Va pour!* O.K. then! – Alright! *Bon, va pour demain, alors!* Oh well, then make it tomorrow! (There is a certain 'needs must' reluctance in the expression.) **7** *Allons donc! (iron.)*: Come on?! – You can't mean it?! *Lui, un doulos?! Allons donc!* Him a snitch?! You must be joking! **8** *Ça va mal, non?! (iron.)*: Are you nuts or something?! – You must be joking!

aller-retour *n.m.* A double slap in the face (fore- and backhand).

allonge *n.f.* 'Sub', advance part-payment of fee.

allongé *n.m.* 'Stiff', corpse. *Le boulevard des allongés* (also: *le jardin des allongés*): The bone yard, the cemetery.

allonger *v.trans.* **1** To hand over, to give (usually money). *Pour avoir la clef de la piaule, il a pas voulu me faire crédit, j'ai dû les allonger tout de suite!* He wouldn't let me have a room on tick and to get the key I had to cough up the money straight away! **2** To 'clout', to land a blow. *Allonger une baffe*: To slap someone in the face. **3** To 'bump off', to gun down. **4** *Se faire allonger (sch.)*: To get 'ploughed', to be failed at an exam.

allonger *v.trans.reflex.* **1** To 'spill the beans', to confess. *Il y a belle lurette qu'il mange à la grande gamelle, il est toujours prêt à s'allonger pour un oui ou pour un non*: He's been a police informer for a long time, always ready to spill the beans at the drop of a hat. **2** To topple, to fall full length. **3** *Se l'allonger*: **a** To 'pull one's wire', to 'wank', to masturbate. **b** *(iron.)*: To count on, to rely on. *S'il s'imagine que je vais l'aider, il peut toujours se l'allonger!* If he thinks I'm going to help him he's got another think coming!

allonges *n.f.pl.* 'Fins and kickers', arms and legs.

alloques *n.f.pl. (abbr. allocations familiales)*: Family allowance. *Toucher des alloques*: To get family benefit.

allouf *n.f.* 'Scratchie', match (also: *alouf*).

allumage *n.m. Avoir du retard à l'allumage* (iron., of person): To be 'slow on the uptake', to be a little dim. (The expression originates from the jargon of motor mechanics and describes an engine where the ignition is retarded.)

allumé *adj.* **1** Titillated, sexually excited. **2** 'Tiddly', 'tipsy', slightly drunk.

allumer *v.trans.* **1** To titillate, to arouse, to excite sexually. *Un rien l'allume!* Just about anything turns him on! **2** To ogle, to eye salaciously. *Allume un peu cette belle môme!* Get a load of that bird!

allumer *v.intrans.* To 'get one's skates on', to hurry up. *Allume! Faut se grouiller!* Get a move on!

allumettes *n.f.pl.* **1** *Sucer des allumettes*: To try to boost one's intelligence. (The theory that phosphorus is an ideal 'brain food' was jocularly misconstrued by a humorist who suggested that his readers suck matchstick heads to increase their intellectual potential.) **2** 'Pins', 'gambs', legs. *Avoir les allumettes en arceaux*: To be bow-legged.

allumeur *n.m.* Accomplice (of gambler/swindler). An *allumeur* (also known as *baron*) is the individual whose task it is to encourage passers-by to participate in illegal gambling by being seen to win.

allumeuse *n.f.* 'Prick-teaser', girl who leads men on for the sheer sake of it.

allure *n.f. Avoir de l'allure*: To look good. *Les choses prennent une mauvaise allure, ça tourne au vinaigre*: Things are turning nasty.

almanach *n.m.* **1** *(pol.)*: Copious criminal record. (The word has a certain built-in jocularity when contrasted with its meaning in standard French and aptly describes a long string of convictions.) **2** *Plaisanterie d'Almanach Vermot*: Weak joke, the kind of feeble witticism on the plane of 'Why did the chicken cross the road?' (The *Almanach Vermot*, France's hardiest 'annual', has always been famous for its rather low-brow literary contents.)

alors *adv.* **1** *Et alors?* So what? *Tu veux partir? Et alors? Moi, je m'en fous!* You want to leave? So what? Go ahead! **2** *Ça alors!* Well I never! – Would you believe it?!

alouf *n.f.* 'Scratchie', match. *Gratter une alouf*: To strike a light.

alpague *n.m.* **1** Jacket, coat. **2** *L'avoir sur l'alpague*: To be blamed for a crime. **3** *Les avoir sur l'alpague*: To be on the wanted list, to be sought after by the police or a rival gang.

alpaguer *v.trans.* To 'nick', to 'collar', to arrest. *Un de ces jours tu vas te faire alpaguer si ça continue!* If you keep this up much longer, the fuzz'll do you!

alpagueur *n.m.* 'Heavy', muscle-man, mobster. (*L'alpagueur* was the title of a 1970s' film with Jean-Paul Belmondo.)

alphonse *n.m.* (Underworld slang): Pimp, ponce, procurer.

alpion *n.m.* Crooked gambler.

alsaco *n.m.* Native of Alsace.

altèque *adj.* **1** (of man): Good-looking, handsome. **2** A-1, very good.

amadouage *n.m.* *(joc.)*: Nuptials, wedding ceremony.

amadouer *v.trans.* **1** To coax, to entice. **2** To cool down, to calm someone down. *Il est entré comme une tornade dans le café, et il a fallu lui payer au moins cinq rhums pour l'amadouer*: He came storming in, and we had to buy him five drinks to simmer him down.

amarrer *v.trans.* To grab hold of, to secure something firmly.

amarres *n.f.pl. Larguez les amarres! (joc.)*: Come on! Let's be off! (This expression, originating from seafaring jargon, has a sort of 'Anchors aweigh!' flavour.)

amateur *n.m. Amateur de rosette*: 'Poufter', 'queer', homosexual. (*Rosette* is a colloquial word for the anal sphincter.)

amazone *n.f.* High-class prostitute who solicits from an expensive motor car.

ambe *n.f.* 'Gamb', 'pin', leg.

ambier *v.intrans.* To run away from someone or something.

âme *n.f.* Small red tag stapled to postal bags describing contents.

amen *n.m. Dire amen à tout*: To be a yes-man.

amener *v.trans.reflex.* **1** To 'roll up', to arrive. *Alors, tu t'amènes?* Come on! Get a move on! *S'amener comme une fleur*: To 'drop in', to arrive uninvited. **2** *Tu peux toujours t'amener! (iron.)*: You can whistle for it! (You don't stand much chance of getting what you want.)

amer *adj. La trouver amère*: To find it no joke, to be cross. *Quand il a découvert que c'était lui qu'on avait balancé, il l'a trouvée amère*: He didn't think it was funny when he discovered that he'd got the sack.

américain *adj. Avoir l'œil américain*: **a** To 'have one's eyes peeled', to have sharp eyesight. **b** To have one's wits about one (when weighing up a situation).

amerlo *n.m.* 'Yank', American (also: *amerloc, amerloque*).

ami *n.m.* **1** *Faire ami-ami*: To 'click', to strike up a friendship easily. **2** *Petit ami*: Boyfriend. *Petite amie*: Girlfriend. (It is worth noting that these innocuous-looking appellations refer to sexual partners, whereas *grand ami/grande amie* have no such connotation and tend, if anything, to mean the opposite, i.e. someone for whom one has little affection.)

aminche *n.m.* Pal, chum, friend (also: *amunche*).

amiral *n.m.* 'Chiv', blade, knife.

amochage *n.m.* Bashing, thrashing, beating-up.

amocher *v.trans.* To bash up, to beat up, to thrash someone. (The implication within the verb is that someone gets 'their face pushed in' and looks a sorry sight afterwards.)

amochir *v.pronom.* To grow ugly.

amorcer *v.trans.* **1** (of business transaction, usually a shady one): To 'set the ball rolling', to get something going. **2** *Amorcer un clille* (Prostitutes' slang): To 'hook a punter', to entice a customer.

amortir *v.trans. Amortir le coup*: **a** To hush things up, to keep matters quiet, to avoid unnecessary publicity. **b** To 'smooth things over', to make as little fuss as possible and minimize the adverse effects of an event.

amortis *n.m.pl. Les amortis*: The thirty- to forty-year-olds. (This teenagers' term was promoted by the 1950s' film *Les Tricheurs*.)

amortisseurs *n.m.pl. (joc.)*: 'Titties', 'boobs', breasts.

amour *n.m.* **1** *Un amour de* . . . (usually of object): A 'darling' . . ., a beautiful . . . *Elle s'est acheté un amour. de petit bibi*: She bought herself the sweetest little hat you could imagine! **2** *Amour vache*: Torrid love affair (the kind where violent scenes alternate with passionate love-making).

amphés *n.f.pl.* (Drugs): Amphetamines.

amphi *n.m. (abbr. amphithéâtre)*: Lecture theatre. *On n'le voit pas souvent dans l'amphi, il sèche pas mal de cours!* He's not often seen at lectures, he skips a fair number of classes!

ampli *n.m. (abbr. amplificateur)*: 'Amp', hi-fi amplifier.

amurer *v.trans.reflex. S'amurer le bec*: To 'clam up', to shut up.

amuse-gueule *n.m.pl. (joc.)*: Cocktail snacks. (As the name suggests, the kind of titbits that alternate happily with the consumption of alcohol.)

amusement *n.m. Je vous souhaite bien de l'amusement (iron.)*: The best of luck! (also: *Je vous souhaite bien du plaisir!*).

amuser *v.trans. Amuser le tapis* (Gamblers' slang): To dither, to hestitate over what card to play.

amuser *v.trans.reflex. Les enfants s'amusent! (iron.)*: Little things please little minds!

amusette *n.f. (iron.)*: **1** 'Kids' stuff', easy task (the kind you could literally do with your eyes closed). **2** Harmless bit of 'slap-and-tickle', flirtation of no consequence. **3** 'Small-time fiddle' (the kind of con-trick that would rouse nothing but disdain from a real villain).

amygdales *n.f.pl.* **1** *Se caler les amygdales*: To 'stuff one's face', to eat a hearty meal. **2** *S'humecter les amygdales*: To 'wet one's whistle', to have a drink. **3** *Se faire lécher les amygdales*: To get a 'smackeroo', to exchange a French kiss. **4** *Avoir les amygdales à l'air*: To have one's throat slit open. **5** *Amygdales sud (joc.)*: 'Bollocks', 'balls', testicles.

ananas *n.m. (mil.)*: 'Pineapple', hand-grenade.

anar *n.m.* Anarchist (also: *anarcho*).

ances *n.f.pl.* (also: *anses*): 'Flappers', ears.

ancêtres *n.m.pl. Les ancêtres (joc.)*: The 'old folk', one's parents.

ancien *n.m. Faire l'ancien* (also: *faire dans l'ancien*): To be in the antique trade, to sell antiques.

andosses *n.f.pl.* (also: *endosses*): Back, shoulders. *En avoir plein les andosses (fig.)*: To be fed up with something.

andouille *n.f.* **1** Fool, idiot. *Faire l'andouille*: To 'arse about', to act the fool. **2** *Andouille à col roulé*: 'Prick', 'cock', penis (also: *chauve à col roulé*).

âne *n.m.* **1** 'Nincompoop', ass, fool. *Quel âne bâté!* What a nurk! **2** *Tenir l'âne par la queue* (of man): To 'have a slash', to pee, to urinate. **3** *Il y a plus d'un âne qui s'appelle Martin! (iron.)*: He's not the only fool who goes by that name! **4** *Comme un âne qui pète (joc.)*: Without so much as a thought. *Faut pas lui en vouloir, il a dit ça comme un âne qui pète*: I wouldn't take offence, he just said it off the top of his head.

ange *n.m.* **1** *Etre aux anges*: To be 'cock-a-hoop', to be delighted. **2** *Rire aux anges*: To laugh to oneself and without apparent reason. **3** *Un ange passe!* (is said of an embarrassing silence). *'Un ange passe' pensa Michel. Il sentit bien qu'il avait fait un impair*: There was a sudden hush and he realized he'd made a boob. **4** *Faiseuse d'anges*: Back-street abortionist.

anglais *adj. Bonbon anglais*: Acid drop.

anglais *n.m.pl. Avoir ses anglais*: To 'have the decorators in', to have a menstrual period. (The more ambiguously expressed *les anglais ont débarqué* is best translated by 'rain stopped play'.)

anglaise *adj.f.* **1** *Filer à l'anglaise*: To take French leave (also: *pisser à l'anglaise*). **2** *Capote anglaise*: 'French letter', condom.

angliche *n.m. & f.* 'Brit', English person (also: *britiche*). To the French such fine distinctions as Welsh, Scottish or Northern Irish are of little consequence.)

angliche *adj.* 'Brit', English.

anguille *n.f.* **1** *Il y a anguille sous roche*: 'Something's brewing' – Something's definitely about to happen. **2** *Anguille de calcif (joc.)*: 'Short-arm', 'cock', penis.

anicroche *n.f.* 'Snag', hitch. *On s'est tapé des vacances sans anicroches*: We had ourselves some really trouble-free holidays.

animal *n.m. Bougre d'animal, va! (joc.)*: You are a card! – You're a right one! (The expression is anything but sarcastic and is always uttered in a happy-go-lucky context.)

anis *n.m. De l'anis! (iron.)*: Not on your nelly! – Not bloody likely! – Certainly not!

anisette *n.f. Anisette de barbillon (joc.)*: 'Adam's ale', 'corporation pop', water. (Tap water, never a popular drink with the French, comes under a variety of humorous appellations, e.g. *sirop de canard, Château-la-pompe*.)

aniterge *n.m.* 'Snot-rag', handkerchief.

anneau *n.m. L'anneau*: The arse-hole, the anal sphincter. *Prendre de l'anneau*: To indulge in passive sodomy.

annif *n.m. (corr. abbr. anniversaire)*: Birthday.

annoncer *v.trans. Annoncer la couleur*: To 'put one's cards on the table', to state one's intentions.

anonyme *n.m. Se faire plomber un polichinelle signé anonyme*: To 'get into the pudding club and not know the cook', to get pregnant and not know who the father is.

anquilleuse *n.f.* Woman shoplifter. (So called because she tries to hide the stolen goods between her legs, or *quilles*.)

anse *n.f.* **1** 'Wing', arm. (The image here, as with the next meaning, reflects the loop configuration of a handle, i.e. that of a basket or a cup.) **2** *(pl.)*: 'Flappers', ears. **3** *Faire sauter l'anse du panier*: To divert housekeeping funds into one's own pocket.

antichambre *n.f. Bagatelles de l'antichambre (joc.)*: Heavy petting, extreme foreplay preceding intercourse.

antif *n.f.* **1** Path, road. **2** *Battre l'antif*: To 'hang about', to loiter.

antifler *v.pronom.* To 'get hitched', to get married.

antigel *n.m. (joc.)*: 'Hooch', 'hard stuff', strong alcohol.

antisèche *n.f. (sch.)*: Crib. *Il est arrivé dans l'amphi bourré d'antisèches; il faut dire qu'en classe il pompait sans cesse aux exam*: He came in loaded down with cribs; mind you, he was always copying off his neighbours in exams.

aoûtien *n.m. Les aoûtiens*: That vast multitude of holidaymakers who, choosing to ignore governmental pleas for *l'étalement des vacances*, take their annual break in August.

apache *n.m.* (Underworld slang): 'Heavy', henchman, gangster. (This is a non-pejorative appellation within the *milieu*.)

apaiser *v.trans. (iron.)*: To 'do in', to murder.

apasqueliner *v.pronom.* To get used to something.

apéro *n.m.* Aperitif.

aplatir *v.trans.* **1** To 'flabbergast', to astound. **2** *(fig.)*: To hit back with a stinging retort. **3** *Aplatir le coup*: To forgive and forget.

aplatir *v.trans.reflex.* **1** To grovel, to be over-subservient. *Il s'est aplati devant le dirlo*: He went boot-licking to the boss. **2** To lie low and hope to be forgotten.

aplomb *n.m.* **1** 'Cheek', nerve. *Tu ne manques pas d'aplomb!* You've got a nerve, mate! **2** *Etre d'aplomb* (of a person): To be 'in fine fettle', to feel in good health.

Apollon *n.m. Apollon du réverbère (joc. corr. Apollon du Belvédère)*: Street-Romeo, would-be Romeo. (Unlike the statue of that name in the Vatican an *Apollon du réverbère* is a *bellâtre*, the kind of vain 'smoothie' men and most women dislike.)

apôtre *n.m.* Finger. (The English 'pinky' is not strictly speaking accurate as it belongs to 'baby-talk'.)

appachonner *v.trans.* To lure, to entice, to attract. (This 1930s' underworld verb usually refers to illegal matters.)

appareil *n.m.* **1** *Etre dans le plus simple appareil*: To be 'in the altogether', to be 'starkers', to be naked. **2** *Remettre l'appareil*: To replace the (telephone) receiver.

appel *n.m.* **1** Wink, 'come on' nod (also a variety of facial expressions appealing to a person one fancies). **2** *Faire des appels du pied*: To 'play footsy', to reach out under a table with one's foot. **3** *Faire un appel de phares*: To flash one's headlights. **4** *Faire un appel au peuple (joc.)*: To scrounge, to ask for money.

appeler *v.trans.reflex.* *Il s'appelle 'Reviens'* (ironical remark about something one is lending): I want it back, you know!

appoint *n.m. Faire l'appoint*: To have the exact change. (The sign *'On est prié de faire l'appoint'* –'Please have the exact change ready' is often displayed on French buses.)

apporter *v.trans.reflex.* To come. *Alors quoi! Tu t'apportes?* Get a move on then! – Are you coming at last?! (also: *s'amener*).

apprenti *n.m.* **1** 'Greenhorn', novice. **2** *Course d'apprentis*: Race for apprentice jockeys.

appuyer *v.trans.* **1** To insist upon, to put pressure behind. *Appuyer une demande*: To bring influence to bear on behalf of a request. **2** *Appuyer sur le champignon*: To accelerate, to get things moving. **3** *Appuyer sur la meule* (Cycling): To pedal hard.

appuyer *v.pronom.* **1** To treat oneself to something. *On s'est appuyé un sacré gueuleton*: We had ourselves a slap-up meal. **2** To have to put up with someone or something unpleasant. *Mon beau-père, ça va encore, mais ma belle-doche*

il faut se l'appuyer! My father-in-law's O.K., but the mother-in-law's a pain in the neck! **3** *S'appuyer une nana*: To 'have it off with a bird', to have intercourse. (This expression has a much more literal connotation than the first two meanings.)

aprèm *n.m. & f. (abbr. après-midi)*: Afternoon. *On se voit cette aprèm?* Will I be seeing you this P.M.?

après *prep.* **1** *Attendre après*: To wait for. *Il attend après sa sœur qu'est au coiffeur*: He's waiting for his sister what's at the hairdresser's. **2** *Monter après une échelle*: To climb up a ladder.

après *adv.* **1** *Cours-lui après!* Run after him! **2** *Et (puis) après?* So what? *Alors je fais du bruit la nuit! Et après?!* So I make a lot of noise at night! You want to make something of it?!

après-ski *n.m.* Warm, fur-lined, ankle-high boots worn, as the name suggests, after skiing sessions. (It has now become fashionable to wear *après-ski* in towns and cities.)

aquarium *n.m.* (Underworld slang): Bistro, café where pimps congregate.

aquijer *v.trans.* (also: *aquiger*): **1** To 'slate', to criticize severely. **2** To bash up, to beat up, to injure.

arabe *adj.* **1** *Fourbi arabe*: 'Tricky business', a very complicated state of affairs. **2** *Téléphone arabe*: 'Grapevine', word-of-mouth transmission of news. *J'ai eu ça par le téléphone arabe*: I heard it through some chaps at work. **3** *Merde arabe!* Blast! (The adjunction of *arabe* would seem to jocularize and soften the expletive.)

aracail *n.m.* 'Sky pilot', 'padre', priest.

araignée *n.f.* **1** *Avoir une araignée au plafond*: To be 'barmy', to be 'bonkers', to be mad. **2** *Faire des pattes d'araignée*: To write in a spidery script. **3** *Faire (des) pattes d'araignée à quelqu'un*: To 'goose', to caress lightly with nails and fingertips.

aramon *n.m.* 'Plonk', cheap red wine. *Il s'est tapé un kil d'aramon*: He downed a litre of vino.

arbalète *n.f.* **1** *(joc.)*: Gun, firearm. **2** Erect cross on tombstone. (These cemetery memorials are indeed reminiscent of a crossbow.) **3** 'Prick', 'cock', penis. *Filer un coup d'arbalète*: To have a bang.

arbi *n.m. (abbr. arbicot)*: Arab, native of North Africa. (This pejorative appellation is equatable with the English 'wog', 'coon'. Also: *bicot*.)

arbif *n.m.* 'Verbal aggro'. *Un méchant coup d'arbif*: A right angry outburst.

arbre *n.m.* **1** Carcass, the human body. **2** *Faire monter (or faire grimper) quelqu'un à l'arbre*: To 'have someone on', to kid, to hoax.

arcan *n.m. (pol.)*: 'Tea-leaf', crook, thief.

arcat *n.m.* Elaborate con-trick often perpetrated by means of a letter. *Monter un arcat*: To set someone up.

arche *n.m.* **1** Trick (at cards). *Prendre l'arche*: To take a trick, to win a round. **2** *Aller à l'arche*: To 'collect some lolly', to fetch some money. **3** *Se fendre l'arche*: To be bored to tears.

archer *n.m.* 'Cop', 'copper', policeman.

archevêché *n.m.* *(pol.)* *L'archevêché*: The Marseilles Police Headquarters (because they are situated close to the Cathedral).

archi This superlative intensifier is often compounded with nouns, adjectives or past participles. *Archicon*: 'As thick as they come'. *Un archipaumé*: A real nobody. *Archisaoul*: 'Blotto', blind drunk.

archicube *n.m.* Former student of the *Ecole Normale Supérieure* or *Ecole Centrale*.

arcpincer *v.trans.* (also: *arquepincer*): To 'nick', to 'collar', to arrest.

ardoise *n.f.* **1** 'Tick', credit. *Mets ça sur mon ardoise!* Put it on the slate for me, will you! *Poser une ardoise*: To eat in a restaurant without any intention of paying the bill. (The technical term for this act which is a criminal offence in France is *grivèlerie*.) *Liquider une ardoise*: To settle a debt. **2** *Prendre une ardoise*: To use a *pissotière*, to go to a street urinal. (Before vitreous enamel, such public conveniences made extensive use of slate.)

arêtes *n.f.pl.* **1** Shoulder blades. **2** Ribs.

areu-areu *n.m.* (Child's language) *Faire areu-areu*: To goo-goo, to gurgle.

argagnasses *n.f.pl.* Menstrual period. *Avoir ses argagnasses*: To have the decorators in.

argasses *n.f.pl.* 'Plates of meat', (large) feet. *Il avait aux argasses la plus mahousse paire de croquenots imaginable*: You should have seen the pair of beetle-crushers he was wearing!

argenté *adj.* *Etre argenté comme une cuiller de bois (iron.)*: To be flat broke (also: *être raide comme un passe-lacet*).

argomuche *n.m.* Slang. *Il jaspine l'argomuche comme un vrai arcan*: He speaks slang as if he'd been a wide-boy all his life.

argoter *v.intrans.* To talk argot, to speak slang.

argougner *v.trans.* (also: *argougnier*): To 'collar', to grab hold of. *Il l'argougna par la cravetouse*: He grabbed him by the tie.

argousin *n.m.* **1** 'Copper', 'cop', policeman. **2** 'Screw', prison-warder. **3** 'Gaffer', foreman.

arguche *adj.* 'Thick', 'dumb', stupid.

arguincher *v.trans.* To 'nick', to 'collar', to arrest.

Argus *Proper name.* *Etre coté à l'Argus (fig.)*: To have made a name for oneself. (*L'Argus*, a motor magazine catering mostly to the trade, gives a year-by-year run-down of second-hand car prices.)

aria *n.m.* Fuss, bother. *Non mais, quel aria!* What a song-and-dance (over nothing)!

aristo *n.m.* *(abbr. aristocrate)*: 'Toff', 'nob', upper-class person.

arlequin *n.m.* **1** 'Bubble-and-squeak', warmed-up left-overs. **2** *(pl.)*: Left-overs from expensive restaurants sold cheaply to down-and-outs.

arlos *n.m.pl.* 'Seconds', rejects, rejected goods.

arme *n.f.* **1** *Etre sous les armes* (also: *être sous les drapeaux*): To be in the army. **2** *Passer (quelqu'un) par les armes*: To execute someone sentenced by a military court. **3** *Passer l'arme à gauche*: To 'croak', to 'snuff it', to die. *Cette garce de vie ne lui a pas fait de cadeaux et on a tous été soulagés d'apprendre qu'il avait passé l'arme à gauche*: Life hadn't been kind to him and it was with some relief that we heard the news that he had passed away. **4** *Il est parti avec armes et bagages!* He cleared off taking everything with him bar the kitchen sink!

armé *past part.* *Etre armé (joc.)*: To have 'the big stick', to have an erection.

Arménouche *n.m. & f.* Armenian.

armoire *n.f.* *Armoire à glace* (also: *armoire normande*): 'Heavy', powerful-looking individual (the kind that would not worry too much about being built like a wardrobe).

arnac *n.m.* 'Copper', 'cop', policeman.

arnaque *n.f.* **1** Con-trick, swindle. *Monter une arnaque*: To set someone (or several people) up. **2** *Un coup d'arnaque*: An underhand blow, a treacherous action.

arnaquer *v.trans.* **1** To 'con', to 'diddle', to swindle. **2** (Gambling slang): To 'fix' a game, to cheat. **3** To grass on, to betray. **4** To 'bash up', to beat up. *Il l'a drôlement arnaqué*: He bashed him up good and proper. **5** To 'collar', to 'nick', to arrest. *Il s'est fait arnaquer à la sortie du guinche*: He got nabbed as he came out of the dance-hall.

arnaqueur *n.m.* Con-man, swindler.

arnau *n.m.* (also: *arno*) *Etre en arnau*: To be in a foul temper (also: *être en renaud*).

arnoucher *v.trans.* To eye, to ogle, to look at with envy.

Aronde *Proper name.* Family saloon car manufactured by Simca between the early 50s and mid-60s.

arpèges *n.f.pl.* *(pol.)*: 'Dabs', set of fingerprints. (There is a certain jocularity stemming from the straight musical meaning.)

arpenteuse *n.f.* 'Hooker', 'prozzy', prostitute.

arpète *n.f.* (also: *arpette*): Apprentice, errand-girl.

arpinche *n.m.* 'Scrooge', mean character.

arpinche *adj.* 'Tight-fisted', mean.

arpion *n.m. L'arpion:* The slang spoken in the rag-and-bone trade.

arpions *n.m.pl.* 'Plates of meat', 'hoofs', feet.

arquepince *n.f. La maison-je-t'arquepince (joc.):* 'The fuzz', the police.

arquepincer *v.trans.* (also: *arcpincer*): To 'nab', to 'collar', to arrest.

arquer *v.intrans.* 1 To walk. *Il était tellement schlass qu'il n'pouvait plus arquer:* He was so drunk he couldn't walk. 2 To 'get the big stick', to have an erection.

arquin *n.m.* 'Chubb-buster', safe-cracker.

arquinche *adj.* (also: *arquiche*): 'Tight-fisted', mean.

arquincher *v.trans.* To 'nab', to 'collar', to arrest.

arraché *n.m. Avoir quelque chose à l'arraché:* To get something by an all-out effort. (This expression originates from the language of weight-lifters.)

arracher *v.trans.* 1 *Arracher du chiendent:* To be 'stood up' by a date, to wait in vain at a rendez-vous. 2 *Arracher les côtes* (Racing cyclists' slang): To keep up speed on a gradient.

arracher *v.intrans.* To 'pull away', to accelerate violently. *Il démarra sur les chapeaux de roues, arracha comme un dingue!* He took off like a streak of lightning, pulling away like a madman!

arracher *v.trans.reflex.* To 'go over the wall', to make a break and escape from prison.

arrangemané *adj.* Infected with V.D., suffering from venereal disease (also: *poivré*).

arrangemaner *v.trans.* 1 To 'con', to 'diddle', to swindle someone. 2 To 'bash', to beat up, to thrash. 3 To give someone 'clap', to infect with V.D.

arranger *v.trans.* 1 *Arranger quelqu'un:* To get the better of someone either through brute strength, by means of a swindle or ultimately by killing him. 2 (of culinary preparation): To do a 'Cordon Bleu' job, to spend hours in the kitchen (not here the connotation of 'rustling something up'). 3 *Arranger quelque chose aux petits oignons (fig.):* To take meticulous care over a task (literally to be as conscious of fine detail as with a delicate recipe).

arranger *v.trans.reflex.* 1 To 'settle a score'. *Qu'ils s'arrangent, après tout c'est leur affaire!* Let them sort it out, it's their business, after all! 2 *Ça s'arrangera!* Things will sort themselves out! 3 *S'arranger de:* To have to be content with. *Il faudra que tu t'arranges de ce*

que j'ai là, je suis vraiment fauché! You'll have to make do with this money, I'm really broke!

arrêter *v.trans.* 1 *Arrêter les frais:* To give something up as a bad job, to stop wasting one's time. 2 *Arrête ton char, Ben Hur! (joc.):* Give over! – Stop bragging!

arrière-saison *n.f. Sentir l'arrière-saison (joc.):* To be getting on in years, to feel old age creeping up on one.

arrière-train *n.m.* 'Bum', 'arse', posterior. *Mon père m'a élevé à coups de pompes dans l'arrière-train:* My dad believed in the old saying 'Spare the rod and spoil the child'.

arrimer *v.trans.* To 'corner', to 'buttonhole', to grab.

arrivé *n.m.* Self-made man (the kind who is not backward in telling you he's made it).

arrivé *past part. Croire que* (also: *s'imaginer que*) *c'est arrivé:* **a** To 'fancy oneself', to hold oneself in high esteem. *Depuis qu'il a décroché ses galons de caporal, il s'imagine que c'est arrivé:* Since they made him corporal, he thinks he's it. **b** To be very gullible, to be credulous. *On peut lui vendre n'importe quoi, il croit que c'est arrivé. Il tombe toujours dans le panneau:* You can sell him anything. He's so gullible, he'll always fall for it!

arriver *v.intrans.* 1 *Arriver pile:* To 'just make it', to arrive in the nick of time. 2 *Arriver dans un fauteuil* (Horse-racing slang): To come in an easy winner, to win with practically no opposition.

arriviste *n.m. & f.* 'Go-getter', ruthless career-minded person.

arrondir *v.trans.* 1 *Arrondir les angles:* To 'smooth things over', to be conciliatory. 2 *Arrondir ses fins de mois:* To do a few odd jobs to make ends meet.

arrondir *v.trans.reflex. Se l'arrondir:* To 'go without', to have to do without. *Si tu t'imagines qu'on va te faire crédit, tu peux toujours te l'arrondir!* If you hope we're going to lend you money, you've got another think coming!

arrosage *n.m. (joc.):* 'Booze-up', celebration where a lot of alcohol is consumed.

arroser *v.trans.* 1 To stand drinks on the occasion of a happy event. *On a arrosé ses galons:* We christened his stripes with a few bevvies. 2 To strafe, to spray with a burst of automatic fire. 3 To bribe (literally to pour money in someone's direction).

arrosoir *n.m. Se parfumer avec un arrosoir (iron.):* To douse oneself in (usually cheap) perfume.

arsonner *v.trans. (pol.):* To 'frisk', to do a body search on someone.

arsouille *n.m.* 'Rogue of a fellow', caddish character. (Originally a pejorative appellation, it has with time and with the advent of the character *Milord l'Arsouille* got the flavour of 'lovable rogue'.)

arsouiller *v.trans.reflex*. To frequent the *'milieu'* (underworld).

Arthur *Proper name.* **1** *Se faire appeler Arthur*: To get told off, to be reprimanded. **2** *Madame Arthur*: Parisian night-club famous for its 'drag' clientèle.

artichaut *n.m.* **1** Wallet, purse. (The word is deemed to have a built-in pun in that it keeps *l'artiche au chaud*.) **2** *Avoir un cœur d'artichaut*: To be flighty and flirtatious (the inference here is that the heart of the person concerned is as difficult to reach as that of a globe artichoke).

artiche *n.f.* **1** 'Brass', 'loot', money. **2** Alibi. *Saler l'artiche*: To 'fix', to cook up an alibi. **3** 'Arse', 'bum', behind. *Se faire botter l'artiche*: To get kicked up the jacksey.

article *n.m.* **1** *Faire l'article*: To do some 'hard sell', to plug one's wares tenaciously. **2** *Etre porté sur l'article (joc.)*: To be a randy so-and-so, to be highly-sexed. **3** *Etre à l'article de la mort*: To be 'not long for this world', to be at death's door. (In contrast to the standard meaning, colloquial French sometimes gives this expression a less serious connotation.)

artiflo *n.m.* (also: *artiflot*): Artilleryman.

artiller *v.trans. & intrans.* **1** To 'have a bang', to 'have it off', to have intercourse. **2** To 'gun' for high profits, to aim for a high return on one's money.

artillerie *n.f.* **1** *(joc.)*: 'Rod', 'shooter', handgun. **2** (Gambling slang): Loaded dice. **3** *(joc.)*: 'Cannonball grub', stodgy food. **4** *La grosse artillerie (joc.)*: 'Big ones', large denomination banknotes. *Sortir la grosse artillerie*: To come out with the heavy readies. (A totally different meaning for this expression sometimes encountered is 'to take strong measures' in order to get one's way.)

artis *n.m.* Slang. (The standard usage is *causer artis*.)

artisse *n.m.* Popular mispronunciation of *artiste*.

artiste *n.m. (pej.)*: 'Geezer', 'bloke', person. *Il me fait suer, cet artiste!* That burk gets on my wick!

artoupan *n.m.* 'Screw', prison-warder.

artous *n.m.pl.* 'Plates of meat', 'hoofs', feet.

as *n.m.* **1** 'Ace', top guy, expert. *Un as de l'aviation*: A crack pilot. *Dans le monde des ordinateurs, c'est un as!* He's the top wallah where computers are concerned! **2** (Waiters' slang): Table number one. (Calls such as *'Une choucroute à l'as!'* answered by *'Ça roule!'* can often be heard in restaurant kitchens in France.) **3** *(pol.)*: Alibi. *Il avait un carré d'as*: He'd fixed himself up with four good alibis. **4** *Aller à l'as (fig.)*: To 'come a cropper', to 'come unstuck', to suffer a setback (also: *aller à dame*). **5** *Bouffer à l'as*: To go hungry, to miss a meal, to go

without food. **6** *Passer à l'as*: **a** To vanish into thin air, to disappear. *Dès qu'il flaira la faillite, il décida de passer à l'as*: As soon as bankruptcy loomed, he did a moonlight. **b** *Passer quelqu'un à l'as*: To by-pass someone in a share-out. **c** *Passer quelque chose à l'as*: To 'pinch', to filch, to spirit something away. **7** *Veiller à l'as*: To 'keep one's eyes peeled', to keep a sharp look-out. **8** *Etre plein aux as*: To be 'rolling in it', to be extremely wealthy. **9** *As de pique*: **a** Nonentity, highly forgettable person. **b** 'Parson's nose' (that part of a fowl indeed looks like an ace of spades upside down). **c** Arse-hole, anal sphincter. **d** *Etre fichu (also: foutu) comme l'as de pique* (of person): To be dressed like a guy, to be as scruffy as they come. (of job): To be bungled, to be badly executed.

ascenseur *n.m. Renvoyer l'ascenseur (joc.)*: To return a favour.

asmoche *n.f.* Absinth. (Although this alcoholic beverage is now illegal, frequent nostalgic references are made to it.)

asperge *n.f.* **1** *Asperge du pauvre*: Leek. **2** *Une grande asperge* (also: *une asperge montée en graine*): 'Bean-pole', tall lanky person. **3** Penis. *Aller aux asperges* (of prostitute): To go soliciting.

asphyxier *v.trans.* **1** To 'flabbergast', to astonish (literally to take the wind out of someone). **2** To 'pull the wool over someone's eyes', to fool. **3** *Etre asphyxié*: To be 'pissed', 'blotto', to be drunk.

aspi *n.m. (abbr. aspirant)*: 'Middy', midshipman.

aspic *adj.inv.* Acid-tongued, back-biting, maligning.

aspine *n.f.* 'Loot', 'brass', money.

aspiquer *v.trans. & intrans.* To indulge in back-biting, to go scandal-mongering.

aspiranche *n.m.* 'Vac', hoover, vacuum-cleaner.

Aspirateur *Proper name. L'Aspirateur (joc.)*: Nickname given to the *Ministère des Finances*.

aspirateur *n.m. Aspirateur à pépées (joc.)*: 'Sexmobile', flashy sports car used to 'pull the birds'.

aspirine *n.f. Avoir un teint cachet d'aspirine* (also: *être bronzé comme un cachet d'aspirine; joc.*): To have a complexion as if one had crawled out from under a slab, to be very pale-skinned.

assabouir *v.trans.* **1** To knock down, to bowl over. *Si tu mets les pieds ici, tu risques de te faire assabouir!* If you so much as come round here, you're likely to get thumped! **2** *(fig.)*: To stun, to astound. *Il a été assaboui par la nouvelle*: He was shattered by the news.

assaisonner *v.trans.* **1** To 'bash up', to beat up, to thrash. **2** To 'tear a strip off someone', to tell off in no uncertain manner. *Un peu que je l'ai assaisonné ton jules de te ramener si tard!* I certainly told that no-good boyfriend of yours what I thought . . . bringing a young girl home so late! **3** To give a dose of 'clap', to pass on V.D. **4** *Se faire assaisonner:* To get sent down for a long stretch, to cop a heavy sentence.

assassiner *v.trans.* **1** To overcharge, to ask exorbitant prices. *C'est un restau où on se fait drôlement assassiner; cinq étoiles, trois fusils, tu vois le genre!* It's one of those eating-places where you get taken for a ride, five stars and all that! **2** To bore someone to death.

asseoir *v.trans.reflex.* **1** *S'asseoir sur:* To 'squash' someone, to put all one's weight in silencing someone. **2** *Je m'assieds dessus!* I don't give a fig! – I couldn't bloody well care less! **3** *Va t'asseoir!* Go to blazes! – Get knotted! – Go away!

assiette *n.f.* **1** *Je ne suis pas dans mon assiette:* I don't feel too bright – I don't feel too good. **2** *Les Assiettes:* The Assizes Court. **2** *L'assiette au beurre:* A cushy job. *Taper l'assiette au beurre:* To ride the gravy train.

assis *past part.* *En rester assis:* To be too stunned to answer.

assommer *v.trans.* To bore. *Quand il raconte ses souvenirs de guerre, il m'assomme:* When he gets going on his war stories, he bores the pants off me.

assommoir *n.m.* **1** 'Grotty pub', down-market drinking establishment. (Zola's novel is probably the originator of this colloquial appellation.) **2** Bore, boring person.

Assottes *n.f.pl.* *Les Assottes:* The Assizes, the Assizes Court.

astap *adj.inv.* *(abbr. à se taper le cul par terre) C'est astap!* **a** It's too ridiculous for words! **b** It's bloody hilarious! (also: *c'est à faire pipi dans un chapeau de paille troué!*).

astibloc *n.m.* Maggot, larva of the blow-fly.

astic *n.m.* (also: *astique n.f.*): Wax polish. *Passer l'astic:* To polish.

asticot *n.m.* **1** Larva of the blow-fly. **2** *(pej.):* 'Bloke', 'geezer', fellow. *C'est un drôle d'asticot:* He's a bit of an odd-ball. **3** *Engraisser les asticots:* To 'be pushing up daisies', to be dead. **4** *Avoir un asticot dans la noisette:* To be 'soft in the head', to be 'bonkers', to be mad.

asticotage *n.m.* **1** Nagging. **2** Teasing.

asticoter *v.trans.* **1** To nag, to pester. *A force de l'asticoter sans cesse, sa femme va le rendre dingue:* With her non-stop bickering, she'll drive him bonkers. **2** To make fun of, to tease.

asticoter *v.trans.reflex.* To squabble, to quarrel. *Ils s'asticotent à longueur de journée, de vrais chiffonniers!* They're constantly at each other's throats.

asting *n.m.* (Algerian *pieds-noirs* slang): 'Biff', blow, punch.

astiquer *v.trans.* **1** To 'bash up', to beat up, to thrash. *Il l'a drôlement astiqué!* He gave him one hell of a pasting! **2** To nag, to pester. **3** To tease.

astiquer *v.trans.reflex.* **1** To 'doll oneself up', to dress up. **2** To row, to quarrel. **3** To 'pull one's wire', to masturbate.

astre *n.m.* *Etre beau comme un astre (iron.):* To be incredibly good-looking. (The expression is nearly always uttered within a tongue-in-cheek context.)

astuce *n.f.* Joke, pun, witticism.

Athénien *n.m.* *C'est ici que les Athéniens s'atteignirent! (joc.):* This is where the crunch comes! – This is the crucial (and funny) bit! (This nonsensical utterance usually occurs within the narration of an interesting or amusing episode.)

atouser *v.trans.* To lead on, to encourage. (This verb originates from the world of card games where the meaning of *atout* is 'trump'.) *S'il ne m'avait pas atousé, j'aurais pas pu le faire:* If he hadn't spurred me on, I'd never have done it.

atout *n.m.* **1** 'Blow', wound. *Il a reçu un méchant atout sur le crâne:* He got a nasty biff on the head. **2** 'Guts', courage. **3** Strength. **4** *Et pan! Atout!* Interjection accompanying a series of well-landed blows. *Et pan! Prends ça! Atout! Atout! Et ratatou!* Take this! . . . and that! **5** *Avoir tous les atouts dans son jeu:* To be 'on a winning wicket', to be in a strong position.

attacher *v.trans.* *Attacher un bidon* (or *attacher une gamelle):* To 'squeal' on someone, to 'give someone away', to betray someone.

attaque *n.f.* **1** *Etre d'attaque:* To be 'full of beans', full of pep, to be raring to go. **2** *Travailler d'attaque:* To work with enthusiasm. **3** *C'est d'attaque:* It's 'ace', it's A-1, it's very good.

attaquer *v.intrans.* To lead (at cards).

atteler *v.trans.* (of pimp): To live off women. *Il attelle (à) plus de huit gonzesses:* He's got over eight girls in his 'stable'.

atteler *v.trans.reflex.* **1** (of couple): To 'shack up', to go and live together. **2** *S'atteler à:* To 'tackle', to set about (a task).

attendri *adj.* 'Tiddly', 'tipsy', slightly drunk.

attention *interj.* *Attention aux épluchures! (joc. & iron.):* Beware of the consequences!

attifer *v.trans.reflex.* To 'dress like a guy', to take no pride in one's attire.

attigé *adj.* (also: *atigé*): Infected with venereal disease. *Planque aux attigés:* Hospital treating V.D. cases.

attiger *v.trans.* (also: *atiger*): **1** To wound. **2** To overcharge. **3** To 'overdo it', to exaggerate. *N'attige pas la cabane!* Pull the other one! Do you think I'm that stupid?! **4** To infect with venereal disease.

attrapade *n.f.* (also: *attrapage n.m.*): Telling-off, severe scolding.

attrape *n.f.* Trick, practical joke. *Magasin de farces et attrapes*: Joke shop.

attrape-couillons *n.m.* Confidence trick, swindle.

attrape-pognon *n.m.* (Gambling slang): 'Fixed' dice or card game.

attraper *v.trans.* **1** To 'haul over the coals', to 'tear a strip off someone', to reprimand. *Un peu que je me suis fait attraper!* I got a right rollicking from her! **2** To 'cop' a prison sentence, to get a term of imprisonment. *Il en a attrapé pour dix ans*: He got sent down for a ten-year stretch.

attributs *n.m.pl.* 'Bollocks', 'balls', testicles (also: *bijoux de famille*).

attrimer *v.trans.* To 'nick', to 'pinch', to steal.

attriquer *v.trans.* To 'fence', to buy stolen goods knowingly.

attriquer *v.trans.reflex.* To 'treat oneself' to something. *On s'est attriqué une bouteille de roteux*: We had ourselves a bottle of champers.

auber *n.m.* 'Dough', 'lolly', money.

auberge *n.m. On n'est pas sorti de l'auberge! (joc.)*: We're not out of the woods yet! – We're not yet out of trouble!

aubergine *n.f.* **1** 'Conk', 'hooter', bulbous nose (the kind of highly-coloured proboscis heralding the heavy drinker). **2** 'Meter-maid', traffic warden. (Until 1980, their uniform was aubergine-coloured.)

auge *n.f. (joc.)*: 'Trough', plate.

Auguste *Proper name. Tout juste, Auguste!* (Rhyming catch-phrase): Right-on! You've said it mate!

aumonières *n.f.pl.* 'Bollocks', 'balls', testicles.

aussi *adv. Aussi sec*: Quick as a flash, suddenly. *Il m'a giflé et aussi sec je lui ai rendu sa baffe*: He slapped me and no messing I landed one on his mush!

autiche *n.f. Faire de l'autiche*: To grumble, to moan, to complain.

auticher *v.trans.* To arouse, to excite sexually.

autobus *n.m.* Part-time prostitute, usually a near-penniless housewife who has to resort to soliciting to make ends meet.

autor *D'autor (adv.exp.)*: **1** 'Off one's own bat', of one's own accord. **2** *Travailler d'autor et d'achar*: To 'graft' non-stop, to work relentlessly, without letting up.

autre *adj. & pron.* **1** *A d'autres! (iron.)*: Pull the other one! – Do you think I'm that stupid? *On ne me le fait pas, mon vieux! . . . A d'autres!* I don't fall for that one! **2** *L'un dans l'autre*: All things being considered – On average. *L'un*

dans l'autre, on n'en est pas mal sorti!* It was a case of swings-and-roundabouts, and we came out even! **3** *Etre l'autre*: To be the 'fall-guy', to be the 'mug', to get the worst of the deal. **4** *Comme dit l'autre (joc.)*: As the saying goes. (The expression has a jocular connotation because no-one has the faintest idea who *l'autre* is.) **5** *En avoir vu d'autres (iron.)*: **a** To have been through worse, to feel undeterred by what one is currently experiencing. **b** (Usually of object): To have 'seen better days', to have considerably deteriorated.

Auverpin *n.m.* Native of the Auvergne.

avachi *adj.* (of person): 'Run-to-seed', fat and flabby.

avachir *v.pronom.* **1** To 'plonk oneself' down any-old-how on a piece of furniture (literally to slump in a position reminiscent of a recumbent cow). **2** To lapse into a 'couldn't-care-less' state of mind. **3** To 'go to seed', to let oneself become fat and flabby.

avaler *v.trans.* **1** *Avaler son extrait de naissance (joc.)*: To 'croak', to 'snuff it', to die (also: *avaler sa chique/le goujon/sa fourchette*). **2** *Avaler une histoire*: To 'fall for something hook, line and sinker', to show oneself to be over-gullible in believing a rather unlikely tale. **3** *Avaler la consigne*: To forget to carry out one's orders. (Some sources suggest that this omission might be intentional.) **4** *Avaler des couleuvres*: To 'swallow one's pride', to have to take abuse in silence. **5** *Avoir avalé le pépin*: To be 'in the pudding club', to be 'preggers', to be pregnant.

avaloir *n.m.* Gullet, throat. *S'arroser l'avaloir*: To 'wet one's whistle', to have a drink (also: *se rincer la gargane*).

avance *n.f. Avoir de l'avance à l'allumage* (of person): To be slightly 'off one's rocker', to be slightly mad.

avantage *n.m. Faire un avantage*: **a** To do someone a good turn, a favour. **b** *(joc. & iron.)*: To give someone orgasmic pleasure.

avantages *n.m.pl.* 'Tits', 'boobs', breasts.

avant-scène *n.f. Il y a du monde à l'avant-scène (joc.)*: She's got a smashing pair of knockers – She's got big breasts (also: *Il y a du monde au balcon*).

avarié *adj. (joc.)*: 'Clapped', infected with venereal disease.

avaro *n.m.* **1** 'Snag', 'hitch', setback. **2** Run of bad luck.

avec *prep. & adv.* **1** *Il y a des pommes de terre avec*: You get spuds with it. (The colloquiality stems from the absence of the complement.) **2** *(iron.)*: *Et avec ça! Un petit coup sur le manche, faut-il vous l'envelopper?* You want jam on it, don't you?! – What more do you want?!

(The expression is said to have originated in its non-ironic form in butchers' shops where a client purchasing a leg of lamb is being treated with old-fashioned business courtesy.)

aveuglette *n.f.* *Agir à l'aveuglette*: To go about one's business in a hit-or-miss fashion.

aveux *n.m.pl.* *Passer à la chambre des aveux spontanés (iron.)*: To be 'put through the third degree', to be given a 'grilling', to undergo forceful police interrogation.

avirons *n.m.pl.* *Les avirons (joc.)*: A knife and fork set. *Lâcher les avirons*: To lay down the shovellers.

avis *n.m.* *M'est avis que*: 'Methinks' (if you ask me my opinion, I think that . . .).

aviser *v.trans.* To 'have a butcher's at', a look at. *Avise un peu cette nana!* Take a dekko at this bird!

avocat *n.m.* **1** (Gambling slang): Card player who carries on for a tired friend at the tables. **2** *Faire l'avocat*: To assist someone in a card-trick routine. **3** *L'avocat bêcheur*: The public prosecutor (in a trial).

avoine *n.f.* **1** 'Grub', 'eats', food. *Prendre son avoine*: To sit down and tuck into a meal. **2** *Avoine de curé (joc.)*: Pepper. (The humour stems from the assumption that the only spice in life a priest is likely to enjoy is dispensed in the form of a condiment.) **3** *Filer* (also: *refiler*) *une avoine à quelqu'un*: To 'bash up', to beat up (literally to give someone the kind of thrashing that separates corn from the sheaf).

avoiner *v.intrans.* (of car): To 'belt along', to go at a fair pace. *On a drôlement avoiné sur l'autoroute!* We were going flat-out on the motorway!

avoir *v.trans.* **1** To 'take in', to fool. *Eh bien, vous m'avez drôlement eu!* You've certainly put one across me! **2** To 'beat hollow', to dismiss through victory. **3** To 'screw', to 'have it off' with someone. **4** To 'reach' someone, to make contact with someone. *J'ai pas pu l'avoir au bigophone*: I couldn't reach him on the blower. **5** *En avoir*: To be 'gutsy', plucky, to be brave. (*En* can refer either to *courage* or *couilles* according to the colloquial emphasis within the expression.) **6** *En avoir jusque-là*: To be 'fed up to the back teeth', to be sick and tired of someone or something. *J'en ai jusque-là de ces histoires à la con!* I've just about had it up to here with these pointless arguments! **7** *En avoir contre quelqu'un*: To bear someone a grudge. **8** *Avoir quelqu'un aux sentiments*: To get what one wants by playing on someone's feelings. **9** *J'en ai pour deux jours!* It'll keep me busy for two days!

azimut *n.m.* **1** *Dans tous les azimuts*: 'Left, right and centre', in all directions. **2** *Il y a de la schtoumoune dans l'azimut* (also: *Il y a de l'entourloupe dans l'azimut*): 'There's aggro brewing' – I can sense trouble ahead.

azimuté *adj.* 'Bonkers', 'nuts', mad.

azor *n.m.* **1** 'Rod', 'shooter', handgun. **2** *Appeler Azor (joc.)*: To whistle for someone, to call for someone's attention with little tact. (*Azor*, like *Médor*, is the archetypal name for dogs in children's stories and twee novels, and is equatable with 'Fido'. The expression '*Pas de ça, Azor!*' is the nearest witty equivalent to 'Not tonight, Josephine!')

B

B.A. *n.f. (abbr. bonne action) Faire sa B.A. (joc. & iron.)*: To do one's daily good deed. (The expression originates from the language of Scouting; in colloquial speech, the good deed can have a variety of tongue-in-cheek meanings.)

B.A. – ba *n.m. C'est le B.A.-ba de la réussite dans les affaires*: It's the ABC of success in business.

baba *n.m.* **1** 'Pussy', 'fanny', vagina. **2** Arsehole, anal sphincter. **3** *L'avoir dans le baba*: To 'have been had', 'diddled', to have been conned.

baba *adj.inv.* 'Bowled over', 'flabbergasted', speechless. *J'en suis resté baba!* I just couldn't say a word! (The image here is of one who is *bouche bée*.)

babafier *v.trans. (joc.)*: To 'bowl over', to 'flabbergast', to dumbfound.

babanquer *v.intrans.* To 'whoop it up', to lead a fast and furious life (also: *bambocher*).

babillard *n.m.* **1** 'Mouthpiece', solicitor. **2** 'Rag', 'sheet', newspaper.

babillarde *n.f.* Letter, item of correspondence. *Il ne fait que lui pondre des babillardes!* He just never seems to stop writing to her! (also: *babille*).

babin *n.m.* 'Gob', 'trap', mouth.

babines *n.f.pl.* (also: *babouines*): 'Chops', lips. *C'était un gâteau fantastique à s'en pourlécher les babines!* It was a real mouth-watering cake! *Se caler les babines* (also: *s'en mettre plein les babines*): To 'stuff one's face', to eat a lot.

babiole *n.f.* **1** 'Knick-knack', thing of little value. **2** Small ailment, minor (health) disorder. (Expressions such as *avoir une babiole au cœur* relate to a serious health disorder where the gravity of the ailment is being played down.)

babyfoot *n.m.* (also: *baby-foot*): Miniature football (the kind of bar game where two or four players operate a number of handles controlling wooden swivelling football players. The standard expression is *faire un babyfoot*).

bac *n.m.* **1** *(abbr. baccalauréat)*: The exam of that name. *Il n'a jamais passé son bac*: He never did

get his A-levels. **2** *(abbr. baccarat)*: Casino card-game of that name.

baccara *n.m.* Spot of bad luck, misfortune. *Etre en plein baccara*: To have a really bad run.

bacchantes *n.f.pl.* 'Tash', whiskers, moustache. (The type referred to here is the long, drooping moustache. The stage production *Ah, les belles bacchantes!* has kept this dated word in the public eye.)

bâche *n.f.* **1** Bed-sheet. *Se mettre dans les bâches*: To 'hit the sack', to go to bed. **2** 'Pancake', flat cap.

bâcher *v.trans.reflex.* To 'hit the sack', to go to bed (literally to get between the sheets).

bâcheur *n.m.* Keeper/proprietor of a low-class hotel.

bâcheuse *n.f.* Landlady, keeper of a lodging house.

bachot *n.m. (abbr. baccalauréat)*: The exam of that name. *Une boîte à bachot (sch.)*: A 'crammer's', a 'cramming shop' (the kind of establishment where backward pupils get some 'force-fed' education).

bachotage *n.m. (sch.)*: Cramming for the *baccalauréat* or (by extension) for any important exam.

bachoter *v.intrans. (sch.)*: To cram, to prepare oneself for an examination (originally the *baccalauréat*).

bachoteur *n.m. (sch.)*: 'Swot', pupil who through need or inclination does a lot of cramming.

bâcler *v.trans.* To 'botch', to skimp, to make a hash of something through haste.

bacon *n.m.* Pig meat, pork.

bacreuse *n.f.* 'Bin', 'poke', pocket.

bada *n.m.* **1** Man's hat. (A woman's hat is known as a *bibi*.) **2** *Porter le bada*: **a** To be suspected of being a police informer. **b** To be made the scapegoat. **3** *Porter le bada de . . .* To have a reputation for . . . (The expression is hardly ever used with a favourable connotation.)

badaboum *n.m.* **1** 'Free-for-all', 'rough-house', brawl. **2** Scandal (the kind that one is unable to hush).

badaf *n.m. (mil. abbr. Bataillon d'Afrique)*: The *badafs* were a disciplinary unit stationed in North Africa, and a *badaf* is a soldier who has served in that regiment (also: *Bat' d'Af'*).

bader *v.intrans.* To 'throw up', to puke, to vomit.

baderne *n.f.* **1** *Une vieille baderne*: A fuddy-duddy, a silly old fool. **2** *Etre baderne-baderne*: To do everything 'by the book', to have a military-type approach to quite day-to-day matters.

badigeon *n.m.* **1** *(joc.)*: 'Warpaint', make-up. *Elle avait un sacré coup de badigeon sur la frime!* She seemed to have been made-up care of Polyfilla! **2** *Donner un coup de badigeon (fig.)*: To do a whitewash job on an embarrassing event.

badigeonner *v.pronom.* *S'en badigeonner*: 'Not to give a fuck', to not care a damn about something (also: *s'en tamponner*).

badigeonneur *n.m. (pej.)*: 'Dauber', untalented painter.

badigoinces *n.f.pl.* 'Smackers', lips. *Activer des badigoinces*: To 'stuff one's face', to eat immoderately.

badour *adj.m.* Good-looking, handsome.

baffe *n.f.* **1** Blow, slap in the face. *Il a chopé une méchante baffe*: He got a right slap across the kisser. **2** 'Tash', moustache.

baffer *v.trans.* To slap someone across the face.

baffi *n.f.* 'Tash', moustache.

baffles *n.f.pl.* 'Lugs', 'lug-holes', ears. *Il était là, baffles et tout*: He was there with his ears flapping.

bafouille *n.f.* Letter, item of correspondence. *Torcher une bafouille*: To dash off a few hasty lines. *Bafouille de chiotte*: Poison-pen letter.

bâfre *n.f. (abbr. bâfrerie)*: 'Good nosh', slap-up meal. (The word has low-brow connotations in that it suggests the kind of meal where one makes a pig of oneself.)

bâfrer *v.intrans. (pej.)*: To eat greedily and in a messy manner. (Expressions such as 'to eat like a pig' or 'to wolf one's food' are not strictly accurate equivalents on their own.)

bâfrer *v.trans.reflex. (pej.)*: To 'stuff one's face', to consume vast quantities of food. (The image that comes to mind here is of near-indecent gluttony.)

bagaf *n.m.* 'Rod', 'shooter', handgun.

bagage *n.m.* **1** *Plier bagage*: To 'pop one's clogs', to 'snuff it', to die. **2** *Avoir un sacré bagage*: To have what it takes 'up top', to be brainy. **3** *Trimbaler des bagages*: To have 'bags under one's eyes', to look worn out through lack of sleep.

bagarrer *v.trans.reflex.* *Se bagarrer avec*: **a** To have a punch-up, to exchange blows with someone. **b** To have a 'barney' with, to row with someone.

bagarreur *n.m.* **1** Brawler, one who doesn't like to miss out on a good punch-up. **2** 'Never-say-die' character, one who fights every inch of the way to get what he wants.

bagatelle *n.f.* **1** *Etre porté sur la bagatelle*: To be a randy so-and-so, to have more than a passing interest in sex. (The expression can refer equally to men and women.) **2** *Les bagatelles de l'antichambre*: 'Heavy petting', sexual foreplay.

bagnard *n.m.* *De la graine de bagnard*: 'Prison fodder', young person likely to end up in jail.

bagnole *n.f.* 'Wheels', car, motor car. (Excepting a gently ironic context, the vehicle in question is more likely to be a 'banger' than something fresh out of a showroom.)

bagof *n.m.* 'Rod', 'shooter', handgun.

bagos *n.m.pl.* (also: *bagots*; *corr. abbr. bagages*): 'Traps', bags, luggage.

bagoter *v.intrans.* **1** To 'loaf', to 'loll about', to loiter with no intent. **2** *(pol.)*: To 'pound the beat', to police an area. **3** To 'put one's skates on', to move niftily. *Il a dû drôlement bagoter pour ne pas manquer son bus*: He had to get cracking to catch the bus.

bagou *n.m.* (also: *bagout*) *Avoir du bagou*: To have the gift of the gab, to have a glib tongue.

bagouler *v.intrans.* To 'natter away', to 'jabber away', to talk endlessly. *Elle bagoulait, mon vieux, impossible d'en placer une!* Crikey, she did go on. I couldn't get a word in edgeways!

bagouse *n.f.* **1** (Jewellery): Ring. **2** Arse-hole, anal sphincter. *Prendre de la bagouse*: To engage in sodomy. **3** *L'avoir dans la bagouse*: To have been 'conned', 'diddled', to have been fooled. **4** *Avoir de la bagouse*: To be a 'jammy bugger', to be a lucky so-and-so. (References to sodomous intercourse are often equated in modern colloquial French with good fortune.)

baguenaude *n.f.* 'Bin', 'poke', pocket.

baguenauder *v.pronom.* To 'loaf about', to wander aimlessly.

baguer *v.trans.reflex.* *Se baguer le nœud* (of man): To 'have a screw', to 'have it off', to have intercourse.

baguette *n.f.* **1** French loaf (the crusty long bread, the pride of all *boulangeries*). **2** *(pl.)*: 'Pins', 'gambs', legs. *Avoir des baguettes style fauteuil Louis XV*: To be bow-legged. (To understand the image, one must picture a chair of that period.) *Mettre les baguettes*: To 'scarper', to 'skedaddle', to go away in haste. **3** 'Prick', 'cock', penis. *Filer un coup de baguette*: To 'have a bang', to 'screw', to have coition with.

bahut *n.m.* **1** One's place of work. (Like the bulky item of furniture the word originally refers to, the faceless employer's large premises lack charisma. *Dans quelle sorte de bahut est-ce que* *tu bosses?* And where do you earn your crust?) **2** *(sch.) Mon bahut:* My lycée, my school. **3** 'Motor', motor car. *Il s'est payé un lampadaire avec son bahut:* He pranged his car on a lamppost. **4** 'Cab', taxi. (The current expression for to flag down a taxi is *frêter un bahut.*)

bahuter *v.trans.* **1** *(sch.):* To 'rag', to tease (also: *chahuter*). **2** To turn a place into a shambles by acting rough.

bahuter *v.trans.reflex.* To 'pull one's wire', to wank, to masturbate.

baigner *v.intrans. Ça baigne dans l'huile:* Things are running smoothly.

baigneur *n.m.* **1** Bum, bottom, posterior. (Expressions such as *mettre la main au baigneur* are sexist and reveal the strong sexual connotation of the word.) **2** *L'avoir dans le baigneur (fig.):* To have been 'conned', 'diddled', to have been duped.

baignoire *n.f.* **1** Small theatre box at the back of the stalls. (Tristan Bernard, the famous humorist and crossword addict, gave this definition to the word *entracte:* '*Vide les baignoires et remplit les lavabos*'.) **2** Form of torture by immersion of the head in water.

bail *n.m. Ça fait un méchant bail qu'on s'est pas vus!* It's a hell of a long time since we met! (also: *Ça fait une paye qu'on s'est pas vus*).

baille *n.f.* **1** Water, any expanse of water (sea, river, etc.). *Ils l'ont filé à la baille:* They tossed him in the soup. **2** Rain. *Il nous est tombé une de ces bailles!* It poured buckets! **3** Water, drinking water. *Etre de corvée de baille:* To be on water-fatigue. **4** *(pej.):* 'Crate', 'tub', aged sea-going vessel.

bain *n.m.* **1** *Etre dans le bain:* **a** To 'know the ropes', to be 'in the know', to be well-informed about the workings of something. *Maintenant que t'es dans le bain, j'te laisse te débrouiller!* Now you know what's what, I'll let you get on with it! **b** To be implicated, to be involved in something unpleasant. *Une sale histoire . . . Il est vraiment dans le bain!* That's a nasty piece of work and he's up to his neck in it! (The expression *mettre quelqu'un dans le bain* can either mean to 'show someone the ropes' or to land someone in trouble – the latter is the more common.) **2** *Envoyer quelqu'un au bain:* To 'send someone packing', to send someone away in a summary manner. **3** *Bain de pieds:* 'Slops', saucerful of spilt tea or coffee. **4** *Le Grand Bain (pol.):* The Central Criminal Archives in Paris.

baïonnette *n.f.* 'Prong', 'prick', penis. *Filer un coup de baïonnette:* To 'have a bang', to have intercourse.

baise-en-ville *n.m. (joc.):* Small overnight bag. (In spite of its obvious vulgarity, the word is steadily drifting into everyday parlance.)

baiser *v.trans.* **1** To fuck, to 'screw', to have coition with. **2** To 'con', to deceive. *Il m'a drôlement baisé avec son histoire à dormir debout!* I was really taken in by his cock-and-bull story! **3** To 'nick', to 'pinch', to steal. *Elle lui a baisé son crapaud:* She lifted his wallet. **4** To 'nick', to 'collar', to arrest. *Il s'est fait baiser à la douane:* He got nabbed at the Customs.

baisette *n.f.* 'Prick', 'cock', penis.

baiseur *n.m.* 'Randy so-and-so', highly-sexed man. (The feminine *baiseuse* in our sexist society refers to an 'easy-lay', a loose woman.)

baiseuses *n.f.pl.* 'Smackers', lips.

baisodrome *n.m. (joc.):* Any location where sexual intercourse is likely to take place frequently.

baisouiller *v.intrans. (iron.):* To make love in a rather unsatisfactory manner. (The connotation here is of the kind of intercourse that leaves one of the partners totally dissatisfied.)

baisse-froc *n.m.* 'Funk', 'yellow-belly', coward.

bakshich *n.m.* **1** 'Backhander', bribe. *Il a toujours eu sa petite caisse à bakshich pour le tirer d'affaire:* He's always had the possibility of dipping into the old slush-fund kitty to steer clear of trouble. **2** (Waiters' slang): 'Tip', gratuity.

bal *n.m.* **1** 'Clink', 'nick', prison. *Etre au bal:* To be doing porridge. **2** *Etre de bal (mil.):* To be in the punishment squad and marching round and round the barrack square. **3** *Donner le bal à quelqu'un:* To 'give someone a dressing-down', to tell someone off in no uncertain manner. **4** *Le bal des 4 z'arts:* Rowdy art students' dance held annually in Paris.

balade *n.f.* **1** Ramble, stroll. **2** 'Spin', short drive in a motor car. **3** *La balade* (Underworld slang): 'The short ride to nowhere' (that ultimate car trip in gangland from which there is no return). **4** *Etre en balade:* **a** To be on the run from prison. **b** To be 'high' (through drugs or alcohol abuse). **c** To be 'out of one's mind', to be in a demented state.

balader *v.trans.* **1** To 'traipse around' with someone, to reluctantly accompany someone (sightseeing, house-hunting, etc.). **2** (of sick person): To go round very obviously ill. *Il balade une méchante grippe:* He's sporting one hell of a cold! **3** *Envoyer balader quelqu'un:* To 'tell someone where to get off', to 'send someone packing', to tell someone off in no uncertain manner. *Quand je lui ai demandé du fric, il m'a envoyé balader:* When I asked him for a loan, he told me to get knotted. **4** *Envoyer balader quelque chose:* To 'chuck something away'. *Il a pris un coup de sang et a tout envoyé balader*: In a fit of anger he turfed the lot out.

balader *v.trans.reflex.* To go for a stroll.

baladeuse *adj. Avoir les pognes baladeuses*: To be 'all hands', to have a tendency to let one's hands wander lecherously.

baladeuse *n.f.* Mains-powered inspection lamp used by mechanics to examine the underside of cars.

balai *n.m.* **1** Last bus or train to run before the nightly closedown. **2** 'Meat-wagon', hearse. **3** *Voiture balai* (Racing cyclists' slang): Ambulance whose job it is to pick up the stragglers too exhausted to finish the race. **4** *Donner un coup de balai (fig.)*: To have a good clear-out. **5** *Du balai!* Hop it! – Get lost! – Go away! **6** *Rôtir le balai*: To lead a fast and furious life. **7** *Con comme un balai*: 'Daft as a brush', silly and stupid.

balaise *n.m.* 'Heavy', muscleman, muscular and stocky figure of a man. (The kind of person who naturally finds work as a bouncer or bodyguard.)

balaise *adj.* **1** (of person): Hefty, muscular. **2** (of object): 'Ginormous', very large. *Elle nous sert toujours des portions balaises!* When she serves us, we get real heaped platefuls!

Balajo *Proper name. Le Balajo (corr. le Bal-à-Jo)*: This famous Paris dance-hall took its name from its original owner.

balançage *n.m.* (Underworld slang): 'Squealing', 'ratting', denunciation (by former accomplice turned informer).

balance *n.f.* 'Sacking', dismissal. *Il est bon pour la balance!* He's just about ready for the push!

balancé *adj.* **1** *Etre bien balancé*: **a** (of man): To be well-built and handsome. **b** (of woman): To be shapely and attractive. **2** *Une vanne bien balancée*: A crisp and witty riposte.

balancement *n.m.* Conviction, prison sentence.

balancer *v.trans.* **1** To 'chuck out', to throw away. *Il y a belle lurette qu'il a balancé ses journaux pornos*: He got rid of his dirty mags ages ago. **2** To 'fire', to 'give the sack', to dismiss. **3** To 'shop', to 'grass' (on someone), to denounce. **4** *Balancer un parpaing* (also: *balancer un coup*): To strike a heavy blow. **5** To answer, to reply. *Et moi aussi sec, je lui ai balancé cette vacherie pour lui clouer le bec!* I didn't let him get away with his nasty crack, and quick as a flash I gave him as good as I'd got. **6** To jilt. *Balancer sa largue*: To jilt one's mistress. **7** *Balancer une bafouille*: To send a letter. **8** *Balancer un pet*: To fart, to break wind. **9** *Balancer ses châsses* (also: *balancer les châssis*): To be on the look-out, to glance briefly left and

right. **10** *Balancer le chiffon rouge*: To 'natter', to talk on and on.

balancer *v.pronom. S'en balancer*: Not to give a damn, to not care 'two hoots' about something, to be totally indifferent to events.

balanceur *n.m.* 'Snitch', 'grass', informer.

balancier *n.m.* 'Fin', arm. (Unlike *brandillon* which is nearly always encountered in the plural, *balancier*, because of its standard French meaning of pendulum, is nearly always in the singular.)

balançoire *n.f.* **1** (*pl.*) *Des balançoires*: 'Poppycock', 'balderdash', nonsense-talk. *Moi, je ne coupe pas dans toutes ces balançoires!* I'm not falling for all those cock-and-bull stories. **2** *Balançoire à Mickey*: 'Jam-rag', sanitary towel.

balandrin *n.m.* 'Bundle', small item of baggage.

balanstiquer *v.trans.* **1** To 'chuck out', to throw away. **2** To 'fire', to 'give the sack', to dismiss. **3** To 'shop', to 'grass' (on someone), to denounce.

balayer *v.trans.* To 'turf someone out of a job', to sack someone.

balayette *n.f.* **1** 'Cock', penis. (Unlike most appellations that refer to the erect organ, *balayette*, in keeping with the standard French meaning, evokes the image of the organ at rest.) **2** *Une moustache en balayette de chiottes (pej.)*: A small, bristly 'Hitler-type' moustache.

balcon *n.m.* **1** *Il y a du monde au balcon!* (Sexist remark): What a pair of knockers! – What big breasts! **2** *'Les cocus au balcon!'*: This humorous jeer is often heard at student marches and its immediate effect is to get the *bons bourgeois* at their windows.

baleine *n.f.* **1** 'Big fat biddy', corpulent woman. **2** *Se tordre* (also: *rigoler*) *comme une baleine*: To 'laugh oneself silly', to double up with laughter. **3** *Gueuler comme une baleine*: To 'kick up a fuss', to voice disapproval vociferously.

balèze *n.m.* 'Heavy', muscleman, muscular and stocky figure of a man. (The kind of person who naturally finds work as a bouncer or bodyguard.)

balèze *adj.* **1** (of person): Hefty, muscular. **2** (of object): 'Ginormous', very large.

ballade *n.f.* **1** 'Bin', 'poke', pocket. *Faire les ballades à quelqu'un*: To 'frisk', to go through someone's pockets.

balle *n.f.* **1** 'Dial', face. (Like *bille* and unlike *gueule*, the word has no pejorative connotation whatsoever. *Fais-lui confiance, il a une bonne balle!* Go on! You can trust him, he's got a kind face!) **2** Monetary unit of French francs. (The word is never used in relation to amounts less than 10 francs, irrespective of the 1958 remonetization.) **3** Bargain, good buy. **4** *Le trou de balle*: The arse-hole, the anus, the anal sphincter. **5** *Un vieux trou de balle*: An old 'fuddy-duddy'. (Unlike *un trou du cul*, which is downright pejorative, this appellation has gentle jocularity.) **6** *Raide comme balle (adv.exp.)*: Quick as a flash, straight away. **7** *C'est ma balle!* That's my business! **8** *Ça fait ma balle!* That suits me down to a T! – That's fine by me!

baller *v.intrans.* *Envoyer baller quelqu'un*: To 'send someone packing', to 'send someone away with a flea in their ear', to dismiss someone in no uncertain manner.

ballets *n.m.pl.* **1** *Ballets roses*: Sexual orgy involving under-age girls. **2** *Ballets bleus*: Sexual orgy involving under-age boys. (*L'affaire des ballets roses* – a famous scandal involving high-ranking politicians and business people got its name through the fact that one of the participants was involved in show-business; the media coined this expression in 1959.)

ballochards *n.m.pl.* 'Tits', 'boobs', breasts.

balloches *n.f.pl.* 'Bollocks', 'balls', testicles.

ballon *n.m.* **1** 'Bum', buttocks, behind. *Enlever le ballon à quelqu'un*: To kick someone up the backside. **2** Belly, stomach. *Se bourrer le ballon*: To 'stuff one's face', to eat vast amounts of food. **3** (*pl.*): 'Titties', 'boobs', breasts. *Elle a une gentille petite paire de ballons*: She's got a pert set of knockers. **4** Balloon-glass (the kind used for wine in cafés throughout France. The request for *un ballon de rouge* is almost a cliché). **5** *Faire du ballon*: To 'do porridge', to serve a term of imprisonment. **6** *Ballon d'essai (fig.)*: 'Feeler', cautious inquisitive remark. **7** *Avoir le ballon*: To 'have a bun in the oven', to be 'preggers', to be pregnant. **8** *Faire ballon*: To miss out on something and suffer disappointment.

ballot *n.m.* 'Nincompoop', fool. (The word has no real pejorative connotation; in fact, it is often uttered as in *bougre de ballot!* You silly boy! with jocular affection. *Mais oui, je t'aime, gros ballot!* Of course I love you, you silly-billy!)

balloté *adj.* *Bien balloté*: **a** (of man): Handsome and well-built. **b** (of woman): Shapely and attractive.

ballustrines *n.f.pl.* 'Bollocks', 'balls', testicles.

balmuche *n.m.* *Balmuche!* Fuck-all! – Not a sausage! – Nothing! (also: *balpeau!*).

balocher *v.intrans.* To 'mooch about and do bugger-all', to wander about in an aimless and idle manner.

baloches *n.f.pl.* **1** 'Bollocks', 'balls', testicles. **2** *En avoir dans les baloches*: To be 'spunky', 'gutsy', to be full of courage.

balocheur *n.m.* 'Slack-arse', 'slacker', idle person.

balourd *adj.* Phoney, fake, false.

balourds *n.m.pl.* **1** Fake I.D.s, forged identity papers. (The expression *marcher sous des balourds*: to go around with false documents, is the most common.) **2** Counterfeit money. *Taper des balourds*: To print falsies.

balpeau *n.m.* (also: *ballepeau*): **1** *Balpeau!* Fuck-all! – Not a sausage! – Nothing! *J'ai cru qu'il allait me donner un pourboire, mais balpeau!* I thought he was going to give me a tip, but I didn't get a bean! **2** *Faire balpeau*: To 'miss out on something' and suffer disappointment. (*Balpeau* is a corrupt *verlen* of *peau de balle*.)

balthasar *n.m.* (also: *balthazar*): **1** 'Blow-out', slap-up meal. **2** Large bottle of champagne equivalent to sixteen standard ones.

baltringue *n.m.* 'Useless git', inefficient person.

baltringue *adj.* Useless, hopeless, inefficient.

baluchard *n.m.* 'Twit', 'nurk', imbecile (also: *baluche*).

baluchon *n.m.* 'Bundle', small item of baggage. *Faire son baluchon*: To pack one's gear, to pack up one's belongings.

baluchonner *v.trans.* To 'nick', to 'filch', to steal items of little value.

baluchonneur *n.m.* **1** Small-time crook. **2** (Prison slang): Friend of incarcerated person who takes him provisions.

balustrades *n.f.pl.* *Envoyer quelqu'un dans les balustrades*: To squeeze someone out, to force someone out of business. (Originally this cycling expression from the heyday of six-day racing literally meant to send another competitor into the side railings and deprive him of a chance of winning.)

bambochade *n.f.* 'Night out on the tiles', drinking spree (also: *bamboche*).

bambochard *n.m.* One who likes to 'whoop it up', reveller.

bamboche *n.f.* 'Night out on the tiles', drinking spree. *La bamboche, il ne connaît que ça!* His idea of fun is to paint the town red!

bambocher *v.intrans.* To 'whoop it up', to 'have a night out on the tiles', to go on a spree.

bambocheur *n.m.* One who likes to 'whoop it up', reveller.

bambou *n.m.* **1** Leg. *Mettre les bambous* (also: *mettre les bouts*): To 'beat it', to run away. **2** *Prendre un coup de bambou*: **a** To get sun-stroke. **b** To 'go off one's rocker', to go suddenly mad. **3** *Avoir le coup de bambou*: To be 'knackered', to be very tired. **4** *Tirer sur le bambou*: To smoke opium.

bamboula *n.m.* 'Darkie', coloured person. (Definitely a racist appellation, it is sometimes uttered without animosity in a 'good old Bwana' patronising spirit.)

bamboula *n.f.* 'Slap-up do', party where a lot of food and drink is consumed.

bambouter *v.trans.* **1** To shatter someone's peace of mind by breaking some bad news to him. **2** To 'give someone the cold shoulder', to deliberately avoid someone. **3** *(sch.):* To give someone a poor grade.

ban *n.m.* Rhythmical round of applause. (Whereas in Great Britain slow hand-clapping indicates audience dissatisfaction, in France it denotes acclaim. *Fermez le ban!* That's enough praise!)

banal *adj.* *Ça, c'est pas banal! (iron.):* That's a turn-up for the book! – This is quite extraordinary!

banane *n.f.* **1** Overrider on motor car bumper. **2** 'Gong', medal, decoration. **3** *Peau de banane (fig.):* Booby-trap, intentionally-laid difficulty aimed at delaying someone's progress.

banc *n.m.* *Etre sur le banc:* To be a down-and-out, to be a vagrant. (*Sur le banc* is the title of a French film with Raymond Souplex and Jeanne Sourza which humorously depicts the colourful life of tramps in Paris.)

banco *n.m.* **1** *Banco!* You're on! – O.K., that's fine by me! *'Tu veux faire une virée en bagnole?!' 'Banco!'* 'You want to go for a spin in the car?!' 'Count me in!' **2** Till, cash register. *Faire le banco:* To nick the takings.

bandaison *n.f.* Erection. *Avoir une méchante bandaison:* To have 'the big stick'. (The word has built-in witticism in relation to *pendaison*.)

bandant *adj.* **1** Titillating, sexually exciting. **2** 'Side-splitting', hilarious. *C'est un truc vraiment pas bandant!* It's what I'd call a pain in the arse!

bandatif *adj.* Titillating, sexually exciting (also: *bandatoire*).

bande *n.f.* *Par la bande:* In a roundabout way, indirectly. *Et comme ça, par la bande, je lui ai demandé où ce qu'elle habitait:* And without seeming to be nosey, I asked her where she lived.

bander *v.intrans.* **1** To 'get the big stick', to have an erection. **2** *(fig.):* To be thrilled to bits, to be very happy. *Il bandait méchant à l'idée de partir en vacances:* He was drooling at the thought of going on holiday. *Ça ne me fait pas bander tout ce boulot!* I'm not too keen on all that extra work!

bander *v.trans.* *Bander la caisse:* To 'do a bunk' with the takings, to disappear with the money.

bandeur *n.m.* Randy so-and-so, man whose main preoccupation is sex.

bandocheur *n.m.* 'Funk', 'yellow-belly', coward.

bannes *n.f.pl.* Bedsheets. *Se glisser dans les bannes:* To 'hit the sack', to go to bed.

bannette *n.f.* **1** 'Pinny', apron. **2** Bed. *Faire bannette:* To 'kip down', to go to bed.

bannière *n.f.* **1** *Etre en bannière:* To be in one's shirt-tails. **2** *C'est la croix et la bannière!* It's a drag! – It's ever so awkward! *C'est la croix et la bannière pour le faire se lever le matin!* Getting him up for work is one hell of a task!

banquer *v.intrans.* **1** To 'cough up', to pay up. *J'en ai marre, c'est toujours moi qui banque!* It's always muggins who foots the bill! **2** *Avoir banqué (fig.):* To have settled one's debt to society (through a prison sentence).

banquette *n.f.* Jaw, chin. *Il a pris un gnon sur la banquette:* He got smacked in the kisser.

banquettes *n.f.pl. Jouer les banquettes (th.):* To play to an empty house.

baptême *n.m. (joc.):* 'Rousting', 'rollicking', beating-up.

baptiser *v.trans.* **1** To water down spirits. (The implication here is that, as with a christening, water is a prime ingredient.) **2** *Avoir été baptisé avec une queue de morue (joc.):* To be overfond of one's tipple, to have a strong liking for alcoholic beverage.

Baptiste *Proper name. Tranquille comme Baptiste:* **a** Cool as a cucumber. **b** Quiet as a mouse.

baquer *v.trans.reflex.* To have a good soak, to take a bath.

baquet *n.m.* Belly, stomach. *Il nous en a filé plein le baquet!* We fair stuffed our faces with his good grub!

barabille *n.f. Mettre la barabille:* To 'stir it', to deliberately cause trouble.

baragouin *n.m.* 'Gabble', gibberish, incomprehensible talk.

baragouiner *v.intrans.* To gabble, to talk what sounds like incomprehensible gibberish.

baraka *n.f. Avoir la baraka:* To have the luck of the devil, to be incredibly lucky.

baraque *n.f.* **1** 'Dump', 'crummy house', hovel. **2** Firm, business. *Moi, je travaille plus pour cette baraque, j'en ai ma claque!* I'm not working for this lousy outfit any more, I'm sick up to here with it! **3** *(pl.):* 'Bollocks', 'balls', testicles. **4** Losing throw at *passe anglaise.* **5** *Faire baraque:* To fail. *Il s'est lancé dans la limonade, mais comme dans tout ce qu'il tâtait à fait baraque!* He tried his luck running a pub, but as with all his ventures he made a cock-up of it! **6** *Casser la baraque (th.):* To 'bring the house down', to be a roaring success.

baraqué *adj. Etre bien baraqué:* To be well-built, to be very muscular.

baratin *n.m.* **1** 'Patter', smooth talking. *Arrêtez votre baratin, j'attends mon ami!* Stop chatting me up, I'm waiting for my boy-friend! **2** Sales talk. (The 1950s film *Le Baratin* with Roger

Nicolas as an enthusiastic *camelot* increased this word's popularity.)

baratiner *v.trans.* **1** To 'chat someone up', to 'sweet-talk' someone. **2** To 'shoot a line', to persuade someone through glib talking (i.e. sales patter).

baratineur *n.m.* **1** 'Smooth-talker', one who is good at chatting up the birds. **2** 'Glib-talker', persuasive person.

barbant *adj.* Boring. *Ce qu'il est barbant, ce mec!* That bloke would bore the pants off anyone! *C'est barbant de vivre à la campagne!* Life in the country's pretty monotonous! (also: *rasant*).

barbaque *n.f.* *(pej.)*: **1** Cheap cut of meat. **2** *De la barbaque*: Low-class prostitutes (literally in the language of the slave-trader 'meat for sale').

barbe *n.m.* Pimp, ponce, procurer.

barbe *n.f.* **1** *Barbe alors!* Damn! – Blast! **2** *C'est la barbe!* What a bore! – It's a pain in the neck! *C'est la barbe, mais il faut que je rentre!* It's a drag, but I have to go home! **3** *Vieille barbe*: Old 'fuddy-duddy', old fogey. **4** *Rire dans sa barbe*: To laugh up one's sleeve. **5** *Faire une barbe à quelqu'un*: To 'take someone for a ride', to fool someone. **6** *Barbe à papa*: Candy-floss.

barbe *adj.inv.* (of person, event or situation): Dreary, boring.

barbeau *n.m.* Pimp, ponce, procurer.

barbelouses *n.f.pl.* (also: *barbelouzes*): Barbed wire.

barber *v.trans.* To 'bore the pants off someone'. (It is interesting to note that an exact equivalent to *barber* is *raser*. See *rasant*.)

barberot *n.m.* Barber, gents' hairdresser (also: *merlan*).

barbichette *n.f.* 'Goatee', small pointed beard. (This word occurs in a child's rhyme and game where two children hold each other's chin and say: *'Je te tiens, tu me tiens par la barbichette; le premier qui rira aura une tapette!'*)

barbillon *n.m.* *(pej.)*: Young pimp.

barbiquet *n.m.* *(pej.)*: Small-time pimp.

barbischnock *n.m.* *(joc.)*: 'Fungus-face', bearded person.

Barbiturique *Proper name.* *Le Barbiturique* is a famous café situated near the School of Pharmacy in Paris. (There is a double dose of humour in the name. See *biture*.)

barbote *n.f.* **1** Body search to which arrested persons or convicts are subjected prior to incarceration. **2** (Underworld slang): Compulsory medical check to which prostitutes have to submit regularly.

barboter *v.intrans.* To be in a muddle, to be confused. *Après que sa bonne femme ait eu mis les bouts, il barbotait en plein cafard*: After his missus

left him he was so depressed and muddled he didn't know which way to turn.

barboter *v.trans.* To 'nick', to 'pinch', to steal. *Il s'est fait barboter sa toquante*: He got his watch nicked.

barboteur *n.m.* **1** Pilferer, petty thief. **2** Kleptomaniac.

barbotin *n.m.* Loot, booty, proceeds from robbery.

barbouille *n.f.* **1** *(Slightly pej.)*: 'Daubing', Sunday painting. **2** *Etre dans la barbouille*: To be 'in a pickle', to be 'bunkered', to be in a difficult situation.

barbouillé *n.m.* 'Greenhorn', young inexperienced person.

barbouillé *adj.* *Se sentir barbouillé* (also: *avoir le cœur/l'estomac barbouillé*): To feel 'queasy', to feel sick. *Après la nouba d'hier soir, c'est pas étonnant si tu te sens barbouillé!* If you're feeling off-colour today, look no further than last night's binge!

barbouiller *v.trans.reflex.* **1** To put make-up on. **2** *Se barbouiller l'estomac*: To upset one's stomach. **3** *Je m'en barbouille!* I couldn't give a damn! – I couldn't care less!

barbouilleur *n.m.* 'Dauber', painter with little talent. (This derogatory appellation was and is often directed at gifted yet misunderstood artists.)

barbouse *n.f.* (also: *barbouze*): **1** 'Face-fungus', beard. **2** Secret agent. (The 1960s film *Les barbouzes* with Lino Ventura firmly established this word in colloquial speech.)

barbu *n.m.* **1** *Le Barbu*: God Almighty, God the Father. **2** King (in pack of cards). *Avec son carré de barbus en main, il pouvait se permettre de rigoler*: With four kings in his hand, he could well afford to laugh.

barca *interj.* (also: *barka*): Lay off! – Cut it out! – Stop it!

barda *n.m.* **1** *(mil.)*: Kit, pack. **2** Personal belongings. *Je l'ai mis à la porte avec tout son barda*: I kicked him out with all his clobber. **3** Banknote of small denomination.

bardane *n.f.* Bedbug. *Pas moyen de dormir, toute la nuit y a eu un congrès de bardanes sous les draps!* I didn't get a wink of sleep all night; the bedbugs were holding a rally!

barder *v.intrans.* *Ça va barder!* Things are going to get hot! – There's trouble brewing! (This expression was made popular in the early 50s as the title of a film starring Eddie Constantine.) *Ça va barder pour toi!* You're going to cop it!

barguigner *v.intrans.* To 'haggle', to bargain. *Ils ont casqué sans barguigner*: They coughed up without quibbling.

barjo *n.m.* 'Mug', 'sucker', fool. *Quel barjo, on pourrait lui faire chercher la clef des champs!* What a burk, you could ask him to fill in the cannon report and he'd try!

barlu *n.m.* **1** 'Tub', steamer, steamship. **2** 'Gang-bang', collective rape.

barnum *n.m.* **1** *Montrer tout son barnum*: To 'flash', to indecently expose oneself. **2** *Quel barnum!* What a cock-up! – What a shambles!

baron *n.m.* Street-hawker's associate whose enthusiastic 'buying' sets the ball rolling.

baronner *v.intrans.* (Hawkers' slang): To get the suckers buying, to act as a *baron*.(See that word.)

baroud *n.m.* **1** 'Scrap', brawl, fight. **2** Hostilities in warfare. **3** *Un baroud d'honneur*: A face-saving last stand. (Meanings of the expression can range from the strictly literal to the figurative where no violent actions are involved.)

barouder *v.intrans.* **1** To go soldiering, to be full-time in the army. **2** To 'scrap', to fight.

barouf *n.m.* 'Hullabaloo', uproar. *Faire un barouf du diable*: To make one hell of a din.

barque *n.f.* *Mener quelqu'un en barque (fig.)*: To 'lead someone up the garden path', to deliberately deceive someone (also: *mener quelqu'un en bateau*).

barquette *n.f.* Sponge cream-cake with a short-crust base.

barrabille *n.f.* Brawl, disturbance. *Mettre la barrabille*: To cause a shindy.

barraqué *adj.* *Etre bien barraqué* (of man): To be hefty, well-built, to be very muscular. (The English 'to be built like a brick shit-house' is derogatory, the French expression is not.)

barre *n.f.* **1** *Avoir le coup de barre*: To be 'knackered', 'whacked', to feel worn out. *Quand on est de nuit, il n'est pas rare d'avoir le coup de barre vers quatre heures du mat'*: When you're on nights, it's not unusual to feel all-in at around 4 a.m. **2** *A toute barre*: At full-pelt, at breakneck speed (also: *A toutes pompes*). **3** *Homme de barre*: Staunch friend. (One who, like the helmsman, can be relied upon to stick by you through thick and thin.) **4** *Zéro la barre!* No dice! –Nothing doing! – Certainly not!

barreau *n.m.* **1** *Barreau de chaise*: Fat cigar. **2** *Mener une vie de barreau de chaise*: To live it up, to lead a fast and furious life.

barrer *v.pronom.* To 'bugger off', to 'buzz off', to go away (usually in haste). *Il faut que je me barre!* I'll have to be off!

barreur *n.m.* 'Chucker-outer', bouncer.

Bar-Tabac *n.m.* *Fier comme Bar-Tabac (joc.)*: As cocky as hell, bursting with pride. (This is a

jocular corruption of the *'Fier comme Artaban'* saying; another witty version is *'Fier comme un petit banc'*.)

bas *adj.* **1** *Les bas morceaux (iron.)*: The 'privates', the private parts. **2** *Etre bas du cul (joc.)*: To be a 'short-arse', to be exceptionally small in stature.

basane *n.f.* **1** 'Hide', (human) skin. **2** 'Birthday suit', 'the altogether', total nakedness. **3** *Tailler une basane*: To make an obscene gesture. (Where the English have a two-finger sign of derision, the French manage with one.)

bascule *n.f.* **1** Squealer, informant. **2** *La bascule à Charlot*: The guillotine (also: *L'abbaye de Monte-à-regret*).

basculer *v.trans.* *Basculer un godet*: To 'wet one's whistle', to have a quick drink.

basduc *n.m.* *(abbr. bas-du-cul)*: 'Short-arse', 'shrimp', pint-size person.

basique *adj.* Unsophisticated, lacking refinement. *L'amour pour lui, c'est un truc assez basique*: He has a crude outlook on love.

basoche *n.f.* *La basoche*: The legal fraternity. *Avant d'être avocat derrière-les-barreaux, il était de la basoche*: Before doing time, he used to make a living as a barrister.

basse *adj.f.* *La terre est basse! (iron.)*: It's all graft in this life! (The expression obviously refers to the weary toil of the farmer.)

basses *n.f.pl.* *Doucement les basses!* **a** Not so loud! – Keep your voice down! **b** There's no need to exaggerate!

bassinant *adj.* Boring. *Quand il se lance dans ses 'souvenirs de guerre', 'y a pas plus bassinant*: I don't know anything more boring than his 'how-I-won-the-war-single-handed' stories.

bassiner *v.trans.* To bore someone stiff.

bassinet *n.m.* *Cracher au bassinet*: To 'fork out', to pay up. *J'en ai marre de douiller, maintenant il va falloir qu'il crache au bassinet!* It's always muggins who pays the bill, from now on he'll have to cough up!

bassinoire *n.f.* 'Pain-in-the-neck', boring person.

basta *interj.* Cut it out! – Lay off! – Stop it!

Bastoche Proper name. *La Bastoche*: The Bastille, the *quartier de la Bastille* in Paris.

baston *n.m.* **1** 'Backhander', slap. *Envoyer un baston*: To give someone a belt round the ear-hole. **2** Punch-up, brawl, fight.

bastonnade *n.f.* Punch-up, brawl, fight.

bastonner *v.trans.* To 'roust', to shower with blows.

bastos *n.f.* Bullet. (*Bastos* is the brand-name of a rather substantial-looking cigarette.) *Il a chopé une bastos dans le plafond*: He got shot through the head.

bastosser *v.trans.* To blast, to shoot at.

bastringue n.m. **1** 'Clobber', 'gear', belongings. *Ils sont partis en vacances avec tout leur bastringue:* They went on holiday with everything bar the kitchen sink. **2** 'Barney', 'shindy', furore. **3** 'Dance-joint', rough-and-ready dance-hall. **4** Juke-box. (The song *'Mes deux thunes dans le bastringue'*, a hit of the 50s, gave the word instant popularity.)

Bataclan *Proper name.* Le Bataclan: This famous Parisian music-hall was renowned for popular audience participation, very much like the Leeds City Varieties.

bataclan n.m. *Et tout le bataclan!* And the whole shebang! – And the whole bloody lot!

bataillon n.m. *Inconnu au bataillon:* This expression meaning 'never heard of him (her) before' is very much a catch-phrase.

bat'd'Af' n.m. *(mil.,* also: *badaf,* abbr. *Bataillon d'Afrique.):* **1** Disciplinary unit stationed in North Africa. **2** Soldier serving in that unit.

bateau n.m. **1** 'Kerb-flat', set of lowered kerb-stones enabling smooth vehicle access from road to private property. **2** *(pl.):* 'Boats', outsize shoes. **3** *(pl.):* 'Plates of meat', feet (usually large ones). **4** 'Eye-wash', cock-and-bull story. *Monter un bateau à quelqu'un:* To pull someone's leg (also: *mener quelqu'un en bateau).* **5** *Du même bateau:* Of the same ilk, very similar. *Ils sont un peu du même bateau!* They're very much birds of a feather! **6** *Du dernier bateau:* 'Bang-up-to-date', very modern. *Il se fringue du dernier bateau:* He wears the very latest gear.

bath adj.inv. **1** 'A-1', first-rate, superb. *Une bath mousmé:* A smashing bird. *C'est une bath affaire!* It's a great opportunity. **2** Bloody awful, appalling. *Pauvre mec, il lui est arrivé un bath machin!* Poor bugger! He's had a rotten setback! (This antiphrastic meaning is only noticeable within context and intonation.)

bathment adv. 'Terribly', incredibly, very.

bathouze adj. (also: *bathouse):* 'A-1', first-rate, superb.

batifoler v.intrans. To frolic, to gambol. *Il n'a jamais voulu se ranger des voitures, il a passé sa vie à batifoler de jupe en jupe!* He never did settle down, he spent his life flitting from one bird to another!

bâtiment n.m. *Etre du bâtiment (fig.):* To be an authority on something, to be an expert at a trade or skill. *Fais-lui confiance, il est du bâtiment!* You can trust him, he knows his onions!

bat-la-dèche n.m. Hobo, tramp.

bâton n.m. **1** *(corr. abbr. bataillon). Il n'est pas de ce bâton:* He's not from this outfit. (Originally an expression confined exclusively to the military, it is occasionally encountered elsewhere.) **2** *Bâton de maréchal (fig.):* High point of a career. *Ça a été son bâton de maréchal:* It was his finest hour. **3** *Bâton creux* (Poachers' slang): Gun. **4** *Mettre les bâtons:* To 'bugger off', to 'buzz off', to go away in haste (also: *mettre les bouts).* **5** *Mettre des bâtons dans les roues à quelqu'un (fig.):* To 'put a spoke in someone's wheel', to thwart someone's endeavours. **6** *Onze, les bâtons!* (Gambling and racing slang): Legs eleven! **7** *Mener une vie de bâton de chaise:* To 'live it up', to lead a fast and furious life. **8** *C'est un vrai bâton merdeux!* I wouldn't touch him with a barge-pole! – He's a despicable character! **9** 'Joystick', 'cock', penis. **10** Unit of 10,000 francs (prior to the 1958 remonetization, the unit is 1,000,000 francs). **11** (Underworld slang): Prohibition from entering a specific area imposed on certain ex-convicts.

bâtonné past part. *Etre bâtonné* (Underworld slang): To be prohibited from entering certain areas. (The legal term for this restriction is *interdiction de séjour.)*

batousard n.m. (also: *batouzard):* Street-trader, travelling hawker.

batouse n.f. (also: *batouze). Faire la batouse:* To work the markets, to have a stall in several markets throughout the week.

battage n.m. *Faire du battage:* To 'plug', to boost, to do a big promotions job.

battant n.m. **1** 'Ticker', heart (also: *palpitant).* **2** Tongue. *Avoir un sacré battant:* To have the gift of the gab. **3** 'Heavy', muscleman (individual whose awe-inspiring muscular physique gets him all the tough jobs. In the boxing fraternity *un battant* is a powerful puncher with plenty of stamina). **4** *Avoir du battant:* To be full of fight, to be not lacking in stamina. **5** *Se remplir le battant:* To 'stuff one's face', to have a good tuck-in. (*Battant* here refers to the stomach but does not have this meaning on its own.)

battant adj.inv. *Battant neuf:* Brand spanking new.

battant adv. 'On the dot', right on time. *Il s'est radiné à huit heures battant:* He got there right on the stroke of eight.

batterie n.f. *Une batterie de cuisine (joc.):* A chestful of medals.

batteur n.m. **1** Percussionist (in a band). **2** 'Fibber', liar. **3** Tout. (The word refers to the kind of shady procurer who introduces nightclub visitors to 'likely ladies'.)

batteuse n.f. Car battery.

battoir n.m. *Battoir à œufs (joc.):* 'Chopper', 'copter', helicopter.

battoirs *n.m.pl.* 'Ham-like mitts', heavy clumsy hands.

battre *v.trans. & intrans.* **1** *Battre quelqu'un à plate(s) couture(s)*: To 'beat someone hollow', to defeat someone convincingly. **2** *Battre quelqu'un comme plâtre*: To give someone a good thrashing. **3** To tell 'tall stories', to fib, to lie. **4** *Battre à Niort*: To deny something vehemently. *Il battait à Niort que c'était pas lui le coupable*: He swore blind he was innocent. **5** *Battre comtois*: **a** To play dumb, to feign ignorance. **b** To state untruths in order to get to the truth. **6** *Battre le dingue*: To feign insanity in order to avoid a sentence on the grounds of diminished responsibility. **7** *Battre son quart* (of prostitute): To be out soliciting.

battu *adj. Avoir un air* (also: *une allure*) *de chien battu*: To have a 'hang-dog look', to look crestfallen and morose.

bauche *n.m.* Safe, strongbox (also: *bauge*).

bauches *n.f.pl.* Playing cards. *Brouiller les bauches*: To 'give the deck a good mix', to shuffle the cards.

bavacher *v.intrans.* To 'yap', to 'natter on and on', to talk endlessly.

bavacheur *n.m.* 'Gasbag', 'yapper', over-talkative person.

bavacheur *adj.* 'Gassy', over-talkative.

bavard *n.m.* **1** 'Mouthpiece', barrister. *Avec un bavard comme le sien, Jo n'avait pas volé son titre de 'roi du non-lieu'*: Joe's clean 'form-sheet' owed much to the skill of his counsel. **2** 'Rod', 'shooter', handgun.

bavarde *n.f.* **1** 'Licker', 'clapper', tongue. **2** Letter, item of correspondence.

bavasser *v.intrans.* To 'yap', to 'natter on', to talk endlessly. *Bavasser, c'était son fort, on l'avait surnommé 'la voix de son maître'*: His endless prattle had earned him the nickname of 'Rent-a-Gob'.

bavau *adj.m.* 'Smashing', good-looking. *Un peu qu'il est bavau, son mec!* Her boyfriend is rather dishy!

bavelle *adj.f.* 'Smashing', good-looking. *Elle est un chouïa bavelle!* She's a right corker!

baver *v.trans. & intrans.* **1** To 'natter', to chatter, to talk endlessly. **2** To 'backbite', to talk behind someone's back. **3** *En baver*: **a** To 'graft', to work very hard. **b** To be green with envy. **c** To be 'hopping mad', to be furious. **d** To be 'flabbergasted', to be astounded. (Another more picturesque alternative with this meaning is *en baver des ronds de chapeau*.) **4** *En faire baver à quelqu'un*: To make someone's life a misery.

bavette *n.f.* **1** Cheap yet tasty cut of beef taken near the sirloin. (The *bavette* and the *araignée* are sought-after morsels appreciated by connoisseurs who attach little importance to the unappetising appearance of those cuts.) **2** *Tailler une bavette*: To have a 'chinwag', to have a 'natter', to have a little chat.

baveuse *n.f.* 'Licker', 'clapper', tongue.

baveux *n.m.* **1** Newspaper. *Il s'est tapé cinq colonnes à la une sur le baveux*: He hit the front-page headlines. **2** Soap. *Comme baveux, tout ce qu'on avait c'était du Marseille!* No fancy soap for us, just the ordinary laundry bar!

bavocher *v.intrans.* **1** To slobber. *Il bavochait à la vue de toute cette boustifaille*: All that grub made his mouth water. **2** To 'natter', to chatter, to talk endlessly.

bavocheux *n.m.* 'Mouthpiece', barrister.

bavonnet *n.m.* 'Gob', 'trap', mouth.

bavour *adj.* Good-looking.

bavure *n.f.* **1** 'Boob', blunder. *Il a fait une de ces bavures!* He really put his foot in it! **2** *C'est net et sans bavure!* It's as plain as a pikestaff! – It couldn't be clearer!

bayard *n.m.* (*pol.*): Bullet-proof shield.

bazar *n.m.* **1** Place of work (factory, office, etc.). **2** School, college. **3** Sexual organs. (This vague euphemism can refer either to the privates – *Il a déballé tout son bazar*: He exposed himself – or to the vagina.) **4** *Tout le bazar*: The whole bag of tricks, everything. *J'en ai marre de tout ce bazar!* I'm fed up with the whole shebang! **5** *Faire du bazar*: **a** To make a din, to make a lot of noise. **b** To 'kick up a row', to remonstrate loudly.

Bazar Proper name. (abbr. *le Bazar de l'Hôtel de Ville*.) This famous Paris department store is better known by its initials B.H.V.

bazarder *v.trans.* **1** To 'chuck out', to get rid of. **2** To sell off cheaply.

beau *adj. Eh bien, nous voilà beaux!* (*iron.*): Well, look at the mess we're in!

beau-dab *n.m.* Father-in-law.

beauf' *n.m.* (*abbr. beau-frère*): Brother-in-law.

Beaujolpif *n.m.* Beaujolais wine (also: *beaujol'*).

beauté *n.f.* **1** *Se refaire une beauté*: To 'put one's face on', to put make-up on. **2** *Faire quelque chose en beauté*: To do something with panache. *Terminer en beauté*: To quit on a winning streak.

bébé *n.m.* **1** *Bébé rose* (*joc.*): 'Greenhorn', novice, inexperienced person. (The interjection *salut, bébé rose!* has connotations of gentle endearment and is best translated by 'Hello there, cheeky chops!') **2** *Gros bébé, va!* (*joc.*): You big softy! – You silly thing!

Bébert Proper name. Bertie, Bert.

bébête adj. 'Dead-easy', simple. C'est un machin tout ce qu'il y a de bébête! There's nothing to it really!

bec n.m. **1** 'Conk', 'hooter', nose. Gommer du bec: To be extremely short-sighted (literally to erase with one's nose when writing). **2** 'Gob', 'trap', mouth. Etre un fin-bec: To be something of a gourmet. Se rincer le bec: To have 'a quick one', to down a drink. Puer du bec: To have foul breath, to suffer from halitosis. **3** Filer un bec: To give a 'peck', to give a quick kiss. **4** Se retrouver le bec dans l'eau: To 'come unstuck', to be left in the lurch. **5** Tomber sur un bec: To 'come a cropper', to come to grief. **6** Bec verseur: 'Prick', 'cock', penis.

bécane n.f. **1** Bike, bicycle. **2** Typewriter. Il martyrisait sa bécane: He was bashing away at his tripe-writer!

bécasse n.f. (pej.): 'Silly moo', stupid girl. (The woodcock is deemed to be an extremely silly bird.)

bécassine n.f. 'Silly little girl'. (Bécassine was a famous cartoon character whose antics have endeared her to children for over fifty years.)

bêchage n.m. 'Swanking', showing off. Il donne dans le bêchage: He likes strutting about.

béchamel n.f. (fig.): 'Sticky situation'. Il se trouvait dans une méchante béchamel: He was in a right old fix.

béchamel adj. 'Show-off', pretentious.

bêche n.f. Jeter de la bêche: To 'throw one's weight about' and behave in an arrogant manner.

bêcher v.trans. To 'have a dig' at someone, to attack someone verbally (usually in their absence).

bêcher v.intrans. **1** To 'throw one's weight about', to swank, to show off. **2** Bêcher d'arrache-pied: To work hard without letting up.

bêcheur n.m. **1** 'Swank', show-off. **2** 'Muck-raker', scandal-monger. **3** 'Slogger', hard-worker. **4** (abbr. avocat bêcheur): Public prosecutor in a trial.

bêcheur adj. **1** 'Swanky', pretentious. Il n'y a pas plus bêcheur que lui, côté bagnole! He's a real Flash Harry when it comes to cars. **2** Evil-minded. **3** Hard-working.

béchigne n.f. 'Pill', rugby ball.

bécot n.m. 'Peck', kiss. Bécot timbreur (joc.): Big wet kiss. (Because it oozes enough moisture to wet a postage stamp.)

bécotage n.m. 'Snogging', 'billing and cooing', necking.

bécoter v.trans. To kiss.

bécoter v.trans.reflex. To exchange a kiss.

bectance n.f. (also: becquetance): 'Eats', 'nosh', food. J'en ai ralbol de cette bectance à la noix! I'm fed up with this rotten grub!

becter v.trans. & intrans. (also: becqueter): **1** To eat. (According to context, the meanings can range from having a bite to eat, to stuffing one's face.) **2** En becter: **a** To be an informer (also: bouffer à la grande gamelle). **b** To live off prostitution (also: bouffer du pain de fesses). **c** To engage in sodomy.

bedaine n.f. 'Corporation', paunch, pot-belly.

bédame interj. You bet! – And how! – Of course!

bédi n.m. (Romany slang): Gendarme, country policeman.

bédoler v.intrans. To have 'the shits', 'the runs', to have a bout of diarrhoea.

bedon n.m. Pot-belly, paunch.

bégaler v.trans.reflex. To 'kid oneself', to deceive oneself.

bégonias n.m.pl. Cherrer dans les bégonias (joc.): To 'come it a bit strong', to exaggerate.

bégueule adj. 'Prim and proper', prudish.

béguin n.m. **1** Sweetheart, loved one. **2** Avoir le béguin pour quelqu'un: To be 'spoony' over someone, to have fallen in love.

béguineuse n.f. Soft-hearted prostitute (the one who on occasion might give her services free of charge. The expression 'Je me le suis fait au béguin' illustrates the genuine feelings of the prostitute in question).

beigne n.f. 'Biff', 'clout', blow. Filer une beigne (à quelqu'un): To give a 'knuckle sandwich', to belt, to hit someone.

bêlant n.m. 'Bleater', perpetual moaner.

Belgico n.m. 'Sprout', Belgian.

belle n.f. **1** 'Decider', deciding game (in sport, cards, etc.). **2** Se faire la belle: To 'break out', to escape from jail. (Freedom to the ex-con is known as la belle, parole or conditional release as la demi-belle; the term for unconditional release is la belle des belles.) **3** Mener quelqu'un en belle: To intentionally lead someone into a trap.

belle adj. **1** L'avoir belle: To be 'onto a cushy number', to have it easy. Vous, les hauts fonctionnaires, vous l'avez belle! You chaps at the Ministry, you're riding on the gravy train! Se la faire belle: **a** To 'lead the life of Riley', to lead an easy life. **b** To 'paint the town red', to go on a spree. **2** L'avoir de belle: To be 'on a winning ticket', to have a highly successful run.

belle-doche n.f. Mother-in-law. (Excepting the inevitable witticisms associated with this status, the word has no pejorative connotations.)

belles n.f.pl. En conter de belles: To tell some 'tall stories', to indulge in some pretty outlandish verbal fantasising.

belote n.f. Belote, rebelote et dix de der! This call at the card game of belote punctuating the disclosure of a winning hand, is sometimes uttered colloquially when verbal reference is made to an overwhelming victory in a different field of endeavour.

ben *adv. (corr. bien)*: Ben quoi?! So what?!

bénard *n.m.* 'Strides', pants, trousers. *Chier dans son bénard*: To get in a blue funk, to be shaking with fear.

bénef *n.m. (abbr. bénéfice)*: Return, profits. *Mini-bénefs*: 'Perks', incidental benefits.

béni oui-oui *n.m.* 'Yes-man', creep (the kind of character who lets the boss pass all decisions on the nod).

bénitier *n.m.* 'Fanny', 'pussy', vagina.

bénouse *n.m.* (also: *bénouze*): 'Strides', pants, trousers.

béquillarde *n.f. La béquillarde*: The guillotine (because its shape is reminiscent of someone on crutches).

béquille *n.f.* 1 'Pin', 'gamb', leg. *Avoir les béquilles en guimauve*: To be 'wonky on one's legs', to feel unsteady. 2 *(pol.)*: Unexpected snag, last-minute hitch.

béquiller *v.trans.* 1 To 'nosh', to eat. 2 *(fig.)*: To go through one's money (literally to eat one's capital).

berdouille *n.f.* 1 Slush, mud (also: *gadoue*). 2 'Corporation', paunch, pot-belly.

bérésina *n.f.* Major 'cock-up', sizeable disaster. (The word originates from the humiliating crossing of the Berezina river by retreating Napoleonic troops in November 1812.)

berge *n.f.* Year. (For obvious reasons, the word is nearly always encountered in the plural. Maurice Chevalier, 1888–1972, in the song '*A 75 berges*' increased that word's popularity with a very personal celebration of his 75th birthday.)

bergère *n.f.* 1 'Lassie', girl, woman. (According to context, the word can refer to one's girlfriend, one's wife or even a prostitute.) 2 Winning switch-card slipped to a gambler by an accomplice in a game of poker.

bergougnan *n.m.* 'Shoe-leather', tough meat.

berline *n.f. (joc.)*: 'Demoted' pram used by *clochards* for collecting the rag-and-bone articles from which they make a living.

berlingot *n.m.* 1 Tetrahedral-shaped boiled sweet for which Carpentras in Provence is famous. 2 Any tetrahedral-shaped container, e.g. *un berlingot de lait*. 3 Boil, carbuncle. 4 'Clit', clitoris. 5 'Banger', decrepit old car.

berlingue *n.m.* Virginity. *Avoir perdu son berlingue (joc. & fig.)*: To have seen a bit of the world, to be anything but a novice.

berlue *n.f.* 1 'Cover', blanket. (Originally, the word referred to bedclothes but has come to

mean the cloth on which dice or card games are played. *Taper la berlue*: To fix a game of dice.) 2 'Front' for illegal activities. *Même avant de se ranger, il s'était toujours trouvé de bonnes berlues*: Even before he 'retired' he was never short of a good cover for his 'activities'. 3 *Filer ses berlues*: To give away the tricks of the trade. 4 *Faire berlue*: To submit to homosexual advances.

berluer *v.trans.* To quiz, to question.

berlurer *v.trans.reflex.* 1 To 'kid oneself', to live in hope. *Si tu t'imagines qu'il va te marida, tu te berlures!* If you think he's going to pop the question, you're kidding yourself! 2 To lead a Walter Mitty type life, to live a life of dreams.

bernard *n.m.* 'Bum', 'arse', bottom.

berne *n.f. Avoir le slip en berne (joc.)*: To be impotent (literally to have one's penis at half-mast).

bernicles *n.f.pl.* 'Specs', spectacles, glasses.

bernique *interj.* No dice! – Not bloody likely! –It's out of the question!

bertelot *n.m.* Vice-squad officer, policeman working for the *Brigade des mœurs*.

berzingue *n.m.* (also: *bersingue*) *Aller à tout berzingue*: To 'go like the clappers', to 'go full-pelt', to go very fast.

bésef *adv. Pas bésef*: Not a lot, very little. *'y a pas bésef de bénefs!* There's not much profit in it!

besogner *v.intrans.* To 'screw', to fuck, to have intercourse.

besoins *n.m.pl. Faire ses besoins*: To 'attend to a call of nature'. (This can refer to either of the excretory functions.)

besouille *n.f.* Belt. *Serrer la besouille d'un cran (fig.)*: To have to make do (literally to have to tighten one's belt).

bessif *adv.* (also: *bécif*): Through coercion. *Aboule le fric, et bessif!* I want the money now and no messing! (This adverb also carries a connotation of immediacy.)

bestiau *n.m. (joc.)*: 'Beastie', creature, animal.

bestiole *n.f.* 'Creepy-crawly', insect.

bêta *n.m.* 1 'Silly git', stupid so-and-so. 2 *Gros bêta, va!* (term of endearment): You silly-billy!

bêta *adj.* 'Thick', silly, stupid. (The feminine *bêtasse* is sometimes encountered.)

bête *n.f.* 1 *Bête à concours*: a *(sch.)*: 'Exam nut', examination fiend, glutton for exams. b 'Sexy bird', beautiful woman. 2 *Faire la bête à deux dos*: To have sex, to have intercourse. 3 *Chercher la petite bête*: To 'go nit-picking', to be 'finicky', to be pernickety. 4 *Faire 'la petite bête qui monte, qui monte'*: To play 'tickles'.

bête *adj.* 1 *C'est bête comme chou!* It's as easy as pie! – It's dead simple! 2 *Pas si bête!* Not on your nelly! – Certainly not! (This expression got a new lease of life when it became the title of a film with Bourvil after the Second World War.)

béton *n.m.* **1** *(sch.)*: Stodge, stodgy food. **2** *Faire du béton*: **a** To live for a long time in the same place. **b** (Football): To play a packed defence, to pull the whole team back on defence.

betterave *n.f.* **1** 'Hooter', red nose. **2** *Une betterave*: A 'bottle of plonk', a bottle of red wine. **3** 'Nurk', 'twit', simpleton.

betting *n.m.* Place where illegal bookmakers congregate on a racecourse. (Gambling is a State monopoly in France.)

beuglant *n.m.* Seedy cabaret, the kind of noisy establishment where second-rate floor shows are the norm.

beuglante *n.f.* Rowdy song (the kind of noisy chant where harmonies are of little importance).

beugler *v.trans. & intrans.* To 'bawl', to shout.

beugne *n.f.* 'Biff', 'clout', blow.

beurre *n.m.* **1** 'Brass', 'loot', money. *Faire son beurre*: To 'make one's pile', to amass a fortune. *Il ne manque pas de beurre!* He's loaded. **2** *Un beurre*: A kind bloke, an easy-going and uncomplicated man. **3** *C'est un beurre que . . .* What a stroke of luck that . . . **4** *Ça fait mon beurre!* That suits me down to the ground! – That's fine by me!

beurré *adj.* 'Pissed', 'sozzled', drunk.

beurrée *n.f. Ramasser une beurrée*: To 'get a skinful', to have too much to drink.

beurrer *v.trans. Se faire beurrer*: To get run over by a car. (The unpleasant image evoked is not for the squeamish.)

beurrer *v.trans.reflex.* **1** To get 'pickled', 'sozzled', to become inebriated. **2** *(fig.)*: To 'take the lion's share', to keep most of the profits for oneself.

bézef *adv. Pas bézef*: Not a lot, very little. *'y a pas bézef de bouffetance!* The cupboard's bare!

bibard *n.m.* **1** 'Old fogey', doddering old man. **2** 'Old soak', perpetually inebriated old man.

bibelots *n.m.pl.* **1** Burglar's tool-kit. **2** 'Wedding-tackle', male sexual organs.

Bibendum *Proper name.* Nickname given to the Michelin logo-figure whose ample proportions seem to be delineated by a series of 'spare tyres'. (The word has become generic for a 'fatso', any outrageously fat man.)

biber *v.trans.* To 'con', to swindle, to cheat. *Il m'a bibé en beauté!* He really pulled a neat one on me!

biberon *n.m.* **1** *(joc.)*: Bottle of booze (any alcoholic beverage). **2** 'Old soak', perpetually inebriated old man.

biberonner *v.trans. & intrans.* To 'tipple', to 'booze', to drink.

bibi *n.m.* **1** *(mil.)*: Private, ordinary soldier. (The word is deemed to be a corrupt abbreviation of *bidasse*.) **2** Woman's hat. **3** Me, myself. *Touche pas, c'est pour bibi!* Hands off, that's mine! **4** *(corr. abbr. bise)*: 'Peck', kiss. **5** *(pl.)*: Skeleton keys. (The kind used for dishonest purposes.)

Bibi *Proper name. Bibi Fricotin* is the colourful 'likely lad' of the cartoon strip of that name.

Bibici *Proper name. La Bibici*: The British Broadcasting Corporation. (Another jocular corruption born during World War II and still very much in existence is *l'abbé baissé*.)

bibine *n.f.* **1** 'Cat's-pee', cheap and rather tasteless wine. **2** Undistinguished warm beverage (the kind that leaves one wondering whether it is tea or coffee).

bibli *n.f. (abbr. bibliothèque)*: Public library.

bic *n.m.* **1** *(pej.)*: Arab (native of North Africa). **2** 'Biro', ball-point pen.

bicause *prep.* Because of. *J'ai fait ça bicause le fric!* I did it for the dough!

biche *n.f.* **1** *Ma biche*: My darling. **2** 'Bird', young woman. (*Les Biches* was a 70s film dealing with lesbianism.)

bicher *v.trans.* To grab hold of, to seize. *Elle m'a biché par l'aileron*: She grabbed my arm.

bicher *v.intrans.* **1** To be 'chuffed', to be as pleased as Punch. *Ça me fait vraiment bicher que t'es des nôtres!* I'm right pleased you've joined us! **2** *Ça biche?* How's tricks? – How's everything? *Ça biche!* Everything's fine!

bichon *n.m. Mon bichon* (term of endearment): My pet, my darling.

bichonner *v.trans.* To pamper, to look after. *Il adore bichonner sa bagnole*: He spends hours polishing up his car.

bichonner *v.trans.reflex.* To put on one's 'best bib-and-tucker', to get dressed-up.

bichotter *v.trans.* **1** To 'nick', to 'pinch', to steal. *Il s'est fait bichotter son crapaud*: He got his wallet lifted. **2** To cuddle, to hug, to hold tight.

biclo *n.m.* Bike, bicycle (also: *bécane*).

bicoque *n.f.* **1** 'Shack', shanty, ramshackle hut. **2** *(joc.)*: House, dwelling. (The jocularity is commensurate with the grandeur of the residence referred to.)

bicot *n.m. (pej.)*: Arab (native of North Africa).

bidard *n.m.* 'Jammy beggar', lucky so-and-so.

bidard *adj.* 'Jammy', lucky.

bidasse *n.m. (mil.)*: Private, ordinary soldier. (The word gained near-immortality with the music-hall song *'Avec l'ami Bidasse'*.)

bide *n.m.* **1** Paunch, belly. *Avoir du bide*: To have something of a spare tyre. *S'en mettre plein le bide*: To stuff one's face. **2** *Ne rien avoir dans le bide*: To be gutless, to lack courage. **3** *Tomber sur le bide (fig.)*: To 'fall flat on one's face', to 'come a cropper', to suffer disappointment. **4** *Tomber sur un bide*: To 'come unstuck', to hit a snag. **5** *Faire un bide (th.)*: To 'have a flop', to get bad reviews.

bidel *n.m.* 'Gaffer', boss.

bider *v.pronom.* To guffaw, to burst out laughing.

bidet *n.m.* **1** 'Nag', poor horse. (The children's rhyming-game ditty *'A cheval sur mon bidet'* has its equivalent in the English 'Ride a cock-horse'.) **2** *Avoir de l'eau de bidet dans les veines*: To lack spunk, to be gutless, to act as a coward. **3** *C'est de la raclure de bidet! (pej.)*: He's a right little runt!

bidochard *n.m. (pej.)*: 'White slaver' (one who recruits and ships women for prostitution).

bidoche *n.f.* **1** Tough meat (cheap and chewy cut). *C'est une bidoche à défoncer les dominos!* This cut is as tough as old boots! **2** *Sac à bidoche (joc.)*: Sleeping-bag. **3** *De la bidoche (pej.)*: New recruits to prostitution. (This contemptuous term belongs to the language of pimps.)

bidon *n.m.* **1** Paunch, belly. **2** 'Con', confidence trick. **3** *Du bidon*: 'Baloney', 'fibs', lies. *C'est pas du bidon, je te jure!* It's the gospel truth! **4** *Faire le nécessaire pour arranger les bidons*: To take one's precautions, to act cautiously.

bidon *adj.inv.* 'Phoney', fake. *Quand il s'est fait alpaguer, il avait des fafs bidon*: When they nabbed him, he had fake I.D.s.

bidonnant *adj.* 'Rib-tickling', hilarious.

bidonner *v.trans. & intrans.* **1** To 'con', to trick. **2** To tell a pack of lies. **3** To 'booze', to imbibe vast quantities of alcohol. *Un peu qu'il bidonne, ce mec!* He's got a fair sloping gullet!

bidonneur *n.m.* **1** 'Bragger', loud-mouthed boaster. **2** 'Con-merchant', habitual trickster.

bidonville *n.m.* Shanty-town.

bidou *n.m.* **1** Post Office foreman. **2** Dice gambling game.

bière *n.f.* **1** *Ça n'est pas de la petite bière!* It's not to be sneezed at! – It's worth taking notice of! *Ne pas se prendre pour de la petite bière*: To be as conceited as hell. **3** *Bière du Père Adam (joc.)*: 'Corporation pop', 'Adam's ale', water (also: *Château-la-pompe*). **4** *Une bière panachée*: A shandy (also: *un panaché*).

bif *n.m.* **1** Steak, beefsteak. **2** 'Note', banknote. **3** Ticket (for a means of travel or a show).

biffe *n.m.* Clochard who earns a meagre pittance by humping dustbins for the *concierge* of a block of flats. (The *biffe* or *biffin* sometimes makes a bit more money on the side by selling 'choice' items to the 'rag-and-bone' trade.)

biffe *n.f. La biffe*: **a** *(mil.)*: The infantry. *Il est dans la biffe*: He's a foot-slogger. **b** The 'rag-and-bone' trade.

biffer *v.trans. Se faire biffer*: To get 'bumped off', to get killed (literally, to get crossed off the list of the living).

biffeton *n.m.* (also: *bifeton* or *bifton*): **1** 'Note', banknote. *Il avait toujours des biffetons plein les vagues, des gros formats en liasses*: He always had his pockets stuffed with cash, and not just oncers! **2** Ticket (for a means of travel or a show). **3** Note, short letter (also: *bafouille*). **4** *(pl.)*: Playing cards (also: *brêmes*). **5** *(mil.)* *Piquer un biffeton*: To hurt oneself deliberately in order to go on sick leave.

biffin *n.m.* **1** *(mil.)*: 'Foot-slogger', infantryman. **2** *Clochard* paid by a *concierge* to put out on the street dustbins for refuse collection. **3** 'Rag-and-bone man', junk dealer.

bifteck *n.m.* **1** *Gagner son bifteck*: To 'earn one's crust', to earn a living. **2** *La course au bifteck*: 'The rat-race', that frantic scramble for survival in the cold world of business.

bigaille *n.f. De la bigaille*: Small change. *Laisse ça comme pourboire, c'est de la bigaille!* Leave that for a tip, it's only coppers!

bigeard *n.f.* French paratrooper's combat cap named after *Bigeard*, a senior French officer famous for his bravery during the Algerian conflict.

bigler *v.trans. & intrans.* **1** To peer at, to eye, to look at. **2** *Bigler en biais*: To have a squint (also: *avoir les yeux en phares-codes*).

bigleux *n.m.* **1** 'Four-eyes', short-sighted person wearing thick glasses. **2** *(pol.)*: Witness to a crime. *Geler les bigleux*: To 'hold' witnesses.

bigleux *adj.* Short-sighted.

biglotron *n.m.* **1** Magnifying spy-hole. (The kind of optical device that enables a house-holder to see who is on the other side of the door.) **2** *(pol.)*: Room where suspects can unwittingly be observed.

bigne *n.m. Le bigne*: The 'slammer', the 'nick', prison.

bignole *n.m. & f.* Concierge, caretaker.

bignolon *n.m.* 'Screw', prison guard.

bignou *n.m.* 'Blower', phone, telephone. *Filer un coup de bignou*: To give (someone) a ring.

bigntz *n.m.* (also: *bignz*): **1** 'Shemozzle', muddle. **2** 'Blow', setback. *Il m'est arrivé un de ces bigntz*: You'll never guess what happened to me! **3** Brawl, rumpus.

bigophone *n.m.* 'Blower', phone, telephone (also: *bignou*).

bigophoner v.trans. & intrans. To 'give a buzz', to give a ring, to telephone.

bigorne n.f. **1** 'Barney', 'bust-up', fight. Il aime la bigorne: He loves a punch-up. **2** La bigorne: 'The fuzz', the police.

bigorné adj. Mal bigorné: **a** 'Grumpy', moody. T'es drôlement mal bigorné aujourd'hui! What's up with you today? Got out of bed the wrong side? **b** 'Off-colour', 'out of sorts', unwell.

bigorneau n.m. **1** 'Twit', simpleton. **2** 'Blower', phone, telephone. Filer un coup de bigorneau: To give someone a ring. **3** (pol.): Tapped telephone. **4** (pl.): Small change. **5** Se taper des bigorneaux: To be hard-up, to be on the bread-line.

bigorner v.trans. **1** To 'bash up', to thrash, to beat up. **2** To 'bump off', to kill. Il s'est fait bigorner au grand casse-pipe: He copped his lot at the war.

bigorner v.pronom. To 'have a scrap', to fight.

bigornette n.f. De la bigornette (Drugs): 'Snow', cocaine.

bigorneur n.m. Brawler, one who is fond of a punch-up.

bigoudi n.m. **1** Un virtuose du bigoudi (joc. & pej.): Ladies' hairdresser. **2** On l'a travaillée au bigoudi trop chaud! (joc. & iron.): She's bonkers! –She's as mad as a hatter!

bigre interj. Gosh! – Crumbs! (The French and the English are equally twee and dated.)

bigrement adv. 'Awfully', very. C'est bigrement cher: It's darned pricey (also: vachement).

bijou n.m. **1** Mon bijou (term of endearment): My sweety-pie – My darling. **2** Bijoux de famille: 'Marriage prospects', privates. Elle l'a botté dans les bijoux de famille: She kicked him in the goolies.

bijoutier n.m. Un bijoutier du clair de lune (iron.): A cat-burglar. (As the appellation suggests, one who acquires jewellery in the early hours of the morning.)

bilan n.m. Déposer son bilan: To 'croak', to 'snuff it', to die.

bilboque n.m. & f. Concierge, caretaker.

bile n.f. Se faire de la bile: To 'fret', to worry. Te fais pas de bile, mon chou! Keep cool, my darling! (also: se faire de la mousse).

biler v.pronom. To 'fret', to worry. Il se bile pour un rien! He gets upset over the slightest little thing!

bileux adj. Awkward and cantankerous.

billard n.m. **1** Operating table. Passer sur le billard: To get 'opened up', to be operated on. **2** Dévisser son billard: To 'croak', to 'snuff it', to die. **3** Boule de billard: 'Pate', bald head. **4** Ça, c'est du billard! It's as easy as pie! – It's dead simple!

bille n.f. **1** 'Mush', 'dial', face. Avoir une bonne bille: To have a friendly mug. Salut, bille de clown! Hello funny-face! (This meaning of the word is seldom encountered in a pejorative context.) **2** 'Mug', fool, simpleton. C'est une bille de première! He's an A-grade twit! **3** Ne plus avoir toutes ses billes: To be 'soft in the head', to be senile. (The English look-alike expression 'to have lost one's marbles' is not an accurate translation.) **4** Reprendre ses billes: To 'back out', to renege on a decision or promise. Si c'est comme ça, moi je reprends mes billes! If that's the way it's going to be, count me out!

bille adj. 'Dumb', stupid. C'est le plus bille du lot! He's the thickest of the bunch!

biller v.intrans. Biller à fond: To 'go full-pelt', to dash along.

billet n.m. **1** Ten-franc note or multiple of 10 francs. (Prior to the 1958 remonetization, the amount was 1000 francs.) **2** Je vous fiche mon billet que . . . You can bet your bottom dollar that . . . You can take it from me that . . . **3** Prendre un billet de parterre: **a** To fall flat on one's face, to fall down. **b** (fig.): To 'come a cropper', to suffer a setback. **4** Prendre un billet d'absence: **a** To 'take French leave', to leave without permission. **b** To 'pass out', to faint.

billot n.m. **1** 'Mug', fool, simpleton. **2** Ma tête sur le billot! Word of honour! (literally 'Cross my heart and hope to die!').

biloter v.pronom. To 'fret', to worry.

binaise n.f. (abbr. combinaison): Ruse, near-deceitful ploy.

binette n.f. 'Mug', face. Méfie-toi! Il a une sale binette! Watch out! I don't like the look of him!

bing n.m. 'Nick', prison. Se taper dix ans de bing: To do a ten-year stretch.

biniou n.m. **1** 'Squeeze-box', accordion. (The biniou is primarily a set of bagpipes associated with Breton folklore.) **2** 'Blower', phone, telephone. Filer un coup de biniou à quelqu'un: To ring someone up.

binoclard n.m. 'Four-eyes', person wearing glasses.

binze n.m. **1** Weird and strange situation. C'est un drôle de binze! It's a right funny set-up! **2** (pl.): Haricot beans. (The word is, in fact, a phonetic corruption of the English.)

bique n.f. Vieille bique (pej.): 'Old cow', cantankerous old woman.

biquer v.trans. To 'screw', to fuck, to have intercourse with.

biquet n.m. Mon biquet: My lovey-dovey – My pet.

birbe n.m. (pej.): **1** 'Burk', 'twit', imbecile. **2** Vieux birbe: Old fogey, doddering geriatric. (With both meanings, the word has a connotative suggestion of one who wilfully or otherwise inflicts boredom.)

biribi *n.m. (mil.)*: Disciplinary battalion. (Originally the word was a place-name in southern Tunisia where ex-cons and recalcitrant soldiers served their time.)

biroute *n.f.* **1** 'Prick', 'cock', penis. **2** Plastic traffic cone.

bisbille *n.f.* (Petty) quarrel. *Ils sont en bisbille à propos d'une affaire d'héritage*: They're at loggerheads over a will.

Biscaye *Proper name. (corr. asile de Bicêtre)*: This old people's home for the destitute near Paris was formerly a hospital and a prison.

biscope *n.f.* Cap. *Avoir la biscope de traviole*: To have one's cap skew-whiff.

biscottos *n.m.pl.* (also: *biscotteaux*): Biceps (and more generally the muscles of the arms and chest). *Rouler les biscottos*: To swagger about. *Il a les biscottos gonflés au gaz de ville! (joc.)*: He's no he-man!

biscuit *n.m.* **1** 'Ticket', traffic offence fine. *Choper un biscuit*: To get booked. **2** *Tremper le* (also: *son*) *biscuit (joc.)*: To 'have it off', to have intercourse.

bise *n.f.* 'Peck', friendly kiss. (The expression *faire la bise à quelqu'un*, an untranslatable typically Gallic act, means to give someone a resounding kiss on each cheek.)

biseness *n.m.* **1** Job, occupation. **2** 'Racket', shady activity. *Faire le biseness*: To be 'on the game', to be a prostitute. (The word is obviously a corruption of the English 'business'.)

bisenesseuse *n.f.* 'Prozzy', 'tart', prostitute.

biser *v.trans.* To 'peck', to kiss.

Bison Futé *Proper name.* The *Opération Bison Futé* is the jocular name given to the re-routing of heavy traffic on Bank Holidays. (The name *Bison Futé* is intended to suggest a wise Indian chief full of good advice.)

bisou *n.m.* 'Peck', lovey-dovey kiss.

bisquant *adj.* 'Niggling', irking, annoying. *C'est un rien bisquant de se faire rabrouer par une nana!* It's bloody irritating being told off by a bird!

bisque *n.f.* 'Aggro', annoyance. *Depuis qu'il est ici, il a eu bisque sur bisque!* Since he got here, his life has been a succession of petty upsets! *Bisque, bisque, bisque! (iron.)*: Temper, temper! (Originally *'Bisque, bisque, rage!'* was a children's taunt often to be heard on playgrounds.)

bisquer *v.intrans. Faire bisquer quelqu'un*: To 'rub someone up the wrong way', to get someone annoyed.

bistingo *n.m. (corr. bistrot)*: French café, public house.

bistouille *n.f.* **1** 'Cheap booze', inferior alcoholic beverage. **2** Coffee laced with brandy (also: *bistrouille*).

bistouquette *n.f.* 'Prick', 'cock', penis.

bistoureur *n.m. (joc.)*: 'Sawbones', surgeon.

bistre *n.m. (abbr. bistrot)*: **1** French café, public house. **2** *Bistrot* proprietor.

bistroquet *n.m.* Bistrot proprietor. *Comme pas mal de boxeurs retraités, son rêve était d'être bistroquet*: Like many a retired boxer, his idea of the last round was to own a bar!

bistrot *n.m.* **1** Untranslatable word for the French 'local'. *C'est le bistrot du coin*: It's the local boozer. **2** 'Mine host', bistrot proprietor.

bistrote *n.f.* Landlady, proprietress of *bistrot*.

bisuth *n.m.* **1** 'Fresher', first-year student. **2** 'Twit', simpleton.

bite *n.f.* **1** 'Prick', 'cock', penis. **2** *Con à bouffer de la bite (pej.)*: As thick as two short planks. **2** *(pol.)*: Truncheon.

biter *v.trans.* **1** To 'screw', to fuck, to have intercourse with. **2** *Se faire biter*: To get 'conned', to be diddled. **3** *Ne rien biter*: To understand fuck-all, not to understand a single thing (about a topic or issue).

bitos *n.m.* Man's hat. *N'avoir rien sous le bitos*: To be 'as dumb as they come', to be stupid.

bitte *n.f.* **1** 'Prick', 'cock', penis. **2** *Etre con à bouffer de la bitte (pej.)*: To be 'as thick as two short planks'. **3** *(pol.)*: Truncheon.

bitter *v.trans.* **1** To 'screw', to fuck, to have intercourse with. **2** *Se faire bitter*: To get 'conned', to be diddled. **3** *Ne rien bitter*: To understand fuck-all, not to understand a single thing (about a topic or issue).

bitume *n.m.* Pavement. *Fouler le bitume* (of prostitute): To go soliciting.

bitumeuse *n.f.* 'Prozzy', 'hooker', prostitute.

biture *n.f.* **1** State of drunkenness, intoxication. *Tenir une sacrée biture*: To be pissed to the eyeballs. **2** *A toute biture*: 'Full-pelt', at full speed.

biturer *v.pronom.* To 'get pissed', 'sloshed', to get drunk. *C'est un pilier de tripot, il se biture à longueur de journée!* He's a right old soak, never a minute off the booze!

bizeness *n.m.* **1** Job, occupation. **2** 'Racket', shady activity. *Faire le bizeness*: To be 'on the game', to be a prostitute. (The word is obviously a corruption of the English 'business'.)

bizut *n.m. (sch.)*: 'Fresher', new student or pupil.

bizutage *n.m. (sch.)*: Rough-and-ready initiation ceremony and ragging inflicted on freshers.

bizuter *v.trans. (sch.)*: To initiate a fresher by putting him through the paces of some rough-and-ready ragging.

bla-bla *n.m.* (also: *bla-bla-bla*): **1** 'Hot air', tall stories. *N'écoute pas tout ce bla-bla-bla*: Don't listen to all that spiel. *Le bla-bla du camelot*: The street-hawker's patter. **2** 'Rubbish', nonsense. *Tout ça, c'est du bla-bla-bla*: It's a load of codswallop.

blablater *v.intrans.* To 'gabble on'. *Il blablate que c'en est une maladie, c'est un vrai moulin à paroles!* What a blethering idiot, he just never stops!

blackbouler *v.trans.* (*sch.*) *Se faire blackbouler*: To get 'ploughed', to be failed at an exam.

blady-penny *n.m.* *Etre sans un blady-penny*: To be 'skint', to be 'stoney-broke', to be penniless.

blague *n.f.* **1** Joke. *Faire une blague à quelqu'un*: To play a practical joke on someone. *Sans blague?!* No kidding?! (This was the catch-phrase of Grock, a famous Swiss clown.) *Blague à part*: Honestly! Joking apart (also: *blague dans le coin!*). *Sale blague*: 'Sick joke'. **2** 'Tall story', lie. *N'écoute donc pas toutes ces blagues!* Don't listen to all that tommy-rot! **3** Blunder. *J'ai l'impression que j'ai fait une blague*: I think I've made a boob. **4** (*pl.*) *Blagues à tabac*: 'Droopy tits', flabby mammaries.

blaguer *v.trans.* To 'pull someone's leg', to tease someone. *Il me blague toujours à propos de mon accent!* He's always having me on about my accent!

blaguer *v.intrans.* To lark, to joke. *Il adore blaguer*: He's always ready for a laugh!

blagueur *n.m.* **1** 'Tease', 'leg-puller', jokester. **2** Prankster, one who enjoys playing practical jokes.

blagueur *adj.* (of person): **1** 'Jokey', humorous. **2** Given to practical jokes.

blair *n.m.* (also: *blaire*): **1** 'Hooter', nose. **2** *Avoir quelqu'un dans le blair* (also: *ne pas pouvoir blairer quelqu'un*): To hate someone's guts. **3** *En avoir plein le blair*: To be fed up to the back teeth. **4** *Se bouffer le blair*: To be 'at loggerheads', to quarrel.

blairer *v.trans.* *Je ne peux pas le blairer!* I can't stomach him! – I can't stand him! (also: *je ne peux pas le piffer!*).

blanc *n.m.* **1** 'Snow', cocaine. **2** White wine. *Un petit blanc*: A glass of white wine.

blanc *adj.* **1** Innocent. *Etre blanc comme neige*: To be totally innocent. (This expression can have a jocular double meaning when applied to a suspected drug-smuggler, *blanc* and *neige* both referring to cocaine.) **2** *Etre à blanc* (abbr. *être saigné à blanc*): To be 'skint', 'broke', to be penniless.

blanc-bec *n.m.* 'Greenhorn', novice, inexperienced person.

blanc-bleu *n.m.* Dependable type, trustworthy fellow. *Lui?! C'est un blanc-bleu!* He's O.K., he's one of us!

Blanche *Proper name.* (*abbr. Place Blanche*, Paris.) *On s'est filé rencart à Blanche à la sortie du métro*: We agreed to meet at *Place Blanche* outside the tube-station.

blanche *n.f.* *Une blanche*: A glass of clear fruit-liqueur.

blanchecaille *n.f.* **1** (*corr. blanchisserie*): Commercial laundry. **2** Laundress, laundry lady. (With the advent of washing machines and launderettes, this occupation seems to have disappeared.)

blanco *n.m.* White wine. *Allez, verse-nous un blanco!* Go on, give us a glass of white plonk! (It is amusing to note that plonk is, in fact, a corruption of *vin blanc*.)

blanco *adj.* *Etre blanco*: To be innocent (of any crime). *Non, il est blanco, lui!* He's O.K., he's got no form at all!

blase *n.m.* **1** 'Handle', name (sometimes nickname). **2** 'Conk', 'hooter', nose.

blaud *n.m.* *C'est pas mon blaud!* It's not my business! – It's nothing to do with me! *Ça c'est ton blaud!* It's your look-out!

blave *n.m.* 'Snot-rag', handkerchief.

blaze *n.m.* **1** 'Handle', name (sometimes nickname). *Qu'est-ce que c'est que ton blaze?!* What is it they call you?! **2** 'Conk', 'hooter', nose.

blé *n.m.* **1** 'Bread', money. **2** *Etre fauché comme les blés*: To be stoney-broke.

bléchard *adj.* (*pej.*; of person): Old and ugly. (Both this word and its alternative *blèche* have no real English equivalent.)

bled *n.m.* **1** 'One-horse town', small village, small town. *Il habite dans un bled perdu*: He lives in some village at the back of beyond. **2** *En plein bled*: 'Out in the sticks', way out in the country.

blédard *n.m.* Country dweller. (According to context the word can have pejorative connotations as in 'country bumpkin'.)

blédine *n.f.* **1** *Bouffer de la blédine avec une paille*: To be 'all gums', to have no teeth. (*Blédine* is the trade-name of a baby food.) **2** *S'en souvenir comme de sa première blédine*: To have no recollection of something.

blême *n.f.* *La blême*: Death (the personification of that great leveller, sometimes written with a capital *B*).

bléno *n.f.* (*abbr. blennorragie*): 'Clap', gonorrhoea (also: *chaude-pisse*).

blette *n.f.* 'Bitch', 'bitchy' character. (As with many colloquial words the appellation becomes even more pejorative when referring to a male.)

blette *adj.* 'Bitchy', snide and malicious.

bleu *n.m.* **1** 'Greenhorn', novice. **2** *Du bleu*: 'Plonk', cheap red wine (also: *du gros rouge qui* *tache*). **3** *N'y voir que du bleu*: **a** To be none the wiser, not to understand what is happening or has happened. **b** To get 'diddled', to be 'conned' (also: *n'y voir que t'chi*). **4** *Passer quelque chose au bleu*: To 'cover up', to hush something up.

bleu *adj*. *Zone bleue*: 'Pink zone', restricted parking zone in city centres.

bleue *n.f.* **1** *La grande bleue*: 'The briny', the sea. **2** *Un paquet de bleues*: A packet of ordinary *Gauloises* or *Gitanes* cigarettes. (The blue pack contrasts with the green and yellow packs containing nicotine-free or Virginia tobacco.) **3** *Oh! La belle bleue!* This near-untranslatable exclamation is a staple utterance at firework displays and can be found with stronger colloquial undertones in a variety of contexts.

bleus *n.m.pl.* *(abbr. bleus de travail)*: Boiler suit, worker's overalls.

bleusaille *n.f.* *De la bleusaille*: 'Greenhorns', inexperienced newcomers. (The expression originates in the world of the military.) *Tout ça, c'est de la bleusaille!* They're still wet behind the ears, that lot!

blinde *n.m.* *Défendre son blinde*: To look after 'number one', to think of one's own interests first.

blinde *n.f.* *A toute blinde*: 'Full-pelt', very fast. *Il a roulé à toute blinde*: He drove like the clappers.

blindé *adj*. **1** 'Thick-skinned', immune to criticism. *Ils peuvent dire ce qu'ils veulent, moi je suis blindé!* They can say what they like, it's all water off a duck's back to me! **2** 'Sozzled', drunk. *Il est complètement blindé*: He's pissed out of his mind.

blinder *v.trans.* To 'pass on the clap', to infect with V.D.

bloblote *n.f.* *Avoir la bloblote*: **a** To 'have the shakes', to be frightened out of one's wits. **b** To have a high temperature, to have a fever.

bloc *n.m.* **1** 'Cooler', solitary confinement cell. *Choper cinq jours de bloc*: To cop five days in solitary. **2** *A bloc (adv.exp.)*: Very, extremely. *Etre bourré à bloc*: To be 'loaded', to be very wealthy. *Etre gonflé à bloc*: To be full of confidence. *Serrer quelque chose à bloc*: To screw something down firmly.

bloche *n.f.* *(abbr. astibloche)*: 'Meaty', maggot.

blond *n.m.* *Salut, beau blond!* *(joc. & iron.)*: Hello sailor!

blonde *n.f.* **1** *Une blonde*: A glass of lager. **2** *Des blondes*: Cigarettes (made from light-coloured tobacco, unlike home-produced *Gauloises* or *Gitanes*).

bloquer *v.trans.* **1** To 'put away', to imprison. **2** *Bloquer un coup* (also: *une baffe*): To 'cop a blow', to 'get biffed', to get hit.

bloquer *v.pronom.* To 'cop', to get punishment. *Il s'est bloqué deux heures de colle*: He copped two hours' detention.

blot *n.m.* **1** Cost, price. *Fourguer quelque chose à bas blot*: To flog something cheaply. **2** *C'est mon blot!* That's my business! – That's my look-out! **3** *Ça ne fait pas mon blot, mais alors, pas du tout!* That doesn't suit me one little bit! **4** *Le même blot*: The same thing. *Ça n'est pas le même blot!* It's a different kettle of fish!

bloum *n.m.* *(Slightly pej.)*: 'Weird headgear', strange hat.

blouser *v.trans.* To 'con', to 'diddle', to swindle. *Je me suis fait blouser*: I've been had. *Il m'a drôlement blousé!* He put one across me!

blouser *v.trans.reflex.* To 'slip up', to 'make a boob', to make a mistake.

blouson *n.m.* **1** *Blouson noir*: 'Yobbo', hooligan. **2** *Blouson doré*: Wealthy yob. (It was the media that coined the appellation which is purely figurative and reflects the hooligan's wealthy background.)

bluffer *v.trans.* *Il m'a bluffé!* He tried it on with me! – He tried to pull the wool over my eyes! (The word is obviously a direct borrowing from the English.)

bob *n.m.* **1** *(abbr. bobinard)*: 'Cat-house', brothel. **2** Fob watch. **3** *(pl.)*: Dice. *Rouler* (also: *pousser*) *les bobs*: To have a game of dice. **4** *Lâcher les bobs (fig)*: To 'throw in the towel', to give up.

bobard *n.m.* **1** 'Tall story', lie. *Ne coupez pas dans tous ces bobards!* Don't fall for all that tommy-rot! **2** 'Crack', nasty comment. *Envoyer des bobards*: To make snide remarks. **3** 'Boob', gaffe, blunder. **4** Joke. *Monter un bobard à quelqu'un*: To 'pull someone's leg'. *Bobard dans le coin!* Seriously though! – Joking apart!

bobèche *n.f.* 'Bean', 'bonce', head. *Avoir la bobèche fêlée*: To be 'nuts', 'bonkers', to be mad. *Se payer la bobèche* (also: *la bobine*) *de quelqu'un*: **a** To 'put one across', to fool someone. **b** To 'poke fun at someone', to make fun of someone.

bobéchon *n.m.* 'Conk', 'nut', head. *Se monter le bobéchon*: **a** To kid oneself. **b** To work oneself into a frenzy (also: *se monter le bourrichon*).

bobinard *n.m.* 'Cat-house', brothel.

bobine *n.f.* **1** 'Conk', head. *Avoir la bobine fêlée*: To be 'bonkers', to be 'nuts', to be mad. **2** 'Mush', face. *Il a une sale bobine*: That's an ugly-looking customer! *Pousser* (also: *faire*) *une drôle de bobine*: To look surprised. **3** Mug, dupe. *C'est une bobine de première*: He's as gullible as they come! **4** Dice game, popular on French racecourses, where punters lose the rest of their money. **5** (Car) breakdown. *On s'est* *retrouvé en bobine avec son vieux tacot*: His 'good little runner' let us down. **6** *Se payer une bobine*: To 'go to the flicks', to go to the movies.

bobinette *n.f.* Dice game (see *bobine*).

Bobino *Proper name*. Famous Paris music-hall.

bobo *n.m.* **1** (Child language): 'Hurt', sore, small pain. *Viens que te fasse un bibi sur ton bobo, mon coco!* Come here, darling, Mummy'll kiss it better! *Ça fait bobo*: It hurts. **2** *Il y a quelques petits bobos par-ci par-là*: There are a few things that need putting right, here and there.

bobonne *n.f.* **1** 'The missus', the wife. *Il faut que j'en parle à bobonne*: I'll have to talk it over with my better half. **2** *Ma bobonne*: My pet, my darling.

bocal *n.m.* **1** Skull. *Il s'est retrouvé avec une olive dans le bocal*: He got shot in the head. *Travailler du bocal*: To be 'nuts', to be 'bonkers', to be mad. **2** Belly, stomach. *Se remplir le bocal*: To 'stuff one's face', to have a good tuck-in. **3** *Echappé de bocal (pej)*: 'Little squirt', runt (also: *raclure de bidet*).

Boche *n.m.* and *f. (pej.)*: 'Kraut', German.

boche *adj. (pej.)*: 'Kraut', German. *Il s'est acheté une bagnole boche*: He bought himself one of them Jerry cars.

Bochie *n.f. La Bochie*: 'Krautland', Germany.

bochisant *n.m.* 'Kraut-lover', Germanophile. (The appellation has pejorative connotations because of its World War II context.)

bock *n.m.* **1** Small glass of beer. (Content of standard balloon glass.) **2** *Avoir du bock*: To have the luck of the devil, to be extremely fortunate. (Jacques Cellard and Alain Rey in their DICTIONNAIRE DU FRANÇAIS NON-CONVENTIONNEL state that the word is found only within the above expression and are in some doubt as to the word's etymology.)

bocon *n.m.* **1** Dose of (unpleasant) medicine. **2** Poison (also: *bouillon de onze heures*). **3** *(fig.)*: Spell of bad luck. *Quel bocon!* What rotten luck!

bocson *n.m.* (also: *boxon*): 'Cat-house', brothel (also: *bocard*).

bœuf *adj.inv.* Incredible, tremendous. *Il a eu un succès bœuf (th.)*: He got rave reviews. *Tu as un toupet bœuf, toi!* You've got a nerve! *Les vacances lui ont fait un effet bœuf*: His hols did him a power of good!

B.O.F. *n.m.* Black-marketeer, profiteering small shopkeeper. (The letters B.O.F. stand for *Beurre-Œufs-Fromages* and refer to those who kept fresh-food shops and whose behind-the-counter dealings brought them great wealth during the *Occupation*.)

bôf *interj*. Typically French untranslatable interjection expressing indifference, doubt or irony.

boire *v.trans.* and *intrans.* **1** *Boire un coup*: To have a drink. *On a bu un coup ensemble*: We had ourselves a few bevvies. *Boire sec*: To 'knock it back', to down a drink in one go. *Boire en Suisse*: To drink on one's own (in order to avoid standing someone else a drink). **2** *Boire du petit lait (fig.)*: To be 'chuffed', to be 'as pleased as Punch' (literally to savour the sweet taste of success. The expression is usually encountered when the recipient of praise feigns modesty). **3** *Il y a à boire et à manger là-dedans*: **a** There's something in it for everyone. **b** It's got advantages and disadvantages.

bois *n.m.* **1** *Etre dans ses bois*: To live in unfurnished digs (literally, as the alternative *être dans ses meubles* further suggests, to have rented accommodation furnished with one's own items). **2** *Etre du bois dont on fait des flûtes*: To be easy-going, to be the amenable type. **3** *Vous allez voir de quel bois je me chauffe!* You'll see what stuff I'm made of! (The expression is usually uttered in anger.) **4** *Casser du bois*: To crash land. (The expression obviously originates from the days when aeroplanes had wooden frames.) **5** *Etre dans les bois* (Football): To be in goal, to act as goalkeeper. **6** *Chèque en bois*: 'Rubber cheque' (the kind that is returned to the payee by his bank as invalid). **7** *'Croix de bois, croix de fer, si je meurs je vais en enfer!'* 'Cross my heart and hope to die' (if what I say is untrue!).

boit-sans-soif *n.m.* 'Old soak', drunkard.

boite *n.f.* **1** Place of work. (The connotations of the word range from the uncommitted to the pejorative according to context.) **2** (*abbr. boîte de nuit*): Night-club. **3** *Boîte à bac*: 'Cram-mer', 'cramming-shop', expensive fee-paying school for the sons of the idle rich. **4** *Mettre une lettre à la boîte*: To post a letter. **5** *Mettre quelqu'un en boîte (fig.)*: To 'pull someone's leg', to 'have someone on', to try and make a fool of someone. *Mise en boîte*: 'Leg-pull', hoax. **6** *Boîte à sel (th.)*: Box-office. **7** *Boîte à dominos*: **a** 'Wooden overcoat', coffin. **b** 'Trap', 'gob', mouth. **8** *Ferme ta boîte!* Shut your gob! – Shut up! **9** *Boîte à ragoût*: 'Bread-basket', belly. **10** *Boîtes à lolo*: 'Tits', 'boobs', breasts. **11** *Boîte à ouvrage*: 'Fanny', 'pussy', vagina.

bol *n.m.* **1** 'Bean', 'bonce', head. *N'avoir rien sur le bol*: To be as bald as a coot. *Ne te casse pas le bol!* Don't fret! – Don't worry! **2** 'Mush', 'dial', face. (With this meaning, the word is always encountered in a pejorative connotation. *Faire un drôle de bol*: To pull a sour face.) **3** Luck. *Un coup de bol*: A stroke of luck. *Manque de bol,* *on s'est fait pincer!* Of all the rotten luck, we got nabbed! **4** *En avoir ras le bol* (also: *ralbol*): To be fed up to the back teeth, to be sick and tired of something. **5** *Prendre un bol d'air:* To get a bit of fresh air.

bolant *adj.* 'Side-splitting', hilarious. *C'est vachement bolant!* It's a right scream!

boler *v.pronom.* **1** To have a bloody good laugh. **2** To have a whale of a time, to enjoy oneself tremendously.

bombarder *v.intrans. and trans.* **1** To 'smoke like a chimney', to smoke too much. **2** To promote (someone) unexpectedly to a very high post. *On l'a bombardé P.D.G.:* He got promoted to managing director out of the blue.

bombardier *n.m.* (Drugs): 'Reefer', cigarette rolled with cannabis. (The current expression is *se taper un bombardier:* to smoke a joint. It is worth noting that *bombardier* can sometimes also refer to the rough hand-rolled cigarette devoid of any illegal substance.)

bombe *n.f.* **1** Binge, 'beano', spree. *Faire la bombe:* To have one hell of a good time. **2** *(abbr. bombe glacée):* Superlative ice-cream dessert. (This confection containing a variety of flavours is reserved for special occasions and ends culinary extravaganzas with a gastronomic bang.)

bombé *n.m. (pej.):* 'Humpie', hunchback.

bomber *v.intrans.* To 'go like the clappers', to 'bomb along', to go very fast.

bomber *v.trans. Bomber une surface à quelqu'un:* To 'flabbergast', to astound someone.

bomber *v. pronom.* To 'have to do without', to miss out on something. *Tu peux toujours te bomber si tu t'imagines qu'on va te payer!* You've got another think coming if it's money you're after! (also: *se l'accrocher, se fouiller*).

bon *adj.* **1** *Etre bon (iron.):* To be a 'sucker', to be a dupe. (The expression *je suis bon, mais ça ne s'écrit pas avec un c!* further highlights the built-in irony of the adjective.) **2** *Etre bon pour:* To be due for, to be in line for something unpleasant. *Il est bon pour la casse:* He's ready for the chop.

bon *n.m.* **1** *Avoir du bon:* To have some good points (in spite of everything). **2** *Avec deux minutes de bon:* With two minutes to spare.

bonbons *n.m.pl.* 'Bollocks', 'balls', testicles.

bond *n.m. Faire faux bond à quelqu'un:* To let someone down.

bondé *adj.* 'Chock-a-block', crammed (with people).

bondieusard *n.m. (pej.):* 'Creeping-Jesus', sanctimonious person. (The female of the species is known as *grenouille de bénitier*.)

bondieuserie *n.f. (pej.):* **1** *La bondieuserie:* Bigotry. **2** *(usually pl.):* Religious ornaments.

bondir *v.trans. Se faire bondir:* To get 'nabbed', to be arrested.

bonheur *n.m. Au petit-bonheur-la-chance (adv.exp.):* Haphazardly. *On a choisi au petit-bonheur:* We took pot-luck!

bonhomme *n.m.* **1** *Aller son petit bonhomme de chemin:* To 'do one's own thing', to go one's own sweet way. **2** *Ça suit son petit bonhomme de chemin:* Things are following their natural course. **3** *Nom d'un petit bonhomme!* (mild expletive): By Jove! – By jiminy!

boni *n.m.* Profit. *C'est autant de boni!* It's that much to the good! (also: *bénef*).

boniche *n.f. (pej. also: bonniche):* Housemaid. (The appellation is a corruption of *bonne-à-tout-faire*).

boniment *n.m.* **1** 'Eye-wash', tall story. *Je n'ai pas coupé à son boniment!* He didn't take me in by talking big! **2** 'Spiel', sales-patter. *C'est un crac du boniment, lui!* He could sell sand to the Arabs!

bonimenter *v.trans & intrans.* **1** To tell tall stories. **2** To 'shoot a line', to lay on the sales-talk.

bonimenteur *n.m.* **1** 'Fast-talker', yarn-spinner. **2** Hawker, street-vendor. *Etre bonimenteur en diable:* To have the gift of the gab.

bonir *v.trans.* **1** *(pol.):* To 'spill the beans', to give away a secret. *Il s'est mis à table et a tout boni:* He turned coppers' nark and gave the whole thing away. **2** To talk, to speak. *Ne pas en bonir une* (also: *ne pas bonir une broque*): To 'stay schtum', to remain silent.

bonisseur *n.m.* Hawker, street-vendor.

bonjour *n.m.* **1** *C'est simple comme bonjour!* It's as easy as pie! – It's dead simple. **2** *Avoir le bonjour (d'Alfred):* To have 'missed the boat', to have missed an opportunity. (The origin of this jocular and highly ironic expression remains a mystery.)

bonnard *n.m.* **1** 'Sucker', dupe. **2** (of person): 'No-chancer', hopeless case. (In both instances the word, a corruption of *bon*, is antiphrastically ironical.)

bonnard *adj.* **1** O.K., fine, good. *C'est bonnard, j'en suis!* That's fine, count me in! **2** *Etre bonnard pour:* To be earmarked by fate for something unpleasant. *On est bonnard pour la vaisselle!* Washing-up time . . . we're in for it again!

bonne *adj.* **1** *Avoir quelqu'un à la bonne:* To have taken a liking for someone. (There is no obvious sexual connotation in the expression, although according to context, it can extend beyond ordinary friendship.) **2** *Prendre quelque* *chose à la bonne*: To take something in good part. *C'est un brave mec, il a pris ça à la bonne!* He's a good lad, he didn't get offended about it!

bonnet *n.m.* **1** *Ne pas se casser le bonnet*: To take life easy, to take life as it comes (also: *ne pas se casser le chou*). **2** *Garder quelque chose sous son bonnet*: To 'keep something under one's hat', to keep something to oneself. **3** *Prendre quelque chose sous son bonnet*: To take the responsibility for something. *Il a dû prendre ça sous son bonnet*: He had to carry the can. **4** *Gros bonnet*: 'Big shot', V.I.P., important person. **5** *C'est bonnet blanc et blanc bonnet*: It's six of one, half a dozen of the other. **6** *Taper le bonnet*: To run a game of *bonneteau*. (*Bonnet* or *bonneteau* is a three-card game, perhaps more accurately described as a three-card trick, in which the innocent player stands little chance of winning.)

bonneteur *n.m.* Three-card trickster, person who runs a game of *bonneteau*.

bonnir *v.trans.* (also: *bonir*): **1** (*pol.*): To 'spill the beans', to give away a secret. **2** To talk, to speak.

bono *interj.* **1** O.K.! – Fine! **2** *Bono macache!* Not on your nelly! – Not bloody likely! – Certainly not!

bonze *n.m.* *Vieux bonze*: 'Old fuddy-duddy', old fogey.

book *n.m.* Bookmaker. (Although bookmaking is illegal in France, quite a few *books* make a fair living.) *C'est un petit book en mal de chance*: He's a small-time bookie on a losing streak.

bord *n.m.* *Sur les bords (adv.exp.)*: 'A touch', slightly. *Il est un peu pédé sur les bords*: He's a bit of a pouf.

bordée *n.f.* 'Beano', binge, spree. *Se payer* (also: *tirer) une bordée*: To paint the town red.

bordel *n.m.* **1** 'Cat-house', brothel. **2** Untidy place. *J'ai été dans sa chambre, quel bordel!* I've been in his room, what a tip! **3** Mess, chaotic state of affairs. *Dans cette usine, il règne un bordel incroyable!* This factory is in a state of utter confusion! **4** *Et tout le bordel!* And the whole shower! – And the whole bloody lot! **5** (Part of string of oaths): *Nom-de-Dieu-de-bordel-de-merde!*

bordelière *n.f.* 'Madame', brothel-keeper.

bordélique *adj.* **1** (of room, etc.): Messy, untidy. **2** (of state of affairs): 'Topsy-turvy', chaotic. **3** *C'est un machin tout ce qu'il y a de bordélique!* It's a bloody nuisance!

bordille *n.f.* **1** 'Mean bastard'. **2** 'Copper', policeman. **3** Copper's nark, informer.

bordurer *v.trans.* To ban, to withdraw someone's permission to be in a specific place. *Il s'était fait bordurer de tous les champs de course*:

He'd been told to steer clear of all race-courses. (The expression *être borduré* can sometimes refer to the legally enforceable *interdiction de séjour* prohibiting ex-cons from entering certain urban areas.)

borgne *n.f.* *La borgne*: Night, night-time.

borgne *n.m.* 'Prick', 'cock', penis. (The word isusually encountered as *le borgne*.)

borgnoter *v.intrans.* (also: *borgnotter*): To 'keep one's eyes peeled', to keep a sharp look-out.

borgnoter *v.trans.reflex.* (also: *borgnotter*): To 'hit the sack', to go to bed (also: *se pager, se pieuter*).

bornasse *n.f. (pej.)*: 'Culture-vulture', 'swot', over-zealous student. (Applies to both male and female.)

borne *n.f.* **1** Kilometre. *Il habite à quelques bornes d'ici*: He doesn't live far from here. **2** *Planter une borne*: To 'have a crap', to 'shit', to defecate.

bosco *n.m.* Bosun, boatswain.

boscot *n.m.* 'Humpie', hunchback.

bosse *n.f.* **1** *Avoir la bosse*: To be a 'jammy so-and-so', to be very lucky. **2** *Avoir la bosse de . . .* To have a real gift for something. *Il a la bosse du commerce*: He's a born businessman. **3** *Avoir roulé sa bosse*: To 'have been around', to have travelled a fair bit during one's life. **4** *Se payer une bosse* (also: *s'en payer, s'en donner une bosse*): **a** To have a bloody good laugh (literally to double up with laughter). **b** To 'stuff one's face', to have a jolly good tuck-in, to get a bellyful of food.

bosseler *v.trans.* To 'bash up', to beat up, to thrash.

bosser *v.intrans.* To 'graft', to work hard.

bosseur *n.m.* 'Grafter', hard worker.

bosseur *adj.* 'Grafting', hard-working.

bossu *n.m.* *Rire* (also: *rigoler) comme un bossu*: To have a bloody good laugh, to be doubled up with laughter.

botte *n.f.* **1** *A toutes bottes*: 'At full-pelt', at full speed. **2** *Lécher les bottes de quelqu'un*: To 'suck up to someone', to flatter someone in a servile manner. (A 'crawler' in colloquial French is known as *un lèche-bottes*.) **3** *En avoir plein les bottes*: To be fed up to the back teeth. *J'en ai plein les bottes de ses histoires de guerre!* I'm sick up to here with his 'How-I-won-the-war' stories! **4** *Chier dans les bottes de quelqu'un*: **a** To 'do the dirty on someone', to play a dirty trick on someone. **b** To be a 'pain in the arse', to be a bloody nuisance to someone. **5** *Cirer ses bottes*: To 'pop one's clogs', to 'snuff it', to die. **6** *Ça fait ma botte*: That suits me down to the ground. – That's fine by me. **7** *A propos de bottes*: For no reason at all, irrelevantly. (A certain jocularity within the expression stems from its non-sensical nature.) **8** *Coup de botte*: 'Tap', attempt at borrowing money. *C'est le roi des coups de bottes!* When it comes to getting subs out of people, he's second to none! 9 *Proposer la botte à quelqu'un*: To 'proposition someone', to suggest sexual intercourse. 10 *Une botte de* (also: *des bottes de*): 'Stacks of', 'masses', lots of. *Elle a loupé des bottes d'occases!* She's missed oodles of opportunities! 11 *Sortir dans la botte (sch.)*: To graduate 'summa cum laude' (with honours). *Chiader la botte*: To aim for a top degree. 12 *Botte de radis*: 'Tootsies', toes.

botter *v.trans.* *Ça me botte!* That suits me down to the ground! – That's fine by me! (also: *Ça fait ma botte!*)

bottin *n.m.* Trades directory. (Sébastien Bottin, 1764–1853, gave his name to the commercial reference-work he created; his *annuaire* has survived to the present day. The *Bottin Mondain* could be described as the French *Who's Who*.)

bottine *n.f.* *Etre de la bottine*: To be a lesbian.

bouboule *n.m.* 'Fatso', corpulent person.

bouc *n.m.* 1 'Goatee', small pointed beard. 2 *Puer comme un bouc*: To 'pong', to stink, to smell foul.

boucan *n.m.* 'Racket', 'din', noise.

bouchaboucha *n.m.* *Bouchaboucha pompeur (joc.)*: 'Plunger' kiss, 'smackeroo', big wet kiss on the lips.

bouche *n.f.* 1 *Bouche cousue!* (also: *motus et bouche cousue!*): Mum's the word! – Keep it to yourself! – It's a secret! 2 *Ta bouche bébé, t'auras une frite!* Shut your face! – Shut up! (This nonsensical catch phrase is more often heard in its abbreviated form *ta bouche bébé!*)

bouche-trou *n.m.* 'Stop-gap'. *J'en ai marre de servir de bouche-trou!* I'm fed up to the back teeth with standing in for you!

bouché *adj.* 'Thick', stupid. *Etre bouché à l'émeri*: To be as thick as two short planks.

bouchée *n.f.* *Ne faire qu'une bouchée de*: To make short work of, to deal with someone or something summarily.

boucher *v.trans.* *Boucher un coin à quelqu'un* (also: *boucher une surface à quelqu'un*): To astound someone. *Ça vous en a bouché un coin, pas vrai?!* That made you sit up, didn't it?!

bouchon *n.m.* 1 Small bistrot (the kind of 'corner caf' that has a very limited clientele). 2 *Sentir le bouchon*: a To be a 'tippler', to be a boozer. b (of item, article): To be long past its prime. 3 *Prendre du bouchon*: To be 'knocking on', to be getting on in years. 4 Youngest of the family. *On est quatre frangins, en comptant bouchon*: We're four brothers, not forgetting Junior. 5 *Mon bouchon*: My pet – My lovey-dovey – My darling. 6 Traffic jam. *On peut s'attendre à des bouchons aux environs de Paris la veille du 14 juillet*: There's likely to be bottle-necks on the approaches to Paris on the 13th July. 7 *Mets-y un bouchon! (iron.)*: Put a sock in it! – Belt up! – Shut up! 8 *Bouchon de carafe (joc.)*: Large and ostentatious diamond (the kind of stone that is reminiscent of the crystal stopper of a decanter). 9 *Envoyer le bouchon*: To exaggerate. *A force d'envoyer le bouchon, personne ne le croit plus!* One tall story after another, no-one believes him now! 10 *C'est plus fort que de jouer au bouchon! (iron)*: Can you beat that?! – Well, that's the limit! 11 *Ramasser un bouchon*: To 'come a cropper', to 'come unstuck', to suffer a setback.

bouchonner *v.intrans.* *Ça bouchonne aux alentours de Paris*: The approaches to Paris are clogged up with traffic.

bouclage *n.m.* 'Cageing', process of imprisonment.

bouclard *n.m.* 'Store', shop. (The word suggests 'lock-up' premises, with no living accommodation.)

bouclarès *adj.inv.* Locked, closed up. (The adjective sometimes has the connotation of 'closed down' as in *les boxons ont été bouclarès*: brothels have been made illegal.)

boucle *n.f.* 1 Imprisonment. *Avec son pédigrée, il était bon pour la boucle*: With his 'form', he was heading straight for the nick. 2 *Boucler la boucle*: a To be back to square one (back to where one started). b To make ends meet, to manage on the money at one's disposal. (The expression originates from the world of aviation where it means to loop the loop.) 3 *La Grande Boucle*: The Tour de France cycling race.

boucler *v.trans.* 1 To lock, to close. *Boucler la lourde*: To lock the door. *Les condés ont bouclé son tapis*: The fuzz closed down his gaming-joint. 2 To 'clap in jail', to imprison. 3 *La boucler*: To shut up. *Ça vous la boucle?!* There's no answer to that! – You don't know what to say, do you?! (also: *ça vous en bouche un coin!*). 4 *Se la boucler*: To 'have to make do', to have to do without (also: *se boucler la ceinture*). 5 *Boucler une affaire*: To wrap up a deal. *C'est une affaire bouclée alors, hein?* It's a deal then?!

bouder *v.intrans.* *Bouder à la vente* (of item or article): To be 'a poor seller', to sell badly.

boudin *n.m.* 1 Cosh, truncheon (also: *goumi*). 2 'Prick', 'cock', penis. 3 Tyre. *On s'est retrouvés en pleine cambrousse avec deux boudins crevés*: We were stranded in the middle of nowhere with two flat tyres. 4 (*pej.*): 'Biddy', ungainly woman. *Chaque fois qu'on sort ensemble, il se lève toujours un affreux boudin!* Whenever we go out on a foursome, he always manages to land the ugliest girl going! **5** 'Prozzie', low-class prostitute. **6** *Avoir du boudin*: To have an unbeatable hand at cards. **7** *Faire du boudin*: To sulk and sulk. **8** *S'en aller* (also: *tourner*) *en eau de boudin*: To 'fizzle out', to come to nothing. **9** *'Tiens – voilà du boudin'*: Humorous yet meaningless words associated with the tune of the slow march of the French Foreign Legion.

boudiou *interj*. 'Gordon Bennett!' – Cripes! – Good heavens! (The word is a euphemistic equivalent to *Bon Dieu!*)

boueux *n.m.pl*. Refuse-collectors. (In non-colloquial language, the singular is *éboueur*, plural *éboueurs*.) *Ça fait une paye qu'on n'a pas vu les boueux*: The dustbin men haven't been round for ages.

bouffarde *n.f*. **1** Smoker's pipe. **2** Fellatio.

bouffe *n.f*. 'Grub', 'nosh', food. *Faire la bouffe*: To do the cooking. *A la bouffe!* Come and get it! – Grub's up!

bouffe-caca *n.m. & f. (pej.)*: 'Mud-slinger', 'muck-raker', scandal-monger.

bouffe-la-balle *n.m*. **1** 'Greedy guts', glutton. **2** 'Fatso', fat person.

bouffer *v.trans. & intrans*. **1** To 'nosh', to eat. *Bouffer à s'en crever la peau du ventre*: To have a good 'blow-out'. **2** *Bouffer des briques* (also: *bouffer des briques à la sauce cailloux*): To 'live on thin air', to 'go hungry', to have to go without food. **3** *Bouffer des pois cassés*: To have foul breath, to suffer from halitosis (also: *puer du bec*). **4** *Bouffer de la taule*: To do 'porridge', to serve a term of imprisonment. **5** *Bouffer du curé*: To be fiercely anticlerical. **6** *En bouffer* (also: *bouffer à la grande gamelle*): To 'grass', to be a police informer.

bouffetance *n.f*. 'Grub', 'nosh', food.

bouffe-tout *n.m*. (also: *bouftou*): 'Greedy-guts', 'guzzler', glutton (also: *bouffe-la-balle*).

bouffi *n.m*. *Tu l'as dit, bouffi!* (The nearest thing in French to rhyming slang): Right on! – You've said it, mate! (also: *Tu parles, Charles!*).

bouge *n.m. (pej.)*: 'Grotty pub', 'dive', low-class public house.

bougeotte *n.f*. *Avoir la bougeotte*: **a** To be fidgety, to have the fidgets. **b** To be constantly on the move, to be unable to settle anywhere.

bougie *n.f*. **1** 'Bean', 'block', head. **2** 'Mush', 'dial', face. *Faire une drôle de bougie*: To pull a face, to look astounded. **3** *Avoir les bougies encrassées (fig.)*: To be 'slow on the uptake', to be rather dim. (*Bougies* are spark-plugs; when they are clogged with dirt, ignition is a problem, hence the imagery of the expression.)

bougnat *n.m*. **1** Auvergnat, native of the Auvergne. **2** Coal-merchant. (The premises from which the *bougnat* trades are very often a small bistrot. The unusual combination of drink and a variety of fuels does not seem to deter the clientèle.)

bougnoul *n.m. (pej.)*: 'Wog', 'coon', coloured person.

bougon *adj*. Grumbling. *Etre d'un naturel bougon*: To be the grumbling kind.

bougonner *v.intrans*. To 'moan', to grumble.

bougre *n.m*. Chap, fellow. *Bon bougre*: Good bloke, decent sort of chap, nice guy. *Ne pas être (un) mauvais bougre*: To be basically a decent fellow. *C'est un sacré bougre!* He's a card! *Bougre de menteur! (joc.)*: You lying hound! *Un pauvre bougre*: A poor sod, a poor devil. *Un sale bougre*: A 'nasty piece of work', an evil bugger.

bougre *adj*. *Bougre d'idiot!* You bloody idiot! – *Quel bougre de temps!* What bloody awful weather! (The adjective is more an intensifier than anything else.)

bougre *interj*. Blimey! – Crikey! (The English and French are equally twee.)

bougrement *adv*. 'Bloody', 'awfully', very. *Il fait bougrement froid!* It's real brass monkey weather!

bougresse *n.f. (pej.)*: 'Scheming cow', calculating woman.

bouiboui *n.m*. (also: *boui-boui*): 'Honky-tonk joint', 'low dive', disreputable public house.

bouic *n.m. (pej.)*: Low-class brothel.

bouif *n.m*. **1** Cobbler, shoe-mender. **2** Snob, conceited person. **3** *Faire du bouif*: To 'swank', to show off.

bouillabaisse *n.f*. *Etre dans une sacrée bouillabaisse*: To be 'in the soup', to be 'in a right old fix', to be in trouble. (*Bouillabaisse* is a highly-seasoned fish soup from Provence.)

bouillasse *n.f*. **1** Mud, slush (also: *gadoue*). **2** *Etre dans la bouillasse*: To be 'in a fine old pickle', to be in trouble.

bouillaver *v.intrans*. To 'screw', to fuck, to have sex.

bouille *n.f*. **1** 'Mush', 'dial', face. *Avoir une bonne bouille*: To look the friendly type. *Faire une sale bouille*: To pull a face. *Avoir la bouille enfarinée*: To look bewildered. **2** *Etre la bonne bouille*: To be 'the fall-guy', to end up being the dupe. **3** *Taper une bouille*: To have a game of *belote*.

bouilleur *n.m*. *Bouilleur de cru*: Profit-conscious landowner who distils (sometimes illegally) his own wine or cider.

bouillie *n.f*. **1** *Réduire quelqu'un en bouillie*: To 'make mincemeat of someone', to beat someone to a pulp. **2** *Avoir de la bouillie dans la bouche*: To 'have a plum in one's mouth', to have a snobbish drawl. **3** *Il est de la bouillie pour* *les chats*: He's a spineless twit. **4** *Bouffer de la bouillie avec une paille*: To be 'all gums', to be toothless.

bouillon *n.m.* **1** *(pej.)*: 'Nosh-house', cheap and uninspiring restaurant. **2** *Gras de bouillon*: Greasy deposits on kitchen walls. **3** *Bouillon de onze heures (iron.)*: Dose of poison. **4** *Tomber dans le bouillon*: To 'fall in the drink', to land in the water. **5** *Boire le bouillon*: To nearly drown (also: *boire la tasse*). **6** *Boire un bouillon (fig.)*: To 'nearly go under', to sustain a heavy financial loss. **7** *Les bouillons* (Newsagents' slang): Unsold papers and periodicals. (The word can sometimes apply to unsold books.)

bouillotte *n.f. (pej.)*: 'Mug', 'dial', face. *Elle a une bouillotte à faire avorter une couvée de singes!* She's got a face like the back of a bus!

bouine *n.f.* 'Biff', 'clout', blow. *Elle lui a filé une de ces bouines!* She thrashed him good and proper!

Boul' *n.m.* (abbr. *Boulevard*): *Le Boul' Mich'*: The *Boulevard Saint-Michel* in Paris.

Boulange *n.f. La Grande Boulange*: The *Banque de France*.

boule *n.f.* **1** 'Bean', 'bonce', head. *Avoir la boule à zéro*: To be as bald as a coot. *Donner un coup de boule*: To butt someone. *Perdre la boule*: To 'go off one's rocker', to go mad. *Y aller de la boule*: To be guillotined. **2** 'Mush', 'dial', face. *Boule de son*: Freckle-face. *Faire une sale boule*: To pull a face. **3** *Se mettre en boule*: To 'get in a huff', to get cross. *Il se met en boule pour un rien*: He gets his back up over nothing. **4** *Boules Quiès*: Ear-plugs. (Another case of a brand-name becoming generic.) **5** *Mystère et boules de gomme! (joc.)*: Search me! – I haven't the foggiest! – It's a mystery to me! **6** *Remonter des boules*: To 'get the readies', to get some money. *Rentrer dans ses boules* : To get one's money back.

boule *adj.* (abbr. *maboule*): 'Nuts', 'potty', mad. *Etre un rien boule*: To be slightly bonkers.

bouledogue *n.m.* 'Rod', 'shooter', handgun.

bouler *v.intrans.* **1** To 'make a balls of things', to mess matters up. **2** *Envoyer bouler quelqu'un*: **a** To bowl someone over. **b** To send someone away with a flea in their ear, to dismiss someone in no uncertain manner.

boulet *n.m.* **1** *Traîner un boulet*: To carry a millstone around one's neck. **2** *Tirer à boulets rouges sur quelqu'un*: To 'go gunning for someone', to pursue someone relentlessly. **3** *Etre sur les boulets*: To be 'all in', to be dog-tired. *Mettre quelqu'un sur les boulets*: To wear someone out.

boulette *n.f.* 'Boob', blunder, mistake. *Faire une boulette*: To 'drop a clanger', to goof.

boulevard *n.m.* **1** *Faire les boulevards*: To go street-hawking, to sell wares from a 'flit-stall' (i.e. without a permit). **2** *Faire les boulevards extérieurs* (Racing slang): To 'go wide', to try and overtake on the outside. **3** *Le boulevard des allongés*: The 'boneyard', the cemetery.

boulonner *v.intrans.* To 'graft', to work hard.

boulot *n.m.* **1** Work. (According to context, it can have a variety of connotations.) *Abattre du boulot*: To get through a pile of work. *S'atteler au boulot*: To 'pitch in', to get down to it. *Décrocher un boulot*: To get a job. *Etre au boulot*: To be 'on the job', to have sex. *Se taper un petit boulot facile* (Underworld slang): To go on an easy job. *Au boulot!* Get cracking! (Start earning your keep!) **2** *C'est pas ton boulot!* It's none of your business!

boulot *adj.* 'Podgy', plump. *Sa femme est plutôt boulotte*: His missus isn't exactly featherlight!

boulot-boulot *adj.inv. Etre boulot-boulot*: To be 'all work and no play', to be over-zealous in one's work.

boulotter *v.trans. & intrans.* **1** To 'gobble', to eat. *Il boulotte des friandises à longueur de journée*: He's never without a sweet in his mouth. **2** To 'blue', to squander. *Elle a boulotté son héritage en deux temps, trois mouvements*: Spend! Spend! Spend! She got through her inheritance double-quick. **3** *Alors, ça boulotte?!* How's tricks?! – How are things? – How's life?! (also: *ça biche?!*).

boum *n.m.* **1** 'Boom', period of prosperity. *Pendant trois ans on a été en plein boum*: For three years, we never had it so good. **2** *Etre en plein boum*: To be up to one's neck in work. **3** Big annual college ball. *Le Boum H.E.C.*: The grand end-of-year 'do' of the *Hautes Etudes Commerciales* College in Paris.

boum *n.f. (abbr. surboum)*: Teenagers' party. (The word had its heyday in the late 50s and early 60s.)

boum *interj. Et boum! Ça roule!* (Waiters' slang): Coming up! (The order has been taken and passed to the kitchens.)

boumer *v.intrans. Ça boume!* Fine! – O.K! *Ça boume?* How's tricks? – How are things?

boumiane *n.m. & f.* Romany, gipsy.

bouquet *n.m.* **1** 'Tip', gratuity. *N'oublie pas de refiler un bouquet au pingouin!* Don't forget to tip the waiter! **2** 'Cut', share of profits (often from illegal gains). **3** Best part, crowning piece. *Et on a gardé ça pour le bouquet . . .* And that's the cherry on the cake! **4** *(iron.)*: *Ça, c'est le bouquet!* That's the last straw! – That's torn it! – That does it! **5** *Avoir les doigts de pied en bouquets de violettes* (of woman): To be in the throes of orgasmic pleasure.

bouquin *n.m.* Book. (The word is a familiar corruption of the English.)

bouquiner *v.trans. & intrans.* **1** To read. **2** To browse through a bookstall.

bouquiniste *n.m.* Second-hand bookseller.

bourbier *n.m.* 'Mess', trouble. *Etre dans un foutu bourbier:* To be in a right old fix. *Tirer quelqu'un du bourbier:* To get someone out of trouble (also: *pétrin*).

bourde *n.f.* 'Boob', blunder, mistake. *Lâcher une bourde:* To drop a clanger.

bourdille *n.m. & f.* **1** 'Mean bastard', evil character. **2** 'Copper', policeman. **3** 'Copper's nark', informer.

bourdon *n.m. Avoir le bourdon:* To be 'down in the dumps', to be depressed. *J'ai eu un sacré coup de bourdon:* I had a fit of the blues.

bourgeois *n.m.* **1** *En bourgeois:* 'In civvies', in plain clothes. **2** *Les bourgeois* (also: *les en bourgeois*): Plain clothes policemen (often from the vice squad). **3** *Faire quelque chose pour épater le bourgeois:* To go out of one's way to shock.

bourgeoise *n.f. Ma bourgeoise:* 'The missus', the wife.

bourgeon *n.m.* Spot, pimple.

bourgeonner *v.intrans.* To be breaking out in pimples.

bourgue *n.m. Le bourgue* (Tramps' slang): The sun (also: *le bourguignon*).

bourlinguer *v.intrans. Avoir bourlingué:* To 'have been around', to have led a very full life.

bourrache *adj.* 'Pissed', 'sozzled', drunk.

bourrage *n.m. Bourrage de crâne:* **a** *(sch.):* 'Cramming', swotting. **b** Brainwashing, indoctrination. **c** *Du bourrage de crâne:* 'Balderdash', eyewash. *N'écoute pas leur publicité, tout ça c'est du bourrage de crâne!* Don't believe all that blurb, their ads are a load of codswallop!

bourre *n.m.* 'Cop', policeman. *Gaffe! V'là les bourres!* Watch out! Here come the fuzz! (also: *bourreman*).

bourre *n.f.* **1** *De première bourre:* 'A.1.', first-rate. *Un gueuleton de première bourre:* A right royal nosh (also: *de première*). **2** *Etre à la bourre:* To be late for something (and rushing to make up time). **3** *Etre à la bourre de* (of bills): To be in arrears (and to be desperately trying to settle them). **4** *Se tirer la bourre:* To compete fiercely. *Ces deux bistrots se tirent la bourre depuis toujours:* Those two pubs have been trying to outdo each other for years. **5** *Des bourres:* 'Tall stories', lies.

bourré *adj.* **1** 'Jampacked', crammed, full-up. *C'était bourré bourré!* It was chock-a-block there! **2** 'Pissed', 'sozzled', drunk. *Il était bourré à mort:* He was pissed as a newt. **3** 'High' on drugs. **4** 'Bonkers', mad. (The word does not refer to madness as such; it is uttered by one who disapproves of another's actions. *T'es bourré, non?!* Have you gone mad or something?!) **5** 'Loaded', rich. *Etre bourré à bloc:* To be rolling in it.

bourreau *n.m.* **1** *Bourreau de travail:* Glutton for work. **2** *Bourreau des cœurs* (of man): Heart-throb.

bourrée *n.f.* 'Beating-up', thrashing. *Filer une bourrée à quelqu'un:* To 'work someone over', to beat someone up.

bourreman *n.m.* 'Cop', policeman. *La Maison Bourreman:* The 'cop-shop', the 'fuzz-house', the police station.

bourre-mou *n.m. Du bourre-mou:* 'Codswallop', 'baloney', untrue statements. *Question politique, les baveux sont pleins de bourre-mou!* When it comes to politics, papers are a load of tripe!

bourrepif *n.m.* 'Smack in the kisser', punch in the face. *Une partie de bourrepif:* A right set-to, a ding-dong fight.

bourrer *v.trans.* **1** To 'bash up', to beat up, to thrash. *Bourrer le pif à quelqu'un:* To push someone's face in. *Je vais lui bourrer la gueule, moi, tu vas voir!* I'm going to put my thumb in his eye and dial a number! **2** To 'screw', to fuck, to have intercourse with. **3** *Bourrer le mou à quelqu'un:* To try and hoodwink someone. **4** *Bourrer la caisse* (also: *la malle*): To tell a pack of lies.

bourrer *v.intrans.* To 'bomb along', to speed. *On a bourré comme des dingues sur l'autoroute!* We fair raced down the motorway!

bourrer *v.trans.reflex.* **1** To 'get pissed', 'sozzled', to get drunk. *Chaque soir dans sa piaule, il se bourre à mort:* Every night in his bed-sit he drinks himself silly. **2** (also: *se bourrer le pif*): To get high on drugs.

bourrés *n.m.pl.* Loaded dice.

bourreur *n.m.* **1** Braggart, boaster. **2** *Bourreur de crâne:* 'Humbugger', one who tries to hoodwink others.

bourreur *adj.m.* 'Show-off', boastful. *Il est bourreur comme pas un!* He's the biggest brag around!

bourrichon *n.m.* **1** 'Brainbox', 'nut', head. *N'avoir rien dans le bourrichon:* To have nothing up top, to be empty-headed. **2** *Monter le bourrichon à quelqu'un:* To fill someone's head with silly ideas. **3** *Se monter le bourrichon:* **a** To kid oneself. **b** To work oneself into a frenzy.

bourricot *n.m.* **1** 'Neddy', donkey. **2** *C'est kif-kif bourricot! (joc.):* It's six of one, half a dozen of the other!

bourrin *n.m.* **1** 'Nag', horse. **2** *(pl.)*: Units of horse-power. *'y a 200 bourrins sous le capot*: He's got 200 horse-power under the bonnet. **3** Randy so-and-so, highly-sexed man. **4** *(pej.)*: 'Prozzy', prostitute. **5** *Bourrin de retour*: 'Old lag', old jailbird, recidivist (the kind of character who seems to boomerang his way in and out of prison).

bourrin *adj.* **1** 'Pig-headed', stubborn. **2** (of man): Randy, highly-sexed.

bourriner *v.intrans.* To 'wench', to flit from one affair to another.

bourrique *n.f.* **1** 'Jackass', 'mutt', stubborn and ignorant person. **2** 'Copper', 'cop', policeman. *Les bourriques*: The fuzz. **3** *Bourrique, va!* (gentle rebuff): You silly-billy!

bourrique *adj.* **1** 'Pig-headed', stubborn. **2** 'Thick', dumb. **3** Mean, nasty.

bourriquer *v.trans.* **1** To fuck, to 'screw', to have coition with. **2** *Se faire bourriquer* (of prostitute): To do a cut-price job, to charge less than the going rate for sex.

bourru *adj.* **1** *Etre bourru*: To be 'nicked', 'collared', to be arrested. *Faire bourru*: To catch unawares, to take by surprise. **2** *Se faire faire bourru*: To be 'conned', 'diddled', to be swindled.

Bourse *Proper name. Etre coté en Bourse (fig. & iron.)*: To have made a name for oneself, to be famous.

bourses *n.f.pl.* 'Bollocks', 'balls', testicles. (The expression *un coup de bourses* has a jocular double-meaning in spoken French where the inference is to the Stock Exchange.)

bouscaille *n.f. La bouscaille*: 'Slush', mud. *Etre en pleine bouscaille (fig.)*: To be in a right old pickle.

bousculé *adj. Bien bousculé*: **a** (of man): Well-built, handsome. **b** (of woman): Curvaceous, shapely. (The expression *mal bousculé* is used only in reference to men where it means scraggy and puny.)

bousculer *v.intrans.* To 'go it a bit strong', to exaggerate. *Dans ses histoires de pêche, qu'est-ce qu'il bouscule!* His angling yarns are all about the one that got away!

bousculer *v.trans. Bousculer les bornes* (Cycling slang): To churn up the miles, to ride long stages (also: *bouffer des kilomètres*).

bousculette *n.f.* Jostling crowd.

bouseux *n.m. (pej.)*: Yokel, country bumpkin (also: *pécore*).

bousillage *n.m.* **1** 'Bumping-off', underworld killings. *Comme règlement de compte, ça a été du bousillage en série!* The crunch came with a right old Valentine's Day style massacre! **2** *Du bousillage*: A 'botch', badly-executed work.

3 *Le bousillage*: Excessive drinking or drug-taking. **4** *(pl.)*: Tattoos.

bousille *n.f.* (also: *bouzille*). *La bousille*: The art of tattooing.

bousiller *v.trans.reflex.* **1** To be fond of the bottle, to drink to excess. **2** To 'get smashed', to take drugs in dangerous doses.

bousilleur *n.m.* **1** *(pej.)*: 'Botcher', 'bungler'. **2** Tattooist, tattoo artist.

bousin *n.m.* **1** Brothel. **2** 'Boozer', 'low dive', cheap-and-nasty pub. **3** 'Hullabaloo', din, loud noise. *Faire un bousin de tous les diables* (also: *faire un bousin à tout casser*): To make one hell of a racket.

bousine *n.f. (pej.)*: 'Banger', 'heap', ramshackle motor car.

boussole *n.f. Perdre la boussole*: **a** To be 'all at sea', to lose one's head. **b** To 'go off one's rocker', to go mad.

boustifaille *n.f. La boustifaille*: 'Grub', food. *Il ne vit que pour la boustifaille!* Life to him is just one big nosh!

boustifailler *v.intrans.* To 'stuff one's face', to 'nosh away', to eat heartily.

boustiffe *n.f. (abbr. boustifaille)*: 'Grub', 'nosh', food. *Ne penser qu'à la boustiffe*: To be 'belly-minded', to have food on the brain.

bout *n.m.* **1** *Etre à bout*: To be 'knackered', 'worn out', to be exhausted. *Pousser quelqu'un à bout (fig.)*: To bring someone to breaking-point. **2** *En connaître un bout*: To 'know a thing or two', to be very knowledgeable (on a specific topic). *Pour ce qui est de la mécanique, il en connaît un bout!* When it comes to cars, he's on the ball! **3** *Mettre les bouts*: To 'buzz off', to 'nip along', to go away. **4** *Au bout le bout! (iron.)*: All in good time! – Don't rush things! **5** *Discuter le bout de gras*: To 'natter away', to chat on idly. **b** To argue away endlessly. **6** (also: *gros bout*): 'Prick', 'prong', penis.

boutanche *n.f. (corr. bouteille)*: Bottle. *Une boutanche de rouquin*: A bottle of plonk.

bouteille *n.f.* **1** *Avoir de la bouteille*: To be 'long in the tooth', to have been around for quite a while. **2** *Prendre de la bouteille*: To be getting on in years, to be ageing noticeably. **3** *C'est la bouteille! (iron.)*: It's as clear as mud! – It's a right old muddle!

boutique *n.f.* **1** *(Slightly pej.)*: Place of work. *J'en ai marre de cette boutique!* I'm fed up working for this outfit! **2** *Plier boutique (fig.)*: To 'pack it in', to give up. *On lui a fait tant de misères qu'il a plié boutique*: He got so much aggro he called it a day. **3** *Etre de la boutique (fig.)*: To 'know the ropes', to know the workings of something (because of past experience). **4** *Et toute la boutique!* And the whole shebang! – The works!

– The lot! **5** *Montrer toute sa boutique*: To indecently expose oneself.

bouton *n.m.* **1** (also: *bouton de rose*): 'Clit', clitoris. (A number of expressions using *bouton* refer to lesbianism. *Maison tire-bouton*: lesbian night-club.) **2** *Cirer toujours le même bouton (fig.)*: To be always harping on at the same subject.

boutonnière *n.f.* **1** 'Clit', clitoris. **2** *Faire une boutonnière à quelqu'un (iron.)*: To knife, to cut someone open.

boutoque *n.f. (corr. boutique)*: Corner shop, small store.

bouzillage *n.m.* **1** Art of tattooing. **2** *(pl.)*: Tattoos (also: *bouzille*).

bouziller *v.trans.* To tattoo.

bouzin *n.m.* **1** *(pej.)*: 'Clap-house', low-class brothel. **2** *(pej.)*: 'Boozer', 'low dive', cheap-and-nasty pub. **3** Hullabaloo, din. *Faire un bouzin à tout casser*: To make one hell of a row.

bouzine *n.f.* **1** 'Puffer', old steam engine. **2** 'Banger', ramshackle motor car. **3** *(pej.)*: Computer. (The kind of 'gubbins' that has incomprehensible workings.) **4** 'Tummy', belly. *Ne rien avoir dans la bouzine*: To be peckish.

boxer *v.trans.* To 'biff', to 'clout', to punch.

boxon *n.m.* 'Cat-house', brothel.

boyautant *adj.* 'Rib-tickling', hilarious.

boyauter *v.pronom.* To split one's sides laughing.

boyaux *n.m.pl.* *C'est à se tordre les boyaux*: It's side-splitting – It's hilarious (also: *c'est boyautant*).

bracelets *n.m.pl.* 'Snips', 'derbies', handcuffs.

braceluche *n.m.* Bracelet.

braco *n.m. (abbr. braconnier)*: Poacher.

bracquemart *n.m.* 'Prick', 'cock', penis.

bradillon *n.m.* 'Fin', 'wing', arm. *Les bradillons en l'air!* Stick 'em up!

braguette *n.f. (pol.)*: Low-class prostitute (the kind that offers 'quickie sex').

braire *v.intrans.* **1** To 'holler', to protest vociferously. **2** *Il me fait braire!* He's a pain in the neck!

braise *n.f.* **1** *De la braise*: 'Brass', 'loot', money. *Il a nib de braise*: He's skint. **2** *Trouver les braises (pol.)*: To uncover vital evidence.

braisé *adj.* 'Loaded', 'flush', very wealthy.

bramer *v.intrans.* **1** To 'bawl', to weep loudly. **2** To 'howl down', to express vociferous disapproval.

brancard *n.m.* **1** *(pej.)*: 'Biddy', 'bit-of-skirt', woman. (The plural, referring to the legs of a woman, highlights the derogatory sexual connotation.) **2** *Ruer dans les brancards*: **a** To have become 'bolshie', to rebel in a fractious manner. **b** To leave one's spouse in a fit of temper.

branche *n.f.* **1** *Avoir de la branche*: To have breeding (literally to have good family antecedents). **2** *Se raccrocher aux branches (fig.)*: To try and save the situation by means of an explanation (after having 'put one's foot in it'). **3** *Vieille branche!* Old cock! – Old bean! *Alors, vieille branche, comment va?!* Well, mate, how's tricks?!

brancher *v.trans.* To put two people in touch with each other. *On l'a branché avec un grossiste*: We put him on to a wholesaler.

brancher *v.trans.reflex.* **1** *Se brancher sur quelqu'un*: To get in touch with someone. **2** *Se brancher sur une affaire*: To get in on something. (The expression can often refer to illegal activities.)

branco *n.m. (abbr. brancardier)*: Stretcher-bearer.

brandillon *n.m.* 'Fin', 'wing', arm. *Il m'a tendu les brandillons*: He reached out to me.

brandon *n.m.* 'Prick', 'cock', penis.

branlage *n.m.* 'Wanking', masturbation.

branlée *n.f.* **1** 'Wanking', masturbation. **2** 'Thrashing', 'bashing', beating-up. *On leur a foutu une de ces branlées!* We knocked the stuffing out of them! **3** *Une branlée de*: 'Heaps of', 'oodles', lots of. *Des jobs comme ça, on en trouve une branlée!* Work like that isn't hard to find!

branler *v.trans.* *Ne rien branler*: To do bugger-all, to be a lazy so-and-so. *Il n'en branle pas une!* He's an idle git! *Alors, qu'est-ce qu'on branle?!* Well, what are we going to do?!

branler *v.trans.reflex.* **1** To 'pull one's wire', to 'wank', to masturbate. **2** *S'en branler*: Not to give a damn about something. *Qu'elle vienne ou pas, je m'en branle!* I couldn't care two hoots whether she comes or not! **3** *Se les branler*: To 'do fuck-all', to 'twiddle one's thumbs', to be idle.

branlette *n.f.* 'Wanking', masturbation. *Se taper une branlette*: To 'pull one's wire'.

branleur *n.m. (pej.)*: **1** 'Slack-arse', idle so-and-so. **2** 'Yobbo', 'wide boy', scrupleless character.

branlure *n.f. (pej.)*: 'Nurk', despicable non-entity. (The very fact that the appellation is feminine makes it even more derogatory.)

branque *n.m.* **1** (Prostitutes' slang): 'Punter', client (also: *miché*). **2** 'Sucker', 'mug', dupe. **3** 'Nutter', 'screwball', mad person.

branque *adj.* 'Bonkers', 'barmy', mad. *Non, mais t'es branque?!* Are you off your head, or something?!

branquignol *n.m.* **1** 'Mug', 'sucker', dupe. **2** 'Loony', 'nutter', madcap character. (*Les Branquignols* was a famous comedy series on radio and in films; its antics were masterminded by Robert Dhéry and the nearest British equivalent to those barmy characters would appear to be the Goons.)

branquignol *adj.* 'Bonkers', 'barmy', mad.

branquignoler *v.intrans.* **1** To 'mosey along', to loaf about idly. **2** To go on a 'little filching spree'. (These petty thefts hardly come under the heading of criminal acts.)

braquage *n.m.* 'Stick-up', hold-up, armed attack.

braque *adj.* 'Bonkers', 'barmy', mad. *Il est légèrement braque sur les bords*: He's slightly nutty.

braquemart *n.m.* 'Prick', 'cock', penis. (The connotation of the word suggests an unusually large organ.)

braquer *v.trans.* **1** To level a gun at someone. **2** To do a 'stick-up', to carry out a hold-up. **3** To 'screw', to fuck, to have coition with.

braquer *v.trans.reflex.* To get 'shirty', to get one's back up, to become irritated and angry. *Faut pas le charrier, il se braque facilement!* Don't pull his leg, he doesn't take kindly to it!

braquet *n.m. Pousser le grand braquet*: To do things in a big way (literally to be in top gear. The word originates from the jargon of racing cyclists and refers to a cog-wheel on a bicycle.)

braqueur *n.m.* 'Triggerman', armed hoodlum.

bras *n.m.* **1** In a number of expressions the English equivalent of *bras* is 'hand' or 'hands'. *Avoir quelqu'un sur les bras*: To have someone on one's hands. *Mes bras sont liés*: My hands are tied. *Etre le bras droit de quelqu'un*: To be someone's right-hand man. **2** *Avoir le bras long*: To have 'plenty of pull', to be influential. **3** *Faire le gros bras*: To play the tough guy, to throw one's weight about. **4** *Mettre le bras jusqu'au coude*: To go all out at something, to spare no effort. **5** *En avoir les bras coupés*: To be 'flabbergasted', to be astounded by something (also: *en avoir les bras qui tombent*). **6** *En avoir plein les bras*: To be 'sick up to here', to be fed up with something. *J'en ai plein les bras de cette affaire!* I'm fed up to the back teeth with all this! **7** *Frapper (quelqu'un) à bras raccourcis* (also: *tomber sur quelqu'un à bras raccourcis*): To 'pitch into someone', to shower someone with blows. **8** *Ça m'est resté sur les bras*: I've been lumbered with it – I'm stuck with it.

brave *n.m. Y a pas d'heure pour les braves!* There's no time like the present for doing what you want to do!

bravo *n.m. Avoir les miches qui font bravo*: To 'have the shits', to be in a blue funk, to be very frightened.

brelettes *n.f.pl. (joc. corr. bretelles)*: Braces.

brelica *n.m.* 'Rod', 'shooter', handgun. (This is a jumbled rendering of the word *calibre*; this linguistic process is known as *verlan* or *verlen*, i.e. putting words *à l'envers*.)

breloque *n.f. Battre la breloque*: To be 'off one's rocker', to 'have a screw loose', to be mad.

brème *n.f.* (also: *brême*): **1** Card, playing-card. *Taper les brèmes*: To have a game of cards. **2** *(pl.)*: I.D. papers, identity documents. **3** *Etre en brème* (of prostitute): To be registered with the police health authorities. **4** *Que des brèmes!* Fuck-all! – Nothing at all!

Bretagne *Proper name. C'est un cousin à la mode de Bretagne*: He's a very distant relative.

bretelle *n.f.* **1** *(pol.)*: Telephone tap-line (also: *jarretelle*). **2** Motorway sliproad.

bréviaire *n.m. (pol.)*: Paris A-to-Z street-plan.

bric *n.m. De bric et de broc*: Of odds and ends, in bits and pieces. *J'ai appris ça de bric et de broc*: I got my information from various sources.

bric-à-brac *n.m.* Odds and ends, bits and pieces. *C'est pas vraiment un antiquaire, il fait du bric-à-brac*: He doesn't really deal in antiques, more in junk.

bricard *n.m. (pej.)*: Senior prison officer.

bricole *n.f.* **1** 'Trifle', thing of no importance. *Mais non, ce n'est qu'une bricole!* It's nothing to worry about! **2** Setback. *Si ça continue, il va lui arriver des bricoles*: If he keeps this up, he's going to come a cropper. **3** *(pl.)*: Odds and ends. **4** *Etre porté sur la bricole* (also: *être porté sur la bagatelle*): To be a randy so-and-so.

bricoler *v.trans. Bricoler une serrure*: To 'tickle' a lock open (to 'pick' it with illegal instruments).

bricoler *v.intrans.* **1** To 'potter about the house', to do odd jobs. **2** (at work): To 'tick over', to do very little. **3** (of criminal): To do easy 'jobs'.

bricoleur *n.m.* **1** *(pej.)*: Jack-of-all-trades (but master of none). **2** Small-time crook.

bride *n.f.* **1** *Avoir la bride sur le cou*: To have a free hand to do as one pleases. **2** Safety-chain. (This can be a thin set of links on an item of jewellery or a heavy burglar-proof device on a front door.) **3** *(pl.)*: 'Bracelets', 'derbies', handcuffs. **4** *Se mettre la bride* (of food, drink or sex): To 'have to go without', to be abstemious.

brider *v.trans.* **1** To keep a close rein on someone, to hold someone back (also: *tenir quelqu'un en bride*). **2** *Brider la lourde*: To close the door. (*Débrider la lourde*: To open the door.)

briffe *n.f.* 'Grub', 'nosh', food. *A la briffe!* Grub's up! – Come and get it!

briffer *v.trans. & intrans.* To 'nosh', to eat. (This verb has no pejorative or complimentary connotation; it relies on context for fuller meaning.)

briffeton *n.m.* Snack-meal, packed lunch.

brigadier *n.m. (th.)*: Stick with which one sounds *les trois coups* indicating that a performance is about to start.

brigand *n.m. Vieux brigand! (joc.)*: You rascal, you!

brignolet *n.m.* Bread. (This word and its corruption *brignoluche* are associated with harsh prison life up to the 30s and 40s.)

brillant *adj.* *C'est brillant, ça!* *(iron.)*: That's smart, that is! – That's no brainwave!

briller *v.intrans.* **1** To be 'in clover', to be doing very well. **2** *Briller par son absence (iron.)*: To be conspicuously absent (but certainly not missed!). **3** *Faire briller (quelqu'un)*: To bring about an orgasm (also: *faire reluire*).

brimborion *n.m.* *(pej.)*: 'Nobody', person of no importance whatsoever.

brin *n.m.* **1** *Un beau brin de fille*: A 'bit of alright', a very nice-looking girl. **2** *Faire un brin de causette*: To 'have a natter', to 'have a chin-wag', to chat for a moment. **3** *Faire un petit brin de toilette*: To have a 'cat-lick', to have a cursory wash.

brindezingue *n.m. & f.* **1** 'Nutter', 'loony', mad character. **2** 'Dipso', perpetually drunk person. (The expression *être dans les brindezingues* further illustrates the meaning.)

brindezingue *adj.* **1** 'Loony', 'barmy', mad. **2** 'Pissed', 'sozzled', drunk.

bringue *n.f.* **1** 'Gawky bird', tall awkward-looking woman. **2** 'Bender', 'binge', drinking spree. *Faire la bringue*: To 'live it up', to lead a fast and furious life.

bringuer *v.intrans.* (also: *faire la bringue*): To lead a fast life, to live it up. *Il bringue d'un bout de l'année à l'autre*: He's constantly whooping it up.

bringueur *n.m.* Character who likes to live it up (for whom life is one never-ending party).

brinqueballer *v.trans.* **1** (of luggage, shopping, etc.): To 'hump', to 'cart around', to carry with difficulty. **2** *Brinqueballer quelqu'un*: To 'cart along', to drag someone against their will.

brinqueballer *v.intrans.* **1** (of fixture): To be loose in its socket. **2** *Ça brinqueballe dans leur mariage*: Their marriage is going through a sticky patch.

brioche *n.f.* **1** 'Pot-belly', paunch. *Prendre de la brioche*: To develop a spare tyre. **2** *(pl.)*: 'Bum', 'backside', behind. **3** *Tortiller de la brioche*: To 'shake it all about', to dance. **4** *Partir en brioche (fig.)*: To 'go to pieces', to totally lose one's composure. **5** *Faire une brioche*: To 'make a boob', to make a blunder (also: *faire une boulette*).

briocher *v.trans.* *(pol.)*: To fill in a very detailed crime-sheet.

brique *n.f.* **1** Sum of one million francs (prior to the 1958 remonetization; after this, *brique* refers to a sum of ten thousand *nouveaux francs*). *Sa nouvelle bagnole lui a coûté dix briques*: His new car cost him ten grand. **2** *Bouffer des briques à la sauce cailloux*: To 'live on thin air', to have to go without food.

briquer *v.trans.* To clean and polish thoroughly. *Il a vachement briqué ses godasses*: He gave his shoes a good bit of spit-and-polish.

briquer *v.trans.reflex.* To get 'dolled up', to get all smartened up.

briquette *n.f.* *C'est de la briquette*: It's of no consequence – It's unimportant.

brisant *n.m.* Wind. *Il souffle un sacré brisant!* There's a right old gale blowing!

briscard *n.m.* (also: *brisquard*): **1** *(mil.)*: Old 'war-horse', old campaigner, veteran. **2** Old stager, old hand. (But one not altogether past his prime.)

brise *n.f.* *Brise d'anus*: Fart, wind.

brise-jet *n.m.* *(joc.)*: 'Prick', 'cock', penis. *N'avoir rien à se foutre sous le brise-jet*: To be 'short of birds', to have no female company. (The jocularity stems from the primary meaning of the word: tap-swirl, that rubber extension which slows the flow of water from a tap.)

brise *adj.* 'Knackered', 'all-in', worn out.

briser *v.trans.* *Les briser à quelqu'un*: To 'get on someone's wick', to be 'a pain in the neck', to be a nuisance.

bristol *n.m.* **1** Invitation card. (The word can sometimes refer to a *carte de visite*.) **2** *(pl.)*: 'Knockers', 'tits', breasts. (Contrary to assumptive etymology, the word has no semantic link with the Cockney rhyming-slang 'bristols'; in French it refers to a firm pair of breasts that seem to have the resilience of top-quality card.)

broc *n.m.* *(abbr. brocanteur)*: Junk-dealer, trader in second-hand goods.

broches *n.f.pl.* 'Choppers', 'gnashers', teeth.

broder *v.intrans.* To 'shoot a line', to exaggerate. (The emphasis is on embellishment for personal glorification. *Quand il parle de la guerre, qu'est-ce qu'il brode!* His 'how-I-won-the-war' stories have to be heard to be disbelieved!)

bromure *n.m.* *(joc.)*: 'Plonk', cheap and nasty wine served in college and army canteens. Its name derives from the dubious hypothesis that it is laced with bromide.

bronze *n.m.* **1** *Couler un bronze*: To 'crap', to 'shit', to defecate (also: *faire des cordes pour la marine*). **2** *L'œil de bronze*: The arse-hole, the anal sphincter. (With this meaning, the appellation is used only when referring to sodomous intercourse.)

bronzé *adj.* *Etre bronzé comme un cachet d'aspirine (joc.)*: To have a 'miner's suntan', to be of pale complexion.

broque *n.f.* **1** *Faire de la broque*: To be a junk-dealer, to sell second-hand goods. **2** *Vol à la broque*: Unusually clever con-trick where the trickster pretends to find an item of jewellery in the gutter and sells his 'find' to an opportunist bystander. **3** *Ne pas valoir une broque*: To be worth 'fuck-all', to be of no value whatsoever. **4** *Ne pas entraver une broque*: Not to understand a blind word of what is being said.

broquille *n.f.* **1** Minute. *Ça fait une heure et des broquilles que je poireaute!* He's kept me waiting well over an hour! **2** *Ne pas entraver une broquille*: Not to understand a blind word of what is being said. **3** *(pl.)*: 'Worms', cheap mince.

brosse *n.f.* **1** *Coupe en brosse*: Crew-cut. **2** *Passer la brosse à reluire*: To 'flannel', to 'soft-soap', to flatter someone. *Pas de brosse à reluire!* Stop the bootlicking!

brossée *n.f.* 'Thrashing', beating-up.

brosser *v.trans.* **1** To fuck, to 'screw', to have intercourse. **2** To 'work over', to thrash.

brosser *v.trans.reflex.* **1** *Se brosser* (also: *se brosser le ventre*): To 'do without food', to go hungry. **2** *Tu peux te brosser!* You can whistle for it! –Don't count on it! *Tu peux te brosser si tu t'imagines qu'il va te prêter du fric!* You've got another think coming if it's money you're after!

brouette *n.f.* **1** 'Jalopy', 'banger', old car. **2** *Brouette norvégienne*: Unusual form of intercourse.

brouillamini *n.m. (abbr. embrouillamini)*: Mix-up, tangle.

brouillard *n.m.* **1** *Foncer dans le brouillard*: **a** To be heading for a host of problems by rushing into the unknown (very much a case of 'leap before you look'). **b** To 'scram', to 'skedaddle', to disappear. **2** *Etre dans les brouillards*: To be 'well-primed', 'sozzled', to be drunk.

brouille *n.f. (pol.) Faire à la brouille*: To take advantage of surprise to make an arrest. *Ils les ont faits à la brouille*: They were caught napping.

brouillé *adj.* **1** *Se sentir brouillé*: To have a 'dicky tummy', to feel queasy (as a result of excessive eating or drinking). **2** *Etre brouillé avec* (of skill): To be hopeless at something. *Il est brouillé avec les math*: He's got no head for figures.

brouille-ménage *n.m. (joc.)*: 'Plonk', cheap red wine.

broussaille *n.f. La broussaille*: The 'short and curly', pubic hair. *Lentilles de broussaille*: 'Crabs', crab-lice.

brousse *n.f. (pej.) La brousse*: 'The sticks', the back-of-beyond, the distant countryside. *Il vit au fin fond de sa brousse*: He never sees town from one year to the next.

brouter *v.trans.* To perform oral sex. (*Brouter le paillasson* refers to cunnilingus and *brouter la tige* to fellatio.)

brouter *v.intrans. Faire brouter l'embrayage*: To drive on 'kangaroo petrol', to release the clutch jerkily.

brouter *v.trans.reflex. Se brouter le museau*: To 'smooch', to exchange long and passionate kisses.

broyer *v.trans. Broyer du noir*: To be 'down in the dumps', to 'have the blues', to be depressed (also: *avoir le cafard*).

brûlé *n.m. Ça sent le brûlé*: That looks fishy – It seems suspicious.

brûlé *adj.* **1** *Etre brûlé*: **a** To have lost one's reputation, one's good name. **b** To find oneself betrayed (to have given oneself away unwittingly). **2** *Une tête brûlée*: A dare-devil.

brûler *v.trans.* **1** To 'bump off', to kill (usually with a firearm). **2** *Brûler un feu rouge*: To go through a set of red traffic lights. **3** *Brûler le dur*: To travel by train without a ticket. **4** *Brûler les planches (th.)*: To be a great hit, to be a tremendous success in a play.

brûler *v.intrans.* To be very near the truth. *Il sentait bien qu'il brûlait, encore deux questions et le malfrat se mettrait à table*: He knew he was getting warmer; another question or two and the suspect would spill the beans.

brutal *n.m.* **1** *Du brutal*: **a** 'Hard stuff', strong liquor (usually of the 'moonshine' variety). **b** 'Rough plonk', cheap and nasty red wine. **c** Coarse bread. (With this meaning, the word is associated with prison life up to the 30s and 40s.) **2** *Le brutal*: The *Métro*, the Paris underground railway.

bûche *n.f.* **1** 'Thickie', 'blockhead', dunce. **2** Match (from a matchbox). **3** Lump found in cheap cigarettes, usually the unchopped stalk of a tobacco leaf. **4** *Ramasser une bûche*: **a** To 'take a spill', to fall over (also: *prendre un billet de parterre*). **b** *(fig.)*: To 'come a cropper', to suffer a serious setback.

bûcher *v.trans. & intrans.* **1** *(sch.)*: To 'swot', to work hard for an exam. *Il faut que tu bûches tes math!* You'll have to get stuck into your maths revision! **2** To 'graft', to work one's fingers to the bone.

bûcheur *n.m.* **1** *(sch.)*: 'Swot', swotter. (With this meaning, the word sometimes takes the connotation of slow learner.) **2** 'Grafter', hard worker.

bucolique *n.f.* Prostitute who seeks out clients mainly in public parks and gardens.

buffecaille *n.m.* 'Bread-basket', 'corporation', belly.

buffet *n.m.* **1** Chest. *Avoir toute une batterie de cuisine sur le buffet*: To have a chestful of medals. **2** 'Bread-basket', belly, stomach. *Se remplir le buffet*: To 'stuff one's face', to eat to satiety.

3 *N'avoir rien dans le buffet (fig.)*: To be gutless, to be a coward.

buis *n.m. Avoir le coup de buis*: To be 'buggered', 'knackered', to be worn out (also: *avoir le coup de pompe*).

bulle *n.f.* **1** *(sch.)*: Nought, zero mark. (The usual expression is *choper* or *attraper une bulle*.) **2** *Coincer sa bulle*: **a** To 'skive', to dodge work successfully. **b** To 'snooze', to 'snatch some shut-eye', to get some sleep (usually while others are working). **3** *Suivre une bulle (pol.)*: To follow up a false lead.

bulletin *n.m. Avaler son bulletin de naissance*: To 'snuff it', to 'croak', to die (also: *avaler son extrait de naissance*).

bureau *n.m. Bureau des pleurs (joc.)*: Complaints counter (in department store, etc.).

burelingue *n.m. (corr. bureau; also: burlingue)*: **1** Office, 'white-collar' place of work. *Il est toujours crevé quand il rentre du burelingue*: He's always whacked when he gets back from work. **2** 'Corporation', pot-belly (because it seems to jut out like a desk).

burette *n.f.* **1** 'Mush', 'dial', face. **2** 'Bean', 'bonce', head. **3** *(pl.)*: 'Bollocks', 'balls', testicles.

buriné *past part. Etre buriné par l'effort*: The standard meaning is to have weathered features through excessive work but the jocularity of the expression stems from its antiphrastic use when referring to someone who doesn't do a stroke of work.

buriner *v.intrans.* To 'graft', to work hard.

burineur *n.m.* 'Slogger', hard worker.

burmas *n.m.pl.* 'Fake gems', paste jewellery.

(*Burma*, a firm dealing mainly in imitation jewellery, has gained fame through generic lexicalization of its name.)

burnes *n.f.pl.* 'Bollocks', 'balls', testicles. *Il me court sur les burnes! (fig.)*: He's a pain in the arse!

burnous *n.m. Faire suer le burnous*: To 'get one's pound of flesh', to be a slave-driver. (This expression originates from the French occupation of North Africa.)

butage *n.m.* (also: *buttage*): Killing, gangland murder.

buté *adj.* 'Pig-headed', stubborn.

buter *v.trans.* To 'bump off', to kill.

buter *v.trans.reflex.* To 'do oneself in', to commit suicide (usually by means of a firearm).

buteur *n.m.* 'Hit-man', hired killer.

butte *n.f.* **1** *La Butte*: Affectionate name given to Montmartre. **2** *Les Buttes (abbr. les Buttes-Chaumont)*: Hilly district of Paris. (The original studios and headquarters of French television were conveniently situated on one of the *buttes*. They evoke the same nostalgic feelings as Crystal Palace does for the British.) **3** *Monter à la butte*: To be guillotined (also: *monter à l'abbaye de Monte-à-regret*).

buvable *adj.* **1** *(joc.) C'est un petit pinard tout ce qu'il y a de buvable!* It's an amusing little wine! **2** *Ne pas être buvable* (of person): To be unbearable. *Tu n'es vraiment pas buvable!* You're really impossible!

buvarder *v.trans.* To blot, to use blotting paper.

buveton *n.m.* Blotting paper.

buveur *n.m. Buveur d'encre*: 'Pen-pusher', menial clerk. (The appellation has in-built jocularity when referring to a journalist.)

C

C *n.f. De la* C: 'Coke', 'snow', cocaine.

ça *dem.pron.* A familiar contraction of *cela*, this pronoun's colloquiality is commensurate with context and usage. **1** Sex, sexual matters. *Faire ça*: To 'have it off'. *Ne penser qu'à ça*: To have a one-track mind. **2** *Ah, ça?!* Who knows?! – God only knows! *Ah, ça?! Te dire s'il va venir?!* Search me! I don't know if he's coming! **3** *Comme ça* (form of 'verbal padding'): So . . . *Alors, comme ça elle me dit . . . et je lui réponds comme ça . . .*: So I says to her . . . and she says to me . . . *Alors comme ça, vous vous mariez?* So you're getting married then? **4** *Et avec ça! (iron.)*: Get away! –Go on with you! – You're joking?! *Il ne picole pas?! Et avec ça!* Him on the wagon? You must be joking! **5** *C'est ça!* Right on! You've got it in one! **6** *C'est tout à fait ça*: That's just the job. – That's just what I want. **7** *Ce n'est pas tout ça, mais. . .*: That's all very well, but . . . *Ce n'est pas tout ça, mais moi, il faut que je rentre*: It's O.K. for you (to talk), but I've got to get home. **8** *Avoir de ça*: To be 'loaded', to have plenty of money (also: *avoir de quoi*). **9** *Il y a de ça!* There's some truth in it! *Il y a de ça! Tu sais, son mariage n'est pas des plus réussis*: You're not far off the truth! She's not all that happily married. **10** *Il n'y a que ça*: There's nothing like it! – You can't beat it! *Un bon cigare à la fin d'un repas, 'y a que ça!* A good cigar at the end of a meal just makes it perfect. **11** *Remettre ça*: To have another. *Alors, on remet ça? C'est ma tournée!* Let's have another drink, it's my round!

cab *n.m. (abbr. cabot)*: 'Mutt', 'pooch', dog.

cabane *n.f.* **1** 'Nick', 'clink', jail. *Faire de la cabane*: To do time. (The word is an abbreviated version of *la cabane aux mille lourdes*.) **2** *(joc.)*: House (often a *résidence secondaire* or weekend dwelling). The tongue-in-cheek jocularity derives from the primary meaning: shack, equated with the grandeur of the residence described. **3** *Attiger la cabane*: To 'lay it on a bit thick', to exaggerate.

cabanon *n.m.* **1** Modest weekend dwelling. (The word originates from the *Côte d'Azur*.)

2 'Nut-house', lunatic asylum. *Il est bon pour le cabanon!* He's just about ready for the happy farm!

cabêche *n.f.* 'Bean', 'brainbox', head. *N'avoir rien dans la cabêche*: To be pig-ignorant.

caberlot *n.m.* **1** Country pub (the kind of back-of-beyond ale-house with a very limited clientele). **2** 'Bean', 'brainbox', head. *Avoir le caberlot en roue libre*: To be 'off one's rocker', to 'have a screw loose', to be more than slightly mad.

cabince *n.f.* **1** Ship's cabin. **2** *(pl.)*: 'Shit-house', 'karzey', lavatory.

câbles *n.m.pl. Faire des câbles pour la marine*: To do 'number two's', to 'shit', to defecate.

cabochard *n.m.* 'Mule', stubborn character.

cabochard *adj.* 'Pig-headed', stubborn. *Il est tout ce qu'il y a de cabochard*: He's as stubborn as a mule.

caboche *n.f.* 'Bean', 'bonce', head. *Avoir une caboche en pain de sucre*: To have an egg-shaped skull. *Avoir la caboche dure (fig.)*: To be 'slow on the uptake', to be dim-witted. *Elle n'a rien dans la caboche*: She's not exactly bursting with O-levels!

cabochon *n.m.* **1** 'Bean', 'bonce', head. *Il a pris un coup de goumi sur le cabochon*: He got himself coshed. *Se monter le cabochon*: **a** To 'kid oneself', to delude oneself. **b** To get 'het-up', to work oneself into a frenzy. **2** 'Nous', intelligence. *Sers-toi de ton cabochon!* Use your loaf! –For heaven's sake, think! **3** 'Biff', clout, blow. **4** Flashy (often phoney) diamond. **5** Car's side-light. (The kind of near-useless lighting device made redundant on modern cars; the *cabochon*, equipped with a tiny bulb, used to protrude like a pimple on car wings.)

cabombe *n.f.* Glim, glimmer, the dim irradiation of a weak lighting device.

cabossé *adj.* **1** (of metal surface): 'Dinged', dented. **2** (of person): Bruised, battered. *Sa gueule cabossée expliquait dix ans de ring*: His lumpy features were a testimony to his boxing past.

cabot *n.m.* **1** 'Mutt', 'pooch', dog. **2** *(mil.)*: 'Corp', corporal. **3** *(th.)*: 'Ham', ham actor.

4 'Swank', show-off. *Quel cabot! Faut toujours qu'il se fasse remarquer!* He's always playing to the gallery!

caboter *v.intrans.* To roam the world (literally to lead the life of a rolling stone).

cabotin *n.m.* **1** 'Ham', ham actor. **2** 'Swank', show-off.

cabotin *adj.* 'Swanky', show-off, vain. *Il est cabotin comme il est pas possible de l'être!* He thinks the world of himself, he does!

cabotinage *n.m.* 'Hamming', playing to the gallery (putting on airs and graces associated with a bad stage performance).

caboulot *n.m.* Modest dance-hall. (The *petit caboulot*, often an open-air establishment in the prettier suburbs of Paris, evokes nostalgic memories of the 30s, 40s and 50s.)

cabriole *n.f. Faire la cabriole (fig.):* **a** To do a 'U-turn', to change one's mind radically about an issue (usually in order to comply with the majority). **b** To 'come unstuck' financially, to go bankrupt. **c** To 'do a bunk', to do a moonlight flit, to run away with the cash. **d** To 'croak', to 'snuff it', to die.

cabriolets *n.m.pl.* 'Derbies', 'bracelets', handcuffs.

caca *n.m.* (Nursery language): 'Biggies', 'number two's', excrement.

caca *adj.inv.* **1** Mucky, dirty. **2** *Couleur caca d'oie:* Pea-green.

cacasse *n.f. Aller à (la) cacasse:* To have anal intercourse.

cacatoire *adj.* 'Shitty', very boring. *J'ai toujours trouvé les math cacatoires!* Maths have always bored the pants off me!

cache-fri-fri *n.m.* 'G-string', pair of mini-briefs.

cachemire *n.m. (joc.):* Duster, dusting cloth.

cache-misère *n.m. (joc.):* Long overcoat hiding tatty clothes.

cacher *v.trans.* **1** To 'wolf', to down vast quantities of food. **2** *Cacher son jeu:* To play one's cards close to one's chest and reveal nothing. **3** *Cacher la merde au chat (joc. & iron.):* To 'sweep something under the carpet', to hide incriminating material and thus avoid problems.

cachet *n.m.* **1** *Avoir du cachet:* To have class, to have style. **2** *Courir le cachet* (of actor): To tout for parts. **3** *Avoir un teint de cachet d'aspirine:* To be as pale as death.

cacheton *n.m. (corr. cachet)* **1** *(th.):* Actor's fee. **2** Payment received by prostitute. **3** Pill, tablet.

cachetonneur *n.m. (th.):* Bit-part actor chasing employment.

cachotterie *n.f.* Petty secret. *Faire des cachotteries:* To make secrets out of trifles.

cachottier *n.m.* 'Cagey character', keeper of petty secrets. *Petit cachottier, va!* You are one for secrets, aren't you!

cachottier *adj.* 'Cagey', secretive (over trivial matters).

cactus *n.m.* **1** 'Hitch', 'snag', difficulty. *'y a comme qui dirait un cactus!* We've got a prickly situation here! **2** *Avoir un cactus dans la poche:* To be 'slow on the draw', to be mean with money.

cadancher *v.intrans.* To 'snuff it', to 'croak', to die.

cadavre *n.m.* **1** 'Dead man', empty bottle of booze. **2** Card-player with a jinx, unlucky gambler.

cadeau *n.m.* **1** Payment received by prostitute. (With this meaning the word derives from the hackneyed expression *'N'oublie pas mon petit cadeau!'*) **2** *Ne pas faire de cadeaux (fig.):* To give nothing away, to be hard and unrelenting (in sport or business matters).

cadenas *n.m. Y mettre un cadenas:* To 'put a sock in it', to 'clam up', to keep silent. *On lui a dit d'y mettre un cadenas:* They told him to keep his trap shut.

cadennes *n.f.pl.* (also: *cadènes*): 'Derbies', 'bracelets', handcuffs.

cadet *n.m. C'est le cadet de mes soucis:* It's the least of my worries.

cador *n.m. (pej.):* **1** 'Mutt', 'pooch', dog. **2** (Underworld slang): 'Big shot', top man, gang leader.

cadran *n.m.* **1** 'Mush', 'dial', face. **2** 'Bum', 'backside', bottom. **3** *Faire le tour du cadran:* To sleep 'round the clock', to sleep a twelve-hour stretch.

cadre *n.m. (pol.) Cadre noir:* High-ranking police officer.

cafard *n.m.* **1** 'Snitch', sneak. *Faire le cafard:* To tell tales. **2** 'Crawler', 'creep', sycophant. **3** *Avoir le cafard:* To be down in the dumps, to be depressed. *C'est un bouquin à vous filer le cafard!* It's a really disheartening novel.

cafardage *n.m.* 'Snitching', sneaking, tale-telling.

cafardant *adj.* Dispiriting, depressing.

cafarder *v.intrans.* To sneak, to tell tales on someone.

cafardeur *n.m.* 'Snitch', sneak, tale-teller.

cafardeux *adj. Etre cafardeux:* **a** To be 'down in the dumps', to be depressed. **b** To be prone to depression.

caf'-conce *n.m. (abbr. café-concert):* Old-time music-hall where patrons could consume alcoholic beverage.

café *n.m.* **1** *Le café du pauvre (joc.):* Love-making, intercourse. **2** *C'est un peu fort de café! (iron.):* That's a bit thick! – That's a bit much! –This is unreasonable!

cafetière *n.f.* 1 'Bean', 'bonce', head. *Travailler de la cafetière*: To be 'bonkers', 'potty', to be mad. *Y aller de la cafetière*: To be guillotined. 2 *Taper sur la cafetière de quelqu'un*: To 'get on someone's wick', to be irritating. 3 'Mush', 'dial', face. *Tirer une drôle de cafetière*: To pull a face. 4 *(corr. cafteur)*: Sneak, tale-teller.

cafeton *n.m.* 1 Café, bistrot. 2 Cup of coffee. *Sers-nous un cafeton bien serré!* Make us a strong cup of coffee, the real stuff!

cafiot *n.m. Un cafiot*: A cup of coffee.

cafouillage *n.m.* Bungling, botching. *Quel cafouillage!* What a cock-up!

cafouiller *v.intrans.* 1 (of engine): To miss, to misfire. 2 (of person): To splutter. 3 To 'make a balls' of something, to mess things up.

cafouilleur *n.m.* 'Bungler', botcher.

cafouilleux *adj.* (of situation): Messy, confused.

cafouillis *n.m.* 'Cock-up', bungled piece of work.

cafter *v.intrans.* (also: *cafeter*): To sneak, to tell on someone.

cafteur *n.m.* (also: *cafeteur*): Sneak, tell-tale. *Sale cafteur, va!* You rotten snitch!

cagade *n.f.* 'Cock-up', 'boob', blunder. *Faire une cagade*: To drop a clanger.

cage *n.f.* 1 'Nick', 'slammer', jail. *On l'a mis en cage*: He got put away. 2 *Cage à poules (iron.)*: 'Pokey digs', cramped lodgings. 3 *(pl.)*: 'Lug-holes', ears.

cageot *n.m. (pej.)*: 'Bag', 'ugly biddy', unattractive woman.

cagna *n.f.* 1 *(mil.)*: Dug-out, shelter. 2 'Den', cramped room. 3 *La Grande Cagna* (Underworld slang): Paris Police Headquarters (also: *la Maison Parapluie*).

cagnard *n.m. Le cagnard*: The sun (the midday kind that warms and roasts you – not surprisingly, a word from Provence).

cagne *n.f. (pej.)*: 'Nag', inferior horse (also: *carne*).

cagnotte *n.f.* 'Kitty', small communal cash-fund.

cagoinces *n.m.pl. Les cagoinces*: 'The karzey', 'the bog', the lavatory.

caguer *v.intrans.* 1 To 'crap', to 'shit', to defecate. 2 *Faire caguer quelqu'un (fig.)*: To be 'a pain in the arse', to be a nuisance to someone.

cahier *n.m. (pol.)*: Crime-sheet.

cahin-caha *adv. Ça va cahin-caha*: We're having our ups and downs. (Things aren't going too smoothly.)

cahoua *n.m.* (also: *caoua*): Coffee. *Son cahoua, c'est pas du jus de chaussette!* He makes a really strong cup of coffee!

caïd *n.m.* 1 (Underworld slang): 'Big shot', top man, gang leader. 2 'Ace guy', brilliant character. *Au vélo, c'est un caïd!* He's really a crack cyclist!

caille *n.f.* 1 'Fair game', innocent young girl. 2 *Ma petite caille*: My lovey-dovey – My pet – My darling. 3 'Hitch', 'snag', setback. *Quelle caille!* What rotten bad luck! 4 *L'avoir à la caille*: **a** To be 'in a lather', to be furious about something. **b** To be disheartened by something. 5 *Avoir quelqu'un à la caille*: To hate someone's guts, to detest someone thoroughly.

cailler *v.intrans.* To be freezing, to feel very cold. *Qu'est-ce qu'on caille ici!* It's real brass monkey weather!

cailler *v.trans. reflex. Se cailler le raisin* (or *le sang*): To worry oneself sick.

caillou *n.m.* 1 Skull. *Avoir le caillou déplumé* (also: *n'avoir plus un poil sur le caillou*): To be as bald as a coot. 2 *(pl.)*: 'Stones', gems. 3 *Casser des cailloux*: To 'do time', to serve a prison sentence. *C'était un caïd, mais maintenant il casse des cailloux*: He used to be a big shot, but now he's sewing mailbags. 4 *Bouffer des briques à la sauce cailloux*: To 'live on thin air', to go hungry.

caisse *n.f.* 1 'Bean', 'brainbox', head. *Se faire sauter la caisse*: To blow one's brains out. *Bourrer la caisse à quelqu'un (fig.)*: To try and fool someone. 2 Chest. *S'en aller de la caisse*: To have T.B., to suffer from tuberculosis. 3 'Heap', 'banger', old motor car. 4 *Caisse à savon (joc.)*: 'Old crate', aeroplane long past its prime. 5 'Glasshouse', 'clink', military jail. *Faire de la grosse caisse*: To do time in the cooler. 6 *Battre la grosse caisse*: To 'blow one's own trumpet', to draw attention to oneself (literally to beat the big drum). 7 *Partir avec la caisse*: To 'do a bunk', to leave with the takings (literally to go off with the till). 8 *Passer à la caisse*: To 'get one's cards', to get the sack. 9 *Tenir une caisse*: To be 'pissed', 'sozzled', to be drunk.

caisson *n.m.* 'Brainbox', head. *Avoir le caisson qui se fait la malle*: To be 'going soft in the head', to be well on the way to senility. *Se faire sauter le caisson*: To blow one's brains out.

calamita *interj. (joc.)*: Strewth! – Crumbs! –Crikey! (This jocular corruption of *calamité* is as twee as its English equivalents.)

calanche *n.f. La calanche*: Death (that great leveller).

calancher *v.intrans.* To 'croak', to 'snuff it', to die.

calbard *n.m. (corr. caleçon)*: 'Jocks', 'drawers', underpants (also: *calcif*).

calbombe *n.f.* (also: *calebombe*): Glim, glimmer, the dim irradiation of a weak lighting device.

calbute *n.m.* 'Jocks', 'drawers', underpants.

calcer *v.trans.* To 'screw', to fuck, to have intercourse with.

calcif *n.m.* (also: *calecif*): 'Jocks', 'drawers', underpants.

calculé *past part. C'est calculé pour!* This humoristic stock-in-trade expression conveys the fact that whatever technical contraption is being discussed 'works because it works'.

calculs *n.m.pl. Se faire des calculs:* To 'worry oneself sick', to make oneself ill with worry (literally to get gallstones; *se faire de la bile* is equally explicit).

cale *n.f.* **1** *Etre sur cales:* **a** (of car): To be up on blocks, to have been jacked up for long-term storage on bricks or wooden blocks. **b** (of person): To be 'out of the running', to have been left out on the touchline of normal activity. **2** *Etre à fond de cale:* To be 'skint', 'broke', to be penniless. **3** *Etre de la cale* (Seamen's slang): To 'know the golden rivet', to be a 'pouf', to be a homosexual.

calé *adj.* **1** 'Gifted', brainy. *Il est calé en math:* He's got a head for maths. **2** *Ça n'est pas calé! (iron.):* I don't call that brilliant! – That's pretty stupid!

calebasse *n.f.* 'Nut', 'brainbox', head. *J'ai une de ces calebasses!* I've got a splitting headache!

calecer *v.trans.* To 'screw', to fuck, to have intercourse with.

calecif *n.m.* 'Jocks', 'drawers', underpants. *Anguille de calecif:* 'Prick', 'cock', penis.

caleçonner *v.intrans. (th.):* To have 'butterflies in one's stomach', to have stage-fright.

calencher *v.intrans.* To 'croak', to 'snuff it', to die.

calendo *n.m.* (also: *calendos*): Camembert cheese. (The very ripe variety is jocularly nicknamed *vient-tout-seul*.)

caler *v.intrans.* **1** (of motor engine): To stall, to come to an abrupt stop. **2** *(fig.):* To falter, to give up. *A la quatrième portion il a calé:* He just couldn't face a fifth helping.

caler *v.trans.reflex.* **1** To settle oneself comfortably (also: *se caler le cul*). *Il s'était bien calé à l'aise près du réchaud:* Next to the heater, he was as snug as a bug in a rug! **2** *Se caler les badigoinces* (also: *se les caler*): To 'stuff one's face', to eat heartily.

caleter *v.intrans.* (also: *calter*): To 'buzz off', to 'skedaddle', to go away.

caleur *n.f. (corr. chaleur) Quelle caleur!* It ain't half hot, Mum! (also: *quelle calor!*).

calfoutre *n.m.* 'Jocks', 'drawers', underpants.

calibre *n.m.* **1** 'Rod', 'shooter', handgun. **2** *Du même calibre* (of persons): To be two (or more) of a kind. *Ils sont tous du même calibre, tes copains, malfrats et compagnie!* You know what I think of your friends . . . crooks the lot of them!

calicot *n.m.* Person in the 'rag-trade' (in the garments industry).

californie *n.f.* Overtime wages.

calin *n.m. Faire un gros calin à quelqu'un:* To cuddle up to someone.

calmer *v.trans.* **1** *(iron):* To knock someone out. *Il l'a calmé d'une droite au menton:* A jab on the chin and he was out for the count. **2** To show someone who's boss, to bring someone into line.

calotin *n.m.* 'Holy Joe', over-zealous church-goer.

calots *n.m.pl.* 'Oglers', 'peepers', eyes. *Rouler des calots:* To 'goggle', to roll one's eyes in astonishment.

calotte *n.f.* **1** 'Clout', 'cuff', slap. *Il lui a filé une de ces calottes!* He belted him round the earhole! **2** *La calotte:* The Catholic clergy and the more ardently zealous. (With this meaning, the word has strong derogatory connotations and the comment *il est de la calotte* is always very disparaging.)

calotter *v.trans.* **1** To 'clout', to box someone's ears. **2** To 'nick', to 'pinch', to steal. *Il a encore calotté mes sèches!* He's swiped my fags again! (With this meaning, the verb has jocular under-tones and never refers to real theft as such.) **3** *Se faire calotter:* To get 'collared', to be arrested by the police. **4** To 'down', to gulp a drink. *Aussi sec, il a calotté un kil de rouge:* He knocked back a bottle of plonk in next to no time.

calouser *v.trans. Calouser le bitume* (of prostitute): To 'walk the streets', to go soliciting.

calouses *n.f.pl.* 'Pins', 'gambs', legs. *Côté nanas, les calouses, c'est son faible!* When it comes to birds, he's a leg-man! (The word seems to relate exclusively to women's legs, as the expression *jouer des calouses:* to show a bit of leg, further illustrates.)

calpette *n.f.* 'Clapper', tongue.

calsif *n.m.* 'Jocks', 'drawers', underpants.

calter *v.intrans.* To 'buzz off', to 'skedaddle', to go away. *Allez, calte!* Scram!

calva *n.m. (abbr. calvados):* Applejack, apple brandy.

calvaire *n.m. Quel calvaire! (joc.):* What a drag! – What a nuisance!

camarade *n.m. Faire camarade:* **a** To 'get pally', to strike up a friendship. *D'entrée, on a fait camarade avec lui:* We got chummy with him from the start. **b** To raise one's hands in surrender.

camarde *n.f.* Death (that great leveller).

camaro *n.m. (corr. abbr. camarade):* 'Buddy', 'chum', friend.

cambriole *n.f. La cambriole:* The brotherhood of burglars.

cambron *n.m.* 'Nick', jail, prison. (In military contexts, the word refers to the 'glasshouse' or 'cooler', i.e. a punishment cell.)

Cambronne *Proper name. Le mot de Cambronne*: Euphemistic equivalent to *merde*. (General Cambronne is reputed to have uttered this expletive when asked to surrender at Waterloo.) *Je lui ai dit le mot de Cambronne*: I told him to get knotted!

cambrouille *n.f. La cambrouille*: 'The sticks', 'the back of beyond', the depths of rural countryside.

cambrousard *n.m.* 'Hayseed', country bumpkin, one who lives right out in the country.

cambrousse *n.f.* 'The sticks', 'the back of beyond', the depths of rural countryside. *Il habite en pleine cambrousse*: He lives miles from anywhere. *Il est tout frais sorti de sa cambrousse*: He's the original country hick.

cambuse *n.f.* Cramped and rather downmarket digs (the kind of accommodation that says little for its occupant. When used to refer to one's own accommodation, the word becomes jocularly modest).

cambut *n.m. Faire un cambut* (Hawkers' slang): To do a switch, to switch goods. (This is a popular con-trick where inferior articles are substituted for those originally purchased by a customer.)

cambuté *adj.* **1** 'Topsy-turvy', jumbled. *Après la perquise, la turne était drôlement cambutée*: The place was in a right old mess after the fuzz turned it inside out. **2** (of person): Upset, distraught. *Elle était toute cambutée à l'idée de ne jamais le revoir*: She was real churned at the thought of never seeing him again.

cambuter *v.trans.* **1** To 'put topsy-turvy', to jumble. **2** To do a switch, to exchange items. *Ils ont cambuté leurs fafs*: They switched I.D.s. **3** To break in. *Cambuter un coffiot*: To crack a safe.

came *n.m.* (*abbr. camelot*): Street-hawker, open-air salesman.

came *n.f.* (*abbr. camelote*): The general and uncharismatic meaning of the word is 'goods'. **1** Merchandise. *Il n'y avait pas lerche de came sur son étalage*: His stall wasn't exactly overloaded with goodies. **2** 'Dope', drugs, narcotics. *Ça fait un moment qu'il tâte de la came*: He's been a junkie since a while back now. **3** 'Brass', 'loot', money. *Il en faut de la came pour une tire comme ça*: You need a hell of a lot of dough for a car like that. **4** *Balancer la came*: To 'juice off', to ejaculate.

camé *n.m.* 'Junkie', drug addict.

camé *adj.* **1** 'High', under the influence of drugs. *Il est camé à la mort*: He's as high as a kite. **2** 'Pissed', 'sozzled', inebriated.

camembert *n.m.* Round and flat traffic beacon (because it is reminiscent of a *camembert* cheese).

camer *v.intrans. Qu'est-ce que ça came!* What a pong! – What a foul smell! (also: *coincer, fouetter*).

camer *v.trans.reflex.* To take drugs, to be an addict.

camp *n.m. Foutre le camp*: To 'piss off', to go away. *Fous le camp!* Bugger off!

campagne *n.f.* **1** *Etre à la campagne*: To be unavailable. (This euphemistic excuse is sometimes uttered in irony.) **2** *Emmener quelqu'un à la campagne*: To show someone who's boss, to assert one's authority in no uncertain manner.

campe *n.f.* (*abbr. campagne*) *La campe*: 'The sticks', the depths of rural countryside.

campêche *n.f. Bois de campêche*: 'Fizzy Lizzy', cheap champagne.

camphre *n.m.* **1** 'Strong booze', hard liquor, strong alcohol. **2** *Ça sent le camphre*: **a** (of file, document, etc.): It's been gathering dust (literally it smells of mothballs). **b** (*pol.*): There's trouble brewing.

camphrer *v.pronom.* To get 'pissed', 'blotto', to get drunk.

camplouse *n.f. La camplouse*: 'The sticks', 'the back of beyond', the depths of rural countryside.

campo *n.m.* 'Break', holiday. *J'ai campo aujourd'hui*: It's my day off today. *Il leur a donné campo*: He gave them time off.

canadienne *n.f. Canadienne en sapin* (*joc.*): 'Wooden overcoat', coffin.

canaillou *n.m. Canaillou, va!* (*joc.*): You rascal, you!

canaque *n.m.* (*pej.*): 'Coon', nigger, coloured person.

canard *n.m.* **1** 'Rag', newspaper. *J'ai lu ça dans le canard du coin*: I got it from the local sheet. *Le Canard Enchaîné*, formerly *le Canard Déchaîné*, took this name after being banned, then heavily censored in the 30s. **2** 'Red herring', misleading piece of news. *Il mord dans n'importe quel canard*: He'll fall for any old story. **3** (*pej.*): 'Nag', 'hack', inferior horse. *Il a tout paumé sur un canard à la gomme*: He lost all his winnings on some third-rate nag. **4** Dunked sugar lump (usually in coffee or brandy). **5** *Froid de canard*: 'Brass monkey' weather, freezing cold conditions.

canarde *n.f. La Grande Canarde*: The Great War.

canarder *v.trans.* To gun down, to shoot.

canari *n.m. Changer l'eau du canari* (*joc.*): To 'have a slash', to pee, to urinate.

canasson *n.m.* 'Hack', 'nag', horse.

cancan *n.m.* Gossip. *Les cancans, c'est son blot!* There'd be no grapevine without her!

cancre *n.m.* 'Duffer', 'blockhead', dunce. *LA FOIRE AUX CANCRES* is a famous satirical novel on education.

cané *n.m.* (also: *canné*): 'Stiff', corpse.

canelles *n.f.pl.* 'Derbies', 'bracelets', handcuffs.

caner *v.intrans.* (also: *canner*): **1** To 'croak', to 'snuff it', to die. *Continue de fumer comme ça et tu caneras d'un chou-fleur aux éponges!* Carry on smoking like that and you'll catch lung-cancer! **2** To 'funk', to back out, to be reluctant to pursue a line of action.

canette *n.f.* Small bottle of beer. (The expression *chasser la canette* refers to the desperate search for refreshing drinks by competitors during a gruelling cycling race. It is an accepted practice that Tour de France competitors go into cafés and swipe as many *canettes* as possible.)

caneur *n.m.* (also: *canneur*): 'Funk', coward.

canevas *n.m.* *Le canevas* (Boxing slang): The canvas, the floor of the ring. *Il est allé quatre fois au canevas avant de se faire compter par l'arbitre*: He hit the deck four times before the ref counted him out.

canif *n.m.* *Donner un coup de canif dans le contrat*: To 'have a fling', to be unfaithful to one's spouse.

canne *n.f.* **1** *(pl.)*: 'Pins', 'gambs', legs. *Mettre les cannes*: To 'scram', to 'scarper', to run away. **2** *Etre en canne* (of criminal): To be prohibited by law from entering certain urban areas. **3** *Avoir la canne*: To 'have the big stick', to have an erection (also: *avoir le gourdin*). **4** *Casser sa canne*: To 'kick the bucket', to 'snuff it', to die.

canon *n.m.* **1** Glass of wine. *Descendre un canon de gros rouge*: To down a glass of plonk. **2** Belly, stomach. *On n'a rien à se mettre dans le canon!* The cupboard's bare! **3** 'Prick', 'cock', penis. *Avoir une balle dans le canon*: To feel as randy as hell.

cantaloup *n.m.* **1** Native of the Auvergne. **2** Coalman, coal-merchant. **3** Proprietor of a small bistrot. (The *bougnat* or *cantaloup* often successfully combines the selling of coal and the retailing of alcoholic beverage.)

canter *n.m.* 'Walkover', easy task. *Ça a été un vrai canter!* It really was 'no contest'! (The word is a direct borrowing from the English 'canter' as opposed to 'gallop'.)

cantine *n.f.* 'Bread-basket', 'tummy', stomach.

cantiner *v.intrans.* (Prison slang): To pool 'outside food resources', parcels and gifts, on a reciprocal basis with fellow cons.

cantoche *n.f.* *(corr. cantine)*: School or works canteen.

canulant *adj.* Dull, tedious, boring. *J'ai un boulot tout ce qu'il y a de canulant*: I've got a real shitty job!

canular *n.m.* **1** Practical joke. *Monter un canular à quelqu'un*: To play a prank on someone. **2** Tall story. *Quel zigoto! On ne sait jamais si ce qu'il dit, c'est des canulars!* He's a right one! You can never tell whether he's pulling your leg!

canuler *v.trans.* To bore the pants off someone.

caoua *n.m.* Coffee (the beverage).

cap *n.m.* *Avoir passé le cap de la cinquantaine*: To have 'chalked up one's half century', to be over fifty years of age.

capilotade *n.f.* *Mettre en capilotade*: To smash to smithereens, to reduce to nothing. (The expression is purely figurative when referring to a person. *Elle l'a mis en capilotade*: She made mincemeat of him.)

capiston *n.m.* *(mil. corr. capitaine)*: Captain.

capitaine *n.m.* *Quel est l'âge du capitaine? (joc.)*: Humorous stock phrase indicating that the mathematical problem posed is practically insoluble.

capital *n.m.* *(joc.)*: Virginity. *Elle a toujours son capital*: Her maiden charms are still firmly under wraps.

capitalo *n.m. & adj. (pej.)*: Capitalist.

capitonnée *adj. f.* *Une môme bien capitonnée*: A 'nice plump chick', a slightly plump yet shapely girl.

capon *n.m.* **1** *(sch.)*: 'Sneak', tell-tale. **2** *Etre capon*: To be 'chicken', 'yellow', to be a coward.

capon *adj.* 'Funky', cowardly.

capone *n.m.* Large cigar (from Al Capone eponymous fame).

caponner *v.intrans.* To 'snitch', to 'sneak', to tell tales.

caporal *n.m.* Cheap and coarse tobacco. *Il fume du caporal plein de bûches*: He smokes the most awful baccy, real warehouse sweepings!

capot *adj.inv.* **1** *Etre capot*: Not to have taken a single trick (in a game of cards, usually *belote*). **2** *Rester capot (fig.)*: **a** To have been totally unsuccessful. **b** To be 'stumped', to be nonplussed. **c** To look a fool.

capote *n.f.* *Capote anglaise*: 'French letter', condom, contraceptive sheath.

capout *adj.inv.* *Faire capout*: **a** To 'bump off', to 'do in', to kill. **b** To take prisoner. (The word is a corruption of the German *kaputt*; its presence in colloquial French can only be attributed to past warfare.)

capsule *n.f.* 'Nut', 'brainbox', head. *Il n'a rien dans la capsule!* He's as thick as two short planks!

capucin *n.m.* *(pej.)*: 'Geezer', 'bloke', man. *Qu'est-ce que c'est que ce capucin?!* Who the bloody hell is this?!

car *n.m.* *(abbr. autocar)*: Coach, long-distance bus.

cara *n.m. (abbr. caractère)*: Personality, character (usually the kind that is difficult to contend with).

carabin *n.m.* 1 'Medic', doctor. 2 Medical student. (The expression *plaisanteries de carabin* can refer either to salacious and risqué stories or practical jokes which could be judged to be in very poor taste, perhaps because French medical students are deemed to have a weird sense of humour.)

carabine *n.f. (joc.)*: 'Prick', 'cock', penis. (The expression *avoir une carabine sous la soutane* refers to a priest or monk who has difficulty in keeping to his celibacy vows.)

carabiné *adj.* Excessive, intense. *Une engueulade carabinée*: One hell of a telling-off. *Une noce carabinée*: A rare old binge.

carabistouille *n.f.* Petty con-trick.

caraco *n.m.* 1 *(pej.)*: 'Dago', Spaniard. 2 'Cock-up', 'boob', blunder.

carafe *n.f.* 1 'Brainbox', head. *Travailler de la carafe*: To be 'off one's rocker', to be mad. 2 'Fathead', 'nincompoop', fool. *Quelle carafe, ce mec!* He's a right Charlie! 3 *Tomber en carafe*: To break down in a motor car. *On est tombé en carafe en pleine cambrousse*: The car let us down miles from nowhere. 4 *Rester en carafe*: a To 'kick one's heels', to wait in vain. b To 'dry up', to get stuck in the middle of a speech, sermon, etc. 5 *Laisser quelqu'un en carafe*: To 'let someone down', to leave someone in the lurch.

carambolage *n.m.* 1 'Pile-up', multiple shunt, serious road accident. 2 *Le carambolage*: 'Banging', 'screwing', intercourse. *Etre porté sur le carambolage*: To be a randy so-and-so.

caramboler *v.intrans. & trans.* 1 (of vehicles): To collide, to crash. 2 To fuck, to 'screw', to have intercourse with. *Il en a carambolé des nanas!* He's had a few women in his time!

carambouille *n.f.* (also: *carambouillage n.m.*): Dishonest business practice where goods are purchased on credit and sold below their true value for a quick profit. By ingenious cross payments several similar schemes can be kept running until the operators have absconded leaving a number of suppliers out of pocket.

carambouilleur *n.m.* Con-man who practises *carambouille*.

carante *n.f.* 1 (Gamblers' slang): Card-table. 2 *Travailler sur la carante* (of street trader): To 'set up shop', to begin trading from an impromptu stall. 3 *Se mettre en carante*: To 'cut up rough', to turn nasty.

carapatage *n.m.* Prompt exit, hurried departure. *Quand les flics sont arrivés, il y a eu du carapatage éclair*: When the fuzz arrived, they all scarpered.

carapater *v.pronom.* To 'make tracks', to move on with speed. *Il va falloir qu'on se carapate si on veut attraper le dur!* We'll have to get our skates on if we want to catch that train!

carat *n.m.* 1 Years (in reference to someone's age). *Elle va sur ses dix-sept carats*: She's sixteen, going on seventeen. (*Prendre du carat* is best translated 'to be getting on in years'.) 2 'Nous', brains, general intelligence. *Pour ce qui est de carat, à la distribution générale on lui avait filé un billet d'absence!* She was at the back of the line when brains were being dished out! 3 (also: *cara*): Personality, character.

Caravelle *Proper name.* Sporty 'coupé' manufactured by Renault in the 1960s.

caravelle *n.f.* High-class prostitute (the kind that caters for the jet-set).

carbi *n.m.* 1 Coal. *On caillait faute de carbi*: The cellar was empty and we were frozen stiff. 2 Coalman, coal-merchant. 3 *(pej.)*: 'Graft', hard work. (The expression *aller au carbi*, a variant of *aller au charbon*, is indicative of the unpleasant nature of the job.) 4 'Brass', 'loot', money (also: *braise*).

carbo *adj.inv.* Discredited, of ill-repute. *Il est carbo dans le quartier depuis qu'on le sait indic*: His name's mud here since we discovered he turned snout.

carboniser *v.trans.* 1 To 'throw a spanner in the works', to cause a project or enterprise to fail. 2 To 'run down', to malign, to discredit someone.

carburateur *n.m. Etre à double carburateur (joc.)*: To be 'AC/DC', to have bisexual tendencies (also: *être à voile et à vapeur*).

carburation *n.f. Trouver la bonne carburation (fig.)*: To find one's rhythm, to settle down to a good working pace.

carbure *n.m. (abbr. carburant)*: 1 'Juice', petrol. *On est tombé en carafe sur l'autoroute faute de carbure*: We ran out of gas and got stranded on the motorway. 2 'Brass', 'bread', money.

carburer *v.intrans.* 1 To 'cough up', to 'fork out', to pay. 2 To booze, to drink heavily. *Elle carbure à la vodka et quelle descente!* Her poison is vodka and she can't half knock 'em back! 3 *Ça carbure bien!* Things are going swimmingly! *Ça carbure mal!* We're having a few problems! *Alors, ça carbure?* How's tricks? – How is business? (The expression *ça va carburer!* can sometimes mean 'things are going to hot up!', i.e. 'we're in for some heated exchanges!')

carcan *n.m. (pej.)*: 1 'Nag', 'hack', broken-down horse. 2 'Battle-axe', nasty old woman.

carder *v.trans. Carder le cuir à quelqu'un*: To 'bash someone up', to give someone a beating.

cardinales *n.f.pl. Avoir ses cardinales*: To 'have the decorators in', to have a menstrual period.

care *n.f. (pej.)*: 'Heap', 'banger', decrepit motor car. *Sa care à la manque lui coûte une fortune*: That tatty motor of his costs him a packet.

caresser *v.trans. Caresser la bouteille* (also: *le goulot*): To be fond of one's tipple, to have an immoderate taste for alcohol.

Carlingue *n.f. La Carlingue*: The Gestapo. (The German Secret Police under the Nazi régime, officially known as the *Geheime Staatspolizei*.)

carluche *n.f.* 'Nick', jail, prison. *On se retrouve en carluche pour moins!* You can end up in the slammer for much less!

carme *n.f.* 'Brass', 'loot', money. *Il fricotait dans la fausse carme*: He dealt in counterfeit notes.

carmer *v.trans. & intrans.* To pay, to pay for something. (According to context, the meaning can be literal or figurative. *Il a carmé la douloureuse*: He paid the bill. *Il a carmé pour son passé*: He's paid his debt to society.)

carmillous *n.m.pl. (joc.)*: 'Cackleberries', eggs.

carmouille *n.f.* Payment (often for illicit transactions). *On l'a fait passer à la carmouille*: He had to cough up the readies.

carnaval *n.m. Quel carnaval! (iron.)*: What a madhouse!

carne *n.f. (pej.)*: **1** 'Shoe-leather', tough and cheap cut of meat. **2** 'Nag', 'hack', inferior horse. **3** 'Battle-axe', nasty old woman. **4** 'Swine', 'rotter', nasty and objectionable fellow.

carottage *n.m.* Filching, small-time theft.

carotte *n.f.* **1** Plug of tobacco. **2** French tobacconist's sign. (This red diamond-shaped sign, familiar to all Frenchmen, is very seldom associated with the plug of chewing tobacco from which it originated.) **3** 'Con-trick', swindle. *Tirer une carotte à quelqu'un*: To con someone out of money. **4** *Les carottes sont cuites! (joc.)*: It's all over bar the shouting! *Ses carottes sont cuites!* He's cooked his goose! – He's had it! – His fate is sealed! **5** Drop-shot (at tennis).

carotter *v.trans.* **1** To 'nick', to 'pinch', to steal. *Il m'a carotté mes sèches!* He's gone and nicked my fags! **2** To 'con', to 'diddle', to swindle. **3** (Prison slang): To hide very small objects by inserting them up one's anus.

carotteur *n.m.* 'Filch', character who misappropriates items of little value. (The word is frequently used when referring to a friend or associate who 'borrows' and never returns.)

carouble *n.f.* 'Twirl', skeleton key (usually for illegal use).

caroubler *v.trans.* To break in, to burgle.

caroubleur *n.m.* 'Break-in artist', burglar.

carpette *n.f.* **1** 'Creep', 'crawler', subservient character. **2** 'Funk', 'quitter', gutless person. (The original meaning of the word: hearth-rug, explains its colloquial extensions.)

carre *n.f.* (Gambling slang): **1** 'Kitty', accumulated stakes. **2** Cash-desk in casino where chips and money are exchanged.

carré *n.m.* **1** *Un carré* (in card game): Four of a kind. *Un carré de barbus*: Four kings. **2** *Lit fait au carré (mil.)*: Bed made up to Service regulations (i.e. with envelope corners, etc.). **3** *Petits carrés*: Game played by schoolboys which entails making small squares with single strokes of the pen; the winner is the one who has the most squares at the end of this giant noughts-and-crosses type pastime.

carré *adj.* **1** (of person): Plain-speaking, forthright. *Il est tout ce qu'il y a de carré!* He doesn't mince his words! **2** *Tête carrée*: Stubborn individual (bordering on the pig-headed). **3** *Partie carrée*: Sex foursome, two-couple sex-party.

carreau *n.m.* **1** (usually *pl.*): 'Oglers', 'peepers', eyes. *Avoir un carreau à la manque*: To have only one good eye. **2** (*pl.*): 'Specs', glasses, spectacles. **3** *En avoir un coup dans les carreaux*: To be 'squiffy', 'tiddly', to be slightly drunk. **4** *Ça ne casse pas les carreaux!* It's nothing to write home about! **5** *Etre sur le carreau*: **a** To be on the dole, to be out of work. **b** To be 'skint', 'broke', to be penniless. **6** *Rester sur le carreau*: To have failed abysmally. **7** *Se tenir à carreau*: To 'watch one's step', to act cautiously.

carrée *n.f.* **1** 'Digs', room. *Il l'a fait monter dans sa carrée pour lui montrer, comme il dit, sa collection de timbres*: He got her up to his pad to 'see his etchings'. **2** 'Block', 'nut', head. *Ça ne tourne pas rond dans sa carrée*: He's going off his rocker.

carrer *v.trans.* **1** To hide. *Vite! Carre ton pognon, v'là les flics!* Quick, stash the dough away, here come the fuzz! **2** *Tu peux te le carrer dans l'oignon! (joc. & iron.)*: You know what you can do with it!

carrer *v.intrans.* To live (somewhere). *Ils carrent ensemble*: They share digs.

carrer *v.trans.reflex.* **1** To 'lie low', to hide (also: *se planquer*). **2** To 'blow', to 'make tracks', to run away. *Carre-toi!* Make yourself scarce!

carreur *n.m.* 'Banker', stake-holder in poker game.

carreuse *n.f. (pol.)*: Professional woman shop-lifter.

carriole *n.f. (joc.)*: 'Jalopy', 'banger', ramshackle motor car.

carrosse *n.m. (joc.)*: 'Black Maria', police wagon.

carrossée *adj.f.* Shapely. *C'est une môme drôlement bien carrossée!* She's got curves in all the right places!

carrosserie *n.f.* Physical build (always with a positive connotation). *Quelle carrosserie, ce mec!* He's your actual Charles Atlas!).

carrousel *n.m.* **1** (*pol.*): Antechamber and waiting-hall of the Paris *Palais de Justice.* **2** *Quel carrousel!* What a madhouse!

carrousel *adj.inv.* 'Blotto', 'tipsy', drunk.

carte *n.f.* **1** *Carte forcée*: 'Hobson's choice' (the choice of taking what is offered or nothing at all). **2** *Carte grise*: Log-book, vehicle registration document. **3** *Carte de France (joc.)*: 'Wet dream', stain on bed-sheet. **4** *On t'enverra des cartes! (joc. & iron.)*: We'll let you know how we get on! (This expression is roughly equivalent to 'Wish you were here, but glad you aren't!') **5** *Etre en carte* (of prostitute): To be registered with the police.

carton *n.m.* **1** Card, playing-card. *Brouiller les cartons*: To shuffle the deck. **2** *Faire un carton*: **a** To 'bump off', to kill. **b** (of man): To 'score', to have intercourse. (The original meaning comes from the world of fairgrounds and amusement arcades where it refers to having a go at the shooting gallery.)

carton *adj.inv.* **1** 'Skint', 'broke', penniless. **2** (of theatrical performance): 'Flopped', unsuccessful.

cartonner *v.intrans.* To play cards, to have a game of cards.

cartonnier *n.m.* 'Card-sharp', dishonest 'pro' card player.

cartouche *n.f.* **1** Carton of cigarettes (i.e. one containing ten packs of twenty). **2** *Avoir brûlé ses dernières cartouches (fig.)*: To be at one's wits' end (literally to have run out of ammunition).

cartouse *n.f.* **1** Card, playing-card. **2** I.D. card, identity papers.

cas *n.m.* *C'est le cas de le dire! (joc. & iron.)*: You can say that again! – That's very true!

casaquin *n.m.* *Sauter* (also: *tomber*) *sur le casaquin de quelqu'un*: **a** To 'pitch into someone', to give someone a thrashing. **b** (*fig.*): To 'gun for someone', to give someone an acrimonious talking-to.

casba *n.f.* (also: *casbah*): 'Digs', 'pad', home. (The word has the same jocular connotation as the famous yet never really uttered 'Come with me to the casbah' film-quote.)

cascader *v.intrans. & trans.* **1** To 'burn the candle at both ends', to lead a fast life. **2** To flit from woman to woman, from one affair to another. **3** To 'pop one's clogs', to 'croak', to die. **4** *Se faire cascader*: To get 'nabbed', 'collared', to be

arrested. **5** To 'go down', to 'do porridge', to serve a prison sentence. **6** (*th.*): To gag one's part, to ad-lib.

cascadeur *n.m.* **1** 'Bed-hopper', womanizer, philanderer. **2** Roisterer, character who likes the high life. **3** Stuntman (in films).

case *n.m.* (*abbr. casier judiciaire*): 'Form', criminal record.

case *n.f.* **1** House. *La case à mes vieux*: My parents' home. **2** 'Nick', 'clink', prison. *Bouffer de la case*: To 'do porridge', to do time. **3** *Avoir une case en moins*: To 'have a screw loose', to 'have a slate loose', to be mad.

caser *v.trans.* To 'screw', to fuck, to have coition with. (The verb usually refers to sodomous intercourse and the expression *'Va te faire caser!'* is best translated by: 'Get stuffed!')

caser *v.trans.reflex.* To 'get hitched', to get married.

casin *n.m.* (*abbr. casino*): Gambling-club, casino.

casingue *n.m.* **1** Caf', bistrot, bar. **2** Inexpensive restaurant.

casque *n.m.* **1** *Prendre son casque*: To 'get a skinful', to get drunk. **2** *Avoir le casque*: To have a hangover.

casque *n.f.* **1** *La casque*: **a** Pay-packet, wages. **b** (*fig.*): Moment of reckoning. **2** *Le coup de casque (joc.)*: Verbal appeal for funds at the end of an emotional speech or a sales-pitch. (The noun is a derivative of *casquer*: to 'fork out', to pay.)

casquer *v.trans. & intrans.* **1** To 'cough up', to 'fork out', to pay up reluctantly. *C'est toujours moi qui casque pour les apéros!* It's always me what pays for the drinks! **2** (*fig.*): To bear the brunt, to take the blame (usually undeservedly).

casquette *n.f.* **1** Gambling losses. **2** *Prendre une casquette*: To 'get pissed', to get drunk. **3** *Travailler de la casquette*: To be 'off one's rocker', to be 'bonkers', to be mad (also: *travailler du chapeau*). **4** *'Un coup pour jeter sa casquette; un coup pour la chercher' (joc.)*: 'Quickie sex', the kind of selfish intercourse where the female partner's satisfaction is totally disregarded.

cassant *adj.* (of person): Very boring. *Qu'est-ce qu'il est cassant, ton jules!* Your boyfriend's a right pain!

casse *n.m.* (*abbr. cassement*): Break-in, burglary. *Faire un casse*: To do a 'job'.

casse *n.f.* **1** *Etre bon pour la casse* (of person): To be 'ready for the scrap-heap', to have outlived one's usefulness. **2** *Pas de casse, j'espère! (joc.)*: No broken bones, eh? – Are you alright, then?

cassé *adj.* **1** 'Pissed', 'blotto', drunk. **2** *Qu'est-ce qu'il y a de cassé?* What's all the kerfuffle about? – Why all this disturbance?

casse-bonbons *n.m.* 'Ear-basher', persistent nagger.

casse-bonbons *adj.inv.* Naggingly boring (also: *casse-burnes*).

casse-cou *n.m.* **1** 'Madcap', dare-devil character. **2** Stuntman (in films).

casse-couilles *n.m.* 'Ear-basher', persistent nagger. (*Casse-bonbons* and *casse-burnes* are euphemistic equivalents.)

casse-cul *n.m.* **1** 'Bum-shaker', rattly old car. **2** 'Pain in the arse', boring person.

casse-dalle *n.m.* Snack meal (also: *casse-graine*).

casse-gueule *n.m.* **1** Dangerous enterprise, perilous exercise. *Aller sur le toit avec un zef pareil, quel casse-gueule!* You're risking your neck on the roof with that kind of wind! **2** War. *Aller au casse-gueule*: To go to the Front (also: *casse-pipe*). **3** 'Rot-gut', cheap alcohol (usually of the moonshine variety).

cassement *n.m.* Break-in, burglary (also: *casse*).

casse-noix *n.m.* Ticket-punch, ticket-clipper.

casse-pattes *n.m.* **1** 'Rot-gut', cheap alcohol (usually of the moonshine variety). **2** (Racing cyclists' slang): Difficult climb, awkwardly changing gradient which breaks the rider's rhythm. **3** Lob (tennis shot that makes the opponent run for the ball thus creating extra fatigue).

casse-pieds *n.m.* 'Pain in the neck', boring person. (The French actor Noël Noël starred in *'Les casse-pieds'*, a film depicting all manner of bores.)

casse-pipe *n.m.* War. *Aller au casse-pipe*: To go to the Front. (Both *casse-pipe* and the expression *casser sa pipe* stem from the use of clay pipes as targets in shooting-galleries.)

casse-poitrine *n.m.* Home-made booze, moonshine alcohol.

casser *v.trans.* **1** *En casser pour deux ronds à quelqu'un*: To tell someone a few home truths, to tell some frank and unpleasant facts. **2** *Ne pas en casser une*: To keep one's trap shut, to say nothing. **3** *Ne rien casser*: To be 'not up to much', to be of little value (also: *ne pas casser quatre pattes à un canard*). **4** *A tout casser*: **a** 'Rip-roaring', fantastic. *On a fait une noce à tout casser*: We had one hell of a binge. **b** 'At the outside', as a maximum. *A tout casser, ça vous coûtera une brique*: It shouldn't set you back more than a grand.

casser *v.intrans.* To break in, to burgle (also: *faire un casse*).

casser *v.trans.reflex.* **1** To 'toddle off', to 'run along', to go away. *Il est cinq heures, il faut que je me casse!* It's five o'clock, I'll have to split! **2** *Ne pas se casser*: To take life easy, to worry very little about day-to-day matters.

casserole *n.f.* **1** Honky-tonk piano, tinny instrument singularly in need of attention. **2** 'Jalopy', 'banger', ramshackle motor car. **3** Trollop, low-class prostitute. **4** (of person): 'Wash-out', failure. **5** 'Snout', 'grass', police informer. **6** *Passer à la casserole (fig.)*: **a** To 'get the chop', to be dispensed with once and for all. **b** To be 'screwed', to be fucked, to have intercourse. (The implication within this meaning is of coerced sex which leaves the partner feeling that she has been 'used'.)

casse-tête *n.m.* 'Puzzler', tricky problem (also: *casse-tête chinois*).

casseur *n.m.* **1** 'Break-in artist', burglar. **2** 'Heavy', muscleman, gang-land enforcer. **3** Car-breaker (one who 'breaks' cars for spares and sells the rest for scrap).

casse-vin *n.m. (joc.)*: Savoury snack, cocktail appetizer.

cassis *n.m.* **1** 'Bean', 'bonce', head. *Il a pris un coup de goumi sur le cassis*: He got coshed. (Expressions such as *en avoir gros sur le cassis*: to be bitterly resentful about something, illustrate the meaning: grey matter, as opposed to skull.) **2** *Cassis de lutteur (joc.)*: 'Plonk', cheap red wine.

cassure *n.f. (th.)*: Actor long past his prime.

castagne *n.f.* **1** 'Belt', 'clout', blow (also: *châtaigne*). **2** 'Free-for-all', brawl. *Il adore la castagne*: He likes a good punch-up.

castagner *v.intrans.* *Ça castagne!* It's all hell let loose! – It's a free-for-all! – Fists are flying!

castagner *v.trans.reflex.* To have a punch-up, to come to blows, to have a fight.

castagnette *n.f.* **1** 'Clip round the ear-hole', sharp clout, stinging blow. **2** *Jouer des castagnettes*: To shake in one's shoes, to tremble with fear.

castapiane *n.f.* 'Clap', gonorrhoea. (The word can sometimes also refer to syphilis.)

castel *n.m.* *Le castel*: 'The big house', 'the nick', prison.

castor *n.m.* **1** Gigolo, kept man. (This jocular nickname arises because, like beavers, *'ils travaillent avec leur queue'*.) **2** 'Nipper', kid, small child. *Lui et sa bonne femme ont une tripotée de castors*: He and his missus have a string of kids. **3** Ship's boy, young cabin attendant.

castu *n.m.* Workhouse, almshouse, hospital-home for the aged poor.

casuel *n.m.* *Faire le casuel*: To let a hotel room for prostitution use.

cataloguer *v.trans.* **1** To 'weigh up', to size up. *A le voir tricoter des fesses, faut pas être grand clerc pour le cataloguer!* It doesn't take three A-levels to guess he's a pouf! **2** *C'est catalogué!* (also:

c'est du catalogué!): It's a cinch! – It's a dead cert! – It's a certainty!

cataplasme *n.m.* Leech-like character, the kind one finds hard to shake off.

cataractes *n.f.pl.* *Lâcher des cataractes*: To 'let loose the weepies', to 'weep buckets', to cry floods of tears.

catastrophe *n.f.* **1** 'Dead loss', useless character. **2** *Faire quelque chose en catastrophe*: To rush something, to act in a flurry (and often to bungle).

catastropher *v.trans.* To astound and distress. *Sa mort nous a catastrophés*: His death was a real blow to us.

cateau *n.f.* 'Prozzy', prostitute.

Catho *Proper name*. *La Catho* (the *Institut catholique*): This independent Catholic college of higher education caters for university students in Paris.

catholique *adj.* (Always used in the negative.) *Ce gars-là ne m'a pas l'air bien catholique*: I don't like the look of him – I wouldn't trust that chap. *Tout ça ne me m'a pas l'air très catholique*: This looks a bit fishy to me – It's a bit suspicious.

catiche *n.f.* 'Prozzy', prostitute (also: *catin*).

catimini *En catimini* (*adv.exp.*): Furtively, with great discretion. *Partir en catimini*: To slip away unnoticed.

causant *adj.* 'Chatty', talkative. *Dis donc, tu n'es guère causant!* What's up with you . . . why the silence?!

cause *n.f.* **1** *Et pour cause*: With some justification – With good reason. *Je voudrais bien t'épouser, mais je peux pas . . . et pour cause: J'suis marida!* I'd love to wed you, gal, but as the song goes: 'My wife won't let me!' **2** *A cause d'à cause!* (*joc.*): Because that's the way it is! (This near-nonsensical expression is used by a cornered speaker who has run out of arguments.)

causer *v.trans. & intrans.* **1** To be able to speak a language. *Il cause couramment l'anglais*: English is a lingo he masters very well. **2** *Qu'est-ce qu'il cause bien!* What a smooth talker! – Doesn't he express himself beautifully! **3** *Cause toujours!* (*iron.*): You've got another think coming! – If you believe that, you're kidding yourself! (Keep talking, but you're not going to convince anybody!)

causette *n.f.* *Faire un brin de causette*: To have a 'chinwag', a 'natter', to have a chat with someone.

cavalant *adj.* Dreary, boring.

cavale *n.f.* **1** 'Gawky bird', tall and awkward-looking woman. **2** *Etre en cavale*: To be on the run from the police.

cavalendour *n.m.* (Underworld slang): Outsider, one not part of the *milieu*.

cavaler *v.trans.* **1** To bore. **2** To pester, to be a nuisance. *Il commence à me cavaler avec ses demandes de prêts*: I'm sick and tired of his constant requests for subs.

cavaler *v.intrans.* **1** To 'leg it', to 'traipse', to have to walk. **2** To dash, to run. *Chaque fois que je le vois, il est en train de cavaler!* Whenever I come across him he's always in a rush. **3** To 'chase skirts', to be always after girls.

cavaler *v.pronom.* To 'make tracks', to 'scarper', to run away.

cavalerie *n.f.* **1** *Grosse cavalerie*: 'Stodge', stodgy and unappetizing food. **2** *Traite de cavalerie*: Wilfully misleading letter of credit enabling the recipient to claim access to funds he does not possess. **3** *Balancer la cavalerie* (of criminal): To pull out of a job and split on accomplices.

cavaleur *n.m.* Randy so-and-so, highly-sexed man.

cavaleur *adj.* Randy, sex-mad, highly-sexed.

cavaleuse *n.f.* 'Man-chaser', highly-sexed woman.

cavalier *n.m.* *Faire cavalier seul*: To 'go it alone', to undertake something unaided.

cave *n.m.* (Underworld slang): **1** Outsider (one not part of the *milieu*). **2** 'Mug', 'sucker', dupe. (The film of the early 60s *'Le cave se rebiffe'* is all about a gangland fool who turns out to be wiser than expected.)

caver *v.trans.* To 'con', to 'rook', to swindle. *Il s'est fait caver en beauté*: He fell for it hook, line and sinker.

cavette *n.f.* (Underworld slang): Young girl not yet 'on the game'. (*Faire la chasse aux cavettes* refers to the recruiting of 'fresh talent' by pimps.)

caviarder *v.trans.* To censor parts of an article or book.

cavillon *n.m.* 'Nurk', nonentity, character totally lacking drive and initiative.

cavillon *adj.* 'Limp', weak-willed.

cavu *n.m.* 'Arse', 'bum', behind.

C.C.C. *n.m.* 'Mac', mackintosh, raincoat. (C.C.C., a famous rainwear firm, gained fame through generic lexicalization of its name.)

cédule *n.m.* Timetable, order of events. (The word is a humorous corruption of the English 'schedule'.)

cégétiste *n.m.* Member of the C.G.T. (*Confédération Générale du Travail*, the Communist-inspired French trade union.)

cégnace *pers.pron.* 'His nibs', him (also: *cézigue*).

céhoène *n.m. & adj.* Phonetic transcription of the spelling of the word *con*.

ceinture *n.f.* 1 *S'en mettre plein la ceinture*: To 'stuff one's face', to eat heartily. 2 *Se serrer la ceinture d'un cran*: To 'go hungry', to do without food. 3 *Faire ceinture*: To have to 'do without', to have to miss out on something. 4 *Ceinture!* You can whistle for it! – Nothing doing! – Certainly not! 5 *La Petite Ceinture*: Paris bus-service following a circular route just within the city boundaries.

ceinturer *v.trans.* To 'nick', to 'collar', to arrest.

celle *dem.pron. Elle est bonne, celle-là!* (of joke): I like it! I like it! (The expression has an antiphrastic meaning when uttered in irony. *Ben, elle est bonne, celle-là, tu me la copieras!* Well, I don't know what you think, but I call it a rotten trick!)

cellote *n.f. (corr. cellule)*: Prison cell.

cencul *n.m. (sch.)*: Vice-principal of a *lycée*. (The word is a corruption of *Censeur*; the man appointed to this post works under the *Proviseur*, known colloquially as *Le Protal*, and is in charge of the school's discipline.)

cendrillon *n.f. Jouer les cendrillons* (of woman): To be a 'perennial wallflower', to be the one who always misses out on social occasions.

cent *num.adj. Je vous le donne en cent!* You'll never guess! (also: *je vous le donne en mille!*).

centre *n.m.* 'Handle', 'monniker', name (also: *blaze*).

centrer *v.trans. Centrer une bulle (sch.)*: To get a nought in an exam.

centriot *n.m.* 'Pet name', familiar nickname.

centrouse *n.f. (corr. abbr. prison centrale)*: Top-security jail, prison housing long-term inmates with serious criminal records.

cep *n.m.* 'Conk', 'hooter', nose.

ce que *adv. exp. Ce qu'il est beau! (iron.)*: Who's a pretty boy, then?!

cerceau *n.m.* 1 'Wheel', steering wheel (of car). 2 *Les cerceaux* (also: *la cage à cerceaux*): The rib-cage.

cercueil *n.m.* Weird and potent beverage, a mixture of beer, aromatic wine and syrup popular with the underworld in the late 40s.

cérébral *n.m.* 'Egghead', intellectual.

cerf *n.m.* 1 *Courir* (also: *cavaler*) *comme un cerf*: To run 'like the clappers', to run very fast. 2 *Se déguiser en cerf*: To 'make tracks', to 'take to one's heels', to run away. 3 *Bander comme un cerf*: To have 'the big stick', to have an erection. 4 *Envoyer le cerf*: To 'tip someone off' about a shrewd gambling move.

cerise *n.f.* 1 'Bean', 'bonce', head. 2 'Mush', 'dial', face. *Se refaire une cerise*: To get back some colour (after an illness). *Faire une drôle de cerise*: To pull a face. 3 Jinx, bad luck. *Avoir la cerise*: To have a run of bad luck. 4 *Le temps des cerises*: The 'good old days', happy bygone times. (The expression gained everlasting recognition as the title of a popular song.)

certal *n.m. (corr. abbr. certificat)*: The *Certificats de licence* are exams which used to make up the *Licence* or French equivalent of the Bachelor of Arts degree.

certif *n.m.* 1 *(abbr. Certificat d'Etudes Primaires)*: Basic school-leaving certificate. 2 Attestation, certificate.

césarienne *n.f.* 1 *Faire une césarienne*: To 'lift', to steal a wallet or purse. 2 *Tu accouches?! Quoi! Ou est-ce qu'il faut te faire une césarienne?* (to reticent person about secret): Come on, out with it! – Go on, tell me, or do I have to drag it out of you?!

césarin *pers.pron.* 'His nibs', him. *Le pinard, il en connaît un rayon, césarin!* There's no denying the old boy knows his wines! (Originally *Césarin* is a Christian name which carries archaic and jocular connotations.)

ceusses *dem.pron. (corr. ceux) Les ceusses qu'ont du fric payent pour ceusses qui n'en ont pas*: Them that have money pay for them that are broke.

cézigos *pers.pron.* They, them. *C'est toujours pour cézigos les bons plats*: It's always them what get the tasty meals.

cézigue *pers.pron.* 'His nibs', him. *La bagnole, c'est pour cézigue, moi je me tape le bus!* 'His lordship' always drives the car, the bus is good enough for the likes of me!

chabanais *n.m.* 1 'Barney', 'hullabaloo', uproar. *Ils ont fait un de ces chabanais!* They raised the roof with their set-to! (Jacques Cellard and Alain Rey in their *DICTIONNAIRE DU FRANÇAIS NON-CONVENTIONNEL* offer conflicting etymologies for this word. The fact that the Rue Chabanais housed a famous *maison de tolérance* could explain the 'disorderly' connotations of the above meaning.) 2 Set of four queens in a hand at cards.

chabler *v.trans. & intrans.* 1 To 'pitch into', to set about someone, to attack an opponent. 2 *Ça va chabler!* All hell is going to be let loose!

chableur *n.m.* 'Scrapper', brawler, one who likes a punch-up.

chabraque *adj.* 'Bonkers', 'cracked', mad (also: *braque*).

chacail *n.m.* (Underworld slang): 'Snitch', 'grass', informer.

chagatte *n.f.* 'Fanny', 'pussy', vagina.

chagrin *n.m.* 'Graft', hard work. (The expression *aller au chagrin* like *aller au charbon* highlights the unpleasant nature of the daily grind.)

chahut *n.m.* 1 'Din', 'hullabaloo', uproar. 2 'Horse-play', rough-house behaviour.

chahutage *n.m.* Rowdy behaviour.

chahuter *v.trans. & intrans.* **1** *(sch.)*: To rag and cause mayhem in a classroom. **2** To taunt and tease. (The suggestion here is more of leg-pulling than anything else.) **3** To indulge in horse-play. *Il faut toujours qu'il chahute les secrétaires*: When he's in the office he's always got to be playing 'big bad wolf' with the secretaries. **4** *Chahuter avec*: To treat with disrespect. *Il n'aime pas qu'on chahute avec la religion*: He doesn't like people to take the mickey out of religion.

chahuteur *n.m.* **1** *(sch.)*: Rowdy and disruptive pupil. **2** 'Tease', leg-puller. **3** *Chahuteur de macchabées (joc.)*: Undertaker's apprentice.

chaille *n.m.* 'Peg', tooth. *Fausses chailles*: 'Choppers', dentures, false teeth.

Chaillot *Proper name. Envoyer quelqu'un à Chaillot*: To send someone off 'with a flea in his ear', to 'send someone packing', to tell someone to go away in no uncertain manner.

chair *n.f.* **1** *Marchand de chair (fraîche)*: White-slaver, recruiter of women for prostitution. **2** *C'est ni chair ni poisson*: It's neither one nor t'other.

chaise *n.f.* **1** *Avoir le cul entre deux chaises (fig.)*: To 'fall between two stools', to be in an ambiguous situation. **2** *Fumer des barreaux de chaises*: To smoke big fat cigars.

chaland *n.m.* (Prostitutes' slang): 'Punter', prospective client. *Attirer le chaland*: To draw in the trade.

chaleur *n.f.* **1** *Etre en chaleur* (of woman): To 'have the hots', to be turned on, to be sexually excited. **2** *Avoir des chaleurs*: To be in a blue funk, to be terrified.

chaleureux *adj.* *(joc.)*: 'Chicken', 'funky', cowardly.

chaloupée *n.f.* *(abbr. valse chaloupée)*: Waltz-like dance popular with the clientele of *guinguettes* near Paris.

chamade *n.f. Battre la chamade*: To be 'all-a-dither', to be confused and distraught. (The usage originates in the expression *avoir le cœur qui bat la chamade* describing palpitations brought on by strong emotions.)

chamailler *v.trans.reflex.* To squabble, to quarrel. *Quand ils étaient gosses, ils n'arrêtaient pas de se chamailler*: As kids they always seemed to be at each other's throats.

chambard *n.m.* 'Hullabaloo', din, uproar. *Faire du chambard*: To kick up a row.

chambardement *n.m.* Upset, upheaval. *Quand il est allé au Service, ça a été un sacré chambardement pour nous*: When he went to do his National Service, what he left behind was chaos.

chambarder *v.trans.* **1** To 'flog', to sell something at a loss. *Ça sentait la faillite, on a tout dû chambarder en vitesse*: The Receiver was just round the corner, so we cleared the shelves in the nick of time. **2** To 'turn upside down', to disrupt. *Il a chambardé tous mes plans*: He played havoc with my project.

chamberlain *n.m.* 'Gamp', 'brolly', umbrella. (To the French, Neville Chamberlain gained eponymous fame through his ever-present umbrella.)

chambouler *v.trans.* **1** To cause havoc, to disrupt (plans, etc.). **2** To unnerve and dismay. *La nouvelle de sa mort m'a complètement chamboulé*: The news of his death gave me quite a turn.

chambrer *v.trans.* To 'have someone on', to 'kid', to tease someone. *Chambrer quelqu'un à froid*: To manage to keep a straight face while pulling someone's leg.

chameau *n.m.* **1** *(pej.)*: 'Sod', 'bastard', evil-minded character. (When referring to a woman, the translation would be 'bitch' or 'cow'.) **2** *Petit chameau, va!* You rascal, you!

champ *n.m.* **1** *Le champ des refroidis*: The 'boneyard', the cemetery (also: *le boulevard des allongés*). **2** *Prendre la clef des champs*: To 'scarper', to 'make off', to run away.

champ' *n.m.* 'Champers', 'bubbly', champagne (also: *roteux*).

champignon *n.m.* 'Gas-pedal', accelerator. *Appuyer sur le champignon* (also: *écraser le champignon*): To 'burn rubber', to accelerate fiercely.

champion *adj.* 'A-1', fantastic. *Pour ce qui est de la cuistance, il est champion*: When it comes to cooking, no-one can beat him.

champion *interj.* Super! – Great!

champoreau *n.m.* Cup of coffee strengthened with rum, brandy or calvados.

Champs *(abbr. Les Champs-Elysées)*: The avenue of that name in Paris (also: *Les Chanzés*).

chançard *n.m.* Lucky blighter, fortunate person. *Quel chançard, il est verni lui! Talk about being lucky, he's a real jammy so-and-so!

chançard *adj.* 'Jammy', lucky, fortunate.

chance *n.f. Il y a des chances!* (iron.): Not bloody likely! – Certainly not! *Moi, lui prêter du fric? Il y a des chances!* You don't really think I'd lend him money, do you?!

chancetiquer *v.trans.* **1** To cause havoc, to disrupt (plans, etc.). **2** To upset, to distress. *Ça m'a drôlement chancetiqué le moral*: It really knocked me for six.

chanceux *adj.* **1** Lucky, fortunate. **2** Hazardous, dangerous. *C'est plutôt chanceux de se balader avec tant de fric sur soi*: I think it's rather risky to go about with so much money.

'**chand** *n.m.* *(abbr. marchand)* *Un 'chand-de-fruits*: A fruit-and-veg seller. *Un 'chand-de-vin*: A bistrot proprietor.

chandelle *n.f.* **1** (Tennis): Lob, ball struck in a high arc. **2** *Tenir la chandelle*: To 'play gooseberry', to be the odd one out in a threesome. (Originally *tenir la chandelle* meant: to be a compliant third, one who, for gain or peace and quiet, chose to close his eyes to what was happening under his roof.) **3** *Avoir la chandelle au nez*: To have a 'dew-drop', to have a snot-drop at the end of one's nose. **4** *Voir trente-six chandelles*: To 'see stars', to be in a daze after a blow. **5** *Faire la chandelle (pol.)*: To be on a stake-out, to stand watch.

changer *v.trans.* *Changer l'eau du canari (joc.)*: To 'go for a pee', to 'wee', to urinate.

changer *v.trans.reflex.* To 'change', to get changed, to change clothes.

chanson *n.f.* **1** *C'est toujours la même chanson!* *(iron.)*: It's always the same old story! (also: *on connaît la chanson!*). **2** *C'est une autre chanson!* That's another kettle of fish! – That's a totally different matter! (also: *c'est une autre paire de manches!*).

chansonnette *n.f.* **1** Con-man's spiel, trickster's patter. *Donner* (also: *pousser*) *à la chansonnette*: To spin a yarn to catch the punter. **2** *(pol.)*: *Avoir quelqu'un à la chansonnette*: To extract a confession by sheer verbal persuasion.

chanstique *n.m.* **1** *Faire un chanstique*: To 'do a switch', to switch goods. (Con-trick where sub-standard articles are substituted for good ones during a transaction.) **2** *Prendre un chanstique* (of enterprise): To 'take a knock', to 'go sour', to fall foul of the predicted course.

chanstiquer *v.trans.* *(corr. changer)*: To switch over, to change.

chanter *v.intrans.* **1** *C'est comme si je chantais!* *(iron.)*: It's like talking to a brick wall! – It's a waste of breath! **2** *Ça me chante!* That's just the ticket! – That suits me! *Moi, je fais ce qui me chante!* I do what I damn well please! **3** *Qu'est-ce que vous me chantez là?!* You don't expect me to swallow that?! – I'm not that gullible! **4** *Angora chanté*: Cunnilingus.

chanterelle *n.f.* *Appuyer sur la chanterelle*: To 'harp on', to go on and on about something (when it would have been wiser and more tactful to remain silent).

chantier *n.m.* **1** *Quel chantier!* What a shambles! – What a cock-up! **2** *Foutre le chantier*: To cause havoc, to create a state of confusion.

chanvré *adj.* (Drugs): 'High' on hash, intoxicated with marijuana.

Chanzés *(corr. Les Champs-Elysées)*: The avenue of that name in Paris (also: *Les Champs*).

chaouch *n.m.* 'Screw', prison warder in a military hard-labour camp. (According to Auguste Le Breton in his *L'ARGOT CHEZ LES VRAIS DE VRAI*, the word originated at Biribi, an infamous military establishment in North Africa.)

chapardage *n.m.* Pilfering, small-time thieving. *Oh, vous savez, dans les supermarchés, 'y a pas mal de chapardage*: Shoplifting's quite a problem in supermarkets, you know!

chaparder *v.trans.* To 'pinch', to 'swipe', to steal.

chapardeur *n.m.* 'Filch', petty thief. *Ton gosse, quel chapardeur!* That kid of yours, what a thieving rascal!

chapeau *n.m.* **1** *Chapeau!* Congrats! – Good show! – Well done! **2** *Faire chapeau* (of boat): To 'turn turtle', to capsize. **3** *Porter le chapeau*: **a** To be suspected of being a police informer. **b** To 'carry the can', to be made the scapegoat. **4** *Prendre un virage sur les chapeaux de roue* (of car): To take a corner on two wheels. **5** *C'est comme si je pissais dans un chapeau de paille troué!* It's like putting a poultice on a wooden leg! – It's totally useless! **6** *Travailler du chapeau*: To 'have bats in the belfry', to be 'bonkers', to be mad. **7** *Etre envoyé au chapeau de paille*: To be deported to a penal colony. (The expression died with the last convict on Devil's Island.) **8** *A plein chapeau* (of radio, hi-fi): Full-blast, at top volume. **9** *Ne t'occupe pas du chapeau de la gamine! (joc. & iron.)*: Keep your nose out of this! – Mind your own business!

chapelet *n.m.* **1** *(pl.)*: 'Derbies', 'bracelets', handcuffs. **2** *Dévider son chapelet*: To 'get it all off one's chest', to speak one's mind to the full. **3** *Défiler son chapelet*: To 'throw up', to 'puke', to vomit.

chapelle *n.f.* **1** *Faire chapelle*: To 'flash', to expose oneself (indecently). **2** *La chapelle aux cinq marches*: The guillotine (also: *L'Abbaye de Monte-à-regret*).

Chapelouse *Proper name.* *La Chapelouse*: The La Chapelle district of Paris.

chapiteau *n.m.* 'Bean', 'bonce', head. *N'avoir pas lourd sous le chapiteau*: To be 'vacant up top', to be pretty dim. (In standard French, *chapiteau* refers to a circus tent.)

chaplard *n.m.* *(corr. chapeau)*: 'Lid', 'headgear', man's hat.

chaque *indef.pron.* Each, each one. *On va vous donner une brouette à chaque*: You'll each get a wheelbarrow. (In colloquial French, *chaque* is sometimes used where *chacun* would normally be expected.)

char *n.m.* **1** 'Crate', 'heap', motor car. **2** *Arrête ton char!* Pull the other one! – You're not fooling me! (This expression, sometimes augmented to *arrête ton char, Ben Hur!* has nothing to do with chariots but is, in fact, a corruption of the word *charre*.)

charabia *n.m.* 'Gabble', 'gibberish', incomprehensible talk.

charançon *n.m.* 'Creep', 'crawler', sycophantic person.

charbon *n.m.* 'Graft', hard work. *Aller au charbon*: To go to work. (The expression stems from the days when known pimps and small-time crooks, having to justify an honest source of income, would go to the docks and take a temporary job unloading coal from barges.)

charbonnier *n.m.* '*Charbonnier est maître chez soi*': 'I do what I please'. (Like many an old saying, this slightly archaic expression seems to be regaining popularity.)

charbougnat *n.m.* 1 Landlord of small bistrot. 2 Retail coal-merchant. (The word is a compound of *charbon* and *bougnat*. The *bougnat*, a native of the Auvergne, often manages successfully to combine the retailing of alcoholic beverage and household fuel.)

charcler *v.trans.* (Underworld slang): To 'bump off', to 'execute a contract', to assassinate.

charcutage *n.m.* Bungled surgical operation.

charcutaille *n.f. (corr. charcuterie)*: Cold cooked meats (also: *cochonaille*).

charcuter *v.trans.* To 'butcher', to bungle a surgical operation. (The verb, when uttered in a jocular vein, refers to an operation without any pejorative implications.)

Charenton *Proper name. Etre bon pour Charenton*: To be ready for the 'happy farm'. (Charenton, a Paris suburb, has within its boundaries one of the largest and best-known mental hospitals in France.)

charge *n.f.* 1 *En avoir sa charge*: To 'have had about as much as one can take', to be at the end of one's tether. 2 *A charge de revanche!* I'll do the same for you, mate! – I'll return the favour!

chargé *adj.* 1 'Loaded', 'pissed', drunk. 2 (Drugs): 'High', under the influence of narcotics.

charger *v.intrans.* To exaggerate. *Charger un brin*: To lay it on a bit thick.

charger *v.trans.reflex.* To get 'rodded up', to carry a handgun.

charibotée *n.f. Une charibotée de*: 'Oodles of', masses of, a great quantity (also: *une tripotée de*).

charivari *n.m. Quel charivari!* What a hullabaloo! – What a row!

charlemagne *n.m. Faire charlemagne*: To quit gambling on a winning streak, to leave a game when one is ahead.

Charles *Proper name. Tu parles, Charles!* a 'You're telling me!' – 'I should jolly well think so!' b 'You must be joking!' – 'What do you take me for?!' (This nonsensical stock rhyming-phrase relies on intonation or context for the degree of irony expressed.)

Charlot *Proper name.* 1 Affectionate nickname given to Charlie Chaplin. 2 Public executioner. *La bicyclette à Charlot*: The guillotine.

charlotte *n.f.* Heavy-duty wire-cutters (usually the kind used for illicit purposes).

charme *n.m.* 1 *Se porter comme un charme*: To feel 'in the pink', to feel as fit as a fiddle. 2 *Chanteur de charme*: Crooner, singer of langorous ballads.

charmeuses *n.f.pl.* Moustache. (The word has not got the slightly pejorative connotation of 'tash'. It is usually encountered in a complimentary context.)

charpie *n.f. Mettre quelqu'un en charpie (fig.)*: To 'make mincemeat of someone', to verbally destroy someone.

charre *n.m.* 1 'Poppycock', 'humbug', rubbish. *Il me sort toujours de ces charres!* He's always coming out with the most incredible stories! *Arrête ton charre!* Give over! – Stop kidding! –Be serious! *Sans charre?!* No kidding?! – Are you serious?! *C'est pas du charre!* It's gospel truth! 2 *Faire des charres à*: a To play the dirty on someone. b To two-time one's spouse or friend, to be unfaithful.

charretier *n.m. Jurer comme un charretier*: To 'turn the air blue', to swear like a trooper.

charrette *n.f.* 1 *(pej.)*: 'Heap', 'banger', ramshackle motor car. 2 Black Maria, police wagon.

charriage *n.m.* 'Mickey-taking', taunting, teasing. *J'en ai ras le bol de son charriage!* I'm sick to the back teeth of his leg-pulling!

charrier *v.trans.* To 'take the mickey out of someone', to 'poke fun', to taunt.

charrier *v.intrans.* 1 To 'kid', to joke. *En compagnie, il ne cesse de charrier*: With friends around, he's a right bundle of laughs. 2 To 'pitch it strong', to exaggerate. *Il charrie un peu à toujours emprunter du fric*: It's really the limit the way he's always asking for a sub. *Charrie pas, dis-moi la vérité!* Stop messing about, let's have the truth!

charrieur *n.m.* 1 'Leg-puller', prankster, jokester. 2 'Munchhausen' character, romancer, teller of tall stories.

charron *n.m. Gueuler au charron*: To 'yell blue murder', to cause a disturbance through vociferous protestations.

charronner *v.intrans.* 1 To 'yell blue murder', to make a vociferous to-do. 2 To land heavy blows (in a punch-up). *Quand il y a de la châtaigne, il charronne comme pas un!* When fists are flying, he's no mean fighter!

chasser *v.intrans.* To be on the lookout for 'talent', to be out chasing the birds, to search for female company.

châsser *v.trans.* To 'ogle', to eye salaciously.

châsses *n.m.pl.* 'Oglers', 'peepers', eyes. *Filer un coup de châsses:* To 'look over', to inspect something. *Avoir les châsses en portefeuille:* To have bags under one's eyes, to look tired.

chassieux *n.m. (pej.):* 'Four-eyes', short-sighted person (the kind who wears very thick glasses).

châssis *n.m.* **1** (of woman): Figure, body (usually a very attractive one). *Elle a un châssis à faire tourner les têtes:* With curves in all the right places, she never walks about unnoticed. **2** (mostly *pl.*): 'Oglers', 'peepers', eyes. *Fermer les châssis:* To 'get a bit of shuteye', to 'have forty winks', to get some sleep. *Avoir un châssis qui dit merde à l'autre:* To have a squint.

chat *n.m.* **1** *Ecriture de chat:* 'Doctor's handwriting', near-illegible scrawl. **2** *Avoir un chat dans la gorge:* To 'have a frog in one's throat', to be a little hoarse. **3** *Pas un chat:* Not a soul, nobody. *Le soir de la première, il n'y avait pas un chat dans la salle:* On that awful first night, we performed in front of rows of empty seats. **4** *Il n'y a pas de quoi fouetter un chat:* It's not worth worrying about. **5** *Avoir d'autres chats à fouetter:* To 'have other fish to fry', to have better things to do. **6** 'Pussy', 'fanny', vagina.

châtaigne *n.f.* **1** 'Biff', blow, punch. *Il a pris une de ces châtaignes!* He got a right knuckle-sandwich! **2** 'Rough-stuff', physical violence. *La châtaigne, il est pas contre!* He's always game for a punch-up!

châtaigner *v.intrans.* To throw punches. *La nuit, à la sortie des bistrots, souvent ça châtaigne dur:* At chucking-out time, you get quite a few fights on the doorsteps of pubs.

châtaigner *v.trans.reflex.* To have a punch-up, to brawl.

châtaignier *n.m. Une infusion de rame de châtaignier (joc.):* A good thrashing, a thorough beating-up.

château *n.m.* **1** *Le château:* 'The nick', 'clink', prison. **2** *Mener la vie de château:* To lead the life of Riley, to live like a lord. (To the criminal fraternity, this expression can have less pleasant connotations when the *château* happens to be the prison.)

château-la-pompe *n.m. (joc.):* 'Adam's ale', 'corporation pop', water.

chatouille *n.f.* Tickle, tickling. *Il craint les chatouilles:* He's as ticklish as hell.

chatouiller *v.trans. Chatouiller une serrure:* To pick a lock.

chatte *n.f.* 'Pussy', 'fanny', vagina (also: *chagatte*).

chattemite *n.f.* 'Pansy', namby-pamby person.

chaud *n.m. Ça ne me fait ni chaud ni froid!* That leaves me cold! – I couldn't care less!

chaud *adj.* **1** *Avoir eu chaud:* To have had 'a narrow squeak', a narrow escape. **2** *Etre chaud pour:* To be keen on, to be enthusiastic about. *Je ne suis pas chaud pour passer des vacances à la maison:* Holidays at home isn't my idea of fun. **3** *Etre un chaud lapin:* To be a randy so-and-so, to have more than a passing interest in sex. **4** *'Chauds, les marrons chauds!'* This ironical and untranslatable taunt is often heard at the ring-side during boxing bouts. The expression puns on the double meaning of *marron* as the chestnut street-vendor's sales-cry.

chaud *adv. Ça va vous coûter chaud!* It's going to cost you a packet! (*Chaud* is really a colloquial alternative to *cher*.)

chaude-pisse *n.f.* 'Clap', gonorrhoea (also: *chaude-lance*).

chaudron *n.m.* **1** Honky-tonk piano, instrument in need of tuning and attention. **2** *(pej.):* Prostitute long past her prime.

chauffard *n.m.* 'Road-hog', reckless driver.

chauffe-Barbès *n.m.* Intense 'how's about it' look, admirative and salacious glance.

chauffer *v.trans.* **1** To 'nick', to 'pinch', to steal. *On lui a chauffé son crapaud:* He got his wallet lifted. **2** *Se faire chauffer:* To get 'nabbed', 'collared', to be arrested.

chauffer *v.intrans. Ça va chauffer!* There's aggro in the air! – Trouble is brewing! – Things are going to get mighty unpleasant here! (also: *ça va barder!*).

chausser *v.trans. Etre difficile à chausser (fig.):* To be the awkward type, to be hard to please.

chaussettes *n.f.pl.* **1** Tyres. *Si tu roules avec ces chaussettes lisses, tu vas te faire pincer par les flics!* If you drive around with these treadbare tyres, the fuzz'll do you! **2** *Mettre ses chaussettes à la fenêtre* (of woman): To be disappointed with a sexual relationship. (According to Jacques Cellard and Alain Rey in their DICTIONNAIRE DU FRANÇAIS NON-CONVENTIONNEL, the expression is usually used with a negative to indicate intense sexual satisfaction.) **3** *Les chaussettes à clous:* The plain-clothes police force. (This expression dates back to the time when all policemen could be recognized by the hob-nailed regulation-type shoes they wore.)

chausson *n.m.* **1** *Etre putain comme chausson* (of woman): To 'be anybody's', to be a right trollop. **2** *Chausson aux pommes:* Apple-filled flaky pastry cake.

chaussure *n.f. Trouver chaussure à son pied:* **a** To come across the ideal thing, to find exactly what one was looking for. **b** To find the ideal partner in life (friend or spouse).

chauve *n.m. Le chauve à col roulé (joc.):* 'Prick', 'cock', penis.

chauve-souris *n.f. Avoir des chauves-souris au plafond:* To 'have bats in the belfry', to be 'bonkers', to be mad.

chbeb *n.m.* 'Nancy-boy', 'young pouf', effeminate homosexual. (The appellation is said to have originated in the *Bat' d'Af'* – see that word – and comes from Arabic.)

chbeb *adj.* Handsome, good-looking.

chef *n.m.* **1** *(joc.): Salut, chef!* Morning, Guv! – Morning, squire! – Hello there! **2** *Se débrouiller comme un chef:* To handle things beautifully, to do just the right thing.

chelem *adj. Etre grand chelem:* To be 'cleaned out', 'skint', to be penniless. (The expression originates from the world of cards in a context of gambling.)

chelinguer *v.intrans.* (also: *chlinguer*): To 'pong', to stink, to smell foul. *Chelinguer du bec:* To have bad breath, to suffer from halitosis.

chemin *n.m.* **1** *Faire son chemin:* To 'get on in life', to make a success of things. **2** *Faire voir du chemin à quelqu'un (fig.):* To 'push someone around', to bully the life out of someone. **3** *Prendre le chemin des écoliers (iron.):* To 'go the pretty way', to take the long way round in order to get somewhere.

chemise *n.f.* **1** *Y laisser jusqu'à sa (dernière) chemise:* To 'go bust', to lose everything. **2** *Changer de quelque chose comme de chemise:* To chop and change. *Changer d'idée comme de chemise:* To change one's mind with the weather, to be inconsistent in one's thinking. **3** *S'en moquer* (also: *s'en foutre*) *comme de sa première chemise:* To 'not care two hoots' about, to feel totally indifferent to something. **4** *Etre comme cul et chemise:* To be 'as thick as thieves', to be bosom pals.

chenaille *n.f.* Sexual intercourse. *Aller à la chenaille:* To 'get one's oats', to have sex.

chenailler *v.intrans.* To 'screw', to fuck, to have intercourse.

chenu *n.m. Du chenu:* 'Quality stuff', top-quality merchandise. *Ne t'y trompe pas, c'est du chenu pour sûr!* Make no mistake, this is the real stuff! (The expression is said to have applied originally to wines.)

chèque *n.m. Chèque en bois:* 'Rubber cheque', cheque returned to payee because of insufficient funds.

cher *adj. Les places seront chères! (iron.):* It'll be a free-for-all at the top! – There'll be strong competition for places!

cher *adv.* **1** *Je ne vaux pas cher aujourd'hui:* I'm feeling out of sorts today – I don't feel too well. **2** *Il n'y en a pas cher comme lui de nos jours:* There aren't many left like him these days.

chercher *v.intrans.* **1** *Tu me cherches?! (iron.):* Are you looking for a fight?! – Do you want a row? (The expression is always used in a vocative context, with the exception of *s'il me cherche, il va me trouver!* Another crack like that and I'll push his face in!) **2** *Il l'a cherché! (iron.):* He's been asking for it! – He got what he deserved! **3** *Où est-il allé chercher ça?* Who put that idea into his head? **4** *Ça va chercher cher:* It'll cost a packet – It'll be expensive. **5** *Aller les chercher* (Underworld slang): To run risks in order to achieve success.

chéro *adj.* (also: *chérot*): 'Pricey', rather dear, a trifle expensive.

cherrer *v.intrans.* **1** To 'lay it on thick', to 'pitch it a bit strong', to exaggerate (also: *cherrer dans les bégonias*). *Alors là, tu cherres un chouïa!* Now that I don't believe! *Cherrez pas!* Pull the other one! – Stop kidding! **2** *Cherrer dans le tas:* To go into a scrap with fists flying.

cherreur *n.m.* (Boxing slang): All-out puncher, fighter who gives his best to the last.

chetard *n.m.* (also: *chtard*): 'Nick', jail, prison.

cheval *n.m.* **1** Butch-looking woman, one singularly lacking in femininity. **2** *Cheval de retour:* 'Old lag', old offender, criminal who seems to regularly boomerang back to jail. (In a humorous context, the appellation can sometimes refer affectionately to someone who cannot keep away from a past occupation.) **3** *Becqueter* (also: *bouffer*) *avec les chevaux de bois:* To miss a meal, to go hungry. **4** (Drugs): Heroin. (A translation of the American 'horse', the word is hardly ever encountered.)

chevalier *n.m.* **1** *Chevalier d'industrie:* Entrepreneur, wheeler-dealer. **2** *Chevalier de la guirlande:* Convict. **3** *Chevalier de la rosette:* 'Faggot', 'queer', homosexual. **4** *Chevalier de la piquouse:* Drug-addict (on hard drugs taken intravenously).

chevalière *n.f.* Arse-hole, anus (in a context of sodomous intercourse).

cheveu *n.m.* **1** *Se faire des cheveux:* To fret, to go grey with worry. **2** *Avoir un cheveu sur la langue:* To have a lisp. **3** *Avoir mal aux cheveux:* To have a hangover, to have a headache after a night of boozing. **4** *C'est tiré par les cheveux* (of argument): It's far-fetched – It's rather contrived. **5** *Il y a comme (qui dirait) un cheveu (fig.):* There's a hitch – There's some sort of snag.

cheville *n.f.* **1** (Underworld slang): Important 'contact', individual whose valuable assistance borders on complicity. (The expression *être en cheville avec* nearly always relates to associations of a dubious nature. *Il est en cheville avec un revendeur marron*: He's in cahoots with some sort of fence.) **2** *Ne pas avoir mal aux chevilles (iron.)*: To be a glutton for compliments. (In the same way that the polishing of fingernails on one's clothing is deemed in 'body-language' to express self-satisfaction, for a Frenchman kicking his ankles translates appreciation at being showered with compliments.)

chevilleur *n.m.* 'Go-between', intermediary (often in a context of illicit activities).

chèvre *n.f.* 'Hot number', 'randy bird', highly sexed woman.

chevreuil *n.m.* **1** 'Funk', coward. **2** 'Snitch', 'grass', police informer.

chiade *n.f.* *Etre en pleine chiade (sch.)*: To be cramming like mad, to be swotting for an exam.

chiader *v.trans. & intrans.* **1** To 'shit', to 'crap', to defecate. **2** *(sch.)*: To swot like mad, to prepare intensively for an exam (also: *bûcher*).

chiadeur *n.m.* *(sch.)*: **1** 'Swotter', swot. **2** 'Plodder', slow learner.

chialer *v.intrans.* To 'blubber', to have the weepies, to sob.

chialeur *n.m.* **1** 'Sniveller', cry-baby. **2** 'Moaner', complainer.

chiant *adj.* **1** Excruciatingly boring. *Il est d'un chiant quand il raconte ses souvenirs de guerre*: He can bore the pants off you with his 'how-I-won-the-war' stories. **2** 'Sickening', depressing. *C'est chiant, j'ai plus un rond, j'ai payé mes impôts*: I'm fed up to the back teeth, I've paid the tax-man and he's cleaned me out! (also: *chiatique*).

chiard *n.m.* 'Brat', 'nipper', child. (In spite of its semantic origin, the word is not always pejorative.)

chiasse *n.f.* 'The runs', diarrhoea. (The expression *avoir la chiasse* can also mean 'to be in a blue funk', to be frightened out of one's wits.)

chiasseur *n.m.* 'Yellow-belly', 'funk', coward.

chiatique *adj.* **1** Excruciatingly boring. **2** 'Sickening', galling in the extreme.

chibis *n.m.* *Faire* (also: *partir en*) *chibis*: To 'go over the wall', to escape from prison.

chibre *n.m.* 'Prick', 'cock', penis. (The word always refers to an erect organ and usually a large one.)

chibrer *v.trans.* To 'screw', to fuck, to have coition with.

chic *n.m.* **1** *Avoir le chic pour (iron.)*: To have an uncanny knack for. *Quel pique-assiette! Il a le chic pour arriver quand on est à table!* What a scrounger, he always manages to time his visits with mealtimes! **2** *Faire du chic*: To 'swank', to show off.

chic *adj.* *Chic alors!* Smashing! – Super! – Great!

chicandier *n.m.* 'Nit-picker', awkward and argumentative person.

chicandier *adj.* 'Nit-picking', fault-finding, awkward.

chicane *n.f.* *Pêcher la chicane*: To be looking for an argument.

chicard *adj.* 'Decent', very fair, kind. *Il n'y a pas plus chicard que lui*: He's as nice as they come.

chiche *interj.* I dare you! – Bet you don't! (This interjection, which is more frequently heard in school yards, is the archetypal French taunt.) *'Chiche que tu lui fasses un poisson d'avril!'* 'Bet you're too chicken to play an April Fool trick on her!'

chiches *n.f.pl.* *Les chiches*: 'The bog', 'the karzey', the lavatory.

chichis *n.m.pl.* **1** Affected manners. *Ce sont des gens à chichis*: They're a rather lah-di-dah crowd. **2** *Faire des chichis*: To 'make a song-and-dance', to make a fuss about something. *Avec tous ces chichis, je ne sais plus où j'en suis*: With all this faffing about, I don't know whether I'm coming or going.

chichite *n.f.* Purely imaginary illness, hypochondriac's complaint.

chichiteux *adj.* 'Mithering', fussy. *Il est d'un chichiteux!* He's a right fusspot!

chicore *n.f.* 'Set-to', 'punch-up', fight. *Il aime la chicore, lui!* He's always ready for a bit of rough stuff!

chicore *adj.* 'Pissed', 'sozzled', drunk.

chicorée *n.f.* **1** *Coiffure chicorée*: 'Afro hairdo', frizzy hairstyle. **2** 'Woolly', pubic hair. *Défriser la chicorée*: To perform cunnilingus. (Both meanings originate from the name of a variety of frizzy-leafed lettuce popular in France.)

chicorer *v.trans.reflex.* **1** To 'have a punch-up', to have a fight. **2** To 'have a set-to', to row vociferously.

chie-dans-l'eau *n.m. (pej.)*: 'Tar', sailor. (This derogatory and would-be witty appellation is usually uttered by the military.)

chiée *n.f.* *Une chiée de*: 'Oodles', 'loads of', vast numbers. *Il y a une chiée de mecs prêts à prendre ta place!* I've got a list as long as my arm of people queuing up for your job! (also: *une tripotée de*).

chiément *adv.* 'Incredibly', fantastically (usually with a positive connotation). *Il a une nana chiément bien*: You should see the smashing bird he goes round with!

chien *n.m.* **1** *Ce n'est pas fait pour les chiens!* *(iron.)*: What do you think it's here for?! – It's not just an ornament, you know! **2** *Faire* (also: *tenir*) *la chronique des chiens écrasés*: To work in the 'dog-bites-man' department of a provincial newspaper. **3** *Recevoir quelqu'un comme un chien dans un jeu de quilles*: To 'give someone the cold shoulder', to make someone feel most unwelcome. **4** *Ne pas attacher son chien avec des saucisses*: To be 'as mean as they come', to be stingy. **5** *Garder à quelqu'un un chien de sa chienne*: To bear a grudge against someone. **6** *Avoir du chien* (of woman): To have 'oomph', to have loads of sex-appeal.

chienchien *n.m.* 'Bowsy-wowsy', 'doggie', dog. *'Ça c'est le chienchien à sa mémère!'* 'Who's a beautiful boy, then?!' (This idiotic rhetorical question is usually uttered by doting owners.)

chiendent *n.m.* 'Hitch', 'snag', difficulty.

chienlit *n.m.* 'Hash', 'cock-up', state of confusion. (The word should be pronounced *chie-en-lit*.)

chiennerie *n.f.* **1** Beastliness. *Ce que je lui reproche le plus c'est sa chiennerie*: I just can't abide his bitchiness. **2** Shameless deed. *Comme chiennerie ça se pose là*: Try and beat that for a rotten trick!

chier *v.trans.* **1** *Chier du poivre*: To 'scarper', to 'make tracks', to run away (usually from the police). **2** *Chier une côtelette* (of human): To give birth. **3** *Il croit qu'il a chié la Colonne Vendôme* (iron.): He thinks he's it – He has a high opinion of himself. **4** *Tu me chies une pendule!* (also: *tu me chies une Tour Montparnasse!* or *tu me chies un haricot!*, etc.): You're a right pain in the arse! (In an escalation of near-scatological expressions, the phrase *tu me fais chier!* has become transitive and the nature of the object heightens the degree of vituperation.)

chier *v.intrans.* **1** To 'crap', to 'shit', to defecate. **2** *Chier dans les bottes à quelqu'un*: To 'do the dirty on', to play a dirty trick on someone. **3** *Faire chier quelqu'un*: To be 'a pain in the arse', to cause someone intense irritation. *Ça me fait chier mais il va falloir que je vende ma bagnole*: I'm really pissed off at the thought of having to sell my car. **4** *Se faire chier*: To experience intense irritation and boredom. **5** *Envoyer chier quelqu'un*: To 'send someone packing', to tell someone to go away in no uncertain manner. **6** *Ça va chier dur!* There's going to be one hell of a set-to! **7** *Il n'y a pas à chier!* You can't get away from it! – There's no denying it! **8** *Ça ne chie pas!* It doesn't matter one little bit! – It's of no consequence. **9** *Chier dans la colle*: To exaggerate.

chierie *n.f.* 'Drag', bloody nuisance. *Quelle chierie, ces embouteillages!* I've never seen such awful traffic jams!

chie-tout-debout *n.m.* *(pej.)*: 'Rake-handle', tall and skinny person.

chieur *n.m.* *(pej.)*: **1** 'Pain-in-the-arse', mitherer. **2** *Chieur d'encre*: 'Pen-pusher', menial clerk.

chieuse *n.f.* *(pej.)*: 'Arsehole', despicable character. (The insult is usually levelled at men and because it is feminine it is all the more derogatory.)

chiffe *n.m.* *(abbr. chiffonnier)*: 'Rag-and-bone man', junk-dealer (also: *chiffetir*).

chiffe *n.f.* 'Drip', spineless person, one who lacks authority and character.

chiffetir *n.m.* (also: *chiftir*): **1** Rag, scrap of cloth. **2** 'Rag-and-bone man', junk-dealer.

chiffonner *v.trans.* To 'bug', to vex, to irritate. *Ça me chiffonne quand on me demande si je suis Français*: It really gets me when people ask whether I'm a foreigner. *Un rien le chiffonne*: He's as touchy as hell.

chiffortin *n.m.* 'Rag-and-bone man', junk-dealer (also: *chiffe*, *chiffetir*).

chigne *n.f.* 'Cry-baby', sniveller.

chigner *v.intrans.* To 'snivel', to 'blubber', to cry.

chignole *n.f.* 'Motor', 'set of wheels', car. *Sa chignole est toujours en carafe*: He always seems to be breaking down with his old banger.

chignoleur *n.m.* Safe-cracker.

chignoleuse *n.f.* 'Hooker', 'tart', prostitute.

chignon *n.m.* **1** Brains. *On l'a retrouvé avec une olive dans le chignon*: They found him with a bullet through his head. *Il n'a pas grand-chose dans le chignon*: He's pretty dim – He's not very bright. *C'est un mou du chignon*: He's a little bit simple. **2** *Se crêper le chignon* (of women): To 'have a ding-dong set-to', to have a violent argument.

chine *n.f.* **1** *De chine (adj.exp.)*: 'Cadged', obtained through sponging or begging. *Toutes les cibiches qu'il fume, il les a de chine*: All the ciggies he smokes he's wangled off friends. **2** *Aller à la chine*: To go 'knocking', to go buying antiques and second-hand goods from door to door.

chiner *v.trans. & intrans.* **1** To 'cadge', to sponge. *Tout ce qu'il a, il l'a chiné*: There's not a thing on him that's not begged or borrowed. **2** To 'take the mickey out of someone', to 'rag someone', to make fun of someone. **3** To 'graft', to work hard. **4** (of rag-and-bone man): To go out collecting.

Chinetoque *n.m. & f.* 'Chink', Chinese person.

chinetoque *adj.* **1** 'Chink', Chinese. **2** Difficult and complicated. *Le mode d'emploi est plutôt* *chinetoque*: That instruction leaflet sounds like gibberish to me.

chineur *n.m.* **1** 'Cadger', sponger. **2** 'Narky teaser', sarcastic ribber. **3** 'Rag-and-bone man', junk dealer.

chiniaiseries *n.f.pl. (joc.)*: 'Orientalia', bric-à-brac objects imported from Asia. (This slightly pejorative word aptly describes the wide range of knick-knacks that clutter our shelves.)

chinois *n.m.* **1** *Du chinois*: 'Gobbledygook', 'double-Dutch', incomprehensible language. *Tout ça, c'est du chinois pour moi!* I can't understand a blind word he's saying! **2** Outsider, stranger. **3** Suspicious character. *Qui c'est ce chinois là-bas?* Who's that geezer over there? *Chinois de paravent*: 'Dodgy type', 'shifty' character. **4** 'Prick', 'cock', penis. *Se polir le chinois*: To 'have a wank', to masturbate. **5** *(pl.)*: 'Tootsies', toes.

chinois *adj.* **1** 'Cagey', awkward. *En affaires, il n'y a pas plus chinois*: In business dealings he's as slippery as an eel. **2** Difficult and complicated. *Fichtre, c'est chinois ce mode d'emploi!* I can't make sense of these instructions!

chinoiser *v.intrans.* To raise pernickety objections.

chinoiseries *n.f.pl.* 'Red tape', pernickety formalities.

chioteur *n.m. (pej.)*: 'Bent cop', crooked policeman who takes backhanders.

chiotte *n.f.* **1** 'Heap', 'banger', motor car. *Ça c'est de la tire, un peu mieux que ta chiotte!* Now that's what I call a car, not like that old crate of yours! **2** *Les chiottes*: 'The karzey', 'the bog', the W.C. *La corvée des chiottes*: Latrine duty. *'Aux chiottes l'arbitre!'* 'We want a referee! We want a referee!' (This derisory chant, more offensive than the English equivalent, can often be heard in football or rugby grounds when the fans feel cheated.)

chiourme *n.f. La chiourme*: Prison staff. (More frequently encountered is the appellation *garde-chiourme*.)

chipé *adj. Etre chipé pour*: To be crazy about, to have a strong liking for. *Il est drôlement chipé pour ma frangine*: He's nuts about my sister.

chiper *v.trans.* **1** To 'swipe', to 'pinch', to steal. **2** *(corr. choper)*: To 'cop', to catch a disease.

chipette *n.f. Ne pas valoir chipette*: To be 'no great shakes', to be worthless. *Ce contrat ne vaut pas chipette*: This contract's not worth the paper it's written on.

chipeur *n.m.* 'Filcher', 'pilferer', petty thief.

chipie *n.f.* 'Sour-puss', spiteful and mean-mouthed woman. *Quelle petite chipie!* She's a right little minx!

chipie *adj.f.* 'Catty', mean-mouthed.

chipolata *n.f. (joc.)*: 'Prick', 'cock', penis. (Unlike *chibre*, the word refers to a rather undersize organ.)

chipotage *n.m.* 'Haggling', quibbling. *Le chipotage, c'est son blot*: He just never stops arguing over trifles.

chipoter *v.intrans.* **1** To haggle. *Au marché faut toujours qu'elle chipote sur les prix*: She's worse than the market-traders when she's out shopping. **2** To quibble. *Quand on se décide à faire quoi que ce soit, il faut toujours qu'il chipote sur les détails*: When it boils down to doing what we said we'd do, he's great at finding stumbling-blocks. **3** To waste time. **4** To nibble, to toy with one's food. *Il faut la voir à table! Elle chipote, elle mange du bout des dents*: She'd drive any cook crazy, picking away at her food.

chipoteur *adj.* 'Pernickety', choosy, fastidious.

chiquage *n.m.* Bluff, make-believe, pretence.

chiqué *n.m.* **1** 'To-do', fuss, commotion. **2** 'Sham', make-believe, pretence. *Tout ça, c'est du chiqué!* This is a load of eyewash! *Faire quelque chose au chiqué*: To bluff one's way through something.

chique *n.f.* **1** *Mou comme une chique* (of person): 'Wet', 'spineless', indecisive (also: *mou comme une chiffe*). **2** *Avoir la chique*: To have searing toothache (emphasized by a bulging cheek). **3** *Avaler sa chique*: To 'pop one's clogs', to 'snuff it', to die. **4** *Pousser sa chique*: To 'crap', to 'shit', to defecate. **5** *Tirer sa chique* (of man): To 'have it off', to have sex (also: *tirer son coup*). **6** *Couper la chique à quelqu'un*: To leave someone speechless. **7** *Faire quelque chose à la chique*: To do something for show, to act in a preposterously ostentatious manner.

chiquement *adv.* **1** Stylishly, smartly. *Elle était chiquement fringuée*: You could have taken her for a model, the way she was dressed. **2** 'Decently', with great loyalty. *Chiquement il m'a prêté sa bagnole*: Like the good guy he is, he lent me his car.

chiquer *v.trans. & intrans.* **1** To 'stuff one's face', to 'nosh', to eat. *Il a tout chiqué!* He scoffed the lot! **2** To bluff, to pretend. *Il a chiqué qu'on ne l'avait pas payé*: He made out he'd never received a penny. *Sans chiquer?!* No kidding?! – Are you serious?! **3** *'y a pas à chiquer!* There's no two ways about it! – There really isn't any choice! *'y a pas à chiquer, va falloir payer le loyer!* It's not 'Will we pay the rent?' but when's the soonest we can do it! **4** *Rien à chiquer!* No way! – Nothing doing! – Certainly not! **5** *Chiquer à tout va*: To deny emphatically. *Il a chiqué à tout va que c'était pas lui qu'avait fait le coup*: He swore blind it wasn't him what had done it.

chiqueur *n.m.* **1** 'Swank', show-off. **2** Small time pimp-cum-crook.

chizbroc *n.m.* **1** 'Hullabaloo', commotion, noise. **2** 'Dust-up', punch-up, fight. **3** *'y a du chizbroc dans l'air*: There's trouble brewing – The atmosphere's as tense as a drumskin.

chlaffe *n.f.* *La chlaffe*: 'Shut-eye', sleep. *Aller à la chlaffe*: To 'turn in', to 'hit the sack', to go to bed.

chlasse *n.m.* (also: *schlasse*): 'Chiv', blade, knife.

chlasse *adj.* (also: *schlasse*): **1** 'Pissed', 'blotto', drunk. **2** 'Knackered', 'buggered', exhausted.

chleu *n.m. & adj.* (also: *chleuh*): 'Kraut', 'Jerry', German.

chlinguer *v.intrans.* To 'pong', to stink, to smell foul. *Ça chlinguait méchant*: It stank to high heaven.

chloffe *n.f.* 'Shut-eye', sleep. *Etre bon pour la chloffe*: To be ready for beddy-byes.

chloroforme *n.m. Du chloroforme en barre (joc.)*: Cosh, bludgeon (also: *goumi*).

chmoutz *n.m. (pej.)*: 'Yid', Jew. (The word, originating from the German *Schmutz*, meaning dirt, is loaded with racism.)

chnaps *n.m.* 'Hooch', 'hard stuff', strong alcohol.

chnoc *n.m.* 'Burk', 'nincompoop', fool. *Vieux chnoc*: Old dodderer.

chnouf *n.f.* 'Snow', cocaine. (The word *chnouf* regained popularity with the 60s film *Razzia sur la chnouf* on the organized repression of drug trafficking.)

chnouffer *v.trans.reflex.* To take drugs, to be a drug addict.

choc *n.m. Amortir le choc (fig.)*: To soften the blow. *Pour amortir le choc, je lui ai annoncé son augmentation*: To help the medicine go down, I told him about his rise.

choc *adj. inv. Prix choc* (of consumer goods): Super bargain price – 'Unrepeatable' cut-price offer.

chochote *n.f.* **1** 'Lah-di-dah' woman, female snob. **2** 'Pouf', 'fairy', effeminate homosexual. **3** *Ma chochote* (term of endearment): My lovey-dovey – My pet – My darling. **4** *Faire sa chochote*: To act as if butter wouldn't melt in one's mouth, to be a demure little hypocrite.

chochoter *v.intrans.* To show affection, to adopt an over-genteel bearing.

chochoteuse *adj.f.* 'Lah-di-dah', affected. (The adjective is particularly pejorative when directed at a man. *Un peu chochoteuse, ce mec-là, tu trouves pas?* He does act rather pouffy, don't you think?)

choco *n.m. (abbr. chocolat)*: **1** 'Choccy', bar of chocolate. **2** Cocoa, chocolate-flavoured drink.

chocolat *n.m.* **1** *Etre chocolat*: To have been 'conned', 'taken in', to have been duped. **2** *Rester chocolat*: To be left in the lurch (and find oneself with no means of assistance). **3** *La turbine à chocolat*: The arse-hole, the anus.

chocotte *n.f.* **1** 'Fang', tooth. *Il a pris un parpaing en pleine poire, et crachait ses chocottes*: The punch landed on his jaw and left him with a mouthful of ivories. **2** *Avoir les chocottes*: To 'have the shakes', to be frightened out of one's wits, to be shaking in one's shoes. *Filer les chocottes à quelqu'un*: To 'give someone the willies', to frighten someone.

chocotter *v.intrans.* To 'have the willies', to 'have the shakes', to be frightened.

choguet *n.m.* Prisoner's gear, prisoner's uniform.

choléra *n.m.* **1** 'Nasty piece of work', evil person. **2** Nasty business, unpleasant state of affairs.

chôme *n.f. La chôme*: Unemployment. *Etre à la chôme*: To be on the dole.

chômedu *n.m. (pej.)*: 'Dole-queue rider', 'scrounger', unemployed person. (The inference here is that the person concerned has no desire to find employment. The expression *toucher ses chômedus* is a pointer to the word's origin.)

chonosof *n.m.* 'Nincompoop', 'twit', imbecile.

choper *v.trans.* **1** To 'nick', to 'pinch', to steal. **2** To grab hold of someone. *Il m'a chopé au passage*: He well and truly buttonholed me! **3** *Se faire choper*: To get 'nicked', 'collared', to be arrested. **4** To get something unpleasant (school detention, parking fine, disease, etc.). *A frayer avec des gonzesses comme ça, tu vas choper une chaude-lance*: With girls like that, you're likely to cop a dose!

chopeur *n.m.* 'Pilferer', small-time thief.

chopin *n.m.* **1** 'Windfall', financial stroke of luck. *Sans ce beau chopin on aurait fait faillite*: Without that money out of the blue, we would have gone bust. **2** Attractive bird, pretty lass, beautiful girl. **3** *Avoir un chopin pour*: To 'have a soft spot' for someone of the opposite sex. *Il a un sacré chopin pour ma frangine*: He's fallen for my sister, hook, line and sinker! **4** *Faire un beau chopin* (of woman): To find a sugar-daddy, to find a wealthy lover.

chopine *n.f.* **1** Small glass of wine served in restaurant. **2** *(joc. corr. pine)*: 'Prick', 'cock', penis.

chopotte *n.f.* (also: *chopote*): **1** Small bottle of wine (usually containing half a litre). **2** 'Prick', 'prong', penis. (The inference here, as with *chibre*, is of a large organ.)

chose *n.m.* **1** 'What's-it', 'thingummy', contraption. **2** *(joc.* of person): 'Thingey', 'what's-his-name'. *J'ai dit à chose qu'il fallait venir:* When I saw him, I told whoever-it-is to come along. **3** 'Prick', 'cock', penis.

chose *n.f.* **1** Sex, sexual matters. *Etre porté sur la chose:* To be a randy so-and-so. **2** *Petite chose (iron.):* 'Cry-baby', over-sensitive person. *Il pleut, et alors?! Petite chose, va!* So it's raining?! You're not made of sugar, are you?! **3** *Dites bien des choses à . . .* Give my regards to . . . **4** *Se sentir tout chose (adv.exp.):* **a** To feel 'off-colour', to feel queasy. **b** To feel lost and bewildered.

chosette *n.f.* Sex, intercourse. *Faire chosette:* To have it off.

chou *n.m.* **1** 'Bean', 'bonce', head. *Je vais lui rentrer dans le chou!* I'm going to knock his block off! *En avoir ras le chou:* To be 'fed-up to here', to be 'fed-up to the back teeth', to be sick and tired of something. *Se creuser le chou:* To rack one's brains. *Ne rien avoir dans le chou:* To have nothing up-top. *Ça m'est sorti du chou:* I clean forgot! – It slipped my mind! *Se monter le chou:* **a** To 'kid oneself', to delude oneself. **b** To 'get into a lather', to work oneself into a frenzy. **2** *Feuilles de chou:* 'Flappers', 'flaps', ears. *Ouvre tes feuilles de chou!* Pin back your lug-holes! – Now listen carefully! **3** *Aller planter ses choux:* To opt out and retire from the rat-race. **4** *Planter un chou* (of train): To break down in the middle of nowhere. **5** *Sauter sur le chou à quelqu'un:* To pounce on someone. **6** *Etre dans les choux:* **a** To be 'in a fix', to be in a difficult situation. *Ton projet, il est dans les choux:* That idea of yours is up the spout! *Grâce à toi, je suis dans les choux!* A fine mess you've got me into! **b** (Horse racing): To be trailing with the tailenders, to be amongst the last past the post. **7** *Chou pour chou:* Word for word, verbatim. *J'ai eu droit à son histoire trois fois, chou pour chou!* He inflicted three carbon-copy narrations of the story on me! **8** *C'est bête comme chou:* It's as easy as pie – It couldn't be simpler. **9** *Faire chou blanc:* To 'draw a blank', to be unsuccessful. **10** *En faire ses choux gras:* To 'make a good thing of it', to do well out of something. **11** *Faites-en des choux raves!* You do what you like with it, it's no skin off my nose! **12** *Mon chou* (term of endearment): My lovey-dovey – My pet – My darling.

chou *adj.* 'Divine', absolutely marvellous. *Son appartement est d'un chou!* She's got the most gorgeous little flat!

chouaga *adj.* 'Smashing', 'great', fantastic.

choucard *adj.* 'A-1', first-rate, superb. *Un peu qu'elle est choucarde, sa nana!* His bird is a bit of alright!

choucarde *n.f.* Any form of electric lighting (wall-lamp, hand-torch, etc.).

chouchou *n.m.* 'Blue-eyed wonder', favourite character. *Il est vite devenu le chouchou de la télé:* He soon became the golden boy of the small screen.

chouchouter *v.trans.* To 'mollycoddle', to make a fuss over someone. *Depuis qu'il est marié, il se fait chouchouter un brin!* Since he got wed, he's got the cushiest life possible!

choucrouteman *n.m.* *(joc.):* 'Kraut', 'Jerry', German.

chouette *n.m.* **1** *Le chouette de . . .* The great thing about . . . *Le chouette de l'affaire, c'est qu'on lui a prêté son propre fric:* The really hilarious thing about it all was that we lent him his own money. **2** *Avoir (quelqu'un) au chouette:* To con someone through high-pressure patter. **3** *(pl.):* Genuine I.D. papers. *Marcher sous ses chouettes:* To go about under one's true identity. **4** *Prendre du chouette:* To indulge in sodomous intercourse.

chouette *n.f. Il était tout à la chouette à l'idée de revoir sa bonne femme:* He was full of the joys of spring at the thought of seeing his missus again.

chouette *adj.* **1** 'Swell', 'great', fine. *C'est une chouette personne, ta frangine:* Your sister is a really nice person. **2** *Avoir quelqu'un à la chouette:* **a** To be 'in someone's good books', to be held in esteem by someone. **b** To 'have a crush on someone', to be enamoured with someone.

chouette *interj.* Good-ho! – Smashing! – Great! *Chouette alors!* Well, that's really super! (The French and English are equally sweet.)

chouettement *adv.* Superbly well. *On a été chouettement reçu chez lui:* He entertained us superbly. *L'affaire a été chouettement réglée:* The whole thing was sweetly expedited.

chouettos *adj.inv. (joc.):* 'Swell', 'great', fine. (The word is pronounced *chouettosse*.)

chou-fleur *n.m. Un chou-fleur:* A cancerous growth, a malignant tumour. *Manque de pot, en fin de carrière il s'est payé un chou-fleur:* It was rotten luck him catching the Big Bug just as he was about to retire.

choufliqueur *n.m.* 'Bungler', 'botcher', slipshod workman. *C'est des choufliqueurs qui nous ont fait cette maison:* That house of ours was jerry-built.

chouïa *n.m.* (also: *chouilla*): **1** *Un chouïa:* 'A teeny-weeny bit', 'a trifle', a little. *Il est un chouïa radin:* He's a bit on the mean side. *Elle nous a donné un chouïa de ragoût:* She dished us out a small portion of stew. **2** *Chouïa chouïa (adv.exp.):* Carefully and quietly. *Chouïa chouïa on s'est débrouillé:* We followed the old adage 'softly, softly, catchee monkey'.

chouïa *adj.inv.* 'Smashing', very attractive.

chouilled *n.m. Un chouilled:* 'A teeny-weeny bit', 'a trifle', a little. *Il est un chouilled radin:* He's a bit on the mean side (also: *chouïa*).

choupaïa *adj.inv.* Good-looking, handsome. *Elle le trouve choupaïa:* She thinks he's smashing.

choupette *n.f.* Mop of hair.

chou-pourri *n.m. (pej.):* 'Perv', sexual pervert.

chouquette *n.f.* **1** 'Dolly bird', sexy young woman. **2** Snobbish and affected young woman. **3** 'Fairy', 'pansy', effeminate homosexual.

chourave *n.f. La chourave:* 'Nicking', 'pinching', petty thieving.

chouravé *adj.* 'Bonkers', 'barmy', mad. *Il est complètement chouravé:* He's totally round the bend.

chouraver *v.trans.* To 'nick', to 'pinch', to steal. *Elle lui a chouravé son crapaud:* She lifted his wallet.

chouraveur *n.m.* Small-time crook, petty thief.

chourin *n.m.* 'Chiv', blade, knife (also: *surin*).

chouriner *v.trans.* To 'knife', to stab (also: *suriner*).

chourineur *n.m.* 'Hit-man', murderer whose 'tool of the trade' is the knife.

choute *n.f.* **1** Snob young lady. *Comme choute elle fait très Marie-Chantal:* She's the archetypal lah-di-dah bird. **2** Darling. *Ma choute:* My lovey-dovey.

chouteries *n.f.pl. Des chouteries:* 'Canoodling', 'snogging', amorous foreplay. *Se faire des chouteries:* To indulge in heavy petting.

chpile *n.m.* **1** *Le chpile:* Gaming, gambling. *Au chpile, c'est un minus!* At the card-table, he's a gutless wonder! **2** *Avoir beau chpile:* To be in a commanding position. (The word is a phonetic representation of the German *Spiel* and the above expression is a mere variation of the non-colloquial *avoir beau jeu*.)

chpoung *n.m.* 'Bloke', 'geezer', fellow.

chproum *n.m.* **1** Temper, anger. *Il est dans un de ces chprouns aujourd'hui:* He's really shirty today! **2** *Faire du chproum:* To 'raise Cain', to complain vociferously.

chrono *n.m. (abbr. chronomètre):* **1** Stop-watch. *On s'est tapé du 160 chrono dans sa bagnole:* We topped 100 mph in his car. **2** Flashy and expensive wrist-watch.

chroumer *v.trans. & intrans.* To strip parked vehicles of resaleable parts and accessories.

chtar *n.m. Le chtar:* 'The nick', 'the clink', prison. (According to context, the word can either refer to a penitentiary or the 'glasshouse', a military place of detention. Also: *chtibe*).

ch'timi *n.m.* Native of the *Pas-de-Calais* and the adjoining *Département du Nord.* (The appellation is friendly and affectionate.)

chtouille *n.f.* 'Clap', gonorrhoea (also: *chaude-pisse*).

chtourbe *n.f.* Trouble, worry. *Maintenant il est vraiment dans la chtourbe:* He's up to his neck in problems now. *Il a des chtourbes à la cambuse en ce moment:* He's having a difficult time at home.

chtrasse *n.f.* **1** Street, road. **2** Hotel bedroom frequented by prostitutes. (The word is a phonetic representation of the German *Strasse* and the jocularity stems from the fact that the room in question has a lot of 'passing trade'.)

chtrope *n.m. & f.* 'Crummy goods', shoddy wares. (The word is often to be heard amongst rag-and-bone dealers.)

chute *n.f.* **1** 'Twist', unexpected turn to a story or joke. **2** *Point de chute:* Favourite haunt, habitual meeting-place.

chuter *v.intrans.* **1** To 'take a tumble', to fall. **2** *(fig.):* To 'come a cropper', to 'come to grief', to suffer a setback.

ciao *interj.* So long! – Cheerio! – Goodbye! (This is a direct borrowing from the Italian and is sometimes spelled *tchaô*.)

cibiche *n.f.* 'Fag', 'ciggy', cigarette.

ciblot *n.m. (mil.):* 'Civvy', civilian. *En ciblot:* In one's civvies (also: *civelot*).

ciboule *n.f. (abbr. ciboulot):* 'Bean', 'bonce', head.

ciboulot *n.m.* **1** 'Bean', 'brainbox', head. *Il n'a plus un tif sur le ciboulot:* He's as bald as a coot. *Il commence à me courir sur le ciboulot!* He's getting on my wick! – He's starting to become a nuisance! **2** 'Nous', brains, intelligence. *Perdre le ciboulot:* To 'go off one's rocker', to lose one's sanity. *Se creuser le ciboulot:* To rack one's brains.

cicatrice *n.f.* 'Clit', clitoris.

cidre *n.m.* **1** *Le cidre:* 'The drink', any expanse of water. *Tomber dans le cidre:* To fall in the soup. **2** *Ça ne vaut pas un coup de cidre (iron.):* It's not worth a toss – It's useless.

cierge *n.m. Allumer les cierges:* To be on the look-out, to keep watch.

ciflard *n.m. (abbr. sauciflard):* Salami-type sausage. (The original *sauciflard* is in fact a corruption of *saucisson sec*, a type of *charcuterie* of which the French are very fond.)

cigare *n.m.* **1** 'Bean', 'brainbox', head. *Avoir mal au cigare:* To have a splitting headache. *Y aller du cigare:* To be executed by guillotine. **2** 'Nous', brains, intelligence. *Avoir quelque chose dans le cigare:* To 'have something up-top', to be brainy. **3** Cosh, bludgeon (also: *goumi*). **4** *Cigare à moustaches (joc.):* 'Prick', 'cock', penis.

cigarette n.f. Cigarette de poitrinaire: 'Skinny Lizzy', sparsely-filled 'roll-your-own' cigarette.

cigler v.trans. & intrans. To 'cough up', to pay. Cigler une amende: To fork out for a fine. Cigler la douloureuse: To settle the bill (in a restaurant).

cigue n.m. 1 Gold twenty-franc piece similar in size and weight to a sovereign. 2 (of age): Score, unit of twenty years. Il a près de quatre cigues: He's knocking on eighty.

cil n.m. 1 Jeter un cil: To have a peep, to have a glance. 2 Avoir les cils cassés: To be 'dead-beat', to feel very tired. 3 Plier les cils: To 'take some shut-eye', to get some sleep.

ciment n.m. 'Stodge', 'stodgy grub', near-in-digestible food (also: béton).

cimetière n.m. Cimetière à bagnoles: Breaker's yard (where unroadworthy cars are brought, stripped of essential parts and recycled as scrap metal).

ciné n.m. Le ciné: 'The flicks', the cinema. Aller au ciné: To go to the pictures.

cinéac n.m. News theatre. (A long-gone relic of our film past, these small cinemas used to show 60-minute programmes of newsreels and comedy cartoons.)

cinéma n.m. 1 Se faire du cinéma: To let oneself be carried away with wishful daydreaming. 2 Faire tout un cinéma: To 'make a song-and-dance about something', to over-react. 3 Tout ça, c'est du cinéma: It's all sham – It's nothing but make-believe.

cinglé n.m. 'Nutter', 'crackpot', mad person.

cinglé adj. 'Bonkers', 'loony', mad.

cinoche n.m. 'Flea-pit', cinema. Aller au cinoche: To go to the flicks.

cinoque adj. 'Bonkers', 'loony', mad (also: cinglé).

cinq num.adj. 1 Les cinq lettres: Euphemistic alternative to merde. (An equivalent expression is le mot de Cambronne.) 2 Un 'cinq-à-sept': Sexy capers. (This could also be described as the busy businessman's shortened naughty weekend.) 3 Il était moins cinq: It was touch-and-go – It was a near thing. 4 En cinq secs (adv.exp.): In a jiffy – Double-quick – Very quickly. 5 Faire cinq-et-trois-font-huit: To trail a gammy leg, to limp. 6 Y aller de cinq: To shake hands with someone. (Literally to proffer a hand, i.e. five fingers.) 7 Je vous reçois cinq sur cinq (Radio operators' and CB enthusiasts' slang): I'm receiving you loud and clear.

cinquante-pour-cent n.m. Mon cinquante-pour-cent (joc.): 'My better half', 'the missus', my wife.

cintième adj. (corr. cinquième): Elle crèche au cintième sur rue: She's got a flat on the fifth floor overlooking the street.

cintrant adj. 'Side-splitting', hilarious, very funny.

cintre n.m. (Racing cyclists' slang): Handlebar. Cramponner le cintre: To pedal flat-out with one's head down.

cintré adj. 1 'Bonkers', 'loony', mad. 2 Cheeky, impudent. Alors, ça t'es drôlement cintré! Well, you've got a nerve!

cirage n.m. Etre dans le cirage: a To be 'in the dark about something', to be unaware of what is happening. b To be in a state of semi-con-sciousness (as a result of a blow, excessive drink, drugs, etc.). Trois bouteilles de roteux et on était tous dans le cirage: Three bottles of champers and we were just about out for the count. c To feel 'down in the dumps', to be overcome by depression. Il est dans le cirage depuis que sa femme l'a quitté: Since his wife left him, he's lost the will to live (also: broyer du noir). d To be in the financial doldrums, to have lost everything.

circuit n.m. Ne pas être dans le circuit: To be out of touch with things, to have lost contact with the workings of business matters, etc. (The positive statement être dans le circuit: to be 'in the thick of it', to be right in the middle of the action, is less frequently encountered.)

circulanche n.f. (corr. circulation): Motor traffic. La circulanche n'était pas coton ce soir-là! It was a right night for traffic jams!

circulation n.f. 1 Disparaître de la circulation: To disappear from the everyday scene. Après son dernier film elle a disparu de la circulation: That last film of hers was a flop and she wasn't ever heard of again. 2 Etre hors de la circulation: To be 'out of the running', to have lost one's power and credibility within everyday life.

circuler v.intrans. Circulez! Keep moving! – Move on! (Stock-in-trade expression of the city policeman telling passers-by to mind their own business.)

cirer v.trans. Cirer les bottes (also: les pompes) de quelqu'un: To 'suck up to someone', to be a 'toady', to act in an obsequious manner.

cirque n.m. 1 Chaos, state of confusion. Quel cirque! What a shambles! 2 (joc.): The Assemblée Nationale (the French House of Commons). 3 Mener popaul au cirque (joc.): To 'have it off', to fuck, to have intercourse.

cisailler v.trans. 1 To 'flabbergast', to astound, to surprise. La nouvelle l'a cisaillé: He was lost for words when he heard the news. 2 (Gambling): To fleece. On l'a proprement cisaillé au poker: They well and truly cleaned him out at poker.

ciseau *n.m.* **1** *Faire ciseaux*: Unorthodox form of sex foreplay involving manipulation of the thumb and forefinger in a pincer-like movement. **2** *Pour le séparer de son fric il faut un ciseau à froid! (joc.)*: He's a mean bastard, nothing will part him from his money!

Cité *Proper name.* **1** *La Cité (abbr. l'Ile de la Cité)*: The oldest *quartier* of Paris, an island on the river *Seine*. **2** *(abbr. Cité Universitaire)*: Student residential complex in France. (The word refers principally to the *Cité Universitaire* built in the early 20th century in the south suburbs of Paris.)

citoyen *n.m. (pej.)*: 'Cove', 'bloke', person. *Qui c'est que ce citoyen?!* Who the hell is that geezer?!

citron *n.m.* 'Bean', 'brainbox', head. *Avoir mal au citron*: To have a splitting headache. *Se creuser le citron*: To rack one's brains.

citron *n.f. (corr. Citroën)*: *Une citron*: A Citroën motor car. *Il a toujours roulé en citron, maintenant il a une deux-pattes*: He's always been a Citroën addict, and now he's running a 2CV.

citrouille *n.f.* **1** 'Block', 'bonce', head. (The use of *citrouille* rather than *citron* suggests a painful, throbbing head, perhaps the result of over-drinking.) **2** 'Nincompoop', 'twit', fool.

civelot *n.m. (mil.)*: 'Civvy', civilian. *Etre en civelot*: To be in 'mufti', in civvies, to be in civilian clothes.

civil *n.m. Et qu'est-ce que vous faites dans le civil? (joc.)*: And what do you do in real life?

claboter *v.intrans.* To 'pop one's clogs', to 'shuffle off', to die.

clac *n.m.* (also: *claque*): 'Cat-house', low-class brothel.

clair *n.m. Jouer le clair de lune de Werther (à quelqu'un)*: To harp on a sentimental chord in order to get one's own way. (The Massenet melody best remembered from that opera has been extensively popularized in film weepies.)

clair *adj. Clair comme de l'eau de roche*: 'Crystal-clear', patently obvious. (The expression *c'est clair comme de l'eau de vaisselle* is an ironic counter-statement meaning that matters look most confused.)

clamser *v.intrans.* (also: *clamecer*): **1** To 'croak', to 'snuff it', to die. **2** *Etre* (also: *se sentir*) *clamsé*: To feel 'dead-beat', to be utterly exhausted.

clandé *n.m.* **1** Illegal brothel. (Prior to 1946, prostitution was controlled through legalized brothels; in spite of that, a number of establishments traded without the sanction of the State and health authorities.) **2** Unlicensed gambling den.

clandès *n.m. Le clandès (abbr. le marché clandestin)*: The black market.

claouies *n.f.pl.* 'Balls', 'bollocks', testicles. *Il me casse les claouies!* He's a pain in the arse! – He's a damn nuisance! (The word is also encountered in the masculine spelled *claouis*. The feminine word is in keeping with the less colloquial *couilles*.)

clape *n.f. La clape*: 'Grub', food. *Il ne pense qu'à la clape*: He's got food on the brain!

claper *v.trans. & intrans.* To 'nosh', to eat. *N'avoir rien à claper*: To be famished.

clapet *n.m.* 'Gob', 'trap', mouth. *Ferme ton clapet!* Put a sock in it! – Shut up!

clapette *n.f.* 'Licker', tongue (also: *clapoteuse, menteuse*).

clapier *n.m.* 'Pokey digs', cramped accommodation.

claquant *adj.* 'Back-breaking', exhausting.

claque *n.m.* (also: *clac*): 'Cat-house', low-class brothel.

claque *n.f.* **1** *La claque (th.)*: Group of spectators receiving financial reward to applaud frantically on the first night of a new play or show. **2** *Avoir une tête à claques*: To have an arrogant mush, to have an insolent-looking face. **3** *En avoir sa claque*: **a** To be fed-up with something. **b** To feel 'shagged', to be 'dead-beat', to feel worn-out.

claqué *n.m.* 'Stiff', corpse.

claqué *adj.* **1** 'Bushed', 'buggered', worn-out. **2** 'Skint', 'broke', penniless.

claque-dents *n.m.* 'Cat-house', brothel.

claque-merde *n.m. (pej.)*: 'Gob', 'trap', mouth. (The word is never used in an alimentary context, but rather where speech is concerned as in *ferme ton claque-merde!* Put a sock in it! – Shut up!)

claquer *v.trans. & intrans.* **1** To 'blow', to 'blue', to spend money furiously. *Elle a tout claqué en deux temps, trois mouvements*: Her motto seems to have been 'spend, spend, spend'. **2** To 'knacker', to wear out, to exhaust. *Rédiger un dico d'argot, ça vous claque!* Compiling a dictionary of slang sure takes it out of you! **3** (of business deal): To 'fall through', to collapse. *Cette affaire nous a claqué dans les mains*: That deal went sour overnight. **4** To 'croak', to 'snuff it', to die. **5** *Claquer le polichinelle* (Prostitutes' slang): To have a miscarriage (usually brought on by dubious abortive methods). **6** *Claquer du bec*: To 'go hungry', to starve.

claquer *v.trans.reflex.* **1** To pull a muscle (whilst engaged in a sporting activity). **2** To 'flog oneself to death', to drive oneself to the limit. *Au boulot il ne se claque pas!* You couldn't say he's working himself into an early grave!

clarinette *n.f. (joc.)*: **1** Rifle. **2** 'Jemmy', crowbar. **3** Any tool for the general handyman. *Passe-moi la clarinette!* Be a good lad, give us that tool over there! **4** 'Prick', 'cock', penis. *Jouer un solo de clarinette baveuse*: To perform fellatio.

class *adv. En avoir class*: To have had more than enough, to be fed-up with something. *Y en a class!* Well that does it, you can count me out of all this rubbish!

classe *n.f. (mil.) Etre de la classe*: To be ready for demob, to have served one's time doing National Service. (The expression *vive la classe!* is often uttered jubilantly by recruits ready to be released.)

classer *v.trans. & intrans.* **1** To file something in the 'to be forgotten' tray. *Des souvenirs comme ça, faut les classer*: Things like that are best forgotten. **2** *Ça vous classe*: It puts you in the right light – It makes you look good. (The expression can become ironical given the right context.)

classique *n.f. Une classique*: A regular and well-loved sporting event.

classique *adj. C'est le coup classique!* It's that same old trick! – It's the usual ploy! *Elle n'est pas venue au rencart, c'est le coup classique!* She didn't turn up, a case of the old heave-ho!

claveter *v.trans.reflex.* To 'flog oneself to death', to drive oneself to the limit.

clavier *n.m.* Set of teeth (often false ones).

clébard *n.m.* **1** 'Mutt', 'pooch', dog. **2** *(mil.)*: Corp', corporal.

cléber *v.trans. & intrans.* To 'stuff one's face', to eat voraciously.

clef *n.f.* (also: *clé*): **1** *Prendre la clef des champs (joc.)*: To 'blow', to bolt, to clear off. **2** *Mettre la clef sous le paillasson (iron.)*: To do a 'moonlight flit', to abscond leaving a string of debts behind. (The expression is only colloquial with this ironical meaning.) **3** *A la clef*: 'Into the bargain', as a bonus. *Et à la clef, il s'est retrouvé contremaître*: And to cap it all, he wangled the foreman's job. **4** *Laisser les clefs sur la porte* (sexual connotation): To be 'asking for it', to be easy game. **5** *Il m'a joué ça en clef de sol (joc. & iron.)*: He gave me a different version (of that story) to yours.

cliche *n.f. La cliche*: 'The shits', 'the runs', diarrhoea.

cliché *n.m.* 'Mush', 'dial', ugly face.

clicli *n.m.* 'Clit', clitoris.

client *n.m.* **1** 'Mug', 'sucker', dupe. **2** 'Cove', 'geezer', strange character. **3** *Etre client*: To be extremely keen about something. *Une semaine de boustifaille gratis, un peu que je suis client!* One week's free grub suits me just fine!

clignotants *n.m.pl.* 'Blinkers', 'peepers', eyes. (In standard French, the word refers to a car's flashing indicators, thus giving in colloquial speech the idea of winking.)

clille *n.m.* Prostitute's client. (The most frequent expression is *éponger un clille*: to 'relieve' a customer.)

clinoche *n.f. (corr. clinique)*: **1** Maternity hospital. **2** Nursing home.

clique *n.f. (pej.)*: **1** Crowd, group of people. *Il ne sort plus qu'avec cette clique!* He never seems to keep any other company than that shower! **2** *Prendre ses cliques et ses claques*: To 'up and go', to pack up and quit.

cliquettes *n.f.pl.* 'Lug-holes', ears.

clito *n.m.* 'Clit', clitoris.

clochard *n.m.* Tramp. (The word according to popular etymology derives from the expression *déménager à la cloche de bois* implying that the individual moved out of his last digs at the dead of night without paying.)

cloche *n.f.* **1** 'Brainbox', head. *Ça sonne creux sous sa cloche*: He's not got much up top. **2** 'Twit', 'nincompoop', fool. (The word is more often than not uttered in a spirit of jocular friendliness. *Bougre de cloche, va!* You sillybilly!) **3** *Déménager à la cloche de bois*: To leave rented accommodation without paying. (The image here is of the lodging-house doorbell having been silenced whilst the door is opened for a hasty midnight exit.) **4** *Sonner les cloches à quelqu'un*: To give someone a ding-dong telling-off. **5** *Se taper la cloche*: To 'stuff one's face', to have a hearty meal.

cloche *adj.* Silly, stupid. *Ce qu'il est cloche!* He's as thick as two short planks! *C'est cloche, mais je ne sais pas ce qu'il faut faire*: I know it sounds silly, but I don't know what to do.

clocher *v.trans.* To 'catch', to hear. *Sans son machin dans l'oreille, il ne cloche que dalle*: Without that hearing-aid of his, he's as deaf as a post.

clocher *v.intrans.* **1** To 'stop in one's tracks', to hesitate. *Je l'ai vu clocher à la nouvelle*: He faltered when he heard the news. **2** *Il y a comme quelque chose qui cloche*: There's a hitch somewhere – Something's wrong. *Qu'est-ce qui cloche?* What's up? – What's wrong?

clochettes *n.f.pl. Avoir des clochettes au cul*: To have a dirty bum, to have not wiped one's behind properly.

clodo *n.m.* Tramp. (The word is an abbreviation of the less common *clodomir*.)

clope *n.m. & f.* 'Ciggy', fag. (The word has rather pejorative connotations in that it more frequently refers to cigarette ends or cigarettes made from recycled tobacco by tramps.)

clopin-clopant *adv. Aller clopin-clopant*: To hobble along. (This not altogether modern expression got a new lease of life in a song by Mireille with a refrain that went *'Et je m'en vais clopin-clopant'*.)

clopinettes *n.f.pl.* **1** 'Nix', 'nowt', nothing. *Bouffer des clopinettes*: To eat next to nothing, to go hungry. *Elle bouffait des clopinettes pour garder la ligne*: She'd starve herself to keep trim. *En fait de fric, il ne nous restait que des clopinettes*: All we had left was very loose change. **2** *Des clopinettes!* No dice! – No way! – Nothing doing!

cloporte *n.m.* Janitor, caretaker in a block of flats. (The appellation is a derogatory equivalent to *concierge*.)

cloque *n.f.* **1** 'Pongy', fart. *Lâcher une cloque*: To break wind. **2** *Etre en cloque*: To 'have a bun in the oven', to be pregnant. *Il l'a foutue en cloque*: He got her in the pudding club.

cloquer *v.trans.* **1** To 'belt', to hit, to land a blow. *Elle lui a cloqué une beigne*: She clocked him one. **2** To give. *Il cloqua deux thunes dans la gapette d'un mendigot*: He slipped some poor devil a few coppers. **3** To put out of sight, to conceal. *Quand il vit que ça tournait au vinaigre, il cloqua son flingue sous le paddock*: When he saw that things were going sour, he hid his shooter under the bed.

cloquer *v.intrans.* To 'let off', to 'fart', to break wind.

cloquer *v.trans.reflex.* **1** To snuggle down into, to settle comfortably in. *Il se cloqua d'autor dans le meilleur fauteuil*: He made a bee-line for the most comfortable armchair and nestled into it. **2** To 'take cover', to hide. **3** *Se cloquer un godet*: To 'knock back', to down a drink. **4** *Se cloquer un bécot*: To exchange a kiss.

close *adj.f. Maison close*: Brothel. (As with *maison de tolérance*, the term has no pejorative connotation.)

clôture *n.f.* *Faire la clôture* (of waiter in bar or restaurant): To do the tail-end of the night-shift. (In contrast *faire l'ouverture* is to be on the early shift when the establishment is opening for business.)

clou *n.m.* **1** *Etre maigre comme un clou*: To be as thin as a rake. **2** *Traverser dans les clous*: To use a pedestrian crossing. (Although 'zebra crossings' are common in France now, a double row of large metal studs used to indicate such protected walkways). **3** *Clou de cercueil (joc.)*: Small cigarillo. **4** *Clous de girofle*: Set of decayed teeth. **5** *Bouffer des clous*: To have nothing to eat, to go hungry. **6** *Ne pas valoir un clou*: To be worth 'fuck-all', to be worthless. **7** *Des clous!* Not on your nelly! – Not bloody

likely! – Certainly not! **8** *Mettre au clou*: To 'hock', to pawn. **9** *Coller quelqu'un au clou*: To sling someone into jail. **10** *Un vieux clou*: An 'old jalopy', a decrepit motor-car.

clouer *v.trans. Clouer le bec à quelqu'un*: To silence someone in no uncertain manner. *Ça lui a drôlement cloué le bec*: She certainly clammed up after that.

clown *n.m. Faire le clown*: To 'arse about', to fool around, to behave in a silly manner. *Cesse de faire le clown!* Stop messing about!

coaltar *n.m.* **1** *Etre dans le coaltar (fig.)*: To be in a 'sticky mess', to find oneself in an awkward situation. **2** 'Plonk', cheap red wine.

cocard *n.m.* 'Shiner', black eye (also: *œil au beurre noir*).

cocarde *n.f.* **1** *Faire quelque chose pour la cocarde*: To do something purely for show. **2** *Avoir sa cocarde*: To have had 'one over the eight', to be 'tipsy', to be slightly drunk.

cocarder *v.trans.reflex.* To 'get tipsy', to have a few drinks too many.

cocardier *adj.* 'Chauvinistic', a trifle over-patriotic.

cocasse *adj.* Droll, amusing (in a silly sort of way). *C'est plutôt cocasse, moi aussi j'ai oublié mes clefs*: You won't believe this, but I've forgotten my keys too!

coccinelle *n.f.* 'Beetle', the Volkswagen motor car that sold for over thirty years without changing its shape (also: *vévé*).

coche *n.m.* **1** *Etre la mouche du coche*: To be a 'meddling busybody', to be an interfering person. **2** *Manquer* (also: *louper*) *le coche (fig.)*: To 'miss the boat', to miss one's chance.

cochon *n.m.* **1** 'Swine', 'sod', despicable character. **2** *Etre plein comme un cochon*: To have 'had a skinful', to be 'pissed', to be drunk. **3** *Etre copains comme cochons*: To be 'as thick as thieves', to be the best of pals. **4** *Etre adroit comme un cochon avec sa queue (iron.)*: To be 'ham-fisted', to be 'all thumbs', to be clumsy. **5** *Jouer un tour de cochon*: To play a dirty trick. **6** *Travail de cochon*: Botched work. **7** *Nous n'avons pas gardé les cochons ensemble! (iron.)*: There's no call to be so familiar with me! **8** *Cochon de payant*: This standard expression is uttered whenever the speaker wishes to emphasize that he is 'one of them that don't get it for nothing'. The nearest English utterance is 'I fought for this country, I pay my rates!'

cochon *adj.* **1** Obscene and vulgar. *Histoires cochons*: Smutty stories. *Aller au ciné-cochon*: To see blue movies. **2** *Quel cochon de. . .!* What bloody awful. . .! *Quel cochon de métier!* What a rotten job to be in! *Quel cochon de temps!* What dreadful weather we're having!

cochonailles *n.f.pl.* Cold cooked meats. (The word refers to what the French usually call *charcuteries*, but has a rather unglamorous and down-market connotation.)

cochonceté *n.f.* 1 'Dirty trick', nasty prank. 2 *(pl.)*: 'Dirty jokes', smutty yarns.

cochonner *v.trans.* To 'mess up', to make a mess of, to bungle.

cochonnerie *n.f.* 1 Filth, dirt. 2 'Filth', 'smut'. *Il ne pense qu'à des cochonneries*: What a dirty mind he's got! 3 'Bad hitch', nasty setback. *Il lui est arrivé une de ces cochonneries*: You'll never believe what ghastly thing happened to her. 4 *(pl.)*: 'Crap', shoddy goods.

coco *n.m.* 1 (Child's language): 'Cackleberry', egg. 2 'Bean', 'bonce', head. *Avoir le coco fêlé*: To be 'slightly cracked', to be a little mad. 3 Gullet, throat. *Dévisser le coco à quelqu'un*: To throttle, to strangle someone. 4 'Tum-tum', belly. *Se remplir le coco*: To 'stuff one's face', to eat heartily. 5 *Du coco en poudre*: Sherbet, fruit-flavoured and slightly effervescent powder. 6 'Juice', petrol. *Fais-moi le plein de coco!* Fill her up, please! 7 *Un drôle de coco*: A 'queer cove', a strange character. 8 *(pl.)*: 'Clodhoppers', shoes. 9 'Red', 'commie', communist. *Il voit des cocos partout*: He sees Reds under the bed. 10 *Des boniments à la noix de coco*: 'Clap-trap', arguments or sales-patter that hold no credence. 11 *Mon coco*: My lovey-dovey – My pet – My darling.

coco *n.f.* 'Coke', 'snow', cocaine.

cocoter *v.intrans.* To 'pong', to stink, to smell foul.

cocotier *n.m.* 1 *N'être pas loin de son cocotier* (also: *être tout juste descendu de son cocotier*): To be 'rather green', to be a trifle naïve about the ways of the (modern) world. 2 *Décrocher le cocotier*: To 'win the big one', to hit the jackpot. 3 *Grimper au cocotier*: To 'fly off the handle', to get into a temper.

cocotte *n.f.* 1 'Floozy', kept woman. 2 'Clap', gonorrhoea. 3 *Faire des cocottes en papier*: To 'twiddle one's thumbs', to while away the hours (literally to indulge in 'office origami'). 4 *Ma cocotte*: My lovey-dovey – My pet – My darling.

cocotte-minute *n.f.* 1 Pressure cooker. 2 *(pej.)*: 'Prozzy', prostitute.

cocu *n.m.* Cuckold. (With the exception of *avoir une gueule de cocu*, this state of marital misfortune is often associated with luck in other areas of life as in *avoir une veine de cocu*: to have the luck of the devil. This could be attributed to the wife's lover being able to influence the husband's promotion prospects within a firm or institution.)

cocufier *v.trans.* To cuckold, to be unfaithful to one's husband.

code *n.m.* 1 *Se mettre en code*: To dip one's headlights. 2 *Avoir les yeux en phares-codes (joc.)*: To have a bad squint. 3 *Moi, je connais le Code!* I know my rights!

cœur *n.m.* 1 *Avoir du cœur au ventre*: To have 'plenty of guts', to be very brave. 2 *Avoir un cœur d'artichaut*: To be a fickle lover, to flit from love to love. (The expression has a certain amount of built-in humour in French where the vegetable referred to is a globe artichoke, and the lover shares his heart in a 'une feuille pour chaque personne' manner.)

coffiot *n.m.* 'Peter', safe, strongbox.

coffioteur *n.m.* Safe-cracker, burglar specializing in breaking into safes.

coffre *n.m.* Chest. *Avoir bon coffre*: To be sound in wind and limb. *Avoir du coffre*: To have something of a he-man physique. (This expression can also mean to be endowed with a deep and powerful voice, particularly where male opera singers are concerned.) *S'en aller du coffre*: To be dying of tuberculosis.

coffrer *v.trans.* 1 To 'collar', to 'pull in', to arrest. 2 To 'put away', to clap in jail. *Se faire coffrer*: To get put in clink.

cogiter *v.intrans. (iron.)*: To 'have a little think', to make a pretence of giving matters what seems like undue consideration.

cogne *n.m. (pej.)*: 'Cop', 'copper', policeman. *Les cognes*: 'The filth'.

cognée *n.f. Jeter le manche après la cognée*: To 'throw in the towel', to give up in disgust (after an initial failure).

cogner *v.trans.* 1 To 'bash', to 'thump', to hit. *Il les a cognés à bras raccourcis*: He beat the living daylights out of them. 2 To stamp official documents. *Il a fait cogner ses fafs*: He got his I.D. papers cleared by the officials. 3 *Cogner les brèmes*: To have a game of cards. 4 *Il m'a cogné de dix raides*: He borrowed ten quid off me. (The implication here is of a very reluctant loan.)

cogner *v.intrans. Ça cogne*: It stinks – It smells foul. *Qu'est-ce que ça cogne!* What a pong!

cogner *v.trans.reflex.* To have 'a punch-up', to come to blows.

cogner *v.pronom.* 1 *Se cogner quelque chose*: **a** To have to do something unpleasant. *Je me suis cogné cinq heures de train*: I've been through five gruelling hours in the train. **b** To treat oneself to something. *On s'est cogné le menu à cinquante francs*: We spoiled ourselves and went for the expensive meal. **c** To help oneself to something. *Je me suis cogné ce qui restait*: I took what was left. 2 *Se cogner de quelque chose*: 'Not to care a rap', to be unconcerned about something. *Je m'en cogne de ce qu'il peut penser!* I don't give a fig about what he thinks!

cognerie *n.f.* *La cognerie:* The 'cop-shop', the police station. (As with *cogne*, the word has derogatory connotations implying that suspects are roughed-up during interrogation.)

cogneur *n.m.* **1** (Boxing): Puncher, solid fighter (the kind of 'pro' who goes determinedly for his opponent regardless of consequences). **2** 'Heavy', gangland enforcer.

cognon *n.m.* *Un cognon:* A 'bout of the fisticuffs', a 'punch-up', a fight.

cognoter *v.intrans.* To 'pong', to stink, to smell foul. *Ça cognote un chouïa!* What a niff! (The expression often refers to body odour in a confined space; an alternative is *ça sent le fauve.*)

coiffé *adj.* **1** *Etre né coiffé:* To be a lucky devil, to have been born lucky. **2** *Etre coiffé de:* To 'have a crush on someone', to be infatuated. *Il est coiffé de ma frangine:* He's spoony over my sister.

coiffer *v.trans.* **1** To 'outstrip', to outclass someone. *Se faire coiffer au poteau (fig.):* To get 'pipped at the post', to be beaten in the race (for a job, promotion, etc.). **2** To head, to be the boss of. *Il coiffe plusieurs services:* He's got a number of departments under him. **3** To 'collar', to arrest. **4** *Coiffer Sainte-Catherine:* To be twenty-five years old and still a spinster. (With the advent of women's lib, this expression has all but disappeared.)

coiffeur *n.m.* *Le grand coiffeur (joc.):* The public executioner (in charge of the guillotine).

coin *n.m.* **1** *Le petit coin:* The 'smallest room', the 'loo', the W.C. **2** *En boucher un coin à quelqu'un:* To leave someone speechless. *Ça t'en bouche un coin, hein?!* There's no answer to that, is there?! **3** *Connaître quelque chose dans les coins:* To 'know the ropes', to know one's way around a problem or topic. **4** *Blague dans le coin!* No kidding! – Honestly! – It's the absolute truth!

coincé *adj.* 'Snookered', 'bunkered', cornered. *Il est drôlement coincé (fig.):* He's really in a Catch 22 situation.

coincer *v.trans.* **1** To 'collar', to 'pull in', to arrest. *Il s'est fait coincer bêtement:* It was so stupid the way he got nicked. **2** *Coincer sa bulle:* **a** To do bugger-all at work, to be a lazy git. **b** To snooze, to sleep.

coincer *v.intrans.* To 'pong', to stink, to smell foul. *Qu'est-ce que ça coince ici!* Coo, what a whiff!

coincetot *n.m.* **1** 'Cubby-hole', small locker or cupboard. *Il a fourré ça dans un coincetot:* He tidied it away in some corner of the room.

2 Quarter, district, area. *Il n'est pas du coincetot:* He's not from these parts.

coinche *n.f.* 'Cushy job', employment where little effort needs to be exerted. *Se dégauchir une bonne coinche:* To get oneself an easy number.

coing *n.m.* **1** *Etre beurré comme un coing:* To be 'pissed', 'sozzled', to be blind drunk. **2** *De la gelée de coing:* **a** 'Physical aggro', bodily assault. **b** 'Aggro', aggravation. *Etre dans de la gelée de coing:* To be 'in the shit', to be deep in trouble.

col *n.m.* **1** *Col bleu:* **a** 'Jolly Jack tar', sailor. **b** Blue-collar worker, shop-floor operative. **2** *Col blanc:* White-collar worker, member of the office staff. **3** *S'envoyer quelque chose derrière le col (joc.):* To toss back a drink, to down a glass of alcoholic beverage. **4** *Faux col:* 'Head', froth on beer. *Donne-nous un demi sans faux col!* Give us a real half pint of beer! (and not all froth!). **5** *Un col à manger de la tarte (joc.):* An old-fashioned stiff collar. **6** *Se hausser (also: se pousser) du col:* To strut about, to swank, to show off.

colbaque *n.m.* (also: *colbac*): 'Collar', scruff of the neck. *Prendre quelqu'un au colbaque:* To 'feel someone's collar', to arrest someone.

colbas *n.f.* 'Digs', 'bed-sit', modest accommodation.

colibard *n.m.* (corr. *colis*): Food parcel. (This word had its greatest vogue during World War II when prisoners relied on such parcels from home in order to survive. It later entered the register of the common-law prisoner.)

colibri *n.m.* **1** 'Bird-brain', 'nincompoop', fool. **2** Unreliable character.

colifichets *n.m.pl.* Baubles and beads, cheap jewellery.

colique *n.f.* **1** (of person): 'Pain in the arse', nuisance. *Quelle colique, ce mec-là!* He's a right pain! **2** *Avoir des coliques bâtonneuses:* To 'have the big stick', to have an erection.

colis *n.m.* **1** 'Duffer', 'nincompoop', idict. **2** *Un gentil petit colis:* A 'bit-of-alright', a nice-looking girl. (This utterance, typical of the male chauvinist, can sometimes have more sinister connotations when relating to prostitution.)

collabo *n.m.* 'Collaborator', one who actively collaborated with the German occupation forces during World War II.

collage *n.m.* *Le collage:* 'Life under the brush', cohabitation. *Etre en collage:* To 'live in sin' (also: *vivre à la colle*).

collant *n.m.* **1** Tights, panty-hose. **2** *Collant publicitaire:* Self-adhesive publicity sticker.

collant *adj.* Tenaciously boring. *Qu'est-ce qu'il est collant!* He's the original limpet-bore!

collante *n.f.* **1** *(sch.)*: Examination advice notice, note sent to students advising them of time and place of exam. **2** Summons issued by the police to witnesses telling them to come forward to give evidence.

colle *n.f.* **1** 'Stodge', stodgy food. **2** 'Stumper', 'poser', brain-teaser. *Philippe, il faut toujours qu'il pose des colles!* He always likes to quiz you with the unanswerable, does Philip! **3** *(sch.)*: Test, written examination. *Passer une colle*: To sit a paper. **4** *(sch.)*: Detention. *Prendre une colle*: To cop detention. **5** *Quelle colle!* **a** (of person): What a bore! **b** (of situation, event): What a drag! **6** *Ménage à la colle*: 'Open marriage', common-law marriage. **7** *Faites chauffer la colle!* (Stock humorous phrase said when someone breaks crockery): Go on, break up the happy home! **8** *Chier dans la colle*: To 'lay it on a bit thick', to exaggerate. **9** *C'est de la colle!* It's bunkum! – Poppycock! **10** *Combat à la colle* (Boxing): 'Duff contest', phoney fight.

collé *adj.* **1** 'Stumped', 'floored', baffled. **2** *(sch.)*: 'Ploughed', failed at an exam. **3** *(sch.)*: 'Kept-in', punished with detention.

collège *n.m.* *(joc.)* *Le collège*: 'The nick', the prison. *Un ami de collège*: A fellow ex-con, an old cellmate. *Ils ont été au collège ensemble*: They did time together.

collègue *n.m.* *Alors, collègue, ça va?! (joc.)*: Well, mate, how are things?!

coller *v.trans.* **1** To 'stump', to baffle someone as to an answer. **2** *Se faire coller (sch.)*: To get 'ploughed', to fail an exam. **3** *Coller une baffe* (also: *un coup, une gifle) à quelqu'un*: To 'clout', to hit someone. **4** To pass on (an infection or a disease). *Tu m'as collé ta grippe!* I've caught your flu! **5** *Coller quelqu'un au bloc*: To 'clap someone in the cooler', to put someone into the punishment cell.

coller *v.intrans.* **1** *Ça colle!* It's on! – It's O.K. by me! – I agree! *Non, mon vieux, ça ne colle pas!* I'm afraid it's not on, old boy. **2** *Il m'a collé au train*: He tailed me – He followed me everywhere.

coller *v.trans.reflex.* **1** To 'shack up', to set up home without being married. **2** *Se coller à la tâche*: To 'pitch in', to get down to a task without further ado. *Je veux des comptes à jour dès ce soir, collez-vous-y!* Get to it, I want those books up to date!

coller *v.pronom.* *Se coller quelque chose*: **a** To treat oneself to something. **b** To land oneself with something unpleasant, to inflict a chore upon oneself. *Il s'est collé le plus fort du boulot*: It was he who chose to do most of the work.

colletar *n.m.* **1** *Etre dans le colletar (fig.)*: To be in a 'sticky mess', to find oneself in an awkward situation. **2** 'Plonk', cheap red wine.

colleter *v.trans.reflex.* To 'scrap', to fight.

colletin *n.m.* (also: *coltin*): 'Graft', hard work. *Aller au colletin*: To go and earn one's crust.

collier *n.m.* **1** 'Tag', label. **2** *Donner un coup de collier*: To 'put one's back into it', to 'give one's all' to something, to work flat out for a short period. **3** *Reprendre le collier*: To 'get back into harness', to resume work. *A la rentrée il va falloir reprendre le collier*: When term starts, it'll be back to the old 9 to 5 routine. **4** *Etre franc du collier*: To be straight, unambiguous in one's attitudes and approach. **5** *Ne pas y aller franco du collier*: To dodge the issue and avoid telling the truth.

collignon *n.m.* 'Cabbie', cab driver.

collimater *v.trans.* To keep a watchful eye on someone or something (also: *garder dans le collimateur*).

collimateur *n.m.* *Garder quelqu'un dans le collimateur*: To 'keep close tabs on someone', to keep someone under intense scrutiny.

colmater *v.intrans.* **1** To 'stump' someone, to leave someone speechless. **2** (Underworld slang): To silence a witness with strong-arm methods.

colmater *v.trans.reflex.* *Se colmater la brèche*: To 'stuff one's face', to eat voraciously.

colo *n.f.* *(abbr. colonie de vacances)*: Children's holiday camp. (*Aller en colo* is part of the schoolboy's routine; these camps are often state-subsidized and run by school staff.)

colombienne *n.f.* (Drugs): Strong hash, top-grade marijuana.

colombin *n.m.* **1** 'Turd', excrement. *Poser un colombin*: To have a crap (also: *planter un étron*). **2** *Les colombins*: 'The shit-house', 'the karzey', the W.C. *Etre de colombins (mil.)*: To be on latrine duty. **3** *Avoir les colombins (fig.)*: To 'have the shits', to be in a blue funk, to be frightened. **4** *Des colombins!* Not on your nelly! – Not bloody likely! – Certainly not!

colon *n.m.* **1** *(mil.)*: Colonel. **2** *Eh bien, mon colon!* *(joc.)*: Well, old cock! – Now then, old fruit! (The utterance is often heard when astonishment is expressed. *En bien, mon colon, tu t'es bien débrouillé!* Well, you certainly did alright for yourself!)

colonne *n.f.* **1** 'Prick', 'cock', penis. (The word is only encountered in the expression *se taper* or *se polir la colonne*: to 'have a wank', to masturbate.) **2** *Il croit qu'il a chié la colonne Vendôme! (iron.)*: He really thinks he's the bee's knees! – He has no mean opinion of himself!

coloquinte *n.f.* 'Bean', 'brainbox', head. *Ça commence à me taper sur la coloquinte*: It's getting on my wick – I'm getting fed up with this. *Ça lui a tapé sur la coloquinte*: He's gone bonkers – He's gone mad.

coltin *n.m.* (also: *colletin*): 'Graft', hard work.

coltiner *v.trans.* **1** To 'lug about', to haul, to carry. *Pas étonnant qu'il soit fatigué avec toute* *cette graisse qu'il coltine!* It's no wonder he always looks shagged, look at the weight of him! 2 *Coltiner des ragots*: To be a scandal-monger.

coltiner *v.trans.reflex.* To 'scrap', to come to blows, to fight.

coma *n.m. Etre dans le coma (joc.)*: To be 'out cold', to be dead drunk.

comac *adj.* (also: *comaque*): 'Whopping', enormous. *Il a un gabarit comac!* He's built like a barn door!

combien *n.m.inv.* 1 *On est le combien?* (also: *le combien sommes-nous?*): What day of the month are we? 2 *Il passe tous les combien l'autobus?* How often is there a bus here?

combinaise *n.f. (abbr. combinaison)*: 1 Scheme, ploy. 2 'Shady deal', underhand commercial transaction.

combinard *n.m.* 'Smart operator', schemer.

combinard *adj.* Scheming, wily, sharp.

combine *n.f.* Ploy, wily scheme. *Il a une combine pour avoir des tickets gratuits*: He knows how to get free tickets.

comédie *n.f.* 1 *Quelle comédie! (iron)*: What a picnic! – What a farce! – What a pretence! 2 *Faire toute une comédie*: To 'make a song-and-dance about something', to over-act in order to get attention. 3 *Envoyer quelqu'un à la comédie*: To 'lay someone off', to suspend someone from work.

cominches *n.f.pl.* (also: *comminches; corr. commissions*). *Les cominches*: The shopping. *Aller aux cominches*: To go to the shops.

comm' *n.f. (abbr. commission)*: 'Kickback', 'cut', financial rake-off. *Il ne travaille qu'à la comm'*: If you want results, you'll have to give him a piece of the action (also: *commisse*).

commande *n.f.* 1 (Underworld slang): 'Job', break-in. 2 'Goldmine scheme', potentially money-spinning ploy. 3 *Avoir une commande* (Underworld slang): To benefit from police immunity (the kind of illegal 'closed-eyes' policy afforded to certain criminals for a ready supply of information). 4 *Une drôle de commande*: A weird set-up, rather unorthodox goings-on. *Connaître la commande*: To be 'in the know', to know the set-up. 5 *Louper la commande*: To 'miss the boat', to miss an opportunity.

comme *adv. & conj.* 1 *C'est tout comme*: It's much of a muchness – It comes to the same thing (also: *c'est du pareil au comme*). 2 *Etre comme-il-faut*: To be a respectable character. *Ce sont des gens tout à fait comme-il-faut*: There's nothing untoward about them at all. 2 *C'est comme ça!* That's the way it is! (and nothing can be done about it!). 4 *Il est un peu comme ça*: He's a bit of a pouf – He's got homosexual leanings. 5 *Comme ci, comme ça*: 'Fair-to-middling', so-so. *Mes vieux se portent comme ci, comme ça*: The old folk are as well as can be expected.

comment *adv. & interj.* 1 *Vouloir savoir le pourquoi du comment*: To want to know all the facts. 2 *Et comment!* And how! – Not half! *Et comment que je l'ai remis à sa place!* I took him down a peg or two, no messing! 3 *Mais comment donc!* By all means! – Certainly!

commérages *n.m.pl.* 'Tittle-tattle', gossip.

commisse *n.f. (abbr. commission)*: 'Kickback', 'cut', financial rake-off (also: *comm'*).

commission *n.f.* 1 *Petite commission*: 'Jimmy Riddle', 'wee', urination. 2 *Grande commission*: 'Biggies', 'number two's', excrement.

commode *n.f.* 1 Honky-tonk piano. 2 *Faire la commode*: To be in the removal business, to be a furniture remover by trade. 3 *Mon cul sur la commode*: Nonsensical expression suggesting the utter ridiculousness of a situation.

commode *adj.* *Ne pas être commode*: To be an 'awkward so-and-so', to be more than a trifle pig-headed. *Ma femme n'est pas commode à vivre!* Living with my wife is no bed of roses!

communale *n.f.* *La communale (abbr. l'école communale)*: Primary school. *On est allé à la communale ensemble*: We used to sit on the same bench at school when we was nippers.

communard *n.m.* 1 'Red', 'commie', communist (also: *coco*). 2 Drink made of black-currant and red wine.

compagnie *n.f.* 1 *Salut la compagnie!* Hello there! (The expression is as lowbrow as the English 'Evenin'' all!') 2 *Tout ça, c'est crapule et compagnie!* They're crooks, the lot of them!

compale *n.f. (corr. composition)*: School paper, written school test (also: *compo*).

comparse *n.m.* Accomplice.

compas *n.m.* 1 *Avoir le compas dans l'œil*: To have the knack of being spot-on in estimating measurements. 2 *Allonger le compas*: To 'step out', to lengthen one's stride. 3 *(pl.)*: 'Pins', 'gambs', legs. *Activer des compas*: To 'skedaddle', to 'make tracks', to run away.

compère *n.m.* 1 Street hawker's associate whose enthusiastic buying sets the ball rolling. 2 (also: *compère-loriot*): Stye, inflammation of a sebaceous gland of the eyelid.

compisser *v.trans.* To 'pee all over something', to urinate on.

complet *n.m.* *Un complet*: 'Club-sandwich', jumbo-size sandwich (filled with a generous assortment of goodies).

complet *adj.* *Ça c'est complet! (iron.)*: Well, that's the last straw! – That's the limit! (Whatever can we expect next?!)

compliment *n.m. Je lui ai retourné le compliment (iron.)*: I gave as good as I got – It was a case of tit-for-tat.

compo *n.f. (abbr. composition)*: School paper, written school test (also: *compale*).

composter *v.trans.* To gun down, to shoot down.

composteur *n.m.* 'Rod', 'shooter', handgun.

compote *n.f.* **1** *Mettre en compote*: To 'beat to a pulp', to give someone a thrashing. **2** *Avoir les pieds en compote*: To have 'Friday-night postman's feet', to be extremely footsore.

compotier *n.m.* **1** 'Brainbox', head. *N'avoir rien dans le compotier*: To have nothing up top (also: *saladier*). **2** *Agiter les pieds dans le compotier*: To 'put one's foot in it and stir', to commit a double gaffe.

comprendre *v.intrans. Un peu que je comprends!* (also: *ça oui, je comprends!*): Rather! – And how! I should jolly well think so! (The expression is loaded with a certain amount of irony.)

comprendre *v.trans.reflex. Je me comprends! (joc.)*: I know what I mean when I say this (even if you don't).

comprenette *n.f.* 'Nous', I.Q., intelligence. *Ne pas avoir la comprenette facile*: To be 'slow on the uptake', to be a little dim.

compression *n.f. Manquer de compression*: To lack 'oomph', to lack go, to have little energy to spare.

compte *n.m.* **1** *Avoir son compte*: **a** To 'have had enough', to be able to take no more punishment. **b** To 'have had what was coming to one', to have got one's just deserts. **2** *Etre laissée pour compte* (of woman): To have been 'left on the shelf', to be still an old maid. **3** *Faire des comptes d'apothicaire*: To be forever totting up trifling amounts of money. **4** *Rendre des comptes*: To 'throw up', to 'puke', to vomit.

comptée *n.f.* Prostitute's earnings.

compte-gouttes *n.m. Les lâcher au compte-gouttes*: To have a penny-pinching approach to money (also: *les lâcher avec un élastique*).

compteur *n.m.* **1** *Mettre le compteur à zéro*: To make a fresh start, to start all over again. **2** *Relever le compteur* (of pimp): To collect a prostitute's earnings.

comptoir *n.m. Durillon de comptoir (joc.)*: 'Bar-belly', paunch. (As the expression implies, through constantly propping up a bar, a habitual boozer might have developed a callous area on his belly.)

comtois *n.m. Battre comtois*: **a** To 'play dumb', to feign ignorance. **b** To state untruths in order to get to the truth. (With this meaning, the expression is sometimes uttered in relation to police enquiries.)

con *n.m.* **1** 'Cunt', 'pussy', vagina. **2** 'Cunt', 'twit', imbecile. *Espèce de con!* You bloody idiot! *Jouer au con*: **a** To 'arse about', to act the fool. **b** To 'act dumb', to feign stupidity. **3** *Quelque chose à la con*: Something utterly stupid. *Il m'a raconté des histoires à la con*: He told me a load of cock-and-bull stories.

con *adj.* 'Thick', 'dumb', stupid. (The fem. *conne* exists but is less frequently used.) *Il est con comme la lune*: He's as thick as two short planks. *Ça c'est vraiment con*: This is really too silly for words. *C'est pas con ça!* That's a bloody good idea!

conard *n.m.* (also: *connard*): 'Burk', 'pillock', idiot.

conasse *n.f. (pej.)*: **1** 'Fanny', 'pussy', vagina. **2** 'Bit-of-skirt', woman. (This sexist appellation is very often used in the plural by the male chauvinist brigade, in expressions such as *il n'y a que les conasses pour aimer ça*: Trust women to like that sort of thing.)

concepiotte *n.f. (corr. concierge)*: Janitor, caretaker of block of flats or office building (also: *concepige*).

concert *n.m. Avoir droit au concert*: To be subjected to vociferous recriminations.

concerto *n.m. Jouer un concerto à quelqu'un*: **a** To 'make a scene', to subject someone to verbal recriminations. **b** To have intercourse with someone. (With this second meaning, the expression has a certain jocularity.)

concocter *v.trans.* To 'cook up', to concoct.

condé *n.m.* **1** Police protection (blind eye to certain illegal activities) offered to certain members of the criminal fraternity in exchange for a constant stream of information on serious crimes. **2** 'Easy fiddle', simple yet profitable con-trick. *Il s'est trouvé un condé fumant*: He's stumbled onto a gem of a fiddle. **3** Plain-clothes policeman.

condisse *n.f.* Proviso, condition. *Je viens à condisse qu'il y ait des nanas*: If there's plenty of birds, I'll come to the party.

conduite *n.f.* **1** *Faire un brin de conduite à quelqu'un*: To walk someone part of the way. **2** *Une conduite à droite/une conduite à gauche*: A right-hand/left-hand drive car. **3** *S'acheter une conduite*: To settle down to a more staid style of life (after a turbulent past).

confection *n.f.* **1** *La confection*: The 'rag-trade'. *Etre dans la confection*: To be in the garment business. **2** *S'habiller en confection*: To wear 'off-the-peg' clothes. (The expressions *s'habiller au 'décrochez-moi-ça'* and *s'habiller au carreau du Temple* are more pejorative and imply that the garments bought are of very poor quality.)

confiance *n.f. Poser la 'question de confiance' (joc.)*: To ask one's female companion whether it will be yes or no to sex. (The humour derives from the political connotation of the expression.)

confidence *n.f. Confidence pour confidence*: One confidence deserves another. *Confidence pour confidence, moi non plus, je n'peux pas le piffer!* Well, as a matter of fact, I can't stand him either!

confiote *n.f. (corr. confiture)*: Jam.

confiture *n.f.* 1 *C'est de la confiture pour les chiens*: It's casting pearls before swine – It's too good for them! 2 *Donner dans la confiture*: To go in for some good old 'soft-soaping', to indulge in base flattery.

confrérie *n.f. La grande confrérie (joc.)*: **a** The big brotherhood of poufs, the homosexual fraternity. **b** The ever-growing army of cuckold husbands.

congai *n.f.* 'Kept woman', mistress. (The expression is said to have originated in Indo-China where the French colonizers found it convenient to cohabit with willing native girls and forget their home-ties.)

conifié *adj.* Driven to a state of stupidity.

conjugo *n.m. Le conjugo*: Marital life, wedlock. *Le conjugo, il en a ralbol*: The ball-and-chain, he's just about had his fill of it.

connaissance *n.f.* Boyfriend, girlfriend. *Alors, tu me présentes ta connaissance?* How's about introducing me to your friend?

connaître *v.trans.* 1 *S'y connaître*: To be a 'dab hand at something', to know something inside-out. *Côté bagnoles, il s'y connaît un brin*: There's not much he doesn't know about cars. 2 *Ne plus se connaître*: To be beside oneself with anger. 3 *Je ne connais que ça!* I'm no stranger to that! – I know that only too well!

connard *n.m.* 'Burk', 'pillock', idiot.

connasse *n.f. (pej.)*: 1 'Fanny', 'pussy', vagina. 2 'Bit-of-skirt', woman. (This sexist appellation is very often used in the plural by male chauvinists to denigrate women in general.)

conneau *n.m.* 'Silly arse', 'twit', imbecile (also: *connard*).

connement *adv.* 1 Stupidly. *Et connement je lui ai prêté du fric*: And like a bloody fool I lent him some money (also: *comme un con*). 2 *Tout connement*: Purely and simply. *C'est tout connement la vérité*: It's the plain and simple truth.

connerie *n.f.* 'Cock-up', stupid action. *Il a fait des conneries récemment*: As of late he's been making a balls of things. *Dire des conneries*: To 'spout a load of nonsense', to talk rubbish. *Pas de conneries!* Stop messing about! – Quit the larking!

connobrer *v.trans.* To 'know the ins-and-outs', to be familiar with something.

conozoff *n.m. (joc.)*: 'Burk', 'nincompoop', idiot.

Conseil *n.m. (abbr. Conseil de révision)*. *Passer le Conseil*: To pass the medical fitness test for the Army. (Although no-one in France enjoys going to do National Service, failing the *Conseil de révision* is very much a slur on one's manhood. Outside the premises where this examination is conducted, those who are passed fit are sold colourful badges bearing the words: '*Bon pour les filles et pour l'Armée*'.)

conséquent *adj.* 'Big', important, of consequence. *C'est un mec conséquent*: He's a big shot.

consigne *n.f.* 1 *Ne connaître que la consigne*: To be a stickler for discipline. 2 *Avaler la consigne*: To disregard orders, to disobey instructions.

consommation *n.f. Pousser à la consommation (joc.)*: To be an over-generous host with food and drink. (Normally, the expression would merely refer to a commission-conscious salesman doing the hard sell.)

consomme *n.f. (abbr. consommation)*: Drink in bar or bistrot. *Jouer les consommes* (also: *faire les consommes*): To have a game of cards or dice to decide who pays the round.

consommé *n.m. Consommé de cartilages (joc.)*: **a** Vice-like grip, crushing handshake. **b** 'Knuckle-sandwich', punch in the face.

constat *n.m. Constat à l'amiable*: 'No-aggro' accident claim form where both parties jot down and sign the irrefutable facts of a minor car scrape. Such small-claims paperwork was the result of the French Ministry of Transport '*Ne nous fâchons pas*' campaign.

constipé *adj.* 1 Sulky, sullen. 2 *Etre constipé du larfeuil (joc.)*: To have 'hedgehogs in one's wallet', to be extremely mean.

contact *n.m.* 1 'Go-between', useful intermediary. *Il a des contacts au Ministère*: He's got friends in high places. 2 *Mettre/couper le contact*: To switch the engine of a car on/off. *Clef de contact*: Ignition key.

contacter *v.trans.* To 'get in touch with'. *Dites-lui de me contacter au bureau*: Tell him to give me a ring at the office.

content *n.m. Avoir son petit content (joc.)*: To 'get one's oats', to enjoy sexual intercourse when one needs it.

continuation *n.f. Bonne continuation!* All the best! (This lowbrow parting repartee is roughly equivalent to 'Carry on chaps!')

contractuel *n.m.* Traffic warden.

contre *n.m. Il y a du pour et du contre*: It's got its pros and cons – There's quite a lot to be said for and against it.

contre *adv.* *Etre contre*: To be against, to be opposed to something. *Ce truc-là, moi je suis tout à fait contre!* I'm dead against this! (The actor-playwright Sacha Guitry is famous for a pun on this word; when asked by a colleague: *'Les femmes, vous êtes pour ou contre?'* he wittily answered: *'Tout contre!'*)

contrecarre *n.m. & f.* 1 Obstacle, hindrance. *Faire du contrecarre à quelqu'un*: To make someone's life difficult, to be a nuisance to someone. 2 Rivalry. *Depuis qu'il est adjoint, il y a de la contrecarre entre eux*: Promotion has meant quite a bit of backbiting between them.

contredanse *n.f.* *(corr. contravention)*: 'Ticket', traffic fine. *Flanquer une contredanse*: To book someone for a motoring offence.

contreficher *v.pronom.* To 'not give a damn', to be totally indifferent to something.

contremarque *n.f.* *Avoir une contremarque pour Bagneux*: To be 'a goner', to be doomed. (In non-colloquial French *contremarque* is a theatre pass-out ticket; *Bagneux* is one of the largest cemeteries serving Paris, hence the jocular paraphrase about someone unlikely to survive.)

contrepéter *v.intrans.* To commit a spoonerism. (There is no denying that *péter* and *contrepéter* are humorously linked in French.)

contrepèterie *n.f.* Spoonerism. (The French have a great fondness for *contrepèteries* and in 1967 Jean-Jacques Pauvert published *L'ALBUM DE LA COMTESSE*, subtitled *RECUEIL DE CONTREPETS CURIEUX ET DÉLECTABLES*.)

contrer *v.trans.* 1 To 'fend off', to thwart, to parry. *Te fais pas de bile, il sait contrer*: Don't worry about him, he can look after himself! 2 To 'beat off', to repel successfully. *Ils contrèrent les Ritals au milieu du terrain*: They got the better of the Ities in mid-field.

contribs *n.f.pl.* *(abbr. Service de Contributions)*. *Les contribs*: The tax office, the Inland Revenue Department.

convalo *n.f.* Convalescence. *Aller en convalo*: To go off to recuperate.

conversation *n.f.* *Ne pas être à la conversation*: To be 'miles away', to be daydreaming.

converse *n.f.* Conversation. *C'est à la converse qu'il lève toutes ses nanas*: It's his gift of the gab that gets him all the birds.

convoque *n.f.* *(abbr. convocation)*: 1 Summons to appear in court or to present oneself at a police station. 2 *(sch.)*: Exam notification.

coordonnées *n.f.pl.* Address and telephone number of person one wishes to reach. *Donnez-moi vos coordonnées* is a very popular expression in business circles.

cop' *n.m.* *(abbr. copain)*: 'Buddy', 'crony', friend.

copaille *n.f.* *(pej.)*: 1 'Nancy-boy', effeminate homosexual. 2 Despicable character, the kind likely to 'grass on friends'. (The word is said to have originally been masculine, but, as is the case with words having a high pejorative connotation, the feminine is more insulting.)

copain *n.m.* 'Buddy', 'crony', friend. *Etre copains comme cochons*: To be the best of mates, to be bosom pals. *Faire copain-copain*: To get pally. *Penser aux petits copains*: To be in favour of the old-boy network.

copeau *n.m.* 1 *Arracher son copeau*: To 'juice off', to ejaculate. 2 *Couper le copeau à quelqu'un*: To silence someone. (In this instance, *copeau* means tongue but is never encountered in other expressions.) 3 *Avoir les copeaux*: To 'have the jitters', to be 'in a blue funk', to be very frightened. 4 *Des copeaux!* Fuck all! – Bugger all! – Nothing at all! *On a pensé qu'on ferait des affaires – des copeaux!* We thought we'd do some business, but it was nothing doing!

copie *n.f.* *Pisseur de copie*: 'Ink-shitter', 'hack', journalist.

copier *v.trans.* *Celle-là, vous me la copierez!* *(iron.)*: I won't fall for that one again! – That trick won't work next time!

copine *n.f.* Woman friend. (This word, the feminine of *copain*, has no sexual connotation whatsoever.)

copiner *v.intrans.* To be 'pally with', to have a friendly relationship with someone.

copinerie *n.f.* 'Palliness', 'mateyness', camaraderie.

coq *n.m.* 1 Gold twenty-franc piece roughly equivalent to a sovereign. 2 *Mener une vie de coq en pâte (joc.)*: To 'lead the life of Riley', to have a cushy time. (A popular corruption of this expression is *mener une vie de coq en plâtre*.)

coquard *n.m.* 'Shiner', black eye.

coque *n.f.* *C'est à la coque!* It's A-I! – It's super! (also: *c'est aux pommes!*).

coquelicot *n.m.* *Avoir ses coquelicots*: To 'have the decorators in', to have one's menstrual period.

coqueluche *n.f.* 'Darling', idol, great favourite. *Il est la coqueluche du Tout Paris*: At present he's the golden boy in Paris.

coquer *v.trans.* To give. *Coquer un bécot*: To plant a kiss. *Coquer la frousse (à quelqu'un)*: To give someone the fright of their life. *Coquer un rencart*: To make a date with someone.

coquet *adj.* *Il va avoir droit à un coquet rapport (iron.)*: That report's going to look just dandy!

coqueter *v.intrans.* To behave in a vain fashion when in the presence of women (literally to behave like a cockerel surrounded by hens).

coquetier *n.m.* *Décrocher le coquetier*: To 'win the big one', to hit the jackpot.

coquette *n.f.* **1** 'Prick', 'cock', penis. **2** 'Flies', button- or zip-opening in trousers.

coqueur *n.m.* 'Snitch', 'grass', informer.

coquillard *n.m.* *S'en tamponner le coquillard*: 'Not to give a damn about something', to feel totally indifferent to something.

coquin *n.m.* **1** 'Fancy man', lover. **2** 'Strong plonk', potent wine. *Ça c'est du coquin!* This is a right fierce vino! **3** *Coquin de sort!* Crikey! –Crumbs! – Oh heck! (This typically Provence expression denotes a mixture of surprise and commiseration.)

coquinou *n.m.* *(joc. corr. coquin)*: *Coquinou, va!* You rascal, you!

cor *n.m.* *Cor au pied*: **a** 'Pain in the arse', 'pain in the neck', bloody nuisance. **b** (Railwayman's slang): Warning detonator placed on track.

corbaque *n.m.* (also: *corbac*): Crow.

corbeau *n.m.* **1** Pejorative appellation for a priest (because of the black cassock). **2** Poison-pen writer. (The typical *corbeau* letter seems to end with the words: *un ami qui vous veut du bien*. This expression in turn seems to have become a sardonic catch-phrase.)

corbi *n.m.* *(abbr. corbillard)*: 'Meat-wagon', hearse.

corde *n.f.* **1** *Parler de corde dans la maison d'un pendu*: To 'put one's foot in it', to mention the unmentionable. **2** *Avoir de la corde de pendu*: To have the luck of the devil. (Popular belief has it that a piece of the tragic rope acts as a good luck charm.) **3** *Se mettre la corde au cou*: To 'put on the ball and chain', to 'get hitched', to get married. **4** *Ça sent la corde!* I can smell a rat! – It looks fishy (suspicious) to me! **5** *Il pleut des cordes*: 'It's pissing down' – 'It's raining cats and dogs' – It's pouring (also: *il pleut des hallebardes*). **6** *Faire des cordes pour la marine*: To 'crap', to 'shit', to defecate. **7** *Ne tirez pas trop sur la corde (avec moi)*: Don't push me too far (if you know what's good for you). **8** *Ça n'est pas dans mes cordes* (also: *ça ne rentre pas dans mes cordes*): It's not (really) my line – I don't think I'm the right person for this. **9** *Prendre un virage à la corde* (Motoring, cycling): To cut a corner close, to cut a corner tight.

corder *v.intrans.* **1** To 'croak', to 'snuff it', to die. **2** *(corr. s'accorder)*: To 'hit it off with someone', to get on splendidly with someone. *On corde bien ensemble, nous deux*: We get on like a house on fire, us two.

corgnolon *n.m.* 'Gullet', throat.

cornac *n.m.* *(joc.)*: Tourist guide. *On a suivi le cornac dans tout Paname*: We traipsed round Paris with the chap from the travel agency.

cornanche *n.f.* (Gambling slang): Mark on playing-card enabling the cheat to recognize it.

Fais gaffe! C'est le roi de la cornanche: Watch out! He'll know that deck inside out after two games.

cornancher *v.trans.* **1** (Gambling slang): To mark cards surreptitiously for cheating purposes. **2** To 'push someone's face in', to thump someone.

cornancher *v.intrans.* **1** To 'croak', to 'snuff it', to die. **2** (of person): To 'pong', to stink, to smell foul.

cornaquer *v.trans.* **1** *(joc.)*: To 'herd', to guide tourists. **2** To initiate. (The word is usually encountered in the context of prostitution.)

cornard *n.m.* *(pej.)*: Cuckold, man whose wife is unfaithful. (*Cornard* has a more pejorative connotation than *cocu*.)

corne *n.f.* **1** *(corr. carne)*: 'Shoe-leather', tough meat. **2** *Faire les cornes*: To 'wave two fingers', to make an insolently mocking gesture. **3** *Avoir un bustier qui fait les cornes (joc.)*: To have a 'perky pair of tits', to have young and rather prominent breasts. **4** *Porter des cornes*: To be a cuckold, to have an unfaithful wife.

corner *v.intrans.* **1** (of person): To 'pong', to stink, to smell foul. **2** To 'shoot one's mouth', to 'blab', to spread gossip.

cornet *n.m.* **1** 'Gullet', throat. *Se rincer le cornet*: To down a drink, to have a swig. **2** 'Belly', stomach. *S'en filer plein le cornet*: To get oneself a bellyful of grub. **3** *(pl.)*: 'Flappers', 'lug-holes', ears.

corniaud *n.m.* *(pej.)*: **1** 'Mutt', 'pooch', mongrel dog. **2** 'Burk', 'twit', imbecile.

cornichon *n.m.* **1** 'Mug', 'twit', simpleton. (Although it is certainly not a complimentary word, *cornichon* is far from pejorative and is even sometimes used in a deliberately affectionate context. *Cornichon, va!* You silly-billy!) **2** 'Blower', phone, telephone. **3** Loud-hailer, megaphone.

corniflot *n.m.* 'Rot-gut', 'tangle-foot', strong alcohol. *Un coup de corniflot*: A tot of the hard stuff.

Corpo Proper name. *La Corpo de Droit*: The Faculty of Law (within a university).

corps *n.m.* **1** *Ça tient au corps* (of food): It's filling. **2** *Un drôle de corps* (of person): 'Odd-bod', 'strange cove', odd character. **3** *Un sacré corps* (of woman): A superb figure. **4** *Avoir servi dans plusieurs corps (joc.)*: To have lead a randy old life. (The witticism lies in the double meaning of *corps*: body and *'corps d'armée'*.)

correct *adj.* (of person): Trustworthy. (This is an adjective that is far more positive than its academic meaning would otherwise suggest; to say of someone *'C'est un type correct'* is to pay quite a sizeable compliment. When applied to an inanimate object, *correct* reverts to its original meaning: 'decent, O.K.'. *Un repas correct*: A fair sort of meal.)

correctance *n.f. (corr. abbr. maison de correction)*: Borstal, reform school. *Etre en correctance*: To be in an approved school.

correctionnelle *n.f. (abbr. tribunal correctionnel). Passer en correctionnelle*: To be summoned to appear in a magistrates' court.

corrida *n.f.* 1 'To-do', violent argument. 2 'Punch-up', 'set-to', free-for-all fight. *Il y a eu une de ces corridas à la sortie du dancing*: There was an almighty punch-up outside the Roxy.

corriger *v.trans.* To beat up. (This verb applies both to men and women and implies punishment of some kind. *Il l'a drôlement corrigée pour ses indiscrétions*: He beat her black-and-blue for opening her big mouth.)

corsé *adj.* 1 (of joke, story): Rather risqué, in bad taste. 2 *Une addition corsée*: A 'steep bill', an extortionate amount demanded for a meal in a restaurant.

corser *v.pronom. Ça se corse!* Things are hotting up! (Things are getting tenser by the minute.)

Corsico *n.m.* Corsican.

corsif *n.m. (corr. corset)*: Girdle, corset.

cortausse *n.f.* 'Thrashing', beating. *Il lui a filé une de ces cortausses*: He beat the other fellow black-and-blue.

corvée *n.f. Quelle corvée!* What a fag! – What a drag! – What a drudge!

cossard *n.m.* 'Lazy git', 'slack-arse', lazy person.

cossard *adj.* 'Bone-idle', lazy.

cosse *n.f. Avoir la cosse*: To feel work-shy, to feel lazy. *Tirer sa cosse*: To do bugger-all.

costard *n.m. (corr. costume)*: Man's suit, suit of clothes.

costaud *n.m.* Athletically-built man, one whose frame is bulging with muscles. (The *costauds des Halles*, even with the advent of forklift trucks, are still much admired for their strong physique.)

costaud *adj.* 1 'Stocky', 'hefty', muscularly built. *Il est vachement costaud*: He's got muscles on his muscles! 2 *Ne pas se sentir costaud*: To feel 'out of sorts', to feel rather weak. 3 *Etre costaud en math*: To have a brain for maths. (*Etre costaud en* . . . can refer to excellence in a variety of subjects and skills.) 4 *Ça, c'est du costaud!* (of object): This is really solid stuff! 5 *C'est plutôt costaud*: a It's rather difficult. *C'est un machin plutôt costaud à expliquer*: It's rather tricky to explain. b It's quite pricey – It's rather expensive. *Notre loyer est plutôt costaud*: The rent here doesn't bear talking about.

costume *n.m.* 1 *En costume d'Adam*: 'Starkers', 'in one's birthday suit', naked. 2 *Se faire faire un*

costume en sapin (joc.): To 'croak', to 'snuff it', to die.

cote *n.f.* 1 Good name, reputation. *Avec sa cote, il peut se permettre de dire ce qu'il pense*: With his standing in the company, he can afford to speak his mind. *Avoir une grosse cote*: To be highly thought of. *Se faire monter la cote*: To 'send up one's own stock', to work on one's good name. *Marcher à la cote*: To trade (abusively) on one's good name. 2 Favouritism. *Avoir la bonne cote (avec quelqu'un)*: To stand in good stead with someone. *Avoir la cote d'amour*: To be someone's 'blue-eyed boy', to be a great favourite with someone. 3 *Cote mal taillée* (of money): 'Friendly split', amicable share-out.

côte *n.f.* 1 *(abbr. vin des Côtes du Rhône). Sers-nous une côte!* Waiter! I'll have a glass of Côtes du Rhône! 2 *Avoir les côtes en long*: To be a 'slack-arse', to be a lazy git. 3 *Se caler les côtes*: To 'stuff one's face', to have a right good tuck-in, to eat heartily. 4 *Etre à la côte*: To be 'skint', 'broke', to be penniless. 5 *C'est à se tenir les côtes*: It's rib-tickling – It's hilarious. 6 *Caresser les côtes à quelqu'un* (also: *chatouiller les côtes à quelqu'un*): To beat someone black-and-blue, to give someone a thrashing.

côté *n.m.* 1 *Le côté du manche*: The winning side. *Choisir le côté du manche*: To 'play it safe', to pick on the winning side. 2 *Etre du mauvais côté de la pente* (also: *être sur le mauvais côté de la pente*): To be (on) the wrong side of forty. 3 *Taper à côté (fig.)*: To be wide of the mark. *Moi, sa petite amie?! Alors là, tu tapes à côté*: Me, his bird?! You must be joking! 4 *Côté cour, côté jardin*: On this side, on that side. (This expression, originally exclusive to the register of the theatre, indicating the right- and left-hand side of the stage, has come to express the existence of two separate entities.)

côtelette *n.f.* 1 *(pl.)*: Ribs, rib-cage (of person). *Il a pris un coup dans les côtelettes*: He got winded. 2 *(pl.)*: 'Mutton-chops', side-burns, side-whiskers. 3 *Pisser sa côtelette*: To give birth.

coton *n.m.* 1 *Filer un mauvais coton*: To look worried and in poor health. 2 *Avoir les jambes en coton*: To feel 'weak at the knees', to be unsteady on one's legs.

coton *adj.inv.* Difficult, arduous. *C'est un problème un rien coton*: It's a rather tough nut to crack.

couac *n.m. Faire couac (joc.)*: To 'croak', to 'snuff it', to die.

couchage *n.m.* Love-making, intercourse. *Le couchage, il est toujours pour*: He's a randy so-and-so!

couche *n.f.* **1** *En avoir* (also: *en tenir*) *une couche*: To be 'as thick as two short planks', to be 'as dumb as they come', to be stupid. (*Couche* here refers to a 'layer', of stupidity.) **2** *Fausse couche* (of person): 'Runt', 'squirt', genetic near-miss (also: *raclure de bidet*).

coucher *n.m. Faire un coucher* (of prostitute): To have an 'all-nighter', to have the same customer throughout the night.

coucher *v.intrans.* **1** *Coucher avec*: To 'sleep with', to have intercourse with. **2** *Avoir un nom à coucher en dehors*: To have one of those unpronounceable names. (The jocularity in this expression stems from the fact that a down-and-out with a long and foreign-sounding name might be refused admission to a hostel.)

coucher *v.pronom. Va te coucher!* Bugger off! –Get lost! – Go away and leave me alone!

coucheries *n.f.pl.* 'Screwing', love-making. *J'en ai marre de toutes vos coucheries!* I'm fed-up with all this bed-hopping of yours!

coucheur *n.m. Mauvais coucheur*: 'Awkward customer', person who is difficult for the sake of it.

couci-couça *adv.* 'Fair to middling' – Not too good, not too bad. *'Et la santé, comment ça va?' 'Couci-couça, faut pas s'en plaindre':* 'How's your health, then?' 'Well, I'm on the mend'.

coucou *n.m.* **1** 'Loony', 'nutter', barmy character. **2** *Vieux coucou*: 'Old kite', old aeroplane.

coude *n.m.* **1** *Jouer des coudes*: To elbow one's way through. (*lit. & fig.*) *C'est un arriviste, lui, il sait jouer des coudes*: He'd walk over his own grandmother to get what he wants. **2** *Se serrer les coudes*: To 'close ranks', to stick together. **3** *Lever le coude*: To 'tipple', to drink immoderately. **4** *Ne pas se moucher du coude*: **a** To have no mean opinion of oneself. **b** To do things in the grand manner. **5** *Se fourrer* (also: *se mettre*) *le doigt dans l'œil jusqu'au coude*: To be 'completely off the mark', to be totally wrong. **6** *Huile de coude*: 'Elbow-grease', hard work.

coudre *v.trans. S'en coudre une*: To roll a cigarette.

couenne *n.f.* **1** 'Hide', skin. *Se racler la couenne*: To have a shave. **2** 'Mutt', 'blockhead', idiot. *Quelle couenne!* He's a right twat!

couenne *adj.* 'Thick', 'dumb', stupid.

couennerie *n.f.* (*joc. corr. connerie*): Stupidity. *Sortir des couenneries*: To come out with a load of balderdash, to talk rubbish.

couic *n.m.* **1** *Faire couic*: To 'croak', to 'snuff it', to die. *Il n'a fait qu'un couic*: He popped off and never even cheeped! **2** *N'y entraver que couic*: To understand bugger-all (also: *n'y entraver que pouic*).

couille *n.f.* **1** 'Bollock', testicle. **2** *Avoir des couilles au cul*: To be 'spunky', 'gutsy', to have courage. **3** *Couille molle*: 'Sap', 'drip', insignificant person. **4** *Partir en couille*: To 'go to pot', to neglect oneself. **5** *C'est de la couille en barre! (iron.)*: It's a load of balls! – What a load of rubbish!

couiller *v.trans.* To 'con', to 'diddle', to swindle. *On s'est fait couiller en beauté*: We was truly done!

couillon *n.m.* **1** 'Twit', blithering idiot, imbecile. *Cesse de faire le couillon!* Stop arsing about! **2** *Jouer un tour de couillon à quelqu'un*: To 'take someone for a ride', to play a trick on someone. **3** *Piège à couillon*: 'Trap', trick that only a fool would fall for.

couillon *adj.* **1** (of person): 'Thick', 'dumb', stupid. *Il est couillon comme pas un*: He's as thick as two short planks. **2** (of thing): 'Bloody stupid', silly. *Un truc comme ça, c'est vraiment couillon!* This is really too silly for words!

couillonnade *n.f.* **1** 'Booboo', 'boob', blunder. *Il ne fait que des couillonnades*: He can't do anything right. *Une couillonnade de plus ou de moins, on n'est pas à ça près*: One more cock-up won't make that much difference. **2** *Dire des couillonnades*: To 'talk a load of bull', to 'spout rubbish', to utter stupidities. *Les couillonnades qu'il nous sort! . . .* You've never heard such bilge!

couillonner *v.trans.* To 'take someone for a ride', to make a fool of someone. *Couillonner quelqu'un en beauté*: To con someone good and proper. *Si on continue comme ça, on va se faire couillonner*: If we go about things like this much longer, we'll come a cropper.

couiner *v.intrans.* To 'whine', to whimper.

couineur *n.m.* 'Eternal moaner', persistent whiner.

coulage *n.m.* Losses through internal pilfering. *Dans une usine il y a pas mal de coulage*: In a factory lots of things seem to grow little legs!

coulant *n.m.* **1** *Du coulant*: 'Cow-juice', milk. **2** *Un coulant*: An over-ripe Camembert cheese. (Another jocular appellation for the above is *un vient-tout-seul*.)

coulant *adj.* 'Easy-going', accommodating. *Dans son genre, il est plutôt coulant ton paternel*: Your dad's no stick-in-the-mud really, is he?!

coulante *n.f.* **1** 'Clap', gonorrhoea, V.D. **2** *Avoir la coulante*: To have 'the runs', to be suffering from diarrhoea.

coule *n.f. Etre à la coule*: **a** To be 'on the ball', to know what's what. **b** To be 'in the know', to be aware of all the facts. **c** To be 'easy-going', to be easy to get on with.

couler *v.trans.* **1** To ruin, to discredit. *Si ça se sait, on est coulé*: If people find out, we might just as well pack up and go. **2** *Se la couler douce*: To 'lead the life of Riley', to enjoy a cushy life. **3** *Couler un bronze*: To 'crap', to 'shit', to defecate.

couleur *n.f.* **1** *En dire de toutes les couleurs*: To say something without mincing one's words. **2** *En voir de toutes les couleurs*: To be led a merry dance. *Sa femme lui en fait voir de toutes les couleurs*: His wife certainly makes him go through hell. **3** *Défendre ses couleurs*: To 'look after Number One', to defend one's (own) interests. **4** *Annoncer la couleur*: **a** (Cards): To call trumps, to call a suit. **b** (Drinks): To 'name one's poison', to choose one's tipple. *Ne pas changer la couleur*: To avoid mixing one's drinks. **c** To 'put someone in the picture', to clue someone up. *Bon, annonce la couleur, où en est-on?* Go on, give us the score! **d** To state one's intentions. **5** *Etre à la couleur*: **a** To be 'on the ball', to know what's what. **b** To be 'in the know', to be aware of all the facts.

couleuvre *n.f. Avaler des couleuvres*: To 'swallow one's pride', to take a verbal hammering without protesting.

couloir *n.m. Le couloir à lentilles (joc.)*: The anal sphincter (also: *la turbine à chocolat*).

coup *n.m.* When one takes a broad look at the word *coup*, it soon becomes obvious that its many diverse uses and combined expressions come under three main categories.

(A): Blow (in the literal and figurative). **1** *En venir aux coups*: To come to blows. **2** *Coup de boule*: 'Head-butt', blow inflicted with the head in opponent's belly. **3** *Le coup du lapin*: Blow on the back of the neck. **4** *Coup de Jarnac*: Treacherous blow, disloyal attack. **5** *Le coup du père François*: Strangulation. **6** *Coup de Trafalgar*: Disastrous turn of events. **7** *Coup de châsse*: 'Quick butchers', peep, quick look. **8** *Coup de filet*: Dragnet, police raid. **9** *Coup de balai*: Clear-out. *Donner un coup de balai (fig.)*: To make room for new ideas. **10** *Coup de torchon*: 'Barney', heated argument. **11** *Tirer un coup*: To fuck, to 'screw', to have intercourse. *Coup de Bourse (joc.)*: Intercourse. (The pun here is on the word *Bourse* meaning both the Stock Exchange and testicle; the standard non-colloquial expression denotes a successful flutter on the Stock Exchange.) **12** *Coup de fil*: 'Buzz', 'ring', telephone call. **13** *Coup dur*: Serious setback. *La vie pour lui a été une succession de coups durs*: It's just been one blow after another for him all his life. **14** *C'est un sale coup (pour la fanfare)*: That's really bad luck, that is! **15** *Faire les quatre cents coups*: To 'burn the candle at both ends', to lead a fast life.

(B): Dose, measure, quantity. **1** *Boire un coup*: To

have a drink. **2** *En avoir un coup* (also: *avoir un coup dans l'aile*): To be 'squiffy', 'tipsy', to be slightly drunk. **3** *En mettre un coup* (of work): To 'do one's darnedest', to 'put one's back into it', to make an extra effort. **4** *Tenir le coup*: To stand the pace, to weather the storm. *Il n'a qu'à tenir le coup comme les autres*: He'll just have to grin and bear it like the rest of us. **5** *Faire quelque chose en trois coups de cuiller à pot*: To do something 'in two shakes of a lamb's tail', double-quick. **6** *Ne pas en ficher un coup*: To do 'fuck-all', to be darned lazy. **7** *Coup de pot*: Stroke of luck. **8** *Prendre un coup de vieux*: To age considerably over a short period of time. **9** *Coup de fusil* (at restaurant): Exorbitant bill. *On a eu droit à un de ces coups de fusil carabinés*: The bill we got looked like the balance of payments deficit! **10** *Coup de pouce*: Help, assistance. *Donner un coup de pouce à quelqu'un*: To give someone a shove in the right direction.

(C): Knack, trick. **1** *Avoir le coup*: To have the knack. *Il a le coup pour draguer les nanas!* He certainly knows how to pull the birds! **2** *Etre au coup*: To 'know the score', to 'know the ropes', to be familiar with the workings of something. **3** *Etre dans le coup*: To be 'in on something', to be involved in something. **4** *Expliquer le coup* (to accomplices): To divulge the plan. **5** *Faire le coup à quelqu'un*: To play the trick on someone. *Il m'a fait le coup du 'portefeuille dans l'autre veston'*: He got money out of me with that age-old 'I forgot my wallet' dodge. **6** *Monter un coup*: To engineer a confidence trick. *On a monté un coup fumant*: That con was a cracker! **7** *Coup d'arnac*: Fraud, swindle. **8** *Le coup classique*: That old, old trick. **9** *Coup fourré*: 'Major cock-up', big blunder.

couparès *adj.inv.* 'Skint', 'broke', penniless.

coup-de-poing *n.m.* **1** *Faire le coup-de-poing*: To lend a hand in a punch-up. **2** *Coup-de-poing américain*: Knuckleduster.

coupe *n.f. Il a vraiment la coupe! (iron.)*: He's just cut out for that!

coupé *adj.* 'Skint', 'broke', penniless. *Etre coupé au trognon*: Not to have two brass farthings to rub together.

coupe-choux *n.m.* Cut-throat razor.

coupe-file *n.m.* Official pass given to V.I.P.s and privileged civil servants (police officials, etc.) enabling the bearer to gain access where others have to wait.

coupe-la-faim *n.m.* (also: *coupe-faim*): Mid-morning or mid-afternoon snack.

coupe-lard *n.m.* 'Chiv', blade, knife.

couper *v.trans. & intrans.* **1** To interrupt (person, conversation). **2** *Couper le sifflet à quelqu'un*: To 'cut someone short', to silence someone.

3 *La couper à quelqu'un* (also: *couper la chique à quelqu'un*): To leave someone agape, to astound someone. *Ça te la coupe, hein?!* That's got you stumped! **4** *Couper les jambes à quelqu'un:* **a** (Sport): To tire, to wear an opponent out. **b** To 'take the wind out of someone's sails', to dishearten someone. *Cette nouvelle m'a coupé les jambes:* When I heard that, my spirits sank. **5** *Se faire couper:* To 'get fleeced', to be swindled. *Etre coupé:* To be bankrupt. **6** *Couper à quelque chose* (of chore): To dodge, to shuffle out of something. *La vaisselle, on ne va pas y couper:* We're dead certs for the washing up. **7** *Couper dans (le truc):* To 'fall for something', to take something at face value. *Je ne coupe pas dans toutes ces giries:* I'm not falling for all that tommy-rot. **8** *Couper la poire en deux:* To 'do a bit of give-and-take', to compromise. **9** *Couper les cheveux en quatre:* To go nit-picking, to split hairs.

couper *v.trans.reflex.* To give oneself away by making contradictory statements.

couperet *n.m.* **1** *Passer au couperet:* To 'get the chop', to 'get axed', to get dismissed from one's job. **2** *Ma tête sous le couperet!* Cross my heart and hope to die! (if what I say is untrue).

coupe-soif *n.m. (joc.):* 'Strong tipple', potent drink (also: *coupe-la-soif*).

coupe-tiffes *n.m.* 'Lock-lopper', barber, gents' hairdresser (also: *merlan*).

Coupole *Proper name. La Coupole:* **a** The *Académie Française.* (Members of that august body are sometimes referred to as *Coupolards.*) **b** The famous Parisian *brasserie* of that name in Montparnasse was and is the popular haunt of artists, thinkers and would-be philosophers.

coupure *n.f.* **1** 'Cock-and-bull story', weak alibi. **2** Confidential info, tip-off. **3** *Coupure! (interj.):* Pull the other one! – I'm not as dumb as you think! **4** *Faire la coupure:* To shift the conversation on to a less embarrassing topic. **5** *Grosse/petite coupure:* Banknote of large/small denomination. *Ils exigèrent la rançon en petites coupures:* They wanted the ransom paid in 'paper-chase money'.

courailler *v.intrans.* To 'go for the birds', to gallivant, to chase women.

courailleur *n.m.* 'Lad-about-town', randy so-and-so.

courant *n.m.* **1** *Le courant:* 'Juice', electricity. *Couper le courant:* To cut off the power. **2** *Courant d'air:* 'Leak', leaked information. *Il y a pas mal de courants d'air au Ministère:* There are quite a few moles at the Ministry! **3** *Se déguiser en courant d'air (joc.):* To 'make oneself scarce', to vanish into thin air. **4** *Se taper des courants d'air:* To 'live on next to nothing', to go

hungry. **5** *Faire courant d'air avec les chiottes:* To have foul breath.

courante *n.f. La courante:* 'The shits', 'the runs', diarrhoea.

courber *v.trans. Se faire courber une aile (fig.):* To be 'cut down to size', to be put in one's place.

courbette *n.f. Faire des courbettes:* To 'bow and scrape', to be over-obsequious.

courette *n.f. Etre en courette:* To be on the run from the police.

coureur *n.m.* 'Randy so-and-so', philanderer.

coureuse *n.f.* 'Easy lay', 'randy bird', promiscuous woman.

courge *n.f. Ne pas avoir un grain de courge à la place du cerveau (joc.):* To 'have something up-top', to be brainy.

courir *v.trans. & intrans.* **1** To 'chase the birds', to womanize. **2** *Pouvoir toujours courir (iron.):* To stand no earthly chance (of obtaining something). *Si c'est du fric qu'il veut, il peut toujours courir!* If it's money he's after, he can go and take a running jump! **3** *Il me court sur l'haricot* (also: *sur le haricot*): He's a pain in the arse – He's a bloody nuisance (also: *il me court*). **4** *Laisser courir:* To let the matter rest, to leave it at that. **5** *Courir trois chiens sans fusil:* To go on a pointless time-consuming chase.

course *n.f.* **1** *Etre dans la course (fig.):* To be 'in the running', to stand a chance. *Ne pas être dans la course:* To be out of touch. **2** *La course au bifteck:* The 'rat-race', the mad rush for survival in modern life. **3** *Course à l'échalotte:* Action of evicting someone by the scruff of the neck. **4** *S'être retiré des courses* (of gangsters): To have retired voluntarily.

course-par-course *n.m.* Establishment providing telexed racing results. (In France, where bookmaking is illegal, there is a State monopoly on racing similar to the British Tote. Off-course bets are placed in the morning in selected franchised cafés.)

courser *v.trans.* To give chase to someone. *Malgré ses cinquante berges, elle les a vachement coursés:* She might just as well have been twenty the way she chased after them.

coursette *n.f.* **1** *Piquer une coursette:* To dash off. **2** *Faire la coursette:* To dash to-and-fro needlessly.

court *adj. L'avoir eue courte et bonne:* To have had a short yet fulfilling life.

court-bouillon *n.m.* **1** *Boire le court-bouillon:* To nearly drown. **2** *Etre dans le court-bouillon:* To be 'in a pickle', to be 'in a stew', to be in trouble. **3** *Avoir la rate au court-bouillon:* To 'have the shits', to be petrified.

court-circuit *n.m.* 'Stabbing pain', lancing spasm.

court-circuiter *v.trans.* To 'short-cut the system'. *Grâce au brave tonton, on a court-circuité son dossier*: It pays to have an uncle in high places, her file went to the top of the pile.

courtille *n.f. Etre un peu de la courtille*: To be 'short of readies', to be in need of cash.

courtines *n.f.pl. Les courtines*: The races. *Flamber gros* (also: *dur*) *aux courtines*: To be a heavy gambler with the gee-gees.

court-jus *n.m.* **1** 'Short', electrical short circuit. **2** *Avoir un court-jus dans la calbombe*: To 'have a screw loose', to be 'bonkers', to be mad.

couru *past part. C'est couru d'avance*: It's a dead cert – It's a sure thing.

cousette *n.f.* **1** Apprentice dressmaker. **2** Travelling sewing-kit.

cousin *n.m. Etre cousins à la mode de Bretagne*: To be vaguely related, to be distant relatives.

cousu *past part. C'est cousu de fil blanc*: It's blatantly apparent. (No-one could possibly be deceived by this hamfisted ploy.)

cousue *n.f.* 'Ciggy', 'fag', cigarette. *Une cousue-main*: A hand-rolled cigarette.

cousu-main *n.m.* 'Dead-cert', certainty. *Comme fric-frac, c'est du cousu-main*: That's no break-in, it's like taking sweets from a kiddy!

coutal *n.m.* 'Shiv', blade, knife.

couteau *n.m.* **1** *(pl.)*: 'Gnashers', 'choppers', teeth. *Trépigner des couteaux*: To be famished. **2** *Un silence à couper au couteau*: A most embarrassed silence (the kind of awkward hush that follows an indiscreet remark).

coûter *v.intrans.* **1** *Coûter les yeux de la tête*: To be exorbitantly expensive. *Mais ça va coûter les yeux de la tête!* You're not going to pay prices like that, are you?! **2** *Pour ce que ça vous coûte! (iron.)*: As if it made any difference to you! (In this example *coûter* does not necessarily refer to money.)

couture *n.f. Etre battu à plate couture*: To get 'trounced', to be 'beaten hollow', to be totally defeated.

couvée *n.f.* **1** 'Brood', host of children (from one family). **2** *Etre moche à faire avorter une couvée de singes* (of person): To be as ugly as sin.

couvercle *n.m.* **1** 'Bean', 'bonce', head. *Travailler du couvercle* (also: *fermenter du couvercle*): To be 'going potty', to be on the verge of insanity. **2** *Trouver le couvercle pour sa marmite*: To find one's partner for life, to find one's spouse. *Chaque marmite a son couvercle*: No-one's unmarriable.

couvert *n.m.* **1** *Mettre le couvert* (Gambling slang): To set the table for a game of cards. **2** *Remettre le couvert*: To start all over again. (The expression can refer to a variety of

activities. The most current usage is in conjunction with sexual intercourse.) **3** *Couvert trois pièces (joc.)*: 'Privates', male sexual organs.

couverte *n.f. (abbr. couverture)*: **1** Blanket. **2** Alibi (very often a phoney one). **3** Respectable front for shady activities.

couverture *n.f.* **1** Respectable front for shady activities. **2** Contrived alibi (the kind one establishes prior to a criminal act). **3** *Tirer la couverture à soi*: To 'grab the lion's share', to hog most of the profits.

couveuse *n.f. Avoir été élevé dans une couveuse (joc.)*: To have been 'brought up in cotton-wool', to have been mollycoddled.

couvrante *n.f.* **1** (Army, scouts' slang): Blanket. **2** Respectable front for shady activities.

couvrir *v.trans.* **1** (Journalism): *Couvrir une affaire*: To 'cover' an event, to report it. **2** To assume responsibility for a subordinate's actions. *Ne vous en faites pas, vous êtes couvert*: Do what I tell you, I'll take the blame if there's any.

coxer *v.trans.* To catch 'red-handed', to arrest someone in the act.

crabe *n.m.* **1** *(mil.)*: 'Corp', corporal. **2** 'Screw', prison warder. **3** *Vieux crabe*: **a** 'Old fogey', old dodderer. **b** *(th.)*: Old actor long past his prime. **4** *(pl.)*: 'Crabs', crab-lice. **5** *Panier de crabes*: 'Dog-eat-dog' situation, inextricable set-up.

crac *interj. Et crac!* **a** Before you could say Jack Robinson! – In a flash (without warning). **b** *(iron.)*: Yaboo sucks! – Put that in your pipe and smoke it! – That's the way it is!

crachat *n.m.* **1** *(joc.)*: 'Gong', military medal. **2** *Se noyer dans un crachat*: To 'make a mountain out of a molehill', to be unable to cope with the simplest situation.

cracher *v.trans. & intrans.* **1** To 'spill the beans', to confess (also: *cracher le morceau*). **2** To 'cough up', to pay up. *Dans un restau comme ça, faut drôlement cracher*: In those four-star places you need a mortgage to eat! **3** *Cracher au bassinet*: To pay protection money. **4** *Cracher jaune*: To be 'rolling in it', to be very wealthy. **5** *Cracher blanc*: To be 'spitting feathers', to be 'parched', to be very thirsty. **6** *Cracher son venin*: To 'juice off', to ejaculate. **7** *Cracher dans le son*: To be guillotined. (Because the severed head falls into a basket of chaff.) **8** *Cracher le feu*: **a** To be a 'live-wire', to be full of zing and pep. **b** *Ça crachait le feu* (of argument): It was a right barney. **9** *Cracher sa valda* (of traffic light): To go to green. (*Pastilles Valda* are green-coloured cough-mints.) **10** *Ne pas cracher sur quelque chose*: To be glad of something. *Il n'a pas craché* *sur mon fric:* He certainly didn't turn his nose up at my money. **11** *Ça va cracher!* Bullets are going to fly!

crachoir *n.m. Tenir le crachoir:* To 'spout', to monopolize the conversation. *Savoir tenir le crachoir:* To have the gift of the gab.

crachouiller *v.intrans.* **1** To shower someone with spittle (also: *postillonner*). **2** *Ça crachouille!* It's drizzling!

crack *n.m.* **1** 'Ace guy', real winner. **2** (Sport): 'Champ', champion.

cracra *adj.* 'Mucky', filthy, dirty. *Môme cracra:* Slut.

cradingue *adj. (corr. crasseux):* Filthy, 'mucky', dirty. *Il est cradingue comme un peigne:* He's really revolting (also: *crado*).

crais *interj.* Watch out! – Look out! – Be careful! (also: *gaffe!*).

cramer *v.intrans.* **1** To 'go up in smoke', to burn. **2** *Etre cramé:* To have been found out. *C'est cramé on n'a plus qu'à se tirer!* The game's up, let's scarper! **3** *Ça sent le cramé:* I can smell a rat – It looks suspicious.

cramouille *n.f.* 'Fanny', 'pussy', vagina (also: *chagatte*).

crampe *n.f. Tirer sa crampe:* To 'screw', to fuck, to have intercourse.

crampon *n.m.* 'Leech', persistent button-holer, tenacious bore.

crampon *adj.* (of person): Tenaciously boring. *Ce qu'il est crampon!* You just can't shake him off, can you?! (also: *cramponnant*).

cramponner *v.trans.* **1** To bore the pants off someone. **2** *Cramponner quelqu'un par l'aile:* To grab hold of someone.

crampser *v.intrans.* To 'croak', to 'snuff it', to die (also: *clamser*).

cran *n.m.* **1** Pluck, courage. *Ne pas manquer de cran:* To be damn gutsy. **2** *Rabattre quelqu'un d'un cran:* To 'take someone down a peg or two', to cut someone down to size. **3** *Ne pas lâcher quelqu'un d'un cran:* To stick to someone's heels, to dog someone's footsteps. **4** *Etre à cran:* **a** To be 'a mass of nerves', to be all tensed-up. **b** To be in a foul temper. **5** *Faire dix jours de cran (mil.):* To be confined to barracks for ten days.

crâne *n.m.* **1** *Bourrer le crâne à quelqu'un:* To fill someone's head with stuff and nonsense. **2** *Crâne de piaf:* 'Nincompoop', 'bird-brain', twit. **3** *(pl.):* 'Scalps', arrests. *C'est un flic de première avec une tripotée de crânes à son actif:* He's a top cop with a list of arrests as long as your arm.

crâner *v.intrans.* To 'swank', to show off, to boast.

crâneur *n.m.* 'Swank', show-off.

crapahu *n.m.* **1** Manoeuvres, military exercises. **2** Tiring gym routine.

crapahuter *v.intrans.* **1** To go on manoeuvres, to carry out military exercises. **2** To have a tough work-out, to do strenuous gym exercises.

crapaud *n.m.* **1** Wallet. *Le coup du crapaud* (Prostitutes' slang): The 'disappearing wallet' trick (when a customer loses more than his inhibitions). **2** *(abbr. fauteuil crapaud):* Low squat heavily-padded armchair.

crapautard *n.m.* (also: *crapotard*): Wallet. *Etre constipé du crapautard:* To be 'stingy', to be mean with money.

crape *n.f. (abbr. crapule):* Rogue, scoundrel.

crapette *n.f. Une crapette:* A game of dice.

crapoteux *adj.* Filthy, 'mucky', dirty.

Crapouillot *Proper name. Le Crapouillot* was a famous satirical magazine born in the trenches of World War I, remembered long after its extinction because of its mixture of fierce humour and superb thinking. It got its name from a small mortar used by the French troops.

crapulados *n.m.* 'Coffin-nail', cheap and nasty cigarillo (also: *crapulos*).

crapuleuse *adj.f. Se la faire crapuleuse:* To 'paint the town red', to live it up in all the best places.

crapuleux *adj.* Dastardly. *Crime crapuleux:* Heinous murder motivated by theft.

craquante *n.f.* Match, matchstick. *Il se curait toujours les chicots avec une craquante:* He'd always be picking his teeth with scratchies.

craque *n.f.* **1** 'Tall story', fantasized tale. **2** White lie. **3** 'Fanny', 'pussy', vagina.

craquer *v.intrans.* **1** To suffer a nervous breakdown. **2** To tell tall stories. **3** *Faire craquer:* To break in, to burgle. **4** *Plein à craquer:* 'Chock-a-block', 'jam-packed', bursting at the seams.

craquette *n.f.* 'Fanny', 'pussy', vagina.

craspec *adj. (corr. crasseux):* 'Mucky', filthy, dirty.

crasse *n.f.* **1** 'Low down action', dirty trick. *Faire une crasse à quelqu'un:* To do the dirty on someone. *Sale crasse:* Sick joke. **2** *La crasse* (Seamen's, airmen's slang): Filthy weather with poor visibility. *On s'est tapé une de ces crasses à trois mille mètres:* We hit some foul bilge 9,000 feet up.

crasseux *n.m. (pej.):* 'Nit-rake', comb (usually a dirty one).

cravache *n.f. Gagner à la cravache (fig.):* To make it with one last spurt of energy.

cravacher *v.intrans.* **1** To 'bomb along', to 'belt on', to go full speed. **2** To work away fast and furiously. **3** To try one's darnedest, to make an all-out effort.

cravate *n.f.* **1** (Wrestling): Headlock. *Faire une cravate à quelqu'un*: To get someone in a stranglehold. **2** *De la cravate*: 'Bunkum', bluff. *Tout ça, c'est de la cravate!* This is just a load of eyewash! **3** *S'en jeter un derrière la cravate*: To 'knock back a bevvy', to down a drink. **4** *Passer à la cravate de chanvre*: To suffer death by hanging.

cravater *v.trans.* **1** To 'buttonhole' someone, to delay someone against their will. **2** To 'feel someone's collar', to arrest someone. **3** To assault, to attack. **4** (Sport): To come to grips with. **5** To 'nick', to 'pinch', to steal. *On m'a cravaté mon larfeuille*: I got my wallet nicked.

cravater *v.intrans.* To 'do a Münchhausen', to tell tall stories.

cravateur *n.m.* **1** 'Mouthpiece', barrister. **2** 'Slick-tongue', smooth-talker.

cravetouse *n.f.* (also: *cravetouze*): 'Neck-gear', tie.

crayon *n.m.* **1** Hair (usually in jocular expressions such as *n'avoir plus un crayon sur la boule*: To be as bald as a coot). **2** *Du crayon*: 'Tick', credit. *Je lui aurais filé dix sacs de crayon, mais il a déjà une sacrée ardoise chez nous*: I'd have lent him the money, but he's already got quite a lot on the slate here.

crayonner *v.intrans.* (of motor car): To 'take off', to accelerate rapidly. *Crayonne, Lulu!* Come on, mate, step on it! (*Crayonner* implies making tracks, leaving burnt rubber tracks behind like two large pencil marks.)

créature *n.f.* (*pej.*): 'Loose woman'. (The word is often used by a wife when talking about 'the other woman'.)

crèche *n.f.* **1** 'Digs', 'bed-sit', flatlet. **2** House, home. *La crèche à ses vieux*: His parents' house.

crécher *v.intrans.* To live, to dwell (somewhere). *Où ce que tu crèches?* Where do you hang out?

crécher *v.trans.reflex.* To 'hit the sack', to 'hit the hay', to go to bed (also: *se pager*).

crédence *n.f.* 'Corporation', pot-belly, large stomach.

crédo *n.m.* 'Tick', credit. *Il me faut ça à crédo*: Put it on the slate!

crémaillère *n.f.* *Pendre la crémaillère*: To give a house-warming party.

crème *n.m.* *Un crème* (abbr. *un café crème*): A cup of white coffee.

crème *n.f.* *La crème* **1** (of person): The very best. *C'est la crème des mecs!* He's the nicest guy you could possibly imagine. *C'est la crème des cons*: He's an 'A-grade' pillock. **2** 'The toffs', 'the upper crust', the upper classes. *Il aime voyager avec la crème*: He likes travelling in

good company. **3** 'The pick of', the very best. *On lui donne toujours la crème*: He always gets first pick. **4** Easy job, easy task. *C'est pas de la crème*: It's not all milk and honey – It's not a bed of roses. *Si tu t'imagines que c'est de la crème, ce boulot!* You're welcome to that job, it's no cushy number!

crémerie *n.f.* **1** The 'local', one's local pub or bar. **2** *Changer de crémerie*: To change job. (The expression can sometimes merely mean to change one's surroundings.)

crêpage *n.m.* *Crêpage de chignon*: 'Argey-bargey', violent to-do. (The row, as the expression suggests, is usually between women.)

crêpe *n.f.* **1** Flat cap (also: *gapette*). **2** 'Nincompoop', 'burk', fool. *C'est le roi des crêpes!* He's really as daft as a brush. **3** *Faire la crêpe* (of motor car): To 'flip over', to end up on its roof.

crêper *v.trans.reflex.* *Se crêper le chignon* (of women): To have a 'ding-dong set-to', to have a vociferous row.

crépi *n.m.* (*joc.*): Heavy make-up (the kind that seems to have been applied with a trowel).

cresson *n.m.* **1** 'Thatch', hair. *N'avoir plus de cresson sur la cafetière*: To be as bald as a coot. **2** *Le cresson*: 'The short-and-curly', pubic hair (also: *le paillasson*). **3** *Du cresson*: 'Loot', 'brass', money (perhaps because of the colour, as in the American 'greenbacks'). **4** *C'est idem au cresson*: It's six of one, half a dozen of the other.

cressonnière *n.f.* The pubis, the pubic region (male or female).

crétin *n.m.* 'Twit', imbecile. *Quelle bande de crétins!* What a shower!

crétiniser *v.trans.* To brainwash with stuff and nonsense.

creuser *v.intrans.* *Ça creuse*: It makes you hungry. *Une journée au bord de la mer, ça creuse*: The sea air certainly builds up your appetite.

creuser *v.pronom.* *Se creuser le citron* (also: *la cervelle* or *la tête*): To 'rack one's brains', to 'put one's thinking cap on', to think hard (about a problem).

creux *n.m.* *Avoir un creux*: **a** To feel famished, to feel very hungry. **b** To 'have a rough patch', to have a bad spell. **c** To have a lull, to have a quiet spell. **d** To 'have a blank', to have a mental lapse, to have forgotten all about something.

crevaison *n.f.* Back-breaking job. *Faire les marchés, quelle crevaison!* Carting fruit and veg for market-traders is enough to drive you into the ground!

crevant *adj.* **1** 'Gruelling', back-breaking, tiring. **2** 'Side-splitting', hilarious. *Il lui est arrivé un truc crevant!* You'll laugh yourself silly when you hear what's happened to him!

crevard *n.m.* **1** 'Goner', near-moribund person. *Avoir une gueule de crevard:* To look like death warmed up. **2** Starveling, emaciated person. **3** Glutton, gluttonous character. *Au restau, quel crevard!* It costs a packet taking him out for a meal! **4** 'Squanderer', spendthrift character.

crève *n.f.* *(joc.):* Bad bout of flu. *Viens pas trop près, j'ai la crève!* Keep away, I've got a stinker of a cold!

crevé *adj.* 'Knackered', 'buggered', exhausted.

crève-la-faim *n.m.* **1** Famished person, starveling. **2** *(joc.):* 'Greedy guts', glutton.

crever *v.trans.* **1** To 'drive someone into the ground', to wear someone out. *Il me crève avec toutes ses jérémiades:* His constant moaning drives me round the bend. **2** *Crever la paillasse à quelqu'un:* To 'do someone in', to commit murder. **3** *Ça crève les yeux:* It's staring you in the face – It's blatantly obvious.

crever *v.intrans.* **1** (Cycling, motoring): To get a puncture. **2** To 'snuff it', to 'croak', to die. **3** *Crever de faim:* To starve, to be terribly hungry. **4** *Crever la faim* (also: *la crever*): To lead a life of poverty. *Depuis que son vieux est mort, elle la crève:* Since her old man died, she's not had two ha'pennies to rub together. **5** *Tu peux toujours crever!* To hell with you! *Qu'il crève!* Sod him! **6** *Marche ou crève!* It's a case of 'do-or-die'. (This expression originally referred to the French Foreign Legion and its near-inhuman training methods.) **7** *Bouffer à en crever:* To 'stuff one's face', to eat immoderately. **8** *Crever de rire:* To split one's sides with laughter.

crever *v.trans.reflex.* *Se crever de boulot:* To 'work oneself into an early grave', to kill oneself with work.

crevette *n.f.* (also: *môme crevette*): 'Pint-size bird', petite woman.

cri *n.m.* **1** *C'est le dernier cri* (also: *c'est du dernier cri*): It's the in-thing – It's the very latest fashion. **2** *Pousser les hauts cris:* To 'make a song-and-dance' about something, to express one's dissatisfaction vociferously. **3** *(abbr. crime):* *C'est du cri que* . . . It's a crying shame that . . . *C'est du cri de la voir sortir avec un zigoto pareil:* It's really not on, her going out with such an awful bloke!

criard *n.m.* **1** 'Brat', noisy infant. **2** 'Squeeze-box', accordion (also: *piano à bretelles*).

criaver *v.trans. & intrans.* To 'nosh', to eat heartily.

cric *n.m.* **1** Car jack. **2** *(joc.):* 'Pick-me-up', glass of strong alcohol. *Le matin avec le caoua il lui faut souvent un coup de cric:* He can't start the day without a coup of brandy laced with coffee!

cricri *n.m.* **1** Cricket, insect of the orthopterous family. **2** Nickname for *Christian, Christiane* or *Christine.* **3** 'Skinny lizzy', emaciated woman. **4** 'Prick', 'cock', penis.

crier *v.intrans.* *Crier aux petits pois:* To complain loudly and bitterly about something.

crignole *n.f.* 'Shoe-leather', cheap and tough cut of meat (also: *barbaque*).

crime *n.m. Ce n'est pas un crime!* There's no harm in that!

crin *n.m.* **1** *Etre à crin:* To be in a foul mood, to be in a lousy temper (also: *être à cran*). **2** *Ce n'est pas un poil qu'il a dans la main, c'est un crin!* He's the archetypal lazy git! (On the assumption that hair grows where there is no friction, it is said of a lazy person: *'Il a un poil dans la main'.* In the jocular mood to talk of a *crin* is the ultimate insult.)

crincrin *n.m.* 'Squeak-box', fiddle, violin. (The commonest usage is *racler le crincrin*.)

criquer *v.pronom.* To 'scram', to 'scarper', to run away.

criquet *n.m.* **1** 'Titch', 'shrimp', pint-size man. **2** Cigarette lighter.

crise *n.f.* **1** *(abbr. crise de fou rire):* Uncontrollable laughter. *Quand il nous a sorti son histoire, ça a été la crise:* He had us rolling in the aisles when he told us what had happened. **2** *Piquer une crise:* To 'fly off the handle', to 'blow one's top', to fly into a temper.

crispant *adj.* (of person): 'Aggravating', exasperating. *Dieu, qu'il est crispant quand il s'y met!* He'd drive a saint to desperation, he would!

crisper *v.trans.* To 'drive someone up the wall', to exasperate someone.

crobar *n.m.* *(corr. croquis):* Sketch, drawing.

crobe *n.m.* *(joc. corr. microbe):* 'Titch', pint-size person.

crocher *v.trans.* *Crocher une serrure:* To pick a lock.

crocher *v.trans.reflex.* To 'scrap', to fight with someone.

croches *n.f.pl.* 'Mitts', (greedy) hands. *Bas les croches!* Keep your thieving hands off!

crochet *n.m.* **1** *Un crochet du droit* (Boxing): A right-hook. **2** *Crochet radiophonique:* Radio talent show. **3** *(pl.):* 'Gnashers', 'choppers', teeth. **4** *Vivre aux crochets de:* To 'sponge', to live off. *Ça fait vingt ans qu'il vit aux crochets de l'Etat:* He's been living off the State these last twenty years. **5** *Avoir le regard en crochets de bottine:* To have an inquisitive look.

crocheter *v.trans. Crocheter une serrure*: To pick a lock.

crochu *adj.* **1** *Avoir des atomes crochus* (of relationship): To 'click' instinctively, to become friends straight away. (It was claimed by scientists in the early 60s that certain atoms linked more readily than others as if they had tiny hooks ready to lock on together.) **2** *Avoir les doigts crochus*: To be light-fingered. *'y en a marre de ses doigts crochus!* I don't want to see those thieving mitts of his again!

croco *n.m. Un sac en croco*: A crocodile-skin bag.

crocs *n.m.pl.* 'Gnashers', 'choppers', teeth. *Avoir les crocs*: To be famished, starving, to be very hungry.

croire *v.trans. & intrans.* **1** *Croire que c'est arrivé*: To think one has 'made it', to believe one has succeeded (when, in fact, it might not quite be the case). **2** *Croire encore au Père Noël*: To be pathetically naïve in one's beliefs. (Ironic by its very nature, the expression is always used in a derogatory statement.) **3** *J'aime mieux croire que d'y aller voir!* I'll take your word for it! – I don't really feel like checking up on this! **4** *Un peu que je te crois!* You bet! – Rather! – I should jolly well think so too! **5** *Crois-tu!* And how! *Quel temps dégueulasse, crois-tu!* It's bloody awful weather, isn't it?! (The expressions *crois-tu!, croyez-vous hein?!* are more typically Belgian than French.)

croire *v.trans.reflex.* To be as conceited as hell. *Un peu qu'il se croit!* He really thinks he's the bee's knees!

croisière *n.f.* **1** *Etre parti en croisière (iron.)*: To have done 'a moonlight flit', to have absconded from one's business responsibilities. **2** *Etre en pleine croisière*: To be on a 'mental trip', to be lost in thought.

croître *v.intrans. Ça ne fait que croître et embellir (iron.)*: It never rains but it pours! – Things are going from bad to worse!

croix *n.f.* **1** 'Burk', 'mutt-head', fool. **2** Illiterate person (i.e. one who signs his name with a cross). **3** (Prostitutes' slang): Awkward customer. **4** (Gangland slang): Outsider, one who is not part of the *milieu*. **5** 'Tricky customer', awkward person. *C'est une vraie croix!* He's a right pain in the neck! **6** *C'est la croix et la bannière*: It's a terrible drag – It's darned awkward. **7** *Mettre une croix dessus*: To 'say goodbye to something', to give something up for lost. **8** *Décrocher la croix de bois*: To get 'bumped off', killed in the war. **9** *Croix de bois, croix de fer (si je mens je vais en enfer)*: Cross my heart and hope to die! (if what I say is a lie). **10** *La croix des vaches*: Punishment inflicted by old-time pimps on recalcitrant prostitutes: deep facial cuts in the shape of a cross, made to fester and leave indelible scars. **11** *Le trafic des croix*: Illegal trade of the Swiss twenty-franc gold coin known popularly as *une croix*.

crompir *n.f.* 'Spud', potato.

cronir *v.trans.* To 'bump off', to kill (also: *buter*).

cronir *v.intrans.* To 'croak', to 'snuff it', to die. *'y a belle lurette qu'ils sont cronis*: They snuffed it yonks ago.

croquant *n.m. (pej.)*: **1** 'Clod-hopper', country bumpkin, peasant. **2** 'Pillock', 'boor', crude and ignorant character.

croquantes *n.f.pl.* 'Choppers', 'gnashers', teeth. *S'aiguiser les croquantes*: To look forward to a good tuck-in.

croque *n.f.* 'Grub', 'nosh', food. *A la croque!* Grub's up! – Dinner's ready!

croque-monsieur *n.m.* Toasted cheese and ham sandwich, a sort of double Welsh rarebit.

croque-mort *n.m.* 'Bone-merchant', undertaker. *Etre bon pour le croque-mort*: To be on the undertaker's waiting-list, to be at death's door.

croquenots *n.m.pl. (pej.)*: 'Clodhoppers', 'beetle-crushers', heavy shoes.

croquer *v.trans.* **1** To 'nosh', to eat. *On n'a rien à croquer!* The cupboard's bare! **2** *Croquer un héritage*: To eat one's way through a legacy, to squander it. **3** *En croquer*: **a** To 'get a share of the action', to be in on something. **b** To 'get a good eyeful', to ogle. **4** *En croquer pour quelqu'un*: To 'have a crush on someone', to be infatuated. **5** *Se faire croquer*: To get 'nicked', 'collared', to be arrested.

croqueuses *n.f.pl.* 'Choppers', 'gnashers', teeth.

croquignole *n.f.* **1** 'Biff', blow, slap in the face. **2** *(pl.)*: 'Bollocks', 'balls', testicles.

croquignole *adj.* **1** Dainty, small and delicate. **2** Ridiculous in a rather pathetic way. *Elle portait un chapeau tout ce qu'il y a de croquignole!* That hat she wore was ever so ridiculous!

crosse *n.f.* **1** *Se mettre en crosse*: To 'get into a huff', to get cross. **2** *Chercher des crosses à quelqu'un*: To deliberately pick a quarrel with someone. *Prendre les crosses de quelqu'un*: To 'stick up for someone', to stand by someone (in a quarrel). **3** *Autant pour les crosses!* It's back to square one! – We'll have to start all over again!

crosser *v.trans. & intrans.* **1** To 'pick quarrels', to be looking for an argument. *A crosser tout le monde, il va récolter de la gelée de coing!* Any more of this getting across people and he'll get his face pushed in! **2** To swagger, to show off. *Avec son nouveau costar, un peu qu'il crosse!* That new suit of his, he doesn't wear it, he parades it!

crosseur *n.m.* 'Aggromaniac', person always eager to pick a quarrel.

crosson *n.m.* 'Swank', show-off.

crottaleux *n.m. (pej.)*: 'Down-and-outer', one who has been left on the scrap-heap of life.

crotte *n.f.* **1** *(interj.)*: Blast! – Drat! (*Crotte* is a milder and more acceptable expletive than *merde!*) **2** *C'est de la crotte de bique*: It's a load of rubbish – It's worthless.

crouille *n.m.* North African Arab. (This is a highly racist and derogatory appellation. Also: *crouillat.*)

croulant *n.m. (joc.)*: Middle-aged person, one who in the eyes of the younger generation is 'past it'. (This contemptuous teenagers' term had its heyday in the late 50s and 60s.)

croum *n.m.* (also: *croume*): 'Tick', credit. *Depuis qu'il a perdu sa place, on ne lui donne plus de croum nulle part*: Since he got the sack, no-one's willing to put anything on the slate for him.

crouni *n.m.* 'Stiff', dead person. *Le boulevard des crounis*: The 'bone-yard', the cemetery.

crounir *v.trans.* To 'bump off', to kill.

crounir *v.intrans.* To 'croak', to 'snuff it', to die.

croupanche *n.m. & f.* Croupier in casino or gaming-club.

croupe *n.f.* 'Bum', buttocks, behind. *Il lui flatta la croupe*: He gave her a friendly pat on the backside. (The word is not necessarily sexist and can sometimes refer to an effeminate homosexual. *Tortiller de la croupe*: To walk with a waddle.)

croupière *n.f.* *Tailler des croupières à quelqu'un*: To make life difficult for someone.

croupion *n.m.* **1** 'Parson's nose', fatty extreme end-portion of the rump of a cooked fowl. **2** *Tirer le croupion*: To get the least attractive lot in a share-out. **3** 'Bum', behind.

croupionner *v.intrans.* To walk with a waddle.

croustance *n.f.* 'Grub', 'nosh', food. *Question croustance, il a un sacré coup de fourchette!* When it comes to stuffing his face, he can certainly shovel it in!

croustillant *adj.* *Histoire croustillante*: Titillating tale (the kind that makes gossip-mongers' mouths water).

croustille *n.f.* *La croustille*: 'Grub', food. *La croustille chez eux, c'est plutôt dégueu!* The stuff they have to eat is pretty awful!

croustiller *v.intrans.* To 'nosh', to eat.

croûte *n.f.* **1** 'Grub', 'eats', food. *La croûte ne valait pas cher*: The grub wasn't up to much. *Casser la croûte*: To have a bite to eat, to have a snack. **2** *Gagner sa croûte*: To 'bring home the bacon', to earn a living. **3** 'Old dodderer', old fogey. **4** 'Daub', inferior painting. *Il s'imagine que ses croûtes valent une fortune*: He's convinced those canvases of his are worth a bomb. **5** *Faire croûte (joc.)*: To be a 'wallflower', to sit

through a whole ball without being invited to dance.

croûter *v.trans. & intrans.* To 'nosh', to eat. *'y a pas lerche à croûter!* There's not much grub in the house!

croûton *n.m.* **1** (Term of endearment): 'Kiddie', small child. *Alors, mon croûton, ça va?!* How's my poppet, then?! **2** *Vieux croûton*: 'Old fogey', old dodderer.

croûtonner *v.pronom.* **1** To get 'browned off', to get 'cheesed off', to suffer the pangs of boredom. **2** To become neurotic through solitude. *Il se croûtonnait à mort dans sa cellotte*: In solitary, he was slowly going out of his mind.

cru *n.m.* *Elle est de mon cru, celle-là!* That's my kind of humour!

cru *adj.* **1** *Avaler quelque chose tout cru*: To 'fall for something hook, line and sinker', to react in a very gullible way. **2** *Manger quelqu'un tout cru (fig.)*: To dispose of someone summarily, to cut someone down to size in an argument.

cruche *n.f.* 'Mutt', 'duffer', fool.

cruche *adj.* 'Thick', stupid. *Je ne suis pas si cruche que ça!* I'm not as green as I'm cabbage-looking!

cube *n.m.* **1** Third-year student in what the French call *'Les Grandes Ecoles'*. (The *Grandes Ecoles* strive to produce, each in its own field, the academic élite of France. The intellectual level is deemed to be superior to that of the universities.) **2** *Une gros cube*: Powerful motorcycle (over 500 c.c.).

cuber *v.intrans.* To 'cost a bomb', to be very expensive. *Des vacances sur la Côte en août, ça peut drôlement cuber!* August on the Riviera can set you back a tidy penny!

cucu *n.m.* (Child language): 'Botty', 'behind', bottom.

cucul *adj.inv.* **1** 'Ninnyish', naïvely stupid. **2** 'Wet', 'spunkless', lacking drive.

cueille *n.f.* 'Dragnet', police raid.

cueillir *v.trans.* **1** To 'pick someone up', to collect someone. *Bon, je te cueille sur le coup des six heures!* O.K. then, I'll call for you at six on the dot! **2** *(pol.)*: To 'nab', to 'collar', to arrest. *On l'a cueilli au saut du lit*: We arrested him at the crack of dawn. **3** *Où t'as cueilli ça?!* Who the hell told you that?! – Where did you pick up that bit of information?!

cuillère *n.f.* **1** 'Mitt', 'paw', hand. *Serrer la cuillère à quelqu'un*: To shake someone's hand. **2** *En trois coups de cuillère à pot*: In two shakes – In a jiffy – Very quickly. **3** *Ne pas y aller avec le dos de la cuillère (iron.)*: **a** To 'lay it on thick', to exaggerate. **b** To spare no-one's feelings, to act ruthlessly. **4** *Etre à ramasser à la petite cuillère*: To be 'knackered', 'jiggered', to be exhausted. **5** *Etre aussi argenté qu'une cuillère de bois (joc.)*: To be 'down on one's uppers', to be 'skint', to be penniless.

cuir *n.m.* **1** Football. *Botter le cuir en touche*: To kick the ball out of play. **2** 'Hide', skin. *Se racler le cuir*: To shave. *Se rôtir le cuir*: To soak up the sun, to sunbathe. *Tanner le cuir à quelqu'un*: To 'knock someone black and blue', to give someone a thrashing. **3** *Faire des cuirs*: To make wrong liaisons or as the French say *'des liaisons mal-t-à-propos'*.

cuirassé *adj.* **1** 'Thick-skinned', impervious to insults. *Je suis cuirassé moi, il faut beaucoup pour me vexer!* It takes a lot to offend me! **2** 'Shielded', unassailable in one's finances. **3** 'Pissed', 'stoned', blind-drunk.

cuire *v.trans. & intrans.* **1** *Etre dur à cuire* (of person): To be 'a tough nut to crack', to be extremely resistant to pressures and tribulations. **2** *Il va vous en cuire!* You'll live to regret it! – You'll be sorry for it!

cuisinage *n.m.* **1** 'Book-cooking', falsifying of accounts. **2** 'Third-degree grilling', tough police interrogation.

cuisine *n.f.* **1** Underhand scheming. *Cuisine électorale*: 'Behind-the-scenes' electioneering. **2** Falsifying of accounts. *Avant de tout passer au fisc, il y a pas mal de cuisine*: The books get well laundered before the taxman sees them. **3** *(pl.)*: Tricks of the trade (those little 'ways and means' that many professions jealously guard). **4** *Pas de cuisine intérieure! (joc.)*: Stop that chattering! – I want some silence!

cuisiner *v.trans.* **1** To 'engineer' something, to scheme. *Il a cuisiné une vacherie du tonnerre!* That dirty trick he cooked up was right nasty! **2** To 'work a fiddle', to falsify accounts. *C'est un as pour cuisiner les notes de frais*: The way he fiddles the old expense account is nobody's business! **3** To 'grill' a suspect, to subject an arrested person to tough interrogation.

cuisse *n.f.* **1** *Avoir la cuisse légère*: To be randy, to be highly-sexed. (The expression refers more often to women than to men.) **2** *Aller aux cuisses*: To 'go and have a bang', to have intercourse.

cuistance *n.f.* **1** *La cuistance*: The 'cookhouse', the kitchen. **2** Cookery, cooking. *Il n'est vraiment pas doué pour la cuistance*: He's not up to much with the old pots and pans. **3** 'Grub', 'eats', food. *Et la cuistance, elle est bonne ici?* Is the nosh up to much here?

cuistot *n.m.* (also: *cuisteau*): 'Gravy-wrecker', cook. *Le cuistot ne vaut pas lerche ici*: You could hardly call him a Chef! (The word originally belonged exclusively to the language of the military and gains jocularity when used in everyday life.)

cuit *adj.* **1** 'Pissed', 'sloshed', drunk. *Il est cuit, archi-cuit!* He's well and truly pickled! (also: *blindé*). **2** *C'est cuit! (fig.)*: The chips are down! – It's all over! **3** *C'est du tout cuit!* It's a dead cert! – It's a foregone conclusion!

cuitarès *adj. Etre cuitarès*: **a** To be 'done for', to have well and truly lost. **b** To have 'blown everything', to be bankrupt.

cuite *n.f.* Drunken stupor. *Tenir une sacrée cuite*: To be 'pissed out of one's mind', to be blind drunk.

cuiter *v.trans.reflex.* To get 'pissed', 'sozzled', to get drunk. *Il se cuite à longueur de journée!* He's never off the bottle!

cujus *n.m. (Slightly pej.)*: 'Geezer', 'bloke', person. *Envoyez le cujus!* Send in that bloke! *V'là le cujus dont je vous parlais*: Here's the chappie I was telling you about.

cul *n.m.* **1** 'Bum', 'backside', behind. **2** *Aller au cul*: To 'screw', to fuck, to have intercourse. **3** *La presse du cul*: Dirty books and mags, pornographic literature. **4** *En avoir plein le cul de quelque chose*: To be fed up to the back teeth with something. **5** *L'avoir dans le cul*: To have 'been had', 'conned', to have been diddled. *Et comme de bien entendu, c'est moi qui l'ai dans le cul!* It's muggins again what carries the can! **6** *Avoir du poil au cul*: To be 'gutsy', 'plucky', to be as brave as they come. **7** *Avoir le cul bordé de nouilles (joc.)*: To have the luck of the devil. (An important subsidiary meaning of *cul* is luck as in *ne pas manquer de cul*, *avoir un cul du tonnerre*, etc.). **8** *Mon cul! (iron.)*: You must be joking! –You don't think I'm that stupid, do you?! **9** *Se crever* (also: *se décarcasser*) *le cul*: To 'sweat one's guts out', to work one's fingers to the bone. **10** *Péter plus haut que son cul (joc.)*: To be snooty, to have ideas above one's station. **11** *Avoir une gueule comme un cul de singe*: To have 'a face like the back of a bus', to be rather ugly. **12** *Faire la bouche en cul de poule*: To pout, to purse one's lips in a demure manner. **13** *Etre bas du cul (joc.)*: To be something of a short-arse, to be rather small in stature. **14** *C'est à se taper le cul par terre! (joc.)*: It's side-splitting! –It's hilarious! **15** *Tirer au cul*: To 'dodge graft', to avoid work (usually by claiming ill-health). **16** *Faire cul sec*: To down a drink in one go. (The image is similar to that in the English 'Bottoms up!')

cul-béni *n.m.* 'Creeping Jesus', over-zealous church-goer. (This derogatory appellation has a feminine equivalent in *grenouille de bénitier*.)

culbutant *n.m.* 'Strides', 'trews', trousers. *Avoir le culbutant en perdition (joc.)*: To have one's trousers at half-mast (also: *culbute n.m.*).

culbute *n.f.* **1** *La culbute*: Fucking, 'screwing', intercourse. *Elle est assez portée sur la culbute*: She's what you'd call a good-time girl! **2** *Faire la culbute*: **a** To double one's money (in a trade deal or at gambling). **b** To 'come a cropper', to take a tumble (both in a figurative and literal context; it is worth noting how, without the ingredient of irony, this expression can have such opposing meanings).

culbuté *adj.* **1** 'Pissed', 'sozzled', drunk. **2** *Bien culbuté* (of person): Physically well-proportioned.

culbutée *n.f.* 'Bike', motorbike (called thus in French because it has overhead valves).

culbuter *v.trans.* **1** To 'screw', to fuck, to have intercourse with. **2** To 'take someone for a ride', to 'diddle', to con someone. *Elle l'a drôlement culbuté*: He fell for her patter hook, line and sinker.

culbuter *v.intrans.* **1** To double one's money (at gambling or in a trade transaction). **2** To 'come a cropper', to 'come unstuck', to suffer a setback.

culbuteur *n.m.* 'Randy so-and-so', over-sexed man.

cul-de-plomb *n.m.* **1** 'Pen-pusher', sedentary office-worker (also: *rond-de-cuir*). **2** Cobbler, shoe-repairer. **3** Pharmacist's assistant.

culment *adv.* *Tout culment*: Just like that! – Without giving it any further thought.

culot *n.m.* **1** 'Sauce', 'nerve', cheek. *Avoir un culot monstre*: To be as bold as brass. **2** 'Junior', last in line of a string of children in a family.

culotte *n.f.* **1** *Tenir une sacrée culotte*: To be 'pissed to the eyeballs', to be blind drunk. **2** *Ramasser une culotte*: To lose heavily at gambling. *Il a ramassé une de ces culottes au pok'*: He lost his shirt at poker. **3** *Se moquer de quelque chose comme de sa première culotte*: To 'not care two hoots about something', to feel totally indifferent. **4** *Une vieille culotte de peau (mil.)*: A strict disciplinarian of the old school. **5** *Culotte de gendarme*: Small patch of blue sky (literally as in English 'Enough to mend a Dutchman's breeches'). **6** *Un morceau dans la culotte*: A prime cut of beef from the rump. (This expression in French 'gay' circles can have a totally different meaning.)

culotté *adj.* **1** 'Spunky', 'game', brave. *Il est culotté comme pas un*: He's as gutsy as they come. **2** 'Cocky', 'cheeky', impudent. *Vous êtes drôlement culotté, vous!* You've got a bloody nerve!

culotter *v.trans.* To swot (for an exam). *Il est en train de culotter ses math*: He's brushing up on his maths.

culotter *v.pronom.* To get 'tanked-up', to get drunk.

culottman *adj.inv.* 'Cocky', 'cheeky', impudent.

cul-terreux *n.m.* *(pej.)*: 'Hayseed', country bumpkin, peasant.

culture *n.f.* *C'est dur, la culture! (joc. & iron.)*: Life is no doddle! (The expression can have a secondary meaning when referring to cultural matters and is used to highlight one's own or someone else's ignorance.)

cumulard *n.m.* 'Moonlighter', person with an 'after-hours' job.

cunuter *v.trans.* To 'tot up', to add up, to count.

curé *n.m.* *Bouffer du curé*: To be fiercely anti-clerical.

cure-dent *n.m.* **1** 'Shiv', blade, knife. **2** *Arriver en cure-dent*: **a** To 'gate-crash' a dinner-party, to come along uninvited. **b** To arrive when the meal is practically over.

cureton *n.m.* *(corr. curé)*: 'Padre', parish priest.

curieux *n.m.* Examining magistrate. (The *juge d'instruction* is a very special magistrate whose task it is to look into possible court cases and to decide whether to pursue the matter. Having taken that decision, he will, with the help of the police and the defence, 'instruct' a case he will not be judging.)

cuti *n.f.* *(abbr. cuti-réaction)*: Skin-test for T.B. The expression *virer sa cuti*: to show a positive reaction in the above-mentioned test, has secondary colloquial meanings: **a** To reach puberty (of man). **b** To 'throw off the fetters', to start living life to the full. **c** To 'turn pouf', to become a homosexual.

cuver *v.trans.* *Cuver une cuite*: To 'sleep it off', to be in a somnolent stupor after a bout of heavy drinking.

cyclard *n.m.* 'Bikie', cyclist. *Piste pour cyclards*: Bike-lane. (Protected lane between pavement and roadway.)

cyclo *n.m.* **1** Bike, bicycle. **2** *(abbr. cyclomoteur)*: 'Moped', light-weight motorized two-wheeler whose engine capacity does not exceed 50 c.c.; a *vélomoteur*, on the other hand, has an engine capacity of more than 50 c.c. but less than 125 c.c.

cyclopage *n.m.* *(sch.)*: 'Bout of the fisticuffs', 'dust-up', brawl.

cyclope *n.m.* 'Prick', 'cock', penis. *Faire chialer* (also: *faire pleurer*) *le cyclope*: To 'juice off', to ejaculate.

cygne *n.m.* *Elle nous a fait le coup du petit cygne*: She turned out not to be the ugly duckling after all!

cylindrée *n.f.* *Grosse cylindrée*: Powerful motorbike (one with a large engine capacity).

cynoque *n.m.* 'Crank', 'nut-case', mad person.

cynoque *adj*. 'Potty', 'bonkers', mad. *T'es complètement cynoque, non?!* You crazy in the head?!

Cyrard *n.m.* Cadet training at the Saint-Cyr Military Academy.

Cythère *Proper name. Embarquement pour Cythère*: Drug addict's 'trip', state of hallucinatory intoxication. (The expression derives from the title of the famous Watteau painting.)

D

D *n.m. Système D. (abbr. système débrouille/système démerde)*: A typically French 'by hook or by crook' way of solving tricky problems. The *Système D.* can apply to fiddly little problems like preventing the steaming-up of a bathroom mirror by wiping it with soapy water, or to ways of conning 'the System'.

dab *n.m.* (also: *dabe*): **1** 'Pop', dad, father. **2** *(pl.)*: 'The old folk' (Mum and Dad). **3** 'The guv'nor', the boss. *Fais gaffe, le dab se méfie de tout le monde*: Watch out, mate, the gaffer doesn't trust a soul!

Dabe *Proper name. Le Dabe*: God Almighty, God the Father. *J'aime pas ceux qui cherchent du suif au Dabe*: I've no time for those who go knocking religion (also: *Dabuche*).

dabe *n.f. Ma dabe*: Mum, mother (also: *dabesse*).

dac *interj.* Right on! – O.K.! – Agreed! (also: *d'acc!*).

dache *A dache (adv.exp.)*: God knows where! –Far away. *Vaut mieux lui téléphoner, il habite à dache*: You'd better give him a ring, he lives miles away. *Envoyer quelqu'un à* (also: *chez*) *dache*: To 'send someone packing', to tell someone to go to hell.

dada *n.m.* **1** (Child language): 'Gee-gee', horse. **2** (Racing slang) *Les dadas*: The horses. *Il a mis toute sa paie sur des dadas à la manque*: He put his whole pay on a string of crummy nags. **3** 'Hobby-horse', pet subject. **4** *Faire dada*: To 'get a leg-over', to have sex.

dadais *n.m.* 'Goof', 'gawk', clumsy idiot. (The word *dadais* is seldom found on its own. The expression *grand dadais* stereotypes the tall, clumsy, accident-prone fool.)

daim *n.m. Vieux daim*: Old beau, ageing male desperately trying to keep his looks.

dalle *n.f.* **1** 'Gullet', throat. *Se rincer la dalle*: To 'wet one's whistle', to have a drink. *Avoir la dalle en pente*: To be 'something of a boozer', to be a tippler. **2** 'Gob', mouth (in the context of food only, as in *crever la dalle*: to go hungry).

dalle *Que dalle (adv.exp.)*: 'Fuck-all', 'sweet Fanny Adams', nothing at all. *N'y entraver que dalle*: To understand bugger-all. *Foutre que dalle*: To 'do fuck-all', to laze about. *Une grosse bagnole comme ça ne vaut que dalle!* Big cars like that are just not worth the money!

dame *n.f.* **1** *Faire la dame*: To 'queen it', to put on airs and graces. **2** *Vot' dame*: 'Your missus', your wife. *Et comment va vot' dame?* And how's your good lady wife? (The use of this expression in colloquial French betrays lack of education. Pierre Daninos in SNOBISSIMO highlights this point when his sergeant, rebuffing him for saying '*Comment va votre femme*', tells him '*Vous ne pourriez pas dire vot' dame comme tout le monde?!*) **3** *Entrer en dame avec quelqu'un*: To 'chat up', to strike up a conversation with someone. **4** *Aller à dame*: **a** To 'hit the deck', to fall down. **b** To 'come a cropper', to suffer a setback. **5** *Dame!* You bet! – And how! – Certainly!

dame-jeanne *n.f.* Jumbo-sized jug holding over six litres.

dame-pipi *n.f.* 'Bog-keeper', lavatory attendant. *C'était une dame-pipi qui ne se prenait pas pour de la merde!* She certainly had ideas above her station!

damer *v.intrans. & trans.* **1** To 'hit the deck', to fall down (also: *aller à dame*). **2** *Damer le pion à quelqu'un*: To outwit someone.

damner *v.trans. Faire damner quelqu'un*: To 'drive someone up the wall', to drive someone crazy. *Ils me feront damner ces gosses-là!* Those kids'll drive me potty!

danger *n.m.* **1** *'y a pas de danger! (iron.)*: Not on your nelly! – Not bloody likely! *Lui prêter du fric? 'y a pas de danger!* What, me lend him money?! You must be joking! **2** *Danger public*: 'Roadhog', dangerous driver.

danse *n.f.* **1** *Entrer dans la danse*: To join in (activity). **2** *Mener la danse*: To 'lead the way', to direct operations. **3** Thrashing, beating-up. *Filer une danse à quelqu'un*: To beat someone black-and-blue. *Ramasser une danse*: To get thrashed good and proper.

danser *v.trans. La danser*: To get thrashed, to be beaten black-and-blue.

danser *v.intrans. Il ne sait pas sur quel pied danser*: He doesn't know if he's coming or going – The pace of life is too hectic for him.

dard *n.m.* 'Prick', 'cock', penis. *Avoir du dard*: To be a randy so-and-so. *Avoir le dard au garde-à-vous*: To 'have the big stick', to have an erection.

dare-dare *adv.exp.* 'Like a shot', in next to no time. *Nettoyez-moi ça dare-dare*: Get this cleaned now, if not sooner!

dargeot *n.m.* 'Arse', 'bum', behind. *Je lui ai filé des coups de pompe dans le dargeot*: I kicked him up the jacksey (also: *dargif*).

daron *n.m.* **1** *Mon daron*: **a** My Dad, my father. **b** 'My old man', my husband. **2** *Mes darons*: 'The old folk', my Mum and Dad. **3** *Le daron*: 'The gaffer', 'the guv'nor', the boss. **4** *Le Vénéré Daron*: God Almighty, God the Father.

daronne *n.f. Ma daronne*: Mum, my mother.

darrac *n.m.* 'Irish screwdriver', hammer.

datte *n.f.* **1** *Ne pas en foutre une datte*: To 'do fuck-all', to sit back and do nothing. **2** *Des dattes!* Not bloody likely! – Not on your nelly! – Certainly not! *Partir en vacances avec elle? Des dattes!* What, take her on holiday with me? You must be joking! (also: *Des clous!*).

daube *n.f.* (*pej.*): **1** 'Potion', dubious medicine. **2** 'Clap', gonorrhoea (originally the word referred exclusively to syphilis).

daubé *adj.* **1** (of foodstuffs): 'Gone-off', unfit for human consumption. **2** Infected with V.D. **3** *C'est pas daubé!* (*iron.*): It's bloody awful!

dauber *v.trans.* **1** To infect with V.D. **2** To rile, to jeer at. **3** To spread malicious gossip about someone.

dauffer *v.trans.* **1** To sodomize, to commit buggery. **2** To 'con', to 'diddle', to swindle. *On s'est drôlement fait dauffer!* We was done!

daufier *n.m.* Ponce, pimp, procurer.

daufière *n.f.* 'Prozzy', prostitute.

dauphin *n.m.* **1** 'Jemmy', crowbar. **2** Ponce, pimp. **3** 'Heavy', muscleman.

Dauphine *Proper name.* Small family saloon car manufactured by Renault in the 50s and 60s.

dé *n.m.* **1** *Le dé à coudre*: The arse-hole, the anal sphincter. *Prendre du dé*: To be a 'pouf', to be a passive homosexual. **2** *Prendre les dés*: To speak up, to talk (and express a point of view forcefully). **3** *Passer les dés*: To 'throw in the sponge', to give in.

débâcher *v.intrans.* (Circus people's slang): To pack up in order to move on (literally to pack up the tarpaulin).

débâcher *v.trans.reflex.* To get up, to get out of bed (also: *sortir des torchons*).

débâcler *v.intrans.* To open a door. *Il a débâclé si vite qu'il les a surpris comme qui dirait 'au flagrant du lit'*: They were still in bed when he burst through the door.

débagouler *v.intrans.* **1** To 'throw up', to 'puke', to vomit. **2** To 'spout on and on', to 'prattle', to talk endlessly.

déballage *n.m.* **1** Airing of differences, venting of feelings. **2** Shedding of clothes. (The word refers exclusively to women and is, more often than not, far from complimentary. The implication here is that the charms revealed are not a pretty sight.)

déballé *adj.* **1** Anxious, worried. **2** Disheartened.

déballer *v.trans. & intrans.* **1** To 'get something off one's chest', to say what one has to say. *Allez, déballe!* Come on, out with it! *Il m'a déballé une histoire à dormir debout*: He came out with a really cock-and-bull story. **2** *Déballer ses outils*: **a** To own up, to confess something. **b** To 'flash', to expose oneself. **3** *Déballer le jars*: To talk argot. **4** *Avoir des nichons qui déballent*: To have 'jelly-boobs', to have ample and not very firm breasts.

déballonné *n.m.* 'Funk', quitter. *Quel déballonné!* What a Cowardy Custard!

déballonner *v.pronom.* **1** To 'get cold feet', to funk, to give in to cowardice. *Au dernier moment il s'est déballonné*: He got the jitters at the last minute (also: *se dégonfler*). **2** To 'come clean', to confess.

débandade *n.f. S'en aller en débandade*: To 'go to pot', to 'go to seed', to neglect oneself.

débander *v.intrans.* To 'lose the big stick', to 'go limp', to lose an erection.

débarbot *n.m.* 'Mouthpiece', counsel for the defence.

débarboter *v.trans.reflex.* To get oneself out of mischief, out of trouble. *En cas de coup dur, il peut se débarboter comme un grand*: When things get tough, he can look after himself.

débarbouiller *v.pronom.* To be able to look after oneself. *C'est sa connerie, qu'il se débarbouille!* It's his cock-up, let him sort it out!

débarcade *n.f.* (Prison slang): Discharge, release.

débardeur *n.m.* String-vest.

débargougner *v.trans.reflex.* To 'off-load', to get rid of something. *Se débargougner les phalangettes à l'hypocrite* (*joc.*): To wipe one's snotty fingers where one shouldn't.

débarqué *n.m.* Un débarqué de frais: An inexperienced person (one who literally has just got off the boat).

débarquer *v.trans. & intrans.* **1** To 'give the push', to 'sack', to dismiss. Il l'a débarqué rapidos: He gave him his cards double-quick. **2** Débarquer à l'improviste: To 'land', to arrive somewhere unannounced. **3** Ma parole, il débarque! Have you ever seen anyone more naïve?! (He's just come off the boat!) **4** Les anglais ont débarqué: She's 'got the decorators in' – She's got her period.

débarras *n.m.* Bon débarras! (joc. & iron.): Good riddance to bad rubbish! (I will be glad never to see him/it again!)

débarrasser *v.trans.* Débarrasse le plancher! Skedaddle! – Scoot! – Clear off!

débaucher *v.trans. & intrans. (joc.):* To 'knock off', to 'call it a day', to stop work. Il nous a débauchés sur le coup des trois heures: He told us to take an early coffee-break!

débectage *n.m.* Quel débectage! What a revolting state of affairs! (also: quelle débectance!).

débectant *adj.* **1** Depressing, disheartening. **2** 'Revolting', disgusting.

débecter *v.trans.* **1** To 'sicken', to disgust. Avec ses vêtements dégueulasses il me débecte: It turns my stomach to see him in those dirty clothes. **2** To 'throw up', to 'puke', to vomit.

déberlinguer *v.trans.* To 'deflower', to initiate a girl in sexual matters.

débile *adj.* 'Crass', 'cretinous', stupid. C'est un machin tout ce qu'il y a de débile! That thing is just too silly for words! (The adjective gains in colloquiality when the two syllables are stressed with a pause in the middle, becoming thus even more derogatory when levelled at individuals, projects, etc.)

débilitant *adj.* Depressing. C'est vraiment débilitant d'en être là: To be reduced to such extremes is sickening!

débinage *n.m.* 'Knocking', disparagement. Le débinage, c'est son blot! She's no beginner when it comes to slating!

débine *n.f.* **1** Utter poverty, complete destitution. Avec la crise, il est dans une de ces débines: The recession seems to be spelling bankruptcy for him. **2** La débine: 'The doldrums', state of depression. C'est la débine pour moi depuis qu'elle est partie! I've been really down in the dumps since she left me! **3** La Grande Débine de '40: The catastrophic military cock-up of 1940 (when Germany invaded France).

débiné *adj.* 'Cut down to size', diminished in self-importance.

débiner *v.trans.* **1** To 'knock', to 'run down', to disparage. Il ne cesse de débiner les copains: He's never got a nice word for his friends. **2** Débiner le truc: To 'snitch', to 'grass', to inform.

débiner *v.pronom.* **1** To 'scram', to 'skedaddle', to run away (also: se calter). **2** (fig.): To be on the downward path healthwise, to be on the verge of a physical breakdown.

débineur *n.m.* One who likes to 'knock' and rile.

débiter *v.trans.* Débiter des âneries (also: des sottises): To 'spout a load of rubbish', to talk a lot of nonsense. Il m'a débité une histoire à n'en pas finir: I was treated to an endless tale of woe.

déblayer *v.trans.* Déblayer le terrain (joc.): To 'scram', to 'skedaddle', to clear off. Allez houste, déblaye! Get lost! – Off with you! – Go away!

débloquer *v.intrans.* **1** To 'talk through the back of one's head', to 'spout a load of rubbish', to talk nonsense. Mais tu débloques, ma parole! To hear you talk, anybody would think you're bonkers! **2** To rave, to talk incoherently. **3** To behave in a madcap fashion (cracking jokes, playing pranks). **4** Débloquer sur quelqu'un: To spread malicious gossip about someone. Il débloque sur ses vieux à qui veut l'entendre: He'll run his family down to all and sundry.

déboire *n.m.* Le déboire (joc.): 'Heaving', vomiting (after a bout of heavy drinking. The word is usually found in the expression après le boire, il y a souvent le déboire!).

déboisé *adj.* Bald. Il est drôlement déboisé: He's as bald as a coot.

déboiser *v.pronom.* To 'go patchy', to lose one's hair.

débonder *v.pronom.* **1** To 'come clean', to come out with some unpalatable truths about oneself. **2** To 'get something off one's chest', to admit the truth.

débotté *n.m.* Saisir quelqu'un au débotté: To 'catch someone on the hop', to take someone unawares.

débouclarès *adj.inv.* Unlocked, open.

déboucler *v.trans.* **1** To unlock, to open. Il a débouclé la lourde: He opened the door. **2** To force open, to break into. Il a débouclé une tripotée de coffiots depuis vingt ans: In twenty years he's cracked more safes than you've had hot dinners!

déboucleur *n.m.* Safe-cracker, criminal specializing in the opening of strongboxes.

débouler *v.intrans.* **1** To tumble down, to roll down. Il était tellement rond qu'il a déboulé les *escadrins*: He was so pissed he rolled down the stairs. **2** To 'scram', to 'skedaddle', to run away. **3** *Débouler à l'imprévu*: To turn up unannounced, to arrive unheralded.

déboulonnage *n.m.* **1** 'Knocking', disparagement. **2** 'Sacking', dismissal.

déboulonner *v.trans.* **1** To 'knock someone off his pedestal', to 'knock someone's prestige for six', to debunk. **2** To 'give the push', to 'give the sack', to dismiss.

débourre *n.m.* 'Crapping', 'shitting', defecation.

débourrer *v.trans. & intrans.* **1** To 'scram', to 'skedaddle', to run away. **2** To 'put off', to dissuade. **3** To 'crap', to 'shit', to defecate.

débourroir *n.m.* Le *débourroir*: 'The shithouse', 'the karzey', the W.C.

débouscailler *v.trans.reflex.* To wipe one's bottom.

débousille *n.f.* Removal of tattoo (also: *débousillage*).

déboussolé *adj.* 'Potty', 'bonkers', mad. *Depuis que sa bergère l'a quitté, il est complètement déboussolé*: Since his wife left him, he doesn't know whether he's coming or going.

debout *adv.* **1** *Ne plus tenir debout*: To be 'knackered', 'dead-tired', to be exhausted. **2** *Ça ne tient pas debout* (of argument): It doesn't hold water – It doesn't make sense. **3** *Avoir quelqu'un tout debout*: To 'con', to 'diddle', to swindle someone. *Il s'est fait avoir tout debout*: He went for that hook, line and sinker.

déboutonner *v.trans.reflex.* **1** To speak one's mind. **2** To 'get something off one's chest', to confess. **3** To 'snitch', to 'grass', to inform.

débrayage *n.m.* Unofficial stoppage, short strike.

débrayer *v.intrans.* To 'down tools', to come out on unofficial strike.

débride *n.f.* La *débride*: Lifting of *interdiction de séjour* restrictions. (The *interdiction de séjour* is an added penalty preventing convicted criminals from entering certain areas where they might team up again with old acquaintances.)

débrider *v.trans.* **1** To unlock, to open. **2** To 'crack a safe', to break into a strongbox.

débrider *v.intrans.* **1** To 'open fire', to shoot. **2** To 'let up', to take a rest.

débringué *adj.* Slovenly dressed.

débris *n.m.* *Un vieux débris*: An 'old fuddy-duddy', one who is long past his prime. *Passe le premier, vieux débris!* (*joc.*): Age before beauty! – Dust before the brush! – You go first!

débrouillard *n.m.* 'Clever Dick', resourceful person.

débrouillard *adj.* 'Full of gumption', 'up to all the dodges', very resourceful.

débrouillardise *n.f.* 'Knack of clever dodges', resourcefulness.

débrouille *n.f.* La *débrouille*: Resourcefulness. *Savoir se tirer d'affaire à la débrouille*: To have an uncanny knack of dodging difficulties.

débrouiller *v.trans.* *Débrouiller quelqu'un*: To help someone sort things out (for himself), to help someone solve his own problems.

débrouiller *v.pronom.* To 'shift for oneself', to fend for oneself, to get by. *Il peut se débrouiller tout seul*: He can look after himself. *Débrouillez-vous tout seul!* Deal with that yourself, it's your pigeon! *Il s'est débrouillé, il nous a dégotté ça en douce*: Somehow or other he managed to wangle it for us.

déca *n.m.* *Un déca*: A cup of decaffeinated coffee.

décalcifier *v.trans.reflex.* (*joc.*): To take off one's underpants. (The humour stems from the fact that what is being withdrawn is a *caleçon* and not *calcium*.)

décale *n.f.* **1** La *décale* (*mil.*): Departure for a period of extended leave. **2** *La Grande Décale* (*joc.*): The massive summer holiday exodus from the cities.

décaler *v.intrans.* **1** To 'set off', to go away. **2** To go off on holiday.

décambuter *v.trans.* To 'pull a gun', to draw a firearm.

décambuter *v.intrans.* To 'make an exit', to leave. *Il s'est fait avoir en décambutant de chez lui*: They nabbed him as he left his digs.

décamper *v.intrans.* To 'bugger off', to 'scram', to leave in haste.

décanillage *n.m.* Disorderly flight, hurried departure.

décaniller *v.intrans.* **1** To 'bugger off', to 'scram', to make a hasty exit. **2** *Décaniller du pieu*: To 'roll out of bed', to get up reluctantly.

décapant *n.m.* (*joc.*): 'Rot-gut', cheap booze (the kind that is nearly as lethal as paint-stripper).

décapotée *n.f.* (*joc.*): Woman wearing a low-cut dress.

décarcasser *v.pronom.* To 'try one's darnedest', to 'give one's all' in order to achieve something. *Il s'est décarcassé pour m'aider*: He leaned over backwards to help me.

décarpillage *n.m.* **1** Inventory of booty before the share-out. **2** 'Stripping', removing of clothes. (As with *déballage*, *décarpillage* has uncomplimentary connotations. Sexist by its very nature, the word suggests that the charms revealed by the lady concerned are not a pretty sight.)

décarpiller *v.trans.* **1** To 'split a booty', to sort out and share the proceeds of a robbery. **2** To undress. *Se décarpiller*: To take one's clothes off.

décarrade *n.f.* **1** Exit, exit door. **2** Start, departure. *Il y avait 102 partants à la décarrade du Tour*: There were 102 starters on the first leg of the Tour de France. **3** 'Break-out', escape from prison. **4** *Etre de décarrade*: To have a day off from work.

décarrer *v.intrans. & trans.* **1** To 'scarper', to 'make off', to run away. **2** To 'set off', to go away. *Si on veut attraper le dur, il faut décarrer à huit heures pile*: If we want to catch that train we'll have to leave spot-on eight! **3** *Décarrer le cleps*: To take the dog for walkies.

décartonner *v.pronom.* To be 'knocking on', to be getting on in years.

décati *adj.* (of person): 'Geriatric', rather aged. *Il est plutôt décati*: He's way past his prime!

décatir *v.pronom.* To be 'getting on in years', to look way past one's prime.

décavé *adj.* **1** 'Down on one's uppers', 'on the rocks', penniless. **2** Old and way past one's prime.

décaver *v.trans.* To 'win the shirt off someone's back', to clean someone out at gambling.

décesser *v.intrans. Ne pas décesser de*: To keep on and on (doing something).

déchanter *v.intrans.* To 'come down a peg or two', to have to lower one's sights (literally, as the French suggests: to have to sing a different tune).

déchard *n.m.* **1** 'Skint' character, penniless person. **2** 'Hobo', down-and-outer.

décharge *n.f.* (abbr. *décharge publique*): Tip, municipal refuse dump. *C'est bon pour la décharge*: It's fit for the scrap-heap.

décharger *v.intrans.* To 'juice off', to ejaculate.

dèche *n.f.* **1** 'Dire straits', utter poverty. *Il est dans une de ces dèches*: He's really below the breadline! **2** 'Incidentals', incidental expenses. **3** 'Leakages', unaccounted cash losses.

décher *v.intrans.* To 'fork out', to pay for something. *Il a dû décher dur pour sa nouvelle bagnole*: He had to pay a packet for his new car.

déchet *n.m.* **1** (of person): 'Wash-out', failure. *Vieux déchet, va!* (joc.): You old crock, you! **2** *'y a pas de déchet* (joc.): It's all profit. (The expression is usually encountered in the context of business transactions.)

dèchetoque *adj.* 'Knackered', old and decrepit.

décheur *n.m.* 'Big spender', spendthrift. *C'est un sacré décheur!* He goes through money like water!

déchirer *v.trans.* **1** *La déchirer*: To 'croak', to 'snuff it', to die. **2** *Déchirer la toile*: To 'fart', to break wind.

déclaveté *adj.* 'Knackered', 'worn-out', exhausted.

décocter *v.intrans.* To 'crap', to 'shit', to defecate.

décoction *n.f. Une décoction de gnons*: A volley of blows. *Il a dégusté une de ces décoctions*: He's still smarting from the trouncing he got.

décoller *v.trans.* To 'bump off', to kill.

décoller *v.intrans.* **1** To be 'pegging out', withering away, to be on the downward path healthwise. **2** *Ne pas décoller*: To stick to someone like a leech. *Il n'a pas décollé de la soirée*: I just couldn't shake him off all evening. **3** *Sans décoller*: Non-stop – Without letting up. *On a travaillé cinq heures sans décoller*: We worked five hours at a stretch.

déconnage *n.m.* **1** 'Tommy-rot', inane statements. **2** 'Ragging', 'larking', exuberant and silly behaviour.

déconner *v.intrans.* **1** To 'spout a load of rubbish', to talk nonsense. **2** To 'arse about', to play the fool. *Cesse de déconner!* Stop messing about! *Il ne déconne plus maintenant qu'il est marié*: Since he got wed, he's on the straight and narrow.

déconneur *n.m.* **1** 'Goofer', blunderer. **2** 'Likely lad', fun-loving guy (the kind of character who seems to be living it up perpetually).

déconophone *n.m.* (joc.): 'Gob', 'trap', mouth. *Ferme ton déconophone!* Put a sock in it! – Shut up!

décoqueter *v.intrans.* To 'crap', to 'shit', to defecate.

décor *n.m.* **1** *Aller dans le décor* (of car): To skid off the road and crash. **2** *Envoyer quelqu'un dans le décor*: To 'send someone flying', to knock someone out of one's way. **3** *Pardonnez le décor!* Forgive the mess! (I know the place is untidy!)

découiller *v.intrans.* To 'have it off', to have intercourse.

décramponner *v.intrans. Ne pas décramponner* (of tenacious bore): To hang on like a limpet.

décrapouiller *v.trans.reflex.* To 'put one's head in the tub', to have a good wash.

décrasser *v.trans.reflex.* **1** (joc.): To 'put one's head in the tub', to have a good wash. **2** (fig.): To 'get a little bit of polish', to lose one's boorish manners.

décrasseur *n.m.* (joc.): 'Rod', handgun.

décrocher *v.trans.* **1** To win, to succeed in obtaining something. *Il a décroché son diplôme du premier coup*: He got his degree first go. *Décrocher la timbale*: To hit the jackpot. **2** To 'wangle', to obtain by hook or by crook. *A coup de pots-de-vin, il a décroché la plus grosse* *commande*: He landed the biggest contract with the help of some good old slush funds! **3** To redeem from pawn. **4** *Décrocher ses tableaux (joc.)*: To 'forage up one's nostrils', to pick one's nose.

décrocher *v.intrans.* **1** To 'pack it in', to retire from work or a sporting career. *La cinquantaine, c'est un bel âge pour décrocher*: It makes sense to quit the rat-race long before you're sixty. **2** *(pol.)*: To shelve an inquiry. **3** To 'tuck in', to eat voraciously. *Qu'est-ce qu'il décroche quand il revient du boulot!* He doesn't half wolf his food when he gets back from work!

décrochez-moi-ça *n.m.* *(joc.) Acheter des vêtements au décrochez-moi-ça*: To buy off-the-peg clothes from a market stall.

décrotter *v.trans.reflex.* **1** *(joc.)*: To 'put one's head in the tub', to have a good wash. **2** *(fig.)*: To 'get a little bit of polish', to lose one's boorish manners.

décuiter *v.pronom.* To 'sober up', to get over a boozing spree.

déculottée *n.f. Une déculottée* (Gambling): A 'trouncing', an unlucky betting spree.

déculotter *v.trans.reflex.* **1** To 'funk', to back out of something. **2** To 'come clean', to own up, to confess.

dedans *adv.* **1** *Etre dedans*: To 'be inside', to be doing time, to be in prison. **2** *Foutre* (also: *mettre) quelqu'un dedans*: To land someone in trouble. (The expression can refer either to hoodwinking or to unintentional deception.) **3** *Donner dedans*: To be 'taken in', to 'fall for something', to be fooled into doing something. **4** *Se fiche dedans*: To 'make a boob', to blunder. **5** *Mettre les pieds dedans*: To 'put one's foot in it', to commit a gaffe. **6** *Rentrer dedans à quelqu'un*: To 'lam into someone', to physically assault someone.

Dédé *Proper name.* *(corr. André)*: Andy, Andrew.

dédé *n.m.* (Child language): 'Botty', 'bum', behind.

dédire *v.pronom. Cochon qui s'en dédit!* (of commercial transaction): It's settled then! – It's a deal! (Originally very much an expression used within farming communities, it has permeated in a jocular vein into everyday colloquial speech.)

dédouaner *v.trans.* **1** To clear someone of a charge. **2** To 'give someone a clean bill of health', to declare someone to be fit and healthy.

défarguer *v.trans.* To exonerate, to clear someone of a charge.

défarguer *v.intrans.* To 'crap', to 'shit', to defecate.

défarguer *v.trans.reflex.* **1** To get rid of incriminating evidence. *Il s'est défargué de son calibre dans les cagoinces*: He got rid of his gun in the karzey. **2** To 'clear one's name', to disculpate oneself. **3** *Se défarguer sur le dos de quelqu'un*: To get someone to 'carry the can', to make someone else responsible for one's own misdeeds.

défargueur *n.m.* Witness for the defence.

défaucher *v.trans.* To give someone a 'financial leg-up', to get someone out of a tight pecuniary predicament. *Pour défaucher les potes, il n'est jamais à la traîne!* If you need a sub, he's not the type to keep you waiting!

défaucher *v.trans.reflex.* **1** To 'make ends meet', to manage on the money one has. *A trois, on se défauchera mieux!* If the three of us pool our money, we should get by! **2** To 'get back on one's feet' financially, to become solvent again.

défausser *v.trans.reflex.* To get rid of incriminating evidence. *Craignant la fouille à la sortie du bal, il s'est défaussé de son ya*: Thinking they'd be frisked as they left the dance-hall, he ditched his blade.

défendre *v.trans.reflex.* **1** To 'be able to hold one's own', to be proficient. *Comme pianiste, il se défend pas mal*: He's no amateur when it comes to tickling the ivories. **2** To earn an honest crust. **3** *Elle se défend encore bien*: She certainly doesn't look her age. **4** (of prostitute): To be 'on the game', to solicit.

Défense *Proper name. La Défense*: High vantage point and densely-populated suburban area of Paris.

défense *n.f.* **1** Lucrative racket, profitable swindle. *Etre tombé sur une bonne défense*: To have cottoned onto a good money-spinner. **2** *Avoir de la défense*: To 'be able to hold one's own', to know how to look after oneself. **3** *Une défense*: Prohibition order preventing a known criminal from entering certain areas. *Avoir trois ans de défense*: To have a three-year ban, to have one's movements legally restricted for three years (also: *interdiction de séjour*).

deffe *n.f.* 'Pancake', flat cap.

défiler *v.pronom.* **1** To 'slope off', to 'slip away', to disappear discreetly. **2** To 'back out of something unpleasant', to dodge an awkward task. **3** To 'lie low', to hide.

déflaque *n.f.* 'Turd', faeces, excrement.

déflaquer *v.intrans.* To 'crap', to 'shit', to defecate.

défonce *n.f. Etre en pleine défonce* (Drugs): To be 'high', to be in a state of extreme intoxication.

défoncé *adj.* **1** 'Pissed', 'sozzled', inebriated. **2** 'High', 'smashed', in a state of extreme drug intoxication.

défoncer *v.trans.* 1 *Défoncer le portrait à quelqu'un*: To 'push someone's face in', to bash someone up. 2 *Se faire défoncer* (of woman): To 'get laid', to have sex. (The expression is sexist and has connotations of coercion.)

défoncer *v.trans.reflex.* 1 To 'sweat one's guts out', to work flat out. *Il va falloir qu'il se défonce pour livrer cette commande*: He'll have to work his fingers to the bone if he wants to get that order off. 2 To get 'smashed', to get high on drugs.

défonceuse *n.f.* 'Prick', 'cock', penis.

déforme *n.f. Tenir la déforme*: **a** To be out of condition, to be suffering from a loss of form. **b** (Gambling): To be on a losing streak.

défouler *v.pronom.* To 'let one's hair down', to shelve one's inhibitions.

défourailler *v.intrans.* 1 To pull a gun and fire. *Il a défouraillé dans le tas*: He showered them with a hail of bullets. 2 To pull one's wallet out, to pay up.

défrimer *v.trans.* To take a 'dekko' at, to take a good look at someone.

défringuer *v.trans.reflex.* To 'take one's togs off', to undress.

défrisé *adj.* 'Down-in-the-mouth', depressed.

défriser *v.trans.* To 'put someone out', to upset someone. *La nouvelle l'a défrisé*: He got upset when he heard the news.

défriser *v.pronom.* To 'lose heart', to get depressed.

défroquer *v.trans.reflex.* 1 To pull one's pants down, to take one's trousers off. 2 *(fig.)*: To 'funk out', to have second thoughts and abandon a project or decision.

défrusquer *v.trans.reflex.* To 'take one's togs off', to undress.

défunter *v.intrans.* *(joc.)*: To 'pop one's clogs', to 'snuff it', to die.

dégager *v.intrans.* 1 To 'pong', to stink, to smell foul. *Le calendo faisandé, ça dégage un chouïa*: Camembert cheese going off doesn't half pong! 2 To 'fart', to break wind. 3 To 'fuck off', to 'piss off', to go away. *Ouste, dégagez!* Off with you!

dégaine *n.f.* *(pej.)*: Gawky look, ungainly appearance.

dégarnir *v.pronom.* To be 'losing one's thatch', to be going bald.

dégâts *n.m.pl.* 1 *Limiter les dégâts (joc.)*: To cut one's losses and avoid unnecessary expenses. 2 *'y a pas de dégâts?! (joc.)*: No bones broken?! (I hope!)

dégauchir *v.trans.* 1 To 'come up with', to discover. 2 To 'wangle', to succeed in obtaining something through unorthodox means. *Il est arrivé à nous dégauchir des places*

assises, le filou! The old so-and-so! He swung it and got us some seats!

dégelée *n.f.* 'Rousting', 'drubbing', thrashing. *Il a dégusté une de ces dégelées!* He got the pasting of his life!

dégeler *v.trans.reflex.* To 'thaw', to 'unbend', to lose one's reserve.

dégingandé *adj.* 'Gawky', 'awkward', clumsy.

déglingue *n.f. La déglingue*: State of deterioration. (*Tomber dans la déglingue* can refer to people, machines, buildings, etc.)

déglingué *adj.* (of machinery): 'Clapped-out', 'broken-down', almost unserviceable.

déglinguer *v.trans.* To 'knacker', to 'foul up', to bring into a state of disrepair.

déglinguer *v.pronom.* (of person): To 'go to pot', to 'get run down', to deteriorate.

dégobillade *n.f.* 'Sick', 'spew', vomit (also: *dégobillon*).

dégobillage *n.m.* 'Puking', 'spewing', vomiting.

dégobiller *v.trans. & intrans.* To 'puke', to 'spew', to vomit.

dégoder *v.intrans.* To 'lose the big stick', to 'go limp', to lose an erection.

dégoiser *v.intrans.* 1 To 'prattle on', to 'waffle', to talk endlessly. 2 To 'shoot one's mouth', to 'blab', to talk carelessly. 3 *Dégoiser sur*: To 'knock', to utter slanderous comments. *Dans cette boîte ils dégoisent tous, les uns sur les autres!* The backbiting that goes on here is nobody's business!

dégommage *n.m.* 1 'Roasting', scolding, telling-off. 2 'Sacking', dismissal. 3 'Rousting', beating-up. 4 'Bumping-off', killing.

dégommer *v.trans.* 1 To 'rap', to tell off, to remonstrate with. 2 To 'fire', to 'sack', to dismiss. 3 To 'dust up', to beat up, to thrash. 4 To 'bump off', to kill.

dégonflade *n.f.* 'Funking', backing-out. *J'espère qu'il n'y aura pas de dégonflade au dernier moment!* I hope no-one gets cold feet at the last minute! (also: *dégonflage*).

dégonflard *n.m.* 'Funk', quitter, character who lacks energy and persistence (also: *dégonflé*).

dégonfle *n.f.* 1 Cowardice. *C'est le roi de la dégonfle!* He's as yellow-bellied as they come! 2 *Jouer la dégonfle* (Football): To kick the ball into touch (in order to enable one's defence to regroup).

dégonflé *adj.* 'Chicken', 'funky', cowardly.

dégonfler *v.trans.* To 'take someone down a peg or two', to 'score off someone', to deflate someone's ego. *Quand il m'a vu avec le patron, ça l'a drôlement dégonflé*: When he saw me with the boss, it really took the wind out of his sails.

dégonfler *v.pronom.* **1** To 'get cold feet', to 'funk', to pull out. **2** To lose one's (arrogant) poise. **3** To 'get something off one's chest', to clear one's conscience. **4** To 'blow the gaff', to 'blab', to divulge a secret.

dégonfleur *n.m.* 'Weather-cock' character, unreliable person.

dégorger *v.intrans. & trans.* **1** To 'pee', to 'wee', to urinate. **2** *Dégorger son panais*: To 'have a change of oil', to fuck, to have sex.

dégoter *v.trans.* (also: *dégotter*): **1** To 'come across', to discover. **2** To 'wangle', to succeed in coming up with something through unorthodox means. **3** To 'lick', to beat, to get the better of someone.

dégoter *v.intrans.* **1** (of person): To 'look the part', to be extremely attractive. **2** *Ça dégote!* It's ace! – It's first-rate!

dégoulinade *n.f.* 'Run', trickle of liquid.

dégoulinante *n.f.* 'Timepiece', clock (because the minutes drip by so slowly).

dégouliner *v.intrans.* To drip, to trickle down.

dégourdi *n.m.* 'Smart guy', clever and resourceful character.

dégourdi *adj.* 'On-the-ball', 'with-it', resourceful. *Il n'est vraiment pas dégourdi*: He's a bit slow on the uptake.

dégourdir *v.trans.* **1** To initiate in sexual matters. **2** *Se dégourdir les jambes*: To 'stretch one's legs', to go for a short walk.

dégourer *v.trans.* (also: *dégourrer*): **1** To malign, to slander. *Il faut toujours qu'il dégoure ses collègues*: He's always running down his workmates. **2** To disgust, to instil a feeling of revulsion.

dégoûtance *n.f. Quelle dégoûtance!* **a** What a revolting so-and-so! – What a disgusting character! **b** What a shocking state of affairs! (also: *quelle dégoûtation!*).

dégoûtarès *adj.* **1** 'Mucky', 'filthy', dirty. **2** Evil, nasty.

dégoûté *adj.* **1** *Faire le dégoûté*: To 'turn up one's nose at something', to show one's dislike. **2** *Ne pas être dégoûté*: Not to be easily put off. *Pour bouffer sa cuisine, il ne faut vraiment pas être dégoûté*: It takes some guts to eat her food!

dégrafer *v.intrans.* To 'scram', to 'scarper', to run away. *Il a dégrafé à toute allure*: He certainly made tracks.

dégrafer *v.pronom.* **1** To 'wriggle loose', to slip niftily out of someone's hold. **2** To 'throw in the towel', to give up.

dégrainer *v.trans.* **1** To 'run down', to speak ill of. **2** To 'deflower', to seduce. *Il en a dégrainé*

des nanas! Where girls are concerned, he's certainly been around!

dégraisser *v.trans.* **1** To 'nick', to 'pinch', to steal. **2** *Dégraisser son morlingue*: To 'spend, spend, spend', to use one's money in a reckless manner. **3** *Dégraisser son panais*: To 'have a change of oil', to fuck, to have sex.

dégraisser *v.trans.reflex.* **1** To 'have it off', to fuck, to have sex. **2** To 'end up in queer street', to go bankrupt.

dégraisseur *n.m. Le dégraisseur*: The tax-man, the man from the Inland Revenue.

dégrène *n.f.* 'Snide tittle-tattle', malicious gossip.

dégrèneur *n.m.* Scandal-monger.

dégringolade *n.f.* 'Tumble', fall. *Sur le trottoir gelé c'était la dégringolade des passants*: The frozen pavement had become a proper little ice-rink! *Dégringolade des prix*: Price slump.

dégringoler *v.trans.* **1** To 'bump off', to kill. **2** *Dégringoler du fric à quelqu'un*: To give someone a 'reluctant sub', to lend someone money under duress. **3** *Dégringoler une mousmée*: To 'score' with a bird, to notch up a sexual conquest.

dégringoler *v.intrans.* **1** To 'fall flat on one's face', to fall down. **2** To rush in at the last minute, to arrive late. **3** *(fig.)*: To 'come a cropper', to fall off one's pedestal in life.

dégringoleur *n.m.* **1** (Racing cyclists' slang): Nippy rider on steep descents. **2** Randy so-and-so, highly-sexed man (one whose aim in life is to notch up as many sexual conquests as possible).

dégripper *v.trans.* **1** To 'ease', to loosen (nut or bolt) by means of a lubricant. **2** *(fig)*: To 'oil the wheels', to make transactions smooth through an injection of funds.

dégripper *v.trans.reflex.* To fight off a tenacious bore.

dégrossi *adj. Mal dégrossi*: 'Loutish', uncouth.

dégrossir *v.pronom.* To acquire finesse and good manners.

dégrouillard *n.m.* 'Live-wire', character who is never at a loss when it comes to sorting problems out (also: *débrouillard*).

dégrouiller *v.pronom.* To 'get a move on', to hurry up. *Dégrouille-toi!* Get your skates on! (also: *se grouiller*).

déguerpir *v.intrans.* To 'scram', to 'skedaddle', to clear off.

dégueu *adj.inv.* (abbr. *dégueulasse*): 'Yukky', 'revolting', disgusting.

dégueulade *n.f.* 'Throwing-up', 'puking', action of vomiting.

dégueulando *adj.inv.* (of melody): Gushing and syrupy. (This word has built-in jocularity to make it resemble the instructions on a musical score.)

dégueulasse *n.m.* *C'est pas le frère à dégueulasse!* *(joc. & iron.)*: This is certainly no rubbish! (The expression is usually uttered when referring to food or drink.)

dégueulasse *adj.* **1** 'Lousy', 'sickening', revolting. **2** 'Yukky', 'mucky', filthy. **3** *C'est pas dégueulasse!* *(joc.)*: It's a bit of alright! – It's not bad! *C'est un petit pinard qui n'est vraiment pas dégueulasse*: It's an amusing little wine!

dégueulasser *v.trans.* To 'muck up', to soil, to make filthy.

dégueulasserie *n.f.* 'Rotten trick', deceitful action. *Il m'a fait une belle dégueulasserie!* He really did the dirty on me!

dégueulatoire *adj.* *(joc.)*: 'Yukky', revolting (literally likely to cause someone to throw up).

dégueulée *n.f.* **1** 'Sick', 'spew', vomit. **2** Torrent of abuse. *Elle lui a lâché une de ces dégueulées*: She gave him a real ear-bashing.

dégueuler *v.trans. & intrans.* **1** To 'puke', to 'spew', to vomit. **2** *Dégueuler sur le compte de quelqu'un*: To 'run someone down', to speak ill of someone.

dégueulis *n.m.* 'Sick', 'spew', vomit.

dégueuloir *n.m.* *(pej.)*: 'Trap', 'gob', mouth.

déguiser *v.trans.reflex.* **1** *Se déguiser en courant d'air* (of person): To do a disappearing trick, to vanish into thin air. **2** *Se déguiser en cerf*: To 'run like the clappers', to 'make tracks', to run away.

dégun *pron.* Somebody, someone. *Il ne voulait pas se faire retapisser par dégun*: He didn't want to be spotted by anybody.

déguster *v.trans.* To 'cop', to be on the receiving end of something unpleasant. *Déguster une infusion de rames de châtaignier*: To get a jolly good hiding. *Qu'est-ce qu'il a dégusté le soir qu'il a découché!* He got a right rollicking from his wife the time he didn't get home till morning!

déhaler *v.intrans.* To 'shift oneself', to leave, to go away.

dehors *n.m.* *Faire le dehors*: To go soliciting, to engage in prostitution (also: *tâter du dehors*).

déhotter *v.intrans. & trans.* (also: *déhoter*): **1** To 'bugger off', to leave. *Déhotter du plume*: To skip out of bed. **2** To 'chuck out', to eject someone forcibly. *Il l'a déhotté à coups de pompes au dargif.* He booted him out of the room.

déhotter *v.pronom.* To 'get cracking', to 'get a move on', to go away in a hurry.

Deibler *Proper name.* *Une coupe à la Deibler (joc.)*: 'Short back and sides', close-crop hairstyle. (The expression has a certain amount of sick

humour in that Deibler was a famous executioner operating the guillotine.)

déjà *adv.* **1** *Comment s'appelle-t-il, déjà?* What did you say his name was? **2** *Et pourquoi qu'il est venu, déjà?* And why was it he came? (In both cases, what is really a superfluous adverb introduces an added element of doubt into a question.)

déjanter *v.intrans.* **1** To 'go off the rails', to lose all touch with reality in a state verging on dementia. **2** To 'lose the big stick', to 'go limp', to lose an erection. (*Déjanter* in standard French refers to the 'parting of the ways' between a tyre and the wheel rim when no air is left in the tyre.)

déjeté *adj.* **1** (of person): 'Over-the-hill', past one's prime. *Il n'est pas déjeté*: He doesn't look his age. **2** (of object): 'Lop-sided', misshapen.

délicat *adj.* *Faire le délicat*: To be 'picky and choosy', to behave in a pernickety manner.

délicatesse *n.f.* *C'est la délicatesse même! (iron.)*: Him and his hob-nailed boots! – Trust him to be tactful!

délinger *v.trans.reflex.* To 'strip', to take one's clothes off.

délire *n.m.* *Faire un délire (th.)*: To get a rave reception, to receive a standing ovation.

déloquer *v.trans.reflex.* To 'strip', to take one's clothes off.

délourder *v.intrans.* To open a door. *Délourde!* Open up! (There is no suggestion of forcible entry with this verb, and *relourder* merely means to close a door.)

déluge *n.m.* *Ça remonte au déluge! (joc.)*: That's going back a bit! – That's ancient history!

demain *adv.* **1** *Demain il fera jour!* Tomorrow's another day! (There's no sense in worrying about the future.) **2** *Ce n'est pas demain la veille! (joc. & iron.)*: You'll grow roots if you're waiting for that to happen!

démanché *n.m.* 'Gawky half-wit', lanky and stupid-looking person.

démanché *adj.* (of person): 'Gawky', ungainly.

démancher *v.pronom.* To 'try one's darnedest', to make an all-out effort. *Il s'est démanché le trou du cul pour nous dégauchir ça*: He went out of his way to get us what we wanted.

demander *v.intrans.* *Je vous demande un peu! (iron)*: Well did you ever?! – Have you ever come across anything so preposterous?!

démanger *v.intrans.* *Gratter quelqu'un où ça le démange*: To ingratiate oneself with someone by pandering to their foibles (literally to scratch someone's back when the need arises).

démantibuler *v.trans.* **1** To 'break', to dismantle for spare parts. **2** To 'bugger up', to render unfit for use. (In both instances the word refers to machinery.)

démaquer *v.pronom.* To 'split up', to separate from one's sexual partner.

déménager *v.intrans.* 1 *Déménager à la cloche de bois*: To 'skip', to leave rented accommodation without paying. 2 To be 'bonkers', 'potty', to be mad. *Tu déménages, ma parole!* You're round the twist!

dément *adj.* 'Incredible', fantastic. *Il m'est arrivé un truc dément*: You won't believe what happened to me!

démerdard *adj.* 'Up to all the dodges', wily, resourceful.

démerde *n.f. La démerde*: 'Knack of clever dodges', art of falling back on one's feet. *Pour ce qui est de la démerde, il s'y connaît!* He can certainly get himself out of a tight corner! (*Le système démerde*, also known as *le système D*, is that typically 'by hook or by crook' French way of solving tricky problems.)

démerder *v.pronom.* 1 To 'shift for oneself', to fend for oneself, to get by. 2 To 'shake a leg', to 'snap to it', to hurry up. *Démerde-toi, on est en retard!* Get cracking, we're late!

démerdeur *n.m.* 1 'Live-wire', 'Clever Dick', resourceful person. 2 'Mouthpiece', barrister.

demeuré *adj.* Mentally-retarded. *Le petit dernier m'a l'air un peu demeuré*: The youngest of the brood looks a bit backward.

demi *n.m.* (*abbr. demi pression*): Glass of keg beer served in cafés and bistrots. (Contrary to optimistic popular belief, *demi* does not refer to a half-litre, the average content of a *demi* being 33 cl.) *Garçon, un demi sans faux-col!* I want a real half (without as much froth as the last one!).

demi-cercle *n.m. Pincer quelqu'un au demi-cercle*: **a** To 'catch someone on the hop', off-guard, to catch someone unawares. **b** To 'get even with someone', to get one's own back. **c** To 'nab', to arrest.

démieller *v.trans.* To 'sort things out', to untangle a complicated issue.

démieller *v.pronom.* 1 To 'shift for oneself', to be able to look after Number One. 2 To get oneself out of trouble.

demi-jambe *n.f.* Fifty francs (as an amount or in the shape of a note).

demi-livre *n.f. Prendre une demi-livre sur le coin de la gueule*: To 'get a bunch of fives up the kisser', to get punched in the face. (A slap is sometimes described as *une demi-livre sans os*.)

demi-molle *n.f. Etre en demi-molle*: To be lukewarm about a venture or a course of action.

demi-mondaine *n.f.* 'Tart', woman of rather loose morals.

demi-monde *n.m.* Twilight society that bridges respectability and the underworld.

demi-pomme *n.m.* (*sch.*): 'Day-boy', non-boarder, pupil who takes only his mid-day meal at school.

demi-portion *n.m.* (*pej.*): 'Squirt', runt, pint-size person.

demi-sac *n.m.* Five franc note. (Prior to the 1958 remonetization, the amount was 500 francs.)

demi-sel *n.m.* 1 Petty thief, small-time criminal. 2 Would-be tough guy, character who would like to let others think he is part of the *milieu*.

demi-tour *interj.* Get knotted! – Get lost! – Go away!

demi-vierge *n.f.* 'Prick-teaser', flirtatious girl who likes to lead men on but never fulfils their expectations.

démoduler *v.trans.* To 'floor', to astound.

demoiselle *n.f.* 1 Daughter. (The expression *vot' demoiselle* is equatable with *vot' dame* as rather 'low-brow'.) 2 Half-bottle of wine.

démolir *v.trans.* 1 To 'bash up', to beat up, to thrash. 2 *Se faire démolir*: To get killed, to die (usually in the context of war. *Il s'est fait démolir en Bochie*: He got bumped off in Krautland).

démolissage *n.m.* Blighting criticism, scathing comments.

démon *n.m. Démon de midi*: 'Seven-year itch', middle-aged man's tendency to seek extra-marital conquests.

démonter *v.trans. Se laisser démonter*: To get 'flummoxed', to be 'put out', to get disconcerted. *Te laisse pas démonter, mon vieux!* Keep your cool, mate!

démordre *v.intrans. Ne pas démordre*: To 'stick to one's guns', to refuse to give up.

démoudre *v.intrans. En démoudre*: To 'prostitute one's talents', to engage in work unworthy of one's qualifications.

démouler *v.intrans.* To 'slip away', to leave promptly and discreetly.

démouscailler *v.pronom.* 1 To 'shift for oneself', to fend for oneself, to get by. 2 To 'shake a leg', to 'snap to it', to hurry up. *Démouscaille-toi!* Pull your finger out! – Get cracking! – Hurry up!

démurger *v.intrans.* To 'make tracks', to 'get a move on', to leave promptly.

déniaiser *v.trans.* To initiate someone in sexual matters.

dénipper *v.trans.reflex.* To 'get one's togs off', to 'strip', to undress.

dénoyauter *v.trans. Dénoyauter un suspect (pol.)*: To interrogate someone skilfully and get to the core of the inquiry.

dent *n.f.* 1 *Avoir la dent*: To be 'famished', to be very hungry. 2 *Il n'y a pas de quoi remplir une dent creuse (iron.)*: These portions are as mean as hell! – You could hardly call this a meal! **3** *Etre sur les dents*: **a** To 'slog one's guts out', to be working non-stop. **b** To be 'knackered', 'buggered', to be exhausted. *Mettre quelqu'un sur les dents*: To be something of a slavedriver, to work someone off their feet. **4** *Avoir les dents dures*: To be 'sarky', to have a biting and sarcastic disposition. **5** *Se casser les dents (sur quelque chose)*: To 'come a cropper', to 'come to grief', over something, to hit failure. **6** *Garder une dent contre quelqu'un*: To harbour a grudge against someone (also: *garder à quelqu'un un chien de sa chienne*). **7** *Etre guéri du mal de dents*: To have 'croaked', to be 'out of one's misery', to be dead. **8** *Mentir comme un arracheur de dents*: To lie through one's teeth (because the amateur tooth-puller is hardly likely to tell his customer how much the extraction is going to hurt).

dentelle *n.f. Avoir les pieds en dentelle*: **a** To have very sore feet. **b** To be unwilling to do something.

dentiste *n.m. Aller au dentiste*: To 'go looking for grub', to go searching for food.

dépagnoter *v.trans.reflex.* To 'skip out of bed', to get up (also: *se dépager*).

dépannage *n.m.* Help, helping hand. *Ton fric m'a été d'un sacré dépannage*: That sub of yours certainly came in handy.

dépanner *v.trans.* To 'lend a hand', to 'help someone out', to give assistance.

dépaqueter *v.intrans.* To 'crap', to 'shit', to defecate.

départ *n.m.* **1** *N'avoir rien au départ (iron.)*: To 'have not much up top', to be rather dim. (The implication is that the person concerned was thrown into life's race with little intellectual ability.) **2** *Piquer un départ (joc.)*: To 'scram', to 'make tracks', to rush away.

dépassé *adj.* 'Old-hat', out-of-date, old-fashioned.

dépasser *v.trans. Ça me dépasse!* It's way above my head! – It's beyond me! – I can't understand it!

dépatouiller *v.pronom.* To 'fall back on one's feet', to get out of a fix. *Il s'est dépatouillé comme un grand*: He certainly got out of that easily.

déphasé *adj.* (of person): 'In the clouds', out of touch with reality.

dépiauter *v.trans.* **1** To skin (an animal). **2** To peel a fruit. **3** *(fig.)*: To tear a literary work to pieces, to express scathing criticisms about it. **4** *Dépiauter un suspect (pol.)*: To 'grill' a suspect, to subject him to in-depth and searching interrogation.

dépiauter *v.trans.reflex.* To 'strip off', to undress.

dépieuter *v.trans.reflex.* To 'skip out of bed', to get up.

déplacement *n.m. Ça vaut le déplacement!* I wouldn't miss this if I was you!

déplaire *v.trans. C'est pas fait pour me déplaire! (iron.)*: It suits me down to the ground! – It's to my liking.

déplanquer *v.trans.* **1** To retrieve an object from a hiding place. **2** To 'get something out of hock', to redeem an item from the pawnbroker's. **3** To take something out of one's pocket.

déplanquer *v.pronom.* To come out of hiding.

déplumé *adj.* **1** Bald, bald-headed. **2** 'Skint', 'broke', penniless.

déplumer *v.pronom.* **1** To go bald, to lose one's hair. **2** To 'go broke', to be on the road to financial ruin. **3** To skip out of bed.

déponé *adj.* 'Down in the dumps', in the depths of depression.

déponer *v.trans.* To bore the pants off someone.

déponer *v.intrans.* To 'crap', to 'shit', to defecate.

déponer *v.pronom.* To 'lose heart', to get discouraged.

déposer *v.trans. Déposer son bilan*: To 'pop one's clogs', to 'snuff it', to die.

Dépôt *Proper name. Le Dépôt*: Place of temporary incarceration within the Paris *Palais de Justice*.

dépoter *v.trans.* **1** To exhume a body. **2** *Dépoter son géranium*: To 'croak', to 'snuff it', to die. **3** To 'drop one's bundle', to have a baby. **4** To drop someone somewhere (after having given him/her a lift).

dépotoir *n.m.* 'Junk-heap', dirty and untidy room.

dépouille *n.f. La dépouille*: 'Mugging', action of robbing defenceless passers-by.

déprime *n.f.* Nervous depression. *Faire une petite déprime*: To have a nervous breakdown.

dépuceler *v.trans.* **1** To deflower a virgin, to make a young girl lose her virginity. **2** To open a package or container for the first time. *Dépuceler une bouteille de roteux*: To pop open a bottle of champers.

députaille *n.f. La députaille (pej.)*: The *députés*, those representatives elected to the *Assemblée Nationale*. (The English equivalent of this derogatory term could be 'that lazy riff-raff we elected'.)

déquiller *v.trans.* To 'bump off', to kill.

der *adj. (abbr. dernier)*: **1** *La der des ders*: The war to end all wars. (This utopic expression, according to the context, can apply to any war.) **2** *Boire le der des ders*: To down the last drink. *C'est le der des ders!* Come on, let's have one for the road! 3 *Jouer le dix de der*: To play for the last trick in a game of *belote* giving the winner an extra ten points.

dérailler *v.intrans.* 1 To 'talk through one's hat', to 'spout a load of rubbish', to utter inanities. 2 To be 'going off the rails', to lose one's sanity.

déramer *v.intrans.* To 'kick the bucket', to 'snuff it', to die.

déramer *v.trans.reflex.* To 'do oneself in', to commit suicide.

déraper *v.intrans. Sans déraper*: Non-stop. *Au boulot, il bosse sans déraper*: When he's at work, it's graft, graft, graft!

dératé *n.m. Courir comme un dératé*: To 'run like the clappers', to run like mad, to race along.

derche *n.m.* 1 'Backside', 'rump', behind. *Il s'est fait botter le derche*: He got kicked up the jacksey. 2 *Se magner le derche*: To 'get a move on', to hurry up (also: *se magner le train* or *la rondelle*). 3 *Faf à derche*: 'Bumf', 'bumfodder', toilet paper. 4 *Faux-derche*: 'Two-faced person', hypocrite (also: *faux-jeton*).

derjo *adv.* (also: *dergeot*): Behind. *La porte étant ouverte, il s'est planqué derjo*: He hid behind the open door.

dernier *n.m. C'est le dernier des derniers*: He's an out-and-out rotter – He's a real swine of a character.

dernière *n.f. La dernière*: a *(abbr. la dernière histoire)*: The latest yarn. *Avez-vous entendu la dernière?* Do you know this one? – Have you heard this joke? b *(abbr. la dernière édition)*: Latest edition of a newspaper (hot off the presses).

dérobard *n.m.* 'Skiver', 'slacker', work-shy person.

dérober *v.intrans.* 1 To slip away. *Dérober en douce*: To slope off unnoticed. 2 To 'dodge the issue', to skilfully avoid giving a straight answer. 3 To 'go back on one's word', to renege on a promise.

dérober *v.pronom.* 1 To 'funk out of something', to avoid an unpleasant task. 2 To 'go on the loose', to 'leave the straight and narrow', to start leading a fast and easy life.

dérondi *adj. (joc.)*: 'Dried-out', sobered-up.

dérondir *v.pronom. (joc.)*: To sober up. *Il est d'humeur massacrante quand il se dérondit*: When he's drying out, he's always in a vile mood.

dérouillade *n.f.* 'Going-over', 'drubbing', thrashing. *Prendre une dérouillade*: To get a pasting.

dérouiller *v.intrans. & trans.* 1 To 'trounce', to 'bash up', to beat up. 2 To be on the receiving end of a bashing, thrashing. *Qu'est-ce qu'il a*

dérouillé! He got the hiding of his life! (It is always necessary to contextualize *dérouiller* in order to be certain whether the person concerned is on the giving or the receiving end.) 3 To be the unlucky one who gets an unpleasant job to do. *C'est moi qu'a dérouillé comme toujours*: It's muggins the fall-guy as usual! 4 *Dérouiller son panais*: To 'have a change of oil', to fuck, to have sex.

dérouiller *v.pronom.* To 'get cracking', to 'get one's skates on', to hurry up.

dérouler *v.trans. Dérouler le tapis (fig.)*: To go into lengthy explanations.

dérouler *v.intrans.* To 'go on a pub-crawl', to go on a drinking spree from bar to bar.

derrière *n.m. Avoir le feu au derrière*: a (of woman): To be a 'hot number', to be more than highly-sexed. b To be 'in a flaming rush', to be in a desperate hurry.

des *partitive article. Il y en a des qui ne rendent jamais ce qu'on leur prête*: There's them that never return what they borrow.

dés *n.m.pl. Lâcher* (also: *passer*) *les dés*: To 'throw in the towel', to give up.

désaper *v.trans.reflex.* To 'strip off', to undress.

désargenté *adj.* 'Skint', 'broke', penniless.

désaxé *n.m.* Psychopath, violently deranged character likely to commit criminal acts.

descendre *v.trans.* 1 To 'knock back', to down a drink. *En cinq secs, il vous descend une rouille*: He can down a bottle of plonk before you can say Jack Robinson. 2 To gun down, to kill with a firearm. 3 To 'shoot someone down', to expose someone to ridicule and humiliation.

descente *n.f.* 1 'Swoop', police raid. 2 *Avoir une sacrée descente*: To 'have a sloping gullet', to be very partial to booze. 3 'Arse-licker', 'crawler', sycophant. 4 *Descente au barbu* (also: *descente à la cave*): 'Hair-pie', cunnilingus.

désentifer *v.pronom.* To give marital life the 'heave-ho', to opt out of married life.

désert *n.m. (mil.)*: Deserter. (The word is pronounced *déserte* to avoid ambiguity.)

déshabillage *n.m.* 1 'Dressing-down', 'roasting', severe telling-off. 2 Scathing review of play or novel.

déshabiller *v.trans.* 1 To 'give someone a roasting', a severe telling-off. 2 To review a play, film or novel scathingly.

désirer *v.trans. Se faire désirer (joc. & iron.)*: a To keep someone waiting. b To be long overdue. *Ce rappel de salaire commence à se faire désirer!* We should have had that back-pay ages ago!

désordre *n.m. Toucher le tiercé dans le désordre* (Racing slang): To get a 'consolation divvy' on a tricast bet. (The object of the *tiercé* is to prognosticate which horses will arrive first, second and third in a given race; failure to do so in the correct order – *'dans le désordre'* – entitles the punter only to a consolation dividend.)

désordre *adj. Ça fait désordre!* It looks darned untidy!

désossé *n.m.* 'Gawk', lanky person. (At the turn of the century, *Valentin le Désossé*, a famous dancer at the *Moulin Rouge*, astounded the cabaret crowds with his indiarubber-man antics.)

désossé *adj.* 'Lanky', tall and skinny. *Il est drôlement désossé!* There's about as much fat on him as on a butcher's pencil!

désosser *v.trans.* To take to pieces. *Désosser une bagnole:* To 'break' a car for spares. *Désosser le jonc:* To separate stolen gems from their gold mountings, the scrap being melted down and the stones recut or reset.

dessalé *adj.* **a** (of man): 'On the ball', 'wide-awake', sharp. **b** (of woman): 'Liberated', totally uninhibited sexually.

dessaler *v.trans.* **1** To initiate someone in the ways of the world. **2** To initiate in sexual matters.

dessaler *v.pronom.* **1** To 'wise up', to come to terms with the hard facts of life. **2** To lose one's inhibitions, one's sexual hang-ups.

desserre *n.f. Etre dur à la desserre:* To be 'stingy', to be mean with money.

dessin *n.m. Faire un dessin à quelqu'un:* To go into minute details when explaining something to someone. *Est-ce qu'il faut te faire un dessin? (iron.):* Do I have to explain it to you in words of one syllable?

dessouder *v.trans.* To 'bump off', to kill.

dessous *n.m.* **1** Prostitute's 'fancy man'. **2** Pimp's second woman. (In an already strange one-to-one, and one-to-many relationship, the pimp's hold over his prostitute is originally based on a kind of faithfulness; often to double his income the small-time pimp will have two women working for him, each believing that she is the only one, both in fact being *un dessous*.) **3** *Dessous de table:* 'Back-hander', 'kick-back', unauthorized payment. **4** *Etre dans le trente-sixième dessous:* To be 'down in the dumps', to feel like ending it all, to have no taste for life.

dessus *n.m.* **1** Kept woman's procurer of finance. *C'est son dessus:* He's her meal-ticket. **2** *Dessus de châsses:* 'Wrinkle-board', forehead.

dessus *adv.* **1** *Tomber dessus:* **a** To come across someone or something unexpectedly. *Il m'est tombé dessus comme j'allais faire les commissions:* He popped up out of nowhere as I was off shopping. **b** To 'go for', to attack physically or verbally. *Il m'est tombé dessus pour avoir oublié le courrier:* He played merry hell with me for forgetting the mail. **2** *Il ne faut pas cracher dessus:* It's not to be sneezed at – It's certainly worth taking seriously. **3** *'y a qu'à souffler dessus (joc.):* There's nothing to it! – It's no great problem!

détail *n.m. Ne pas faire de détail:* **a** To act in a 'ham-fisted', in a clumsy manner. **b** To 'put one's back into something', to spare no effort.

détaler *v.intrans.* To 'scram', to 'scarper', to run away. *Détaler comme un lièvre:* To run like the clappers.

dételer *v.intrans.* **1** To 'jack it in', to 'pack it in', to give up a strenuous occupation. **2** To 'kick over the traces', to leave one's marital partner. **3** *Sans dételer:* 'At a stretch', continuously, without stopping.

détente *n.f. Etre dur à la détente:* **a** To be 'a trifle dim', to be 'slow on the uptake', to understand with difficulty. **b** To be 'stingy', to be 'tight-fisted', to be mean with money.

déterré *n.m. Avoir une gueule* (also: *une mine*) *de déterré:* To 'look like death warmed up', to look pale and unwell.

détrancher *v.trans.* To eye someone inquisitively.

détrancher *v.pronom.* **1** To have a quick peep, to take a surreptitious look. **2** (Gambling slang): To change one's mind about a bet.

détraqué *adj.* **1** Physically 'shattered', in very poor health. **2** 'Bonkers', 'potty', mad.

détréper *v.pronom.* To become drained of people. *Paris se détrèpe drôlement en juillet-août:* Paris is a bit of a ghost town in July and August.

détresse *n.f. Y aller du coup de la détresse:* To 'come the old soldier', to harp on someone's feelings of sympathy.

détroncher *v.trans.* To eye someone with an inquisitive look. *Sur le quai de la gare, il détronchait les arrivants:* He took a close look at all those leaving the train.

détroncher *v.pronom.* To 'look over one's shoulder', to look back at something or someone.

deuche *n.f.* (abbr. *deux-chevaux*): Citroen 2 CV motor car. (A not uncommon misconception is that this famous 'sit-up-and-beg' French motoring contraption is powered only by a 2 hp engine. In fact, for taxation purposes in France, road fund licences are issued for vehicles on the basis of *'chevaux fiscaux'*. These units bear no relation to the traditional concept of brake horse-power.)

deuil *n.m.* **1** Risk of arrest. *Il y avait du deuil à sortir après le couvre-feu:* Being out of doors after curfew was asking for trouble. **2** *Faire son deuil de quelque chose* (also: *en faire son deuil*): To resign oneself to the loss of something. *Ce fric-là, tu peux en faire ton deuil!* You can kiss goodbye to that money! **3** *Porter le deuil*: To lodge an (official) complaint. **4** *Avoir les ongles en deuil*: To have dirty fingernails.

deusio *adv.* (also: *deuxio*): Secondly, in the second place. *Primo, j'ai pas envie d'y aller, deusio, j'ai pas le temps*: For starters, I couldn't be bothered going, and apart from that I haven't the time.

deux *num.adj.* **1** *Ne faire ni une ni deux*: To 'make no bones about something', to be straightforward and frank. **2** *Ça fait deux*: It's a totally different kettle of fish – These are two entirely different matters. **3** *On sera deux! (iron.)*: Two of us can play that game! – You're going to have some opposition! **4** *Piquer des deux*: To 'get one's skates on', to hurry up. **5** *En moins de deux*: In two ticks – Promptly – Very quickly. **6** *Il était moins de deux*: It was touch-and-go –It was a near thing. **7** *de mes deux (adj.exp.)*: Bloody awful. *J'en ai marre de cette bagnole de mes deux*: I'm sick to the back teeth with that perishing car! (*de mes deux* implies *couilles*, hence the strongly pejorative connotation of the expression). **8** *Atteler à deux*: **a** (of pimp): To have two prostitutes working. **b** To 'have a sandwich', to have a sexual threesome (two girls and one man).

deuxio *adv.* (also: *deusio*): Secondly, in the second place.

deux-pattes *n.f. (joc.corr. deux-chevaux)*: Citroen 2CV motor car. (Contrary to popular belief, this frog-like economy motor car is not powered by a 2 horse-power engine. The French for taxation purposes have graded motor vehicles in *chevaux fiscaux* categories and the 602 cc engine certainly develops more power than a lawnmower!)

devant *n.m.* 'Belly', stomach. *Bâtir sur le devant (joc.)*: To 'get a corporation', to develop a pot-belly. *Se faire arrondir le devant*: To 'join the pudding-club', to get pregnant.

devant *adv.* *S'arracher de devant*: To 'scarper' in order to avoid aggro, to leave when trouble's brewing.

devanture *n.f.* *Une belle devanture*: 'A smashing pair of boobs', large and firm breasts. (This sexist term is always uttered in a jocular context.)

déveine *n.f.* Run of bad luck. *Etre dans la déveine*: To be down on one's luck. *Quelle déveine!* What rotten luck!

développement *n.m.* **1** *Mettre le grand développement (fig.)*: To 'give one's darnedest', to make an all-out effort. (This expression originates from the world of cycling and the *grand développement* refers to the highest gear-ratio available.) **2** *Suivre les développements*: To 'keep tabs on something', to keep track of what is happening.

dévider *v.intrans. & trans.* **1** To 'waffle on', to talk endlessly on vacuous topics. **2** *Dévider le jars*: To talk slang.

dévider *v.trans.reflex.* To reel out a lengthy and verbose tale of woe.

dévisser *v.trans.* **1** *La dévisser* (also: *dévisser son billard*): To 'kick the bucket', to 'croak', to die. **2** To 'come across', to find. *Où qu' t'as dévissé ça?* And where did you dig that up from?

dévisser *v.trans.reflex.* **1** To 'bugger off', to go away. **2** *Avoir un blaze qui se dévisse (joc.)*: To have a double-barrelled name.

dévoreuse *n.f.* 'Man-eater', 'randy bird', highly-sexed woman.

dézinguer *v.trans.* **1** To 'knacker', to 'bugger up', to damage. **2** To 'bump off', to kill.

diable *n.m.* *Habiter au diable (Vauvert)*: To live 'out in the sticks', to live miles away from anywhere.

diabolo *n.m.* Soft drink – a mixture of lemonade and fruit or peppermint syrup, the most popular being the *diabolo menthe*.

diam *n.m. (abbr. diamant)*: 'Rock', gem, diamond.

Diane *Proper name.* *Un prix de Diane*: A 'pretty filly', a 'good-looking lass', an attractive young girl. (The *Prix de Diane* is a famous flat race for fillies run at the *Longchamp* race-course.)

diapason *n.m.* *Se mettre au diapason*: To 'get attuned', to get in the swing of things.

diapo *n.m. (abbr. diapositive)*: 'Slide', colour photographic transparency.

dico *n.m.* 'Dic', dictionary.

didine *n.f. (joc.)*: 'Fanny', 'pussy', vagina.

didis *n.m.pl.* (Child language): 'Pinkies', fingers.

didite *n.f.* (Horse racing slang): Dead-heat. (This is a phonetic corruption of the English.)

Dieu *Proper name.* The plethora of swear locutions invoking the name of God is hardly relevant to a dictionary dealing with modern colloquial French. It is worth noting, however, that expressions involving the mild substitute *bleu* for *dieu* seem to be regaining popularity: *parbleu*, *sacrebleu* have a quaint comical connotation making them acceptable today.

difficile *adj.* *Faire le difficile*: **a** To be 'picky and choosy', to be 'finicky', to be difficult to please. **b** To 'play the awkward bugger', to be obstreperous.

digérer *v.trans.* *Ne pas digérer quelque chose*: To react angrily to an affront or setback. *Il n'a pas digéré ça*: He really couldn't stomach that.

digue *n.f.* 'Fuck-all', nothing. *Etre venu pour la digue*: To have gone on a fool's errand, to have made a wasted journey. *Que digue!* No way! – Nothing doing! – Certainly not!

digue-digue *n.f. Tomber* (also: *partir*) *en digue-digue:* To 'black out', to faint.

dimanche *n.m.* **1** *Etre né un dimanche (iron.):* To have 'a lazy streak', to be an idle so-and-so. **2** *Etre en dimanche:* To be 'dolled-up', to be all dressed-up.

dindon *n.m. Dindon de la farce:* 'Fall-guy', 'mug', dupe.

dindonner *v.trans.* To 'pull a fast one on someone', to 'con', to swindle.

dîne *n.f.* 'Grub', 'eats', food. *A la dîne!* Grub's up! – Come and get it! – Dinner is ready!

dingue *n.m.* 'Nut-case', 'crackpot', mad person. *Aller à la tôle aux dingues:* To go to the 'loony-bin', to be interned in a mental asylum.

dingue *n.f.* **1** 'Jemmy', crowbar. **2** *Prendre une dingue:* To have a bout of tropical fever.

dingue *adj.* 'Bonkers', 'loony', mad.

dinguer *v.intrans.* **1** *Envoyer dinguer quelqu'un:* **a** To thump someone and send him sprawling. **b** To 'send someone off with a flea in his ear', to send someone away with a torrent of abuse. **2** *Envoyer dinguer quelque chose:* To 'chuck something out', to throw something away.

dire *v.trans. & intrans.* **1** *Ne pas envoyer dire quelque chose à quelqu'un:* To tell someone something straight to their face. **2** *A qui le dites-vous?! (iron.):* Don't I know it! – You're telling me! – I certainly am aware of that! **3** *Je ne vous le fais pas dire!* Need I say more?! – I'm not putting the words into your mouth. **4** *Vous m'en direz tant!* This colloquial expression combining gentle irony and mild astonishment can best be translated by the single word: Really! with its various shades of meaning, e.g. You don't say! – Now you're talking! **5** *Qu'il dit! (iron.):* Says he! – So he says! – That's his story! **6** *Ça me dit!* I like it, I like it! – It suits me down to the ground! **7** *Il y a comme qui dirait un défaut:* I smell a rat! – Something's not quite right.

dirlo *n.m.* **1** *(sch.):* 'Head', headmaster. **2** 'Gaffer', boss, director of business firm (also: *dirlingue*).

discagogo *n.m.* Jukebox. (*Le Discagogo* was a famous Parisian discotheque of the 60s.)

disciplote *n.f. (mil.):* Discipline. *Les disciplotes* (also: *les compagnies de disciplote*): Disciplinary battalions formerly stationed in North Africa whose intake of National Servicemen seemed heavily loaded with men having either a criminal record, a background of juvenile violence or a reputation for being untrainable.

discutailler *v.intrans.* To 'thrash things out', to try and resolve problems through discussion.

discuter *v.trans.* **1** *Discuter le coup:* To 'thrash things out', to have a frank exchange of views. **2** *Discuter le bout de gras:* To 'chew the fat', to natter away amicably.

disque *n.m.* **1** *Change de disque!* Stop harping on! – Give it a rest! – Please change the subject! **2** *Le disque:* The anal sphincter (in the context of sodomous intercourse).

disserte *n.f. (sch.):* Essay, dissertation.

distance *n.f. Pouvoir tenir la distance:* To 'have what it takes', to be resilient. (The word originates from the language of the long-distance runner.)

distribe *n.f. (abbr. distribution):* **1** *(mil.):* Issue of army rations. **2** 'Hand-out', share-out. *A la distribe des méninges, il a manqué son tour! (iron.):* He was at the back of the queue when brains were being dished out!

distribution *n.f.* **1** *(joc.):* 'Bashing-up', beating, thrashing. **2** *La distribution des prix (joc.):* Judgement, sentence from court of law.

divisionnaire *n.m. (abbr. Commissionnaire divisionnaire):* Police superintendent.

dix *n.m. Piquer le dix:* To pace up and down in a confined space. (The expression originates from prison slang.)

dix *num.adj.* **1** *Dix sur dix!* You got it in one! – Right first time! **2** *Dix de der!* Exclamation at *belote* indicating that one has clinched the last trick with a bonus of ten points.

doc *n.m.* 'Quack', 'doc', doctor.

doche *n.f.* **1** *Ma doche:* 'The old woman', my mother. **2** *Les doches:* 'The old folk', my parents.

doches *n.f.pl.* **1** 'Bones', dice. *Passer les doches (fig.):* To 'throw in the towel', to give up. (The expression originates from the language of the gambler who after a bad throw decides reluctantly to pass the dice-cup to another player.) **2** Dominoes. *Boîte à doches:* **a** 'Gob', 'trap', mouth. **b** 'Bone-box', coffin. **3** *Avoir ses doches:* To 'have the decorators in', to have a menstrual period.

docteur *n.m.* 'Doc', medic. (It is considered rather low-brow to say *docteur* instead of *médecin*, particularly in ungrammatical expressions like *aller au docteur.*)

docu *n.m.* **1** *(abbr. document):* Paper, document. **2** *(abbr. documentaire):* Documentary film.

dodo *n.m.* **1** 'Beddy-byes', sleep. *Faire dodo:* To get some shut-eye. *Aller au dodo:* To 'hit the sack', to go to bed. (The word may have originated in the nursery but it has long since been in general colloquial usage.) **2** *Dodo ninette:* Sex, sexual intercourse. *Ne pas donner dans le dodo ninette:* To have a low sex-drive.

doigt *n.m.* **1** *Se fourrer le doigt dans l'œil (jusqu'au coude)*: To 'have got it all wrong', to have made a major blunder. **2** *Mon petit doigt m'a dit que . . . (joc.)*: A little bird told me that . . . –'I heard through the grapevine that. . . . (The expression belongs originally to the *langage bêtifiant* inflicted on children but seems to have drifted into adult drivel.)

dolluches *n.f.pl.* 'Greenbacks', dollars.

dombeur *n.m.* 'Jemmy', crowbar.

domicile *n.m.* *Livrer à domicile (joc.)*: To have some 'nookie' away from home, to have intercourse at the home of one's lady friend.

dominos *n.m.pl.* **1** 'Gnashers', 'choppers', teeth. (The expression *avoir un jeu de dominos complet* can mean either to have all one's own teeth, or to be kitted out with a full set of dentures.) **2** Bones. (*Boîte à dominos* can be either a jocular word for coffin, or refer to the mouth using the meaning of 'teeth'.)

dondon *n.f.* *Grosse dondon (pej.)*: 'Big lump', 'fat biddy', corpulent woman.

donnant *Donnant donnant (adv.exp.)*: 'You scratch my back, I'll scratch yours' – 'If you help me, I'll help you'.

donne *n.f.* **1** Largesse, financial generosity. *Pour la donne, il est toujours là*: He's not backward when it comes to dipping into his pocket. **2** *Etre de la donne*: To be on the losing side in a financial transaction.

donner *v.trans.* **1** To inform on, to denounce someone. **2** (Cards): To deal. *C'est à vous de donner*: It's your turn to deal. (In this case the verb is only transitive by implication.) **3** *C'est donné! (iron.)*: It's cheap at the price! – I wouldn't call that expensive! **4** *On t'en donnera! (iron.)*: You'll be lucky! – You're setting your sights a bit high!

donner *v.intrans.* **1** *Donner dans*: **a** (also: *donner dans le panneau*): To 'fall for something hook, line and sinker', to be totally fooled by a ploy. **b** To become, to undergo a change of character. *Depuis la mort de sa femme, il donne dans le grincheux*: He's become a real misery guts since his missus passed away. **2** *Donner à pleins tubes*: To give one's all, to make an all-out effort.

donner *v.trans.reflex.* **1** *S'en donner* (of pleasurable activity): To 'get some in', to get one's fill. *On va s'en donner du bon temps!* We're going to let our hair down! **2** *Se donner peur*: To panic without reason.

donner *v.pronom.* *Se la donner*: To have one's suspicions, to be 'cagey', to be wary about something. *On se la donnait qu'il était flic*: It was thought he might be a cop working undercover.

donneur *n.m.* **1** 'Squealer', informer. **2** *Ne pas être donneur*: To be 'tight-fisted', to be mean where money is concerned.

donzelle *n.f.* 'Bird', 'lassie', young girl.

dopant *n.m.* (Drugs): 'Upper', stimulant.

doper *v.trans.* To boost someone's morale, to give someone words of encouragement.

doré *adj.* Lucky, fortunate (also: *verni*).

dorer *v.trans.* **1** *Dorer la pilule*: To 'gild the lily', to 'sugar the pill', to make something look enticing. **2** *Se faire dorer la pilule*: **a** To get a good sun-tan. **b** To let life take care of itself, to take things easy.

dorme *n.f.* *La dorme*: 'Kip', 'shut-eye', sleep. *Aller à la dorme*: To hit the sack.

dorto *n.m.* *(abbr. dortoir)*: 'Dorm', dormitory.

dorure *n.f.* *Une dorure*: A 'walk-over', an easy task.

doryphore *n.m.* 'Jerry', 'Kraut', German. (The ravages of the Colorado beetle are equated with those of the Hun in World War II.)

dos *n.m.* **1** *Avoir bon dos*: To be an 'easy touch' for favours, to find it difficult to turn down requests. (The implication here is that he who has *'bon dos'* usually lives to regret his generosity.) **2** *L'avoir dans le dos*: To have been 'diddled', to have been 'conned' out of something. **3** *En avoir plein le dos*: To be 'sick to the back teeth' with something, to be unable to stand any more of something. **4** *Passer la main dans le dos de quelqu'un*: To 'butter up', to flatter someone. **5** *Scier le dos à quelqu'un*: To be 'a pain in the neck' to someone, to be a confounded nuisance. **6** *Ne pas y aller avec le dos de la cuiller*: To 'lay it on a bit thick', to exaggerate. **7** *Donner du dos*: To engage in sodomy.

dose *n.f.* **1** *En avoir* (also: *en tenir*) *une dose*: **a** To have had 'one over the eight', to be drunk. **b** To suffer from a violent bout of a particular disease. **2** *Forcer la dose*: **a** To 'go over the top', to overdo something. **b** To 'lay it on a bit thick', to make exaggerated claims.

dossière *n.f.* **1** 'Bum', 'botty', behind. *Jouer de la dossière*: To walk with a waddle, with undulating hips. **2** *La dossière*: The arse-hole, the anal sphincter (in the context of sodomous intercourse).

dos-vert *n.m.* Pimp, ponce, procurer.

douanier *n.m.* Glass of *absinthe*. (Although *absinthe* became illegal during World War I, because it had hallucinatory side-effects, the word and a few hoarded bottles survived into the early 1940s.)

doublage *n.m.* 'Double-cross', deception.

double *adj.* *Mener en double*: To 'lead someone up the garden path', to try and deceive someone.

doublé *n.m.* *Toucher un doublé (joc.)*: To have twins.

double-mètre *n.m.* *(joc.)*: 'Bean-pole', 'gawk', tall and thin person.

doubler *v.trans.* 1 To 'double-cross', to deceive. *Doubler un truand comme lui, c'est vraiment chercher la castagne*: Trying to put one across a crook like him is really asking for trouble. 2 To 'two-time', to be unfaithful to one's sexual partner.

double-six *n.m.* 1 *(pl.)*: 'Grinders', molars. 2 *Rendre le double-six à quelqu'un*: To show someone who's boss, to prove oneself to be more than someone else's equal.

doublure *n.f.* 1 *(th.)*: Understudy. 2 'Stand-in', stuntman prepared to take the knocks for a film star. 3 'Front-man', person who lets his name be used by others for nefarious activities.

douce *adj.* 1 *En douce (adv.exp.)*: 'Softly-softly', quietly, discreetly. *Faire quelque chose en douce*: To do something on the Q.T. *Filer en douce*: To slip away unnoticed. 2 *Se la couler douce*: To 'lead the life of Riley', to have a cushy life.

doucettement *adv.* 'Softly-softly', slowly. *Ça va doucettement*: Things are ticking over – Business is slow but steady. *Il se remet doucettement*: He's slowly on the mend.

douche *n.f.* 1 Downpour, heavy rainfall. *Prendre une douche*: To get soaked to the skin. 2 'Rollicking', reprimand. 3 *Douche écossaise*: Raising and dashing of hopes. *Avec ce patron on a toujours droit au régime de la douche écossaise*: You never know where you stand with this boss of ours!

doucher *v.trans.* 1 To 'cool someone off', to bring someone back to reality. 2 To shake someone's confidence. *Ça l'a drôlement douché de voir le bilan*: Seeing the accounts made him a trifle less cocky. 3 *Avoir été douché*: To have 'got one's fingers burnt', to have suffered a severe financial loss.

doudounes *n.f.pl.* 'Knockers', 'boobs', breasts. (This sexist word suggests rather flabby mammaries.)

douillard *adj.* 1 'Loaded', stinking rich. 2 'Well-thatched', endowed with a fine head of hair.

douille *n.f.* 1 'Dough', 'brass', money. *Côté douille c'est pas brillant!*: Finances aren't very bright, I'm afraid! 2 *La douille:*'Forking-out', paying up. *Pour ce qui est de la douille, il est plutôt radin*: He's a mean bastard when it comes to settling bills. 3 *(pl.)*: 'Thatch', head of hair. *Il est toujours à se fourrager les douilles*: He's forever scratching an itch in his hair.

douiller *v.trans.* To 'cough up', to 'fork out', to pay. *Douiller la douloureuse*: To settle the bill.

douillettes *n.f.pl.* *(joc.)*: 'Balls', 'bollocks', testicles.

doul *n.m.* *(abbr. doulos)*: 'Squealer', police informant.

douleur *n.f.* 1 'Pain-in-the-neck', obnoxious character. 2 *Comprendre sa douleur (iron.)*: To realize to what extent one has been conned. 3 *Oh douleur! (joc.)*: Bloody Nora! – Good grief!

doulos *n.m.* 1 'Lid', man's hat. 2 'Snitch', 'grass', police informant.

douloureuse *n.f.* 'Tab', bill (in restaurant, hotel). *Passe-moi la douloureuse!* What's the damage then?!

douter *v.trans.indirect.* *Ne douter de rien*: To be 'as cocky as hell', to be brimming with self-confidence. *Tu ne doutes de rien!* You must be joking!

douteux *adj.* *Des sous-vêtements douteux*: Grubby underwear.

doux *adv.* *Filer doux*: To tread warily and toe the line, to conform. *Depuis qu'il vit chez sa belle-doche, il doit filer doux*: Since moving in with the mother-in-law, he's learnt to keep a low profile.

douzaine *n.f.* *On en trouve à la douzaine*: They are a pretty common sight. (The irony of the expression is more blatant in the negative. *On n'en trouve pas à la douzaine!* They don't grow on trees you know!)

douze *n.m.* 'Cock-up', gaffe, blunder. *Faire un douze*: To put one's foot in it.

drag *n.f.* (Drugs): 'Joint', 'reefer', hand-rolled cigarette containing marijuana.

drage *n.f.* 'Quack remedy', suspect 'miracle potion', dubious medicine.

dragée *n.f.* 1 *Avaler la dragée*: To 'swallow the pill', to fall for something. 2 *Tenir la dragée haute à quelqu'un*: **a** To 'string someone along', to keep someone waiting for something a long time. **b** To make someone pay dearly for something. *Elle lui tient la dragée haute*: She's got him just where she wants – He's certainly paying the price for her favours. 3 Pistol bullet. *Il s'est cloqué une dragée dans le plafond*: He pumped a red-hot pip in his nut.

draguer *v.trans.* To be out trying to 'pull the birds', to be on the look-out for pick-ups.

dragueur *n.m.* 'Wolf', persistent womanizer.

drapeau *n.m.* 1 Unpaid bill. *Planter un drapeau*: To leave without paying. 2 'Shimmy', shirt. 3 *Etre en drapeau* (of car): To have broken down.

draps *n.m.pl.* *Etre dans de beaux draps (iron.)*: To be 'in a right old fix', to be up to one's neck in trouble.

dreauper *n.m.* 'Cop', 'copper', policeman. (The word is an example of *verlen* where the already colloquial word *perdreau* is written syllabically back-to-front.)

drelinguer *v.intrans.* To 'ding-a-ling', to ring a doorbell. (*Dreling, dreling!* is the onomatopoeic transcription in cartoons of a doorbell ringing.)

dresser *v.trans.* *Dresser quelqu'un*: To make someone toe the line, to get someone to conform. *Moi je vais le dresser, ce zigoto!* That nurk's going to do what I want him to!

driver *v.trans. & intrans.* **1** To give someone a lift, to drive someone somewhere. *Il m'a drivé chez ma belle-doche*: He dropped me at my mother-in-law's. **2** To be an active boss, a driving managerial force. **3** *Il drive une dizaine de polkas* (of pimp): He's got ten birds beavering away for him.

droguer *v.intrans.* *Faire droguer quelqu'un*: To keep someone hanging about, to keep someone waiting.

droit *adv.* *Marcher droit*: To 'toe the line', to do what one is told.

droit-commun *n.m.* *Un droit-commun*: A common criminal (as opposed to a political internee).

droite *n.f.* *Tenir sa droite* (Motoring): To stay on the right-hand side of the road.

drôle *adj.* **1** Weird, strange. *Un drôle de paroissien*: A 'queer cove', a bizarre character. **2** 'Great', extraordinary. *C'est un drôle de mec!* He's a really fantastic bloke! **3** *Se sentir tout drôle*: To feel queasy, to feel physically unwell.

drôlement *adv.* **1** Extremely, very. *Elle est drôlement bath, cette nana!* She's jolly attractive, that girl! **2** *Il s'est fait avoir et drôlement!* (*iron.*): He got well and truly done!

droper *v.trans.* To 'leave in the lurch', to let someone down badly.

droper *v.intrans.* To put some zest in what one is doing, to inject some tempo into an activity.

drouille *n.f.* *De la drouille* (Market traders' slang): Useless junk, unsaleable wares. (The word can sometimes in department stores refer to sub-standard sales goods.)

duce *n.m.* **1** Pre-arranged sign of connivance between partners in a con or a fiddle. **2** (*pol.*): Secret information given to a member of the Force by an informant. *Envoyer le duce*: To give a tip-off.

duchnock *n.m.* (*joc.*): 'Nincompoop', cretin. (The noun is often written with a capital, thus

inferring that it could, in fact, be a proper name.)

dudule *n.m.* (*joc.*): 'Whatsisname', 'thingummy', that person. (As with *duchnock*, this slightly derogatory term is sometimes elevated to the status of proper name.)

dur *n.m.* **1** *Un dur*: A tough guy, one who is not easily frightened. *Jouer au dur*: To play the heavy. **2** *Le dur*: The train. *Brûler le dur*: To travel without a ticket. **3** *Du dur*: 'Readies', hard cash (as opposed to cheques, promissory notes, etc. Originally, *du dur* referred to gold coins – to many, the most reliable currency). **4** *Les durs*: 'Hard', hard labour. *Monter aux durs*: To get sentenced to a term of penal servitude. (The distinction between prison and *travaux forcés* has all but disappeared; the difference to hardened criminals until recently was of great importance.)

dur *adj.* **1** 'Tough', difficult. *Ça n'est pas dur à piger*: It's easy to guess. **2** *Etre dur à cuire*: To be 'something of a tough nut', to be resilient to all manner of stresses and strains. **3** *Etre dur de la feuille*: To be 'hard of hearing', to be a little deaf. **4** *Etre dur à la desserre* (also: *à la détente*): To be 'tight-fisted', to be mean. **5** *L'avoir dur pour*: To 'have a crush on', to be infatuated with someone.

dur *adv.* *Croire dur comme fer à quelque chose*: To take something for gospel truth, to believe firmly in something.

duraille *adj.* 'Tough', rather difficult. *C'est plutôt duraille ce que tu me demandes*: You're not exactly asking for a small favour! (also: *durillard*).

durand *n.m.* *Le durand*: The sun (usually in the context of a hot, sultry day).

dure *n.f.* **1** *La dure*: Bare ground, the hard earth (as in the expression *coucher à la dure*: to sleep rough). **2** *De la dure*: 'Shoe-leather', tough meat.

durillon *n.m.* *Durillon de comptoir* (*joc.*): 'Corporation', pot-belly (literally a corn on one's belly from having been a bar-prop most of one's life).

durite *n.f.* *Péter une durite* (*joc.*): To 'blow one's top', to very nearly burst a blood vessel whilst in a fit of anger.

Dyna *Proper name.* Family saloon car manufactured by Panhard between the 50s and late 60s.

dynamite *n.f.* 'Snow', cocaine. *Marcher à la dynamite*: To be totally addicted to cocaine.

dynamité *n.m.* 'Junky', drug addict.

dynamité *adj.* 'High', 'smashed', drugged.

E

eau *n.f.* **1** *N'avoir pas inventé l'eau chaude (joc. & iron.)*: To be 'slow on the uptake', to be rather dimwitted (also: *ne pas avoir inventé le fil à couper le beurre*). **2** *Tomber à l'eau* (of plan, project): To 'fall through', to come to nothing. **3** *Mettre de l'eau dans son vin*: To 'lower one's sights', to accept more humble aspirations. **4** *Il y a de l'eau dans le gaz*: There's a 'fly in the ointment' – There seems to be something of a problem. **5** *Nager entre deux eaux*: To 'sit on the fence', to avoid committing oneself. **6** *Croyez ça et buvez de l'eau! (iron.)*: If you believe that, you'll believe anything! **7** *De la plus belle eau (adj.exp.)*: Of the worst kind. *C'est une ordure de la plus belle eau!* There's no doubt he's a real swine! **8** *De l'eau de bidet*: 'Bugger-all of value' (something barely worth contempt). **9** *Partir* (also: *tourner*) *en eau de boudin*: To 'fizzle out', to come to nothing. **10** *Un roman à l'eau de rose*: A 'dewy' novelette (the kind of syrupy fiction devoured by low-brow sentimentalists).

ébats *n.m.pl.* 'Randy goings-on', sexy frolics.

ébaubir *v.trans.* To 'flabbergast', to astound (also: *abalober*).

ébéno *n.m.* 'Chips', joiner.

ébonite *n.f. La passoire d'ébonite*: 'The blower', the phone, the telephone.

éboulé *adj.* 'Passed away', deceased.

ébouriffant *adj.* 'Fantabulous', extraordinary.

ébouser *v.trans.* (also: *ébouzer*): **1** To 'bump off', to kill. **2** To 'crush', to reduce someone to silence.

ébréché *adj.* 'Tiddly', 'tipsy', slightly drunk (also: *éméché*).

écailler *v.trans.* **1** To 'clean out', to fleece at gambling. **2** To 'diddle', to 'con' someone out of money.

écart *n.m.* (Racing slang): Number of consecutive bad races plaguing a jockey. *Briser son écart*: To get a change of luck. (This expression has extended into everyday colloquial speech, and to the compulsive womanizer it means to have a lucky break where relationships are concerned.)

échalas *n.m.* **1** 'Bean-pole', skinny person. **2** *(pl.)*: 'Pins', 'gambs', legs. *Mettre les échalas*: To go away, to leave (also: *mettre les bouts*).

échalote *n.f.* **1** *L'échalote*: The arse-hole, the anal sphincter. *Prendre de l'échalote*: To engage in passive sodomy. **2** *La course à l'échalote*: Act of chucking someone out by the scruff of the neck and the seat of the pants. **3** *Se faire dévisser les échalotes*: To 'have it all taken away', to have a hysterectomy.

échappé *n.m. Échappé de bocal (pej.)*: 'Squirt', 'runt', physically under-developed person (also: *raclure de bidet*).

écharpiller *v.trans. Se faire écharpiller*: To get thrashed good and proper, to get beaten up.

échasses *n.f.pl.* 'Pins', 'gambs', legs.

échassière *n.f.* Bar-room tart (prostitute who solicits customers from a high bar-stool).

échauder *v.trans.* To 'con', to 'diddle', to swindle. *Se faire échauder*: To get fleeced.

échelle *n.f.* **1** *Grimper* (also: *monter*) *à l'échelle*: To 'fall for something', to 'get taken in', to be hoaxed. **2** *Après ça, il n'y a plus qu'à tirer l'échelle! (iron.)*: Top that! – That's the limit! – You can't improve on that!

échiner *v.pronom.* To 'work oneself into the ground', to overdo it work-wise.

échineur *n.m.* Virulent critic.

échouer *v.intrans.* To 'land', to end up somewhere. *En fin de compte il a échoué en Suisse*: He finally settled in Switzerland.

éclairer *v.trans. & intrans.* To 'fork out', to pay up. *Les éclairer*: To 'show the colour of one's money', to prove one is solvent. *Il avait dû les éclairer avant de taper les cartons*: They made sure he had some loot before letting him in on the game. **2** *Eclairer sur la couleur*: To 'give the low-down on something', to explain.

éclater *v.pronom.* (Drugs): To 'have a trip', to suffer drug-induced hallucinations.

écluser *v.trans. & intrans.* To 'knock back', to 'swig', to drink. *Ecluser sec*: To down drinks in quick succession.

écluses *n.f.pl. Ouvrir les écluses:* To 'open the floodgates', to burst into tears.

éconocroques *n.f.pl. (corr. économies):* 'Nest-egg', savings. *Côté éconocroques, il a su se débrouiller:* He certainly made the best of the good times and stashed money away.

économies *n.f.pl. Faire des économies de bout de chandelle:* To scrimp and save in pointless ways.

écoper *v.intrans.* To be on the receiving end of something unpleasant. *Il a écopé d'une infusion de rame de châtaignier:* He got thrashed good and proper. *Il a écopé de dix ans de durs:* He copped ten years hard labour. *Tu vas écoper!* You're for the high jump! – You're going to get what you deserve!

écorcher *v.trans.* 1 *Ecorcher un nom:* To 'make a hash' of someone's name, to mispronounce it. 2 *Se faire écorcher:* To 'get fleeced', to be overcharged. *Pour ce qui est de la douloureuse, on s'est fait drôlement écorcher!* With that bill, we really got taken for a ride!

écosser *v.trans. & intrans.* 1 To 'shell out', to 'fork out', to pay up. 2 *En écosser:* To engage in prostitution. (The expression can sometimes also refer to 'hard graft' of any nature.)

écouter *v.intrans. 'Ecoute! Ecoute!' (joc.):* 'Don't go away!' (This was the famous catchphrase of comedian Roger Nicolas who in his early film career was typecast as a *camelot* or street-hawker.)

écouter *v.trans.reflex. Trop s'écouter:* To mollycoddle oneself to the extent of becoming a hypochondriac.

écoutilles *n.f.pl.* 'Flappers', 'lug-holes', ears (also: *étagères à mégot*).

écrabouiller *v.trans.* To crush, to squash to a pulp. *Il s'est fait écrabouiller par une bagnole:* He got run down by a car.

écrase-merde *n.m.pl. (joc.):* 'Beetle-crushers', 'boats', large-size shoes (also: *pataugas*).

écraser *v.trans.* 1 *Ecraser le coup:* **a** To 'give in', to give up. **b** To 'let bygones be bygones', to put something down to experience (and do nothing more about it). 2 *Ecrase!* Pack it in! –Belt up! – Shut up! 3 *En écraser:* To 'sleep like a log', to be fast asleep. *Qu'est-ce qu'il en écrase!* He's dead to the world! 4 *En écraser cinq:* To shake hands.

écraser *v.pronom.* 1 To 'clam up', to adopt a silent attitude. 2 To 'keep a low profile', to steer clear of involvement.

écrémer *v.trans.* 1 To take 'first pick', to choose the best items. 2 To 'fleece', to leave penniless. *Ecrémer les clilles:* To 'take the customers for a ride', to overcharge them heavily.

écrouler *v.pronom.* To collapse wearily (usually in an armchair).

écumeur *n.m. Ecumeur de marmite:* 'Sponger', 'hanger-on', parasite-like character.

écurie *n.f.* 1 'Regular pigsty', filthy dwelling. 2 *Sentir l'écurie:* To be in a hurry to get home. 3 *Se croire dans une écurie:* To behave in an uncouth manner. *Entrer comme dans une écurie:* To come in without greeting anyone.

édicule *n.m. (joc.):* Urinal, gents' public convenience.

édredon *n.m. (pol.):* Promise made to felon to tempt him to turn 'supergrass', and inform on past accomplices.

éducation *n.f. Ça manque à ton éducation! (iron.):* You've a few things to learn yet!

effacer *v.trans.* 1 To 'polish off', to 'knock back', to consume (food or drink). *Il a effacé un morcif comme ça!* He scoffed a giant portion! 2 To 'cop a blow', to be on the receiving end of physical violence. *Il a effacé une de ces mandalles!* The slap he got sent him reeling. (The expression *en effacer une* often indicates that someone has been hit by a bullet.)

effaroucher *v.trans. (joc.):* To 'nick', to 'pinch', to steal.

effet *n.m. Si c'était un effet de votre bonté . . .* It would be rather nice if you could . . . (This expression is loaded with supercilious irony.)

effeuiller *v.trans. Effeuiller la marguerite:* To 'strip', to perform a striptease. (Originally *effeuiller la marguerite* was literally to pick the petals off the flower with the 'she loves me, she loves me not' ditty.)

effeuilleuse *n.f.* 'Stripper', striptease artiste.

égoïner *v.trans.* 1 To exclude. *Il s'est retrouvé égoïné:* He found himself out on a limb. 2 To 'bump off', to kill. 3 To 'screw', to fuck, to have coition with.

égoutter *v.trans. Egoutter son cyclope (joc.):* To 'have a slash', to 'pee', to urinate.

élastique *n.m. Les lâcher avec un élastique:* To be 'tight-fisted', to be mean with money.

électeur *n.m. Carte d'électeur (joc.):* 'Prick', 'cock', penis. *Glisser sa carte d'électeur:* To 'have a fuck', to 'screw', to have coition (also: *mettre son bulletin dans l'urne*).

électraque *n.f. L'électraque:* 'Juice', electricity. *Mettre l'électraque:* To switch the light on.

emballage *n.m.* 1 *(pol.):* Raid, round-up of suspects. 2 'Dressing-down', telling-off, reprimand. 3 *Piquer un emballage* (Racing cyclists' slang): To spurt ahead.

emballarès *adj.inv.* 'Nicked', 'collared', arrested.

emballé *adj.* Keen, enthusiastic. *Etre vraiment emballé pour quelque chose:* To be dead keen on something.

emballer *v.trans.* 1 To fire with enthusiasm, to thrill. *Ça ne m'emballe pas!* I'm not too keen on this! **2** To 'chat up', to make a conquest. **3** *Se faire emballer*: **a** To get 'nicked', 'collared', to be arrested. **b** To 'get a roasting', to be told off in no uncertain manner. **4** *Emballé, c'est pesé!* *(joc.)*: How's that?! – Well, that's certainly a success! (This seemingly nonsensical utterance reflects originally the jocular mood of the market trader who, having made a sale and weighed it, gives the customer the packed goods with a flourish and this quip.)

emballer *v.pronom.* **1** To 'get carried away', to be overcome by enthusiasm. **2** To 'fly off the handle', to lose one's temper. *Ne t'emballe donc pas!* Keep your cool!

emballes *n.f.pl.* Faire des emballes: To 'create', to 'kick up a fuss', to make vociferous recriminations.

embaquer *v.pronom.* (Gambling slang): To get onto a losing streak.

embarbouiller *v.pronom.* To get in a muddle, to become confused. *Il s'embarbouille pour un rien*: He gets all of a dither over nothing.

embarquer *v.trans.* **1** To 'lift', to 'pinch', to steal. *Il a embarqué mes sèches*: He's gone and nicked my fags! **2** To 'collar', to arrest. **3** *Embarquer une nana*: To 'chat up a bird', to walk away with a female conquest.

embarras *n.m.pl.* Faire des embarras: **a** To 'put on a performance', to make a fuss over nothing. **b** To put on airs and graces, to 'swank', to show off.

embastiller *v.trans.* To 'clap into jail', to imprison.

embéguiné *adj.* Etre embéguiné de quelqu'un: To be 'soft on', to be 'spoony about', to be infatuated with someone.

embellemerdé *adj. (joc.)*: Saddled with an awkward mother-in-law.

embellie *n.f.* 'Lucky break', stroke of luck.

emberlificoter *v.trans.* To 'muddle', to confuse someone (in order to get what one wants).

emberlificoter *v.pronom.* To get all tangled up in explanations.

embêté *adj.* **1** 'Narked', bothered. *Je suis drôlement embêté*: I'm in a right old stew. **2** 'Fed-up', bored.

embêtement *n.m.* 'Hitch', 'bother', problem.

embêter *v.pronom.* Tu ne t'embêtes pas, toi!/vous ne vous embêtez pas, vous! *(iron.)*: You've got it made! – You're certainly doing well for yourself!

embigner *v.trans.* To 'clap into jail', to imprison.

embistrouiller *v.trans.* To be a flaming nuisance to someone.

embobiner *v.trans.* **1** To wheedle, to cajole. *Avec les bonnes femmes, il se laisse toujours embobiner*: Women always get the better of him.

2 To 'hoodwink', to 'bamboozle', to trick someone.

emboîtage *n.m. (th.)*: Performance greeted with jeers by the public.

emboîter *v.trans.* **1** To 'rib', to engage in 'leg-pulling', to try and make a fool of someone. **2** *(th.)*: To hiss and boo.

emboucaner *v.trans.* **1** To 'aggravate', to irritate. *Il fait tout ce qu'il peut pour nous emboucaner*: He goes out of his way to be a bloody nuisance. **2** To 'stink out', to permeate with a foul smell. *Sa cuistance nous emboucane tous les midis*: Every lunch-time this place smells to high heaven with his foul cooking. **3** To poison. *Ils s'étaient emboucanés avec des conserves à la mords-moi-le-machin*: They got a bad case of the collywobbles through eating duff preserves.

embouché *adj.* Mal embouché: 'Foul-mouthed', pouring forth streams of abuse.

embourber *v.trans.* **1** To 'shunt', to crash into. *Il a embourbé un platane avec sa bagnole*: He pranged his car against a tree. **2** *Embourber* (also: *s'embourber*) une nana: To 'have it off with a bird', to have coition. **3** *S'embourber quelque chose*: To get lumbered with an unpleasant task. *Je me suis embourbé toute la vaisselle*: It's muggins who got all the washing-up.

embouteillage *n.m.* 'Snarl-up', traffic jam.

embouteiller *v.pronom.* To get stuck in a traffic jam.

emboutir *v.trans.* To 'prang', to crash into, to collide with another vehicle.

emboutissage *n.m.* 'Shunt', collision of motor cars.

embrayer *v.intrans.* **1** To 'start grafting', to start work. **2** To 'get cracking', to get on one's way. *On a embrayé dès l'aube*: We set off at dawn. **3** To start explaining something. *Aussi sec, il embraya sur sa maladie d'estomac*: Straight away, he set about giving us an in-depth account of his stomach complaint. **4** To be getting on friendly terms with a woman. (Perhaps because of the motoring origin of this word, the various meanings imply a progressive action as with the letting in of a clutch.)

embringuer *v.trans.* To 'rope in', to involve reluctant participants in an undertaking they might later regret.

embringuer *v.pronom.* **1** To 'get mixed up with', to get involved. *Il s'est embringué dans une sale histoire*: He got himself tangled up in a really nasty business. **2** *Ça s'embringue mal* (of plan, project): It's got off to a bad start.

embrouille *n.f.* **1** *De l'embrouille*: 'Muddle', mess, confusion. *Faire de l'embrouille*: To cause a real mix-up. *Sac d'embrouille*: **a** Inextricable mess, state of utter confusion. **b** Person who creates chaos wherever he or she is. (The confusion within the person is reflected in matters handled.) **2** 'Dirty trick', underhand deed. *Faire une embrouille à quelqu'un*: To do the dirty on someone.

embrouiller *v.trans. Ni vu ni connu, je t'embrouille!* Stock jocular phrase uttered when faced with an inexplicable state of muddle, the nearest colloquial equivalent being: 'Now you see it, now you don't!'

embrouilleur *n.m.* Clever trickster, near-con-man whose handling of business affairs follows the old adage 'divide and rule'.

embusqué *n.m.* **1** One who has a 'cushy number', character who through favouritism is landed with an easy job. **2** 'Skiver', 'shirker', character who dodges work successfully.

embusquer *v.trans.reflex.* **1** To land oneself a 'cushy number', to get an easy job with no responsibilities and little work. **2** To 'skive', to shirk active work successfully.

éméché *adj.* 'Tiddly', 'tipsy', slightly drunk. *Il était légèrement éméché sur les bords*: He'd had one over the eight.

émeraudes *n.f.pl. (joc.corr. hémorroïdes):* Piles.

émeri *n.m. Etre bouché à l'émeri (joc.):* To be 'as thick as two short planks', to be as stupid as they come.

émietteuse *n.f.* 'Hooker', 'prozzy', prostitute.

éminence *n.m. Un éminence:* A pair of Y-fronts, male underpants. (Like many popular registered trade-names, the *slip Eminence* has given its name to a consumer item.)

emmanché *n.m. (pej.):* **1** 'Clumsy clot', bumbling imbecile. **2** Passive homosexual.

emmancher *v.trans.* To sodomize (the verb is usually found in a passive construction).

emmancher *v.pronom. Ça s'emmanche bien/mal* (of plan, project): Things are getting off to a good/bad start.

emmener *v.pronom. S'emmener promener (joc.):* To 'slope off', to leave someone else to cope with a difficult or unpleasant task.

emmerdant *adj.* 'Shitty', boring.

emmerde *n.f.* 'Hitch', 'snag', trouble. *Faire des emmerdes à quelqu'un*: To give someone hassle.

emmerdé *adj.* 'In the shit', deep in trouble.

emmerdement *n.m.* Serious problem, grave difficulty. *Avoir des emmerdements d'argent*: To be badly in debt.

emmerder *v.trans.* **1** To be 'a pain in the neck', to be a nuisance to someone. *Tout ce travail m'emmerde*: I'm fed up to the back teeth with all this bloody work! **2** To 'hassle', to pester. *Il m'emmerde à longueur de journée avec toutes ses questions*: His day-long barrage of questions

drives me potty! **3** *Je t'emmerde!* Go to hell! –Get lost! – Leave me alone!

emmerder *v.pronom.* **1** To 'get bored stiff', to be bored to tears. *'Ah, ce qu'on s'emmerde ici!'* is a derisory chant sung by expectant and disappointed audiences, roughly equivalent to the well-known 'Why are we waiting!' **2** *Ne pas s'emmerder (iron.):* To be on to a good thing (and know it). *Alors, toi, tu ne t'emmerdes pas!* You've got it made, haven't you?!

emmerdeur *n.m.* **1** 'Pain in the neck', crashing bore. **2** 'Mitherer', pesterer.

emmiellement *n.m.* 'Fly in the ointment', 'hitch', spot of bother. *Il a eu une foultitude d'emmiellements avec son nouveau restau*: He's been plagued by snags with his new eating-house.

emmieller *v.trans.* This is just a euphemistic variant of *emmerder*, as *miel* is of *merde*.

emmielleuse *n.f.* 'Sticky beak', interfering woman.

emmistoufler *v.trans.* To pester, to bother, to irritate someone.

emmouscaillement *n.m.* (mostly *pl.*): Trouble, worries.

emmouscailler *v.trans.* To bother, to irritate. *Ça m'a drôlement emmouscaillé*: It really got up my nose.

émos *n.f.* (also: *émosse*) *Une émos:* A shock, an emotional blow.

émotionner *v.trans.* To upset someone. *Ça m'a émotionné de te revoir comme ça*: I was all cut up seeing you again like this!

émoustillant *adj.* 'Titillating', sexually arousing.

émoustiller *v.trans.* To titillate, to arouse sexually.

empaffé *n.m. (pej.):* **1** 'Pouf', 'pansy', passive homosexual. **2** 'Pillock', 'nincompoop', idiot.

empaffer *v.trans.* To commit buggery, to sodomize.

empaillé *n.m.* **1** 'Stuffed-shirt', person filled with a feeling of his own importance. **2** 'Nincompoop', 'burk', imbecile.

empalmer *v.trans.* To 'nick', to 'pinch', to steal. (The word originates from the language of card-sharps where it describes a swift legerdemain for cheating purposes.)

empalmeur *n.m.* **1** 'Card-sharp', crooked gambler. **2** 'Con-man', trickster.

empapaouté *n.m. (pej.):* **1** 'Fairy', 'pansy', passive homosexual. **2** 'Mug', 'twit', imbecile.

empapaouter *v.trans.* To commit buggery, to sodomize. (The word is particularly insulting in expressions such as *Va te faire empapaouter!* Get stuffed!)

empaqueté *n.m. (pej.):* **1** 'Burk', 'twit', imbecile. **2** 'Clumsy oaf', ham-fisted person. **3** 'Pansy', passive homosexual.

empaqueté *adj.* **1** 'Dim', 'dumb', stupid. **2** Clumsy. *Il est bougrement empaqueté*: He's all fingers and thumbs.

empaqueter *v.trans.* **1** To 'con', to 'diddle', to swindle. (The word is usually found in the passive. *Il s'est fait empaqueter comme un gosse!* He got done, it was like taking sweets off a kiddy!) **2** To 'nick', to 'pinch', to steal. **3** To 'collar', to arrest.

empaumer *v.trans.* **1** To 'con', to 'diddle', to swindle. **2** To 'collar', to arrest.

empêcheur *n.m. Empêcheur de tourner en rond* (*joc.*): 'Killjoy', meddling busybody.

empégaler *v.trans.* To 'pop', to 'hock', to pawn.

empéguer *v.trans.* To 'take someone for a ride', to 'pull a fast one on someone', to dupe. *Je m'suis fait empéguer!* I was done! – I've been had!

empeigne *n.f. Avoir une gueule d'empeigne*: To have an 'ugly mush', to have a sour and unpleasant face.

empiffrer *v.trans.reflex.* To 'gobble up', to 'stuff one's face', to eat immoderately.

empiler *v.trans.* To 'rook', to 'con', to swindle. *Il s'est fait empiler en beauté*: He got done good and proper.

empileur *n.m.* **1** 'Card-sharp', crooked gambler. **2** 'Con-merchant', trickster.

emplacarder *v.trans.* To 'clap into jail', to put in prison.

emplafonner *v.trans.* **1** To 'butt', to ram into someone. (The word can also apply to vehicles colliding.) **2** To 'roust', to beat up. *Il s'est fait emplafonner dans une manif'*: He got duffed up at a demo. **3** To 'whip', to 'nick', to steal. *Il avait emplafonné la recette du jour*: He'd knocked off the day's takings.

emplâtre *n.m.* **1** 'Milksop', weakling. **2** 'Clumsy oaf', blundering idiot. **3** 'Biff', 'clout', blow. **4** *Marcher à l'emplâtre*: To lead a life of constant petty crime. **5** *Avoir une gueule d'emplâtre*: To have 'a face like the back of a bus', to have unphotogenic features.

emplâtrer *v.trans.* **1** To 'butt', to ram someone. **2** To 'duff up', to beat up. **3** To 'knock off', to 'make away with', to steal.

emplumé *adj.* 'Thick', 'dumb', stupid.

empoignade *n.f.* 'Dust-up', 'set-to', brawl.

empoigne *n.f.* **1** *Foire d'empoigne*: 'Free-for-all', brawl, all-out fight. **2** *Acheter quelque chose à la foire d'empoigne* (*joc.*): To get something from 'off the back of a lorry', to come into possession of goods of dubious origin.

empoigner *v.trans.* To 'collar', to 'nick', to arrest. *Ils se sont laissé empoigner en douceur*: There was no aggro when they got nabbed.

empoigner *v.trans.reflex.* To have a set-to. *Ils se sont empoignés à la sortie du bal*: They were at each other's throats when they left the dance.

empoisonnant *adj.* **1** 'Narking', irritating. **2** 'Mind-deadening', incredibly boring.

empoisonnements *n.m.pl.* 'Snags', 'hitches', set-backs.

empoisonner *v.pronom.* To get bored to sobs, to die of boredom.

empoisonneur *n.m. Empoisonneur public*: Character who manages to antagonize all and sundry.

empoté *n.m.* **1** 'Clumsy clot', bumbling imbecile. **2** 'Work-shy git', idle so-and-so.

empoté *adj.* **1** 'All fingers-and-thumbs', very clumsy. **2** 'Work-shy', idle.

empoupé *adj.* 'Dolled-up', 'tarted-up', overdressed.

emprosé *n.m.* (*pej.*): **1** 'Pouf', 'pansy', passive homosexual. **2** 'Pillock', 'nincompoop', idiot.

emproser *v.trans.* **1** To commit buggery, to sodomize. **2** To 'do' someone, to 'con', to fool someone.

emprunt *n.m. Emprunt forcé* (*joc.*): Hold-up, armed robbery.

èms *n.f. de l'èms*: 'Muzak', piped music.

èmsien *n.m.* Musician. *V'là les èmsiens!* Here come the band!

en *pers.pron. En être*: To be 'one of them', to be gay, to be homosexual.

en-bourgeois *n.m.* Plain clothes policeman, one who does not normally wear a uniform. (An alternative humorous spelling of this word is *hambourgeois*.)

encadrer *v.trans.* **1** To 'pitch into', to 'go for', to attack. **2** (Motoring): To crash into, to collide with. *Il a encadré un feu rouge*: He crashed into some traffic lights. **3** *Ne pas pouvoir encadrer quelqu'un*: To be unable to stomach someone. *J'peux pas l'encadrer!* I can't stand the sight of him! **4** *Tu peux (te) le faire encadrer!* (*iron.*): You know what you can do with it?! (Stuff it up your jumper!)

encaisser *v.trans.* **1** To 'take punishment', to receive blows. *Il a drôlement encaissé dans les cinq premiers rounds*: He soaked up a hell of a lot of punishment in the first five rounds. **2** To swallow insults. *Il a tout encaissé sans rien dire*: He took this flood of abuse without a murmur. **3** *Ne pas pouvoir encaisser quelqu'un/quelque chose*: To be unable to stomach someone or something. **4** *Encaisser des salades*: To 'fall for something hook, line and sinker', to show oneself to be extremely gullible.

encalbécher *v.trans.* To 'butt', to charge into someone with one's head.

encaldosser *v.trans.* To commit buggery, to sodomize.

encanner v.trans. To 'pinch', to 'swipe', to steal.

encarrade n.f. **1** Act of entering. *Elle a fait une encarrade remarquée*: Her arrival was a real conversation-stopper. **2** *L'encarrade*: Entrance (to a dance-hall, cinema, etc.).

encarrer v.trans. & intrans. **1** To get in, to enter. **2** To 'send someone away with a flea in their ear', to tell someone off. *Se faire encarrer chez Plumeau*: To be told to 'get knotted', to be sent on one's way in no uncertain manner.

encartée n.f. 'Hooker', prostitute registered with the police and health authorities. (One who is *en carte*, and has to submit regularly to the '*visite*'.)

encaustique n.f. *Passer l'encaustique (joc.)*: To 'butter up', to flatter (also: *passer la brosse à reluire*).

enceintrer v.trans. To 'get someone in the pudding-club', to make pregnant.

encensoir n.m. *Donner des coups d'encensoir*: To 'soft-soap', to flatter. *Casser l'encensoir sur le nez de quelqu'un*: To go overboard with flattery.

enchariboter v.trans. **1** To 'bore stiff', to bore to tears. **2** To 'badger', to pester.

enchaudelancer v.trans. *(joc.)*: To 'give a dose of clap', to infect with gonorrhoea.

enchère n.f. *Pousser les enchères (joc.)*: To indulge in heavy petting.

enchetarder v.trans. To 'clap into jail', to imprison (also: *enchtiber*).

enchifrené adj. 'Bunged-up', suffering from flu.

enchnouffé n.m. 'Junkie', drug addict.

enchoser v.trans. **1** To be 'a pain in the neck to someone', to be a nuisance. *Tu commences à m'enchoser!* You're getting to be a pain in the arse. **2** *Je t'enchose!* Bugger off! – Go to hell! (The vulgarity of the verb stems from the fact that the word *chose* refers euphemistically to *merde*.)

enchrister v.trans. To 'clap into jail', to imprison.

enchtourber v.trans. To 'get someone in the shit', to put someone in a difficult situation.

encloquer v.trans. To 'get someone in the pudding-club', to make pregnant.

encorner v.trans. To cuckold. (The popular image of the spouse of an unfaithful woman is that he has grown a set of invisible horns, hence this verb. It is worth noting that the not so male-chauvinist French, when talking of the female counterpart, merely describe her as '*la pauvre!*')

encouragement n.m. *Un peu d'encouragement (joc.)*: Some 'Dutch courage', a tipple to settle unsteady nerves.

encrasse n.m. *(pej.)*: Young inexperienced pimp (also: *barbiquet*).

encre n.f. **1** *Se faire un sang d'encre*: To worry oneself sick about something. **2** *C'est la bouteille à l'encre!* It's a hopeless muddle! – I can't make head nor tail of this!

encrister v.trans. To 'clap into jail', to put in prison.

encroumé adj. 'Hocked to the eyeballs', deeply in debt.

encroûté n.m. **1** 'Stick-in-the-mud', character who is deeply set in his ways. **2** 'Old fogey', old dodderer.

encroûter v.pronom. **1** To 'get into a rut', to become staid. **2** To start 'doddering', to become an old fogey.

enculade n.f. Sodomous intercourse (also: *enculage*).

enculage n.m. 'Screwing', sexual intercourse.

enculé n.m. *(pej.)*: **1** 'Bum-boy', 'queer', homosexual. **2** 'Pillock', 'twerp', idiot.

enculer v.trans. **1** To sodomize, to commit buggery. **2** *Va te faire enculer!* Get stuffed! –Bugger off! – Go to hell!

enculeur n.m. *Enculeur de mouches (joc.)*: 'Hair-splitter', quibbler (also: *pinailleur*).

enculodrome n.m. *(joc.)*: Meeting place for wild and randy parties (also: *baisodrome*).

endêver v.intrans. To be 'seething', to be furious. *Faire endêver quelqu'un*: To 'get someone's goat', to irritate someone profoundly. *Il adore faire endêver sa belle-doche*: He gets a real kick out of driving his mother-in-law round the twist.

endimanché adj. 'Dolled-up', 'in one's best bib and tucker', all dressed-up.

endoffé n.m. *(pej.)*: **1** 'Faggot', 'queer', homosexual. **2** 'Pillock', 'twerp', imbecile.

endoffer v.trans. To sodomize, to commit buggery.

endormeur n.m. 'Crashing bore', incredibly boring person.

endormi n.m. 'Beak', magistrate, judge.

endormir v.trans. **1** (Boxing): To knock out cold, to knock out for the count. **2** To 'bore the pants off someone', to be extremely boring. **3** To 'pull the wool over someone's eyes', to con someone.

endormir v.pronom. *S'endormir sur le rôti* (also: *sur le mastic*): To 'slack on the job', to dawdle over one's work.

endosses n.f.pl. Back, shoulders. *En avoir plein les endosses*: To be 'worn out and fed up', to be tired. *Mettre quelque chose sur les endosses de quelqu'un*: To get someone to 'carry the can', to make someone responsible for something (also: *faire porter le bada à quelqu'un*).

endroguer *v.trans.* To 'pull the wool over someone's eyes', to con someone.

endroit *n.m. Le petit endroit:* 'The loo', 'the smallest room', the lavatory.

enfant *n.m.* **1** *Faire l'enfant:* To 'act dumb', to pretend to be stupid. **2** *Il n'y a plus d'enfants!* (catch phrase): They know it all nowadays! – There's no innocence left in today's society. **3** *Enfant de chœur:* Incredibly naïve person. **4** *Un enfant de la balle (th.):* Second-generation artiste, person who, as the saying goes, was 'born in a trunk'. **5** *L'enfant se présente mal (fig.):* Things aren't looking too good – Prospects are bleak.

enfariné *adj.* **1** *Etre enfariné:* To be 'in a fix', to be in trouble (also: *être dans le pétrin).* **2** *Avoir la gueule enfarinée:* **a** To look like 'death warmed up', to be as pale as a sheet. **b** To seem bewildered.

enfifré *n.m. (pej.):* **1** 'Faggot', 'queer', homosexual. **2** 'Pillock', 'twerp', imbecile.

enfifrer *v.trans.* To sodomize, to commit buggery.

enfilade *n.f.* Run of bad luck. *Rien ne marche pour lui en ce moment, il s'est tapé une enfilade terrible:* He's had a spate of rotten luck lately, nothing seems to be going right for him.

enfilé *n.m. (pej.):* 'Pansy', 'queer', passive homosexual.

enfiler *v.trans.* **1** To 'screw', to fuck, to have coition with. *Va te faire enfiler!* Get stuffed! **2** To 'con', to swindle, to dupe. *Il s'est fait enfiler de première:* He got done good and proper! **3** *Enfiler des perles (joc.):* To 'do bugger-all', to loaf about.

enfiler *v.pronom.* **1** To get through quite a lot of food or drink. *Il s'est enfilé une tripotée d'apéros:* He was knocking back Martinis as if they were going out of fashion! **2** To be lumbered with an unpleasant task. *Il a dû s'enfiler la vaisselle, la lessive et le ménage:* He got stuck with all the household chores.

enflaquer *v.trans.* To 'mither', to pester someone.

enflé *n.m. (pej.):* 'Pillock', 'nincompoop', imbecile (also: *enflure).*

enfler *v.trans.* **1** To get someone in the 'pudding club', to make pregnant. **2** *Se faire enfler:* To 'get done', 'double-crossed', to be the victim of a swindle.

enflure *n.f. (pej.):* 'Pillock', 'nincompoop', imbecile.

enfoiré *n.m. (pej.):* **1** 'Faggot', 'queer', homosexual. **2** 'Pillock', 'twerp', idiot.

enfoiré *adj.* (of person): Silly, stupid.

enfoirer *v.trans.* **1** To 'stuff', to 'screw', to have coition with. **2** To 'con', to 'diddle', to swindle.

enfoncé *past part.* 'Licked', well and truly beaten. *Enfoncés les copains, c'est moi qu'ai décroché la*

timbale! I wiped the floor with them and won outright!

enfoncer *v.trans.* **1** To 'lick', to get the better of someone. *Ils se sont fait enfoncer dans les grandes largeurs:* They got beaten hollow. *Ça enfonce tout!* That caps it all! – That certainly beats the competition! **2** To 'con', to 'diddle', to swindle. *Un peu qu'il s'est fait enfoncer!* He got done good and proper! **3** *Enfoncer des portes ouvertes:* To 'whip a willing horse', to act forcefully where no force is needed.

enfouiller *v.trans.* **1** To put something in one's pocket. **2** To 'pocket', to keep something for oneself. *C'était le dirlo qui enfouillait les bénéfs:* It's the manager who was syphoning off all the profits.

enfouraillé *adj.* 'Rodded-up', armed with a handgun. *(Défourailler* means to fire a gun.)

enfourailler *v.trans.reflex.* To get 'rodded-up', to arm oneself with a handgun. (The implication here is that the gun is tucked away out of sight.)

enfourner *v.trans.* **1** To 'wolf', to gobble one's food. **2** To 'screw', to fuck, to have coition with. **3** *Il lui a enfourné un lardon:* He got her in the 'pudding club' – He made her pregnant.

enfourner *v.trans.reflex.* To 'pile into', to crowd into. *Ils s'enfournèrent dans sa petite bagnole:* They packed themselves like sardines in his Mini.

engaille *n.f.* 'Bait', tempting and misleading offer.

engailler *v.trans.* To 'con', to 'pull the wool over someone's eyes', to deceive.

engailleur *n.m.* 'Con-man', trickster.

engelure *n.f. (pej.):* **1** 'Pain in the neck', crashing bore. **2** 'Mitherer', pestering nuisance.

engerber *v.trans.* To 'nab', to 'nail', to arrest. *Il s'est fait engerber sans moufter:* He got run-in without so much as a squeak.

engin *n.m.* 'Joystick', 'cock', penis.

englandé *n.m. (pej.):* **1** 'Faggot', 'queer', homosexual. **2** 'Pillock', 'twerp', idiot.

englander *v.trans.* **1** To sodomize, to commit buggery. **2** *Se faire englander:* To be 'taken in', to be deceived.

Engliche *n.m. & f.* 'Brit', British person.

engourdir *v.trans.* To 'lift', to 'nick', to steal. *Il lui a engourdi son larfeuil:* He pinched his wallet.

engrainer *v.trans.* To entice, to tempt someone into something (usually a bitterly regretted decision). *Il m'a engrainé dans une sale affaire:* He roped me into some nasty business.

engrais *n.m.* (Gambling slang): 'Lefties', money forgotten on table by an absent-minded gambler.

engrenages *n.m.pl.* *Les engrenages de quelque chose*: The 'ins-and-outs', the workings of something.

engrosser *v.trans.* To 'get someone in the pudding club', to make pregnant.

engueulade *n.f.* 'Rollicking', 'roasting', severe telling-off. *Il m'a filé une engueulade maison*: He gave me one hell of a slating.

engueuler *v.trans.* To 'haul over the coals', to 'give someone a dressing-down', to tell off in no uncertain manner. *Il s'est fait engueuler comme du poisson pourri*: He got a right rollicking (also: *passer un savon à quelqu'un*).

engueuler *v.trans.reflex.* To have a 'barney', to have a row. *S'engueuler ferme*: To have a slanging match.

enguirlander *v.trans.* To 'haul over the coals', to 'give someone a dressing-down', to tell off in no uncertain terms.

énième *adj.ord.* (also: *ennième*): Umpteenth. *Faut-il que je te répète ça pour la énième fois?* How many more times do I have to tell you this?

enjamber *v.trans.* To fuck, to 'screw', to have intercourse with (literally, to 'get a leg over').

enjambeur *n.m.* 'Super-stud', highly-sexed man.

enjuponné *adj.* 1 Under the thumb of a matriarchal influence. 2 'Pissed', 'pickled', inebriated. (The only reference to this acceptation of the word is to be found in *L'ARGOT CHEZ LES VRAIS DE VRAI* by that prolific exponent of modern colloquial French, Auguste Le Breton.)

enkroumé *adj.* 'Hocked to the eyeballs', deeply in debt.

enkroumer *v.pronom.* To get into debt.

enlever *v.trans.* 1 *Se faire enlever*: To 'get hauled over the coals', to get told off sharply. 2 *Enlevé, c'est pesé!* (Jocular exclamation expressing gleeful triumph): Howzat! – How's that then?!

énormité *n.f.* 1 'Bunkum', preposterous statement. *Il sort toujours de ces énormités!* He's always spouting the most incredible bilge! 2 'Howler', ginormous blunder.

enquiller *v.trans. & intrans.* 1 To get in, to gain access. *Enquiller par la tabatière*: To break in through the skylight. 2 To 'shaft', to 'screw', to have intercourse with.

enquiller *v.pronom.* 1 To slip in, to enter unnoticed. 2 To 'find a cosy niche', to slot oneself into a cushy position.

enquilleuse *n.f.* Woman shoplifter.

enquiquinant *adj.* 1 'Irksome', tiresome. *C'est drôlement enquiquinant, mais il faut que je me taille*: I know how you feel, but I'll have to go. 2 Incredibly boring.

enquiquinement *n.m.* (often *pl.*): 'Hitch', 'bother', difficulty.

enquiquiner *v.trans.* 1 To 'needle', to 'aggravate' someone, to irritate. 2 To bore someone to tears.

enquiquiner *v.pronom.* To get really bored. *Il s'enquiquine à mourir au bureau!* He's bored to death with office life.

enquiquineur *n.m.* 1 'Mitherer', pesterer. 2 Crashing bore, incredibly boring person.

enragé *n.m.* Die-hard extremist.

enrichir *v.trans.* *Ce n'est pas que ça enrichisse, mais ça soulage!* This jocular catchphrase is usually uttered when returning from the W.C., and has, to our knowledge, no English equivalent.

enrouler *v.intrans.* To get on with what one is doing speedily, efficiently and with apparent ease. (The word originates from the language of racing cyclists.)

ensuqué *adj.* Dazed, dizzy, out of touch with what is happening. (The cause of this state can be tiredness, inebriation, or drug abuse.)

ensuquer *v.trans.* 1 To 'get on someone's wick', to irritate someone. 2 To 'wear out', to tire someone out.

entamer *v.trans.* *Entamer son capital (joc.)*: To lose one's virginity, to experience sex for the first time.

entapé *adj.* *Bien entapé*: 'Togged-up', nattily dressed.

entaulage *n.m.* (also: *entôlage*): 'Con-trick', swindle. *Quel entaulage!* What a rip-off!

entauler *v.trans.* (also: *entôler*): 1 To 'nick', to 'pinch', to steal. 2 To set up a successful con-trick. 3 To 'clap into jail', to put into prison.

entendre *v.pronom.* *Je m'entends! (joc.)*: I know what I mean (even if it sounds gibberish to you!).

entendu *n.m.* *Faire l'entendu*: To 'play the clever Dick', to act important.

entendu *past part.* 1 *(interj.)*: Right ho! – O.K. – Agreed! 2 *Comme de bien entendu! (iron.)*: As luck would have it! – Isn't that just typical?!

enterrement *n.m.* 1 *Avoir une gueule d'enterrement*: To 'have a face as long as a fiddle', to look glum. 2 *Un enterrement de première classe (joc.)*: A 'spontaneous ripple of apathy', a 'thumbs-down' verdict to a project, etc.

enterrer *v.trans.* 1 To shelve permanently (a project, etc.). *C'est mort et enterré!* It's a dead duck! 2 *Enterrer sa vie de garçon*: To have a stag party to celebrate the end of one's bachelor days.

entiché *adj.* *Etre entiché de*: To be 'spoony over', to be infatuated with.

enticher *v.pronom.* To get 'spoony over', to get 'stuck on', to become infatuated with.

entiflage *n.m.* 'Hitching', action of getting married.

entifler *v.pronom.* 1 To get in, to gain access, to enter. 2 To 'get hitched', to get married.

entoiler *v.trans.* To 'clap into jail', to imprison.

entôleur *n.m.* 1 Card-sharp. 2 'Con-man', trickster.

entôleuse *n.f.* Thieving prostitute, one who steals money from a sleeping client.

entonner *v.trans.* 1 To 'guzzle', to 'shovel down food', to eat voraciously. 2 To 'knock back', to 'swig', to down vast amounts of booze fast and furiously.

entonnoir *n.m.* 1 'Gullet', throat. *Avoir une sacrée descente d'entonnoir*: To be something of a boozer. 2 'Soak', heavy drinker. 3 *(pl.)*: 'Lug-holes', ears.

entortiller *v.trans.* To 'get round someone', to talk someone into doing something. *Se faire entortiller*: To 'have the wool pulled over one's eyes', to be taken in by specious talk.

entortiller *v.pronom.* To get embroiled in tangled explanations.

entourer *v.trans.* To 'con', to 'diddle', to swindle. *Fais gaffe de ne pas te faire entourer!* Watch out you don't get taken for a ride!

entourloupe *n.f.* 'Fast one', sharp ruse, trickery. *Se faire placer une entourloupe maison*: To get well and truly done (also: *entourloupette*).

entourlouper *v.trans.* To 'take someone for a ride', to 'play a con-trick on someone', to try and swindle someone.

entourloupette *n.f.* 'Fast one', sharp ruse, trickery.

entournures *n.f.pl.* *Etre gêné aux entournures*: To be 'short of readies', to lack ready cash.

entraîneuse *n.f.* 'Prozzy', prostitute. (Originally the word referred to the attractive 'good-time' girls whose job in nightclubs was to get customers to buy expensive drinks.)

entraver *v.trans.* 1 To understand, to perceive as intelligible. *Entraver le jars*: To understand argot. *N'entraver que pouic*: To understand fuck-all (of what someone is saying). 2 To understand, to comprehend. *Il n'entravait pas qu'il était en train de clamecer*: He didn't realize he was croaking.

entre *prep.* *Entre quat'z-yeux*: Between you, me and the gatepost – Between ourselves.

entrebigler *v.trans.* To glimpse, to catch sight of.

entrecogner *v.trans.reflex.* To 'have a punch-up', to brawl.

entrecôte *n.f.* *Se taper une entrecôte*: To 'get a leg over', to have intercourse.

entrée *n.f.* 1 *L'entrée des artistes (joc.)*: 'The jacksey', the anal sphincter. 2 *D'entrée*: Straight away, immediately. *D'entrée on a été copains*: We were buddies from the word go.

entréper *v.trans.* (of hawker, street-vendor): To raise an audience, to get a crowd of onlookers (literally to rustle up the *trèpe*).

entreprendre *v.trans.* 1 To try and get someone round to one's way of thinking. 2 To 'buttonhole', to hold someone in conversation against his will. *Il m'a entrepris à la sortie de la messe*: I couldn't get away; he collared me as I left church.

entre-sort *n.m.* Hawker's patch, street-vendor's stall.

entretenir *v.trans.* *Elle se fait entretenir*: She's a kept woman.

entrèver *v.trans.* 1 To understand, to perceive as intelligible. 2 To understand, to comprehend.

entripaillé *adj. (joc.)*: 'Paunchy', pot-bellied.

entrouducuter *v.trans. (joc.)*: 1 To sodomize, to commit buggery with. 2 To 'con', to 'diddle', to swindle. *Il s'est drôlement fait entrouducuter*: He really got taken for a ride.

entubage *n.m.* 'Con-trick', 'swindle', fraud.

entuber *v.trans.* 1 To sodomize, to commit buggery with. 2 To 'con', to swindle.

entubeur *n.m.* 'Con-man', trickster.

envapé *adj.* Out of touch with reality. (The word can refer to a state of daydreaming, or to dizziness resulting from excessive drinking or the taking of powerful drugs.)

enveloppe *n.f.* *La petite enveloppe (joc. & iron.)*: 'Backhander', inducive payment from 'slush funds'.

envelopper *v.trans.* 1 To 'nick', to 'lift', to steal. *On lui a enveloppé son larfeuil au bistrot*: He got his wallet pinched at the pub. 2 *Se faire envelopper*: a To get 'conned', 'diddled', to be duped. b To get 'collared', 'nabbed', to be arrested. 3 *Un petit coup sur le manche, faut-il vous l'envelopper?! (iron.)*: You want jam on it, don't you?! – You don't seriously expect me to do more?! (This jocular and rather sarcastic utterance is said to have originated in butchers' shops where a special customer is made to feel that nothing is too much trouble.)

enviandé *n.m. (pej.)*: 1 'Pouf', 'pansy', homosexual. 2 'Nurk', 'pillock', idiot. 3 *Espèce d'enviandé!* You fucking bastard! (This highly insulting utterance contains a direct reference to sodomy.)

enviander *v.trans.* To 'con', to 'diddle', to swindle.

envie *n.f.* 1 *Ce n'est pas l'envie qui me manque! (iron.)*: Do you think I'd hesitate?! – I'd go ahead and do it if I could! 2 *Avoir envie* (Child language): To want to do a wee-wee, to need to go to the W.C.

envoyer *v.trans.* **1** *Les envoyer*: To 'show the colour of one's money', to pay up (also: *envoyer la soudure*). **2** *En envoyer une*: To 'chip in with a tune', to contribute something to a sing-song. **3** *Je ne le lui ai pas envoyé dire!* No messing, I told him straight! *Ça c'est envoyé!* That's telling him!

envoyer *v.pronom.* **1** General meaning: to consume and enjoy something. **a** *S'envoyer un godet*: To down a drink. **b** *S'envoyer un gueuleton*: To have a slap-up meal. **c** *S'envoyer une nana*: To 'get a leg over', to 'screw a bird', to have coition. *S'envoyer en l'air*: To have sex. **2** General meaning: to have to do something unpleasant. *S'envoyer tout le boulot*: To have to do all the work. *S'envoyer la vaisselle*: To be landed with the washing-up.

épagneul *n.m.* *Avoir une gueule d'épagneul fidèle*: To have a forlorn and pensive expression.

épahules *n.f.pl.* (*joc. corr. épaules*): 'Shouldies', shoulders. *Avoir les épahules en bouteille de Bordeaux* (of man): To be of puny build.

épais *adv.* *En avoir épais sur la coupole*: To be 'sick and tired of something', to be fed up to the back teeth with a situation.

épaisseur *n.f.* *En tenir une épaisseur*: To be 'as thick as two short planks', to be more than a trifle dim (also: *en tenir une sacrée couche*).

éparpiller *v.trans.* *En éparpiller de première*: To 'sleep like a top', to be fast asleep.

épatamment *adv.* 'Spiffingly', splendidly. (The French and English are equally twee and dated.)

épatant *adj.* 'Groovy', 'smashing', great.

épate *n.f.* **1** Swanking. *Faire de l'épate*: To 'throw one's weight about', to show off. *Faire quelque chose à l'épate*: To 'make a splash', to do something with panache. **2** *Faire des épates*: To 'kick up a fuss', to create a commotion.

épater *v.trans. & intrans.* **1** To 'stagger', to astound. *Eh ben, ça, ça m'épate!* Well, I'm flabbergasted! **2** To 'swank', to show off.

épaule *n.f.* **1** *Donner un coup d'épaule*: To 'give a push in the right direction', to help someone or something on its way. **2** *En avoir par-dessus les épaules (de quelque chose)*: To be 'fed up to the back teeth with something', to be sick and tired of something. **3** *Faire quelque chose par-dessus l'épaule*: To do something in an off-hand and perfunctory manner.

épaulé-jeté *n.m.* Mighty heave. (The term comes directly from the language of weight-lifters. *Il l'a foutu à la baille d'un épaulé-jeté*: He tossed him in the drink effortlessly.)

épée *n.f.* **1** 'Big shot', important person in the *milieu*. **2** 'Ace', expert at a skill. *Pour ce qui est de la mécanique, c'est une épée*: He knows engineering inside out. **3** *Epée de plumard*: 'Superstud', highly-sexed man.

éperdument *adv.* *Se foutre de quelque chose éperdument*: 'Not to give a fuck about something', to feel totally indifferent towards something.

épice *n.f.* *Marchand d'épices (pej.)*: 'Chink', person of oriental extraction.

épicemar *n.m.* (*joc.*): Grocer. *J'ai acheté ça à l'épicemar*: I bought it at the corner-shop.

épicerie *n.f.* *Changer d'épicerie*: **a** To change one's surroundings. **b** To change one's job.

Epinal *Proper name.* *C'est tout Epinal! (iron.)*: He doesn't miss a cliché! (The expression is usually uttered when reference is made to a cheap piece of journalism.)

épinards *n.m.pl.* **1** *Plat d'épinards*: Gaudily-painted landscape, canvas high in colour and low in quality. **2** *Mettre du beurre dans les épinards*: To make financial matters easier. *Les heures supplémentaires, ça met du beurre dans les épinards*: Overtime certainly helps stretch the house-keeping. **3** *Aller aux épinards* (of pimp): To be 'in financial clover', to live in the lap of luxury.

épingle *n.f.* **1** *Tirer son épingle du jeu*: To 'pull out in time', to save one's stakes in a tricky venture. **2** *Monter quelque chose en épingle*: To make a song-and-dance about something, to draw attention to it. **3** *Etre tiré à quatre épingles*: To be 'dressed to the nines', to look a proper fashion-plate. **4** *Ramasser des épingles* (*joc. & iron.*): To go looking for the 'golden rivet', to practise passive sodomy.

épingler *v.trans.* To 'nick', to 'collar', to arrest. (*LE CAPORAL ÉPINGLÉ*, a novel by Jacques Perret and later a successful film, narrates the story of a French prisoner of war during the Second World War.)

épique *adj.* *Ça a été vraiment épique! (joc. & iron.)*: What a carry-on! – What a to-do over nothing!

épluchure *n.f.* (*Fais*) *gaffe aux épluchures!* Watch out! – Watch your step! – Take care!

éponge *n.f.* **1** *Passer l'éponge*: To 'let bygones be bygones', to decide to forget the past. **2** *Jeter l'éponge*: To 'throw in the towel', to give in. (As with the English, the expression originates in the language of boxing.) **3** *Une vieille éponge*: An 'old soak', a habitual drunk. **4** *Avoir les éponges mitées*: To have T.B., to suffer from tuberculosis. (In this expression, the word *éponges* refers to the lungs.)

éponger *v.trans.* 1 To 'relieve someone of his money' (either through theft, gambling or deceitful business practices). 2 *Eponger un clille* (of prostitute): To have intercourse.

époque *n.f.* *Ça fait époque*: It's certainly dated – It's more than old-fashioned.

époques *n.f.pl.* *Avoir ses époques*: To have one's 'thingies', to have a menstrual period.

épousseter *v.intrans.* To 'scram', to 'bugger off', to make a hasty withdrawal. *Epoussette!* Piss off!

époustouflant *adj.* 'Stunning', 'staggering', astounding. *La nouvelle est vraiment époustouflante!* This is really news!

époustoufler *v.trans.* To 'flabbergast', to astound. *Ça m'a drôlement époustouflé!* You could have knocked me down with a feather!

épouvantail *n.m.* 'Abortion', abominable work of art.

équerre *n.f.* *Etre à l'équerre* (of person): To be 'on the level', to be an honest and truthful person. *J'ai senti tout de suite qu'il n'était pas à l'équerre avec moi*: I felt straight away he was being shifty with me.

équiper *v.trans.reflex.* To 'get rodded-up', to arm oneself with a handgun.

équipier *n.m.* (Underworld slang): 'Fellow hood', accomplice.

éreintant *adj.* 'Fagging', 'back-breaking', exhausting.

éreintement *n.m.* 'Slating', scathing criticism.

éreinter *v.trans.* 1 To 'jigger', to tire out, to exhaust. *Ce boulot m'éreinte un tantinet!* This job isn't half back-breaking! 2 To 'drive someone round the twist', to irritate someone to distraction. 3 To 'carp at', to 'pull to pieces', to criticize severely.

éreinteur *n.m.* *(th.)*: 'Scalp-hunter', severe critic.

ergoter *v.intrans.* To 'quibble', to 'niggle', to argue over small details.

erreur *n.f.* 1 *'y a comme qui dirait une erreur!* *(iron.)*: I'd say we've got a major cock-up here! 2 *Erreur d'aiguillage (joc.)*: Wrong direction taken by visitor, dossier, etc.

esballonner *v.pronom.* To go over the wall, to escape from jail.

esbigner *v.pronom.* To 'skedaddle', to 'scram', to disappear hastily. *S'esbigner en douce*: To slip away unnoticed.

esbrouffant *adj.* 'Mind-boggling', unbelievable. *C'est vraiment esbrouffant!* It's really incredible!

esbrouffe *n.f.* 1 *De l'esbrouffe*: 'Swanking', action of showing off. *Faire de l'esbrouffe*: To chuck one's weight about. 2 *Faire quelque chose à l'esbrouffe*: To succeed in something by bluffing one's way along. 3 *Vol à l'esbrouffe*: 'Shuffle-and-snatch' pickpocket robbery (one where an accomplice jostles a passer-by whilst the thief makes off with the money).

esbrouffer *v.trans.* To overawe, to impress with grandiose behaviour.

esbrouffeur *n.m.* 1 'Swank', show-off. 2 Pickpocket's accomplice.

escadrin *n.m.* Steps, stairs, staircase.

escagasser *v.trans.* 1 To dumbfound, to leave speechless. *Ça m'a drôlement escagassé!* I really didn't know what to say! 2 To 'knock out cold', to leave unconscious. 3 To 'bump off', to kill. (The general meaning of the verb is to silence; it originates from Provence.)

escalope *n.f.* 1 'Licker', tongue. *Rouler une escalope*: To give a 'French kiss' (also: *rouler une galoche*). 2 Divot, piece of turf scooped out by a golf club. 3 *(pl.)*: 'Flappers', 'lugs', ears.

escampette *n.f.* *Prendre la poudre d'escampette*: To 'skedaddle', to 'make tracks', to disappear hastily.

escaner *v.trans.* To 'con', to 'diddle', to swindle. (The word originates from Provence.)

escarette *n.f.* *Se faire l'escarette* a To 'scram', to 'skedaddle', to disappear hastily (also: *se faire la paire*). b To go over the wall, to escape from jail (also: *faire le mur*).

escargot *n.m.* 1 'Slow-coach', person who always arrives late. 2 'Blower', phone, telephone.

escarpe *n.m.* 'Heavy', thug, underworld enforcer.

escarpins *n.m.pl.* *(joc.)*: 'Boats', large shoes. (The humour comes from the original meaning of the word: dainty, delicate shoes. Georgette Marks, in her dictionary, quotes the example *escarpins en cuir de brouette*: Galoshes.)

esclaffade *n.f.* Guffaw, boisterous outburst of laughter.

escobar *n.m.* Steps, stairs, staircase.

escoffier *v.trans.* (Underworld slang): To 'bump off', to kill.

escogriffe *n.m.* *(pej.)*: 'Gawk', tall and angular character. *Et v'là que ce grand escogriffe vient pour m'emprunter du fric!* And then that tall pillock has the nerve to ask me for a loan.

esgourder *v.trans.* To listen attentively.

esgourdes *n.f.pl.* 'Lugs', 'flappers', ears. *Ouvre bien tes esgourdes!* Pin back your lug-holes! – Now listen carefully!

espadoches *n.f.pl.* *(corr. espadrilles)*: Rope-soled sandals.

espagnol *adj.* *'C'est comme dans une auberge espagnole'* *(joc. & iron.)*: 'You gets what you pays for!' (Popular myth has it that in such establishments one only got served the food one brought along. Subsequently the meaning of the expression has shifted slightly.)

espèce *n.f. Espèce de crétin!* You stupid pillock! *Espèce d'idiot!* You blithering idiot! (Preceded by *espèce de*, terms of abuse become even more virulent.)

espérance *n.f. Avoir des espérances (joc.)*: To be in the 'pudding club', to be 'preggers', to be pregnant. (The original meaning of the expression is that the person concerned is very likely to inherit a large sum of money.)

espérer *v.intrans. & trans.* 1 *Espérer après quelqu'un*: To wait for someone (usually in vain). 2 *J'espère! (iron.)*: I should bloody well think so! 3 *Espère un peu! (joc. & iron.)*: You've got another think coming! – You must be joking!

Espingo *n.m.* 1 'Dago', Spaniard. 2 *L'espingo*: Spanish, the Spanish language.

espion *n.m. (sch.)*: Discipline monitor in a French *lycée*. (The jocularity of the word stems from the corruption of the word *pion*, the colloquial term for a *surveillant d'externat* whose main function is to exercise discipline in the absence of teachers.)

espionnite *n.f. (joc.)*: 'Spy-fever', near-neurotic obsession with spies and spying. *De ce côté-ci du rideau de fer, il y en a pas mal qui souffrent d'espionnite*: 'Reds under the bed' seems to be a current obsession over here.

espoir *n.m.* 1 'Hopeful', likely candidate for success. *C'est un espoir français de la boxe*: He's likely to be one of tomorrow's top French boxers. 2 *Les espoirs anglais et français ont fait match nul*: In the junior internationals the French and English football teams had a draw.

esprit *n.m. Avoir l'esprit mal tourné*: To have a one-track mind (and a dirty one at that!).

esquimau *n.m.* 1 Wind-cheater with a fur-lined hood. 2 'Choc-ice', chocolate-coated ice-cream sold in cinemas.

esquintant *adj.* 'Fagging', 'back-breaking', exhausting.

esquinter *v.trans.* 1 To 'bugger up', to damage. *Il m'a esquinté ma bagnole neuve*: He went and pranged my new car. 2 To 'jigger', to tire out.

esquinter *v.trans.reflex.* To try one's darnedest, to do one's best (and wear oneself out in the process). *Et dire que je me suis esquintée à vous élever tous les deux!* And to think how I tried to bring you two up properly!

essayer *v.intrans. Tu peux toujours essayer! (iron.)*: Just you try (and you'll see what happens to you!).

essence *n.f. Essence de panard (joc.)*: 'Toe-jam', sticky sweat produced by feet.

essorer *v.trans.* To 'wring someone dry', to make someone penniless.

essoreuse *n.f.* 1 'Prozzy', prostitute. 2 Noisy motorbike. (This meaning is only attested in François Caradec's DICTIONNAIRE DU FRANÇAIS ARGOTIQUE ET POPULAIRE.)

essuyer *v.trans.* 1 *Essuyer le coup*: To show one's feelings of disappointment at a setback. 2 *Essuyer les plâtres*: To suffer teething problems in a new venture. (Originally the meaning of the expression was literal and referred to the problems experienced by someone moving into newly-built premises.) 3 *Essuyer les planches (th.)*: To have the difficult task of 'warming up an audience' at a variety show.

estafette *n.f.* Small box-van. (Like many trade-names, this Renault product became generic in the 60s and 70s.)

estampage *n.m.* 'Con-job', confidence trick.

estamper *v.trans.* To 'con', to 'diddle', to swindle. (The verb is often encountered in the context of overcharging in a restaurant.)

estampeur *n.m.* 'Con-merchant', trickster, swindler. (As with *estamper*, the word is often encountered in the context of overcharging in a restaurant.)

estanco *n.m. (corr. estaminet)*: 'Watering-hole', pub, licensed drinking establishment.

estom *n.m. (abbr. estomac)*: 'Belly', stomach.

estomac *n.m.* 1 *Avoir l'estomac dans les talons*: To feel famished, to be ravenous, to feel very hungry. 2 *Avoir quelque chose sur l'estomac*: To feel resentful about something. *Ça m'est resté sur l'estomac*: It still rankles with me. 3 *Avoir de l'estomac*: To be 'gutsy', to have what it takes in the face of adversity. 4 *Faire quelque chose à l'estomac*: To bluff one's way through.

estomaquer *v.trans.* To 'bowl over', to 'flabbergast', to dumbfound.

estoquer *v.trans.* 1 To wallop good and hard, to smack with vigour. 2 To 'pull a fast one' on someone, to diddle someone with a neat con-trick.

estourbir *v.trans.* 1 To 'biff over the head', to knock out cold, to render unconscious. 2 To 'bump off', to kill.

estrasse *n.f.* Road, street. (The word is a direct borrowing from the German *Strasse*.)

établi *n.m. Aller à l'établi*: To go to the 'sweat-shop', to go to work.

étage *n.f. Monter à l'étage* (of prostitute): To have sex.

étagères *n.f.pl. Etagères à mégots*: 'Flappers', ears. (This jocular term aptly describes the French habit of leaving half-consumed cigarettes parked behind the ear.)

étal *n.m.* *(abbr. étalage) Fauche à l'étal*: Market-filching, petty thieving from stalls.

étaler *v.trans. En étaler*: To 'swank', to show off.

étaler *v.pronom.* **1** To fall flat on one's face, to go sprawling. **2** To 'blab', to 'blabber', to talk indiscreetly. (In the context of the underworld, the verb can mean to 'snitch', to inform on an accomplice.)

étape *n.f. Brûler les étapes*: To rush things.

état *n.m. Etre dans tous ses états*: To be 'all of a dither', to be 'in a real state', to be extremely upset.

étau *n.m.* 'Pussy', 'fanny', vagina. *Descente à l'étau*: Cunnilingus.

été *n.m. Se mettre en été*: To 'put one's summer togs on', to get into lightweight clothing.

éteignoir *n.m.* **1** *(joc.)*: 'Conk', 'snout', nose. **2** 'Wet blanket', killjoy. **3** *(pl.)*: 'Blinkers', 'peepers', eyes.

étendards *n.m.pl. (joc.)*: Undergarments strung along a washing-line.

étendre *v.trans.* **1** To knock out cold. *Le champion l'a étendu en cinq secs*: The champ had him out for the count in no time at all. **2** *Se faire étendre*: **a** *(sch.)*: To get 'ploughed' at an exam, to be failed in an examination. **b** (Gambling slang): To get 'cleaned out', to lose all one's money. **c** To get 'bumped off', to get 'done in', to be killed. *Son paternel s'est fait étendre en '14 avec les copains*: His old man got his chips with the other poor buggers in World War I.

éterniser *v.pronom. S'éterniser chez quelqu'un*: To outstay one's welcome, to stay longer somewhere than one should.

éternité *n.f. Ça fait une éternité qu'on ne s'est pas vus!* It seems like ages since we met!

éternuer *v.intrans. Eternuer dans le son* (also: *dans la sciure*): To die of decapitation under the guillotine (because the severed head fal!s into a bran tub).

Etienne *Proper name. A la tienne, Etienne!* Mud in your eye! – Here's looking at you! – Bottoms up! (This rhyming catch-phrase is often used when toasting someone with a drink.)

étincelles *n.f.pl.* **1** *Faire des étincelles*: To be sparklingly witty. **2** *Ça a fait des étincelles!* Sparks were certainly flying! (This expression is usually uttered in the context of a verbal confrontation.)

étiquettes *n.f.pl.* 'Flappers', 'lugs', ears.

étoffe *n.f. Ne pas manquer d'étoffe*: To 'have what it takes', to be a person of resilient character.

étoffer *v.pronom.* **1** To 'fill out', to put on some flesh, to lose one's puny constitution. **2** To 'broaden one's horizons', to gain experience.

étoile *n.f.* **1** *Coucher à la belle étoile*: To 'sleep rough' (out in the open). **2** *Voir les étoiles en plein*

midi: To 'see stars', to be dazed by a blow (also: *voir trente-six chandelles*).

étouffe-chrétien *n.m. (joc. & iron.)*: 'Stodge', 'heavy grub', indigestible food.

étouffer *v.trans.* **1** To 'nick', to 'pinch', to steal. *On m'a étouffé mon larfeuil*: Someone's made off with my wallet. **2** *Etouffer le coup*: To 'let bygones be bygones', to forget old scores (also: *écraser le coup*). **3** *En étouffer un*: To 'knock back', to down a drink. *Etouffer un perroquet*: To have a pastis. **4** *Ce n'est pas la politesse qui l'étouffe! (iron.)*: He could certainly do with a few lessons in manners!

étouffeur *n.m. L'étouffeur de fric (joc.)*: The tax-man, the man from the Inland Revenue.

étourdir *v.trans.* **1** To wear down, to tire out. **2** To 'nick', to 'pinch', to steal.

étourneau *n.m.* 'Scatter-brain', 'dizzy' forgetful person.

étrangler *v.trans.* To down drinks in quick succession. *Il en a étranglé quatre ou cinq d'affilée*: He knocked back four or five glasses in a row.

étrangleuse *n.f.* 'Neck-gear', tie.

être *v.intrans.* **1** *Etre de*: To be lumbered with an undesirable task. *Etre de garde*: To be on watch-duty. *C'est mon tour d'être de vaisselle!* As luck would have it, it's my turn to do the washing-up again! **2** *L'être*: To be a cuckold, to have an unfaithful wife. **3** *En être*: To be 'one of them', to be a 'pouf', to be a homosexual. **4** *Etre un peu là*: **a** To have a he-man physique, to be of a powerful build. **b** To have 'something up-top', to be really brainy. **c** To be 'loaded', to have plenty of money. **5** *Je suis comme je suis!* That's the way I am and you're not going to change me! **6** *J'y suis!* I've twigged! – I understand now what you mean!

étrenne *n.f.* **1** *Avoir l'étrenne de quelque chose*: To be the first to use something. *La nouvelle machine à écrire, j'en veux l'étrenne!* Bags I get first bash at that new typewriter! **2** *Il a eu ça pour ses étrennes! (iron.)*: He got what was coming to him! – He got his just deserts!

étrenner *v.trans. & intrans.* **1** To 'have first go at', to be the first to use something. **2** (Stall-holder, market-trader's slang): To get the first sale of the day. *Etrennez-moi!* Get the first bargain of the day! **3** To 'cop', to be on the receiving end of something unpleasant. **4** To get thrashed, to get 'drubbed', to be beaten up. **5** To get a 'wigging', to get told off, to be reprimanded. *Qu'est-ce qu'il a étrenné quand sa mère a su ça!* When his mum heard about it, he got the rollicking of his life.

étrier *n.m.* **1** *Avoir le pied à l'étrier*: To be set for success. *Mettre à quelqu'un le pied à l'étrier*:

To 'give someone a leg-up', to help someone with their finances or career. **2** *Ne pas perdre les étriers*: To 'stay cool', to keep one's wits about one.

étriller *v.trans.* **1** To 'wallop', to 'bash up', to beat up. **2** To 'tear a strip off someone', to reprimand severely. **3** (Gambling slang): To 'clean out', to fleece.

étriper *v.trans.* **1** To 'make mincemeat of someone', to shower someone with blows. **2** To 'give someone the rollicking of their life', to tell someone off in the strongest possible manner.

étron *n.m.* Turd, excrement. *Planter un étron*: To 'have a crap', to defecate.

étudié *past part.* *C'est étudié pour* (of contraption, device): That's the way it works! (Don't ask me how, but it does!) The comedian Fernand Raynaud made this expression memorable by including it in one of his famous one-man sketches.

étui *n.m.* 'Belly', stomach. *Avoir l'étui en creux*: To feel famished.

eulpif *adj.inv.* **1** 'Natty', smart and stylish. **2** 'Nifty', nimble, agile.

eurêka *n.m.* *(joc.)*: 'Rod', 'shooter', handgun. (The humour in this word stems from the fact that *Eurêka* is the registered trade-name of a toy gun that fires wooden darts tipped with rubber suckers.)

eustache *n.m.* Jack-knife, clasp-knife.

euzigues *pers.pron.* Them, themselves. *C'est à euzigues de décider*: It's up to them to make their minds up.

évangile *n.m.* *Ça, c'est vérité d'évangile!* It's as true as I'm standing here! – It's the gospel truth! (also: *parole d'évangile*).

évaporée *n.f.* 'Feather-brain', dotty and absent-minded young woman.

évaporer *v.pronom.* To 'skedaddle', to 'make tracks', to disappear.

Eve *Proper name.* *Ne connaître quelqu'un ni d'Eve ni d'Adam*: Not to know someone from Adam. (There is a jocular corruption of this expression: *Ne connaître quelqu'un ni des lèvres ni des dents* which carries its own humorous message.)

événement *n.m.* *C'est pas un événement!* It's nothing to write home about! – It's hardly what you'd call news!

éventail *n.m.* *Avoir les pieds en éventail*: To laze about (literally to have put one's feet up and opted out of work).

exam *n.m.* *(sch.)*: Test, exam, examination.

excédent *n.m.* *Avoir de l'excédent de bagages (joc.)*: To be more than a little over-weight.

excès *n.m.* *Faire de l'excès de zèle*: To 'crawl', to act in a sycophantic manner.

exclusivité *n.f.* *Il m'a joué ça en exclusivité*: I got a blow-by-blow report on his 'trials and tribulations'. (Originally the expression *'en exclusivité'* referred to the showing of new films in leading Paris cinemas before their general release.)

excuser *v.trans.* *Excusez-moi de vous demander pardon!* This jocular and slightly tongue-in-cheek expression became famous in the 60s through Fernand Raynaud, one of the top French comedians of the period. Raynaud's forte was in portraying the subservient underdog in French society.

exécuter *v.pronom.* To 'cough up', to pay up reluctantly.

exécution *n.f.* *Exécution!* Let's be having you! – Jump to it! – Hurry up and get on with it! (Do what you've been told!)

existence *n.f.* *C'est pas une existence! (iron.)*: This is no way to make a living! – If this is life, count me out!

exo *n.f.* *Une exo (th.)*: A complimentary ticket. *Il nous a filé une demi-douzaine d'exos*: He gave us six comps for the show.

expédier *v.trans.* **1** To 'sell someone down the river', to cheat someone out of something. **2** To 'send someone packing', to get rid of someone. **3** To 'bump off', to kill (literally to send someone to kingdom come). **4** *Expédier son repas*: To 'wolf one's food', to eat with great haste.

expliquer *v.pronom.* To be 'on the game', to practise prostitution.

expliquer *v.trans.reflex.* **1** To 'have it out' man-to-man, to have the nearest thing to a slanging match. **2** To 'have a set-to', to come to blows.

explorateur *n.m.* *(pol.)*: Cat-burglar operating mainly in small hotels.

expo *n.m.* *(sch.)*: Exposé, oral dissertation.

expo *n.f.* *(abbr. exposition)*: Show, exhibition (annual trade-fair, etc.).

exprès *adj.inv.* *C'est comme un fait exprès!* It's almost as if it was done on purpose!

extinction *n.f.* *Avoir une extinction*: To have lost one's voice.

extra *n.m.* **1** Waiter employed part-time by a restaurant when there is a rush on. **2** *(th.)*: 'Extra', actor who is given very minor or non-speaking parts. **3** *Faire un extra*: To take on an after-hours job.

extra *adj.inv.* 'Ace', 'A-1', first-rate. *Comme bière, ça c'est de l'extra!* This is real beer, this is!

extrait *n.m.* *Avaler son extrait de naissance*: To 'croak', to 'snuff it', to die.

F

fabriquer *v.trans.* **1** To do (with a pejorative connotation, mostly in the interrogative). *Qu'est-ce que tu fabriques là?!* What the hell are you up to? **2** To 'nick', to 'pinch', to steal. **3** *Etre fabriqué* (also: *se faire fabriquer*): **a** To be 'diddled', to get swindled. **b** To be made a fool of, to be made to look a fool. **c** To get 'collared', to be arrested. *Il a été fabriqué sur le tas*: He was caught red-handed.

Fac *n.f. La Fac*: The University.

façade *n.f.* **1** 'Show', 'make-believe', pretence. **2** *Se refaire la façade* (of woman): To 'put one's face on', to apply make-up.

facho *n.m. & adj.* Fascist, right-wing(er).

facile *adv.* Easily, effortlessly. *Il a gagné la course facile*: He won that race easy, it was no contest!

façon *n.f.* **1** *Faire des façons*: To 'stand on ceremony', to be over-officious. **2** *Sans façon!* No thanks, really!

fada *n.m.* 'Screwball', 'nutter', loony character. (The word orginates from Provence.)

fada *adj.inv.* 'Potty', 'barmy', mad.

fadasse *adj.* Insipid, lacking in character.

fade *n.m.* **1** 'Whack', 'cut', share of booty. *Toucher son fade*: To take one's split. **2** 'Whack', share of bill. *Y aller de son fade*: To chip in with one's share of the costs. **3** Orgasmic pleasure, sexual satisfaction. *Prendre son fade*: To 'come', to have a climax. **4** *Avoir son fade*: **a** To have had one's fill (of blows, bad luck, etc.). **b** To be 'blotto', to be 'pissed out of one's mind', to be blind drunk.

fadé *adj.* 'Knackered', 'buggered', exhausted.

fader *v.trans.* **1** To 'do in', to kill. **2** To punish, to treat severely. *Le juge l'a drôlement fadé*: He certainly got a stiff sentence from the judge. **3** To 'fuck up', to ruin, to make a mess of. **4** To give someone his 'whack', his cut, his share in a successful venture.

faf *n.m.* (also: *faffe*): **1** Slip of paper. **2** 'Note', banknote. **3** (*pl.*): 'I.D. papers', identity documents. *Taper aux fafs* (*pol.*): To check I.D.s.

fafiots *n.m.pl.* 'Flimsies', 'notes', banknotes.

fagot *n.m.* **1** 'Guy', dowdily dressed person. **2** *Une bouteille de derrière les fagots*: A really super bottle of wine. (The implication here is that this rare vintage has been saved for a special occasion.)

fagoté *adj.* Frumpishly, dowdily dressed. *Il était drôlement mal fagoté*: He was certainly no fashion-plate.

faiblard *adj.* **1** (of person): **a** Puny, weak. **b** 'Slow on the uptake', rather backward. **2** (of argument): Feeble, weakish.

faible *adj.* **1** *Se trouver faible*: To 'keel over', to 'pass out', to faint. **2** *C'est plutôt faible!* (of joke): I don't think that's very funny! – I can't see the humour in this!

faignant *n.m.* (*corr. fainéant*): **1** 'Lazy-bones', 'slacker', idle person. **2** 'Funk', coward.

faignasse *n.f.* (*pej.*): 'Lazy bugger', idle so-and-so.

faim *n.f. Rester sur sa faim* (*fig.*): To be expecting more and not get it.

faire *v.trans. & intrans.* **1** To 'nick', to 'pinch', to steal. *On m'a fait mon larfeuil*: Someone's pinched my wallet. **2** To 'have someone on', to 'hoodwink', to mislead. *On l'a fait de première*: He was bamboozled good and proper. **3** *Faire à l'influence*: To 'try and pull rank', to try and impose one's seniority. **4** *Faut pas me la faire!* Don't come the old soldier with me! – Don't try it on, it won't work! **5** To 'look', to seem. *Ça fait chic!* It looks trendy! *Il fait bien son âge!* He certainly looks his age! **6** (of commercial traveller): To be an agent in a given area. *Il fait la région parisienne*: He reps in and around Paris. **7** *A vous de faire!* (Cards): It's your go! – It's your turn! **8** *Il faut le faire!* (*joc. & iron.*): It's not as easy as it sounds! **9** *Ça commence à bien faire!* That's about as much as I can stand! **10** *Laisser faire et voir venir*: To 'leave things be', to let things take their natural course. *Je vais laisser faire et voir venir!* I'm going to have a little think about it all!

faire-part *n.m. Avoir une gueule en faire-part de deuil*: To have 'a face as long as a fiddle', to look as glum as hell.

faisan *n.m.* 'Con-man', swindler, crook.

faisandé *adj.* **1** 'Rotten to the core', highly disreputable. **2** 'Phoney', false.

faisander *v.trans.* **1** To 'con', to 'diddle', to swindle. **2** *Se faire faisander*: To get 'nicked', 'collared', to be arrested.

faiseur *n.m.* 'Chiseller', 'diddler', crook.

faiseuse *n.f. Faiseuse d'anges*: Back-street abortionist.

fait *past part. C'est bien fait pour lui!* Serves him bloody well right!

falot *n.m. (mil.)*: Court martial, military tribunal.

falots *n.m.pl.* 'Oglers', 'peepers', eyes.

falzar *n.m.* 'Trews', 'strides', trousers.

fameux *adj.* **1** 'Fab', 'A-1', first-rate. *Ce petit pinard, mon vieux, il est fameux!* That little wine of yours is no plonk! **2** *Elle est fameuse, celle-là! (iron.)*: You must be joking! – Do you expect me to believe that?!

famille *n.f.* **1** *La grande famille (iron.)*: The great 'pouf fraternity', the clique of male homosexuals (also: *la famille tuyau de poêle*). **2** *Elle nous a servi un petit gueuleton des familles*: She did us really proud with some good, honest grub. (*des familles* could best be translated as honest-to-goodness and unpretentious in statements similar to the one above.)

fana *n.m. (abbr. fanatique)*: Enthusiast, one who practically goes overboard about a hobby, etc. *C'est un fana de la moto*: He's potty about motorbikes.

fanal *n.m.* 'Bread-basket', 'belly', stomach.

fandard *n.m.* 'Trews', 'strides', trousers.

fanfan *n.m. (corr. enfant)*: 'Kiddlywink', 'kiddy', child.

fanfare *n.f.* **1** 'Song-and-dance', fuss about nothing. **2** *En avant la fanfare! (joc.)*: Off we go again! (This rather hackneyed expression is often used by scoutmasters and other youth group leaders.) *C'est un sale coup pour la fanfare!* What rotten luck!

fanta *n.m.* Fizzy orange or lemon drink. (Like many brand-names, *Fanta* has become generic for any carbonated fruit drink.)

fantabos *n.m. (mil.)*: 'Foot-slogger', infantry-man. (The word is a corruption of *fantassin* and pronounced *fantabosse*.)

fantaise *adj. (corr. de fantaisie)*: Not in keeping with the norm. *Il avait un uniforme plutôt fantaise*: You could hardly call what he was wearing a uniform!

fantaisies *n.f.pl.* Sex foreplay.

fantassins *n.m.pl.* 'Crabs', crab-lice (also: *morbaques*).

fantoche *n.m.* **1** 'Fly-by-night', disreputable character. **2** *En fantoche*: In a highly irregular way, not in keeping with the norm.

fantoche *adj.* **1** (of clothes): 'Loud', very colour-ful. **2** 'Potty', silly. *Il a toujours des idées fantoches*: He's always got pie-in-the-sky ideas.

faramineux *adj.* 'Incredible', fantastic. *Ça va vous coûter un prix faramineux*: It'll cost you a bomb! *Il a réussi un coup faramineux*: He's pulled off the almost unbelievable!

faraud *n.m.* 'Pill', 'pillock', arrogant and bossy twit. *Quel faraud!* He's always throwing his weight about!

faraud *adj.* Boorishly arrogant.

farce *adj.inv.* 'Rib-tickling', hilarious, very funny. *Je trouve le tout drôlement farce!* The whole matter's a hoot! (In the merry-go-round of language, this slightly dated adjective seems to be regaining popularity.)

farces *n.f.pl. Faire ses farces*: To 'sow one's wild oats', to gain experience in sexual matters.

farcir *v.trans.* **1** To 'screw', to fuck, to have sex with. **2** To 'con', to 'diddle', to swindle. **3** To 'bump off', to kill (literally to fill someone with lead).

farcir *v.pronom.* According to context, the verb means either getting the better of someone or something, or coming out a loser from a similar confrontation. **1** *Il s'est farci les deux frangines*: He scored with both sisters. **2** *On s'est farci un gueuleton sensationnel*: We had ourselves one hell of a slap-up meal. **3** *Ce mec-là, il faut se le farcir!* That guy is just one big pain in the neck! **4** *On a dû se farcir la vaisselle!* It was us poor buggers who had to do the washing-up!

fard *n.m. Piquer un fard*: To turn bright red, to blush.

farfadet *n.m.* Slightly potty character, the kind of person who is just a genial extrovert. *Quel farfadet!* What a fruitcake!

farfelu *n.m.* 'Nutty character', mild eccentric.

farfelu *adj.* 'Potty', 'slightly barmy', gently eccentric.

farfouiller *v.intrans.* To rummage. *Il a encore farfouillé dans mes affaires!* He's been through my things again!

farfouillettes *n.f.pl. Les Galeries Farfouillettes*: The *Galeries Lafayette*. This gentle corruption of the name of one of Paris's oldest department stores is far more revealing than might be obvious at first sight, going back to those good old days when you could rummage at leisure through the store.

fargue *n.f.* Charge, accusation, indictment. *Il s'est trouvé avec une ribambelle de fargues*: His charge-sheet read like a crime book-of-words.

farguer *v.trans.* To charge, to indict. *On l'a fargué au saut du lit:* He was charged before he even got his slippers on.

farguer *v.intrans.* To swank about, to posture.

farguer *v.trans.reflex.* To 'get rodded up', to 'pack a shooter', to arm oneself with a handgun.

fargueur *n.m.* Prosecution witness.

faridon *n.f.* 1 *Faire la faridon:* To 'whoop it up', to have a good time (eating and drinking). 2 *Etre de la faridon:* To be 'skint', 'broke', to be penniless.

farine *n.f.* 1 *Etre de la même farine:* To be of the same ilk. 2 *C'est la grosse farine!* It's a complete mystery (to me and to everyone)!

faro *n.m.* Three-card con-trick in which the punter has to guess where a specific card is placed.

fatal *adj. C'est fatal! (joc. & iron.):* I could see it coming! – I knew what was going to happen!

fatiguée *adj.f. Baiser à la fatiguée:* To have 'Aussie' sex.

fatiguer *v.trans.* 1 To 'wear down', to tire out. *Dieu, qu'il me fatigue!* He'd drive a saint to drink! 2 *Fatiguer les oreilles à quelqu'un:* To talk someone into submission, to talk and talk until the listener couldn't give a damn about what is being said.

fatiguer *v.intrans. Il fatigue plus du cul que des bras (iron.):* He doesn't exactly exert himself! (This sarcastic remark is usually uttered when referring to someone in a pen-pushing occupation.)

fatma *n.f.* 'Biddy', 'bird', woman.

fatras *n.m.* 1 'Hotch-potch', jumble of things. 2 'Mix-up', confusion. 3 'Cock-up', blunder.

faubourg *n.m.* 'Botty', young woman's behind. (This amusing voyeur's term was coined by Auguste Le Breton back in 1937, and is still very much in favour.)

fauche *n.f.* 'Nicking', 'filching', stealing. *Il est plutôt porté sur la fauche:* He's got what you could call itchy fingers.

fauché *adj.* 'Skint', 'broke', penniless. *Etre fauché comme les blés:* To be stoney-broke.

faucheman *adj.inv.* 'Skint', 'broke', penniless. *Etre faucheman:* To be in Queer Street.

faucher *v.trans.* 1 To 'nick', to 'pinch', to steal. *On lui a fauché sa montrouse:* Someone pinched his wristwatch. 2 *Se faire faucher:* To 'snuff it', to 'croak', to die. *Il s'est fait faucher à la fleur de l'âge:* He cashed in his chips rather early in life.

faucheur *n.m.* 'Filcher', petty thief.

faucheuse *n.f. La faucheuse:* The guillotine (also: *l'abbaye de Monte-à-regret*).

fausse *n.f. de la fausse:* 'Dud notes', counterfeit money.

faute *n.f.* 1 *Faute de mieux on couche avec sa femme!* Needs must where the devil drives! (If the naïve Anglo-Saxon users of the expression *faute de mieux* knew its rhetorical ending they might avoid using it.) 2 *C'est la faute à pas-de-chance:* It's just one of those things! – Accidents like that just happen!

fauter *v.intrans.* (of woman): To fall victim to temptation, to give in and have sex. (This sexist and twee verb still has its users.)

fauteuil *n.m.* (Racing slang) *Arriver dans un fauteuil:* To win 'hands down', to have an easy victory (also: *gagner les doigts dans le nez*).

faux *n.m. Un faux:* A fake, a forgery.

faux *adj.* 1 *Etre faux comme un jeton* (of person): To be as phoney as they come. 2 *C'est faux, faux, archi-faux!* It's a pack of bloody lies!

faux-col *n.m.* 1 Head of froth on glass of beer. *Je veux un demi, un vrai, sans faux-col!* I want a real half, not two inches of froth! 2 *Avoir un faux-col à manger de la tarte:* To display a haughty, holier-than-thou attitude. (Originally the starched collar worn by men forced their heads into an aloof position.)

faux-cul *n.m.* 'Two-faced person', hypocrite.

faux-poids *n.m.* Underage prostitute.

faveur *n.f. Faire une faveur:* To perform oral sex.

favo *n.m. Le favo* (Racing slang): The favourite, the horse tipped as most likely to win.

favouille *n.f.* 'Bin', pocket. (This is a corruption of the already colloquial *fouille*.)

fayot *n.m.* 1 Haricot bean. *Cesse de bouffer des fayots, ça devient gênant!* I'd give those beans the wind of change if I were you! (In colloquial French, *fayots* are also known as *musiciens*.) 2 *Aller becter des fayots:* To 'do porridge', to get a term of imprisonment. 3 'Crawler', 'creep', sycophant. (Specific extensions of this meaning are: 'swot', hard-working pupil in the slang of schools and colleges; or: re-enlisted man in military jargon.)

fayot *adj.inv.* 'Crawling', 'fawning', over-obsequious.

fayotage *n.m.* 'Flannelling', obsequious flattering.

fayoter *v.intrans.* To 'suck up to someone', to crawl obsequiously to someone. *Pour la promo ici, faut drôlement fayoter:* If you want to get anywhere here promotion-wise, it's flannel, flannel all the way!

fée *n.f.* 1 *La fée électricité (joc.):* 'Juice', electricity. (This expression became popular between the wars as the result of a publicity campaign. Today it merely retains humorous connotations.) 2 *La fée blanche:* 'Snow', cocaine.

feignant *n.m.* *(corr. fainéant)*: 'Slack-arse', 'slacker', idle person.

feignant *adj.* *(corr. fainéant)*: 'Slacking', idle. *Il est feignant comme pas un!* He's the most idle bugger I've come across!

feignasse *n.f.* 'Idle skiver', lazy so-and-so. *Quelle feignasse!* What a bloody slacker! (The ending *-asse* in a word referring to a man has an even greater pejorative connotation than normally because it is feminine.)

feinte *n.f.* 'Dodge', clever ruse.

feinter *v.trans.* **1** To 'pull the wool over someone's eyes', to fool someone. **2** To 'con', to 'diddle', to swindle.

fêlé *adj.* 'Cracked', 'bonkers', mad.

félouse *n.m.* *(corr. fellagha)*: Algerian guerrilla (or freedom fighter, depending on one's political stance, in the late 50s and 60s).

fêlure *n.f.* *Avoir une fêlure*: To 'have a screw loose', to be 'cracked', to be mad.

femelle *n.f.* *(pej.)*: 'Female', 'biddy', woman (also: *fumelle*).

femme *n.f.* **1** *Bonne femme*: Wife. *Ma bonne femme*: The missus. **2** *Les bonnes femmes (pej.)*: Women in general (with all their faults!) *Ah, les bonnes femmes, mon vieux!* You don't need to tell me how infuriating women can be! **3** *Femme du capitaine*: Inflatable rubber dummy.

femmelette *n.f.* *(pej.)*: **1** 'Cissy', weakling, man who cannot stand pain. **2** 'Pouffy character', effeminate homosexual.

fendant *adj.* 'Side-splitting', hilarious.

fendard *n.m.* (also: *fendart*): 'Trews', 'strides', trousers. (The origin of the word can be found in the verb *fendre*: to split.)

fendre *v.pronom.* *Se fendre de quelque chose*: To 'stump up', to 'fork out', to pay reluctantly for something. *Et c'est moi qui ai dû me fendre d'une tournée*: And it was muggins who had to pay for a round of drinks.

fenêtre *n.f.* *Il faut passer par là ou par la fenêtre! (iron.)*: I don't think you've got much option! – It's a case of Hobson's choice!

fente *n.f.* 'Fanny', 'pussy', vagina.

féodal *adj.* 'Fantabulous', 'super', incredible. (This adjective best illustrates the twee attempts at innovative language of the late 50s and early 60s.)

fer *n.m.* **1** *Mauvais fer*: 'Ugly customer', dangerous character likely to resort to violence. **2** *Fer à repasser*: **a** (Racing slang): 'Nag', 'loser', useless horse. **b** *Nager comme un fer à repasser*: To have no ability whatsoever when it comes to swimming. **3** *Il y a du fer à prendre!* There's money to be made here!

fer-blanc *n.m.* *Pacotille en fer-blanc*: 'Tinpot goods', worthless merchandise.

ferblanterie *n.f.* *De la ferblanterie*: 'Gongs', rows of medals, chestful of military decorations.

fermer *v.trans.* *La fermer* (also: *fermer sa gueule*): To 'clam up', to shut up. *La ferme!* Put a sock in it!

fermeture *n.f.* *Faire la fermeture* (in café, restaurant): To work the last hours of the evening shift. (*Faire l'ouverture*: To 'open up shop'.)

ferraille *n.f.* **1** *De la ferraille*: 'Coppers and silver', small change. **2** *Mettre à la ferraille (fig.)*: To 'scrap', to discard.

ferré *adj.* *Ferré en*: 'Well up on something', proficient in. *Il est drôlement ferré en math*: He's tops at maths.

ferrer *v.intrans.* *Ferrer dur*: To 'knuckle down', to 'put one's back into it', to make a start in earnest.

ferté *n.f.* *La bonne ferté*: Fortune-telling. *Dire la bonne ferté*: To tell someone's future.

fesse *n.f.* **1** *Poser ses fesses*: To sit down. *Pose tes fesses!* Take a pew! **2** *Serrer les fesses*: To be 'in a blue funk', to be frightened. **3** *Coller aux fesses de quelqu'un*: To 'stay hot on someone's trail', to follow someone like a leech. *Les avoir aux fesses*: To have the fuzz on one's tail. **4** *N'y aller que d'une fesse*: To do something half-heartedly. **5** *Occupe-toi de tes fesses!* Mind your own bloody business! **6** *Ça coûte la peau des fesses*: It costs a bomb – It's very expensive. **7** *Histoires de fesses*: 'Country matters', sexual goings-on. **8** *Journal de fesses*: 'Girlie mag', soft-porn magazine. (The umbrella term for such publications is *la presse du cul*.) **9** *Le pain de fesses*: Prostitution. **10** *Mes fesses!* My arse! – Not bloody likely!

festonner *v.intrans.* To lurch about in a drunken stupor (also: *faire des festons*).

fêtard *n.m.* 'Night-owl', character who enjoys whooping it up till the early hours of the morning.

fête *n.f.* **1** *Ne pas être à la fête*: To be 'getting a rough ride', to have a tough time. **2** *Ce n'est pas tous les jours fête!* Christmas comes but once a year! (so enjoy yourself!). **3** *Faire sa fête à quelqu'un*: To 'duff up', to 'bash someone up', to give someone a rousting. *Ça va être ta fête!* You're going to cop it!

feu *n.m.* **1** *Du feu*: A light (flame to light a cigar, pipe or cigarette). *Donne-moi du feu!* Give us a light! **2** *(pl.)*: 'Lights', traffic lights. *Brûler les feux*: To 'shoot the lights', to go through a set of traffic lights on red. **3** *Donner le feu vert (fig.)*: To give the go-ahead. **4** 'Rod', 'shooter', handgun. **5** *Coup de feu*: Rush, busiest period (in a shop, pub or restaurant). *Fiche-nous la paix, on est en plein coup de feu!* Come back later, we're rushed off our feet! 6 *Il n'y a pas le feu à la maison!* (joc. & iron.): What's the rush? – There's no hurry! 7 *Avoir le feu aux fesses*: a To be 'in a mad rush', to be in a hurry. b (of woman): To 'feel randy', to have a craving for sex. 8 *Cracher le feu*: To be 'full of beans', to be bursting with energy. 9 *N'y voir que du feu*: 'Not to twig', to understand bugger-all about what is happening.

feuille n.f. 1 'Flapper', ear. *Etre dur de la feuille*: To be hard of hearing. 2 *Feuille de chou*: 'Local rag', unimportant newspaper (one with a tiny circulation. The origin of the appellation lies in the green shade of the newsprint used in the 30s by some small provincial news-sheets). 3 *Recevoir sa feuille de route*: To 'croak', to 'snuff it', to die (literally to get one's marching orders to a better world). 4 *Feuille de vigne*: 'G-string', minimal briefs worn by striptease artist. 5 *Voir les feuilles à l'envers* (of woman): To have intercourse. (The expression is usually used in the past tense to indicate that a woman has lost her virginity.)

feuillées n.f.pl. (mil.): 'Temporary lats', field latrines used during army manoeuvres.

fève n.f. *Tirer* (also: *trouver*) *la fève*: To 'come out tops', to strike it lucky. (The expression is a direct reference to the *galette des rois* – a large flaky pastry pie in which a white bean is hidden. The lucky person is the one who finds it in his slice.)

Fiacre Proper name. *Le Fiacre*: Popular 'gay' night-club in Paris.

fias n.m. 1 Arse-hole, anal sphincter. 2 'Odd-ball', weird character. (With both meanings, the word is pronounced *fiasse*.)

fiasse n.f. (abbr. *pouffiasse*): 'Biddy', 'moo', woman. (This sexist and pejorative appellation sometimes refers to prostitutes.)

ficelé adj. 1 *Etre drôlement ficelé* (of person): To be frumpishly, dowdily dressed. 2 *Ça m'a l'air mal ficelé!* (of task, project): It certainly looks like a botched job!

ficelle n.f. 1 'Neck-gear', tie. 2 (pl.): Ropes surrounding boxing ring. 3 Long thin French loaf, equivalent in weight to half a *baguette*. 4 (pol.): 'Tail', officer or officers following a suspect's every move. 5 (mil.): Stripe indicating rank in army. 6 (th.): Hackneyed trick of the trade. *C'est un vieux de la vieille sur les planches, il connaît toutes les ficelles*: You can't teach an old campaigner like him any new tricks, can you?! 7 'Twister', trickster. *Une vieille ficelle*: A 'wily old bird', an 'old hand', character who really knows it all. 8 *Tirer les ficelles*: To 'pull strings', to manipulate. *Vous savez, c'est lui qui tire les ficelles!* He's the one

who really calls the shots, you know! 9 *Trop tirer sur la ficelle*: To 'come it a bit strong', to try it on a bit too much. 10 *Connaître les ficelles*: To 'know the ropes', to know the where-and-how of something. 11 *Voir la ficelle*: To 'see the bare bones', to be able to see the truth behind it all. 12 *Casser la ficelle*: To 'get unhitched', to get a divorce.

ficelle adj.inv. 'Crafty', sly, cunning. *Pour être ficelle, il l'était!* He was as sharp as they came!

ficher v.trans. & intrans. (This verb is the euphe-mistic equivalent of *foutre*, and a surprising alternative infinitive form *fiche* is quite often to be found.) 1 To be up to (with pejorative connotation), to do (very little). *Et qu'est-ce qu'il fiche ici quand il se donne la peine de venir?!* And can you tell me what he does here, if and when he bothers to clock in? *Ne rien ficher* (also: *ne pas en ficher un coup*): To 'do bugger-all', to 'sit on one's backside', not to do a stroke of work. 2 To 'bung', to 'stick', to put. *Où est-ce que vous avez fiché ma valise?* Where did you dump my suitcase? 3 *Ficher quelqu'un dedans*: To 'land someone in it', to get someone into trouble. 4 *Ficher quelqu'un à la porte*: To chuck some-one out. 5 *Ficher le camp*: To 'bugger off', to 'piss off', to go away. 6 *Ficher la frousse* (also: *ficher la trouille*): To frighten the wits out of someone. 7 *Je t'en fiche* (also: *je vous en fiche*) *mon billet!* You can bet your bottom dollar on this! – You can take it from me that . . . 8 *Envoyer faire fiche quelqu'un*: To send some-one away with a flea in his ear. *Va te faire fiche!* Go to hell! 9 *Faire quelque chose à la va-te-faire-fiche*: To do something 'any old how', to do something in a slapdash manner (also: *à la va-comme-je-te-pousse*). 10 *Je t'en fiche!* You must be joking! – Nothing of the sort! – Not remotely likely! 11 *Ça la fiche mal!* That doesn't look good! – That certainly makes a bad impression! *Ça la fiche mal, un patron qui fait de la taule!* A director in the clink certainly doesn't enhance the company image.

ficher v.pronom. 1 *Se ficher de*: a 'Not to give a fuck', not to care a damn about something. *Il se fiche éperdument de ce que vous pouvez bien lui dire*: He couldn't care two hoots what you say. b To 'poke fun at', to 'pull someone's leg', to make fun of someone or something. *Je sais qu'il se fiche de moi derrière mon dos!* I know he's always taking the mickey out of me! 2 *Se ficher dedans*: a To 'make a boo-boo', to make a blunder. b To 'land oneself in it', to get oneself into trouble. 3 *Se ficher en l'air*: a To get killed. *Il s'est fichu en l'air sur l'autoroute*: He got shunted to kingdom come on the motorway. b To 'bump oneself off', to commit suicide.

4 *Se ficher sur la gueule*: To 'have a ding-dong set-to', to 'have a punch-up', to have a fight. **5** *Se ficher par terre*: **a** To fall flat on one's face, to go sprawling. **b** To 'come a cropper', to fall foul of one's luck.

fichets *n.m.pl.* 'Darbies', 'bracelets', handcuffs.

fichtre *interj.* **1** Expressing surprise. Cripes! –Crumbs! – Good gracious! *Fichtre! Toi ici?!* Fancy meeting you here! **2** Expressing admiration. *Une Rolls?! Fichtre! Tu ne te refuses rien!* A Rolls, no less?! You've certainly got on in life! **3** Expressing annoyance. Damn! –Blast! – Hell! *Fichtre, alors! Foutez-moi la paix pendant l'heure du déjeuner!* Bloody hell! Isn't a man entitled to his lunch break?! **4** Expressing pain. Ow! – Ouch! *Fichtre! T'aurais pu te couper les ongles!* Ouch! Those nails of yours aren't half sharp! **5** Used as an 'intensifier' within a sentence. (In the affirmative) Ra-ther! – You bet! – Too right! (In the negative) No fear! – Not bloody likely! *Je n'en sais fichtre rien!* I'll be hanged if I know!

fichtrement *adv.* 'Confoundedly', 'deucedly', extremely. *J'en ai fichtrement assez!* I'm fed up to the back teeth with this!

fichu *adj.* **1** 'Bally', 'bloody', awful. *Quel fichu temps!* What rotten weather we're having! *Il a un fichu caractère, tu sais!* He's got a lousy temper. **2** 'Done-for', doomed. *Il est fichu, c'est la fin, vous savez!* He's a goner, you know, he's not long for this world! **3** Capable. *Ne pas être fichu de faire quelque chose*: To be incapable of doing something useful. *Il n'est même pas fichu de faire la vaisselle*: He can't even be relied on to do the dishes. **4** *Il est fichu de ne pas venir*: It's just as likely he won't turn up. **5** *Etre mal fichu*: To 'feel out of sorts', to be 'off-colour', to be unwell.

fidèle *adj.* *Avoir un air de chien fidèle*: To have an expression of mute admiration.

fief *n.m.* *(joc.)*: Territory, area of influence. *C'est moi qui arrose, ici c'est mon fief!* The drinks are on me, this is my local!

fiel *n.m.* *Donner dans le fiel*: To 'have a touch of the sour grapes', to stoop to caustic comments in a context of jealousy.

fiente *n.f.* *Soigner des bobos à la fiente de pigeon*: To believe in old-wives' remedies.

fier *n.m.* *Faire le fier*: To 'play the high and mighty', to put on airs and graces.

fier *adj.* **1** 'Hoity-toity', 'stuck-up', arrogant. **2** 'Deuced', confounded. *C'est un fier crétin!* He's an A-grade pillock! **3** *Devoir à quelqu'un une fière chandelle*: To be deeply indebted to somebody.

fier-à-bras *n.m.* Bully who likes to throw his weight about a bit. *Faire le fier-à-bras*: To 'come the heavy', to play the tough guy.

fiérot *n.m.* *Faire le fiérot*: To 'strut about', to play the important person.

fiérot *adj.* 'Stuck-up', 'full of oneself', arrogant.

fiesta *n.f.* **1** 'Binge', 'booze-up', drinking spree. **2** 'Nosh-up', feast. (The expression *faire la fiesta* refers to the 'good time had by all' at an eating and drinking session.)

fieu *n.m.* 'Laddie', chap, fellow. *Un bon fieu*: 'A good sort', a decent chappie.

fièvre *n.f.* **1** *Tenir une fièvre de cheval*: To be running a high temperature. **2** *Fièvre de Bercy* *(joc.)*: Stupor, state of inebriation. (The humour within the expression stems from the fact that the Paris wine docks are at Bercy.)

fiévreux *n.m.* 'Raving nut', lunatic, madman. *Etre chez les fiévreux*: To be in 'the loony bin', in 'the happy farm', to be a patient in a mental hospital.

fiévreux *adj.* 'Bonkers', 'loony', mentally deranged.

Fifi *Proper name.* Diminutive of the Christian name *Delphine*.

fifi *n.m.* **1** *(corr. F.F.I.: Forces Françaises de l'Intérieur)*: Armed branch of the French *Résistance* freedom fighters during World War II. **2** Sparrow. **3** *Le fifi de*: The darling, the apple of someone's eye. *Le fifi du prof*: Teacher's pet.

fifille *n.f.* Daddy's little darling daughter.

fifine *n.f.* 'Jam-rag', sanitary towel.

fiflot *n.m.* *(mil.)*: 'Foot-slogger', infantryman.

fifre *n.m.* *(pej.)*: 'Gawky twit', tall and lanky idiot.

fifre *indef.pron.* **1** *Ne faire que fifre*: To 'do sweet F.A.', to 'do bugger-all', to be idle. **2** *Que fifre!* Not on your nelly! – Nothing doing! – Certainly not!

fifrelin *n.m.* (Usually in a negative clause): 'Next to nothing', very little. *Ça ne vaut pas un fifrelin*: It's not worth a brass farthing. *Je n'ai pas un fifrelin*: I'm skint (also: *roupie de sansonnet*).

fifti *n.m.* Half, 50 per cent. *Faire fifti-fifti*: To go halves. (When referring to monetary matters, an equivalent to *fifti-fifti* is *afanaf*, also a corruption of the English half-and-half.) *Rencart à deux plombes fifti!* Meet you at two-thirty!

figaro *n.m.* **1** Barber, men's hairdresser (also: *merlan*). **2** *Faire figaro* (Waiters' slang): To 'miss out on a tip', to get no gratuity.

figé *adj.* (of person): **1** 'Frozen stiff', blue with cold. **2** 'Paralytic', in a drunken stupor. **3** 'Smashed', drugged to the eyeballs.

fignedé *n.m.* **1** 'Arse', 'bum', behind. **2** *L'avoir dans le fignedé*: To have been 'conned', 'diddled', to have been swindled.

figue *n.f.* **1** 'Pussy', 'fanny', vagina. **2** *(pl.)*: 'Bollocks', 'balls', testicles. *Avoir les figues* molles: To have 'flat batteries', to have little or no sex drive. **3** *Mi-figue, mi-raisin*: Neither one thing nor the other. *Un ton (de voix) mi-figue, mi-raisin*: A sarcastic bitter-sweet intonation. *Etre mi-figue, mi-raisin*: To 'sit on the fence', to be cagey. **4** *Faire la figue à quelqu'un*: To show one's contempt with a gesture of the hand. (Basically, to join the tips of one's fingers in the shape of a fig; this gesture is intended to imply that the recipient is a coward.) **5** *Figue molle*: 'Wet' person, one who lacks drive, personality and initiative.

figuier *n.m.* *Tronc de figuier (pej.)*: Arab native of North Africa.

figure *n.f.* **1** *Se casser la figure*: **a** To have an accident. **b** *(fig.)*: To 'come a cropper', to fall foul of someone or something. **2** *Casser la figure à quelqu'un*: To 'push someone's face in', to beat someone up. **3** *Se payer la figure de quelqu'un*: To 'make a fool of someone', to make someone look an idiot (also: *se payer la fiole de quelqu'un*). **4** *Avoir une figure de papier mâché*: To 'look like death warmed up', to be a sickly shade of pale. **5** *Faire une figure d'enterrement*: To look as gloomy as hell, to be extremely morose. **6** *Figure de fifre! (pej.)*: Monkey-face!

fil *n.m.* **1** 'Tape', finishing line. *Etre coiffé sur le fil*: To get pipped at the post. (Although the expression originated in the sporting world, it is often used figuratively in other contexts.) **2** *Le fil (abbr. le filage)*: Card-sharp's manipulation of a deck enabling him to cut the pack where he wishes. **3** *Avoir le fil*: To be 'on the ball', to be sharp. **4** *Avoir un fil à la patte*: To have matrimonial ties. *Se mettre un fil à la patte*: To get 'spliced', 'hitched', to get married. **5** *Un vrai fil*: A mere slip of a girl, a hyper-slender woman. **6** *Donner du fil à retordre à quelqu'un*: To 'lead someone a merry dance', to give someone a lot of trouble. **7** *Sécher sur le fil*: To be 'stood up', to be kept waiting. **8** *Coup de fil*: 'Buzz on the phone', telephone call. *Il m'a donné un coup de fil*: He gave me a tinkle. *'Y a ta mère au bout du fil*: It's your Mum on the phone. **9** *C'est cousu de fil blanc* (of plot): You can see right through it – It's not a very discreet ploy. **10** *Ne pas avoir inventé le fil à couper le beurre*: To be more than a trifle dim (also: *ne pas avoir inventé la poudre*).

filage *n.m.* **1** *(pol.)*: 'Tail', discreet shadowing and surveillance of suspect. **2** Card-sharp's manipulation of a deck enabling him to cut the pack where he wishes.

filard *n.m.* **1** Character who is easily led astray, weak mind easily influenced. **2** 'Blab', 'blabbermouth', one who cannot keep a secret.

filasse *adj.* *Avoir une crinière filasse*: To have a 'mousey' thatch, to have tow-coloured hair.

filature *n.f.* *(pol.)*: 'Tail', discreet shadowing and surveillance of suspect. *Prendre quelqu'un en filature*: To put a tail on someone.

file *n.f.* *Etre en double file* (of car): To be double-parked.

filer *v.trans.* **1** *(pol.)*: To 'tail', to shadow a suspect. *On l'a filé en douce dès son arrivée*: We put a tail on him from the word go. **2** *Filer le train à quelqu'un*: **a** To follow someone around, to accompany someone everywhere. **b** To 'twig', to follow the gist of what someone is saying. **3** To 'blow the gaff on someone', to 'snitch', to inform. *Il m'a filé comme le dégueulasse qu'il est!* Like the rotten swine he is, he went and told on me! **4** *Filer du chouette*: To commit buggery, to practise sodomy. **5** To 'hand over', to give. *File-moi du fric!* Give me some dough! **6** To administer something unpleasant. *Filer une beigne/filer une baffe*: To punch, to slap. *Filer une danse*: To bash up, to beat up. *Elle m'a filé la chtouille*: I caught a dose of clap off her. **7** *Filer en cabane*: To 'clap into jail', to put into prison. **8** *Filer un mauvais coton*: To be in poor health.

filer *v.intrans.* **1** To 'scram', to 'skedaddle', to rush away. **2** *Filer à l'anglaise*: To 'take French leave', to slip away (also: *filer en douce*). **3** *Filer doux*: To 'change one's tune' to a humbler one, to 'knuckle under', to become docile and submissive.

filer *v.trans.reflex.* **1** To get into, to slip into. *Il s'est filé dans le cagibi*: He hid in the box-room. *Se filer dans les toiles*: To 'hit the sack', to go to bed. **2** To get involved in something unpleasant. *Il a été se filer dans une sale affaire*: He got mixed up in some nasty business.

filet *n.m.* **1** *Ne pas avoir le filet*: To 'have the gift of the gab', to be a smooth and prolific talker. **2** *L'artiste travaille sans filet! (joc.)*: Things like that don't frighten me! (This piece of verbal bravado originates from the world of trapeze artists where a safety net is a salutary precaution.)

filetouze *n.m.* String shopping bag (also: *filetoche*).

fileuse *n.f. (pej.)*: 'Grass', 'snitch', informant.

filin *n.m.* Phone call. *Il m'a envoyé un petit filin*: He gave me a buzz.

fille *n.f.* **1** *Jouer la fille de l'air*: To 'beetle off', to 'scram', to clear off. *Quand il a su qu'on le cherchait, il nous a joué la fille de l'air*: When he heard we were onto him, he was off and away. **2** *La plus belle fille du monde ne peut donner que ce qu'elle a*: You mustn't expect more than is humanly possible. (This statement is usually uttered when a discontented person is being told that nothing more can be done to please him.)

fille-mère *n.f.* Unmarried mother. (A less offensive modern equivalent is *mère célibataire*.)

fillette *n.f.* 1 Half-bottle of wine. 2 *Chausser du quarante-sept fillette (joc.)*: To have incredibly large feet. (The humour here stems from the juxtaposition of the word *fillette* with what could practically be called 'outsize' shoe measurements.)

filochard *n.m.* 'Wily dog', cunning so-and-so. (*Filochard* is one of the characters in Louis Forton's famous series of cartoon strips *La Bande des Pieds-Nickelés*.)

filoche *n.f.* (*pol.*): 'Tail', discreet shadowing and surveillance. *Pas de bile! La filoche, ça me connaît!* Have no fear! I'll tail him, he won't know I'm there!

filocher *v.trans. & intrans.* 1 (*pol.*): To 'tail', to shadow a suspect. 2 To 'shirk', to dodge some unpleasant duty. 3 To 'put one's skates on', to hurry up.

filon *n.m.* 1 'Spot of luck', 'lucky break', fortunate occurrence. 2 'Plum', 'cushy number', easy task. *Il a décroché un sacré filon*: He's certainly landed the plummest job around. *Tenir le filon*: To be onto a good thing.

filoneur *n.m.* (also: *filonneur*): 'Shirker', idle so-and-so. (The kind of character who always seems to land the jobs where little work is entailed.)

filou *n.m.* 1 'Con-man', trickster, deceitful character. 2 (term of endearment): *Filou va!* You are awful . . . but I like you!

filouter *v.trans.* To 'con', to 'diddle', to swindle. *Il les a filoutés en beauté!* He certainly took them for a ride!

filouterie *n.f.* 'Diddle', small-time con-trick. *La filouterie, c'est son blot!* He's never without some con-job up his sleeve!

fils *n.m.* 1 'Chappie', laddie. (This cordial form of address has condescending undertones. *Salut fils!* Hello there, young man!) 2 *Fils à papa*: 'Daddy's boy', spoilt son of a rich father.

fin *n.m. C'est le fin du fin!* It's the cat's whiskers! – It's the bee's knees! – It's first-rate!

fin *n.f.* 1 *La fin des haricots*: 'The last straw', the limit. *Ça, c'est vraiment la fin des haricots!* Well, that does it, count me out! 2 *Avoir des fins de mois difficiles*: To 'find it difficult to make ends meet', to be short of money. 3 *Faire ses fins de mois*: To engage in part-time prostitution to make ends meet. 4 *Liquider les fins de série*: To 'weed out the weak', to get rid of the weaklings. (Originally this expression referred only

to the selling off at reduced prices of items that were not 'going well'.) 5 *Faire une fin* (of footloose and fancy-free person): To turn over a new leaf and get married. 6 *Faire une belle fin*: a To end one's footloose and fancy-free days in style by a wealthy and opportune marriage. b To 'go out in a blaze of glory', to die in style. 7 *Sentir la fin de saison*: To 'be getting past it', to have aged noticeably.

fin *adj. Avoir l'air fin*: To 'look a proper Charlie', to look stupid. *Ce que t'as l'air fin, mon pauvre vieux! (iron.)*: If you could only see yourself! (you'd realize how silly you are).

fin *adv.* Completely, absolutely. *Etre fin prêt*: To be ready to go. *Etre fin ratiboisé*: To be 'skint', to be stoney-broke. *Etre fin saoul*: To be 'pissed', 'sozzled', to be dead drunk.

finasser *v.intrans.* 1 To outsmart, to outwit. *Lui au moins, il sait finasser avec le fisc*: At any rate, he doesn't come out second-best when arguing with the tax-man. 2 To 'play the smart-alec', to act the know-all.

finasserie *n.f.* 1 Small-print escape clause in contract. 2 *Faire des finasseries*: To try and dodge the issue, to find a multitude of reasons why something can't be done.

finasseur *n.m.* 'Smart-alec', character who can always talk himself out of a tricky situation.

finaud *n.m.* Character who is always 'on the ball', shrewd and cunning person.

finaud *adj.* 'Smart', shrewd, clever. *Gaffe! Il est finaud!* Don't take him at face value, he doesn't miss a trick!

fin-de-mois *n.f.* Part-time prostitute. (Some seemingly respectable *mères de famille* find it necessary to 'make ends meet' in this way.)

fine *n.f.* Top quality distilled alcohol. *Une fine à l'eau*: Brandy and water.

fine *adj. Fine mouche*: 'Crafty customer', artful and cunning person. *C'est une fine mouche, tu sais!* She doesn't miss a trick!

fini *adj.* 1 'Utter', complete, total (usually in a derogatory context). *C'est un salaud fini!* He's an out-and-out rotter! 2 *C'est fini, n-i-ni!* That's the end of it – It's all over! (This semi-jocular expression rhythmically spells it out that all is well and truly over. It is sometimes uttered: *n-i-ni, c'est fini!*)

finir *v.intrans.* 1 *Finir en eau de boudin*: To 'fizzle out', to 'fall through', to come to nothing (also: *finir en queue de poisson*). 2 *Des histoires à n'en plus finir*: a Interminable (and boring) stories. b An unending sequel of misfortunes.

fion *n.m.* 1 Arse-hole, anus. *L'avoir dans le fion*: To have been 'had', 'conned', to have been tricked. 2 Luck (the kind others do not think you deserve). *Il a un de ces fions!* He's got the luck of the devil! **3** *Avoir le fion pour (faire) quelque chose*: To have the knack for something. **4** Brush, broom. *Donner un coup de fion dans la taule*: To give the place a bit of a clean. **5** *Donner le coup de fion*: To give the finishing touches to something.

fion *n.f.* Bottle of booze (refers usually to a full rather than to an empty bottle of strong alcohol). **2** 'Bean', 'bonce', head. *Il a pris un coup de goumi sur la fiole*: He got coshed. **3** *(pej.)*: 'Mush', 'dial', face. *Il a une de ces fioles!* He's got a face as ugly as sin! *J'en ai marre de ta fiole*: I can't stand the sight of you! **4** *Ma fiole*: Me, myself. *Ta fiole*: You. *C'est bon pour ta fiole*: It's good enough for you.

fioritures *n.f.pl.* *Donner dans les fioritures*: To waste time and effort on frills and pointless details.

fiotte *n.f.* *(pej.)*: 'Nancy-boy', 'pansy', effeminate homosexual. *J'en ai ralbol de ses mines de fiotte*: I can't stand his pouffy airs and graces!

fisc *n.m.* *Le fisc*: The tax-man, the Inland Revenue. *Frauder le fisc*: To fiddle one's taxes.

fissa *adv.* Quickly, speedily. *Faire fissa*: To be 'quick about it', to lose no time. *Faut faire fissa, si on veut pas louper le dur*: We'll have to get a move on if we want to catch that train.

fissure *n.f.* **1** *Colmater les fissures (iron.)*: To put on some heavy make-up. **2** *Avoir une fissure*: To be 'slightly cracked', to be 'bonkers', to be mad.

fiston *n.m.* **1** Son. *C'est mon fiston*: This is my lad. **2** (Term of endearment): Laddie, sonny-boy.

fistot *n.m.* *(mil.)*: First-year naval cadet.

fistule *n.f.* *Avoir (de) la fistule*: To have the luck of the devil, to be incredibly fortunate.

fixe *n.m.* Basic wage (without overtime or gratuities). *Son fixe n'est déjà pas cochon, mais avec les pourliches il fait son beurre*: His basic isn't to be sneezed at, but what with tips and extras he's in the good times.

fixé *past part.* *Etre fixé*: To know where one stands. *Maintenant qu'elle est partie, vous êtes fixé*: Now she's gone and left, you know how much you meant to her.

fixer *v.trans.reflex.* To 'get a fix', to inject oneself with a drug.

flac *n.m.* *Il y en a flac!* That does it! – I'm sick and tired of all this! (also: *il y en a marre!*).

flacdal *n.m.* 'Gutless wonder', 'spineless' person, character without will and personality.

flacdal *adj.inv.* 'Wet', spineless. *Ce qu'il est flacdal, ton mec!* He's a proper drip, that boyfriend of yours!

Flacmann *Aller chez Flacmann*: To 'have a crap', to 'shit', to defecate. (*Flacmann* is a fictitious proper name coined from the verb *flaquer*.)

flacon *n.m.* **1** *Prendre du flacon*: To be 'getting on in years', to be getting old. *Avoir du flacon*: To be 'long in the tooth', to be slightly past it. **2** *Renifler du flacon*: To have foul breath (also: *puer du bec*).

flafla *n.m.* *Faire du flafla* (also: *faire des flaflas*): To 'put on airs and graces', to over-act with ingratiating mannerisms.

flafla *adj.inv.* *Etre flafla*: To be 'pooped', to feel 'knackered', to be dog-tired (also: *être flagada*).

flag *n.m.* *(abbr. flagrant délit)*: **1** *Etre pris en flag*: To be 'caught red-handed', to be caught in the act. **2** Tribunal dealing with offenders caught in the act. *Passer en flag*: To be judged by the Tribunal des flagrants délits. (The *Tribunaux Correctionnels* dealing with such undisputed cases administer a summary justice that sometimes appeals to hardened criminals because the tribunal has little time to get to know of previous convictions. The inevitable sentence is therefore often lighter than the offender might have expected had the court known of his past record.)

flagada *adj.inv.* 'Knackered', 'buggered', exhausted.

flagdas *n.m.pl.* Haricot beans. *Avoir bouffé des flagdas (joc.)*: To be 'full of wind', to be prone to farting.

flageolet *n.m.* **1** 'Prick', 'cock', penis. *Avoir le flageolet à la portière*: To 'have the big stick', to have an erection. **2** *(pl.)*: 'Bean-poles', 'sticks', thin legs.

Flahute *n.m. & f.* 'Flem', Flemish person.

flair *n.m.* *Avoir le flair blair*: To 'have a nose for finding things out', to have an intuitive mind.

flambard *n.m.* 'Swank', show-off. *Faire son flambard*: To 'throw one's weight about', to show off.

flambe *n.f.* *La flambe*: Betting, gambling (usually where high stakes are concerned).

flambé *past part.* *Etre flambé*: To have been 'rumbled', to have been found out.

flambeau *n.m.* **1** *Passer le flambeau*: To let someone else 'carry the flame', to pass responsibility to someone else. **2** *Avoir du flambeau* (Gambling slang): To have the luck of the devil.

flamber *v.intrans.* **1** To gamble recklessly. *Les pontes du milieu, ça aime flamber dur*: The big-shots of the underworld like throwing their money around in casinos. **2** To 'spend, spend, spend', to burn the financial candle at both ends.

flambeur *n.m.* **1** Heavy gambler. **2** Spendthrift man-about-town. (The image in both instances is of a character who has money to burn.)

flamme *n.f. Etre tout feu, tout flamme*: To be 'full of zip', to have plenty of enthusiasm.

flan *n.m.* **1** 'Bosh', 'baloney', nonsense. *Tout ça, c'est du flan!* What a load of codswallop! **2** *Du flan!* Not on your nelly! – Not bloody likely! – Certainly not! **3** 'Con tactics', devious lies. *Faire du flan*: To tell a pack of lies. **4** *Faire quelque chose au flan*: **a** To con one's way through (or into) something. **b** To have a go (at something) 'on the off chance', to try one's luck. **5** *Venir au flan*: To 'come on the off chance', to chance it. **6** *Travail au flan*: Pilfering, petty thieving. **7** *En rester comme deux ronds de flan*: To be 'knocked all of a heap', to be 'flabbergasted', to be dumbfounded.

flanc *n.m.* **1** *Etre sur le flanc*: **a** To be 'knackered', 'buggered', to be exhausted. **b** To be 'off sick', to have a 'sick-note', to be off work for health reasons. **2** *Mettre sur le flanc*: To exhaust, to wear out mentally and physically. *En vacances, il nous met tous sur le flanc*: Holidaying with him leaves you longing for a rest! **3** *Tirer au flanc*: To 'come the old soldier', to 'swing the lead', to malinger. **4** *Se battre les flancs*: **a** To rack one's brains. **b** To 'flog oneself needlessly', to get into a useless frenzy of activity.

flanchard *n.m.* 'Quitter', 'shirker', character who gives up too readily.

flanchard *adj.* 'Sickly', weakish, unwell.

flanche *n.m.* **1** 'Job', gainful criminal act. *Monter un flanche du tonnerre*: To mastermind a superb heist. **2** *C'est pas ton flanche!* It's none of your (bloody) business! **3** Game, gambling session. *Aller au flanche*: To go gambling. **4** Hawker's, street vendor's patter.

flanche *n.f. Une flanche*: 'Squeal', informant's betrayal.

flancher *v.trans.* **1** To 'chicken out', to 'get cold feet', to funk out of something. **2** *(sch.)*: To get 'ploughed', to fail an exam. **3** To gamble, to have a bet.

flancheur *n.m.* **1** 'Funker', 'quitter', character who cannot be relied on. **2** Card-sharp.

flandrin *n.m. (pej.)*: 'Gawk', tall and lanky fool.

flanelle *n.f. Faire flanelle*: **a** To sit in a *bistrot* and while away the hours without ordering many drinks. (In waiters' slang, the expression relates more to the inactivity of the bar staff than the meanness of the customers.) **b** (of travelling salesman): To have an unproductive working day.

flaneuse *n.f.* 'Sit-you-down', easy-chair.

flânocher *v.intrans.* To 'mooch', to loaf about. *Le dimanche, chez lui, il flânoche toute la journée*: Sundays he spends pottering around at home.

flânocheur *n.m.* 'Loafer', idle and lazy person.

flanquer *v.trans.* **1** To 'bung', to 'stick', to put. *Où t'as flanqué mon pardosse?* Where the hell did you throw my coat? **2** *Flanquer quelqu'un dedans*: To 'land someone in it', to get someone into trouble. **3** *Flanquer quelqu'un à la porte*: To 'send someone packing', to chuck someone out. **4** *Flanquer la frousse à quelqu'un*: To 'put the wind up someone', to frighten the wits out of someone.

flanquer *v.trans.reflex.* **1** *Se flanquer dedans*: To 'land oneself in it', to get oneself into trouble (usually through an error of judgement). **2** *Se flanquer en l'air*: To 'top oneself', to 'do oneself in', to commit suicide.

flanquette *n.f. A la bonne flanquette*: Without much ado, without too much ceremony. (*Flanquette* is a corruption of *franquette*, the more popular expression being really *à la bonne franquette*.) *Viens donc bouffer chez nous à la bonne flanquette!* Why don't you come for a nice simple meal with us?

flapi *adj.* 'Buggered', 'knackered', worn-out.

flapir *v.trans.* To 'wear down', to tire out. *Huit heures d'affilée, ça m'a flapi!* Eight hours' graft on the trot, I've had it!

flaquer *v.intrans.* **1** To 'crap', to 'shit', to defecate. **2** To 'funk', to be fearful and give in.

flash *n.m.* (Drug addicts' slang): Engulfing rush, overwhelming and overpowering primary effect following the intravenous injection of a narcotic. (Words such as 'bang', 'flash', English in origin, are part and parcel of the international drug scene.)

flasquer *v.intrans.* To 'crap', to 'shit', to defecate.

flaupée *n.f. Une flaupée de*: 'Oodles of', 'masses of', a great quantity. *Ils ont une flaupée de gosses*: They've got a string of kids.

flauper *v.trans.* To 'bash up', to beat black and blue.

flèche *n.m.* **1** Because originally *flèche* referred to the smallest coin in circulation, it is nearly always used in the negative implying impecuniosity. *Pas un flèche!* Not a penny! *Etre sans un flèche*: To be stoney-broke. **2** 'Fagend', cigarette butt.

flèche *n.f.* **1** *Décocher une flèche*: To make a snide remark. **2** *Avoir les pieds en flèche*: To walk knock-kneed. **3** *Marcher en flèche*: To walk ahead of the rest. **4** 'Hide', tough meat. **5** Trick, dishonest scheme. **6** Gang, association of criminals. *Faire flèche*: To team up (for dishonest purposes).

flécher *v.intrans.* To team up, to work in collaboration with someone (usually on illegal activities).

flemmard *n.m.* (also: *flémard*): 'Weary Willy', 'lazybones', idle character.

flemmard *adj.* (also: *flémard*): Idle, lazy.

flemmarder *v.intrans.* (also: *flémarder*): To 'mooch', to laze about. *Le dimanche, il fait bon flemmarder*: Sunday's just the day for taking it easy.

flemme *n.f.* Laziness. *Avoir la flemme de faire quelque chose*: To have no enthusiasm for doing something. *Tirer sa flemme*: To 'take life easy', to laze about and do very little.

fleur *n.f.* 1 'Prezy', present. *Gardez ça, c'est une fleur!* Keep your money, have it on me. 2 Favour. *Faire une fleur à quelqu'un*: a To do someone a favour. b To let someone off lightly. 3 *S'envoyer des fleurs*: To 'give oneself a pat on the back', to indulge in self-congratulation. 4 *Comme une fleur*: 'Without a hitch', easily. *L'avion s'est posé comme une fleur*: The landing was as smooth as silk. 5 *S'amener* (also: *arriver*) *comme une fleur*: To 'breeze in', to arrive somewhere oblivious of the effect one has created. 6 *Etre fleur*: To be 'broke', to be penniless. *Vraiment 'y a pas! J'suis fleur!* Nothing doing! I'm really skint! 7 *Etre fleur bleue*: To be 'starry-eyed', to be of a highly romantic disposition. 8 *Fleur de nave (vinaigrette)*: 'Pill', 'pillock', imbecile. 9 *Perdre sa fleur*: To lose one's virginity. 10 *Fleur de tunnel (joc.)*: 'Dark bird', coloured woman. 11 *Fleurs blanches*: Vaginal discharge. 12 *Beau comme un paf en fleur* (slightly pej.): 'Dolled-up', dressed-up. 13 *La fleur des pois*: 'The tops', 'the pick of the bunch', the very best. 14 *La Fleur!* 'Thingey', 'what's his name'. (This fanciful and friendly nickname is used in a jocular context.) *Par ici, la Fleur!* Hey, you over there, come this way!

fleurette *n.f. Conter fleurette*: To murmur sweet nothings.

flibuster *v.trans. & intrans.* To 'nick', to 'pinch', to steal.

flibusterie *n.f.* High-handed con-trick. *Ça, c'est de la flibusterie, ou je ne m'y connais pas!* A cheekier con I have never seen!

flibustier *n.m.* 'Wide-boy', 'con-merchant', confidence trickster.

flic *n.m.* 'Cop', 'copper', policeman. (The word is not strictly derogatory and only the context can situate its colloquiality.)

flicaille *n.f. La flicaille (pej.)*: 'The fuzz', the 'aggro boys in blue', the police in general.

flicard *n.m. (pej.)*: 'Cop', 'copper', policeman.

flic-flac *n.m.* 1 Onomatopoeic transcription of the pitter-patter of raindrops. 2 Resounding double slap across the face.

flingot *n.m. (corr. flingue)*: 'Rod', 'shooter', handgun.

flingoteur *n.m.* Trigger-happy gangster.

flingue *n.m.* 'Rod', 'shooter', handgun. *Quand les flics sont entrés, il a vite remisé son flingue*: When the fuzz burst in, he quickly stashed away his gun.

flingué *adj.* 'Broke', 'skint', penniless.

flinguer *v.trans.* 1 To shoot someone down, to hit someone with gunfire. 2 To 'screw', to fuck, to have sex with.

flingueur *n.m.* 'Mechanic', hired killer, assassin. (The film *Les Tontons flingueurs* seems to have revitalized the word in noun and adjectival form.)

flippant *adj.inv.* 1 (Drug addicts' slang): 'Mind-blowing', exhilarating. 2 'Side-splitting', hilariously funny.

flippé *adj.* 1 Drugged to the eyeballs. 2 'Potty', 'bonkers', mad. 3 'Down in the dumps', depressed.

flipper *n.m. Faire une partie de flipper*: To have a game on the electric pinball machine. (The word is pronounced *flipperre*.)

flipper *v.intrans.* (Drug addicts' slang): To be 'on a trip', to be 'smashed', to be drugged to the eyeballs.

flopée *n.f. Une flopée de*: 'Oodles of', 'masses of', a great quantity. *Il a toujours une flopée de nanas au train*: There's always a string of birds chasing after him.

floppée *n.f.* 'Walloping', 'thrashing', beating-up.

flopper *v.trans.* To 'bash up', to 'wallop', to beat up.

flot *n.m. Etre à flot*: To be 'flush', to be 'well off', to be prosperous. *Remettre quelqu'un à flot*: To 'put someone back on his feet', to extend someone a financial helping hand.

flottant *n.m. Un flottant*: A pair of baggy trousers.

flottante *adj. La population flottante (pol.)*: The monthly count of drowned persons logged by the police. (This example of macabre humour was first noted by Jacques Arnal in his glossary *L'ARGOT DE POLICE*.)

flottard *n.m.* Student of the *Ecole Navale*.

Flotte *n.f. La Flotte*: The *Ecole Navale*.

flotte *n.f.* 1 General meaning of water. *Qu'est-ce qu'il tombe comme flotte!* It's pouring buckets! *Le jour où il a fait du bateau, il est tombé à la flotte*: The day he went sailing, he fell in the soup. *Aux repas chez lui, on n'a droit qu'à de la flotte*: The only thing you're likely to get with meals at his place is corporation pop! 2 *Une flotte de*: 'Oodles of', 'masses', a vast quantity of. *Des filles comme elle, il y en a des flottes*: Girls like her come ten-a-penny.

flotter *v.intrans. Il flotte*: It's pouring – It's raining. *Qu'est-ce qu'il a flotté pendant nos vac!* It didn't half come down on our hols!

flotteurs *n.m.pl.* 'Boobs', 'knockers', breasts.

flouer *v.trans*. To cheat (out of money), to swindle. *On s'est fait flouer en beauté!* We've been done good and proper!

floueur *n.m*. 'Con-merchant', trickster.

flouse *n.m*. (also: *flouze*): 'Bread', 'loot', money.

flouser *v.trans. & intrans*. (also: *flouzer*): 1 To 'con', to 'diddle', to swindle. *Il nous a flousés de première!* We fell for his patter hook, line and sinker! 2 To do a 'pongy', to 'fart', to break wind.

flubard *n.m*. 1 'Funk', 'yellow-belly', coward. *Comme flubard, il se pose un peu!* Yellow's his middle name! 2 'Blower', phone, telephone.

flube *n.m*. 1 'Info', piece of information. 2 Stroke of luck. *Il a eu un de ces flubes!* You won't believe the luck he's had! 3 *Avoir les flubes*: To 'have the shits', to be 'in a blue funk', to be petrified. *Il lui a foutu les flubes*: He scared the pants off him.

fluber *v.intrans*. 1 To 'have the frights', to be scared stiff. 2 To 'fake', to 'sham', to pretend.

flurer *v.trans*. *Flurer le pet*: To go looking for trouble by poking one's nose into other people's business.

flûtant *adj*. 'Dashed', 'bally', darned. *C'est flûtant, mais faut que je rentre!* I know it's rotten, but I've got to go home!

flûte *n.f*. 1 Small French loaf (also: *ficelle*). 2 'Prick', 'cock', penis. 3 *(pl.)*: 'Sticks', 'gambs', legs. *Se manier les flûtes*: To 'skedaddle', to 'scram', to run away (also: *jouer des flûtes*). 4 *Ne pas être du bois dont on fait les flûtes*: To 'have a mind of one's own', to be strong-willed. *Je ne suis pas du bois dont on fait les flûtes, moi!* You won't get round me that easily!

flûte *interj*. Bother! – Dash! – Darnation! *Flûte, alors!* Strewth! (The French and English are equally twee.)

Fluviale *n.f*. *La Fluviale (abbr. la Brigade Fluviale)*: The River Police.

focard *n.m*. *(pej.)*: 'Brat', 'kid', child.

focardise *n.f*. Stupidity, stupid act or word. *Sortir des focardises*: To come out with a load of bull.

focardité *n.f*. Weird comment, inane statement.

fofolle *n.f*. 'Birdbrain', scatty female.

fofolle *adj.f*. 'Hare-brained', scatty, flighty and unreliable.

foi *n.f*. *Il n'y a que la foi qui sauve! (iron.)*: If you believe that, you'll believe anything!

foie *n.m*. 1 *Avoir les jambes en pâté de foie*: To 'feel weak at the knees', to feel unsteady on one's legs. 2 *Bouffer le foie à quelqu'un*: To 'make mincemeat of someone', to make a fierce verbal onslaught on someone (also: *bouffer la rate à quelqu'un*). 3 *Avoir les foies* (also: *avoir les foies blancs*): To be 'in a funk', to be frightened.

foin *n.m*. 1 *Etre bête à manger du foin*: To be 'as thick as two short planks', to be as dumb as they come. 2 *Faire la rentrée des foins*: To 'shovel one's food in', to eat like a pig. 3 *Avoir du foin dans ses bottes*: To 'have some loot stashed away', to have some money put away for a rainy day. *Mettre du foin dans ses bottes*: To feather one's nest. 4 *Faire ses foins*: To 'make a packet', to make large profits. 5 *Faire du foin*: a To 'make a din', to be very noisy. b To 'kick up a fuss', to 'make a song-and-dance about something', to complain bitterly and vociferously about something. *Il a fait un foin de tous les diables pour un petit rien*: What a fuss he kicked up over nothing, really!

foirade *n.f*. 1 Irrepressible outburst of mirth (also: *marrade*). 2 'Funking', cowardly behaviour. 3 'Cock-up', utter mess. *Avec lui, on a eu droit à la foirade monstre*: What with his meddling touch, everything went wrong! 4 *Avoir la foirade*: To 'have the shits', 'the runs', to have a bout of diarrhoea.

foirage *n.m*. 'Total flop', fiasco, complete failure.

foire *n.f*. 1 Bedlam, state of crush and confusion. *Les grands magasins la semaine d'avant Noël, c'est toujours la foire*: It's utter chaos trying to shop in a big store the week before Christmas. 2 *Faire la foire*: To 'paint the town red', to live it up. *Quand on a su la nouvelle, on a fait une foire du tonnerre*: We had one hell of a binge when the good news came through. 3 *Foire d'empoigne*: Free-for-all where the weakest go to the wall. *Acheter quelque chose à la foire d'empoigne*: To get something from 'off the back of a lorry', to acquire illegally. 4 *La foire aux croûtes (iron.)*: The 'daub-show', exhibition of atrocious paintings. 5 *S'entendre comme larrons en foire*: To 'be as thick as thieves', to be the best of pals. 6 *La foire n'est pas sur le pont!* (also: *Il n'y a pas la foire sur le pont!*): Cool it, there's no rush! 7 'The shits', 'the runs', diarrhoea. 8 'Blue funk', intense fear.

foirer *v.intrans*. 1 To 'crap', to 'shit', to defecate. *Foirer dans la brise (fig.)*: To cause intense embarrassment. 2 (of plan, project): To misfire, to fall through.

foireur *n.m*. 1 'Gay-spark', reveller. *C'est un foireur de première*: He certainly enjoys living it up! 2 Accident-prone character. 3 'Jonah', character who seems to bring bad luck.

foireux *n.m*. 1 Character who suffers from recurring bouts of colic. 2 'Funk', coward.

foireux *adj*. 1 Suffering from diarrhoea. 2 'Funky', cowardly. *Depuis son accident, il est un rien foireux*: Since his accident, he isn't half jittery.

foiridon *n.f*. *Faire la foiridon*: To 'whoop it up', to have a good time and spend money as if it was going out of fashion.

foiron *n.m.* 'Bum', 'bottom', behind. *Rouler du foiron*: To wiggle one's bottom, to walk with undulating hips.

fois *n.f.* **1** *Des fois*: Occasionally, sometimes. *Des fois on le rencontre au théâtre*: You can sometimes see him at the theatre. *Si des fois vous le voyez, dites-lui bien des choses de ma part*: When you see him next, give him my best wishes. **2** *Non mais, des fois! (iron.)*: Don't make me laugh! – Not bloody likely! – Certainly not! *Sortir avec lui? Non mais des fois, pour qui tu me prends?!* Me go out with him? You must be joking!

foisonner *v.intrans.* To 'pong', to stink. *Dis donc, ça foisonne un brin ici!* Cor, it doesn't half whiff here!

folichon *adj.* Funny but not all that funny really. *Comme livre, on peut trouver plus folichon!* You could say I've read funnier books! *C'est pas folichon de passer les vacances à la maison*: It's no barrel of laughs spending one's hols at home. (Because of its pejorative connotation, *folichon* is usually found in a negative statement.)

folichonner *v.intrans.* To 'gad about', to fool around with women.

folingue *n.m.* 'Nutter', 'crackpot', extrovert and slightly loony character.

folingue *n.f.* 'Fairy', 'nancy-boy', effeminate homosexual.

folingue *adj.* 'Nutty', 'potty', slightly mad. *Il est gentil mais plutôt folingue*: He's nice, but only just this side of fruit-cake!

folklo *adj.inv. (pej.)*: 'Old-hat', old-fashioned.

folklorique *adj.* Outlandishly colourful.

folle *n.f.* 'Fairy', 'pansy', effeminate homosexual. (The appellation *grande folle* is used to describe the histrionic, limp-wristed gay.)

folle *adj.* *Avoir une patte folle*: To have 'a gammy leg', to be afflicted with a permanent limp.

follement *adv.* 'Terribly', 'incredibly', very. *C'est follement bête*: It's too stupid for words. *C'est follement drôle*: It's a scream! *S'amuser follement*: To have a rare old time.

follette *n.f.* 'Bird-brain', scatty woman.

follingue *n.m.* 'Nutter', 'crackpot', extrovert and slightly loony character.

follingue *n.f.* 'Fairy', 'nancy-boy', effeminate homosexual.

follingue *adj.* 'Nutty', 'potty', slightly mad. *Comme situation, on n'aurait pas pu trouver plus follingue*: You just couldn't picture a sillier situation.

foncer *v.intrans.* **1** To 'get one's skates on', to 'get cracking', to hurry up. *Il va falloir qu'on fonce pour tout finir ce soir*: We'll have to pull our finger out if we want to be finished by tonight. **2** To 'bomb along', to 'belt along', to go very

fast. *Le soir en semaine, on peut drôlement foncer sur l'autoroute*: You can certainly pelt down the motorway mid-week in the evenings. **3** *Foncer dans le brouillard (fig.)*: To leap headlong into the unknown. **4** To 'lash out', to pay. *J'en ai vraiment marre de toujours foncer pour lui!* I'm sick and tired of always having to fork out for him!

fonceur *n.m.* **1** 'Come-hell-or-high-water' type, character who is afraid of nothing. *On peut lui faire confiance, c'est un fonceur!* We're safe with him, he'll get us through! **2** Smuggler.

fond *n.m.* **1** *Avoir un bon fond*: To be good-natured. **2** *Etre à fond de cale*: To be 'skint', to be 'down on one's uppers', to be penniless. **3** *A fond de train*: 'Full-pelt', at full speed. *Aller à fond de train*: To 'belt along', to 'bomb along', to go very fast. *Travailler à fond de train*: To work flat-out.

fondre *v.intrans.* To 'shed some fat', to lose weight.

fonds *n.m.* *Etre en fonds*: To be in the money. *Ne pas être en fonds*: Not to be very flush. *Rentrer dans ses fonds*: To get back one's outlay.

fondu *n.m.* **1** 'Screwball', 'nutter', mad person. **2** *Faire un fondu*: To drop out of circulation, to disappear. (The expression originates in the world of film-makers where it refers to a visual fade-in/fade-out.)

fondu *adj.* 'Bonkers', 'potty', mad. *Etre un rien fondu*: To be slightly round the twist.

fontaine *n.f.* *Faire couler la fontaine (fig.)*: To 'open the floodgates', to shed abundant tears (also: *ouvrir les écluses*).

fonte *n.f.* *Une fonte*: 'Weight', dumbbell. *Manier la fonte*: To 'pump iron', to do a bit of weightlifting.

foot *n.m.* Soccer, football. *On va faire du foot?* Shall we go and kick a ball around?

footing *n.m.* *Faire du footing*: To go jogging.

forçat *n.m.* *Les forçats de la route* (Racing cyclists' slang): The competitors in the *Tour de France* race.

forcé *adj.* 'Heavy-handed', lacking subtlety.

forceps *n.m.pl.* *Mettre les forceps* (also: *accoucher quelqu'un avec des forceps*): To 'drag it out of someone', to question someone repeatedly for information. *Alors, tu accouches, ou il faut te mettre les forceps?* Out with it, don't be so bloody cagey!

forcer *v.trans.* *Forcer la dose*: To 'overdo it', to be too forceful in one's approach.

forcing *n.m.* Burst of energy. *Faire le forcing*: To 'put on the pressure', to take on a dominant and forceful role at work or in a discussion. *Dans le porte-à-porte, sans forcing on ne gagne pas sa croûte*: Door-to-door repping means slogging your guts out or being on the breadline.

forcir *v.intrans.* To start 'bulging at the seams', to put on weight.

forge *n.f. Avoir les poumons en soufflets de forge:* To be puffing and wheezing.

format *n.m.* 'Note', banknote. *Un grand format:* A big 'un, large denomination banknote.

forme *n.f.* State of mental or physical fitness. *Je suis en pleine forme:* I'm feeling on top of the world! *Il ne tient pas la forme en ce moment:* He's a bit out of condition these days!

formidable *n.m.* Half-litre tankard of beer.

formidable *adj.* **1** 'Super', 'smashing', fantastic. *C'est un mec formidable, tu sais!* He's really a great guy! **2** *Etre formidable (iron.):* To be a cheeky so-and-so, to have an inflated idea of someone else's gullibility. *Moi, te prêter la voiture? . . . non, mais t'es formidable!* Me lend you the car? . . . you must be bloody joking! *C'est formidable!* Well I never! – Would you believe it? *C'est formidable vraiment, on lui dit bonjour et il se fâche!* It's really too silly for words . . . you greet him and he gets cross!

formide *adj. (abbr. formidable):* 'Great', 'super', fantastic.

fort *n.m.* **1** *Un fort des Halles:* Muscular, burly porter working in the *Halles de Paris.* (Like Covent Garden Market in London, *Les Halles de Paris* are now a thing of the past, and the picturesque characters humping heavy loads have been superseded by fork-lift trucks.) *Avoir un gabarit de fort des Halles:* To have the physique of a weightlifter. **2** *Un fort en gueule:* A 'loud-mouth', a person who speaks his mind a little too vehemently. **3** *Fort en thème (sch.):* 'Egg-head', brainy pupil. (The appellation has slightly pejorative connotations.)

fort *adj.* **1** 'Smart', clever, brilliant. *Lui faire signer ça, c'était vraiment fort!* Getting him to sign that was a neat move! **2** *C'est un peu fort ça! (iron.):* That's a bit thick! – That's coming it a bit strong! – That's hard to believe! *C'est vraiment trop fort!* This is really too much!

fort *adv.* **1** *Y aller fort:* **a** To 'lay it on thick', to exaggerate. **b** To 'pull no punches', to be thick-skinned and ruthless. *Je trouve que tu y es allé un peu fort avec elle:* I still think you could have spared her feelings. **2** *Ça ne va pas fort:* **a** Times are hard – Business isn't too bright. **b** Health is a problem. *Depuis qu'il est à la retraite, ça ne va pas fort:* Since he retired, his health is certainly not what it used to be. *Ça ne va pas fort, on dirait!* You look a bit peaky today!

fortanche *n.f. La bonne fortanche:* Soothsaying. *Dire la bonne fortanche:* To tell someone's fortune.

fortancheur *n.m.* Fortune-teller.

fortiche *n.m. & f.* **1** Smart person, clever individual. **2** *Faire le fortiche* (also: *jouer au fortiche*): To 'act the clever-clogs', to 'play the smart-aleck', to swank about.

fortiche *adj.* **1** 'Burly', 'brawny', muscular. **2** 'Smart', clever, brilliant. *Elle se croit un rien fortiche, Eileen!* She thinks she's the bee's knees, she does! **3** Hard to understand. *C'est un problème plutôt fortiche:* I'd say this is something of a puzzler.

fortifs *n.f.pl.* (also: *fortifes*): *Les fortifs* were old defence works surrounding Paris. (Although the *fortifications* are very much a thing of the past, frequent nostalgic mention of them is to be found in novels about 'the good old days'.)

fosse *n.f. La fosse aux ours* (Prison slang): The exercise yard.

fossile *n.m. Vieux fossile:* 'Old fuddy-duddy', 'geriatric fuss-pot', mithering old man.

fossiliser *v.pronom.* To settle for the rut of routine.

fou *adj.* **1** 'Great', stupendous, tremendous. *Il a eu un succès fou:* He made a great impact. *Il a une chance folle:* He's got the luck of the Irish. *C'est fou ce qu'il a l'air jeune!* He looks terribly, terribly young! **2** *Etre tout fou:* To be 'nutty', 'bonkers', to be slightly mad.

fouaron *n.m.* 'Arse', 'bum', behind.

foucade *n.f. Une foucade:* A 'bee in one's bonnet', a short-lived crazy idea.

fouchtra *n.m.* **1** *Un fouchtra:* A native of the Auvergne (also: *auverpin*). **2** Dialect spoken by the *auvergnats. Pour se faire bien remarquer, il aime causer fouchtra:* He likes to show off by talking the local lingo.

foudre *n.f. Avoir le coup de foudre pour quelqu'un:* To fall head over heels in love with someone.

fouet *n.m. L'opération coup de fouet* (Motor mechanics' slang): New lease of life given to a tired engine where only cylinder sleeves and pistons are changed. (A jocular extension of the meaning is the revamping of a person's sex life either through a change of partner or medical rejuvenation.)

fouettard *n.m.* 'Bum', behind. (This word can have pejorative or non-pejorative connotations according to context. *Se faire botter le fouettard:* To get kicked up the backside. *L'avoir dans le fouettard:* To 'have been had', to have been conned. *Elle avait un petit fouettard à faire rêver:* She had a smart little sit-me-down.)

fouetter *v.intrans.* **1** To 'pong', to stink, to smell foul. *Qu'est-ce que ça fouette ici!* Cor! What a niff! **2** To be 'in a blue funk', to be petrified with fear.

foufou *n.m.* 'Madcap', 'harebrain', slightly dotty character.

foufou *adj.m.* 'Fruitcake', 'potty', slightly mad.

fouignedé *n.m.* **1** 'Arse', 'bum', behind. **2** *L'avoir dans le fouignedé*: To have been 'conned', 'diddled', to have been swindled.

fouignozof *n.m.* (also: *fouignosof*): 'Fanny', 'pussy', vagina.

fouille *n.f.* **1** 'Sack', 'bin', pocket. *Avoir les fouilles pleines* (also: *En avoir plein les fouilles*): To be 'flush', to be 'rolling in it', to have lots of money. *Vaisselle de fouille*: Small change, coins. **2** *C'est dans la fouille* (of transaction): It's in the bag – We've got a deal – It's clinched. (This expression can sometimes be found in other contexts, e.g. where someone is successfully swayed.) **3** *(pol.)* *La fouille*: The frisking of a suspect.

fouille-merde *n.m.* *(pej.)*: **1** Council workman who empties cesspits. **2** 'Muck-raker', scandalmonger. **3** 'Dick', 'private-eye', private investigator.

fouiller *v.trans.reflex.* **1** To rack one's brains, to search one's mind. **2** *Tu peux toujours te fouiller!* *(iron.)*: Not on your nelly! – You've got another think coming! – Certainly not!

fouillouse *n.f.* 'Sack', 'bin', pocket.

Fouilly-les-Oies *Proper name.* 'Hick-town', little place in the back of beyond. (This is a jocular nickname to describe an unimportant little town, another one being *Trifouillis-les-Oies*.)

fouinard *n.m.* **1** 'Conk', 'hooter', nose. **2** 'Nosey-Parker', indiscreet and prying character. *Gaffe! Voilà le fouinard!* Watch out! Here comes Big Ears!

fouinard *adj.* 'Nosey', prying, over-inquisitive.

fouinasser *v.intrans.* **1** To poke one's nose in other people's business. **2** *(pol.)*: **a** To go looking for clues. **b** To sift through evidence.

fouine *n.f.* *(pej.)*: **1** 'Mush', 'dial', face. **2** 'Nosey-Parker', indiscreet and prying character.

fouinedé *n.m.* **1** 'Fanny', 'pussy', vagina. **2** 'Bum', 'bottom', behind.

fouiner *v.intrans.* **1** To poke one's nose into other people's business. **2** *(pol.)*: **a** To go looking for clues. **b** To sift through evidence. **3** To go bargain-hunting. *Il aime fouiner chez les brocanteurs*: He just loves rummaging in junk shops.

fouineur *n.m.* **1** 'Nosey-Parker', indiscreet and prying character. **2** Persistent and tenacious police officer. **3** Bargain-hunter.

fouineur *adj.* 'Nosey', prying, inquisitive.

foulant *adj.* 'Fagging', 'back-breaking', very tiring. (The word is more commonly used in the negative with the implication that someone is making a song-and-dance about it all.) *'y a pas de quoi gueuler au charron. Il est pas foulant, ton boulot!* I don't know why you keep moaning about that job of yours, it's a doddle!

foule *n.f.* *Ameuter la foule*: To 'kick up a fuss', to 'make a song-and-dance about something', to make bitter and vociferous recriminations.

fouler *v.trans. Fouler le bitume* (of prostitute): To go soliciting (also: *faire le trottoir*).

fouler *v.pronom. Ne pas se fouler*: To 'do bugger-all', not to overtax one's energy. *On ne peut pas dire qu'il se foule, lui!* You could hardly say he's going to rupture himself! (The expression *ne pas se fouler* can often be used in conjunction with *la rate* or *les méninges*, in this last instance with the meaning 'not to overtax one's brains'.)

foultitude *n.f.* **1** *La foultitude*: Masses of people, a crowd. **2** *Une foultitude de*: 'Heaps of', 'masses', lots of. *Il a une foultitude de soucis*: He's got a stack of worries.

four *n.m.* *(th.)*: 'Flop', failure. (The expression *faire un four*, although usually used in the theatrical world, is seeping into everyday language with the meaning of having one's repartee received in silence.)

fouraille *n.f.* 'Rod', 'shooter', handgun.

fouraillé *adj.* 'Rodded-up', armed.

fourailler *v.trans.* To 'screw', to fuck, to have sex with (also: *fourrer*).

fourailler *v.intrans.* **1** To 'go through', to rummage (in order to find something). **2** To let off a shot, to fire a gun.

fourbi *n.m.* **1** *(mil.)*: 'Kit', military pack. **2** 'Gear', personal belongings. **3** *(pej.)*: 'Doodah', 'gubbins', contraption. *Et comment que ça marche, ce fourbi-là?* How the hell do you get this thing to work? **4** 'Sticky mess', complicated situation. *Quel sale fourbi!* This is a real cock-up, isn't it?! *C'est tout un fourbi!* What a mix-up! *Il nous a laissé un de ces fourbis arabes!* He really left us holding the baby! **5** *Tout le fourbi*: 'The whole shebang', 'the whole shooting match', the whole set-up.

fourche *n.f. Au bout d'une fourche! (iron.)*: Not on your nelly! – Not bloody likely! – Certainly not! *Te prêter du fric! Comptes-y mon gars, au bout d'une fourche!* Me lend you money? You must be joking!

fourchée *n.f.* 'Gobful', large mouthful.

fourchette *n.f.* **1** *(mil.)*: 'Pig-sticker', bayonet. **2** 'Paw', 'mitt', hand. *Manger avec la fourchette du Père Adam*: To eat with one's fingers. **3** 'Diver', 'snitch', pickpocket. **4** *Avoir un bon coup de fourchette*: To 'ply a good knife and fork', to be a hearty eater. **5** *Jouer de la fourchette*: To tuck into one's food with enthusiasm. **6** *Coup de fourchette* (All-in wrestling): Index-and-middle-finger prong attack directed at the opponent's eyeballs. **7** *Avoir avalé sa fourchette*: To be 'as stiff as a poker', to sit up in a frozen prim and proper attitude.

fourgat *n.m.* 'Fence', receiver of stolen goods (also: *fourgue*).

fourgon *n.m. Se taper le fourgon*: To hitch a free ride in a train's goods waggon.

fourgonner *v.trans. and intrans.* **1** To 'cook up', to 'fix', to arrange something illicit. **2** To 'poke about', to rummage.

fourgue *n.m.* 'Fence', receiver of stolen goods.

fourguer *v.trans.* **1** To sell 'hot goods', to dispose of stolen wares. **2** To 'flog', to sell something cheaply. *Alors il m'a fourgué une bagnole à la manque!* I paid next to nothing for that banger of his! (The inference is often that the goods sold are shoddy or worthless.) **3** To 'push' drugs, to sell narcotics.

fourlineur *n.m.* 'Diver', pickpocket (also: *fourlineux*).

fourmi *n.m.* **1** *Avoir des fourmis dans les jambes*: To have pins-and-needles in one's legs. **2** *Avoir des fourmis (rouges) dans le calcif*: To 'have ants in one's pants', to be incessantly fidgety.

fournée *n.f. Une fournée de (pej.)*: 'A bunch of', 'a batch', another lot of people. *Il nous a encore amené une fournée de touristes*: He brought us another lot of bloody tourists.

fourrage *n.m. Du fourrage (joc.)*: Lettuce, green salad.

fourrager *v.trans.reflex. Se fourrager la tignasse*: To scratch one's head.

fourreau *n.m.* 'Trews', pants, trousers.

fourrer *v.trans.* **1** To 'bung', to 'stick', to put. *Je vais lui fourrer mon pied au cul!* I'm going to kick him up the backside! *Fourrer quelqu'un en taule*: To clap someone in jail. *Fourrer son nez dans les affaires des autres*: To poke one's nose into other people's business. *Il est toujours fourré chez nous*: He seems to have set up home at our place! **2** To 'screw', to fuck, to have sex with. **3** *Fourrer quelqu'un dedans*: To 'land someone in it', to get someone into trouble.

fourrer *v.trans.reflex.* **1** *Se fourrer le doigt dans l'œil (jusqu'au coude)*: To make a ginormous mistake, to be totally wrong about something. **2** *Ne pas savoir où se fourrer*: To feel extremely embarrassed. **3** *S'en fourrer jusque-là* (with accompanying gesture): To stuff oneself with food until one's eyes pop out. *Je m'en suis fourré jusque-là!* I'm full up to here!

fourrière *n.f.* **1** 'Pound', dogs' and cats' refuge, place where stray animals await their fate. **2** *(pol.)*: Compound, place where impounded motor vehicles are kept by the police till the owners pay up to retrieve them.

foutable *adj.* 'Worth a bang', sexually attractive. (This male chauvinist adjective reflects more

contempt than admiration for the woman concerned.)

foutaise *n.f.* **1** 'Hogwash', 'tommyrot', rubbish. *Tout ça, c'est de la foutaise!* This is a load of codswallop! **2** 'Trifle', unimportant matter.

foutoir *n.m.* **1** Incredibly untidy place. **2** 'Cathouse', brothel.

foutral *adj.* 'Fantabulous', fantastic. *Un succès foutral*: One hell of a success.

foutre *n.m.* 'Spunk', sperm, semen.

foutre *v.trans.* **1** To 'bung', to 'chuck somewhere', to put. *On l'a foutu en taule*: He was clapped into jail. *Il a foutu ça dans un coin*: He chucked it in a corner. *On l'a foutue à la porte*: She got the sack. *Foutre quelque chose en l'air*: To throw something away. **2** To do (usually with derogatory connotations). *Qu'est-ce que tu fous ici?* What the hell are you doing here? *Il n'a jamais rien foutu de sa vie*: He's never done a stroke of work. **3** *Foutre un coup de poing sur la gueule de quelqu'un*: To punch someone in the face. **4** *Foutre le camp*: To 'bugger off', to leave (usually in haste). **5** *Foutre la paix à quelqu'un*: To leave someone in peace. *Fous-moi la paix!* Leave me alone!

foutre *v.trans.reflex.* **1** *Se foutre par terre*: To fall flat on one's face, to fall to the ground (also: *se foutre la gueule par terre*). **2** *Se foutre dedans*: To 'make a cock-up', to make a mistake. *Il s'est drôlement foutu dedans avec la dernière commande*: He made a real balls of that last order. **3** *Se foutre en l'air*: To 'top oneself', to 'do oneself in', to commit suicide.

foutre *v.pronom. Se foutre de quelqu'un*: To 'take the mickey out of', to poke fun at someone.

foutre *interj.* Cripes! – Bloody hell! (A less potent alternative is fichtre!)

foutrement *adv.* 'Confoundedly', deucedly, extremely.

foutrer *v.intrans.* To 'juice off', to ejaculate, to experience orgasmic pleasure.

foutriquet *n.m.* *(pej.)*: 'Squirt', 'whippersnapper', small and insignificant character.

foutu *adj.* **1** 'Blasted', damned. *Quel foutu temps!* What bloody awful weather! **2** *Il n'est jamais foutu de faire ce qu'on lui demande!* He can never do what you bloody well ask him!

foutument *adv.* 'Confoundedly', deucedly, extremely.

fracas *n.m.pl. Envoyer promener quelqu'un avec pertes et fracas*: To 'send someone packing', to tell someone to go to hell.

fraîche *n.f.* **1** *De la fraîche*: 'Adam's ale', 'corporation pop', water. **2** 'Loot', 'bread', money. *Ne lui confie surtout pas ta fraîche*: I wouldn't lend him any money if I was you.

fraîche adj. *Elle est fraîche, celle-là! (iron.)*: That's a bit stiff! – That's going it a bit strong! – Well would you believe it!

fraîchement adv. Coolly, unenthusiastically. *On l'a reçu fraîchement*: He got a pretty cool reception.

frais n.m. *Mettre quelqu'un au frais*: To 'slam someone in the cooler', to clap someone into jail.

frais n.m.pl. **1** *En être pour ses frais*: To get bugger-all for one's efforts, to get nothing for one's pains. *Avec elle, il en a été pour ses frais*: You could say it was a case of no joy and little change from his evening out with her. **2** *Se mettre en frais*: To 'put oneself out', to go to vast (personal) expense to please. **3** *Arrêter les frais*: To give up. *Arrête les frais!* That's enough! **4** *Faire quelque chose aux frais de la princesse*: To get something on the old expense account (State, institution or firm). *Lui, il voyage toujours aux frais de la princesse*: All his travelling is pretty buckshee. **5** *Faire ses frais (iron.)*: To do alright for oneself. *'y a pas à dire, il fait ses frais*: There's no denying, business seems to be going well for him.

frais adj. *Etre frais (joc. & iron.)*: To be in a proper mess. *Eh bien, je suis frais!* Well, I'm in a fine fix! (also: *me voilà frais!*).

fraise n.f. **1** 'Mush', 'mug', face. *Le dirlo fait une sale fraise aujourd'hui*: The boss looks real grumpy today. **2** *Ramener sa fraise*: **a** To arrive somewhere unexpectedly. **b** To 'put one's oar in', to meddle and interfere. *Dans les discussions, il faut toujours qu'il ramène sa fraise!* Whatever the discussion, he's always got the answer! **3** *Envoyer quelqu'un sur les fraises*: To 'send someone off with a flea in their ear', to tell someone to go away in no uncertain manner. **4** *Sucrer les fraises*: To have the shakes, to be afflicted with pronounced trembling. **5** *Aller aux fraises* (of motor vehicle): To 'crash into the scenery', to go off the road.

fralin n.m. Brother. *Il s'est ramené avec son fralin et ses fralines*: He came along with his brother and sisters (also: *frangin*).

framboise n.f. *Avoir les framboises*: To 'have the shits', to be frightened out of one's wits.

franc adj. 'Sure', safe, without risk. *Comme affaire, il n'y a pas plus franc*: This deal's as safe as houses. *Ce n'est pas (très) franc*: It looks dodgy – It seems dicey – I think it's dangerous.

Francaoui n.m. Derogatory name given to the metropolitan French by the *'pieds-noirs'* (European settlers in Algeria prior to independence).

francaoui n.m. *Le francaoui*: 'Froggy', the French lingo, French (the language).

Franchecaille Proper name. *La Franchecaille*: 'Frogland', France.

franco adj.inv. **1** Honest, safe, trustworthy. *C'est un mec tout ce qu'il y a de franco*: He's a bloke you can really trust. **2** (of venture): Sure, safe, without risk.

franco adv. Without second thoughts, without hesitation. *Il faut y aller franco*: Let's not beat about the bush!

François Proper name. *Le coup du Père François*: **a** (lit.): Deadly stranglehold involving the breaking of the cervical vertebrae. **b** (fig.): 'Below-the-belt' blow, unfair attack.

frangin n.m. **1** Brother. *Mon petit frangin*: My kid brother. **2** 'Mate', 'pal', friend. *On est sortis avec des frangins*: We went out with a few of the guys. **3** *Le petit frangin*: 'Prick', 'cock', penis.

frangine n.f. **1** 'Sis', sister. *Je te présente ma frangine*: Meet my sister. **2** *Les frangines (pej.)*: Women in general. *Ah, les frangines, je te jure!* Isn't that just typical of women!

franquette n.f. *A la bonne franquette*: 'Without to-do', without ceremony. *Recevoir quelqu'un à la bonne franquette*: To invite someone without making a song-and-dance about everything. (The informality implied can sometimes have a pejorative connotation. *Faire quelque chose à la bonne franquette*: To do something any-old-how.)

frappada adj. 'Potty', 'bonkers', mad.

frappadingue n.m. **1** 'Nutter', 'potty character', one who projects a mad image. **2** 'Psycho', psychopath, madman.

frappe n.f. **1** 'Yobbo', destructive ruffian. **2** 'Pouf', 'pansy', effeminate homosexual.

frappé adj. 'Slightly touched', 'mildly bonkers', rather mad.

frapper v.trans. To 'tap someone for money', to ask someone for a loan. *Il m'a frappé de tout ce que j'avais en poche*: After giving him a sub, I was just about broke.

frapper v.pronom. To 'get into a flap', to be 'all of a flutter', to panic. *Ne te frappe donc pas!* Don't get all het-up over nothing!

frayer v.trans. & intrans. **1** To 'haunt', to frequent. **2** To 'knock about with', to go out with. *Il frayait avec des nanas plutôt moches*: He used to be seen with some rather ugly girls.

Frégate Proper name. Family saloon car made by Renault in the late 50s and 60s.

frelot n.m. **1** Brother. *Mon petit frelot*: My kid brother. **2** *Le petit frelot*: 'Prick', 'cock', penis.

frelotte n.f. **1** 'Sis', sister. **2** 'Funk', coward.

freluquet n.m. (pej.): 'Squirt', 'runt', small person.

fréquenter v.trans.reflex. To 'pull one's wire', to 'have a wank', to masturbate.

frère *n.m.* 1 Pal, 'mate', friend. *T'es un frère!* You're a real brick! 2 'Feller', 'geezer', chap. *Qu'est-ce qu'il me veut, ce frère?* What's up with that bloke? (What does he want with me?) 3 *Ne pas être le frère à dégueulasse:* To be O.K., to be really quite alright. (The expression does not necessarily refer to a person. *Ce pinard, il n'est pas le frère à dégueulasse:* This little wine is no plonk!) 4 *Petit frère:* 'Prick', 'cock', penis. *Dérouiller son petit frère:* To 'pull one's wire', to 'wank', to masturbate.

frérot *n.m.* 1 'Kid brother', younger brother. 2 'Prick', 'cock', penis.

fréter *v.trans.* *Fréter un bahut:* To hire a cab, to take a taxi.

frétillant *adj.* 1 Bubbling over with enthusiasm. 2 Sexually titillated.

frétillante *n.f.* 1 'Randy bird', sexually-inclined woman. 2 Dog's tail.

frétillon *n.m.* 'Fidget', restless character.

fric *n.m.* 'Bread', 'brass', money. *Abouler son fric:* To come out with the readies. *Etre plein de fric:* To be rolling in it.

fricassée *n.f.* 1 Large amount of squandered money. 2 'Dusting', 'drubbing', thrashing. *Il a ramassé une de ces fricassées:* He got the pasting of his life. 3 *Fricassée de museaux (joc.):* Passionate exchange of kisses.

fricasser *v.trans.* To 'blue', to squander one's money. *Il a tout fricassé:* He blew the lot.

fricasser *v.trans.reflex.* *Se fricasser le museau:* To exchange passionate kisses.

fric-frac *n.m.* Break-in, burglary (also: *casse*).

fricfraquer *v.trans. & intrans.* To break in, to burgle.

frichti *n.m.* 1 'Grub', 'eats', food. *Etre de frichti:* To be lumbered with the cooking. 2 'Bubble-and-squeak', warmed-up leftovers.

fricot *n.m.* 1 (*pej.*): 'Grub', 'eats', food. *J'en ai marre de son fricot:* I'm fed up with the awful grub she keeps dishing up. 2 'Cushy number', soft job, undemanding occupation.

fricotage *n.m.* 1 'Stew-up', unappetizing food. 2 'Wangling', 'string-pulling', small-time power-game of manipulating people. *Tout ce fricotage ne me dit rien qui vaille!* All this double-dealing stinks! 3 'Screwing', sexual intercourse.

fricoter *v.trans. & intrans.* 1 (*lit*): To stew up, to cook up. *Qu'est-ce que tu nous fricotes ce soir?!* So what are we eating tonight?! 2 To wangle, to fiddle. *On se demande bien ce qu'il fricote, celui-là:* It makes you wonder what he's up to. 3 To 'make a bit on the side', to make some money on the sly. 4 To 'shirk', to dodge the real work. 5 To 'blue', to 'blow', to squander money. *Son héritage, il l'a tout fricoté:* It was

'spend, spend, spend' with all he inherited. 6 To have a sexual relationship with. *Ça fait belle lurette qu'il fricote avec elle:* He's been knocking about with her for yonks.

fricoteur *n.m.* 1 'Wangler', 'string-puller', character who spends his time manipulating events and people. 2 'Shirker', work-shy character.

friction *n.f.* (*joc.*): 'Pasting', 'drubbing', thrashing. *Il lui a passé une de ces frictions!* He beat the living daylights out of him!

Fridolin *n.m.* 'Kraut', 'Jerry', German.

fri-fri *n.m.* 'Fanny', 'pussy', vagina.

frigo *n.m.* 1 'Fridge', refrigerator. 2 (*pl.*): Frozen foodstuffs. 3 *Le frigo (pol.):* The morgue. 4 *Mettre au frigo (fig.):* To 'shelve' provisionally, to postpone something temporarily.

frigousse *n.f.* *La frigousse:* Quality food. *Il est plutôt porté sur la frigousse:* He's very partial to good grub.

frigousse *adv.* *En avoir frigousse de quelque chose:* To be 'fed-up to the back teeth', to be sick and tired of something.

frimage *n.m.* (*pol.*): 1 Taking of 'mugshots', photographing of criminals. 2 Confrontation between suspect and witness.

frimard *n.m.* 1 'Extra', actor with a non-speaking part in a film. 2 'Con-artist', trickster.

frime *n.f.* 1 'Physog', 'dial', face. *Vise un peu cette frime!* Gor! Look at that ugly mush! *Il a fait une de ces frimes quand je lui ai annoncé la nouvelle:* He certainly pulled a face when I gave him the news. 2 'Looks', appearance. *Il a une drôle de frime, cet arbre:* What a weird-looking tree! 3 'Sham', pretence. *Tout ça c'est de la frime:* It's a load of bunkum. *Faire quelque chose pour la frime:* To do something for appearances' sake. *Sa ricaine, c'est pour la frime:* That big Yank car of his is just for show. 4 *Pour la frime:* Uselessly, in vain. *Tout ça, ça a été pour la frime:* It's all been a bloody waste of time. 5 *Tomber en frime:* To break down. 6 *Laisser en frime:* To abandon. 7 *Faire de la frime* (Films): To act as an extra, to take silent parts (crowd scenes, etc.) to make ends meet.

frimer *v.trans. & intrans.* 1 To 'ogle', to 'eye', to stare at. *Cesse de me frimer comme ça!* Stop staring at me all the time! 2 To 'sham', to pretend. *Quand il va au toubib, faut toujours qu'il frime un peu pour couper court au boulot:* He likes to come the old soldier with the doc to get his sicknote quick and easy. 3 *Frimer bien:* To 'cut a dash', to look smart.

frimousse *n.f.* Fresh and pleasant face.

fringale *n.f.* 1 Pangs of hunger. *J'ai une de ces fringales!* I'm absolutely famished! 2 *Avoir la fringale de quelque chose:* To 'be dying for something', to be eager for something. *J'ai la fringale de tes doux bras! (joc.)*: I'm missing you something rotten!

fringant *n.m.* Would-be 'man-about-town'. *Faire le fringant*: To strut and stride about like a peacock.

fringuer *v.trans.reflex.* To 'tog oneself up', to get dressed. *Quand j'ai vu qu'il se ramenait, j'ai dû me fringuer en vitesse!* When I saw him coming I had to jump into my clothes double-quick! *Se fringuer chez Poubelles-Sœurs (joc. & iron.)*: To dress like a scarecrow.

fringues *n.f.pl.* 'Gear', 'clobber', clothes. *Mettre ses fringues du dimanche*: To get into one's Sunday-best. *Fringues de coulisses (joc.)*: 'Smalls & stalls', women's underwear.

fringueur *n.m.* **1** 'Tat', second-hand clothes dealer. **2** Theatrical costumier. **3** *(joc.)*: Men's tailor.

frio *adj.* Frosty, very cold. *Qu'est-ce qu'il fait frio!* It's certainly brass-monkey weather today! (also: *frisquet*).

fripe *n.f.* **1** 'Grub', 'eats', food. *Qu'est-ce qu'il y a pour la fripe ce soir?* What's cooking tonight? *A la fripe!* Grub's up! – Come and get it! **2** Cooking, preparing of meals. *Ce soir je suis de fripe!* I'm on cook-house duty tonight!

fripes *n.f.pl.* 'Tats', 'rags', old clothes. *A t'entendre on croirait que tu n'as que des fripes!* To hear you talk one would think you hadn't got a thing to wear!

fripouillard *n.m. (joc.)*: 'Cad', 'rotter', immoral so-and-so.

fripouille *n.f.* 'Scallywag', 'layabout', good-for-nothing character. *C'est la dernière des fripouilles*: He's an out-and-out rotter!

fripouillerie *n.f.* Blackguardism, dishonest action. *J'en ai ralbol des fripouilleries de ton frère*: I'm sick to the back teeth with all the dirty tricks that bloody brother of yours gets up to!

friquet *n.m.* 'Grass', 'snitch', informer. (The word refers more to the inmate of a prison who, for favours, betrays fellow-cons to Authority.)

frire *v.trans. Rien à frire! (joc. corr. rien à faire!)*: Not on your nelly! – Not bloody likely! – Certainly not! *Partir avec ce temps? Rien à frire!* What, go out in this weather? You must be joking!

frisbi *adj.inv.* 'Nippy', frosty, very cold.

Frisé *n.m. Les Frisés*: 'The Jerries', 'the Krauts', the Germans.

frisquet *adj.* 'Frosty', chilly, rather cold. *Il fait frisquet*: It's nippy – There's a nip in the air. *On lui a réservé un accueil plutôt frisquet*: He certainly got a chilly reception.

frisson *n.m. Le grand frisson*: Orgasmic pleasure.

frit *adj.m.* **1** 'Nicked', 'collared', arrested. **2** 'Gone', 'finished', done for. *Maintenant il est frit!* Now he's really had his chips! **3** *C'est frit!* It's all over!

frite *n.f.* **1** *(pej.)*: 'Mush', 'dial', face. *Vise cette sale frite!* Take a look at that ugly customer! **2** 'Zizz', painful blow on the behind given with a flick of the wrist. (This typically French schoolboy prank is particularly painful to the recipient as the speed with which the fingernails meet their target creates a hot and searing pain.) **3** *En être* (also: *en rester*) *comme deux ronds de frites*: To be 'all of a heap', to be 'flabbergasted', to be dumbfounded. **4** *Tomber dans les frites*: To 'keel over', to 'pass out', to faint (also: *tomber dans les pommes*). **5** *Ta gueule, bébé, t'auras une frite!* Button up your face! – Belt up! – Shut up!

fritouse *n.f.* **1** Chip-pan. **2** *De la fritouse*: 'Fry-up', fried cooking. **3** Crackling, interference (on radio or telephone).

friture *n.f.* Crackling, interference (on radio or telephone). *Qu'est-ce qu'il y a comme friture, aujourd'hui!* What a terrible line we've got today!

Fritz *n.m.* 'Kraut', 'Jerry', German.

fritz *n.m. Le fritz*: 'Kraut', the German language.

Frizous *n.m.pl. Les Frizous*: 'The Krauts', 'the Jerries', the Germans.

froc *n.m.* **1** 'Trews', trousers. **2** *Baisser son froc*: To 'funk out', to give in under duress. (This pejorative expression relates to a humiliating defeat.)

frocaille *n.f. (pej.) La frocaille*: The clergy.

frocs *n.m.pl.* 'Clobber', 'togs', clothes.

froid *n.m.* **1** *Froid de canard*: 'Brass monkey weather', icy conditions. **2** *Etre en froid*: Not to be on speaking terms. *V'là quinze jours qu'ils sont en froid*: They've been ignoring each other for a fortnight now. **3** *Battre (quelqu'un) à froid*: To 'give someone the cold shoulder', to avoid someone with ostentation. **4** *Démarrer à froid*: To 'get down to the nitty-gritty' straight away, to get down to the business in hand without wasting any time. (The expression originates in the language of motoring where it refers to the starting-up of a cold engine.)

fromaga *n.m.* Cheese (also: *fromgif*).

fromage *n.m.* **1** 'Cushy number', easy and highly profitable occupation. *Il s'est bloqué un de ces fromages!* He's certainly landed the plum of plums! **2** *(En) faire tout un fromage*: To 'kick up a fuss', to 'make a song-and-dance about something', to create a verbal commotion. **3** *Laisser aller le chat au fromage*: Not to put up much of a fight, to give in easily. **4** *(pl.)*: 'Tootsies', toes.

fromager *v.trans.* (Underworld slang): To engineer a 'heist', to organize a robbery.

fromeller *v.trans.reflex.* To rub oneself down, to dry oneself.

fromgif *n.m.* Cheese (also: *frometon*).

frotte n.f. **1** Avoir la frotte: To have a persistent itch. **2** La frotte et l'astique (mil.): 'Bull', 'spit and polish', the meticulous cleaning of one's army kit.

frotté past part. Etre frotté de: To have 'a smattering of', to have a superficial knowledge of. Pour ce qui est de la cuistance, il en est plus que frotté: Be fair! There's no denying he can cook.

frottée n.f. **1** 'Drubbing', thrashing. **2** (fig.): Painful and humiliating defeat. En finale de la Coupe, on vous a filé une sacrée frottée: Last Cup Final, we beat the living daylights out of you!

frotte-frotte n.m. Une partie de frotte-frotte: 'Some hanky-panky', sexy goings-on (also: une partie de frotti-frotta).

frotter v.trans. **1** To 'dust up', to beat up, to thrash. **2** Frotter les oreilles à quelqu'un: To 'give someone a clout round the ear-hole', to box someone's ears. **b** To give someone a severe telling-off. **3** En frotter une: To 'have a whirl', to 'have a shuffle', to have a dance with someone (also: en suer une).

frotter v.intrans. To dance closely entwined. Les jours de bal, ça frotte ferme au village: At the village hop, couples really let their hair down.

frotter v.trans.reflex. **1** To attack, to engage in contact (physical or verbal). Qu'il ne se frotte pas à moi! He'd better keep his distance if he knows what's good for him! **2** To 'beat the dummy', to 'wank', to masturbate.

frotteuses n.f.pl. 'Blighters', matches.

frottin n.m. Faire un frottin (also: faire une partie de frottin): To 'rip the baize', to have a game of billiards.

frotting n.m. Dancing. On se paie le frotting ce soir? How's about a night out at the old dance-hall?

frou-frou n.m. (also: froufrou): **1** 'Skelly', skeleton key. **2** Des frou-frous: Indiscreet chit-chat about amorous goings-on.

froussard n.m. 'Funk', 'yellow-belly', coward.

froussard adj. 'Funky', 'spunkless', cowardly.

froussardise n.f. 'Funk', cowardice.

frousse n.f. La frousse: 'The jitters', 'funk', cowardice. Flanquer la frousse à quelqu'un: To scare the pants off someone.

frusquer v.trans.reflex. To 'tog up', to get dressed.

frusques n.f.pl. 'Togs', 'clobber', clothes. Prends tes frusques et calte! Get your clobber on and scram!

frusquin n.m. Tout le frusquin (also: tout le saint-frusquin): 'The whole shebang', the lot, everything.

fu-fute adj.inv. (Usually in the negative): Bright, clever. Il n'est pas fu-fute, ton frangin: That brother of yours is as thick as two short planks.

fuite n.f. **1** 'Leak', indiscretion. (In the late 50s, l'affaire des fuites, a notorious scandal involving leaked information, gave the word a new lease of life.) **2** La fuite: **a** (mil.): Demob day. **b** (sch.): 'Break-up day', the last day of term. **c** The great holiday exodus on the roads.

fuiter v.intrans. To 'scram', to 'skedaddle', to leave in haste (also: se fuiter).

fumant adj. **1** 'Fuming', seething, furious. Gare tes miches! Il est fumant aujourd'hui! I'd give him a wide berth if I were you! He's in a foul temper today! **2** 'Smashing', fantastic. Elle est fumante, celle-là! (of story): Top that!

fumante n.f. **1** Une fumante: An incredible bit of news. **2** (pl.): 'Sweaties', socks.

fumasse n.f. Rage, anger. Etre en fumasse: To be fuming, to be seething with anger.

fumasse adj. Weird and droll. Elle est fumasse, celle-là! Well I never! – Would you believe it?!

fumée n.f. **1** De la fumée: 'Aggro', physical violence. **2** Envoyer (also: balancer) la fumée: **a** To shoot, to fire a gun. **b** To 'juice off', to ejaculate.

fumelle n.f. 'Biddy', 'bird', woman.

fumer v.intrans. **1** To be 'in a huff', 'in a paddy', to be angry. **2** Ça va fumer! All hell is going to be let loose! (You can expect some violent reactions!) **3** Fume, c'est du belge! Put that in your pipe and smoke it! – You know what you can do . . . get stuffed! (The action of smoking here is an obscene reference to fellatio.)

fumeron n.m. **1** '40-a-day' man, chain-smoker. **2** (pl.): 'Plates of meat', 'hoofs', feet. Avoir le fumeron sensible: To have delicate tootsies, to have sensitive feet. **3** (pl.): 'Gambs', legs. La môme avait de sacrés fumerons: She had a smashing pair of legs. **4** Avoir les fumerons: To 'have the shits', to be 'in a blue funk', to be very frightened.

fumette n.f. La fumette (Drugs): Cannabis smoking.

fumier n.m. 'Shyster', despicable character.

fumiste n.m. **1** 'Slack-arse', 'lazy bugger', idle so-and-so. **2** 'Leg-puller', practical joker. Comme fumiste, il se pose un peu! When it comes to hoaxes and leg-pulling, he's his own master.

fumisterie n.f. **1** 'Codswallop', 'rubbish', worthless goods. **2** 'Baloney', 'ballyhoo', inane comments.

funérailles n.f.pl. Funérailles! Cripes! – Crikey! – Blimey! (This mild and rather twee interjection originates from the south of France.)

furat n.m. **1** 'Nosey Parker', over-inquisitive person. **2** (pol.): Tenacious officer whose ferret-like inquiries lead him to culprits.

Furax Proper name. *C'est signé Furax!* (joc.):
There's no prizes for guessing who did that!
(*Signé Furax* was a famous radio comedy
series of the 50s and early 60s.)

furax adj. 'Livid', furious. *Il est un rien furax
depuis qu'elle l'a quitté*: He still hasn't simmered
down since she left him.

furibard adj. 'Livid', furious. *Ça, pour être
furibard, je le suis!* If you're still guessing, yes I
am bloody angry!

furieusement adv. 'Awfully', 'terribly', very.
J'en ai furieusement envie: I'm dying for it.

fusain n.m. 1 (pej.): Gawky priest, pencil-like
figure of a cleric. 2 (pl.): Spindly legs.

fusant n.m. 'Pongy', fart. *Lâcher un fusant*: To
'let off', to break wind.

fuseaux n.m.pl. 1 'Pegs', 'gambs', legs. *Se manier
les fuseaux*: To 'skedaddle', to hurry off.
2 'Drainpipes', tight-fitting trousers. 3 Skiing
trousers.

fusée n.f. 1 'Technicolor yawn', 'liquid laugh',
violent burst of vomit. 2 'Loaded fart',
diarrhoeal burst of anal wind. (In both cases,
lâcher une fusée is the accepted colloquial usage.)

fuser v.intrans. To 'do a pongy', to 'fart', to break
wind.

fusible n.m. *Péter un fusible*: To 'blow one's top',
to explode into uncontrollable anger. (The
alternative *péter une durite* suggests the
bursting of a blood vessel.)

fusil n.m. 1 'Gut', 'belly', stomach. *Se coller
quelque chose dans le fusil*: To have a bite to eat.
Se bourrer le fusil: To 'stuff one's face', to eat
immoderately. 2 *Coup de fusil*: Exorbitant
restaurant bill. (*Coup de fusil* can sometimes
refer to a restaurant known for its exorbitant
prices.) 3 *Un logement en coup de fusil*: A
'corridor flat', a long and narrow dwelling.
4 *Repousser du fusil*: To have foul breath, to
suffer from halitosis. 5 *Décharger son fusil*: To
'juice off', to ejaculate.

fusiller v.trans. 1 To 'bump off', to kill. 2 To
'bugger up', to damage beyond repair. *Il a
complètement fusillé le moulin de ma bagnole!*
When he had my car, he burnt out the engine!
3 (Gambling slang): To 'clean out', to take
someone for every penny he's got. *Qu'est-ce
qu'on s'est fait fusiller aux bobs!* He even took
the shirts off our backs in that game of dice!
4 To 'spend, spend, spend', to fritter money
away. *Il a tout fusillé*: He blew the lot. 5 *Se
faire fusiller*: To get overcharged in a restaurant.

futal n.m. 'Trews', trousers.

futé adj. (Usually in the negative): 'Bright',
clever, brilliant. *Ça c'est vraiment pas futé!*
That's not very clever now, is it?

futur n.m. (joc.) *Mon futur*: 'My intended', my
future husband. *Je te présente ma future!* Meet
the lady who's twisted my arm!

G

gabardine *n.f. (pol.)*: Unofficial 'carte blanche', verbal assurance from senior quarters that officers involved in an inquiry may, for the purposes of the case, act outside the law.

gabarit *n.m.* 'Type', 'kind', sort. *Ça c'est mon gabarit!* That's just up my street! – That's just what I fancy! *Ils sont du même gabarit:* They're two of a kind.

gabegie *n.f.* **1** 'Tangle', muddle, mess. *Quelle gabegie depuis qu'on est sans secrétaire!* We're really up the spout without a secretary! **2** Criminal waste (through mismanagement). *Quelle gabegie!* What a wicked waste! **3** 'Dirty work', 'foul play', trickery.

gabelou *n.m.* 'Customs man', customs officer.

gabier *n.m. Gabier de mes deux* (Naval slang): 'Nincompoop', imbecile.

gabouiller *v.intrans.* To 'make a boo-boo', to commit a gaffe.

gâche *n.f.* **1** Job, employment. *Quelle gâche!* What a rotten job! *Une bonne gâche:* A 'cushy number', a well-paid occupation necessitating little work. *Lui, au moins, il s'est trouvé une bonne gâche:* When it comes to cushy jobs, he's certainly landed the plummest! **2** Room, space. *'y avait de la gâche:* There was room to spare.

gâcher *v.intrans.* To 'graft', to work hard. *Où qu'on gâche aujourd'hui?* And where are we slogging our guts out today?

gâchette *n.f.* 'Hit-man', hired killer. (In the film *Les Tontons Flingueurs* a character is described as *première gâchette*, thus indicating that he is the top trigger-man to a high-ranking member of the underworld.)

gâcheuse *n.f.* Affected character, effete person. (When directed at a man, the word is distinctly pejorative as it casts doubt on his masculinity.)

gâchis *n.m. Quel gâchis!* What a cock-up! – What a mess!

gadin *n.m.* **1** 'Tumble', fall. (The expression *ramasser un gadin* can either mean to fall down or to suffer a setback.) **2** 'Bean', 'bonce', head.

Prendre un gnon sur le gadin: To get biffed over the head. *Y aller du gadin:* To be guillotined.

gadjé *n.m.* **1** (Gypsy slang): One who is not a *Manouche*, not one of the tribe. **2** 'Mug', 'sucker', dupe.

gadoue *n.f.* (also: *gadou*): **1** 'Slush', mud. **2** *Une gadoue (pej.):* Low-class prostitute.

gadouille *n.f.* 'Mess', 'mix-up', state of chaos.

gaffe *n.m.* **1** 'Screw', prison warder. **2** (Underworld slang): 'Crow', look-out, confederate on sentry duty. **3** *Faire gaffe:* To be on one's guard, to be careful. *Fais gaffe!* Watch it! – Look out! *Gaffe à tes os!* If you don't want to get hurt, stand clear!

gaffe *n.f.* **1** 'Boo-boo', 'boob', blunder. *Faire une gaffe:* To drop a clanger. *Il a fait la gaffe des gaffes!* He didn't just put his foot in it, it was a case of both! *Manier la gaffe:* To be a regular goofer. (*Gaston la Gaffe*, a famous bungling cartoon character of the 60s and 70s, epitomizes the uncontrollable goofer.) **2** *Avaler sa gaffe:* To 'pop one's clogs', to 'shuffle off', to die.

gaffer *v.intrans.* **1** To 'make a boob', to make a blunder. **2** To 'crow', to keep a look-out. *On a eu beau gaffer, on les a pas vus venir dans la brume:* We kept our eyes peeled, but they still caught us unawares with all that mist.

gaffer *v.pronom.* To be wary of, to be on one's guard. *Je me suis bien gaffé de l'inviter à dîner, tu connais son appétit!* I took no chances inviting him to dinner, he'd eat us out of house and home!

gaffeur *n.m.* 'Goofer', gaffe-prone individual.

gaga *n.m.* 'Yoghurt brain', old dodderer.

gaga *adj.* 'Soft in the head', doddering, in a state of senile decay.

gagne-pain *n.m. (joc.)*: 'Bum', 'bottom', behind. (The word originates from the language of prostitution.)

gagneur *n.m.* 'Do-or-die' character, tenacious and successful trier.

gagneuse *n.f.* 'Good little earner', prostitute who keeps her pimp in clover.

gai *adj.* **1** *Etre un peu gai*: To be 'tiddly', to 'have had one over the eight', to be slightly inebriated. **2** *Ça, c'est gai, alors! (iron.)*: That's all we needed! – What rotten luck!

gail *n.m.* (also: *gaille*): **1** 'Mutt', 'pooch', dog. **2** 'Nag', horse. *Il a tout flambé aux gails*: He blew the lot on the gee-gees.

galapiat *n.m.* 'Layabout', 'good-for-nothing', useless character.

gale *n.f.* **1** 'Evil minx', nasty-minded and persistent pest. *Elle est méchante comme la gale!* She's as mean as they come! **2** *Ne pas avoir la gale aux dents*: To be a glutton, to have a voracious appetite.

galéjade *n.f.* 'Cock-and-bull story', improbable tale. *Il faut toujours qu'il nous sorte des galéjades!* He's always spouting the most incredible rubbish!

galéjer *v.intrans.* To make up 'cock-and-bull stories', to tell tall stories.

galère *n.f. Vogue la galère! (iron.)*: Who cares?! – Come what may!

galerie *n.f.* **1** *Poser pour la galerie*: To 'swank', to show off (also: *essayer d'épater la galerie*). **2** *Amuser la galerie*: To 'keep everyone in fits', to 'keep everyone rolling in the aisles', to have someone in fits of laughter.

Galeries *n.f.pl. Les Galeries*: The Galeries Lafayette (large department store in Paris).

galetouse *n.f.* (also: *galetouze*): **1** *(mil.)*: Mess-tin. **2** 'Loot', money. *Côté galetouse, elle a pas à se plaindre!* She's certainly not short of a bob or two! **3** (Film-makers' slang): Unedited reel of film. *Enroulé! C'est dans la galetouse!* O.K., lads! I think we've got a take!

galettard *adj.* 'Stinking rich', wealthy. *Pour être galettards, ils le sont*: They're rolling in it (also: *galetteux*).

galette *n.f.* **1** 'Brass', 'loot', money. *Avoir de la galette*: To be in the money. *C'est une grosse galette!* (of person): He's loaded! *Par ici la galette!* Remember who your friends are! (when it comes to sharing out the goodies). **2** *(mil.)*: Beret. **3** *(mil.)*: 'Backbreaker', thin and hard mattress. **4** 'Duffer', 'pillock', nincompoop. **5** (Film-makers' slang): 'Can', unedited reel of film (also: *galetouse*). **6** *(pl.)*: 'Poached egg' boobs, flat chest.

galetteux *adj.* 'Stinking rich', wealthy.

galipette *n.f.* **1** 'Gambol', somersault. **2** 'Caper', frolic. *Faire des galipettes*: **a** To 'lark about', to fool about. **b** To lead a free-and-easy randy life.

galoche *n.f. Rouler une galoche*: To give someone a 'smackeroo', to kiss on the lips. *Il lui a roulé une galoche princière*: After that kiss, she sure was gasping!

galon *n.m. Prendre du galon*: **a** To 'come up in the world', to get on in life. **b** To 'be getting on in years', to grow old.

galonnard *n.m. (mil.)*: Officer. *Les galonnards*: The top brass.

galop *n.m.* **1** 'Rocket', 'roasting', reprimand. *Attends qu'il rentre, je vais lui filer un de ces galops!* As soon as he gets through that door, he'll hear a few home truths from me! **2** *Faire quelque chose au petit galop (les mains basses)*: To 'take something in one's stride', to do something effortlessly.

galopin *n.m.* **1** 'Cheeky brat', insolent kid. **2** 'Half', small glass of beer more commonly known as the *bock*. (The *bock* is the smallest merchandisable volume of beer sold on tap.)

galoupe *n.m.* (also: *galoup*): 'Dirty trick', underhand deed. *Faire un galoupe à quelqu'un*: **a** To 'do the dirty on someone'. **b** To have an affair, to be unfaithful to someone.

galtouse *n.f.* **1** *(mil.)*: Mess-tin. **2** 'Brass', 'lolly', money. **3** (Film-makers' slang): Unedited reel.

galuche *n.f.* 'Ciggy', *Gauloise* cigarette.

galurin *n.m.* 'Lid', man's hat (also: *bitos*).

gamahuche *n.f.* Oral sex.

gamahucher *v.intrans.* To practise oral sex.

gamberge *n.f.* **1** 'Grey matter', brain. *Avoir la gamberge qui fait roue libre*: To have an over-active brain running wild. **2** Idea, thought. **3** Worry, concern.

gamberger *v.intrans.* **1** To think. **2** To 'fret', to worry. **3** To 'twig', to understand. *Il n'a rien gambergé*: He didn't get my drift. **4** To daydream. (An alternative for this meaning alone is *gambergeailler*.)

gambette *n.f.* **1** *La gambette*: 'Loose living', dissolute life. *Etre porté sur la gambette*: To be a randy so-and-so. **2** *(pl.)*: 'Pins', 'gambs', legs. *Tricoter des gambettes*: **a** To 'cut and run', to 'skedaddle', to run away. **b** To 'shake it all about', to dance.

gambille *n.f.* **1** *La gambille*: 'Stomping', dancing. **2** *(pl.)*: 'Pins', 'gambs', legs. *J'ai vraiment les gambilles en coton*: I'm really feeling weak at the knees.

gambiller *v.intrans.* To 'stomp', to 'shake it all about', to dance.

gamelle *n.f.* **1** *Ramasser une gamelle*: **a** To 'bite the dust', to fall flat on one's face. **b** *(fig.)*: To 'come unstuck', to 'come a cropper', to suffer a setback. **2** *S'accrocher une gamelle*: To 'have to do without', to miss one's turn.

gamin *n.m.* 'Kid', son. *Mon gamin vient de se marier*: My lad's just got married.

gamine *n.f.* **1** 'Kid', daughter. **2** *T'occupe pas de la gamine! (iron.)*: Keep your nose out of this! – Mind your own business!

gamme *n.f.* **1** *Faire ses gammes*: To 'drill', to practise, to get through the unglamorous exercises leading to better things. **2** *Faire des gammes*: To do some light 'pawing' (to let one's fingers run up and down one's partner's body). **3** *Chanter sa gamme à quelqu'un*: To give someone a few home truths. **4** *Changer de gamme*: To 'change one's tune', to take a different (and often more down-to-earth) line of argument. **5** *Et toute la gamme! (joc.)*: And the whole shooting match! – And everything! *On a eu droit aux flics, aux pompiers et toute la gamme!* We got the fuzz, the fire brigade boys, the ambulance, the lot!

ganache *n.f.* 'Nincompoop', 'pillock', idiot. *Une vieille ganache*: A silly old fuddy-duddy.

gandin *n.m.* **1** Elegant well-dressed person. **2** Over-dressed swank. **3** Knave (in pack of cards).

gandin *adj.* **1** Elegant, well-dressed. **2** Over-dressed.

gano *n.m.* (also: *ganot*): **1** 'Nest-egg', stashed savings. **2** Booty, plundered spoils.

gant *n.m.* **1** *Retourner quelqu'un comme un gant*: To 'twist someone round one's little finger', to be so forceful as to sway someone into changing their mind. **2** *Prendre des gants (avec quelqu'un)*: To take great care not to offend or upset someone. *Il n'a pas pris des gants pour lui dire ses quatre vérités!* He wasn't out to spare her feelings when he told her a few home truths! **3** *Ça me va comme un gant*: It suits me to a T – That suits me down to the ground – That's certainly O.K. by me. **4** *Se donner des gants*: To take the credit for doing something. *Comme toujours il s'est donné des gants*: Like the modest so-and-so he is, he pulled the blanket to himself yet again! **5** *Savonner quelqu'un au gant de crin*: To give someone a sharp telling-off. **6** *Mes-gants, tes-gants*: Me (myself), you. **7** *En être pour ses gants*: To be 'the fall-guy', to be the sucker. *J'en ai été pour mes gants!* It's muggins who carried the can!

gapette *n.f.* 'Pancake', flat cap.

garage *n.m.* **1** (Prostitutes' and pimps' slang): 'Knocking-shop', hotel room. **2** 'Dead-end' post, out-of-the-way job where unpopular employees can be shunted off to. **3** Place of no-return where documents of a sensitive nature can be left to gather dust.

garce *n.f.* **1** 'Bitch', spiteful woman. **2** *Quelle garce de vie!* What a rotten life this is!

garce *adj.* 'Bitchy', spiteful. *Dans le genre garce on ne fait pas mieux*: Bitch could be her middle name!

garçon *n.m.* **1** 'Kid', son. *C'est mon garçon!* That's my boy! **2** Bachelor. *Enterrer sa vie de garçon*: To 'have a stag party', to celebrate the end of one's bachelor days.

garçonnière *n.f.* 'Bachelor-pad', single man's flat. (The word describes a small, often well-appointed flatlet used to entertain lady friends.)

garde *n.f.* **1** *Faire donner la garde (joc.)*: To 'call the fuzz', to summon the police. **2** *S'enferrer jusqu'à la garde (fig.)*: To get oneself embroiled in a tangle of explanations. (In this instance, *garde* referred originally to the hilt of a sword.)

garde-à-vous *n.m.* *Etre au garde-à-vous* (also: *avoir le zigouigoui au garde-à-vous*): To 'have the big stick', to have an erection.

garde-chiourme *n.m.* *(joc.)*: **1** 'Gaffer', fore-man. **2** *(sch.)*: Invigilator. (The jocularity of the word stems from the original meaning of prison warder in a penal colony.)

garder *v.trans.* *Garder à quelqu'un un chien de sa chienne*: To harbour a grudge against someone (also: *avoir une dent contre quelqu'un*).

garder *v.pronom.* *Se garder à carreau*: **a** To 'keep a low profile', to avoid confrontation. **b** To stand on one's guard, to be wary.

gardon *n.m.* *Etre frais comme un gardon*: To be 'as fresh as a daisy', to feel in tip-top condition.

gare *n.f.* **1** *Envoyer quelqu'un à la gare*: To 'send someone packing', to 'send someone away with a flea in their ear', to tell someone to go to hell. **2** *A la gare!* Push off! – Shove off! – Get lost!

gare *interj.* **1** Fingers! – Keep your mitts off! – Don't touch! **2** Watch it! – Look out! – Be careful!

garer *v.trans.* **1** To 'salt away', to 'stash', to hide something. *Je m'en vais garer un petit peu de fric, on ne sait jamais!* You can never be too careful, I'm putting something away for a rainy day! **2** *Garer ses miches*: To 'get out of harm's way', to stand clear of something dangerous or unpleasant. **3** *Etre garé en double file*: To be 'in a mad rush', in a fearful hurry. (Originally the expression referred to a double-parked car, hence the swift movement of its driver.)

garer *v.pronom.* *Se garer des voitures* (Underworld slang): To retire from active service, to pension oneself off.

gargane *n.f.* 'Gullet', throat. *Avoir une sacrée gargane*: To 'have a sloping gullet', to be a boozer (also: *avoir une sacrée descente*).

gargariser *v.pronom.* **1** To 'wet one's whistle', to 'have a tipple', to have a little drink. **2** To 'hit the bottle', to 'booze', to drink heavily. **3** To 'crow', to exult, to wallow in self-congratulation.

gargiches *n.m.pl.* Snails (that culinary delicacy of which the French are so fond). This word is never found in the singular.

gargote *n.f. (pej.)*: **1** Caf', cheap and unglamorous eating-place. **2** 'Lousy grub', cheap and nasty food.

gargotier *n.m. (pej.)*: Proprietor of a run-down caf'.

gargue *n.f.* 'Gob', mouth. *Ferme ta gargue!* Keep your trap shut!

garni *n.m.* **1** Furnished accommodation. *Vivre en garni*: To live in furnished digs. **2** 'Knocking-shop', hotel room. (Originally the *garni* was an inexpensive hotel let by the week or the month to regulars. With the closing of brothels and the outlawing of prostitution, prostitutes started using them to ply their trade, giving them a bad name. Also: *garno*.)

garni *adj.* *Etre bien garnie* (of woman): To be 'well-stacked', to 'have everything in the right places', to be physically well-endowed.

garnots *n.m.pl.* *Les garnots*: The police department whose task it is to collate and check all information appertaining to hotels (also: *la police des garnis*).

garouse *n.f.* (also: *garouze*): Station, railway station.

gars *n.m.* **1** 'Laddie', 'geezer', chap. *C'est un drôle de gars!* He's a right funny feller! **2** 'Sonny', son. *Mon gars est au Service*: My lad's doing his National Service. **3** 'Hubby', 'old man', husband. (Pierre Daninos in SNOBISSIMO highlights the affected affection shown by the upper classes for that word. *Mon gars est allé faire ses dix-huit trous*: My old man's gone for a round of golf.)

Gascon *n.m.* *Promesse de Gascon*: Promise one makes with no intention of keeping it. *J'en ai marre de ses promesses de Gascon*: I'm sick and tired of his 'if ever you're in Katmandu, do look us up' invites.

gaspard *n.m.* **1** Rat. *Dans notre cave 'y a des gaspards gros comme des greffiers*: We've got whopping big rats in our cellar. **2** Cunning bastard, evil scheming character. **3** *Avaler le gaspard*: To take Holy Communion.

gaspi *n.m.* *Le gaspi*: The wasting of energy resources. (In 1979 and the early 80s, the French were introduced to *la chasse au gaspi*, a Gallic equivalent of the British 'Save it' campaign promoted at the same time.)

gâté *past part.* *Ne pas être gâté*: **a** To be 'short on luck', to have suffered many setbacks. **b** To have an ungainly appearance. (In both instances, the expression is cruelly ironic and is used to refer to an individual for whom no pity is really felt.)

gâteau *n.m.* **1** Profits. *Avoir sa part du gâteau*: To have a share of the takings. *Partager le gâteau*: To split the profits. *Avec lui, pas*

question de partager le gâteau! Watch out, he'll keep the lot! **2** *C'est du gâteau!* It's a piece of cake! – It's a walkover! – It's dead easy! *Comme bracage, c'est du gâteau!* It's no hold-up, it's like taking sweets off a kid! **3** *Papa-gâteau*: **a** Over-indulgent father. **b** 'Sugar-daddy', wealthy older lover.

gâterie *n.f.* *Faire une gâterie*: To indulge in oral sex.

gau *n.m.* Nit, louse.

gauche *n.m.* *Il y a du gauche!* This isn't quite kosher! – I smell a rat! – I have my doubts about this!

gauche *n.f.* **1** *En mettre à gauche* (of money): To 'put aside for a rainy day', to save. **2** *Passer l'arme à gauche*: To 'pop one's clogs', to 'kick the bucket', to die. **3** *Jusqu'à la gauche*: Completely, utterly, totally. *On est avec toi jusqu'à la gauche*: We'll stick by you through thick and thin. *Emmerder quelqu'un jusqu'à la gauche*: To go out of one's way to be a pain in the neck to someone.

gauchisant *n.m.* 'Leftie', 'near-Commie', character with Left-wing political ideas.

gauchisant *adj.* Left-wing orientated.

gaudriole *n.f.* **1** A bit of 'how's your father?!', 'hanky-panky', randy horse-play. *Il ne pense qu'à la gaudriole*: He's got sex on the brain! **2** *(pl.)*: Smutty jokes and stories. *Débiter des gaudrioles*: To come out with coarse jokes.

gauffrer *v.trans.* (also: *gaufrer*): To 'nick', to 'collar', to arrest. (This verb is nearly always used in the passive. *Il s'est fait gauffrer*: He got nabbed red-handed.)

gauffrer *v.trans.reflex.* (also: *gaufrer*): To 'have a good tuck-in', to eat plenty of excellent food. *Qu'est-ce qu'on s'est gauffré!* We certainly had our fill of tip-top grub!

gaufre *n.f.* **1** 'Mush', 'dial', face. *Vise cette gaufre!* *(joc.)*: Look at that god-awful face! *Se sucrer la gaufre*: To 'powder one's nose', to put powder on one's face. **2** 'Pancake', flat cap. **3** 'Grub', 'eats', food. *Viens donc à la gaufre chez nous ce soir*: Come and have a bite with us tonight. **4** 'Bloomer', 'boob', mistake. *Il a encore fait une de ces gaufres*: He's gone and put his foot in it again. *Ramasser une gaufre*: **a** *(lit.)*: To fall flat on one's face, to fall down. **b** *(fig.)*: To 'come unstuck', to 'come a cropper', to suffer a setback (also: *ramasser une gamelle*). **5** *Moule à gaufres*: 'Duffer', 'nincompoop', idiot.

gaule *n.f.* 'Prick', 'cock', penis. *Avoir la gaule*: To 'have the big stick', to have an erection (also: *avoir le gourdin*).

gauler *v.trans. & intrans.* **1** To 'screw', to fuck, to have intercourse with. **2** To 'have a slash', to 'pee', to urinate. **3** *Se faire gauler*: To get 'collared', to get 'nicked', to be arrested. *Il s'est bêtement laissé gauler*: It was sheer stupidity the way he got nabbed.

gauleur *n.m.* **1** 'Randy so-and-so', over-sexed man. **2** 'Rook', thief. *Méfie-toi, c'est un vilain gauleur!* If you don't watch him, he'll have the clothes off your back!

gaupe *n.f.* 'Tart', loose woman.

gaveau *n.m.* Piano. *Tâter du gaveau*: To 'tickle the ivories', to play the piano. (*Gaveau* is the name of a famous piano factor which has become generic for that instrument.)

gaviot *n.m.* 'Gullet', throat.

gavousse *n.f.* 'Les', 'dyke', lesbian (also: *gougne*).

gavroche *n.m.* 'Imp', Parisian street urchin.

gavrocherie *n.f.* Cheeky and witty repartee typical of the Parisian *gavroche*.

gaye *n.m.* (also: *gay, gaille*): **1** 'Mutt', 'pooch', dog. **2** 'Nag', horse. *Les gayes c'est sa vie*: If he couldn't go to the races, he'd die of boredom.

gaz *n.m.* **1** *Mettre les gaz* (also: *ouvrir les gaz*): To 'put one's foot down', to accelerate violently. *Aller à plein(s) gaz*: To 'go full-pelt', to 'zoom along', to travel at high speed. **2** *Eteindre son gaz*: To 'snuff it', to 'pop one's clogs', to die. **3** *Lâcher un gaz*: To 'do a pongy', to 'fart', to break wind. **4** *Il y a de l'eau dans le gaz*: There's a fly in the ointment – There's a hitch – We have a problem here. **5** *(corr. gars)*: 'Geezer', bloke. *C'est pas le mauvais gaz!* He's not a bad sort really!

gazé *past part.* 'Pickled', 'sozzled', drunk.

gazer *v.intrans.* **1** To 'do a pongy', to 'fart', to break wind (also: *louffer*). **2** To 'pong', to stink. **3** To 'go full-pelt', to go full-speed. *On a drôlement gazé sur l'autoroute*: We belted down the motorway. **4** To 'go without a hitch', to go smoothly. *Ça gaze?* How's tricks? *Ça gaze à bloc!* Things are going great guns! **5** *Ça va gazer pour toi!* You're going to cop it! – You're definitely in trouble!

gazier *n.m.* *(pej.)*: 'Geezer', 'bloke', fellow. *Qu'est-ce que c'est que ce foutu gazier?* Who the hell is that burk?

gazon *n.m.* **1** 'Mop', 'thatch', hair. *Avoir le gazon mité*: To have 'a patchy thatch', to be balding. *Se faire tondre le gazon*: To get 'cropped', to get shorn, to have a close haircut. **2** The 'short and curly', female pubic hair. *Mouiller son gazon*: To urinate.

G.D.B. *n.f. Avoir la G.D.B. (la gueule de bois)*: To 'have a hangover', to 'feel under the weather after a binge', to suffer the after effects of an excessive drinking bout.

géant *n.m. Les géants de la route*: Journalese nickname given to the professional riders in

road cycling races. An alternative when the going is hard is: *Les forçats de la route*.

Gégène *Proper name*. Nickname for *Eugène*.

gégène *n.m. (mil.)*: General.

gégène *n.f.* **1** Electricity generator. **2** *La gégène*: Torture by electricity. **3** *(corr. répétition générale)*: Dress rehearsal in theatre, music-hall, etc.

gelé *adj.* **1** 'Paralytic', 'blotto', dead-drunk. **2** 'Bonkers', 'crazy', mad. *T'es complètement gelé?* Are you off your rocker or something?

gelée *n.f.* **1** *Gelée de coing*: 'Mess', 'fix', trouble. *Etre dans la gelée de coing*: To be 'in the shit', to be deep in trouble. *Récolter de la gelée de coing*: To get one's face pushed in. **2** *Etre dans la gelée* (Racing slang): To get 'bunched', to be impeded by a group of horses.

gencive *n.f. Prendre un coup dans les gencives (fig.)*: To get a slap in the face, to be humiliated.

gendarme *n.m.* **1** Bossy woman. **2** Bloater, smoked herring. **3** *(th.)*: Rod with which *les trois coups* announcing the beginning of a performance are struck. **4** 'Turd', faeces, excrement. *Planter un gendarme*: To 'crap', to defecate.

gêner *v.pronom.* **1** *Ne pas se gêner (iron)*: To do something outrageous, oblivious of the effects. *Ne vous gênez pas!* Don't mind me! (Just pretend I don't exist!). *Et il ne s'est pas gêné, vous savez!* He couldn't have given a damn about the rest of us (the way he went on). **2** *Je vais me gêner?!* (also: *avec ça que je vais me gêner!*): You can bet your life I will! – You see if I don't! *Prendre mes vacances en juillet, avec ça que je vais me gêner!* What, me miss taking my holidays in July? – you must be joking!

génial *adj. C'est génial!* That's great! – That's fantastic! (This rather pretentious utterance had its vogue in the 60s and 70s; the equatable antonym is *débile*.) *Génial, ce dîner!* That dinner of yours was out of this world, darling!

genou *n.m.* **1** *Faire du genou*: To 'play footsie', to give a fellow-guest amorous knee-nudges. **2** *Etre sur les genoux*: To 'feel knackered', to be dead-beat (also: *être sur les boulets*). **3** *Son caillou, c'est de la peau de genou!* He's as bald as a coot!

genre *n.m.* **1** *Se donner du genre* (also: *faire du genre*): To 'put it on', to overact the part. *Quand il reçoit, il aime se donner du genre*: When he's hosting, he likes to put on airs and graces. **2** *Faire mauvais genre*: To give a bad impression. *Ça fait mauvais genre de partir comme ça*: It really looks bad going off like that. **3** *Ce n'est pas du tout mon genre!* This definitely isn't me! (It's not what would appeal to me.) **4** (Antique dealers' slang): 'Would-be' article, imitation.

Ça, mon vieux, c'est du genre! This isn't the real thing. (It's a copy.)

gens *n.m.pl. Les gens sont méchants!* This catchphrase made famous by the comedian Fernand Raynaud expresses naïve astonishment at Life's cruel ways.

géo *n.f. (sch.) La géo*: Geography.

géranium *n.m. Dépoter son géranium*: To 'pop one's clogs', to 'kick the bucket', to die.

gerbe *n.f.* **1** Year in jail (usually in the plural). *Il a écopé de cinq gerbes*: He copped five years in the nick. **2** *La gerbe*: 'Wanking', masturbation. **3** *Une gerbe*: A violent spurt of vomit.

gerber *v.trans. & intrans.* **1** To 'get sent down', to be sentenced to a term of imprisonment. *Il a gerbé cinq piges*: He got done for five years. **2** To 'juice off', to ejaculate. **3** To 'throw up', to 'puke', to vomit.

gerbier *n.m.* 'Beak', judge, magistrate.

gerboise *n.f.* 'Nancy-boy', 'pouf', effeminate homosexual.

gerce *n.f. (pej.)*: 'Biddy', 'bird', woman.

gertrude *n.f.* 'Biddy', 'bird', woman. *Tiens, le v'là avec sa gertrude!* There he goes again with his bit-of-skirt! (*Gertrude* is less pejorative than *gerce* and roughly equivalent to 'judy'.)

gésier *n.m.* **1** 'Gullet', throat. **2** 'Tum', stomach.

gestape *n.f. La gestape*: The Gestapo (also: *la gestapette*).

gi *adv.* Yeah – Yes. *Gi-go!* Right-on! – O.K.! (There is a certain humour in this utterance because of the word *gigot*.)

gibboque *n.m.* Game of billiards. *Faire un gibboque*: To 'rip the baize', to do a few frames.

gibecière *n.f.* 'Tum', 'belly', stomach. *Se bourrer la gibecière*: To 'stuff one's face', to eat immoderately.

gibier *n.m.* **1** *Sentir le gibier*: To 'pong', to smell foul. **2** *Effacer le gibier* (of prostitute): To short-change the pimp. (The implication here is that the lady lies about the number of 'customers' she has had.)

giclée *n.f.* **1** Burst of machine-gun fire. *Envoyer une giclée*: To fire a burst (also: *balancer la purée*). **2** 'Spunk', spurt of semen. *Tirer une giclée*: To 'juice off', to ejaculate.

gicler *v.intrans.* **1** To let off a burst of gunfire. **2** To 'scram', to 'skedaddle', to run away. *Allez, gicle!* Piss off! – Get lost! **3** *Gicler des mirettes*: To 'turn on the water-works', to cry.

gicleur *n.m.* **1** 'Gob', 'trap', mouth. *Ferme ton gicleur!* Shut your cake-hole! **2** 'Prick', 'cock', penis. (The standard meaning of *gicleur*: carburettor-jet, explains the above colloquial usages.)

gidouillette *n.f.* 'Tum-tum', 'tummy', stomach (also: *gidouille*).

gifle *n.f. Tête à gifles*: Arrogant face. *Avoir une tête à gifles*: To have an arrogant mush, one that seems to be asking for clouts.

gig *n.f.* 'Gig', one-nighter, one-night concert. (The French have adopted the English pop- and jazz-world colloquialism.)

gigal *n.m.* Jobbing plumber.

gigo *interj.* Right on! – O.K.!

gigolette *n.f.* **1** Young lass, young girl. **2** 'Floosie', 'easy bird', girl with happy-go-lucky morals.

gigolpince *n.m.* Gigolo, fancy-man.

gigoter *v.intrans.* To 'shake a leg', to have a dance.

gigots *n.m.pl. (joc.)*: Thighs. *Vise ces gigots!* Get a load of those gammons! (The word smacks of male chauvinism as it refers mostly to women.)

gigouilleur *n.m.* Painter-decorator.

gigue *n.f.* **1** 'Bean-pole lassie', gawky girl. **2** *(pl.)*: 'Pins', 'gambs', legs.

gilet *n.m.* **1** *Pleurer dans le gilet de quelqu'un*: To 'weep on someone's shoulder', to pour out one's troubles to someone. **2** *S'en fourrer dans le gilet*: To 'booze', to drink heavily (also: *s'en filer derrière la cravate*).

Ginette *Proper name.* Nickname for *Geneviève*.

gingin *n.m.* 'Nous', gumption, common-sense. *Ne pas manquer de gingin*: To know the ropes.

girafe *n.f. Peigner la girafe (joc.)*: To waste one's time doing useless tasks. *On peut faire ça ou peigner la girafe!* We might just as well do that as anything else! (The ironic humour of the expression is such that San-Antonio, alias Frédéric Dard, entitled one of his novels EN PEIGNANT LA GIRAFE.)

giries *n.f.pl.* **1** Affected mannerisms. *Faire des giries*: To put on airs and graces. **2** 'Moans and groans', perpetual complaining. *Avec elle, c'est toujours des giries*: With her, whatever the problem, it's moan, moan, moan!

giroflée *n.f. Une giroflée à cinq feuilles*: A slap across the face. (Some dictionaries erroneously translate this expression by 'a bunch of fives', i.e. a blow with the fist, when in fact it is a blow with the open hand.)

girond *n.m.* (also: *giron*): 'Nancy-boy', 'pouf', effeminate homosexual.

girond *adj.* Handsome, good-looking.

gironde *adj.f.* Buxom and titillating. *C'est une nana drôlement gironde*: She's got everything in the right place – and lots of it!

girouette *n.f. Tourner comme une girouette*: To be as changeable as a weather-vane, to lack persistence. *Gaffe! C'est une vraie girouette!* Watch him! You never know which way he'll turn!

gisquette *n.f.* 'Filly', pretty young woman.

gîter *v.intrans.* To 'hang out', to live somewhere. *Où que tu gîtes?* Where are your digs?

giton *n.m.* 'Nancy-boy', young effeminate homosexual.

givré *adj.* **1** 'Pissed', 'sozzled', drunk. *Dès trois heures il est complètement givré:* Gone lunchtime, you can be sure he's had a skinful! **2** 'Bonkers', 'doolally', mad. *Il est un tantinet givré:* He's rather touched.

givrer *v.pronom.* To get 'pissed', 'sozzled', to get drunk (also: *se poivrer*).

glace *n.f.* *Passer devant la glace* (also: *se bomber devant la glace*): To 'be done out of something', to miss out on one's share of the proceeds (usually from illegal activities).

glagla *adj.inv.* *Etre glagla:* To be frozen stiff, to be shivering with cold. (The expression *les avoir à glagla* can also mean to be shaking with fear.)

glaglater *v.intrans.* To shake, either because of intense cold or fear.

glaiseux *n.m.* *(pej.):* 'Hick', peasant countrydweller.

gland *n.m.* **1** 'Prick', 'cock', penis. *Effacer le gland:* To fuck, to have intercourse. *Se cogner le gland:* To 'beat the dummy', to 'wank', to masturbate. **2** 'Pill', 'pillock', imbecile.

glander *v.intrans.* To 'mooch', to laze about, to be idle. (The expression *qu'est-ce que tu glandes?* What are you doing? implies that the person concerned is doing very little.)

glandeur *n.m.* **1** 'Lazy git', idle so-and-so. **2** 'Superstud', highly-sexed man. *C'est un sacré glandeur!* He's a real ladies' man!

glandilleux *adj.* **1** 'Tricky', difficult. **2** 'Dicey', dangerous. *C'est trop glandilleux, je préfère passer la main:* Count me out, it's a bit too risky for me.

glandouiller *v.intrans.* **1** To wait (to be kept waiting). *Il m'a fait glandouiller trois heures:* He kept me hanging around for three hours. **2** To 'moon about', to fritter one's time away.

glandouilleur *n.m.* 'Lazy git', idle fellow.

glandouilleux *adj.* **1** 'Tricky', difficult. **2** Abstruse, incomprehensible.

glandu *adj.inv.* (of person): 'Thick', stupid. *Il est un rien glandu:* He's as dumb as they come.

glaner *v.trans. & intrans.* To 'go nicking', to go on a pilfering spree in shops.

glasse *n.m.* *Un glasse:* A drink, a full glass of alcoholic beverage. *On a pris un glasse ensemble:* We had a couple of bevvies.

glaude *n.f.* 'Bin', 'poke', pocket. *Tireur de glaudes:* 'Diver', pickpocket.

glaviot *n.m.* 'Oyster', 'gob', clot of spittle (also: *mollard*).

glavioter *v.intrans.* To 'hoik', to spit. *Glavioter des éponges:* To suffer from T.B.

glissade *n.f.* (Card-sharps' slang): Nifty legerdemain.

glisse *n.f.* *Faire de la glisse à quelqu'un:* To do someone out of his share of the takings (criminal or otherwise).

glisser *v.trans. & intrans.* **1** *Glisser quelque chose en douce à quelqu'un:* To tell someone something 'on the q.t.' (in confidence). **2** *Laisser glisser:* To 'let the matter rest', to take no further action. *Laisse glisser, vaut mieux oublier tout ça!* Let sleeping dogs lie! **3** To 'slip a length', to fuck, to have intercourse. *Il l'a glissée un soir qu'elle avait trop picolé:* He had it off with her one night she was fair sozzled. **4** *Glisser un fil* (of man): To 'splash one's boots', to 'pee', to urinate. **5** *La glisser:* To 'sling one's hook', to 'shuffle off', to die.

glissoire *n.f.* *La glissoire:* 'Gullet', throat. *S'en filer quelques-uns dans la glissoire:* To down a few drinks.

globe *n.m.* **1** 'Corporation', pot-belly. *Se faire arrondir le globe:* To 'get in the pudding-club', to become pregnant. **2** (*pl.*; also: *globes arrondis*): 'Boobs', 'knockers', large and firm breasts.

gloria *n.m.* Brandy-laced coffee.

glouglou *n.m.* Onomatopoeic transcription of the gurgling sound made by a liquid being poured.

glousser *v.intrans.* To chuckle.

glousseuse *n.f.* 'Easy-lay', a simple mind in a sexy body.

gluant *adj.* Leech-like. *Qu'il est gluant!* What a barnacle!

gluck *n.m.* Luck, good fortune. *Il a un de ces glucks!* He was born lucky!

gnace *n.m.* (also: *gniasse*): 'Geezer', 'guy', fellow. *C'est un drôle de gnace:* He's a funny sort of person.

gnaf *n.m.* (also: *gniaf*): Cobbler, shoe-repairer.

gnangnan *n.m.* **1** 'Milksop', 'namby-pamby' character, weak-willed person. **2** Perpetual moaner.

gnangnan *adj.* **1** 'Soppy', 'namby-pamby', weak-willed. **2** 'Whingey', wailing, moaning.

gniard *n.m.* **1** 'Geezer', 'guy', fellow. **2** 'Brat', 'kid', child.

gnière *n.m.* *(pej.):* 'Geezer', 'bloke', fellow. *Qui c'est que ce gnière?* Who the hell's that git?

gnognote *n.f.* 'Tripe', 'trash', rubbish. *Tout ça, c'est de la gnognote!* This is a load of codswallop! *Goûtez-moi ça, c'est pas de la gnognote!* Taste it, this is the good stuff!

gnôle *n.f.* (also: *gniole*): 'Hooch', 'the hard stuff', strong alcohol. *On a fait le trou normand avec quelques coups de sa gnôle:* We got some respite in that eating bout by downing some of his home-made brew.

gnon *n.m.* 'Biff', 'bonk', blow. *Je lui ai filé un de ces gnons*: I cracked him a corker. *Se flanquer un gnon*: To knock oneself inadvertently.

gnouf *n.m.* 'Clink', 'nick', jail. *Il s'est retrouvé au gnouf*: He got slammed in the cooler.

Gob' *Proper name. Les Gob'*: The *Quartier des Gobelins* in Paris.

gobe-la-lune *n.m.* 'Sucker', 'gull', credulous person. *Quel gobe-la-lune!* He's the easy target if ever there was!

gobelot *n.m.* 'Tippler', happy-go-lucky drunk.

gobelotter *v.intrans.* To 'tipple', to be fond of the bottle.

gober *v.trans.* To 'go for something hook, line and sinker', to fall for something. *Il gobe n'importe quoi*: He'll believe anything.

gober *v.pronom.* To 'fancy oneself', to have no mean opinion of oneself.

goberger *v.pronom.* **1** To 'stuff one's face' with good grub, to overindulge in good food. **2** To 'lead the life of Riley', to 'do oneself well', to enjoy life to the full.

gobette *n.f.* 'Booze', alcoholic drink (consumed too generously). *Tâter de la gobette* (also: *donner dans la gobette*): To be something of a tippler.

gobeur *n.m.* 'Gull', 'sucker', credulous person. *On fait pas mieux comme gobeur!* He's the easy target if ever there was!

gobie *n.m.* (*pej.*): 'Wog', 'coon', coloured person.

gobilles *n.f.pl.* 'Peepers', 'oglers', eyes.

godaille *n.f.* *Aimer la godaille*: To have a taste for the good life.

godailler *v.intrans.* **1** To 'live it up', to lead a merry-old-life. **2** To 'laze about', to take life easy. **3** To 'have the big stick', to have an erection. (With this meaning, an alternative verb is *goder*.)

godant *adj.* Exciting, sexually titillating.

godasses *n.f.pl.* 'Boats', large shoes. *Il ne quitte jamais ses grosses godasses*: He goes everywhere in those big clodhoppers of his.

godelureau *n.m.* (*pej.*): 'Smart-aleck', character who rather fancies himself.

godemiché *n.m.* Dildo, surrogate penis. (The word results from the compounding of *gode* and *miché*.)

goder *v.intrans.* **1** To be excited, to be sexually titillated. **2** To 'have the big stick', to have an erection. **3** *Goder pour* (*fig.*): To 'have one's sights on', to be keen on something. *Il gode pour une petite Alfa rouge*: He's dead keen on a little Alfa Romeo sports car.

godet *n.m.* *Un godet*: A drink, a glass of alcoholic beverage. *Ecluser un godet*: To knock back a jar (or two!).

godeur *n.m.* 'Randy so-and-so', highly-sexed man.

godeur *adj.* 'Randy', highly-sexed.

godiche *n.f.* Malaria, paludal fever.

godiche *adj.* **1** 'Gawky', awkward, clumsy. **2** 'Simple', silly and naïve. *Je ne suis pas si godiche que j'en ai l'air*: I'm not as green as I'm cabbage-looking, you know!

godichon *n.m.* **1** 'Gawk', clumsy character. *Quel godichon!* He's the original bull in a china shop! **2** 'Nincompoop', simpleton.

godille *n.f.* *A la godille*: **a** 'Any-old-how', without any method. *Faire quelque chose à la godille*: To go about something in a sloppy, disorderly manner. **b** Aslant, sideways. *Il m'a regardé à la godille*: He gave me a side-glance.

godiller *v.intrans.* To 'have the big stick', to have an erection (also: *avoir le gourdin*).

godillot *n.m.* 'Clodhopper', 'beetle-crusher', heavy shoe. (Originally *godillots* were Army-issue shoes and got their name from a certain A. Godillot who manufactured them.)

godillot *adj.* 'True-blue', faithful to the last.

godmiché *n.m.* (also: *godemiché*): Dildo, surrogate penis.

godo *n.f.* 'Les', 'dyke', lesbian.

gogne *n.f.* **1** 'Bean', 'bonce', head. **2** (*joc.corr. cigogne*): Stork.

gogo *n.m.* **1** 'Gull', 'sucker', gullible person. *Il s'y connaît pour aguicher les gogos*: He really gets the suckers rolling in. **2** *A gogo* (*adv. exp.*): 'Oodles', 'loads of', an abundance. (That well-known British film classic *Whisky Galore* became *Whisky à gogo* when shown in France.)

gogues *n.m.pl.* *Les gogues*: 'The karzey', 'the bog', the lavatory. *Etre de (corvée de) gogues (mil.)*: To be on latrine duty.

goguette *n.f.* *Etre en goguette*: **a** To be 'out on the spree', to be having a good time. **b** To 'have had one over the eight', to be slightly tipsy.

goinfrer *v.pronom.* **1** To 'stuff oneself like a pig', to eat sloppily and immoderately. *Vise comme il se goinfre!* It's not a plate he needs, it's a trough! **2** To profiteer, to make unreasonable profits.

gomme *n.f.* **1** *La gomme*: The 'hoity-toity', the 'upper-crust', the élite of society. **2** *Gomme à effacer les sourires* (*joc.*): 'Cosh', rubber truncheon (also: *goumi*). **3** *Aller à toute gomme*: To 'drive like the clappers', to go full-pelt. **4** *A la gomme* (*adj.exp.*): 'Phoney', 'bogus', worthless. *J'en ai ralbol de ses excuses à la gomme*: I'm sick and tired of his cock-and-bull excuses.

gommé adj. (of alcoholic beverage): Sweetened with cane-syrup. *Un blanc gommé*: A glass of white wine with a dash of syrup.

gommeux n.m. 'Toff', 'swell', member of the social élite who rather fancies himself. (The word was fashionable up to the 1940s.)

gonde n.f. Door (also: *lourde*).

gondolant adj. 'Creasing', 'side-splitting', hilarious. *Il lui est arrivé un truc gondolant*: What happened to him is just too funny for words!

gondoler v.pronom. To 'crease oneself', to double up with laughter. *Qu'est-ce qu'on s'est gondolé quand on l'a vu en uniforme!* We were in stitches when we saw him out of his civvies!

gonds n.m.pl. *Sortir de ses gonds*: To 'fly off the handle', to 'hit the ceiling', to have an outburst of rage. (The translation 'unhinged' is a trifle too strong, but helps to understand the image.)

gone n.m. 'Nipper', 'kid', child. (Contrary to the assertions of certain lexical sources, this word hailing from Lyon is non-pejorative as is proven in the San-Antonio novel SAN-ANTONIO CHEZ LES GONES.)

gonflant adj. 'Side-splitting', hilarious.

gonfle n.f. **1** *Avoir la gonfle*: To be in the 'pudding-club', to be pregnant. **2** *Salut, la gonfle! (joc.)*: Hi there, fatso!

gonflé adj. **1** 'Cocky', 'cheeky', arrogant. **2** Plucky, courageous. *Il faut être drôlement gonflé pour se risquer là-bas!* You need guts to go in places like that! **3** (of engine): 'Souped-up', modified to produce more power. (The modification, contrary to the suggested image, does not relate to the size of the cylinders, but to carburation.)

gonfler v.pronom. To 'put on airs and graces', to strut about full of one's own importance.

gonze n.m. 'Bloke', 'geezer', chap (also: *gonzier*).

gonzesse n.f. (pej.): **1** 'Biddy', 'bird', woman. **2** 'Nancy-boy', 'pouf', effeminate homosexual. **3** 'Funk', coward.

gorgeon n.m. Drink, glass of alcoholic beverage. *Écluser un gorgeon*: To 'knock back a bevvy'.

gorille n.m. 'Heavy', muscleman, underworld enforcer. (With the increased vulnerability of prominent figures, the status has been raised to that of bodyguard.)

gosier n.m. *Avoir le gosier en pente*: To be a bit of a tippler, to be overfond of one's drink. (The expression *avoir le gosier blindé* suggests a cast-iron gullet able to down the fieriest alcohol.)

gosse n.m. & f. **1** 'Nipper', 'kid', child. *On est venus avec les gosses*: We brought the kids along. **2** Immature person. *Quel gosse!* He's never grown up! **3** *Beau gosse*: Young male who is very conscious of his good looks.

gosseline n.f. 'Filly', pretty young woman.

gouailler v.intrans. To 'chaff', to banter, to jeer at. *Il faut toujours qu'il gouaille*: He's always got to take the mickey out of someone.

gouailleur n.m. 'Mickey-taker', jeerer.

goualante n.f. **1** Song. *Y aller de sa goualante*: To burst out in song. **2** Wail, cry of pain or anguish. (The expression *pousser une goualante* can either mean 'to sing' or 'to let out a wail'.)

gouale n.m. **1** Blackmail. *Faire du gouale à quelqu'un*: To extort blackmail money. (There could well be a linguistic link with *chanter* and *chantage* here.) **2** Protection racket, extortion of funds. **3** *Donner du gouale*: To 'raise Cain', to 'kick up a fuss', to complain vociferously.

goualer v.intrans. & trans. **1** To sing a song (also: *en pousser une*). **2** To moan, to let out a cry of pain. **3** To 'sing', to confess to criminal activities.

gouallerie n.f. 'Chaff', banter, cocky repartee.

gouape n.m. **1** 'Yob', 'yobbo', lout. **2** *La gouape*: The 'down-and-outs', the flotsam and jetsam of society. (The expression *faire la gouape* has a broader meaning than 'to become a drifter'; the connotation of debauchery is often there by implication.)

goudou n.f. 'Les', 'dyke', lesbian.

gouge n.m. 'Layabout', idle character.

gouge n.f. *N'avoir pas une gouge*: To be 'broke', to be penniless. (Originally *gouge* referred to a five-franc piece, but successive devaluations and demonetizations have made it redundant.)

gougnafier n.m. (also: *gougniafier*): 'Duffer', 'goof', prize idiot.

gougnoter v.trans. & intrans. To engage in lesbian intercourse.

gouine n.f. 'Les', 'dyke', lesbian.

goule n.f. **1** 'Gob', 'trap', mouth. **2** 'Gullet', throat. *Avoir une sacrée goule* (also: *avoir la goule en pente*): To be something of a tippler.

goulée n.f. **1** 'Guzzle', big gulp. **2** Drag, inhalation of cigarette-smoke. *Tirer une goulée*: To inhale a lungful.

goulot n.m. **1** 'Gob', 'trap', mouth. **2** 'Gullet', throat. (The expression *repousser du goulot*: to have foul breath, could be under either heading according to the source of the halitosis.)

goumi n.m. 'Cosh', rubber truncheon.

goupille n.f. 'Trick', knack, simple solution to a problem.

goupiller v.trans. **1** To fix, to repair. **2** To 'fix', to wangle. *Je ne sais pas comment t'as goupillé tout ça, mais merci quand même!* I don't know how you pulled that one, but thanks a million!

goupiller v.pronom. *Ça se goupille mal*: Things don't look too good! – I don't like the way this is going!

goupilleur *n.m.* Wily wangler. *Quel goupilleur!* He's the real Mr. Fix-it!

goupillon *n.m. (joc.):* 'Prick', 'cock', penis.

goupillonner *v.intrans.* To have 'a bit of nookie', to have intercourse.

gourance *n.f.* **1** Mistake, error. *Il y a gourance ici!* You've got it wrong! **2** *(pl.):* Doubts, suspicions. *J'en avais des gourances!* I thought as much! – I had my suspicions, you know!

gourbi *n.m.* **1** 'Digs', accommodation. *Il s'est trouvé un gourbi tout ce qu'il y a de soin-soin:* He found himself a smashing little pad. **2** 'Clobber', 'kit', possessions. *Prends ton gourbi et calte!* I want you out with all your stuff! **3** *Faire gourbi:* To 'club together', to pool resources.

gourde *n.f.* **1** 'Bean', 'bonce', head. *Il n'a rien dans la gourde!* He's not got much up-top! **2** *(pej.):* 'Dumb broad', slow-witted woman.

gourde *adj.* 'Dim', 'thick', rather stupid. *Dieu, qu'elle est gourde!* She's bloody gormless!

gourdichon *n.m.* 'Nincompoop', 'twit', imbecile.

gourdin *n.m.* 'Prick', 'cock', penis. *Avoir le gourdin:* To 'have the big stick', to have an erection.

gourer *v.trans.* To 'con', to deceive. *Il m'a drôlement gouré!* I was certainly taken in!

gourer *v.pronom.* **1** To 'get it wrong', to make a mistake. *Comme de bien entendu, on s'est gouré de numéro:* As luck would have it, we went to the wrong address. **2** *Se gourer de:* To 'have an inkling', to suspect. *Je m'en suis bien gouré!* I thought as much!

gourgandine *n.f. (pej.):* 'Loose woman', 'hussy', promiscuous woman.

gourmand *n.m.* 'Haggler', tough bargainer, one who wants to cream off most of the profits.

gourmand *adj.* **1** (of business person): Keen on profit margins. **2** *Pierrot gourmand:* 'Greedy-guts', gluttonous eater. (The term comes from a famous brand of boiled sweets, which used a plump-faced *Pierrot* to promote its name.)

gourmandise *n.f. Faire une gourmandise:* To indulge in oral sex.

gourme *n.f. Jeter sa gourme:* To 'sow one's wild oats', to rid oneself at a young age of sexual inhibitions.

gourrance *n.f.* **1** Mistake, error. **2** *(pl.):* Doubts, suspicions.

gouspin *n.m.* 'Scamp', young rascal.

gousse *n.f.* 'Les', 'dyke', lesbian (also: *gouine*).

gousser *v.trans.reflex.* To indulge in lesbian love.

goût *n.m.* **1** *Avoir perdu le goût du pain:* To have 'popped one's clogs', to have died. The macabre humour of the expression is further highlighted in the utterance *je m'en vais lui faire perdre le goût du pain!* **2** *Ça a un goût de*

revenez-y: I like it! I like it! (I wouldn't mind more of the same.)

goutte *n.f.* **1** 'Nip', tot, drink of strong alcohol. (The expression *boire la goutte* can either mean to have a 'short' or to drown.) **2** *Se noyer dans une goutte d'eau:* To 'make a mountain out of a molehill', to flap needlessly. **3** *Avoir les fesses en gouttes d'huile:* To have a saggy bum.

gouzi-gouzi *n.m. Faire gouzi-gouzi* (Child language): To play tickles.

goyau *n.m. (pej.):* Low-class prostitute.

grabater *v.pronom.* To 'hit the sack', to 'turn in', to go to bed.

grabuge *n.m.* **1** 'Rumpus', 'stir', commotion. **2** 'Set-to', exchange of blows. **3** Damage (direct consequence of the above two).

gradaille *n.f. (mil.): La gradaille* is a pejorative blanket-word referring to N.C.O.s and officers from the ordinary soldier's point of view.

grade *n.m. En prendre pour son grade:* To 'get a dressing-down', to get 'slated', to be reprimanded. *'y a pas à chier, tu vas en prendre pour ton grade!* He'll tear a strip off you, and no messing!

graille *n.f.* 'Grub', 'eats', food. *Aller à la graille:* To 'go to the trough', to get down to a meal. (The implication is that the meal is not particularly appetising.) *A la graille!* Come and get it! – Grub's up!

grailler *v.intrans.* To 'tuck in', to 'stoke up', to eat. *Avec lui qu'est-ce qu'on graille bien!* When he takes you out for a meal, you're sure of a right good spread! (*Grailler* and *graille* are related to *graillon*, but need not necessarily be as pejorative as that word.)

graillon *n.m.* Greasy and unpalatable food. *Ça sent le graillon!* What a greasy pong!

grain *n.m.* **1** *Avoir un grain:* To 'have a screw loose', to be 'doolally', to be slightly mad. **2** *Avoir son grain:* To be 'tipsy', 'tiddly', to be slightly drunk. **3** *Veiller au grain:* To try and steer clear of trouble. (With this meaning, the word originates from the language of seafarers.) **4** *Mettre son grain de sel quelque part:* To 'stick one's oar in', to make an uncalled-for remark.

graine *n.f.* **1** *Monter en graine* (of child): To 'shoot up', to grow quickly. *Ah, les gosses ça monte vite en graine!* Kids, before you know it, they've grown up! **2** *En prendre de la graine:* To 'take a' leaf out of someone's book', to follow someone's example. **3** *De la mauvaise graine* (of person): A 'nasty piece of work', a disreputable character. **4** *Casser la graine:* To have a bite to eat.

grainer *v.intrans.* To 'have a bite', to have a meal.

graisse *n.f.* **1** 'Dough', 'brass', money. *Affurer la graisse*: To be 'raking it in', to be making loads of money. **2** *Faire de la graisse*: To 'make up cock-and-bull stories', to tell lies about personal exploits. **3** *Boniments à la graisse de chevaux de bois*: Glib and far-fetched sales-patter.

graisser *v.trans. Graisser la patte à quelqu'un*: To 'grease someone's palm', to bribe someone.

graisser *v.intrans.* **1** To 'pitch it strong', to exaggerate. **2** To 'shoot a line', to do the hard sell, to make an all-out sales effort.

Grande Boulange *n.f. La Grande Boulange*: The *Banque de France* whose main activity, as with the Bank of England, is to print and control the flow of currency.

Grande Maison *n.f. La Grande Maison*: The *Préfecture de Police* in Paris (also: *La Maison Parapluie*).

grappin *n.m. Mettre le grappin sur*: To 'get one's hooks into', to get hold of. *Ils ont mis le grappin sur la fortune du vieux*: They certainly got their teeth into the old man's money. *Elle a mis le grappin sur un beau parti*: You could say she landed the husband of the year!

gras *n.m.* **1** *Du gras*: 'Brass', 'loot', money. *Avec tout ce gras, on va se payer de belles vacances*: With all this lovely lolly, we're going to have ourselves some super hols! **2** *Discuter le bout de gras*: To 'jaw', to natter away.

gras *adv. Pas gras de*: Not a lot, very little. *De bons restaux par ici, 'y en a pas gras!* Really good restaurants here, you can count them on the fingers of one hand!

gras-double *n.m.* 'Spare-tyre', 'pot-belly', paunch.

gras-du-bide *n.m.* 'Fatso', fat person.

grasse *adj. Se la faire grasse*: To 'live like a lord', to spend money like water (also: *se la faire grassouillette*).

gratin *n.m. Le gratin*: The 'tops', the best, the élite (in any field of endeavour or category of objects). *Il fraye toujours avec le gratin du beau monde*: He's always hobnobbing with the toffs. *La Rolls, c'est vraiment le gratin des bagnoles*: You could say that Rolls Royce is a motoring superlative.

gratiné *adj.* Incredible, extraordinary. *Il tenait une cuite gratinée*: He was pissed to the eyeballs. *Une histoire gratinée*: Some shocking 'tittle-tattle', a scandalous piece of news.

gratouille *n.f.* Itch, scratch. *Avoir la gratouille*: To be itchy all over.

gratouiller *v.trans.* To scratch in order to relieve an itch.

gratte *n.f.* **1** Itch, persistent itching. *Sa gratte me tape sur les nerfs!* His constant itch-scratching

drives me up the wall! **2** Guitar. **3** *De la gratte (sch.)*: 'Seconds', second helping of food. *Allons, sois pas vache, donne-nous de la gratte!* Come on, don't be mean, give us another helping! **4** *Une gratte (abbr. gratification)*: A bonus, a bonus payment in a pay packet. **5** *Faire de la gratte*: To graft hard for some extra cash.

grattée *n.f.* 'Drubbing', thrashing, beating-up.

gratte-papier *n.m. (pej.)*: 'Ink-shitter', 'pen-pusher', menial office clerk.

gratter *v.trans.* **1** To beat, to get the better of someone. *Il pensait me gratter, mais je l'ai eu au finish*: He thought he could beat me, but I showed him who was boss. **2** To 'show a clean pair of heels', to pass someone, to overtake. *Il a été gratté d'une longueur* (Racing slang): He was beaten by a length. **3** *Gratter les fonds de tiroir*: To scrape the bottom of the financial barrel. **4** *Gratter du jambonneau*: To play the mandolin or the guitar. **5** *En gratter pour*: To be 'spoony on', to 'have a crush on', to be infatuated with. *Je crois qu'elle en gratte pour ma pomme*: I think she's doolally on me.

gratter *v.intrans.* To work, to be employed. *Il gratte chez Renault*: He's got a job with Renault. *Dans ce boulot il faut drôlement gratter*: If you want to keep that job you've got to graft.

gratter *v.trans.reflex.* **1** To hesitate, to want to think things over. *Je me gratte pour savoir si je pars en vacances*: I'm not quite sure I want to go on holiday. **2** *Pouvoir toujours se gratter (iron.)*: To 'have another think coming', to be under a serious misapprehension. *Il peut toujours se gratter s'il pense que je vais lui prêter du fric!* He doesn't stand a cat-in-hell's chance of getting any money off me! **3** *Se gratter la couenne*: To be bored to sobs. (This is a jocular reference to shaving as in the synonymous expression *se raser*.)

Gravelotte Proper name. *Ça tombait comme à Gravelotte*: It was raining cats and dogs. (It would take an unusually learned linguist to associate this expression with the fierce military exchanges that took place in 1870 in that Moselle village.)

gravosse *n.m. & f.* Fat person.

gravosse *adj.* Fat, overweight.

grec *n.m.* **1** Card-sharp. **2** 'Con-man', swindler. (A well-orchestrated confidence trick is sometimes known as *un vol à la grecque*.) **3** *Le grec*: The 'deli', the local delicatessen store. **4** *Va te faire voir chez les Grecs!* Get stuffed! – Get knotted! – Go away!

greffier *n.m.* **1** 'Mog', 'moggy', cat. **2** 'Pussy', 'fanny', vagina.

grelot *n.m.* **1** 'Blower', phone, telephone. *Je lui ai passé un coup de grelot*: I gave him a ring. **2** *Attacher le grelot (fig.)*: To 'get into the driving seat', to take the initiative. **3** *(pl.)*: 'Bollocks', 'balls', testicles. **4** *Avoir les grelots*: To 'have the shits', to be frightened. *Flanquer les grelots à quelqu'un*: To 'put the wind up someone', to give someone a scare. **5** *Avoir des grelots au cul*: To have a dirty behind (also: *avoir des clochettes au cul*).

grelotte *n.f.* *Avoir la grelotte*: To 'have the shakes', to be frightened.

grelotteur *n.m.* 'Funk', coward.

greluche *n.f.* 'Biddy', 'bird', woman. (*Ma greluche* more often means 'the missus', my wife, than girlfriend.)

greluchon *n.m.* Gigolo, fancy man.

grenouillage *n.m.* **1** Scandalous 'tittle-tattle', nasty gossip. *Les bonnes femmes, le grenouillage, elles ne connaissent que ça!* Trust women to indulge in some good old lace-curtain gossip! **2** Plotting, intrigue. *Le grenouillage électoral*: Election back-stabbing.

grenouille *n.f.* **1** 'Biddy', 'bird', woman. *Et qui m'a foutu une grenouille pareille?!* Women, honestly! I wonder where he picks them?! **2** 'Prozzy', prostitute. *Il a un joli petit cheptel de grenouilles*: He's daddy to a fine little team of breadwinners. **3** *Grenouille de bénitier (pej.)*: 'Church-hen', over-zealous female church-goer (also: *punaise de sacristie*). **4** Cash-box, funds. *Faire sauter* (also: *manger*) *la grenouille*: To 'scoop the till', to make off with the takings. **5** *Jeter une pierre dans la mare aux grenouilles*: To 'put the cat amongst the pigeons', to cause an unnecessary disturbance.

grenouiller *v.intrans.* To indulge in scandalous 'tittle-tattle', to go scandal-mongering.

grenouillette *n.f.* *Pousser à la grenouillette (pol.)*: To lead a suspect into believing during interrogation that more is known about him than is really the case.

grenouilleur *n.m.* **1** Gossip-monger. **2** Schemer, one who likes intrigue.

grenu *n.m.* *Le grenu*: The unpleasant side of truth.

griffard *n.m.* 'Mog', 'moggy', cat.

griffe *n.f.* **1** 'Mitt', 'paw', hand. *En fin de compte, on s'est serré la griffe*: After the arguing, we shook hands and made our peace. **2** *(pl.)*: 'Plates of meat', 'hoofs', feet. *Aller quelque part à griffes*: To 'hoof it', to have to go somewhere on foot. **3** *La griffe*: The army. *Il se tourne les pouces à la griffe en attendant la quille*: He's just twiddling his thumbs waiting to get back into Civvy Street.

griffer *v.trans.* **1** To grab, to snatch. *On a griffé un bahut au passage*: We grabbed a cab. **2** To

'nick', to 'pinch', to steal. *Il m'a griffé mon larfeuil*: He swiped my wallet.

griffer *v.trans.reflex.* To 'have a blow', to 'wank', to masturbate.

grifton *n.m. (mil.)*: 'Foot-slogger', infantryman.

grigou *n.m.* **1** 'Skinflint', 'scrooge', miser. **2** *Vieux grigou, va! (joc.)*: You cunning old bastard!

grigri *n.m.* **1** Lucky charm. **2** Item of jewellery dangling from a neck-chain.

grille *n.f.* *Avoir une haleine de grille d'égout*: To have foul breath, to suffer from halitosis.

griller *v.trans.* **1** *En griller une*: To 'have a fag', to have a smoke. **2** To inform on, to denounce. *Il m'a grillé comme le salaud qu'il est!* The rotten sod went to the fuzz and did me! **3** To 'brand', to give a bad name, to compromise. *Si on nous voit ensemble, t'es grillé!* If they see you with me, we'll be tarred with the same brush! **4** *C'est grillé!* That's blown it! – That's torn it! – We've been found out! *C'est grillé! Faut pas compter vendre notre camelote ici!* It's curtains for us here, we don't stand a chance of getting any sales now! **5** To 'race past', to pass someone in a race, to overtake. *Il l'a grillé dans la ligne droite*: He showed him a clean pair of heels in the straight. **6** *Griller un feu rouge*: To 'burn the lights', to go through a set of traffic lights on red.

griller *v.pronom.* **1** To 'burn one's boats', to cut off one's escape options. **2** To 'get tarred with a bad brush', to lose one's good name. *Avec une histoire comme ça, il s'est grillé*: A story like that will have sunk him for ever.

grilleur *n.m.* Unscrupulous philanderer (one who will make a bee-line for anybody's wife).

grillot *n.m.* **1** 'Cuckoo-in-the-nest' character, unscrupulous opportunist. **2** *(pol.)*: Compromising document.

grill-room *n.m.* *Le grill-room (joc.)*: The crematorium.

grimace *n.f.* *Manger la soupe à la grimace*: **a** To eat in grim silence (because everyone is sulking). **b** To have to eat up the bitter fare life has dished out.

grimbiche *n.f.* 'Bird', 'lass', young woman.

grimpant *n.m.* 'Trews', 'pants', trousers.

grimper *v.trans.* **1** To 'mount', to 'screw', to have intercourse with. *Il y a belle lurette qu'il la grimpe*: He's been having it off with her for yonks! **2** *Grimper à l'arbre*: To 'fall for something', to be taken in by an unlikely story. *Et comment qu'il l'a fait grimper à l'arbre!* He certainly got him to swallow that 'hook, line and sinker'!

grimpette *n.f.* **1** *(joc.)*: Steep climb. *Quand l'ascenseur fait des siennes, c'est la grimpette* *jusqu'au sixième*: When the lift packs it in, it's 'Everest here we come', to the top floor! **2** (Prostitutes' slang): 'Quickie', short session with a customer. (There is a double entendre intended because of the first meaning of *grimper* and the proverbial climb up the steps to the *hôtel de passe* bedroom.)

grincement *n.m. Il va y avoir des pleurs et des grincements de dents!* We're in for the weepies and argy-bargy with this!

grinche *n.m.* Crook, thief.

grinche *n.f. La grinche*: Thieving, larceny. *De père en fils ils vivent de la grinche*: Breaking and entering runs in the family!

grincher *v.trans. & intrans.* To 'nick', to 'pinch', to steal.

gringue *n.m. Faire du gringue à*: To 'sweet-talk', to flirt with.

grippe *n.f. Prendre en grippe*: To take a dislike to.

gripper *v.pronom.* To grind to a halt. (The colloquial usage is purely figurative; the literal meaning refers to badly lubricated machinery which has ceased to function.) *Entre Moscou et New York, ça se grippe ces temps-ci*: East-West relations are going through a difficult patch.

grippe-sou *n.m.* 'Skinflint', miser.

grippette *n.f.* **1** Mild bout of flu. **2** 'Pussy', 'fanny', vagina.

gris *n.m.* Shag, strong fine-cut tobacco for pipe-smokers and those who roll their own cigarettes.

gris *adj.* **1** 'Tiddly', 'tipsy', slightly drunk. **2** *En voir de grises*: To 'go through a rough patch', to have a tough time.

grisbi *n.m.* 'Loot', 'brass', money. *Touchez pas au grisbi!* Lay off the gelt! (This expression gained overnight national recognition in France when a feature film based on Albert Simonin's novel of the same title got cinema-goers in their droves to see it.)

grisole *adj.* 'Pricey', 'dear', expensive. *Tout compte fait, ça va être grisole*: All said and done, it'll cost a packet!

grive *n.f. La grive*: The army. *Faire sa grive*: To do one's national service (also: *la griffe*).

griveton *n.m. (mil.)*: 'Foot-slogger', infantryman (also: *grivier*).

groggy *adj.* Dizzy, dazed by blows. *Il devait se retenir aux cordes, tant il était groggy*: He soaked up so many blows, he could barely stand in the ring.

grognasse *n.f. (pej.)*: 'Biddy', 'bit of skirt', woman. *Les grognasses et la logique, ça fait deux*: You can't expect logic from a woman!

groin *n.m.* **1** 'Conk', 'hooter', nose. *Il faut toujours qu'il foute son groin partout*: He's always poking his bloody nose into other people's

business! **2** 'Mush', 'ugly mug', unappealing face.

grôle *n.m.* Nit, louse.

grolles *n.f.pl.* **1** 'Boats', shoes. **2** *Avoir les grolles*: To 'have the shits', to be 'in a funk', to be frightened out of one's wits. *Une nouvelle comme ça leur a flanqué les grolles*: That news certainly put the wind up them! (also: *avoir les jetons*).

gros *n.m.* **1** *Le gros*: The wholesale trade. *Il fait le gros*: He deals wholesale. **2** *(pl.)*: 'The nobs', 'the upper-crust', the wealthy. *C'est jamais les gros qui trinquent*: It's always the poor what cop it! **3** *Du gros (rouge) qui tache*: 'Plonk', cheap red wine. **4** *Faire son gros*: To 'crap', to 'shit', to defecate.

gros *adj.* Exaggerated. *Ça c'est un peu gros!* This is a bit far-fetched!

gros *adv.* **1** *Gagner gros*: To be a big earner, to have a hefty pay-packet. **2** *En avoir gros sur le cœur*: To feel resentful about something. **3** *En avoir gros sur la patate*: To have a load of worries.

gros-cube *n.f. (corr.abbr. moto à grosse cylindrée)*: Powerful motorcycle.

gros-cul *n.m.* **1** 'Baccy', shag, strong fine-cut tobacco for pipe-smokers and those who roll their own. **2** H.G.V., heavy goods vehicle. *Il n'y avait rien que des gros-culs sur l'autoroute*: The motorway was jam-packed with artics and big lorries.

grosse *n.f. Faire de la grosse*: To 'do time', to do a stretch in jail. *Il a dérouillé cinq ans de grosse*: The poor bugger copped five years porridge.

grossium *n.m.* 'Big-shot', rich and influential person.

grouille *n.f. Les balancer à la grouille*: To spend money recklessly. *A force de les balancer à la grouille, elle s'est retrouvée sans un*: Her 'spend, spend, spend' approach left her broke.

grouiller *v.pronom.* To 'get cracking', to 'get a move on', to hurry up. *Grouille-toi!* Chop, chop! – Jump to it!

groumer *v.intrans.* To 'bellyache', to 'moan', to complain in a bitter manner.

groumeur *n.m.* Perpetual moaner. *C'est un groumeur de première*: We call him Mr. Grouch!

groumeur *adj.* 'Grumpy', perpetually dissatisfied.

grouper *v.trans.* **1** To 'nick', to 'pinch', to steal. **2** *Se faire grouper*: To get 'nicked', 'collared', to be arrested.

grue *n.f.* **1** 'Tart', loose woman (the kind who frequents bars and likes to sit on a stool showing off her long legs). **2** *Faire le pied de grue*: To 'hang about', to be kept waiting.

gruère *n.m. (joc.)*: Gruyère cheese.

guelte *n.f.* Sales commission.

guenipe *n.f.* Low-class prostitute.

guenon *n.f. (pej.)*: 'Bag', 'hag', ugly woman.

guêpe *n.f.* **1** 'Bitch', bitchy woman (one whose every comment has a sting in the tail). **2** *Pas folle, la guêpe!* There's a canny mind! – There's a wily person! (This jocular expression can sometimes refer to oneself as well as to another.) *Lui prêter du fric?! Pas folle la guêpe!* Me lend him money?! I'm not that dumb! **3** *Avoir la guêpe* (Drugs): To feel a dire need for a 'fix'.

guêpier *n.m. Se fourrer* (also: *tomber*) *dans un guêpier*: To get into a load of trouble (literally to stir up a hornets' nest).

guette-au-trou *n.m.* 'Peeping Tom', character who gets a kick out of spying through a keyhole. (In the feminine, the appellation can jocularly refer to a midwife.)

gueulante *n.f.* Yell, shout. *Pousser une gueulante*: To bawl. (An implication within the meaning is that it is a cry of protest or anger.)

gueulard *n.m.* **1** 'Bawler', vociferous character. **2** 'Loudmouth', 'brag', braggart. **3** 'Greedy guts', 'guzzler', glutton.

gueulard *adj.* **1** 'Loud', vociferous. **2** 'Loud-mouthed', 'braggy', self-congratulatory. **3** Greedy, gluttonous.

gueule *n.f.* (A) General meaning: mouth. **1** *Etre fort en gueule*: **a** To have a loud and booming voice. **b** To be 'foul-mouthed', to constantly use coarse language. **2** *Un coup de gueule:* An angry verbal outburst. *Leur vie est faite de coups de gueule*: Their life is just one perpetual slanging match. **3** *Ta gueule!* Shut your cake-hole! – Shut up! (also: *la ferme!*). **4** *Avoir la gueule de bois*: To 'have a hangover', to suffer the after-effects of a drinking bout. **5** *Etre une fine gueule*: To be something of a gourmet. **6** *Etre porté sur la gueule*: To be in the habit of over-indulging where food is concerned.

(B) General meaning: face. **1** *Avoir une sale gueule*: **a** To look 'down in the mouth', to look ill. **b** To 'have an ugly mush', to be afflicted with an ugly face. *Avoir une gueule à coucher dehors*: To have a face like the back of a bus (literally to have features that would even get you turned away from a hostel for down-and-outs). **2** *Faire la gueule*: To sulk, to act sullen and disapproving. *Quand il est sorti, il poussait une de ces gueules*: You should have seen the way he was scowling when he came out of the office. **3** *Se fendre la gueule*: To 'split one's sides laughing', to have a jolly good laugh (also: *se fendre le parapluie*). **4** *Se payer la gueule de quelqu'un*: To 'take the mickey', to poke fun at someone. **5** *Casser la gueule à quelqu'un*: To

'push someone's face in', to bash someone up. **6** *Se flanquer la gueule par terre*: **a** *(lit.)*: To fall flat on one's face, to fall to the ground. **b** *(fig.)*: To 'come a cropper', to 'come unstuck', to suffer a major setback. **7** *Les Gueules Cassées*: War veterans whose faces were disfigured in the war. (The appellation has become very familiar through a charity known by that name and indirectly sponsored by the *Loterie Nationale*.)

(C) General meaning: looks, appearance. **1** *Avoir de la gueule* (not necessarily of person): To look good. *C'était un spectacle qui avait vraiment de la gueule*: As a show it really stood out. *C'est une fille qui a de la gueule*: She really has what it takes! – There's a good-looking girl! **2** *Ça prend une sale gueule*: Things are looking grim – Matters are taking a turn for the worse.

gueulements *n.m.pl. Pousser des gueulements*: To 'raise Cain', to 'yell blue murder', to utter vociferous recriminations.

gueuler *v.intrans.* **1** To 'bawl', to 'bellow', to shout. *Gueuler au charron*: To 'raise Cain', to yell blue murder. **2** To protest vociferously (also: *rouspéter*).

gueuleton *n.m.* 'Nosh', slap-up meal. *On s'est tapé un de ces gueuletons!* We really treated ourselves to a four-star meal!

gueuletonner *v.intrans.* To 'have a nosh-up', to feast, to eat a lavish meal.

gueuloir *n.m.* 'Trap', 'gob', mouth.

gueusaille *n.f. (pej.) La gueusaille*: 'The riff-raff', the rabble. (The term can refer to all those we despise because of their poverty, their actions, etc.)

gueuse *n.f. Courir la gueuse*: To go out 'on the drag', to go gallivanting, to go out looking for women. (To many, this expression is twee and dated, and its revival is limited to a jocular context.)

gugusse *n.m.* 'Nincompoop', blithering idiot.

guibolle *n.f.* 'Pin', 'gamb', leg. *Il s'est retrouvé avec une guibolle dans le plâtre*: He ended up in plaster (after breaking his leg). *Tricoter* (also: *jouer*) *des guibolles*: To 'make a break', to hare off. *Ne pas tenir sur ses guibolles*: To be shaky on one's pins (through ill-health or over-drinking). *Se sentir mou des guibolles*: To feel weak-kneed.

guiche *n.f.* **1** Kiss-curl, ringlet of hair on forehead (also: *accroche-cœur*). **2** Amorous advance. *Faire une guiche*: To make a salacious move.

guichet *n.m.* **1** *Jouer à guichets fermés (th.)*: To play to a full house. **2** 'Trap', 'gob', mouth. *Refiler du guichet*: To have foul breath, to suffer from halitosis. **3** *Le petit guichet (joc.)*: The arse-hole, the anal sphincter (in a context of sodomous intercourse).

guignard *n.m.* **1** Unlucky so-and-so, character who seems to be plagued by bad luck. **2** 'Jonah', person who seems to generate bad luck.

guignard *adj.* **1** Unlucky. *Il est drôlement guignard!* He never gets a decent break! **2** 'Jinxy', bringing bad luck.

guigne *n.f.* 'Hoodoo', bad luck. *Avoir la guigne:* To have a run of bad luck. *Porter la guigne à quelqu'un:* To 'jinx' someone, to bring someone bad luck. *Ah ça, la guigne, on peut dire qu'il la porte!* He's as lucky as a barrow-load of broken mirrors!

guignol *n.m.* **1** Buffoon, one who overdoes the clowning. *Cesse de faire le guignol!* Stop arsing about! **2** Burlesque and chaotic state of affairs. *Quel guignol!* (also: *C'est un vrai guignol!*): What a performance! – What a ridiculous shambles! **3** Tribunal, court of law. *Passer au guignol:* To come up in front of the bench. **4** *(th.):* Prompt-box (where the prompter sits). **5** *(pl.):* *Les guignols:* 'The fuzz', the police. (Most of these meanings are directly related to the original meaning of *guignol*, with their Punch and Judy implications.) **6** 'Ticker', heart. *'y a son guignol qui fait des siennes:* The poor bugger's got a dicky ticker.

guignon *n.m.* 'Hoodoo', bad luck. *Avoir le guignon:* To be down on one's luck, to be clean out of luck.

guiguite *n.f.* (Child language): 'Willy', penis.

guili-guili *n.m.* (Child language): Tickle, tickling. *Bébé aime qu'on lui fasse guili-guili!* Diddums wants some tickles!

guilledou *n.m. Courir le guilledou:* To gad about, to go gallivanting.

guimauve *n.f.* **1** Over-sentimental ballad. *Tout son oseille il se l'est fait en roucoulant de la guimauve:* He made a packet crooning his syrupy songs. **2** Cheap sentimental novelette, literary twaddle. **3** 'Limp prick', impotent penis.

guimbarde *n.f.* 'Jalopy', 'bone-shaker', ram-shackle motor car. *On lui a fauché sa vieille guimbarde:* Someone pinched his old banger.

guimpette *n.f.* 'Pancake', flat cap (also: *gapette*).

guinche *n.m.* Unpretentious dance-hall. (Long before the age of the disco, the *guinche*, born of the *bal musette*, drew its faithful clientèle, fond of the tango and the waltz.)

guinche *n.f.* 'Shuffle', dance.

guincher *v.intrans.* To 'stomp', to dance.

guincheur *n.m.* Dancer. *C'est un guincheur de première:* He's a great little mover.

guindal *n.m.* 'Drink', glass of alcoholic beverage. *Ecluser un guindal:* To down one. *Avoir un guindal dans le pif:* To have had one too many.

guinde *n.f.* 'Wheels', 'motor', motor car. *Il passe souvent au guignol avec sa manie de faucher des guindes:* His taste for joy-riding regularly lands him in court.

guiser *v.intrans.* To 'screw', to fuck, to have intercourse.

guisot *n.m.* **1** 'Prick', 'cock', penis. **2** *(pl.):* 'Pins', 'gambs', legs.

guitare *n.f.* **1** Bidet. **2** *Pincer toujours la même guitare (fig.):* To keep on harping at the same thing, to go on and on about the same topic. **3** *Avoir une belle guitare* (of woman): To have a shapely figure.

guitoune *n.f.* **1** *(mil.):* Sentry-box. **2** Work-man's hut. **3** *(joc.):* 'Poky bed-sit', cramped flatlet.

gusse *n.m.* *(pej.):* 'Geezer', 'bloke', person. *Qui c'est, ce gusse?!* Who the hell is this nurk? (also: *gugusse*).

gy *adv.* **1** Yeah, yes. **2** *Faire gy:* To be on one's guard. *Fais gy!* Look out! – Take care! (also: *faire gaffe*).

gym' *n.f. (abbr. gymnastique):* **1** *La gym':* 'P.T.', gym, gymnastic exercises. **2** *Au pas de gym':* 'On the double', 'double-quick', at a brisk pace.

H

H *n.m. de l'H*: Heroin. *Depuis un certain temps, il se came à l'H*: He moved on to the hard stuff a while ago, and takes his trips on heroin.

habillé *n.m.* Uniformed policeman. *Les habillés*: 'The boys in blue'. *Après un interrogatoire en règle, ils l'ont refilé aux habillés*: After some thorough grilling, he was handed over to the uniformed branch.

habillé *past part. Etre habillé d'une peau de vache* (of villainous character): To 'look the part', to be as evil-looking as one is deemed to be.

habiller *v.trans.* (Police slang): To prepare a factual and irrefutable case against an apprehended culprit. This includes a comprehensive list of the charges, sworn testimonies, past criminal record and where possible, a signed confession. *Ils l'ont bien habillé, avec un casier comme le sien c'était couru*: What with his form, they made sure they got him to court with a watertight case.

habiller *v.pronom. S'habiller de quatre planches*: To 'get a wooden overcoat', to 'snuff it', to die.

habitants *n.m.pl.* Lice. *Avoir des habitants*: To have 'little friends', to be lice-ridden.

habitué *n.m.* 'Regular', regular customer.

hachesse *adj.inv.* 'Pissed', 'blotto', drunk. (In their *DICTIONNAIRE DU FRANÇAIS NON-CONVENTIONNEL*, Jacques Cellard and Alain Rey find the origin of the word in the military abbreviation *H.S.* short for *Hors Service*. The nearest English equivalent would be U/S, short for unserviceable.)

hallebardes *n.f.pl. Il tombe des hallebardes*: It's raining cats and dogs – It's pouring.

hambourgeois *n.m.* Plain-clothes officer, non-uniformed policeman. (The word is a pun on *en bourgeois*.)

han *n.m.* Cry accompanying a sudden and vigorous effort. *Pousser des han(s)*: To grunt and groan with effort.

hanneton *n.m. Ça n'est pas piqué des hannetons* (joc.): It's hunky-dory! – It's first-rate.

hareng *n.m.* **1** Ponce, pimp (also: *maquereau*). **2** (Racing slang): 'Nag', 'gawky steed', horse unlikely to win a race. **3** *La mare aux harengs* (joc.): 'The briny', the sea.

haricot *n.m.* **1** *Aller bouffer des haricots*: To 'do porridge', to 'do time', to go to jail. *L'hôtel des haricots*: 'The nick', 'the clink', jail. **2** *(pl.) Des haricots* (joc.): 'Peanuts', a meagre amount of money. *Je ne travaille pas pour des haricots, moi!* When I work, I want paying! **3** 'Bean', 'bonce', head. *Il commence à me courir sur le haricot!* He's really getting on my wick! **4** *(pl.)*: 'Tootsies', toes. **5** *La fin des haricots* (joc.): The limit, the end. *Côté fric, c'est la fin des haricots!* We've just about run out of money!

harnacher *v.trans.* To 'fix', to arrange by devious means. *Il a harnaché tout ça à sa façon*: He had it all rigged up to suit his purpose.

harnacher *v.trans.reflex.* To 'put on one's gladrags', to dress oneself for a special occasion.

harnais *n.m.* **1** *Reprendre le harnais*: To 'get back into harness', to go back to work. **2** *(pl.)*: 'Togs', clothes.

harnaquer *v.trans.* **1** To 'con', to 'diddle', to swindle. *Dans ces pays-là, ils ne pensent qu'à vous harnaquer*: In those countries, pulling a fast one on the tourists is a national pastime. **2** (Gambling slang): To 'fix' a game, to cheat. **3** To 'grass on someone', to betray. **4** To 'duff up', to 'bash up', to beat up. **5** To 'collar', to 'nick', to arrest. *C'est couru, au train où il va, il est bon pour se faire harnaquer par les cognes*: The way he's going about it, it won't be long before the fuzz pull him in.

harnaqueur *n.m.* 'Con-man', swindler.

harpie *n.f.* 'Cow', 'bitch', nasty woman.

harpigner *v.trans.* **1** To grab, to seize. **2** To 'nick', to 'pinch', to steal.

harpigner *v.trans.reflex.* To 'get into a tussle', to come to blows.

harponner *v.trans.* **1** To 'nab', to 'collar', to arrest. *Il s'est fait harponner bêtement*: The way he got pulled in was just too silly for words!

2 To 'buttonhole someone', to grab someone and talk him into the ground. *Si on fait pas un détour, on va encore se faire harponner par lui*: We'd better give him a wide berth, or it'll be 'yap, yap, yap' for the next half hour.

haute *n.f. La haute (abbr. la haute société)*: 'The upper crust', 'the smart set', the aristocracy of power and wealth. *Il est de la haute, lui*: He's a right toff.

hauteur *n.f.* **1** *Etre à la hauteur*: To be 'on the ball', to be 'all there', to know all the tricks. *Lui, au moins, il est à la hauteur!* There's no denying he's got what it takes! **2** *Prendre la hauteur du soleil (joc.)*: To 'have a swig', to raise a bottle to one's lips.

hebdo *n.m. (abbr. hebdomadaire)*: 'Weekly', magazine or newspaper appearing once a week.

herbe *n.f. de l'herbe*: 'Grass', cannabis.

Hérisson *Proper name. Le Hérisson*: A popular joke and cartoon periodical which had its greatest following in the 50s and 60s. Printed on cheap green paper, it was not renowned for its high-brow jokes.

hérisson *n.m. (pol.)*: 'Awkward customer', difficult suspect (literally, one who, like the hedgehog, is prickly to handle).

héro *n.m. de l'héro*: 'Horse', heroin.

heure *n.f.* **1** *L'heure H*: The moment of decision. **2** *A l'heure tapante*: 'On the dot', 'dead on time', punctually. **3** *Je ne te* (also: *je ne vous) demande pas l'heure qu'il est! (iron.)*: Mind your own bloody business! – Keep your questions to yourself! **4** *Avant l'heure, c'est pas l'heure; après l'heure, c'est plus l'heure! (iron.)*: Being early is no good either, you have to be on time! (This popular catchphrase is often uttered in a jocular context.)

hic *n.m. Voilà le hic!* Aye, there's the rub! *Il y a un hic*: There's a snag!

hier *adv. Je ne suis pas né d'hier!* I'm not as green as I'm cabbage-looking! – I'm not as stupid as you think! *Ça ne date pas d'hier*: It's ancient history!

hirondelle *n.f.* **1** 'Freeloader', 'gate-crasher', character who goes to parties uninvited. **2** Bicycle-riding policeman. (This picturesque appellation aptly describes the policeman on his bicycle with his flapping cape.) **3** *Les hirondelles volent bas! (iron.)*: There's trouble brewing!

histoire *n.f.* **1** 'Tale', silly story. *Une histoire à la mie de pain* (also: *une histoire à dormir debout*): A cock-and-bull story. *Tout ça, c'est des histoires!* It's a load of codswallop! *C'est toute une histoire!* You'll never believe this! **2** *La belle histoire! (iron.)*: So what! – Who cares! **3** *Histoire de*: Just for the sake of. *Histoire de rire*: Just for a laugh. **4** *(pl.)*: 'Fuss', trouble, problems. *Avoir des*

histoires: To be 'in stuck', to be in trouble. *Chercher des histoires à quelqu'un*: To go out of one's way to thwart someone. **5** *Avoir ses histoires*: To 'have the decorators in', to have a menstrual period.

hiviot *n.m.* (also: *hivio*): Winter.

holdopeur *n.m. (joc.)*: 'Stick-up specialist', armed-robbery gangster (also: *braqueur*).

homard *n.m. Pinces de homard (joc.)*: Bicycle clips.

hommasse *n.f.* 'Butch-looking' woman. (The word is often used when referring to a lesbian with masculine features.)

hommasse *adj.* (of woman): 'Butch', masculine-looking.

homme *n.m.* **1** *Mon homme*: My 'hubby', my 'better half', my husband. **2** *Messieurs les hommes* (Underworld slang): The tough guys. (The appellation has 'macho' connotations within the *milieu*.) **3** *Homme-orchestre*: 'Jack-of-all-trades', character who can turn his hand to almost anything. **4** *Ça ne nourrit pas son homme (joc.)*: There's no money in it.

hommelette *n.f. (joc.)*: **1** 'Weed', weakling. **2** 'Nancy-boy', 'pansy', effeminate homosexual. (The word, a pun on *omelette*, is pejorative.)

homo *n.m.* 'Fag', 'queer', homosexual. (In recent years, *homo* has lost its derogatory connotation as it has become the abbreviation for *homophile* instead of *homosexuel* and is an accepted term within the gay community.)

homo *adj.inv.* 'Pouffy', 'queer', homosexual.

hôpital *n.m. C'est l'hôpital qui se moque de la charité (iron.)*: It's a case of the pot calling the kettle black.

horaire *n.m.* Hourly-paid worker.

horripilant *adj.* 'Infuriating', 'maddening', exasperating. *C'est horripilant cette manie qu'il a de se bouffer les ongles!* His persistent nail-biting drives me bonkers!

horripiler *v.trans.* To 'infuriate', to 'madden', to exasperate.

hosto *n.m.* Infirmary, hospital.

hôtel *n.m.* **1** *Hôtel de passe*: 'Knocking-shop', hotel used by prostitutes (also: *maison de passe*). **2** *Coucher à l'hôtel du cul tourné*: To sulk in bed, to sleep back-to-back with one's partner.

hotte *n.f.* **1** 'Wheels', 'motor', motor car. **2** 'Cab', taxi-cab.

hotu *n.m. (pej.)*: 'Pillock', 'nincompoop', idiot.

housard *n.m.* (also: *houzard*): Voyeur's peep-hole in hotel or public convenience.

houste *interj. Allez houste!* Hop it! – Be off with you!

H.S. *adj. (abbr. Hors Service)*: 'U/S', unserviceable, out of order.

hublots *n.m.pl. (joc.)*: **1** 'Peepers', 'lamps', eyes. **2** 'Specs', 'glasses', spectacles.

huile *n.f.* **1** 'Big shot', 'big nob', top person. *Les huiles*: 'The upper crust', the high and mighty of society. **2** *de l'huile*: 'Brass', 'loot', money (perhaps because it oils the works). **3** *Mettre de l'huile sur le feu (fig.)*: To 'stir it', to make matters worse (when people are arguing). **4** *Ça baigne dans l'huile!* Things are going swimmingly! – Everything's just fine! **5** *Huile de coude*: 'Elbow grease', hard work. **6** *à l'huile (adj.exp.)*: 'Lousy', useless, worthless. *Il m'a sorti des excuses à l'huile*: He came out with a load of phoney excuses.

huit *n.m.inv. Faire des huit*: To go zig-zagging about. (The expression originates from the track-marks made by a swerving vehicle.)

huit *num.adj. Les trois huit*: Shift work. *Faire les trois huit*: To work shifts.

huître *n.f.* **1** 'Gob', clot of phlegm (also: *glaviot*). **2** 'Burk', 'nincompoop', blithering idiot. **3** *Etre plein comme une huître*: To be 'pissed as a newt', to be blind drunk.

humecter *v.trans.reflex.* To 'wet one's whistle', to have a drink (also: *s'humecter le gosier*).

humeur *n.f. Etre d'une humeur massacrante*: To be in a foul mood.

huppé *adj.* **1** 'Loaded', 'stinking rich', very wealthy. **2** 'Hoity-toity', 'uppity', affected with a sense of superiority.

huppés *n.m.pl. Les huppés*: 'The swells', 'the nobs', the wealthy and powerful.

hure *n.f.* 'Mush', 'mug', face. *Se gratter la hure*: To 'scrape the stubble', to have a shave.

hurfe *adj.inv.* (also: *hurf*): 'A-1', 'tip-top', first-rate. *On s'est payé un gueuleton drôlement hurfe*: We had ourselves a slap-up meal.

hurleur *n.m.* Loudspeaker.

hurluberlu *n.m.* 'Scatterbrain', erratically absent-minded person.

hussarde *A la hussarde (adv.exp.)*: Inconsiderately, without manners. (The expression *faire l'amour à la hussarde* describes the rough-and-tumble manner of an inconsiderate lover.)

hypocrite *adj. Faire quelque chose à l'hypocrite*: To do something without warning. *Il nous a fait ça à l'hypocrite*: He sprung this on us.

hystérique *n.f.* 'Nympho', nymphomaniac.

I

I *n.m.* **1** *Etre droit comme un I*: To be as straight as a ramrod. **2** *Mettre les points sur les i*: To dot the i's and cross the t's. *Il faut toujours lui mettre les points sur les i!* You have to explain everything to him.

ici *adv. Je vois ça d'ici! (joc. & iron.)*: I can just picture it! – I can just imagine the events!

icigo *adv.* Here. *C'est icigo qu'on s'est rencontrés*: This is where we met.

I.D. *n.f.* **1** *(abbr. Indication Durée) Appeler avec I.D.*: To make an ADC call, to book a telephone call through the operator whose brief it is to inform you immediately after completion of its cost. **2** *Une I.D. 19, une I.D. 21*: Well-known models of cars manufactured by Citroën from the late 50s through to the 70s.

idée *n.f.* **1** *Se faire des idées*: To 'imagine things', to have illusions about oneself or matters in general. *Mais non, tu te fais des idées, on t'aime bien!* You've got it all wrong, we're very fond of you! **2** *Se changer les idées*: To have a break (in order to forget one's worries). *Un voyage, ça te changera les idées*: You should go away for a bit, a change is as good as a rest! **3** *Avoir de la suite dans les idées*: To know what one wants, to be forceful in following one's original train of thought. **4** *Avoir une idée de derrière la tête*: To have 'a niggly inkling', to have a lurking suspicion. **5** *Quand il a une idée dans la tête, il ne l'a pas ailleurs!* He's as pig-headed as they come! **6** *A mon idée*: 'To my mind', in my opinion. *A mon idée, tout ça va nous causer des emmerdements!* If you ask me, this is going to bring us a load of trouble! **7** *Une idée de*: 'A teeny bit', 'soupçon' of, a very small quantity. *Il y a une idée de cognac dans votre sauce*: I reckon there's some brandy in that sauce of yours!

idem *adj. C'est idem au cresson*: It's six of one, half a dozen of the other – It's very much the same thing.

I.J. *Proper name. (abbr. Service de l'Identité Judiciaire) L'I.J.*: The department dealing with criminal records at Police Headquarters.

illico *adv.* 'Right away', straight away, instantly. *Il me faut ça illico!* I want this now, if not sooner! (also: *presto*).

image *n.f.* 'Note', banknote. *Si t'es sage, t'auras des images! (joc.)*: If you play your cards right, you'll get some money! (If you do what you are told you will be rewarded.)

imbitable *adj. (joc.)*: **1** (of person): 'Insufferable', unbearable. **2** (of problem, situation): 'Unfathomable', incomprehensible.

imbuvable *adj.* (of person): 'Impossible', insufferable. *Il est vraiment imbuvable, ton mari*: I can't stand the sight of that husband of yours!

impair *n.m.* **1** Gaffe, 'boob', blunder. *Faire un impair*: To put one's foot in it. *Quand tu fais un impair, toi, c'est la belle gaffe*: When you boob, you really put both feet in it! **2** Dirty trick. *Faire un impair à quelqu'un*: To do the dirty on someone.

impasse *n.f. (sch.)*: Calculated exam risk whereby a student shortcuts his (revision) work-load by not studying part of the syllabus. *Il a fait de ces impasses et n'a pas été recalé!* The lucky devil! He passed his exam in spite of skipping most of the programme.

impayable *adj.* 'Priceless', hilarious, very funny. *Sur scène, il est impayable*: On the stage, he's just too funny for words.

impec *adj. (abbr. impeccable)*: 'Super-duper', fantastic, incredibly good.

impensable *adj.* Out of the question. *Un truc pareil, c'est impensable!* No way will I accept that kind of thing!

imper *n.m. (abbr. imperméable)*: 'Mac', mackintosh, raincoat.

imposer *v.trans. En imposer à quelqu'un*: To make someone feel inferior. *En uniforme, qu'est-ce qu'il en impose!* When he's out of his civvies, he certainly loves strutting!

incendier *v.trans.* To 'haul someone over the coals', to reprimand. *Il s'est drôlement fait incendier par sa belle-doche*: His mother-in-law gave him one hell of a rocket.

incollable *adj.* (of person): 'Unstumpable', unbeatable. (This non-pejorative word is usually uttered when referring to someone who knows all the answers.)

incondisse *n.m.* *(corr.abbr.* *inconditionnel)*: Character who will never compromise. *Les incondisses de la droite*: The Right-wing diehards.

inconnoblé *adj.* Unknown, never heard of (also: *inconnobré*).

incruster *v.pronom.* To 'take root', to outstay one's welcome.

indécrottable *n.m.* 'Boor', oaf, uncouth character.

indécrottable *adj.* 'Boorish', 'oafish', coarse. *Il est indécrottable, il sent encore sa campagne*: City life certainly hasn't added any lustre to his manners!

indérouillable *adj.* 1 (of machinery): 'Jammed', stuck fast. 2 (of woman): Un-titillating, sexually uninspiring.

index *n.m.* *Mettre à l'index*: To blacklist. *On est bon pour une mise à l'index générale*: It looks like a general boycott.

indic *n.m.* *(abbr. indicateur de police)*: 'Grass', police informant.

indicatif *n.m.* 1 Signature tune. 2 *Change d'indicatif!* Stop harping on! – Don't go on and on about the same thing!

indien *n.m.* *(pej.)*: 'Cove', 'geezer', suspect person.

indigestion *n.f.* *En avoir une indigestion (fig.)*: To be 'fed up to the back teeth with', to have had more than enough of something. *J'en ai une indigestion de ses jérémiades!* I've had all I can take of her moaning!

indiqué *past part.* *C'est pas indiqué! (iron.)*: I don't recommend it! – It doesn't sound like a good idea!

infirme *adj.* *Etre infirme des méninges*: To be 'soft in the head', to be rather simple-minded.

influence *n.f.* *Faire quelque chose à l'influence*: To 'pull strings', to bring pressure to bear.

info *n.f.* *(abbr. information)*: 1 'Tip', useful bit of news. 2 *Les infos*: The news (on radio or television).

infourgable *adj.* Unsaleable. *Tout ce fourbi est infourgable*: We'll never flog all this clobber.

ingénue *n.f.* *Jouer les ingénues* (of woman): To put on a 'butter-wouldn't-melt-in-her-mouth' act, to play the innocent.

innocents *n.m.pl.* *Aux innocents, les mains pleines! (iron.)*: Some people have all the luck!

inox *n.m.* *(abbr. acier inoxydable)*: Stainless steel.

inspecteur *n.m.* *Inspecteur des travaux finis (joc. & iron)*: Work-shy character (literally the kind of person who turns up when the job is finished only to utter words of wisdom).

installer *v.intrans.* *En installer*: To 'throw one's weight about', to 'swank', to show off.

instantané *n.m.* 'Snap', snapshot, photograph.

Institut Proper name. *(abbr. Institut Médico-Légal)*: *L'Institut* is an up-market name for the Paris city morgue.

inter *n.m.* 1 *L'inter (abbr. l'interurbain)*: Regional telephone service manned by operators. 2 *(abbr. France-Inter)*: National radio station broadcasting light music and chat programmes. 3 *(abbr. intermédiaire)*: Go-between (usually where shady activities are concerned).

interdit *adj.* *Interdit de séjour*: Prohibited (through a court order) from entering certain urban areas. (The *interdiction de séjour* is an added penalty preventing convicted criminals from entering certain areas where they might team up again with old acquaintances. *Un interdit de séjour*: One who has been served with such a restrictive order.)

intéresser *v.trans.* *Cause toujours, tu m'intéresses! (joc. & iron.)*: You can say what you like, I'm not listening! (This antiphrastic statement is usually uttered under one's breath with profound sarcasm.)

intérêt *n.m.* *'y a intérêt à*: It would be wise (to do this). *Chez eux, 'y a intérêt à pas manquer la bouffe*: If you know what's good for you, you're there at mealtimes!

intime *n.m.* *Se fourrager l'intime (joc.)*: To have a good crotch-scratch.

intoxico *n.m.* 'Junkie', drug addict (also: *toxico*).

intrigue *n.f.* *Nouer une intrigue*: To begin an (amorous) affair.

introduire *v.trans.* *L'introduire à quelqu'un*: To 'take someone in', to con someone. *Se la laisser introduire*: To get taken for a ride.

invalo *n.m.* Invalid, handicapped person.

Invaloches Proper name. *Les Invaloches*: The *quartier des Invalides* in Paris.

invitation *n.f.* *Ça a été l'invitation à la valse! (iron.)*: There was certainly aggro in the air! (The ironic jocularity of the expression stems from the fact that a popular tune of that name has echoed through dance-halls for many decades.)

invite *n.f.* 1 'Invite', invitation. 2 *Faire des invites*: To make (amorous) advances.

I.P. *n.m.* *(abbr. Inspecteur Principal)*: Chief Inspector of police.

isoloir *n.m.* Urinal, lavatory cubicle. (The humour stems from the original meaning of polling booth.)

italique *n.m.* *Avoir les jambes en italique (joc.)*: To be bandy-legged.

Italo *n.m.* 'Itie', Italian (also: *Italgo, Rital*).

itou *adv.* Likewise, also. *Moi itou!* Me too! *Pour pas se faire remarquer on a fait itou*: So as to blend in with the scenery, we did like the others.

Ivans *n.m.pl. Les Ivans*: The 'Russkies', the Russians.

ivoire *n.m. Taquiner l'ivoire (joc.)*: To 'tickle the ivories', to play the piano.

ivrogne *n.m. Serment d'ivrogne*: 'New Year's resolution', promise that has little chance of being kept.

J

J.3 *n.m. & f.* Teenager. (This World War II appellation has not altogether died out, although few remember that it was a ration card grouping. *Les J.3*, a successful play and novel, did a lot to perpetuate its use.)

jab *n.m.* Punch in the stomach.

jabot *n.m.* **1** 'Belly', stomach. *Se remplir le jabot*: To 'have a good blow-out', to 'have a tuck-in', to fill one's belly. **2** *Se pousser du jabot*: To 'strut about', to 'put on airs', to show off (also: *enfler le jabot*).

jaboter *v.intrans.* To 'yap', to 'jaw', to talk endlessly.

jacasse *n.f.* 'Gas-bag', 'chatterbox', over-talkative person.

jacasser *v.intrans.* To 'yap', to 'jaw', to talk endlessly.

jacassin *n.m.* 'Chit-chat', light conversation of no great significance. (It could be said that Pierre Daninos gave the word a new lease of life when he wrote his novel *LE JACASSIN*.)

jack *n.m.* (Cabbies' slang): Taximeter.

jacob *n.m.* Clay pipe (originally the kind which had a bowl moulded in the shape of a head).

jacot *n.m.* 'Jemmy', crowbar.

jacques *n.m.* **1** 'Jemmy', crowbar. **2** 'Prick', 'cock', penis. **3** *Faire le jacques*: To 'act the giddy goat', to play the fool. *Cesse donc de faire le jacques!* Stop arsing about!

jactage *n.m.* 'Yackety-yack', 'rabbiting', meaningless chatter.

jactance *n.f.* *La jactance*: The gift of the gab. *La jactance, c'est son blot!* He could talk the hind legs off a donkey!

jacter *v.intrans.* **1** To speak, to talk. *Jacter argot*: To talk slang. **2** To 'yap', to 'jabber on', to talk volubly. *Qu'est-ce qu'elle jacte, elle!* She must have been vaccinated with a gramophone needle! **3** To malign, to talk ill of.

jaffe *n.f.* 'Tuck', 'grub', food. *Ici la jaffe est bonne*: We get reasonable nosh here! *On s'est tapé une de ces jaffes! We had a slap-up meal!*

jaja *n.m.* 'Plonk', red wine. *Ecluser un jaja*: To knock back some vino.

jalmince *adj.* (*corr. jaloux*): Jealous.

jambe *n.f.* **1** *Avoir les jambes en manches de veste*: To be 'bandy', to be bow-legged. **2** *Tricoter des jambes*: To hare along. **3** *Tirer la jambe*: **a** To limp. **b** To 'come the old soldier', to feign ill-health. **4** *Ça vaut mieux qu'une jambe cassée (joc.)*: It's better than a kick in the pants. **5** *Une partie de jambes en l'air*: A bit of 'how's-your-father?', sexual intercourse. **6** *Tenir la jambe à quelqu'un*: **a** To prolong a conversation unnecessarily. **b** To bore the pants off someone. **7** *Faire quelque chose par-dessus la jambe*: To do something 'any old how' (in an off-hand, careless manner). **8** *S'en aller sur une jambe*: To have only one (alcoholic) drink. **9** *Ça te fait une belle jambe! (iron.)*: Fat lot of good it does you! – That's not much good, is it?! **10** *N'aller que d'une jambe* (of business): To be in dire straits. *Chez eux, ça ne va que d'une jambe*: The old firm's on its last legs. **11** *Faire jambe de bois*: To leave without paying. **12** *La jambe! (interj.)*: Bugger off! – Piss off! – Get lost! **13** 100-franc note. *Une demi-jambe*: 50 francs, a 50-franc note.

jamber *v.trans.* To bore the pants off someone. *Qu'est-ce qu'il me jambe!* He's a right pain!

jambeur *n.m.* 'Bore', boring person (also: *jambard*).

jambon *n.m.* **1** Mandolin. *Gratter du jambon*: To play that instrument. **2** (*pl.*): 'Hams', thighs. *Une partie de quatre jambons* (also: *quatre jambons au même clou*): Sexual intercourse.

jambonné *past part.* *Etre bien jambonnée* (of woman): To have a nice pair of legs. *D'accord, elle est bien jambonnée, mais quelle gueule!* Nice legs, shame about the face!

jambonneaux *n.m.pl.* 'Hams', thighs.

jante *n.f.* *Rouler sur la jante*: **a** To be 'dead-beat', to feel worn-out. **b** To be 'loony', 'bonkers', to be drifting into madness. (The expression originates from the register of cycling, a flat tyre bringing the rim of a wheel in contact with the road.)

jaquette *n.f. Etre de la jaquette (flottante)*: To be a 'queer', to be homosexual. (The witticism lies in the strategically-placed slit in the coat-tails.)

jar *n.m.* (also: *jars*): Slang. *Dévider le jar*: To speak argot.

jardin *n.m.* 1 *Le jardin des refroidis*: The 'boneyard', the cemetery (also: *le boulevard des allongés*). 2 *Va voir au jardin si j'y suis! (iron.)*: Go and get lost! (while I have a private conversation). 3 *Faire du jardin*: To 'run down', to speak ill of. 4 *Aller au jardin*: To get involved in a confidence trick.

jardiner *v.trans. & intrans.* 1 To 'pull to pieces', to 'run down', to disparage. 2 To 'shoot a line', to 'draw the long bow', to exaggerate.

jardinier *n.m. Etre comme le chien du jardinier*: To be a 'wet blanket', to be something of a kill-joy.

jarret *n.m. Couper les jarrets à quelqu'un (fig.)*: To 'take the wind out of someone's sails', to dash someone's spirits.

jaser *v.intrans.* 1 To 'yap', to 'jabber on', to talk volubly. 2 To 'blab', to divulge a secret. 3 To 'run down', to talk ill of.

jaspin *n.m.* 'Chit-chat', idle conversation (also: *jaspinage*).

jaspiner *v.intrans.* 1 To speak, to talk. *Il jaspine comme un de la haute*: He talks like a toff. 2 To 'chew the fat', to chat.

jaspineur *n.m.* 1 'Yapper', perpetual 'chinwagger', character who just never stops talking. 2 'Mouthpiece', barrister.

jauger *v.trans. (fig.)*: To 'weigh up', to evaluate.

jaune *n.m.* 1 'Scab', 'blackleg', person who works after a strike has been called. 2 'Cowardy-custard', funk. 3 Cuckold.

jaune *adv. Rire jaune*: To 'laugh on the wrong side of one's face', to venture a half-hearted laugh when confronted with adversity.

jaunet *n.m.* 1 *(pej.)*: 'Chink', Chinese person. 2 (30s and 40s slang): 20-franc gold piece.

jaunisse *n.f. En faire une jaunisse*: To be green with envy.

java *n.f.* 1 'Bender', 'beano', spree. *Partir en java*: To paint the town red. *On a fait une de ces javas*: We whooped it up. 2 Thrashing, 'rousting', beating-up. *Filer une java*: To work someone over. 3 'Break-out', escape from jail.

javanais *n.m.* 'Av-slang'. (*Javanais* is a cant, a special humorous, would-be secret language born in the 1860s and still alive and kicking today. Its principle is to introduce certain syllables like *pi*, *av* or *va* into words to create an element of confusion for the non-speaker; *jardin* becomes *javardin*; *oiseau* becomes *oipiseau*. Another distortive process, known as *verlen*, is to invert letters and syllables; *calibre* becomes *brelica*, etc.)

javotte *n.f.* 'Yapper', 'chatterbox', over-talkative woman.

jazz-tango *n.m., n.f. & adj. Etre (un) jazz-tango*: To be A.C./D.C., to lead a mixed hetero and homosexual life (also: *être à voile et à vapeur*).

jean-foutre *n.m. (pej.)*: 1 'Lazy git', idle fellow. 2 'Pillock', 'nincompoop', idiot.

jean-jean *n.m.* 'Ninny', simpleton.

jeannette *n.f.* Sleeve-board, small ironing board.

jean-nu-tête *n.m. (joc.)*: 'Prick', 'cock', penis.

jecte *n.f.* Tear, tear-drop.

je-m'en-foutisme *n.m.inv.* 'Don't-give-a-damn', 'couldn't-care-less' attitude (also: *je-m'en-fichisme*).

je-sais-tout *n.m. Un je-sais-tout*: A 'know-all', a character who seems to have an answer to everything.

jèse *n.m.* Jesuit.

jésus *n.m.* 1 Sweet young child. 2 *Etre en jésus*: To be 'starkers', to be stark naked. 3 Type of *saucisson*, dry sausage, manufactured in Lyon.

jet *n.m. Parler à jet continu*: To 'spout', to talk non-stop.

jetard *n.m.* 'Clink', 'nick', prison (also: *chtard*).

jetée *n.f.* 100 francs and multiples thereof. *Une demi-jetée*: Fifty francs.

jeter *v.trans.* 1 To 'bounce', to 'chuck out', to kick someone out. *Il s'est fait jeter en beauté!* He got the heave-ho, no messing! 2 *Jeter quelqu'un dedans*: To 'drop someone in it', to land someone in trouble. 3 *S'en jeter un derrière la cravate*: To toss back a drink. 4 *Jeter son venin* (also: *jeter la purée*): To 'juice off', to ejaculate. 5 *N'en jetez plus, la cour est pleine! (joc. & iron.)*: Whoa with the compliments! – That's more than enough praise! (This expression is usually directed at someone bestowing lavish praise or compliments. It originates from the world of street-singers who, when times were hard, performed in the backyards of apartment blocks hoping that the flat-dwellers would throw them a few coins. A glut of coins seems an unlikely occurrence!) 6 *En jeter*: To 'graft', to work hard. *Pour en jeter, il en jette, il ne craint pas la besogne, lui!* You've got to hand it to him, he's no shirker! 7 *La jeter mal*: To 'look bad', to give a bad impression. *Elle la jetait mal dans ses fringues rapiécées*: She certainly looked no fashion model in her stitched-up hand-me-downs! 8 *Ça, c'est jeté!* That's the stuff to give 'em! – That's telling them!

jeton *n.m.* 1 Knock, blow. *Filer un jeton*: To 'biff', to hit someone or something. *Prendre un jeton* (of car): To get 'pranged', to receive a dent. 2 *(pej.)*: 'Geezer', 'bloke', person. *Qui c'est, ce jeton avec qui t'étais hier?* Who's that character I saw you with yesterday? *Vieux jeton*:

'Old fuddy-duddy', geriatric man. *Faux jeton*: 'Two-timer', two-faced character. **3** *Etre faux comme un jeton*: To be 'phoney to the core', to be as devious as they come. **4** *Avoir un jeton avec quelqu'un*: To 'click' (on the amorous plane) with someone. **5** *Prendre un jeton*: To get a salacious eyeful, to ogle a sexy sight. (The voyeurish origin of this expression lies in the days when many *hôtels de passes* had peepholes and eager lechers could get their money's worth of *un jeton de mate*.) **6** *Avoir les jetons*: To 'have the shits', to be 'in a blue funk', to be frightened. **7** *Flanquer les jetons à quelqu'un*: To 'put the wind up someone', to frighten someone.

jetouille *n.f.* *Avoir la jetouille*: To 'have the shits', to be frightened (also: *chtouille*).

jeu *n.m.* **1** *Vieux jeu*: 'Old hat', old-fashioned. *Tout ça, c'est vieux jeu!* This is just too dated for words! **2** *Ce n'est pas de jeu!* That's not cricket! – That's quite unfair! **3** *Cacher son jeu* (*fig.*): To 'play one's cards close to one's chest', to be secretive about one's actions. **4** *Faire le jeu* (of prostitute): To be 'on the game'. **5** *Faire le grand jeu*: To have a 'no holds barred' sex-romp.

jeudi *n.m.* *Dans la semaine des quatre jeudis* (*joc. & iron.*): 'In a month of Sundays', 'once in a blue moon', probably never. *On verra ça dans la semaine des quatre jeudis!* Yes, and pigs might fly before we see that!

jeunabre *n.m.* (*pej.*): Youth, young person. *Les jeunabres d'aujourd'hui, faut se les farcir!* The young these days are a pain in the neck!

jeunabre *adj.* 'Wet behind the ears', young and immature.

jeune *adj.* Not quite enough, insufficient. *Dix briques pour se lancer, c'est un peu jeune*: Ten grand for setting up in business isn't really much.

jeunesse *n.f.* *Une jeunesse*: A 'biddy', a young and immature girl.

jeunot *n.m.* 'Greenhorn', character who is still wet behind the ears.

jeunot *adj.inv.* Young and inexperienced.

jèze *n.m.* Jesuit.

ji *adv.* Yeah, yes. *Ji-go!* Right-on! – O.K.!

jinjin *n.m.* **1** 'Nous', 'grey matter', brain. *N'avoir rien dans le jinjin* (also: *avoir un courant d'air dans le jinjin*): To have nothing up top. **2** 'Plonk', cheap red wine.

Job *Proper name.* Brand of cigarette-paper for smokers who 'roll their own'. (Like many brand-names, it has become generic for any make.)

job *n.m.* **1** Job, position, employment. *Mon vieux est à son job*: My old man's out earning a crust. **2** (*abbr. jobard*): 'Gull', 'noodle', simpleton. **3** *Monter le job à quelqu'un*: To 'take someone in', to dupe someone. *Se monter le job*: To 'kid oneself', to imagine things.

jobard *n.m.* **1** 'Gull', 'mug', simpleton. *Des jobards comme lui, on n'en fait plus*: You won't find more gullible than him! **2** 'Nutter', loony character.

jobard *adj.* **1** Puzzled, disconcerted. **2** Naïve and ridiculous. **3** 'Loony', 'potty', mad.

jobarder *v.trans.* To dupe, to fool.

jobré *adj.* 'Cracked', 'unhinged', mad.

jockey *n.m.* *Faire jockey*: To go without food, to diet for financial reasons. (*Le régime jockey* is the kind of strict diet to which only dedicated weight-watchers will adhere because it cuts out fats and carbohydrates.)

joice *adj.* 'Cheery', pleased, happy. *Elle était toute joice à l'idée de lui faire une vacherie*: The idea of playing a dirty trick on him brought a grin to her face.

joie *n.f.* *Fille de joie*: Prostitute. (The appellation is very much a bourgeois term describing the 'ladies of the night'.)

joint *n.m.* **1** 'Reefer', 'joint', cigarette containing hashish. **2** *Trouver le joint*: To find a solution (to a problem or difficulty). *A force de chercher, on trouve le joint*: Where there's a will there's a way! **3** *Péter un joint de culasse*: To blow one's top and by so doing, appear to be on the verge of madness. (The English expression 'to blow a gasket' is equally apt and colloquial.) **4** *Aller au joint*: To 'have a fuck', to have intercourse.

jojo *n.m.* **1** 'Pain in the arse', 'awkward bugger', tricky character. **2** *Un affreux (petit) jojo*: A 'Dennis-the-menace' character, an awful brat. **3** *Faire le jojo*: To 'act the clever dick', to 'play the smart-aleck', to behave like a regular know-all. **4** *Faire son jojo*: To act the 'Holy-Joe', to put on a puritan front.

jojo *adj. inv.* Fine, beautiful, good, etc. (This adjective is more often than not tainted with a degree of irony, and seldom found without a preceding negative or moderator.) *Sa nana n'est vraiment pas jojo*: That bird of his looks a right little scrubber. *Comme patacaisse, c'était jojo*: That was a right royal cock-up!

joli *n.m.* (*iron.*) *Ça, c'est du joli!* That's a bloody disgrace! *Comme de coutume, il a fait du joli!* In that inimitable way of his, he's made a balls of it!

joli *adj.* (*iron.*): Just fine! – Nice! *Eh ben, me v'là joli!* Another fine mess you've got me into! *En voilà un joli salaud!* He's a right prime bastard!

joliment *adv.* *Je me suis joliment emmerdé*: I had a bloody awful time! *Je suis joliment content*: I'm as pleased as Punch!

jonc *n.m.* **1** Gold. **2** 'Brass', 'dough', money. **3** *Se peler le jonc*: To be bored stiff. (Georgette Marks, in her DICTIONARY OF SLANG AND COLLOQUIALISMS, lexicalizes this expression as: to be chilled to the bone.) **4** 'Joystick', 'cock', penis.

joncaille *n.f.* **1** 'Brass', 'gelt', money. **2** *De la joncaille*: Assorted items of gold jewellery.

joncailler *n.m.* Small-time jeweller (more a *bijoutier* than a *joaillier*).

jongler *v.intrans.* **1** To 'miss out on something', to be deprived of what one should be receiving. *On nous a fait jongler du dessert*: When it came to getting our afters, we had to lump it. *Si on se méfie pas, il va nous faire jongler nos parts*: If we don't keep tabs on the share-out, our loot'll end up in his pocket. **2** *Savoir jongler avec les chiffres*: To have a canny way with figures (to be able to balance the diciest accounts).

jongleur *n.m.* 'Con-man', trickster.

jongleuse *n.f.* 'Light-fingered' check-out girl (in supermarket, department store; the kind of person who is adept at some fiddling at the day's accounts).

jorne *n.m.* Day, working day or unit of twenty-four hours. *On a encore cinq jornes à tirer ici*: It'll be another five days graft before we're finished here.

Joseph *Proper name. Faire son Joseph*: To play the 'Holy-Joe', to put on virtuous airs.

Joséphine *Proper name. Faire sa Joséphine*: To put on virtuous airs (also: *jouer sa Sainte Nitouche*).

jouasse *n.f.* (Drugs): 'Kick', powerful thrill experienced after a 'take'.

joue *n.f. Se caler les joues*: To 'stuff one's face', to have a jolly good tuck-in.

jouer *v.intrans. & trans.* **1** *Jouer des compas*: To 'beetle off', to 'skedaddle', to move niftily away. (There is a plethora of expressions using the verb *jouer* with that same meaning: *jouer des flûtes, des guibolles*; also: *jouer rip, jouer la fille de l'air*, etc.) **2** *Jouer l'homme* (Football): To go for the player (not the ball). **3** *Jouer sur le velours* *(fig.)*: To take no risks. (The expression originates in the language of gambling.) **4** *Jouer 'parlez-moi d'amour' (joc.)*: To give repeated peals on a doorbell as if scanning the first bars of that famous tune. **5** *A toi de jouer! (fig.)*: The ball's in your court! – It's up to you to make a move now!

joufflu *n.m.* 'Sit-me-down', 'botty', behind.

jouge *n.m. En moins de jouge*: Before you could say Jack Robinson – In two shakes of a lamb's tail – Straight away (also: *en deux temps, trois mouvements*).

jouir *v.intrans.* To 'come', to have an orgasm.

jouissance *n.f.* **1** Orgasm. **2** *Je te souhaite bien de la jouissance! (iron.)*: You're welcome to it! (I don't reckon you are going to enjoy that.)

jouissant *adj.* 'Titillating', sexually exciting.

jouisseur *n.m.* Fun-loving character who savours the many pleasures of life as if they were sexual experiences; *jouisseuse* has a more sexual connotation.

jour *n.m.* **1** *Le jour J*: 'Make-or-break day', the day of reckoning, the day of decision. **2** *Etre long comme un jour sans pain*: **a** To be as long as a wet weekend. **b** (of person): To be as tall as a lamp-post. **3** *C'est clair comme le jour*: It's as clear as daylight – There's not the shadow of a doubt (also: *c'est clair comme de l'eau de roche*). **4** *Ce n'est pas tous les jours dimanche!* Life isn't a bowl of cherries! **5** *Au jour d'aujourd'hui*: Mediocre journalese expression roughly equivalent to: 'at this moment in time'. **6** *Demain il fera jour!* (about task one is reluctant to continue with): Tomorrow is another day! **7** *Etre dans ses mauvais jours*: To be having one of one's 'off-days'. **8** *Ça craint le jour!* (of goods that seem to have fallen off the back of the proverbial lorry): It's hot stuff, you know! (It could do with not being seen.)

journaleux *n.m.* *(pej.)*: 'Ink-shitter', 'hack', journalist.

journanche *n.f.* Day. (Not just day-time, but also, sometimes, a period of 24 hours.)

joyeuses *n.f.pl.* 'Goolies', 'cobblers', testicles.

juge *n.m. Juge de paix*: 'Rod', 'shooter', handgun. *Passé minuit, il se sentait tout nu sans son juge de paix*: Gone midnight, he felt none too happy if he wasn't packing a rod.

jugeotte *n.f.* **1** *De la jugeotte*: 'Nous', 'savvy', gumption. *Avoir de la jugeotte*: To have a bit of common-sense. *Il ne manque pas de jugeotte, lui!* He's not slow on the uptake! **2** *Passer en jugeotte*: To come up in front of the judge, to be on trial.

juif *n.m. Le petit juif*: The 'funnybone', the extremity of the elbow which, when struck, delivers a painful and tingling sensation.

Jules *n.m.* **1** 'Feller', regular boyfriend. **2** 'Hubby', husband. **3** Ponce, pimp. **4** 'Jerry', 'tinkler', chamber-pot. **5** *(mil.)*: Latrine pail. *Etre de Jules*: To be on slopping-out duties.

Julie *n.f.* **1** 'Regular bird', girlfriend. **2** 'Bit-on-the-side', 'fancy-woman', mistress. **3** 'Missus', 'better-half', wife. **4** *Faire sa Julie*: To act the 'proper little madam', to put on prudish airs and graces.

julot *n.m.* **1** 'Geezer', 'bloke', chappie. **2** Real man, person who, when friendship demands it, can be relied on. **3** Pimp, ponce, procurer.

jumelle *adj. Une maison jumelle*: A 'semi', a semi-detached house.

jumelles *n.f.pl.* **1** 'Tits', 'boobs', breasts. **2** 'Jacksey', 'sit-me-down', behind. **3** 'Goolies', 'nuts', testicles.

jupé *adj.* 'Pissed', 'sozzled', drunk.

jupon *n.m. Courir le jupon*: To 'chase the birds', to be a womanizer.

juponné *adj.* 'Pissed', 'sozzled', drunk.

jus *n.m.* **1** Water. **a** Rain (also: *jus de parapluie*). *Qu'est-ce qu'il tombe comme jus!* It ain't half raining! **b** 'The drink', 'the soup' (the sea, a lake, a river). *Tomber au jus*: To fall overboard. *Tout le monde au jus!* Let's all have a swim! **2** Coffee. *Siroter un jus*: To sip a quiet cup of coffee. *Jus de chaussette*: Bitter and nasty coffee. *Jus de chapeau*: Watery coffee. **3** 'Juice', 'gas', petrol. *Donner du jus*: To 'step on it', to open the throttle. *Aller plein jus*: To 'belt along', to bomb along. **4** 'Juice', electricity. *Mettre/couper le jus*: To switch on/off. *Court-jus*: Short-circuit. **5** 'Spunk', sperm. *Lâcher le jus*: To 'juice off', to ejaculate. **6** *Avoir du jus de navet dans les veines*: To be 'spunkless', 'spineless', to be weak-willed. **7** *Laisser mijoter* (also: *mariner*) *quelqu'un dans son jus*: To 'let someone stew in his own juice', to let someone sweat it out (of the mess he got himself into). **8** *Y mettre du jus*: To put some vim (and zest) into it, to 'pull out all the stops', to try one's darnedest. **9** Lengthy 'blurb', verbose text. *Se noyer dans le jus (sch.)*: To waffle on and on. **10** Long-winded speech, lengthy allocution. *Dévider un jus*: To spout at length. **11** *Valoir le jus*: To be worth-while. *Ça vaut le jus, je t'assure!* I can tell you it's well worth it! **12** *C'est le même jus*: It's six of one

and half a dozen of the other – It's the same thing. **13** *Jeter du jus*: To 'look swell', to look great. *Qu'est-ce qu'elle en jette!* She's a sight for sore eyes! **14** *C'est du peu au jus! (mil.)*: Demob day is just around the corner! **15** *Etre dans son jus* (of an antique): To be in its original (untampered-with) state.

jusqu'au-boutiste *n.m.* (also: *jusqu'auboutiste*): 'Last-ditcher', die-hard, character who never gives in or up.

juste *adj.* **1** Barely enough. *Un poulet pour six, ça me paraît un peu juste!* There won't really be enough to go round, if we're six sharing a chicken! **2** *Ça a été juste!* That was a close shave! – That was a narrow escape! **3** *Comme de juste (joc. & iron.)*: As luck would have it. *Comme de juste, j'étais sorti sans argent!* Trust me to go out without my wallet! **4** *Tout juste, Auguste!* (Rhyming catchphrase): Right on! – You've said it mate!

juter *v.intrans.* **1** To 'spout', to 'blather', to talk on and on. **2** To 'throw one's weight about', to 'swank', to show off. **3** To 'juice off', to ejaculate. **4** *Ça me fait drôlement juter!* It makes me really envious!

juteuse *n.f.* (abbr. *histoire juteuse*): **1** 'Hot gossip', scandalous tittle-tattle. **2** 'Naughty story', risqué joke.

juteuse *adj.* 'Juicy', scandalous.

juteux *n.m. (mil., corr. adjudant)*: Warrant officer (also: *adjupète*).

juteux *adj.* 'Swish', smart, elegant.

J.V. *n.m. (abbr. jeune voyou)*: 'Yob', 'yobbo', hooligan. (This journalese appellation had a great vogue in the 60s and 70s.)

jy *adv.* Yeah, yes. *Jy-go!* Right-on! – O.K.!

K

kangourou *n.m.* 'Jocks', 'Y-fronts', jockey shorts. (The *slip kangourou*, one of the first Y-fronts to be sold in France, became generic for this item of clothing.)

kasba *n.f.* (also: *kasbah*): **1** Home, house. *Viens boire un verre à la kasba*: Why don't you drop in for a drink? **2** (*pej.*): 'Shack', 'dump', hovel.

kékouok *n.m.* This jocular phonetic transcription of 'cake-walk', a popular World War II dance, is used by Raymond Queneau in his novel PIERROT MON AMI.

kick *n.m.* **1** Kick-start lever on motorbike. **2** 'Kick', surge of pleasure experienced by drug addict.

kif *n.m.* (Drugs): 'Hash', hashish, Indian hemp.

kif-kif *adj.inv.* *C'est kif-kif (bourricot)*: It's six of one, half a dozen of the other – It makes no odds – It's the same thing. *C'est pas du kif*: It's a different kettle of fish – It's quite a different matter.

kiki *n.m.* **1** 'Gullet', throat. *Serrer le kiki à quelqu'un*: To wring someone's neck, to throttle someone. **2** *C'est parti, mon kiki!* (Jocular interjection): That's it! – There we go! (This friendly rhyming expression is usually uttered when things have got off to a good start.)

kil *n.m.* 'Litre of plonk', bottle of cheap red wine. *On s'est payé un kil à trois*: The three of us downed a bottle of vino (also: *kilbus*).

kilo *n.m.* **1** 'Litre of plonk', bottle of cheap red wine. (The fact that 100 cl. of water weigh 1 kilogram explains this colloquial meaning.) **2** (*sch.*): A half-day's detention. **3** (*mil.*): 24 hours in the cooler, one day's detention in a punishment cell. **4** *Déposer un kilo*: To 'have a crap', to 'shit', to defecate (also: *poser un étron*).

kino *n.m.* *Le kino*: 'The flicks', the cinema. *On s'est payé une toile au kino*: We took in a movie at the old flea-pit.

kir *n.m.* Pleasant drink of white wine and blackcurrant cordial. (This drink was made famous by the *chanoine Kir* of Dijon.)

klaxon *n.m.* Hooter, horn. (Named after a famous make of car horns.)

klaxonner *v.trans. & intrans.* To hoot, to honk one's horn.

klébard *n.m.* (*pej.*): 'Mutt', 'pooch', dog (also: *clebs*).

k.o. *adj.inv.* 'Knackered', 'buggered', exhausted. *Quand je rentre du boulot, j'suis k.o.*: When I get home from work, I'm all in.

kopeck *n.m.* (also: *kopek*) *Ne pas avoir un kopeck*: To be 'skint', 'broke', to be penniless.

kroum *n.m.* (also: *kroume*): 'Tick', credit. *Il va nous falloir du kroum si on veut se payer ça*: We'll need some good old H.P. to buy that.

krounir *v.intrans.* To 'croak', to 'snuff it', to die.

kyrielle *n.f.* **1** 'String', long series. *Une kyrielle d'injures*: A long flow of insults. **2** *Une kyrielle de mômes*: A 'tribe' of children.

L

la *n.m.inv.* *Donner le la (fig)*: To set the tone of a meeting or discussion.

là *adv.* **1** *Là, là!* (Soothing words to a child): There, there, there (everything will be alright). **2** *Tout est là*: **a** That's the whole point – That's what it's all about. **b** That's the beauty of it – That's what makes it great. **3** *Etre un peu là* (of person): **a** To be utterly reliable. *Quand on a besoin de lui, un peu qu'il est là!* When you need him, you can be sure he won't let you down. **b** To be 'ace', to be an expert at something. *En mécanique-auto, il est un peu là*: When it comes to car mechanics, he's unbeatable. **4** *Ils ne sont pas là*: I'm broke – I'm skint – I haven't a penny. **5** *Avoir quelqu'un là*: 'Not to give a sod about someone', to not care a damn about someone.

là-bas *adv.* 'You-know-where', place a speaker would rather not refer to by name (mental home, prison, etc.).

labeur *n.m. (joc. & iron.)*: 'Job', employment that brings in the hard-earned cash and little job-satisfaction. *Aller au labeur*: To plod off to work.

labo *n.m.* 'Lab', laboratory.

lac *n.m.* **1** *Etre dans le lac*: To be 'in the soup', to be in trouble. **2** *Tomber dans le lac*: To fall into a trap. (*Lacs*, from the Latin *laqueus* meaning 'snare', also gave the French word *lacet*, but popular etymology sees the victim falling into a lake.) **3** 'Fanny', 'pussy', vagina. *Descente au lac*: Cunnilingus.

lacet *n.m.* *Marchand de lacets*: Gendarme.

lâcher *v.trans.* **1** *Lâcher quelqu'un*: To 'leave someone in the lurch', to 'walk out on someone', to let someone down. **2** *En lâcher un*: To 'do a pongy', to 'fart', to break wind. **3** *Les lâcher*: To 'cough up', to 'fork out', to pay. *Les lâcher avec un élastique*: To be 'stingy', to be mean (also: *être dur à les lâcher*). **4** *Lâcher l'écluse*: To 'pee', to 'wee', to urinate. **5** *Lâcher les dés*: **a** To 'throw in the sponge', to give in. **b** To be conciliatory (also: *passer les*

dés). **6** *Lâcher le paquet*: To 'squeal', to 'spill the beans', to confess. **7** *Lâcher la rampe*: To 'pop one's clogs', to 'shuffle off', to die.

lâcheur *n.m.* **1** 'Quitter', undependable character (person who is likely to let you down). **2** *(joc.)*: 'Funk', person who 'gets cold feet' but can't be blamed for it. *Lâcheur va, t'aurais dû rester, on a picolé jusqu'à trois heures du mat'!* You're a right cissy to have left so early, we were still knocking drinks back at three in the morning!

lacsatif *n.m. (joc.)*: 10-franc note. (Prior to the 1958 remonetization, the face-value of the note was 1000 francs.)

lacson *n.m.* 'Pack', packet. *Un lacson de pipes*: A pack of fags.

laguiole *n.m.* 'Chiv', blade, knife.

laidasse *n.f.* 'Ugly cow', unattractive woman.

laine *n.f.* **1** 'Woolly', woollen garment. *Si tu sors, n'oublie pas ta laine*: If you have to go out, mind you take a sweater. **2** *Se laisser bouffer la laine sur le dos*: To suffer scroungers in silence. **3** *Avoir la jambe de laine*: To peg along wearily (also: *avoir les jambes en coton*). **4** 'Woolly', 'pussy', pudenda.

laissé-pour-compte *n.m.* Bachelor long past his prime (one who like the proverbial spinster has been 'left on the shelf').

laisser *v.trans.* *En prendre et en laisser*: To 'take it all with a pinch of salt', to retain a healthy dose of scepticism about something.

lait *n.m.* **1** *Avoir encore du lait dans le nez*: To be 'still wet behind the ears', to lack maturity. **2** *Boire du (petit) lait* (where complimentary comments are concerned): To 'lap it all up', to take it all in eagerly. **3** *Ça se boit comme du petit lait* (of innocuous-looking yet potent alcoholic drink): It's so good it just slips down your gullet. **4** *Etre soupe au lait*: To be quick-tempered. *Monter comme une soupe au lait*: To flare up (usually over trifles). **5** *Grosse vache à lait (pej)*: Big, fat, soft biddy (plump, bovine-like female). **6** *Etre une vache à lait* (of man or woman): To be a 'soft-touch', to be generous to the point of stupidity where subs and gifts are concerned.

7 *Lait de poule* (Drink): Egg-flip. **8** *Lait de chameau* (also: *lait de tigre*): Pernod, pastis (because it has a bite to it).

laitue *n.f.* **1** 'Fresh meat', novice prostitute. **2** 'Pussy', 'fanny', pudenda. **3** *Brouter les laitues* (Racing slang): To be left at the post.

laïus *n.m.* Verbose speech. *Faire du laïus*: To speechify.

laïusser *v.intrans.* To 'spout', to 'waffle on', to talk on and on.

laïusseur *n.m.* 'Spouter', one who enjoys the sound of his own voice.

lambin *n.m.* 'Slow-coach', dawdler.

lambin *adj.* Slow (to the point of laziness). *Mais qu'il est lambin!* He needs a kick up the backside to get him moving!

lambiner *v.intrans.* To 'dawdle', to 'dilly-dally', to go slowly.

lamdé *n.f.* **1** Lady, woman. **2** 'Missus', wife.

lame *n.f.* **1** 'Chiv', blade, knife. **2** 'Ace guy', super character. **3** *Pisser des lames de rasoir* (of man): To have the 'gons', to suffer from gonorrhoea (also: *avoir la chaude-pisse*).

lamedus *n.m.pl.* 'Hot goods', stolen wares.

lamentation *n.f.* *Le mur des lamentations (joc. & iron.)*: The complaints counter (in department store, etc.).

lamer *v.trans.* To knife, to stab.

lamfé *n.f.* **1** Woman. **2** 'Missus', wife.

laminer *v.trans.* To 'bump off', to eliminate, to kill.

lampe *n.f.* **1** 'Gullet', throat. *S'humecter la lampe*: To 'wet one's whistle', to have a drink. **2** 'Belly', stomach. *S'en coller plein la lampe*: To have a real good fill, to eat a hearty meal. **3** *Lampe à souder*: 'Tippler's conk', red nose. **4** *Avoir une lampe à souder dans le slip (joc.)*: To be randy, to be over-sexed.

lampée *n.f.* 'Swig', large gulp of drink.

lampion *n.m.* **1** 'Gullet', throat. *S'en mettre un coup dans le lampion*: To take a swig, to down a drink. **2** *(pl.)*: 'Oglers', 'peepers', eyes. **3** *L'air des lampions*. This stamping of feet by an audience or crowd to the strains of a popular tune is roughly equivalent to slow hand-clapping and the chanting of 'Why are we waiting?'

lampiste *n.m.* Underling who generally 'carries the can' for other people's mistakes. Originally, the *lampiste* in the railways was the least important employee and an ideal scapegoat, hence the expression: *C'est toujours les lampistes qui trinquent.*

lance *n.f.* **1** Downpour, heavy rain. *On a tous eu droit à une sacrée lance*: We all got soaked to the skin. **2** 'Corporation pop', tap water. **3** 'Pee', 'wee', urine. **4** 'Clap', gonorrhoea (also: *chaude-pisse*).

lancecailler *v.intrans.* (of man): To 'have a slash', to 'pee', to urinate.

lancement *n.m.* *Rampe de lancement (joc.)*: 'Love-pad', bed.

lance-parfum *n.m.* Tommy-gun, machine-gun. (The expression *envoyer le parfum* is literally to spray a target with bullets.)

lance-pierres *n.m.* *Manger avec un lance-pierres*: To 'wolf one's food', to gobble one's grub in haste.

lancequinade *n.f.* Steady downpour of rain.

lancequine *n.f.* Heavy drizzle, rain.

lancequiner *v.intrans.* **1** To rain. **2** (of man): To 'have a slash', to 'pee', to urinate.

lancer *v.intrans.* *Ça me lance*: I've got this stabbing pain.

Landerneau *Proper name.* *Ça va faire du bruit dans Landerneau*: It'll certainly set tongues wagging around here! (Landerneau, a small town near Brest, used to be the butt of music-hall jokes between the wars, as was the case for Wigan and its phantom pier.)

langouse *n.f.* 'Licker', tongue. *Faire un bisou langouse*: To give a passionate 'French kiss'.

langouste *n.f.* **1** 'Biddy', 'bird', young woman. **2** 'Prozzy', prostitute.

langue *n.f.* **1** *Avaler sa langue*: **a** To 'keep mum', to hold one's tongue. **b** To stifle a yawn. **c** To 'snuff it', to 'croak', to die. **2** General meaning: chatter, gossip. *Avoir la langue bien pendue*: To have the gift of the gab. *Ne pas avoir sa langue dans sa poche*: To have a glib tongue, to be quick on the verbal draw. *Se mordre la langue*: **a** To stop short of saying something. **b** To regret having said something. *Faire aller les langues*: To set tongues wagging. *Etre mauvaise langue*: To be a gossip-monger. *Etre une langue de vipère*: To be mean-mouthed. **3** *Donner sa langue au(x) chat(s)*: To give up guessing (where a question or riddle is concerned). **4** *Avoir la langue qui fourche*: To make a slip of the tongue. *Zut, ma langue a fourché!* No, that's not what I meant to say! **5** *Faire une langue fourrée*: To exchange a 'French kiss'. **6** *Langue fourrée princesse*: Cunnilingus. **7** *Tirer la langue*: **a** To be near the end of one's tether, to show signs of exhaustion. **b** To be starving. **c** (of health or finances): To be in a bad way. **8** *Faire tirer la langue à quelqu'un* (of employee or subordinate): To drive someone too hard. **9** *La langue verte*: Argot, slang.

languir *v.pronom.* *Se languir de quelqu'un*: To pine, to yearn for someone.

lanlaire *n.m.* *Va te faire lanlaire!* Go to hell! – Go to blazes! – Get lost! (The word *lanlaire* is in fact a phonetic transcription of the strains of a long-forgotten popular tune.)

lansquinade *n.f.* Steady downpour of rain.

lansquine *n.f.* Heavy drizzle, rain.

lansquiner *v.intrans.* **1** To rain. **2** (of man): To 'have a slash', to 'pee', to urinate.

lanterne *n.f.* **1** Window. **2** *(pl.):* 'Glims', 'lamps', eyes. *Ouvre un peu tes lanternes!* For Pete's sake keep your eyes on what you're doing! **3** 'Bread-basket', 'belly', stomach. *S'en fourrer* (also: *s'en mettre*) *plein la lanterne*: To 'have a good blow-out', to have a right good tuck-in, to eat heartily. **4** *Lanterne rouge* (Professional cyclists' slang): Booby-prize tag awarded (in the same spirit as the 'wooden spoon') to the cyclist who is last overall in a major 'stages' race.

lanterner *v.intrans.* To 'dilly-dally', to waste time.

lapalissade *n.f.* Patently obvious and fatuous remark.

lape *n.f.* (also: *lap* or *lappe*) *Etre bon à lape*: To be bloody useless, to be good for nothing. *Ça ne vaut que lape*: It's not worth a brass farthing!

lapin *n.m.* **1** *Un sacré lapin*: **a** 'One hell of a guy', an ace character. **b** A 'tricky bugger', an awkward fellow. **2** *Un drôle de lapin*: A 'queer cove', an oddball (is usually said of someone who is difficult to weigh up). **3** *Un chaud lapin*: A 'randy bugger', a 'horny so-and-so', an over-sexed man. **4** *Mon petit lapin* (Term of endearment): My little pet. **5** *Mon vieux lapin!* 'Me old mate'! **6** *Le coup du lapin*: **a** *(lit.):* A 'chocolate chop', a wallop behind the ears (with G.B.H. intentions). **b** *(fig.):* A treacherous blow. **7** *Poser un lapin*: To fail to turn up for an appointment (intentionally or otherwise). *Becqueter du lapin*: To get stood up. **8** *Ça sent le lapin!* It smells a bit fuggy here! (also: *Ça sent le fauve*). **9** *Ça ne vaut pas un pet de lapin*: It's worth bugger-all! – It's worthless!

lapine *n.f. Une vraie (mère) lapine*: A 'conveyor-belt mum', a mother with a seemingly never-ending string of children.

lapiner *v.intrans.* To be in a state of near-permanent pregnancy.

lapuche *n.f. Etre bon à lapuche*: To be bloody useless. *Ça ne vaut que lapuche*: It's no earthly good.

larbin *n.m.* (*pej.*): 'Flunkey', 'lackey', servant.

lard *n.m.* **1** *Faire du lard*: To 'run to fat' (by doing bugger-all), to grow fat and idle. **2** *Gros lard*: 'Fatso', grossly overweight man. **3** *Sauter sur le lard à quelqu'un*: To pounce on someone. **4** *Rentrer dans le lard à quelqu'un*: To 'lam into', to aggress someone. **5** *Mettre le lard au saloir* (*joc.*): To 'hit the sack', to get between the sheets. **6** *Sauver son lard* (*fig*): To 'save one's bacon', to save one's skin. **7** *Se racler le lard*: To

'scrape the stubble', to have a shave. **8** *Tête de lard*: **a** 'Fat-head', fool. **b** 'Pig-head', obdurate character. **9** *Prendre tout sur son lard*: To be 'ready to carry the can', to take full responsibility for something. **10** *Ne pas savoir si c'est du lard ou du cochon*: Not to know what to make of something.

lardé *n.m.* 'Porker', pig.

larder *v.trans.* To 'get under someone's skin', to get on someone's nerves.

lardeusse *n.m.* (also: *lardeus*): Coat, overcoat.

lardoir *n.m.* 'Chiv', blade, knife.

lardon *n.m.* 'Brat', 'kid', child.

lardosse *n.m.* Coat, overcoat.

lardu *n.m. Le lardu*: 'The cop-shop', the police station. (*Un lardu* has also come to mean a superintendent or a policeman in general.)

larfeuil *n.m.* Wallet (also: *crapaud*).

large *n.m.* **1** *Prendre le large*: To 'make oneself scarce', to 'vamoose', to clear off. **2** *Gagner le large*: To 'get out of harm's way', to steer clear of trouble. **3** *Donner du large à quelqu'un*: To 'give someone a wide berth', to carefully avoid someone.

large *adj.* **1** *L'avoir large*: To have 'the luck of the devil', to be extremely fortunate. **2** *Ne pas être large du dos*: To be 'tight-fisted', to be mean.

large *adv. Ne pas en mener large*: To feel deflated and down-in-the-mouth, to be crestfallen.

largement *adv. Avoir largement le temps*: To have oodles of time in front of one. *Avoir largement de quoi vivre*: To be O.K. for money.

largeot *n.m.* Baggy pair of trousers.

largeot *adj.* (of man): Broad, well-built.

largeur *n.f. Dans les grandes largeurs (adv.exp.):* Completely, utterly (usually with a negative connotation). *Se foutre de quelqu'un dans les grandes largeurs*: To take the mickey out of someone in no uncertain manner. *Emmerder quelqu'un dans les grandes largeurs*: To go all-out to be a pain in the neck to someone. *Se gourer dans les grandes largeurs*: To be wildly out, to get it all wrong.

largonji *n.m.* (Butchers' slang): This intricate 'gobbledygook-like' secret language resembles *javanais* with its latched-on syllables, and further confuses the non-speaker with the use of *verlen*.

largue *n.f.* 'Prozzy', 'hooker', prostitute.

larguer *v.trans.* **1** To give someone the 'heave-ho', to get rid of someone. **2** To 'chuck away', to 'dump', to throw something out. **3** *Les larguer*: To 'cough up', to 'fork out', to pay. **4** *Larguer les amarres* (*joc.*): To 'slope off', to 'slip away', to leave.

Laribo *Proper name.* The *Hôpital Lariboisière* in Paris.

larmichette *n.f.* 'Wee dram', 'tiny drop', small quantity of alcoholic drink. (*Une larmichette*, like the expression *'une larme, un soupçon'*, is usually uttered *with gentle irony* as the quantity of drink requested is anything but modest.)

larron *n.m. S'entendre comme larrons en foire*: To be 'as thick as thieves', to be the best of pals.

lasane *n.f.* Letter, item of correspondence (also: *bafouille*).

lascar *n.m.* 'Geezer', 'bloke', guy. *Un sacré lascar*: A 'likely lad' (the kind of chap who always comes out tops). *Un rude lascar*: A 'tough customer', someone hard to deter.

latte *n.f.* **1** Foot. *Filer un coup de latte à quelqu'un*: To kick someone up the jacksey. *Prendre un coup de latte*: **a** *(lit.)*: To get kicked in the shins. **b** *(fig)*: To get 'nobbled', to fall victim to a treacherous move. **2** *(pl.)*: 'Treaders', shoes. *Traîner ses lattes*: To 'mooch about', to wander aimlessly. **3** *Marcher à côté de ses lattes (fig.)*: To be 'down on one's uppers', to be 'broke', to be penniless. **4** *Y aller d'un coup de latte*: To ask for a 'sub', to try and get a loan. **5** *Deuxième latte (mil.)*: 'Buck-private', ordinary soldier.

latter *v.trans.* **1** *(lit.)*: To kick someone up the backside. **2** *(fig.)*: To tap someone for a loan. *Comme de bien entendu, je me suis fait latter*: Being the mug I am, I loaned him the money.

laubé *adj.* Beautiful, appealing. (The word is always used in a negative context.) *Après dix ans dans le ring, il n'était vraiment pas laubé*: Not a pretty sight! Ten years boxing had seen to that!

lavabe *n.m.* 'Lav', 'bog', lavatory.

lavasse *n.f.* **1** *De la lavasse*: **a** 'Dishwater', thin and tasteless soup. **b** Watered-down 'plonk', diluted wine. **2** 'Wash-out', gutless character.

lavdu *n.m.* (also: *lavedu*): 'Mug', 'sucker', dupe. (The word refers primarily to someone not belonging to the *milieu*.)

lavé *adj.* **1** 'Knackered', 'buggered', exhausted. **2** 'Skint', 'cleaned-out', penniless. **3** *Chèque lavé*: Forged cheque (one where the amount or the name of the payee has been altered).

lavement *n.m.* 'Pain-in-the-arse', tenacious bore.

laver *v.trans.* **1** To sell off cheaply and quickly dubious merchandise (stolen goods). **2** *Laver la tête à quelqu'un*: To 'give someone a dressing-down', to tell someone off in no uncertain manner. **3** *Laver son linge sale en famille*: To keep a private quarrel out of the public eye.

lavette *n.f.* **1** 'Spineless character', person who totally lacks will and energy. (When referring to a man the word is highly pejorative.) **2** 'Willie', limp penis. (The original meaning of *lavette* is dish-mop.)

laveur *n.m.* 'Fence', receiver and merchandiser of stolen goods.

lavouge *n.f.* 'Laundry', washing.

lavougner *v.intrans.* To 'do the dishes', to wash up.

lavure *n.f.* **1** 'Dishwater', thin and tasteless soup. **2** Watered-down 'plonk', 'wishy-washy' red wine. **3** 'Wash-out', gutless character who fails at everything.

laxé *n.m. (corr. lacsatif)*: 10-franc note. (Prior to the 1958 remonetization, the face-value of the note was 1000 francs.)

laxons *n.m.pl.* 'Undies', underwear.

lazagne *n.f.* **1** Letter, item of correspondence. **2** Wallet (also: *porte-lazagne*).

Lazaro *Proper name*. The *Saint-Lazare* prison-cum-hospital in Paris where prostitutes were interned and treated when suffering from venereal disease.

lazaro *n.m.* 'Nick', 'clink', prison.

laziloffe *n.m.* Venereal disease. (The word can refer either to syphilis or gonorrhoea.)

laziloffe *adj.* Infected with V.D.

leaubé *adj.* Beautiful, appealing. (The word is always used in a negative context. *Pas leaubé le mec après son accident de bagnole!* Not a pretty sight! He looked terrible when they pulled him out of the car after the crash.)

lèche *n.f. De la lèche*: 'Boot-licking', sycophantic attitude. *Il fait toujours de la lèche au prof!* He's always sucking up to the teachers.

léché *adj.* Meticulously executed. (The word originally referred to paintings and the standard usage was *une peinture léchée*: a highly detailed canvas.)

lèche-bottes *n.m.* 'Arse-crawler', sycophant (also: *lèche-cul*).

lécher *v.trans.* **1** To 'suck up to someone', to behave in a sycophantic manner. **2** To carry out a delicate task with the utmost care and attention.

lécheur *n.m.* 'Arse-licker', 'toady', flatterer (also: *lèche-cul*).

lèche-vitrines *n.m. Faire du lèche-vitrines*: To go window-shopping.

lecture *n.f. Etre en lecture* (of prostitute): To be 'on the job', to be with a customer. (The alternative expression *être sous presse* has an amusing *double entendre*.)

léger *n.m. Faire du léger*: **a** (Underworld slang): To do an easy 'job', to take the least risks possible. **b** To act with the utmost delicacy, to handle tricky matters with kid gloves.

légionnaire *n.m.* Litre-bottle of 'plonk'.

légitime *n.f. Ma légitime*: My 'ball-and-chain', 'the missus', my wife.

légobiffin *n.m.* Soldier of the French Foreign Legion.

légume *n.f. Une grosse légume*: A 'bigwig', a 'big cheese', a V.I.P. *On a été de corvée ici aujourd'hui avec toutes les grosses légumes*: We were on our toes all day with the top brass on official visit.

légumes *n.m.pl. Perdre ses légumes*: To shit in one's pants, to have an involuntary anal discharge through fear, etc.

légumier *n.m.* 'Limo', V.I.P.'s limousine.

lendemain *n.m. Etre triste comme un lendemain de fête*: To look as though one had 'lost a shilling and found sixpence', to look glum.

lentilles *n.f.pl. Trieuse de lentilles*: 'Les', 'dyke', lesbian.

Léon *Proper name. Gros Léon* (Underworld slang): 'Mr Big', top man in the *milieu*.

Lépine *Proper name. Concours Lépine*: Annual exhibition, convention-cum-competition where small-time inventors find a platform for their 'Heath Robinson' type creations. Some are quite serious; others, like the visors for eating grapefruit, slightly more extravagant.

lerche *adj.* 'Pricey', dear, expensive. (As with the adverb, one seldom finds this adjective with a positive connotation.) *Elle n'avait rien de lerche, sa robe*: That dress of hers looked what it was – a cheapie!

lerche *adv.* 'Oodles', masses of, lots of. (This adverb is nearly always found in a negative context. *'y a pas lerche de fric*: There's not a lot of money in the kitty.)

lessivage *n.m. Le lessivage de crânes*: The brainwashing of the masses.

lessive *n.f.* **1** Brisk clear-out sale in shop or department store. **2** *Passer à la lessive*: To get a free pardon.

lessivé *adj.* **1** 'Knackered', 'buggered', exhausted. *Je suis vraiment lessivé!* I feel completely washed-out! **2** 'Cleaned-out', utterly penniless. **3** *C'est lessivé!* It's curtains! – All is lost!

lessiver *v.trans.* **1** To 'flog', to sell off cheaply. **2** *Tout lessiver*: To 'spend, spend, spend', to blow the lot, to spend all one's money in a frantic spree. **3** *Se faire lessiver*: To lose all one's money (either in a financial venture or at gambling).

lessiveuse *n.f. (joc.)*: 'Puffer', steam-engine.

lest *n.m. Lâcher du lest*: To make concessions in a genuine attempt to save the day.

lettre *n.f.* **1** *Les cinq lettres*: Dainty euphemism for the swear-word *merde*, a popular equivalent being *le mot de Cambronne*, an unusual in-memoriam for that famous general. **2** *Prendre quelque chose au pied de la lettre*: To 'do some-

thing by the book', to act on instructions without giving them a personal interpretation. **3** *Passer comme une lettre à la poste* (of recommendation, decision subject to some form of scrutiny or censorship): To go through without a hitch.

levage *n.m. Faire un levage*: **a** To 'chat up a bird', to sweet-talk a potential girlfriend. **b** (of prostitute): To make a pick-up, to hook a customer.

lever *n.m. Faire un lever* (of prostitute): To hook a client.

lever *v.trans.* **1** To 'lift', to 'nick', to steal. **2 a** To 'chat up', to sweet-talk a potential girlfriend. **b** (of prostitute): To 'hook' a client, to make a pick-up. **3** To 'nab', to 'collar', to arrest. **4** *Lever un lièvre*: **a** (of idea): To come up with something interesting. **b** To uncover a hitherto well-kept and embarrassing secret. **5** *Faire quelque chose au pied levé*: To do something at the drop of a hat. *Il m'a pris au pied levé*: He caught me on the hop.

leveur *n.m.* 'Tea-leaf', 'filch', thief.

leveuse *n.f.* 'Prozzy', 'hooker', prostitute.

lèvres *n.f.pl. Ne connaître quelqu'un ni des lèvres ni des dents*: To not know someone from Adam.

levrette *n.f. Se faire baiser en levrette*: To get caught unawares, to fall victim to a treacherous attack. (The expression can also mean to have been neatly conned.)

lézard *n.m.* 'Lazybones', idle fellow. *Faire le lézard*: To bask idly in the sun.

lézarder *v.intrans.* To laze about, to be totally idle.

liant *n.m. Avoir du liant*: To be a 'good mixer', to be a good socializer. *Manquer de liant*: To be uncouth.

liant *adj.* Over-friendly. *Il est un peu trop liant à mon goût*: He tends to throw himself at people a bit.

lichade *n.f.* 'Swig', gulp of booze.

lichedu *n.m.* 'Pain-in-the-neck', bloody nuisance, awkward person.

licher *v.trans. & intrans.* To 'tipple', to down alcoholic drink (also: *lichailler*).

lichetrogner *v.trans. & intrans.* To 'booze', to drink alcoholic beverage to excess. (Whereas *licher* can refer to a connoisseur of fine wines, *lichetrogner* is associated with the heavy drinker.)

lichette *n.f.* 'Wee dram', 'teeny drop', small quantity of alcoholic drink.

licheur *n.m.* 'Boozer', 'tippler', habitual drinker.

liège *n.m. Sentir le liège (joc.)*: To be something of a boozer, to have more than a passing fancy for alcohol.

lier *v.trans. Etre fou à lier*: To be 'bonkers', to be raving mad.

lièvre *n.m.* **1** 'Bright spark', character who is quick on the uptake. **2** (Racing slang): 'Pace-maker', horse whose task it is to lead the field from the start of the race. **3** *Courir comme un lièvre*: To 'run like the clappers', to hare along. **4** *Lever un lièvre*: **a** To come up with an interesting idea. **b** To uncover a hitherto well-kept and embarrassing secret.

ligne *n.f.* **1** (of person): Figure. *Avoir la ligne*: To be slim, svelte. *Garder la ligne*: To keep in trim. *Faire attention à sa ligne*: To be a dedicated weight-watcher. **2** *A la ligne!* Period! – End of discussion! **3** *Tirer à la ligne* (of journalist): To 'pad out', to spin out an article. **4** *C'est pas dans ma ligne!* It's not quite up my street! – It's not really my line of work!

ligoter *v.trans.* To read. *Ligote-moi cet article!* Have a butchers at this news item!

limace *n.f.* **1** (also: *limasse*): 'Shimmy', shirt. **2** (*pl.*): 'Smackers', lips.

limande *n.f.* **1** *Etre plate comme une limande*: To have 'poached egg boobs', to be flat-chested. **2** 'Prozzy', 'hooker', prostitute. **3** 'Belter', slap in the face. *Il a pris une sacrée limande*: He got a right smack across the face.

limé *adj.* Diluted with lemonade. *Un demi limé*: A half of shandy. (A more popular drink in France is the *blanc limé*: white wine with a drop of lemonade.)

limer *v.intrans.* To 'screw', to fuck, to have intercourse.

limogeage *n.m.* 'Firing', 'sacking', dismissal of an employee.

limoger *v.trans.* **1** To demote. **2** To 'fire', to 'sack', to dismiss someone. *Après toutes ses gaffes, il s'est fait limoger en beauté*: He got his cards with his pay-packet after that last bloomer!

limonade *n.f.* **1** *La limonade*: The licensed victualling trade. *Etre dans la limonade*: To run a pub. **2** *Tomber dans la limonade*: To 'fall in the drink', to fall into the water. (The expression *être dans une sacrée limonade* can mean to be 'in the soup', to be in deep trouble.)

limonadier *n.m.* (*joc.*): Landlord, publican.

limouse *n.f.* (also: *limouze*): 'Shimmy', shirt (also: *limace*).

linge *n.m. Le beau linge*: 'The toffs', the well-to-do. *C'est une boîte où il n'y a que du beau linge*: It's a night-club that only caters for the upper-crust.

lingé *adj. Etre bien lingé*: To be 'togged-up', to be 'decked-out', to be well-dressed.

linger *v.trans.* To 'rig out', to dress. *On ne linge pas une gonzesse avec du prêt-à-porter*: You can't really get a bird to look her best with off-the-peg gear.

linger *v.trans.reflex.* To get 'togged-up', 'rigged-out', to get dressed.

lingue *n.m.* 'Chiv', blade, knife.

linguer *v.trans.* To 'stick', to stab.

lino *n.m.* (*abbr. linoléum*): Lino.

linotte *n.f. Une tête de linotte*: A 'dizzy-lizzy', a hare-brained person.

lion *n.m.* **1** 'Tiger', lion of a man, courageous chap. **2** *Se défendre comme un lion*: To 'hold one's own' with vigour and energy, to fight off attacks (physical or verbal) in a swashbuckling manner. **3** *Avoir bouffé du lion*: **a** To be 'full of beans', to be full of energy. **b** To be in a go-getting mood.

lip *n.f.* 'Timex', timepiece, watch. (Like Timex, *Lip* has become a generic term for any wrist-watch.)

lippe *n.f. Pousser sa* (also: *faire la*) *lippe*: To pout.

liquette *n.f.* 'Shimmy', shirt (also: *limace, limouse*).

liquider *v.trans.* **1** To get rid of, to remove someone from office. **2** To 'bump off', to kill.

lisbroquer *v.intrans.* To 'pee', to 'wee', to urinate.

Lisette *Proper name. Pas de ça, Lisette!* Not on your nelly! – Nothing doing! – It's out of the question! (This jocular catchphrase, dating back to the 1830s, is as popular as it ever was.)

lisses *n.f.pl.* 'Nylons', stockings.

lit *n.m.* **1** *Lit en portefeuille*: 'Apple-pie bed'. **2** *De la graine de bois de lit* (*joc.*): 'Brat', 'kid', child.

litron *n.m.* **1** Litre of 'plonk', bottle of cheap red wine. **2** *Tenir le litron*: To be able to 'hold one's liquor', to have a good resilience to alcohol.

lobé *adj.* 'Ace', 'A-1', first-rate. (This adjective is nearly always found within a negative statement.) *Sa nana c'est le genre pas lobé!* That bird of his looks bloody awful!

locdu *n.m.* **1** 'Weirdo', 'oddball', strange person. **2** 'Nutter', 'loony', mad person. **3** 'Slack-arse', 'slacker', workshy person. **4** Ugly person. (The feminine *locdue* exists but is seldom used.)

locdu *adj.* **1** (of person): Weird, strange, bizarre. **2** 'Bonkers', 'potty', mad. **3** Workshy, idle. **4** Ugly, unappealing. **5** (of goods): 'Tatty', shoddy.

loche *n.m.* 'Cabbie', taxi-driver.

locomotive *n.f.* **1** *Fumer comme une locomotive*: To 'smoke like a chimney', to be a heavy smoker. **2** In the vernacular of up-market restaurateurs and night-club owners, *une locomotive* is the most popular sort of customer, one who brings a lot of trade in his wake, and whose friends and associates like to spend liberally.

loge *n.f. Etre aux premières loges* (*fig*): To have 'a ringside seat' where an argument or a titillating spectacle is concerned.

logé past part. Etre logé à la même enseigne: To be 'in the same boat', to have common troubles with someone.

loi n.f. Avoir la loi: To 'have the upper-hand', to get the best of a deal or situation.

loilpé adj. Etre à loilpé: To be 'starkers', 'in one's birthday suit', to be stark naked (also: être à poil).

loin adv. Revenir de loin: To 'have had a close shave', to have had a lucky escape.

loinqué n.m. 'Cubby-hole', corner.

loinqué adv. In the distance, far away.

lolo n.m. **1** (Child language): Milk. **2** (pl.): 'Titties', 'boobs', breasts (also: boîtes à lolo). **3** Ça, c'est du lolo! That's a bit of alright! –Yes, I like that!

long En long, en large et en travers (adv.exp.): Through and through, thoroughly. Il m'a conté ça en long, en large et en travers! He gave me the whole story without sparing one bloody detail!

longe n.f. Year (when counting a term of incarceration). Il a écopé de cinq longes: He got sent down for a five-year stretch.

longitude n.f. Prendre une longitude: To 'put one's feet up', to take a rest.

longue adj.f. **1** Les avoir longues: **a** To be ravenous, to be extremely hungry. **b** To be hungry for success, to be driven by ambition. **2** De longue (adv.exp.): 'For ages', for a long time. Je le connais de longue: I've known him for yonks.

longuet adj. (of speech, etc.): A trifle long and boring, a bit on the long side.

lope n.f. **1** 'Wet lettuce', weak-willed character. **2** 'Funk', coward. **3** 'Nancy-boy', effeminate homosexual.

loqué adj. 'Togged', dressed. Etre bien loqué: To be decked-out, to be well-dressed.

loquer v.trans. To dress. Il dépense un fric fou pour loquer ses nanas: He spends a bomb on his girlfriends' wardrobes.

loquer v.trans.reflex. To 'get one's rags on', to get dressed.

loques n.f.pl. 'Togs', 'clobber', clothes.

losange n.m. Mener une vie en losange: To have a happy, permissive no-holds-barred marriage where each partner has his and her lover.

lot n.m. **1** Gagner le gros lot: To 'hit the jackpot', to strike it rich. (Originally Gros Lot referred to the top prize in the draw of the Loterie Nationale.) **2** Un beau petit lot (joc.): A 'right little cracker', a 'shapely bird', a pretty woman.

loti adj. Etre bien loti: To 'have come out tops', to have been favoured by chance. Etre mal loti: To 'have had a rough deal', to be badly off. Dans

cet hôtel, on n'est pas trop mal lotis!: We can't really complain about the hotel we got!

lotos n.m.pl. Rouler (also: ribouler) des lotos: To 'goggle', to stare in astonishment. (The expression avoir des yeux en boules de loto, i.e. like bingo balls, indicates the origin of the headword.)

loubac adj. 'Bonkers', 'potty', mad. T'es loubac, non?! You crazy in the head?!

loubar n.m. (also: loubard): 'Yob', 'yobbo', young tearaway.

loubarde n.f. Electric light. (The word can refer to an ordinary bulb, a flashlight or the headlamp of a vehicle.)

loubé n.m. Un loubé: 'A teeny bit', a small quantity. File-nous un loubé de rab! I'm famished, give us a bit more grub!

loubiats n.m.pl. White beans (the dried variety you have to boil for hours on-end).

loucedé adj. En loucedé (adv.exp.): 'Softly-softly', quietly, discreetly. Filer en loucedé: To slip away unnoticed (also: en loucedoc).

louche n.m. Flairer du louche: To 'smell a rat', to get suspicious.

louche n.f. 'Mitt', 'paw', hand. Se serrer la louche: To shake hands (also: cuillère).

louchébème n.m. (also: louchébem). **1** Butcher. **2** Le louchébème: Butchers' cant, secret language, also known as largonji, where components become rearranged.

loucher v.intrans. Loucher sur: To eye (with envy), to covet. Un peu qu'il louche sur ta bagnole! He doesn't half fancy your car!

loufdingue n.m. 'Loony', 'nut-case', mad person.

loufdingue adj. 'Potty', 'bonkers', mad.

louffe n.m. 'Pongy', silent fart. Lâcher un louffe: To let one ripple.

louffer v.intrans. To do a 'pongy', to 'fart', to break wind.

louffiat n.m. (also: loufiat): Waiter (in café, restaurant).

loufoque n.m. 'Mild nutter', gentle eccentric with loony ideas.

loufoque adj. 'Cracked', 'loony', mad. C'est loufoque comme machin, mais j'aime! It's a right nutty one, but I like it!

loufoquerie n.f. 'Daftness', 'barminess', eccentricity.

louftingue n.m. 'Loony', 'nut-case', mad person (also: cinoque).

louftingue adj. 'Potty', 'bonkers', mad.

Louis Proper name. Avoir des jambes Louis XV (joc.): To be 'bandy', to be bow-legged (literally to have 'cabriole legs' like the chairs of that period).

louise n.f. 'Pongy', silent fart. Lâcher une louise: To let one ripple.

loulou n.m. **1** (abbr. loulou de Poméranie): 'Pom', Pomeranian (toy dog of that breed). **2** Mon *loulou:* 'My lovey-dovey', 'my pet', my darling. **3** *(pl.):* 'Yobbos', hooligans. (With this meaning the word is never found in the singular. According to Auguste Le Breton, it refers principally to those bored teenagers who take pleasure in disrupting and vandalizing.)

louloute *n.f.* **1** 'Biddy', 'bird', woman. **2** *Ma louloute:* 'My lovey-dovey', 'my pet', my darling.

loup *n.m.* **1** *Etre connu comme le loup blanc:* To be known to all and sundry, to have a far-reaching reputation (good or bad). **2** *Faire un loup:* To 'make a cock-up of something', to blunder. **3** *Mon gros loup:* 'Duckie', 'my lovey-dovey', darling.

loupage *n.m.* 'Botching', action of messing things up.

loupe *n.f.* Idleness, laziness. *Etre de la loupe:* To be a lazy git.

louper *v.trans.* To miss. *Louper une occase:* To let a good opportunity go by. *On a loupé le dur:* We missed our train. *Louper son entrée (th.):* To 'fluff it', to make a hash of one's entrance on stage.

loupiot *n.m.* 'Brat', 'kid', child.

loupiotte *n.f.* Weak light (small bulb, torch, etc.).

lourd *n.m.* **1** 'Moneybags', very wealthy man. **2** *(pej.):* 'Hayseed', 'yokel', country bumpkin.

lourd *adj.* **1** 'Thick', 'dumb', dull-witted. *Un peu qu'il est lourd, ton cousin!* That cousin of yours is a bit slow on the uptake! **2** *En avoir lourd sur la patate:* **a** To 'have a load on one's mind', to be burdened with worries. **b** To be full of resentment. **3** *Il fait lourd:* It's close – The weather is muggy.

lourd *adv.* Lots of, much. (With the exception of *gagner lourd:* to 'make a packet', to earn a lot, this adverb is nearly always to be found in a negative turn of phrase. *Il n'en fait pas lourd:* He does bugger-all. *Il n'en reste pas lourd:* There's not much left. *Ça ne vaut pas lourd:* It's really worthless.)

lourde *n.f.* Door. *Bouclez la lourde!* Shut that door!

lourdeur *n.m.* 'Break-in artist', burglar.

lourdière *n.f. Concierge,* caretaker of a block of flats.

lourdingue *n.m.* 'Dumbo', dull-witted character.

lourdingue *adj.* **1** Weighty, heavy. **2** 'Dumb', 'slow on the uptake', rather stupid.

lousdé *adj. En lousdé (adv.exp.):* 'Softly-softly', quietly, discreetly. *Se barrer en lousdé:* To slip away unnoticed (also: *en lousdoc*).

loustic *n.m.* **1** 'Would-be wit', facetious character. **2** *(pej.):* 'Geezer', 'bloke', chap. *Qui*

m'a foutu un loustic pareil?! Where the hell did you find that nurk?! (The word is a phonetic corruption of the German *lustig:* funny.)

lové *n.m.* 'Loot', 'brass', money. (This *manouche* word is generally found in the plural, but expressions such as *ne pas manquer de lové:* to be O.K. for money, are not uncommon.)

loyale *adj.f. Faire quelque chose à la loyale:* To be straight, to act in an honest manner.

Luc *Proper name. Fêter Saint-Luc:* To have sodomous intercourse. (This expression is lexicalized by Jacques Cellard and Alain Rey in their DICTIONNAIRE DU FRANÇAIS NON-CONVENTIONNEL, *luc* being the inversion of *cul*.)

lucarne *n.f. La lucarne enchantée (joc.):* The arse-hole, the anal sphincter (in a context of sodomous intercourse).

lucarnes *n.f.pl.* **1** 'Peepers', 'oglers', eyes. **2** 'Specs', 'glasses', spectacles.

Luco *Proper name. Le Luco:* The Luxembourg gardens in Paris.

luette *n.f. Se rincer la luette:* To 'wet one's whistle', to have a drink.

lune *n.f.* **1** *Etre dans la lune:* To be 'up in the clouds', to be day-dreaming. **2** *Promettre la lune:* To make wild promises. *Il veut que je décroche la lune avec les dents:* What he's asking for is near impossible. **3** *Avoir des lunes:* To be a moody person, to be subject to erratic moods. **4** *Avoir ses lunes:* To have a menstrual period. **5** *Etre con comme la lune:* To be 'as thick as two short planks', to be very dim-witted. **6** *Se faire taper dans la lune:* To submit to sodomy.

luné *adj. Etre bien/mal luné:* To be in a good/bad mood. *T'es vraiment mal luné aujourd'hui!* You're really in a foul mood today!

lunette *n.f.* **1** 'Granny's doughnut', lavatory seat. **2** *Mettre la tête à la lunette:* To get the chop, to be guillotined.

lupanar *n.m.* 'Knocking-shop', 'cat-house', brothel.

lurette *n.f. Il y a belle lurette (adv.exp.):* 'Yonks ago', a long time since, quite a long time ago.

lustucru *n.m.* 'Noodle', simpleton, fool. (The origin of the word, according to Kastner and Marks in their GLOSSARY OF POPULAR AND COLLOQUIAL FRENCH, lies in the phonetic representation of *l'eusse-tu cru?* – Would you have believed it? The fact that a French firm manufacturing pasta trades under the name *Lustucru* is probably unconnected.)

luttanche *n.f.* 'Barney', fight.

luxe *n.m. C'est pas du luxe! (iron.):* It's the bare minimum! – Anything less would be an insult!

lyre *n.f. Toute la lyre:* 'The whole bag of tricks', the lot. (In the register of card-players, *la lyre*, short for: *et toute la lyre!* refers to a winning flush.)

M

maboul *n.m.* **1** 'Loony', 'crackpot', mad character. **2** *Etre un maboul de quelque chose*: To be an aficionado, an enthusiastic devotee of a sport or other leisure activity. *C'est un maboul du ballon rond*: He's absolutely nuts about soccer.

maboul *adj.* **1** 'Bonkers', 'potty', mad. **2** Eccentric.

mac *n.m.* **1** *(abbr. maquereau)*: Ponce, pimp, procurer. **2** *(corr. mec)*: 'Geezer', 'bloke', fellow. *C'est un sacré mac!* He's one hell of a guy! (This word has strong 'macho' connotations.) **3** 'Jock', 'Mack', Scotsman.

macab *n.m.* *(abbr. macchabée)*: 'Stiff', dead person.

macache *adv.* **1** 'Bugger-all', none. *On a macache de fric*: We're broke. *J'ai essayé, mais macache!* I tried to but it was a case of nothing doing! **2** *(interj.)*: Not on your nelly! – Certainly not!

macadam *n.m.* **1** Sidewalk, pavement. *Faire le macadam* (of prostitute): To walk the streets, to go soliciting. **2** *Piquer un macadam*: To take a calculated and spectacular tumble whilst on a pedestrian crossing in order to cash in on an unfortunate motorist's insurance policy.

macaron *n.m.* **1** Insignia worn by the recipient of a *décoration* (*Légion d'honneur*, etc.). This small button-sized badge is highly valued by those who sadly cannot sport, in everyday public life, medals received. **2** Official 'disc', windscreen badge adorning the cars of the high and mighty and guaranteed to repel the eagle eye of any traffic warden. **3** 'Wheel', steering-wheel. *Etre un as du macaron*: To be a crack driver. *Il manie le macaron comme un grand!* He certainly doesn't drive like a kid!

Macaroni *n.m.* 'Itie', Italian.

macaroni *n.m.* 'Prick', 'cock', penis. *S'allonger le macaroni* (also: *se taper sur le macaroni*): To 'pull one's wire', to 'wank', to masturbate.

macchabée *n.m.* 'Stiff', dead person.

machin *n.m.* **1** 'Thingy', 'whatsisname', that person. *J'ai encore vu machin hier*: I saw that bloke again yesterday. **2** (also: *machin-chose*): 'Thingummy', thing. *Passe-moi le machin sur la table!* Give me the doodah on the table!

machine *n.f.* **1** *Une machine*: A plot, an intrigue. *Il n'a rien compris à toute votre machine*: He never even realized what you were up to. **2** *Une grande machine (th.)*: A 'spectacular', a large and expensive production. **3** *Machine à coudre (mil.)*: Tommy-gun, machine-gun. **4** *La machine à raccourcir (joc.)*: The guillotine.

mâchouiller *v.trans. & intrans.* To chew absentmindedly.

mâchuré *adj.* 'Blotto', 'pissed', drunk.

Madeleine *Proper name. Pleurer comme une Madeleine*: To 'cry one's heart out', to be in floods of tears.

madoué *interj.* (Euphemistic corruption of *mon Dieu!*): In the same way that the dated 'Ye gods!' appears to be coming back into fashion, *madoué!*, a Breton colloquialism, seems to be gaining favour throughout France.

magasin *n.m. Votre magasin est ouvert! (joc.)*: Your flies are undone! – Your trousers are unzipped! (To this witticism, the usual retort is: *Pas de danger, le vendeur est à l'intérieur!*)

magaze *n.m.* Shop.

magner *v.pronom. Se magner le train* (also: *le derche*): To 'put one's skates on', to get a move on, to hurry up. (The verb is often encountered without the complement, particularly in the imperative. *Magne-toi, ou on va louper le dur!* Get cracking, or we'll miss our train!)

magnes *n.f.pl.* Airs and graces. *Faire des magnes*: To 'act', to behave in an affected manner. *J'en ai marre de ses magnes!* His madam-manners get on my wick!

magnéto *n.m.* *(abbr. magnétophone)*: Tape-recorder.

magnéto *n.f.* Alternator (on motorcar).

magot *n.m.* 'Pile', 'stashed loot', savings. *Epouser un joli petit magot*: To marry into money.

magouille *n.f.* 'Backbiting', intrigues within a firm or establishment. *J'en ai plein le dos de leurs* *magouilles*: I'm sick and tired of this man-eat-man atmosphere!

mahousse *n.m.* 'Hulk', hunk of a man.

mahousse *adj.* 'Ginormous', very big. *On a bouffé une dinde mahousse*: We had a whopping big turkey.

maigre *n.m.* *Faire maigre (joc.)*: To have a lean time where sex is concerned.

maigre *n.f.* *Une fausse maigre*: A woman with a bony frame and features, but with all the vital statistics in the right places.

maigrichon *n.m.* Puny and skinny character.

maigrichon *adj.* 'Skinny', on the thin side. *Elle est plutôt maigrichonne, celle-là!* There's about as much meat on her as on a butcher's pencil!

mailloche *n.f.* Thumping and bashing. *Il aime la mailloche*: He likes a good punch-up.

mailloche *adj.* Hard-hitting, brutal, violent. *Comme catcheur, il y a pas plus mailloche*: You won't find a fiercer fighter in the wrestling game.

main *n.f.* **1** *Avoir la main heureuse*: To 'have a knack with things', to be lucky by nature. **2** *Avoir la main baladeuse*: To 'have wandering hands', to have a tendency to 'paw'. **3** *Avoir un poil dans la main*: To be an 'idle git', to be a lazy so-and-so. **4** *Etre en main* (of prostitute): To be with a client. **5** *Se faire la main*: To 'try one's hand at something', to practise. **6** *Ça fait ma main!* It suits me to a T! – That's fine by me! **7** *Faire une main tombée*: **a** To make a swoop for, to 'pinch', to steal. **b** To give a woman a sly stroke on the behind. **8** *Se prendre en main (joc.)*: To 'pull one's wire', to masturbate. **9** *Se prendre par la main*: To pluck up courage, to act in a confident manner. **10** *Ne pas y aller de main morte*: To 'make no bones about something', to be ruthlessly frank and aggressive. **11** *Passer la main dans le dos à quelqu'un*: To 'butter up', to flatter someone. *Il aime bien se passer la main dans le dos*: He likes to pat himself on the back. **12** *Avoir un enfant de la main gauche*: To have an illegitimate child. **13** *Ne pas se moucher de la main gauche (iron.)*: To 'fancy oneself', to have no mean opinion of oneself. **14** *C'est du cousu main*: It's done to a turn – It's perfectly done. **15** *Passer la main*: **a** To 'give in', to let someone else handle things. **b** To 'let things ride', to be amenable. **16** *La main de ma sœur dans la culotte d'un zouave*: This jocular catch phrase has no specific meaning, but implies that whatever has been said or done is highly ridiculous.

maintenir *v.pronom.* *Ça se maintient* (In answer to a question inquiring about someone's health): 'So-so', 'fair-to-middling', no better no worse.

mais *adv.* *Non mais des fois! (iron.)*: Don't make me laugh! – You must be joking!

maison *n.f.* **1** (abbr. *maison close* or *maison de passe*): 'Cat-house', brothel. *Maison d'abattage*: Low-class brothel (usually situated near a harbour or army barracks). **2** *La Grande Maison*: 'The cop-shop', the police station. **3** *La maison des mille lourdes*: 'The big house', 'the nick', prison. **4** *La maison tire-boutons*: Lesbianism. **5** *Gros comme une maison (adv.exp.)*: Plainly, clearly, obviously. *Gros comme une maison, j'ai vu qu'il allait me demander du fric*: I just knew he was going to ask me for a loan!

maison *adj.inv.* 'Ace', first-rate, really out of the ordinary. *Une engueulade maison*: One hell of a telling-off. *On a fait un gueuleton maison*: We had ourselves a slap-up meal!

mal *n.m.* **1** *Avoir* (also: *se donner*) *un mal de chien*: To have the devil of a job. *Elle se donne un mal de chien pour élever ses enfants*: She sweats her guts out to bring up her kids. **2** *Avoir mal aux cheveux*: To 'have a hangover', to feel the after-effects of a drinking bout. **3** *Etre guéri du mal de dents (iron.)*: To be 'out of one's misery', to be dead. **4** *En avoir mal au ventre*: To feel sick at the thought of something. **5** *Un pantalon à la mal au ventre*: Old-fashioned trousers with frontal pockets.

mal *adv.* **1** *La foutre mal*: To 'look bad', to give a bad impression. *Vraiment, tu la fous mal toujours en pullover*: You really let the side down, always wearing baggy pullovers. **2** *Ça va mal, non?! (iron.)*: Are you alright?! – You must be joking! **3** *Tu vas mal, toi!* You're going it a bit strong! –You're exaggerating! **4** *Tu me fais mal, toi!* You give me the pip! – You make me sick! **5** *Se trouver mal sur quelque chose (joc.)*: To 'nick', to 'pinch', to steal something.

malabar *n.m.* **1** 'Hulk', hunk of a man. **2** Bank-note of large denomination.

malabar *adj.* **1** 'Ginormous', huge, large. **2** 'Ace', first-rate.

malade *adj.* **1** *Etre malade du pouce (iron.)*: To be 'tight-fisted', 'stingy', to be mean. **2** *Non mais, tu es malade?!* Are you out of your tiny little mind?! – You must be joking!

maladie *n.f.* **1** *En faire une maladie*: To be 'down in the dumps', to be very upset over something. *Il n'y a vraiment pas de quoi faire une maladie!* I really don't see what all the fuss is about! **2** *La maladie de neuf mois (joc.)*: Pregnancy.

malaga *n.m.* *Un malaga de boueux*: A glass of 'plonk', a measure of cheap red wine.

malapatte *n.m.* 'Butter-fingers', clumsy oaf.

malapatte *adj.* 'All fingers-and-thumbs', clumsy.

mal-baisée *n.f.* Grouchy and dissatisfied woman. (The male chauvinist assumption here is that unsatisfactory sex is at the root of the problem.)

mal-blanchi *n.m. (pej.)*: 'Coon', 'wog', coloured person.

malchançard *n.m.* 'Jonah', unlucky person (one who is afflicted with bad luck or brings it to others).

maldonne *n.f. Il y a maldonne*: **a** We're not on the same wavelength! – There's a misunderstanding here. **b** There's a hitch – There's a snag. (Originally *maldonne* referred to a misdeal in a card-game.)

malfrat *n.m.* Crook, criminal.

malfretaille *n.f. La malfretaille*: Small-time crooks. (The word is used in a derogatory manner by law-enforcement officers and the 'big boys' of the underworld.)

malheur *n.m.* **1** *Faire un malheur*: To lose control of oneself. *Retenez-moi ou je fais un malheur!* I won't be able to restrain myself much longer! **2** *Jouer de malheur*: To 'be out of luck', to be plagued by misfortune. **3** *Ne parlez pas de malheur!* Don't even think about it, it'll bring bad luck!

malheureux *adj.* **1** 'Pitiful', paltry. *Et tout cela pour une malheureuse petite bêtise!* And all that for a trivial lapse! *Et vous travaillez pour une malheureuse paye comme ça?!* And you mean to say you work for a pittance like that?! **2** *C'est malheureux pour lui!* It's hard lines on him! – It's tough for him! **3** *Si c'est pas malheureux (quand même)!* Isn't it a rotten shame?! – Doesn't it make you sick?! – What rotten luck! **4** *Avoir la main malheureuse*: To be plagued with bad luck.

malice *n.f. Se faire malice tout seul* (of woman): To masturbate (also: *se faire une malice*).

malin *adj.* **1** *Faire son petit malin*: To 'play the smart-aleck', to try and show off one's intellectual capacities. **2** *C'est malin! (iron)*: That's really clever (of you)! – What a stupid thing to do!

malle *n.f.* **1** 'Trap', 'gob', mouth. *Ferme ta malle!* Shut your cake-hole! – Shut up! *S'en fourrer plein la malle*: To 'stuff one's face', to eat immoderately. **2** *(mil.)*: 'Cooler', 'slammer', prison. **3** *Se faire la malle*: To 'beetle off', to 'hook it', to decamp. **4** *Boucler sa malle*: To 'pop one's clogs', to 'snuff it', to die. **5** *La malle à quatre nœuds (joc. & iron.)*: 'Pauper's wallet' (literally, the Dick Whittington neckerchief bundle with all his worldly possessions).

mallette *n.f. Faire mallette et paquette*: To walk out after a bust-up, to jilt.

mallouzer *v.trans.* (also: *mallouser*): To 'walk out on', to jilt someone.

malparade *n.f.* Ineffective dodge away from a blow.

Malva *Proper name. Aller chez Malva*: To have a run of bad luck. (This personification of ill-fate is not what it seems; *malva* is, in reality, the result of *verlen* on *va mal*.)

mama *n.f.* 'Brood-hen', mother with a string of children.

mamelons *n.m.pl.* 'Bristols', 'knockers', firm breasts.

mamelue *adj.f.* 'Well-stacked', endowed with ample and firm breasts.

mamie *n.f.* (Child's language): 'Gran', 'grannie', grandmother.

mamours *n.m.pl. Faire des mamours (à quelqu'un)*: **a** To caress and smother with kisses. **b** To indulge in base flattery.

manchard *n.m.* Tramp, beggar.

manche *n.m.* **1** 'Burk', 'nincompoop', idiot. *Il s'est débrouillé comme le manche qu'il est*: He went about it all like the fool he is. *Etre dégourdi comme un manche*: To be a clumsy oaf. **2** 'Prick', 'cock', penis. *Avoir le manche*: To have 'the big stick', to have an erection. *S'astiquer le manche*: To 'wank', to masturbate. **3** *Etre du côté du manche*: To be well in with the high-and-mighty. **4** *Branler dans le manche* (of person or venture): To be 'shaky', to be on the proverbial last legs. **5** *Tomber sur un manche*: To 'come a cropper', to suffer a setback. **6** *Manche à balai*: **a** Joystick, control lever in aircraft. **b** 'Prick', 'cock', penis (also: *manche à couilles*). **c** 'Beanpole', gawky person.

manche *n.f.* **1** *Tirer quelqu'un par la manche*: To 'buttonhole', to pester someone. *Se faire tirer par la manche*: To need persuading. **2** *Avoir quelqu'un dans sa manche*: To be 'well in with someone', to be on excellent terms with someone. **3** *Avoir les jambes en manches de veste*: To be bandy, to be bow-legged (also: *avoir des jambes Louis XV*). **4** *Faire la manche*: To go round begging. **5** *C'est une autre paire de manches!* That's a different kettle of fish! – It's another matter!

manche *adj.* Gauche, clumsy.

manchette *n.f.* **1** Karate chop, fierce blow with the stretched hand and forearm. **2** Banner headline in newspaper. **3** *(pl.)*: 'Ringlets', 'bracelets', handcuffs.

manchot *adj. Ne pas être manchot*: **a** To be 'handy', to be clever with one's hands. **b** To be 'all there', to be 'sharp', to be clever and quick-witted.

mandagat *n.m. (corr. mandat)*: 'Money-order', postal money transfer.

mandalle *n.f.* 'Clout', slap in the face.

mandarin *n.m.* 'Egghead', intellectual.

mandarines *n.f.pl.* 'Fried-egg boobs', 'titties', small breasts.

mandibules *n.f.pl. Claquer des mandibules*: To be famished, to be starving.

mandoline *n.f.* **1** Bidet. **2** Bed-pan. **3** *Se faire un solo de mandoline* (of woman): To masturbate.

mandrin *n.m.* 'Prick', 'cock', penis. *Avoir le mandrin*: To have 'the big stick', to have an erection.

manettes *n.f.pl.* **1** (Cycling slang): Bicycle pedals. *Pousser sur les manettes*: To pedal away fast and furiously. **2** *Perdre les manettes*: To 'go to pieces', to lose control of oneself.

mangave *n.f.* **1** Begging, the act of soliciting money in a public place. **2** Food, sustenance.

mangaver *v.trans. & intrans.* **1** To beg for alms. **2** To 'nosh', to eat.

mangeaille *n.f.* 'Grub', 'eats', food. *Côté mangeaille, ça va*: The nosh here is reasonable.

manger *v.trans. & intrans.* **1** *Ça se laisse manger!* This is pretty good grub by any standard! **2** *On en mangerait!* If it's as good as it looks, count me in! **3** *Manger avec les chevaux de bois*: To 'skip it', to 'skip a meal', to go without food. **4** *Manger de la vache enragée*: To have to rough it, to be forced into a life of near total indigence. **5** *Manger son blé en herbe*: To destroy a financial venture for the sake of a quick profit. **6** *Manger à tous les râteliers*: To be an opportunist (by serving several masters or by receiving payments from different and often conflicting parties). **7** *Manger la consigne*: **a** To forget or ignore advice given. **b** To 'pop one's clogs', to 'snuff it', to die. **8** *Manger le morceau*: To 'spill the beans', to own up, to confess. **9** *En manger*: To be a 'snitch', to be a police informer. **10** *Se manger le pif*: To 'have a barney', to 'have a bust-up', to quarrel. **11** *Il y a là à boire et à manger*: **a** There's more to it than meets the eye. **b** There are pros and cons.

mange-tout *n.m.pl. Les mange-tout*: 'The Krauts', 'the Jerries', the Germans. (This World War II nickname for the Germans refers principally to the colour of the *Wehrmacht*'s uniform reminiscent of the *mange-tout* French bean. Also: *les vert-de-gris*.)

manier *v.pronom. Se manier le derche* (also: *le train*): To 'put one's skates on', to get a move on, to hurry up. *Manie-toi le train!* Don't just stand there! (*Se manier* is often found on its own in the imperative where *le train, le derche* would be cumbersome.)

manière *n.f.* **1** *Avoir la manière*: To have the (right) touch. *Il a la manière, lui au moins!* He at any rate knows how to go about things! **2** *Etre*

pour la manière forte: To favour strong-arm tactics. **3** *Faire des manières*: To 'act lah-di-dah', to put on airs and graces. **4** *En voilà des manières!* That's a fine way to behave!

manieur *n.m. Manieur de fonte (joc.)*: Weight-lifter.

manif *n.f.* (*abbr. manifestation*): 'Demo', demonstration.

manigance *n.f.* 'Hanky-panky', 'jiggery-pokery', underhand practice. (*Manigance* is more often than not found in the plural, perhaps because underhand practices are several and co-ordinated. *J'en ai marre de leurs manigances*: I'm sick and tired of all this string-pulling.)

manigancer *v.trans.* To scheme, to intrigue. *Je me demande ce qu'il est en train de manigancer!* I wonder what underhand business he's up to now!

manigancer *v.pronom.* **1** *Je me demande ce qui se manigance!* I wonder what's cooking! – I wonder what's going on. **2** *Comment ça se manigance, ce machin?* How the devil does that thing work?

manitou *n.m. Un grand manitou*: A 'big-shot', a 'kingpin', an important person. *Dans cette affaire, il est le grand manitou*: In this operation he's the chief cook and bottle-washer!

manivelle *n.f. Démarrer à la manivelle*: To be 'slow on the uptake', to need prompting.

manivelles *n.f.pl.* **1** (Cycling slang): 'Pins', 'gambs', legs. **2** Arms, limbs in general. *Jouer des manivelles*: To race along.

mannequins *n.m.pl. Les mannequins*: 'The fuzz', the 'cops', the police.

mannezingue *n.m.* Wine-merchant and bistrot proprietor. (The establishment he runs gives customers the opportunity of sampling wine by the glass before purchasing bottles.)

manoche *n.f.* (*corr. manille*): This card game was particularly popular between the wars. *Se tailler* (also: *se taper*) *une manoche*: To have a game of manille.

manœuvre *n.f. Y aller à la manœuvre*: To make a great show of a flurry of activity. *Et ça y va à la manœuvre! (joc. & iron.)*: They're certainly pulling their finger out!

manouche *n.m.* **1** (also *n.f.*): Romany, gipsy. **2** *Le manouche*: The 'gipsy lingo', a language spoken by gipsies.

manque *n.m.* **1** (Drug addiction): 'Cold turkey', withdrawal symptoms. **2** *Manque de pot!* What rotten luck! (This expression is not always used as an interjection. *Manque de pot, j'ai dû rentrer*: It was just my (bad) luck I had to go home.)

manque *n.f. A la manque* (*adj.exp.*): 'Dud', 'sham', worthless. *Il a toujours sa bagnole à la* *manque*: He's still driving around in his old banger.

manqué *n.m.* 'Wash-out', failure.

mansarde *n.f.* 'Bean', 'bonce', head. *Yoyoter* (also: *travailler*) *de la mansarde*: To have 'bats in the belfry', to be a trifle mad.

maousse *n.m.* **1** 'Hulk', hunk of a man. **2** *Lâcher un maousse*: To let off a mighty fart.

maousse *adj.* 'Ginormous', very large. *Il fume des cigares maousses*: He's never without a whacking big cigar.

mappemondes *n.f.pl.* 'Knockers', 'boobs', globe-like breasts.

maq *n.m. (abbr. maquereau)*: Ponce, pimp, procurer.

maqué *past part.* 'Shacked-up', cohabiting. *Depuis le temps qu'ils sont maqués, il aurait pu régulariser la situation*: You'd have thought he'd pop the question, them living under the brush all that time.

maquer *v.pronom.* To 'shack up' (with), to start cohabiting.

maquereau *n.m.* **1** Ponce, pimp, procurer. **2** 'Con-man', confidence trickster.

maquereautage *n.m.* **1** Pimping, living off immoral earnings. **2** Diverting and capitalizing of funds.

maquereauter *v.intrans.* **1** To ponce, to live off immoral earnings. **2** To divert funds (for one's own benefit).

maquerelle *n.f.* 'Madam', brothel-keeper.

maquerotin *n.m. (pej.)*: Small-time pimp. (The word is pejorative in that it is used by the 'macho' element in the underworld when referring to the upstarts who have no other means of support.)

maquillage *n.m.* **1** Faking, manufacturing of fake documents. **2** Respraying of body-work and changing of number-plates on stolen cars.

maquille *n.f. Faire de la maquille*: **a** To give 'hot' cars a change of looks and number-plates (as well as fresh documents). **b** To fake I.D. papers and other documents. **c** To mark playing cards.

maquiller *v.trans.* **1** *Maquiller une bagnole*: To give a stolen car new looks, number-plates and log-book. **2** *Maquiller des fafs*: To fake I.D. papers. **3** *Maquiller des brèmes*: To mark cards (for cheating purposes). **4** *Qu'est-ce que tu maquilles?!* What the hell are you up to?

maquiller *v.pronom. Je me demande ce qui se maquille*: I wonder what's going on here.

maquilleur *n.m.* **1** 'Cheat', trickster. **2** 'Fraud', swindler.

marabout *n.m. (mil.)*: 'Sky-pilot', 'padre', clergyman from the Services.

marant *n.m.* **1** 'Card', jokester. **2** 'Prankster', practical joker. *C'est un drôle de petit marant!* He's quite a leg-puller in his own way!

marant *adj.* **1** 'Killing', screamingly funny, hilarious. *Qu'il est marant!* What a card! – He's a scream! **2** Funny, strange, bizarre.

marasquin *n.m.* 'Ketchup', blood.

maraude *n.f. Faire la maraude* (of taxi): To be touting for trade by driving around rather than queueing with other cabs at a taxi-rank.

marauder *v.intrans.* (of cabbie): To be touting for trade.

maravédis *n.m. Etre sans un maravédis*: To be 'skint', 'broke', to be penniless.

maraver *v.trans.* **1** To 'bash', to beat up. **2** To 'bump off', to kill.

marca *n.m.* Market, market-place. *Il fait le légume sur les marcas*: He sells veg on the markets.

marchand *n.m.* **1** *Marchand de bobards*: 'Con-man', confidence trickster. **2** *Marchand de lacets*: Gendarme, country policeman. **3** *Marchand de participes*: **a** 'Chalkie', schoolteacher. **b** 'Egg-head', academic pedant. **4** *Marchand de quat'* *(abbr. marchand des quatre saisons)*: Barrow-boy, costermonger. **5** *Marchand de sommeil*: Hotel proprietor. **6** *Marchand de soupe (pej.)*: **a** Restaurateur catering for the masses rather than with quality in mind. **b** Headmaster of a crammer. **7** *Marchand de viande* (also: *marchand de bidoche*): International pimp, white-slaver.

marchande *n.f. Marchande d'ail*: 'Les', 'dyke', lesbian.

marchandise *n.f.* **1** 'Doings', excrement. **2** *Balancer la marchandise*: To 'juice off', to ejaculate.

marche *n.f. Faire une marche arrière (fig.)*: To pull out of a deal.

marché *n.m. S'en tirer à bon marché*: To 'get off lightly', to avoid punishment.

marcher *v.intrans.* **1** To accept, to consent to. *D'accord, je marche, comptez sur moi!* O.K., I'm with you, count me in! **2** To 'be taken in', to fall for something. *Il marche à tous les coups*: He's as gullible as they come. *Faire marcher quelqu'un*: To 'pull someone's leg', to lead someone along. **3** *Ça ne marche pas pour moi!* That doesn't suit me at all! **4** *Marcher à côté de ses lattes*: To be 'down on one's uppers', to be 'broke', to be penniless (also: *marcher sur les empeignes*). **5** *Marcher sur les pieds de quelqu'un*: To 'tread on someone's corns', to offend someone. **6** *Marcher à la dix heures dix*: To have a 'ten-to-two' gait (with the tips of one's feet pointing outwards). **7** *Avoir appris à marcher sur un tonneau*: To be 'bandy', to be bow-legged.

marcheur *n.m.* 'House-breaker', burglar.

marcheuse *n.f.* 'Prozzy', prostitute.

marcottin *n.m.* (also: *marcotin*). *Un marcottin*: A month. *Ça fait bien onze marcottins que je l'ai pas vu!* It's going on a year since I last saw him!

mardoche *n.m.* Tuesday.

mare *n.f.* 1 *La Grande Mare* (Racing slang): The water jump (originally the one at the Auteuil racecourse in Paris). 2 *La mare aux harengs*: **a** The Atlantic Ocean. **b** 'The briny', any sea or ocean.

margoulette *n.f.* 1 'Mush', 'dial', face. *Casser la margoulette à quelqu'un*: To 'push someone's face in', to sock someone in the jaw. 2 'Gob', mouth. *Ça vous emporte la margoulette* (of highly-spiced food or very potent drink): It burns a hole in your mouth.

margoulin *n.m.* 1 'Con-man', swindler. 2 Black marketeer.

marguerite *n.f. Effeuiller la marguerite*: **a** To play 'she loves me, she loves me not' (by plucking daisy petals). **b** To undress a woman.

Marianne *Proper name*. The French Republic, its personification in the shape of a woman, as Britannia is to the British.

marida *n.m.* 'Wedding-knot', marriage. *Aller au marida*: To 'get hitched', to 'get spliced'.

marida *adj.* 'Hitched', 'spliced', married.

marida *v.pronom.* To 'get wed', to get married.

marié *past part. Etre marié à la mairie du 21ᵐᵉ arrondissement (joc. & iron.)*: To be 'shacked up', to 'live under the brush', to cohabit. (The humour arises from the fact that there are only twenty *arrondissements* in Paris.)

Marie-Chantal *Proper name*. Popular personification of the typical uppity young lady in France. (The male counterpart is *Gérard*. In the 50s and 60s there was a spate of *Gérard et Marie-Chantal* jokes.)

Marie-couche-toi-là *n.f. (pej.)*: 'Easy-lay', promiscuous girl.

mariée *n.f. Se plaindre que la mariée est trop belle*: To be a jammy bugger and moan about it, to complain about getting too much of a good thing.

marie-jeanne *n.f.* (Drugs): 'Mary-Jane', marijuana.

marie-louise *n.f.* 'Pongy', silent fart.

marie-salope *n.f.* 'Bloody Mary', tomato juice strengthened with vodka.

marin *n.m. Marin d'eau douce (joc. & iron.)*: 'Landlubber', person who is unaccustomed to seafaring.

marine *n.m. (abbr. pantalon marine)*: 'Bell-bottoms', heavily-flared trousers.

marine *n.f. Faire des cordes pour la marine (joc.)*: To 'crap', to 'shit', to defecate.

marine *adj. (abbr. bleu marine)*: Navy-blue.

mariner *v.intrans.* To 'wait and wait', to be kept waiting.

mariole *n.m.* 1 'Smart-aleck', 'clever clogs', would-be know-all. 2 'Nincompoop', fool. *Cesse de faire le mariole!* Stop arsing about! (and drawing attention to yourself).

mariole *adj.* Stupid, foolish.

marionnette *n.f.* 'Fall-guy', scapegoat.

marle *n.m.* 1 'Wise head', character who knows his business. 2 (also: *marlou*): Pimp, ponce, procurer.

marle *adj.* 'Wily', cunning.

marlou *n.m.* Pimp, ponce, procurer.

marlouserie *n.f.* Sly con-trick.

marmaille *n.f. Une marmaille*: 'A load of kids', a string of children.

marmelade *n.f.* 1 *En marmelade*: 'Bashed-up', smashed-up. *Mettre quelqu'un en marmelade*: To beat someone to a pulp. 2 *Etre dans la marmelade*: To be 'in a jam', to be 'in the soup', to be in a fix.

marmitage *n.m.* 1 *(mil.)*: Strafing, heavy bombing or shelling. 2 'Hiding', severe and painful punishment.

marmite *n.f.* 1 'Prozzy', 'tart', prostitute (literally, the pimp's meal-ticket.) 2 *Grande marmite*: Top-security jail. 3 *Faire bouillir la marmite*: To 'keep the pot boiling', to be the bread-winner.

marmiter *v.trans. Se faire marmiter* (of inmate): To be caught red-handed breaking a prison regulation and get sentenced to 'solitary'.

marmot *n.m.* 1 'Nipper', 'kid', child. *Un sale marmot*: A brat. 2 *Croquer le marmot*: To 'kick one's heels', to become impatient through having to wait.

marmouset *n.m.* 1 'Nipper', 'kid', child. 2 Fœtus, aborted embryo.

marner *v.intrans.* To 'graft', to work hard.

marneur *n.m.* 'Grafter', character who 'works his guts out', hard worker.

maronner *v.intrans.* 1 To 'bleat', to 'belly-ache', to grumble. 2 To 'wait and wait', to be kept waiting.

marotte *n.f.* 1 'Bee-in-one's-bonnet', obsession. 2 'Fad', passing whim.

maroufler *v.intrans.* To indulge in some underhand and profitable activities under the cover of one's job. (The original and literal meaning of *maroufler*: to lay a canvas on a board or other flat surface by means of glue, points to the colloquial meaning.)

marqua *n.m.* Market, market-place.

marqué *n.m. Un marqué*: A month of imprisonment. *Tirer trois marqués de ballon*: To do a three-month stretch.

marquer *v.trans.* 1 *Marquer le pas*: **a** To bide one's time. **b** To miss out where promotion is concerned. 2 *Marquer un point*: To 'notch up a victory', to strike an advantage. 3 *Marquer le coup*: To be unable to hide one's feelings, emotions when confronted with startling facts or news.

marquer *v.intrans. & trans.* **1** To 'score', to notch up a sexual victory. **2** *Marquer midi (joc.)*: To 'have the big stick', to have an erection. **3** *Marquer mal*: **a** To look out of place. **b** To make a bad impression.

marquouse *n.f.* (also: *marquouze*): Mark on playing cards for cheating purposes.

marquouser *v.trans.* To mark cards.

marrade *n.f. Une marrade*: 'A giggle', a good old laugh.

marrant *adj.* **1** 'Killing', screamingly funny, hilarious. *Il est d'un marrant!* He's a right card! **2** 'Funny', strange, bizarre.

marre *adv.* Enough, more than enough. *En avoir marre*: To 'have had a bellyful of', to be fed up to the back teeth with. *J'en ai plus que marre de ses giries!* I'm sick and tired of his perpetual moans and groans!

marrer *v.pronom.* **1** To have a jolly good laugh. *Se marrer comme un bossu*: To be doubled up with laughter. **2** *Il me fait marrer! (iron.)*: He must be joking, who does he think he is?! *Vous me faites marrer avec vos grèves!* I don't know what you're up to with all your bloody strikes!

marron *n.m.* Blow, punch. *Prendre un marron sur la gueule*: To get a knuckle-sandwich up the kisser. *Secouer la poêle à marrons*: To get a drubbing, to get thrashed. *Chauds, les marrons, chauds!* This jocular and ironic expression is often uttered by spectators and bystanders enjoying a good punch-up in or out of the ring.

marron *adj.inv.* **1** 'Sham', bogus. **2** 'Shady', disreputable. **3** *Etre fait marron*: **a** To be 'conned', 'diddled', to be swindled. *On a vraiment été faits marron*: We were taken in good and proper. **b** To get 'nabbed', 'collared', to be arrested.

marronnant *adj.* 'Aggravating', irritating, annoying.

marronner *v.intrans.* To 'grouse', to grumble, to complain.

Marsiale *Proper name. La Marsiale*: Marseilles. *Un de la Marsiale*: A native of that city.

marsouin *n.m.* 'Jack-tar', sailor.

marteau *n.m. Avoir un coup de marteau*: **a** To feel 'knackered', 'shattered', to feel suddenly very tired (also: *avoir le coup de marteau*). **b** To be 'cracked', 'bonkers', to be mad.

marteau *adj.inv.* 'Cracked', 'loco', mad. *Il est complètement marteau!* He's gone off his rocker!

martique *n.m. & f.* Native of Marseilles.

masquard *n.m.* 'Hard-luck-Joe', character who never seems to get a lucky break.

masquard *adj.* Unlucky, plagued by bad luck.

masque *n.f.* Run of bad luck.

massacrante *adj.f. Etre d'une humeur massacrante*: To be 'in a rotten mood', to be in a foul temper.

massacre *n.m. Un jeu de massacre*: A venture where few come out unscathed. (The standard meaning of *jeu de massacre* is the Aunt Sally stall at a fun-fair.)

massacrer *v.trans.* To give an abysmal rendering (of play, poetry, musical work). *Il nous a massacré du Mozart toute la soirée*: We were treated to an evening of chopsticks Mozart!

massacreur *n.m.* Infernal interpreter (where music or acting is concerned).

masse *n.f.* **1** *Une masse* (also: *des masses de*): 'Loads of', 'oodles', a vast quantity of. **2** *La masse*: 'The kitty', pooled financial resources. *Sans la masse, on aurait crevé la dalle*: Without our piggy-bank, we'd have gone hungry. **3** *C'est le coup de masse!* (of bill, price): It's the limit! – It's exorbitant! **4** *Recevoir le coup de masse (fig.)*: To be 'hit for six', to be stunned by an emotional blow. **5** *Tomber comme une masse*: To 'go out like a light', to fall asleep as one's head hits the pillow. **6** *Etre à la masse*: To be 'cracked', 'barmy', to be mad. (The expression *à la masse* originates in the language of electricians, and literally means that an appliance is 'live' and therefore dangerous to touch.)

masser *v.intrans.* To 'graft', to toil, to work hard.

massue *n.f.* **1** *Argument massue*: Sledge-hammer logic. **2** *Coup de massue*: **a** 'Floorer', knockout blow. **b** 'Crusher', emotional shock (news, unkind comment). **c** 'Fleecer', outrageously heavy bill (in hotel, restaurant).

mastard *n.m.* **1** 'Hulk', stocky figure of a man. **2** Bulky item, large object.

mastard *adj.* **1** 'Hunky', near muscle-bound. **2** 'Ginormous', very large.

mastègue *n.f.* 'Grub', 'eats', food. *La mastègue est de première ici*: The nosh here is first-rate.

mastéguer *v.trans. & intrans.* To eat. (Both the noun *mastègue* and the verb *mastéguer* originate from Provence.)

mastic *n.m.* **1** 'Mix-up', muddle. *Tu parles d'un mastic!* That was one hell of a cock-up! **2** 'Printers' pie', typographical mix-up. (It is amusing to note that the non-colloquial meaning of 'cock-up', according to Garmonsway, is: 'a superior letter or number, as "r" in D".) **3** *Cherrer dans le mastic*: To 'lay it on a bit thick', to exaggerate. **4** *Faire le mastic* (of waiter in café): To sweep up after closing time. **5** *Bouder le mastic*: To 'pick at one's food', to nibble at a plateful. **6** *S'endormir sur le mastic*: To leave a job unfinished.

masticotte *n.f. Avoir une bonne masticotte*: To have the gift of the gab, to have a loquacious disposition (also: *avoir la langue bien pendue*).

masticotter *v.intrans.* To 'gab', to talk on and on.

mastoc *n.m.* 'Bull-in-a-china-shop' character, very clumsy person.

mastoc *adj.inv.* **1** Bulky, very large. **2** (of person): 'Heavy', 'lumpish', ungainly in manner.

mastodonte *n.m.* **1** 'Hulk', hunky figure of a man. **2** 'Whopper', large object. **3** 'Artic', articulated heavy goods vehicle.

mastroquet *n.m.* Bar-keeper, publican. *Le mastroquet est vraiment sympa*: The landlord here is a genial bloke.

m'as-tu-vu *n.m.* **1** *(th.)*: 'Ham', conceited actor. **2** 'Wally', character whose crass and low-brow behaviour makes him the laughing-stock of those who think they have better taste.

mat' *n.m. (abbr. matin)*: Morning. *On s'est levé à six heures du mat'*: We got up at 6 a.m. *Au petit mat'*: At the crack of dawn.

mataf *n.m.* 'Jack-tar', sailor.

mataguin *n.m. (corr. matin) Le mataguin*: 'The crack of dawn', first thing in the morning.

mate *n.f. Prendre un jeton de mate*: To get a salacious eyeful (also: *se rincer l'œil*).

mate *n.f. La mate (abbr. l'Ecole Maternelle)*: Infant school.

matelas *n.m.* Packed wallet, one filled with a wad of notes. *Avoir les matelas*: To be 'loaded', to be 'rolling in it', to be extremely rich.

mater *v.trans. & intrans.* **1** To watch closely, to observe. *Mate un peu ça!* Take a butcher's at this! **2** To 'ogle', to eye salaciously.

matérielle *n.f. Assurer sa matérielle*: To 'make ends meet', to earn one's living.

mateur *n.m.* 'Voyeur', salacious ogler.

matheux *n.m. (sch.)*: 'Crack' at maths, pupil who is gifted for mathematics.

mathurin *n.m.* 'Jack-tar', sailor.

matière *n.f. Matière grise*: 'Grey matter', intelligence. *Avoir de la matière grise*: To have what it takes up-top.

matin *n.m. Un de ces quatre matins (joc.)*: One of these days. *Un de ces quatre matins, tu vas prendre un pain sur le coin de la gueule!* One of these days, laddie, you'll get what's coming to you! (also: *un de ces quatre*).

matinée *n.f. Faire la grasse matinée*: To 'have a lie-in', to get up late.

matois *n.m.* 'Canny devil', shrewd person (also: *fin matois*).

matois *adj.inv.* 'Canny', shrewd.

maton *n.m.* **1** 'Screw', prison warder. **2** 'Grass', prison inmate who hopes to gain favour by informing on others.

matou *n.m.* **1** 'Tom', tom-cat. **2** *(joc. & iron.)*: Randy so-and-so, sexy lover.

matouser *v.trans. & intrans.* (also: *matouzer*): **1** To watch closely, to observe. **2** To 'ogle', to eye salaciously.

matraque *n.f.* **1** *Mettre la matraque*: **a** To use strong-arm tactics. **b** To resort to drastic measures. **2** *Coup de matraque*: 'Fleecer', 'stinger', outrageously heavy bill (in hotel, restaurant). **3** *Avoir la matraque*: **a** To have a winning hand at poker. **b** To have 'the big stick', to have an erection.

matraquer *v.trans.* **1** To make someone pay dearly for something he may or may not have done. **2** (in restaurant): To 'clobber', to grossly overcharge. **3** (of judge): To be heavy-handed when sentencing someone. **4** To use strong-arm tactics. **5** To hammer an advertising message home to the public.

matraqueur *n.m.* 'Heavy-handed yob', bully who enjoys resorting to violence.

matricule *n.m. En prendre pour son matricule*: To 'cop it', to be on the receiving end of something unpleasant. *Ça va barder pour ton matricule!* You're in for it!

matuche *n.m.* **1** 'Cop', 'copper', policeman. *Les matuches*: The fuzz. **2** 'Screw', prison warder. **3** *(pl.)*: Loaded dice.

Maub' *Proper name. La Maub'*: The *Place Maubert* and its surrounding *quartier* in Paris.

mauvais *adv. Ça sent mauvais!* I can smell a rat! – There's trouble brewing!

mauvaise *adj.f. L'avoir mauvaise*: To 'take a dim view of', to find something no joke.

mauviette *n.f.* **1** Puny figure, weakling, skinny character. **2** 'Drip', spineless character.

maxi *n.m. (abbr. maximum)*: **1** *Ecoper le maxi*: To 'cop a heavy sentence', to get a long term of imprisonment. **2** *Donner le maxi*: To try one's darnedest, to give one's all. **3** *Se taper le maxi*: To drive flat-out (in a car, on a motorbike, etc.).

maxi *n.f.* Maxi-skirt, fashion's antonym to the mini.

mayonnaise *n.f.* **1** 'Cock-up', mix-up. *On s'est retrouvé dans une sacrée mayonnaise*: We landed ourselves in one hell of a mess. **2** *Monter en mayonnaise*: To 'get all worked up about something', to become more and more angry.

mazagran *n.m.* Tall glassful of black coffee. (This seemingly unappetizing beverage – it is drunk cold – is still reasonably popular.)

mazette *n.m.* 'Drip', 'spineless character', person lacking will and initiative.

mazette *interj.* Cripes! – Blimey! – Crumbs! (This interjection expressing astonishment is as dated in French as its English counterparts.)

mec *n.m.* **1** 'Geezer', 'bloke', fellow. *Un sacré mec*: One hell of a guy. *Un drôle de mec*: A queer cove (someone you can't really weigh up). *Un pauvre mec*: A nobody, a real nonentity. *Pauvre mec!* You burk! *C'est le mec des mecs*: He's tops – He's a first-rate guy. **2** *Le grand Mec*: God Almighty. **3** *(corr. maquereau)*: Pimp, ponce, procurer.

mécanique *n.f.* **1** 'Gadget', contraption. **2** *(pl.)*: Shoulders. *Rouler des mécaniques* (also: *rouler les mécaniques*): To 'strut about', to walk around in a cocky, rooster-like manner.

mécano *n.m.* Mechanic.

méchamment *adv.* 'Bloody', 'damned', hellishly. *C'est méchamment bon!* It's scrumptious! (This adverb is more often than not used with a positive connotation.)

méchant *n.m.* One who is both cantankerous and violent. *Faire le méchant*: To act the bully-boy. *Cesse de faire le méchant!* Why don't you be nice for a change!

méchant *adj.* 'Great', splendid. *Il m'a donné un méchant coup de main*: He certainly came to my rescue.

mèche *n.f.* **1** *Etre de mèche avec quelqu'un*: To be 'in cahoots with', to be in league with someone. *Ils sont de mèche, ces deux-là*: Those two characters are hand-in-glove. **2** *Eventer la mèche*: **a** To 'let the cat out of the bag', to let a secret slip out. **b** To get wind of a secret. **3** *Sentir la mèche*: To 'smell a rat', to get suspicious. **4** *Il n'y a pas mèche de*: There's not a lot of it about. *Il n'y a pas mèche de toubibs ici!* Medics are pretty thin on the ground in, these parts! **5** *Pas mèche!* Nothing doing! – No way! – It's impossible! **6** *et mèche*: And on top of that – and a bit more. *Des comme ça j'en ai vu et mèche*: I've seen quite a few like that in my time!

mécol *pers.pron.* Me, myself. *La bouffe qui reste, c'est pour mécol!* The grub what's left is for me!

mecton *n.m.* (also: *mecqueton*): 'Geezer', 'bloke', chap.

médaille *n.f.* *Porter la médaille*: **a** To 'carry the can', to shoulder the responsibility. **b** To 'get framed', to fall foul of fabricated evidence.

médoche *n.f.* *(corr. médaille)*: 'Gong', medal (also: *méduche*).

Médor *Proper name.* Archetypal dog's name found in many novelettes and children's stories. Suitable English equivalents would be Rover or Fido.

méduser *v.trans.* To 'flabbergast', to 'stagger', to dumbfound.

mégot *n.m.* **1** 'Dog-end', 'fag-end', cigarette butt. **2** *Des mégots*: 'Peanuts', trifling amounts of money.

mégotage *n.m.* **1** *Du mégotage*: 'Odd-jobbery', unimportant activities. **2** *(pl.)*: 'Mean moves', stingy actions.

mégoter *v.intrans.* **1** To go collecting 'dog-ends' (in order to make up 'second-hand'

cigarettes). **2** To behave in a stingy manner, to bicker over trifling amounts of money. *Il passe son temps à mégoter sur les notes de frais*: He likes to go through expense claims with a fine toothcomb. *Il ne mégote pas sur la qualité, lui*: He believes in giving customers value for money.

mégoteur *n.m.* **1** 'Bickerer', awkward and argumentative character where money is concerned. **2** 'Small-fry', small-time operator (also: *mégoteux*).

mégotier *n.m.* Down-and-out who makes a meagre living from the recycling of *mégots*. (In a limited number of cases, *mégotier* can also have the meanings of *mégoteur*, meanings which are figurative rather than literal.)

mélanco *adj.* Sad, melancholic.

mélasse *n.f.* *Etre dans la mélasse*: To be 'up a gum-tree', to be 'in the soup', to find oneself in a difficult situation.

melba *n.f.* *Coupe melba*: Head-shaving inflicted on women alleged to have cohabited with Germans during World War II. This barbarous act of retaliation was perpetrated by many angry French people after the *Libération*.

mélécass *n.m.* **1** Mixture of blackcurrant liqueur and clear brandy. (This deceptively potent drink is still very popular.) **2** *Une voix de mélécass*: A raucous voice denoting habitual inebriation.

mêler *v.pronom. De quoi je me mêle?* (iron.): What's it got to do with you? – What business is it of yours? (*De quoi tu te mêles?* – *De quoi il se mêle?*, etc. have a similar meaning, but lack the ironical edge of the first person singular.)

méli-mélo *n.m.* 'Mish-mash', 'jumble', mix-up. *Quel méli-mélo!* You've never seen such a mess!

mélo *n.m.* *(abbr. mélodrame)*: 'Blood-and-thunder' drama. *Sa vie, faut toujours qu'elle en fasse un mélo!* You could sell her life-story to Mills & Boon! *Faire du mélo*: To over-dramatize.

melon *n.m.* **1** 'Bean', 'bonce', head. **2** 'Goof', 'fat-head', simpleton. **3** Bowler hat. **4** 'Coon', Arab. **5** *Avoir les pieds en cosses de melon*: To be an 'idle git', a lazy so-and-so (literally to have feet and toes curled in the shape of slices of melon skin, in a typically idle, recumbent posture).

membre *n.m.* *(abbr. membre viril)*: Penis.

membrer *v.intrans.* To 'graft', to work hard.

membrineuse *n.f.* 'Licker', 'clapper', tongue (also: *menteuse*).

même *n.m. C'est du pareil au même!* (joc. & iron.): Same difference! – It comes to the same thing!

mémé *n.f.* **1** 'Gran', 'granny', grandmother. **2** *(iron.)*: Woman long past her prime, but who fails to acknowledge it.

mémère *n.f.* **1** 'Mammy', mother. **2** *Faut pas pousser mémère dans les orties! (joc. & iron.)*: Don't push me to the limit! – Don't strain my patience!

ménage *n.m. Se mettre en ménage*: To 'shack up and live under the brush', to cohabit.

ménagerie *n.f. Ça sent la ménagerie!* What a pong! – What a stink! (This expression is usually uttered when referring to a confined space shared by a lot of people.)

mendigot *n.m.* Tramp, beggar.

mendigoter *v.intrans.* To go begging, to ask for charity.

mener *v.trans.* **1** *Mener quelqu'un en barque (fig.)*: To 'lead someone up the garden path', to mislead someone. **2** *Ne pas en mener large*: To 'have one's heart in one's boots', to look and feel sorry for oneself. **3** *Mener Popaul au cirque* (also: *mener le petit au cirque*): To 'have a screw', to fuck, to have intercourse.

ménesse *n.f.* **1** 'Biddy', 'bird', woman. **2** *Ma ménesse*: My missus, the wife. **3** *(pej.)*: 'Pouf', 'pansy', effeminate homosexual. **4** *(pej.)*: 'Funk', coward.

mengave *n.f.* **1** Begging, the act of soliciting money in a public place. **2** 'Grub', food. *La mengave chez eux est de première!* The nosh at his place is pretty good!

Ménilmuche *Proper name.* The *quartier* of *Ménilmontant* in Paris.

méninges *n.f.pl. Les méninges*: 'Grey matter', the brains. *Se creuser les méninges*: To rack one's brains. *Ne pas se casser les méninges*: **a** To take the easy way out (one that involves little reflection). **b** To take life as it comes (without worrying unduly about anything). *MÉNAGE TES MÉNINGES* is the title of a well-known novel by San-Antonio. *Fais un peu travailler tes méninges!* Use your loaf! – Can't you think for yourself?!

méningite *n.f. Ne pas se donner une méningite (joc. & iron.)*: To not overtax one's brain, to go for the easy solution.

menotte *n.f.* (Child language): 'Mitt', hand.

menouille *n.f.* Small change, coins (also: *vaisselle de fouille*).

mental *n.m. Le mental*: 'Grey matter', the brain. *Ne pas se creuser le mental*: **a** To take the easy way out (one that doesn't involve too much thinking). **b** To take life as it comes (without worrying unduly about anything).

mental' *n.f.* In the *milieu*, the notion of *mentalité*, for which this word is an abbreviation, carries a lot of weight. According to Auguste

Le Breton this 'honour amongst thieves' has certainly waned in recent years.

menteuse *n.f.* 'Licker', 'clapper', tongue.

mentir *v.intrans. Mentir comme un arracheur de dents*: To lie through one's teeth.

menu *n.m. Qu'est-ce qu'il y a au menu?! (joc.)*: What's cooking? – What's the plan for today?

mépris *n.m. Traiter quelque chose par le mépris*: To believe in stoic contempt as a cure to an illness.

mequer *v.intrans.* To issue orders left, right and centre (literally to act the big boss).

mequeton *n.m.* 'Geezer', 'bloke', fellow.

mer *n.f. Ce n'est pas la mer à boire! (joc.)*: It's dead easy! – There's nothing to it! – It's very simple!

merdaillon *n.m. (pej.)*: **1** 'Arrogant nurk', pretentious and bombastic person. **2** 'Evil brat', obstreperous child.

merde *n.f.* **1** 'Shit', 'crap', excrement. **2** *Une merde* (of person): A 'turd', a despicable character. **3** 'Crap', rubbish, useless stuff. *Qu'est-ce que vous voulez que je foute avec toute cette merde?!* What do you expect me to do with all this junk?! **4** *Ne pas se prendre pour de la merde*: To think the world of oneself. **5** *Semer la merde*: To get everyone in a panic. **6** *Etre dans la merde (jusqu'au cou)*: To 'be in the soup', to 'be (deep) in it', to be in a (right old) fix. **7** *Traîner quelqu'un dans la merde*: To resort to smear tactics. **8** *Merde alors!* This expletive is only translatable in its spoken context. It is very much a case of who says what; on certain lips, it can be jocular and near-meaningless, on others, near-blasphemous. **9** *Dire merde à quelqu'un*: **a** To tell someone to 'get knotted', to tell someone where he can go (i.e. to hell!). **b** To wish someone luck. (It is interesting to note that coming in contact with excrement, i.e. walking in animal faeces, is deemed in France to bring luck, probably a consolation for having soiled one's shoes! Likewise, wishing someone *merde* is considered as a good luck omen, the ultimate being to wish someone *Merde puissance treize*: Good luck to the power of thirteen.) **10** *Oui ou merde?!* For God's sake, make your mind up! **11** *Faire sa merde*: To 'strut about', to act important. **12** (Typographers' slang): Printers' ink. **13** (Aviation slang): 'Pea-soup', thick mantle of fog. **14** (Drugs): 'Hash', hashish. **15** *Piquer une merde (sch.)*: To get 0/20.

merder *v.intrans.* To 'fuck things up', to 'make a hash of things', to fail abysmally.

merderie *n.f.* 'Shitty' object, ugly item.

merdeux *n.m (pej.)*: **1** 'Arse-hole', unpleasant character. **2** *Faire son merdeux*: To act the high and mighty (also: *ne pas se prendre pour de la merde*).

merdeux *adj.* 'Shitty', nasty. *Un bâton merdeux* (of person): An evil bugger, character you wouldn't like to handle under any circumstance, even with the proverbial barge-pole.

merdier *n.m.* 'Shit', 'right old fix', difficult situation. *On n'est pas encore sorti de ce merdier!* We're not out of this mess by a long chalk!

merdique *adj.* 1 'Shitty', awkward. 2 Boring. *Un discours merdique*: A 'no-light-in-the-tunnel' speech. 3 Confused, uncertain. *Une situation merdique*: An awkward state of affairs (one where all solutions are unsatisfactory).

merdouille *n.f.* *(pej.)*: 'Nurk', weak-willed and unpleasant nonentity.

merdouiller *v.intrans.* To 'dither off course', to become embroiled in details and waver from one's intended course of action.

mère-maca *n.f.* 'Madam', brothel-keeper (also: *mère-maquerelle*).

mère-poule *n.f.* Over-protective character. (When the word refers to a man, it tends to have a pejorative connotation.)

mérinos *n.m.* *Laisser pisser le mérinos (joc. & iron.)*: To bide one's time and stand clear where an awkward decision might prove a sorry one.

merlan *n.m.* 1 'Lock-lopper', hairdresser. 2 Pimp, ponce, procurer.

merle *n.m.* *Un vilain merle*: A 'nasty piece of work', an evil so-and-so.

merlette *n.f.* Under-age prostitute.

merlifiche *n.m.* 1 'Quack', character selling miracle cures at fairs. 2 'Clown', buffoon.

mérovingien *adj.* *(joc. & iron.)*: 'As old 'as the hills', ancient.

mésigue *pers.pron.* Me, myself.

messe *n.f.* *Faire* (also: *tenir*) *des messes basses*: To mutter under one's breath. *Je n'aime pas toutes ces messes basses!* I wish you two would stop whispering!

messieurs-dames *n.pl.* 1 'Queers', 'poufs', homosexuals. *Son bistrot a une clientèle de messieurs-dames*: His pub's a watering-hole for the gay brigade! 2 *'Bonsoir messieurs-dames!'*: Stock popular greeting uttered when entering or leaving a public place; it is roughly equivalent to the English 'Evenin' all!'.

métallo *n.m.* *(abbr. ouvrier métallurgiste)*: Metal-worker.

météo *n.f.* *La météo*: 'The weather', the weather report.

métèque *n.m.* *(pej.)*: 1 'Coon', 'wog', coloured man. 2 Any foreigner with the slightest trace of colouring in his skin.

méthode *n.f.* *Avoir la méthode*: To 'have a few tricks up one's sleeve', to know how to cope with certain problems.

métier *n.m.* *Etre du métier*: To 'know the ropes', to be more than familiar with the running of something.

mètre *n.m.* *Piquer un cent mètres (joc.)*: To 'skedaddle', to 'make tracks', to run away.

métro *n.m.* 1 *Le Métro*: 'The Tube', the underground railway system in Paris. *"Métro, boulot, dodo"*. Standard and disillusioned comment uttered by those only too conscious of the rut of their lives. 2 Throng, crowd of people. *Avant les fêtes il y a un sacré métro dans les grands magasins*: Before Christmas the stores are jam-packed with shoppers.

mettre *v.trans.* 1 *Les mettre (abbr. mettre les bouts)*: To 'beat it', to 'scram', to hare away. 2 To 'lay', to fuck, to have coition with. (This rather pejorative acceptation of the verb becomes even more so in the passive where it seems to refer exclusively to anal intercourse. The expression *se faire mettre* is more often than not found with a figurative meaning: to get conned, to be had.) 3 *Mettre quelqu'un dedans*: To 'pull a fast one' on someone, to con someone. 4 To inflict something very painful on someone *(lit. & fig.)*: *Qu'est-ce qu'il lui en a mis!* She didn't half cop it! 5 *En mettre (un coup)*: To 'graft', to work fast and furiously for a short spell. 6 *Y mettre du sien*: a To 'put one's shoulder to the wheel', to put some personal effort into something. b To 'meet someone halfway', to show the willingness and ability to be conciliatory. 7 *Y mettre les doigts*: To have 'sticky fingers', to pinch, to steal. 8 *Mettre à disposition (pol.)*: To haul someone in front of a magistrate. 9 *Ote-toi de là que je m'y mette!* (Jocular and ironic catch phrase): Move over! – Buzz off! 10 *Mettons que* (also: *Mettez que*): Let's say that . . . *Mettons que tu l'épouses, ça ne va pas résoudre le problème*: Getting married to her won't solve your problem.

mettre *v.trans.reflex.* 1 *Se mettre avec quelqu'un*: To 'shack up with someone', to start co-habiting. 2 *Se mettre bien*: a To 'dress to the nines', to put one's best clothes on. b To 'do oneself proud', to deny oneself nothing. 3 *S'en mettre jusque-là*: a To 'stuff oneself to the gills', to eat voraciously. b To get one's fill (of any pleasurable activity).

meublé *n.m.* 1 *Un meublé*: 'Digs', furnished accommodation. 2 *La police des meublés*: Division of the police force whose task it was to collect the day-to-day information from hotels via the now-defunct card registration system.

meubles *n.m.pl.* 1 *Etre dans ses meubles*: To live in 'unfurnished' digs (i.e. to have all one's own furniture). *Se mettre dans ses meubles*: To move into a place of one's own. **2** *Sauver les meubles (fig.)*: To rescue something from a financial disaster.

meuf *n.f.* (also: *meuffe*): 'Biddy', 'bird', woman.

meule *n.f.* **1** 'Bike', motorbike. **2** *(pl.)*: 'Crunchers', molars. **3** *(pl.)*: 'Cheeks', 'bum', buttocks.

meumeu *adj.inv.* 'Hunky-dory', first-rate. *On s'est tapé un gueuleton tout ce qu'il y a de meumeu*: We treated ourselves to a really slap-up meal.

mézigue *pers.pron.* Me, myself. *Les sèches, c'est pour mézigue!* Those fags are mine!

miam-miam *interj.* Yum-yum! – Yummy-yummy! – It's very good!

miauler *v.intrans.* **1** To 'moan and groan', to complain. **2** To 'open the floodgates', to 'have a bout of the weepies', to cry.

miché *n.m.* **1** (Pimps' slang): 'Punter', client of a prostitute. **2** 'Mug', 'sucker', dupe (also: *micheton*).

miches *n.f.pl.* **1** 'Cheeks', 'bum', behind. *Il s'est fait botter les miches*: He got kicked in the jacksey. *Mettre ses miches en veilleuse* (of prostitute): To retire from 'the game', to give up soliciting. **2** *Avoir les miches à zéro*: To 'have the shits', to be 'in a blue funk', to be petrified.

michetonner *v.intrans.* (of prostitute): To go soliciting.

michetonneuse *n.f.* **1** Housewife resorting occasionally to prostitution to make ends meet. **2** Kept woman. **3** 'Easy-lay', 'randy bird', promiscuous woman.

michto *adj.* (Romany slang): 'Fine', beautiful.

mickey *n.m.* 'Mickey Finn', doctored drink.

micmac *n.m.* **1** 'Mess', 'jumble', complicated state of affairs. *Et qu'est-ce que je dois faire avec tout ce micmac?* And how do you expect me to unravel all this? **2** 'Hanky-panky', 'jiggery-pokery', fiddle (where business matters are concerned).

micro *n.m.* **1** 'Trap', 'gob', mouth. *Ferme ton micro!* Put a sock in it! – Shut up! **2** *Micro polisson (joc.)*: 'Joystick', 'prick', penis.

midi *n.m.* **1** *Voir midi à sa porte*: To see things in one's own light. *Chacun voit midi à sa porte*: There's no accounting for tastes! **2** *Ne pas voir clair en plein midi*: To be blind to the obvious, not to see what is staring one in the face. **3** *Faire voir à quelqu'un les* (also: *des) étoiles en plein midi*: To 'clock someone on the jaw' (and in so doing, make him see the proverbial stars). **4** *Chercher midi à quatorze heures*: To 'go nit-picking', to find complications where none exist. *Ne pas chercher midi à quatorze heures*: To be of a 'go-ahead' disposition, to be a straightforward person. **5** *C'est midi!* It's curtains! – It's

too late now! **6** *Marquer midi*: To 'have the big stick', to have an erection.

midinette *n.f.* Dressmaker's apprentice, young girl training and working at the lowest level in the Paris *Haute Couture* industry. (The expression *avoir une âme de midinette*: to be romantically gullible, reflects the 'one-day-my-Prince-will-come' mentality of the Cinderellas in a luxury trade.)

mie *n.f.* **1** *Mie de pain mécanique* (also: *mie de pain à ressorts*): 'Little strangers', body lice. (As the alternative suggests, this expression can also refer to fleas.) **2** *à la mie de pain (adj.exp.)*: 'Dud', worthless. *Un mec à la mie de pain*: A 'drip', a 'wash-out', a spineless character.

miel *n.m.* **1** *Un miel* (of 'job', enterprise verging on the illegal): A doddle, an easy task. *C'est du miel!* It's as easy as pie! (also: *c'est un pur miel!*). **2** *Miel!* Oh sugar! – Drat! – Damn and blast! (*Miel!* is a euphemistic alternative to the expletive *merde!*)

miette *n.f.* **1** *Ne pas en perdre une miette*: To 'have one's ears flapping', to catch every bit of the tittle-tattle going, to listen intently to sensitive gossip. **2** *Ne pas s'en faire une miette*: 'Not to care a rap', not to give a damn about something. **3** *Faire des miettes*: To suffer from eczema.

mieux *adv. & n.m.* **1** *Qui dit mieux?! (joc. & iron.)*: Any advance on that?! (This expression and its English equivalent originate from the vocabulary of auctioneering, and have drifted into colloquial language with a sarcastic undertone where, for instance, 'tall stories' are concerned.) **2** *On ne peut pas mieux!* You can't top that! **3** *Tout ce qu'il y a de mieux*: 'The tops', nothing but the best. **4** *Etre au mieux avec quelqu'un*: To be 'well in with someone', to be on the best of terms with someone. **5** *Faute de mieux*: For want of anything better. (The ancillary clause to this 'Needs-must-when-the-Devil-drives' expression is the surprising . . . *on couche avec sa femme*.) **6** *A-qui-mieux-mieux*: In competition, in close rivalry (trying to outdo the opposition). *Ce sont des adeptes du qui-mieux-mieux*: They belong to the 'one-up-on-the-Joneses' brigade.

mignard *n.m.* 'Nipper', 'kid', young child.

mignard *adj.* 'Sweet', dainty and pretty.

mignon *n.m.* 'Pansy', 'pouf', homosexual. (The name given to the gay courtiers under Henri III seems to have drifted back into fashion.)

mignonnette *n.f.* Phoney or would-be 'dirty postcard' sold outside Parisian night-clubs to tipsy tourists. (More often than not, these very soft-porn photographs are reproductions of well-known nude paintings housed in the Louvre!)

mignoter *v.trans.reflex.* To 'mollycoddle oneself', to try to lead a cushy and unperturbed life.

mijaurée *n.f.* 'Stuck-up', affected and conceited woman. *Faire sa mijaurée* (of man or woman): To put on languid airs and graces.

mijoter *v.trans.* To scheme (literally, to concoct some devious plans). *Je me demande ce qu'il peut bien mijoter*: I'd like to know what dirty trick he's up to!

mijoter *v.pronom. Qu'est-ce qui se mijote? (fig.)*: What's cooking? – What's brewing? – What's up?

milico *n.m. (corr. milicien)*: Member of the French militia working hand-in-glove with the Germans under the Pétain régime during World War II.

milieu *n.m. Le milieu*: The French underworld. (Strange as it may seem, the word has no real pejorative connotation and is accepted by members of the criminal fraternity as an almost complimentary appellation.)

militaire *adj. A l'heure militaire (adv.exp.)*: On the dot – Exactly – Precisely. *Je serai là à cinq heures, heure militaire!* Have no fear, I'll be there at five on the button!

mille *n.m. Le mille*: The bull's-eye. *Taper dans le mille (fig.)*: To 'hit the nail on the head', to be spot-on. *Et pan dans le mille!* That's the stuff! –That's told him good and proper!

mille *num.adj.inv.* **1** *Gagner des mille et des cents*: To earn money hand-over-fist. **2** *Je vous le donne en mille!* You'll never guess in a hundred years!

mille-feuille *n.m.* **1** Thick wad of banknotes. **2** 'Fanny', 'pussy', vagina. **3** *C'est du mille-feuille!* It's as easy as pie! – It's a doddle! (also: *c'est du gâteau*).

millimètre *n.m. Faire du millimètre*: To 'skimp', to economize in a miserly fashion.

milord *n.m.* Wealthy 'toff', rich and aristocratic man. (This word regained popularity with the Edith Piaf song *'Milord'*.)

mimi *n.m.* **1** 'Puss', pussy, cat. **2** 'Pussy', 'fanny', vagina. **3** (Term of endearment): 'Pet', darling. *Mon mimi*: My lovey-dovey. **4** *Faire mimi* (Child language): To cuddle, to stroke. (The word, as its first meaning suggests, is a corruption of *minet*, itself a colloquial alternative for *chat*.)

mimi *adj.inv.* Sweet, too sweet for words.

mimines *n.f.pl.* 'Mitts', hands (usually small and dainty ones).

minable *n.m.* 'Useless git', 'pathetic nurk', individual who looks as if he'll never achieve anything.

minable *adj.* Pathetically inadequate.

mince *adj. C'est plutôt mince! (iron.)*: It's not much to show for! – I don't call that much!

mince *interj.* Euphemistic equivalent to the expletive *merde!* expressing surprise, admiration, incredulity. *Mince alors!* Crumbs! – Golly! – By Jove! *Mince de rigolade!* What a lark! – How funny! *Mince de bouffe!* Some nosh!

mine *n.f.* **1** *Faire la mine*: To 'pull a face', to pout, to scowl. **2** *Faire des mines*: To simper. **3** *Faire mine de*: To pretend to do something. *Il fit mine de partir*: He got to his feet as if he were leaving. *Faire mine de peler des œufs (joc.)*: To look the picture of innocence. **4** *Mine de rien, il est parti en douce*: He sloped off casually as if he hadn't noticed a thing. **5** *Payer de mine*: To 'look the part', to look good. (This expression is usually used in the negative in sentences such as *il ne payait vraiment pas de mine avec son physique de gratte-papier*: You couldn't guess he was an athlete by looking at him.) **6** *Avoir bonne mine (iron.)*: To 'look a proper Charlie', to be left looking foolish in an embarrassing situation.

minet *n.m.* **1** 'Puss', pussy, cat. **2** Fashion-conscious young man. **3** Effeminate gigolo. **4** 'Fanny', 'pussy', vagina.

minette *n.f.* **1** Fashion-conscious young girl (with a taste for the flashy rather than the strictly elegant). **2** *Faire minette*: To practise cunnilingus.

mini *n.f.* **1** Mini, the small popular British Leyland car of the 60s, 70s and 80s. **2** *(abbr. mini-jupe)*: Mini-skirt.

minium *n.m. Passer sa grille au minium*: To 'have the decorators in', to have a menstrual period. (*Minium* is the red lead paint applied to metalwork as a rust-proofer prior to undercoating and glossing.)

minot *n.m.* 'Brat', 'kid', child.

minou *n.m.* 'Puddy-tat', pussy, cat. (Strictly speaking, the word does not belong to the language of children, but to the imbecile patter inflicted on infant and beast alike. *Mon minou* has the ancillary meaning: My lovey-dovey, my pet.)

minouche *n.f.* (Term of endearment): 'Sweetie-pie', 'precious', darling.

minus *n.m. (abbr. minus habens)*: **1** 'Genetic near-miss', runt. **2** 'Insignificant nurk', useless nonentity.

minute *n.f.* **1** *Ne pas être à la minute*: Not to be pressed for time. **2** *Entrecôte minute*: Minute steak. (Unlike the English, there is no potential pun in this term.) **3** *(interj., also: minute papillon!)*: Half a mo! – Not so fast! – Wait a minute! (The expression originates from a café on the Boulevard St. Germain; *Papillon* was the nickname of an elusive and always hurried waiter, sporting a dicky-bow tie, whose epitaph in English might have read: 'At last God caught his eye!')

mioche *n.m. & f.* 'Brat', 'kid', infant.

mirante *n.f.* 'Glass', looking-glass, mirror.

mirer *v.trans.* To 'take a gander at', to look at. *Mire un peu ça!* Take a butchers at this!

mirettes *n.f.pl.* 'Mince-pies', 'blinkers', eyes. *Faire des mirettes à quelqu'un:* To 'give someone the glad eye', to flutter one's eyelids at someone.

mirifique *adj.* 'Fantabulous', 'stupendous', fantastic.

mirliton *n.m.* **1** *Des plaisanteries de mirliton:* Weak jokes, the sort English schoolboys might find in crackers. **2** *Des vers de mirliton:* Pathetic verse of the kind usually found in third-rate greeting cards.

miro *adj.inv.* 'Mope-eyed', short-sighted in the extreme. (The alternative *miraud, miraude* is also encountered.)

mirobolant *adj.* 'Staggering', 'stupendous', astounding.

miroir *n.m. Miroir aux alouettes (fig.):* Enticing booby-trap (literally a flashy item that will take in a few suckers).

mironton *n.m.* **1** 'Cove', 'geezer', guy. *Un drôle de mironton:* An 'oddball', a queer cuss. **2** *Dévisser le mironton:* To have a miscarriage.

mise *n.f.* **1** *Sauver la mise à quelqu'un:* To 'get someone off the hook', to go to someone's rescue and save the day. **2** *Mise en l'air:* **a** Break-in, burglary. **b** 'Con', confidence trick. **3** *Mise en boîte:* 'Ragging', 'leg-pulling', teasing. **4** *Mise à pied:* 'Sacking', 'firing', act of dismissing someone from a job. **5** *Faire de la mise en scène (à quelqu'un):* To put on an act in order to pull off a coup or simply to get one's own way. *Elle lui a fait une de ces mises en scène quand il est rentré:* She certainly pulled out all the stops – tears, pleas, the lot – when he got home.

miser *v.intrans. & trans.* **1** *Miser sur:* To 'bank on', to count on something. *Alors, je peux miser sur toi?!* You won't let me down, will you? **2** To 'lay', to 'poke', to have coition with.

misérable *n.m.* **1** *(joc.):* Five-franc note (during the 60s and 70s, so-called because on it figured prominently the effigy of Victor Hugo, author of the tear-jerking LES MISÉRABLES). **2** *Jouer les misérables:* To have a run of bad luck.

misère *n.f.* **1** *Pleurer misère:* To plead poverty (in a whining fashion). **2** *Quelle misère!* What a life! (we lead). **3** *Ça vous tombe dessus comme la misère sur le pauvre monde:* This catch phrase, very much in the vein of 'it never rains but it pours', expresses persistent 'bolt-out-of-the-blue' bad luck. A more colloquial alternative is: *Ça vous tombe dessus comme la vérole sur le bas-clergé breton.* **4** *Faire des misères à quelqu'un:* To 'give someone a bad time', to

taunt and torment. **5** *Une misère:* A mere trifle. *Il a eu sa baraque pour une misère:* That house of his he got practically given. **6** *Misère!* Oh dear! (This interjection, particularly popular in Provence, can be tainted with irony or jocularity according to context and intonation, and is often used in expressions such as: *Misère de nous autres!* We're the poor buggers!)

mistigri *n.m.* **1** 'Puss', pussy, cat. **2** (Cards): Jack of clubs in certain games of patience.

miston *n.m.* **1** 'Punter', prostitute's client. **2** 'Brat', 'kid', infant. (This meaning of the word is more often than not encountered south of Lyon.)

mistonne *n.f. (pej.):* 'Biddy', 'bit of skirt', woman.

mistouflard *n.m.* 'Down-and-out', pauper completely down on his luck.

mistoufle *n.f.* **1** *La mistoufle:* The depths of poverty. *Etre dans la mistoufle:* To be down-and-out. **2** *Faire des mistoufles à quelqu'un:* To make someone's life a misery.

mitaines *n.f.pl.* **1** 'Gloves', boxing gloves. *Croiser les mitaines:* To have a punch-up (ironically, it seems, of the bare-knuckle kind). **2** *Enlève tes mitaines!* Pull your finger out and deal properly! (This sarcastic interjection can usually be heard in card-playing circles where the dealer is making an unnecessary 'meal' of it all.)

mitan *n.m.* **1** Middle, geographical centre of a given place. **2** The *milieu*, the French underworld.

mitard *n.m.* 'Cooler', disciplinary prison cell. *Faire du mitard:* To be in solitary.

mitarder *v.trans.* To 'slam in the cooler', to clap into jail (usually into a punishment cell).

mite *n.f.* **1** *Bouffé aux mites:* **a** (of thing): 'Knackered', 'buggered', worn-out. **b** (of person): 'Bonkers', 'potty', mad. **2** *Avoir des mites dans le portefeuille (fig.):* To be 'tight-fisted', to be as mean as hell with money.

mité *adj. Avoir les éponges mitées:* To suffer from T.B., to have tuberculosis.

miter *v.intrans.* To 'blubber', to whimper.

miteuse *n.f.* **1** 'Lass', slip of a girl. **2** Over-sentimental woman, one who sheds a tear at the drop of a novelette.

miteux *n.m. (pej.):* **1** 'Narrow-minded nurk', characterless nonentity. **2** 'Brat', infant, child.

miteux *adj.* **1** (of dwelling): 'Dingy', shabby. **2** (of person): 'Pathetic', totally lacking charisma and personality.

mitraille *n.f.* 'Clinkers', 'coppers', small change (literally, worthless leadshot).

mitrailleuse *n.f.* **1** 'Gasbag', character who jabbers non-stop. **2** Letter-franking machine.

mob *n.f. (abbr. mobylette)*: 'Moped', ultra-light motorbike whose engine capacity does not exceed 50 cc. Like many a successful commercial product, *Mobylette*, manufactured by *Motobécane*, has become generic for any moped.

mobilard *n.m. (abbr. garde mobile)*: Member of a special riot police squad.

mochard *adj.m.* 'Not a pretty sight', verging on the ugly.

moche *adj.* 1 Ugly, unattractive. *Qu'elle est moche!* She's got a face like the back of a bus! *Etre moche à pleurer*: To be as ugly as sin. 2 'Rotten', unethical. *C'est vraiment moche ce que t'as fait!* What you did is wrong and you know it! 3 *Ça n'est (vraiment) pas moche!* This is really good! (This negative expression is one of the most positive ways of expressing admiration.)

mochement *adv.* 'Rottenly', badly. *Il a été mochement traité*: He really didn't deserve that.

mochetée *n.f.* Ugly woman whose prime remains a mystery.

Moco *n.m.* Native of Provence. The Jean Gabin film *Pépé le Moco* did a lot to revitalize the word.

Mocobo *Proper name. La Mocobo*: The *Place Maubert* and its surrounding *quartier* in Paris (also: *Maub'*).

mœurs *n.f.pl. (pol.) Les mœurs* (also: *la brigade des mœurs*): The vice squad. (Perhaps because of its rare use in everyday French, this word seems to have acquired a sibilant ending and is pronounced as if it was spelled *mœurse*.)

moineau *n.m.* 1 *Avoir une cervelle de moineau*: To have a 'bird-brain', to be empty-headed. 2 *(pej.)*: 'Bloke', 'geezer', fellow. *Et qui c'est, ce moineau-là?!* And who the devil's that character?! *Un drôle de moineau*: A 'queer cuss', a weird bloke (one not to be trusted). *Un vilain moineau*: A 'bad egg', a 'nasty piece of work', an unpleasant and untrustworthy person.

moins *Les moins-de-vingt-dents (joc. & iron.)*: The old fogeys. (Pierre Daninos, in his witty and amusing study *SNOBISSIMO*, highlights this expression when referring to wealthy and over-dressed old ladies. It is obviously a pun on *les moins-de-vingt-ans*.)

moins *adv. Il était moins une!* (also: *il était moins cinq*): It was touch-and-go! – It was a close thing!

mois *n.m. Tous les trente-six du mois (joc. & iron.)*: 'Once in a blue moon' – Hardly ever. *Du rôti, on en bouffe tous les trente-six du mois!* In this place, the 29th of February is just about the only time you can expect a decent roast!

moisi *n.m. Ça sent le moisi! (fig.)*: This sounds fishy to me! – I don't like the look of this!

moisi *adj. C'est pas moisi*: It's first-rate – It's very good.

moisir *v.intrans.* To have a long wait. *Moisir en prison*: To rot in jail.

moite *adj. Les avoir moites*: To 'have the shits', to be 'in a blue funk', to be frightened.

moiter *v.intrans.* To 'have the shits', to be 'in a blue funk', to be frightened.

moitié *n.f. Ma moitié*: 'The missus', 'my better half', my wife.

mollard *n.m.* 'Gob', ball of spit, expectoration.

mollarder *v.trans. & intrans.* To 'blow an oyster', to 'gob', to expectorate.

mollasse *n.f.* 'Wet' person, spineless character. (When referring to a man the appellation is even more pejorative.)

mollasse *adj.* 'Wet', 'spineless', apathetic.

mollasson *n.m.* (also: *molasson*): 1 'Softie', wet and spineless individual. 2 'Lazy git', idle person.

molletière *adj. Avoir besoin de bandes molletières*: To self-congratulatory in a deprecating manner. (In the now famous register of body language, the heel-to-ankle tapping gesture can be equated with the polishing and gazing at one's fingernails registering the 'I'm-wonderful-and-I-know-it, but-I-won't-make-a-fuss-about-it' message, hence the need for protective bandages.)

molletogommes *n.m.pl.* Calves and ankles.

mollets *n.m.pl.* 1 *Avoir des mollets de coq*: To have 'spindleshanks', to have legs like matchsticks. 2 *Se masser les mollets (fig.)*: To display self-deprecating yet blatant immodesty.

mollo *adv.* 1 'Softly-softly', without undue haste. *Y aller mollo*: To play it by ear. 2 *(interj.)*: Hold your horses! – Not so fast!

mollusque *n.m.* 'Spineless git', character who lacks fibre in every sense of the word.

molosse *n.m.* 'Hulk', hunk of a man.

môme *n.m. & f.* 1 'Kid', child. *Les mômes sont partis en vacances*: The kids have gone on their hols. 2 Adolescent, teenager. *Une belle môme*: A 'corker', a really pretty girl. (The male equivalent is *un beau gosse* not *un beau môme*.)

mômerie *n.f.* 1 *La mômerie*: Kids in general, youngsters. 2 'Kids' stuff', trivial matters worthy only of youths and immature people. *J'en ai marre de toutes ces mômeries!* I'm sick and tired of all this childish arguing!

mômichon *n.m.* 'Brat', 'kid', infant.

momie *n.f. (joc. & iron.)*: 'Old fogey', 'old fuddy-duddy', geriatric person.

monacos *n.m.pl.* 1 'Loot', 'lolly', money (and lots of it). *Avoir des monacos*: To be loaded. 2 'Change', coins, loose change.

Mondaine n.f. *La Mondaine* (pol.; *abbr. la Brigade mondaine*): The vice squad.

monde n.m. **1** *En faire un monde*: To 'make a song-and-dance about something'. *N'en fais donc pas un monde!* I wish you'd keep things in perspective! **2** *Se faire un monde de quelque chose*: To 'make a mountain out of a molehill', to exaggerate the importance of something. **3** *Il y a du monde au balcon!* (joc.): What a pair of knockers! – What large and beautiful breasts! (This typically male-chauvinist utterance is usually accompanied by wolf-whistles.)

moniche n.f. 'Fanny', 'pussy', vagina (also: *monichette*).

monnaie n.f. **1** *Rendre à quelqu'un la monnaie de sa pièce*: To 'give as good as one got', to engineer tit-for-tat reprisals. **2** *Payer quelqu'un en monnaie de singe*: To 'bilk', to skilfully avoid paying a debt. **3** *Commencer à rendre la monnaie* (iron.; of woman): To 'be getting on' where physical attributes are concerned (in effect, if the woman were a prostitute, she would have to give a partial refund).

monôme n.m. (sch.): 'Rag-parade', students' carnival-like march where exam nerves can find an outlet.

monseigneur n.f. (abbr. *pince-monseigneur*): 'Jemmy', crowbar.

monsieur n.m. **1** *Jouer au monsieur*: To 'act the swell', to 'dandy about', to put on gentlemanly airs and graces. **2** *Un joli monsieur* (iron.): A 'thoroughly nasty piece of work', an evil character.

monsieur-dame n.m. 'Pansy', 'pouf', homosexual.

monstre n.m. *Un petit monstre*: A 'right little terror', a horrible child.

monstre adj. 'Whopping', huge, enormous. *Il y avait un trèpe monstre*: There was one hell of a crowd.

mont n.m. *Promettre monts et merveilles*: To 'promise the moon', to make wild promises.

montage n.m. Well-planned con-trick.

montagne n.f. **1** 'Hulk', hunk of a man. **2** *S'en faire une montagne*: **a** To make a mountain out of a molehill. **b** To 'make heavy weather' of something, to exaggerate the importance of an inflicted task. **3** *Montagnes russes*: **a** Big Dipper (in amusement park). **b** (joc.): 'Switchback' road, hilly route.

montant n.m. *Avoir du montant*: To 'have what it takes', not to lack gumption.

montante adj.f. 'Easy to bed', promiscuous. *Une nana montante*: An easy-lay.

mont-de-piété n.m. State-run 'pop-shop', official pawnbroker's. *Engager quelque chose au mont-de-piété*: To 'hock', to pawn something.

monte n.f. (Prostitutes' slang): 'Quickie', short sex-session in a hotel or *maison de passe*, hence *monte* because of the steps. (A Paris prostitute once complained that she had had *'quinze montes ce matin'*, to which her sympathetic friend retorted *'Ah, tes pauvres petits pieds!'*)

monté past part. **1** *Etre très monté contre quelqu'un*: To be 'up in arms', to be furious with someone. **2** *Etre bien monté*: **a** (iron.): To be 'in hot water', to be in deep trouble. **b** (of man): To be 'well-tooled', to have virile genitals.

monte-en-l'air n.m. 'Cat-burglar', character who shins up drainpipes to gain access.

monter v.trans. & intrans. **1** To go (up) to, to travel to. *On est monté à Paris*: We travelled to Paris. (The climb is a geographical ascension from south to north.) **2** To 'screw', to fuck, to have coition with. **3** (Prostitutes' slang): To 'hook' a customer (also: *faire une monte*). **4** *Faire monter quelqu'un*: To 'send someone up', to make someone look a fool. **5** *Monter le coup à quelqu'un*: To 'con', to deceive someone.

monter v.pronom. *Se monter pour un rien*: To 'get worked up', to get excited over nothing.

montgolfière n.f. **1** 'Nympho', nymphomaniac. **2** (pl.): 'Bubbies', 'bristols', full and self-supporting breasts. (The *montgolfière*, the invention of the Montgolfier brothers, was one of the first hot-air balloons.) **3** (pl.): 'Balls', 'bollocks', testicles. (The reference to *montgolfières* in respect of testicles is, more often than not, made in a jocular vein, implying either an over-sexed brain or advanced V.D.)

Montparno Proper name. The *Boulevard Montparnasse* in Paris and the *quartier* of that name in its vicinity.

montre n.f. **1** *Verre de montre*: 'Bum', 'backside', behind. *Casser son verre de montre*: To 'fall on one's fanny', to crack one's bum on the ground. *Il commence à me casser le verre de montre!* He's getting on my wick! – He's becoming a pain in the arse! **2** *Faire quelque chose pour la montre*: To do something for show.

montrouze n.f. 'Timex', 'timepiece', watch.

Mont Valo Proper name. *Le Mont Valo*: The *Mont Valérien*, well-known hillock topped by a military fort on the western outskirts of Paris.

monumental adj. (of faux pas): 'Whopping', 'whacking', enormous. *Faire une connerie monumentale*: To put one's foot in it good and proper.

moque n.f. (Prison slang): 'Pot', chamber pot (also: *tinette*).

moquer v.intrans. To 'pong', to stink, to smell foul.

moquer *v.pronom. Se moquer du tiers comme du quart*: 'Not to care two hoots', to not give a damn about something.

moquette *n.f. Faire moquette (iron.)*: To 'lie low' and take a few knocks to avoid aggro and confrontation, with an 'anything-for-a-quiet-life' approach. (Unlike the English use of the word, *moquette* in French refers more generally to wall-to-wall carpeting.)

moral *n.m.* **1** *Avoir le moral*: To be 'in good heart', to be in good spirits (to feel well and truly confident). **2** *Avoir le moral à zéro*: To be 'down in the dumps', to feel very depressed. **3** *Remonter le moral à quelqu'un*: To cheer someone up.

morbac *n.m.* (also: *morbaque*): **1** 'Crab', crab-louse. **2** *(pej.)*: 'Runt', 'little squirt', small and irritating person.

morceau *n.m.* **1** *Gober le morceau (fig.)*: To 'swallow the bait', to 'fall for something hook, line and sinker', to be duped (also: *avaler le morceau*). **2** *Un beau morceau* (chauvinist utterance): A 'bit of alright', a 'nice bit of skirt', an attractive woman. **3** *C'est un sacré morceau*: It's a tough nut to crack – It's a difficult task. **4** *Emporter le morceau*: To clinch the deal. **5** *Cracher le morceau*: To own up, to confess. **6** *Casser le morceau à quelqu'un*: To break unpleasant news in an ungentle manner. *Et sec, il lui a cassé le morceau!* He let him have it straight from the shoulder, no messing!

morcif *n.m.* (*corr. morceau*): This word used to apply predominantly to food, as in *manger un morcif*: to have a quick snack, but with time has come to replace *morceau* in the expressions involving that word.

mordante *n.f.* **1** Rasp, file. **2** Hacksaw.

mordants *n.m.pl.* 'Shears', scissors.

mordicus *adj.inv.* (of person on a specific issue): Unswayable. *Elle est mordicus, son gosse, elle le garde!* When it comes to her kid she won't budge, she wants custody!

mordicus *adv.* Doggedly, stubbornly. *Il soutient mordicus que c'est la vérité*: He sticks to his guns and insists it's the truth.

mordiller *v.trans. & intrans.* To nibble, to take tentative and playful bites at something. *Elle lui mordillait les oreilles*: She was nibbling his ear-lobes.

mordre *v.trans. & intrans.* **1** To 'twig', to understand. *Tu mords ce que je veux dire?* Do you get my drift? **2** *Mordre à*: To 'take to' an academic subject, to comprehend and progress in it. *Il ne mord vraiment pas aux math*: He really isn't getting on with his maths. **3** *Mords-moi ça!* Take a butchers at that! – Have a look at this! **4** *Ça ne mord pas avec moi!* I don't fall for that!

– I'm not that gullible! **5** *C'est à se les mordre!* It's too funny for words! – It's bloody hilarious! **6** *à la mords-moi le machin (adj.exp.)*: **a** 'Dodgy', tricky, dangerous. **b** Stupid, ridiculous. *J'en ai marre de ses histoires à la mords-moi le machin*: I'm sick and tired of his codswallop!

mordu *n.m. Un mordu*: A 'fan', a character who has 'the bug' where a hobby, sport or interest is concerned. *Un mordu de la moto*: A 'bikie', a motorbike fanatic.

mordu *adj.* Mad about something, bitten by 'the bug'. (The word often refers to hobbies and sports.)

morfal *n.m.* **1** 'Greedy-guts', glutton. **2** 'Grabber', greedy person where profits are concerned (also: *morfalou*).

morfal *adj.* **1** Greedy, gluttonous. **2** 'Grabbing', grasping where money and profits are concerned (also: *morfalou*).

morfale *n.f.* 'Grub', 'eats', food.

morfaler *v.trans. & intrans.* To 'guzzle', to 'stuff one's face', to eat voraciously (also: *se morfaler*).

morfalobullard *n.m. (mil.)*: 'Canteen locust', soldier with a voracious appetite.

morfile *n.f.* 'Grub', 'eats', food.

morfiler *v.trans. & intrans.* To 'guzzle', to 'stuff one's face', to eat voraciously.

morfler *v.trans.* To 'cop', to get (to be on the receiving end of something unpleasant). *Il a morflé deux bastos dans le baquet*: He got shot twice through the gut. *Morfler une chaude-lance*: To 'catch clap', to get gonorrhoea.

morganer *v.trans. & intrans.* **1** To 'gobble up', to eat. **2** To 'grass', to inform on. *Comme la lavette qu'il est, il a morgané à bloc!* The spineless git spilled the beans on the lot of us!

moricaud *n.m. (pej.)*: 'Coon', 'wog', any dark-skinned male. (The feminine *moricaude* exists but is not often encountered.)

morlingue *n.m.* **1** Purse. **2** Wallet. *Etre constipé du morlingue* (also: *avoir des oursins dans le morlingue*): To be 'tight-fisted', to be 'stingy', to be mean. (Originally, *morlingue* referred exclusively to a purse, but with demonetization and the passing of time, paper money has come into its own and ousted the heavy gold coin in favour of the banknote.)

mornifle *n.f.* **1** 'Tingler', slap across the face. **2** *De la mornifle*: Loose coins, small change. **3** 'Brass', 'loot', money. *Leur restau maintenant, ça vaut un paquet de mornifle*: I reckon their restaurant must be worth a tidy sum nowadays!

mornifleur *n.m.* Counterfeiter, manufacturer of counterfeit money.

morphino *n.m.* 'Junkie', character who is addicted to morphine.

morpion *n.m.* **1** Crab-louse. **2** *(pej.)*: 'Brat', infant, child. *Vos morpions commencent à me courir!* Those bloody kids of yours are a pain in the neck! **3** *Jouer aux morpions*: To play noughts-and-crosses (on a much larger scale than the original; five noughts or five crosses need to be in line for a score and a game can fill a whole sheet of squared paper).

mors *n.m.* *Prendre le mors aux dents*: **a** To take the initiative. **b** To 'fly off the handle', to blow up with anger.

mort *n.m.* *Faire le mort*: To 'lie low' in order to avoid reprisals. (In the game of bridge, the expression means 'to play dummy'.)

mort *adj.* **1** *C'est mort!* (of project, undertaking): It's had it! – It's all over! (The expression *c'est mort et enterré*: It's dead and buried, implies more the 'long past, long forgotten' nature of the event.) **2** *Encore une de morte!* (Boozers' slang): Another dead man! – Another empty bottle!

mort *À mort* *(adv.exp.)*: Extremely, to the extreme. *Elle m'en veut à mort!* She hates my bloody guts!

mortibus *adj.inv.* *(joc.)*: 'Snuffed', 'croaked', dead.

morticole *n.m.* *(joc.)*: 'Quack', 'medic', doctor.

morue *n.f.* **1** *(pej.)*: 'Trollop', 'loose woman', promiscuous female. **2** *Avoir été baptisé avec une queue de morue (joc.)*: To be something of a tippler, to have more than a liking for alcoholic beverage. (The expression is jocular in that *morue* in France is considered more as a salt-preserved fish, likely therefore to provoke thirst.)

morveux *n.m.* *(pej.)*: **1** 'Brat', 'kid', child. **2** 'Whipper-snapper', officious nonentity. *Qui est-ce qui m'a foutu un petit morveux pareil?* Where the hell did that nurk spring up from?

mot *n.m.* **1** *Se donner le mot*: To 'get in cahoots', to conspire. **2** *Avoir deux mots à dire à quelqu'un*: To have a few (usually unpleasant) things to say to someone. **3** *Avoir des mots avec quelqu'un*: To 'have a barney' with, to quarrel with someone. **4** *Ne pas mâcher ses mots*: 'Not to mince one's words', to speak one's mind forcefully. **5** *Le mot de Cambronne*: Euphemistic alternative to *merde* (also: *les cinq lettres*). **6** *Pas un mot à la reine mère!* (Jocular catch phrase): Mum's the word! – Keep it quiet!

motale *n.f.* (also: *motal*): 'Bike', motorbike.

motard *n.m.* **1** 'Bikie', character who rides a motorbike (more the Hell's Angel leather-clad type than the gentle commuter). **2** *(pol.)*: Speed-cop (one who patrols on a motorbike).

motte *n.f.* **1** *La motte*: Half. *Faire la motte*: To 'go fifty-fifty', to go halves. **2** 'Fanny', 'pussy',

vagina. **3** Arse-hole, anus. *Se faire défoncer la motte*: To engage in passive sodomy.

motus *n.m.* *Motus et bouche cousue!* Mum's the word! (*Motus* is often used as a straight interjection without the ancillary *et bouche cousue*. *Motus! Tout sera pour le mieux!* You keep quiet and no-one will be the wiser!)

mou *n.m.* **1** *Du mou*: Animal lungs cooked as pet-food. (Butchers in France are often asked for *'du mou pour mon chat'*.) **2** *Rentrer dans le mou à quelqu'un*: To 'lay into someone', to hit someone hard where the fists are likely to meet little muscular resistance. **3** *Bourrer le mou à quelqu'un* *(fig.)*: To 'fill someone's head with stuff and nonsense', to try and deceive someone. *Voilà des mois que tu me bourres le mou!* You've been having me on for months!

mou *adj.* (of person): 'Wet', 'gutless', soft. *Il est d'un mou, ton frangin!* That brother of yours is the original spineless wonder!

mou *adv.* *Y aller mou*: To go it 'softly-softly', to 'play it by ear', to act in a circumspect manner.

mouchard *n.m.* **1** *(sch.)*: 'Sneak', tell-tale. **2** *(pol.)*: 'Grass', 'snitch', informer. **3** (Prison slang): Spy-hole in cell door. **4** (Lorry drivers' slang): 'Spy-in-the-cab' device, time-recording instrument reporting on an H.G.V.'s movements (speed, length of trips, etc.).

moucharder *v.trans. & intrans.* To 'snitch', to inform on.

mouchardeur *n.m.* *(sch.)*: 'Sneak', tell-tale.

mouche *n.f.* **1** *(sch.)*: 'Sneak', tell-tale. **2** (Prison slang): 'Snitch', informer. **3** *Fine mouche*: 'Canny customer', cunning and resourceful individual. *C'est une fine mouche, tu sais!* She wasn't born yesterday! **4** *Gober des mouches*: To be 'stood gawping', to have a look of bewildered amazement on one's face. **5** *Quelle mouche t'a piqué?!* *(fig.)*: What's eating you?! – What on earth is the matter with you?! **6** *Ne pas avoir peur des mouches*: To no coward, to have guts, to be courageous. **7** *Faire la mouche du coche*: To act the busybody and antagonize everyone. **8** *Mouche à merde*: Scandal-monger, character who delights in spreading nasty rumours. **9** *Tuer les mouches à quinze pas (joc.)*: To suffer from 'terminal halitosis', to have really bad breath. **10** *C'est à cause des mouches!* (Ironical catch phrase): Ask me another! – What answer do you expect?! **11** *Attraper les mouches* (of woman): To 'lie back and think of England', to be anything but a willing participant during intercourse. **12** *Pattes de mouche*: Spidery scrawl, illegible handwriting. **13** *Enculeur de mouches*: 'Finicky nurk', over-fussy and exacting character.

moucher *v.trans.* **1** To 'take someone down a peg or two', to snub. *Et comment qu'il l'a mouché!* You should have seen the way he pushed his nose in it! **2** To 'tick off', to tell off. *Il s'est drôlement fait moucher!* He was sent off with a flea in his ear! **3** To 'bash up', to 'rollock', to beat up. **4** (Sport): To 'thrash', to beat good and proper.

moucher *v.pronom.* *S'en moucher:* Not to give a fuck about something, not to care two hoots, to not give a damn about something. *Et comment que je m'en mouche!* And see how I care! (also: *s'en moucher du coude* or *du pied*).

moucheron *n.m. (pej.):* 'Brat', 'kid', young child.

mouchique *adj.* **1** 'Spiffing', 'A-1', superb. **2** Bloody awful, useless. (Attempts at explaining the conflicting meanings of the word rely more on dubious etymology than substantiated text analysis. Only the context can verify the meaning.)

mouchodrome *n.m. (joc.):* 'Pate', bald head (also: *mouchedrome*).

mouchoir *n.m.* **1** *Arriver dans un mouchoir* (Cycling and horse-racing slang): To make it a close finish, to arrive grouped at the tape. **2** *Mets ça dans ta poche avec ton mouchoir par-dessus! (joc. & iron.):* Put that in your pipe and smoke it! – It's a case of take it or leave it!

moudre *v.trans. En moudre:* **a** (Cycling slang): To pedal on in a steady and relentless way. **b** (Pimps' slang): To engage in prostitution. (This highlights the 'daily grind' aspect of the job.)

Mouffe *Proper name. La Mouffe:* The *rue Mouffe-tard* in Paris and the *quartier* in its immediate vicinity.

mouflet *n.m.* 'Kid', infant, child. *Elle se balade toujours avec une tripotée de mouflets:* She's always got a string of kids with her. (*Mouflette* is seldom encountered, but refers usually to a young woman with child-like features.)

moufter *v.intrans.* To 'crib', to 'grumble', to protest. (This verb is hardly ever found within a positive statement. The accepted usage is *ne pas moufter:* to 'keep mum', to stay quiet.)

mouillage *n.m. Faire du mouillage:* To dispense 'slush-funds', to use accumulated money for corrupt purposes.

mouiller *v.trans.* **1** To implicate, to compromise. *Surtout, ne me mouillez pas dans cette affaire!* For heaven's sake keep me out of all this! *Il a été salement mouillé dans l'affaire des piastres:* He was up to his neck in the Indo-Chinese currency racket. **2** *Se mouiller la meule:* To 'wet one's whistle', to have a drink. **3** *Mouiller son froc (fig.):* To 'have the shits', to be 'in a blue funk', to be frightened out of one's wits. **4** *En mouiller pour quelqu'un:* To be

sexually attracted to someone. (An ancillary meaning to this expression jocularly highlights someone's 'feelings' for a coveted object. *Il en mouille drôlement pour ta bagnole:* He's just obsessed by your new car.)

mouiller *v.intrans.* **1** To be 'in a cold sweat', to be frightened. **2** To 'drool at the thought of something', to strongly desire something. (Originally the verb related to salacious fore-thoughts, but with time the meaning has broadened.) **3** (Gamblers' slang): To 'put one's money where one's mouth is', to dip into one's pocket in the hope of pulling off a coup.

mouiller *v.trans.reflex.* To compromise oneself, to become implicated. *Il s'est drôlement mouillé pour nous:* He really stuck his neck out on our behalf.

mouilles *n.f.pl.* 'Cheeks', 'bum', behind. *Il s'est fait botter les mouilles:* He got kicked up the backside.

mouillette *n.f.* **1** 'Soldier', sippet of bread ready for dunking. **2** 'Licker', tongue. **3** *Y aller de la mouillette:* To jump headlong into lengthy explanations. **4** *Aller à la mouillette:* To take unnecessary risks.

mouisant *adj.* Debilitating, depressing.

mouisard *n.m.* 'Down-and-outer', character without the proverbial penny to his name (or the hope of getting one).

mouise *n.f.* **1** Never-ending streak of bad luck. **2** Poverty. *Depuis qu'il est mort, ils sont dans la mouise:* Since he snuffed it, they're virtually on the breadline.

moujingue *n.m.* **1** 'Kid', child, infant. **2** *Se tricoter un moujingue:* To get 'preggers', to become pregnant. **3** *Tricoter le moujingue:* To have a 'dipstick abortion', to terminate a pregnancy in a most unmedical manner.

moujingue *adj.* 'Titchy', tiny, small.

moukala *n.m.* 'Piece', 'rod', handgun. *Il ne sort jamais sans un moukala dans sa fouille:* He's always rodded-up when he goes out.

moukère *n.f.* 'Biddy', 'bird', woman.

moule *n.m.* **1** *Moule à gaufres:* 'Burk', 'twit', imbecile. **2** *Après lui, on a cassé le moule! (joc. and sometimes iron.):* They don't make them like him any more!

moule *n.f.* **1** 'Fanny', 'pussy', vagina. **2** 'Pillock', 'burk', imbecile.

mouler *v.trans.* **1** To 'quit', to leave. *Il vient de mouler sa nana:* He's just ditched his bird. **2** To leave, to deposit. *Moule ça là mon gars, je m'en occuperai plus tard!* Dump it there laddie, I'll see to it later! **3** *En mouler* (of prostitute): To ply that trade (also: *en moudre*). **4** *Mouler un bronze:* To 'plant a turd', to 'crap', to defecate (also: *couler un bronze*).

moulin *n.m.* **1** Motor, engine (of car, aeroplane, etc.). *Le moulin a chauffé une fois de trop, et on s'est retrouvé en carafe*: We broke down when that bloody engine overheated one last time. **2** 'Chatterbox', character who jabbers endlessly (also: *moulin à paroles*). **3** Profitable enterprise, 'going concern' that brings in a steady stream of money. (According to the 'who-says-what' law, it can refer to a shop, a string of nightclubs or a 'fleet' of prostitutes, the staple expression being *avoir des moulins qui tournent*.) **4** *Alors, on entre ici comme dans un moulin?! (iron.)*: This is not a public place, you know! (The English ironical 'Come in, it's a shop!' is equally meaningful.) **5** *Envoyer quelqu'un au moulin*: To get someone out of the way for a while (literally, to send someone on any old errand in order to get rid of him).

mouliner *v.intrans.* (Cycling slang): To pedal away at a fair pace.

moulinet *n.m. Faire des moulinets*: To 'dive in' with flailing fists, to rush into a fight.

moulinette *n.f.* 'Trap', 'gob', mouth. *Il a une de ces moulinettes!* He can certainly talk the hind legs off a donkey!

moulinex *n.m.* 'Mixer', any electrical appliance that grinds, pulps, liquidizes, etc. (Like many a brand-name, *Moulinex* has become generic.)

moulu *adj.* 'Knackered', 'buggered', exhausted. *Ah, j'suis vraiment moulu!* Heck! I'm all in!

moumoute *n.f.* **1** 'Sheepie', sheepskin coat or jacket. **2** Toupee, hairpiece, wig. **3** 'Pussy', 'fanny', vagina. **4** *Ma moumoute* (term of endearment): My lovey-dovey – My pet – Darling.

mouquère *n.f.* 'Biddy', 'bird', woman.

mouron *n.m.* **1** Hair (usually tufts of hair). **2** *Du mouron*: Worries. *Se faire du mouron*: To 'fret', to worry (very often, unnecessarily). **3** *C'est pas du mouron pour ton serin!* (Ironical catch phrase): This isn't really for you! (This expression is ambivalent in that the ancillary can either be 'It's not good enough for you' or 'You don't deserve it'.)

mouronner *v.pronom.* To 'fret', to worry (usually unnecessarily).

mouscaille *n.f.* **1** 'Shit', excrement. **2** Filth, dirt. **3** (*fig.*): Bad luck, lasting misfortune. *Etre dans la mouscaille*: To be 'in the shit', to have a run of bad luck. **4** *Avoir quelqu'un à la mouscaille*: To 'have it in for someone', to hate that person. *Avoir quelque chose à la mouscaille*: To have a phobia about something.

mousmé *n.f.* (also: *mousmée*): 'Biddy', 'bird', woman. *Il n'est jamais à court de mousmés!* He's got a right little harem!

mousquetaire *n.m.* Up-and-coming young sportsman. (This expression refers, more often than not, to tennis and cycling.)

mousse *n.f.* **1** Hair. *N'avoir plus de mousse sur le caillou*: To be as bald as a coot. **2** *Se faire de la mousse*: To 'get things out of proportion', to worry unnecessarily.

mousser *v.trans. & intrans.* **1** To 'get into a lather', to foam with rage. **2** *Faire mousser quelqu'un*: **a** To 'rub someone up the wrong way' and get him in a right old temper. **b** To bring a smile to someone's lips by praising him highly. *Ça l'a drôlement fait mousser de devenir notre dirlo*: He was cock-a-hoop at becoming our boss. **3** *Faire mousser quelque chose*: To crack something up to what it isn't really. *C'est un vrai camelot, il fait toujours mousser la marchandise*: There's a bit of the street-hawker in him the way he bulls his goods.

mousseux *n.m.* Sparkling white wine, cheap imitation of champagne. *Radin comme il est, il nous a servi du mousseux!* The mean bugger, he served us some of that fizzed-up cats'-pee!

moussu *adj.* (of man): Hairy. (This adjective refers to the hair sported by 'macho' chests.)

moustache *n.f. Cigare à moustache (joc)*: 'Joystick', 'cock', penis.

moustagache *n.f. (joc.)*: 'Tash', moustache.

moutard *n.m. (Slightly pej.)*: 'Brat', 'kid', infant. (Because it is a masculine noun, *moutard* generally refers to a young boy. In the plural, however, it refers indifferently to either sex. *Il faut toujours qu'elle vienne avec ses moutards!* She always comes round with her bloody kids!)

moutarde *n.f. Avoir la moutarde qui monte au nez*: To be on the verge of 'blowing one's top', to be seething with anger. *Quand j'ai vu ça, la moutarde m'est monté au nez*: When I saw that, I nearly blew a gasket! (Anyone who has sampled very strong mustard will realize that the literal and figurative meanings are closely related.)

moutardier *n.m.* **1** 'Big nob', V.I.P. (With this meaning the word is only to be found in the expression *se croire le premier moutardier du pape*: to have no mean opinion of oneself.) **2** 'Arse', 'bum', behind.

mouton *n.m.* **1** (Police slang): 'Snitch', 'grass', informer. **2** (Prison slang): 'Stoolie', 'stool-pigeon', inmate whose brief it is to wheedle information from a recalcitrant prisoner. **3** (*pl.*): 'Fluffies', bits of dusty fluff that tend to accumulate under large items of furniture. **4** *Mouton à cinq pattes*: **a** Freak, outlandish character. **b** 'Five-leaf clover', item that is near-impossible to find. **5** *Etre un mouton de Panurge*: To lack initiative, to follow the herd.

6 *Revenir à ses moutons* (of lengthy explanations): To get back to the matter in hand.

moutonner *v.trans. & intrans.* **1** To 'pump' someone for information. **2** To 'grass', to inform on someone. **3** *Ça moutonne!* (of sea): The white horses are out! – It's getting rough!

mouvement *n.m.* **1** *Etre dans le mouvement*: To be 'zing up to date', to be on cue where fashions and trends are concerned. *Se sentir hors du mouvement*: To feel out of things. **2** *Allez, un bon mouvement!* (Verbal appeal to one who is undecided): Come on, be a sport! (Don't be such a stick-in-the-mud!)

mouver *v.trans.reflex.* *Mouve-toi!* Don't just stand there! (Get a move on!)

moyen *n.m.* **1** *Arriver par ses propres moyens*: To get somewhere 'under one's own steam'. **2** *Utiliser les moyens du bord*: To 'make do', to use the means to hand. **3** *Employer les grands moyens*: To resort to the proverbial sledgehammer to crack a nut. **4** *Oter ses moyens à quelqu'un*: To cramp someone's style, to put someone off his stride (also: *couper ses moyens à quelqu'un*). **5** *Tâcher moyen de*: To try to find a way (to do something). *On va tâcher moyen de vous tirer de ça!* We'll pull out all the stops to get you out of this! **6** *Il n'y a pas moyen de moyenner*: There's not a bloody thing we can do!

muche *n.f.* **1** 'Thingummy', 'whatsit', thing (also: *trucmuche*). **2** Little known in its own right, *muche* is more often than not found as a humorous suffix sometimes replacing the normal ending of a word as in *Ménilmuche* for *Ménilmontant*, or just tacked on as in *argomuche* for *argot*.

Muette *Proper name. La Muette*: The *quartier* of that name in Paris.

muette *n.f.* **1** *La muette*: One's conscience. **2** *La grande muette* (*mil.*): The army.

muffée *n.f.* Drunken binge. *Prendre une bonne muffée*: To get a skinful.

mufle *n.m.* (*pej.*): **1** 'Mush', 'dial', face. **2** 'Cad', 'rotter', man with no manners where ladies are concerned.

muflerie *n.f.* Caddish behaviour. *Pour ce qui est de la muflerie, il s'y connaît*: He's the original rough diamond inside and out!

munitions *n.f.pl.* (*joc.*): 'Larder-bounty', reserves of foodstuffs.

mur *n.m.* **1** Pickpocket's accomplice. (Character who 'screens' the main culprit.) **2** *Faire le mur*: To escape from custody. **3** *Raser les murs* (usually of wanted person): To move along in a swift and unobtrusive manner. **4** *On ne peut pas tirer de l'huile d'un mur*: You can't get blood out of a stone. **5** *Etre sourd comme un mur*: To be as

deaf as a post. (It would appear that French walls, unlike British ones, don't have ears!)

6 *Franchir le mur du çon* (*joc. & iron.*): To 'have a screw', to fuck, to have intercourse. (The jocularity stems from the seemingly optional cedilla.)

mûr *adj.* 'Well-primed', 'sozzled', drunk.

mûre *n.f.* 'Biff', 'clout', blow. *Prendre une mûre sur le coin de la frite*: To get a knuckle-sandwich. (The figurative reference to the fruit relates to the colour of the bruising inflicted.)

mûrir *v.pronom.* To get 'pickled', to get drunk.

museau *n.m.* **1** 'Mush', 'dial', face. **2** 'Kisser', 'gob', mouth. **3** 'Hooter', 'conk', nose. (The reason for the three anatomical definitions lies in the non-colloquial nature of the word where animals are concerned.) **4** *Une fricassée de museau*: A 'smooch-session' (one peppered with passionate kisses).

musée *n.m.* **1** *Le musée des allongés* (also: *le musée des refroidis*): The 'cold-meat parlour', the morgue. **2** *Avoir une tête à sortir du Musée Grévin*: To be afflicted with horrendous features. (The *Musée Grévin* is to Parisians what Madame Tussaud's is to Londoners. Both waxworks museums have a Chamber of Horrors.)

museler *v.trans.* To 'gag', to silence someone.

musette *n.m.* *Le musette*: Accordion music, the kind much favoured by the clientèle of the *bal musette*.

musette *n.f.* **1** (*joc.*): Bag, handbag. **2** *Garde ça dans ta musette!* (*fig.*): Keep it under your hat! – Don't talk about this! **3** *Tenir une sacrée musette*: To 'have a skinful', to be drunk. **4** *Qui n'est pas dans une musette* (*adj.exp.*): Incredible, remarkable. *Il a reçu une engueulade qui n'était pas dans une musette*: He got a rare old talking-to. **5** *Bal musette*: Dance-hall typical of the Paris suburbs which catered for a weekend working-class clientèle. Such establishments smacked more of cheap wine, simple food and sawdust than the sophistication of the elegant ballroom.

musicien *n.m.* **1** 'Flannel-artist', flatterer. **2** 'Con-man', confidence trickster.

musiciens *n.m.pl.* (*joc.*): Haricot beans (because of their wind-instrument after-effects).

musico *n.m.* Musician. (More the fiddle-scraper than the concert virtuoso.)

musique *n.f.* **1** 'Flannel', flattery. *Je l'ai vu venir, lui et sa musique!* I could spot him a mile off, him and his soft soap! **2** *De la musique*: A bunch of lies. *On lui pose une question et il vous sert de la musique*: You ask him a direct question and he gives you a load of bull! **3** 'Con', confidence trick. *Monter une musique*: To set up a rip-off.

4 Blackmail. (It is worth mentioning that *chantage* is the non-colloquial word.) **5** 'Fuss', row. *Quand il a appris ça, il nous a fait une de ces musiques*: When they broke the news to him, he flew off the handle. *Il va y avoir de la musique au kiosque!* (of marital row): It's going to be a right old ding-dong! **6** *Baisse un peu la musique!* Pipe down, will you! – Don't talk so loudly! **7** *Connaître la musique!* To 'know the ropes', to know one's way around. *Pas de danger avec lui, il connaît la musique*: I wouldn't worry about him, he knows what to do! **8** *C'est réglé comme du papier à musique* (of project, plan): It's planned to the very last detail. (As detailed and accurate as a musical score.) **9** *Changer de musique*: **a** To change the subject. *Change de musique veux-tu?!* I wish you wouldn't harp on! **b** To change one's tune, to take another stance. *Il a vite changé de musique quand il a vu les résultats*: When he heard the news, his about-turn was a lesson in instant diplomacy. **10** *En avant la musique!* On with the show! (This jocular, slightly ironical catch phrase is usually uttered when a reluctant go-ahead is given to a project.)

musiquette *n.f.* **1** 'Muzak', piped music (the kind dispensed in supermarkets). **2** Short and repetitive burst of music used by the telephone service to inform a subscriber that lines are engaged, a number is unobtainable, etc. (These 'peals' are just about as exhilarating as those of an ice-cream van.) **3** Blackmail. *Il tire un gentil pactol de toutes ses musiquettes*: He certainly makes a living out of his 'I'll-hush-it-up-for-you' game.

Mutu *Proper name. La Mutu*: The *palais de la Mutualité*. This famous hall, which caters for all manner of mass functions, pop concerts, boxing promotions, etc. is often used for political gatherings, hence the expression *une manif à la Mutu* (also: *la Mut'*).

mystère *n.m.* **1** Elaborate and tasty ice-cream confection. **2** *Mystère et boule de gomme!* (*joc. & iron.* catch phrase): Search me! – Heaven knows what it's all about!

N

na *interj.* So there! – And see if I care! (Originally confined to 'childspeak', this interjection, because of its pouting jocularity, seems to have seeped through elsewhere.)

nabot *n.m.* 'Runt', 'squirt', dwarf-like person. (This pejorative word often comes up in insulting interjections. *Eh va donc, eh nabot!* Crawl back into the woodwork!)

nageoire *n.f.* 1 Arm and elbow (because of the fin shape). 2 'Mitt', 'paw', hand.

nager *v.intrans.* 1 To be 'all at sea', to be 'completely out of one's depth', to be lost as to what to do. *En math, il nage complètement:* When it comes to maths, it's all above his head. 2 *Nager dans l'encre:* To be helpless. 3 *Savoir nager:* To be 'on the ball', to know most of the answers, to be resourceful.

nana *n.f.* 'Bird', young woman. *Il s'est trouvé une nouvelle nana, tu sais!* Have you met his latest? (Originally this word was very pejorative and referred primarily to working prostitutes. Auguste Le Breton claims that we owe the word to Emile Zola.)

nanan *n.m.* 1 (Child language): 'Good grub', tasty food. (This baby-talk word usually refers to desserts, sweets, etc. *C'est du nanan ça!* This is yummy-yummy!) 2 'Doddle', easy task. *Pas de problème, mon vieux, ça, c'est du nanan ou je ne m'y connais pas!* I'd say this is a piece of cake, wouldn't you?!

nanar *n.m.* (also: *nanard*): 1 'Nincompoop', 'twit', imbecile. 2 (*pl.*): End-of-season lines, and goods somewhat past their prime which only a super salesman could flog.

nanar *adj.* (also: *nanard*): 1 (of person): 'Soft', stupid, rather silly. 2 Uninspiring, lacking charisma. 3 'Worthless', of little value.

Nantoche *Proper name.* Nanterre, suburb on the west of Paris. Its university saw the first signs of the 1968 student uprising.

nap *n.m.* (*abbr. napoléon*): Twenty-franc gold coin roughly equivalent to a sovereign. (Some people still use the even more dated *louis* when referring to a twenty-franc gold piece.)

naphtalinard *n.m.* (*mil.*): Re-enlisted officer (literally one who, like a battleship, has been taken out of mothballs).

naphtaline *n.f.* 1 *Ça sent la naphtaline! (joc. & iron.):* It's a bit past it! – Don't you think it's a bit old?! *Mettre en naphtaline:* To shelve indefinitely. (Although mothballs are a thing of the past, they seem to have gained lexical fame.) 2 (Drugs): 'Coke', cocaine.

naphtaliné *adj.* (of person): 'Past it', long past his prime. (Like *naphtalinard*, the word is a jocular send-up on the idea of mothballs.)

napo *n.m.* Neapolitan (native of Naples).

nappe *n.f.* 1 *Trouver la nappe mise:* To marry where money is (not necessarily for money's sake). 2 *Mettre la main sur la bonne nappe:* To 'strike it rich', to get onto a good thing financially.

nardu *n.m.* *Commissaire de police*, police superintendent.

narines *n.f.pl.* *Prendre quelque chose dans les narines:* To 'get one's just deserts' (usually of the unpleasant variety), to get what was coming to one. *Et prends ça dans les narines!* This should take you down a peg or two!

nase *n.m.* 'Conk', 'hooter', nose. *Il faut toujours qu'il foute son nase partout:* He's always poking his nose into other people's business!

nase *n.f.* *La nase:* Syphilis.

nase *adj.* 1 (of person): 'Blotto', 'sozzled', drunk (perhaps because a red nose is indicative of the generous consumption of alcohol). 2 'Bonkers', 'potty', mad. 3 (of mechanical contraption): 'Knackered', 'buggered', worn-out. *Le moulin était complètement nase:* The engine was really clapped-out.

naseau *n.m.* 'Conk', 'hooter', nose. *Prendre un pain sur le naseau:* To 'get a knuckle-sandwich', to get punched in the face.

nasebroque *n.m.* 'Wino', alcoholic (the down-and-outer rather than the executive dipso).

nasebroque *adj.* 'Blotto', 'sozzled', drunk.

natchaver *v.pronom.* To 'bugger off', to vanish into thin air.

nationale *n.f.* **1** (*abbr. route nationale*): 'A' road, main trunk-road. (Even in these days of motorways, the best-known *nationale* is the *nationale* 7, made famous by the Charles Trénet song of that name.) **2** *La nationale* (*abbr. la Sûreté Nationale*): Branch of the French Secret Service.

nattes *n.f.pl.* Faire des nattes (*pol.*): To make a statement which it is near-impossible to unravel. (Some barristers handling underworld cases like to rephrase the evidence in ambiguous terms.)

nature *n.f.* **1** *Une nature*: **a** A 'one-in-a-million' character (the kind of person you will never forget). **b** One who speaks his/her mind without fear of consequences. **c** 'Gull', gullible so-and-so, naïve person. **2** *Petite nature (iron.)*: **a** 'Cotton-wool' character, one who complains about the slightest inconvenience or ailment. *Quelle petite nature, celui-là!* He certainly believes in mollycoddling himself! **b** Fainthearted, squeamish character. **3** *Etre une force de la nature*: To be 'a real ball of fire', to be a powerhouse of energy. **4** *Disparaître dans la nature*: To 'vanish into thin air', to disappear.

nature *adj.* **1** *Etre nature*: **a** To be as honest and straight as one looks. **b** To be a bit of a rough diamond. **2** *Boire quelque chose nature*: To drink something neat. *Lui, il aime le pastis nature*: He never puts water in his Pernod. *Un café nature*: Straight coffee (one that isn't laced with brandy or rum).

nature *adv.* (*abbr. naturellement*): Obviously, naturally. *Et moi nature, je lui ai filé du fric*: And me being the fool I am, I gave him a sub.

naturel *n.m.* *Ça part d'un bon naturel, tu sais!* He really means well (in spite of what you might think!).

naturellement *adv.* *Naturellement et comme de bien entendu!* This tautological and slightly ironical repartee is really self-explanatory, and its colloquiality is rather well translated in Georgette Marks's *DICTIONARY OF SLANG AND COLLOQUIALISMS* by 'absoballylutely'.

naturlich *adv.* (also: *naturliche*): Obviously, naturally, of course.

nave *n.m.* 'Nincompoop', 'twit', imbecile. (The jocular extension *fleur de nave* was given a vigorous new lease of life by San-Antonio's novel *FLEUR DE NAVE VINAIGRETTE*.)

navet *n.m.* **1** 'Clot', 'nincompoop', imbecile. *Quel navet, ce mec-là!* He's as thick as two short planks! **2** (of film, play, operetta): 'Flop', abysmal production. *On voit moins de navets à Cannes cette année*: The films you see at the

Cannes festival are a darned sight better now! **3** *Avoir du sang de navet dans les veines*: To be 'as wet as a lettuce', to lack the 'get-up-and-go' spirit. **4** *Des navets!* Not bloody likely! – You must be joking! – Certainly not! **5** (*mil.*): 'Boneyard', cemetery.

naveton *n.m.* 'Chump', 'burk', fool. *C'est un naveton de première*: He's as gullible as they come.

naviguer *v.intrans.* Savoir naviguer (*fig.*): To have the knack for steering clear of trouble.

n.d.D. *interj.* (*abbr. nom de Dieu!*): Darnation! –Damn and blast! (This relatively innocuous form of swearing is obviously only to be found in veiled reported-speech sequences.)

né *past part.* Je ne suis pas né d'hier! (*iron.*): I'm not as green as I'm cabbage-looking! (literally, as in English, 'I wasn't born yesterday').

nécessaire *n.m.* Overnight bag for erring husbands or wives. (It is also sometimes known as *un baise-en-ville*.)

nécrops *n.m.* (*pol.*): Post-mortem. *Faire un nécrops*: To carry out a P.M. examination.

nèfles *n.f.pl.* **1** *Des nèfles*: 'Bugger-all', very little. *Bref, tout ce boulot ça a été pour des nèfles?!* What you're trying to tell me is that we've worked for peanuts! (Because, literally, *nèfles* are medlars i.e. a very 'low-market' fruit, the expression *récolter des nèfles*: to have very little to show for one's efforts, retains a certain agricultural flavour.) **2** *Avoir des nèfles plein la gueule*: To be a mass of bruises. (Medlars are at their tastiest when discoloured and going rotten.) **3** *Des nèfles!* Not on your nelly! – Not bloody likely! – You must be joking! (if you think that).

négifran *n.f.* 'Biddy', 'bird', woman. (This word is merely a *verlen* corruption of *frangine*.)

nègre *n.m.* **1** Ghost-writer, one who does the literary donkey-work for a famous and otherwise busy author. **2** *Faire le nègre*: To be landed with all the chores. **3** *Faire comme le nègre, continuer*: To carry on with what one is doing. (The origin of what could loosely be called an ironical catch phrase is to be found in the seemingly pointless comment uttered by Marshal Mac-Mahon, President of the French Republic in the 1870s. When visiting a military academy he asked a junior recruit what his functions were and when told *'Je suis le nègre'*, i.e. one acting as a temporary batman, Mac-Mahon, always lost for a word, simply said: *'Eh bien, continuez!'*, the French equivalent to the military: 'Carry on as you were!') **4** *Parler petit nègre*: To speak broken French. (*Petit nègre* is the French counterpart to pidgin English.) **5** *C'est comme un combat de nègres dans* *un tunnel (joc. & iron.)*: I defy anyone to make head or tail of all this!

négresse *n.f.* **1** 'Bounder', flea (the variety that frequents humans rather than animals). **2** Bottle of 'plonk', of cheap dark red wine. (This word only seems to have survived in the expression *étouffer une négresse*: to down a bottle of plonk.) **3** (Restaurateurs' slang): Large capacity chip-fryer. (The only lexicographical reference to this meaning of the word is to be found in François Caradec's *DICTIONNAIRE DU FRANÇAIS ARGOTIQUE ET POPULAIRE.*)

négrier *n.m.* Employer who relies on 'black labour' to keep his firm going, i.e. employees for whom he has to bear no State charges and who, in turn, evade taxation.

neige *n.f.* (Drugs): 'Coke', 'snow', cocaine. (The otherwise unambiguous expression *être blanc comme neige*: to be totally innocent of anything, has in the world of drug trafficking a more sinister double-entendre.)

nénés *n.m.pl.* 'Titties', 'bristols', breasts.

nénesse *n.f.* **1** 'Biddy', 'bird', woman. **2** Wife. *Ma nénesse*: The missus.

nénette *n.f.* **1** 'Bean', 'bonce', head. *Se casser la nénette*: To rack one's brains and try one's darnedest to solve a problem. *En avoir pardessus la nénette*: To be 'fed up to the back teeth' with something, to be sick and tired of something. **2** 'Biddy', 'bit-of-skirt', woman. *C'est une petite nénette tout ce qu'il y a de meumeu!* She's a dinky little raver with everything in the right place! (With this meaning, *nénette* is a typically male-chauvinist utterance, and the association with 'a bit of fluff' can be better understood when one knows that *Nénette* is a brand-name car-duster used by salesmen in showrooms.)

nerf *n.m.* **1** *Avoir les nerfs à cran* (also: *avoir les nerfs en boule* or *en pelote*): To be 'all on edge', to be extremely tense. *Tout ça m'a mis les nerfs à cran*: This whole business has made me really uptight. **2** *Porter sur les nerfs à quelqu'un*: To 'get on someone's wick', to irritate and make angry. *Tu commences à me porter sur les nerfs!* I'm getting rather tired of you! **3** *Y mettre du nerf*: To 'put some vim into it', to get some zest into whatever one is doing. (This expression is practically always found in the second person singular or plural of the imperative. *Mets-y du nerf, bon sang!* For Pete's sake, get a move on!) **4** *Le nerf de la guerre*: 'Loot', 'brass', money (literally what makes war-mongering financially possible). **5** *Ne pas avoir un nerf*: To be 'skint', to be penniless. (Unlike the previous entry for this word, the reference is to '*argent*

monnayé', i.e. real money in notes and coins, and the word is pronounced *nerffe*.)

nervi *n.m.* **1** 'Yobbo', hooligan. **2** 'Heavy', mobster.

nettoyage *n.m.* **1** (Gambling slang): 'Fleecing' (literally the 'cleaning-out' of a punter on a losing streak). **2** (Underworld slang): 'Contract job', paid assassination.

nettoyer *v.trans.* **1** (Gambling slang): To 'clean out' a punter on a losing streak. *Il m'a nettoyé au pok', facile!* He trounced me at poker, it was like taking sweets off a kid! **2** *(mil.)*: To 'mop up', to clear an area where enemy forces are concerned. **3** (of disease): To 'wipe out', to kill. *Il a attrapé une petite saloperie qui l'a nettoyé en deux jours*: He caught some rotten little bug and it polished him off in 48 hours. **4** To 'rub out', to 'bump off', to kill.

neuf *adj.* **1** *Etre tout neuf* (of person): To be 'a bit green', to lack experience. **2** *Quoi de neuf?!* *(joc. & iron.)*: What's up doc?! – What's the news?! (This expression is often used with a jocular double-entendre by antique-dealers where a 'what's new?' query takes a novel twist.)

neuille *n.f.* Night. *Il est rentré à la neuille*: He came home when it was dark. *Ça fait trois neuilles que je n'ai pas pioncé*: I haven't slept a wink in three nights.

Neuneu *Proper name.* Neuilly-sur-Seine. This suburb on the west of Paris has for over a hundred years played host to an annual and gigantic fun-fair known as the *fête à Neuneu*, a good-hearted and popular entertainment now slightly out of character with the up-market population of this urban area.

neunœil *n.m.* One-eyed man.

neutron *n.m.* *Des idées à la 'mords-moi-le-neutron' (joc. & iron.)*: 'Pie-in-the-sky' ideas. (The *mords-moi-le-neutron* expression is a euphemistic and jocular corruption of '*mords-moi-le-nœud'*.)

neveu *n.m.* *Un peu, mon neveu!* Not half! – You bet! – I should jolly well think so! (This jocular catch phrase, in spite of its built-in nonsense rhyme, is in no way relatable to English rhyming slang.)

nez *n.m.* **1** *Avoir du nez* (also: *avoir bon nez*): To be well-inspired where making a decision is concerned. *On peut dire que tu as eu du nez de ne pas y aller*: You certainly made the right choice in keeping away! **2** *Avoir le nez creux*: To have an uncanny knack at guessing right first time. (When uttered, this expression is often accompanied by the 'bodyspeak' gesture of tapping the side of one's nose with the index finger.) **3** *Avoir quelqu'un dans le nez*: To be unable to 'stomach' someone, to have a strong antipathy towards someone. *Depuis sa vacherie je l'ai dans le nez*: I can't stand the sight of him since he did the dirty on me! 4 *Avoir un verre dans le nez*: To have had 'one over the eight', to be 'tipsy', to be slightly drunk. 5 *Se piquer le nez*: To get 'pickled', to get drunk as a matter of habit. 6 *A vue de nez*: At a rough guess. *A vue de nez, je dirais qu'elle a la cinquantaine*: My guesstimate is she's well into her fifties! 7 *Tirer les vers du nez à quelqu'un*: To 'pump' someone, to extract information from a reluctant party. 8 *Se casser le nez*: **a** To find no-one at home. **b** To 'come a cropper', to fail. 9 *Se bouffer le nez*: To 'squabble', to quarrel. 10 *Ça va nous tomber sur le nez!* We're sure to 'cop it' – We're certainly in for some trouble! 11 *Ça lui pend au nez!* He's got it coming to him! (The expression is quite often used in the past tense as if to prove the foresight of the speaker in a 'He had it coming to him!' stance.) 12 *Les doigts dans le nez*: With the greatest of ease. *Il a gagné la course les doigts dans le nez*: He romped home to victory.

niac *n.m.* 'Chink', Chinese. (Originally not pejorative or racialist, this appellation during the *Guerre d'Indochine* became as derogatory as the American 'gink' when referring to Communist Koreans or Vietnamese.)

Niaca *Proper name*. Person who is always ready to volunteer the kind of simple and easy solution no-one else is deemed to have thought of. *Niaca* is in fact a jocular corruption of *il n'y a qu'à*.

niard *n.m. (pej.)*: 1 'Brat', 'kid', child. 2 'Geezer', 'bloke', chap.

niasse *n.m. (pej.)*: 'Geezer', 'bloke', fellow. *Qui m'a foutu un niasse pareil?* I'd like to know who hired that nurk!

nib *adv.* 'Bugger-all', nothing. *Etre bon à nib*: To be bloody useless. (This expression can refer to a person or thing.) *Tout ce fatras est bon à nib*: All this clobber's not worth a sausage. *Avoir nib d'oseille*: To be 'skint', 'broke', to be penniless. *Faire quelque chose pour nib de nib*: To do something for sweet F.A.

nibe *interj.* Put a sock in it! – Shut up!

nibé *n.m.* Small-time con-trick. (The word is used contemptuously by hardened criminals when referring to petty larcenies committed by the 'small-fry' in the underworld.)

niche *n.f. A la niche, Médor! (joc. & iron.)*: Go back to sleep! – Nobody asked your advice! (In novelettes and children's stories, *Médor* is the archetypal name for a dog.)

nichemards *n.m.pl.* 'Knockers', 'bristols', breasts.

nicher *v.trans.* To store away. *Je ne sais pas où j'ai niché ça!* I don't know where the hell I've put it! (As the above expression illustrates, the original intention is not to hide something purposely, although the net result is that the item is seldom found again.)

nicher *v.intrans.* To 'hang out', to live, to dwell. *Où que tu niches ces temps-ci?* And where's your pad these days?

nicher *v.pronom.* To find oneself in a place where one is unlikely to be discovered. *Dieu sait où il se niche!* Heaven knows where he is now! (This verb can sometimes refer to 'impossible' geographical locations. *Te dire où ça se niche? Alors là?!* Don't ask me where that place is! I've never the foggiest!)

niches *n.f.pl.* Pranks. *Faire des niches à quelqu'un*: To play gentle and innocuous tricks on someone.

nichons *n.m.pl.* 'Knockers', 'boobs', breasts.

nickel *adj.inv.* 1 'Spick-and-span', very clean. *Chez eux c'est vraiment nickel*: It's all shipshape and clean as a whistle where they live. 2 *C'est nickel-nickel!* It's hunky-dory! – It's super-duper! – It's first-rate!

nickelé *adj. Avoir les pieds nickelés*: **a** To be a 'jammy bugger', to have the luck of the devil. (The *Pieds-Nickelés*, the creation of the humorous cartoonist Louis Forton, are three happy-go-lucky characters who boomerang from rags to riches and back to rags in every episode. Their ability to fall back on their feet and laugh at adversity was and is their trademark as their hilarious cartoon capers are forever being revived.) **b** To sit tight, to refuse to budge. (This expression is often used in a work context when referring to an obstreperous employee.)

nickeler *v.trans.* To clean with some proverbial 'spit-and-polish'.

nicodème *n.m.* 'Noodle', 'chump', simpleton.

niçois *adj.inv. Etre niçois*: To 'stand pat', to refuse to increase one's stakes at a game of poker.

nième *adj.ord.* (Pronounced *ennième*). *Pour la nième fois*: For the umpteenth time. *C'est la nième fois que je me tape ce trajet*: I feel like a yo-yo going there all the time.

nien *n.m.* 'Cold turkey', drug addict's withdrawal symptoms.

niente *n.m. & f.* 'Nonentity', insignificant and inefficient person. (This word applies only to men and as with many colloquial terms becomes even more pejorative in the feminine.)

niente *pron.* 'Nix', nothing.

nière *n.m. (pej.)*: 1 'Geezer', 'bloke', fellow. *Un nière à la manque*: An incompetent nurk. 2 Accomplice, confederate.

niflette *n.f.* (Drugs): 'Snow', cocaine. (This word is an abbreviation of *reniflette* which is more descriptive of the manner in which the addict takes his drug, i.e. by sniffing it.)

niguedouille *n.m.* 'Noodle', 'nincompoop', simpleton.

ninas *n.m.* 'Whiff', cheroot, inexpensive small cigar. (Originally a brand name, the word has become generic for cigarillos.)

nini *n.m.* 'Nincompoop', 'ninny', fool.

niôle *n.f.* 'Hooch', 'the hard stuff', strong alcohol. *Vous prendrez bien un petit coup de niôle?* How about a short?!

Niort *Proper name. Aller* (also: *battre*) *à Niort*: To deny vehemently.

nippe *n.f.* Item of clothing. (The expression *n'avoir plus une nippe à se mettre*, a very feminine complaint, goes perhaps to prove that 'I haven't got a thing to wear' knows no frontier.) The word is mildly pejorative – *Il n'a que des nippes*: He goes around in rags – being typical of its usage.

nippé *adj.* Dressed. *Etre bien nippé*: To be 'togged-up', to be well rigged-out. (Strangely, *nippé* is more often than not encountered with a positive connotation, whereas *fringué* is more likely to be in a pejorative context.)

nipper *v.trans.reflex.* To 'tog oneself up', to 'rig oneself out', to dress. *A le voir, on dirait qu'il se nippe aux puces*: He seems to be a bespoke customer of the Oxfam shop where togs are concerned!

nique *n.f. Faire la nique à quelqu'un*: To jeer at someone. *A sa façon, il nous a fait la nique*: It was really his way of waving two fingers at us!

niquer *v.trans. & intrans.* To 'screw', to fuck, to have coition with.

nisco *interj.* Nix! – No way! – Nothing doing!

niston *n.m.* 'Laddie', 'lad', young boy. (This friendly appellation is very typical of Provence where it originated.)

niston *adj. Etre niston*: To 'stand pat', to refuse to increase one's stakes at a game of poker. (Auguste le Breton in his *L'ARGOT CHEZ LES VRAIS DE VRAI* states that this word is eponymous with a famous poker player whose shrewd gaming tactics made him a byword for careful gambling.)

nistonne *n.f.* 'Lassie', 'slip of a girl', young and slender woman.

nobler *v.trans.* To know, to be acquainted with someone.

nobler *v.pronom. Comment tu te nobles?* What's your name? (In its pronominal form this verb is always found in the interrogative; no-one would say *'Je me noble'* or *'Il se noble'*.)

noblesse *n.f. La noblesse (joc. & iron.)*: The *milieu*, the French underworld.

nocdu *adj.* (of person): Ugly. (This somewhat rare adjective is the product of an intricate *largonji* corruption mentioned in Esnault's *DICTIONNAIRE DES ARGOTS*.)

noce *n.f.* 1 'Shindy', 'bender', spree. *Faire la noce*: To go on a spree, to live it up. 2 *Etre à la noce* (*fig.*): To be having the time of one's life. *Ne pas être à la noce*: To feel far from happy. 3 *N'avoir jamais été à pareilles noces*: To have 'jam on it' for a change, to enjoy the kind of good fortune one has never had before. 4 *Faire la noce* (of prostitute): To be 'on the game', to ply that trade. (Only the underworld context will enable a reader to differentiate this meaning from the first entry.)

nocer *v.intrans.* To 'make whoopee', to live it up (also: *faire la noce*).

noceur *n.m.* 'Hell-raiser', character who believes life is for making whoopee.

noceuse *n.f.* 'Easy-lay', fast woman. (Unlike its masculine counterpart this word seems to refer solely to sexual matters.)

nœil *n.m* (*joc.*): Eye. (The jocularity stems from the phonetic transcription of *un œil*, and this really excludes the plural *nœils* as its true jocular equivalent is *zyeux* from *les yeux*.)

Noël *Proper name. Il croit encore au Père Noël* (*joc. & iron.*): He'll believe the moon is made of cheese! – He's as gullible as they come!

nœud *n.m.* 1 'Prick', 'cock', penis. 2 *Peau de nœud*: 'Bugger-all', nothing at all. *On a fait tout ça pour peau de nœud!* We went to all that trouble for sweet Fanny Adams! 3 *Tête de nœud*: 'Pillock', 'burk', blithering idiot. 4 *Faire quelque chose à la mords-moi-le-nœud*: To make a real cock-up of things, to make a mess of whatever task one has been entrusted with.

noille *n.f.* (also: *noye*): Night. *Il n'est pas rentré de la noille*: He was out on the tiles all night.

noir *n.m.* 1 *Avoir le noir*: To 'have the blues', to feel 'down in the mouth', to be depressed (also: *avoir le cafard*). 2 *Le noir (abbr. le marché noir)*: Black-market trading. *Acheter quelque chose au noir*: To purchase something under the counter. 3 *Travailler au noir*: To be employed in an illegal situation where tax and other State controls are concerned. (The notion of 'black labour' seems to know no frontiers.) 4 *Un petit noir*: A small cup of black coffee (literally, a cup of 'demi-tasse'!).

noir *adj.* 'Sloshed', 'lit-up', blind-drunk.

noircicot *n.m.* (also: *noircicaud*): 'Darkie', coloured person. (Although, sadly, most references to coloured people are racialist and derogatory, this word is by no means as disparaging as 'coon' or 'wog'. Also: *noirpiot*.)

noircif *n.m. Le noircif*: Black-market trading.

noircir *v.pronom.* To get 'blotto', to get blind-drunk.

noire *n.f.* 1 *La noire*: Night, literally the darkest one imaginable devoid of moon and stars. 2 (Drugs): Raw opium (the crude unrefined variety).

noirpiot *n.m. (pej.)*: 'Darkie', coloured person (also: *noircicot*).

noisettes *n.f.pl.* 'Nuts', 'balls', testicles.

noite *n.f.* Night. (This word is a corruption of the English 'night' and can also be pronounced *à la française*.)

noité *adj.* Endowed with a fleshy behind, as opposed to a flabby one. (Not surprisingly, the adjective refers more to women than to men. *Elle est drôlement bien noitée!* You should see the neat little pack she wiggles when she walks!)

noix *n.f.* 1 'Nut', 'bonce', head. *Il a pris un sacré coup de goumi sur la noix*: He got neatly coshed behind the ears. 2 'Mush', 'dial', face. 3 *(pl.)*: 'Cheeks', buttocks, behind. *Sortir quelqu'un à coups de pompes dans les noix*: To boot someone out. *T'aurais dû voir cette paire de noix!* You should have seen that neat little 'sit-me-down' of hers! *Serrer les noix (fig.)*: To 'have the shits', to be 'in a blue funk', to be very frightened. 4 *(pl.)*: 'Nuts', 'balls', testicles. *Tu me fais mal aux noix!* You get on my tits, you do! – You really are a bloody nuisance! 5 'Noodle', 'chump', fool. *Une vieille noix*: A silly old fuddy-duddy. *Quelle noix ce mec-là!* Have you ever seen a bigger nurk?! 6 *à la noix (adj.exp.)*: Useless and meaningless. *Des boniments à la noix*: 'Eyewash', 'baloney', preposterous statements. (The extended expression *à la noix de coco* is more specific and means 'phoney', fake, false.)

nom *n.m.* 1 *Nom d'un chien!* Cripes! – By jove! (This expression and others such as *Nom d'une pipe! – Nom d'un petit bonhomme! – Nom de nom!*, etc. are euphemistic variations on the now quite bland *Nom de Dieu!*) 2 *Petit nom*: Christian name, forename. (*Petit nom* is more often than not found in an interrogative clause. *Quel est ton petit nom?* What do they call you? Such a turn of phrase is indeed low-brow and belongs to the world of amorous badinage.) 3 *Un nom à charnière* (also: *un nom à rallonge*): A double-barrelled name. 4 *Un nom à coucher dehors (avec un billet de logement)*: A right jaw-twister of a name. (This jocular and ironical expression is that and nothing more. It has no real pejorative connotation.) 5 *Ça n'a pas de nom!* Well I never! – It's beyond words! – It's incredible!

nombril *n.m.* 1 *Etre décolletée jusqu'au nombril*: To have a 'morning, judge!' cleavage, to wear a garment that shows a lot of breast. 2 *Se prendre pour le nombril du monde*: To 'think the world of oneself', to have an inflated idea of one's own importance.

non *adv. Non, c'est non!* N-O spells no! – When I say no I mean it!

non-lieu *n.m.* Withdrawal of a legal case, magistrate's decision not to proceed with a trial where evidence for the prosecution is insufficient. (As is the case elsewhere, the old adage 'there's no smoke without fire' is reflected in the moral slur of the *non-lieu*. Where criminals are concerned, the opposite is true and a well-known *truand* revelled in the title bestowed by the Press: *'le roi du non-lieu'*.)

nonnette *n.f.* 'Dolly', bandaged finger.

nono *adj.inv. La zone nono*: The unoccupied zone in France during World War II.

noraf *n.m. (pej.)*: Native of Algeria, Tunisia or Morocco.

nord *n.m. Perdre le nord*: **a** To be 'all at sea', to lose one's head. *Il perd le nord pour un rien*: He's at sixes and sevens over trifles. **b** To 'go off one's rocker', to go mad.

nordaf *n.m. (pej.)*: Native of Algeria, Tunisia or Morocco.

Normand *n.m. Une réponse de Normand*: An evasive answer, a non-committal reply. (Where provincial folklore imagery is concerned, the natives of Normandy have the reputation of sitting on the fence with a *'peut-être-ben-qu'oui, peut-être-ben-que-non'* approach to direct questioning.)

nouba *n.f.* 'Shindy', 'bender', spree. *Faire la nouba*: To 'have a whale of a time', to live it up.

nougat *n.m.* 1 *Un vrai nougat* (of task, undertaking): 'A walkover', a doddle. (This expression is more usually associated with illegal activities, hence the second meaning.) 2 *Toucher son nougat* (of booty): To 'get one's cut', to 'get one's whack' in a share-out. 3 *(pl.)*: 'Plates of meat', 'trotters', feet. (The image is not a savoury one as the sticky nature of *nougat* emphasizes the filthiness of the feet in question.)

nougatine *n.f. C'est de la nougatine!* (of illicit activity): It's as easy as pie! – It's a doddle!

nouille *n.f.* 'Noodle', 'drip', spineless fool.

nouille *adj.* (of person): Wet, spineless. *Ce qu'il est nouille, celui-là!* He's a real drip!

nounou *n.f.* (Child language): Nanny, children's nurse.

nounours *n.m.* 'Teddy', teddy bear.

nourrice *n.f.* 1 *Mettre un objet en nourrice* (Antique-dealers' jargon): To place an item on a sale-or-return basis with a colleague. 2 *Oublier les mois de nourrice* (Usually of woman): To have a 'discount scheme' when referring to one's age, to pretend to be younger than one really is. **3** *Sans compter les mois de nourrice* (of time lapsed generally): . . . and a little bit more. *On travaille ensemble depuis cinq ans sans compter les mois de nourrice*: We've been teamed up for five years at the very least.

nourrir *v.trans. Ça ne nourrit pas son homme! (joc. & iron.)*: It's not worth doing! – There's no profit in it!

nourrisson *n.m. (fig.)*: One who is extra to requirements (in a business, etc. Literally, an extra mouth to feed). *Leur taule a croulé, 'y avait trop de nourrissons*: Their firm went bust, there were too many hangers-on.

nouvelles *n.f.pl.* **1** *Vous aurez de mes nouvelles!* You've not heard the last of this! – You'll be hearing from me! (This colloquial expression could, in plain English, be translated by: 'You'll be hearing from my solicitor!') **2** *Vous m'en donnerez des nouvelles!* (of highly-praised item): I'm sure you'll be delighted! *C'est un petit pinard dont vous me donnerez des nouvelles!* I think you're really going to like this wine!

novice *n.m. Ne pas être un novice*: To be an 'old hand', to 'know the ropes', to be familiar with the workings of something.

noyau *n.m. Un matelas rembourré aux noyaux de pêche*: A hard and lumpy bed.

noye *n.f.* Night. *Ce qu'il fait de ses noyes, je m'en fous!* I don't give a damn what he gets up to at night!

noyer *v.trans. Noyer le poisson*: To cloud and confuse the issue with an avalanche of irrelevant facts.

noyer *v.trans.reflex. Se noyer dans un crachat*: To 'make a mountain out of a molehill', to give matters an exaggerated importance and to worry about them.

nuit *n.f. Etre de nuit*: To be 'on nights', to work the night shift.

nuitard *n.m.* (Postmen's slang): 'Nightie', one who sorts mail at night.

nuiteuse *n.f.* 'Lady of the night', prostitute plying her trade after dusk.

nuiteux *n.m.* (Taxi drivers' slang): One who does the night shift.

numéro *n.m.* **1** 'Character', 'card', person who stands out from the crowd. *Quel numéro, celui-là!* You won't see two like him! *Un drôle de numéro*: A bit of an oddball. **2** *Maison à gros numéro*: 'Cat-house', brothel. **3** *Vendre au numéro* (Artists' jargon): To have a ready market where certain canvas sizes are concerned. **4** *Quel numéro!* (of prowess): What a feat! – What an exploit! **5** *Un bon numéro*: 'Some valuable info', good advice. **6** *Avoir tiré le bon numéro*: To have struck it lucky. (The expression originates from the days when conscripts were designated for National Service by a lottery system.) **7** *Je retiens votre numéro!* You've not heard the last of this! – You'll be hearing from me! (Although the expression suggests hate and animosity, it is usually uttered with restrained jocularity.) **8** *Le numéro cent*: The 'karzey', the 'bog', the W.C. (The appellation is said to have its origin in the misreading of the word 'loo' on the door of a battle-weary field-latrine during W.W.I.)

numéroter *v.trans. Tu peux numéroter tes abatis!* I'm going to make mincemeat of you! – You're in for a thrashing! (These menacing words can be literally explained in that the threatened person should 'number his limbs' for piecing together after a good hiding.)

nunu *n.m. (joc.)*: Nudist.

O

obitus *n.m.* Death. (There appears to be no register-keyed equivalent to this part-scientific, part-jocular term. 'Demise' and 'passing-over', 'croaking' and 'snuffing it' miss the *carabin* flavour.)

objection *n.f. Objection, votre Honneur! (joc. & iron.)*: I do beg your pardon! (Forgive me for saying so, but I disagree!)

objet *n.m. Les objets trouvés*: The lost property office.

obligado *adv. Faire quelque chose obligado*: To be bulldozed into doing something, to do something under compulsion.

obligations *n.f.pl. Etre dégagé des* (also: *de ses*) *obligations militaires*: To be within the law where National Service is concerned. (Either to have served one's time as a soldier or received an exemption.)

occase *n.f. (abbr. occasion)*: **1** Opportunity, favourable circumstance. *Heureusement qu'on a profité de l'occase*: It was a lucky thing we took advantage of the situation. *A l'occase*: Should the opportunity arise. *A l'occase, venez nous voir si vous êtes par ici!* Pop in and see us whenever you're around! **2** Bargain. *C'est une occase à ne pas manquer*: It's too good a buy to miss. **3** *D'occase*: Second-hand. *Toutes ses voitures, il les achète d'occase*: You'll never see him drive a new car.

occasion *n.f.* **1** *Faire d'occasion*: To 'look the worse for wear', to look old. (In an ironical context, this can also apply to a person.) **2** *Il a perdu une bonne occasion de se taire*: Silence is a virtue! – He'd have been better off holding his tongue.

occupe *n.f. L'occupe*: The German occupation of France during World War II.

occuper *v.pronom.* **1** *S'occuper de ses affaires*: To mind one's own business. *C'est mes oignons, occupe-toi de tes affaires!* Keep out of it, this is my pigeon! **2** *T'occupe!* Mind your own bloody business! (The very brevity of this riposte gives it extra 'bite'.) **3** *Savoir s'occuper*: To 'know

one's way around', not to be lacking initiative when it comes to the crunch.

odeur *n.f. Ne pas être en odeur de sainteté avec quelqu'un (iron.)*: To be 'in someone's bad books', to be rather unpopular with someone.

œil *n.m.* **1** *Avoir quelqu'un à l'œil*: To keep a close eye on someone. *Je veux que vous m'ayez ce lascar à l'œil!* Don't let that bugger out of your sight! **2** *Avoir quelqu'un dans l'œil* (Racing and cycling slang): To see a fellow competitor forge ahead. **3** *L'avoir dans l'œil (fig.)*: To have been 'conned', 'diddled', to have been duped. **4** *Risquer un œil*: To 'take a peep', to glance furtively at something. **5** *Se rincer l'œil*: To 'feast one's eyes', to get a salacious eyeful. **6** *Pisser de l'œil* (often of woman): To 'have the weepies', to 'turn on the waterworks', to cry. **7** *Ne dormir que d'un œil*: To take a wary 'forty winks', to drift into a state of superficial sleep because danger is lurking. **8** *Ouvrir l'œil et le bon*: To 'keep one's weather eye open', to keep a sharp lookout. **9** *Monter un œil à quelqu'un*: To 'give someone a shiner', a black eye. **10** *Avoir un œil qui dit merde à l'autre (joc.)*: To have a pronounced squint (also: *avoir les yeux qui se croisent les bras*). **11** *Tourner de l'œil*: To 'pass out', to faint. **12** *Etre frais comme l'œil* (of person): To be (and look) as fresh as a daisy. **13** *Obéir au doigt et à l'œil*: To be hyper-obedient (literally to jump to attention at the quiver of an eyebrow). **14** *Faire un œil de crapaud mort d'amour*: To look 'spoony', to have a lovesick expression on one's face. **15** *Taper dans l'œil à quelqu'un*: **a** To make a deep impression on someone. **b** To 'click' with someone, to take someone's fancy. **16** *S'en battre l'œil*: 'Not to care a rap about something', to be totally unconcerned. **17** *Mon œil!* You must be joking! (This ironical interjection is usually accompanied by the pulling down with the index finger of the lower eyelid. This 'bodyspeak' gesture emphasizes the 'I'm not as gullible as you think' quality of the remark.)

18 *L'œil du bidet (pol.)*: 'Dick', private eye. (This pejorative appellation for a private detective reflects explicitly the snooping that constitutes a fair proportion of his business.) **19** *L'œil de bronze*: The anus, the anal sphincter (where sodomous intercourse is concerned).

œillade *n.f.* *Faire* (also: *lancer*) *une œillade*: To give someone the glad eye. *Il faut toujours qu'il lance des œillades en loucedé!* As soon as your back's turned he'll wink his way into any bird's heart!

œillères *n.f.pl.* *Avoir des œillères*: To be narrow-minded (literally, to wear blinkers where life and society are concerned).

œillet *n.m.* **1** Anus, anal sphincter (where sodomous intercourse is concerned; also: *œil de bronze*). **2** *(pl.)*: 'Mince-pies', 'blinkers', eyes. *Cliquer des œillets* (of woman): To 'flutter', to bat eyelashes in an enticing manner. *Gicler des œillets*: To 'open the flood-gates', to weep.

œuf *n.m.* **1** 'Pill', 'pillock', fool. *Faire l'œuf*: To arse about. *Cesse de faire l'œuf!* Stop mucking about! **2** *Aux œufs*: 'A-1', 'champion', first-class. *Comme boulot, c'est aux œufs!* That's what I'd call a plum job! **3** *Casser son œuf*: To have a miscarriage. **4** *Avoir des œufs sur le plat*: To have 'poached-egg-on-toast boobs', to have an insignificant bust. **5** *Marcher (comme) sur des œufs*: **a** *(lit.)*: To walk carefully (because of pain). **b** *(fig.)*: To tread warily. **6** *Sortir de l'œuf*: To be 'as green as they come', to be totally lacking experience (where life is concerned). **7** *Etouffer quelque chose dans l'œuf*: To 'nip something in the bud', to abort an enterprise or rumour in its early stages. **8** *Etre chauve comme un œuf*: To be as bald as a coot. **9** *Tondre des œufs*: To be a 'skinflint', to be as mean as they come. **10** *Qui vole un œuf vole un bœuf*: Once a thief, always a thief! **11** *Aller se faire cuire un œuf*: To 'get knotted', to go to blazes. *Va te faire cuire un œuf!* Get stuffed! (The expression *aller se faire cuire un œuf*, because of its very nature, is quite interjection-loaded.) **12** *Plein comme un œuf*: 'As tight as a tick', as drunk as a lord. **13** *L'avoir dans l'œuf*: To have been 'conned', 'diddled', to have been swindled. **14** *(pl.)*: 'Nuts', 'balls', testicles. **15** *Œuf corse! (joc.)*: Absoballylutely! – Of course!

œuvre *n.f.* *C'est pour mes bonnes œuvres! (iron.)*: It's for my own little nest-egg! – It's just for me! (There is a certain jocularity in this statement as '*bonnes œuvres*' usually relates to charitable funds raised through public collection.)

offense *n.f.* *'y a pas d'offense!* No harm done! – It's quite alright! (This is an honest-to-goodness lowbrow French *formule de politesse* and does

not have the 'don't mind me' sarcastic angle suggested by some sources.)

officemar *n.m.* *(mil.)*: Officer.

officiel *n.m.* *De l'officiel*: 'The real McCoy', the genuine stuff. *Ces biftons, c'est de l'officiel, tu peux me faire confiance!* These are real notes, not Mickey-Mouse money – you can trust me!

officiel *adj.* Sure, certain. *C'est officiel!* It's a dead-cert!

ogino *adj.* *Bébé ogino*: Unplanned baby, infant born to a mother who miscalculated her menstrual cycle according to the Ogino contraception method. (The *méthode Ogino*, eponymous with that medical practitioner, did more to boost France's birth-rate than any governmental incentive, hence the ironical *bébé ogino* tag.)

ognard *n.m.* Arse-hole, anus (also: *ogne, ogneul!*).

oie *n.f.* **1** *Oie blanche*: Innocent and gullible young woman (one totally ignorant of the facts of life). **2** *Des boniments à la graisse d'oie*: 'Bull', 'bullshit', preposterous statements.

oignard *n.m.* Arse-hole, anus. *L'avoir dans l'oignard (fig.)*: To have been 'conned', 'diddled', to have been swindled.

oignon *n.m.* **1** 'Turnip', fob-watch. **2** Arse-hole, anus. *L'avoir dans l'oignon*: To have been 'conned', 'diddled', to have been duped. *Quand il a repris son fric, c'est nous qu'on l'a eu dans l'oignon*: It really fucked us up when he withdrew his subsidies! **3** Luck, good fortune. *Avoir de l'oignon*: To have the luck of the devil. (Expressions such as *avoir l'oignon qui décalotte*, synonymous with the previous one, tend to emphasize what Albert Simonin states in his NOUVEAU DICTIONNAIRE DE L'ARGOT, namely the link between sodomy and good fortune. Simonin is of the opinion that many successes can be linked to past homosexual liaisons. A similar bias can be found in *cocu*; see that word.) **4** *En rang d'oignons*: In a neat row. *On avait l'air vraiment fin là, tous en rang d'oignons!* There we were standing like a neat row of dummies! (It would appear that the expression comes from the language of the vegetable garden, and usually refers to people.) **5** *Ce n'est pas* (also: *ce ne sont pas*) *mes oignons!* It's none of my business! *Je fais ce qui me plaît, c'est mes oignons!* What I do is my business! *Occupe-toi de tes oignons!* Keep your nose out of it! **6** *Aux petits oignons*: 'First-rate', 'smashing', superb. *Son système, il est aux petits oignons!* You can't fault the way he organizes things! **7** *Arranger quelqu'un aux petits oignons (iron.)*: To 'give someone a proper dressing-down', to tell someone off in no uncertain manner. **8** *Course à l'oignon*: Act of chucking someone out by the scruff of his neck and the seat of his pants. **9** *Un oignon à réclamers* (Racing slang): A selling-stakes nag (the kind of steed unlikely to ever really make it on the courses).

oiseau *n.m.* **1** *(pej.)*: 'Obdurate nurk', pigheaded fool. *Un drôle d'oiseau*: An 'awkward customer'. **2** *Donner à quelqu'un des noms d'oiseau*: To 'call someone names', to shower abuse on someone.

olibrius *n.m.* Brash and breezy show-off, pompous extrovert. *Cesse de faire l'olibrius!* Stop arsing about! (It would appear that Olibrius, a governor of the Gauls around 300 A.D., gained eponymous fame for his erratic behaviour.)

olive *n.f.* **1** 'Slug', bullet. *Il s'est cloqué une olive dans le plafond*: He shot himself through the head. **2** 'Pill', rugby ball. *Tâter de l'olive*: To play rugger. **3** *(pl.)*: 'Bollocks', 'balls', testicles. **4** *Changer ses olives d'eau*: To 'have a slash', to 'pee', to urinate.

ollé-ollé *adj.inv.* *(joc.)*: **1** (of story, joke): 'Risqué', 'close to the knuckle', slightly smutty. **2** (of woman): Fast and flighty. *Elle est ollé-ollé, sa nana!* His bird's a right bit of ooh-la-la!

olpette *adj.* **1** 'Natty', smart, stylish. **2** 'Nifty', nimble, agile.

ombre *n.f.* **1** *Marcher avec son ombre*: To 'skulk', to move stealthily. **2** *Il y a une ombre au tableau (fig.)*: The picture's not really very clear! – All's not well! **3** *Etre à l'ombre*: To be 'inside', to be in prison. *Il y a belle lurette qu'ils l'ont mis à l'ombre*: They put him in the nick yonks ago.

ombrelle *n.f.* *Avoir un bec d'ombrelle*: To have an 'ugly mush', an unpleasant face. (This expression could relate to bygone days when parasols, umbrellas and walking-sticks often had knobs in the form of a caricatured head.)

omelette *n.f.* **1** *Faire une omelette*: To 'make a hash of things', to mess things up. *Comme gaffe ça a été une sacrée omelette!* That boob of his left him with egg on his face! **2** 'Cissy', soppy figure of a man. (With this meaning, the word is a would-be pun on *hommelette*.)

on *indef.pron.* To translate *on* by 'one' is to lose the colloquiality of this 'we' pronoun. (Expressions such as *on a bien rigolé!* translate best as 'We had a bloody good laugh!' The popular French saying *On c'est un con qui n'a pas de nom* gives this pronoun its real semantic pitch.)

ongle *n.m.* **1** *Payer rubis sur l'ongle*: To pay 'cash on the nail', to settle a debt promptly and in full. **2** *Avoir les ongles en deuil*: To have dirty fingernails. (This expression is self-evident to the French for whom all correspondence relating to mourning is edged in black.)

onze *num.adj.* **1** *Bouillon d'onze heures* (also: *de onze heures*): Dose of poison. **2** *Prendre le train onze* (also: *le train d'onze heures*): To 'go by Shanks's pony', to 'hoof it', to have to go on foot. (The origin of this expression remains a mystery; it might well be the last train left at 22.59!)

O.P. *n.m.* *(abbr. Officier de Police)*: Police officer (in or out of uniform).

opé *n.f.* 'Op', surgical operation. *On lui a fait une opé*: They did surgery on him.

opérer *v.trans. & intrans.* **1** To 'knife', to stab someone. **2** To 'screw', to fuck, to have coition with. **3** *Il m'a opéré de dix sacs*: He conned me out of ten quid. (The deviation from the standard meaning is jocular and suggests the 'painless removal' of funds or valuable items.) **4** To 'operate', to ply a trade (usually an illegal one). *Il opère sur les champs de courses et fait son beurre au bonneteau*: He works the racecourses with the old three-card trick. **5** *Opérer en douce*: To go about one's business in a furtive and clandestine way.

ophtalmo *n.m.* *(abbr. ophtalmologiste)*: Eye-specialist.

or *n.m.* **1** *Rouler sur l'or*: To be 'rolling in it', to be stinking rich. *Je ne roule pas sur l'or, tu sais!* I'm sorry, I haven't got money to burn! (also: *être cousu d'or*). **2** *Je ne le ferais pas pour tout l'or du monde!* I wouldn't do it for all the tea in China! **3** *C'est de l'or en barre* (of project, venture): It's as safe as houses. **4** *Etre franc comme l'or* (of person): To be frank and outspoken. *Lui, il est franc comme l'or!* He's as straight as a die and won't give you any bull! **5** *Avoir un caractère d'or*: To have a lovely nature, to have a pleasant and amenable disposition. **6** *Parler d'or*: To speak words of wisdom. **7** *C'est en or!* (of project, venture): It's a doddle! – It's a walkover! – It's as easy as pie! **8** *L'avoir en or*: To be a lucky so-and-so.

orage *n.m.* *Il y a de l'orage dans l'air!* There's trouble brewing!

orange *n.f.* **1** 'Biff', blow. *Choper une orange sur le coin de la gueule*: To get a knuckle-sandwich. **2** *(pl.)*: Small and firm breasts. *Elle a une sacrée paire d'oranges sur l'étagère!* She's got the kind of knockers to hang your hat and coat on!

orbite *n.f.* *En placer un sur orbite*: To 'sow one's wild oats' successfully, to get a girl pregnant. (There is tongue-in-cheek humour in the *hors bite* pun.)

orchestre *n.m.* **1** *Faire l'homme-orchestre*: To have to act the 'Jack-of-all-trades', to be forced to do all manner of chores. **2** *Déboucher son orchestre*: To 'blow a turd', to 'crap', to defecate.

ordinaire *n.m.* **1** *De l'ordinaire*: Two-star petrol, 91 octane-rated car fuel. (The French do not differentiate between three- and four-star petrol; *du super* refers to 94-plus octane-rated fuel.) **2** *En faire son ordinaire (joc. & iron.)*: To have to 'make do with something' (usually a desirable item or commodity). *Mate un peu cette nana, j'en ferais bien mon ordinaire!* I wouldn't complain if I had a bird like that every night!

ordonnance *n.f. Je prends ça sur ordonnance! (joc. & iron.*; of alcoholic drink): This is just the medicine for me!

ordres *n.f.pl. Marcher aux ordres*: To submit through fear to someone's rule of iron. (This is very much an underworld expression, one that reflects the importance of sheer brute force.)

ordure *n.f. Une belle ordure*: A 'right shit', a 'nasty piece of work', a most obnoxious person.

oreille *n.f.* **1** *Glisser quelque chose dans le tuyau de l'oreille à quelqu'un*: To whisper something to someone. **2** *Faire la sourde oreille*: To turn a deaf ear. **3** *Se faire tirer l'oreille*: To show unwillingness to do something (not, as some lexicographers suggest, 'to dig one's heels in'). **4** *Dormir sur ses deux oreilles*: **a** *(lit.)*: To sleep soundly. **b** *(fig.)*: To rest easy, not to worry. *Pour ce qui est de tout ça, vous pouvez dormir sur vos deux oreilles!* On that score, rest assured you've nothing to worry about. **5** *Partir l'oreille basse*: To 'go off with one's tail between one's legs', to leave crestfallen.

oreiller *n.m.* **1** *Consulter son oreiller*: To 'sleep on something', to avoid making a hasty decision. **2** *Se raccommoder sur l'oreiller* (of strifing couple): To make it up in bed.

original *n.m.* 'Card', character who stands out from the crowd.

original *adj. Ça c'est original! (joc. & iron.)*: **a** (of joke): That's a hackneyed chestnut! **b** (of solution): Whoever thought of that didn't invent the wheel!

orme *n.m. Attendez-moi sous l'orme! (iron.)*: You can wait for me but I shan't come! (There is a little of the pastoral 'waiting till the cows come home' in this expression, with the proviso in this instance that they won't.)

orphelin *n.m.* **1** 'Fag-end', cigarette-butt. **2** Unclaimed item in lost-property office. **3** (Junk-cum-antique-dealers' slang): Odd item (one of a pair or a set that will be difficult to sell on its own).

orphelines *n.f.pl.* 'Bollocks', 'balls', testicles.

orteils *n.m.pl. Avoir les orteils en éventail (joc.)*: To be 'high on a come', to be in the throes of orgasmic pleasure (also: *avoir les doigts de pied en bouquets de violettes*).

orties *n.f.pl. Faut pas pousser mémère dans les orties! (joc.)*: Hold on! – Keep things in perspective! – Don't exaggerate!

os *n.m.* **1** 'Hitch', unexpected snag. *Il y a comme un os!* I can feel there's something wrong here! *Tomber sur un os*: To hit a snag. (San-Antonio probably gave the word, with this meaning, literary status when he wrote the novel *Un os dans la noce*. The expression *il y a un os dans le fromage* belongs to the register of the police force, and means that enquiries have come to a halt.) **2** (Underworld slang): 'Evil customer', dangerous character (one definitely to be steered clear of). **3** 'Bone-shaker', 'banger', clapped-out car. *Il s'est fait fourguer le dernier des os*: They flogged him a right heap of rust! **4** *Ne pas faire de vieux os* (never in the present tense): Not to be long for this world. *Au train où il va, il ne fera pas de vieux os!* If he keeps this up, he'll soon be for the knacker's yard! **5** *Sauver ses os*: To save one's skin. **6** *Se rompre les os pour faire quelque chose (fig.)*: To break one's back in order to do something. **7** *Se casser un os (fig.)*: To 'come unstuck', to 'come a cropper', to fail. **8** *Etre trempé jusqu'aux os*: To be 'soaked to the skin', to be wet through. *Etre gelé jusqu'aux os*: To be frozen to the marrow. **9** *L'avoir dans l'os*: To have been 'had', 'conned', to have been duped. *Et comment qu'il l'a eu dans l'os!* They took him good and proper! **10** *Jusqu'à l'os*: Through and through. *Il nous a blousés jusqu'à l'os*: He completely pulled the wool over our eyes. **11** *Ça vaut l'os!* It's well worth it! – It's certainly worthwhile! **12** *Gagner son os*: To earn a crust. *Pour gagner son os, ces temps-ci, faut se lever tôt!* It's all graft these days if you want to earn a living! **13** *Os à moelle*: **a** 'Conk', 'hooter', nose (the runny kind). **b** 'Prick', 'cock', penis. (The expression *faire juter l'os* is generally lexicalized as having two meanings, according to which part of the anatomy it refers to: **a** To blow one's nose. **b** To ejaculate. *Avoir l'os* is more accurately translated by 'to have the big stick', to have an erection.) **14** *Mes os*: Me, myself. *Tes os*: You, yourself. *Ses os*: Him, himself. *Amène tes os!* Come here! *Fais gaffe à tes os!* Watch out!

oseille *n.f.* **1** *La soupe à l'oseille*: The bitter fare dished out by life. *Avoir eu droit à la soupe à l'oseille*: To have had a tough time in life. (As in the next example, the literal meaning of *oseille*: sorrel, probably the bitterest of edible vegetables, gives the flavour of the expressions.) **2** *La faire à l'oseille (à quelqu'un)*: To 'cod', to deceive someone. *Faudrait voir à ne pas nous la faire à l'oseille*: Don't try those little tricks on us! **3** 'Brass', 'loot', money. *Faire son oseille*: To make one's pile.

oseillé *adj.* 'Loaded', 'worth-a-packet', rich. *Elle est drôlement oseillée:* She's stinking rich.

osier *n.m.* 'Brass', 'loot', money. *Avoir un champ d'osier:* To be made of money.

osselets *n.m.pl.* 1 *Faire gaffe à ses osselets:* To be careful. *Fais gaffe à tes osselets!* Watch out! 2 *Tu commences à me courir sur les osselets!* You're getting on my wick! – You're starting to be a nuisance!

osseux *adj.* Awkward and irritable.

osto *n.m.* (also: *hosto*): Hospital.

ostrogoth *n.m.* Abrupt and uncouth character.

ôter *v.trans.reflex. Ote-toi de là que je m'y mette! (joc. & iron.):* Move over! – Make room for your betters (i.e. Me!).

ôticher *v.trans.* 1 To titillate, to excite sexually. 2 To charm, to woo.

ôticher *v.pronom. S'ôticher de:* To 'go spoony over', to fall in love with.

ouah-ouah *n.m.* (Child language): 'Bowsy-wowsy', 'bow-wow', dog.

ouais *adv.* Yep! – Yeah – Yes.

ouallou *interj.* No way! – Nothing doing! – This is just impossible!

ouatères *n.m.pl. Les ouatères:* 'The karzey', 'the bog', the W.C. (This word is, in fact, a truncated and phonetic representation of 'water closets'.)

ouatte *interj.* Not bloody likely! – You must be joking! – Don't you believe it! (As with the previous entry, it is a case of a phonetic representation of an English word, in this instance the ironic and indignant 'What?!')

oubli *n.m. Marcher à l'oubli:* To walk aloof, oblivious of other people (in many cases, in order to avoid embarrassing questions). *Depuis que je lui ai prêté du fric, il marche à l'oubli et j'en suis pour mes frais:* I'll never get that sub back off him, he just floats by whenever we meet, it's a lost cause!

oublier *v.intrans. Oublier de respirer (joc.):* To 'snuff it', to 'pop one's clogs', to die.

oublier *v.pronom.* 1 To be 'taken short', to 'wet oneself', to urinate in one's pants. (Sadly, more often than not, the expression refers to the elderly rather than to young children.) 2 To 'burp', to belch. 3 To 'fart', to break wind.

oubliettes *n.f.pl. Mettre aux oubliettes:* To shunt from one's memory, to take an active hand in forgetting something. *Tout ce qui s'est passé entre nous est mis aux oubliettes:* I've put the lid on our past.

ouf *interj. Avant de pouvoir diré ouf!* Before you could say Jack Robinson! – Quick as a flash.

ouiche *interj.* Not bloody likely! – You must be joking! – Don't you believe it! *Ah ouiche!* Not on your nelly!

ouiouine *n.f.* (Prostitutes' slang): 'Jam-rag', sanitary towel.

ouiquende *n.m. (joc.):* Week-end.

ouiquendard *n.m. (joc.):* Week-end tourist.

ouistiti *n.m.* 1 *(pej.):* 'Young whipper-snapper', youthful know-all. (One very often encounters this word in conjunction with 'the boss's son', perhaps because this parentage makes him feel a cut above the rest.) 2 Skeleton-key used by burglars in hotels and apartment blocks.

ourdé *adj.* 'Sloshed', 'sozzled', drunk. *Etre ourdé à zéro:* To be pissed out of one's tiny little mind.

ourdée *n.f. Tenir une sacrée ourdée:* To be 'pissed to the eyeballs', to 'have had a skinful', to be well and truly drunk.

ours *n.m.* 1 'Rough diamond', gruff individual. *C'est un ours mal léché!* He really has no manners! 2 *(mil.):* 'Cooler', 'glasshouse', prison cell (literally one where the inmate, like a captive bear, paces endlessly up and down). 3 (Writers' and publishers' slang): 'Boomerang-manuscript', one that is rejected by all possible takers. 4 *(pl.):* Menses, menstrual period. *Avoir ses ours:* To 'have the decorators in'.

oursin *n.m. Avoir des oursins dans le morlingue:* To be 'tight-fisted', to be mean. (The literal meaning is 'to have sea-urchins in one's purse', hence the reluctance to dip into it.)

ourson *n.m.* 'Kid', child. (Unlike many words referring to children, *ourson* is definitely non-pejorative.)

ousque (corr. *où est-ce que*): Where? *Ousque t'habites?* Where do you have your digs?

ouste *interj.* (also: *houste*): Come on! – Hurry up! *Allez ouste, foutez-moi le camp!* Come on, clear off!

outil *n.m.* 1 'Chiv', blade, knife. 2 'Prick', 'cock', penis. *Déballer ses outils:* To 'flash', to expose oneself, to expose one's genitals. (This expression, according to Georgette Marks's *DICTIONARY OF SLANG AND COLLOQUIALISMS,* is also lexicalized as: to confess.) 3 'Clumsy nurk', fumbling imbecile. *Ah j'te jure, quel outil, celui-là!* Have you ever seen a more gormless ham-fisted twit?!

outillé *past part. Etre bien outillé:* To be well 'tooled-up', to have large genitals.

outiller *v.trans.* To 'knife', to stab.

ouverture *n.f.* 1 (Café, restaurant slang): Opening-time. *Faire l'ouverture:* To do the early-morning shift. 2 *Avoir l'ouverture retardée:* To be 'slow on the uptake', to find it difficult to understand things straightaway. (This expression is a borrowing from the language of the parachutist.)

ouvrage *n.m.* **1** Break-in, burglary. **2** *Boîte à ouvrage*: 'Fanny', 'pussy', pudenda.

ouvre-boîte *n.m.* (Prison slang): Key.

ouvrier *n.m.* (Underworld slang): Burglar, house-breaker.

ouvrir *v.trans.* **1** *L'ouvrir*: To 'blab', to 'blabber', to confess. **2** *L'ouvrir sur quelqu'un*: To 'knock' someone, to talk disparagingly about someone.

ovale *n.m.* 'Botty', woman's behind. *Avoir un bel ovale*: To have a shapely sit-me-down.

oxygène *n.m. Ne pas manquer d'oxygène*: To be a cheeky so-and-so (also: *ne pas manquer d'air*).

P

pacha *n.m.* **1** (Navy slang): 'Skip', 'skipper', captain. **2** *Mener une vie de pacha*: To lead the kind of life even 'Riley' might envy, to live in the lap of luxury.

pacson *n.m.* **1** Package, parcel. **2** 'Wad', pile of banknotes. *Son rêve, c'était de toucher le pacson aux courtines*: He always hoped he'd make a packet at the races (also: *pacsif*).

paddock *n.m.* (also: *padoc*): Bed. *Aller au paddock*: To 'hit the hay', to go to bed.

padoquer *v.trans.reflex.* To 'hit the sack', to 'kip down', to go to bed.

paf *n.m.* **1** 'Prick', 'cock', penis. **2** *Etre beau comme un paf (joc. & iron.)*: To 'cut a dash', to look very handsome. (For reasons unknown to the authors, this expression is directly linked to the first meaning, an alternative being: *être beau comme une bite en fleur*.) **3** 'Hitch', unexpected snag. *Tomber sur un paf*: To 'come a cropper', to suffer a setback (also: *tomber sur un os, sur un bec*).

paf *adj.inv.* **1** 'Pissed', 'sozzled', drunk. **2** 'Bonkers', 'potty', mad. *T'es complètement paf, non?!* Are you crazy or something?!

paffer *v.pronom.* To 'get plastered', to get drunk.

pagaille *n.f.* **1** 'Shambles', 'muddle', mess. *T'aurais dû voir cette pagaille!* You should have seen the confusion! **2** *En pagaille*: 'Oodles', lots of. *Il y avait des vélos en pagaille*: There were masses of bikes about.

page *n.m. Le page*: 'The sack', 'the straw', bed. *Se filer au page*: To slip in between the sheets (also: *pageot*).

page *n.f.* **1** *Etre à la page*: To be bang-up-to-date where news or fashion are concerned. *C'est un mec à la page, lui!* No messing, he's in the know! **2** *Tourner la page*: To turn to sodomous intercourse (to 'turn over a new leaf' where sexual matters are concerned).

pager *v.trans.reflex.* To 'hit the sack', to 'kip down', to go to bed (also: *se pageoter*).

pagnot *n.m. Le pagnot*: 'The sack', 'the straw', bed.

pagnoter *v.trans.reflex.* To 'turn in', to 'kip down', to go to bed.

paillasse *n.f.* **1** Low-class 'prozzy', prostitute long past her prime. **2** *Crever la paillasse à quelqu'un*: To knife someone in the guts, to stab someone in the belly.

paillasson *n.m. (pej.)*: **1** 'Easy-lay', 'promiscuous bird', easily wooed woman. **2** Low-class 'prozzy', prostitute long past her prime. **3** 'Doormat', character who submits to all indignities where pride and personality are concerned. *Chez lui, c'est un vrai paillasson*: She wears the pants at home, he lets her walk all over him. **4** 'Snowshoe', clapped-out tennis racket. **5** 'Woolly', woman's pubic hair. *Brouter le paillasson*: To perform cunnilingus.

paille *n.f.* **1** *Tirer à la courte paille*: To draw straws (in order to decide who will be lumbered with an unpleasant task). **2** *Etre sur la paille*: To be 'down on one's uppers', to be penniless. *Mettre quelqu'un sur la paille*: To drive someone out of business. **3** *Feu de paille*: 'Flash in the pan', promising start eventually tailing off into failure. **4** *Homme de paille*: 'Puppet', front-man who is more often than not made to 'carry the can' when the undertaking he manages, runs into difficulties. **5** *Le chapeau de paille*: Deportation to the penal colony of French Guiana. (According to Auguste le Breton it is a direct reference to the hat worn by the 'Papillon-like' convicts during their term of hard-labour.) **6** *Passer la paille de fer*: **a** To get down to some hard graft, to put in some hard work. **b** (of musicians): To serenade diners from table to table in a restaurant. **7** *Allumer la paille (pol.)*: To 'swoop', to deploy men in force. **8** *Une paille (iron.)*: A mere trifle. *Il s'est payé une tire pour vingt briques, une paille!* That twenty-grand car to him is just a drop in the ocean! **9** *Il y en a pour une paille!* We're in for quite a long wait! (This expression can also be found as *il y en a pour une paye* implying that the wait can last until next payday.) **10** *Faire des* *pailles*: To be unfaithful to one's spouse (also: *faire des paillons* or *faire des traits*).

paillons *n.m.pl.* *Faire des paillons*: To be unfaithful to one's spouse.

pain *n.m.* 1 'Sock', 'clout', blow. *Prendre un pain sur le coin de la gueule*: To get a 'knuckle-sandwich', to get punched in the face. 2 *Un pain* (Music): A wrong note. *Aux répétitions, les pains tombaient dru*: Band practice was enough to make you gnash your teeth! 3 *Le pain de fesse (joc.)*: Profits from prostitution. 4 *Pain au lait*: 'Prick', 'cock', penis. 5 *Pain dur*: 'Crummy enterprise', worthless venture. 6 *Etre bon comme du bon pain*: To be 'the salt of the earth', to have a heart of gold. 7 *Ça se vend comme des petits pains*: It sells like hot cakes – These goods don't stay long on the shelf. 8 *Ça mange pas de pain*: There's no risk entailed – This venture is self-supporting. (This expression got a new lease of life when it became the title of a San-Antonio novel.) 9 *Ne pas manger de ce pain-là*: To be 'dead against', to be firmly opposed to something. *Je ne mange pas de ce pain-là*! I'd rather starve than do that! 10 *Perdre le goût du pain (iron.)*: To 'croak', to 'snuff it', to die. *Je vais lui faire perdre le goût du pain!* He's going to get the thrashing of his life from me! (Contrary to logic, in direct speech the expression loses a lot of its virulence.)

paire *n.f.* 1 *Les deux font la paire!* (of people): They're two of a kind! – These two are well-matched. 2 *Avoir une paire de lunettes contre le soleil (joc. & iron.)*: To 'have a pair of shiners', to have got two black eyes. 3 *C'est une autre paire de manches!* It's another kettle of fish! – It's a totally different proposition! 4 *Se faire la paire*: To 'skedaddle', to 'scram', to go away in haste.

paître *v.intrans.* *Envoyer paître quelqu'un*: To 'send someone packing', to tell someone to go away in no uncertain manner (also: *envoyer péter quelqu'un*).

paix *n.f.* *Foutre la paix à quelqu'un*: To 'leave someone alone', to not disturb someone. *Fousnous la paix!* Stop bothering us!

pajer *v.trans.reflex.* To 'hit the hay', to go to bed.

pajot *n.m.* *Le pajot*: 'The sack', 'the straw', bed.

pajoter *v.trans.* *Pajoter quelqu'un*: To 'put someone up', to give someone a bed for the night.

pajoter *v.trans.reflex.* To 'hit the hay', to go to bed.

palace *adj.* 'Splendiferous', 'stunning', superb. *Il nous a payé un gueuleton palace*: He treated us to a slap-up meal.

palanquée *n.f.* *Une palanquée de*: 'Oodles', 'masses of', a vast quantity. *Il y avait une palanquée de tordus qui l'attendaient à la sortie*:

There were all these burks waiting for her outside!

palass *n.m.* (also: *palasse*): 'Gas', 'waffle', meaningless patter. *Faire du palass*: To 'give a load of eyewash', to talk a lot of baloney.

palasser *v.intrans.* To have 'verbal diarrhoea', to 'waffle', to talk on and on.

palasseur *n.m.* 'Gas-bag', 'waffler', incessant talker.

pâle *n.m.* 'Stiff', dead person.

pâle *adj.* 'Off-colour', 'poorly', ill. *Etre pâle des genoux*: To 'feel knackered', to be 'all in', to feel very tired. *Se faire porter pâle*: To get a sick-note.

paletot *n.m.* 1 *Paletot sans manches* (also: *paletot de sapin*): 'Wooden overcoat', coffin. 2 *Avoir quelqu'un sur le paletot*: To be 'saddled with', to be 'lumbered with' someone. *Je me suis retrouvé avec la plus moche sur le paletot!* As usual, I got landed with the 'I-don't-fancy-yours' biddy! 3 *Prendre tout sur le paletot*: To 'carry the can' (voluntarily), to assume full responsibility. *Je prends tout sur le paletot!* I'll take the blame! 4 *Tomber sur le paletot*: To 'plonk oneself', to arrive unheralded and uninvited. *Ma belle-doche nous est tombée sur le paletot pour une quinzaine*: The mother-in-law swooped on us for a brief fortnight's stay! (*Tomber sur le paletot à quelqu'un* can sometimes have the meaning of *sauter sur le paletot à quelqu'un*.) 5 *Sauter sur le paletot à quelqu'un*: **a** To 'pitch into', to 'wade into', to assault someone. **b** To shower someone with abuse and violent criticism.

palette *n.f.* 'Mitt', 'paw', hand. *Range tes palettes!* Keep your hands to yourself! (Stop pawing me!)

pâlichon *adj.* 'Pale round the gills', slightly pale.

palissandre *n.m.* *Avoir la bouche en palissandre*: To have 'a mouth and tongue like the bottom of a parrot's cage', to be suffering from the after-effects of excessive drinking.

pallaque *n.f.* Low-class 'prozzy', prostitute long past her prime.

pallass *n.m.* (also: *pallasse*): 'Gas', 'waffle', meaningless patter.

pallasser *v.intrans.* To have 'verbal diarrhoea', to 'waffle', to talk on and on.

pallasseur *n.m.* 'Gas-bag', 'waffler', incessant talker.

palmé *adj.* *Les avoir palmées*: To be an idle so-and-so, to be as lazy as they come (also: *avoir un poil dans la main*).

palombe *n.f.* 'Bird', girl, woman.

palper *v.trans.* To 'draw', to receive money. *Qu'est-ce qu'il palpe dans son nouveau boulot!* He certainly makes a packet in that new job of his!

palper *v.trans.reflex.* *Tu peux toujours te palper!* *(iron.)*: You can 'whistle for it!' – If you expect that, you've got another think coming!

palpitant *n.m.* 'Ticker', heart. *Son palpitant bat la breloque:* He's got a dicky ticker.

palpouser *v.trans.* **1** To 'paw', to touch salaciously. **2** To 'draw', to receive money.

paluche *n.f.* 'Mitt', 'paw', hand. *Un petit coup de paluche nous aiderait bien!* We'd appreciate it if you could lend a hand! *Gare tes paluches!* Keep your hands to yourself! (Stop pawing me!)

palucher *v.trans.* To 'paw', to touch salaciously (also: *envoyer les paluches*).

palucher *v.trans.reflex.* **1** To 'beat the dummy', to 'wank', to masturbate **2** *Se palucher de:* To be 'cock-a-hoop', to be 'over the moon', to be proud of oneself about something. *Il se paluchait d'être arrivé le premier:* He was certainly crowing over being the first one to arrive. **3** *Se palucher sur:* To have illusions about. *On se paluchait guère sur ses talents!* We had our doubts as to his ability!

pana *n.m.* **1** (Junk dealers' slang): 'Stayer', 'white elephant', unsaleable item (also: *rossignol*). **2** *(th.):* Non-acting part. *Faire un pana* (Films): To be an extra.

panache *n.m.* **1** *Avoir son panache:* To have had 'one over the eight', to be 'boozed up', to be drunk. **2** *Faire panache:* To go 'arse-over-tit' off a bike.

panaché *n.m.* Shandy, lager-and-lemonade drink. *Un demi panaché:* A half of shandy.

panaché *adj. (pej.):* 'Cooned', of mixed ethnic parentage.

panade *n.f.* Destitution consequent on a run of bad luck. *Quelle panade!* What a life! *Etre dans la panade:* To be down and really out on one's luck.

panais *n.m.* **1** 'Prick', 'cock', penis. *Dérouiller son panais:* To 'wank', to masturbate. **2** *(pej.):* 'Cunt', 'burk', blithering idiot.

Paname *Proper name.* (also: *Panam*): Paris. (This is the affectionate nickname given to the capital by poets and songwriters.)

panard *n.m.* **1** 'Hoof', foot. *Traîner ses panards:* To 'mooch about', to walk aimlessly. **2** *Prendre son panard:* To 'come', to have an orgasm (also: *prendre son fade* or *son pied*).

pandore *n.m.* 'Cop', 'copper', policeman. *Gaffe, v'là les pandores!* Watch out, here come the fuzz!

paneton *n.m. (corr. panier):* Basket.

panier *n.m.* **1** (Auctioneers' and junk-dealers' slang): 'Bundle', job-lot. **2** 'Botty', 'bum', woman's behind. *Elle a un gentil petit panier!* She's got a smashing little sit-me-down! *Mettre la main au panier:* To put one's hand up a skirt. (The expression *panier à crottes*, although totally devoid of charm, refers generally to a woman's behind.) *Secouer* (also: *faire sauter*) *le*

panier à crottes: To have a dance. **3** *Panier percé:* 'Hole-in-the-pocket' character, spendthrift person. **4** *Faire sauter l'anse du panier (iron.):* To 'fiddle accounts', to divert funds. (Originally, as the expression suggests, the fiddle was one involving pennies rather than pounds and operated by light-fingered maids.) **5** *Faire le panier à deux anses:* To go for a 'loving-cup' walk, to have a woman on each arm. **6** *Le dessus du panier* (of person or object): The 'cream of the cream', the 'pick of the bunch', the very best. **7** *Panier de crabes:* 'Hornets' nest', situation loaded with aggro and partisan feelings where it would be dangerous to take a hand. **8** *Panier à salade:* 'Black-Maria', police van used to ferry prisoners and suspects. **9** *Mettre dans le même panier:* To 'tar with the same brush', to consider people or items to be of equally low standing or value. **10** *Con comme un panier:* Bloody stupid. (The Yorkshire/Lancashire 'daft as a brush' is no equivalent as it is jocular and non-pejorative.) **11** *Coucouche panier!* **a** *(joc.):* Off to bed! **b** *(joc. & iron.):* Down, Rover! (This expression is often used by women to over-enthusiastic suitors.)

paniquard *n.m.* 'Jitterbug', panic-monger.

paniqué *adj.* **1** 'Panicked', frenzied with fear. **2** 'Bonkers', 'potty', mad. *T'es paniqué ou quoi?!* Are you crazy in the head?! – What's got into you?!

pannade *n.f.* Destitution consequent on a run of bad luck. *Etre dans la pannade:* To be down and really out on one's luck.

panne *n.f.* **1** Breakdown (general meaning). *Tomber en panne* (of car): To 'conk out', to have a breakdown. *On est resté en panne plus de cinq heures:* It took more than five hours to get the car on the road again. *Avoir une panne d'essence:* To run out of petrol. *Panne d'électricité:* Blackout, power-cut. **2** *Laisser quelqu'un en panne:* To 'leave someone in the lurch', to let someone down. **3** 'Blackout', lapse of memory. **4** *(th.):* 'Bit part', walk-on walk-off part (one that no true actor would really fancy). **5** (of picture): 'Daub', monstrosity (the 'painting-by-numbers' variety). **6** Financial breakdown. *Etre dans une panne noire:* To be in dire poverty. **7** (Junk dealers' slang): 'Stayer', 'white-elephant', unsaleable item.

panné *adj.* 'Stoney-broke', penniless.

panneau *n.m. Tomber dans le panneau:* To fall right into a trap (one that has been carefully laid).

pannetée *n.f. Une pannetée de:* 'Oodles of', a vast quantity.

pano *n.m. (abbr. regard panoramique) Filer un coup de pano:* To give a sweeping glance to unfamiliar surroundings.

panoplie *n.f. (joc.)*: 'Full set of tools', genitals (also: *service trois pièces*).

panouillard *n.m. (th.)*: **1** Bit-part actor. **2** 'Extra', figure-in-the-crowd person (in films).

panouille *n.f.* **1** 'Stick-in-the-mud', individual very much stuck in his ways. **2** 'Burk', 'nincompoop', fool. **3** *(th.)*: Bit-part acting, life of small roles.

pan-pan *n.m.* (also: *panpan*): **1** 'Biff', bang, wallop. *Cucul pan-pan*: 'Smack-botty'. (The word belongs to the *langage bêtifiant* inflicted on children.) **2** *Faire zizi pan-pan (joc.)*: To have 'whang-bam-thank-you-ma'am' sex, to have a quick one-night stand.

panse *n.f.* 'Corporation', paunch, pot-belly. *Se faire péter la panse*: To 'have a good blow-out', to have a hearty meal.

pante *n.m. (pej.)*: 'Mug', 'sucker', dupe. *On s'est trouvé un vrai pante!* We found ourselves the ideal Charlie!

panthère *n.f.* **1** *Ma panthère*: The 'old battle-axe', my wife. (As the image might suggest, the wife in this instance is all tooth-and-claw, eager to keep her man; the expression is non-pejorative.) **2** *Lait de panthère*: Pernod, pastis (because of its bite and its milky colour when mixed with water).

pantouflard *n.m.* 'Stay-at-home character' (person who relishes the uncommitted fireside life one leads in slippers).

pantoufle *n.f.* **1** (of person): 'Drip', 'wash-out', weak-willed character. **2** *Raisonner comme une pantoufle*: To 'talk through one's hat', to argue nonsensically. **3** *Jouer comme une pantoufle*: To 'be terrible at', to play badly (a sport or game). *Il joue au tennis comme une pantoufle!* He wouldn't know one end of a racket from the other! (also: *jouer comme un pied*).

pantoufler *v.intrans.* **1** To lead a 'stay-at-home' existence, shunning commitments and avoiding the abrasive side of life. **2** To take on a cushy no-responsibility job.

Pantruchard *n.m.* Parisian, native of Paris.

pantruchard *adj.* Parisian, from Paris.

Pantruche *Proper name.* Friendly nickname given to Paris by its true natives. (*Paname* in a way carries more nostalgia by implication than *Pantruche*.)

panuche *n.f.* Destitution consequent on a run of bad luck. *Ils sont dans une de ces panuches!* They've really hit rock-bottom!

papa *n.m.* **1** (Child language): 'Dad', 'Daddy', father. **2** Expressions such as *Salut papa!* directed at a man older than oneself, carry a certain ironic jocularity and could be compared to the English 'Morning, squire!'. **3** *Un bon gros papa (joc. & iron.)*: A good old fatso

(literally the counterpart to the 'fat Mamma'). **4** *de papa (adj.exp.)*: Old-time, of bygone times. *Il en est encore aux chemins de fer de papa!* To him, travel is all steam engines and wooden carriages! **5** *Papa gâteux (joc. & iron.)*: 'Sugar daddy', near-geriatric beau, aged suitor who lavishes gifts. (The jocularity stems from the suffix-deviation from *papa gâteau*.) **6** *à la papa (adv.exp.)*: In a simple and leisurely way. *On a fait une petite virée en bagnole à la papa*: We went for a nice quiet drive. *Faire l'amour à la papa*: To have intercourse 'in the missionary position'. **7** *Gros papas*: 'Big ones', banknotes of large denomination. *Quand il joue, il balance les gros papas!* When he goes gambling, notes are just confetti to him!

papaout *n.m.* 'Faggot', 'queer', homosexual (the kind who submits to sodomy; see *empapaouter*).

papeau *n.m. (corr. chapeau)*: 'Lid', 'decker', hat.

papelard *n.m.* **1** Paper (any kind: writing-paper, wrapping-paper, etc.). **2** Newspaper. *Il aime bien voir son nom dans le papelard*: He likes to see his name in print. **3** *(pl.)*: I.D. papers, identity documents. *Montre tes papelards!* Let's see your papers! (also: *aboule tes fafs!*). **4** Reputation. *Il a un mauvais papelard dans ce coin-ci!* His name is mud in these parts!

paperasse *n.f.* 'Red-tape', useless paperwork. *J'en ai marre de toutes ces paperasses!* These forms will be the death of me!

paperasserie *n.f.* 'Red-tapery' (that mountain of paperwork that stands in the way of enterprise).

paperassier *n.m.* Civil servant-like figure who lives on the perpetuation of paperwork.

paperassier *adj.* Over-fond of paperwork.

papier *n.m.* **1** 'Copy', article written by journalist. *Pondre* (also: *faire*) *un papier*: To write an article. **2** 10 francs. (Sometimes the note, but more often than not a multiple of that amount as redefined in the 1958 currency.) *Ça lui a coûté 500 papiers*: It cost him 5000 francs.) **3** (Racing slang): 'Form-sheet' (where runners and riders are listed and the horses' past performance is given to the punter). *Faire son papier*: To make out one's bet. **4** *(pl.)*: Playing cards. *Taper les papiers*: To have a game of cards. **5** *(pl.)*: 'Papers', I.D. documents. *Avoir des papiers en règle*: To have legit papers. **6** *Papier à douleur (iron.)*: 'Stinger', unexpectedly heavy bill which the recipient will be reluctant to pay. **7** *Connaître le papier*: To 'know the score', to be well-informed about something. *Pas de problème! Lui, il connaît le papier!* Don't give it another thought, he knows the ropes! **8** *Avoir un bon papier*: To have a 'good name', an unblemished reputation. **9** *Etre dans les petits papiers de quelqu'un*: To be 'in someone's good books', to be appreciated by someone. **10** *Rayer quelqu'un de ses papiers*: To give someone the 'big elbow', 'the push', to get rid of someone. *Rayez ça de vos papiers!* I'd give up any thought of that if I were you! **11** *Faire voler du papier timbré*: To issue writs left, right and centre. (In France, most legal documents bear an adhesive stamp representing the State's levy.) **12** *C'est réglé comme du papier à musique*: **a** It's as regular as clockwork. **b** It's as sure as fate. (The predictable and precise nature of sheet music is reflected in this expression.) **13** *Se faire passer au papier de verre (joc.)*: To have a skinhead haircut, to have one's skull shaved. **14** *Avoir une gueule* (also: *une figure*) *de papier mâché*: To look 'pale around the gills', to have a washed-out complexion.

papillon *n.m.* **1** *Papillons d'amour*: 'Crabs', crablice. **2** *Minute papillon!* Whoa there! – Not so fast! (See *minute*.)

papogne *n.f.* 'Mitt', 'paw', hand. *Gaffe! Il a une sacrée paire de papognes!* I'd stay clear of his dukes if I were you! (This word is a corruption of *pogne*.)

papouille *n.f.* **1** Action of pawing and fondling. **2** Naïve and inexperienced kiss. (*Faire des papouilles* is usually understood to mean 'back-row snogging'.)

papouiller *v.trans.* **1** To cuddle, to fondle amorously. **2** To kiss hesitantly.

pâquerette *n.f.* **1** 'Fanny', 'pussy', vagina. (Auguste Le Breton claims to have lexicalized this meaning in expressions such as *aller cueillir la pâquerette derrière un talus*: To have sex.) **2** *Tiges de pâquerette*: 'Pins', 'gambs', skinny legs. **3** *Cueillir les pâquerettes* (Racing-cyclists' slang): To ease off during a long and gruelling stage. (Obviously, this decision to take things easy is a concerted one, often taken by the tired competitors where over-enthusiastic efforts seem pointless.) **4** *Aller dans les pâquerettes* (of motor car): To go 'into the scenery', to come off the road.

paqueson *n.m.* **1** Package, parcel. **2** 'Wad', pile of banknotes. *Toucher le paqueson*: To 'land the big one', to strike it rich.

paquet *n.m.* **1** *Faire ses paquets*: To pack up and leave. *On lui a dit de faire ses paquets, comme ça sans le prévenir*: Out of the blue, he heard he'd got the sack. **2** *Avoir son paquet*: To be 'blotto', to be 'pissed', to be drunk. **3** *Recevoir son paquet*: **a** To get 'bashed-up', 'pitched into', to get beaten up. **b** To 'get a rollicking', to be severely told off. (The expression *lâcher son*

paquet à quelqu'un, like the above, has two meanings: **a** To 'lam into someone', to let fists fly. **b** To 'give someone a piece of one's mind', to tell someone in no uncertain manner what one thinks of him/her.) **4** *Lâcher le paquet*: To 'spill the beans', to let out a secret inadvertently. **5** *Mettre le paquet*: To make an all-out effort in order to achieve something. (This expression originally belonged to the language of the racing cyclist, but with time and a growing interest in this sport, it has become more widespread in its use.) *Si tu veux réussir dans la vie, faut mettre le paquet!* Sitting on your backside won't get you anywhere in life! **6** *Risquer le paquet*: **a** To 'chance it', to take quite a risk. (In racing and gambling circles, the meaning is very literal in that the punter is staking a 'bundle'.) **b** To 'go the whole hog', to go 'all the way', to make a no-holds-barred effort to achieve something. **7** *Etre un paquet de nerfs*: To be 'a bundle of nerves', to be extremely tense and nervous. **8** *Faire dégringoler* (also: *descendre*) *le paquet*: To induce an abortion, to act in a totally unmedical way to terminate a pregnancy. **9** *Etre fichu comme un paquet de linge sale* (usually of woman): To look a proper sight (literally to be dressed like a bundle of old clothes. *Un paquet* is often encountered as meaning a frump, an uninspiring and badly-dressed female). **10** *Le paquet* (Rugby): The pack.

para *n.f.pl.* Parallel bars (in a gymnasium).

parachuté *n.m.* Person who has been brought in from far afield to take up a position that might otherwise have gone to a 'local lad'. (The word is often encountered in a political context where a strong candidate has been brought in from Central Office to win a difficult seat.)

parachuter *v.trans.* To land an outsider in a plum job. (The expression is very often used in politics when favoured politicians are given easy seats to contest in a General Election.)

parade *n.f.* *Faire quelque chose pour la parade*: To do something for show.

paradis *n.m.* **1** *Le paradis (th.)*: 'The gods', the upper gallery. **2** *Tu ne l'emporteras pas en paradis!* You won't get away with it!

paraître *v.intrans.* *A ce qu'il paraît!* So it would seem! *A ce qu'il paraît, on dîne à huit heures*: I'm told we're eating at eight.

parallèle *n.m.* *Le parallèle*: The black market (literally the kind of parallel trading which inevitably exists where there are two levels of exchange – the official and the unofficial).

parapluie *n.m.* **1** 'Cover', fictitious and 'legit' occupation enabling a criminal to justify his earnings. **2** Alibi. **3** *Porter le parapluie*: To 'carry the can', to shoulder the responsibility. **4** *La Maison Parapluie*: The 'cop-shop', the police. **5** *Avoir l'air d'avoir avalé un parapluie*: To look as stiff as a poker, to be stiff and starchy. **6** *Fermer son parapluie*: To 'pop one's clogs', to 'snuff it', to die.

paravent *n.m.* **1** 'Front', 'legit' occupation enabling someone to pursue activities he is keen to keep out of the limelight. **2** Person whose brief it is to polarize attention and thus quash possible rumours concerning another.

parc *n.m. Le parc des refroidis (joc. & iron.)*: The 'bone-yard', the cemetery (also: *le boulevard des allongés*).

parcours *n.m.* Venture, undertaking. (The word carries no positive connotation, perhaps because it is generally associated with the *parcours du combattant*: the obstacle course that recruits have to negotiate with full pack during their army training.)

pardessus *n.m. Pardessus sans manches*: 'Wooden overcoat', coffin.

pardeusse *n.m. (corr. pardessus)*: **1** Coat, overcoat. **2** *Se faire faire un pardeusse en sapin*: To 'croak', to 'snuff it', to die.

pardon *interj.* Wow! – Crumbs! (This interjection, described by Caradec as *exclamation superlative*, can probably best be translated by the low whistle denoting astonishment on the part of a bystander. *Pardon! Ça c'est de la voiture!* Now that's what I call a motor car!)

paré *adj.* 'Cushy', easy. *Un boulot paré*: A doddle of a job.

pare-brise *n.m.inv.* 'Specs', 'glasses', spectacles.

pare-chocs *n.m.pl.* 'Knockers', 'bristols', breasts.

pareil *n.m. C'est du pareil au même!* It's six of one, half a dozen of the other! – It's as broad as it's long! – It's the same thing!

pareil *adv.* Colloquial alternative to *comme*. *Il a fait pareil que moi!* He did the same what I did! *C'est pareil à ce que j'ai dit!* It's like what I said!

pareille *n.f. Je lui ai rendu la pareille!* I gave him as good as I got! – I got my own back on him!

pare-lance *n.m.* 'Brolly', umbrella. (The primary colloquial meaning of *lance* is 'rain'.)

parer *v.intrans. Parer le coup à* (also: *pour*) *quelqu'un*: To shield, to protect someone.

parer *v.intrans. Parer à la manœuvre (joc. & iron.)*: To handle a problem, situation efficiently. (Originally a true nautical expression, it has found its way into colloquial language.) *V'là la belle-mère! Il va falloir parer à la manœuvre!* Here comes the old battle-axe! Stand by to repel boarders!

parfait *adj. Parfait!* Capital! – Good show! – Splendid!

parfaitement *adv. Parfaitement!* Quite so! – Of course! – Exactly!

parfum *n.m. Etre au parfum*: To be 'in the know', to know all about an issue. *Mettre quelqu'un au parfum*: To 'fill someone in' (on something), to 'give someone the low-down on', to inform someone.

parfumer *v.trans.* To 'fill someone in' (on something), to 'give someone the low-down on', to inform someone. *On avait été parfumés qu'il viendrait*: We'd been tipped off he was coming.

parigot *n.m. & adj.* Parisian, from Paris. *C'est une gentille parigotte*: She's a sweet miss from Paris.

Parisien *Proper name. Le Parisien*: According to whether the context is pre- or post-World War II, this title refers to either *Le Petit Parisien* or *Le Parisien Libéré*, both popular and mass-circulation newspapers.

parisien *adj. C'est bien chaud, bien parisien! (iron.)*: That's typically French! (This rather condescending acknowledgement originally appeared in the hackneyed jargon of radio commentators.)

parlant *n.m. Le parlant*: The 'talkies', films with soundtrack.

parler *v.intrans.* **1** To 'squeal', to 'spill the beans', to confess and give the game away. *Ils l'ont fait parler sans trop de difficulté*: He sang like a bird, all he needed was a bit of gentle persuasion! **2** *Tu parles de . . . ! (iron.)*: Talk about . . . ! *Tu parles d'une pagaille!* You should have seen that mess! *Vous parlez d'une histoire!* What a scandal! **3** *Tu parles Charles!* According to context, this jocular and ironic catch phrase can either mean 'You're telling me!' – 'I should jolly well think so!' or 'You must be joking!' – 'What do you take me for?!'

parlote *n.f.* 'Waffle', empty chatter. *Avoir la parlote*: To 'have been vaccinated with a gramophone needle', to be a chatterbox. *Ça n'est que de la parlote!* It's all talk!

paroisse *n.f. Changer de paroisse (joc.)*: **a** To 'change digs', to 'move out', to go to new accommodation. **b** To 'change watering-hole', to 'haunt a different pub', to become a regular in a different bar.

paroissien *n.m. Un drôle de paroissien (pej.)*: A 'queer cove', a strange character.

parole *n.f.* **1** *Donner sa parole*: To give one's word, to promise. *Parole d'homme!* Word of honour! (The word *homme* emphasizes the 'macho' reliability of the oath.) **2** *C'est parole d'évangile!* You can take my word for it! (Literally: It's the gospel truth!) **3** *Parole!* (at card-game): Pass! – No bid! **4** *Porter la parole (iron.)*: To effect punitive measures on a rebellious party or group of individuals. (This underworld expression is frequently found in conjunction with racketeering pressure groups where the odd-man-out needs to be taught a lesson.)

parpagne *n.f. La parpagne (joc.corr. la campagne)*: 'The sticks', the countryside.

parpaing *n.m.* 'Biff', blow with the fist. *Prendre un parpaing sur le coin de la gueule*: To get a knuckle-sandwich.

parrain *n.m.* Witness (in a court of law).

partant *adj. Etre partant*: To 'be game', to be ready to do something. *On est partants!* We're game! – You can count on us! *Je suis vraiment pas partant!* Count me out!

parterre *n.m.* **1** *Prendre un billet de parterre*: **a** To fall flat on one's face, to fall down. **b** *(fig.)*: To 'come a cropper', to suffer a setback. **2** *Jouer pour le parterre (fig.)*: To 'swank', to show off.

parti *past part. C'est parti, mon kiki! (joc.interj.)*: That's it! – Off we jolly well go! (This humorous rhyming catch phrase usually punctuates the successful start of a venture or action.)

parti *adj.* 'Sozzled', 'sloshed', drunk. *Un peu qu'il était parti à la fin de la noce!* He was blind-drunk by the end of the wedding-do!

particule *n.f. Avoir la particule*: To have 'a handle to one's name', to belong to the aristocracy. (The *particule* referred to here is usually *'de'*, always readily associated with members of the nobility. The nearest social equivalent for the English speaker is the 'double-barrelled name'.)

particulier *n.m. (pej.)*: 'Geezer', 'bloke', person. *Où avez-vous pêché ce particulier?!* Where did you dredge up this nurk?! *Un drôle de particulier*: A queer cove.

particulière *n.f. C'est sa particulière*: It's his bird – She's his steady girlfriend.

partie *n.f.* **1** Party, one where the enjoyment is often of a salacious nature as in: *partie fine, partie de jambes en l'air*: Orgy. (In the 50s and early 60s, the word did not have such a loaded implication as it was an abbreviation of *surprise-partie*, the in-word for teenagers of that period.) **2** *Les parties (abbr. les parties nobles)*: 'Marriage prospects', the genitals. *Prendre un coup de latte dans les parties*: To get kicked in the groin.

partir *v.intrans. (iron.)*: To 'shuffle off', to 'snuff it', to die. (A certain morbid jocularity is attached to this verb in the paraphrase of the hackneyed *'partir, c'est mourir un peu'* which became *'mourir, c'est partir beaucoup!'*)

partition *n.f. Connaître la partition*: To remain undeterred where an enterprise is concerned (because, literally, one knows the score).

partouzard *n.m.* 'Swinger', randy so-and-so who enjoys attending *partouzes*.

partouze *n.f.* (also: *partouse*): Party ending in salacious fun-and-games.

partouzer *v.intrans.* (also: *partouser*): To participate in a *partouze*.

parts *n.f.pl. Prendre les parts de quelqu'un*: To take sides with someone, to support someone in a dispute.

pas *n.m.* **1** *Emboîter le pas à quelqu'un*: **a** *(lit.)*: To follow close behind someone. **b** *(fig.)*: To copy someone in a subservient manner. *Une fois lancée la bonne idée, ils se sont tous donné le mot pour lui emboîter le pas*: Once it was clear the idea was viable, manufacturers trod a trail of copycat patents. **2** *Ça ne se trouve pas sous le pas d'un cheval! (iron.)*: 'It doesn't grow on trees, you know!' – It's pretty scarce! **3** *Mettre quelqu'un au pas (fig.)*: To make someone 'toe the line', to force someone to obey an order. *Et comment qu'il l'a mis au pas!* He certainly told him where he stood, no messing! **4** *Sauter le pas*: To 'take the plunge', to make a drastic decision. **5** *Mauvais pas*: 'Scrape', difficult situation. *Je l'ai tiré d'un mauvais pas!* I got him out of that mess he was in!

pas-de-porte *n.m. Demander un pas-de-porte*: To ask for key-money (to demand payment from an incoming tenant when leaving rented accommodation allegedly for improvements effected. In many cases, in fact, this transitional payment is due to the pepper-corn rent of the flat/dwelling).

pas-grand-chose *n.m.* 'Bad egg', 'ne'er-do-well', worthless person. (The French and the English are equally dated, and betray the speaker's age.)

pasque *conj. (corr. parce que)*: 'Cos', because.

passade *n.f.* Fleeting romance, short-lived love-affair.

passage *n.m.* **1** *Attendre quelqu'un au passage*: To have a grudge against someone and literally lie in wait for an opportunity to get one's own back (also: *garder à quelqu'un un chien de sa chienne*). **2** *Passage clouté*: Zebra crossing, pedestrian crossing (because originally in France the path was delineated by large chrome-plated studs). **3** *Passage à tabac*: 'Drubbing', beating-up of an individual by several.

passe *n.f.* **1** *Passe anglaise* (Gambling): 'Craps', game of dice. **2** *Faire une passe* (of prostitute): To have a 'quickie', to take a client for a short sex-session. **3** *Maison de passe*: 'Cat-house', 'knocking-shop', hotel-cum-brothel. (The expression *faire la passe*, when referring to a hotel proprietor, means that he lets out some rooms for use by prostitutes.)

passé *n.m. Avoir un passé*: To have 'form', to have some kind of criminal record.

passe-lacet *n.m. Etre raide comme un passe-lacet*: To be 'skint', 'broke', to be penniless.

passe-passe *n.m.inv. Tour de passe-passe*: 'Jiggery-pokery', trickery. (It is difficult to ascertain whether the expression *tour de passe-passe* comes from the language of the stage magician or the professional card-sharp. Whatever the origin, it effectively conveys the legerdemain tactics employed in both cases.)

passer *v.trans.* **1** *Passer quelque chose à quelqu'un*: **a** To 'rough up', to beat someone up (also: *passer quelqu'un à tabac*). **b** To give someone a 'roasting', a 'wigging', to give someone a severe telling-off. *Qu'est-ce qu'elle lui passe quand il rentre à deux heures du mat'!* When he gets home at 2 a.m. she's waiting for him rolling-pin at the ready! (also: *passer un savon à quelqu'un*). **2** *Passer quelque chose à l'as*: To 'spirit something away', to make something disappear for one's own benefit. (The in-transitive expression *passer à l'as*, directly related to the conjurer's legerdemain, illustrates the 'now-you-see-it, now-you-don't' aspect of the disappearing trick.) **3** *Le faire passer*: To engineer an abortion (usually through 'back-street' methods). **4** *Cela me passe! (corr. cela me dépasse!)*: That's got me stumped! – That beats me! *Comment qu'ils se débrouillent avec si peu de fric, cela me passe!* I just can't understand how they manage on so little money! **5** *Ça lui passera!* (of pet liking, obsession): He'll grow out of it! – He'll get over it!

passer *v.intrans.* **1** *Passer à travers (quelque chose)*: To miss out on something good. **2** *Passer au travers (de quelque chose)*: To escape something unpleasant. *Comme de bien entendu, il est passé au travers de tous ces emmerdements!* As luck would have it, the jammy bugger got away scot-free! **3** *Y passer*: To go through an un-pleasant experience. **a** (of woman): To be forced into sexual intercourse. **b** To 'croak', to 'snuff it', to die. *Tout le monde y passe, vous savez!* We all have to go sometime, you know! **4** *Sentir passer quelque chose*: To smart, to suffer where physical punishment is concerned. **5** *Passer sous une voiture*: To get run over. **6** *Passer sous le nez* (of opportunity): To slip by. *Ça lui est passé sous le nez!* He let a good thing go by! **7** *Il faut passer par là ou par la fenêtre! (iron.)*: It's a case of Hobson's choice! – Really you have no alternative!

passe-sirop *n.m. (joc.)*: Phone, telephone. (Georgette Marks in her *FRENCH-ENGLISH DICTIONARY OF SLANG AND COLLOQUIALISMS* defines it further with the picturesque 'spittle-strainer'. An alternative is *passoire d'ébonite*.)

passion *n.f. Homme à passions*: 'Randy so-and-so', highly-sexed male. *Femme à passions*: 'Hot-stuff', 'thunder-thighs', highly-sexed woman. (Unlike *femme à passions*, which has only one meaning, *homme à passions* can also denote one who is 'kinky' where sexual matters are concerned.)

passoire *n.f.* **1** Sieve-like memory. *Quelle passoire qu'il a!* He'd forget his own name, given half a chance! **2** 'Spend, spend, spend' character, spendthrift person. **3** Clumsy goal-keeper, one who seems to let the ball through every time.

pastaga *n.m.* **1** Pernod, pastis. **2** 'Fix', 'muddle', mess. *On s'est retrouvé dans un sacré pastaga!* We really landed ourselves in the soup there!

pastèque *n.f.* 'Bum', 'bottom', behind (because of the fruit's segment-like configuration).

pastille *n.f.* **1** 'Pip', 'slug', bullet from handgun (also: *praline*). **2** 'Biff', blow. *Prendre une pastille dans la gueule*: To get socked. **3** Anus, anal passage (in a context of sodomy).

pastiquer *v.trans.* To smuggle goods.

pastiquette *n.f.* **1** (Gambling): 'Craps', game of dice (also: *passe anglaise*). **2** (Prostitutes' slang): 'Quickie', brief sex-session with a client.

pastiqueur *n.m.* One who makes a living from smuggling.

pastis *n.m.* 'Fix', muddle, mess. *Quel pastis!* What a cock-up! *Tu m'as foutu dans un sacré pastis!* Another fine mess you've got me into!

pasto *n.m.* Dead-end street, dingy alley leading nowhere. (It is worth noting that the English use of cul-de-sac is far more up-market than the French; no self-respecting Frenchman lives in a *cul-de-sac*. If the street concerned leads no-where, it is *une impasse*.)

patachon *n.m. Mener une vie de patachon*: To lead the 'night-life of Riley', to whoop it up more than is customary and mostly in the evenings.

patapouf *n.m.* (also: *gros patapouf*): 'Fatso', 'greaseball', short and plump individual.

pataquès *n.m.* 'Liaison' blunder, what the French also jocularly refer to as *une liaison mal-t-à-propos*'. (Kastner and Marks in their *GLOSSARY OF COLLOQUIAL AND POPULAR FRENCH* give an amusing anecdotic explanation as to the origin of this word.)

patate *n.f.* **1** 'Tater', 'spud', potato. *Des patates en purée*: Mash. **2** 'Bean', 'bonce', head. *Prendre un gnon sur la patate*: To get coshed. *En avoir lourd* (also: *gros*) *sur la patate*: **a** To have a load on one's mind. **b** To be filled with resentment (to find something hard to stomach). **3** 'Schnozzle', burgeoning nose (also: *nez en patate*). **4** 'Hayseed', 'hick', country bumpkin. **5** 'Clot', 'chump', fool. *Va donc, eh, patate!* Go (and) get knotted! **6** 'Biff', blow from a fist. *Prendre une patate sur le coin de la gueule*: To get a knuckle-sandwich. **7** *Des patates!* Not bloody likely! – You must be joking! (also: *des clous!*).

patati *Et patati et patata!* This onomatopoeic expression evokes the empty tittle-tattle of endless conversations.

patatras *interj.* Originally the onomatopoeic transcription of a 'crash-bang', this word has drifted into spoken language in the guise of a 'and-what-do-you-think-happened?!' exclamation. *On pensait avoir la commande et patatras! c'était foutu!* We thought we had the order and wham bang! it was back to square one!

patatrot *n.m.* (also: *patatro*) *Faire un patatrot*: To 'scram', to 'skedaddle', to run away.

pataugas *n.m.pl.* (Pronounced *pataugasse*): 'Clod-hoppers', 'beetle-crushers', heavy rubber-soled shoes. (This is another case of a trade-name becoming generic; *Pataugas* manufacture shoes for farmers and hunting sportsmen.)

pâté *n.m. Boîte à pâté*: 'Shit-box', rectum and anal passage. (This obscene expression only occurs where sodomous intercourse is referred to in derogatory terms.)

pâtée *n.f.* 'Pasting', beating-up, thrashing. *Prendre une pâtée*: To get duffed up.

patelin *n.m. (Slightly joc.)*: 'One-horse town', village. *Où que c'est, ce patelin-là?!* Do they put places like that on the map?! *Ça c'est mon patelin*: This is my home-town. (There is nothing pejorative in this word, and the jocularity is highlighted sometimes by the size of the town. *Son patelin à lui, c'est Lyon!*)

paternel *n.m. Mon paternel*: 'My old man', my father (also: *pater*).

pâteux *adj.* 'Under-the-weather', 'weak-at-the-knees', a little unwell. *Se sentir pâteux*: To feel out of sorts.

patin *n.m.* **1** 'Clapper', 'licker', tongue. *Rouler un patin*: To give a French kiss. **2** Brakes. *Filer un coup de patin*: To slam on the brakes, to brake violently. **3** *(pl.)*: 'Hoofs', 'plates of meat', feet. *Traîner ses patins*: To 'mooch about', to 'loaf around', to walk about aimlessly. (A *traîne-patins* is a hobo, drifter-cum-vagabond.) **4** *Faire le patin*: To go shoplifting. **5** *Chercher des patins à quelqu'un*: To pick a quarrel with someone. **6** *Prendre les patins de quelqu'un* (in quarrel): To take sides with someone, to take up the cudgels on someone's behalf.

patiner *v.trans.* To 'paw', to stroke with salacious intentions.

patiner *v.pronom.* To 'skedaddle', to 'make tracks', to run away.

pâtissemar *n.m. (corr. pâtissier) Aller chez le pâtissemar*: To go to the cake-shop.

patoche *n.f.* 'Mitt', 'paw', hand.

patoche *adj.* Clumsy. *Qu'il est patoche!* What a butter-fingers!

patouillard *n.m.* 'Tub', slow steamer long past its prime.

patouille *n.f.* **1** Sludge, mud. **2** Light caress. *Faire des patouilles*: To fondle. **3** *La patouille*: 'The briny', the sea.

patraque *n.f.* 'Timex', timepiece, watch. *Quelle heure est-il à ta patraque?* What time do you make it?

patraque *adj.* **1** (of person): 'Out-of-sorts', 'poorly', unwell. *Se sentir patraque*: To feel under the weather. *Avoir un palpitant patraque*: To have a 'dicky ticker', to have cardiac problems. **2** (of machinery, equipment, etc.): 'Wonky', worn-out.

patriotard *n.m.* 'Flag-waver', chauvinist.

patriotard *adj.* Chauvinistic, over-patriotic.

patro *n.m (abbr. patronage)*: Church-run youth-club association.

patron *n.m. Le patron*: 'The guv'nor', the boss. With this general acceptation of 'the top man' in different professions/work-spheres, a *patron* can be: **a** (Hospital slang): A senior consultant. **b** (Naval slang): 'The skipper', a captain on board a ship. **c** *(pol.)*: A chief superintendent. The words *le patron/la patronne* have a less serious meaning in familiar speech with reference to a married couple, their English equivalents being 'my old man'/'the missus'. *Je vais demander à la patronne si on a le temps d'aller boire un coup*: I'll just check with my old woman if we've time to nip off to the pub.

patte *n.f.* **1** 'Pin', 'gamb', leg. *Aller à pattes*: To 'hoof it', to have to walk. *Aux pattes!* (Let's) scram! *Ne pas être solide sur ses pattes*: To be unsteady on one's pins. *Tirer la patte*: To limp. **2** *En avoir plein les pattes*: To be 'all-in', to feel worn-out. **3** *Ça ne casse pas quatre pattes à un canard!* *(joc. & iron.)*: It's no great shakes! – I don't rate it very highly! **4** *Lever la patte* (of man): **a** To have a 'slash', to urinate (literally to cock a leg). **b** To get a 'leg-over', to 'screw', to have coition. **5** *Marcher sur trois pattes* (of conventional motor car): To fire on only three cylinders. (An offspring of the above literal meaning, the figurative describes a venture or undertaking that is not running smoothly.) **6** *Traîner la patte*: To 'come the old soldier' (literally to exaggerate a limp in order to get compassion). **7** *Tirer dans les pattes de quelqu'un*: **a** To 'put a spoke in someone's wheel', to hamper someone's progress. **b** To 'stab someone in the back', to speak ill of someone. **8** *Etre fait aux pattes* (also: *se faire faire aux pattes*): To get 'nabbed', to be 'collared', to get arrested. **9** 'Mitt', 'paw', hand. *Arriver les pattes vides*: To come empty-handed. *Bas les pattes!* (Woman's retort): Stop pawing! – Keep your hands to yourself! **10** *Faire patte de velours (fig.)*: To 'draw in one's claws', to be extra gentle with someone. **11** *Faire (des) pattes d'araignée à quelqu'un*: To 'goose', to caress lightly with nails and fingertips. **12** *Faire des pattes de mouche*: To write in a spidery script. **13** *Graisser la patte à quelqu'un*: To 'grease someone's palm', to bribe someone. **14** *Faire quelque chose aux pattes*: To 'lift', to 'pinch' something. **15** *Avoir le coup de patte*: To 'have the knack', to be skilful at something. **16** *Pattes de lapin* (Hairstyle): Short sideboards. **17** Feet (without colloquial overtones). *Retomber sur ses pattes*: **a** To 'fall on one's feet', to come off better than one might have expected. **b** To 'get off scot-free', to escape ill-fate or retribution, sometimes through good fortune, but more often than not through connivance. **18** *Se fourrer dans les pattes de quelqu'un*: To disturb someone (literally to get in someone's way). **19** *Mettre une affaire sur pattes*: To start up a business, to get an enterprise under way. **20** *Avoir des pattes d'oie*: To have 'crow's feet', 'laugh-lines', to have wrinkles around the eyes.

patuche *n.f. (corr. patente)*: Market-trader's licence.

paturons *n.m.pl.* 'Hoofs', 'plates of meat', feet. *Jouer des paturons*: To 'make tracks', to 'beat it', to bolt off. (This word has a jocular connotation because of its equine origin, *paturon* being the horse's pastern.)

paume *n.f. La paume*: Deportation to the penal colony of French Guiana (also: *le chapeau de paille* – see *paille*).

paumé *n.m.* **1** 'Wash-out', down-trodden individual. **2** Down-and-outer, one who has hit rock-bottom.

paumé *adj.* **1** Dazed, bewildered. **2** 'Knackered', 'buggered', exhausted. **3** 'Skint', 'broke', penniless.

paumer *v.trans.* **1** To lose. *On avait paumé nos billets, mais ils nous ont laissés passer*: We couldn't find our tickets, but they let us through. *Paumer son temps*: To waste one's time. **2** (of disease): To 'catch', to be infected with. *Il a paumé la chtouille au régiment*: He got clap when he was in the army. **3** *Se faire paumer*: To get 'nabbed', 'collared', to be arrested.

paumer *v.pronom.* **1** *(lit.)*: To get lost, to lose one's way. **2** *(fig.)*: To 'bark up the wrong tree', to be completely off course.

paupière *n.f. S'en battre la paupière*: Not to give a damn, not to care two hoots (also: *s'en battre l'œil*).

paupol *n.m.* 'Prick', 'cock', penis. *Mener paupol au cirque*: To 'have it off', to have intercourse.

pauvre *adj.intensifier.* **1** *Pauvre con!* You bloody idiot! *Pauvre petit! (iron.)*: Who's an unlucky boy then!? **2** *La pauvre!* (Pronounced *povre*.) This Provence expression is usually uttered when the news of a husband's unfaithfulness is being discussed by other women. Whereas the converse brings knowing smiles to the *mauvaises langues*, the cuckolded woman is an object of pity. (See *cocu*.)

pauvretés *n.f.pl.* Inanities, stupid statements. *Sortir des pauvretés*: To spout a load of bilge.

pavé *n.m.* **1** *Etre sur le pavé*: **a** To be out of work, to be redundant. **b** To be near-destitute and homeless. *Jeter quelqu'un sur le pavé* (of home or employment): To turf someone out. **2** *Brûler le pavé* (of car): To 'scorch along', to drive at break-neck speed. **3** *Fusiller le pavé*: To blow one's nose 'manually' by closing one nostril with the index finger and literally firing snot at the ground. **4** *C'est clair comme un pavé dans la gueule d'un flic! (iron.)*: It's as plain as a pikestaff! – It's patently obvious. **5** *N'avoir plus de pavés dans la cour (joc.)*: To be 'gummy', to be toothless. **6** *Il en a eu pour cinq pavés*: It cost him five grand. (When referring to post-1958 currency, the sum involved for *un pavé* is 10,000 francs; the loose monetary translation of 'grand' is in fact linguistically quite correct.)

pavé *past part. C'en est pavé* (of goods, etc.): 'It's littered with them' – There's no shortage. *Des bagnoles d'occase ces temps-ci, c'en est pavé!* Second-hand cars these days are thick on the ground!

paveton *n.m. (corr. pavé)*: Cobblestone. (Racing cyclists, when referring to the Paris-Lille race, talk about the *pavetons* which gave it the nickname of *l'enfer du Nord*; the competition is routed over the toughest cobblestone roads yet to be resurfaced.)

pavillon *n.m. Baisser (le) pavillon*: **a** To surrender, to give in when the going gets too tough. **b** *(joc. & iron.)*: To get a 'half-mast' penis, to lose an erection.

pavillons *n.m.pl. (joc.)*: 'Flappers', 'lug-holes', ears. *Ouvre tes pavillons!* Will you listen?!

pavoiser *v.intrans.* **1** To be 'all-smiles', to show one's glee. **2** To 'splash out', to go on a spending spree. (The implication here is very much that purchases are being made on the strength of a financial success without there being an actual exchange of money.) **3** To 'sport a shiner', to have a very obvious black eye. **4** (Boxing slang): To 'have one's claret tapped', to bleed profusely from facial injuries. **5** To 'have the decorators in', to have a menstrual period.

pavomme *n.f. (corr. pomme)*: Apple. (This, and the next four words, are 'av-slang' colloquializations of a standard French word.)

pavot *n.m. (corr. pot)*: 'Arse', 'bum', behind. *Virer quelqu'un à coups de pompe dans le pavot*: To boot someone out.

pavoule *n.f. (corr. poule)*: 'Biddy', 'bird', woman.

pavour *n.m. (corr. pour)*: 'Leg-pull', practical joke.

pavute *n.f. (corr. pute)*: 'Prozzy', prostitute.

paxon *n.m. (also: pacson)*: **1** Package, parcel. **2** 'Wad', pile of banknotes. *Toucher le paxon*: To 'hit the jackpot', to get a big pay-out.

payant *adj.* Worthwhile, profitable. *Il s'est monté un petit truc tout ce qu'il y a de payant*: He rigged himself up a profitable little sideline.

paye *n.f. Ça fait une paye qu'on s'est pas vus!* 'Long time no see!' (Literally: I haven't seen you since last payday!) *Il y en a pour une paye d'ici qu'on le revoit!* It'll be ages before we see him again!

payer *v.intrans.* **1** *Avoir payé*: To have paid one's debt to society, to have done time and wiped the slate clean. *J'ai payé, c'est fini! Maintenant foutez-moi la paix!* I'm out now, been paroled, why can't you leave me alone?! **2** *Je suis payé pour! (le savoir)*: I should know! (It's my business to know!) **3** *C'est payant!* (also: *ça paie!*): It's a scream! – It's a laugh! – It's hilarious! (Strange as it may seem, the adjective *impayable* has the meaning of 'too funny for words', 'hilarious'. A famous comedian, when told by his optimistic yet near-bankrupt producer: *'Mon cher, vous êtes impayable!'*, retorted sadly, *'Hélas, oui, je le sais!'*)

payer *v.trans.reflex.* **1** *Se payer quelque chose*: **a** To treat oneself to something. *Il se paye une bagnole neuve tous les six mois*: He gets himself a new car twice a year. **b** To go through a gruelling experience, to have to put up with something very unpleasant. *On s'est payé une grippe carabinée!* We were all down with a dose of that awful flu! **2** *S'en payer*: To 'whoop it up', to have the time of one's life.

pays *n.m.* **1** Fellow-countryman, one who hails from the same county, town or village. *On est pays*: We come from the same parts. **2** *Faire voir du pays à quelqu'un*: To 'lead someone a merry dance', to take someone on a time-consuming and useless journey.

paysage *n.m.* **1** *Partir dans le paysage* (of vehicle): To 'crash into the scenery', to come off the road. **2** *Cela ferait bien dans le paysage!* That would be just the ticket! – It would certainly be the right thing!

paysan *n.m. (pej.) Quel paysan!* What a boor! – What a crude fellow! (Parisian motorists find the *'Paysan, va!'* insult a potent one when riling a clumsy motorist from the provinces.)

peau *n.f.* **1** *Une peau (pej.)*: A 'prozzy', a low-class prostitute. *Une vieille peau*: One long past her prime. **2** *Avoir quelqu'un dans la peau*: To be 'hooked on someone' (very much in the vein of the American song 'I've got you under my skin'). **3** *Porter à la peau de quelqu'un*: To turn someone on, to titillate, to arouse someone's sexual desires. *Elle nous porte tous à la peau au bureau!* At the office she's made lechers of us all! **4** *Se sentir bien dans sa peau*: To feel on top of the world and in the happiest frame of mind. *Se sentir mal dans sa peau*: To feel ill at ease. **5** *Traîner sa peau*: To 'mooch about', to laze around. **6** *Faire peau neuve*: To turn over a new leaf, to amend one's ways. **7** *Mettez-vous dans ma peau!* Put yourself in my shoes! **8** *Avoir la peau trop courte*: To be a 'lazybones', to be an idle so-and-so (also: *les avoir palmées*). **9** *Faire quelque chose pour la peau*: To get bugger-all for one's efforts, to work for no recompense at all. **10** *Y laisser sa peau*: To die, to fall victim to. (This expression can also have a figurative, less traumatic secondary meaning. *Encore une hausse et nous y laisserons tous notre peau!* Another price rise and we've had it!) **11** *Faire la peau à quelqu'un*: To 'do someone in', to kill someone (usually through stabbing). **12** *J'aurai sa peau!* I'll have his guts for garters! (The strong literal meaning 'I'll kill him!' is very seldom encountered.) **13** *Une peau de vache*: A 'bastard', a mean and hateful character. *Faire la peau de vache*: To behave like a heel. (*Peau de vache!* and other expressions starting with *peau de* are all associated with verbal insults: *Peau de fesses!* You pillock! New ones come and go with the fluctuations of language.) **14** *Peau de balle (et balai de crin!)*: Bugger-all! – Damn all! *On a touché peau de balle!* We didn't get a penny for our efforts! (The latch-on *et balai de crin* bit of the expression turns it into a jocular catch phrase; the French have a penchant for such nonsense rhyme-like phrases.) **15** *En peau de lapin* (of person): 'Two-bit', of no significance. *Un politicien en peau de lapin*: An 'all-talk-and-no-action' politician. **16** *En peau de saucisson* (of goods): 'Tatty' and worthless. *Une valoche en peau de saucisson*: A crappy little suitcase (literally, in this instance, made of the cheapest imitation leather). **17** *Une peau de banane (fig.)*: Booby-trap. *Il est tombé sur une de ces peaux de banane!* He fell right in it!

peau-rouge *n.m.* (Underworld slang): Fearless 'heavy'. (The *milieu* has this complimentary appellation for those who show total disregard for personal safety – the bravest among the *apaches*.)

pébroque *n.m.* 1 'Brolly', umbrella (also: *parejus*). 2 (*fig.*): Alibi (very often a shady one). 3 'Cover', fictitious and 'legit' occupation enabling a criminal to justify his earnings.

pécaïre *interj.* Oh dear! – Alas! (This expression from Provence, unlike others, has failed to attain national recognition.)

pêche *n.f.* 1 'Biff', 'clout', blow. *Prendre une pêche sur le coin de la gueule*: To get a 'knuckle-sandwich'. 2 *Avoir la pêche*: To 'feel on top of the world', to feel happy and confident (also: *avoir le moral*). 3 *Poser une pêche*: To 'crap', to 'shit', to defecate (also: *poser un étron*). 4 *Aller à la pêche*: To go looking for a job, searching for employment (in a rather hit-and-miss manner).

pêchecaille *n.m.* Angler, fisherman.

pêchecaille *n.f.* Angling, fishing.

pêcher *v.trans.* *Où as-tu été pêcher ça?* Where the hell did you dig that up? (This jocular question, usually referring to objects, becomes ironic and derogatory when referring to a person. A third meaning, relating to trains of thought, could loosely be translated by 'I wonder who gave you that idea?')

pécole *n.f.* 'Clap', gonorrhoea.

pécore *n.m.* 'Hayseed', 'yokel', country bumpkin. (This word is certainly not complimentary, but exudes a certain bonhomie lacking in the seldom-used feminine which is downright offensive.)

pécu *n.m.* (also: *pécul*): 1 'Bum-fodder', toilet paper. (*Pécu* is an abbreviated corruption of *papier-cul*; it is sometimes even more succinctly transcribed as *P.Q.*) 2 'Bumf', useless paperwork. 3 (*sch.*): 'Paper', essay.

pécufier *v.intrans.* 1 To 'waffle', to talk on and on in a self-conscious and boring manner. 2 To write a load of pompous tripe (the kind 'B-grade' speeches are made of).

pécunier *adj.* *Des problèmes pécuniers*: Financial problems. *Du point de vue pécunier, ça va!* I'm alright where money's concerned! (Unlexicalized in traditional dictionaries, *pécunier* is rife in spoken French where *pécuniaire* should be used; there is no feminine, as it would overlap phonetically with the correct adjective. Colloquial grammar rejects *des problèmes pécuniaires* because it does not 'sound right' gender-wise.)

pédago *n.m.* *Instituteur*, primary-school teacher in France.

pédago *n.f.* Pedagogy. *La pédago, c'est pas son fort!* I wouldn't call him a born teacher!

pédale *n.f.* 1 *Perdre les pédales*: To 'get in a tizz-wizz', to 'get flustered', to lose self-control when under pressure. 2 *Lâcher les pédales*: To 'throw in the sponge', to give up. (Both expressions come from the register of cycling.) 3 *Une pédale*: A 'pouf', a 'pansy', a homosexual. *Etre de la pédale*: To be 'one of them'. (The hip-swaying motions of the cyclist pedalling uphill and the feminine bum-wiggle of the 'fairy' are the link where the origin of this word is concerned.)

pédaler *v.intrans.* 1 To 'hare along', to travel at high speed. *On a pédalé comme des fous avec son tacot pour arriver à l'heure!* We certainly made that banger of his hum to get there on time! 2 To hurry, to work with haste. 3 *Pédaler dans la semoule*: To be hampered in one's progress.

pédaleur *n.m.* *Pédaleur de charme*: Gushing and smarmy individual who tends to overwhelm those on whom he is trying to make an impression. (There is no implication that the man concerned is homosexual, but his mannerisms are irritating.)

pédalo *n.m.* Amusement-park pedal-boat.

pédé *n.m.* 'Fag', 'queer', homosexual.

pédibus *adv.* 'On Shanks's pony' – On foot. *On a dû y aller pédibus*: We had to hoof it. (The origin of this word is to be found in the 'dog Latin' expression *pedibus cum jambis*.)

pédigrée *n.m.* *Avoir un pédigrée* (*pol.*): To have 'form', to have a criminal record.

pédoque *n.m.* 'Pouf', 'homo', homosexual.

pedzouille *n.m.* (also: *pedezouille*): 1 'Hayseed', 'yokel', peasant. 2 Gormless and uncouth character.

pégal *n.m.* *Le pégal*: The *mont-de-piété*, the State-run 'pop-shop', the municipal pawn-brokers.

pègre *n.f.* *La pègre*: The underworld. (This Marseilles word does not have the aura of *le milieu*. *Faire partie de la pègre* is uncomplimentary; *appartenir au milieu* somehow seems more acceptable.)

pégrer *v.trans.* To 'nab', to arrest. *Il s'est fait pégrer en beauté*: He got neatly collared!

pégrillot *n.m.* 1 'Borstal graduate', novice criminal. 2 Small-time crook (one that the *milieu* regards as riff-raff).

peigne *n.m.* 1 'Jemmy', crowbar. 2 *Sale comme un peigne* (of person): Filthy, dirty. *Il est sale comme un peigne!* He's a walking dustbin!

peigne-cul *n.m.* 'Pain-in-the-neck', nuisance, awkward character.

peignée *n.f.* 1 'Scrap', punch-up, fight. *Se filer une peignée*: To have a bout of the fisticuffs. 2 'Drubbing', thrashing. *Il a reçu une de ces peignées!* He got the beating of his life!

peigner *v.trans.reflex.* To 'have a bout of the fisticuffs', to 'scrap', to have a set-to (also: *se filer une peignée*).

peinard *adj.* **1** Without a care in the world. *Depuis qu'ils travaillent tous les deux, ils sont peinards*: With two wages coming in, they don't have much to worry about. *Faire quelque chose en père peinard*: To do something without undue haste and concern. *Je l'ai vu qui pédalait en père peinard*: I saw him cycling along at a leisurely pace. **2** Safe from trouble, out of danger. *Se tenir* (also: *rester*) *peinard*: To 'lie doggo', to 'keep a low profile', to stand clear of trouble.

peinardement *adv.* **1** In a carefree manner. **2** Safely, without fear of consequences.

peine *n.f. C'était bien la peine! (iron.)*: And what a waste of time it turned out to be!

peine-à-jouir *n.m. (joc.)*: **1** 'Nurk', character who finds it difficult to comprehend things. **2** *(pol.)*: Suspect whose reluctant admissions have to be extracted piecemeal. (The appellation is a jocular borrowing from the language of sexual intercourse, where it refers to a character who cannot reach an orgasm easily.)

peinture *n.f. Je ne peux pas le voir en peinture!* I can't stand the sight of him!

peinturlurer *v.trans.* **1** To slap on paint without regard to colour schemes where decorating is concerned. **2** (of artist): To 'daub', to apply colours to canvas or board in a 'painting-by-numbers' manner.

pékin *n.m. (mil.) Etre habillé en (tenue de) pékin*: To be 'in civvies', to be out of uniform.

pelé *n.m. Trois pelés (et un tondu)*: A 'rag-tag and bobtail gathering', a very small crowd of people. (This expression is always uttered with jocular irony.)

pelé *adj.* (Gambling slang): 'Cleaned-out', 'relieved' of money.

peler *v.trans.* (Gambling slang): To 'fleece'. *Il m'a pelé de ma paie!* He did me out of my whole wage packet, the rotten sharp!

peler *v.intrans.* **1** To shiver with cold. *Qu'est-ce qu'on pelait l'hiver dernier!* Last winter we had a dose of brass-monkey weather! **2** *Peler le jonc à quelqu'un*: To be a 'pain-in-the-arse', to be a nuisance to someone. *Il commence à me peler le jonc!* He's getting on my wick!

pèlerin *n.m. (Slightly pej.)*: 'Geezer', 'bloke', fellow. *Qui m'a foutu un pèlerin pareil?!* Where the hell did you get that nurk?!

pèlerines *n.f.pl. Les pèlerines*: 'The fuzz', the police.

pelle *n.f.* **1** *A la pelle*: 'Oodles', 'masses of', vast quantities. *Des comme lui, on en trouve à la pelle!* Blokes like him come ten-a-penny! **2** *Ramasser une pelle*: **a** To 'take a tumble', to fall down. **b** *(fig.)*: To 'come a cropper', to 'come unstuck', to suffer a setback. **3** *Rouler une pelle*: To give a 'French kiss' (also: *rouler une galoche*).

pelloche *n.f. (corr. pellicule)*: Film, roll of film for a camera.

pellot *n.m. Etre sans un pellot*: To be 'skint', 'broke', to be penniless.

pelotage *n.m.* 'Pawing', heavy petting.

pelote *n.f.* **1** 'Nest-egg', savings. *Arrondir sa pelote*: To 'feather one's nest'. **2** *Aller à la pelote (mil.)*: To have to join a punishment-drill platoon. (*Pelote* is an abbreviated corruption of *peloton disciplinaire*.) **3** *Envoyer quelqu'un aux pelotes*: To 'send someone packing', to send someone away in no uncertain manner. **4** *Une pelote d'épingles*: A 'crosspatch', an irritable and peevish character. **5** *(pl.)*: 'Bollocks', 'balls', testicles.

peloter *v.trans.* **1** To 'paw', to caress salaciously. **2** *(joc.)*: To 'rub up the right way', to 'flannel', to flatter.

peloteur *n.m.* **1** 'Pawer', randy character (literally one who is 'all hands'). **2** 'Apple-polisher', flatterer.

pelousard *n.m.* Racegoer, the kind you will find on the *pelouses* backing his fancies rather than in a betting-shop.

pelure *n.f.* **1** Coat, overcoat. *Ote ta pelure!* Hang your coat up! (and make yourself comfortable). **2** *(fig.)*: 'Hide', back. *Les flics nous sont tombés sur la pelure à la sortie du ciné!* The cops pounced on us as we left the flicks. **3** 'Flimsy', sheet of typing copy-paper. **4** *(pej.)*: 'Nurk', man of no intellectual substance.

pénard *adj.* **1** Without a care in the world. **2** Safe from trouble, out of danger. (See *peinard*.)

penco *n.m. (sch.)*: Boarder. (This word is an abbreviated corruption of *pensionnaire*.)

pendant *prep. Pendant ce temps-là sur le pont supérieur . . . (joc.)*: Meanwhile, back at the ranch . . . (Both the French and the English are said to originate in the 'flatulent' language of cheap romantic fiction.)

pendantes *n.f.pl.* Earrings.

pendard *n.m. (joc.)*: 'Rascal', rogue. *Pendard, va!* You rascal, you! (As the example shows, the word is, if anything, endearing and should not be translated as 'bounder'.)

pendouiller *v.intrans.* To 'dangle', to hang loosely.

pendre *v.intrans. Ça te pend au nez! (joc. & iron.)*: Like two and two make four, you're sure to cop it! (When the context is deemed to be particularly humorous, this expression often has the appendage: *comme un sifflet de deux ronds*.)

pendu *n.m.* **1** *Avoir une veine de pendu*: To have the luck of the devil. (Why this should be, is baffling, unless the poor devil survived!) **2** *Ne pas parler de corde dans la maison d'un pendu*: To steer clear of a sensitive topic of conversation.

pendule *n.m.* 'Ditherer', character whose course of action is always in doubt.

pendule *n.f.* **1** Person whose movements are as predictable and regular as clockwork. **2** Parking meter. **3** Meter in taxicab. **4** *En faire une pendule*: To 'make a song-and-dance' about it, to kick up a fuss about something.

pénible *adj.* (of person): 'Wearing', difficult to put up with. *Qu'il est pénible, ton fils!* I don't know how you can put up with that son of yours!

péniches *n.f.pl.* 'Boats', outsize shoes.

péno *n.m.* Penitentiary, top-security jail.

péno *n.f.* *(sch.)*: 'Lines', extra work given to unruly or indolent pupils.

pensant *Bien pensant (adj.exp.)*: Devout. (This expression, relating exclusively to Catholics, is not, strictly speaking, derogatory. It carries, however, a certain tongue-in-cheek irony.)

pense-bête *n.m.* Memory-jogger, 'knot-in-a-handkerchief' type memory-tickler.

pensio *n.m.* (*sch.*; *abbr. pensionnaire*): Boarder.

pension *n.f.* *Etre en pension (iron.)*: **a** To be 'in the nick', to be in jail (literally, in English, to be a boarder at H.M. prisons). **b** (of young prostitute): To be learning the trade in a brothel.

pépé *n.m.* (Child language): 'Gramps', grandad, grandfather.

pépée *n.f.* 'Bird', 'bit of skirt', woman. *Il aime courir les pépées*: He's a bit of a ladies' man. (Very much a male chauvinist word; in spite of its condescension, it has no pejorative connotation.)

pépère *n.m.* **1** 'Gramps', grandpa, grandfather. **2** 'Old codger', easy-going old man. (This word is more often than not used in a friendly, vocative context. *Alors, comment ça va, pépère?* Well, dad, how's things?)

pépère *adj.* **1** 'Easy-going', amenable. *Il est tout ce qu'il y a de pépère, le directeur!* That boss of ours is no stickler for rules! **2** 'Whopping', large. *Il s'est tapé un sandwich plus que pépère*: He was chomping his way through a ginormous sandwich.

pépère *adv.* In a happy-go-lucky manner, gently. *Les affaires vont pépère*: Business is ticking over nicely. *On a roulé pépère*: We drove at a leisurely pace.

pépètes *n.f.pl.* *Des pépètes*: 'Mazuma', 'lolly', money. *Il est plutôt regardant, côté pépètes!* He's a tight bastard with money!

pépette *n.f.* **1** *(pej.)*: 'Biddy', 'bird', woman. *Les pépettes, il ne connaît que ça!* He's

sex-mad! **2** *(pl.)*: 'Readies', cash, money. (With this meaning, the word *pépettes* is a corruption of *pépites* meaning 'nuggets'.)

pépie *n.f.* *Avoir la pépie*: To be 'dying for a drink', to be thirsty (usually for an alcoholic beverage). *J'ai une de ces pépies!* I could murder a pint! *Ne pas avoir la pépie*: To 'spout on and on', to talk volubly (literally, not to feel the need to wet one's whistle as one prattles on).

pépin *n.m.* **1** 'Brolly', umbrella. **2** 'chute, parachute. **3** 'Hitch', snag. *On a eu quelques pépins en cours de route*: We had to stop several times on the way. **4** Accident, serious setback. *Il leur est arrivé un de ces pépins*: They've come badly unstuck. **5** *Avoir un pépin dans la timbale*: To have 'bats in the belfry', to be 'potty', to be mad. **6** *Avoir le pépin pour quelqu'un*: To have a crush on someone, to be infatuated with someone. **7** *Avaler le pépin (joc.)*: To 'get in the pudding club', to get pregnant.

pépite *n.f.* *N'avoir plus une pépite*: To be 'skint', 'broke', to be penniless.

péquenaud *n.m.* *(pej.)*: **1** 'Yokel', peasant. **2** Gormless and uncouth character.

percale *n.m.* 'Baccy', tobacco.

perche *n.f.* **1** *Une grande perche*: 'Beanpole', tall and thin person. **2** *Tendre la perche à quelqu'un (fig.)*: **a** To extend a helping hand. **b** To help bring about a desired topic of conversation.

percher *v.intrans.* To 'hang out', to live somewhere. *Où c'est que tu perches?* Where's your pad? (The rhetorical question *Je me demande où il peut bien percher!* means 'I wonder where the hell he is now!')

perchoir *n.m.* *(joc.)*: 'Prick', 'cock', penis.

perco *n.m.* Coffee percolator.

percuté *adj.* 'Cracked', 'bonkers', mad.

perdre *v.trans.* **1** *Ne pas en perdre une*: 'Not to miss a thing', to hear and see everything that is happening. *En été, quand ils s'engueulaient, on n'en perdait pas une!* When they had rows in the summer, our ears used to flap! **2** *Tu ne perds rien pour attendre!* I'll get you! (You just wait!)

perdreau *n.m.* Plain-clothes police-officer. *Les perdreaux*: The fuzz. (In the plural, no distinction seems to be made between plain-clothes and uniformed policemen.)

père *n.m.* **1** *Père tranquille*: Easy-going character, one who takes life in his stride. **2** *Jouer les pères nobles*: To 'come the heavy father' (literally, to act the 'Victorian pater' in a rather 'hypocritical-to-one's-past' manner). **3** *Un placement de père de famille*: A gilt-edged investment, one that may only bring low interest but is as 'safe as houses'. **4** *Croire (encore) au père Noël*: To be a bit on the naïve side. **5** *Le père presseur*: The tax-man. (This is

a jocular pun-like corruption of *percepteur*.)
6 *Ton père était-il vitrier?!* *(iron.)*: Get out of the light will you?! **7** *Le père fouettard*: 'Arse', 'bum', behind. *Je l'ai sorti à coups de pompes dans le père fouettard*: I booted him out, no messing! *L'avoir dans le père fouettard (fig.)*: To have been 'diddled', 'conned', to have been fooled. **8.** *Le père frappart*: 'Prick', 'cock', penis. *Etrangler le père frappart*: To 'pull one's wire', to 'wank', to masturbate.

performances *n.f.pl.* *Performances indoor (joc.)*: Sexual prowess. *Côté performances indoor, c'est du modeste!* He's no contender for the sex-Olympics!

périf *n.m.* (abbr. *le boulevard périphérique*). *Le périphérique* is the motorway ring-road encircling Paris.

périmé *n.m.* 'Old codger', character out of touch with the times.

péripatéticienne *n.f.* *(joc.)*: 'Prozzy', 'hooker', prostitute.

périscope *n.m.* **1** *(joc.)*: 'Prick', 'cock', penis. (The word is humorous because of the 'Up periscope!' naval terminology familiar to all W.W. II film-buffs.) **2** *Jeter un coup de périscope*: To 'have a shufty', to glance discreetly at.

perle *n.f.* **1** 'Treasure', gem of a person. *Quand on a une perle comme ta femme, on ne la trompe pas!* I can't understand you gallivanting, with a wife like yours! **2** *(sch.)*: 'Howler', terrible mistake in homework or exam. *Relever des perles*: To jot down some prize gems. **3** *Passer son temps à enfiler des perles*: To waste time, to while away hours doing nothing. (The expression *il n'est pas venu ici pour enfiler des perles* is slightly misleading in that it means: he didn't come here without a purpose.) **4** Fart. *Lâcher une perle*: To 'let one rip'. *Ecraser une perle*: To do a 'pongy', to let off a silent fart. **5** Prostitute catering for the kinky.

perlot *n.m.* 'Baccy', tobacco. (This rather dated word seems to be making a comeback with the increase in 'roll-your-own' smokers.)

perlouse *n.f.* (also: *perlouze*): **1** Pearl. *Un collier de perlouses*: A string of pearls. **2** 'Pongy', fart.

perme *n.f.* (mil.; abbr. *permission*): Leave. *Quand il a une perme, il fait valser les biftons*: When he goes on leave, he blows everything he's got!

perniflard *n.m.* Pernod. (This is a jocular corruption of that word, even if the *pastis* is of another brand.)

Pérou *Proper name. Ce n'est pas le Pérou!* It's nothing to write home about! – It's of no great importance! *Et tu appelles ça un salaire?! Ce n'est vraiment pas le Pérou!* I wouldn't call that a salary, sounds more like charity!

perpète *à perpète (adv.exp.)*: **a** For ever and ever. *Il est bonnard pour s'en occuper à perpète*:

He's going to be landed with that chore for ever. *Etre condamné à perpète*: To get 'life', to be sentenced to life imprisonment. **b** Far away. *Habiter à perpète*: To live 'at the back of beyond', to live miles and miles away.

perquise *n.f.* *(abbr. perquisition)*: House-search (usually by the police with a warrant).

perroquet *n.m.* Alcoholic drink, a mixture of *pastis* and *sirop de menthe*. (The expression *étouffer* (also: *étrangler*) *un perroquet*, originally from Marseilles and Provence, has, with the popularity of this drink, travelled further afield.)

perruche *n.f.* 'Bit of skirt', 'biddy', woman. (Very much a male chauvinist word.)

perruque *n.f.* **1** *Avoir une perruque en peau de fesse (joc. & iron.)*: To be as bald as a coot. **2** *Une vieille perruque*: An 'old fogey', an old fuddy-duddy. **3** *Faire de la perruque*: To do a job 'on the side', to work after hours with the firm's equipment for one's personal gain.

persil *n.m.* **1** The 'short and curly', pubic hair. *Descente au persil*: 'Hair-pie', cunnilingus. **2** *Aller au persil* (of prostitute): To go soliciting. (This expression and *faire son persil* have drifted from the world of hookers and pimps into everyday slang with the straighter meanings of 'to go to. work' and 'to make a living'.)

persilleuse *n.f.* *(joc.)*: 'Prozzy', prostitute.

pescale *n.m.* **1** Fish. **2** Pimp, procurer (also: *poiscaille*).

pésetas *n.f.pl.* *(joc.)*: 'Nuggets', 'readies', money.

peseux *adj.inv.* 'Loaded', 'stinking rich', very wealthy.

pestouille *n.f.* Run of bad luck (also: *scoumoune*).

pet *n.m.* **1** Fart. *Lâcher un pet*: To 'let one rip', to break wind. **2** Danger, risk, peril. *En '42 il y avait du pet à sortir sans ausweis*: If Jerry caught you without I.D. on the streets, during the war, you were in trouble. **3** 'Row', disturbance. *Faire du pet*: To kick up a fuss. *Flurer le pet à quelqu'un*: To pick a quarrel with someone. **4** *Faire le pet*: To be on the look-out (where danger is concerned), to be on watch. **5** *(interj.)*: Pet! Look out! – Careful, someone's coming! **6** *Porter le pet*: **a** To complain. **b** To lay a charge against someone. **7** *Avoir un pet de travers*: **a** To 'feel out of sorts', to be unwell. **b** To be awkward and unco-operative. **8** *Ça ne vaut pas un pet de lapin!* It's not worth a brass farthing! – It's worthless!

pétant *adj.* (of time): Exactly, precisely. *Je te veux là à l'heure pétante!* I want you to be there on the dot!

Pétaouchnock *Proper name.* 'Thingsville'. (As in the English equivalent, *Pétaouchnock* is the jocular and ironic name for the kind of back-of-beyond town no-one ever seems to have heard of.)

pétarader *v.intrans.* To 'fly off the handle', to blow up with anger. (Originally, *pétarade* was the burst of farts let off by a horse springing into action, and with the advent of the motor car described the misfiring of an engine as it is being revved up; *pétarader* is a figurative extension of these meanings.)

pétard *n.m.* **1** 'Hullabaloo', uproar. *Faire du pétard*: To kick up a fuss. *Etre en pétard*: To be flaming angry. *Se filer en pétard*: To 'fly off the handle'. **2** Danger, risk, peril. *Quand il y a du pétard, 'faut pas compter sur lui!* Don't count on him when things hot up! **3** 'Arse', 'bum', behind. (With this meaning, the word has a built-in pejorative connotation as in *'Vise un peu ce pétard!'* Look at that fat arse!) **4** 'Rod', 'shooter', handgun.

pétarder *v.trans.reflex.* **1** To 'have a set-to', to have a fight. **2** To 'have a slanging match', to have a violent argument with someone.

pétardier *n.m.* 'Irascible fireball', character who flies off the handle at the slightest provocation.

pétardier *adj.* 'Fiery', irascible.

pétasse *n.f. (pej.):* 'Biddy', 'bit of skirt', woman. *Côté pétasses, ne lui en parle pas, il en a ralbol!* Don't mention women to him, he'll fly off the handle!

pet-de-nonne *n.m.* Fritter-cum-doughnut. (This rather bland item of pastry is about as inspiring as its name!)

pété *adj.* 'Pissed', 'sozzled', drunk.

pétée *n.f.* **1** *Une pétée de:* 'Oodles', 'masses of', a vast quantity. *Le lundi il y a toujours une pétée de mecs qui cherchent du boulot:* Early on Mondays, there's always a queue of blokes looking for work. **2** *Tirer* (also: *filer*) *une pétée:* To 'have a screw', to fuck, to have sex. (As some dictionaries are prompt to point out, *pétée* is the ejaculation of sperm.)

pet-en-l'air *n.m.* Waist-length wind-cheater, 'bum-freezer' type overgarment.

péter *v.intrans. & trans.* **1** To 'fart', to break wind. **2** *Péter dans la soie:* To live in the lap of luxury. **3** *Péter plus haut que son cul:* To be 'snooty', to have ideas above one's station. **4** *Péter le feu:* To be 'full of beans', to be bursting with energy. **5** *La péter:* To 'have to skip a meal', to go hungry. *Souvent on a dû la péter quand on faisait les petits théâtres!* Many a time our tummies rumbled when we were touring in rep! **6** To break. *Je suis sûr que c'est toi qui as pété ma radio!* I'm as sure as hell it's you who broke my tranny! *C'est d'un fragile, ça m'a pété dans les doigts!* It's so bloody brittle, it just snapped in my hand! **7** *Bouffer à s'en faire péter la sous-ventrière:* To have a good 'blow-out', to 'stuff one's face', to have a marathon

eating session. **8** *Ça va péter!* Things are going to hum! – There's going to be one hell of a row! *Pour sûr, ça va péter si elle rentre encore si tard!* She's going to get a right rollicking if she comes home late again! **9** *Il faut que ça pète!* It's make-or-break now! (The expression *il faut que ça pète ou dise pourquoi!* meaning 'Things had better get cracking!' is rather more subtle.) **10** *Péter dans la main* (of business deal): To 'fall through', to break down. *Avec cette foutue crise, v'là une gentille petite affaire qui nous a pété dans la main!* If it hadn't been for this bloody recession, we'd have had a booming little business on our hands! **11** *Envoyer péter quelqu'un:* To 'send someone packing', to send someone away in no uncertain manner. *T'aurais dû voir comme je l'ai envoyé péter!* I sent him on his way, no messing!

pète-sec *n.m.* 'Martinet', stickler for discipline.

pète-sec *adj.inv.* Abrupt and officious.

péteux *n.m.* **1** 'Pretentious nurk', self-important fool. **2** 'Funk', coward. (The feminine *péteuse* exists but refers only to men, and intensifies the pejorative connotation.)

péteux *adj.* **1** 'Snobby', pretentious. **2** 'Funky', cowardly.

pètezouille *n.m.* (also: *pètzouille*): **1** 'Yokel', 'hayseed', peasant. **2** Gormless and uncouth character.

petiot *n.m.* **1** 'Titch', small character. **2** 'Kid', child. *Les petiots:* The kiddlywinks.

petiot *adj. (joc.):* 'Titchy', 'teeny', small.

petit *n.m.* **1** *Le petit:* 'The kid', the child. *C'est le petit aux Martin:* It's the Martins' offspring. **2** *Mon petit* (Term of endearment): My pet – Precious – Darling. **3** *Faire des petits (fig.):* To multiply, to grow in numbers. *Dès qu'il y a un mécontent, ça fait des petits:* Before you know it, from one disgruntled character you've got a whole horde! **4** 'Prick', 'cock', penis. *Emmener le petit au cirque (joc.):* To have 'a leg-over', to 'have it off', to have sex. *Prendre* (also: *envoyer*) *du petit:* To get sodomized. (Certain dictionaries lexicalize *petit* with reference to the previous example as being the anal sphincter where sodomous intercourse is concerned.)

petit *adv.* At a slow pace. *En ce moment côté affaires, ça va petit!* Business is just about chugging along!

petite *n.f.* **1** *Mettre en petite:* **a** To 'swipe', to 'pinch', to steal petty items. *Devant un étalage, elle pouvait pas résister de mettre des trucs, des machins en petite:* Shoplifting was like a craving with her; in front of a stall temptation would prove too strong. **b** To 'salt away', to put money aside for a rainy day. **2** One-gramme 'fix' of heroin; the standard expression where drug-addicts are concerned is *prendre une petite*.

petit-lait *n.m. Boire du petit-lait* (of compliment): To 'lap it all up', to be delighted with what one hears.

petit-nègre *n.m.* 'Pidgin' French, the kind of broken French deemed to be spoken by 'the natives' in the colonies. Expressions such as *'Alors, ti veux zouli tapis, mon zami?!'* and *'Moi, y en avoir beaucoup argent!'* are typical of the genre.

pétochard *n.m.* 'Yellow-belly', 'funk', coward.

pétochard *adj.* 'Funky', cowardly.

pétoche *n.f.* 'Funk', fear. *Avoir une pétoche de tous les diables*: To 'have the shits', to be in a blue funk.

pétoire *n.f.* 1 *(Slightly pej.)*: Moped or light motorcycle (more often than not, the noisy two-stroke type). 2 'Rod', 'shooter', handgun.

peton *n.m.* (of child or woman): Small, delicate foot. (The word gained near-permanent overnight fame with the Maurice Chevalier song, *'Valentine'*, who, we are told, had *'un petit menton, deux petits petons'* and two rather attractive, if small, *'tétons'*.)

pétouille *n.f.* 'Funk', fear. *Avoir la pétouille*: To 'have the shits', to be in a blue funk.

pétoulet *n.m.* 'Bum', backside, behind. *L'avoir dans le pétoulet (fig.)*: To have been taken for a ride, to have been duped.

pétrin *n.m.* 'Spot', fix, lumber. *Etre dans un sacré* (also: *joli*) *pétrin*: To be 'up a gum-tree'. *Tu m'as mis dans un de ces pétrins!* Another fine mess you got me into! (The 'straight' meaning of *pétrin*: kneading-trough, helps to understand its colloquial extension, the sticky contents of the above being equatable with a problem or situation one cannot get clear of.)

pétrole *n.m.* 'Hooch', strong alcohol (usually the privately and illegally distilled variety). *File-moi un coup de pétrole!* Give us a swig of the hard stuff!

pétrolette *n.f. (joc.)*: Moped or light motorcycle.

pétroleuse *n.f.* 'Raver', 'randy bird', highly-sexed woman.

pétrus *n.m.* 'Arse', 'bum', behind. *Je ne l'ai jamais vu autrement qu'assis sur son pétrus!* I can't say I've ever seen him do a stroke of work! *L'avoir dans le pétrus (fig.)*: To have been 'diddled', 'conned', to have been fooled.

pétrusquin *n.m.* 1 'Arse', 'bum', behind. 2 'Hayseed', peasant. 3 'Nurk', 'twit', imbecile. 4 *(mil.)*: 'Civvy', civilian.

peu *n.m.* 1 *Ça a été du peu au jus!* It was a close shave! – It was a near thing! (I'm glad I got away scot-free!) 2 *Excusez du peu! (iron.)*: Is that all?! – You are modest!

peu *adv.* 1 *Un peu*: Very much, a lot. (Strange as it may seem, the colloquial meaning of *un peu* is the exact opposite of the straight acceptation.) *Il est un peu bon, ton gâteau!* That cake of yours tastes smashing! *'C'est cher, la Côte d'Azur?' 'Un peu!'* 'Is the Riviera expensive?' 'Not half!' (Although, strictly speaking, there is no rhyming slang in French, the expression: *Un peu, mon neveu!* could loosely be translated by 'And how! – You bet'. The *mon neveu* is totally meaningless, as is *Auguste* in *Tout juste, Auguste!*) 2 *Un peu beaucoup (iron.)*: Far too much. *Son père, sa mère, sa sœur et le beau-frère, c'est un peu beaucoup!* With her mother, her father, her sister and that brother-in-law, there wasn't room to swing a cat! 3 *Très peu pour moi! (iron.)*: Definitely not for me! *Une soirée devant la télé, très peu pour moi!* Sat sitting watching the telly till the dot disappears isn't my cup of tea!

pèze *n.m.* (also: *pèse*): 'Brass', 'loot', money. *Etre au pèze*: To be 'rolling in it', to be very rich.

pharmaco *n.m.* Chemist, one who owns or works in a chemist's shop.

phéno *adj. (abbr. phénoménal)*: 'Fab', fantastic.

phénomène *n.m.* 'Coughdrop', 'card', mild eccentric. *C'est un drôle de phénomène!* He's a bit of an oddball!

philo *n.f. (abbr. philosophie)*: One of the three course options that used to be open to students preparing the *second baccalauréat*. *'On a fait notre philo ensemble'* could loosely be translated: 'We did our A-levels together'.

phono *n.m. (abbr. phonographe)*: 'Gram', gramophone.

phosphorer *v.intrans.* To think hard. (The verb originates in the popular near-myth that phosphorus is food for the brain, and many an unfortunate child has been told to eat his fish with a *'ça te rendra intelligent'* injunction.)

photo *n.f. Tu veux ma photo?! (iron.)*: Do you want me to sign you an autograph?! (This sarcastic expression is usually uttered by a woman when the salacious or admiring glances of a male have started to annoy her.)

photographier *v.trans. Se faire photographier*: To 'get spotted', to be noticed.

phrasicoter *v.intrans.* To 'speechify', to string out pompous and near-meaningless sentences.

phrasicoteur *n.m.* 'Pompous waffler', character who seems to like the sound of his own voice.

piaf *n.m.* 1 Sparrow. 2 Small bird (to the un-ornithologically-minded). *Avoir une cervelle de piaf*: To have a bird-brain. (Edith Piaf was given her stage-name because of her diminutive stature and bird-like features. To mention this is particularly relevant in view of the fact that a rival artiste bore the nickname of *la môme moineau*.) **3** *Un drôle de piaf (pej.)*: An 'oddball', a 'queer cove', a weird character.

piano *n.m.* **1** *Piano à bretelles (joc.)*: Accordion (also: *piano du pauvre*). **2** 'Print', fingerprint. *Passer au piano*: To have one's dabs taken. **3** Set of teeth, 'one's own' or dentures. (The expression *n'avoir plus toutes ses ratiches dans le piano* not only conjures up the image of 'ivories', but also the dark gaps of the black keys.)

piaule *n.f.* **1** Room. *La piaule à ma sœur*: My sister's bedroom. **2** 'Digs', rented accommodation.

piauler *v.trans.reflex.* **1** To 'hit the sack', to go to bed. **2** To go back home (after a night on the tiles).

pic *à pic (adv.exp.)*: Just at the right time. *Cette augmentation est tombée à pic*: That rise couldn't have come at a better time. *Il est arrivé à pic, le dur allait partir*: The train was about to leave, he got there in the nick of time.

picaillons *n.m.pl.* **1** 'Chips', 'brass', money. *Avec les picaillons qu'il a, il ne manque pas d'amis!* With that kind of brass, he's not short of friends! **2** Small change, coins of low denomination.

pichpin *n.m. C'est du pichpin!* (of task, project): It's a doddle! – It's dead easy! (*Pichpin* is a simple corruption of pitchpine, one of the easier timbers to work with.)

pichtegorne *n.m.* (also: *pichtogorne*): 'Plonk', cheap red wine.

picole *n.f. La picole*: 'Boozing', 'tippling', alcohol over-indulgence. *Il s'est laissé aller à la picole*: He's got a drink problem.

picoler *v.trans. & intrans.* To 'booze', to 'knock it back', to drink alcohol immoderately.

picoleur *n.m.* 'Boozer', heavy drinker.

picolo *n.m.* Wine, usually red, rather lacking in character. (Like the musical instrument, it's no 'big noise' in the wine world.)

picoter *v.trans.* To tease and anger in a pinpricking manner.

picotin *n.m. N'avoir plus un picotin*: To be 'skint', 'broke', to be penniless. *Ça ne vaut pas un picotin*: It's not worth a sausage! – It's worthless!

picouse *n.f.* 'Jab', injection.

picrate *n.m. (pej.)*: 'Bottom-of-the-barrel' plonk, cheap and rough-tasting red wine.

pictance *n.f. (joc.)*: Quantity of booze, of alcoholic drink. (This word is a jocular compounding of *picton* and *pitance*.)

picter *v.intrans.* To 'booze', to 'knock it back', to drink alcohol immoderately. *Pour ce qui est de picter, il s'y connaît!* He's certainly got a sloping gullet!

picton *n.m.* 'Plonk', cheap red wine.

pie *n.f. Voiture pie*: 'Panda car', police squad car. (The origin of the term lies in the black and white colour sported by police vehicles in France up to the 1970s.)

pièce *n.f.* **1** *Pièce de dix ronds (joc. & iron.)*: 'Jacksey', anus, anal sphincter (where sodomous sex is concerned). **2** *Service trois pièces (joc.)*: 'Privates', genitals. **3** *Rendre à quelqu'un la monnaie de sa pièce*: To 'give as good as one got', to engineer tit-for-tat reprisals. **4** *On n'est pas aux pièces (iron.)*: There's no fire! – Why the rush?! (The literal meaning of *être* or *travailler aux pièces* is 'to be on piecework' in a factory.)

pied *n.m.* **1** *Faire du pied à quelqu'un*: To 'play footsie', to make amorous foot-play advances. **2** *Se tirer des pieds*: **a** *(lit.)*: To 'skedaddle', to 'scram', to move away niftily. **b** *(fig.)*: To get out of a scrape in the nick of time. **3** *S'être levé du pied gauche*: To be in a foul mood (because one has got out of bed on the wrong side). *Partir du pied gauche* (of venture, undertaking): To make a bad start. **4** *Lever le pied*: **a** To ease off the accelerator pedal, to reduce one's speed in a motor car. **b** To take things at a more leisurely pace (and let others do the rushing about). **c** (of shady entrepreneur): To do a 'moonlight flit', to disappear with the takings. **5** *S'en aller les pieds devant*: To 'pop one's clogs', to 'snuff it', to die. **6** *Faire des pieds et des mains pour . . .* : To 'try every trick in the book', to worry more about the ends than the means where success is concerned. *Il a fait des pieds et des mains pour un petit rôle de rien du tout*: For a two-bit part in that play he literally flogged his granny! **7** *Ça lui fera les pieds!* (That will) serve him jolly well right! *C'est bien fait pour tes pieds!* Well you asked for it, didn't you?! **8** *Etre bête comme ses pieds*: To be 'as thick as two short planks', to be totally stupid. *Quel pied!* What a nurk! – What a fool! **9** *Prendre son pied* (also: *aller au pied*): To have a 'come', to experience an orgasm. (The origin of the expression could be sought in the picturesque *avoir les pieds en bouquets de violettes* which is both descriptive and humorous.) **10** *Ça, c'est le pied!* This is great! – This is fantastic! (In this instance *pied* has taken a far more metaphorical meaning.) **11** *En avoir son pied de quelque chose*: To be fed up to the back teeth with something. **12** *Aller au pied* (Underworld slang): To 'split the takings', to have a share-out. **13** *Il y a du pied dans la chaussette!* There's no rush! – We've plenty of time!

pied-de-biche *n.m. Tirer le pied-de-biche*: To go begging from house to house. (In this instance, a *pied-de-biche* is the cloven-foot door-knocker.)

This expression died in the late 30s, and in modern French a *pied-de-biche* is purely and simply a crowbar.)

pied-de-figuier *n.m.* *(pej.)*: Arab, native of North Africa. (Definitely a racist word, in use when the French held colonial power.)

pied-noir *n.m.* Non-Arab native of Algeria. (Since independence the word has lost its *raison d'être*.)

piège *n.m.* **1** *Piège à macaroni (joc.)*: Beard, the serviette-like 'face-fungus' that tells one what its owner has been eating. **2** *Piège à cons (fig.)*: 'Trap', confidence trick (the kind only the fools of this world could fall for).

piéger *v.trans.* *(fig.)*: To lay a trap for someone and succeed in the undertaking. *Il s'est drôlement fait piéger*: He fell for it hook, line and sinker.

Pierre Proper name. *Pierre, Paul et Jacques*: Tom, Dick and Harry.

pierreuse *n.f.* Prostitute down on her luck. (*La Pierreuse* is a well-known porno song much liked and sung in the world of the *carabins*.)

pierrot *n.m.* **1** 'Sparrer', sparrow. **2** *Un drôle de pierrot*: A 'weird 'un', a queer fellow, someone not to be trusted.

piétaille *n.f.* *(pej.)* *La piétaille*: The riff-raff of underlings.

pieu *n.m.* *Le pieu*: 'The sack', bed. *Aller au pieu*: To 'hit the hay', to 'kip down', to go to bed.

pieuter *v.intrans.* To sleep, to spend the night (somewhere). *J'ai eu la chance de pouvoir pieuter chez eux*: I was lucky they offered me a bed for the night.

pieuter *v.trans.reflex.* To 'hit the sack', to go to bed.

pif *n.m.* **1** 'Conk', 'hooter', nose. (Expressions involving *pif* such as *à vue de pif, avoir un coup dans le pif, se casser le pif*, etc. can all be found under the heading *nez*.) **2** *Faire quelque chose au pif*: **a** To do something on a 'guesstimate' basis (relying on good old intuition rather than facts and figures). **b** To 'take potluck' in doing something, to take a chance by backing a hunch (also: *faire quelque chose au pifomètre*).

piffer *v.trans.* *Ne pas pouvoir piffer quelqu'un*: To be unable to stand (the sight of) someone. *Ce mec-là, je peux vraiment pas le piffer!* That guy really gets up my nose! *Eux, ils peuvent vraiment pas se piffer!* These two are just like cat and dog!

piffrer *v.trans.reflex.* To 'stuff one's face', to guzzle, to eat immoderately. (*Se piffrer* is a truncated form of *s'empiffrer*.)

pifomètre *n.m.* *Faire quelque chose au pifomètre*: **a** To do something on a 'guesstimate' basis (relying on good old intuition rather than facts and figures). **b** To 'take potluck' in doing

something, to take a chance by backing a hunch. (The *pifomètre* is a jocular neologism based on *pif*: nose, modulated with a pseudo-technical ending in the same 'ho-ho' spirit as the English 'crapometer'.)

pige *n.f.* **1** Year. (The word can be used in conjunction with someone's age, but occurs more often in relation to time elapsed and in the context of prison sentences. *Ça va bientôt faire dix piges que je l'ai pas vu*: It's going on ten years since I saw him. *Il a écopé de quinze piges*: He got fifteen years' porridge.) **2** *Faire la pige à quelqu'un*: To 'lick' someone, to 'go one-up on', to surpass someone. *Côté méninges, un peu qu'il vous fait la pige!* When it comes to brains, he's in a totally different league! **3** *Etre (payé) à la pige* (of journalist, novelette-cum-soap-opera writer): To write on a 'penny-a-line' basis. (Alphonse Allais boasted of having once conned an absent-minded editor out of a fair amount of money, whilst working *à la pige*, with an avalanche of easy-to-write 'one-word' lines that went *'Vous?!' 'Oui!' – 'Ah, non!' – 'Si!' – 'Ça alors!' – 'Mais oui!'*, etc.)

pigeon *n.m.* 'Gull', 'sucker', dupe. *Se faire plumer comme un pigeon*: To get 'done' good and proper.

pigeonner *v.trans.* To 'take for a ride', to 'con', to dupe.

piger *v.trans.* **1** To 'twig', to 'grasp', to understand. *Pour sûr, à la longue il a pigé tout ton machin*: It was a dead-cert he'd cotton on to what you were doing. **2** To 'take a butchers', to 'take a shufty', to look at. *Pige-moi un peu la gueule qu'elle fait!* Look at the face she's pulling! **3** (of disease): To 'cop', to 'go down with', to catch. *Il a pigé une bléno maison*: He caught a right dose of clap. **4** To 'cop', to get sentenced to a term of imprisonment. *Avec leurs pédigrées ils vont piger le maxi*: With their form, they're in line for a full plate of porridge! **5** *Se faire piger*: To get 'nabbed', 'collared', to be arrested.

pigette *n.f.* *Etre* (also: *travailler*) *à la pigette* (of small-time journalist): To work on a 'penny-a-line' basis.

pigiste *n.m.* 'Penny-a-liner', freelance hack chasing work. (See *pige*.)

pignocher *v.intrans.* **1** To 'pick at one's food', to leave half of it on one's plate (because one has no appetite). **2** To 'nibble', to eat between meals.

pignocher *v.trans.reflex.* To 'have a bout of the fisticuffs', to have a punch-up, to have a set-to. (The origin of the verb lies in the noun *gnon*: blow.)

pignole *n.f.* *La pignole*: 'Wanking', masturbation. *Se taper une pignole*: To 'pull one's wire', to masturbate.

pignouf *n.m.* 'Ignorant nurk', character totally lacking manners.

pilant *adj.* 'Creasing', 'side-splitting', hilarious.

pile *n.f.* **1** Thrashing. **a** *(lit.)*: 'Pasting', walloping. *Il lui a filé une de ces piles à la fin du round*: He knocked the living daylights out of him right on the bell. **b** *(fig.)*: *En '45 les Chleus ont pris la pile des piles!* Just before the end of the war we knocked the stuffing out of Jerry! **2** Unit of 100 francs in pre-1958 currency. *Cinq piles, c'est vraiment pas cher pour toutes ces cibiches!* I'd say you're getting these fags at a reasonable price! (Like the English 'pony', *pile* belongs to the grey language area shadowing the underworld. The word would have no meaning to the middle classes of the 40s and 50s.)

pile *adv.* **1** Precisely, exactly. *Je dois commencer à huit heures pile*: I've got to start at eight on the dot. *Ça fait pile ce que je te dois!* Here's what I owe you, now we're quits! **2** *Ça tombe pile*: It couldn't have happened at a better time! *Vous arrivez pile!* Am I glad you're here! **3** *S'arrêter pile*: To 'stop dead', to come to an abrupt halt. (There would appear to be a link between the adverbial *pile* and the wrist-smacking flip-over involved in the tossing of a coin.)

piler *v.trans.* **1** *Etre à piler*: To be too terrible for words. *Ça, c'est vrai, son dernier film, il est à piler!* You have to agree with the critics, who slated his latest film! *Il est à piler, ce mec-là!* What a dreadful chap! **2** *La piler*: To 'go hungry', to have to go without food.

piler *v.intrans.* **1** (Cycling slang): To 'grind away', to toil up a steep hill. **2** To 'slog one's guts out', to work relentlessly. **3** (of vehicle): To come to an abrupt stop. *Et comment qu'on a pilé au feu rouge!* We certainly screeched to a halt when the lights changed (also: *s'arrêter pile*).

piloches *n.f.pl.* 'Gnashers', 'choppers', teeth. *Allez, on va se mettre quelque chose sous les piloches!* Come on, let's have a bite to eat!

pilon *n.m.* **1** 'Drumstick', cooked leg of poultry. **2** 'Stump', wooden leg. **3** Beggar. (As the expression *faire le pilon* suggests, the poor vagabond in question plays on the compassion of passers-by where his 'war-wound' is concerned. With this meaning the word has all but disappeared.)

pilonner *v.intrans.* To go begging, to go soliciting alms.

pilule *n.f.* **1** *Avaler la pilule* *(fig.)*: To 'fall for something', to be gullible. *Et comment qu'il a avalé la pilule!* He fell for it hook, line and sinker! **2** *Dorer la pilule*: To 'sugar the pill', to give a silver lining to a grey cloud, to make things look better than they really are. **3** *Se*

dorer la pilule: To get a suntan. (In this instance, *pilule* refers to the face.) **4** *Envoyer quelqu'un se faire dorer la pilule*: To tell someone to 'get stuffed', to tell someone off in no uncertain manner. (Auguste Le Breton, in his *L'ARGOT CHEZ LES VRAIS DE VRAI*, sees in the expression a connection with buggery, much in the vein of the naval 'golden rivet'.) **5** *Prendre une (sacrée) pilule*: To get a real thrashing, to be beaten up. **6** *Prendre la pilule (fig.)*: To 'come a cropper', to suffer a serious setback.

piment *n.m.* *Avoir du piment*: To have flair, to have a sixth sense for sniffing out trouble or an opportunity. (Although the literal meaning of *piment* can be seen as nose, it is never found in any other expression. Also: *avoir du nez*.)

pinaillage *n.m.* 'Hair-splitting', quibbling. *Il est plutôt porté sur le pinaillage*: He always queries things to the smallest detail.

pinailler *v.intrans.* To 'split hairs', to quibble. *Toute sa vie il n'a jamais cessé de pinailler*: Nothing ever seems to be right for him.

pinailleur *n.m.* 'Nit-picker', quibbler.

pinailleur *adj.* 'Nit-picking', hair-splitting and argumentative. (The feminine *pinailleuse* is hardly ever encountered.)

pinard *n.m.* 'Vino', wine (more the 'plonk' than the 'château' variety).

pinardier *n.m.* Wine-barge ferrying 'plonk' to the Bercy docks in Paris (sometimes oceangoing tanker transporting wine from overseas).

pince *n.f.* **1** 'Mitt', 'paw', hand. *Serrer la pince à quelqu'un*: To shake someone's hand. **2** *(pl.)*: 'Plates of meat', 'hoofs', feet. *Aller (quelque part) à pinces*: To 'hoof it'. **3** *Etre chaud de la pince* (of man): To be a randy so-and-so. **4** *Bonne pince!* Great! – That's clever of you! **5** *Mettre les pinces à quelqu'un (pol.)*: To 'put someone in bracelets', to handcuff someone.

pinceau *n.m.* **1** 'Gamb', 'pin', leg. *Tricoter des pinceaux*: To 'make tracks', to move speedily. **2** *(pl.)*: 'Plates of meat', 'hoofs', feet. *S'emmêler les pinceaux*: To fall over one's feet. *Se décrasser les pinceaux*: To wash one's tootsies. **3** 'Joystick', 'cock', penis. *Avoir un sacré coup de pinceau*: To be a 'superstud'. **4** *Etre verni au pinceau à merde*: To have the luck of the devil.

pince-cul *n.m.* **1** 'Hop', cheap dance hall or venue definitely lacking in charisma. **2** 'Do', party. (There is a blend of gentle humour when *pince-cul* or *pince-fesses* refers to a private party where, unlike a tatty dance-hall, one is not likely to have one's bottom pinched.)

pincée *n.f.* *Une pincée* (of money): A fair amount, a sizeable sum. (The word has jocular and ironic connotations in that, in formal

French, it means 'a mere pinch'. *Il s'est fait une sacrée pincée dans le trafic des devises*: He made a packet in currency rackets.)

pince-monseigneur *n.m.* 'Jemmy', crowbar.

pincer *v.trans.* **1** To 'collar', to 'buttonhole', to take someone aside (forcibly or otherwise). **2** To 'nab', to arrest. *On s'est fait pincer avec la came*: We got caught red-handed with all the gear. **3** (of disease): To 'cop', to catch. **4** To 'twig', to 'catch on', to understand. *Tu pinces?! Do you get it?!* **5** *En pincer pour*: To 'have a crush on', to be infatuated with. *Elle en pince pour ma pomme!* I definitely think she's doolally on me!

pince-sans-rire *n.m.* 'Dry joker', one who indulges in dry humour, keeping a stiff upper lip when others are bent double laughing.

pincettes *n.f.pl.* **1** 'Gambs', 'pins', legs. *Tricoter des pincettes*: To run (away) like the clappers, to make tracks. **2** 'Bracelets', handcuffs (also: *poussettes*). **3** *Ne pas être à prendre avec des pincettes*: To be seen to be in a foul temper. *Je ne sais vraiment pas ce qu'il a aujourd'hui, il n'est pas à prendre avec des pincettes!* I don't know what's got into him today, he's like a bear with a sore head!

pine *n.f.* 'Prick', 'cock', penis. *Revenir avec la pine sous le bras*: To suffer a humiliating set-back where sex is concerned.

piné *adj.* 'Spot-on', 'A-1', first-rate. *Ça, c'est piné!* If this isn't success, I don't know what is!

piner *v.trans.* To 'screw', to fuck, to have coition with.

pingler *v.trans.* (*corr. épingler*): **1** To catch red-handed. **2** To 'nab', to 'collar', to arrest.

pingoter *v.intrans.* To 'stomp', to dance.

pingots *n.m.pl.* 'Hoofs', 'plates of meat', feet.

pingouin *n.m.* *Etre habillé en pingouin (joc.)*: To be wearing 'tails', to be dressed in a tail-coat outfit (including starched white shirt which gives one a penguin-like appearance).

pingouins *n.m.pl.* 'Hoofs', 'plates of meat', feet.

pingre *n.m.* 'Skinflint', miser.

pingre *adj.* 'Tight', mean.

pinter *v.trans. & intrans.* To 'booze', to drink unwise amounts of alcohol. *Qu'est-ce qu'il pinte, celui-là!* He doesn't half knock 'em back! *On a pinté de sa saloperie d'alcool maison!* We had a few too many of his rotten home-brew!

pinter *v.trans.reflex.* To get 'pissed', 'canned', to get drunk.

piochage *n.m. (sch.)*: 'Swotting', painstaking revision for an exam.

pioche *n.f. Une tête de pioche*: A 'pig-head', an obdurate person. *Quelle tête de pioche, celui-là!* He won't budge, you know! – He's as stubborn as they come!

piocher *v.trans. & intrans.* **1** (*sch.*): To 'swot', to study hard. **2** To 'graft', to work hard. **3** To research something thoroughly. *Piochez-moi ça, je veux tout savoir*: I want all the facts, leave no stone unturned!

piocheur *n.m.* **1** (*sch.*): 'Swot', over-zealous student. **2** 'Grafter', hard worker. **3** Investigative journalist.

pioger *v.intrans.* To 'have digs', to live somewhere. *Où que tu pioges?* Where do you hang out?

pion *n.m.* **1** (*sch.*): Invigilator-cum-assistant-master whose main function in the French *lycées* is to see to basic disciplinary matters. (As the word suggests, he is a mere pawn on the chess-board of education.) **2** *N'avoir plus un pion*: To be 'skint', 'broke', to be penniless. *Désolé, mon vieux, j'ai plus un pion!* Sorry, no sub, I haven't got a bean!

pion *adj.inv.* 'Pissed', 'blotto', drunk.

pioncer *v.intrans.* To 'kip', to sleep. *C'est pas tout, mais faut que j'aille pioncer!* That's all very well, but I must get some shuteye!

pionnard *n.m.* **1** Habitual boozer, heavy drinker. **2** Drunk, drunkard.

pionner *v.pronom.* To get 'sozzled', 'sloshed', to get drunk (also: *se pionnarder*).

pioupiou *n.m.* **1** (Child language): 'Birdie', bird. **2** (*mil.*): Private, soldier.

pipe *n.f.* **1** 'Ciggy', 'fag', cigarette. *Sois pas vache, file-nous des pipes!* Go on, be a mate, give us a few smokes! (also: *cibiche*). **2** 'Gob', mouth. *Se fendre la pipe*: To burst out laughing. **3** *Avoir un coup dans la pipe*: To have had 'one over the eight', to be 'tipsy', to be slightly drunk. **4** *Casser sa pipe*: To 'kick the bucket', to 'snuff it', to die. **5** *Par tête de pipe*: 'Per head', per person. *Combien ça va nous coûter par tête de pipe?* What do you reckon we'll each have to pay? **6** *Faire* (also: *tailler*) *une pipe*: To gamaroosh, to practise fellatio.

pipé *adj. Dés pipés*: Loaded dice.

pipelet *n.m.* (*pej.*): **1** Caretaker in a block of flats, the famous French *concierge*. (This derogatory word, of which the feminine *pipelette* is far more current, originated in Eugène Sue's *Mystères de Paris*.) **2** 'Nosey-parker', inquisitive and gossipy character.

piper *v.trans. Ne pas pouvoir piper quelqu'un*: To find someone unbearable (also: *ne pas pouvoir piffer quelqu'un*).

piper *v.intrans. Ne pas piper*: To 'stay stum', to 'keep one's trap shut', to remain silent. (Although intransitive, the verb is really transitive by implication as the standard expression is *ne piper mot*.)

pipette *n.f.* 'Ciggy', 'fag', cigarette. (With this meaning, *pipette* is very much part of the 30s and 40s.) **2** *Vol à la pipette*: Theft of petrol by syphoning it out of parked cars. (With the explosion of fuel prices, the expression has had a new lease of life.)

pipeur *n.m.* (Gambling): Cheat, crooked player.

pipeuse *n.f.* Low-class prostitute (the kind who practises fellatio).

pipi *n.m.* **1** (Child language): 'Wee-wee', 'pee', urine. *Faire pipi*: To do 'number ones'. **2** *Pipi de chat*: **a** Cheap and nasty white wine. **b** 'Tripe', rubbish. **3** *C'est comme si je faisais pipi dans un chapeau de paille troué! (iron.)*: One might just as well put a poultice on a wooden leg!

pipi-room *n.m. Le pipi-room (joc.)*: The loo, 'Aunt Jane's', the lavatory. (This rather twee made-up franglais word refers more often to public conveniences than to the domestic W.C.)

piquage *n.m.* 'Collaring', arrest.

piqué *n.m.* 'Loony', 'nutter', mad person. (The word can only be evaluated according to context and its meanings can range from gentle eccentric to raving lunatic.)

piqué *adj.* **1** 'Bonkers', 'potty', mad. (With this meaning the adjective refers only to people.) **2** *Ça n'est pas piqué des hannetons!* (also: *des vers*): **a** This certainly isn't old-hat! – Well, this is new! **b** This is great! **c** That's a turn-up for the book! – What a surprise!

pique-gaufre *n.m. (joc.)*: 'Conk', 'hooter', nose.

pique-lard *n.m.* 'Chiv', blade, knife.

piquer *v.trans.* **1** To 'jab', to inject. (The verb is only really encountered with this meaning when it refers to the 'putting to sleep' of a pet dog or cat. *Elle a dû faire piquer son chien*: She had to have her dog put down.) **2** To stab, to knife. **3** To 'cop', to catch (a disease). *Il a piqué une chtouille maison!* He caught a right dose of clap! **4** *Piquer une sale note (sch.)*: To get a rotten mark. (In schools and colleges, the verb *piquer* with reference to an assessment can sometimes have a positive connotation with *piquer un quinze sur vingt*: To get a first-class mark.) **5** *Piquer un 100 mètres*: **a** To 'skedaddle', to 'make tracks', to run away. **b** *(fig.)*: To be off and away when something unpleasant has occurred. **6** *En piquer un*: To 'have a kip', to 'take some shuteye', to steal a few minutes for a snooze (also: *piquer un roupillon*). **7** To 'nick', to 'pinch', to steal. *Elle m'a piqué tout mon fric*: She filched all my dough. **8** To 'nab', to 'collar', to arrest. *A ce train-là, on va se faire piquer par les cognes!* If we keep this up, the fuzz'll do us! **9** *Piquer le dix* (Prison slang): To pace up and down a cell like a bear in a cage.

piquer *v.intrans. Piquer à quelque chose*: **a** To 'get the hang of something', to understand the workings of something. **b** To get 'hooked' on, to have a compulsive liking for something.

piquer *v.trans.reflex.* **1** (Drugs): To 'mainline', to inject intravenously. **2** *Se piquer le nez*: To 'get pickled', to get drunk. (The expression reflects the habitual nature of the act whereby the subject is well on the road to dipsomania.)

piqueur *n.m.* 'Filch', light-fingered individual (one whose thieving habits are limited to objects of little value).

piquette *n.f.* **1** Cheap and nasty wine (literally the nearest thing to vinegar). **2** *Filer une piquette à quelqu'un (fig.)*: To 'beat someone hollow', to trounce someone (at cards, dominoes, etc.). *Il a ramassé une de ces piquettes!* If he'd been gambling he'd have lost his shirt!

piquouse *n.f.* (also: *piquouze*): 'Shot', 'jab', injection.

pire *adj. C'est plus pire!* It's worse than that! (Literally, this jocular corruption of grammar could be translated by: It's even worser!)

pissat *n.m.* 'Cat's-pee', lousy white wine (also: *pipi de chat*).

pisse-copie *n.m. (pej.)*: 'Ink-shitter', lousy hack, journalist with no literary pretensions.

pisse-froid *n.m.* 'Cold fish', character who seems to have no emotions. (There is a suggestion that the 'cold fish' in question might be also something of a 'wet blanket'.)

pissenlits *n.m.pl. Bouffer les pissenlits par la racine*: To be 'pushing up (the) daisies', to be long gone, to be dead and buried.

pisser *v.trans. & intrans.* **1** To 'pee', to urinate. **2** *En pisser dans son froc*: To be overcome by laughter (the kind of laughter typical of the yokel statement: 'When I laughs I wets meself!'). **3** *Ne plus se sentir pisser*: To be so full of oneself as to be impermeable to ridicule.

pisseuse *n.f. (pej.)*: Pre-teen girl. (This derogatory word is uttered by the male counterpart shortly before heterosexual attraction becomes an obsession. *On ne veut pas de pisseuses ici!* We certainly don't want any bloody girls here!) **2** (of man): 'Funk', coward. (Terms of abuse are always more derogatory to males when they are feminine. See *chieuse*.)

pisseux *adj.* 'Dingy', dull and depressing.

pissotière *n.f.* 'Piss-house', public convenience.

pistache *n.f. Prendre une pistache*: To get 'pissed to the eyeballs', to get really drunk. *Avoir sa pistache*: To be well and truly plastered.

pistacher *v.pronom.* To get 'pissed', 'sozzled', to get drunk.

pistard *n.m.* (Cycling slang): Track-racer, one who races in a stadium as opposed to the open road.

pister *v.trans.* To 'dog', to tail, to follow someone closely (and unobserved).

pisteur *n.m.* Night-club tout, one whose job it is to fill the seedier joints.

pistole *n.f.* 1 'Chokey', 'slammer', prison. 2 Prison cell offering above-average comfort to inmates willing and able to pay for this privilege. (This facility was discontinued in 1939.)

pistolet *n.m.* 1 Bedpan for use in male wards. (The pistol-like shape gave it its name.) 2 *Un drôle de pistolet*: A queer so-and-so (the kind of person one does not know how to handle).

piston *n.m.* 'String-pulling', back-stairs influence. *Sans piston, il n'aurait jamais réussi*: Without the old-boy network, he'd still be waiting for promotion. (The expression *coup de piston* refers to a single bit of 'backstage' help.)

pistonner *v.trans. & intrans.* To 'pull strings', to 'work the old-boy network' for someone. (The verb refers exclusively to the backstage manipulations involved in promotions, etc.)

pistonneur *n.m.* Powerful 'string-puller', person who holds influence and uses it where another's promotion prospects are concerned.

pitaine *n.m. (mil.)*: Cap'n, captain.

pitancher *v.trans. & intrans.* To 'booze', to drink alcohol immoderately.

pitancheur *n.m.* 'Boozer', heavy drinker.

pitchoun *n.m.* 'Kiddlywink', 'kid', child.

pitchoun *adj.* 'Teeny-weeny', 'titchy', very small. (This word and the noun from which it comes originate from Provence.)

piton *n.m.* 'Conk', 'hooter', nose (usually a large one).

pive *n.m.* 'Plonk', cheap red wine (also: *piveton*).

pivoine *n.f. Piquer sa pivoine*: To go red, to blush (because a *pivoine*: poppy is bright red).

P.J. *Proper name. La P.J. (La Police Judiciaire)*: The non-uniformed branch of the police, roughly equivalent to the C.I.D. (Criminal Investigation Department).

placard *n.m.* 1 'Chokey', 'clink', prison. 2 Amount paid by a pimp to another for the purchase of a prostitute. (As with footballers, the 'transfer fee' is commensurate with the lady's potential.)

placarde *n.f.* 1 Public square in village or small town. 2 'Pitch', area where a hawker or market-trader does business. 3 Hiding-place. *Il a dû trouver une bonne placarde vu qu'il est pas chez les flics*: He must have picked a good place to lie low as the fuzz haven't got him. 4 Job, position, employment.

placarder *v.trans.* 1 (of pimp): To get prostitutes 'on the game'. (The verb refers primarily to the man who sets the evil ball of prostitution rolling.) 2 To find someone a cushy job.

placardier *n.m.* 'Meat-merchant', pimp who procures for others women likely to become prostitutes.

plafond *n.m.* 1 'Bean', 'bonce', head. *Se cloquer une olive dans le plafond* (also: *se faire sauter le plafond*): To 'top' oneself, to shoot oneself through the head. *Avoir une araignée dans le* (also: *au*) *plafond*: To be 'bonkers', 'barmy', to be mad. 2 *Etre bas de plafond*: To be 'a bit dim', to have a rather limited intellect. 3 *Sauter au plafond*: **a** To be 'over the moon', to jump for joy. **b** To fall about in astonishment. **c** To 'hit the roof', to 'blow one's top', to flare up in anger.

plafonnard *n.m.* 'Bean', 'bonce', head.

plaga *à plaga (adv.exp.) Etre à plaga*: **a** To feel 'knackered', 'buggered', to be exhausted. *Toutes ses noubas l'ont mis à plaga*: No wonder he's jiggered with all this boozing and gallivanting. **b** To be 'skint', 'broke', to find oneself penniless. *Avec tous ces aminches, il s'est vite retrouvé à plaga*: With all those friends and hangers-on, he soon found himself in Queer Street.

plaie *n.f.* (of person): 'Plague', 'pest', nuisance.

plaindre *v.pronom. Se plaindre que la mariée est trop belle*: To still find something to complain about when Lady Luck is on one's side.

plaisir *n.m. Souhaiter à quelqu'un bien du plaisir (iron.)*: To wish someone 'the best of British', to wish someone the best of luck (where none can really be expected).

plan *n.m.* 1 *(Il n') y a pas plan!* Not bloody likely! – Nothing doing! – Certainly not! 2 *En plan (adv.exp.)*: **a** (of person): In the lurch. *Il m'a laissé en plan*: He left me to fend for myself. *Je me suis retrouvé en plan*: I found myself out in the cold. **b** (of plan, project): 'Shelved', unfinished. *Bref, ses grandes idées sont restées en plan!* To put it in a nutshell, his great dreams are there gathering dust!

planche *n.f.* 1 Flat-chested woman (also: *planche à pain* or *planche à repasser*). 2 *(sch.)*: Mock exam (originally an oral test, because one had to go up to the blackboard). 3 *(pl.)*: 'The boards', the stage. *Monter sur les planches*: To take up a career in acting. *Brûler les planches*: To enjoy a tremendous success on the stage. 4 *Faire la planche*: **a** To 'lie low', to try and remain undetected. **b** *(fig.)*: To 'keep a low profile', to avoid getting involved in anything.

5 *Avoir du pain sur la planche*: To have a lot of work on one's plate. **6** *S'habiller de quatre planches*: To 'get a wooden overcoat', to 'snuff it', to die.

plancher *n.m.* **1** *Débarrasser le plancher*: To 'clear off', to go away. *Débarrasse-moi le plancher!* Hop it! – Buzz off! **2** *Aller au plancher* (Boxing): To hit the canvas, to go down. *Il est allé trois fois au plancher avant de se faire compter*: He went down three times before he was counted out. **3** *Le plancher des vaches* (*joc.*): Terra firma. *Ne lui parlez pas d'avion, il n'a jamais quitté le plancher des vaches!* He'd rather walk, he's too frightened of flying!

plancher *v.intrans.* **1** (*sch.*): To have a mock exam (written or oral). **2** (*sch.*): To 'cram', to swot for an examination. **3** *Plancher pour quelqu'un*: To 'carry the can', to take the blame for someone (against one's will).

planer *v.intrans.* **1** To be 'miles away', to be lost in one's daydreams. **2** To be out of touch with reality. *Le pauvre, il plane toujours à cinq mille mètres!* I don't think he's got the faintest (idea) what's going on! **3** (Drugs): To be 'high', to be in a state of dazed beatitude after a 'fix'.

planque *n.f.* **1** 'Stash', hiding-place where a precious object is stored. **2** 'Nest-egg', savings. *Il a une gentille petite planque pour ses vieux jours*: When he pulls out, he'll be able to live on what he's got stashed away. **3** Hide-out, hiding-place. **4** Place, spot (one that holds pleasant memories). **5** 'Cushy number', 'plum job', undemanding employment. *Il est jardinier chez des vieux, c'est la planque des planques!* The job he's got as gardener for some old toffs must be the plummest thing going! **6** *Etre en planque* (*pol.*): To be on a 'stake-out', to keep a place under surveillance after a tip-off.

planqué *n.m.* **1** Character who has a 'cushy number', person who through favouritism has landed an easy job. **2** 'Skiver', 'shirker', person who dodges work successfully.

planquer *v.trans.* To hide, to secrete someone or something away.

planquer *v.trans.reflex.* **1** To hide, to find a hiding-place. **2** (*fig.*): To 'lie low', to 'keep a low profile', to avoid being buttonholed for an unpleasant task. **3** To 'shoehorn' oneself into a cushy job.

planquouse *n.f.* **1** (of object): 'Stash', hiding-place. **2** Hide-out, hiding-place. **3** 'Cushy job', 'plum' occupation, employment where little effort is required.

planter *v.trans.* **1** To stab, to knife. (The verb is nearly always found in the passive, as in *Il s'est fait planter à la sortie du bal*: He got chivved coming out of a dance-hall.) **2** *En planter un*:

To get a girl 'in the club', to make a woman pregnant. *Elle s'est fait planter un polichinelle signé anonyme*: The poor girl's preggers and doesn't even know who to blame! **3** *Planter un drapeau*: To leave without paying (in café, restaurant).

planter *v.trans.reflex.* **1** (of motorist): To come off the road and crash into the scenery. **2** (of light aircraft): To crash-land.

plaque *n.f.* *Mettre à côté de la plaque*: To have missed the point of an argument or discussion, and make a fool of oneself by giving an irrelevant answer.

plaquer *v.trans.* To 'ditch', to 'walk out on', to leave. *Il a plaqué sa femme pour une petite jeunesse de rien du tout*: He left his missus and went off with some chick he'd picked up. *Avoir envie de tout plaquer*: To feel like 'chucking everything in', to feel like opting out. *En ce moment, j'ai envie de tout plaquer!* Just now I feel like saying 'Stop the world, I want to get off!'

plastronner *v.intrans.* To 'crow', to 'strut about', to show off.

plat *n.m.* **1** *Faire du plat*: **a** (in amorous relationship): To 'smooch up to', to sweet-talk. **b** To 'butter-up', to 'soft-soap', to flatter. *Les clients, il faut toujours qu'il leur fasse du plat*: When he's there, the customers all get a fair bit of flannel. **2** *En faire tout un plat* (of event, happening): To make a mountain out of a molehill. (There are two possible interpretations where this expression is concerned, according to whether too much is made of a good or bad thing.) *Ne pas faire un plat de quelque chose*: To play something down. **3** *Envoyer du plat à quelqu'un*: To 'tip someone the wink', to signal discreetly to an accomplice to be on his guard. **4** *Etre à plat*: To be 'knackered', 'buggered', to be exhausted. *V'là quinze jours que je me sens à plat*: I've been feeling under the weather these last two weeks. *Toute cette histoire m'a vraiment mis à plat!* This whole business has taken it out of me! **5** *Mettre à plat*: To 'stash away', to save and hoard money. **6** *Prendre un plat* (Diving): To come a belly-flopper. **7** *Repiquer au plat*: **a** (*lit*): To come back for 'seconds', to have another helping of food. **b** (*fig.*): To come back for more. *Du jour qu'il a mis les pieds au P.M.U. il n'a cessé de repiquer au plat*: Since the day he set foot in the bookie's, it's become a real habit with him. **8** *Il en fait un de ces plats!* (of weather): Phew! What a scorcher! **9** *Plat de nouilles*: 'Drip', 'wet nurk', spineless individual.

platée *n.f.* (*joc.*): 'Troughful', plate heaped full with food (not necessarily of the most appetizing variety). *File-lui sa platée qu'il nous foute la* *paix!* For heaven's sake give him his grub, perhaps he'll leave us in peace!

plates-bandes *n.f.pl. Marcher sur* (also: *piétiner*) *les plates-bandes de quelqu'un:* To poach on someone's preserves (literally to encroach on someone's territory).

platine *n.f. Quelle platine!* What a gasbag! (The advent of stereograms and music centres has all but killed the 'vaccinated with a gramophone needle' image and thus the platinum stylus has entered colloquial speech.)

plâtre *n.m.* 'Brass', 'loot', money. *Etre au plâtre:* To be 'loaded', to be stinking rich.

plat-ventre *n.m.* (Diving): 'Belly-scorcher', belly-flop.

plein *n.m. Faire le plein:* To take a tankful, to fill a petrol tank with fuel.

plein *adj.* **1** 'Pissed to the eyeballs', 'sozzled', rolling drunk. **2** *Plein aux as:* 'Rolling in it', stinking rich. **3** *En avoir plein le dos* (also: *les bottes* or *le cul*): To be sick and tired of someone or something.

plein *adv.* **1** *Plein de:* 'Oodles', plenty of. *Avoir plein de fric:* To be 'loaded', to have lots of money. **2** *A plein tube:* **a** As loud as hell. *Il branche toujours sa chaîne hi-fi à plein tube:* When he plays his music centre, you have to put earplugs in! **b** 'Full-pelt', at top speed. *A plein tube qu'on a traversé la ville!* We certainly burnt rubber crossing the town!

pleurer *v.intrans.* **1** To moan and complain. **2** *Ne pleurer que d'un œil:* To shed 'crocodile tears'.

pleurs *n.m.pl. Le bureau des pleurs:* 'Moan-counter', complaints department.

pli *n.m.* **1** *Mettre quelqu'un au pli:* To make someone 'toe the line' very forcefully. **2** *Ça ne fait pas un pli!* It's all cut-and-dried! – It's a sure thing! *Ça ne fait pas un pli, il va se retrouver à la porte!* It's a safe bet he'll get the sack in the near future!

plomb *n.m. Avoir du plomb dans l'aile* (of person or enterprise): To be faltering, to be on a downward spiral. *Sa bonne petite affaire d'il y a dix ans a du plomb dans l'aile:* That profitable little money-spinner he set up ten years ago has just about had it now.

plombard *n.m.* Plumber.

plombe *n.f.* **1** Hour (time of day). *Je te verrai à trois plombes pile!* I'll see you at three o'clock sharp! **2** Hour (time spent). *Ça fait plus de deux plombes que je fais le pied de grue à t'attendre!* I'd say it's two hours I've been stood here waiting for you!

plombé *adj.* Infected with V.D.

plomber *v.trans.* **1** To 'wing', to wound by gunshot. **2** To gun down, to kill. **3** To infect with V.D.

plomber *v.intrans. Plomber du bec* (also: *du goulot*): To have foul breath, to suffer from halitosis.

plomber *v.trans.reflex.* (Underworld slang): To exchange a flurry of shots.

plonge *n.f.* Washing-up. *Faire la plonge:* To do the dishes.

plongeon *n.m. Faire le plongeon:* To 'lose a packet' at gambling, the Stock Exchange, etc. and go under.

plonger *v.intrans.* **1** To 'take pot-luck' in making a decision (literally to take the plunge). **2** To enter a venture, legal or otherwise, knowing full well the risks involved. **3** To 'go down', to get 'nicked', to be incarcerated.

plongeur *n.m.* 'Washer-upper', one who washes dishes in a restaurant.

plouc *n.m. (pej.):* **1** 'Bonehead', 'nincompoop', simpleton. **2** 'Hayseed', 'yokel', country bumpkin.

ploum *n.m. (abbr. Auverploum):* Native of the Auvergne.

plucher *v.trans. (corr. éplucher):* To peel vegetables.

pluches *n.f.pl.* **1** (Vegetable) peelings. **2** *La corvée de pluches:* 'Spud-bashing', the interminable 'fatigue' of peeling potatoes.

pluie *n.f. Ne pas être tombé de la dernière pluie:* To have one's wits about one. *Je ne suis pas tombé de la dernière pluie, tu sais!* I wasn't born yesterday!

plumard *n.m. Le plumard:* 'The hay', 'the sack', (one's) bed. *Aller au plumard:* To turn in.

plumarder *v.trans.reflex.* To 'hit the sack', to get between the sheets, to go to bed.

plume *n.m. Le plume:* 'The hay', 'the sack', (one's) bed. *Pour le tirer du plume le matin, quelle histoire!* Getting him off to work in the morning is some task!

plume *n.f.* **1** 'Jemmy', crowbar. **2** *(pl.):* Hair. *Perdre ses plumes:* To be going bald. **3** *Voler dans les plumes de quelqu'un:* **a** To 'go for', to assault someone. **b** *(fig.):* To fly at someone, to remonstrate furiously. **4** *Passer à la plume:* To get a 'bashing', a 'belting', to get beaten up. **5** *Y laisser des plumes:* **a** (of physical altercation): To come out bruised and battered. **b** (of row, argument): To get lambasted, to come out of it something of a loser. **c** (of financial venture): To 'lose a packet', to lose heavily.

Plumeau Proper name. *Envoyer quelqu'un chez Plumeau:* To tell someone to 'get knotted', to 'go to blazes', to tell someone off in no uncertain manner (also: *envoyer quelqu'un se faire voir chez Plumeau*).

plumer *v.trans.* To 'fleece', to 'rip off', to make outrageous profits from someone. *Il s'est fait plumer au pok':* He got taken to the cleaners in a little game of poker. *Les pigeons sont là pour être plumés!* Suckers are here to be taken!

plumet *n.m.* *Avoir* (also: *tenir*) *son plumet*: To have had 'one over the eight', to be tipsy, to be slightly drunk.

P.L.V. *(abbr. pour-la-vie)*: For ever-and-ever. (Like 'SWALK': Sealed-with-a-loving-kiss, this lowbrow amorous pledge is very much an open secret and could be found up to the 60s carved on tree-trunks with a heart and the initials of the plighted. A few ill-advised males might still sport it tattooed on their forearms or hairy chests!)

P.M.U. *(abbr. Pari Mutuel Urbain)*: The Tote. (In a country where private bookmakers have been outlawed, the state-run *Pari Mutuel Urbain* has a monopoly where on- and off-course betting is concerned. Because there are no betting shops as such, the *P.M.U.* does business in selected *cafés* but only in the morning prior to race-meetings.)

pneu *n.m.* *(abbr. pneumatique)*: **1** Tyre. **2** Express letter dispatched through a network of air-ducts in bullet-shaped containers propelled by compressed air. This ingenious and speedy method of delivering notes has all but disappeared, as has the expression *petit bleu* reflecting the colour of the lightweight envelopes.

pochard *n.m.* 'Soak', habitual heavy drinker.

pochard *adj.* 'Boozy', drunk.

pocharder *v.pronom.* To 'get pickled', 'sozzled', to get drunk.

poche *n.m.* *(abbr. livre de poche)*: Paperback. *Attends que ça sorte en poche, c'est moins cher!* I wouldn't buy it in hardback, wait for the cheap reprint! (Strictly speaking, *Livre de Poche* is a registered tradename but has come to mean any paperback, as has *poche*.)

poche *n.f.* **1** *Faire les poches à quelqu'un*: To go through someone's pockets. **2** *En être de sa poche*: To be 'out of pocket', to have had to dip into one's own resources to finance a venture. **3** *Y avoir été de sa poche*: To have had to 'stump up', to have been landed with a bill to pay. **4** *Avoir quelqu'un dans sa poche*: To be sure of someone's total obedience. **5** *Mettre quelqu'un dans sa poche*: To 'beat someone into a cocked hat', to 'wipe the floor with someone', to be more than a match for someone. **6** *C'est dans la poche!* It's in the bag! – It's a dead-cert! –It's a sure thing! **7** *Connaître quelque chose comme le fond de sa poche*: To know something like the back of one's hand. **8** *Mets ça dans ta poche et ton mouchoir par-dessus! (iron.)*: Put that in your pipe and smoke it! – That's the way things are (whether you like it or not!).

poché *adj.* *Œil poché*: 'Shiner', black eye.

poche-revolver *n.f.* Hip-pocket (although it's the most uncomfortable place to carry a gun!).

pochetée *n.f.* 'Burk', 'twit', imbecile.

pochette-surprise *n.f.* *Avoir eu son permis de conduire dans une pochette-surprise (iron.)*: To be a lousy driver. (The *pochette-surprise* is to the French what the Christmas cracker is to the British, its contents a constant source of bewilderment as to how anyone can be thrilled with what falls out!)

poème *n.m.* *C'est un poème!* (of food, drink): It's too good for words! (Statements making use of the above expression, when referring to a person, can sometimes be tinged with irony and come to mean the exact opposite. *Alors, celui-là mon vieux, c'est tout un poème!* You've no idea what a loony he is!)

pogne *n.f.* **1** 'Mitt', 'paw', hand. (Expressions such as *avoir à sa pogne*, *passer la pogne* and others not lexicalized under this heading, can be found under *main*.) **2** *Prendre la pogne*: To take the initiative. *Il a bien fallu que je prenne la pogne, on peut pas compter sur des lavettes comme vous!* I just had to make a move, seeing you're all such ditherers! **3** *Homme à pogne*: **a** Muscular figure, strong male. **b** Masterful and strong-willed man. **4** *Se faire une pogne*: **a** To 'wank', to masturbate. **b** To crow over someone's downfall.

pogner *v.trans.reflex.* To 'wank', to 'pull one's wire', to masturbate.

pognon *n.m.* 'Bread', 'dough', money.

poids *n.m.* **1** *Prendre du poids*: To be getting on in years. (With this meaning the word refers to age in general and is never used in connection with any specific number of years. *Un faux-poids* in the language of pimps is an under-age prostitute.) **2** *Ne pas faire le poids*: To be lacking experience. (The expression *faire le poids* can sometimes mean: to have reached the age of legal majority.) **3** *Deux poids (et) deux mesures*: Double standards. *Pas moyen de discuter, avec lui il y a toujours deux poids deux mesures!* You'll never win an argument with him, he's always right in his book, even if it's not always the same one!

poids-mort *n.m.* 'Passenger', character who tags along in a project or enterprise and is more a burden than anything else to his partners.

poigne *n.f.* *A poigne (adj.exp.)*: Firm-minded, masterful. *Lui, au moins, c'est un homme à poigne!* Let's face it, he's not one to dilly-dally!

poignet *n.m.* **1** *Ne pas se fouler le poignet (joc. & iron.)*: Not to 'wear one's fingers to the bone', to take things easy, to treat work in an off-hand manner. **2** *La veuve Poignet (et ses cinq filles)*: 'Wanking', masturbation.

poil *n.m.* **1** *Un poil*: A teeny-weeny bit. *Il s'en est fallu d'un poil!* It was as near as damn it! – It was a close thing! **2** *Au poil*: Perfect, absolutely superb. *Le dîner qu'elle nous a servi était vraiment au poil*: There's only one word to describe the meal she served us – fantastic! (also: *au petit poil*). **3** *Au poil!* Great! – Smashing! – Fantastic! *Tu viens ce soir?* . . . *Au poil!* You coming tonight? . . . Great! **4** *Au quart de poil*: Exactly, to perfection. *Le moulin de ma bagnole est réglé au quart de poil*: The engine on my car is tuned spot-on. (This is not so much a case of splitting hairs as of getting details right to the breadth of a hair.) **5** *A poil*: 'In one's birthday suit', 'starkers', naked. *Se mettre à poil*: To strip off. **6** *Etre à poil et à plume*: To be 'AC/DC', to have bisexual tendencies. **7** *Avoir un poil dans la main*: To be consistently work-shy. **8** *Avoir du poil au cul*: To be 'gutsy', 'plucky', to be brave (also: *ne pas avoir froid aux yeux*). **9** *Tomber sur le poil de quelqu'un*: **a** *(fig.)*: To 'go for' someone, to lam into someone. **b** To 'land on' someone, to arrive at an inopportune moment. *Dès qu'on est seuls, il nous tombe sur le poil*: We can never enjoy a few minutes together, without him landing on our doorstep. **10** *Etre de bon/mauvais poil*: To be in a good/bad mood. *Le lundi il est toujours de mauvais poil!* After the weekend, he's as grumpy as hell! **11** *Reprendre du poil de la bête*: **a** (of patient): To 'pick up again', to get better. **b** To take heart after a setback. **12** *Poil au nez! – Poil au cul! – Poil au pied!*, etc. These expressions, in interjectory form, are usually uttered by hecklers. The aim of the would-be wit is to get the last syllable of any given sentence to rhyme with the last word of these interjections, giving something like: . . . *c'est ce que nous avons décidé! – Poil au nez!* or . . . *le temps qu'il nous faut. – Poil au dos!* The ultimate for receptive audiences and hecklers alike is to get an *'u'* ending when the inevitable *Poil au cul!* is greeted by roars and jibes.

poilant *adj.* 'Killing', screamingly funny, hilarious. *C'est un film poilant, tu devrais y aller!* You should go, that film'll have you in stitches!

poiler *v.pronom.* **1** To 'laugh oneself silly', to have a jolly good laugh. **2** To 'have a whale of a time', to enjoy oneself thoroughly.

poil-poil *adj.inv.* 'Super-duper', 'A-1', first-class. *C'est un restaurant tout ce qu'il y a de poil-poil*: It's a really smashing little eating-place! (also: *au poil*).

poil-poil *adv.* (also: *en douce poil-poil*): 'Softly-softly', on the Q.T., quietly and furtively. *A deux heures du mat' c'est poil-poil qu'on a dû monter l'escalier*: At 2 a.m. we had to tip-toe upstairs.

poilu *n.m.* French soldier of the Great War. (The heroism and gallantry of those manning the trenches will live on long after the last of these old soldiers has faded away; they are as immortal as Napoleon's *grognards*.)

poilu *adj.* 'Gutsy', 'plucky', brave.

point *n.m.* **1** Franc. (Successive devaluations and the introduction of the *nouveau franc* have robbed this word of any exact value. It is usually to be found in that grey area of language hobnobbing with the underworld.) **2** *Commencer à rendre des points*: To be getting on in years and past one's professional prime. (This expression could be seen as having a similar meaning to *rendre la monnaie*. See *monnaie*.) **3** *Point de chute*: 'Haunt', regularly-frequented place. *Quel est son point de chute?* Where am I likely to find him? **4** *Point noir*: Arse-hole, anus (also: *as de pique*).

point-de-côté *n.m.* **1** 'Pain-in-the-neck', 'awkward cove', difficult person. **2** Persistent creditor.

pointe *n.f.* **1** 'Chiv', blade, knife. **2** *Etre (chaud) de la pointe*: To be a randy so-and-so, to have more than a penchant for women. **3** *Avoir sa pointe*: To have had 'one over the eight', to be 'tipsy', to be slightly drunk. **4** *Pousser une pointe*: **a** (of motor vehicle): To 'burn rubber', to spurt ahead. **b** To move along niftily (either to escape or to join someone). **5** *Heure de pointe*: Peak-time (when trading, traffic, etc. is at its busiest).

pointé *past part.* *Rester pointé*: To be kept in police custody.

pointer *v.trans.* To 'poke', to fuck, to have coition with.

pointer *v.pronom.* To 'turn up', to arrive. *Si on veut prendre le dur de huit heures, va falloir que je me pointe chez toi à sept heures*: If we want to catch the rapid o'clock train, I'll have to be at your place at seven on the dot! *Oublier de se pointer à la mairie (joc.)*: To leave one's prospective marriage partner in the lurch.

poire *n.f.* **1** 'Bean', 'bonce', head. *Se payer la poire de quelqu'un*: To 'have someone on', to 'take the mickey out of someone', to make a fool of someone (also: *se payer la tête de quelqu'un*). **2** 'Mush', 'dial', face. *Avoir une sale poire*: **a** To be afflicted with an ugly face. **b** To look sinister and awe-inspiring. *Faire sa poire (anglaise)*: To 'put on airs and graces', to have an affected mien. **3** 'Mug', simpleton. *On ne fait pas mieux comme poire!* You'd have to go a long way to find someone as thick as him! **4** 'Gull', 'sucker', dupe. *Dans toutes vos histoires c'est toujours moi la poire!* I've had it up to here with all your ideas, it's always muggins what cops it! **5** *Couper la poire en deux* (in argument concerning finance): To split the difference and compromise. **6** *Ma poire*: Me, myself. *Ta poire*: You, yourself, etc.

poireau *n.m.* **1** 'Mug', 'sucker', gullible fool. **2** 'Prick', 'cock', penis. *Souffler dans le poireau*: To practise fellatio. **3** *Le poireau (joc.)*: The *Mérite Agricole*, decoration given by the French

Government to those who have distinguished themselves in the field of agriculture. **4** *Faire le poireau*: To 'cool one's heels', to be kept waiting.

poireauter *v.intrans.* To 'kick one's heels', to be kept hanging about, to waste time waiting.

poirer *v.trans.* To 'collar', to grab hold of, to catch. *Se faire poirer*: To get 'nabbed', to get collared by Authority.

poiscaille *n.m.* Fish, any fish.

poison *n.m. Un poison* (of person): A 'pest', a nuisance of a character.

poissant *adj.* **1** 'Aggravating', irksome. *Ah qu'il est poissant celui-là, j'aimerais bien m'en débarrasser!* What a pain (he is), I wish I could get rid of him! **2** 'Jinxy', directly associated with bad luck.

poissard *n.m.* **1** Jinxed person, one who is plagued by misfortune. **2** 'Jinx', one whose very presence seems to bring on bad luck.

poissard *adj.* 'Jinxy', directly associated with bad luck.

poisse *n.m.* Pimp, procurer. (As with *maquereau*, there is a semantic link between fish and procuring, *poisse* being an abbreviated corruption of *poisson*; see that word.)

poisse *n.f.* **1** 'Jinx', bad luck. *Avoir la poisse*: To be plagued by misfortune. *Etre dans la poisse*: To be in the soup. *Porter la poisse*: To jinx, to blight, to bring bad luck. **2** 'Limpet', tenacious bore.

poisser *v.trans.* **1** *Se faire poisser*: To get 'nabbed', 'collared', to be arrested. **2** *Poisses-en un autre!* Pull the other one, I'm not falling for that! (literally: 'Try and find a more gullible mug!').

poisson *n.m.* **1** Pimp, procurer. (As G. Sandry and M. Carrère point out in their DICTIONNAIRE DE L'ARGOT MODERNE, many slang words for pimp are names of fish species, to wit, *barbeau, barbillon, brochet, hareng, merlan, maquereau*, etc.) **2** *Faire des yeux de poisson frit*: To raise one's gaze skywards and show the whites of one's eyes to express cynical contempt, boredom, etc. (also: *faire des yeux de merlan frit*). **3** *Engueuler (quelqu'un) comme du poisson pourri*: To 'bawl someone out', to 'give someone a dressing-down', to tell someone off. **4** *Changer son poisson d'eau*: To 'pee', to 'wee', to urinate (also: *changer l'eau du canari*). **5** *Noyer le poisson*: To cloud and confuse the issue with an avalanche of irrelevant facts. **6** *Faire une queue de poisson* (of vehicle): To cut in (in front of another, after having overtaken). **7** *Finir en queue de poisson* (of play, musical piece, story): To come to an abrupt and unexpected end.

poitrine *n.f. Avoir une poitrine de vélo* (*joc. & iron.*): To have a 'bird-cage' chest, to be anything but musclebound.

poitringle *adj.* Consumptive, suffering from T.B. (also: *tubard*).

poivrade *n.f. Tenir une poivrade*: To be 'pissed to the eyeballs', 'sozzled', to be drunk. *Marcher à la poivrade*: To be a dipso, to be totally dependent on alcohol.

poivre *n.m.* **1** 'Drunk', inebriated person. **2** *Chier du poivre*: To 'run like the clappers', to race away.

poivré *adj.* **1** (of bill, invoice): Unexpectedly high. *J'ai reçu une douloureuse tout ce qu'il y a de poivrée!* The bill I got was a right stinger! **2** Infected with V.D.

poivrer *v.trans.* To infect with V.D.

poivrer *v.trans.reflex.* (also: *se poivrer la gueule*): To 'get pissed', to get drunk.

poivrier *n.m. Vol au poivrier* (*pol.*): 'Mugging' of drunks, robbing of persons under the influence of alcohol.

poivrot *n.m.* 'Soak', drunkard.

Polak *n.m.* (also: *Polack*): Pole, native of Poland.

polak *adj.* (also: *polack*): Polish, from Poland.

polar *n.m.* 'Whodunnit', detective novel usually in paperback form.

polar *adj.* Over-studious, perpetually poring over books.

polard *n.m.* 'Prick', 'cock', penis.

police *n.f.* **1** *Police secours*: The emergency services of the police force available to the public through the French equivalent of a 999 call. **2** *Faire ses polices* (of prostitute): To undergo regular official medical checks.

polichinelle *n.m.* **1** *Un secret de polichinelle*: An 'open secret', the kind that seems to confirm the French saying *'Les secrets les mieux gardés sont ceux que chacun devine'*. **2** *Mener une vie de polichinelle*: To lead a fast, loose and disorganized life. **3** *Avoir un polichinelle dans le tiroir*: To 'have a bun in the oven', to be 'preggers', to be pregnant. **4** *(Faire) claquer le polichinelle*: To have a miscarriage (usually brought about by back-street abortive methods).

polio *n.m.* Polio victim, person who contracted poliomyelitis.

polir *v.trans. Se polir le chinois* (*joc.*): To 'beat the dummy', to 'wank', to masturbate.

politesse *n.f. Faire une politesse*: To engage in oral sex.

politicard *n.m.* (*pej.*): Small-time would-be politician.

polka *n.f.* (*pej.*): **1** 'Biddy', 'bit-of-skirt', woman. **2** (Pimps' slang): Prostitute.

polker *v.intrans.* (Usually of person): To 'pong', to smell (often because of advanced B.O.).

polochon *n.m.* Bolster, long narrow pillow or cushion. *Une partie de polochon*: **a** A pillow-fight. **b** (*fig.*): A meaningless skirmish with no serious consequences. **c** A 'bit of nookie', a short (sex) session in bed.

polope *interj.* (also: *pollope*): **1** Watch out! – Look out! – Careful! **2** No way! – Nothing doing! – Certainly not!

pomaquer *v.trans. & intrans.* **1** To lose at gambling. **2** To mislay, to lose something.

pommade *n.f.* **1** 'Blarney', flattering talk. *Passer la pommade à quelqu'un*: To 'soft-soap' someone. **2** *(fig.)*: 'Tight corner', 'pickle', trouble. *Etre dans la pommade*: To be up a gum-tree. **3** *Quelle pommade!* What a bore!

pommader *v.trans.* To 'soft-soap', to 'flannel', to flatter (also: *passer la pommade*).

pommadin *n.m.* *(Slightly pej.)*: 'Lock-lopper', hairdresser (from the days when barbers used to apply liberal doses of haircream to their clients).

pomme *n.f.* **1** 'Bean', 'bonce', head. **2** 'Mush', 'mug', face (perhaps because of the rosiness of round cheeks). *Sucer la pomme à quelqu'un*: To give someone 'a smacker' on the cheek, to kiss. *Ne fais pas cette pomme!* Stop pulling that sour face! **3** *Pomme de terre*: **a** 'Spud', 'potato', large hole in sock. **b** 'Tall story'. *Monter une pomme de terre*: To spin one hell of a yarn. **4** 'Mug', fool, simpleton. *Et moi, bonne pomme, je lui ai prêté des sous!* And me being the sucker I am, I went and lent him some money! *Une pomme à l'eau*: An incredibly gullible person. **5** *Etre haut comme trois pommes*: To be 'knee-high to a grasshopper', to be very small. **6** *Tomber dans les pommes*: To 'keel over', to 'pass out', to faint. **7** *Aux pommes*: 'A-1', first-class. *C'est aux pommes!* It's super-duper! **8** *Recevoir des pommes cuites* (of actor): To 'get the bird', to be given a hostile reception (literally to be pelted with projectiles that considerate members of the audience have taken the precaution to cook). **9** *Ma pomme*: Me, myself. *Ta pomme*: You, yourself. *Sa pomme*: Him, himself. (*Ma pomme* was the name of a song made famous by Maurice Chevalier, also the title of a film featuring that artist. The song did a lot to promote the usage of this term.) **10** *Des pommes!* Not bloody likely! – Nothing doing! – Certainly not! *Faire quelque chose pour des pommes*: To do something for bugger-all.

pomme *adj.inv.* 'Green', simple, inexperienced.

pommé *adj.* 'Super-duper', fantastic.

pompe *n.f.* **1** 'Hoof', foot. *Je l'ai viré à coups de pompe au cul*: I booted him out of the room. **2** *(pl.)*: 'Dogs', 'boats', shoes (not necessarily outsize ones). **3** *(pl.)*: 'Gambs', 'pins', legs. *Filer à toutes pompes*: To 'skedaddle', to 'scram', to run off at full-speed. **4** *Marcher à côté de ses pompes*: To be 'down on one's uppers', 'broke', to be penniless. **5** *Avoir un coup de pompe*: To feel 'knackered', 'jiggered',

to be exhausted. **6** *Balancer* (also: *filer*) *un coup de pompe à quelqu'un*: To 'touch someone for a sub', to corner someone for a loan. **7** *Deuxième pompe (mil.)*: Private, ordinary soldier.

pompé *adj.* 'Knackered', 'buggered', exhausted.

pompelard *n.m.* **1** Fireman. **2** *Faire un pompelard*: To gamaroosh, to practise fellatio.

pomper *v.trans.* **1** To 'booze', to drink heavily. *Pour son déjeuner, qu'est-ce qu'il pompe comme rouge!* You should see the amount of plonk he gets through at lunch! **2** To 'tap someone for money', to ask for a loan. *Il est encore venu me pomper de dix sacs*: He borrowed another ten quid off me. **3** *Il me pompe (l'air), celui-là!* He's a real pain in the neck! – He's a nuisance!

pomper *v.intrans. (sch.)*: To cheat at an exam by means of secreted notes or by copying from a fellow student's paper. *J'ai toujours pompé en math!* I've never sat a maths paper without outside help! (Although basically intransitive, the verb can sometimes be found in a transitive context as in *Il a tout pompé*: He copied the lot.)

pompette *adj.* 'Squiffy', 'tipsy', slightly drunk.

pompeuses *n.f.pl.* 'Smackers', lips.

pompier *n.m.* **1** *Fumer comme un pompier* (of person): To smoke like a chimney. **2** *Faire un pompier*: To practise fellatio.

pompier *adj.* **1** 'Square' and rather pretentious. **2** In painting, the *style pompier*, famous at the turn of the century, is one in which the artist goes slightly overboard where sentimentality towards the *genre* subject is concerned.

pomplard *n.m.* **1** Fireman. **2** *Faire un pomplard*: To gamaroosh, to practise fellatio.

pompon *n.m.* **1** *Avoir le pompon*: To 'take the biscuit', to 'be the tops', to be the very best. *A lui le pompon!* He's the best! (without a shadow of a doubt). *Ça c'est le pompon!* **a** It's the bee's knees! – It's the very best! **b** That's the last straw! – That's the limit! **2** *Avoir touché le pompon*: To be 'favoured by Lady Luck'. (French sailors in the armed forces have a red pompon on top of their caps. It is an accepted tradition that a girl will enjoy some good luck if she can touch the pompon; obviously young recruits try to make the most of this.) **3** *Avoir son pompon*: To be 'squiffy', 'tipsy', to be slightly drunk.

pomponnette *n.f. Boire à la pomponnette*: **a** To swallow some wine, beer, etc. in big gulps. **b** To drink straight from the bottle.

ponction *n.f. Faire une ponction (iron.)*: To transfer funds from one account to another (this withdrawal can sometimes be seen as an illegal syphoning-off).

pondeuse *n.f. Une bonne pondeuse*: A 'child-toboggan', a woman with a large brood. (This uncomplimentary and condescending label is not necessarily derogatory.)

pondre *v.trans.* **1** To 'drop the bundle', to give birth. **2** To come up with an idea, an invention, an artistic creation. *Vise un peu ce qu'il nous a pondu!* Just have a look at his latest!

ponette *n.f.* Pimp's moll. (Auguste Le Breton in his *L'ARGOT CHEZ LES VRAIS DE VRAI* claims that the word derives from *poney*, the French spelling of pony, and as with many words lexicalized in his dictionary, he names the inventor of this now little-used neologism.)

pont *n.m.* **1** *Faire le pont*: To enjoy an extra day's holiday between a weekend and a Bank Holiday. (Unlike most British Bank Holidays, French *jours fériés* sometimes fall on Tuesdays or Thursdays, and it makes good holiday sense to give staff the Monday or Friday off to bridge an unworkable day.) **2** *Pont arrière (joc.)*: 'Bum', 'bottom', behind.

ponte *n.m.* **1** V.I.P., important person. **2** (Drugs): 'Mr. Big', trafficking tycoon. **3** 'Punter', gambler.

pontife *n.m.* 'Bigwig', character who rightly or wrongly rather fancies himself.

pontifier *v.intrans.* To 'waffle' portentously, to pontificate.

Pont-Neuf *Proper name. Se porter comme le Pont-Neuf*: To be as fit as a fiddle. (This expression carries a certain amount of gentle irony and humour as the *Pont-Neuf*, started in 1588, is the oldest bridge in Paris.)

Popaul *n.m.* 'John Thomas', 'prick', penis.

Popof *n.m. Les Popofs*: 'The Ruskies', the Russians.

popote *n.f.* **1** *(mil.)*: 'Mess', mess-room. *Faire la tournée des popotes* (of general or high-ranking officer): To go on an inspection tour of barracks. (An important stop is always the soldiers' canteen where recruits are asked point-blank the traditional *'Alors, soldat, la soupe est bonne?'*) **2** Cooking. *On a dû faire notre popote*: We had to do our own grub. *Faire popote ensemble*: To share the kitchen chores.

popote *adj.* (of person): 'Stay-at-home', over-homely. *Il s'est trouvé une nana très popote*: His latest bird is the proud-little-housewife kind!

popotin *n.m.* **1** 'Botty', 'bum', behind. *Trémousser du popotin*: To 'shake it all about', to dance. **2** *Se magner le popotin*: To 'get one's skates on', to 'get a move on', to hurry up. **3** *Avoir du popotin*: To be 'jammy', to be lucky. *Quand on tape des cartons qu'est-ce qu'il a comme popotin!* When we play cards he seems to have the luck of the devil!

popu *adj.inv. (abbr. populaire)*: **1** Common, vulgar. *C'est un restaurant plutôt popu*: It's more an eating-house than a real restaurant. **2** *Le Front popu*: The left-wing alliance which united French Communists and Socialists in the mid-thirties.

populo *n.m.* **1** Crowds, people 'en masse'. *Vers six heures, qu'est-ce qu'il y a comme populo dans le métro!* At six o'clock in the Underground, you can't move for people! **2** *Le populo*: 'The great unwashed', the plebs. *Les fêtes foraines, ça plaît aux gosses et au populo*: Fun-fairs appeal to kids and the common herd.

popus *n.m.pl. Les popus (abbr. les places populaires)*: The cheaper seats in a place of entertainment (e.g. 'the gods' in a theatre or music-hall).

poquer *v.intrans.* To 'pong', to stink, to smell foul.

porcif *n.f. (corr. portion)*: 'Helping', portion (of food).

porno *n.m. Le porno*: Pornographic material (in book or film form). *Il ne lit que des pornos*: All he ever reads is dirty books.

porno *adj.inv. Des films porno*: Blue movies. *Des photos porno*: 'Dirty postcards', pornographic pictures.

porte-biffetons *n.m.* Wallet.

porte-coton *n.m. (joc.)*: Deputy, assistant of little standing given menial tasks.

porte-flingue *n.m.* 'Heavy', bodyguard (usually in the underworld).

porte-guigne *n.m.* 'Jonah', 'jinx', character who brings bad luck.

porté *adj.* **1** *C'est mal porté*: It's bad style – It's not the thing to do. *C'est bien porté*: It's the 'in' thing. **2** *Etre porté sur la bagatelle* (also: *sur le truc*): To be 'randy', to be highly-sexed.

porter *v.trans. En porter* (also: *porter des cornes*): To be a cuckold, to have an unfaithful wife.

porter *v.intrans.* **1** *Porter sur les nerfs à quelqu'un*: To 'get on someone's wick', to 'aggravate', to be irritating to someone. **2** *Porter à droite, à gauche*: To 'dress' on the right, on the left. (*Porter à gauche* can also have the meaning: To be a randy so-and-so. Why the way in which a man wears his trousers should have a bearing on his sexuality is a mystery.)

porter *v.pronom. Un/une . . . qui se porte bien*: A rare old . . . *Recevoir un savon qui se porte bien*: To get a telling-off one won't forget in a hurry.

porte-viande *n.m.* 'Meat-wagon', trolley used in hospitals to ferry patients.

Portigue *n.m.* Portuguese, native of Portugal (also: *Porto*).

portigue *adj.* Portuguese, from Portugal.

portillon *n.m. (joc.)*: 'Gob', 'trap', mouth. The expression *ça se bouscule au portillon* is said of a person who splutters in an effort to churn out words as fast as his/her mind ticks over.

portrait *n.m.* 'Mush', 'dial', face. *Etre le portrait (tout) craché de quelqu'un*: To be 'the spitting image' of someone, to bear an uncanny likeness to someone. *Rentrer dans le portrait à quelqu'un*: To give someone a 'knuckle-sandwich', to sock someone in the jaw. *Se faire abîmer le portrait*: To get one's face pushed in.

portugaises *n.f.pl.* 'Lug-holes', 'flappers', ears. *Avoir les portugaises ensablées*: To be a trifle deaf. (*Portugaises* are a variety of oysters and the shell of this mollusc closely resembles an ear.)

pose *n.f. Etre à la pose*: To put on airs and graces. *Faire (quelque chose) à la pose*: To do something with swank, in a show-off manner. *Même le plus simple machin, il le fait à la pose*: Life's one big stage for him, he acts out the simplest things.

poser *v.trans. & intrans.* 1 *Faire poser quelqu'un*: To 'keep someone hanging around', to keep someone waiting. 2 *Ça vous pose*: It gives you standing. *Ça les pose drôlement d'avoir une téloche!* Having a telly seems to put them a cut above the rest! 3 *Poser ça là*: To 'down tools', to stop working.

poser *v.pronom. Se poser là*: **a** To be 'really up to it', to be very capable. *Comme cuistot il se pose un peu là!* He's no mean cook, I can tell you! **b** *(iron.)*: To be totally useless, to be inept. (Only the full context involving this expression, or the intonation in a conversation, reveals whether it is 'straight' or ironic.)

poser *v.trans.reflex. Se poser chez quelqu'un*: To 'land' oneself on someone, to arrive at someone's home unexpectedly (and unwanted).

poseur *n.m.* 'Swank', show-off.

position *n.f. Etre dans une position intéressante*: To be in the (pudding) club, to be preggers, to be pregnant (also: *être dans une situation intéressante*).

posséder *v.trans. Posséder quelqu'un*: To 'lead someone up the garden path', to fool someone. *Et comment que je l'ai possédé!* He fell for my spiel hook, line and sinker!

possible *adj. Si c'est possible!* Well I never! – What a surprise!

poste *n.m.* 1 *(abbr. poste de radio)*: Wireless. *On en a causé dans le poste*: They mentioned it on the radio. 2 *Etre fidèle au poste*: To be 'still around', to be alive and kicking.

postère *n.m. (abbr. postérieur)*: 'Backside', 'bum', behind.

postiche *n.f.* 1 'Set-to', verbal assault. 2 (Fairground slang): Crowd-pulling patter.

Faire la postiche: To give a bit of the 'Roll up, roll up!' to the crowds.

postillon *n.m.* Droplet of saliva. *Envoyer des postillons*: To splutter in someone's face.

postillonner *v.intrans.* To 'splutter', to shower with droplets of saliva.

postillonneur *n.m.* 'Splutterer', one who showers others with droplets of saliva.

pot *n.m.* 1 'Arse', 'bum', behind. (Few expressions containing the word *pot* have literal meanings. Most, like *se manier le pot*: to 'put one's skates on', to hurry up and *en avoir plein le pot*: to be fed-up, are figurative derivations.) 2 Luck, good fortune. *Avoir un sacré pot*: To have the luck of the devil. *Un coup de pot*: A lucky break. *Manque de pot!* Hard cheese! – Hard luck! (There is a strange correlation between sodomy as in *se faire casser le pot* and good fortune, which would suggest as with *cocu* (see that word) that sexual favours and good luck are closely intertwined.) 3 Drink, alcoholic beverage. (Although some lexicographers describe the drink as being a 'short', the very nature of the straight meaning of the word suggests it is a long drink, i.e. wine or beer. *Prendre un pot avec quelqu'un*: To have a jar with someone.) 4 (Gambling slang): 'Pot', kitty, pool of money staked at cards, etc. 5 *Faire son pot*: To 'make one's pile', to amass a tidy sum of money. 6 *Payer les pots cassés*: To 'carry the can', to pay the consequences (often literally, on the financial plane). 7 *Pot de colle*: 'Limpet-bore', tenacious button-holer (also: *crampon*). 8 *Pot de yaourt (joc.)*: Bubble-car. (In the 50s, the most popular bubble-car in France was manufactured by Isetta. These vehicles with their large glass area and striking white colour quickly earned this nickname.) 9 *Etre sourd comme un pot*: To be as deaf as a post. 10 *Tourner autour du pot*: To 'beat about the bush', to tackle a problem or a situation in a dilly-dally manner. 11 *Etre bête comme un pot*: To be 'as thick as two short planks', to be as dumb as they come. 12 *Ne pas bousculer le pot de fleurs*: To 'keep things on an even keel', to 'avoid upsetting the apple-cart', to refrain from causing trouble. 13 *Ne t'occupe pas du pot!* Leave it to me! – Let me worry about it! 14 *Pot aux roses*: Sensitive secret. *Découvrir le pot aux roses*: To stumble on a bit of scandal. (Because of a possible hiatus, the 't' in *pot* is pronounced as a liaison in colloquial contexts.)

potable *adj. (joc.)*: 1 (of alcoholic beverage): 'Not too bad', drinkable, quite palatable really. 2 *(fig.)*: Not so bad after all, alright really.

potache *n.m. (sch.)*: Pupil of a *lycée* or other secondary education establishment.

potage *n.m.* **1** *Servir le potage à la seringue (joc. & iron.)*: To act in a miserly way. (The imagery of the expression is illustrated in the film *Porte des Lilas* featuring Georges Brassens; in that film the proprietor of a very low-class *bistrot* is seen serving *vin rouge* with a syringe and when a customer fails to pay, the beverage is sucked back into the dispensing instrument.) **2** *Etre dans le potage*: **a** To be 'in the soup', 'in a fix', to be in trouble. **b** To be 'out cold', to be unconscious. **3** *Tomber dans le potage*: **a** To fall into the water (a river, the sea, a lake). **b** To swoon, to faint. **4** *Envoyer* (also: *balancer*) *le potage*: To 'gun down', to shoot to kill.

potard *n.m.* **1** One who owns or works in a chemist's shop. **2** One who studies pharmacology.

potasser *v.trans. & intrans.* **1** *(sch.)*: To 'swot', to study hard. *Il potasse pour son exam*: He's cramming for his exam. *Il faut que tu potasses tes math!* You'll have to work at maths! **2** *Potasser un problème*: To 'put one's thinking cap on', to have a good think over a problem.

potasseur *n.m.* **1** *(sch.)*: 'Swot', assiduous student. **2** Person who goes thoroughly into the ins and outs of a problem.

potauf *n.m.* *(abbr. pot-au-feu)*: Dish of boiled beef and vegetables.

pot-au-feu *n.m.* Hard-working prostitute, one that a pimp might describe as 'a good little earner'.

pot-au-feu *adj.inv.* (often of woman): 'Stay-at-home', over-homely.

pot-de-chambre *n.m. T'occupe pas du pot-de-chambre!* Keep your nose out of this! – Mind your own business!

pot-de-vin *n.m.* 'Back-hander', bribe. *Leur chiffre d'affaires, ils le doivent à des pots-de-vin*: Without slush-funds they wouldn't have that kind of turnover.

pote *n.m.* 'Buddy', 'pal', friend. *Salut mon pote!* Watcher mate!

poteau *n.m.* **1** 'Chum', 'pal', friend. **2** *(pl.)*: 'Tree-trunks', fat legs. (Because legs are usually seen as a feminine attribute, this derogatory meaning applies to women.) **3** *Mettre quelqu'un au poteau (fig.)*: To put someone up against the wall, to put someone in the firing line, to make someone take the brunt of it all. **4** *Au poteau!* Down with. . . ! *L'arbitre au poteau!* Ref out! Ref out! (With the growth of soccer violence, such chants can often be heard on the terraces.)

potée *n.f. Une potée de*: 'Oodles', a vast quantity of. *Des cinglés, on en a une potée ici!* We've got loonies by the bucketful here! (also: *une tripotée de*).

potin *n.m.* **1** 'Din', 'racket', loud noise. *Faire un potin de tous les diables*: To make an almighty din. **2** *(Usually pl.)*: 'Tittle-tattle', gossip. *Ça a fait un sacré potin*: It turned out to be quite a scandal. *Les potins, elle adore ça*: She's a real gossip-monger.

potiner *v.intrans.* To engage in tittle-tattle, to gossip.

pou *n.m.* **1** *Chercher des poux à quelqu'un*: To deliberately pick a quarrel with someone (as the image suggests, in a 'nit-picking' way). **2** *. . . comme un pou* (comparative with a superlative implication). *Etre moche comme un pou*: To be as ugly as sin. *Etre sale comme un pou* (of person): To be as filthy as they come. *Etre fier comme un pou*: To be crowing with pride. *Bicher comme un pou (dans la crème fraîche)*: To be 'cock-a-hoop', to be beside oneself with pride and elation.

poubelle *n.f.* **1** 'Tip', dirty and very untidy dwelling. (*Poubelle*, eponymous with the *Préfet de la Seine* who made dustbins compulsory in 1884, really refers in colloquial French to any filthy confined space.) **2** *(joc.)*: 'Bone-shaker', 'banger', motor vehicle with little to commend it where comfort or performance are concerned.

pouce *n.m.* **1** *Manger sur le pouce*: To snatch a (quick) bite, to have the kind of snack-meal where no knives or forks are involved. **2** *Donner un coup de pouce à quelqu'un/quelque chose*: To give someone or something a push in the right direction, to lend a helping hand. **3** *Donner le coup de pouce*: To give the finishing touch to something. **4** *Filer le coup de pouce* (of dishonest shopkeeper): To tip the scales by some skilful legerdemain. **5** *Et le pouce (iron.)*: And a little bit more. *'Elle doit avoir trente ans, non?!' 'Trente ans et le pouce!'* 'She's thirty, isn't she?' 'More like knocking on forty I'd say!' **6** *Mettre les pouces*: To 'give in', to give up. **7** *Pouce!* Pax! – I give in! (A hardy relic of Roman times, this interjection coupled with a thumbs-up sign has survived in school playgrounds and also drifted into everyday language.)

poucettes *n.f.pl.* 'Bracelets', handcuffs.

poudre *n.f.* **1** *Ne pas avoir inventé la poudre (iron.)*: To be a trifle dim, to be the type 'who won't set the Thames on fire'. **2** *Poudre de perlimpinpin*: 'Quack-remedy', 'miracle medicine' of the cure-all variety, hardly likely to be found in pharmacies.

pou-du-ciel *n.m.* Small private aircraft of the 'Tiger Moth' type.

pouèt-pouèt *n.m.* (also: *pouette-pouette*): **1** *(interj.)*: Honk! Honk! (Onomatopoeic transcription of the honking of a motor car horn, more the vintage type than the modern saloon.) **2** *Faire pouèt-pouèt (à quelqu'un)*: To 'sweet-talk' someone, to make up to someone with amorous intentions. (The popularity of this expression can be traced to a pre-1940s song where the lyrics went: '*Je lui fais pouèt-pouèt, elle me fait pouèt-pouèt, on se fait pouèt-pouèt*' . . ., etc. – hardly highbrow stuff!)

pouèt-pouèt *adj.inv. & adv.* (also: *pouette-pouette*): 'So-so', not very reliable. *Les affaires vont pouèt-pouèt*: Business is just about chugging along.

pouf *n.m. Faire un pouf*: To 'do a bunk', to go bankrupt and abscond.

pouffant *adj.* 'Creasing', 'too funny for words', hilarious.

pouffiasse *n.f. (pej.)*: **1** 'Biddy', 'bit of skirt', woman. **2** Low-class prostitute.

pouic *adv. Que pouic*: 'Bugger-all', very little. *Je n'y entrave que pouic!* I can't make head nor tail of this! *On n'y voit que pouic avec cette purée de pois*: You can't see a thing with this fog.

pouilladin *n.m.* Penniless nonentity.

pouillerie *n.f.* **1** Squalor, utter poverty. **2** *Des pouilleries*: Objects of little or no commercial value. (With this meaning, the word refers usually to the kind of items only a very hard-pressed junk-dealer might be interested in.)

pouilleux *n.m.* 'Down-and-outer' (as the word suggests, one who is ridden with lice).

pouilleux *adj.* **1** Filthy, dirty. **2** 'Down-and-out', in the depths of poverty.

poulaga *n.m.* 'Cop', 'copper', policeman. *La Maison Poulaga*: **a** The 'cop-shop', the police station. **b** 'The fuzz', the police.

poulaille *n.f. La poulaille*: 'The law', 'the fuzz', the police.

poulailler *n.m. (th.) Le poulailler*: 'The gods', the upper gallery.

poulain *n.m.* Up-and-coming sportsman, promising young athlete.

poulbot *n.m.* Paris street-urchin. (This modern-day successor to *gavroche* is eponymous with Francisque Poulbot, the painter, 1879–1946, who made his name by painting the impish *titi parisien*.)

poule *n.f.* **1** 'Bird', girlfriend. *Touche pas, c'est ma poule!* Keep off, she's my woman! **2** *(pej.)*: 'Biddy', 'bit-of-skirt', woman of loose morals (the 'easy-lay' variety). *Poule de luxe*: High-class tart. **3** *Ma poule*: 'My lovey-dovey', 'my pet', my darling. **4** *Poule mouillée*: **a** A 'Softie', 'weed', sissy-like character. **b** Funk, coward. **5** *La poule* (also: *la Poule*): 'The fuzz', the police.

Pouleman *La Maison Pouleman(n)*: **a** 'The law', 'the fuzz', the police. **b** The 'cop-shop', the police station.

poulet *n.m.* **1** 'Cop', 'copper', policeman. **2** 'Cringer', unpleasant letter. (Originally, a *poulet* was a love-letter, and the colloquiality stems from the antiphrasis.) **3** *Mon poulet*: 'My ducky', 'my lovey-dovey', my darling. **4** *C'est du poulet!* It's as easy as pie! – It's dead simple. **5** *Mon cul, c'est du poulet?!* (iron): You must be joking!

pouliche *n.f.* **1** 'Filly', pretty young woman. **2** Young prostitute.

poupée *n.f.* 'Biddy', 'bird', woman.

poupougne *n.m. & f. Faire poupougne (de la main)*: To 'wave two fingers', to make an obscene gesture, usually to another motorist.

poupoule *n.f.* **1** *Ma poupoule*: 'My chickadee', my darling. **2** *Jouer viens poupoule*: To honk one's horn rhythmically (as if to the strains of that well-known song).

pour *n.m. C'est du pour!* (iron.): It's a load of waffle – I wouldn't believe it! (The irony of this expression is that it is an antiphrasis of the seemingly obvious. To express adamant affirmation one says: *C'est pas du pour! Lui, patron de bistrot?! C'est du pour!* He's never owned a pub, don't you believe it!)

pour *prep. Etre pour*: To be completely in favour of. *Du pinard aux repas, lui il est pour*: You won't see him eating without a bottle of plonk. (Sacha Guitry, the actor and film director when asked '*Les femmes, vous êtes pour ou contre?*' once wittily replied '*Tout contre!*')

pourliche *n.m. (corr. pourboire)*: 'Tip', gratuity.

pourri *n.m.* 'Bastard', evil and utterly corrupt individual. (In his novel MESSIEURS LES HOMMES, San-Antonio has a character called Paul-le-pourri whose nickname has a deeper meaning since he suffers from facial eczema.)

pourri *adj.* **1** *Un temps pourri*: Foul weather. **2** *Etre pourri* (of child): To be 'spoilt something rotten', to have been granted every wish regardless of trouble or cost. **3** *Etre pourri d'argent*: To be 'stinking rich', to be 'rolling in it', to be very wealthy. **4** *Ne pas être pourri* (of person): To be 'as fit as a fiddle', to be the picture of health.

poussah *n.m.* 'Fatso', very corpulent person.

pousse-au-crime *n.m.* **1** 'Hooch', cheap and strong alcohol. (This jocular label is very much in the spirit of 'mother's ruin'.) **2** 'Plonk', red wine.

pousse-café *n.m.* 'Chaser', small glass of alcohol taken to round off a hearty meal, usually after the traditional cup of coffee.

pousser *v.trans. & intrans.* **1** To 'go too far', to overdo things. *Une fois ça va, deux fois peut-être,* *mais faut pas pousser avec moi!* Once is alright, twice is enough, but don't push me too far! (There is a would-be humorous extension to *faut pas pousser* in the expression: *Faut pas pousser grand-mère dans les orties*.) **2** *En pousser une* (also: *pousser une goualante*): **a** To burst out into song. **b** To moan, to complain. **c** To let out a cry of pain. **3** *A la va-comme-je-te-pousse*: 'Any-old-how', in a slapdash manner, without care and attention.

poussette *n.f.* **1** (Drugs): 'Hype', hypodermic syringe. **2** (Racing cyclists' slang), illegal assistance given to a faltering competitor by team-mates or enthusiastic onlookers. **3** (of dishonest shopkeeper): Skilful legerdemain operated to tip the scales.

poussières *n.f.pl.* . . . *et des poussières* (of money): . . . and a little bit more. *Ça m'a coûté dix briques et des poussières*: It cost me just over ten grand.

poussin *n.m.* **1** *(mil.)*: Air Force cadet. **2** Very young sportsman in any discipline. (The *poussin* category caters for the 6 to 9 year-olds.)

P.P.H. *n.m. (abbr. passera pas l'hiver)*: 'Old-timer', old person (literally one not long for this world. Unlike the English, the French expression is gently jocular).

P.Q. *n.m. (abbr. corr. papier-cul)*: **1** 'Bum-fodder', toilet paper. **2** 'Bumf', useless paperwork. **3** *(sch.)*: 'Paper', essay (also: *pécul*).

P.4 *n.f.* Cheap cigarette. (For many years the *P.4* have been the smoke of the less affluent; these cigarettes, also known as *parisiennes*, come in packs of four, hence their name.)

praline *n.f.* **1** 'Slug', bullet. **2** 'Clit', clitoris. **3** 'Biff', punch, blow.

précautions *n.f.pl. Prendre ses précautions*: To use a condom during intercourse.

prêchi-prêcha *n.m.* Pontificating waffle.

Préfectance *Proper name. (abbr. corr. Préfecture de police)*: Police Headquarters.

première *De première (adj.exp.)*: 'A-1', first-rate. *La bouffe qu'il nous a servie était de première!* That grub he served us was top-hole!

prendre *v.trans.* **1** To 'cop it', to 'catch it', to get told off in no uncertain manner. *Qu'est-ce que tu vas prendre!* You're (in) for it! – You'll get the roasting of your life! **2** *Ça ne prend pas avec moi!* I'm not falling for that one! – That trick won't work with me! **3** *Qu'est-ce qui te prend?* What's eating you? – What's the matter? **4** *J'en prends et j'en laisse!* I take it all with a pinch of salt! *Il faut en prendre et en laisser!* You can't believe all you hear!

presse *n.f. Etre sous presse* (of prostitute): To be busy with a client. (This expression has a jocular double-entendre as the straight meaning describes a book being printed.)

presse-bouton *adj.inv.* Automatic, clockwork-like, devoid of human involvement. *Bientôt l'amour sera une affaire presse-bouton!* One day, I reckon, even sex will be microchip-controlled!

presto *adv.* 'Right-away', straight away, instantly.

prétentiard *n.m.* 'Stuck-up' character, snob.

prétentiard *adj.* 'Stuck-up', 'snobby', pretentious.

prévence *n.f. (corr. détention préventive)*: Remand in custody, incarceration pending trial (also: *prévette*).

prévent *n.m. (abbr. préventorium)*: Sanatorium where cases of early-diagnosed T.B. are treated.

prévôt *n.m.* (Prison slang): 'Trusty', inmate entrusted with minor administrative tasks.

primeur *n.f. (joc.)*: Virginity. *Elle n'a plus sa primeur!* She's seen the ceiling a good few times!

princesse *n.f. Aux frais de la princesse*: On the old expense account (on the State, the firm, etc.).

prise *n.f.* **1** (Drugs): 'Take', 'fix', dose of narcotic, usually cocaine. **2** *Prise de bec*: 'Barney', 'bust-up', quarrel. **3** *Etre en prise directe avec*: To be in close touch, in close contact with. (The original meaning of *prise directe* comes from the world of motor vehicles where it refers to 'direct drive'.)

pristo *n.m.* (Prison slang): Inmate.

prix *n.m.* **1** *Prix de Diane*: 'Filly', pretty lass, beautiful young girl. (The *prix de Diane* is one of the classics where French race-meetings are concerned and this flat race is open to fillies only.) **2** *Prix à réclamer*: Unattractive female, one that is unlikely to inspire the male population. (As with *prix de Diane*, *prix à réclamer* originates from the world of horse-racing; the original meaning is 'selling race', where less successful horses compete for a prize and hopefully a new owner.)

pro *n.m. & adj.* (of sportsman): 'Pro', professional.

probloque *n.m.* (also: *probloc*): Landlord, proprietor of rented accommodation.

procu *n.m. (abbr. Procureur de la République)*: Member of the Bar of considerable standing whose function in French Courts is to prosecute on behalf of the State.

prof *n.m. (sch., abbr. professeur)*: Teach', teacher.

profonde *n.f.* 'Bin', pocket.

prolo *n.m. (pej.)*: 'Prole', 'pleb', proletarian.

promenade *n.f.* 'Doddle', 'walkover', easy victory.

promener *v.trans. Promener ses tatanes (dans le coin)*: To 'mooch about', to loaf around a past habitual haunt.

promener *v.intrans. Envoyer promener quelqu'un*: To 'send someone packing', to tell someone to go away. *Envoyer tout promener*: To 'throw it all in', to opt out of everything.

promener *v.trans.reflex. Se promener partout* (of objects): To be 'kicking about', lying around, to be all over the place.

propé *n.f. (sch., abbr. propédeutique)*: Introductory study-year at University sanctioned by an exam of the same name. (To the chagrin of a few, this 'weaning-year' disappeared from the French system in the late 60s.)

propre *n.m. En voilà du propre! (iron.)*: Well that's a fine state of affairs! *Ça serait du propre! (iron.)*: That would just about put the lid on it! (You couldn't do much worse!)

propre *adj. Me voilà propre! (iron.)*: Well that's me in a fine mess, thank you very much!

propriétaire *n.m. Viens faire le tour du propriétaire!* Come along and I'll show you round the place!

proprio *n.m. (abbr. propriétaire)*: Landlord. (The feminine *propriote* is quite widely used.)

prose *n.m.* **1** 'Bum', behind. *Prendre du prose*: To engage in sodomy. **2** Good luck, good fortune. (As exemplified in other words, success and sexual favours seem to go hand-in-hand.)

prostipute *n.f.* 'Prozzy', 'hooker', prostitute. (The word is a jocular compounding of *prostituée* and *pute*, itself in popular etymology an abbreviation of *putain*.)

protal *n.m. (sch., corr. proviseur)*: Headmaster of a *lycée*.

prout *n.m.* **1** 'Pongy', fart. *Lâcher un prout*: To break wind. **2** *Prout! (Ma chère!) (joc. & iron.)*: Hello sailor! (Like its English counterpart, this interjection expressing derision is more often than not directed at effeminate characters.)

prouteur *n.m.* 'Funk', coward.

prouteur *adj.* 'Funky', cowardly.

provisoire *n.f. Etre en provisoire*: To be out on bail. (This is a contraction of *être en liberté provisoire*.)

prune *n.f.* **1** 'Slug', bullet. *Il s'est cloqué une prune dans la tirelire*: He shot himself through the nut. **2** 'Biff', blow. *Avoir de la prune*: To pack a punch. **3** 'Ticket', motoring fine. *Se faire coller une prune*: To 'get booked', to get fined. **4** *(pl.)*: 'Nuts', 'balls', testicles. **5** *Pour des prunes*: 'For sweet F.A.', for nothing, in vain. *On a bossé quinze jours et tout ça pour des prunes!* We slogged our guts out for a fortnight and got fuck-all for our troubles! *Ça compte pour des prunes!* It counts for nothing! **6** *Des prunes!* No dice! – Nothing doing! – Certainly not! **7** *Poser une prune*: To 'have a crap', to 'shit', to defecate.

pruneau *n.m.* 'Slug', bullet (usually from a handgun).

pschtt *n.m. Faire un pschtt*: To 'wow' in admiration, to make an admiring noise in that onomatopoeic

manner. *(Perrier's* advertising agents in France capitalized on this expression with the slogan *'l'eau qui fait pschtt'*.)

psy *n.m.* 'Shrink', psychiatrist.

puant *n.m. (joc.)*: Cheese (one of the smelly variety).

puant *adj.* Objectionably 'stuck-up' and arrogant. *Il est d'un puant!* You've never seen such a conceited nurk!

pub *n.f. La pub*: The advertising industry. *Je crois qu'il travaille dans la pub*: I think he's something in advertising.

puce *n.f.* **1** 'Shrimp', diminutive person. (The word nearly always seems to carry a friendly connotation.) **2** *Saut de puce* (Airline slang): 'Short hop', short haul flight. **3** *Secouer ses puces*: To make a move and get out of bed (or a comfortable armchair). **4** *Secouer les puces à quelqu'un*: To give someone a good ticking-off, to tell someone off in no uncertain manner.

pucelage *n.m.* Virginity. (The words *puceau* and *pucelle*, referring to persons who have never experienced sex, are associated in the popular mind, in spite of clear etymological evidence, with the idea that the only 'visitor' to the pubic region might have been a flea.)

pucier *n.m.* Bed. (In contrast with its obvious origin, the word is not really pejorative.)

pue-la-sueur *n.m. (pej.)*: Labourer, unskilled worker.

puits *n.m. Puits de science*: Walking encyclopedia (not a 'know-all' but one with a very wide-ranging knowledge).

punaise *n.f.* **1** *(pej.)*: Bitchy and cantankerous woman. **2** *Punaise de sacristie (pej.)*: 'Church-hen', over-zealous woman church-goer. **3** *Punaise!* Damn! – Blast! (This exclamation is a soft alternative to *putain*, and more often encountered in Provence than anywhere else.)

pur *n.m. Un pur* (Underworld slang): Reliable and trustworthy fellow (in a different social context, one of the 'true-blue' variety). *Etre un pur in the milieu* is indeed great praise).

purée *n.f.* **1** *Etre dans la purée*: To be 'in the soup', to be in a fix (usually where financial matters are concerned). **2** *Purée de nous autres!* Heaven help us! – Luck is never on our side! (This expression originated in Algeria with the *pied-noir* community. With the exodus of the European settlers, it is moving into everyday colloquial French.) **3** *Balancer la purée*: **a** To fire a hail of bullets. **b** To 'juice off', to ejaculate.

purge *n.f.* 'Bashing', thrashing, beating-up. *Il lui a filé une de ces purges!* He gave him the tanning of his life!

purotin *n.m.* 'Skint' character (one who seems just a step away from being a down-and-outer because he is *dans la purée*).

putain *n.f.* 1 'Prozzy', prostitute. 2 *Putain de* . . . (intensifier). *Quel putain de temps!* What bloody awful weather! *Cette putain de guerre!* This damn war!

putain *adj.inv.* (usually of man). *Etre putain*: To be a 'toady', a 'crawler', to be a sycophant.

putasserie *n.f. Quelle putasserie!* What a shit! –What a lousy state of affairs!

putassier *adj.m.* Debauched.

pute *n.f.* 'Prozzy', 'hooker', prostitute.

putois *n.m. Gueuler comme un putois*: To squeal like a stuck pig, to scream blue murder.

P.V. *n.m. (abbr. Procès-Verbal)*: Fine. *Se faire coller un P.V.* (of motorist): To get a ticket. (Contrary to what the word suggests, *Procès-Verbaux* come in written form.)

Q

quai *n.m. Au bout du quai les ballots!* Get knotted! – Get lost! (This near-nonsensical catch phrase is loaded with derision and contempt.)

quand-est-ce *n.m.* (also: *quantès*): Round of drinks paid by a new employee to his workmates. (This compound noun is a truncation of *Quand est-ce que tu paies à boire?*)

quarante-quatre *n.m. Filer à quelqu'un un quarante-quatre maison*: To give someone a good kick up the jacksey. (Where French shoe sizes are concerned, 44 is definitely on the large side, hence the humour of the expression. See *fillette*.)

quart *n.m.* **1** *(mil.)*: Tin mug (because it holds ¼ litre). **2** *Le quart*: The 'cop-shop', the police station. **3** (also: *quart d'œil*): 'Super', police superintendent. **4** *Faire le quart* (of prostitute): To go soliciting (also: *battre son quart*). **5** *Partir au quart de tour*: **a** (of car): To start first time. **b** To 'skedaddle', to move off at the double. **6** *Régler quelque chose au quart de poil*: To get something working to perfection.

quart-de-brie *n.m.* Long, pointed nose (because it is reminiscent of a wedge of that cheese).

Quartier *Proper name. Le Quartier*: The Latin Quarter in Paris.

quatorze *num.adj. C'est reparti comme en 14!* Here we go again! – We're in for more of the same! (The irony of the expression has rather macabre origins as *quatorze* refers to 1914. The utterance became popular at the beginning of World War II when it turned out the French, amongst others, were in for more trouble from Germany.)

quatre *num.adj.* **1** *Se mettre en quatre*: To 'put oneself out', to put oneself to a lot of trouble. **2** *Un de ces quatre (matins)*: One of these (fine) days.

quat' *num.adj. (abbr. quatre)*: In colloquial speech a 'plural' z-sound is introduced in front of words beginning with a vowel, as in *quat'z-idiots*. *Entre quat'z-yeux*: In private, in confidence. *Entre quat'z-yeux, je peux te dire la*

vérité! Between you, me and the gatepost, this is what really happened!

Quat'z-Arts *n.m.pl. Le bal des Quat'z-Arts* is one of the most popular events in the Paris students' calendar and is organized by those attending the *Ecole des Beaux-Arts* where painting, engraving, sculpture and architecture are taught.

quelque part *adv.* 'You-know-where', euphemistic blanket-word for places one would rather not mention by name. *Il peut se le mettre quelque part!* He can stuff it up his jumper! *Aller quelque part*: To go and 'wash one's hands' (i.e. to go to the loo).

quelqu'un *indef.pron.* **1** *C'est quelqu'un!* He's really somebody! (He's out of the ordinary.) *Se croire quelqu'un*: To be stuck-up, to be conceited. **2** *C'est quelqu'un!* Well I never! – This is incredible! (In this instance, the colloquiality stems from the fact that *quelqu'un* stands for *quelque chose. C'est quelqu'un tout de même de ne pas savoir où coucher!* It's really the limit not knowing where to find a bed!)

quenaupe *n.f.* Smoker's pipe.

qu'en-dira-t-on *n.m.inv. Le qu'en-dira-t-on*: 'Tittle-tattle', idle gossip. *Se moquer des qu'en-dira-t-on*: To have no time for what people say.

quenotte *n.f.* (Child language): 'Toothy-peg', tooth.

quenottier *n.m. (joc.)*: 'Tooth-puller', dentist.

quenouille *n.f. Partir en quenouille* (of project, undertaking, etc.): To 'go steadily downhill', to deteriorate progressively.

quéquette *n.f.* 'Prick', 'cock', penis. (Initially from the language of children, *quéquette* has a 'wee-willy' connotation, i.e. a limp penis.)

quès *n.m. C'est du quès!* It's six of one, half a dozen of the other! – It's the same thing! (also: *c'est du kif!*)

qu'es-aco? *adv.phrase.* **1** What's that? **2** What's eating you? – What's the matter?

question *n.f.* Question . . . (also: *question de . . .*): When it comes to . . ., When the issue is . . .

R

rab *n.m.* **1** (of food): 'Seconds', second helping. *S'il en reste dans la marmite, je prendrais bien du rab!* If there's any grub going spare, I wouldn't mind another helping! (The expression *du rab de rab* in school and army canteens is what pupils and recruits will ask for when really hungry.) **2** *En rab*: Surplus to requirements. *J'ai deux places de théâtre en rab!* I've got two theatre tickets if anybody wants them! **3** *Faire du rab*: To do overtime, to work extra hours for bonus pay (also: *rabiot*).

rabat *n.m.* **1** *(abbr. rabatteur)*: Night-club tout, one whose brief it is to steer in the big spenders. **2** *Rabat de col*: 'Kickback', financial bribe.

rabattre *v.trans.* *Rabattre les oreilles à quelqu'un*: To 'witter on' about something to someone, to harp on *ad nauseam*. (This is a corruption of the accepted expression *rebattre les oreilles à quelqu'un* which is losing ground to the colloquial one.)

rabattre *v.intrans.* To come back, to return (often with unfriendly intentions).

rabattre *v.pronom.* **1** (of motorist, etc.): To swerve back onto the correct side of the road to avoid oncoming traffic. **2** To return to an old haunt, to come back to familiar surroundings.

rabibocher *v.trans.* **1** To 'tinker up', to repair in a 'D.I.Y./Heath Robinson-ish' manner. **2** To 'patch up a quarrel', to reconcile discording parties.

rabibocher *v.trans.reflex.* To 'patch things up', to make it up after a quarrel.

rabiot *n.m.* **1** (of food): 'Seconds', second helping. **2** *En rabiot*: 'Going spare', surplus to requirements. **3** *Faire un peu de rabiot*: To do some overtime.

rabioter *v.trans. & intrans.* **1** To make a bit extra on the side by creaming off some of the profits. **2** *(sch. & mil.)*: To 'wangle' something extra (food, leave, etc.).

rabioteur *n.m.* *Un rabioteur*: A 'Mr Fix-it', character whose winning ways always seem to help him come out on top.

râble *n.m.* *Sauter* (also: *tomber*) *sur le râble de quelqu'un*: To 'catch someone unawares', to surprise someone (literally to pounce on him from behind).

râbler *v.trans.* To 'pitch into', to 'go for', to attack someone.

raboter *v.trans.* To 'pinch' from someone, to steal something from someone. *Chaque vendredi elle me rabote ma paie!* Come payday she nicks the lot from me!

rabouin *n.m.* **1** 'Gyppo', gypsy. (The feminine *rabouine* exists but is not often encountered.) **2** *Le Rabouin*: The devil (Mephistopheles).

raccommoder *v.trans.reflex.* To 'patch things up', to make it up after a quarrel. *Se raccommoder sur l'oreiller* (of lovers): To make it up after a tiff (in the most congenial way).

raccord *n.m.* *Se faire un raccord (joc.)*: To freshen one's make-up.

raccourcir *v.trans.* *Se faire raccourcir*: To get 'topped', to be guillotined. (The expression has a blend of dubious built-in humour.)

raccroc *n.m.* *Faire le raccroc*: **a** (of prostitute): To go soliciting. **b** (of business person hard-pressed for trade): To go out touting.

raccrocher *v.trans.* **1** (of prostitute): To 'hook', to solicit. **2** To 'buttonhole', to detain and delay someone in conversation.

raccrocher *v.intrans.* **1** To 'hang up', to put the phone back on the receiver. **2** (of endeavour, enterprise): To 'pack it in', to give up.

raclée *n.f.* 'Pasting', 'trouncing', thrashing. *Filer une raclée à quelqu'un*: To beat someone black and blue.

racler *v.trans.* *Racler les fonds de tiroir (fig.)*: To 'scrape the barrel', to have to resort to last-choice options.

racler *v.trans.reflex.* To 'scrape the stubble', to shave.

raclette *n.f.* *Coup de raclette (pol.)*: Successful swoop or raid where the forces of law and order round up all those wanted for questioning.

racloir *n.m.* 'Stubble-scraper', razor (more the cut-throat type than the patent safety model).

(Colloquial grammar places *de* after *question* when it is followed by a verb.) *Question pinard, il s'y connaît!* He certainly knows his way around the wine-list! *Question boulot, compte pas sur moi!* If it's work you want doing, don't look at me! *Question de faire le mur, faut pas y penser!* Going over the wall is out of the question!

queue *n.f.* **1** 'Prick', 'cock', penis. **2** *Queue de cervelas* (Prison slang): Monotonous daily walk round the exercise-yard. **3** *A la queue-leu-leu*: In close single-file. (*Marcher à la queue-leu-leu* evokes the image of elephants filing past in a trunk-to-tail chain.) **4** *Faire des queues*: To be unfaithful to one's spouse. **5** *Laisser une queue* (in hotel, restaurant): To leave without paying the bill. **6** *Bouffer des queues de cerises*: To be down on one's luck (literally to be so impoverished that any foodstuff will do). **7** *Faire une queue de poisson* (of vehicle): To cut in (in front of another, after having overtaken). **8** *Finir en queue de poisson* (of play, musical piece, story): To come to an abrupt and unexpected end.

queue-de-pie *n.f.* 'Tails', dress-suit jacket.

queutard *n.m.* 'Randy so-and-so', over-sexed man.

queuter *v.trans. & intrans.* To 'screw', to fuck, to have coition.

quille *n.f.* **1** Bottle of booze, of alcoholic beverage (because it is skittle-shaped). *Une quille de roteux*: A bottle of champers. **2** *(pl.)*: 'Pins', 'gambs', legs. *Ne pas tenir sur ses quilles*: To be shaky on one's pins. **3** *La quille*: Demob day for national servicemen. (Before their return to civvy street, young conscripts can be heard shouting '*Vive la quille!*' after a last boozy night out.) **4** *(non-pej.)*: 'Gal', 'bird', young woman.

quiller *v.trans.* To 'gull', to 'cod', to fool.

quimper *v.trans. & intrans.* **1** To 'chat up', to woo. *Si tu veux quimper des frangines, fringue-toi mieux!* If you want to pull the birds, get yourself properly togged-up! **2** (Prison slang): To 'cop' a sentence. *Avec son pédigrée, il va quimper chéro!* With his form, he's in for one hell of a stretch! **3** *Quimper pour*: To fall for, to be the victim of someone or something. *Il*

quimpe pour n'importe quel baratin! He'll fall f[or] any patter! **4** *Laisser quimper*: To drop, to giv[e] up (as a bad job). *Laisse quimper, mon vieu[x]* Pack it in, mate!

quincaille *n.f.* *(joc. & iron.)* *De la quincaill[e]* Jewellery (of the expensive kind; this near[ly] derogatory word seems tainted with envy).

quincaillerie *n.f.* *De la quincaillerie*: **1** 'Loos[e] change', coins of small denomination. **2** *(joc. &* *iron.)*: 'Gongs', string of medals. **3** *(joc. &* *IRON.(*: Expensive jewellery. (See *quincaille*.) **4** Computer hardware.

quine *adv.* *En avoir quine de*: To be fed up with. *J'en ai quine de son moulin à paroles!* I'm sick and tired of his constant chattering!

quinquets *n.m.pl.* 'Glims', 'lamps', eyes. (These colloquial English translations are quite accurate. Sandry and Carrère in their *DICTIONNAIRE DE L'ARGOT MODERNE* describe *quinquets* as '*yeux brillants*'. The *PETIT LAROUSSE* lexicalizes *quinquet* as an oil-lamp, named after its inventor. *Allume tes quinquets!* Keep a sharp look-out!)

quinquin *n.m.* **1** 'Tootsie', toe. **2** 'Kiddlywink', child. **3** '*Le p'tit quinquin*': Title of a popular song of Northern France. (Although the strains of this well-known melody instantly provoke recognition of the refrain to any Frenchman, the words have little relevance outside the area where it originally flourished.)

quiqui *n.m.* 'Gullet', throat. *Serrer le quiqui à quelqu'un*: To wring someone's neck, to throttle someone.

quitte *adj.* *Etre quitte*: To have paid one's debt to society, to have done time (in prison) and be back on the straight and narrow.

quoi (A) *(rel.pron.)*: **1** *Avoir de quoi*: To be 'well-padded', to be well-off where money is concerned. **2** *Il n'y a pas de quoi!* Don't mention it! (There's no need to thank me.) (B) *(interr. pron.)*: *De quoi (je me mêle)?!* And what's it got to do with you?! (This defiant and aggressive expression is usually directed at interfering busybodies.) (C) *(interj.)*: *On est là, quoi!* Well, here we are! *Enfin, quoi, c'est la vie!* Well, that's life!

raclure *n.f.* *(pej.)*: **1** (of person): 'Scum', despicable character. **2** *Raclure de bidet*: 'Squirt', runt. (As the expression suggests, the genetic near-miss in question wasn't worth bearing.)

racolage *n.m.* **1** (of prostitute): Touting, soliciting. **2** *Faire du racolage* (of desperate individual): To recruit, to enlist support regardless of the candidate's value. *C'est un piteux racolage, la chasse aux affreux*: You really have to scrape the bottom of the barrel when you're touting for mercenaries.

racoler *v.trans.* **1** (of prostitute): To solicit. **2** To go touting for customers (where business would otherwise take care of itself).

racoleur *n.m.* **1** Night-club tout. **2** Pimp, procurer.

racoleuse *n.f.* 'Prozzy', prostitute.

radada *n.m.* *Aller au radada* (also: *faire une partie de radada*): To 'have it off', to have sex.

radar *n.m.* *Marcher au radar* (of drunk): To walk 'by guesswork', to totter along with arms stretched out like feelers.

radasse *n.f.* *(pej.)*: 'Biddy', 'bit of skirt', woman (the kind who is not too fussy about those she goes out with).

rade *n.m.* **1** Bar (in pub or café). *Prendre un verre au rade*: To have a drink at the bar. **2** (Prostitutes' slang): Pavement. (*Faire le rade* can have two meanings, either to solicit perched on a bar stool, or more prosaically to 'pound the beat'.)

rade *n.f.* *Etre en rade*: To be 'stranded', to be left to cope on one's own. *Tomber en rade*: **a** (of motorist): To break down. **b** (*fig.*, of plans, projects, etc.): To 'grind to a halt', to come to nothing. (These expressions make colloquial use of the French word for harbour; a maritime-flavoured translation of *être laissé en rade* could be 'to be left high and dry' – like a ship at low tide.)

rader *v.intrans.* (of prostitute): To go soliciting.

radeuse *n.f.* 'Prozzy', prostitute. (Two popular etymologies jostle for recognition where this word is concerned; one, that the prostitute solicits from a *bistrot* perched on a stool at the *rade*; the other that she walks the streets; see the second meaning of *rade n.m.*)

radin *n.m.* 'Scrooge', 'skinflint', miser.

radin *adj.* 'Mingy', 'stingy', mean.

radiner *v.intrans.* (also: *v.pronom.*): To come back sharpish, to return quickly. *On a radiné fissa quand on a appris la nouvelle*: We got back like a flash when we heard the news. *T'en vas pas, je me radine!* Hold on, I'll be with you in a jiffy!

radinerie *n.f.* 'Stinginess', meanness.

radis *n.m.* **1** 'Tootsie', toe. *Se laver les radis*: To wash one's feet. (When in the plural, as in this expression, *radis* refers to feet rather than toes.) **2** *Ne pas avoir un radis*: To be 'skint', 'broke', to be penniless. *Je n'ai pas un radis!* I haven't got a bean! *Ça ne vaut pas un radis!* It's not much cop! – It's worthless!

raffut *n.m.* **1** 'Din', 'racket', noise. **2** 'Hullabaloo', uproar. *Il a fait un de ces raffuts quand on lui a présenté l'addition*: He certainly kicked up a fuss when they gave him the bill. *Un raffut de tous les diables*: A devil of a row.

rafiot *n.m.* (also: *raffiot*) *Un vieux rafiot*: An 'old tub', a decrepit old ship.

rafistolage *n.m.* Makeshift repair.

rafistoler *v.trans.* To 'patch up', to mend in a haphazard way.

ragaga *n.m.* *Faire du ragaga*: To 'buzz around like a blue-arsed fly', to make a show of being busy with little result.

rageant *adj.* 'Narking', 'aggravating', irritating. *Je sais que c'est rageant mais je n'y peux rien!* I know it's a bind, but what can I do?!

ragot *n.m.* **1** Semi-truth or out-and-out lie passed on by wagging tongues. **2** *(pl.)*: 'Tittle-tattle', idle or malicious gossip. *Faire des ragots*: To spread rumours.

ragoter *v.intrans.* **1** To 'tittle-tattle', to gossip. **2** *(pol.)*: To rake in tittle-tattle information when other leads have fizzled out.

ragougnasse *n.f.* 'Slop', 'uninspiring grub', unappetizing food.

ragoût *n.m.* **1** *Boîte à ragoût*: 'Belly', stomach. **2** *Prendre un ragoût de semelles* (*joc.*): To 'get booted out of somewhere good and proper', to be forcibly evicted.

ragoûtant *adj.* (always with a negative): 'Appetizing', enticing. *Après quinze jours au gnouf, il était vraiment pas ragoûtant!* After a fortnight in the slammer, no-one would have touched him with a barge-pole!

raide *n.m.* **1** 1000-franc note (in the 30s and 40s when it represented a 'steep' amount). **2** 'Hooch', rough and ready booze strong in alcohol content.

raide *adj.* **1** 'Paralytic', 'blind-to-the-world', dead-drunk. **2** 'Skint', 'flat-broke', penniless. *Désolé, mon vieux, je suis raide comme un passe-lacet!* No can do! I'm as hard-up as you! **3** Incredible, difficult to believe. *Elle est raide, celle-là! Lui, directeur, on aura tout vu!* Well, would you believe it, they made him a director, whatever next?! **4** *En conter des raides*: To tell 'close-to-the-knuckle' stories, risqué jokes. **5** *En avoir vu de raides*: To have been in a few tight corners in one's time. **6** *Raide comme balle* (*adv.exp.*): **a** Quick as a flash. **b** 'As sure as hell', without a doubt.

raidir *v.trans. Se faire raidir* (Gambling slang): To 'get cleaned out', to lose everything at the tables (also: *se faire raiguiser*).

raie *n.f.* **1** *Avoir une gueule de raie*: To have an 'ugly mush', to have a face like the back of a bus. **2** *(abbr. raie des fesses)*: 'Bum', behind. (The word is never encountered with this literal meaning, but only as part of injurious statements such as *je lui pisse à la raie des fesses* expressing utter contempt.)

raisin *n.m.* 'Claret', blood. *Prendre un coup de raisin*: To 'blow one's top' (literally to go apoplectically red with anger).

raison *n.f. Se faire une raison*: To make the best of a situation, to accept the inevitable.

rajouter *v.intrans. En rajouter*: To 'pile it on', to exaggerate. *Ne crois pas tout ce baratin, il faut toujours qu'il en rajoute!* I wouldn't believe all he says, it's liberally laced with optimism!

râlant *adj.* 'Galling', infuriating.

râler *v.intrans.* To 'bellyache', to 'gripe', to grumble. *Râler sec* (also: *râler comme un pou*): To make a song-and-dance about something.

râleur *n.m.* 'Grumbler', character who is perpetually complaining.

râleur *adj.* 'Grumpy', 'snarly', constantly displeased.

ralléger *v.intrans.* **1** To 'land', to arrive. **2** To come back, to return.

rallonge *n.f.* **1** Rise, increase in salary. **2** *(mil.)*: Extended leave. **3** Extension of prison sentence consequent to the uncovering of further misdemeanour. **4** 'Chiv', blade, knife. **5** *Un nom à rallonge*: A double-barrelled name.

rallonger *v.trans.* To 'knife', to stab.

ramarrer *v.trans.* To meet up with someone again.

ramasser *v.trans.* **1** *Se faire ramasser*: **a** To get 'nabbed', 'collared', to get picked up by the police. **b** To 'get a rocket', to get a sound telling-off. **c** *(sch.)*: To 'get ploughed', to fail an exam. **2** *Ramasser une bûche* (also: *ramasser une pelle*): **a** To take a tumble, to fall down. **b** To 'come a cropper', to 'come unstuck', to suffer a setback. **3** *Etre à ramasser à la petite cuillère*: To be 'dead-beat', to be tired-out.

ramastique *n.f.* Confidence-trick where a passer-by is sold a worthless item of jewellery dropped by accomplice Number 1, picked up by Number 2 and highly praised by Number 3 posing as an expert.

ramastiquer *v.intrans.* To live off the con-trick known as *ramastique*.

rambin *n.m.* **1** *Faire du rambin*: **a** To behave in an over-ingratiating manner. **b** To 'chat up', to court a woman. **2** *Marcher au rambin*: To slalom through everyday problems with a bundle of excuses always at the ready.

rambiner *v.trans.* To patch up differences between opposing parties. *Depuis qu'ils sont mariés, on passe notre temps à les rambiner!* Since they got hitched, we seem to spend our time acting as mediators!

rambiner *v.trans.reflex.* To patch up differences (in many cases, to kiss and make up).

rambour *n.m.* **1** *(corr. rendez-vous)*: 'Date', appointment, meeting. **2** *(pl.)*: 'Info', information. *Aller aux rambours*: To scout one's ear to the ground', to scout around for information.

ramdam *n.m.* **1** 'Din', 'racket', loud noise. **2** Uproar, furore. *Faire du ramdam*: To kick up a fuss.

rame *n.f.* **1** *Avoir la rame*: To feel lazy. **2** *Ne pas en fiche* (also: *en foutre*) *une rame*: To 'do bugger-all', to sit back and twiddle one's thumbs.

ramée *n.f. Pas une ramée*: 'Bugger-all', very little. *Ne pas (en) fiche une ramée*: To do fuck-all. *Ne pas en savoir une ramée*: To be as ignorant as they come.

ramener *v.trans. Ramener sa fraise* (also: *la ramener*): **a** To poke one's nose in other people's business. **b** To 'swank', to show off. **c** To protest vehemently.

ramener *v.trans.reflex.* To 'turn up', to arrive somewhere. *Ramène-toi!* Let's be having you!

ramer *v.intrans.* **1** To 'graft', to 'slog one's guts out', to work very hard. **2** To 'have a bang', to 'screw', to have coition with.

rameuter *v.trans.* To make loud noises in order to get others to rally round. *En cas de problèmes, on peut toujours rameuter la famille!* If the going gets tough, we can always S.O.S. the family!

ramier *n.m.* 'Lazy-bones', work-shy character.

ramier *adj.* 'Slacking', idle, lazy.

ramolli *n.m.* **1** Doddering old fogey. **2** Halfwit, near-imbecile. (The full expression *un ramolli du bulbe*, referring either to a doddering geriatric or a near-idiotic person, reveals that it is the brain that has gone soft.)

ramolli *adj.* **1** 'Shagged', worn-out, exhausted. **2** Doddering. **3** Half-witted.

ramollir *v.pronom.* To be going 'soft in the head', to lose one's intellectual faculties.

ramollo *n.m.* **1** 'Jellyfish', archetypal weakling. **2** *Se taper un ramollo*: To 'pull one's wire', to 'wank', to masturbate.

Ramona *Proper name. Chanter Ramona à quelqu'un*: To play hell with someone, to go into loud and lengthy recriminations. ('*Ramona*' is the title of a popular song of the 30s with a lingering melody and plaintive lyrics.)

ramoner *v.trans.* **1** To 'poke', to 'screw', to have coition with. **2** *Se faire ramoner*: **a** (Gambling slang): To get 'cleaned out', to lose all one's money. **b** To get bawled out, to be told off in no uncertain manner.

rampant *n.m.* (Airmen's slang): 'Ground-wallah', 'penguin', member of the ground-staff.

rampe *n.f.* **1** *Tenir bon la rampe*: To be 'still going strong', to act as if still in one's prime. **2** *Lâcher la rampe*: To 'pop one's clogs', to 'snuff it', to die.

rampeur *n.m.* 'Crawler', 'arse-licker', toady character.

ramponneau *n.m.* 'Biff', 'clout', blow.

ramponner *v.trans.* To 'clout', to 'thump', to punch.

rancard *n.m.* (also: *rancart*): **1** 'Date', appointment, arranged meeting. *On s'est filé un rancard*: We arranged to meet. **2** (often *pl.*): 'Info', information.

rancarder *v.trans.* To 'gen someone up', to 'put someone in the picture', to inform someone. *T'en fais pas, j'suis rancardé!* Don't fret, I've been clued up! (where that's concerned).

rancarder *v.trans.reflex.* To try and get 'genned up', to make enquiries.

ranger *v.trans.reflex.* **1** To settle down (after having led a rather fast and furious life) often in order to get married. **2** *Se ranger des voitures* (Underworld slang): To 'pull out of the game', to retire in time and invest one's capital in 'legit' operations.

rantanplan *n.m.* *Faire quelque chose au rantanplan*: To bluff one's way through (literally as the onomatopoeic transcription suggests, to bang the big drum in order to divert attention and succeed in one's endeavour).

raousse *n.m.* 'Shindy', celebration where drinks flow freely. *Il a donné un de ces raousses!* He threw one hell of a party!

raousse *interj.* Out! – Get out! (This is a gallicization of the colloquial German utterance *'raus!*)

raousser *v.trans.* To 'turf out', to 'chuck out', to eject someone from somewhere (also: *raouster*).

rapapilloter *v.trans.reflex.* To 'patch things up', to make it up after a quarrel.

râpé *past part.* *C'est râpé!* It's curtains! – It's off! (What was envisaged is no longer possible.)

raper *n.m.* (Pronounced *rapère*): Bicycle-mounted policeman (also: *hirondelle*).

râper *v.trans.* To 'poke', to 'screw', to have coition with.

râpeuse *n.f.* 'Licker', tongue.

rapiat *n.m.* 'Skinflint', 'meanie', stingy character.

rapiat *adj.* 'Stingy', 'mingy', mean with money.

rapide *n.m.* **1** Character who is sharp, quick to understand. **2** Opportunist. *C'est un rapide, lui!* He doesn't miss a trick!

rapide *adj.* (of person): **1** 'Quick on the uptake', prompt to understand. **2** Opportunist.

rapide *adv.* (*abbr. rapidement*): 'Pronto', at the drop of a hat, quickly. (This abbreviation is itself a contraction of the jocular expression *'Rapide, vite fait sur le gaz!'*)

rapidos *adv.* 'In two shakes of a lamb's tail', 'in a jiffy', very quickly. *On a dû mettre les bouts rapidos!* We had to scarper double quick!

rapière *n.f.* (*joc.*): 'Chiv', blade, knife.

rapiotage *n.m.* Slapdash repair, one that doesn't hide the slipshod methods involved.

rapioter *v.trans.* To fix, to mend in a haphazard and 'Heath-Robinson-ish' manner. *Il va falloir qu'on rapiote le poulailler*: We'll have to patch that henhouse of ours soon!

raplaplat *adj.* (also *raplapla*): 'Knackered', 'jiggered', exhausted. *Pas ce soir, mon vieux, j'suis raplaplat, on a bossé comme des dingues!* I can't make it tonight, I'm all in, we slogged our guts out at work today!

rappliquer *v.intrans. & v.pronom.* **1** To 'show up', to 'turn up', to arrive (often with some sense of urgency). *Les clilles ont rappliqué en masse, à ces prix c'est normal!* At those prices customers were falling over themselves, and who could blame them?! **2** To come back, to return. *Si tu veux garder ton job, t'as intérêt à rappliquer avant qu'on embauche un autre mec!* If you value your post you'd better come back before we take on someone else! (Although strictly speaking the verb *rappliquer* is just as likely to occur in its pronominal form as the intransitive, *se rappliquer* seems to refer more to a 'hasty arrival', than a 'leisurely return'.)

rapport *n.m.* **1** *Etre de bon rapport* (of prostitute or shady enterprise): To be 'a little goldmine'. *C'est une nana de bon rapport!* She's a good little earner! (also: *c'est une gagneuse*). **2** *Rapport à*: 'Cos', because of. *On a pas pu venir rapport aux gosses!* We couldn't make it because of the kids.

rapporter *v.trans.* To be profitable, to be worthwhile financially. (Although the verb is seldom followed by a direct object confirming the 'worthwhile' nature of the activity discussed, it is transitive 'by implication'. *Une affaire comme la sienne ça rapporte*: A business like hers is a regular little goldmine!)

rapporter *v.intrans.* (*sch.*): To tell tales.

rapporteur *n.m.* (*sch.*): 'Sneak', tell-tale. (The feminine *rapporteuse* exists, but is seldom encountered.)

raquer *v.trans. & intrans.* To 'cough up', to have to pay up. *Comme de bien entendu j'ai dû raquer les consos!* It was muggins who had to fork out for the drinks!

raquettes *n.f.pl.* 'Plates of meat', 'trotters', feet.

rare *adj. Se faire rare:* To 'keep a low profile', to steer clear of certain places in order to avoid meeting someone. *Tu te fais rare ces jours-ci!* We don't seem to see much of you these days!

rare *adv.* Not often, seldom. *C'est rare s'il revient si tôt!* He doesn't often come back that early!

rarranger *v.trans.* **1** To put things straight (again), to tidy things up. *Va falloir que je rarrange mon bureau!* I'm going to have to sort my office out. It sure needs it! *Rarranger son emploi du temps:* To reorganize one's timetable. **2** *Se faire rarranger:* **a** To 'get bashed up', to be beaten black and blue. **b** To 'cop it', to get a sound telling-off. **c** To 'get conned', to get well and truly swindled. **d** To 'catch a dose of clap', to get infected with V.D.

ras *n.m. En avoir ras le bol* (also: *ras le bord*): To be sick and tired of something, to be fed up (literally to have had it 'up to here').

rasant *adj.* Deadly boring (perhaps because shaving is such a tediously repetitive task). *C'est vraiment rasant d'écouter ses 'souvenirs de guerre'!* It's a real drag having to listen to his 'how-I-won-the-war' stories!

rase *n.f. Quelle rase!* What a bore! – What a nuisance!

raser *v.trans.* To bore the pants off someone.

raser *v.pronom.* To be bored stiff.

raseur *n.m.* 'Limpet-bore', tenaciously boring person.

rasibe *n.m.* Razor, wet razor (also: *rasif*).

rasibus *adj.inv.* 'Skint', 'broke', penniless.

rasibus *adv. (joc.):* **1** *Couper rasibus* (hair, grass, etc.): To cut very short. *Il s'est fait tailler les tifs rasibus:* He got himself a crew-cut. **2** Suddenly, without warning. *La veille il se portait comme une fleur et puis rasibus son palpitant lui a joué relâche!* One day he was as fit as a fiddle, the next his ticker packed it in and that was it! **3** *Rasibus!* Not on your nelly! – Not bloody likely! – Certainly not!

rasoir *adj.inv.* Deadly boring.

rassis *n.m. Se taper* (also: *se coller*) *un rassis:* To 'pull one's wire', to 'have a wank', to masturbate.

rasta *n.m. (abbr. rastaquouère):* 'Flashy dago'. (This pejorative appellation conjures up the image of an expensively yet badly dressed man of Latin origin, hair plastered down with cream, sporting a trilby and a pencil-line moustache – very much in the mould of the archetypal spiv.)

rat *n.m.* **1** *Rat de bibliothèque:* Bookworm. **2** *Rat d'hôtel:* Cat-burglar operating in hotels. **3** *Gueule* (also: *face*) *de rat:* 'Weasel-face', evil-looking character. **4** *Etre fait comme un rat:* To be cornered, to be in a tight spot. **5** *S'ennuyer comme un rat:* To be bored to tears. **6** *Mon petit rat:* My lovey-dovey – My pet – My darling. (In total contrast with all the other meanings of *rat*, *mon petit rat* is a surprising term of endearment.)

rat *adj.inv.* 'Mingy', 'stingy', mean.

rata *n.m. (sch. & mil.):* 'Stodge', unappetizing grub, filling and rather tasteless fare. (The 'grub's up' bugle-call, familiar to French national servicemen, was given the following lyrics: *C'est pas d'la soupe c'est du rata! C'est pas d'la merde mais ça viendra!*)

ratagasse *n.m.* Second-rater. (Gaston Esnault in his DICTIONNAIRE DES ARGOTS traces the etymology to *raté* with the pejorative suffix *-asse*, the word originating from the world of cycle-racing.)

ratatiné *adj.* (of aged person): Withered and stooping.

ratatiner *v.trans.* **1** To squash 'flat as a pancake'. **2** To 'bump off', to kill. *Ils se sont tous fait ratatiner en 14–18:* They all copped it in the Great War.

ratatout *interj.* (Cards): *Atout, ratout et ratatout!* Trump, trump and trump again!

rate *n.f.* **1** *Se dilater la rate:* To 'laugh oneself silly', to split one's sides with laughter. **2** *Ne pas se fouler la rate:* To take things easy, not to break one's back with work.

raté *n.m.* (of person): 'Wash-out', failure.

râteau *n.m.* 'Cootie-rake', comb. *Donne-toi un coup de râteau!* Put a comb through your hair!

râtelier *n.m. Manger à tous les râteliers:* To be on several and often conflicting payrolls.

rater *v.trans. Ne pas en rater une:* To 'put one's foot in it' every time, to always make a mess of things.

ratiboiser *v.trans. & intrans.* **1** To 'nick', to 'pinch', to steal. *Elle lui a ratiboisé son larfeuil:* She lifted his wallet. *Ratiboiser sur les notes de frais:* To do a fiddle on the old expense accounts. **2** *Se faire ratiboiser* (Gambling slang): To get 'cleaned out', to lose all one's money at the tables.

ratiche *n.f.* **1** 'Chiv', blade, knife. *Il a pris un coup de ratiche dans le baquet:* He got stabbed in the guts. **2** 'Peg', tooth. *Pépé n'a plus toutes ses ratiches:* Gramps has lost most of his chompers!

ratichon *n.m. (pej.):* 'Crow', priest.

ratier *n.m.* Inmate, prisoner.

ratière *n.f.* 'Nick', 'clink', jail.

ration *n.f.* **1** *Avoir sa ration*: To have had one's fill of something unpleasant. *Arrête de cogner, il a sa ration!* Stop hitting him, I don't think he can take any more! **2** *Recevoir sa ration*: To get what is coming to one (to get one's just deserts).

ratissage *n.m. (pol.)*: Dragnet operation.

ratissé *adj.* 'Cleaned-out', penniless.

ratisser *v.trans.* **1** To 'nick', to 'pinch', to steal. **2** *Se faire ratisser*: **a** To 'be done', to get 'conned', to be swindled. **b** To be arrested during a *ratissage*.

raton *n.m. (pej.)*: Arab native of North Africa. (This highly derogatory word is roughly equivalent to the English 'wog' or 'coon'.)

ratonnade *n.f.* Muscle-loaded witch-hunt against immigrant North-African workers; an English sociolinguistic equivalent could be 'paki-bashing'.

ravagé *adj.* 'Bonkers', 'loony', mad.

ravageur *n.m.* (also: *ravageur de frifri*): 'Superstud', randy and promiscuous male.

ravageuse *n.f.* (also: *souris ravageuse*): 'Easy-lay', girl with few scruples where sex is concerned.

ravalement *n.m. Faire son ravalement* (of woman; *joc.*): To slap on the make-up. (Primarily *ravalement* describes the 'face-lift' given to buildings and tenements; the implication in the expression is that the lady needs to apply the make-up with a trowel.)

ravaler *v.trans.* **1** (Antique-dealers' slang): To have to buy in, to buy back goods that have failed to reach their reserve price in an auction. **2** *Ravaler sa façade* (also: *se ravaler la façade*): To 'go to work on one's face', to slap make-up on.

ravalo *n.m.* (Antique-dealers' slang): Item of furniture, etc. entered into an auction, which failed to reach its reserve price and was 'bought back' by the dealer concerned.

ravelure *n.f. (pej.)*: Old hag, woman whose good looks are a thing of the past but who has failed to acknowledge the judgement of time.

ravigotant *n.m.* 'Pick-me-up', alcoholic drink that gives the quick 'lift' one is looking for.

ravigotant *adj.* Refreshing, rejuvenating.

ravigoter *v.trans.* To 'buck up', to put new life into someone or something. *C'est une compagnie qu'on pourrait facilement ravigoter!* This is a little business that just needs a shot in the arm!

rayon *n.m.* **1** *En connaître un rayon*: To 'know something inside-out', to be in the know at something. **2** *En mettre* (also: *en filer*) *un rayon* (of work, enterprise): To 'get stuck-in', to 'put one's back into it', to work hard at the task. **3** *C'est mon rayon!* **a** That's my line! – I'm quite knowledge-able about that! **b** That's just up my street! – That suits me perfectly! **c** That's my business! (and none of yours!)

razif *n.m.* Razor, wet razor (also: *razibe*).

rébecca *n.m. Faire du rébecca*: **a** To 'kick up a fuss', to protest vehemently. **b** To go with fists flying into an argument. (*Une séance de rébecca*: a bout of the fisticuffs.)

rebectage *n.m.* **1** Legal appeal (to a higher court). **2** 'Kiss-and-make-up' reconciliation. **3** Convalescence. *Il est parti dans le Midi pour un peu de rebectage*: He's gone to Provence to charge up his batteries.

rebectant *adj.* (also: *rebecquetant*): **1** 'Mouth-watering', delicious and appetizing. **2** Morale-boosting, encouraging.

rebecter *v.trans.* (also: *rebecqueter*): **1** To engineer a reconciliation. **2** To nurse back to health. **3** To prop up financially, to help out of a tight monetary spot.

rebecter *v.pronom.* (also: *rebecqueter*): To get back on one's feet physically or financially.

rebecter *v.trans.reflex.* (also: *rebecqueter*): To 'kiss and make up', to 'make it up', to become reconciled.

rebecteur *n.m.* (also: *rebecqueteur*): 'Doc', 'medic', doctor.

rebelote *interj. (iron.)*: Here we go again! – It's the same thing all over again! (see *belote*).

rebichoter *v.trans.* To identify a suspect. *Connu comme le loup blanc, il risquait de se faire rebichoter par le premier cogne en vadrouille*: His mush, the pride of any mug-file, would get him recognized by any copper.

rebiffe *n.f.* (Underworld slang): **1** Vengeance, revenge. *Méfie-toi, il donne dans la rebiffe, lui!* I'd be careful if I were you, he's the kind to bear grudges! **2** *Aller à la rebiffe* (also: *faire de la rebiffe*): To 'jib', to revolt (also: *se rebiffer*).

rebiffer *v.intrans. Rebiffer au truc*: To have another shot at something, to have another go.

rebiffer *v.pronom.* To 'jib', to revolt. (Jean Gabin starred in a film called *Le cave se rebiffe* where a stooge-like character played by Maurice Biraud rebels in a counterfeiting plot when his con-men mentors least expect it.)

recal *adj.* (*abbr. récalcitrant*): 'Bolshie', rebellious.

recaler *v.trans.* To fail someone at an exam. *Il s'est fait recaler en beauté*: He muffed his exam good and proper!

recharger *v.trans.* **1** (also: *recharger les wagonnets*): To 'fill 'em up', to order another round of drinks. **2** *Recharger ses accus*: To take a well-deserved rest (literally, to recharge one's batteries).

rechasser *v.trans.* To 'eye', to look at (often with salacious intentions). *Sur la plage il aime bien rechasser les nanas en monokini*: When he's on the beach he likes to get an eyeful of all the topless birds.

réchauffé *n.m. C'est du réchauffé!* It's old-hat! – It's hackneyed!

réclame *n.f. Faire sa propre réclame*: To 'blow one's own trumpet', to boast unashamedly.

réclamé *n.m.* Unattractive female, one that is unlikely to inspire the male population. (See *prix à réclamer*.)

récluse *n.f. (abbr. réclusion*; prison slang): 'Hard', hard labour. (Both in Britain and in France, the notion of hard labour or *travaux forcés* has disappeared from the modern penal system.)

recoller *v.trans.reflex.* (of sexual partners): To 'make it up', to get together again. *Ils passent leur vie à s'engueuler et à se recoller*: Their life seems to be one big row with frequent kiss-and-make-up breaks.

récolter *v.trans.* (of prison sentence): To 'cop', to get, to receive. *Il a récolté le maxi*: He got the stiffest sentence possible.

recommencer *v.intrans. On efface tout et on recommence! (joc. & iron.)*: I think we'll start from scratch again! (This expression is sometimes devoid of jocularity when uttered in a 'let-bygones-be-bygones' context.)

reconnaître *v.trans. Je te reconnais bien là!* That's you all over! – That's typical of you!

reconnaître *v.trans.reflex. Ne plus s'y reconnaître*: To be 'all at sea', to be utterly and totally confused.

reconnobler *v.trans.* To 'peg', to 'place', to recognize (also: *reconnobrer*).

recta *adv.* **1** 'On the dot', 'bang on time', punctually. *Dans les affaires les factures se règlent recta*: A good businessman always pays cash-on-the-nail. **2** 'Spot-on', accurately. *Oui, dans le mille mon vieux! Recta! Tu as deviné juste!* Yes, you got it in one! – Your guess was bang on target! **3** *Recta!* (as an intensifier): And how! *Et recta! Il s'est fait virer de la boîte!* He got the push from the old firm and was out before he knew what hit him!

rectifier *v.trans.* **1** (Gambling slang): To 'clean out' (usually through card-sharp trickery). **2** To 'bump off', to kill. *Dans le mitan, les donneurs on les rectifie d'autor!* If you grass in the underworld you don't live to a ripe old age! **3** *Se faire rectifier le portrait (joc. & iron.)*: To get one's face pushed in. (The kind of 'plastic surgery' inflicted by fists and boots gives the expression its dubious humour.)

rectifieur *n.m.* **1** 'Heavy', muscleman, mobster. **2** 'Hitman', gangland assassin.

récupérer *v.trans. (joc. & iron.)*: To 'swipe', to 'nick', to steal.

redingote *n.f. Redingote de sapin (joc.)*: 'Wooden overcoat', coffin.

redresse *n.f. A la redresse (adj.exp.)*: 'On the ball', 'wide-awake', energetic and resourceful. *C'est un mec à la redresse, lui!* There's no denying he knows the ropes! *Faire à la redresse*: To act the tough guy.

redresser *v.trans.* To 'peg', to 'spot', to recognize. *Les portiers de casinos s'y connaissent pour redresser la mauvaise clientèle*: You need a sharp eye to keep out the riff-raff when you're a doorman at a gaming-club.

refaire *v.trans.* To 'con', to 'diddle', to swindle. (The verb is used more often than not in the passive. *J'ai été refait en beauté!* I was done good and proper!)

refaire *v.trans.reflex.* **1** *Se refaire au jeu* (Gambling slang): To win back one's losses. **2** *Se refaire une santé*: To convalesce.

refile *n.m.* (also: *refil*): **1** Returned goods, item returned to a shop-keeper for a refund. *Elle boucle ses fins de mois avec le coup des refiles bidons*: She makes ends meet by operating the 'phoney refund' con-trick. **2** *Aller au refile*: To 'puke', to 'throw up', to vomit (also: *accrocher les wagons*). **3** *Passer au refile*: To 'cough up', to pay up under duress.

refiler *v.trans.* **1** *Refiler quelque chose à quelqu'un*: **a** To hand something to someone. *Il m'a refilé ton courrier*: He gave me your mail. **b** To return something to someone, to give something back to someone. *Refile-moi d'abord le fric que tu me dois!* I want that money you owe me first! **c** To 'fob something off' on someone. *Il m'a refilé toutes ses fripes!* I was lumbered with all his hand-me-downs! **d** To infect someone with a disease. *Tes gosses nous ont refilé les oreillons!* We all went down with the mumps thanks to your kids! **2** *En refiler*: To engage in passive sodomy (also: *refiler de la jaquette*).

refouler *v.intrans.* To 'stink', to smell foul. *Refouler du corridor*: To have foul breath, to suffer from halitosis.

refourgue *n.f. La refourgue*: The selling of stolen goods to a 'fence'.

refourguer *v.trans.* To sell stolen goods.

refrain *n.m.* **1** *C'est toujours le même refrain! (iron.)*: It's (always) the same old story! **2** *Change de refrain!* Stop harping on! – Give it a rest! – Change the subject!

refroidi *n.m.* 'Stiff', corpse, dead person.

refroidir *v.trans.* To 'bump off', to kill (also: *dessouder*).

refus *n.m. C'est pas de refus!* I don't mind if I do! – I wouldn't say no to that!

refuser *v.trans.reflex. Ne rien se refuser*: To satisfy one's every whim. (When uttered about someone else, the expression is always ironical and loaded with envy. *Eh ben, mon vieux, tu ne te* *refuses rien!* I can see you're not going short of the good things in life!)

régaler *v.intrans. C'est moi qui régale!* This treat is on me! – (of drinks): It's my shout!

régaler *v.trans.reflex.* 1 To enjoy a spicy sex-session. 2 (of business transaction): To 'make a killing', to make vast profits.

regard *n.m. Suivez mon regard! (fig. & iron.):* Do I have to spell it out?! – Can't you guess who I'm talking about?! (As the literal meaning suggests, the person in question is just 'within earshot'.)

regardant *adj.* Over-thrifty, rather mean.

regarder *v.trans. Vous (ne) m'avez (pas) regardé?! (iron.):* What do you take me for?! (Do you really think I'm that stupid?!)

régime *n.m. Régime jockey:* 'Weight-watcher's diet', low-calorie dietary intake.

régler *v.trans.* 1 *Avoir un compte à régler (avec quelqu'un):* To 'have a bone to pick' with someone. *Régler de vieux comptes:* To settle old scores. 2 *Régler son compte à quelqu'un:* To 'bump someone off', to kill someone.

réglo *adj.inv.* 1 'In order', fair, correct. *Il avait des fafs réglo:* His I.D. papers were O.K. 2 (of person): 'Straight', 'on the level', honest. *C'est un mec tout ce qu'il y a de réglo!* He's as straight as a die! (also: *régul*).

réglo *adv.* 'As per usual', normally.

regonfler *v.trans. Ça l'a regonflé (fig.):* It put new life into him.

regriffer *v.trans.* To snatch back, to retrieve something.

régul *adj.inv. (abbr. régulier):* 1 'In order', fair, correct. 2 (of person): 'Straight', 'on the level', honest (also: *réglo*).

régul *adv. C'est régul-régul:* It's 'by the book' – It's as per regulations.

régulier *adj.* 1 'In order', fair, correct. 2 (of person): 'Straight', 'on the level', honest. 3 *A la régulière:* Without trickery. *Il a gagné à la régulière:* He beat me fair and square.

régulière *n.f.* 1 'Steady', regular girlfriend. 2 Wife (or common-law wife). *Ma régulière:* The missus.

reine *n.f.* 1 'Queen', 'pansy', effeminate homosexual. (As in the English 'cottage queen', there is a suggestion that the person in question has a little sex empire.) 2 *La reine des . . . (pej.intensifier): Son père est la reine des vaches!* Her father's a sadistic swine! (Expressions such as *le roi des cons*, etc. carry a superlative connotation, but the feminine where men are concerned makes the statement even more insulting.) 3 *La petite reine:* The bicycle. (This is an affectionate appellation for the humble bike that sporting journalists covering cycle races use when in need of a hackneyed cliché!)

reine-mère *n.f. Pas un mot à la reine-mère! (joc.):* Mum's the word! – Don't breathe a dickey-bird! – Keep it secret!

reins *n.m.pl.* 1 *Avoir les reins solides:* To have a strong financial backbone (to be able to resist quite a few business set-backs). 2 *Casser les reins à quelqu'un:* To 'break someone', to ruin someone's career. 3 *Avoir quelque chose sur les reins:* To be lumbered with something. 4 *Les avoir dans les reins:* To have the police on one's tail.

relâche *n.f. Faire relâche:* a To take things easy (by taking time off). b To have a menstrual period. (The expression comes from the world of the theatre where it means that there will be no performances for a short while.)

relance *n.f.* 1 'Yet-another-sub' loan-request. *Faire de la relance:* To go 'sub-scrounging'. 2 *Aller (also: venir) à la relance:* a To try to rekindle a friendship (usually an amorous one). b To come looking for trouble after having been turned down in relation to a request.

relancer *v.trans.* 1 To remind someone of a promise made. 2 To 'badger', to pester someone. 3 (at card game): To raise the bid. *Je te relance de 100 Frs!* I'll raise you 100 Francs!

relarguer *v.trans.* (Prison slang): To let out, to release from jail.

relaxe *n.m.* 'Easy-chair', reclining chair.

relaxe *n.f.* (also: *relax*): Rest and relaxation.

relaxe *adj.inv.* (also: *relax*): 'Unflappable', easygoing. *C'est un mec tout ce qu'il y a de relaxe:* He's the most unruffled chap you could expect to meet.

relègue *n.f. (abbr. relégation):* Deportation. (Before the reform of the judicial system, recidivists used to be sent to the penal colony of French Guiana.)

relever *v.trans. Relever le compteur* (of pimp): To collect the day's takings.

relingé *adj.* Kitted out in brand-new clothes.

reloquer *v.trans.reflex.* To put one's clothes back on.

relourder *v.intrans.* To close a door. (*Lourde* in colloquial French means door.)

reluire *v.intrans.* 1 To 'come', to experience an orgasm. (The verb is more often than not encountered with *faire*, but expressions such as *un micheton qu'a bien relui, c'est un client pour l'avenir!* are not uncommon.) 2 *Ça m'a fait reluire de le savoir en taule!* It pleased me no end to hear that he was doing porridge! 3 *Passer la brosse à reluire:* To flatter in a 'crawling' manner. (The 'apple-polishing' imagery is also present in the French expression.)

reluquer *v.trans.* 1 To 'eye', to observe intently (and with envy). 2 To eye salaciously, to 'ogle', to leer at. *Reluque un peu cette nana!* Take a butchers at that smashing bird!

remballer *v.trans*. *Remballer ses outils*: To put one's trousers on again (literally to pack one's 'tools' away after sex).

rembarrer *v.trans*. To 'take down a peg or two', to put someone in their place. *Chaque fois que je vais à son bureau, je me fais rembarrer comme un malpropre!* Every time I go to see him, he just wipes the floor with me!

rembin *n.m*. **1** Feeble excuse, weak pretext and explanation (one that is not likely to satisfy the person to whom it is made). *Marcher au rembin*: To go through life with a ready stock of excuses. **2** 'Date', appointment, arranged meeting. **3** *Faire du rembin*: To 'chat up', to court a woman.

rembiner *v.trans*. To 'patch things up', to reconcile warring parties.

rembiner *v.intrans*. (also *v.pronom*.): To 'come back sharpish', to return quickly. *Il a* (also: *il s'est*) *rembiné fissa*: He got back double-quick.

rembour *n.m*. **1** 'Date', appointment, arranged meeting. *Filer un rembour*: To make a date. **2** *Aller au rembour*: To 'cough up', to pay back monies owed (under duress).

rembrayer *v.intrans*. To get 'stuck in' again, to go back to work.

remède *n.m*. **1** *Remède de bonne femme*: 'Home remedy', old wives' cure. **2** *Remède de cheval*: 'Kill-or-cure' medication. **3** *Remède à l'amour* (*joc.*): Ugly woman (literally the kind to give homosexuality a good name!).

remettre *v.trans*. **1** *Remettre ça*: **a** To have another go, to have another try at something. (With this meaning, the expression is nearly always tainted with reproval. *Ne remets pas ça!* Will you stop it! *A peine sorti de taule pour coups et blessures, il remettait ça avec le mec du gaz*: He was only just out of jail for G.B.H. when he got done for bashing up the man who came to read the gas-meter.) **b** (of drinks): To pour some more. *Garçon, remets-nous ça!* Barman, fill 'em up! **2** *En remettre*: To 'try and go one better', to exaggerate. *Il faut toujours qu'il en remette!* He can never stick to the truth when he's telling a story! **3** *Remettre quelqu'un*: To recognize, to remember someone. *Désolé mon vieux, je ne vous remets pas!* I'm sorry but I really can't place you!

remiser *v.trans*. **1** To put away, to put to one side (without any real intention of retrieving). *Remiser son calibre au râtelier* (of mobster): To pull out of the underworld rat-race. **2** *Remiser quelqu'un*: To 'take someone down a peg or two', to put someone in their place. *Je l'ai drôlement remisé!* I told him where he stood, no messing!

remmancher *v.trans*. **1** To give something a new lease of life. **2** To patch things up between dissenting parties.

remontant *n.m*. 'Pick-me-up', strong drink (that will put some life into you).

remonte *n.f*. Renewal of 'staff' in brothel. (When state-supervised brothels closed after World War II, the word fell into disuse. It has to a certain extent been resurrected with reference to the touting for fresh talent in the film and TV industries.)

remonter *v.trans*. **1** To 'buck up', to cheer up. *Ça m'a drôlement remonté d'avoir de tes nouvelles!* Hearing from you did me no end of good! **2** To overtake competitors in a race. **3** *Faire remonter*: To 'flash' something new, to acquire something and show it off. **4** *En faire remonter*: To reverse a compromised financial situation (literally to be able to come up with the readies). **5** *Remonter le courant*: To come out tops against the odds.

remordre *v.intrans*. *Y remordre*: To 'have another bash at something', to have another try. *Depuis qu'il est à la retraite, le jardinage, j'ai l'impression qu'il est en train d'y remordre*: Since retiring, he seems to have taken to gardening again.

remoucher *v.trans*. To 'peg', to 'spot', to recognize.

rempiffer *v.pronom*. To put weight on again.

rempilé *n.m*. (*mil.*): Re-enlisted man.

rempiler *v.intrans*. **1** (*mil.*): To re-enlist. **2** To 'go back to square one', to start all over again.

rempli *adj*. 'Loaded', stinking rich.

remplir *v.trans.reflex*. To 'make one's pile', to get stinking rich.

remplumer *v.pronom*. **1** To 'pad out again', to put on weight (after having lost it through illness, etc.). **2** To 'pick up again', to get back into good health. **3** To 'get out of Queer Street', to get back on one's feet financially.

remue-fesses *n.m*. (*joc.*): 'Hop', dance, function where there is dancing (also: *pince-fesses*).

renâcler *v.intrans*. To 'jib', to balk at. *Renâcler à la besogne*: To do one's darnedest to steer clear of work.

renard *n.m*. **1** *Un fin renard*: A 'sly 'un', a crafty so-and-so. **2** *Tirer au renard*: To 'skive', to dodge work skilfully. **3** *Lâcher un renard*: To 'puke', to 'throw up', to vomit (also: *lâcher une fusée*).

renaud *n.m*. 'Huff', 'paddy', anger. *Se mettre en renaud*: To fly off the handle.

renauder *v.intrans*. To 'gripe', to complain. *Il passe son temps à renauder*: With him it's moan, moan, moan all the time!

renaudeur *n.m*. 'Moaner', persistent complainer.

rencard *n.m.* (also: *rencart*): **1** 'Date', appointment, arranged meeting. *(Se) filer un rencard*: To arrange to meet. **2** (often *pl.*): 'Info', information.

rencarder *v.trans.* To 'gen someone up', to 'put someone in the picture', to inform someone.

rencarder *v.trans.reflex.* To try and get 'genned up', to make inquiries.

rencontre *n.f.* **1** *Faire à la rencontre*: To engineer a meeting and pretend it is pure chance. **2** *Vol à la rencontre*: 'Hustle-bustle' three-man pocket-picking trick.

rendève *n.m.* (*abbr. rendez-vous*): 'Date', appointment, arranged meeting.

rendez-moi *n.m. Vol au rendez-moi*: 'Cash-till boomerang' con-trick. (This fraudulent operation is worked by a 'client' who, having offered a large note to the cashier, receives his change and by a sleight-of-hand recovers the bank-note as well.)

rendre *v.intrans.* **1** To 'puke', to 'throw up', to vomit. **2** *C'est un truc qui rend*: **a** It's something that really brings a profit. **b** It's something that certainly works. (It does the trick.) **3** *Ne pas rendre*: 'Not to be taken in', to not be fooled. *Je ne rends pas à toutes ses salades!* I don't fall for all that patter of his! (also: *ça ne prend pas avec moi!*).

rendu *n.m.* **1** *Un rendu*: Returned goods (in a shop or department store). **2** *C'est un prêté pour un rendu! (joc.)*: It's tit for tat! – I'm only giving as good as I got! – It's a fair retaliation!

renfouiller *v.trans.* To put something back in one's pocket. *Je lui ai dit de renfouiller son pèze*: I told him to let me pay.

rengaine *n.f. C'est toujours la même rengaine! (iron.)*: It's (always) the same old story! *'Prête-moi du fric, prête-moi du fric!'* – *avec lui c'est toujours la même rengaine!* 'Lend us some money' seems to be a jingle with him!

rengracier *v.intrans.* **1** To come to terms with fate, to accept the inevitable. **2** To forgive and forget, to let bygones be bygones.

reniflant *n.m.* 'Sniffer', 'beak', nose.

renifle *n.f.* **1** *La renifle*: 'The fuzz', the police. **2** (Drugs): Sniff of cocaine.

renifler *v.trans.* **1** *Renifler le coup*: To 'smell a rat', to sense trickery ahead. **2** *Ne pas pouvoir renifler quelqu'un*: To find someone unbearable. *Ce mec-là, je peux pas le renifler!* I just can't stand that bloke! **3** *Renifler la comète*: To 'sleep rough', to sleep in the open air (also: *refiler la comète*).

renifler *v.intrans.* **1** To 'pong', to stink, to smell foul. *Renifler des nougats*: To have smelly feet. *Ça renifle!* What a pong! **2** *Renifler sur quelque chose*: To 'turn one's nose up at something', to show scorn for something.

reniflette *n.f.* (Drugs): 'Coke-sniff', nasal 'take' of cocaine.

renquiller *v.intrans.* **1** To go back into. *A peine sorti du bistro, il a renquillé voyant qu'il pleuvait*: He'd only just left the bar when he quickly backtracked realizing it was raining. **2** (*mil.*): To re-enlist.

renseignements *n.m.pl. Aller aux renseignements (joc.)*: To have a quick feel of a girl's sit-me-down.

rentes *n.f.pl. Penser à ses rentes*: To keep an eye on one's piggy-bank. *Tu penses à mes rentes?!* (of prostitute): Don't forget my little present! – I want paying!

rentre-dedans *n.m. Faire du rentre-dedans à quelqu'un*: To 'make a pass at', to make amorous advances to someone.

rentrer *v.intrans. Rentrer dedans à quelqu'un* (also: *rentrer dans le lard* or *le chou à quelqu'un*): To 'lam into someone', to attack someone violently *(lit. & fig.)*.

renversant *adj.* 'Mind-boggling', 'staggering', amazing.

renverser *v.trans.* **1** To 'bowl over', to dumbfound, to surprise. *La nouvelle de sa mort m'a renversé*: You could have knocked me down with a feather when they told me he was dead! **2** *Renverser la vapeur (fig.)*: To make an about-turn, to change one's mind or tactics completely.

renverser *v.intrans.* **1** To come to terms with fate, to accept the inevitable (also: *rengracier*). **2** To start behaving in a totally different manner (one that could not be seen as an improvement).

réparouze *n.f.* (*corr. réparation*): Repair (usually a botched job).

repassage *n.m.* 'Con-trick', swindle.

repasser *v.trans.* **1** To 'con', to 'diddle', to swindle. (The verb is often used in the passive with *faire* as in *Je me suis fait repasser en beauté!* I fell for that hook, line and sinker!) **2** To 'bump off', to kill.

repasser *v.intrans. Pouvoir repasser (iron.)*: To 'have another think coming', to be expecting too much. *Si c'est du fric que tu veux, tu peux toujours repasser!* If it's money you're after, you can whistle for it!

repasseur *n.m.* **1** 'Con-man', swindler. **2** (Underworld slang): Unscrupulous accomplice.

repêchage *n.m.* (*sch.*): 'Rescue' of a borderline candidate through upping his marks by the fraction he needs.

repêcher *v.trans.* **1** (*sch.*): *Repêcher un candidat*: To take sympathetic action where a borderline candidate is concerned. *S'il n'avait pas été* *repêché en dernière année, ç'aurait été trois ans de sa vie foutus!* If he hadn't been given a pass at his finals, it would have meant three wasted years! **2** To help someone out of a mess, to give someone a helping hand.

repérer *v.trans.* To 'keep an eye on', to watch closely. *Se faire repérer:* To get spotted.

répertoire *n.m. Sortir tout son répertoire (iron.):* To come out with a flood of abuse.

repiquer *v.intrans. Repiquer au truc:* **a** To 'have another shot at something', to have another go. **b** To go back to one's old ways. (This can be seen as a positive or negative move.)

répondant *n.m. Avoir du répondant:* **a** To have 'quite a bit on the side', to have a fair amount of money stashed away. **b** (of woman): To have curves (and lots of them) in all the right places.

répondre *v.intrans. Je t'en réponds! (iron.):* You can bet your life on it! – I should jolly well think so!

report *n.m.* (Racing slang): Accumulator bet.

repos *n.m. De tout repos* (of task, job): 'As easy as pie' (demanding very little energy).

repousser *v.intrans.* To stink, to 'pong', to smell foul. *Ça repoussait drôlement dans la chambrée!* The dormitory smelt like a zoo-cage! *Repousser du goulot:* To have foul breath, to suffer from halitosis.

repoussoir *n.m.* Ugly person (usually a woman).

reprendre *v.intrans. On reprend à deux heures:* We start work again at two.

reprise *n.f.* 'Key-money', amount paid by an incoming to an outgoing tenant, allegedly for fixtures and fittings.

requimpe *n.f.* Coat, overcoat.

requin *n.m.* 'Shark', ruthless individual where business matters are concerned.

requinquant *n.m.* 'Pick-me-up', strong drink (that will put some life into you).

requinquant *adj.* 'Boosting', heartening, uplifting.

requinquer *v.trans.* **1** To 'spruce up', to smarten. *Ils sont en train de requinquer une vieille bicoque pour leurs vacances:* They're giving their holiday-home a face-lift. **2** To 'buck up', to cheer up. *Viens plus souvent, ta visite m'a bien requinqué!* Don't leave it so long next time, your visit did me a power of good!

requinquer *v.pronom.* To 'pick up again', to get back to good health. *Je vais me requinquer au bord de la mer!* I'm going to get some sea-air to put me back on my feet again!

rescapé *n.m. Rescapé de bidet:* 'Genetic near-miss', runt (also: *raclure de bidet*).

respectueuse *n.f.* 'Prozzy', prostitute.

respirer *v.trans. C'est dur à respirer!* It's hard to swallow! – It's hard to believe!

respirette *n.f.* (Drugs): 'Coke-sniff', nasal 'take' of cocaine.

resquillage *n.m.* 'Wangling', action of obtaining by deceitful manipulation.

resquille *n.f. Faire de la resquille:* To 'wangle', to obtain by deceitful manipulation. *Tout ce qu'il a chez lui, il se l'est fait à la resquille:* There's not a thing in his house he got the honest way.

resquiller *v.intrans.* To obtain things by deceitful manipulation.

resquilleur *n.m.* 'Wangler', character who obtains what he wants by deceitful means. *Comme resquilleur on ne fait pas mieux!* He's the original Mr Fixit!

ressang *n.m. Etre à ressang:* To be 'really sore', to be angry.

ressaut *n.m.* Anger. *Aller à ressaut:* To 'fly off the handle', to have an angry outburst. *Mettre quelqu'un à ressaut:* To get someone's back up.

ressauter *v.intrans.* To 'kick up a fuss', to protest vehemently.

ressentir *v.pronom. S'en ressentir pour quelqu'un:* To be 'sweet on someone', to have an amorous liking for someone. (The French and English expressions are equally twee.)

ressort *n.m. De l'eau à ressorts (joc.):* Fizzy water.

restau *n.m.* 'Eating-house', inexpensive restaurant. *Le restau U (abbr. restaurant universitaire):* 'Refec', university students' canteen (also: *restif*).

rester *v.intrans.* **1** To 'hang out', to live somewhere. *Où ce que tu restes ces temps-ci?* Where's your pad these days? **2** *Y rester:* To 'croak', to 'snuff it', to die. *S'il prend le volant, bourré comme il est, on va tous y rester!* Sozzled as he is, if he gets into the driver's seat we'll all end up in kingdom come!

resucée *n.f.* Rehashed news, umpteenth version of a story. *En mal de copie, les baveux du lundi ne servent que des resucées!* With no-news weekends, Monday papers just dish out pepped-up rehash!

rétamé *adj.* **1** 'Blotto', 'blind-to-the-world', dead-drunk. **2** 'In Queer Street', 'cleaned-out', bankrupt.

rétamer *v.trans.* **1** (Gambling slang): To 'clean out', to take someone for all the money he's got. **2** To 'bump off', to kill. *Ils se sont tous fait rétamer en 14–18:* They all got killed in the Great War.

rétamer *v.trans.reflex.* To get 'blotto', 'sozzled', to get really drunk. *Tous les jeudis il se rétame en beauté!* Every payday he hits the bottle something fierce!

retape *n.f. Faire (de) la retape* (of prostitute): To 'pound the beat', to go soliciting.

retaper *v.trans.* **1** To do a 'botched' repair, to mend something in a haphazard manner. *Chaque fois qu'il fait du vent, on doit retaper le poulailler:*

Every time it blows a gale we have to plug holes in the henhouse. **2** To 'buck up', to cheer up. *Ça m'a drôlement retapé de te voir aujourd'hui!* Seeing you today did me a power of good! **3** *Se faire retaper (sch.)*: To 'get ploughed', to get failed at an exam.

retaper *v.pronom.* **1** To 'pick up again', to get back to good health. **2** To 'come out of Queer Street', to become solvent again. **3** To get kitted out with brand-new clothes.

retapissage *n.m. (pol.)*: Identification parade. *Passer au retapissage*: To be confronted with a plaintiff.

retapisser *v.trans.* To identify, to recognize a person. *Je ne peux vraiment pas le retapisser!* I really can't figure (out) who he is!

retard *n.m.* **1** *Avoir du retard*: To be 'late', to fear one is pregnant. **2** *Etre en retard d'affection (joc.)*: To have 'gone short', to be sex-starved.

retenir *v.trans.* **1** *Je la retiens celle-là* (of joke, good story): I like it! I like it! – That's a good one, that is! **2** *Pour ce qui est de la politesse, je te retiens! (iron.)*: When it comes to manners, you're no copybook!

retombées *n.f.pl. Il va y avoir des retombées!* There's going to be some nasty repercussions!

retourne *n.f. Les avoir à la retourne*: To be 'born tired', to be 'bone-idle', to be lazy.

retourner *v.trans. Ça m'a vraiment retourné!* It gave me quite a turn! – I was really upset by it!

retourner *v.intrans.* **1** *Retourner dans les brancards*: To 'get back in harness', to go back to work. **2** *En retourner*: **a** To engage in sodomous intercourse. **b** To engage in prostitution. *Il avait une demi-douzaine de polkas qui en retournaient sur le Sébasto*: He had six little scrubbers working away on the Boulevard Sébastopol. **c** To 'grass', to act as an informer to the police.

rétro *n.m.* **1** *(abbr. rétroviseur)*: Rear-view mirror. **2** 'Sit-me-down', 'bum', behind. *Prendre un coup dans le rétro*: To get kicked up the jacksey.

rétro *adj.inv.* **1** *(abbr. rétrograde) Comme décision, c'est plutôt rétro!* I wouldn't call that a very positive decision! **2** *(abbr. de la rétrospective) La mode rétro*: Revival fashion, ways of dressing based on resurrected styles.

retrousser *v.trans. En retrousser*: To be 'raking it in', to be making a lot of money.

retrouver *v.trans.reflex.* **1** To manage to make ends meet and make a little on top too. (The verb becomes more ironical when the profits get bigger.) **2** *Comme on se retrouve!* Fancy meeting you here!

rêve *n.m. Ce n'est pas le rêve!* (of person): He's no picture postcard! – He's nothing special to look at!

revenant *n.m. Mais, c'est un revenant! (iron.)*: Well look who's here! – You're a stranger in these parts!

revendre *v.trans. En avoir à revendre* (of gift, talent): To have enough and to spare. *Sur le plan de la débrouillardise, il en a à revendre!* When it comes to falling back on his feet again, he's not short on tricks!

revenez-y *n.m. Avoir un petit goût de revenez-y*: Not to be lacking in appeal. *Les voitures de sport avec lui ont un petit goût de revenez-y!* Fast cars have always been the love of his life!

revenir *v.trans.* **1** *Il a une gueule qui ne me revient pas!* I don't like the look of him! (I don't trust him!) **2** *Il s'appelle Reviens! (joc.)*: I want it back, you know! (This near-ironical expression is uttered by a lender to a borrower who is not in the habit of returning loaned items.)

revoyure *n.f. A la revoyure! (joc.)*: See you later, alligator! – I'll see you soon, I hope!

revue *n.f. Etre de la revue*: **a** To have to 'go without', to miss out on something. **b** To have been 'done', 'conned', to have been fooled. **c** To be 'for the high jump', to be in for some punishment. *Je vais être encore de la revue!* It's muggins who'll cop it again!

rez-de-chaussée *n.m. (joc.)*: 'Tools', 'privates', private parts. *Avoir le rez-de-chaussée en deuil*: To be impotent (also: *avoir le slip en berne*).

rhabiller *v.trans.reflex. Aller se rhabiller*: To go away 'with one's tail between one's legs', to leave crestfallen. *Va te rhabiller!* Go to hell! –Get lost! (The vision of a footballer being sent off the pitch back to the dressing-room can best illustrate the literal emphasis of this expression.)

rhume *n.m. Prendre quelque chose pour son rhume (iron.)*: To 'get a piece of someone's tongue', to 'cop it', to get told off in no uncertain manner.

ribambelle *n.f. Une ribambelle de*: 'Heaps of', a string of. *Elle a une ribambelle de gosses!* It's unbelievable the number of kids she's got! *Il m'a sorti une ribambelle d'injures!* He called me all the names under the sun.

ribote *n.f.* 'Binge', 'booze-up', all-out drinking bout. *Faire la* (also: *partir en*) *ribote*: To go on a pub-crawl.

riboter *v.intrans.* To booze one's way through life.

riboteur *n.m.* 'Boozer', heavy drinker.

ribouis *n.m.pl.* **1** 'Clodhoppers', 'beetle-crushers', shoes. **2** 'Hoofs', 'plates of meat', feet.

ribouldingue *n.f.* 'Beano', spree. (A combination of a good blow-out and a binge. *Faire la ribouldingue* could be translated as: to paint the town red. In the comic-strip series *Les Pieds-*

Nickelés, Ribouldingue is the name of one of the three outrageous fun-loving characters.)

ribouler *v.intrans.* 1 To 'whoop it up', to lead a fast and furious life where over-eating and drinking are concerned. 2 *Ribouler des calots*: To gawp, to gaze (at someone or something) in amazement.

riboustin *n.m.* 'Rod', 'shooter', handgun.

Ricain *n.m.* 'Yank', American.

ricain *adj.* 'Yankee', American.

ricaine *n.f.* *(abbr. voiture américaine)*: 'Yank', large American car.

ric-à-rac *adv.* (also: *ric-rac*): 1 (of financial settlement): 'On-the-nail', in full (and on time). *J'ai dû casquer ric-à-rac pour toutes tes conneries!* I had to settle on-the-spot and in full for all your tomfoolery! 2 'Touch-and-go', by the narrowest of margins. *Ça a été ric-rac de prendre le dur à Saint Lago!* We only just made it to the train at Saint-Lazare station!

richard *n.m.* 'Loaded geezer', very wealthy man.

riche *adj.* *(iron.)*: 'Not-up-to-much', of little merit. *Elle est riche, cette idée!* I don't think much of that crackpot idea of yours!

richelieu *n.m.* Ten-franc note. (Prior to the 1958 remonetization it was a one thousand franc note; it got its name because Cardinal Richelieu figures on it. See *misérable*.)

rideau *n.m.* 1 *Faire rideau* (also: *passer au rideau*): To 'do without', to 'have to go without', to miss out on something. *Pour la bouffe, les gars, il va falloir faire rideau!* I think you'll have to tighten your belts, lads, because there's no grub! 2 *Rideau!* Well, that does it! – I don't want to hear another word! 3 *Ça a été rideau* (of project, etc.): That was it – That was the end of it. *Quand la banque a cessé de payer, ça a été rideau.* It was curtains when the bank withdrew its support. 4 *Tomber en rideau*: To break down in a motorized vehicle. *On est tombés en rideau à dix kilomètres de Paris!* The car died on us seven miles from Paris! 5 *En lever de rideau (joc.)*: For starters – To begin with. *En lever de rideau, on s'est tapé la vaisselle!* Washing up was the first item on the agenda!

rider *n.m.* 'Top togs', 'Sunday best', natty suit.

ridère *adj.inv.* (of man): 'Swish', smart, elegant.

rien *indef.pron.* 1 *Pour trois fois rien* (of purchase): 'For next-to-nothing', very cheaply. *Son mobilier s'est vendu pour trois fois rien en salle des ventes*: In auction, his furniture went for a song. 2 *En un rien*: 'In no time at all', very quickly. *En un rien on survolait déjà l'Atlantique*: It seemed like minutes and we were well on our way to America. 3 *Ce n'est pas rien!* It's quite something! *Faire le tour du monde en bateau, ce n'est pas rien!* Sailing round the world is no

mean feat! 4 *De rien!* No trouble at all! – Don't mention it! (This polite retort to words of gratitude is rather low-brow.) 5 *Rien de rien*: 'Fuck-all', 'bugger-all', nothing at all.

rien *adv.* *(Antiphrastic intensifier)*: 'Not half', very. *Elle est rien moche!* She's as ugly as sin! *C'est rien bath de passer des vacances avec toi!* It's really super spending hols with you!

rien-du-tout *n.m.* 'Bad egg', 'wrong 'un', scoundrel.

rif *n.m.* 1 Fire. *Quand ça caille en plein air, rien ne vaut un bon rif!* There's nothing like a big crackling fire when you're freezing out in the open! *File-nous du rif!* Give us a light! 2 *Monter* (also: *aller*) *au rif (mil.)*: To go into battle (literally into the firing-line). 3 *Chercher du rif à quelqu'un*: To 'go looking for aggro', to pick a quarrel with someone. 4 *Mettre quelqu'un en rif*: To 'needle someone', to get someone angry. 5 *De rif*: Through sheer brute force. *Et de rif, on l'a obligé à fermer son bistrot!* After we leaned on him a bit, he had to close his joint! 6 *De rif et d'autor*: 'Snappily', without further ado.

riffauder *v.trans.* 1 To set fire to, to ignite. 2 To cook. *Elle nous a riffaudé des nouilles*: She boiled us some noodles.

riffauder *v.intrans.* To go up in flames, to burn (away).

riffer *v.trans.reflex.* To 'scrap', to 'have a bout of the fisticuffs', to fight.

rififi *n.m.* 'Rough-stuff', violent set-to. (Auguste Le Breton claims to have lexicalized this word; his novel DU RIFIFI CHEZ LES HOMMES, a best-seller in the *Série Noire* and a highly-acclaimed film, gave the word permanent status. *Dès qu'il y a du rififi dans l'air, il se dégonfle*: As soon as the going gets rough, he's nowhere to be seen.)

riflard *n.m.* 'Brolly', 'gamp', umbrella.

riflette *n.f.* *La riflette*: War, warfare.

riflot *n.m.* (also: *riflo*) 'Idle-rich' character. *Avoir des goûts de riflot*: To have expensive tastes.

riflot *adj.inv.* (also: *riflo*) 'Swish', 'natty', elegant.

rigadins *n.m.pl.* 1 'Clodhoppers', 'beetle-crushers', shoes. 2 'Hoofs', 'plates of meat', feet.

rigodon *n.m.* *Faire du rigodon*: To 'um-and-ah', to dither, to be unable to make one's mind up (also: *danser la valse hésitation*).

rigolade *n.f.* 1 Laughter, merriment. 2 'Fun-and-games', larking about. *Sans rigolade, on aurait crevé d'ennui au régiment!* National Service would have been a drag without all that horsing about! 3 Sexy capers. *Il ne pense qu'à la rigolade!* He's got sex on the brain! 4 *Prendre* *quelque chose à la rigolade*: Not to take something seriously. *Il n'a pas pris ça à la rigolade!* He certainly didn't take it as a joke! **5** *Ce n'est pas de la rigolade!* It's no laughing matter! **6** *Une vraie rigolade* (of task, undertaking): Mere child's play.

rigolard *n.m.* **1** 'Larker', one who doesn't take life too seriously. **2** Practical joker.

rigolard *adj.* **1** 'Screamingly funny', hilarious. **2** (of person): 'Larkish', fond of practical jokes.

rigolboche *adj.* 'Side-splitting', hilarious.

rigoler *v.intrans.* **1** To laugh. *On a bien rigolé au théâtre hier soir*: We laughed all through last night's play. **2** To 'pull someone's leg', to 'have someone on', to try and fool someone. *Tu veux rigoler!* You must be joking! – You can't be serious! *Il a dit ça pour rigoler!* He just said it for a joke! – He didn't mean it! **3** *Aimer rigoler*: To be fond of sexy capers, to like gallivanting. *Les nanas c'est sa vie, il a toujours aimé rigoler*: Birds seem to be a way of life with him, he's always been one for a bit of slap-and-tickle.

rigoleur *n.m.* **1** 'Larker', one who doesn't take life too seriously. **2** Practical joker. **3** 'Lad-about-town', randy so-and-so.

rigoleur *adj.* **1** Jolly, jovial. **2** Fond of 'slap-and-tickle', randy.

rigollot *n.m.* Mustard poultice. (In a country fond of home-remedies, even the old-fashioned mustard poultice lives on, and the easy-to-administer paper-based *rigollot* has brought its inventor-manufacturer eponymous fame.)

rigolo *n.m.* **1** 'Card', amusing character. (In its usual context, the word often conveys an ironic connotation, with an implication that the person may think he is funny, but his sense of humour is not appreciated. *Des rigolos comme toi, on s'en passe!* Your kind of funny person I can do without!) **2** 'Fly-by-night', unreliable person. **3** 'Rod', 'shooter', handgun. **4** 'Jemmy', crowbar.

rigolo *adj.* **1** Funny (hilarious). *C'est d'un rigolo!* It's an absolute scream! *Il est drôlement rigolo, ton frangin!* Your brother's a hoot! **2** Funny (peculiar). *C'est rigolo, mais je ne lui fais pas confiance*: It's funny, but I don't trust him. *Il lui est arrivé un truc rigolo*: A strange thing happened to him. (The feminine *rigolot(t)e* exists but is seldom encountered.)

rigouillard *adj.* **1** (of person): Fond of 'larking about', 'full of the joys of spring' where women are concerned. **2** 'Side-splitting', hilarious, very funny.

rigoustin *n.m.* 'Rod', 'shooter', handgun.

rikiki *n.m.* **1** 'Squirt', runt, under-sized person. **2** (Child language): 'Pinky', small finger.

3 (Child language): 'Willy', 'cock', penis. **4** Cheap (cooking) brandy.

rikiki *adj.* 'Teeny-weeny', tiny, very small.

rilax *adj.inv.* 'Unflappable', easy-going. (This phonetic spelling reflects the English origin of the word.)

rimer *v.intrans. Ne rimer à rien*: To make no sense. *A quoi ça rime, tout ça?* What's all this in aid of?

rimmel *n.m.* Mascara, cosmetic for colouring eyelashes and eyebrows. (The word *rimmel* has been lexicalized from the name of the manufacturer of the most widely sold brand.)

rince *n.f.* Round of drinks. *C'est à toi de remettre la rince!* It's your shout!

rince-cochon *n.m.* Drink made up of white wine, lemon juice and soda water. (This concoction is deemed to be efficacious when a hangover is the problem.)

rincée *n.f.* **1** Sudden downpour of rain. *On a pris une de ces rincées!* We got soaked to the skin! **2** 'Pasting', thrashing, volley of blows. *Quand il est rentré à trois heures du mat', bobonne lui a filé une de ces rincées!* His missus gave him the old rolling-pin treatment when he traipsed home at 3 a.m.!

rincer *v.trans.* (In colloquial usage, the verb is nearly always encountered in the passive.) *Se faire rincer*: **a** To get drenched, to get soaked to the skin. **b** To be 'stood a few drinks', to consume lots of alcohol at someone else's expense. **c** (Gambling slang): To get 'taken to the cleaners', to lose all one's money more 'by crook than by hook'. **d** To get 'worked over', to be beaten up.

rincer *v.intrans.* To stand a round of drinks. *C'est moi qui rince!* It's my shout!

rincer *v.trans.reflex.* **1** *Se rincer l'œil*: To 'feast one's eyes', to get a salacious eyeful. **2** *Se rincer la dalle*: To 'wet one's whistle', to have a drink.

rincette *n.f.* 'Chaser', small glass of alcohol taken at the end of a hearty meal, usually after the traditional cup of coffee.

rinçure *n.f. (abbr. rinçure de tonneau)*: Weak 'plonk', cheap watered-down wine.

riné *n.m. Le riné*: 'The flicks', the cinema.

ringard *n.m.* **1** *(th.)*: 'Two-bit' actor, performer whose talent is very much in doubt. **2** 'Gormless nurk', apathetic nonentity. **3** (Prostitutes' slang): 'Punter', client. (This appellation is uncomplimentary but not derogatory.)

ringard *adj.* **1** *(th.)*: 'Tatty', of poor quality. (The adjective can refer to productions, performances, décor, etc.) **2** (of person): 'Wet', 'useless', totally lacking in energy and spirit. *Il est d'un ringard, ce mec!* He's the original spineless wonder! (The feminine *ringarde* exists, but is seldom encountered.)

ripaille *n.f.* 'Blow-out', big 'tuck-in', mammoth eating session.

ripailler *v.intrans.* To feast, to eat and drink with no regard for moderation.

ripailleur *n.m.* One who is forever living it up where good food and drink are concerned.

ripatons *n.m.pl.* 'Hoofs', 'plates of meat', feet.

ripe *n.f.* 1 *Faire la ripe*: To roam the countryside. 2 *Jouer ripe*: To 'skedaddle', to 'make tracks', to run away.

riper *v.trans.* 1 To 'nick', to 'pinch', to steal. *On lui a ripé son larfeuil*: Someone lifted his wallet. 2 (Gambling slang): To 'clean out', to relieve a punter of all his money (usually by card-sharp methods). 3 *Etre bon à riper la lune* (of person): To be bloody useless, to be good for nothing.

riper *v.intrans.* 1 To 'buzz off', to move away niftily. 2 *Allez, ripe!* Go piss up a rope! – Get lost!

ripeur *n.m.* Dustman, refuse collector. (Excepting the driver, the refuse collection team includes the *ripeur* who brings out the bins, and the *biffin* who empties them into the cart after having put aside items worth selling to the rag-and-bone man.)

ripopée *n.f.* 1 Weak 'plonk' (cheap wine that has been watered down). 2 *Une ripopée de* (*fig.*; of ideas, etc.): A hotchpotch, an incoherent jumble. *Il a toujours une ripopée de bonnes idées dans la calebasse!* His mind's always bursting with innumerable pie-in-the-sky ideas!

riquette *n.f.* (*joc.*): 'Joy-stick', 'cock', penis. *Emmener la riquette au cirque*: To 'have it off', to have intercourse.

riquiqui *n.m.* 1 'Squirt', runt, under-sized person. 2 (Child language): 'Pinky', small finger. 3 (Child language): 'Willy', 'cock', penis. 4 Cheap (cooking) brandy.

riquiqui *adj.* 'Teeny-weeny', tiny, very small.

rire *v.intrans.* *Histoire de rire*: 'Just for kicks', just for a laugh. *Histoire de rire, on lui a fauché son falzar!* For a bit of fun and games we nicked his pants!

Riri *Proper name.* Popular nickname for anyone called *Henri* (also: *Riton*).

risettes *n.f.pl.* Amusing anecdotes (usually the kind connected with the most unlikely people. Jacques Arnal in his *L'ARGOT DE POLICE* quotes a few *risettes* relating to famous criminals).

risquer *v.intrans.* *Risquer de*: To stand a chance. *Verni comme il est, il risque de gagner le gros lot!* He's such a jammy bugger, I wouldn't be surprised if he won the top prize!

Rital *n.m.* 'Dago', Italian. (René Cavanna's novel *LES RITALS* did a lot to further the popularity of this word.)

rital *adj.* 'Wop', 'dago', Italian. *Il a un penchant pour les bagnoles ritales*: When it comes to cars, he prefers them Italian jobs!

ritournelle *n.f.* *C'est toujours la même ritournelle!* (*iron.*): It's always the same old story!

river *v.trans.* *River son clou à quelqu'un*: To silence someone with a cutting riposte.

roberts *n.m.pl.* 1 'Knockers', 'boobs', breasts. 2 'Oglers', 'peepers', eyes. *S'écarquiller les roberts*: To screw up one's eyes (in order to distinguish something).

robinet *n.m.* 1 'Yapper', incessant talker. *Quel robinet d'eau tiède!* What a wet waffler he is! 2 'Gob', mouth (where speech is concerned only). *Ferme ton robinet!* Shut your cakehole! 3 *Ouvrir les robinets*: To 'open the floodgates', to burst into tears (also: *ouvrir les écluses*).

rôdailler *v.intrans.* To loiter (usually 'with intent').

rôdeuse *n.f.* 'Prozzy', 'street-walker', prostitute.

rogatons *n.m.pl.* 'Leftovers', scraps of food that might end up as 'bubble-and-squeak'.

Roger-Bon-Temps *n.m.* 'Good-time Charlie', man-about-town who likes to whoop it up.

rogne *n.f.* 1 'Foul mood', state of bad temper. *Quoi qu'on fasse, il est toujours en rogne!* There's no pleasing him, he always seems to have got out of bed the wrong side! *Se mettre en rogne*: To get into a huff. *Il tient une de ces rognes!* He's in a stinking mood today! 2 *Chercher des rognes à quelqu'un*: To (try and) pick a quarrel with someone.

rogner *v.intrans.* To grumble loudly, to moan vociferously.

rognons *n.m.pl.* (*joc.*): 'Bollocks', 'balls', testicles.

rognure *n.f.* (*pej.*): 1 'End-of-the-road prozzy', prostitute long past her prime. 2 (of man): 'Genetic near-miss', runt-like character.

rogomme *n.m.* 1 'Hooch', strong spirits (usually the moonshine variety). 2 *Une voix de rogomme*: A beery voice, the slurred and croaky speech of a drunkard.

roi *n.m.* *Le roi des . . .* (*iron.*): A prize so-and-so when it comes to . . . (Expressions such as *le roi des cons*, *le roi des pommes* emphasize the superlative nature of the insult.)

romaine *n.f.* *Etre bon comme la romaine*: **a** To be 'as good as gold', to be kindness personified. **b** (*iron.*): To be the likely mug for an unpleasant task. **c** (*iron.*): To be 'for the chop', to be 'for the high jump', to be heading for punishment.

roman-fleuve *n.m. (iron.)*: Never-ending tale. (In colloquial French, the word refers to verbose explanations, lengthy tales of woe.)

romano *n.m.* Romany, gypsy (also: *romanigo, romanuche*).

rombier *n.m. (Slightly pej.)*: 'Geezer', 'bloke', fellow.

rombière *n.f. (pej.)*: 'Middle-aged moo', woman devoid of youth and charm. *Une vieille rombière*: A silly old cow.

roméo *n.m.* Drink of rum cut with iced water. (*Roméo* is a pun on *rhum et eau*.)

rompre *v.trans. Tu me les romps!* You're a pain in the arse! (also: *tu me casses les couilles!*).

rompu *past part.* 'Knackered', 'buggered', exhausted.

ronchon *n.m.* 'Grouch', perpetual grumbler.

ronchon *adj.* 'Grouchy', grumpy.

ronchonner *v.intrans.* To 'grouch', to grumble.

rond *n.m.* **1** 'Brass', 'loot', money. *Ça a dû te coûter des ronds!* It must have cost you a packet! *J'ai eu ça pour deux ronds!* I got it for next to nothing! *Ne pas avoir un rond*: To be 'skint', 'broke', to be penniless. *Il n'a jamais le rond!* He never has two brass farthings to rub together! **2** *Ne pas être . . . pour deux ronds*: Not to be in the least . . . *Il n'est pas méchant pour deux ronds!* There's not an ounce of meanness in him! **3** *Faire des ronds dans l'eau*: To while away the hours doing bugger-all, to be idle. **4** *En rester comme deux ronds de flan*: To be 'knocked all of a heap', to be 'flabbergasted', to be dumbfounded. **5** *Le rond* (also: *la pièce de dix ronds*): The arse-hole, the anal sphincter. *Prendre du rond*: To engage in sodomous intercourse. (The expression *se manier le rond* refers more generally to the behind and can be translated as to 'put one's skates on', to get a move on, to hurry up.)

rond *adj.* 'Sozzled', 'sloshed', drunk. *Il est rond comme une bourrique*: He's pissed out of his tiny little mind.

rond *adv. Tourner rond*: To go 'without a hitch', to run smoothly. *Depuis qu'on a des commandes, ça tourne rond à l'usine*: Since orders have been coming back in again, we seem to be holding our own at the factory. (The expression *ça ne tourne pas rond* when referring to a person suggests an unbalanced state of mind. *Ça ne tourne pas rond avec lui, ces temps-ci!* He's seemed to be going off his rocker lately!)

rond-de-cuir *n.m.* 'Pen-pusher', clerk (usually a civil servant. The origin of the appellation lies in the round leather cushion used to minimize the 'buff-and-shine' to which trouser seats are subjected).

ronde *n.f. La ronde*: The (planet) Earth.

rondelle *n.f.* **1** *La rondelle*: The arse-hole, the anal sphincter. (The word is nearly always used in a context of sodomous intercourse.) **2** *Se manier la rondelle*: To 'put one's skates on', to get a move on, to hurry up (also: *se manier le train*).

rondin *n.m.* 'Turd', faeces. *Planter un rondin*: To have a crap.

rondins *n.m.pl.* 'Knockers', 'bristols', breasts.

rondouillard *n.m.* 'Podge', 'fatso', tubby person.

rondouillard *adj.* 'Podgy', 'tubby', small and fat.

ronflaguer *v.intrans.* **1** To snore away. **2** To sleep. *J'ai ronflagué chez des potes hier soir*: I kipped down at some friends' last night.

ronfle *n.f. La ronfle*: 'Kip', some 'shuteye', sleep.

ronfler *v.intrans.* **1** (of business): To be 'going great guns' (literally to be doing a roaring trade. There is a link between the whirring noise of busy machinery and brisk trading). **2** *Ça va ronfler!* Things are going to hum! – There's going to be one hell of a to-do! (also: *ça va barder!*).

ronflette *n.f.* 'Snooze', short nap. *Après la bouffe, ça fait du bien de pousser une ronflette*: After a good meal, nothing beats a bit of shuteye! (also: *roupillon*).

ronfleur *n.m.* 'Blower', phone, telephone.

rongeur *n.m.* 'Clock', meter in taxi.

roploplots *n.m.pl.* 'Boobs', 'knockers', breasts.

roquet *n.m.* 'Whippersnapper', small arrogant man.

Roquette *Proper name. La Roquette*: Women's prison in Paris. (The *Prison de la Roquette* has always suffered from a certain notoriety because its inmates – prostitutes, brothel-keepers, etc. – formed a hard core of recidivists.)

rosalie *n.f. (mil.)*: 'Pig-sticker', bayonet.

rosbif *n.m.* 'Brit', British person. (The 'roast beef' origin gives the alimentary connotation so well reciprocated in English by the appellation 'frog' where Frenchmen are concerned; neither is truly pejorative.)

rosbif *adj.inv.* British. *Dans le temps, les voitures rosbif c'était de la bonne camelote!* In the old days British cars used to be a cut above the rest!

rose *n.f.* **1** *Envoyer quelqu'un sur les roses*: To 'send someone off with a flea in his ear', to tell someone off in no uncertain manner. **2** *Ça n'a pas été des roses!* It wasn't all plain sailing! – It wasn't that easy! **3** *Bouton de rose*: 'Clit', clitoris. **4** *Faire feuille de rose*: To perform anilingus.

rosette *n.f.* Arse-hole, anus (where sodomous intercourse is concerned. The expressions *amateur de rosette* and *chevalier de la rosette* refer respectively to active and passive homosexuals).

rossard *n.m.* **1** 'Idle git', lazy fellow. **2** 'Nasty piece of work', evil character.

rossard *adj.* **1** Idle, lazy. **2** Nasty, evil.

rosse *n.f.* **1** 'Nag', horse long past its prime. **2** 'Nasty so-and-so', evil-minded person. (Like many pejorative appellations, this feminine word becomes more derogatory when directed at a male.)

rosse *adj.* **1** 'Catty', 'bitchy', mean and nasty. **2** Sharp-tongued, sarcastic. (This adjective is often used in a non-derogatory context when each meaning is mellowed by intonation. *Dans le fond, tu n'es pas si rosse que ça!* You're not as nasty as you make yourself out to be!)

rossée *n.f.* 'Bashing-up', thrashing, beating.

rosser *v.trans.* **1** To 'bash up', to beat black and blue. **2** To 'beat into a cocked hat', to trounce.

rosserie *n.f.* **1** Snide remark. *Elle passe son temps à dire des rosseries!* Nasty gossip seems to be her trade in life! **2** Dirty trick, underhand deed. *Il m'a fait une de ces rosseries!* You wouldn't believe the dirty one he pulled on me!

rossignol *n.m.* **1** Irritating squeak, persistent noise within a motor-driven contraption. **2** Skeleton key (for illegal purposes). **3** (Antique-dealers' slang): 'White elephant', unsaleable item.

rot *n.m.* 'Burp', belch.

roter *v.intrans.* **1** To 'burp', to belch. **2** *En roter*: To 'get the rough end of the stick', to have a tough time.

roteuse *n.f.* *(joc.)*: Bottle of champagne.

roteux *n.m.* 'Champers', 'bubbly', champagne.

rôti *n.m.* *S'endormir sur le rôti*: **a** To 'dawdle over one's work', to treat it in a lackadaisical fashion. **b** To show little ardour where love-making is concerned.

rotin *n.m.* *Ne pas avoir un rotin*: To be 'skint', 'broke', to be penniless.

rôtissoire *n.f.* *(joc.)*: Crematorium (also: *grill-room*).

rotoplots *n.m.pl.* 'Boobs', 'knockers', breasts.

rotules *n.f.pl.* *Sur les rotules*: 'Done-in', 'buggered', exhausted. *Quand les beaux-parents viennent en visite, ça nous met sur les rotules!* When the in-laws leave after a 'short stay', we're all completely knackered!

roubignolles *n.f.pl.* **1** 'Bollocks', 'balls', testicles. **2** *En avoir plein les roubignolles*: To be 'fed up to the back teeth', to be sick and tired of something. **3** *Avoir les roubignolles bien accrochées*: To be gutsy in the face of danger, to be brave (also: *avoir les couilles au ventre*).

roublard *n.m.* 'Crafty beggar', cunning so-and-so. *Quel roublard, celui-là!* He's a right con-artist!

roublard *adj.* 'Crafty', cunning.

roublardise *n.f.* **1** Craftiness, cunning nature. *La roublardise, c'est son blot!* He knows every trick in the book! **2** Dirty trick. *Sans toutes ces roublardises, il n'aurait pas réussi!* Playing dirty got him where he is today!

rouchie *n.f.* *(pej.)*: **1** Kept woman. **2** Low-class prostitute.

roucouler *v.intrans.* **1** To sing soppy and syrupy love-ballads. (Crooning is a possible translation but is less pejorative.) **2** To whisper lovey-dovey sweet nothings. (The billing-and-cooing image is extended in these colloquial meanings.)

roucouleur *n.m.* (also: *roucouleur de charme*): 'Crooner', vocalist specializing in languorous melodies.

roudoudou *n.m.* Children's confection. (This can either be barley sugar in a small non-edible container or a sticky concoction consisting of sugar and liquorice.)

roue *n.f.* **1** *Etre dans la roue*: To be 'in the running', to be in on a success. (This expression and the following three originate from the language of racing cyclists.) **2** *Sucer la roue à quelqu'un*: **a** To ride in a fellow-competitor's wind-stream, to stick to his rear wheel in a leech-like manner. **b** *(fig.)*: To stick closely to someone and copy his every move with the intention of beating him at the finish. **3** *Montrer sa roue arrière*: To 'show a clean pair of heels', to leave the opposition standing. **4** *Faire roue libre*: To take life easy (as the literal meaning suggests, 'to free-wheel along'). **5** *Mettre des bâtons dans les roues à quelqu'un*: To 'put a spoke in someone's wheel', to hamper someone's progress. **6** *Pousser à la roue (fig.)*: To give (someone) a push in the right direction. **7** *Faire la roue*: To 'strut about', to show off (like the peacock whence the expression originates). **8** *Graisser les roues* (of motorist): To 'have one for the road', to have one more drink before driving off. **9** *Etre la cinquième roue du carrosse*: To be surplus to requirements (to have as little active use as a spare wheel on a stage-coach).

rouflaquette *n.f.* **1** Kiss-curl. **2** *(pl.)*: 'Chops', sideburns, side-whiskers.

rouge *n.m.* **1** *Du rouge*: Red wine. *Vous prendrez bien un petit rouge?* How about a glass of red wine? *Gros rouge*: 'Plonk', cheap and rough red wine. (The appellation *du gros rouge qui tache* gives a good idea of the coarse nature of this 'vino'.) **2** 'Commie', 'Red', Communist. *Les* *rouges, c'est son obsession, il en voit partout!* He seems obsessed with 'Reds under the bed' ideas! **3** *Mettre le rouge:* To 'kick up some aggro', to create a disturbance (usually through sheer physical violence. The expression *le rouge est mis* belongs either to the language of horse-racing where it indicates that no more on-course betting is possible, or to the world of T.V. and film productions where it means that a scene is being shot in a studio).

rougnotter *v.intrans.* To 'pong', to stink, to smell foul.

rouille *n.f.* Bottle of wine. (The logical implica-tion would be that the wine is red, and not necessarily upmarket, but Auguste Le Breton, San-Antonio and others use it when referring to champagne.)

roulant *n.m. (abbr. personnel roulant):* Railway staff employed on board trains.

roulante *n.f. (mil.):* Field-kitchen.

roulé *adj. Etre bien* (also: *pas mal) roulée* (of woman): To be 'well-stacked', to 'have every-thing in the right places', to have a shapely figure. (When referring to a man, *bien roulé* can be equated with the *beau gosse* image and a he-man physique.)

rouleau *n.m.* **1** *Etre au bout de son rouleau:* **a** 'Not to be long for this world', to be nearing the end. **b** To be 'at the end of one's tether', to be at one's wits' end. **c** To have overspent, to be out of funds. **2** *(pl.):* 'Balls', 'bollocks', testicles. **3** *Baver sur les rouleaux à quelqu'un* (also: *casser les rouleaux à quelqu'un):* To 'get on someone's wick', to be 'a pain in the neck to someone', to be a nuisance.

roulée *n.f.* **1** 'Ciggy', 'fag', cigarette (the 'roll-your-own' kind. Manufactured cigarettes are known as *cousues).* **2** 'Drubbing', beating, thrashing. *Filer une roulée à quelqu'un:* To beat someone black-and-blue.

rouler *v.trans.* **1** To beat at sport (often through greater tactical skill than sheer strength). **2** To 'con', to 'diddle', to swindle. *Se faire rouler:* To get done. **3** *La rouler:* To 'burn the candle at both ends', to lead a fast and furious life. **4** *Les rouler:* To 'roll the bones', to throw the dice. **5** *Se les rouler:* To 'twiddle one's thumbs', to while away the time doing nothing. **6** *En rouler une:* To (hand-) roll a cigarette. **7** *Rouler un patin:* To give a 'smackeroo', to exchange a 'French kiss'. **8** *Rouler les* (also: *des) mécaniques:* To 'act the tough guy', to strut about.

rouler *v.intrans.* **1** To 'prattle on', to talk non-stop with little intellectual effort. **2** *Rouler sur l'or:* To be 'rolling in it', to be very wealthy. **3** *Rouler des miches:* To walk with a wiggle.

(The expression is often used where the undulating and effeminate walk of homosexuals is concerned.) **4** *Ça roule!* **a** You're on! – Great! – That's O.K. by me! **b** (Waiters' slang): Coming up! (In the hustle and bustle between the kitchen and the dining area, this expression can often be heard and is an acknowledgement that a menu item is being prepared.)

rouletabille *n.m.* 'Rolling stone', character who forever seems to be on the move.

roulettes *n.f.pl.* **1** *Marcher* (also: *aller) comme sur des roulettes* (of project, enterprise): To 'go swim-mingly', to go without a hitch. *Ça a marché comme sur des roulettes!* It was all plain sailing! **2** *Etre à la roulette:* To be 'on the ball', to be with it, to be not lacking in the 'get-up-and-go' spirit. **3** *Les vaches à roulettes:* 'The fuzz', the police (those that are motorized, because they are 'on wheels').

rouleur *n.m.* **1** 'Here-today-gone-tomorrow' character, one who never seems to be able to settle. **2** 'Gasbag', character who prattles on and on. **3** *(abbr. rouleur de mécaniques):* 'Swank', show-off (one who struts about). *Il se prend au sérieux, ce rouleur!* That pompous burk certainly takes himself seriously! **4** 'Con-man', swindler.

rouleuse *n.f.* Trollop, slut.

roulotte *n.f. Vol à la roulotte (pol.):* Stealing from parked cars.

roulottier *n.m.* **1** One who operates *vol à la roulotte.* **2** Car-thief. (Unlike the joy-rider who abandons vehicles when he has no further use for them, this criminal operates within a framework of forged logbooks and sells his spoils.)

roulure *n.f.* Trollop, slut.

roupane *n.f.* **1** Policeman's cape (the kind that helped give *hirondelles* their nickname; see that word). **2** Woman's skirt.

roupes *n.f.pl.* 'Bollocks', 'balls', testicles (also: *roupettes).*

roupie *n.f.* **1** 'Bogey', 'snot', nasal discharge. **2** *De la roupie de sansonnet:* Worthless rubbish. **3** *Vieille roupie (pej.):* 'Old hag', scruffy old woman. (With this meaning the word seems to have drifted out of usage in the late 30s.)

roupillade *n.f.* **1** 'Snooze', short nap. **2** 'Kip', sleep.

roupiller *v.intrans.* To sleep, to get some sleep.

roupillon *n.m.* 'Kip', 'snooze', short nap. *Piquer un roupillon:* To take forty winks.

roupillonner *v.intrans.* To sleep, to get some sleep.

roupiot *n.m.* Young apprentice or shop assistant.

rouquemoute *n.m.* Red wine. (The word has no real pejorative connotation, unlike *picrate, gros rouge,* etc.)

rouquemoute n.m. & f. 'Redhead', man or woman with red hair.

rouquin n.m. 1 'Redhead', ginger-haired person. 2 Du rouquin: 'Plonk', red wine. File-nous un coup de rouquin! Give us a glass of vino! (It is interesting to note that the word 'plonk' is, in fact, a corruption of vin blanc.)

rouscaille n.f. Vociferous recriminations. Dans les affaires d'héritage, il y a toujours de la rouscaille! It's usually dog-eat-dog when a will is opened!

rouscailler v.intrans. To grumble vociferously.

rouscailleur n.m. 'Grouch', persistent and vociferous grumbler.

rouspétance n.f. Argumentative quarrelling. Il est plutôt porté sur la rouspétance! He's a cantankerous bugger if ever was!

rouspéter v.intrans. To 'create', to 'bellyache', to grumble. A l'hôtel, il passe son temps à rouspéter! Nothing seems to please him when he's in a hotel!

rouspéteur n.m. 'Bellyacher', grumbler.

rousse n.f. La rousse: 'The fuzz', 'the cops', the police. Gaffe, il travaille pour la rousse, lui! Steer clear of him, we reckon he's a snitch!

roussi n.m. Ça sent le roussi! There's trouble brewing! – I can sense aggro in the air!

roussin n.m. 1 'Cop', policeman. 2 C.I.D. officer, plain-clothes policeman. 3 'Snitch', 'copper's nark', police informant.

rouste n.f. 'Pasting', 'walloping', thrashing. Filer une rouste à quelqu'un: To beat someone black-and-blue.

rousti adj. 1 'Snookered', cornered. Avec les condés devant et derrière on était bien roustis! There was no way out, the fuzz had us well and truly hemmed in! 2 'Done for', ruined (financially or reputation-wise). Encore une connerie comme ça et il est rousti! Another slip-up and his reputation's gone for a burton!

roustir v.trans. 1 To 'con', to 'diddle', to swindle. 2 To 'nick', to 'pinch', to steal.

roustissure n.f. De la roustissure: 'Trash', worthless goods (also: camelote).

roustons n.m.pl. 'Bollocks', 'balls', testicles.

routier n.m. 1 Long-haul lorry driver. 2 Restaurant catering for the above. (These eating-houses have quite a reputation for good food at an honest price; lorry drivers are not easily led up the garden path when it comes to grub! The French way of distinguishing an excellent restaurant routier from merely a good one is to be on the lookout for extensive oil stains on the parking area.) 3 Vieux routier: 'Old stager', 'old hand', character who is skilled at something through long experience.

royal adj. Ficher à quelqu'un une paix royale: To let someone get on with what he is doing without interfering or interrupting him.

royalement adv. Se foutre (also: se ficher) royalement de quelque chose: 'Not to give a fuck', to not give a damn about something. Il se fout royalement de tout ce que tu peux lui dire! He won't take a blind bit of notice of whatever you say to him!

ruban n.m. 1 Road (the highway). Se taper un bon bout de ruban: To have to hoof quite a few miles. 2 Faire le ruban (of prostitute): To go soliciting. (With this meaning of pavement, the word is only used in the context of prostitution.)

rubrique n.f. Il en connaît une rubrique! (also: il en sait des rubriques!) He knows every trick in the book!

ruche n.f. 'Conk', 'hooter', nose. Se taper la ruche: To 'stuff one's face', to have a hearty meal (the implication being that a lot of alcohol is consumed).

rude adj. 1 En avoir vu de rudes: To have had a tough time. Au régiment on en a vu de rudes! Barrack-room life was no doddle! 2 Elle est rude, celle-là (of story, item of news): That's a bit stiff! – I can't believe that! 3 'Smashing', first-rate. On a fait un rude gueuleton: We had a really super meal.

rudement adv. 'Awfully', extremely, very. Il fait rudement froid! It's real brass-monkey weather!

rue n.f. 1 Faire la rue de Lappe: To 'have gone on a fool's errand', to have nothing to show for one's efforts. (The rue de Lappe in Paris in the quartier de la Bastille used to attract the less desirable elements of society, hence the expression.) 2 Ça fait la rue (Michel): It's all square, then?! – The matter's settled! (Gaston Esnault in his DICTIONNAIRE DES ARGOTS claims that the expression is a truncation of Ça fait la rue Michel-le-Comte!, itself a pun on Ça fait le compte!)

ruer v.intrans. Ruer dans les brancards: To 'kick against the pricks', to rebel.

ruminer v.trans. To 'mull over', to think long and hard about something.

rupin n.m. 'Swell', 'toff', one of the 'upper crust'. (The French and the English are equally dated.)

rupin adj. 1 'Swish', smart, elegant. 2 'Well-heeled', well-off, rich. Une Rolls, ça fait rupin! A Rolls-Royce certainly makes you look wealthy.

rupiner v.intrans. 1 (sch.): To do well at an exam. 2 To 'slog one's guts out', to work very hard.

rupinskoff n.m. 'Swell', 'toff', one of the 'upper crust'. (Both in noun and adjective form the word has a flavour of wealthy Russian aristocracy.)

rupinskoff *adj.* **1** 'Swish', smart, elegant. **2** 'Well-heeled', well-off, rich.

Ruscoff *n.m.* (also: *Ruskoff*): 'Ruskie', Russian.

ruscoff *n.m.* (also: *ruskoff*): Russian, the Russian language. *Parler ruscoff comme père et mère*: To speak fluent Ruskie.

russe *adj. Chaussettes russes*: Makeshift socks. (This appellation, current in the world of down-and-outers, describes the bandage-like rags worn by those who have to resort to any means to ward off sub-zero temperatures.)

rustine *n.f.* **1** Puncture-patch, rubber patch for tyre repair. (This is another instance of a very successful brand-name becoming generic.) **2** 'Buttonholer', 'limpet-bore', tenacious and boring person (one who like the adhesive patch is hard to shake off).

S

sable *n.m.* **1** *Etre sur le sable*: To be 'on the rocks', to be in a state of ruin and destitution. **2** *Avoir du sable dans les yeux* (of child): To be 'ready for beddy-byes', to be showing signs of drowsiness. (This expression and *le marchand de sable est passé* are part of that register that can only be described as *le langage bêtifiant* directed at children by would-be adults.)

sabler *v.trans.* *Sabler le champagne*: To have some champers, to drink some bubbly in order to celebrate an occasion.

sabord *n.m.* **1** *Mille sabords!* Thunder and lightning! – By jove! (This jocular and dated exclamation was given a totally new lease of life by *Le Capitaine Haddock*, the bearded seawolf in the *Tintin* cartoon comic-strip stories.) **2** *Coup de sabord*: Searching look. *On a jeté un coup de sabord avant d'entrer*: We had a quick butchers before going through the door.

sabot *n.m.* **1** 'Old tub', seagoing vessel long past its prime. **2** Inefficient and worthless bit of machinery. **3** 'Bungler', 'botcher' (literally a character who unwittingly 'sabotages' whatever task he undertakes). **4** (Gambling): 'Shoe', box from which cards are dispensed to players in games such as baccarat. **5** *Il joue comme un sabot!* He can't play for toffee! **6** *Voir venir quelqu'un avec ses gros sabots* (iron.): To be no mug where trickery is concerned. *Je l'ai vu venir avec ses gros sabots!* I could see what his little game was! (He certainly wasn't fooling me!) **7** *Ne pas avoir les deux pieds dans le même sabot*: **a** To be 'always on the go', to be full of energy. **b** To be 'on the ball', not to be lacking the spirit of enterprise.

sabouler *v.trans.reflex.* To get 'togged up', to get dressed with elegance in mind.

sabre *n.m.* 'Mutton-dagger', 'cock', penis. *Donner un coup de sabre*: To 'have it off', to have coition.

sabrer *v.trans.* **1** To fuck, to 'screw', to have coition with. (As this 'macho' verb would suggest, little importance seems to be given to the partner's participation and pleasure.) **2** To 'strike out', to cross something out of a text. *Il a sabré mon article dans les grandes largeurs!* You should see the way he wielded the editorial blue pen! **3** To 'blast', to give someone a (public) dressing-down. **4** To 'botch', to 'bungle', to make a mess of something (through haste and lack of care). *Depuis qu'il est marié il sabre tout son boulot!* Since he got hitched, his work seems to have gone to pieces!

sabreur *n.m.* **1** 'Superstud', 'randy so-and-so', man whose only motivation in life is sex. **2** 'Bungler', 'botcher', character who always seems to make a mess of his work.

sac *n.m.* **1** 'Belly', stomach. *S'en mettre plein le sac*: To 'stuff one's face', to have a hearty meal. **2** Unit of ten francs or ten-franc note. (Prior to the 1958 remonetization, the amount was 1000 francs. According to certain sources inflation in the mid-70s resulted in an upgrading of the *sac* to 100 *nouveaux francs*.) **3** *Etre au sac* (also: *avoir le sac*): To be 'stinking rich', to be 'rolling in it', to be very wealthy. (Expressions such as *épouser un sac*: to marry a wealthy girl, and terms like *gros sac*: wealthy so-and-so, confirm the money image of this meaning of the word.) **4** *Faire son sac*: To 'make one's pile', to amass a fortune. **5** *L'affaire est dans le sac!* **a** It's in the bag! – It's a dead-cert! – It's a sure thing! **b** *(iron.)*: She's preggers! – She is pregnant. **6** *Avoir son sac*: To 'have had a skinful', to be drunk. (The boozing image is further illustrated in the term *sac à vin*: 'wino', dipsomaniac.) **7** *Etre fichu comme un sac*: **a** (of person): To be 'dressed like a guy', to be frumpily attired. **b** (of work, plans, etc.): To be in a right old mess, in total disarray. **8** *Vider son sac*: To 'get something off one's chest', to speak one's mind. **9** *Mettez ça dans votre sac!* **a** Keep it under your hat! – Keep this to yourself! – Don't mention this to anyone! **b** Put that in your pipe and smoke it! – Accept that fact if you can! (There's little else you can do!) **10** *Travailler le sac* (Boxing): To have a workout with the punchbag. **11** *Mettre dans le même sac (fig.)*: To 'tar with the same brush', to 'lump together', to judge in the same manner. **12** *Avoir la tête dans le sac*: To be completely out of funds, to be near to financial ruin. **13** *Cracher dans le sac*: To be guillotined (also: *cracher dans le son*). **14** *Sac à malice(s)*: 'Tricky customer', cunning so-and-so (character who always seems to have something left in his bag of tricks). **15** *Sac d'embrouilles*: Inextricably jumbled issue or situation (literally a tangled web. Also: *sac de nœuds*). **16** *Sac à viande (joc.)*: Sleeping-bag. **17** *Sac d'os*: 'Bag of bones', skinny person. *Quel sac d'os!* I've seen more meat on a butcher's pencil!

saccagne *n.f.* (also: *sacagne*): 'Chiv', blade, knife.

saccagner *v.trans.* (also: *sacagner*): To 'stick', to knife, to stab.

sachem *n.m. (joc.)*: 'Big white chief', top man, leader. *Quand le sachem a parlé, 'faut y aller de l'ouvrage!* When the big boss has spoken, it's 'jump to it and do what you're told'! (Even this American Indian word seems to have entered colloquial French.)

sachets *n.m.pl.* 'Smellies', 'coffee-strainers', socks.

sacotin *n.m. (corr. sac)*: Unit of ten francs or ten-franc note. (Prior to the 1958 remonetization, the amount was 1000 francs. According to certain sources, inflation in the mid-70s resulted in the upgrading of *sac* and *sacotin* to 100 *nouveaux francs*.)

sacouse *n.m.* (also: *sacouze*): Bag, handbag.

sacquer *v.trans.* **1** To 'give someone the big E', to give someone the push, to sack someone. **2** *(sch.) Se faire sacquer*: To get 'ploughed', to be failed at an examination.

sacré *adj.intensifier.* **1** Expletive expressions such as *bordel de merde! – nom de nom!* become more potent when preceded by *sacré*. **2** According to the context, *sacré* can crystallize admiration as in *une sacrée idée*: one hell of a good idea; envy as in *avoir un sacré pot*: to have the luck of the devil; or contempt as in *une sacrée fripouille* (of man): an out-and-out swine.

sacrer *v.intrans.* To curse and swear (also: *jurer comme un charretier*).

sacristain *n.m.* **1** *(pej.)*: 'Bloke', 'geezer', fellow. *Un drôle de sacristain*: A bit of a weirdo, a strange character (one certainly not to be trusted). **2** *Sauter le sacristain (pol.)*: To steal money from a church alms-box by inserting a stick tipped with glue.

safran *n.m. Aller au safran*: To throw one's money away. (The only work to lexicalize this expression is HARRAP'S FRENCH-ENGLISH DICTIONARY OF SLANG AND COLLOQUIALISMS. A likely explanation as to the origin of this

expression could be found in the prohibitive cost of the spice extracted from the dried stigmas of *Crocus sativus*.)

sagouin *n.m.* **1** 'Out-and-out rotter', dishonest and treacherous character. **2** 'Botcher', unskilled and careless 'craftsman'. **3** 'Dirty old man', lecherous male. (The feminine *sagouine* exists but is seldom encountered.)

saignant *adj.* (of argument, discussion): 'Heated', fierce.

saigner *v.trans.* **1** To 'stick', to stab to death. *Il se vantait d'avoir saigné un malfrat dans un bouge*: He was boasting how he'd chivved a heavy in some down-town caf'. **2** *(fig)*: To 'bleed dry', to extort money from someone.

saigner *v.intrans. Ça va saigner!* **a** It'll be an all-out battle! (literally, blood will flow!). **b** It's going to be one hell of a slanging match!

saindoux *n.m.* 'Fatso', fat person.

Sainte-Anne *Proper name. Etre bon pour Sainte-Anne*: To be fit for the 'loony bin', to be 'bonkers', to be mad. (*Sainte-Anne* is the name of a famous Paris mental hospital. *Un échappé de Sainte-Anne* is one whose state of mental health is even more perilously poised – both expressions are used with ironic overtones.)

Sainte-Catherine *Proper name. Coiffer la Sainte-Catherine* (of woman): To have reached the age of 25 in a state of spinsterhood. (*Sainte-Catherine* is the patroness of virgins and on her name-day, the 25th November, it is customary to adorn her statue with a new headdress.)

Sainte-Nitouche *n.f.* Demure 'little madam', hypocritical little 'goody-goody' girl. (The 'butter-wouldn't-melt-in-her-mouth' image comes from a truncation of the ironic *Sainte qui n'y touche*.)

Sainte-Touche *n.f. La Sainte-Touche*: Payday (because on that day *on touche sa paye*).

Saint-Frusquin *n.m.* **1** Personal effects. *Avec tout son Saint-Frusquin dans ma piaule, on ne peut pas bouger!* With all his clobber in my bedsit, there isn't room to swing a cat! **2** 'Privates', male sexual parts. *Il s'est fait pincer par les mœurs pour avoir déballé son Saint-Frusquin dans le métro*: He got done for 'flashing' in the tube-station. **3** *Tout le Saint-Frusquin*: The 'whole caboodle', the 'whole shebang', every damn thing.

Saint-Galmier *Proper name. Avoir les épaules en bouteille de Saint-Galmier (joc.)*: To have narrow sloping shoulders. (The *eau minérale* of *Saint-Galmier* is sold in distinctive long-necked bottles, hence the jocular and ironic reference made to them when describing a gawky individual.)

Saint-Georges *n.m.* Unorthodox form of coitus, graphically described by Guillaume Apollinaire in LES ONZE MILLE VERGES.

Saint-Ger *Proper name. (abbr. Saint-Germain-des-Prés)*: The *quartier* of that name in Paris.

Saint-Glinglin *Proper name.* Fictitious saint whose name-day obviously does not appear in any calendar. *A la Saint-Glinglin*: 'When pigs have wings' – Never. *Tu peux attendre jusqu'à la Saint-Glinglin pour te faire payer!* You'll be waiting till doomsday to get paid!

Saint-Jean *Proper name. Etre en Saint-Jean*: To be 'starkers', to be naked. *Employer toutes les herbes de la Saint-Jean*: **a** To 'leave no stone unturned', to explore every avenue. **b** To 'try every trick in the book', to go for every possible solution.

Saint-Lago *Proper name. (corr. Saint-Lazare)*: **1** The railway station of that name in Paris. **2** The *Prison Saint-Lazare*.

Saint-Lundi *Proper name. Faire la Saint-Lundi (joc.)*: To take Monday off. (To claim sick-leave after one hell of a weekend.)

Saint-Martin *Proper name. Ce n'est pas la même Saint-Martin!* It's a different kettle of fish! – It's not the same thing!

Saint-Trou-du-cul Fictitious saint's-day which obviously never occurs. *A la Saint-Trou-du-cul*: 'Not in a blue moon', never (also: *Saint-Truc*).

salade *n.f.* **1** 'Mix-up', confusion. *Quelle salade!* It's a proper shambles! (also: *salade russe*). **2** *En salade*: In a 'higgledy-piggledy' way, in a disorderly manner. *Il nous a présenté ses arguments en salade*: The case he put to us was a jumble of facts and angles. **3** (also *pl.*): 'Bullshit', 'baloney', nonsense. *J'en ai marre de toute cette salade!* I'm sick to the back teeth of all this tommyrot! *Je ne crois à toutes ses salades!* I don't believe all the bilge he's spouting! **4** *(pl.)*: 'Nasty tittle-tattle', evil gossip (the inference being that it is 'a pack of lies'). *Il est toujours à balancer des salades sur ses meilleurs 'copains'*: He's always doing the dirty on his so-called pals. **5** *Faire des salades*: **a** To 'stir it', to create trouble (usually by passing on malicious gossip). **b** To put up a barrage of excuses (in order to avoid chores, etc.). **6** *Passer une salade à quelqu'un*: To give someone 'a real wigging', a good telling-off. **7** *Bonnir sa salade à quelqu'un*: To 'give someone the full spiel', to spin someone a right old yarn. (The assumption is that the recipient falls for it hook, line and sinker.) **8** *Vendre sa salade*: To 'know one's onions', to know one's trade or business inside-out. **9** *Savoir vendre sa salade*: To have the gift of the gab (literally to be able to sell

sand to the Arabs). **10** *Avoir une salade au cul*: To have something unpleasant lurking in one's past. (This is not so much a case of skeletons in the cupboard as the Damoclean consequences to recent misdemeanours.)

saladier *n.m.* **1** 'Trap', 'gob', mouth. *Refouler* (also: *taper*) *du saladier*: To have bad breath, to suffer from halitosis. (With this meaning, the word is seldom found in other contexts.) **2** 'Stirrer', gossip-monger. (The feminine *saladière* is often encountered.) **3** *Faire un saladier de*: To 'make a meal of something', to go on and on about a fact or issue not worth a second thought.

salamalecs *n.m.pl. Faire des salamalecs*: To 'bow and scrape', to behave in an over-obsequious manner.

salaud *n.m.* 'Bastard', 'rat', swine of a character. (According to context and intonation, the word can be derogatory or jocularly ironic. *C'est un beau salaud!* He's a real shyster! *Tu es un sacré petit salaud!* You're a right little twister!)

sale *adj. Ça n'est pas sale!* It's bloody good! (The colloquiality of the expression stems from the fact that the adjective is always used with a negative.) *Six semaines de vacances, mon vieux, ça n'est pas sale!* You're onto a good thing there, what with those six weeks annual paid leave!

salé *n.m.* (also: *petit-salé*): 'Brat', kid, child. (The near-pejorative connotation of *salé* and *petit-salé* stems from the fact that in standard French *petit-salé* is salted pork.)

salé *adj.* **1** (of bill): 'Stiff', exorbitant. **2** (of joke, story): 'Blue', 'close-to-the-knuckle', rather obscene.

salement *adv.* Awfully, extremely, very. *Ce qu'il nous a fait manger était salement bon!* The grub he gave us wasn't half good! (The colloquiality of this adverb stems from its antiphrastic use.)

saler *v.trans.* **1** To 'salt away', to 'stash', to put away for a rainy day. **2** To 'soak', to 'sting', to overcharge. *On bouffe bien chez lui, mais qu'est-ce qu'il sale la note!* He's a top-class restaurateur, but the bills he dishes out afterwards aren't all that sweet!

saleté *n.f.* **1** 'Dirty trick', underhand act. *Elle n'a pas cessé de lui faire des saletés!* She's played him one rotten trick after another! **2** Smutty talk or story. *Il faut toujours qu'il nous sorte une saleté à table!* He's always coming out with blue jokes at mealtime!

saligaud *n.m.* 'Bastard', 'rat', swine of a character. (According to context and intonation, the word can be derogatory or jocularly ironic. *Comme saligaud on ne fait pas mieux!* When it comes to shysters, he beats the lot! *Bougre de petit saligaud!* You rascal, you!)

salingue *n.m.* 'Dirty dog', salacious individual, one whose mind is constantly occupied with smutty thoughts.

salingue *adj.* **1** 'Mucky', dirty, filthy. **2** 'Smutty', salacious. *Il vend des photos salingues*: He sells dirty postcards.

salir *v.trans.* *La salir*: To 'lay it on thick', to exaggerate. *Entre nous, mon vieux tu la salis, tu te fous de nous!* Don't you think you're going it a bit strong with us?!

salive *n.f.* *Perdre sa salive*: To 'waste one's breath', to talk to no avail.

salle *n.f.* **1** *Jouer à la salle (fig.)*: To 'play to the gallery', to 'act the ham' in a loud conversation. **2** *Salle à manger*: 'Gob', 'trap', mouth (obviously where food is concerned; it is not always clear whether this appellation refers to the mouth as an aperture or to the inside, i.e. to the teeth. The jocular *salle à manger démontable* is more explicit in its reference to dentures, false teeth).

saloir *n.m.* *Mettre la viande au saloir (joc.)*: To 'hit the sack', to go to bed.

salonnard *n.m.* 'Upper-cruster', character who enjoys nothing better than rubbing shoulders with fellow 'pseuds' at cocktail parties, etc.

salopage *n.m.* 'Botching', 'bungling'. *Pour le salopage, il s'y connaît!* When it comes to making a hash of things, he's your man!

salopard *n.m.* 'Bastard', 'rat', swine of a character. (According to context and intonation, the word can be derogatory or jocularly ironic. *Quel salopard!* What a shyster! *Tu es un gentil petit salopard, toi!* You're a right little rogue!)

salope *n.f.* **1** Slut, woman with loose morals and few admirers. **2** 'Shyster', swine of a character. (As with most terms of abuse, the feminine gender adds insult to injury when the word is directed at a man.)

saloper *v.trans.* To 'botch', to 'bungle', to make a mess of something. *Si vous le laissez faire, il va tout nous saloper!* If you give him a free hand, he'll muck everything up!

saloperie *n.f.* **1** 'Shoddy goods', sub-standard wares. *Cette saloperie de bagnole est encore en panne!* That useless car's off the road again! **2** 'Dirty trick', underhand act. *Il m'a fait une de ces saloperies!* He really did the dirty on me!

salsifis *n.m.pl.* Fingers. (The word has not got the gentle connotation of 'pinkies' in English, a typical expression being *se rincer les salsifis*: To 'wash one's hands', i.e. to go to the lavatory.)

salutas *interj. (joc.)*: **1** Hi there! – How do?! – Hello! **2** Tatty-bye! – Toodle-oo! – Goodbye!

samedi *n.m.* *Etre né un samedi*: To be 'born lazy', to have an idle streak.

sana *n.m.* *(abbr. sanatorium)*: Hospital-cum-health-resort for T.B. sufferers (see *préventorium*).

sandwich *n.m.* *Etre pris en sandwich*: To be 'caught between two fires', to be cornered.

sang *n.m.* **1** *Attraper un coup de sang*: To 'fly off the handle', to have a fit of temper (literally to go red in the face). **2** *Ne pas avoir de sang dans les veines*: To be 'gutless', 'funky', to be a coward (also: *avoir du sang de navet*). **3** *Se cailler le sang* (also: *se faire du mauvais sang*): To 'fret', to worry. *Se ronger le sang*: To worry oneself sick. **4** *Se refaire du sang*: To 'get back into the pink' (healthwise). **5** *Avoir le sang chaud*: To be a randy so-and-so. **6** *Ça m'a retourné les sangs!* That gave me quite a turn! – It really upset me!

sangsue *n.m.* 'Wallet-leech', hanger-on where money is concerned.

sans *prep.* *Etre sans un*: To be 'skint', 'broke', to be penniless.

sans-un *n.m.* Penniless character (also: *sans-le-sou*).

Santaga *Proper name.* *La Santaga*: The *Prison de la Santé* in Paris.

santé *n.f.* **1** *Avoir une petite santé*: To be something of a hypochondriac. *Soigner sa petite santé*: To (molly)coddle oneself. **2** *Se refaire une santé*: To be 'on the mend', to get back in tip-top condition healthwise. **3** *Avoir de la santé*: To have a very patient nature. *Il faut avoir de la santé pour supporter une nana comme la sienne!* You need a pair of wings and three Valiums to live with a wife like his! **4** *En avoir une santé (iron.)*: To 'have a nerve', to be totally unabashed. *Tu en as une santé, toi!* You're a cheeky so-and-so, aren't you?!

Santoche *Proper name.* *La Santoche*: The *Prison de la Santé* in Paris.

sape *n.m. (abbr. sapement)*: 'Stretch', prison sentence. (Authors and lexicographers choose to differ on the gender of this word, but on the basis of *sape* being an abbreviation of *sapement*, the masculine seems in order.)

sapé *past part.* Dressed. *Etre bien sapé*: To be togged-up.

sapement *n.m.* 'Stretch', prison sentence.

saper *v.trans.* To 'send down', to sentence to a term of imprisonment.

saper *v.trans.reflex.* To 'get togged up', to get dressed. *Il s'est sapé en dimanche*: He put on his glad rags.

sapes *n.f.pl.* 'Togs', clothes.

sapin *n.m.* *Ça sent le sapin!* He's not long for this world! (The implication here is that the smell of pine, the wood of cheap coffins, could well be heralded by that person's sickly complexion.)

saquer *v.trans.* **1** To 'give someone the big E', to give someone the push, to sack someone. **2** *(sch.)*: *Se faire saquer*: To get 'ploughed', to be failed at an examination.

sarbacane *n.f. (joc.)*: Rifle. (The humour stems from the straight meanings of the word: peashooter, blowgun.)

sarcif *n.m. (corr.abbr. saucisson)*: Dry, salami-type sausage sold in *charcuteries*.

sarco *n.m. (joc.; abbr. sarcophage)*: 'Wooden overcoat', coffin.

sardine *n.f. (mil.)*: N.C.O.'s stripe, insignia of rank in the lower echelons of the Forces.

sardoches *n.f.pl. (joc.)*: Sardines.

satané *adj.* 'Infernal', confounded, damned.

sataner *v.trans.* To bash, to pummel, to hit violently.

sataner *v.trans.reflex.* To 'have a bout of the fisticuffs', to have a fight.

saton *n.m. Coup de saton*: Kick. *Il a pris un coup de saton dans les joyeuses*: He got kicked in the goolies.

satonner *v.trans.* **1** To 'bash', to pummel, to hit violently. **2** To 'boot someone', to kick someone repeatedly.

sauce *n.f.* **1** 'Soup', heavy downpour of rain. *Recevoir une sauce*: To get soaked to the skin. **2** Motor-fuel (petrol or diesel). *Mettre la sauce*: To 'burn some rubber', to accelerate violently. **3** *Coup de sauce* (Sporting slang): Burst of energy. *Répondre à chaque coup de sauce* (Cycling slang): To counter every sprint. **4** *Balancer la sauce*: **a** To 'juice off', to ejaculate. **b** To fire off, to shoot (a gun). **5** *Etre dans la sauce*: To be 'in the soup', 'in a pickle', to be in a fix. **6** *Allonger* (also: *rallonger*) *la sauce* (of tale, narration): To 'spin it out', to make it last and last. **7** *Faire de la sauce* (Musicians' slang): To 'fill in' with some spontaneous free composition. **8** *Mettre à toutes les sauces*: To put someone or something to every possible use. *Le pauvre, on le met à toutes les sauces!* Poor bugger! He seems to be at everyone's beck and call!

saucée *n.f.* **1** 'Downpour', heavy shower. **2** 'Rocket', talking-to, reprimand.

saucer *v.trans. Se faire saucer*: **a** To 'get soaked to the skin', to get drenched by a downpour of rain. **b** To 'get the rough edge of someone's tongue', to get told off in no uncertain manner.

sauciflard *n.m. (corr. saucisson)*: Dry, salami-type sausage sold in *charcuteries*.

saucisse *n.f.* **1** 'Silly sausage', 'nincompoop', fool (also: *andouille*). **2** *Ne pas attacher son chien* (also: *ses chiens*) *avec des saucisses*: To be as mean as they come. **3** *Rouler une saucisse*: To give a 'French kiss'. **4** 'Prozzy', low-class prostitute. **5** 'Prick', 'cock', penis.

saucisson *n.m.* **1** (Musicians' slang): Tune or song of little merit (literally one that seems to have come into existence like sausages off a conveyor-belt). **2** 'Biddy', rather unattractive woman (one whose figure is as remarkable as that of a sausage). *Etre ficelée comme un saucisson* can either mean to be bulging in the wrong places, or to be trussed up like a *saucisson sec*). **3** *(pol.)*: 'Stinker', difficult case (one that will take a lot of unravelling).

saucissonnard *n.m.* (slightly *pej.*): 'Picnicker-cum-weekender' (the kind who sets up table on the roadside and leaves the grass verges littered with refuse).

saucissonné *adj.* Dressed in tight and badly-fitting clothes.

saucissonner *v.trans.* **1** To truss up, to tie up firmly like the *saucisson sec* sold in *charcuteries*. **2** To 'collar', to arrest. (The implication here is that the suspect is shackled or tied up.)

saucissonner *v.intrans.* To have a bite to eat (the kind of picnic-like quick-meal so aptly described by the expression *manger sur le pouce*).

saumâtre *adj.* Not at all to one's liking, nasty. *Elle est saumâtre, celle-là! (iron.)*: Well, I like that!

saumure *n.f. La saumure*: 'The briny', the sea. *Piquer une tête dans la saumure*: To take a dive into the ocean.

sauret *n.m.* Pimp, procurer. (The word is an alternative for *hareng saur*. See *maquereau*.)

saut *n.m.* **1** *Faire le saut*: **a** To 'take the plunge', to make a decision (usually after quite a bit of hesitating). **b** To 'jump the gun', to go ahead with a decision or project before weighing up the pros and cons. **2** *Faire un saut chez quelqu'un*: To pop round to someone's place, to pay someone a fleeting visit.

sautée *n.f. Grande sautée*: Gawky nurk. (The appellation is usually directed at a man, and because it is feminine it is even more derogatory.)

sauter *v.trans.* **1** To 'nab', to 'collar', to arrest (literally to pounce on someone's back). **2** To 'screw', to fuck, to have intercourse with. **3** *Sauter le pas*: **a** To 'take the plunge', to make a decision (usually after quite a bit of hesitating). **b** To 'jump the gun', to go ahead with a decision or project before weighing up the pros and cons. **4** *La sauter*: To 'go hungry', to be starving (literally to skip a meal).

sauter *v.intrans.* **1** To 'hit the ceiling', to 'fly off the handle', to have an angry outburst. **2** *Il faut que ça saute!* Get to it! – I want some action! **3** *Allez, et que ça saute!* Look lively (about it)!

– Make it snappy! **4** *Sauter (du train) en marche*: To practise coïtus interruptus.

sauterelle *n.f.* 'Biddy', 'bird', woman.

sauterie *n.f.* **1** 'Hop', informal dance. **2** Any party, with or without music.

sauteur *n.m.* Unreliable so-and-so (the kind of bounder one cannot trust).

sauvage *adj. Grève sauvage*: Wildcat strike.

sauvette *n.f. Vendre à la sauvette*: To sell goods in the street (often without a licence).

savate *n.f.* **1** Tough meat (literally, as the standard meaning suggests, 'shoe-leather'). **2** 'Bungler', 'botcher', poor workman. **3** *Traîner la savate*: To 'loaf about' jobless (with no serious intention of finding employment).

savater *v.trans.* To 'kick someone up the jacksey', to boot someone in the behind.

saveur *n.f. Coup de saveur*: Searching look. *On a jeté un coup de saveur avant d'entrer*: We had a quick butchers before going through the door.

savoir *v.trans. & intrans.* **1** *Savoir! (abbr. c'est à savoir!)*: That remains to be seen! (The northern English 'appen! is the nearest elliptical equivalent to this usage of *savoir*.) **2** *Ne vouloir rien savoir*: To 'dig one's heels in', to be obstreperously unwilling to conform. **3** *Elle pleurait tout ce qu'elle savait*: She was crying her eyes out.

savon *n.m.* **1** 'Rocket', 'roasting', severe reprimand. *Je lui ai passé un de ces savons!* I certainly tore a strip off him! **2** 'Trade', job, occupation. *Il vend des bagnoles d'occase, et pourtant c'est pas son savon!* He's down to selling second-hand cars which certainly wasn't his calling!

savonner *v.trans. Savonner la tête à quelqu'un*: To 'give someone a right rollicking', to tell someone off in no uncertain manner.

savonnette *n.f.* **1** Bald tyre (one that is as smooth and slippery as a bar of soap). **2** *Donner dans la savonnette*: To engage in sodomy. (The expression is deemed to have originated in the army where the action of bending down to pick up a bar of soap in the communal showers could have surprising consequences!)

sbire *n.m. (pej.)*: **1** 'Cop', policeman. **2** 'Screw', prison warder. **3** 'Heavy', bodyguard to an important person in the underworld. **4** Insignificant underling.

scaille *A la scaille (adv.exp.)*: 'On the cheap', at little expense. *Il ne se sape pas à la scaille, lui!* He certainly doesn't get his clothes from Oxfam!

scalp *n.m. (pol.)*: Arrest of a criminal. *Il a plusieurs beaux scalps à son actif*: He pulled in quite a few big-name villains in his time.

schbeb *n.m.* 'Nancy-boy', 'young pouf', effeminate homosexual. (The appellation is said to have originated in the *Bat' d'Af'* – see that word – and comes from the Arabic.)

schlaf *n.f.* 'Shut-eye', sleep. *Aller à la schlaf*: To 'turn in', to 'hit the sack', to go to bed.

schlague *n.f.* **1** 'Birch', instrument used for beating (castigation). **2** 'Thrashing', beating, castigation. **3** 'Rocket', 'roasting', severe reprimand.

schlass *n.m.* 'Chiv', blade, knife.

schlass *adj. (also: schlasse)*: **1** 'Pissed', 'blotto', drunk. **2** 'Knackered', 'buggered', tired out.

schlinguer *v.intrans.* To 'pong', to stink, to smell foul. *Il schlingue un brin, ton calendos!* That Camembert cheese of yours certainly whiffs!

schloffe *n.f.* 'Shut-eye', sleep. *Etre bon pour la schloffe*: To be ready for beddy-byes.

schmoutz *n.m. & f. (pej.)*: 'Yid', Jew. (This is an anti-semitic word if ever there was, as it is a phonetic representation of the German *Schmutz* meaning filth.)

schmoutz *adj. (pej.)*: 'Yid', Jewish.

schnaps *n.m.* 'Hooch', 'hard stuff', strong alcohol.

schnock *n.m.* 'Burk', 'nincompoop', fool. *Vieux schnock*: Old dodderer.

schnouf *n.f.* 'Snow', cocaine.

schnouffer *v.trans.reflex.* To take drugs, to be a drug addict.

schpile *n.m.* **1** *Le schpile*: Gambling, gaming. *Au schpile, c'est un as!* At the tables, he's no learner! **2** *Avoir beau schpile*: **a** To have a winning hand at cards. **b** *(fig.)*: To have one's opponents 'snookered', to be in a commanding position. **c** To be 'on to a good thing', to 'have it made', to be sure of success.

schproum *n.m.* **1** 'To-do', commotion. *Faire du schproum*: To 'raise Cain'. **2** Temper, anger. *Il est dans un de ces schprooms!* He's in a right lather!

schtar *n.m. (also: schtard)*: **1** 'Clink', 'nick', prison. **2** Disciplinary cell. **3** 'Glasshouse', military punishment block.

schtibe *n.m.* 'Clink', 'nick', prison.

schtilibem *n.m.* 'Nick', 'clink', prison. (Auguste Le Breton in his *L'ARGOT CHEZ LES VRAIS DE VRAI* identifies the word as coming from the language of the gypsies and mentions Georges Arnaud's book of poems *SCHTILIBEM 41* to that effect.)

schtouillard *n.m.* **1** One who has caught a dose of *schtouille*. **2** 'Funk', cowardly character.

schtouille *n.f.* **1** 'Clap', V.D., gonorrhoea. **2** 'Funk', fear. *Il avait une de ces schtouilles à l'idée d'aller au front*: He was in a blue funk at the thought of going to the Front.

sciant *adj.* Deadly boring. *C'est un film tout ce qu'il y a de sciant!* It's a movie that'll send you to sleep!

scier *v.trans.* **1** To 'give the boot' to someone, to 'sack', to dismiss someone. **2** To 'bump off', to kill. **3** *Tu me scies (le dos)!* You're a bloody pain in the arse! – You're a damn nuisance!

scion *n.m.* 'Chiv', blade, knife. *Donner un coup de scion:* To 'knife', to stab.

scionnage *n.m.* 'Chivving', 'knifing', stabbing.

scionner *v.trans.* To 'knife', to stab.

sciure *n.f. Avoir de la sciure dans la caboche:* To 'have nothing up top', to be as dumb as they come.

score *n.m.* **1** *(joc.):* Score (in anything but a sporting context, where colloquial usage is concerned). *Côté nanas, il s'est payé un beau score!* He notched up a few smashing birds, I can tell you! **2** 'Stretch', prison sentence.

scotch *n.m.* **1** Whisky. **2** 'Sellotape', transparent adhesive tape. (As with its English equivalent, *Scotch,* a brand-name, has become generic for any transparent adhesive tape.)

scoubidou *n.m.* **1** *(joc.):* 'Doo-dah', 'whatsit', thing. (This word gained tremendous momentum with the song *'Des pommes, des poires, des scoubidous'* which launched the crooner Sacha Distel into a successful career.) **2** Key-holder made of plaited coloured flex in the manner and spirit of a corn-dolly. (The *scoubidou* craze did a lot for the electrical flex industry!)

scoumoune *n.f.* Run of bad luck.

scribouillard *n.m. (pej.):* 'Pen-pusher', menial office-worker.

scribouiller *v.trans.* To write with little concern for legibility.

scrogneugneu *n.m.* 'Old fuddy-duddy', doddering old martinet. (Where military men are concerned, a 'Colonel Blimp' type.)

scrogneugneu *adj.* Grumpy and officious.

Sébasto *Proper name. Le Sébasto:* The *Boulevard Sébastopol* in Paris.

sec *n.f.inv. En cinq sec (abbr. en cinq secondes):* 'In two ticks', 'in two shakes of a lamb's tail', as quick as a flash.

sec *adj.inv.* **1** *Etre à sec:* **a** To be 'skint', 'broke', to be penniless. *Je me suis fait mettre à sec au pok'!* I got cleaned out in a friendly little game of poker! **b** To have run out of words or ideas (literally to have dried up). **2** *L'avoir sec:* To 'be fuming', to be furious (also: *l'avoir mauvaise*). **3** *Rester sec (sch.):* To be 'stumped for an answer' (literally to be left high and dry in front of an exam paper).

sec *adv.* **1** 'Neat', exactly. *Ça lui a coûté toute sa paye sec:* It just about cost him all his pay-packet. *Ecoper huit ans sec* (Prison slang): To get an eight-year stretch (actual incarceration, not a suspended sentence). **2** *Boire sec:* **a** To down (a drink) rapidly. **b** To drink

heavily. *Au régiment il buvait sec, ce mec-là!* When he was in the Forces, he used to knock 'em back something terrible!

sécateur *n.m. Baptisé au sécateur (joc.):* 'Yid', Jewish.

seccotine *n.f.* 'Limpet-bore', tenacious and boring person. (*Seccotine* is the name of a well-known strong adhesive which like many brand names has become generic in colloquial French.)

séchage *n.m. (sch.):* Exam 'blackout', mental block at an examination.

sèche *n.f.* 'Ciggy', 'fag', cigarette. *Griller une sèche:* To have a smoke. *Gaffe! C'est un piqueur de sèches!* Keep your cigs out of sight, his favourite brand is 'other people's'!

sèche *adj. Tomber en panne sèche:* To run out of petrol.

sécher *v.trans.* **1** *(sch.): Sécher un cours:* To 'cut' a lecture, to give a class a miss. **2** *Sécher un pot:* To 'down' a drink. *On a séché un kil de rouge ensemble:* We had ourselves a bottle of plonk. **3** *La sécher:* To be 'spitting feathers', to be very thirsty.

sécher *v.intrans.* **1** *(sch.):* To 'black out' in an exam, to suffer from a mental block at an examination. **2** *Sécher (sur le fil):* To wait and wait in vain (literally to be left dangling, as on a washing-line).

séchoir *n.m.* (Prison slang): 'Cooler', punishment cell.

sécor *n.m. & adj.* Corsican, from Corsica. (This is a *verlen* corruption of *corse*.)

sécot *adj.* Tall and skinny.

secouée *n.f.* **1** 'Rocket', 'telling-off', reprimand. **2** *Une secouée de:* 'Oodles', vast quantities of. *Il y a toujours une secouée de mecs pour des turbins comme ça!* There's no shortage of volunteers for jobs like that!

secouer *v.trans.* **1** To 'nick', 'to 'pinch', to steal. *Il m'a secoué mes sèches!* He whipped my fags! **2** To 'give someone a dressing-down', to tell someone off in no uncertain manner. *Après sa dernière connerie, il s'est drôlement fait secouer le paletot!* After that last bloomer of his, he got the rocket he deserved!

secouer *v.trans.reflex.* **1** To 'snap out of it', to 'pull oneself together', to shake oneself out of a state of lethargy or depression. **2** To 'get a move on', to snap out of a state of idleness.

secouette *n.f. (joc.):* 'Wanking', masturbating.

secousse *n.f.* **1** *Ne pas en foutre une secousse:* To do 'bugger-all', to not do a stroke of work, to stay idle out of choice. **2** *L'hôtel des cent mille secousses (joc.):* The 'knocking-shop'. (As the name suggests, the kind of hotel where sleep is not the clientèle's aim!)

sécu *n.f. La sécu (abbr. la Sécurité Sociale)*: The Department of Health and Social Security.

sécurisé *adj.* Relaxed and confident (after having been given some sound and sensible advice).

sègue *n.f. Se taper une sègue*: To 'pull one's wire', to 'have a wank', to masturbate. (Cellard and Rey in their *DICTIONNAIRE DU FRANÇAIS NON-CONVENTIONNEL* attest the usage of this word, and mention its presence in G. Guégan's *UN SILENCE DE MORT.*)

sein *n.m.* **1** *Le coup du troisième sein. Faire le coup du troisième sein* is a humorous expression describing the ploy where a mother breast-feeding a hungry baby offers it more from the first breast, which is still empty. **2** *Tu me fais mal aux seins!* You get on my tits! – You're a bloody nuisance!

sélect *adj.inv.* 'Top-notch', high-class.

self *n.m. (abbr. self-service)*: **1** Supermarket, self-service shop. **2** Self-service cafeteria-cum-restaurant. **3** Self-serve petrol station.

selon *prep. C'est selon!* Depends! – It depends on the circumstances!

semer *v.trans.* **1** To 'shake off', to 'give someone the slip', to manage to get away from someone. **2** *Semer la merde*: To 'stir it', to cause chaos and acrimony.

semeur *n.m. Semeur de virgules* (slightly *pej.*): 'Chalkie', teacher. (The kind of pedagogue held in low esteem by the rest of the community.)

semi *n.m. (abbr. semi-remorque)*: 'Artic', articulated heavy goods vehicle.

semoule *n.f.* **1** *Lâcher* (also: *envoyer*) *la semoule*: To 'juice off', to ejaculate. **2** *Pédaler dans la semoule*: To be hampered in one's progress, to be getting nowhere, to achieve nothing. (The expression is said to have originated among racing cyclists and vividly describes the heavy-legged weariness of a tired competitor.)

sens *n.m. Se taper un coup de sens unique*: To down a glass of 'plonk'. (The origin of the expression can perhaps be found in the red and white colours of the wine and its container, reminiscent of a 'No-Entry' sign.)

sensass *adj. (abbr. sensationnel)*: 'Great', 'super', fantastic (also: *formide*).

sent-bon *n.m. (joc.) Du sent-bon*: Scent, perfume (also: *du senti-bon*).

sentiment *n.m. Avoir quelqu'un au sentiment*: To go it 'the tear-jerking way', to play on someone's feelings. *Chaque fois qu'il est dans la dèche, il se fait les aminches au sentiment*: Whenever he's broke, he goes round his pals for a sub with the old heartbreak routine.

sentinelle *n.f.* 'Turd', faeces. *Planter une sentinelle*: To 'have a crap', to 'shit', to defecate.

sentir *v.trans.* *Ne pas pouvoir sentir quelqu'un/ quelque chose*: To hate the sight of someone or something.

sentir *v.intrans.* **1** *Ça sent mauvais!* I don't like the look of this! (literally: it stinks!). **2** *Ça sent la patate!* I smell a rat! – I can sense some devious moves ahead!

sentir *v.pronom. S'en sentir pour quelqu'un/quelque chose*: To be keen on someone or something. *Je ne m'en sens pas pour bosser aujourd'hui!* I don't feel much like grafting today!

sentir *v.trans.reflex. Ne pas se sentir (pisser)*: To be totally unaware of what is happening, to act as if nothing were amiss. (The expression is never used in the first person, but always directed at others with a considerable amount of irony. *Lui prêter du fric?! Il ne se sent pas!* Me lend him money?! He must be out of his tiny little mind!)

sérail *n.m. Passage en sérail*: 'Gang-bang', collective rape (also: *passage en série*).

serbillon *n.m. Envoyer le serbillon*: To 'tip the wink to someone', to 'give someone a tip-off', to warn someone.

série *n.f.* **1** *Série Noire*: Famous collection of paperback 'whodunnits' with distinctive black covers published by Gallimard. *Un série-noire* has become generic for any detective novel. **2** *Une série noire*: A run of bad luck.

sérieux *n.m.* Litre glass of beer (a sort of 'super-pint' for the keen beer drinker).

serin *n.m.* 'Nincompoop', 'ninny', gullible fool (one who might easily fall for a *miroir aux alouettes!*).

seriner *v.trans.* To 'harp on and on' about something, to try and drive something home to a reluctant learner. (The parrot or canary-like nature of the tuition explains the origin of the verb.)

seringue *n.f.* **1** Firearm (anything ranging from a handgun to a sub-machine-gun). **2** *Chanter comme une seringue*: To sing way out of tune. **3** *Avoir le coup de seringue*: To feel 'knackered', 'buggered', to be exhausted (also: *avoir le coup de pompe*).

seringuer *v.trans.* To fire a hail of bullets at someone.

serpent *n.m. Serpent-à-lunettes (joc.)*: 'Four-eyes', spectacle-wearer.

serre *n.m. (also: ser)*: **1** (Gambling slang): Secret signal between card-sharps at a table. (In this context, the expression *faire/envoyer le serre* means to give the go-ahead for a concerted move aimed at distracting an honest player.) **2** *Faire* (also: *envoyer*) *le serre*: To 'tip the wink' to someone, to warn someone. (Auguste Le Breton in his *L'ARGOT CHEZ LES VRAIS DE VRAI* identifies *serbillon* and by implication *ser(re)* as the chalked rune-like warning left by tramps to indicate to fellow down-and-outs the good and not-so-good 'ports of call'.)

serré *adj.* 'Short of readies', a little low on cash. *Je t'aiderais bien, mais en ce moment j'suis un peu serré dans les entournures!* I'd gladly help you out but I'm pretty tight where cash is concerned!

serrer *v.trans.* Expressions such as *serrer la cuillère, les fesses, la pince, la vis,* etc. will be found under the heading of the direct object. **1** To strangle, to throttle. *Il y est allé du cigare pour avoir serré sa belle-doche:* He got guillotined for doing his mother-in-law in. **2** To 'pitch it strong', to 'lay it on thick', to exaggerate. *Il nous a drôlement serré ses vertus!* If you go by what he said, he's a clone of Superman and Albert Einstein!

serrer *v.trans.reflex.* Se la serrer: **a** To shake hands (also: *se serrer la pince*). **b** To go hungry, to go without food (also: *se serrer la ceinture*).

serreur *n.m.* **1** Strangler. **2** Münchhausen-type character, one who indulges in gross exaggeration.

servi *past part.* Etre servi *(iron.):* To be landed with more than one bargained for. *Lui qui voulait travailler, il va être servi!* If it's work he's after, he's going to get one hell of a surprise!

service *n.m.* **1** Le service *(abbr. le service militaire):* National service. *Il a fait son service dans la marine!* He did his 'army-days' in the navy! **2** *Etre service-service:* To do everything 'by the book', to be a stickler for rules and regulations. **3** *Le service trois-pièces (joc):* 'Privates', private parts.

serviette *n.f.* Un coup de serviette: A police raid (also: *coup de torchon*).

servietter *v.trans. (pol.):* To 'nick', to 'collar', to arrest.

servietter *v.intrans. (pol.):* To 'swoop', to organize a dragnet operation.

seul *adj.* Ça ira tout seul! It will be all plain sailing! – It will be quite straightforward! *Ça n'a pas été tout seul!* It was no doddle!

seulabre *adj.* 'On one's tod', on one's own, alone. (Sometimes the word is written *seulâbre* – with a circumflex accent on the â.)

seulet *adj. (f. seulette):* **1** Alone. **2** Lonely.

sézig *pers.pron.* (also: *sézigue*): Him, himself. *C'est sézig qui a tout casqué!* It was his lordship who coughed up for the lot!

shampooing *n.m. Passer un shampooing à quelqu'un:* To 'give someone a rocket', to tell someone off in no uncertain manner. *Il s'est fait passer un shampooing maison!* They certainly tore a strip off him!

shooter *v.trans.reflex.* (Drugs): To 'mainline', to inject oneself with narcotics.

shooteuse *n.f.* 'Hype', hypodermic syringe.

show-bise *n.m.* Le show-bise: Show-business.

sibiche *n.f.* 'Ciggy', 'fag', cigarette. *File-moi une sibiche!* Give us a smoke!

sidéré *past part.* 'Knocked-out', 'flabbergasted', astounded.

sidi *n.m. (pej.):* **1** Native of North Africa. (The appellation is as derogatory and racist as 'coon'.) **2** 'Geezer', 'bloke', fellow. *Qui m'a fichu un sidi pareil?!* Where on earth did you get such a gormless nurk?!

siècle *n.m.* Ça fait un siècle que je ne t'ai pas vu! I haven't seen you for yonks! – It seems like ages since I saw you!

sienne *n.f.* **1** Y aller de la sienne: **a** To take the cue and tell one's own joke or funny story. **b** To stand one's round of drinks. **2** *Faire des siennes:* **a** To 'be up to one's old tricks', to be back in the bad old routine. **b** To act in a selfish and obstreperous manner.

sifflard *n.m. (corr. abbr. sauciflard):* Saucisson sec, dry sausage of the salami type.

siffler *v.trans.* To 'knock back a drink', to down a beverage with eagerness and haste.

siffler *v.intrans.* C'est comme si je sifflais! *(iron.):* It's like talking to a brick wall! – Whatever I say is of no avail!

sifflet *n.m.* 'Gullet', throat. *Se rincer le sifflet:* To 'have a quick one', to down a drink. *Couper le sifflet à quelqu'un:* **a** To slit someone's throat. **b** To 'score off someone', to shut someone up with an unanswerable retort.

sifflote *n.f.* Syphilis.

sigue *n.m.* **1** Gold twenty-franc piece similar to a sovereign. **2** *(Slightly joc.):* 'Score', unit of twenty (for a person's age). *Il a près de deux sigues:* He's knocking on forty.

silencieux *n.m.* 'Piece', 'shooter', handgun (one fitted with a silencer).

simili *n.m. (abbr. simili cuir):* Leatherette, imitation leather. *Il reconnaissait les tocards à leurs valises en simili:* He could weigh up a customer by the quality of his suitcase.

simple *adj.* C'est simple comme bonjour! It's as easy as pie! – It's ever so simple!

sincère *adj.* (Antique dealers' slang): Untouched, unrestored.

singe *n.m.* **1** 'Gaffer', 'guv'nor', boss. *Il va falloir que j'en cause à mon singe!* I'll have to ask the boss about it! **2** 'Bully beef', corned beef. (Amongst the hypotheses as to the origin of the appellation, Cellard and Rey in their DICTION-NAIRE DU FRANÇAIS NON-CONVENTIONNEL suggest 19th-century tales of woe where French soldiers serving on the Ivory Coast were reduced to eating monkey-meat. Less far-fetched is the present authors' version whereby the contents of a certain brand of corned beef bore a jovial monkey on the label.)

3 *Ce n'est pas à un vieux singe qu'on apprend à faire des grimaces!* (iron.): Don't try and teach your grandmother to suck eggs!

sinoque *n.m. & f.* 'Loony', 'nutter', mad person.

sinoque *adj.* 'Bonkers', 'potty', mad.

sinoquet *n.m.* 'Bean', 'bonce', head (more usually the 'contents' than the 'container'. *Travailler du sinoquet:* To be 'bonkers', 'barmy', to be mad).

siouplaît *(joc.abbr. s'il vous plaît?!)*: 'Beg (your) pardon?!' (The jocular irony comes from the sarcastic intonation, in the same way that the English 'Thank you!' can, with appropriate stress and intonation, come to mean anything but the expression of grateful thanks.)

siphon *n.m.* 'Bean', 'bonce', head. (The implication here is that the contents are in the same state of 'fizz' as those of a soda-water dispenser. See *siphonné*.)

siphonné *adj.* 'Bonkers', 'potty', mad. *Il est complètement siphonné!* He's as nutty as a fruit-cake!

siphonner *v.intrans.* **1** To 'talk through one's hat', to 'spout a load of rubbish', to talk a lot of nonsense. **2** To 'go off the rails', to be on the steady slope of mental derangement. *Un célibataire qui perd sa mère a souvent tendance à siphonner:* Hardened bachelors who lose their mothers often lose their marbles too!

sirop *n.m.* **1** *(abbr. sirop de canard,* or *de grenouille,* also *sirop de parapluie)*: 'Adam's ale', 'corporation pop', water. **2** Water surface (lake, river, sea). *Aller au sirop:* To 'fall into the soup'. **3** 'Watering-hole', low-class pub. *Comme plus d'un boxeur, près de la retraite, il ne pensait qu'à avoir son propre sirop!* Like many a punch-drunk boxer, he fancied owning a little pub of his own! **4** 'Booze', liquor, alcoholic beverage. *Avoir* (also: *tenir) un coup de sirop:* To have had 'one over the eight', to be 'tipsy', to be slightly drunk. *Quand sa bonne femme l'a plaqué, il s'est mis au sirop:* When his missus left him he took to drink. **5** 'Sticky mess', 'fix', awkward situation. *On s'est retrouvés dans un de ces sirops après la grève!* The strike left us in one hell of a mess! **6** *Tomber dans le sirop:* To 'keel over', to 'pass out', to faint.

siroter *v.trans. & intrans.* **1** To sip with relish, to savour a drink in a leisurely manner. **2** To 'tipple', to be over-fond of one's drink.

siroteur *n.m.* 'Tippler', 'boozer', over-enthusiastic drinker.

sisite *n.f. Faire sisite* (Child language): To sit, to sit down.

situation *n.f. Etre dans une situation intéressante:* To be 'in the pudding club', to be 'preggers', to be pregnant.

six-quatre-deux *A la six-quatre-deux (adv.loc.)*: 'Any-old-how', in a slap-dash manner. *Elle nous a fait de la boustifaille à la six-quatre-deux!* She knocked us up some pretty awful grub!

skoumoune *n.f.* Run of bad luck.

slalom *n.m. Faire du slalom* (of vehicle): To weave in-and-out of the traffic.

slibar *n.m. (corr. slip) Un slibar:* 'Jocks', a pair of Y-fronts. *Etre un chaud du slibar:* To be a randy so-and-so.

smalah *n.f.* (also: *smala; slightly pej.*): Large family. (The word coming from the Arabic has more the connotation of 'tribe'. It does not just refer in colloquial French to a string of children, but also to a host of dependent relatives. *Il nous est tombé sur le poil avec toute sa smalah!* They all descended on us, Uncle Tom Cobbleigh and all!)

smicard *n.m. (Slightly pej.)*: Low-wage earner, one who only gets the *S.M.I.C.* (*Salaire Minimum Interprofessionnel de Croissance.* Previously this low wage was known as *S.M.I.G.* or *Salaire Minimum Interprofessionnel Garanti* and *smigard* was the equivalent of *smicard.*)

sniffer *v.trans. & intrans.* To take narcotics nasally.

snober *v.trans.* **1** To 'lord it' over someone, to act the high-and-mighty. **2** To 'give someone the cold shoulder', to avoid talking to someone (through a feeling of superiority).

soce *n.f. (abbr. société): 'Salut la soce!':* 'Evenin' all!' (The French and English are equally lowbrow.)

social *n.m.* 'Crony', 'chum', friend. *Il est brave, lui! C'est un social à moi!* He's a mate of mine and a good bloke too!

socialo *n.m.* 'Lefty', one whose sympathies lie with the Socialists.

sœur *n.f.* **1** 'Bird', 'lass', woman (usually a pretty one, the only exception being in the plural where disparaging generalizations are uttered. *Les sœurs, c'est toujours pareil!* Well, you know what women are like!). **2** 'Pansy', 'nancy-boy', effeminate homosexual. **3** *Et ta sœur?!* (iron.): What's it to do with you?! – Is it any of your business?! (This near-nonsensical repartee is sometimes followed by the rhyming and even more nonsensical *Elle bat le beurre!*)

soie *n.f.* **1** *Péter dans la soie* (also: *coucher dans des draps de soie)*: To 'lead the life of Riley', to 'live it up', to have an opulent lifestyle. **2** *Avoir quelque chose sur la soie:* To be burdened with a problem. *Il m'est tombé un de ces pataquès sur la soie!* You'll never believe the shit I've landed myself in! **3** *Avoir quelqu'un sur la soie:* To have someone 'on one's back', to be persistently tracked down by someone. *Depuis quinze jours* *il a les mecs du fisc sur la soie*: For a fortnight, I think he's had the Inland Revenue on him!

soif *n.f.* **1** *Il fait soif!* It's thirsty weather! – I'm parched! **2** *Jusqu'à plus soif*: To one's heart's desire, to satiety. *Des nanas comme ça, je m'en taperais jusqu'à plus soif!* Birds like her, you could bring me a lorry-load any day!

soiffard *n.m.* 'Dipso', character who is perpetually drunk. (The feminine *soiffarde* exists and, with the rise in sex-equality, seems to be gaining momentum.)

soigné *adj.* 'A-1', 'smashing', first-class. *Il s'est tapé une engueulade soignée de sa belle-doche!* He got a right rocket from his mother-in-law! *J'ai un rhume tout ce qu'il y a de soigné!* Keep your distance, I've got a stinking cold!

soigner *v.trans.reflex.* To 'mollycoddle oneself', to 'do oneself well', to look after oneself well (where personal comforts are concerned).

soin-soin *adj.inv.* 'Tip-top', 'A-1', first-rate. (The alternative *soi-soi* is more indicative of the near-certain origin of the term: *soigné-soigné*. *La boustifaille chez lui est vraiment soin-soin!* The nosh he serves is really top-hole!)

soissonnais *n.m.* (also: *soissonnais rose*): 'Clit', clitoris. (The *soissonnais* is a variety of kidney bean comparable in shape to the organ. It is interesting to note that the appellation *trieuse de lentilles*, implicating another leguminous seed, refers to lesbians in colloquial French.)

soixante-neuf *n.m.* Reciprocal form of oral sex. (The pictorial jocularity obviously stems from the *'tête-bêche'* positions of the figures 6 and 9.)

soldat *n.m.* **1** *Faire soldat*: To 'share-and-share alike' (as barrack-room buddies would). **2** *Jouer au petit soldat*: To 'play the little Napoleon', to bulldoze others about in an authoritative manner.

soleil *n.m.* **1** *Piquer un soleil*: To turn bright red, to blush. **2** *Ça craint le soleil!* (of goods): They're best kept out of sight! (because they have been stolen).

solo *adj.inv. & adv.* Alone, on one's own.

somme *n.m. Piquer un petit somme*: To 'take forty winks', to 'have a catnap', to have a snooze.

sommeil *n.m. Marchand de sommeil*: **a** Keeper of a low-class hotel (only one step away from the doss-house). **b** *(joc.)*: Hotel-proprietor. (To have a witty flavour, the appellation must be used when referring to the owner/manager of a high-class establishment.)

sommier *n.m. Matraqueur de sommiers (joc.)*: Randy so-and-so (literally one who gives bed-springs a tough time).

sommiers *n.m.pl. (pol.) Les sommiers*: Place where criminal records and police files on individuals are kept. (The *casier judiciaire* only records sentences imposed, whereas files at the *sommiers* can be far more instructive where abortive investigations and *non-lieu* findings are concerned.)

son *n.m. Cracher* (also: *éternuer*) *dans le son*: To be guillotined. (The sick humour is made vividly explicit because the chopped-off head falls into a tub of bran which soaks up the blood.)

son *n.m. Les son-et-lumière (joc. & slightly pej.)*: 'The old fogeys', the way-over-sixties. (The French film of the late 50s, *Les Tricheurs* with Jacques Charrier and Laurent Terzief, gave this and other slightly derogatory age-group appellations a tremendous platform. The *son-et-lumière* are literally the 'grand old ruins' worthy of sightseers.)

son This possessive adjective, its feminine *sa* and plural *ses*, are sometimes equivalent in colloquial French to the definite article, *le*, *la* or *les*. *Comme toujours, il fait son crétin!* As always, he's playing the fool!

sonnage *n.m.* 'Tapping', borrowing.

sonne *n.f. La sonne*: 'The fuzz', 'the law', the police. (Like the word *cogne n.m.*, this derogatory appellation portrays the strong-arm techniques allegedly used by the law-enforcers.)

sonné *adj.* **1** 'Dizzy', dazed (through a volley of blows). **2** 'Bonkers', 'loony', mad. (The implication here is that a shock of some sort could be responsible for this state of mind.) **3** *Il a cinquante ans bien sonnés!* He's fifty, knocking on sixty!

sonner *v.trans.* **1** To 'bash', to pummel, to beat up. *Qu'est-ce qu'il s'est fait sonner dans le dernier round!* The other chap beat the living daylights out of him at the end of the fight! **2** To 'give someone a rocket', to tell someone off in no uncertain manner (also: *sonner les cloches à quelqu'un*). **3** To 'strike someone dumb', to stun someone into silence with an apt and scathing repartee. **4** *On ne t'a pas* (also: *on ne vous a pas) sonné! (iron.)*: Who asked you for your advice?! – Keep your comments to yourself!

sonneur *n.m.* **1** 'Heavy', muscleman, one whose job it is to go banging heads together and pushing people's faces in. **2** *Ronfler comme un sonneur (de cloches)*: To snore away. (The expression *dormir comme un sonneur de cloches*: to 'sleep like a log', and the above, go a long way to confirming that bellringers after a boozing ding-dong session were able to sleep it off at leisure!)

Sophie *Proper name. Faire sa Sophie*: **a** To 'put on airs and graces', to simper. **b** To be delicately reluctant at complying with perfectly normal requests.

sorbonne *n.f.* 'Bean', 'bonce', head (literally the seat of knowledge). *'y en a plus qu'il en faut dans sa sorbonne!* He's got what it takes up top!

sorcier *adj.inv. Ça n'est pas (bien) sorcier!* There's not much to it! – There's nothing very difficult about that!

sorgue *n.f. La sorgue*: Night (when it is dark. Some dictionaries see it as meaning dusk or evening).

sorguer *v.intrans. Sorguer (à la paire)*: To have to 'rough it' at night, to spend a sleepless night looking for somewhere to rest.

sorlingue *n.m.* 'Chiv', blade, knife. *Il a pris un coup de sorlingue dans les tripes*: He got stabbed in the guts.

sorlots *n.m.pl.* 'Dogs', 'boats', shoes. (Without being pejorative, the word is hardly evocative of dainty footwear.)

sort *n.m. Faire un sort à quelqu'un*: To get rid of, to eliminate someone. *Faire un sort à quelque chose*: To 'polish something off', to make short work of something. *Son cassoulet toulousain, on lui a fait un sort!* By the time we'd eaten our fill, that cassoulet stew was a thing of the past!

sortable *adj. Ne pas être sortable (joc. & iron.)*: To be unfit to be seen in good company. *Tu n'es vraiment pas sortable, mon vieux!* The way you go about, you'll get us turfed out of any party!

sortie *n.f.* **1** Outburst of temper, fit of verbal rage. *Faire une sortie à quelqu'un*: To 'give someone a right rollicking', to pitch into someone. **2** *Etre de sortie (joc. & iron.)*: To be 'nowhere to be found' (literally to be as present as if it was one's day off. When referring to anything but persons, the expression becomes even more ironical as in *Son intelligence, elle est de sortie!* I wouldn't count on his grey matter, it left without forwarding address! *Mes économies, elles sont de sortie!* My savings?! They've just about sunk without trace!).

sortir *v.trans.* **1** To 'boot out', to 'chuck out', to dismiss someone. *C'est à coups de pompe au derche qu'on l'a sorti!* A few well-aimed kicks up the backside got him out! **2** To 'pitch a yarn', to come out with a rather incredible story. *Il nous en a sorti de belles!* You should have heard what he told us!

sortir *v.intrans.* **1** To 'stick one's neck out' (where a criminal venture is concerned), to take a risk of some sort. **2** *En sortir* (also: *sortir du trou*): To have finished 'porridge', to have come out of prison. **3** *D'où sortez-vous? (iron.)*: **a** Where were you dragged up? – Haven't you any manners?! **b** Fancy you not knowing that! (Where have you been all this time?) **4** *Il n'y a*

pas à sortir de là! You can't get away from that! – There's no disputing this! *Je ne sors pas de là!* I'm sticking to that! – You won't get me to shift! **5** *Merci, je sors d'en prendre! (iron.)*: Thanks all the same but I've had my lot! – It's the kind of experience I don't want to have again!

sortir *v.trans.reflex. S'en sortir*: To 'get oneself out of a tight spot', to escape from a difficult situation.

sossot *adj.* (of person): 'Ninnyish', rather simple. (The feminine *sossotte* exists and, like the masculine, has no real pejorative connotation.)

sot-l'y-laisse *n.m.inv.* 'Parson's nose', rump of a cooked fowl. (The assumption is that, according to a would-be connoisseur, this is a tasty morsel that only a fool would overlook.)

sou *n.m.* **1** *Etre près de ses sous*: To be 'tight', to be a 'skinflint', to be mean with money. **2** *Etre fichu comme quatre sous* (of person): To be dressed like a guy (also: *être fichu comme l'as de pique*). **3** *En rester comme deux sous de frites*: To be 'all of a heap', to 'have the wind taken out of one's sails', to be dumbfounded. **4** *Ne pas être . . . pour deux sous*: Not to be one bit . . ., not to be in the least . . . *Il n'est pas méchant pour deux sous!* There isn't an ounce of meanness in him!

soucoupe *n.f.* **1** Bill in café or restaurant (because the 'billet doux' informing the client how much he owes is delivered in a saucer – a worthy receptacle for a tip. Cellard and Rey in their DICTIONNAIRE DU FRANÇAIS NON-CONVENTIONNEL mention that up to 1940, amounts owed in *bistrots* were actually inscribed on the saucer itself). **2** (Cycling slang): 'Chain-wheel', sprocket-wheel to which the pedals are attached. (Gaston Esnault in his DICTIONNAIRE DES ARGOTS exemplifies the use of this word in the expression *appuyer sur la soucoupe*: to use the larger chain-wheel in order to develop maximum pedal-ratio.) **3** *(pl.)*: 'Flappers', 'lug-holes', ears.

soudure *n.f.* 'Brass', 'loot', money. *Envoyer la soudure*: To 'cough up', to pay up. *Faire la soudure*: **a** To have just about enough money to tide one over. **b** To overlap where work-shifts are concerned.

soufflant *n.m.* 'Rod', 'shooter', handgun.

soufflant *adj.* 'Mind-blowing', incredible. *Il lui est arrivé un coup soufflant!* You'll never believe what happened to him!

souffle *n.m.* 'Gall', 'cheek', impudence. *Tu ne manques pas de souffle, toi!* You cheeky beggar, you!

soufflé *past part.* 'Bowled over', 'flabbergasted', dumbfounded.

souffler *v.trans.* **1** To 'nick', to 'pinch', to steal. *Encore une bonne idée qu'on s'est fait souffler!* That's another bright idea we got whipped from under our noses! **2** *Souffler le mirliton*: To 'give a blow-job', to perform fellatio.

souffler *v.intrans. Laisse-moi souffler!* Give us a breather! – Give me some respite!

soufflerie *n.f. La soufflerie*: The 'blowers', the lungs, the pulmonary system. *Cracher sa soufflerie*: To suffer from T.B., to have tuberculosis.

soufflet *n.m.* **1** *(pl.)*: 'Bellows', lungs. *Avoir les soufflets mités* (also: *cracher ses soufflets*): To suffer from T.B., to have tuberculosis. **2** *Soufflet à punaises (joc.)*: 'Squeeze-box', concertina. (When referring to an accordion, the appellation *piano à bretelles* is more readily used.)

soufrante *n.f.* (also: *souffrante*): 'Scratchie', match. (There is a would-be pun within this word referring back to the days when matches beyond the phosphorus tip were impregnated with sulphur giving the ignited flame a greater chance of survival. These 'kitchen' matches were never favoured by smokers for obvious reasons!)

souhait *n.m. A tes* (also: *à vos*) *souhaits!* Bless you! (When a person has sneezed twice in succession, it is customary to wish him, tongue-in-cheek, on the second occasion *à tes amours!*)

soulager *v.trans.* **1** To bring someone to a sexual climax. **2** *Soulager quelqu'un de quelque chose (joc.)*: To 'lift' something, to pinch something from someone (literally to relieve him of the burden of ownership).

soulager *v.trans.reflex.* To 'answer a call of Nature', to go to the W.C. *Il s'est soulagé contre un arbre*: He had a slash.

soûlard *n.m.* 'Soak', 'boozer', drunk. (The feminine *soûlarde* exists but is used mostly when referring to the near-sexless flotsam-and-jetsam more partial to meths than commercial booze.)

soûlardise *n.f.* 'Boozing', heavy drinking. *La soûlardise, c'est son blot!* When it comes to knocking 'em back, he's your man!

soûlaud *n.m.* (also: *soûlot*): 'Soak', 'boozer', drunk.

soûlerie *n.f.* Drunken binge.

soulever *v.trans.* To 'lift', to 'pinch', to steal. *Elle m'a soulevé mon crapaud!* She pinched my wallet!

souliers *n.m.pl. Etre dans ses petits souliers (iron.)*: To be ill-at-ease, to feel uncomfortable. (Wearing tight shoes is hardly conducive to comfort!)

soûlographie *n.f. La soûlographie (iron.)*: 'Boozing', heavy drinking. (There is a certain built-in jocularity in an appellation which elevates alcohol consumption to a skill or science.)

soupçon *n.m. Une larme, un soupçon! (joc.*, of drink): Just a wee dram! – A teeny drop only! (This otherwise rather twee expression regained colloquial vitality through *Le Capitaine Haddock*, the boozing sea-hound friend of *Tintin* in the cartoon books by Hergé; Haddock's modest request when being offered a drink was *'Une larme, un soupçon!'*, in other words a brimming glass!)

soupe *n.f.* **1** 'Grub', food. *Etre de soupe (mil.)*: To be on cookhouse fatigue. *Aller à la soupe*: To go for one's nosh. **2** 'Slush', wet and very soft snow. **3** *Un gros plein de soupe (pej.)*: A big fat slob. (The derogatory nature of the appellation lies not so much in contempt for outsize people, as in the erroneous assumption that they are big-heads and that they 'throw their weight about'!) **4** *Etre trempé comme une soupe*: To be 'wringing wet', to be soaked to the skin. **5** *Etre soupe au lait*: To get into a huff at the drop of a cross word (literally to rise at the slightest provocation like milk on the boil). **6** *Manger (de) la soupe à la grimace*: To weather a marital storm and eat in stony silence. **7** *Servir la soupe (th.)*: To hold a very minor part in a production (to be something like a standard-bearer in a Shakespearean drama). **8** *Etre le dernier pour la soupe (joc. & iron.)*: To miss out where the better things of life are concerned. (This expression is very much in tune with the hackneyed story of the private complaining to his sergeant that he did not often get a leave-pass, adding: 'My name is Wimpole' – to this the sergeant replied 'If your name had been Arse-hole, Bum-hole or Cunt-hole you'd have had a chance, but being Wimpole you come last!') **9** *Par ici la bonne soupe! (iron.)*: (If it's a fight you're after) come and get it! (This belligerent taunt is usually uttered by hotheads, boastful bullies and the like.) **10** *Marchand de soupe (pej.)*: **a** Restaurateur. (As the appellation suggests, hardly the keeper of a three-star establishment.) **b** Headmaster of a crammer. (Academic whose objective seems to be a healthy turn-over of pupils, i.e., large profits rather than the imparting of knowledge.) **c** Any businessman whose primary objective is a large turn-over and quick profits. **11** *Faire de la soupe* (Musicians' slang): To prostitute one's talents by working for a sub-standard band or outfit churning out Muzak-like tunes for popular consumption. **12** *Donner la soupe à quelqu'un*: To show a clean pair of heels to an adversary in the race for success. **13** *Avoir soupe de . . .*: To be fed-up with . . ., to have had enough of someone or something. *J'en ai soupe de sa fiole!* I'm sick and tired of seeing his face around! **14** *La soupe sera bonne! (joc. & iron.)*: This incongruous remark is directed at anyone who is picking his nose or scratching his behind. **15** (also *pl.*): Abominable substances ingurgitated by perverts and the scatologically-minded.

souper *v.intrans.* *En avoir soupé de* . . . : To be fed-up with . . ., to be sick and tired of. . . . *J'en ai soupé de sa litanie de goualantes!* I've just about had enough of his moan, moan, moan routine!

soupeur *n.m.* Scatological pervert whose pre-occupation is with the consumption of abominable substances. (Reference to such matters is made in Auguste Le Breton's *L'ARGOT CHEZ LES VRAIS DE VRAI*, and Jacques Cellard's and Alain Rey's *DICTIONNAIRE DU FRANÇAIS NON-CONVENTIONNEL.*)

sourd *n.m.* **1** *Gueuler comme un sourd*: To shout one's head off (probably because one cannot hear one's own voice). **2** *Cogner* (also: *frapper*) *comme un sourd*: To hit, to beat violently without respite. (The assumption could be that the one who is violent cannot or will not hear the cries of pain.)

sourdine *n.f.* **1** *La sourdine*: The secret police (perhaps because of its 'softly, softly' approach!). **2** *Mets-y une sourdine!* Put a sock in it! – Quieten down will you! (The English 'Put a sock in it!' is deemed to come from the days when wind-up gramophones could be muted by inserting a sock or cloth in the horn.)

sourdingue *n.m. & f.* Deaf person.

sourdingue *adj.* 'Hard-of-hearing', deaf.

souricière *n.f.* (*pol.*): 'Baited trap' laid by the forces of law-and-order.

souris *n.f.* **1** 'Bird', 'bit-of-skirt', woman. (The appellation is not derogatory *per se*, and like many other such words, relies on the context for interpretation.) **2** *Les souris grises*: Nickname given to the female members of the German Wehrmacht during World War II.

sous-bite *n.m. (mil.)*: Lieutenant. (The assumption here is presumably that the *bite* or direct superior is the *capitaine*.)

sous-fifre *n.m.* 'Side-kick', 'second fiddle', underling.

sous-mac *n.m.* (also: *sous-maque*): Brothel-keeper.

sous-off *n.m. (abbr. sous-officier)*: N.C.O., 'non-com', non-commissioned officer.

sous-tasse *n.m.* Unfortunate individual who usually ends up by paying the bill where a round of heavy boozing is concerned.

(François Caradec in his *DICTIONNAIRE DU FRANÇAIS ARGOTIQUE ET POPULAIRE* makes the word out to be feminine and defines it as the gullible 'punter' who foots a prostitute's drinks bill.)

soustraction *n.f. (joc.)*: Bill in café or restaurant. (The jocularity stems from the antonymic nature of the word as opposed to the traditional *addition*.)

sous-ventrière *n.f.* *Bouffer à s'en (faire) péter la sous-ventrière*: To have 'a right blow-out', to eat fit to burst.

sous-verge *n.m.* 'Second fiddle', menial underling.

souvenance *n.f.* *En avoir souvenance* (slightly joc. & iron.): To remember something 'at a pinch'. (The rather archaic expression *j'en ai souvenance* can be equated with Maurice Chevalier's refrain 'I remember it well!' in the song of that name.)

spé *n.m.* *Le spé* (Prostitute's slang): Anal intercourse. *Faire le spé* (also: *faire le spécial*): To submit to sodomy.

spé *adj.inv.* *Math spé (sch.)*: Advanced maths studied after the *baccalauréat*.

spécial *adj.* *Avoir des goûts spéciaux*: To have a penchant for sodomous intercourse.

spécialo *n.m. (corr. spécialiste)*: Consultant, specialist medical practitioner.

speed *adj.inv.* *Etre speed* (Drugs): To be addicted to amphetamines and show outward signs of this dependence.

spontex *n.m.* 'Old soak', habitual drunkard. (*Spontex* is the well-known brand-name of a household sponge, like many others has drifted into colloquial language.)

sport *n.m.* *Il va y avoir du sport! (iron.)*: It's not (all) going to be plain sailing! – We're in for some aggro!

sport *adj.inv.* *Etre sport*: To be 'a good sport', to accept a challenge with grace and an open mind.

spountz *n.m.* Gullible 'cinéphile' whose only aim in life is to become a star of the screen. (Marcel Pagnol's film *Le spountz*, with Fernandel in the title-role, gave this word a good platform in the colloquial French of the 30s and early 40s.)

sténo *n.f.* **1** (*abbr. sténographie*): Shorthand, stenography. **2** (*abbr. sténodactylo*): Shorthand typist.

step *n.m.* 'Conk', 'hooter', nose. *Avoir un step à repiquer les choux*: To have one hell of a beak.

stick *n.m.* (Drugs): 'Joint', 'reefer', cigarette containing marijuana.

stop *n.m.* **1** 'Stoplight', brake light on motorized vehicle or trailer. **2** *Le stop (abbr. l'autostop)*: Hitch-hiking. *Il va falloir qu'on fasse du stop si on* *veut être à l'heure!* We're going to have to thumb a lift if we want to be home on time!

stoppeur *n.m. (abbr. autostoppeur)*: Hitch-hiker.

stores *n.m.pl. Baisser les stores*: To 'get some shuteye', to take a nap. (The image here is of a shop rolling down the steel shutters.)

strasse *n.f.* **1** Street. (This is a direct borrowing from the German *Strasse*.) **2** Room (usually in a less-than-reputable hotel. The implication here is that the room has as many people passing through it as a street).

stress *n.m. Vivre dans le stress*: To lead a near-neurotic life of perpetual worrying. (The word is obviously a direct borrowing from the English.)

strobus *n.m.* (Junk/antique dealers' slang): 'White elephant', unsaleable item. (François Caradec's *DICTIONNAIRE DU FRANÇAIS ARGOTIQUE ET POPULAIRE* is the only work to formally lexicalize this otherwise seldom encountered word.)

stropiat *n.m. (pej.)*: 'Crutchie', cripple. (This word is probably a derogatory corruption of *estropié*.)

stups *n.m.pl. Les stups (abbr. les stupéfiants)*: Narcotics. (The French word *stupéfiants* is in keeping with the dazed look of addicts after a 'take'.)

suante *n.f. (pej.)*: Week (another week of toil and sweat).

subodorer *v.trans.* To 'get an inkling', to become aware of something. *J'ai subodoré ses tours de vache!* I got wind of his dirty tricks!

subtiliser *v.trans.* To 'lift', to 'filch', to steal.

sucer *v.trans.* **1** To perform oral sex. **2** *Sucer la pomme à quelqu'un*: To give someone a kiss on the cheek.

suçon *n.m.* 'Love-bite', suction mark left on the neck by an amorous and over-enthusiastic partner.

sucre *n.m.* **1** 'Doddle', easy task. *C'est un vrai sucre!* It's as easy as pie! **2** *C'est de sucre!* There's nothing to beat it! *Un weekend à la cambrousse, c'est du sucre!* Spending Saturday and Sunday in the country is tops! **3** *Recevoir son morceau de sucre (iron.)*: To 'get one's just deserts', to get the reward one has been expecting. (This expression originated in the world of the theatre and describes the expected round of applause that a famous actor gets when he first comes on stage.) **4** *Ne pas être en sucre (iron.)*: To be hardier than might be assumed. (The jocular implication here is that the person concerned is no lump of sugar likely to dissolve in the rain.) **5** *Casser du sucre sur le dos de quelqu'un*: To 'backbite', to 'run someone down', to speak ill of someone in his/her absence.

sucrée *n.f. Faire la* (also: *sa*) *sucrée* (of woman or effeminate character): To simper, to put on demure airs and graces.

sucrer *v.trans.* **1** To 'nick', to 'pinch', to steal. (The emphasis is not so much on theft *per se* as on the taking away of something the owner feels entitled to. *Il m'a sucré ma place sur la plage!* He pinched that nice spot I'd got myself on the beach!) **2** To 'nab', to 'collar', to arrest. (With this meaning the verb is usually found in the passive. *Il s'est fait sucrer par la Maison Pouleman à cent mètres de la prison*: He only managed to get a hundred yards from the prison before being nicked by the fuzz.) **3** To 'duff up', to 'rough up', to beat. (The implication where this meaning is concerned is that the beating is inflicted by a member of the police force.) **4** *Sucrer un texte (th.)*: To use the (editorial) blue pencil, to 'cut up' a text, to perpetrate some edits. (The implication in this instance is that the cuts are unjustified and 'rob' the text.) **5** *Sucrer les fraises*: To 'have the shakes', to suffer from violent trembling (through age, illness or fear).

sucrer *v.trans.reflex.* **1** To take the lion's share of something. (Because it usually relates to ill-gotten gains, the act can be seen as a double misappropriation.) **2** *Se sucrer la gaufre*: To powder one's face. (The image here is of powder applied to a face like icing sugar to a waffle.)

sucrette *n.f. Aller à la sucrette*: To dip into the old 'slush funds' for one's own benefit (generally to take out money to which one is not really entitled).

suée *n.f.* **1** 'Graft', 'grind', hard work. **2** Fright (cold sweat). **3** *Une suée de*: 'Oodles', masses of. *Des bosseurs comme lui, j'en connais pas une suée!* You don't come across grafters like him that often!

suer *v.trans. En suer une (joc. & iron.)*: To 'have a shuffle', to have a dance. *Alors, poupée, on en sue une?!* How's about a quick waltz around the hall?!

suer *v.intrans.* **1** *Faire suer quelqu'un*: To be 'a pain in the arse', to be a bloody nuisance to someone. **2** *Faire suer le bournous*: To get one's pound of flesh where someone else's hard work is concerned. (Originally the expression referred to the attitude of the *pieds-noirs*, the European settlers in North Africa, towards the colonized natives.)

suffoquer *v.trans.* To 'flabbergast', to leave speechless. *Des histoires comme ça me suffoquent!* I just don't know what to say when I hear things like that!

suif *n.m.* **1** Argument, quarrel, bitter disagreement. *Chercher du suif à quelqu'un*: To pick a quarrel with someone. *Se mettre en suif*: To 'fly off the handle', to have a fit of temper. *Etre en suif*: To be in a foul mood. **2** Uproar, commotion. *Faire un suif (du diable)*: To kick up (one hell of) a fuss. **3** 'Rocket', 'roasting', telling-off. *Flanquer un suif à quelqu'un*: To 'haul someone over the coals'. **4** *Se faire du suif*: To worry oneself sick about something.

suiffard *n.m.* Dandy, 'swell', nattily dressed man. (The French and the English are equally twee and dated.)

suiffer *v.trans.reflex.* To 'have a slanging match', to have a vociferous row.

suiffeur *n.m.* 'Awkward so-and-so', character who will pick a quarrel with anyone.

suisse *n.m.* *Faire suisse* (also: *boire en suisse*): To find a quiet place to have a drink on one's own (in order to avoid having to stand a round of drinks).

suite *De suite (abbr. tout de suite)*: 'In a tick' – 'In a jiffy' – Shortly. *Il va revenir de suite!* He'll be back in a sec!

sujet *n.m.* 'Biddy', 'bit-of-skirt', woman. (The appellation is more often than not used in the world of prostitution where *un gentil petit sujet* usually refers to a docile and pretty potential hooker.)

sulfater *v.trans.* To 'pepper' with shot, to gun down with a shotgun. (*Sulfater* and *sulfateuse* relate to the spraygun used to douse vines with anti-mildew agent.)

sulfateuse *n.f.* Tommy-gun, sub-machine-gun (because it lets off a steady stream of bullets. See *sulfater*.)

sultane *n.f.* Mistress. (The appellation has not got the connotation of 'kept woman' but stresses more the isolation and esteem in which she appears to be held.)

sup *adj.inv. (abbr. supplémentaire)* *Faire des heures sup*: To put in some overtime.

Supélec *Proper name. (sch.)*: This is the students' abbreviated appellation of the *Ecole Supérieure d'Electricité*.

super *n.m. (abbr. supercarburant)*: High-octane fuel equivalent to four-star petrol. *'Qu'est-ce que vous voulez, de l'ordinaire ou du super?'* 'What will it be then, two-star or four-star?'

superflip *n.m.* Intense state of mental depression bordering on neurosis.

supposition *n.f.* *Une supposition que* . . . Now let's imagine that . . . *Une supposition que tu me vendes ta bagnole, qu'est-ce que je fous si elle tombe en panne?!* O.K., so you sell me your car, what do I do then if it breaks down?!

suppositoire *n.m.* *Suppositoire d'autobus (joc. & iron.)*: Bubble-car. (In the 50s and 60s when petrol was not at a premium, these mini-vehicles were generally viewed with derision and contempt. See *pot à yaourt*.)

sûr *adj.* *C'est (du) sûr et certain!* It's a dead-cert! – It's a sure thing!

surbine *n.f.* **1** Isolation cell in top security jail from where it is impossible for a prisoner to communicate with other inmates. **2** Police surveillance of a suspect. *Depuis que ses potes étaient en taule il avait hérité d'une surbine vingt-quatre heures sur vingt-quatre*: From the minute his pals were in clink, the police decided to tail him round the clock.

surbiner *v.trans.* To keep a watchful eye on, to observe closely with anything but sympathetic intentions.

surboum *n.f.* 'Super do', party where drinking, dancing and having a good time are the order of the evening. (The word had its heyday in the late 50s and 60s.)

Sûrepige *Proper name. (corr.abbr. Sûreté Nationale)*: State security police.

surface *n.f.* **1** *Avoir de la surface*: To be 'comfortably off', to have a sound financial base. **2** *Refaire surface*: **a** To 'be back in the money', to get back in the swing of things where financial matters are concerned. **b** To 'surface' again, to come back after a long absence. *Alors comme ça, on refait surface?!* Well, well, long time no see! Where have you been all these years? **3** *En boucher une surface à quelqu'un*: To leave someone speechless, to astound someone.

surgé *n.m. (sch.abbr. surveillant général)*: Non-teaching senior member of staff in *lycée* or *collège* whose task it is to deal with discipline within those establishments.

surgelé *n.m.* **1** *Un surgelé (abbr. un plat surgelé)*: A deep-freeze meal. **2** *Les surgelés*: Deep-freeze goods which are on sale in supermarkets.

surin *n.m.* 'Chiv', blade, knife.

suriner *v.trans.* To 'chiv', to stab, to knife.

surineur *n.m.* Hoodlum whose favourite weapon is a flick-knife.

surnombre *n.m.* Nickname.

surpatte *n.f. (abbr.corr. surprise-partie)*: 'Super do', party where drinking, dancing and having a good time are the order of the evening.

surplace *n.m.* *Faire du surplace (fig.)*: To get nowhere, to be in a stalemate situation.

surprenante *n.f.* **1** Illegal and rigged lottery. **2** *Faire quelque chose à la surprenante*: To catch someone unawares, to do something without warning.

surrincette *n.f.* 'One for the road' after-dinner drink. (The *rincette* or *pousse-café*, as the name suggests, is part of the meal; the *surrincette* might prove unwise!)

survolté *n.m.* 'Supercharged' character whose energy never seems to let up.

survolté *adj.* 'Het-up', 'worked-up', over-tense.

swing *adj.inv.* 'Hep', 'hip', fashionable. *Etre swing*: To be really on the ball.

sympa *adj. (abbr. sympathique)*: Lovable, likeable, friendly. *C'est un mec tout ce qu'il y a de sympa!* You couldn't find a nicer guy!

syphlotte *n.f.* Syphilis.

système *n.m.* **1** 'Thingumajig', gadget, device. *Et comment ça marche votre système?* And how does that contraption of yours work? **2** *Système D (abbr. système débrouille, also: système démerde)*: Resourceful and ingenious way of overcoming a seemingly arduous problem. *Pratiquer (also: employer) le système D* does not necessarily refer to wangling, it can relate to any task practical or otherwise. See *'D'*. **3** *Taper (also: courir) sur le système à (also: de) quelqu'un*: To 'get on someone's wick', to 'get someone's goat', to irritate someone. (With this meaning the word is an abbreviation of *système nerveux*.)

systusse *n.m. (corr. système)*: **1** Way of 'wangling' something, of achieving what one wants. **2** 'Thingumajig', 'doo-dah', contraption or device.

T

tabac *n.m.* **1** *(abbr. bureau de tabac)*: Tobacconist's. (In France the licence to sell tobacco nearly always goes with that of selling alcoholic drinks, and the *Café-Tabac* with its distinctive red diamond-shaped sign is part of the typical French scenery.) **2** *Fumer du tabac de Chine (joc. & iron.)*: To smoke 'o.p.'s', to cadge 'smokes' from other people. (The jocularity of the expression stems from the pun on *Chine* with the meaning of 'cadging', not 'China'.) **3** *Un mauvais tabac*: A 'bad business', a bad state of affairs. *C'est un mauvais tabac d'être à court de fric le 20 du mois!* It's a sorry thing to have run out of housekeeping money after only three weeks! **4** 'Rocket', 'roasting', telling-off. *Passer un tabac à quelqu'un*: To tear a strip off someone. **5** *Faire tout un tabac*: To 'make a song-and-dance about something', to kick up a fuss. **6** *Passer quelqu'un à tabac*: To give someone 'the third degree', to beat someone up. (The *passage à tabac* is always associated with alleged police brutality.) **7** *Coup de tabac* (Naval slang): 'Spot of rough weather', storm. **8** *Se donner un tabac terrible*: To give oneself no end of trouble, to spare oneself no effort. **9** *Faire un tabac terrible (th.)*: To have a rip-roaring success in a stage production. **10** *C'est du même tabac!* It's six of one, half a dozen of the other! – It's much of a muchness! – It's the same thing!

tabacco *n.m.* *(corr. bureau de tabac)*: Tobacconist's.

tabassage *n.m.* 'Third degree', alleged police manhandling of a suspect.

tabassée *n.f.* 'Bashing-up', beating-up, thrashing.

tabasser *v.trans.* To 'duff up', to beat up.

tabasser *v.trans.reflex.* To have a punch-up, to have a fist-fight.

tabernacle *n.m.* 'Garret', 'brainbox', head. (This appellation, only lexicalized by A. Rey and J. Cellard in their DICTIONNAIRE DU FRANÇAIS NON-CONVENTIONNEL, is not limited to the language of the thirties.)

table *n.f.* **1** *Se mettre à table* (also: *passer à table*): To 'grass', to 'turn nark', to inform on someone to the police. **2** *Manger à la table qui recule*: To go hungry, to have to go without food.

tableau *n.m.* **1** *Un vieux tableau (pej.)*: An old 'has-been', a painted old hag. **2** *Ça ne fera* (also: *Ça ne ferait) pas mal dans le tableau!* That would just fit the bill! – That would be just right! (also: *Cela fera/ferait bien dans le paysage!*). **3** *Tableau!* Just picture the scene! *J'entre dans la piaule et je la trouve au plume avec un copain – tableau!* I open the bedroom door and find her in bed with a pal of mine. Need I say more?! **4** *Jouer* (also: *miser) sur les deux tableaux (fig.)*: To 'hedge one's bets', to play for safety by avoiding total commitment to one side or the other in a financial enterprise or in an argument. **5** *Etre gagnant sur tous les tableaux*: To be a winner 'all along the line', to have successfully 'hedged one's bets' and come out a winner on every count. **6** *C'est au tableau!* 'It's in the offing!' – It's in the reckoning! *Un coup fourré comme ça, c'était au tableau!* A cock-up like that was to be expected all along! **7** *Avoir . . . au tableau*: (Fighter pilots'/hunters' slang): To have scored . . . victories (to have bagged so much 'game'). *C'est un as, il a quinze Messerschmitt au tableau!* He's a crack pilot, to-date he's shot down fifteen Jerry aircraft! **8** *Décrocher ses tableaux (joc.)*: To go 'scrumping for snot', to pick one's nose.

tablettes *n.f.pl.* *(joc.)* *Rayez ça de vos tablettes!* Get any such thought out of your mind! – Such a thing is definitely not on!

tablier *n.m.* *Rendre son tablier*: To 'ask for one's cards', to give notice, to leave one's employment. (The expression originates from the world of domestic service, but is used in other employment contexts.)

tabourets *n.m.pl.* 'Chompers', 'gnashers', teeth. *N'avoir plus de tabourets dans la salle à manger*: To be all gums, to be toothless. (To understand this term, one must picture an extracted molar resembling a stool with its legs.)

tac *n.m.* **1** 'Cab', taxi-cab. **2** *Répondre du tac au tac*: To give a verbal riposte at the drop of a hat.

tacot *n.m.* 'Jalopy', 'bone-shaker', ramshackle motor-car.

taf *n.m.* (also: *taff*): **1** 'Cut', share of ill-gotten gains (theft, etc.). *Aller au taf*: To split the booty. **2** *Avoir le taf*: To 'have the shits', to be 'chicken', to be afraid. **3** *Prendre son taf*: **a** To 'come', to experience an orgasm. **b** To feel elation because of one's success or someone else's failure. **4** *Sur le taf*: On the spur of the moment. **5** *Y mettre le taf*: To 'put one's back into it', to make an all-out effort to achieve something.

tafanard *n.m.* 'Botty', 'bum', behind (usually where salacious thoughts or acts are concerned).

tafeur *n.m.* (also: *taffeur*): 'Funk', coward.

taffer *v.intrans.* To 'have the shits', to be 'yellow', to be frightened.

tafia *n.m.* (also: *tafiat*): 'Booze', drink, alcoholic beverage.

tafiater *v.intrans.* To 'booze', to drink vast quantities of alcohol.

tagada *n.m.* **1** 'Botty', 'bum', behind (usually where salacious thoughts or acts are concerned). *La vie pour lui n'est qu'une grande partie de tagada!* Sex seems to be his only pre-occupation in life! **2** *Le tagada tsoin-tsoin*: The 'oompah-oompah' musical beat of brass bands and other syncopated music.

taille *n.f.* **1** *Pierre de taille*: 'Skinflint', mean person. **2** *Faire sa taille*: To earn a 'fair crust', to make a decent living.

taillé *past part.* *Etre bien taillé* (of man): To have a handsome and powerful physique.

tailler *v.trans.* **1** *Tailler une bavette (à quelqu'un)*: To have a natter (with someone). **2** *Tailler une pipe*: To perform fellatio.

tailler *v.pronom.* To 'scarper', to 'skedaddle', to leave (usually in haste). *Salut, les mecs, il faut que je me taille!* Cheerio then, I'll have to dash!

tala *n.m.* *Les talas*: Devout churchgoers. (The appellation is jocularly derogatory in that it is a contraction of *les gens qui vont à la messe*. The word also exists as an adjective – *ce sont des gens très talas!* You won't go down well in that house if you mock religion!)

talbin *n.m.* 'Note', banknote. *Il ne se déplace jamais sans talbins gros format*: He never goes anywhere without a wad of big notes.

talc *n.m.* (Drugs): 'Snow', 'coke', cocaine (because it is a fine white powder).

talentueux *adj.* Gifted, blessed with a gift (usually artistic).

talmouse *n.f.* Violent slap in the face (also: *talmoche*).

talmouser *v.trans.* To hit violently in the face (usually by way of a slap).

taloche *n.f.* 'Clout', 'cuff', blow with the flat of the hand. (The word is usually encountered in conjunction with disobedient children; where adults are concerned, the word *talmouse* is more likely. *Il lui a filé une sacrée taloche à son moujingue*: He gave that kid of his a whacking clout round the ear-hole.)

talocher *v.trans.* To 'clout', to 'cuff', to give a blow with the flat of the hand.

tambouille *n.f.* **1** Cooking, cookery, the preparation of food. (Without being pejorative, this word is not exactly complimentary and refers to humble efforts far removed from *haute cuisine*. *Faire la tambouille*: To cook up some nosh.) **2** 'Grub', 'eats', food.

tambour *n.m.* **1** *Raisonner comme un tambour*: To 'spout a load of tommy-rot', to 'talk through one's hat', to utter inanities. **2** *Il n'y a pas de quoi faire passer le tambour de ville!* It's nothing to make a song-and-dance about! – It's hardly worth a mention! (Unlike his English counter-part who rings a bell to get the public's attention, the French village newsbearer, as the name suggests, beats a quick roll on the drum before an announcement.)

tampon *n.m.* **1** *(mil.)*: Batman, orderly. **2** *Coup de tampon*: Punch, blow with the fist. **3** *(pl.)*: 'Dukes', fists. *'Gaffe à ses tampons, c'est un solide cogneur!'* 'Watch his hands, he packs a powerful punch!'

tamponner *v.trans.* **1** To 'thump', to 'wallop', to beat up. **2** To 'bang', to 'screw', to have coition with.

tamponner *v.trans.reflex.* *Se tamponner (le coquillard) de quelque chose*: Not to 'give a fuck about something', not to 'care two hoots', to not give a damn about something. *Je m'en tamponne de ses idées à la mords-moi-le-machin!* I don't give a fig about his cock-eyed plans and ideas! (also: *s'en battre l'œil*).

tamponnoir *n.m.* 'Plug', sanitary tampon.

tam-tam *n.m.* **1** 'Till', cash register. **2** (Under-world slang): 'Good name', renown where trustworthiness and reliability are concerned. **3** *Faire du tam-tam*: To 'make a lot of ballyhoo', to 'make a song-and-dance about something', to make a fuss. (The expression obviously originates from a 'the natives are restless' situation.)

tandem *n.m.* 'Twosome', association of two people within a business venture or an amorous entanglement.

tangent *n.m.* **1** *(sch.)*: Borderline candidate at an examination. **2** *Ça va être du tangent!* It'll be touch-and-go! – It's going to be a near-thing!

tangente *n.f. Prendre la tangente*: **a** To 'scarper', to 'skedaddle', to run away. **b** To wriggle out of a difficult situation by taking an acceptable compromise.

tango *n.m.* Drink of lager sweetened by a shot of grenadine syrup. (This concoction is not unlike the traditional lager-and-lime.)

tannant *adj.* **1** (of person): 'Badgering', pestering. **2** (of person, task or event): 'Deadly', very boring.

tannée *n.f.* 'Thrashing', 'walloping', beating-up.

tanner *v.trans.* **1** To 'badger', to go on and on at someone. *Il me tanne (les oreilles) à longueur de journée à propos de sa nana!* His only topic of conversation with me seems to be his woman! **2** To 'bash up', to 'beat up', to thrash.

tanneur *n.m.* 'Badgerer', persistent bore (character who always seems to harp on the same string).

tant *adv.* **1** *Tant et plus*: 'Any amount', a lot. *Il gagne du fric tant et plus!* He's making money hand-over-fist! **2** *Tant qu'à faire, il vaut mieux se raccommoder!* It seems just as sensible to make it up! **3** *Vous m'en direz tant! (iron.)*: You don't say! (Well, I understand it all now!)

tante *n.f.* **1** 'Nancy-boy', 'pouf', effeminate homosexual. **2** *Les tantes! (interj.)*: The bastards! *Le fisc m'a encore filé une amende. Ah les tantes!* I've just had another fine from the tax-people, sod the rotten buggers! **3** *Ma tante*: The pawnshop. *J'ai dû larguer ma montre chez ma tante!* I had to hock my watch!

tantine *n.f.* (Child language): Auntie, aunt.

tantôt *n.m.* **1** Afternoon. *Je te verrai ce tantôt!* I'll see you this p.m.! **2** *A tantôt!* See you later, alligator!

taouée *n.f.* 'Ciggy', 'fag', cigarette. (The only attested reference to this word is to be found in Jean Genet's NOTRE-DAME DES FLEURS and is lexicalized in J. Cellard's and A. Rey's DICTIONNAIRE DU FRANÇAIS NON-CONVENTIONNEL.)

tapage *n.m.* 'Cadging', borrowing of money. *Le tapage, c'est son blot!* Whenever you see him, he's always after a sub!

tapant *adj.* (of time): 'On the dot', precisely. *Arriver à l'heure tapante*: To arrive bang on time. *A minuit tapant, il faut qu'on décarre!* We'll have to leave on the stroke of midnight!

tape *n.f.* 'Knock', setback, failure. *Ramasser* (also: *prendre*) *une tape*: To 'come a cropper', to 'come unstuck', to suffer a setback.

tapé *adj.* **1** 'Bonkers', 'potty', mad. *T'es tapé, non?!* You crazy in the head or something?! **2** *Réponse bien tapée*: Stinging retort (one that leaves the recipient speechless. *Elle est bien*

tapée, celle-là! That's the style! – That's the stuff to give 'em!)

tape-à-l'œil *n.m.inv.* Show-off behaviour. *Faire du tape-à-l'œil (à quelqu'un)*: To 'swank', to show-off.

tape-à-l'œil *adj.inv.* 'Flashy', 'showy', ostentatious.

tape-cul *n.m.* **1** 'Boneshaker', 'old crate', ramshackle motor-car. **2** *Faire du tape-cul*: To go horse-riding. (The image conjured up by this expression is of a rider shaken up by a horse's trot.) **3** *Quel tape-cul!* What a load of codswallop! – What rubbish! – How stupid!

tapée *n.f. Une tapée de*: 'Oodles of', masses, vast quantities of. *On a une tapée de problèmes en ce moment!* Life's problems, problems, problems at the moment! *Avec le chômage ces temps-ci, on peut trouver une tapée de mecs pour un boulot comme ça!* What with unemployment and everything, people for jobs like that are pretty thick on the ground!

taper *v.trans.* **1** To 'tap', to 'touch' someone for a sub, to cadge money off someone. **2** *Taper une lettre*: To 'tap out', to type a letter. **3** *Taper des talbins*: To print counterfeit money. **4** *Taper une belote*: To have a game of *belote*. (The expression is true to reality; this game of cards full of French histrionics gives a deck of cards a tough time.)

taper *v.intrans.* **1** *Taper sur*: To 'pitch into', to 'lam into', to go for someone with fists flying. **2** *Taper sur les nerfs* (also: *sur le système*) *à quelqu'un*: To 'get on someone's wick', to be a real nuisance to someone. **3** *Taper dans l'œil à quelqu'un*: **a** To make an impression on someone. **b** To 'click' with someone of the opposite sex. **4** *Taper aux fafs (pol.)*: To ask for I.D. papers, to request identification documents. **5** *Ça tape!* It's fair blazing down! – We've got some super sunshine! **6** *Taper le 180 km./h.* (of car): To top 100 m.p.h. easily. **7** *Taper de*: To 'pong', to stink, to smell foul. *Il tape des panards que c'en est affreux!* His feet smell something rotten!

taper *v.pronom.* **1** *Se taper quelque chose*: **a** To have to do something unpleasant. *C'est encore moi qui dois me taper la vaisselle!* I can see it'll be muggins who does the washing-up again! **b** To treat oneself to something nice. *On s'est tapé un gueuleton tout ce qu'il y a de meumeu!* We had ourselves a super nosh! *Je me taperais bien cette nana!* I wouldn't mind laying this chick! **2** *Se taper de quelque chose*: **a** Not to 'give a fuck', not to 'care a rap' about something. *Ses histoires de nanas, je m'en tape royalement!* I don't give a fig about his goings-on with women! **b** To have to do without something. **3** *Se taper* *le cul par terre*: To 'laugh oneself silly', to be overcome by mirth. **4** *Se taper la colonne*: To 'pull one's wire', to 'wank', to masturbate.

tapette *n.f.* **1** 'Clapper', tongue. (With this meaning, the word relates to speech as in *avoir une sacrée tapette*: to have been 'vaccinated with a gramophone needle', to be an endless yapper.) **2** 'Pouf', 'pansy', effeminate homosexual.

tapeur *n.m.* 'Habitual cadger', inveterate borrower.

tapin *n.m.* **1** 'Prozzy', 'hooker', prostitute. **2** Soliciting, prostitution. *Elle fait le tapin dans les boîtes de nuit*: She finds her clients in night-clubs.

tapinage *n.m.* Soliciting, prostitution.

tapiner *v.intrans.* (of prostitute): To go soliciting.

tapineuse *n.f.* 'Prozzy', 'hooker', prostitute.

tapir *n.m.* *(sch.)*: Pupil receiving extra (paid) tuition in the form of private lessons. (The appellation also has a connotation of 'teacher's pet' which, in the context of monies paid by parents, makes sense.)

tapis *n.m.* **1** 'Dive', low-class drinking-hall. *Au début de sa carrière elle chantait dans des tapis près de Montmartre*: Long before she was a star, she sang in the clip-joints near Montmartre. **2** *Aller au tapis* (Boxing): To hit the canvas, to suffer a knockdown. **3** *Tenir le tapis*: To act the 'star' at a gathering or party. **4** *Amuser le tapis*: To act the 'bundle of fun' at a party, to keep the company laughing.

tapis *adj.inv.* *Etre tapis*: To be 'skint', 'broke', to be penniless.

tapissage *n.m.* *(pol.)*: Identification of a suspect (also: *retapissage*).

tapisser *v.trans.* To identify, to recognize a person (also: *retapisser*).

tapisserie *n.f.* *Faire tapisserie* (of girl at a dance): To be a 'wallflower', to be unpartnered throughout the evening.

taquet *n.m.* Punch, blow with the fist. *Il lui a filé un taquet sur le coin de la gueule*: He gave him a knuckle-sandwich.

taquiner *v.trans.* *Taquiner le goujon*: To do a spot of angling.

tarabiscoté *adj.* Over-decorated (with a proliferation of needlessly detailed work).

tarabistouille *n.f.* Intentional 'cock-up' sometimes contrived for 'conning purposes'.

tarabistouiller *v.trans.* To bring about a confused state of affairs, sometimes with the purpose of pulling a fast one in the world of business.

tarabuster *v.trans.* **1** To bully, to inflict verbal and physical violence. **2** To 'badger', to pester. *Il va me tarabuster jusqu'à ce que je baisse pavillon!*

I can see he's going to plague me until I give in! **3** *Se tarabuster l'esprit*: To 'rack one's brains', to search and search through one's mind.

taratata *interj.* Fiddlesticks! – Baloney! –Rubbish! (This interjection is equatable with 'pull the other one!')

tarauder *v.trans.* **1** To bully, to inflict verbal and physical violence. **2** To 'badger', to pester.

tarbouif *n.m.* (also: *tarbouiffe*): 'Conk', 'hooter', nose.

tard *adv.* *Il se fait tard!* It's getting a bit late!

tarde *n.f.* Night, night-time. *A la tarde* (also: *sur la tarde*): At dusk, at nightfall.

tarderie *n.f.* *(pej.)*: **1** 'Old biddy', unkempt and slovenly old woman. *Vise un peu cette tarderie!* She's a right old mess, she is! **2** (of object): 'Load of crap', decrepit and totally useless item. **3** *(pl.)*: Troublesome thoughts (the kind that keep you awake at night).

tardigrade *n.m.* 'Stick-in-the-mud' reactionary, character for whom 'progress' is always in the wrong direction.

targette *n.f.* **1** *(pl.)*: 'Clodhoppers', 'beetle-crushers', large shoes. (The word becomes all the more colloquial when it refers to normal or dainty footwear.) **2** *Coup de targette*: Request for 'sub', borrowing of money.

tarin *n.m.* 'Conk', 'hooter', nose.

tarte *n.f.* **1** 'Biff', blow (usually a slap in the face). **2** *C'est de la tarte!* 'It's a piece of cake!' – It's as easy as pie! **2** (of task): It's (dead) simple! *Lui faire payer l'addition, ça va pas être de la tarte!* Getting him to pay the bill's going to be no doddle! **3** *Avoir de la tarte* (Gambling slang): To have the luck of the devil.

tarte *adj.inv.* **1** Ugly. *Sa dernière nana est d'un tarte!* That latest bird of his is some eyesore! **2** 'Crummy', 'lousy', worthless. **3** (of person): 'Thick', stupid. **4** (of happening): Stupid, silly. *Il lui arrive toujours des histoires tarte!* The daftest things seem to happen to him!

Tartempion *Proper name.* 'Whatsisname', 'Thingy'. (This jocular appellation is more often than not derogatory. *Des machins comme ça, c'est bon pour Tartempion!* You give stuff like that to any Tom, Dick or Harry!)

tarter *v.trans.* To give (someone) a slap in the face.

tartignolle *adj.* (also: *tartignol*): **1** Ugly in a silly and gawky way. **2** 'Crummy', 'lousy', worthless. **3** (of person): 'Thick', stupid. *Il est vraiment tartignolle, ton beauf!* That brother-in-law of yours is as thick as two short planks!

tartinage *n.m.* 'Cadging', borrowing. (This kind of appeal for a 'sub' usually comes with a lengthy tale of woe.)

tartine *n.f.* **1** Lengthy and boring account, verbal or otherwise. *Ses rapports, il faut se les farcir, quelles* *tartines!* You really need a couple of hours to get through one of his boring reports! *En faire une tartine*: To waffle about something. **2** *En connaître une tartine*: To know a hell of a lot about something, to be extremely well informed on a subject.

tartiner *v.trans. & intrans.* **1** To 'waffle', to talk and talk about something. **2** To write a lengthy article or report where the main purpose of the exercise seems to be to put as many words on paper as possible. **3** To appeal for a 'sub', usually with a long tale of woe.

tartiner *v.pronom. S'en tartiner*: To 'not give a fig' about something, not to 'care two hoots', to be totally indifferent to something. *Ses histoires à la mords-moi-le-machin, je m'en tartine!* His cock-and-bull stories really leave me cold!

tartines *n.f.pl.* **1** Footwear (usually the more dainty and delicate variety). **2** 'Plates of meat', feet.

tartir *v.intrans.* **1** To 'crap', to 'shit', to defecate. **2** *Faire tartir quelqu'un*: To bore the pants off someone. **3** *Se faire tartir*: To be bored stiff. *Qu'est-ce qu'on se fait tartir à ces soirées mondaines!* Those posh evening dos are just one big yawn! **4** *Envoyer tartir quelqu'un*: To 'send someone packing', to show someone the door in no uncertain manner.

tartisses *n.f.pl. Les tartisses*: 'The karzey', 'the bog', the W.C.

tartissure *n.f.* Trace of excrement.

tartouze *adj.* (also: *tartouse*): **1** 'Crummy', 'lousy', pretty worthless. **2** Stupid, rather silly.

tas *n.m.* **1** 'Ugly biddy', ungainly woman. **2** *Gros tas*: 'Fatso', corpulent person (also: *gros plein de soupe*). **3** *Bonsoir tout le tas!* Evenin' all! (Like the English, the French has a slight touch of irony.) **4** *Tas de ferraille*: 'Heap', 'banger', decrepit motor car. **5** *Etre sur le tas*: To be at one's job, to be at work. **6** *Se retrouver sur le tas*: To find oneself out of work. (This expression, diametrically in contradiction with *être sur le tas*, conjures up the image of the 'scrap-heap of life'.) **7** *Sécher sur le tas*: To be 'left cooling one's heels', to wait in vain. **8** *Prendre quelqu'un sur le tas*: To catch someone red-handed. *Etre fait sur le tas*: To be caught in the act. **9** *Taper dans le tas*: **a** To 'lash out blindly', to hit out at the first available target. **b** To choose at random. **c** To make a wild guess. **10** *Piquer dans le tas*: To pick freely, to choose at random. **11** *Faire le tas* (of prostitute): To be 'on the job', to go soliciting (also: *faire le trottoir*). **12** *Une grève sur le tas*: A 'sit-down' strike (occupation/take-over of factory). **13** *Un tas de/des tas de*: 'Heaps of', 'oodles', vast quantities of. **14** *Sur le tas!* 'Pronto!' – Straight away! – Immediately!

tasse *n.f.* **1** Drink consumed in a café. *T'as bien le temps de prendre une tasse?* Come on, have a quick one! **2** *La grande tasse*: 'The briny', the sea. **3** *Boire la tasse*: **a** To swallow a considerable amount of water while swimming. **b** To drown. **c** *(fig.)*: To 'go under', to go bankrupt. **4** *En avoir sa tasse de quelque chose*: To be sick and tired of something, to be fed up to the back teeth with something. **5** (Homosexuals' slang): 'Cottage', urinal where male gays congregate (also: *théière*).

tassé *adj. Bien tassé*: **a** (of food, drink): Generously served. *On s'est tapé deux scotchs bien tassés*: We had ourselves a couple of well-poured whiskies. (The expression *un café bien tassé* does not relate to the quantity in the cup but to the large amount of coffee grounds through which water is made to filter.) **b** (of time lapsed) *Deux heures bien tassées*: Two solid hours.

tasseau *n.m.* (also: *tassot*): 'Conk', 'hooter', nose. (This word is usually used in an uncomplimentary context. Also: *tarin*.)

tassée *n.f. Une tassée de*: 'Oodles', vast quantities of.

tasser *v.intrans. Qu'est-ce que je lui ai tassé!* I didn't half let him have it! – I gave him what for! – I gave him a severe punishing! (this can be physical or verbal).

tasser *v.trans.reflex.* To 'stuff one's face', to consume vast quantities of food and drink. *On s'est tassé un sacré petit gueuleton!* We had ourselves a really slap-up meal!

tasser *v.pronom. Ça va se tasser!* It'll all come out in the wash! – Things will sort themselves out! *T'en fais pas, tout finira par se tasser!* I wouldn't bother, things will right themselves eventually!

tata *n.f.* **1** (Child language): Auntie, aunt. **2** *(pej.)*: 'Poufter', 'nancy-boy', effeminate homosexual.

tatanes *n.f.pl.* 'Boats', 'trotter-cases', shoes. *Je l'ai sorti à coups de tatanes!* I booted him out good and proper!

tâter *v.intrans. Tâter de quelque chose*: **a** To give something a try. **b** To have a penchant for something. (With this meaning, *en tâter* usually refers to less mentionable activities. *La rondelle, il en tâte*: I believe he's partial to the 'gay' life!)

tâter *v.trans.reflex.* To 'have a little think' before making a decision, to weigh up the pros and cons.

Tâtes-z-y *La mère Tâtes-z-y*: A randy yet unattractive female. (This uncomplimentary appellation makes a phonetic witticism of *la mère qui y tâte*.)

tâteur *n.m.* 'Jack-of-all-trades' (and master of none), character who seems to want to try his hand at everything with little success.

tâteuse *n.f.* (Underworld slang): Skeleton key.

tatoué *n.m.* 'Heavy', tough guy (perhaps because the macho musclemen have their brawn adorned with tattoos).

tatouille *n.f.* **1** 'Walloping', thrashing. **2** 'Dressing-down', telling-off.

tatouiller *v.trans.* **1** To 'wallop', to 'thrash', to beat up. **2** (*fig.*): To 'tear a strip off', to tell off in no uncertain manner.

taulard *n.m.* 'Jailbird', recidivist who seems to be on a shuttle service where prisons are concerned.

taule *n.f.* **1** 'Nick', 'clink', jail. *Etre en taule* (also: *faire de la taule*): To 'do bird', to do time. **2** *La grande taule*: Police headquarters in a major city. **3** *Ma taule, ta taule, sa taule*: My, your, his home/house. *Bon, je rentre à la taule!* Well, I'll be off home then! (The fact that prison and home are referred to, in this case, by the same word could be more than coincidental.)

taulier *n.m.* Owner/proprietor of restaurant, hotel or pub. (The appellation is not exactly up-market, and gains in humour when the person runs a high-class establishment.)

taulière *n.f.* **1** 'Madam', brothel-keeper. **2** Proprietress of a hotel, pub, restaurant (usually of little repute).

taupe *n.f.* **1** (Students' slang): Class of advanced mathematics. (Those attending the course aim to compete for the *Grandes Ecoles*.) **2** *Vieille taupe (pej.)*: Old hag, old woman.

taupin *n.m.* Student attending *taupe*.

taxi *n.m.* **1** Mode of transport (plane, car, etc.). *Il a pris un taxi pour les States*: He took a plane for the U.S.A. *Son vieux taxi est toujours en panne*: That old banger of his always seems to be in for repairs. **2** 'Prozzy', prostitute. (The word is usually used by pimps when referring to their 'personnel'. *J'ai encore deux petits taxis qui m'arrondissent mes fins de mois!* I've still got a couple of good little earners to keep me in clover!) **3** (Underworld slang): 'Go-between', intermediary.

T.C.F. *(abbr. Touring-Club de France)*: Motoring organization roughly equivalent to the A.A. or the R.A.C. (Those belonging to this Association are sometimes called *técéfistes*.)

tchao *interj.* 'Toodle-oo!' – 'So long!' – Cheerio! (This is a phonetic representation of the Italian *ciao*!)

tchi (also: *t'chi*) *Que tchi*: 'Fuck-all', 'bugger-all', nothing. *Sans loupiotte, on ne voyait que tchi!* With no light on, you couldn't see a blind thing!

tchin-tchin *interj.* Here's mud in your eye! – Cheers! – Good health to you! (This boozers' interjection exists, in fact, in English and is said by Gaston Esnault in his DICTIONNAIRE DES ARGOTS to originate from Cantonese pidgin English.)

té *interj. (corr. tiens!)*: What a question to ask! – Of course! (This interjection originating from Provence seems to be filtering through to the rest of France.)

técolle *pers.pron.* You, yourself. *Des bagnoles comme ça, c'est pas pour técolle!* Cars like that aren't for the likes of you!

teigne *n.f.* 'Pest', nasty person whose evil-minded niggling is more than just a nuisance. (As with most terms of abuse, this word, because it is feminine, becomes all the more insulting when directed at a male.)

teigneux *n.m.* 'Nasty piece of work', unpleasant character who tends to take umbrage at the slightest provocation.

teigneux *adj.* Cantankerous in a nasty sort of way.

teint *n.m. Bon teint (adj.exp.)*: **a** (of person): 'As true as they come', very honest. **b** (of goods, etc.): 'Honest-to-goodness' and reliable.

teinté *adj.* 'Pissed', 'blotto', drunk. *Un peu qu'il était teinté!* You could see he'd been painting the town red!

teintée *n.f.* **1** 'Binge', heavy drinking spree. **2** 'Skinful', (state of) drunkenness. *Il tenait une de ces teintées!* He was pissed to the eyeballs!

télé *n.f. (abbr. télévision) La télé*: 'The box', the telly. *Depuis qu'il est passé à la télé, qu'est-ce qu'il se prend au sérieux!* Just the once on T.V. and now he lords it over us!

téléfon *n.m.* Phone, telephone.

télégraphe *n.m. Donner du* (also: *faire le*) *télégraphe*: To 'tip the wink', to warn someone.

téléguidé *past part. C'était téléguidé, ça!* You could guess he was being manipulated when that decision was taken!

téléguider *v.trans.* To be the steering force behind someone's actions.

télémuche *n.m.* 'Blower', phone, telephone.

téléphone *n.m.* **1** *Le téléphone*: The 'smallest room', the W.C. (The expression *aller au téléphone* can be seen as a polite way of saying that one needs to attend to an urgent Call of Nature.) **2** *Le téléphone arabe*: The 'grapevine', that mysterious and near-instantaneous way by which news seems to filter through. **3** *Le téléphone polisson*: Fellatio.

téléphoner *v.intrans.* **1** To do 'number twos', to go to the W.C. (The verb's jocularity becomes apparent when extended in the euphemistic *'Je vais aller téléphoner.'*) **2** *Téléphoner dans le ventre*: To 'have a bang', to have intercourse. **3** *C'était téléphoné! (iron.)*: **a** (of contrived joke): You

could see what the punchline was going to be!
b (Sporting context): It was easy to guess what
was going to happen!

téléphonite *n.f.* 'Telephonitis', irrepressible
need to be always on the telephone.

téloche *n.f. (corr. abbr. télévision) La téloche*:
'The box', the telly. *La téloche, c'est son opium!*
The gogglebox seems to be a fascination for
her!

tempérament *n.m.* **1** *Avoir un sacré
tempérament*: To be a 'goer', not to be lacking
vim and zest when a strenuous effort is
required. **2** *Se crever* (also: *s'esquinter*) *le
tempérament*: To 'knock oneself up', to wear
oneself out. **3** *Ne pas manquer de tempérament*:
To 'have a nerve', to be as cheeky as they
come.

température *n.f.* *Prendre la température*: To
make (discreet) inquiries.

temps *n.m.* **1** *Tirer son temps*: To 'do one's
stretch', to 'do time', to serve a prison
sentence. (A subsidiary connotation to this
expression is that the prisoner concerned
adopts an obedient 'low-profile' attitude in
order to steer clear of trouble and get full
remission.) **2** *En deux temps, trois mouvements*:
In two shakes (of a lamb's tail)' – 'In a jiffy' –
Straight away. *J'ai dû rappliquer en deux temps,
trois mouvements!* I had to get back double-
quick!

tendeur *n.m.* 'Randy so-and-so', over-sexed
man.

tenir *v.trans.* **1** *En tenir une*: **a** (also: *tenir une
sacrée cuite*): To be 'pissed to the eyeballs', to
be roaring drunk. **b** (also: *en tenir une couche*):
To be 'as thick as two short planks', to be
extremely stupid. **2** *En tenir pour quelqu'un*: To
be 'spoony on', to be infatuated with someone.
3 *Tiens-toi bien!* (also: *tenez-vous bien!; joc. &
iron.*): Just listen to this! – (The implication is
that the person addressed has to brace himself
for the news.)

tenir *v.intrans.* *Ça tient au corps!* (of food): It
certainly fills you up! (This expression usually
refers to stodge-like edibles.)

tennis-barbe *n.m.* This popular student pastime
consists in trying to spot as many bearded men
as possible in the street. The reason it is called
tennis-barbe is that the scoring is done on the
lines of the game of tennis: 15–30–40–deuce,
etc.

tentiaire *n.m. (abbr. pénitentiaire):* 'Pen',
penitentiary.

tenu *past part. Tenu!* (referring to wager): You're
on! – I'll take you up on that!

tenue *n.f. De la tenue!* 'Manners, manners!'
– Behave yourself!

terminus *n.m. Terminus! (joc.)*: 'Hop out!' – This
is as far as I can drive you! (Originally this
interjection was only used by conductors on
trams and buses.)

terrain *n.m.* **1** *Déblayer le terrain*: To 'make
tracks', to 'clear off', to leave in haste. **2** *Tâter
le terrain*: To sound things out discreetly (to
make sensible enquiries to avoid putting a foot
wrong).

terre *n.f. Donner dans la terre jaune*: To be partial
to sodomous intercourse.

terre-neuve *n.m.inv. Jouer les terre-neuve*: To be
always going out of one's way to help the
'lame-ducks' of this world.

terreur *n.f.* 'Frightener', 'heavy', member of the
underworld whose function it is to enforce.

terreux *n.m.* 'Hick', 'hayseed', country bumpkin.

terrible *adj.* 'Incredible', fantastic, wonderful. *Il
a un bagout terrible!* He can talk the hind leg off a
donkey! *Sa nana, elle est terrible!* That bird of
his, what a dazzler! (The colloquiality of this
adjective comes from its antiphrastic usage.)

terrible *adv. (abbr. terriblement)*: 'Terribly',
enormously, incredibly.

terrine *n.f.* **1** 'Bean', 'bonce', head. *Prendre un
coup sur la terrine*: To get biffed on the block.
(Expressions such as *se payer la terrine de
quelqu'un* are nothing more than a colloquial
variation on the same with *tête*.) **2** 'Mush',
'mug', face. (This appellation is always used in
a derogatory context as in *avoir une sale terrine*:
to have a face like the back of a bus.) **3** *Terrine
de gelée de con*: 'Burk', 'nurk', imbecile.

terroir *n.m. Sentir le terroir*: **a** (of person): To be
obviously from a particular region (because of
one's accent and/or use of certain idioms).
b (of person): To look out of place within city
life. **c** (of produce): To have that genuine
home-grown flavour.

têtard *n.m.* **1** 'Babby', 'brat', very young child.
2 'Bibber', tippler (one who, like a suckling
babe, drinks straight from the bottle).
3 'Mug', 'sucker', dupe. *Etre toujours le
têtard*: To be always the one who cops it. *Faire
têtard*: To 'con', to 'take in', to deceive.

têtard *adj.m.* 'Pig-headed', stubborn.

têtasses *n.f.pl.* 'Droopy boobs', flabby breasts.

tête *n.f.* **1** *Avoir la tête de l'emploi (iron.)*: To
'look the part'. *Les croque-morts n'ont pas toujours
la tête de l'emploi, c'est souvent des rigolos!*
Undertakers aren't always the mournful
buggers we expect them to be! **2** *Faire une
drôle de tête*: To look sour and discontented.
Faire la tête à quelqu'un: To sulk. **3** *Faire la
mauvaise tête*: To be 'pig-headed', to be
obstreperous and reluctant to comply. **4** *Avoir*

ses têtes: To 'have one's (little) favourites', to let oneself be ruled by likes and dislikes where relationships at work are concerned. **5** *Avoir une tête à coucher dehors avec un billet de logement*: To have an 'ugly mug', to have an unattractive face (in fact, to have the kind of features that would even get you turned away from a welfare hostel). **6** *Faire un prix à la tête du client*: To quote a price according to the likely means of a customer. *Au garage, les prix sont un peu à la tête du client!* If you drive a Rolls, they'll charge the earth for repairs! **7** *Tête de pipe*: Portrait-photograph. *J'ai vu sa tête de pipe dans le canard!* I've seen his mug somewhere in a paper! **8** *Tête de . . . !* (insult intensifier): You bloody . . . ! *Tête de courge, va!* You blithering idiot! **9** *Tête de lard* (also: *tête de cochon, tête de mule*): Pig-headed character. **10** *Affaire tête de lard (pol.)*: Dead-end enquiry, one where witnesses and accused alike make the police's job more arduous by refusing to co-operate. **11** *Se payer la tête de quelqu'un*: To 'take the piss out of someone', to 'take the mickey', to poke fun at someone. **12** *Etre tombé sur la tête*: To be 'bonkers', 'potty', to be mad. *T'es tombé sur la tête, quoi?!* You crazy in the head?! **13** *Piquer une tête dans le bouillon*: **a** To 'take a header', to dive into the water. **b** *(fig.)*: To 'go under', to become bankrupt. **14** *Petite tête!* (jocular form of address): *Salut, petite tête!* Mornin' mate! *Alors, comment ça va, petite tête?!* Well, how's tricks?! **15** *Cause à mon cul, ma tête est malade!* (sarcastic retort): 'Get knotted' – I don't want to hear what you've got to say! **16** *La tête et les jambes*: The combination of brains and brawn. (The expression *courir avec la tête et les jambes* originates from the racing cyclist's slang and refers to competitors who use critical judgement when exerting physical effort. In the 1960s, a television quiz-cum-competition with that name teamed up scholars and sportsmen to compete for prizes.) **17** *Tenir la tête* (Gambling slang): To act as judge and arbiter at the tables. (August Le Breton in his *L'ARGOT CHEZ LES VRAIS DE VRAI* explains that this 'refereeing' activity is often given to a 'cleaned-out' player by a gambling baron; the position carries a small commission on stakes.) **18** *Tête d'oreiller (corr. taie d'oreiller)*: Pillowcase.

téter *v.intrans.* To 'tipple', to 'booze', to be over-fond of drinking.

tétère *n.f. (corr. tête)*: 'Bean', 'bonce', head.

tétés *n.m.pl.* 'Boobies', 'boobs', breasts (also: *tétons*).

teuf-teuf *n.m.* **1** (Child language): 'Putt-putt', motor-car. **2** Vintage or veteran car (probably because of their 'Chitty-chitty-bang-bang'

image in modern society). **3** (Child language): 'Puff-puff', steam engine.

tévé *n.f. (corr. abbr. télévision)*: Television (the medium). *Passer à la tévé*: To appear on T.V. (Unlike *téloche* and *télé*, *tévé* does not refer specifically to 'the box', the electrical appliance.)

texto *adv. (abbr. textuellement)*: 'Word-for-word', verbatim. *C'est ce qu'il m'a dit, texto!* Those were his very words!

tézigue *pers.pron.* You, yourself. *Des emmerdes comme ça, c'est pas pour tézigue!* I would steer clear of cock-ups like that if I were you!

thé *n.m.* **1** *Marcher au thé*: **a** To be a 'dipso', to be dependent on alcohol. **b** (Drugs): To be addicted to marijuana. **2** *Tasse à thé*: 'Cottage', urinal where homosexuals congregate. **3** *Prendre le thé*: To engage in homosexual activities (of males only).

théière *n.f.* **1** 'Bean', 'bonce', head (probably because the spout is seen as the nose). **2** 'Cottage', urinal where homosexuals congregate.

thème *n.m.* **1** *Etre un fort en thème*: To have what it takes 'up-top', to be brainy. **2** *Faire thème*: To 'keep mum', to keep quiet.

thomas *n.m.* **1** 'Jerry', 'po', chamber-pot. **2** *Aller voir la mère Thomas*: To 'go and have a crap', to 'shit', to defecate.

thune *n.f.* Five-franc piece (long before the remonetization of 1958). Although no longer used when referring to money, the appellation has gained near-immortality with the popular song *'Mes deux thunes dans le bastringue'* – the *bastringue* being a jukebox.

thurne *n.f.* (Students' slang): 'Hall digs', room in hostel.

ti *pers.pron. Alors, viens-ti?* Well, are you coming? *T'as-ti tout ce qu'il te faut?* Well, have you got all your gubbins? (This interrogative particle is seen in popular etymology as a corruption of *tu*; it has a rather 'yokelish' flavour and is used in modern colloquial French usually with jocular undertones.)

ticket *n.m.* **1** 'Note', banknote (usually one of small denomination). **2** *Avoir un ticket avec quelqu'un* (amorous context): To have 'clicked' with someone, to enjoy instant appeal with a possible partner. **3** *Prendre un ticket*: To get a salacious eyeful (also: *prendre un jeton*). **4** *Un drôle de ticket*: A queer 'un, a strange character.

ticson *n.m.* (also: *tickson; corr. ticket*): Ticket (for a show, public transport, etc.).

tienne *poss.pron.* '*A la tienne, Etienne!*' 'Bottoms up!' – 'Cheers!' – To your good health! (This is not rhyming slang as in English; *Etienne* is as meaningless as *Auguste* in *'Tout juste, Auguste!'*)

tierce *n.f.* (Underworld slang): Small gang, team of criminals. (As the appellation suggests, there might well only be three.)

tiers *n.m. Se moquer du tiers comme du quart:* Not to give a damn, not to care a rap for anybody or anything.

tiffier *n.m.* (also: *tifier*): 'Lock-lopper', barber, gents' hairdresser.

tifs *n.m.pl.* Hair. *Manquer de tifs sur la calebombe:* To have a patchy thatch.

tige *n.f.* **1** 'Ciggy', 'fag', cigarette. *File-moi une tige!* Give us a smoke! **2** *(pl.;* also: *tiges de pâquerettes):* 'Spindle-shanks', skinny legs. **3** 'Prick', 'cock', penis. *Faire une tige:* To perform fellatio. **4** *Vieille tige* (Friendly term of familiarity.) *Salut, vieille tige!* Hello, old cock! (This appellation is said to have originated amongst airmen and referred to 'old hands' at the flying game.)

tiges *n.m.pl. Les tiges:* The 'fuzz', the cops. (This rather dated appellation refers to policemen patrolling areas on bicycles. They were also known as *hirondelles.*)

tignasse *n.f.* 'Mop', shock of untidy hair. *Passe un peigne dans ta tignasse!* I wish you'd straighten your hair!

tilt *n.m. Faire tilt:* **a** To 'twig', to 'grasp something', to understand. **b** To 'hit the mark', to be 'spot-on' where judgement is of the essence. **c** To 'flip', to break down completely where nerves are concerned. (With this last meaning, the origin of the expression can be explained: it refers to pinball machines where an electrically-wired pendulum brings the game to a halt when the machine is manhandled too roughly.)

timbre *n.m. Avoir le timbre fêlé:* To be 'bonkers', 'potty', to be mad (literally to be 'cracked').

timbré *adj.* 'Cracked', 'bonkers', mad.

tinche *n.f. Faire la tinche:* **a** To go begging for alms. **b** To 'pass the hat round', to have a 'whip-round' for someone.

tinée *n.f. Une tinée de:* 'Oodles', a great number of. (The expression can refer either to people or objects.)

tinette *n.f.* **1** Ramshackle motor vehicle. (The word is, if anything, affectionate and refers to a trusted vehicle, the survivor of bygone better times.) **2** *(pl.) Les tinettes:* 'The bog', the karzey', the W.C. **3** *Faire (une) tinette sur:* To pass disparaging comments on (someone or something).

tintin *n.m.* **1** *Faire tintin:* To 'get bugger-all', to have to do without, to be deprived of something. **2** *Tintin!* Nothing doing! – Not a hope! – There's not an earthly chance of that!

tintouin *n.m.* **1** Bother, worry. *C'est un zigoto qui nous a donné du tintouin!* This bloke spelled trouble right from the start! **2** *Et tout le tintouin!* And the whole bag of tricks! – And everything else!

tiquer *v.intrans.* To show signs of surprise (usually dissatisfaction, disappointment or disapproval, but in certain instances signs of interest). *Il n'a pas tiqué quand je lui ai annoncé la nouvelle:* He didn't bat an eyelid when I broke the news to him.

tir *n.m. Allonger le tir:* To have to pay more than expected. *Si tu veux ma bagnole, il va falloir que t'allonges le tir!* If you want that car of mine, you'll have to bid higher!

tirage *n.m. Du tirage:* 'Friction', state of awkward tension between people. *Depuis qu'il bosse ici, il y a du tirage avec les employés:* Since he joined the staff, the workforce have been extremely unco-operative.

tirailleur *n.m. Travailler en tirailleur:* To work freelance.

tire *n.f.* **1** 'Motor', car, motor car. **2** *La tire* (also: *le vol à la tire):* 'Dipping', the picking of pockets.

tire-au-cul *n.m.* 'Idle git', shirker, character who always successfully dodges chores and hard work (also: *tire-au-flanc*).

tire-bouchon *n.m. (pol.):* Highway patrol vehicle entrusted with the clearing of *'bouchons'* or 'bottlenecks' occurring at peak travelling times.

tirebouchonnant *adj.* 'Creasing', 'side-splitting', hilarious.

tirebouchonner *v.trans.reflex.* To 'split one's sides laughing', to laugh one's head off.

tire-bouton *n.m.* 'Les', 'dyke', lesbian. (Expressions such as *maison tire-bouton* and *ménage tire-bouton* refer disparagingly to lesbian twosomes.)

tirée *n.f.* 'Long haul', long journey (in respect of miles rather than time).

tire-fesses *n.m.* 'Ski-pull', ski-lift. (As the jocular appellation suggests, this T-shaped contraption supports the behind and pulls a skier up a slope.)

tire-jus *n.m.* 'Snot-rag', handkerchief.

tirelarigot *A tirelarigot (adv.exp.):* 'To one's fill', to satiation. *Le vin nouveau, on en boit à tirelarigot!* The new wine from the year's crop goes down a treat, we drink gallons of it!

tirelire *n.f.* **1** 'Bean', 'brainbox', head. **2** 'Dial', 'mush', face. **3** 'Trap', 'gob', mouth. **4** 'Belly', stomach. **5** 'Pussy', 'fanny', vagina. (The money-box image permeates every meaning.)

tirer *v.trans.* **1** To 'nick', to 'pinch', to steal (also: *voler à la tire).* **2** To spend time (and quite a lengthy period) doing something unpleasant. *Encore quinze jours à tirer et on part en vacances!* Another fortnight's grind and it's 'holidays here we come!' *Il a tiré cinq piges de dur:* He did five

years' porridge. **3** *En voilà une autre de tirée!*
(of day, month or year): And that's another one
gone! **4** *Tirer la couverture à soi:* To get the
most of something for oneself (either kudos or
worldly goods). **5** *Tirer l'échelle:* To 'call it a
day', to have to give up. *Après une connerie
comme ça, il n'y a plus qu'à tirer l'échelle!* After
a boob of that magnitude, there doesn't seem to
be any point in going any further! (also: *tirer la
ficelle*). **6** *Tirer la langue:* To be near exhaustion
(literally to have one's tongue lolling out
through sheer fatigue). **7** *Tirer les vers du nez à
quelqu'un:* To 'pump' someone, to winkle
information out of someone. **8** *Tirer un coup:*
To 'have a bang', to 'have it off', to have
coition. **9** *Tirer un fil* (of man): To 'splash one's
boots', to 'have a pee', to urinate.

tirer *v.intrans.* **1** To 'dip', to steal. **2** *Tirer au cul*
(also: *tirer au flanc* or *au renard*): To 'dodge a
chore', to steer clear of hard work. **3** *Tirer sur
la ficelle:* To 'go it a bit strong', to exaggerate.
(There is a possible parallel with the English
'pull the other one!' retort.)

tirer *v.trans.reflex.* **1** To 'bugger off', to 'slope
off', to go away. *Bon, il faut que je me tire,
demain je bosse de bonne heure!* I'll have to drift,
I'm on mornings tomorrow! **2** *Se tirer
d'épaisseur:* To get out of 'stuck', to get out of
trouble. **3** *Se tirer la bourre:* **a** To 'have a
punch-up', to have a fight. **b** To have a
flaming row. **4** *Ça se tire!* We can see the light
at the end of the tunnel! – We're nearing the
end! (The expression is usually used when
referring to times one is not enjoying.)

tireur *n.m.* **1** 'Dip', pickpocket. **2** 'Randy so-
and-so', highly-sexed man.

tireuse *n.f.* Wine-dispensing tap. (Going to a
shop where wine is sold *à la tireuse* has always
been a wise and economical custom. The wine
is often extremely good, and bottling and
labelling charges are thus avoided.)

tiroir *n.m.* **1** 'Tummy', stomach. *Avoir un
polichinelle dans le tiroir:* To be 'preggers',
'expecting', to be pregnant. **2** *(abbr. tiroir-
caisse):* 'Till', cash-register. **3** *Tiroir à lentilles*
(also: *tiroir aux lentilles*): Anal sphincter.

tisane *n.f.* **1** Water (river, lake, sea). *Tomber dans
la tisane:* To fall in the soup. **2** 'Pasting',
'thrashing', beating-up. *Il a pris une de ces
tisanes!* He got beaten black-and-blue!

tisaner *v.trans.* To 'bash up', to 'beat up', to
thrash.

titi *n.m.* Street urchin; cheeky, wily and
resourceful young boy. (The *titi parisien* is often
affectionately referred to in popular songs and
was immortalized by the French painter
Francisque Poulbot, 1879–1946, whose name

also became eponymous with that Gavroche-
like character.)

toboggan *n.m.* **1** 'Gullet', throat. *Se graisser le
toboggan (joc.):* To 'knock 'em back', to tipple.
2 *Toboggan à enfants (pej.):* Prolific mother, or
woman likely to have a large family.

toc *n.m.* **1** 'Nerve', self-assurance. *Manquer de toc:*
To lack confidence. *Reprendre du toc:* To regain
aplomb. **2** *Du toc:* Fake goods, sham
merchandise. *Ses bijoux, mon vieux, c'est du toc!*
That jewellery of hers is really just paste! **3** *Des
tocs (abbr. des papiers tocs):* False I.D.s, fake
identity papers. *Marcher sous des tocs:* To go
about with forged papers. *Marcher sous un toc:*
To go under an assumed name.

toc *adj.m.* **1** 'Trashy', 'sham', rubbishy.
2 'Bonkers', 'potty', mad. **3** (of criminal):
Vindictive, violent and dangerous. (With this
meaning, the adjective refers to the kind of
thug who is likely to end his days in a hospital
for the criminally insane.) **4** Ugly, afflicted
with unattractive features. **5** 'Thick', stupid.
6 Unlucky, plagued by bad luck.

tocante *n.f.* 'Timex', 'timepiece', watch.

tocard *n.m.* **1** (Racing slang): 'Worthless nag',
horse devoid of any ability. **2** 'Loser', character
with no record of success in life.

tocard *adj.* **1** Ugly, rather unsightly. **2** Stupid,
rather ridiculous. **3** Unlucky, plagued by bad
luck.

tocasse *n.f. (pej.):* Low-class prostitute.

tocbombe *adj.* 'Bonkers', 'potty', mad.

toctoc *adj.inv.* 'Bonkers', 'potty', mad. (There is
a certain element of jocular imagery in this
adjective suggesting the index finger tap-
tapping on the head indicating that someone is
behaving in an irrational manner.)

toile *n.f.* **1** *(pl.):* Sheets, bed-sheets. *Se glisser
dans les toiles:* To 'hit the sack', to go to bed
(also: *torchons*). **2** *Se payer une toile:* To 'catch a
movie', to go and see a film. (In this case, the
toile is obviously the cinema screen.)
3 *Déchirer la toile:* To 'let one rip', to 'fart', to
break wind.

toise *n.f.* 'Bashing', 'drubbing', thrashing. *Filer
une toise à quelqu'un:* To beat the living
daylights out of someone.

toison *n.f.* **1** 'Mop' of hair. **2** 'Woolly', pubic
hair.

tôlard *n.m.* 'Jailbird', recidivist who seems to be
on a shuttle-service where prisons are
concerned.

tôle *n.f.* **1** 'Nick', 'clink', jail. *Il vient de sortir de
tôle:* He's only just out of prison. **2** Home, the
place where one lives. *Bon, faut que je rentre à
ma tôle!* Well, I'll have to get back to my digs!
(It is interesting to note that prison and home

are, in this instance, referred to by the same word.)

tôlier *n.m.* Owner/manager of restaurant, hotel or pub. (The appellation is not exactly up-market, and gains in humour when the person runs a high-class establishment.)

tôlière *n.f.* **1** 'Madam', brothel-keeper. **2** Proprietress of a hotel, pub, restaurant (usually of little repute).

tomate *n.f.* **1** Red 'mush', rubicund face. **2** 'Hooter', 'conk', red nose (usually indicative of over-indulgence in alcoholic beverage). **3** Aperitif drink consisting of *pastis* and grenadine syrup. **4** 'Noodle', 'nincompoop', fool. **5** *Des tomates!* Not on your nelly! – Not bloody likely! – Certainly not! (also: *des clous!*).

tombé *n.m. (joc.)*: Easy victory. (This word, stemming from the language of wrestling, is a translation of the English 'fall', as in 'two falls or a knockout'.)

tombeau *n.m.* **1** Trustworthy person where secrets are concerned. (Your secret will go to the grave with him.) **2** *Rouler à tombeau ouvert*: To drive at breakneck speed.

tomber *v.trans.* **1** To 'floor', to knock down. **2** To 'bowl over', to astound. **3** To woo, to win over. (With this meaning, the verb can refer to sexual prowess. *Il l'a tombée fastoche!* He scored with her easy!) **4** *Tomber la veste*: **a** To take one's jacket off (because of the hot weather, exertion, etc.). **b** *(fig.)*: To 'get stuck in', to participate in some hard graft. (The image here is of rolling up one's sleeves in order to 'muck in' with one's minions. *Il est pas fier lui, notre patron, il a tombé la veste pour nous aider!* He's no boardroom smoothie, our boss, he came and grafted with us!)

tomber *v.intrans.* **1** To get 'nicked', 'picked up', to be arrested. **2** To get sentenced. **3** *Laisser tomber* (of item of conversation): To 'drop it', to change topic. **4** *Laisser tomber quelqu'un*: **a** To 'let someone down', to fail to support someone in his hour of need. **b** To 'ditch' someone, to jettison someone when he or she is of no further use. **5** *Qu'est-ce qu'il tombe!* It ain't half chucking it down! – It's pouring buckets! **6** *Tomber sur quelqu'un*: To come down on someone (like a ton of bricks), to reproach someone violently. **7** *Tomber sur un bec*: To 'hit a snag', to suffer a setback. **8** *Tomber quelque part*: To 'land', to end up somewhere. *On est tombé dans un patelin perdu!* We finished up in some God-forsaken place! **9** *Je ne sais pas d'où il est tombé!* I don't know where he sprang from! – He's a total stranger as far as I'm concerned. **10** *Tomber pile*: To arrive in the nick of time.

tombereau *n.m.* **1** *(joc.)*: 'Heap', car, motor car. **2** *(pej.)*: 'Ugly biddy', graceless girl (the kind you dread to 'cart around').

tombeur *n.m.* **1** 'Heavy', muscleman, individual whose sheer physical strength enables him to enforce orders. **2** *(abbr. tombeur de filles* or *de femmes)*: 'Macho Casanova', manly seducer.

tonalité *n.f. Il n'a pas attendu pour avoir la tonalité! (joc. & iron.)*: He didn't exactly wait to get an answer/a reaction to what he had said! (In standard French *la tonalité* refers to the dialling-tone on the telephone.)

tondre *v.trans. Se faire tondre*: **a** To 'get shorn', to get a hair-cut. **b** *(fig.)*: To 'get fleeced', to 'get cleaned out', to lose all one's money at gambling.

tondre *v.intrans. Tondre sur un œuf*: To 'act the skinflint', to behave like a miser.

tondu *n.m. (joc.)*: 'Baldie', bald-headed man. (This humorous appellation got an extra boost from the comic cartoon-strip *'Tif et Tondu'*.)

tondu *adj.* 'Cleaned-out', 'skint', penniless through reckless gambling or careless spending.

tonneau *n.m.* **1** *Faire un tonneau* (of car): To turn a somersault. (There appears to be no accurate word in English to describe this roll-over-somersault action, where a driver having lost control, the vehicle turns a 360° spiral course on its side. The expression originates from the 'victory roll' executed by aviators.) **2** *Être du même tonneau*: **a** (of people): To be 'birds of a feather', to be singularly alike. (When used with a pejorative implication, the 'tarred with the same brush' image is more apt.) **b** (of things): To be 'much of a muchness', to be so alike as to be indistinguishable.

tonnerre *n.m.* **1** *Du tonnerre*: 'Fab', fantastic. *Il s'est payé une bagnole du tonnerre!* He bought himself a really smashing motor car! **2** *Tonnerre de Dieu!* Well, blow me! – Strewth! – Stone the crows! (This expletive and its English equivalents can be judged as equally dated.) **3** *Habiter au tonnerre de Dieu*: To live 'at the back-of-beyond', far away.

tonton *n.m.* **1** (Child language): 'Nunkie', uncle. **2** *Tonton macout(t)e*: Name given to the infamous henchmen of the Duvalier 'dynasty' on Haiti.

tonus *n.m.* 'Vim', zest, energy. *Ne pas manquer de tonus*: To be 'full of beans'.

top *n.m.* 'Time-pip'. *'Au quatrième top, il sera exactement . . .'* : 'At the third stroke, it will be exactly . . .'

topaze *n.m.* Grafting minion. (No doubt, Marcel Pagnol's *Topaze* has become eponymous with the hard-working, obsequious little men of our time.)

topo *n.m.* **1** Draft plan. **2** *(sch.) Faire un topo*: To give an exposé, to deliver a small 'paper'.

3 *Donne-moi le topo!* Give me the lowdown! – Give me the vital and detailed information! *Avant qu'on parte, il nous a donné le topo*: He filled us in (on the mission/work) before we left.

Topol *Proper name. (abbr. le Boulevard Sébastopol) Le Topol*: The arterial road of that name in Paris and the *quartier* in its vicinity.

toquade *n.f.* 'Whim', passing fancy. (The word has a subtle connotation of amorous entanglements. *Giselle, c'est une toquade, rien de plus!* She was nothing more than a flighty moment in his life!)

toquant *n.m.* 'Ticker', heart. *Son toquant bat la chamade!* He's got a dicky ticker!

toquante *n.f.* 'Timex', 'timepiece', watch.

toqué *adj.* **1** 'Touched', 'potty', mad. **2** *Etre toqué de*: To be 'spoony over', 'sweet on', to be besotted with.

toquer *v.pronom. Se toquer de*: **a** To 'go spoony over', to 'get doolally about', to fall head-over-heels in love with someone. **b** (of idea, project, etc.): To 'go mad over', to go crazy about. *Il s'est toqué de politique ces temps-ci!* Recently he's been bitten by the politics bug!

torche *n.f. Se mettre en torche*: **a** (of parachute): To 'candle', to fail to unfurl. **b** (*fig.*): To 'come unstuck', to 'come a cropper', to suffer a serious setback. *Nos ventes sont en torche!* Our sales-figures have taken a nose-dive!

torché *adj.* **1** *Mal torché*: **a** (of person): Uncouth, ill-mannered. *En voilà un mal torché!* What an uncivilized nurk! **b** (of work, task): 'Botched', bungled. **2** *Bien torché* (of task, sometimes of a work of art): Neatly executed. *Il nous sort des dessins bien torchés!* He's been churning out some really crisp drawings!

torche-cul *n.m.* **1** 'Bum-fodder', toilet-paper. **2** (*pej.*): 'Rag', trashy newspaper (one whose ultimate function when the day is gone is easy to guess!).

torchée *n.f.* **1** (*lit. & fig.*): 'Pasting', thrashing. **2** (*mil.*): Short but violent fight where one of the adversaries is trounced good and proper. **3** *Une torchée de*: 'Oodles', masses of. *Des bagnoles comme ça, t'en trouveras des torchées!* Bangers like that are ten-a-penny! (also: *une chiée de*).

torcher *v.trans.* **1** To 'scamp', to botch (a job or task). **2** (of unimportant newspaper article, etc.): To 'knock off', to 'dash off', to write in haste with little care for style. **3** *Se faire torcher*: To 'get trounced', to be soundly defeated.

torcher *v.pronom. Se torcher de quelque chose*: 'Not to give a fuck about', not to care two hoots about something. *Vos histoires à la con, je m'en torche!* I don't care a rap about those silly stories of yours!

torchon *n.m.* **1** (*pl.*): Sheets, bed-sheets. *Se mettre dans les torchons*: To 'hit the sack', to go to bed.

2 'Rag', trashy newspaper (the kind that collects as much mud as it slings). **3** Scruffy-looking report (one that looks as though it has been used to wipe the floor). **4** 'Slut', dirty and slovenly woman. (This appellation is quite hardy; when referring to their maid, the Josserand family in Zola's *POT-BOUILLE* call her *'ce torchon d'Adèle'*.) **5** *Coup de torchon*: **a** 'Clean sweep', drastic change (by a 'new-broom' character who intends to sweep very clean). **b** (*pol.*): 'Swoop', dragnet operation. **c** 'Punch-up', fight. *Ils se sont filé un sacré coup de torchon en sortant du notaire*: They got to blows after the reading of the will. **d** (also: *coup de tabac*): 'Spot of bad weather' at sea. **6** *Le torchon brûle!* It's a 'daggers-drawn' situation! (Originally the expression referred exclusively to smouldering rows and dissensions within a marriage, but is now used more widely when referring to any state of violent disagreement.)

torchonner *v.trans.* To 'scamp', to botch (a job or task).

tordant *adj.* 'Creasing', 'side-splitting', hilarious.

tord-boyaux *n.m.* 'Rot-gut', the kind of 'hooch' that is likely to make your hair curl because of its rough nature and strong alcohol content.

tordre *v.trans.reflex. (abbr. se tordre de rire)*: To split one's sides laughing. *C'est à se tordre de le voir allumer un mégot en plein vent!* The sight of him lighting a fag-end against the breeze is enough to make you crease up with laughter!

tordu *n.m.* **1** 'Odd-bod', 'weirdo', character with a warped sense of values. **2** 'Pillock', 'burk', imbecile. **3** 'Nutter', 'nutcase', mad character. **4** 'Weed', puny and insignificant person.

tordu *adj.* (of person): **1** 'Odd', weird, strange. **2** Stupid, silly. (The insulting interjection *'Va donc, eh tordu!'* relates only to this meaning of the adjective.) **3** 'Bonkers', 'loony', mad. **4** 'Weedy', puny.

torgnole *n.f.* **1** Slap, open-handed blow in the face. **2** 'Trouncing', thrashing, severe beating. *Il a pris une de ces torgnoles dans le ring!* He got beaten black-and-blue against the ropes!

torgnoler *v.trans.* **1** To slap in the face. **2** To 'whip', to 'trounce', to beat.

torpille *n.f.* **1** 'Sub', cadged money. *Marcher à la torpille*: To go through life on borrowed money. **2** *Torpille humaine (joc.*): 'Prick', 'cock', penis.

torpiller *v.trans.* **1** To 'torpedo', to attack scathingly a plan, project, proposition, etc. *C'est toujours pareil, mes bonnes idées il les torpille d'autor!* It's always the same thing, all my good ideas get shot down in flames! **2** To 'cadge', to get a 'sub' out of someone. **3** *Se faire torpiller*:

To 'get conned out of some money', to be the victim of a fraud. **4** To 'screw', to fuck, to have coition.

torpilleur *n.m.* **1** Character whose greatest delight in life is to fire critical broadsides where projects, 'good ideas', etc. are concerned. **2** 'Sponger', 'cadger', near-professional borrower. **3** 'Rep', door-to-door salesman.

torsif *adj.* 'Rib-tickling', 'side-splitting', hilarious.

tortillard *n.m.* **1** 'Puffer', small rural train, the kind that stops at every station on the line. (This affectionate appellation probably stems from the meandering line of the tracks.) **2** Expresso coffee. (The connection between the puffing steam-engine and the coffee percolator is apparent.)

tortiller *v.trans.* *Tortiller une lazane* (also: *une bafouille*): To write a letter.

tortiller *v.intrans.* **1** *Tortiller du cul* (of woman or effeminate homosexual): To walk with a wiggle, with an undulating hip-movement. **2** *Il n'y a pas à tortiller (du cul)!* **a** There's no denying it! – It's got to be said! **b** There's no getting out of it! – It has to be done!

tortore *n.f.* 'Grub', 'eats', food. *On s'est payé une tortore tout ce qu'il y a de mar-meu!* We had ourselves a right super nosh!

tortorer *v.trans. & intrans.* To eat. (The verb has pleasant connotations and is more often than not used in a context of plentiful and good food.)

tôt *adv.* *Ce n'est pas trop tôt! (iron.)*: And about time too! – And not before time!

total *n.m. (abbr. au total; adv.exp.)*: In short – To sum it all up. *On a pris la mauvaise route, roulé quinze kilomètres, total on s'est perdus!* We took the wrong turn, drove about ten miles and in a word – we was lost!

totale *n.f.* Hysterectomy. *On lui a fait une totale*: She had it all taken away.

toto *n.m.* **1** Nit, head-louse. **2** Jocular nickname used when addressing someone whose first name one does not know. *Allez, Toto, ça va les affaires?!* Well, chum, how's tricks?! **3** *Mon toto*: My pet, my darling.

totoche *n.f.* 'Bean', 'bonce', head.

Totor *Proper name.* Jocular corruption of the forename *Victor*.

toubib *n.m.* 'Doc', 'medic', doctor. (Richard Gordon's novel DOCTOR IN THE HOUSE and the subsequent film were renamed in French *Toubib or not toubib* thus introducing the French masses to a Shakespearean pun!)

touche *n.f.* **1** *(pej.)*: Looks. *Vise un peu cette touche!* Have a butchers at that ugly mush! **2** 'Drag', share of a communal cigarette. (The

word can be heard in circles where finances and circumstances make smoking a luxury, i.e. amongst schoolchildren, servicemen and prisoners.) **3** *Avoir une touche avec quelqu'un*: To have 'clicked' with someone (amorous context). *Il a une méchante touche avec ta sœur!* I think your sister fancies him something rotten! *Essayer de faire une touche avec quelqu'un*: To make a pass at someone. (The word is a direct borrowing from the jargon of the angler where the bobbing and momentary submersion of the float indicate more than passing interest on the part of a fish.) **4** *Rester sur la touche (fig.)*: To be left out of things. **5** *Botter quelqu'un en touche*: To get rid of someone (literally to kick someone into touch. Both this expression and the preceding one stem from the language of rugby). **6** *Se faire une touche*: To 'wank', to masturbate.

touché *adj.* 'Touched', 'potty', mad. *Son frangin est un peu touché sur les bords!* That brother of hers has a screw loose!

touche-pipi *n.m.* *Une partie de touche-pipi (joc.)*: Some 'hanky-panky', some sexy goings-on.

toucher *v.trans.* **1** (of money): To 'pocket', to get, to receive. *Il a touché un pacson quand on l'a viré de la boîte!* He certainly got a golden handshake when they gave him the push at the firm! **2** *Pas touche! (abbr. touche pas ça!)*: Keep your mitts off! – Don't touch that! **3** *Avoir l'air de ne pas y toucher* (also: *ne pas avoir l'air d'y toucher*): To 'look as if butter would not melt in one's mouth', to be the picture of innocence.

toucher *v.intrans.* *Toucher à . . .* (of age): To be 'knocking on' . . . *Il touche à la cinquantaine*: He's the wrong side of forty.

toucher *v.pronom.* *S'en toucher*: 'Not to give a fuck', 'not to care a rap' about something. *La retraite quand on a vingt ans, on s'en touche!* A pension when you're twenty is the last thing to cross your mind!

toucher *v.trans.reflex.* **1** To 'wank', to masturbate. **2** *Tu te touches?!* Are you crazy or something?! (The implication in such a rhetorical remark is that the person concerned is deemed to be out of touch with reality through excessive masturbation.)

toufiane *n.f.* (also: *touffiane*): Opium.

touillage *n.m.* **1** *(lit.)*: Stirring, action of mixing substances with a cooking implement. **2** *(fig.)*: Shady manipulations, near-illegal dabbling within a commercial enterprise or transaction.

touiller *v.trans. & intrans.* **1** *(lit.)*: To stir. *Elle est toujours à touiller son chocolat!* She stirs her hot cocoa endlessly! **2** *(fig.)*: To 'dabble', to 'pull strings' in shady dealings.

touilleur *n.m. (pej.)*: Disreputable character who makes his money from shady dealings.

toupet *n.m.* 'Nerve', 'cheek', impudence.

toupie *n.f.* **1** *Une vieille toupie*: A 'silly old trout', a stupid old woman. (The word is nearly always encountered in interjectory form. *Vieille toupie, va!* You stupid old bag!) **2** *Etre une véritable toupie* (of person): To be gormless, to have no will of one's own (literally to spin at anyone's whim).

tour *n.m.* **1** *Faire le tour du cadran*: To 'sleep the clock round', to sleep a twelve-hour stretch. **2** *Jouer un tour de cochon à quelqu'un*: To 'do the dirty' on someone, to play a dirty trick on someone. **3** *Le Tour*: The *Tour de France* cycling race.

tour *n.f.* *La Tour de l'Horloge (pol.)*: The *Conciergerie*, the former prison of that name now the Paris Headquarters of the French C.I.D. where suspects are held and interrogated. (The official address is 36 Quai des Orfèvres; the *Quai des Orfèvres* is another name for these police headquarters.)

tourlousine *n.f.* (also: *tourlouzine*): **1** Blow (slap, punch, kick, etc.). **2** 'Rousting', thrashing, beating. *Je m'en vais lui filer une de ces tourlousines!* I'm going to lead him a fair dance when I lay my hands on him!

tournailler *v.intrans.* To lurk around. (To 'loiter with intent' even if the action has no criminal undertones.) *Ça fait un mois qu'il me tournaille autour des jupes!* For a month now he's been sniffing around me and I've just about had enough!

tournanche *n.f.* Round of drinks. *C'est ma tournanche!* It's my shout! – These drinks are on me!

tournant *n.m.* **1** *Avoir* (also: *rattraper*) *quelqu'un au tournant*: To get one's own back on someone (literally to catch up with someone where and when it matters). *Le salaud, il m'a eu au tournant!* The swine, he didn't let me get away with that! **2** *Faire un sale tournant à quelqu'un*: To 'do the dirty on someone', to play a dirty trick on someone. **3** *Etre dans un sale tournant*: To be mixed up in some nasty business. **4** *Prendre quelque chose sur le tournant de la gueule*: **a** *(lit.)*: To get a 'knuckle-sandwich', to get punched in the jaw. **b** *(fig.)*: To 'come a cropper', to 'come unstuck' in a dramatic sort of way.

tournante *n.f.* Key (often in a context where it is used for dishonest purposes).

tournebouler *v.trans.* *(fig.)*: **1** To 'bowl over', to astound. **2** To leave in a turmoil, to leave in a state of disorientated distress. *Ça m'a tourneboulé de le voir dans un lit d'hôpital!* It gave me quite a turn to see him in his little hospital bed!

tournée *n.f.* **1** 'Round', round of drinks. *C'est ta tournée, mon vieux!* It's your shout this time! *Tu vas nous payer une tournée, hein!* You're

going to stand us some drinks, what?! **2** *Faire la tournée des grands ducs*: To 'paint the town red', to go out and have a merry old time (eating, drinking, etc.).

tourner *v.trans.* *Tourner la page*: To engage in passive sodomy.

tourner *v.intrans.* *Ça tourne!* (of business activities): Things are going O.K.! (The implication here is that factory machinery and the wheels of finance are turning happily.)

tournicoter *v.intrans.* **1** (of business activities): To run unevenly. *Ces temps-ci, côté affaires, ça tournicote!* What with the recession things aren't going too merrily! **2** To lurk around. (To 'loiter with intent' even if the action has no criminal undertones.)

tourniquet *n.m.* Military tribunal. *Passer au tourniquet*: To get court-martialled.

tournis *n.m.* *(lit.)*: State of dizziness. *A regarder les coureurs sur le vélodrome, ça m'a donné le tournis!* Watching the riders whizz round the track has made me giddy!

tourte *n.f.* 'Twit', 'burk', imbecile.

tousser *v.intrans.* **1** To 'grouch', to 'grumble', to complain. *Il a toussé méchant quand je l'ai mis à la porte!* He played merry hell with me when I turfed him out! **2** (of motor): To misfire, to run unevenly. **3** (of gun): To fire. (Sandry and Carrère in their DICTIONNAIRE DE L'ARGOT MODERNE lexicalize the expression *tousser des deux poches*: to fire a pair of pistols secreted in pockets.) **4** *Tousser jaune*: To be 'loaded', to be stinking rich (also: *cracher jaune*. Literally to be coughing up gold).

tout *pron.* **1** *Comme tout (adv.exp.)*: Extremely, very. *Il est gentil comme tout!* He's jolly nice! **2** *C'est pas tout ça . . . !* That's not the point! *C'est pas tout ça, mais qu'est-ce que je vais lui dire?!* That's as may be, but what do I tell him?!

toutim *n.m.* (also: *toutime*): **1** *Le toutim*: 'The lot', everything. *Il est parti camper avec une bagnole pleine de casseroles et le toutim!* He went off camping loaded with everything bar the kitchen sink! **2** *Et tout le toutim*: Etcetera. *Il m'a raconté son enfance, sa jeunesse, ses études, l'armée et tout le toutim!* He buttonholed me to tell me the story of his life!

tout-le-monde *Monsieur tout-le-monde*: The man-in-the-street. (This near-proper-name appellation has no pejorative connotation whatsoever.) *Si vous demandez à Monsieur tout-le-monde ce qu'il pense des impôts – il est contre!* If you ask Mr Average how he views taxes, he'll tell you he's dead against them!

toutou *n.m.* **1** (Child language): 'Bow-wow', 'doggy', dog. **2** *A la peau de toutou*: 'Crummily', in a trashy manner.

Tout-Paris *n.m. Le Tout-Paris*: The Parisian smart-set. (*Le Tout-Paris* usually encompasses beautiful women, politicians, film stars, sportsmen, etc. At a recent dog-show a journalist reported the presence of *Le Toutou-Paris!*)

toxico *n.m. (abbr. toxicomane)*: 'Junkie', drug-addict.

tracassin *n.m.* **1** *Le tracassin*: State of fretting, worrying. *Il a le tracassin, son affaire bat de l'aile!* His business is going to pot and he's got the jitters! **2** 'Morning rise', early-morning sexual erection.

tracer *v.intrans.* To 'go like the clappers', to travel at a fair old speed. *Sa nouvelle bagnole, un peu qu'elle trace!* That new car of his can certainly burn rubber!

tracer *v.pronom.* To 'skedaddle', to 'make tracks', to move away niftily.

tracsir *n.m. (corr. trac)*: 'Funk', 'nerves', fear. (Originally *trac* meant stage-fright. It has broadened to encompass exam nerves and any form of apprehension where personal performance is concerned.)

traction *n.f. (abbr. traction avant)*: Family saloon car manufactured by Citroën between the 30s and the late 50s.

Trafalgar *Proper name. Coup de Trafalgar*: 'Bolt-from-the-blue' catastrophe, sudden and unexpected setback. (Lord Nelson's naval victory over the French and Spanish fleets on 21 October 1805 was probably Napoleon's worst setback.)

trafic *n.m. (joc.)*: Small 'wheeling-and-dealing', insignificant transaction.

trafiqué *adj.* **1** (of wine): 'Interfered with', adulterated. (The implication here is that the wine could have been *chaptalisé*, in other words, had its alcoholic content raised by the surreptitious adding of sugar to the must prior to fermentation.) **2** (of motor): 'Souped-up', made more powerful by adjustments to carburation, etc. *Sa Mercedes a un moulin trafiqué; avec sa chignole il se tape maintenant du 240 sur l'autoroute!* He hotted up his Merc and now he can top 160 m.p.h. on the motorway!

trafiquer *v.trans. & intrans.* To be doing. *Qu'est-ce que tu trafiques?!* How's tricks?! – What are you up to these days?!

train *n.m.* **1** 'Arse', 'bum', behind. *Botter quelqu'un dans le train*: To kick someone up the jacksey. *Avoir le feu au train*: To 'have ants in one's pants', to be itching to get moving, to be in a great hurry. **2** *Se magner le train*: To 'get one's skates on', to hurry up. **3** *Filer le train à quelqu'un*: To dog someone's footsteps, to follow someone closely. *On lui a dit de filer le train au malfrat*: He was told to tail that suspect.

4 *Remettre quelqu'un au train* (Underworld slang): To 'twist someone's arm', to compel someone to do something (literally to get someone to go along with one's wishes). **5** *Manquer le train (fig.)*: To 'miss the boat', to fail to get what one might be entitled to. **6** *N'être pas en train* (also: *ne pas se sentir en train*): To 'feel out of sorts', to feel below par. **7** *Etre dans le train*: To be 'on the ball', to be 'in the swing of things', to be right-up-to-date with trends, etc. **8** *Faux train* (Cycling and horse-racing slang): Brisk but not exceedingly fast pace set by a group of riders to enable the champion to be in the running for the critical final furlong. **9** *Sauter du train en marche (joc.)*: To have coïtus interruptus.

traînard *n.m.* **1** Straggler, one who persistently lags behind. **2** *Ramasser* (also: *faire*) *un traînard*: To 'come a cropper', to fall flat on one's face. (This expression is only encountered with the literal meaning of falling down.)

traînasser *v.intrans.* To 'dawdle', to let things drag on, to waste time.

traîne *n.f. Etre à la traîne*: **a** To be a 'slow-coach', to be straggling behind. **b** To be 'behind the times', to be out of step with everyday life. **c** To be 'skint', to be behind with one's payments.

traînée *n.f. (pej.)*: **1** 'Loose woman', trollop, woman whose personal hygiene is as much in question as her morals. **2** 'Prozzy', low-class prostitute.

traîne-lattes *n.m.* 'Hobo', tramp (the kind of layabout who has drifted into dire poverty).

traîner *v.intrans.* **1** To 'mooch', to loaf about. *Il traîne du matin au soir depuis qu'il est au chômage!* Since going on the dole, he just loafs around all day! **2** *Ça traîne les rues! (fig.)*: There's a lot of it about! – It's not an uncommon thing!

traintrain *n.m.* Routine. *Le traintrain quotidien*: The daily grind.

traître *adj.* Dangerous (in a treacherous sort of way). *Gaffe, c'est un escalier tout ce qu'il y a de traître!* Steady as you go, these steps are a real deathtrap!

traits *n.m.pl. Faire des traits* (of husband or wife): To 'wander from the straight-and-narrow', to be unfaithful. *Sa gonzesse, un peu qu'il lui fait des traits!* He's been two-timing his missus for as long as I can remember!

tralala *n.m.* **1** 'Showy' get-up. *Arriver en grand tralala*: To go somewhere overdressed. (The 'dressed-to-the-nines' image is acceptable according to context.) **2** *Faire du* (also: *tout un*) *tralala*: To 'make a song-and-dance about something', to make a big fuss about personal achievements. *Quand sa fille s'est mariée, elle a fait tout un tralala!* When their daughter got wed, she turned it into a state occasion! **3** *Et tout le tralala*: 'And the whole show' – 'And all the works' – And all the paraphernalia.

tranche *n.f.* **1** 'Mush', 'dial', face. *Avoir une sale tranche*: To have an ugly mug (also: *tronche*). **2** 'Burk', 'nincompoop', imbecile. *Faire la tranche*: To act the silly-billy. **3** *En avoir une tranche*: To be 'as thick as two short planks', to be as dumb as they come (also: *en avoir une couche*). **4** *S'en payer une (bonne) tranche*: To 'have the time of one's life', to enjoy a moment to the full.

trancher *v.trans.* To 'screw', to fuck, to have coition with.

transat *n.m. (abbr. transatlantique)*: **1** 'Liner', ocean liner. **2** Deck-chair (originally because they were on the decks of liners for sun-loving passengers).

transbahuter *v.trans.* To 'hump', to 'lug about', to carry. *Il m'a fallu transbahuter tout son bastringue!* I had to cart all his clobber for him!

transfo *n.m. (abbr. transformateur)*: Electricity transformer.

trapu *adj. (sch.)*: 'Tough', difficult. *On s'est payé un exam tout ce qu'il y a de trapu!* That paper we sat was a right stinker!

traquer *v.intrans.* To 'freeze', to have the frights, to be incapable of uttering a word (usually in a context where personal performance is of paramount importance, i.e. on stage, at an interview, at an exam, etc. Also: *avoir le trac*).

traquette *n.f.* 'Funk', 'nerves', fear. (*Traquette*, a corruption of *trac*, originally meant stage-fright. It has broadened to encompass exam nerves and any form of apprehension where personal performance is concerned.)

traqueur *n.m.* 'Funk', 'yellow-belly', coward.

travail *n.m.* **1** *Faire un petit travail* (of burglar): To go out on a 'job', to go and commit a burglary. **2** *Un travail*: A 'botch', badly executed work. *Qu'est-ce que c'est que ce travail?* What in heaven's name is this monstrosity?

travailler *v.intrans.* **1** *Travailler du chapeau*: To 'go off one's rocker', to be 'round the bend', to be mad. **2** *Travailler de la jaquette*: To practise passive sodomy. (To understand this expression, it is necessary to refer to *jaquette*. *Etre de la jaquette flottante* means to be a male homosexual. The witticism lies in the strategically-placed slit in the tails.)

travailleuse *n.f.* *Une bonne travailleuse*: A 'good little earner', a prostitute whose good looks and eagerness to work make her a commercial success.

travelo *n.m. (also: travelot)*: 'Drag-queen', transvestite (also: *trav*).

travers *n.m.* **1** *Etre en plein travers*: To be 'going through a sticky patch', to find that everything is against one. **2** *Passer au travers*: **a** To come out unscathed from a period of misfortune. **b** To miss out on something good one would otherwise have received.

traversin *n.m.* **1** *Coup de traversin*: 'Kip', 'snooze', some sleep. *Prendre un coup de traversin*: To get some shuteye. **2** *Une partie de traversin*: Some 'nookie', sexy capers.

traviole *De traviole (adv.exp.)*: 'Skewwhiff', awry, askew. *Quand il a pinté, son galure est de traviole!* You can always tell when he's drunk by the way he wears his hat!

travs *n.m.pl. (abbr. travaux forcés)*. *Les travs*: Hard labour, penal servitude. *Fricoter dans les faux talbins jadis, ça valait les travs à perpète!* In the old days, counterfeiting meant Devil's Island for life!

trèfle *n.m.* **1** 'Dough', 'brass', money. (The colour of clover and the green of banknotes are the common denominator; the American 'greenbacks' testifies to the imagery.) **2** 'Baccy', tobacco. **3** *(corr. trèpe) Du trèfle*: Crowds, masses of people. *Il y a du trèfle sur le Boul' Mich' le dimanche!* The Boulevard St-Michel is fair packed with people on Sundays! **4** *As de trèfle*: Anus, anal sphincter.

treillage *n.m.* *A chaque treillage/au premier treillage*: Each time/the first time. *Au premier treillage il a décroché un job du tonnerre!* First time lucky, he got himself a smashing job!

tremblement *n.m.* *Et tout le tremblement*: 'And the whole shebang' – 'And all that jazz' – And everything. *Il a pris sa canne à pêche, son fusil de chasse, ses machins de golf et tout le tremblement, pour ses grandes vacances!* He took his shooting and fishing clobber, his golf things and the whole bag of tricks for his summer hols!

tremblote *n.f.* *Avoir la tremblote*: To 'have the shakes', to be 'in a blue funk', to be frightened. *Ça vous fiche la tremblote, d'être dans un bled comme ça à dix heures du soir!* I wouldn't fancy meeting a stranger at ten o'clock at night in those parts!

trempe *n.f.* 'Thrashing', 'drubbing', beating-up. *Il s'est ramassé une sacrée trempe!* He got the beating of his life! (also: *trempée*).

trempette *n.f.* *Faire trempette*: **a** To 'go for a quick dip', to go into the water (sea, river, pool) without really intending to swim. **b** To have a quick wash. **c** To 'dunk' bread, biscuits or cake into a warm beverage.

trente-et-un *n.m.* *Se mettre sur son trente-et-un*: To get all 'togged-up', to put on one's best clothes. (*Trente-et-un* is a corruption of *trentain*, a very fine cloth described in the *PETIT ROBERT* as *un* *drap de luxe dont la chaîne était composée de trente centaines de fils.*)

trente-six *num.adj.* **1** *Faire les trente-six volontés de quelqu'un*: To be at someone's every beck-and-call, to give in to someone's every whim. **2** *Le trente-six du mois (joc.)*: 'Once in a blue moon', very seldom. *Le loyer, il vous le paiera tous les trente-six du mois!* If you reckon on his paying the rent, you've got another think coming!

trèpe *n.m. Du trèpe*: Masses of people, crowds. *En juillet sur les plages, un peu qu'il y a du trèpe!* Beaches are thick with people, come July!

trésor *n.m.* **1** *(joc.)*: 'Pussy', 'fanny', vagina. *Se briquer le trésor*: To have a thorough wash. **2** *Mon petit trésor!* My pet! – My lovey-dovey! – My darling!

tréteau *n.m. (pej.*; racing slang): 'Nag', 'loser', bad horse.

tri *n.m. (abbr. triporteur)*: Delivery trike, tricycle used by grocers, butchers, etc. for the delivery of their wares.

triage *n.m. A chaque triage/au premier triage, etc.*: Each time/the first time, etc. *A chaque triage, c'est cézigue qui casque!* Each time it's muggins who has to pay!

tricard *n.m.* Ex-con, one who is *interdit de séjour*, i.e. whose presence in certain (urban) areas is prohibited.

tricard *adj.m.* (of ex-convict): Prohibited from living in or entering certain (urban) areas.

triche *n.f. La triche*: Cheating. *Son menu 'tout compris', quelle triche!* That all-inclusive menu of his, what a swindle!

tricoche *n.f. (pol.)*: Investigation undertaken by policemen, often during working hours, on behalf of private individuals. (This unofficial use of official powers and services is obviously quite illegal.)

tricocheur *n.m.* Policeman who undertakes 'private jobs', making use of his official status and facilities.

tricoter *v.intrans.* **1** To do some underhand wheeling-and-dealing. **2** *Tricoter des gambettes*: **a** To 'stomp', to dance. **b** To 'nip off', to go away hastily.

tricotin *n.m.* **1** 'Cosh', truncheon. **2** *Avoir le tricotin*: To have 'the big stick', to have 'a hard', to have an erection.

trictrac *n.m.* 'Fiddle', 'shady deal', near-illegal transaction.

trieuse *n.f. Trieuse de lentilles*: 'Les', 'dyke', lesbian. (The expression's imagery comes from the finger-flicking action of someone sorting lentils prior to cooking.)

trifouiller *v.intrans.* To 'poke about', to rummage. *Les douaniers, ça aime trifouiller dans*

les valoches! The customs bods get a kick out of rifling through bags!

Trifouillis-les-Oies *Proper name.* This jocular and fictitious place-name is used when referring to a practically unknown, 'back-of-beyond' small town or village.

trimard *n.m.* (also: *trimar*): **1** 'Grafter', hard-working individual. **2** Tramp, vagabond. **3** The open road leading to 'pastures new'. **4** The life of the country drifter.

trimarder *v.intrans.* **1** (of vagabond, country drifter): To walk in search of pastures new. **2** To 'graft', to work for a crust. (The image is very much one of 'work-for-keep' where the 'here-today-gone-tomorrow' drifter does a few odd jobs for a meal and a bed.)

trimardeur *n.m.* **1** Tramp, drifter, vagabond. **2** Nomadic worker.

trimardeuse *n.f.* 'Prozzy', low-class prostitute.

trimbalage *n.m.* 'Carting', 'humping about', carrying of (usually heavy) goods.

trimbaler *v.trans.* **1** To 'cart', to 'hump', to carry a (often heavy) load. **2** *Qu'est-ce qu'il trimbale! (fig.)*: Isn't he thick?! – What a stupid person! (also: *il trimbale une de ces couches!*).

trimer *v.intrans.* To 'graft', to work hard. *Qu'est-ce qu'il nous a faits trimer!* He worked us right into the ground!

tringle *n.f.* **1** *Se mettre la tringle*: To have to 'go without', to have to go short of something. *Côté bouffetance, on a dû se mettre la tringle!* When it came to grub, we all had to tighten our belts! **2** *En avoir tringle de*: To be sick and tired of something. *Ecoute, mon vieux, on en a tringle de tes histoires à la con!* Listen chum, we've just about had it up to here with your arsing about! **3** *Avoir la tringle*: To have 'the big stick', to have 'a hard', to have an erection. *Donner un coup de tringle*: To 'screw', to fuck, to have coition with.

tringleur *n.m.* 'Shafter', fornicator, randy man (also: *tringlomane*).

tringlot *n.m.* (also: *trainglot*): Soldier of the *train des équipages*, the equivalent of the British Army Service Corps.

trinquer *v.intrans.* To 'get it in the neck', to 'cop it', to get the worst of something. *Côté impôts, c'est toujours les fumeurs qui trinquent!* Come Budget-day, it's always us smokers what bear the brunt!

tripaille *n.f.* **1** Guts, bowels. **2** 'Droopy boobs', flabby breasts.

tripatouillage *n.m.* **1** Tampering, unwarranted intervention. **2** 'Fiddling', 'cooking' of books. *Ses tripatouillages lui ont valu cinq ans de dur*: He did five years' porridge for all that 'fixing' of books!

tripatouiller *v.trans. & intrans.* **1** To tamper, to interfere with. *Depuis qu'il a tripatouillé (avec) ma machine, elle est foutue!* Since he got his sticky mitts on my machine, it's just about knackered! **2** To 'cook the books', to fiddle accounts.

tripatouilleur *n.m.* **1** 'Jack-of-all-trades, master-of-none' dabbler. *Comme tripatouilleur, on ne fait pas mieux!* He's always poking his fingers into gubbins he doesn't know a thing about! **2** 'Fiddler', 'sticky-fingered' book-keeper (one who acts dishonestly).

tripes *n.f.pl.* **1** Guts, bowels. (With this meaning, the word is used more often than not in a figurative way as in the English: 'I'll have your guts for garters'.) *Dégueuler tripes et boyaux*: To be as sick as a dog. *J'aurai tes tripes!* I'll get you! **2** 'Droopy boobs', flabby breasts.

tripette *n.f. Ne pas valoir tripette*: To be worth bugger-all, to be practically worthless. *Un contrat avec cézigue, ça ne vaut pas tripette!* An agreement with him isn't worth the paper it's written on!

tripotage *n.m.* Near-underhand transaction. *Le tripotage des comptes, c'est son blot!* He's just the kind of bloke who'd cook the books!

tripotée *n.f.* **1** 'Bashing-up', 'thrashing', beating-up. *Si je le rencontre, il va prendre une de ces tripotées!* If I ever catch up with him, he won't know what's hit him! **2** *Une tripotée de*: 'Oodles', 'bags of', vast quantities of. *Des occases comme ça on en trouve pas uñe tripotée!* You don't come across bargains like that every day!

tripoter *v.trans.* To 'interfere with' sexually, to perpetrate an act of gross indecency. (The word is more often associated with the 'dirty old man' than with sexy goings-on at an office party.)

tripoter *v.pronom. Il se tripote un tas de choses bizarres ces temps-ci!* There have been quite a few funny goings-on lately!

triquard *n.m.* Ex-con, one who is *interdit de séjour*, i.e. whose presence in certain (urban) areas is prohibited.

triquard *adj.m.* (of ex-convict): Prohibited from living in or entering certain (urban) areas.

trique *n.f. La trique*: Prohibition imposed on ex-convicts to prevent them from living in or entering certain (urban) areas. (The official appellation is *interdiction de séjour*.) *Pour ce qui est de Pantruche, il a été frappé de trois ans de trique*: After doing time, he was ordered to keep clear of Paris for three years.

trique *n.f.* **1** 'Cosh', truncheon. *Il a pris un coup de trique sur le coin de la gueule*: He got biffed on the nut. **2** *Mener quelqu'un à la trique* (*fig.*): To rule someone with a rod of iron. **3** *Etre sec comme une trique* (also: *comme un coup de trique*): To be the 'lean and mean' type, to be aggressively thin. **4** 'Prick', 'cock', penis. *Avoir la trique*: To have 'the big stick', to have 'a hard', to have an erection.

triquer *v.intrans.* To have 'the big stick', to have 'a hard', to have an erection (also: *bander*).

trisser *v.pronom.* To 'make tracks', to 'skedaddle', to run away. *Ecoute, il va falloir que je me trisse!* Listen, chum, I'll have to be on my way!

tristounet *adj.inv.* A trifle sad. *Ça n'a pas l'air de carburer, tu m'as l'air tristounet ces jours-ci!* What's up?! You don't seem your usual jolly self these days!

trocson *n.m.* Caf', bistrot. (This word is a corruption of *troquet* which is itself a truncation of *bistroquet*, coming originally from *bistrot*.)

trogne *n.f.* (*pej.*): 'Mush', bloated face. (The appellation usually refers to the rubicund face of the alcoholic. *Une trogne comme la sienne dit tout, côté biberon!* You don't need three A-levels to guess that tippling remodelled his features!)

trognon *n.m.* **1** 'Bean', 'bonce', head. *Se casser le trognon*: To rack one's brains. *Y aller du trognon*: To get guillotined (also: *y aller du cigare*). **2** *Avoir quelqu'un jusqu'au trognon*: To 'do' someone, to 'con' someone through and through. *Il m'a eu jusqu'au trognon, celui-là!* He stitched me up good and proper, the bastard! **3** *Un petit trognon*: A mere slip of a girl, a 'petite' lady. **4** *Mon (petit) trognon*: My lovey-dovey – My pet – My darling.

trombine *n.f.* 'Mush', 'dial', face.

tromblon *n.m.* (*joc.*): **1** Old gun, 'geriatric' firearm. (Originally *tromblon* referred to the blunderbuss, probably the most inaccurate firearm ever devised.) **2** 'Conk', 'hooter', nose. **3** 'Bean', 'bonce', head. **4** 'Topper', top-hat, the kind of head-gear worn by the Mad Hatter in 'Alice in Wonderland'. **5** *Filer un coup de tromblon*: To have 'a bang', to 'screw', to have coition with.

trompette *n.f.* **1** 'Mush', 'dial', face (not often a pleasant one). **2** 'Conk', 'hooter', nose. (The *nez en trompette* is the kind of turned-up nose where nostrils seem to feature prominently.) **3** 'Gob', 'trap', mouth. (The appellation *la trompette du quartier* refers to the gossiping busybody whose 'secrets' are soon on every-one's lips.)

tronc *n.m.* **1** (also: *tronc de figuier*): Native of North Africa. (This racist term is equatable with the English 'wog' or 'coon'.) **2** 'Belly', stomach. *S'en filer plein le tronc*: To 'stuff one's face', to eat a hearty meal. **3** 'Bean', 'bonce', head. *Ne pas se casser le tronc*: To take life as it comes. (With the meaning of *tête*, this appears to be the only expression where the word is encountered.)

tronche *n.f.* **1** 'Mush', 'dial', face. *Faire la tronche*: To 'pull a face', to sulk in a sullen manner. **2** 'Bean', 'bonce', head.

troncher *v.trans.* To 'screw', to fuck, to have coition with. *Troncher les nénettes, il n'a que ça en tête!* You could say he's got sex on the brain!

troncheur *n.m.* 'Randy so-and-so', highly-sexed man.

trône *n.m.* *(joc.)* *Le trône*: 'The loo', the W.C. (As Jacques Cellard and Alain Rey point out in their DICTIONNAIRE DU FRANÇAIS NON-CONVENTIONNEL the term has no real vulgar connotation.)

troquet *n.m.* **1** Bistrot, small-time corner café. (The word is a truncation of *bistroquet*, itself a colloquialization of *bistrot*.) **2** Bistrot proprietor.

trot *n.m.* *Au trot!* *(adv.exp.)*: At the double! –Double-quick! *Tout le monde dans la cour au trot!* Jump to it, lads, I want you on parade . . . now!

trotte *n.f.* *Une bonne trotte*: A fair old distance. *D'ici à chez lui, ça fait une trotte*: It's no five-minute walk from here to his place!

trotter *v.pronom.* To 'make tracks', to 'skedaddle', to move away rapidly.

trottin *n.m.* Young errand girl. (The word is as dated as the concept and only owes its continuing existence to a couple of nostalgic songs.)

trottinant *n.m.* 'Hoof', 'trotter', foot (also: *trottinet*).

trottiner *v.intrans.* (of prostitute): To go soliciting.

trottinette *n.f.* *(joc.)*: 'Wheels', 'motor', motor car. (The twee jocularity stems from the original meaning of the word; a *trottinette* is a child's scooter.)

trottoir *n.m.* *Faire le trottoir* (of prostitute): To go soliciting.

trou *n.m.* **1** 'Dump', dead-end of a place. *Il est allé se terrer dans un trou perdu*: He's gone to ground in some godforsaken place. (The word does not always have this near-pejorative connotation; the expression *un petit trou pas cher*, in the lingo of tourists, refers to that inexpensive holiday place we always search for and seldom find.) **2** 'Clink', 'nick', prison. *Aller au trou*: To 'go down', to do time. (In the film of the 60s, *Le Trou*, the title gained a deeper meaning in that the plot was all about prisoners trying to burrow their way to

freedom.) **3** *Etre dans le trou*: To be 'six foot under', to be dead. **4** *Trou de balle*: Arse-hole, anal sphincter. *Se dévisser* (also: *se décarcasser*) *le trou*: To 'try one's darnedest', to nearly break one's back doing something. **5** *Boire comme un trou*: To have 'a sloping gullet', to drink like a fish. **6** *Boucher un trou*: To 'make do with something', to use an expedient for want of something better. *On l'a pris au bureau pour boucher un trou*: We just took him on in the office as a stop-gap. **7** *En boucher un trou à quelqu'un*: To leave someone speechless, to astound someone (with an unexpected action, some surprising information, etc.). **8** *Faire son trou*: To 'make one's way in the world', to elbow oneself into a position of prominence. (There is a certain hint of 'finding one's niche' in this expression.) **9** *Ne pas avoir les yeux en face des trous*: To have a cock-eyed view of things, to be unable to see things as they are. (The expression often occurs in a context of drunken stupor.)

trou-du-cul *n.m.* 'Arse-hole', 'burk', idiot.

trou-du-cul *adj.inv.* 'Bloody stupid', idiotic.

troufignard *n.m.* **1** Arse-hole, anal sphincter. **2** 'Bum', behind. *Se faire botter le troufignard*: To get kicked up the backside (also: *troufignon*).

troufigner *v.intrans.* To 'pong', to stink, to smell foul.

troufion *n.m.* *(mil.;* also: *trouffion*): National Serviceman. (The word never refers to conscripted N.C.O.s or higher ranks.)

trouillard *n.m.* 'Funk', 'yellow-belly', coward.

trouillard *adj.* 'Funky', 'yellow', cowardly.

trouille *n.f.* 'Funk', fear. *Foutre la trouille à quelqu'un*: To put the wind up someone.

trouiller *v.intrans.* To be 'in a blue funk', to be very frightened.

trouillomètre *n.m.* *(joc.)* *Avoir le trouillomètre à zéro*: To be 'in a blue funk', to be petrified with fear. (The *trouillomètre* is a fictitious device humorously assumed to gauge resistance to fear.)

trouilloter *v.intrans.* **1** To 'have the shits', to be 'in a blue funk', to be very frightened. **2** To 'pong', to stink, to smell foul. (There is some logic in assuming that the second meaning is related to the first.)

troupe *n.m.* *(abbr. tabac de troupe).* *Du troupe*: Rough-and-ready tobacco issued to the Services at a very nominal price. (*Troupes* – the word is feminine – were the most uncharismatic cigarettes issued to servicemen. In recent years, branded 'smokes' are regularly available to Army personnel at subsidized prices.)

troupe *n.f.* *En avant, mauvaise troupe!* Let's be 'avin' you! – Get a move on! (This jocular expression is said to have originated in the world of mercenaries as far back as the 15th century, then drifted colloquially into the language of boy scouts and finally entered the realm of everyday speech.)

trousse *n.f.* 'Fanny', 'pussy', vagina (also: *trésor*).

troussequin *n.m.* *(corr.abbr. pétrousquin)*: 'Bum', 'bottom', behind. *Se faire botter le troussequin*: To get kicked up the backside. *L'avoir dans le troussequin*: To have been 'conned', 'diddled', to have been fooled.

trouver *v.trans. La trouver mauvaise*: To 'find it a bit much', to be very displeased with treatment meted out. *Il l'a trouvé mauvaise quand on lui a dit qu'il était de vaisselle*: He didn't exactly jump for joy when he discovered he was doing the washing-up.

truand *n.m.* Gangster, member of the underworld.

truander *v.trans.* To 'con', to 'diddle', to swindle.

truanderie *n.f.* 'Con-job', illegal activity whose objective it is to do someone out of money.

truc *n.m.* 1 'Fiddle', ruse, trick. *Couper dans le truc*: To 'fall for it', to fall into a trap. (This expression is nearly always found in the negative. *Pas bête! J'ai pas coupé dans le truc!* I'm no mug, I didn't fall for that dodge!) 2 'Hang', 'knack', know-how. *Connaître les trucs du métier*: To know the tricks of the trade (those ingenious solutions fathered by the *Système D*). 3 'Doodah', 'thingummy', (indeterminate) thing. *Sa cave est pleine de trucs et de machins qui ne servent à rien!* His cellar's cluttered with loads of useless junk! 4 *Piquer au truc*: To get a liking for something. *Repiquer au truc*: a To take up where one had left off. *Il a la musique dans le sang, il a repiqué au truc fastoche!* Getting back into music was no problem, it was always in him! b To fall back into one's (bad) old ways. *La picole, c'est tenace, il a repiqué au truc à la sortie du trou!* It's hard to kick the boozing habit; he was back on the bottle the day he left the nick! 5 *Faire le truc* (of prostitute): To go 'on the job', to go soliciting. 6 *Ça fait mon truc!* That suits me down to the ground! – That's fine by me! 7 *Etre porté sur le truc*: To be 'a randy so-and-so', to have more than a casual interest in sexual matters.

trucmuche *n.m.* 'Doodah', 'whatsit', indeterminate thing.

truffe *n.m.* 1 'Conk', 'hooter', bulbous nose. (The word derives its imagery from that most expensive delicacy, the truffle.) 2 'Burk', 'nincompoop', idiot. *Comme truffe, on ne fait pas mieux!* He's just about as thick as they come!

truffé *past part. (fig.)*: 'Riddled with', full of. *Ses rapports sont truffés de fautes*: His memos are just a catalogue of spelling mistakes.

trumeau *n.m. (pej.)*: 'Ugly biddy', graceless woman. *Vieux trumeau*: 'Old bag', 'old hag', ugly old woman.

truquage *n.m. (th.) Travailler dans le truquage*: To work in 'special effects' (in that department where trick cinematography gives the illusion of reality).

truquailler *v.intrans.* To lead a rather 'hand-to-mouth' life, to live off expedients. (The image that comes to mind is that of a drifter who has to turn his hand to all manner of odd jobs to scrape a living.)

truquer *v.trans.* To 'rig', to fake.

truqueur *n.m.* 1 'Artful dodger', 'bright spark' whose ability to steer clear of work and trouble constantly amazes everyone. 2 'Con-artist', confidence trickster.

truqueuse *n.f.* 'Prozzy', prostitute.

truster *v.trans. & intrans.* To take over completely, to monopolize. *Cesse de truster bobonne, on veut danser aussi!* O.K. she's your wife, but can't the rest of us have a dance with her?!

tsoin-tsoin *adj.inv.* 'Tip-top', 'A-1', first-rate (also: *soin-soin, soi-soi*).

tuant *adj.* 1 (of work): 'Back-breaking', 'killing', exhausting. 2 (of person): Exasperating. (With this meaning, the adjective is used when referring to someone who 'drives you up the wall'.)

tubard *n.m.* 1 Racing tip (the kind of 'straight from the horse's mouth' information that is usually worth ignoring!). 2 'Lunger', T.B. sufferer, one afflicted with tuberculosis. (The feminine is *tubarde*.) 3 Hawker, busker, beggar, anyone who makes a living in the corridors of the *Métro*.

tubard *adj.* Tubercular, suffering from T.B.

tube *n.m.* 1 'Belly', stomach. *S'en filer plein le tube*: To 'stuff one's face', to eat immoderately. 2 *Le tube*: The *Métro*, 'the tube', the underground (railway). 3 'Blower', phone, telephone. *Donnez-moi un coup de tube dès qu'il y a du nouveau!* Give me a buzz if there's any change! 4 (Racing slang): 'Tip', confidential piece of 'inside information'. 5 'Lunger', T.B. sufferer, one afflicted with tuberculosis. 6 'Hit', 'hit-single', highly successful record. *Il a un disque avec tous les tubes de Sinatra*: He's got an L.P. of Frank Sinatra's greatest hits. 7 *A plein(s) tube(s)*: a 'Full-pelt', 'flat-out', at full speed. *On a monté l'autoroute à plein tube!* He drove us up the motorway with his foot to the floor! b *Débloquer* (also: *déconner*) *à pleins tubes*: To 'talk through the back of one's head', to 'spout a load of rubbish', to talk a lot of nonsense.

tuber *v.trans. & intrans.* 1 To 'give (someone) a ring', to phone, to telephone. 2 To give (someone) 'some info', 'the low-down', to give some information. (With this meaning, the verb is often heard on racecourses where tipsters try to make a living.)

tubeur *n.m.* (Racing slang): Professional tipster.

tuer *v.trans.* **1** To tire out, to exhaust someone. *Les anniversaires de gosses, ça me tue!* The kids' birthday parties leave me shattered! **2** To bore (the pants off) someone. *Quand il cause affaires ce mec-là, il me tue!* When he starts talking shop, he bores me stiff!

tuile *n.f.* **1** Unit of 10,000 francs (1,000,000 francs prior to the 1958 remonetization. Also: *brique*). **2** *(fig.)*: Nasty blow, bad setback. (This meaning of the word is said to originate from the incident where Pyrrhus, king of Epirus, met his death while entering Argos in 272 B.C.; a woman threw a roof-tile which hit him on the head and fatally injured him.)

tumec *n.m.* 'Plonk', 'vino', (cheap) red wine. (Georgette Marks in Harrap's DICTIONARY OF SLANG AND COLLOQUIALISMS appears to be the only person to lexicalize this word, which is a jocular transcription of *tue-mec*, itself equatable with *étouffe-chrétien*.)

tune *n.f.* Five-franc piece (see *thune*).

tunnel *n.m.* **1** *(th.)*: Lengthy monologue or soliloquy, the kind of 'to be or not to be' tirade where the actor must make it on his own. **2** Arse-hole, anal sphincter. *Prendre du tunnel*: To engage in sodomous sex. **3** *Etre dans le tunnel*: To be 'in the soup', in a fix, to be in a tricky situation. (As the image would suggest, with 'no light at the end of the tunnel'.)

turbin *n.m.* **1** 'Graft', work. (According to context, the word can relate to 'hard graft', the 'daily grind', any licit or illicit activity and is often used with a humorous connotation as in *Faut que j'aille au turbin!* I'll have to go and earn my crust!) **2** 'Dirty trick', disloyal act. *Faire un turbin à quelqu'un*: To do the dirty on someone.

turbine *n.f. Turbine à chocolat (joc.)*: Arse-hole, anal sphincter.

turbiner *v.intrans.* To 'graft', to 'slog', to work hard.

turbineur *n.m.* 'Grafter', hard worker.

turbineuse *n.f.* 'Prozzy', prostitute (the kind of 'good little earner' whose eagerness to work helps keep her pimp in clover).

turf *n.m.* **1** *Le turf*: The world of horse-racing. *Il ne loupe pas une réunion, le turf c'est sa vie!* You'll find him at every race meeting; he's got gee-gees in the blood! **2** *Aller au turf*: **a** (of prostitute): To go soliciting (whether she is a *Prix de Diane* or a *réclamer!*). **b** *(joc.)*: To go to work. *Si je vais pas au turf, on va devoir se serrer la ceinture!* If I don't head for the old sweat-shop, we'll be on short rations!

turfeuse *n.f.* 'Prozzy', prostitute.

turlu *n.m.* 'Blower', phone, telephone. *Il m'a filé un coup de turlu*: He gave me a ring.

turlupiner *v.trans.* To 'fret', to 'bother', to worry. *Et pourtant, il y a quelque chose qui me turlupine à son sujet!* I can't quite put my finger on it, but I have some niggling doubts about him!

turlutte *n.f. Faire (une) turlutte*: To perform fellatio.

turlututu *interj.* Fiddlesticks! – Poppycock! – Rubbish!

turne *n.f.* **1** Room, bedroom (usually with the connotation of 'digs'). **2** 'Dump-of-a-place', dirty and very disorganized house.

tutoyer *v.trans. Se faire tutoyer*: To 'get hauled over the coals', to be told off in no uncertain manner. (With this 'verbal assault' meaning, the verb is only found conveying a passive sense.)

tutu *n.m.* **1** (Child language): 'Botty', 'bottom', behind. *Si tu manges pas ta soupe, tu vas avoir tutu pan-pan!* If baby doesn't eat his din-dins, he'll get smack-botty! **2** 'Blower', phone, telephone. **3** 'Plonk', 'vino', cheap red wine (the often maligned *vin ordinaire* served in small restaurants).

tutu-panpan *n.m. Une partie de tutu-panpan*: 'A bit of the other', sexual intercourse.

tuyau *n.m.* **1** 'Tip', 'bit of info', inside information. *Il m'a filé un tuyau de première pour la 3ème à Longchamp*: He gave me a red-hot tip for the 3.30 race. **2** *Pantalon en tuyau de poêle*: 'Drainpipe' trousers (those tight leg-hugging trousers that spelled the end of ironed creases). **3** *La famille tuyau de poêle*: **a** Any rather unconventional couple (either because of their disorientated approach to everyday life or because they believe in free-love). **b** The world of male homosexuality.

tuyauter *v.trans.* To 'tip the wink to someone', to 'tip someone off', to pass on some inside information. *Question bouffetance, il est toujours bien tuyauté!* He's always got the low-down on the best eating-places! *Désolé, mec, mais on t'a mal tuyauté!* I'm sorry, chum, but you seem to have got hold of the wrong end of the stick!

tuyauter *v.trans.reflex.* To get 'genned up', to seek some information about something. *J'ai essayé de me tuyauter à son sujet!* I tried to find out a bit more about him!

tuyauterie *n.f. La tuyauterie*: **a** The 'waterworks', the urinary system (also: *la plomberie*). **b** The lungs, the respiratory system. (Some dictionaries see the word as referring to the intestinal passage, but there appears to be little textual substantiation of this meaning.)

tuyauteur *n.m.* **1** (Racing slang): Racing pundit who markets 'red-hot tips'. **2** Person who dispenses (interesting) information, professionally or otherwise.

type *n.m.* 'Bloke', 'chap', fellow. (According to context, the appellation can be derogatory, innocuous or complimentary.) *Pauvre type, va!* You silly burk! *C'est un type que j'ai rencontré à la gare*: I met this bod in the station. *Elle a épousé un type vraiment sensass!* She got herself a really super husband! *Tu es un chic type!* You're a trump!

typesse *n.f.* 'Biddy', 'bird', woman. (This feminine version of *type* has all but disappeared in the 8os.)

typo *n.m. (abbr. ouvrier typographe)*: Typesetter, compositor. *C'est un sacré typo, Dave!* Sharp's the word for that typesetter of ours on the dictionary!

tyrolien *n.m. (abbr. sac tyrolien)*: Rucksack, haversack.

tyrolienne *n.f. Pousser* (also: *lâcher*) *une tyrolienne*: To let out a cry of pain.

U

U *adj.inv. Restau U (abbr. Restaurant Universitaire)*: 'Refec', government-subsidized student restaurant.

un *n.m. Le un (th.)*: Act 1. *On a répété la troisième (scène) du un*: We rehearsed Act 1, Scene 3.

un *indef.pron. & num.adj.* 1 *L'un dans l'autre*: 'All in all', all things being considered. *L'un dans l'autre, on ne s'en est pas trop mal tiré!* You could say that the swings more than made up for the roundabouts! 2 *Et d'un! (Et d'une!)*: **a** Firstly, in the first instance. *Et d'un, c'est moi qui gagne les sous, et de deux, t'es trop jeune!* For a start, I'm the breadwinner, and anyway, you're underage! **b** So much for that! – That settles it! 3 *De deux choses l'une!* It's either this or that! *De deux choses l'une, tu restes ici ou tu viens avec nous!* There's no umming and ahing, you either come with us or stay at home! 4 *Ne faire ni une ni deux*: To have a go without further ado, to make one's mind up and act straight away. 5 *Il était moins une!* It was a narrow squeak! – It was a close thing! 6 *Etre sans un*: To be 'broke', 'skint', to be penniless. 7 *En* + verb + *un/une*: There are a number of set expressions in colloquial speech 'riding' an obvious ellipsis, such as: *En griller une (cigarette)*: To have a smoke. *Ne pas en rater une (sottise)*: To put one's foot in it every time. *En coller un (marron)*: To land a punch, etc.

une *n.f. La une*: The front page of a newspaper. (The expression *cinq colonnes à la une* refers to a banner headline, the kind that spreads across five columns of page one. The most famous current affairs programme on French television was called *Cinq Colonnes à la Une*, and dealt with the major stories of the week.)

unième *adj.ord. Le unième du mois (joc.)*: The 'foist' of the month (the first day).

unif *n.m.* Uniform.

unique *adj. (iron.)*: 'Priceless', unbelievable. *Alors là vraiment, mon vieux, tu es unique!* You're really the limit! (In colloquial French, the expression is always loaded with sarcasm, unlike the 'straight parlance' meaning.)

unité *n.f.* 'Grand', unit of one million francs prior to the 1958 remonetization. (Since the advent of the *Nouveau Franc* the sum of 10,000 francs is its equivalent but lacks the charisma of old. Even in the 1980s, sums of money become superlative when described as *'cinquante millions de nos anciens centimes'*.)

urf *adj.inv.* 'Classy', 'swell', first-rate. *Il s'est levé une nana tout ce qu'il y a de urf!* You should see the smashing bird he's pulled! (Opinions vary drastically as to the origin and nature of this adjective; on the latter issue, it is safer to presume the adjective to be invariable.)

urger *v.intrans. Ça urge!* It can't wait! – It's got to be done now! (*Cela/ça urge* is the only expression where this impersonal verb is encountered.)

user *v.trans. User sa salive*: To 'talk and talk', to talk non-stop (usually in vain, in other words, to waste one's breath).

usine *n.f.* 1 *Aller à l'usine (joc.)*: To go to work. (To have any in-built humour, the expression must refer to 'non-factory' work.) 2 *Usine à bachot*: 'Crammer', 'cramming-shop', fee-paying school for the idle offspring of the rich (also: *boîte à bac*).

usiner *v.intrans.* To 'graft', to work hard. *Un peu que ça usine dans son magasin!* You won't see any slackers in his shop!

utilités *n.f.pl. Jouer les utilités (th.)*: To have a 'walk-on' part (the nearest up-market thing to *faire de la figuration*).

V

va (Imperative of *aller*): **1** *Va pour* . . . : O.K. for
. . . *Va pour trois briques!* Alright, I'll settle for
three grand! **2** *Va donc!* (Insult intensifier): *Va
donc, eh couillon!* You stupid idiot, you! (More
current in everyday speech is *va!* with no
specific connotation; its sole function is to
emphasize a statement. *Je t'aime bien, va!* You
know I love you! *Tu es méchant, va!* You're
really bad to me! *Il est gentil, va!* He's a nice
boy! Sometimes it is merely a 'rhetorical prop'
like the Liverpudlian 'you know!'. *C'est pas
difficile, va!* It's not difficult, you know!) **3** *À la
va-vite (adv.exp.)*: In a slapdash manner, in a
rushed and careless way. **4** *A la va-comme-je-
te-pousse (adv.exp.)*: In a 'happen-what-may'
careless manner. *Elle nous a servi à bouffer à la
va-comme-je-te-pousse!* She dished up the grub
just any-old-how!

vacant *adj.* 'Skint', 'broke', penniless. *Compte pas
sur lui, côté larfeuille il est vacant!* I wouldn't
bank on him, mate, I think he's skint!

vacciné *adj.* **1** Forearmed through previous
experience. *Après deux mariages, côté bonnes
femmes, je suis vacciné!* Having been hitched
twice, I know what to expect from women!
2 *Avoir été vacciné avec une aiguille de phono*:
To be 'something of a gasbag', to be an endless
prattler. **3** *Avoir été vacciné avec une queue de
morue*: To have a 'sloping gullet', to be fond of
one's tipple, to have more than a liking for
alcoholic beverage. (The origin of the expression lies in the salt-fish nature of cod in days
gone by, when *morue salée* was a popular
cheap dish likely to bring on thirst.)

vachard *adj.* **1** (of person): 'Idle as the day is
long' (probably as energetic as a cow). **2** (of
person): 'Nasty', awkward. **3** (of problem):
'Tricky', near-insoluble. *Ils sont vachards, ces
mots croisés!* This crossword puzzle leaves me
stumped!

vachardise *n.f.* **1** Laziness, state of complete and
complacent idleness. **2** 'Rotten trick', nasty
action. *Depuis qu'on est ici, il n'a cessé de nous*
faire des vachardises! From the day we moved
here, he tried every dirty trick in the book!

vachasse *n.f. (pej.)*: 'Big fat biddy', very plump
and unattractive female.

vache *n.f.* **1** *(pej.)*: 'Copper', policeman. *Les
vaches*: 'The fuzz'. (This seemingly injurious
appellation, as well as the expression *Mort aux
vaches!*, has nothing to do with the bovine
species. *Mort aux vaches!* is said to have
originated after 1870 in occupied Alsace-
Lorraine where the German military police
force, *die Wache* (the watch), focused discontent
among the occupied, and the jeer was originally *Mort à la Wache!*) **2** (also: *peau de vache*):
'Pig of a character', very awkward so-and-so.
3 *Coup de pied en vache (fig.)*: Dirty trick, sly
and malicious act. **4** *Vache à lait*: 'Sucker',
wealthy dupe, the kind of rich gullible fool
who keeps cadgers and hangers-on in food and
money. **5** *Vache laitière (pej.)*: 'Big fat biddy'
(the kind of 'silly moo' whose ample mammaries are her dominant feature). **6** *Etre plein
comme une vache*: To be 'pissed to the eye-balls',
to be rolling drunk. **7** *Il pleut comme vache qui
pisse!* It's raining cats and dogs! **8** *Bouffer de la
vache enragée*: To have to rough it, to go
through a tough period in life. (The image here
is of the impoverished individual whose meat
rations, when he can afford them, are of the
'shoe-leather' variety.) **9** *Oh, la vache!* Damn
and blast! – Drat! (This exclamation and its
English equivalents are equally innocuous and
dated.) **10** *Vache de . . . !* This colloquial
intensifier can either be damning as in *Quel
vache de temps!* What bloody (awful) weather! or
loaded with admiration as in *C'est un vache de
mec!* He's one hell of a guy! **11** *La croix des
vaches*: Punishment inflicted by old-time pimps
on recalcitrant prostitutes or by members of the
underworld on a traitor. These deep facial cuts
in the shape of a cross made with a razor blade,
were encouraged to fester and leave a scar by
the application of a chemical.

vache adj. 1 (of person): Weak, all limp. *Je me sens tout vache aujourd'hui!* I'm really feeling weak at the knees today! 2 (of person): 'Beastly', 'mean', nasty. *Son père est drôlement vache avec lui, côté discipline!* His father's a right Colonel Blimp! *Sois pas vache, prête-moi des sous!* Come on, be a pal, lend us some money! *Tu es vraiment vache, ces temps-ci!* You're a right swine these days! 3 (of problem, poser): 'Stinking difficult', awkward and loaded with (intentional) snags. *Ses questions d'examen sont toujours vaches!* The papers he sets are right stinkers! 4 *Un vache . . . , une vache . . . :* An incredible . . . (When the adjective precedes the noun, it acts as an intensifier nearly always with a positive connotation. *Une vache nana:* A smashing bird. *Il m'est arrivé une vache histoire!* You won't believe what happened to me!) 5 *Amour vache:* Tempestuous sort of love affair (the kind where the partners seem to be exchanging as many blows as kisses).

vachement adv. Extremely, very. (As Jacques Cellard and Alain Rey point out in their *DICTIONNAIRE DU FRANÇAIS NON-CONVENTIONNEL*, this adverbial intensifier has lost all pejorative connotation and strengthens any statement, good or bad. *Il est vachement méchant!* He's really evil! *Elle est vachement belle!* She's jolly pretty! This adverb is very much a product of the liberated 60s.)

vacherie n.f. 1 'Rotten trick', nasty action. *Comme de bien entendu, elle m'a encore fait une vacherie!* As you might well expect, she pulled another dirty trick on me! 2 'Hitch', 'snag', nasty turn of events.

va-de-la-gueule n.m. 'Loudmouth', 'bigmouth', rumbustious type who verbally bulldozes people.

vadrouille n.f. 1 Hike, long walk. *Quand j'étais scout, on se tapait de sacrées vadrouilles!* In my scouting days, we used to tackle some fair walks! 2 'Spree', 'out-on-the-town' jollification. *Je ne compte pas sur lui aujourd'hui, il est encore parti en vadrouille!* I don't expect him back today, he's off on another binge! 3 (also: *vadrouilleuse*): 'Licker', tongue (often in a sexual context).

vadrouiller v.intrans. 1 To roam, to wander aimlessly. 2 To enjoy a 'life on the tiles', to be forever gadding it.

vadrouilleur n.m. 1 Hiker, eager walker. 2 'Gad-about-town', character who enjoys living it up.

vague n.m. *Etre dans le vague:* **a** To be 'in the clouds', to be miles and miles away in one's mind (also: *planer*). **b** To be 'in the dark' about something, not to be in the know. *Te dire où il est, je suis plutôt dans le vague!* I haven't the foggiest where he is!

vague n.f. 'Bin', pocket. *N'avoir rien dans les vagues:* To be penniless.

vaguer v.trans. To rifle through someone's pockets. (With the increased fear of terrorist violence, the verb has also come to mean 'to frisk'.)

vaguotte n.f. Jacket, short coat (also: *vaguette*).

vaillant adj. 'Full of beans', sprightly, full of energy. *Tu n'as pas l'air très vaillant ce matin!* You don't look full of the joys of spring this bright and cheery morning!

vaisselle n.f. 1 *De la vaisselle de fouille:* 'Change', loose change, coins. 2 *Se balader avec toute sa vaisselle* (mil.): To parade a chestful of medals.

valade n.f. 'Bin', pocket.

valda n.f. 1 Bullet (from a handgun). 2 Green light at traffic junction. (*Pastilles Valda* are green bullet-shaped throat lozenges. It is often claimed that a *titi parisien* on his bicycle was heard to quip *'Alors, tu la craches, ta Valda?'* whilst waiting for the traffic lights to turn green. The sole French right to this street wit is disputed by Pierre Daninos in *SNOBISSIMO*.)

valdingue n.m. 'Tumble', fall. *Ramasser* (also: *prendre*) *un valdingue:* **a** To suffer a heavy fall (and usually get hurt in the process). **b** (*fig.*): To 'come a cropper', to suffer a serious (financial) setback.

valdingue n.f. (corr. *valise*): 1 Suitcase. 2 *La Grande Valdingue:* Death. (The saying *'partir c'est mourir un peu'* was once wittily paraphrased *'mourir c'est partir beaucoup'!*)

valise n.f. *Faire la* (also: *sa*) *valise:* To 'bugger off', to 'beat it', to go away. (The expression has the connotative value of to pack up and leave in disgust.)

valoche n.f. (corr. *valise*): 1 Suitcase. 2 *Avoir des valoches sous les yeux:* To have bags under one's eyes (also: *valouse, valouze*).

valoir v.intrans. *Ça vaut!/Ça valait!* It is/It was unique! *Des engueulades comme les leurs, ça valait!* The rows they had were just like something on telly!

valouser v.trans. To 'send packing', to 'turf out', to dismiss (also: *valiser*).

valse n.f. 1 'Drubbing', 'thrashing', beating-up. *Je lui ai filé une de ces valses!* I gave him the thrashing of his life! 2 *Invitation à la valse:* Bragging taunt to 'come and settle it outside', the kind of request no self-respecting male can rightly turn down. 3 *Faire la valse à quelqu'un:* To 'walk out on someone', to let someone down. 4 *Valse lente* (also: *valse hésitation*): Reluctance to pay for a round of drinks (a sort of 'short hands, deep pockets shuffle').

valser *v.intrans.* **1** *Envoyer valser quelqu'un*: To send someone reeling with a violent blow. **2** *Faire valser les biffetons*: To 'spend, spend, spend' (literally to throw money about like confetti).

valseur *n.m.* 'Bum', 'bottom', behind. (Originally the word referred exclusively to the wiggling female posterior but is used now when referring to either sex.)

valseuses *n.f.pl.* 'Balls', 'bollocks', testicles.

vamper *v.trans.* (of woman): To turn on the charm, to try on a seduction act.

vanne *n.f.* **1** 'Blow', serious setback. *Il lui est arrivé une série de vannes l'année dernière*: Last year for him was a never-ending series of catastrophes. **2** Snide remark, cutting and hurtful repartee. *Encore une de ses vannes et je lui fous ma main sur la gueule!* Just one more remark like that and I'll push his face in! **3** Witty riposte, clever, amusing and off-the-cuff remark. *Il faut toujours qu'il lance des vannes, cézigue!* He's the type who's always cracking jokes! **4** 'Braggy claim', boast. (The word is sometimes encountered in the masculine with this meaning.)

vanné *adj.* 'Buggered', 'knackered', exhausted. *Après les fêtes, je suis toujours vanné, moi!* I don't know how it is with you, but the festive season leaves me shattered!

vanner *v.trans.* To 'knacker', to 'jigger', to exhaust. *Ah, les gosses m'ont vanné aujourd'hui!* I'm proper worn out with the kids today!

vanner *v.intrans.* **1** To fire snide and cutting remarks. **2** To 'wisecrack', to shower liberally quips and merry ripostes. **3** To 'talk big', to brag.

vanneur *n.m.* **1** Boisterous wit, character who endlessly reels off jokes and clever repartee. **2** 'Brag', boaster.

vape *n.f.* **1** *La vape*: The Turkish baths, steam baths (also: *vapes*). **2** *Etre dans la vape*: **a** To feel 'woozy', to feel faint (usually through excessive drinking). **b** To be stuck in a 'rut of bad luck'. *V'là quinze jours qu'on est en pleine vape!* The last fortnight's been a catalogue of disasters!

vapes *n.f.pl.* **1** (abbr. *vapeurs*). *Tomber dans les vapes*: To 'flake out', to faint. (*Vapes* refers directly to 'the vapours'.) *Etre dans les vapes*: **a** To be 'out cold', to be unconscious. **b** (*fig. & iron.*): To be totally out of touch with reality (not so much 'not with it' as incapable in the eyes of others of coping or making coherent comments). **2** (abbr. *bains de vapeur*): Turkish baths.

vapeur *n.f.* **1** *Renverser la vapeur*: To make a 'U-turn', to have a complete change of mind on a specific issue. (The image obviously derives from the days of the steam engine.) **2** *Filer à toute vapeur*: To 'make tracks', to dash away. **3** *Avoir* (also: *prendre*) *ses vapeurs*: To get 'hot under the collar', to become angry.

vaporisateur *n.m.* (*joc.*): Tommy-gun, machine-gun.

variations *n.f.pl.* *Variations sur un thème connu!* (*iron.*): Yeah, yeah, yeah, we've heard it all before!

varloper *v.intrans.* **1** To go window-shopping. **2** (*pol.*): To drift about casually collecting information.

varlot *n.m.* Time-wasting customer, the kind who can seldom decide on a purchase.

vase *n.m.* **1** *Le vase*: The arse-hole, the anal sphincter. **2** *Avoir du vase*: To have the luck of the devil. *Il a eu un vase terrible ces temps-ci au P.M.U.!* Lately he's had an incredible winning streak with the gee-gees! (It is interesting to note that sodomy and good fortune are often associated in modern colloquial French as exemplified in expressions such as *avoir du fion, avoir un cul terrible*.)

vase *n.f.* **1** Rain. *Il nous est tombé une de ces vases!* It just poured buckets! **2** 'Corporation pop', 'Adam's ale', water. **3** *Etre dans la vase*: To be 'in the shit', 'in the soup', to be in a fix.

vaseline *n.f.* **1** *Passer la vaseline à quelqu'un*: To 'soft-soap' someone, to be over-obsequious. **2** *Prendre de la vaseline* (also: *donner dans la vaseline*): To be partial to passive sodomy.

vaser *v.intrans.* **1** To 'pour', to rain heavily for quite a while. *Et comment qu'il a vasé pendant nos vacs!* The rain just never let up during our hols! **2** (*sch.*): To make a mess of an examination. (The inference is not of failing, but of making a 'hash' of what could otherwise have been a good paper.)

vaseux *adj.* **1** (of idea, answer): 'Woolly', unclear. *Il m'a fait des excuses plutôt vaseuses*: His explanations were pretty muddled. **2** (of comment, repartee): 'Weak', lacking bite and imagination. *Il nous a sorti son répertoire d'astuces vaseuses!* We were treated to his catalogue of feeble party jokes! **3** *Se sentir vaseux*: **a** To feel 'muddle-headed', to be rather confused. **b** To feel 'off-colour', to be unwell.

vasistas *n.m.* 'Mush', 'dial', face. (In standard French the word refers to a fanlight or small opening window situated above a doorway; it is a corruption of the German *was ist das?* During the occupation of France in World War II, a witty repartee to this German query was: *Petite fenêtre!*)

vasouiller *v.intrans.* **1** *(sch.)*: To 'waffle' in an examination paper, to side-step an answer through a combination of ignorance and nerves. **2** To 'dither', to hesitate. **3** To 'make a balls of it', to make a mess of things.

va-te-laver *n.f.* Slap, slap across the face. *Effacer une va-te-laver*: To get smacked in the face.

vatères *n.m.pl.* *Les vatères*: 'The karzey', 'the bog', the W.C. (The alternative spelling *ouatères* is a direct phonetic indication of the colloquial corruption of water-closet.)

va-vite *n.f.* *A la va-vite (adv.exp.)*: In a 'slapdash' manner, hurriedly and with little care. *Elle nous a fait de la tambouille à la va-vite*: She knocked us up some grub double-quick.

veau *n.m.* **1** (Racing slang): 'Nag', inferior race-horse. **2** Car definitely lacking in accelerating power, the kind of vehicle that just trundles along at a leisurely pace. **3** (also: *tête de veau*): 'Burk', 'nincompoop', fool. **4** *Pleurer comme un veau*: To 'blubber', to 'cry one's eyes out', to weep.

vécés *n.m.pl.* *Les vécés*: 'The karzey', 'the bog', the W.C. (This is an unusual phonetic representation of W.C.)

vécu *past part.* *Avoir (beaucoup) vécu*: To have 'been around', to have seen life.

veilleuse *n.f.* **1** *Mettre quelque chose en veilleuse*: To keep something (a business, sporting activity) just 'ticking over', to all but stop something. (This is a direct reference to a low-level flame or pilot-light.) **2** *La mettre en veilleuse*: To 'hold one's tongue', to remain silent.

veinard *n.m.* Lucky devil. *Sacré veinard!* You jammy bugger!

veinard *adj.* Lucky, fortunate.

veine *n.f.* Luck, good fortune. (This colloquial meaning of the word is said to have originated from the language of mining where encountering a vein of ore is equatable with success.) *Avoir une veine de cocu*: To have the luck of the devil. *C'est bien ma veine! (iron.)*: Just my luck! *Pas de veine!* Tough! – Hard luck! *Une veine que tu sois là!* It's a stroke of luck you being here!

Vel' d'Hiv' *Proper name.* *Le Vel' d'Hiv'* (abbr. le *Vélodrome d'Hiver*): Paris indoor cycling track originally used for six-day races. (Replaced today by a skyscraper, this once-famous stadium was often the location for public meetings and concerts but gained infamous notoriety during World War II as a temporary detention centre for Jews prior to their deportation to concentration camps.)

vélo *n.m.* **1** 'Bike', bicycle. *On a fait du vélo hier*: We took our bikes out yesterday. **2** *Faire un vélo de. . .*: To 'kick up a fuss', to create a to-do over a minor incident.

velours *n.m.* **1** Profit. *Comme investissement, ça a été tout velours!* That venture showed nothing but profit! *Petit velours*: 'Perk', small 'on-the-side' reward. **2** 'Doddle', easy success. *Ça a été un vrai velours!* It was just plain sailing! **3** *Jouer sur le velours*: **a** To 'gamble on a cert', to be sure of winning. (Some sources attest the expression as meaning to gamble only one's winnings, making sure that the original stake is never eroded.) **b** To 'be on to a sure thing', to be certain of achieving success.

vendange *n.f.* *(joc.)*: 'Haul', loot, proceeds from a break-in. *La vendange a été bonne!* We did ourselves a few profitable jobs!

vendre *v.trans.* **1** To 'shop', to inform on someone. **2** *Vendre un piano*: To 'blind someone with words', to try and fool someone with a verbal avalanche. (The implication here is that the larger the object, the more effort must go into the sales-patter.)

vendu *n.m.* *(pej.)*: 'Double-crosser', traitor to a cause.

venette *n.f.* 'Funk', fear. *On lui a filé une de ces venettes!* We certainly put the wind up him!

venin *n.m.* *Lâcher son venin*: To 'juice off', to ejaculate.

venir *v.intrans.* *Voir venir quelqu'un (fig. & iron.)*: To 'see what someone is driving at', to not be fooled by someone's manoeuvering. *Je l'ai vu venir avec ses gros sabots!* He certainly wasn't going to fool me!

vent *n.m.* **1** *Du vent*: 'Waffle', empty talk. *Toutes ses promesses, mon vieux, c'est du vent!* I wouldn't believe in his pie-crust promises if I were you! **2** *Vendre du vent*: To sell fictitious goods (merchandise that does not exist). **3** *Faire du vent*: To 'create', to make a big to-do about very little. **4** *Avoir du vent dans les voiles*: To have had 'one too many', to be tipsy, to be slightly drunk. **5** *Etre dans le vent*: **a** To be 'with it', trendy, to be fashionable. **b** (of book, song, etc.): To be popular with the public. **6** *Du vent!* Get lost! – Off with you! – Go away!

ventouse *n.f.* **1** Tenacious bore. **2** Motor vehicle that seems to have parked once and for all (as typified in English by Tony Hancock in a sketch where a road has been resurfaced several times round a stationary vehicle).

Vénus *Proper name.* *Recevoir un coup de pied de Vénus*: To 'cop a dose', to catch V.D.

ver *n.m.* **1** *Nu comme un ver*: 'Starkers', 'in one's birthday suit', stark naked. **2** *Tuer le ver*: To take a 'rouser', to take an early-morning drink for the purpose of killing a hang-over. (Popular myth has it that alcohol consumed on an empty stomach first thing in the morning will destroy any worms in the intestines.) **3** *Avoir le ver solitaire*: To be a 'guzzler', to be forever 'stuffing one's face', to have an immoderate appetite for food. (The tapeworm is a bogey parasite to French hypochondriacs.) **4** *Ça n'est pas piqué des vers!* It's smashing! – It's fantastic! (The parasite in question here is the woodworm, and anything free of that pest is therefore in prime condition.) **5** *Tirer les vers du nez à quelqu'un*: To 'pump' someone for info (literally to 'worm' information out of someone).

verdine *n.f.* **1** Gypsy caravan. (According to certain sources, the kind of rickety trailer that would fail any police inspection.) **2** *(pol.)*: 'Snag', 'hitch', difficulty (occurring within an inquiry). **3** 'Cock-up', 'mix-up', confused situation.

verdouze *n.f.* **1** *La verdouze*: Greenery (the bucolic pastures dreamt of by the city-dweller). *La verdouze, il n'y a que ça pour se relaxer!* There's nothing like a bit of the countryside for soothing the nerves! **2** (Sometimes *pl.*): 'Greens', green vegetables.

verjo *n.m.* (also: *verjot*): 'Jammy bugger', lucky so-and-so.

verjo *adj.m.* (also: *verjot*): 'Jammy', lucky, fortunate.

verlen *n.m.* (also: *verlan*): 'Gobbledygook' sounding secret language where syllables are pronounced in the wrong order, e.g. *brelica*: *calibre*. The very name of this secretive form of speech is self-explanatory, *verlen*: *l'envers*. ('Back slang' is not an exact equivalent.)

vermicelle *n.m.* **1** Hair. *Il n'a pas lourd de vermicelle sur la caboche!* You could certainly say he's going thin on top! **2** 'Woolly', 'pussy', female pubic hair.

verni *adj.* 'Jammy', lucky, fortunate. *Etre verni au pinceau à merde*: To have the luck of the devil. (There is a strange correlation between the word *merde* and good fortune in modern colloquial French.)

verre *n.m.* **1** *(pl.)*: 'Specs', 'glasses', spectacles. *Sans mes verres, je n'y vois que tchi!* I'm as blind as a bat without my specs! **2** *Verre de montre*: 'Bum', behind. *Casser son verre de montre*: To 'crack one's arse'. **3** *Manier quelqu'un comme du verre filé*: To 'handle someone with kid gloves', to treat someone with great care and respect. (To replace *verre filé* by *verre cassé* in the expression is figuratively incorrect. The precautionary care needed when handling spun glass is far removed from the cautionary care needed for broken glass.) **4** *Pisser du verre pilé*

(of man): To have 'clap', to suffer from gonorrhoea (also: *pisser des lames de rasoir*).

verse *n.f.* *La verse*: Rain, rainfall. (The term might have originated from *l'averse*: shower of rain.) *Il est tombé une de ces verses!* It poured buckets!

vert *n.m.* *Se mettre au vert*: To settle down to a life of leisure away from the rat-race.

vert *adj.* **1** (of story, joke): 'Blue', risqué and smutty. *En sortir des vertes et des pas mûres*: To come out with some pretty close-to-the-knuckle stuff. **2** *Etre* (also: *se retrouver*) *vert*: To have been 'conned', 'diddled', to have been fooled. **3** *Langue verte*: Another appellation for *argot*. (To claim a definitive origin here, in view of conflicting opinions, seems unwise.)

vert-de-gris *n.m.* 'Kraut', 'Jerry', German. (This World War II appellation has its origin in the colour of the Wehrmacht's uniform.)

verte *n.f.* 'Smutty story', risqué joke.

vertu *n.f.* *Ce n'est pas une vertu!* (iron., of woman): She's no angel! (The virtue here is sexual morality.)

vesse *n.f.* 'Pongy', noiseless and smelly fart.

vesser *v.intrans.* **1** To 'fart', to break wind. **2** *Vesser du bec*: To have foul breath, to suffer from halitosis.

veste *n.f.* **1** Setback, failure. *Prendre* (also: *ramasser*) *une veste*: To come seriously unstuck. **2** *Tomber la veste*: To get 'stuck in', to lend a hand (literally to take off one's jacket in order to work more freely and perspire less).

vestiaire *n.m.* *Vestiaire!* (iron.): On your bike! – Off with you! – Go away! (A sort of sarcastic irony lurks within this interjection which would otherwise merely be a head waiter's request for the hats, coats, etc. of clients in an expensive establishment.)

véto *n.m.* (corr.abbr. *vétérinaire*): 'Vet', veterinary surgeon.

veuve *n.f.* **1** *La veuve*: The guillotine (also: *la bicyclette à Charlot*). **2** *La veuve poignet (et ses cinq filles)*: 'Wanking', male masturbation. **3** *Une (bouteille de) veuve*: A bottle of champers. (The renowned brand of champagne *Veuve Clicquot* is gaining eponymous ground in modern colloquial French.)

Vévé *Proper name.* *Une vévé*: A Volkswagen car. (The strange phonetics of this word can be explained by the fact that the VW initials do not exactly roll off the tongue in French where W is pronounced *'double-v'*.)

viande *n.f.* **1** *(joc.)*: 'Carcass', human body. *Amène ta viande!* Come here! *T'as intérêt à planquer ta viande!* If I were you, I'd lay low! **2** *Viande froide*: 'Stiff', corpse, dead body. **3** *Marchand de viande*: White-slaver, procurer of innocent women for prostitution. **4** *Ma viande*: Me, myself. *Ta viande*: You, yourself. *Sa viande*: Him/her. *C'est pas pour ta viande!* It's not for the likes of you!

viander *v.pronom.* To get oneself killed (in a car crash, accident, etc.).

vibure *n.f.* Speed, great haste. *A toute vibure*: 'Like shit off a stick', double-quick. *Il a dû filer à toute vibure!* He certainly had to put his skates on!

vice *n.m.* **1** Hidden snag, unforeseen circumstance likely to cause problems. *Dans votre affaire, il y a comme qui dirait un vice!* I can smell a rat in that little fiddle of yours! **2** *Avoir du vice*: **a** To 'know all the ropes', to be full of cunning and expediency. **b** To be 'cocky', 'cheeky', to be impudent. **3** *Prendre son vice où l'on peut*: To get one's pleasure (usually sexual) how and where one can.

vicelard *n.m.* 'Dirty old man', salacious character.

vicelard *adj.* **1** Salacious. (The connotation is nearly that of depraved.) **2** Sly, cunning, likely to deceive wilfully.

vicelardises *n.f.pl.* Kinky sexual practices (only in a heterosexual context).

Vichy *Proper name. Etre invité en pastille de Vichy*: To act as a stop-gap at a dinner-party, to be invited as an afterthought. (*Pastilles de Vichy* are a well-known brand of indigestion tablets usually taken after a hearty meal, hence the meaning of the expression.)

vidage *n.m.* 'Sacking', 'chucking-out', dismissal.

vidé *adj.* **1** 'Knackered', 'buggered', exhausted. **2** 'Skint', 'broke', penniless.

vider *v.trans.* **1** To 'sack', to 'give the boot to', to dismiss someone. *Ses tripotages l'ont fait vider!* His little fiddles got him the push! **2** To 'knacker', to exhaust. *Les gosses m'ont vidé aujourd'hui!* I'm just about done in today looking after the kids! **3** *(fig.)*: To 'clean out', to squeeze dry (where money is concerned). **4** *Vider un glass/un kil*: To have a glass, to down a bottle of wine. **5** *Vider son sac (fig.)*: To 'get something off one's chest', to speak one's mind after some hesitation. **6** *Vider ses burettes* (of man): To 'have it off', to have sex.

videur *n.m.* 'Bouncer', stockily-built doorman in restaurant, nightclub, etc. whose job it is to eject unwanted and recalcitrant customers.

vieille *n.f.* **1** *La vieille*: The 'old lady', mother. *Ma vieille et ma femme ne s'entendent pas!* My wife and her mother-in-law don't get on! **2** *Ma vieille*: 'Old girl'. (This term of familiarity is less frequent than its masculine equivalent.)

vient-tout-seul *n.m. (joc.)*: Ripe camembert cheese (the kind that is so runny that it oozes out when left cut open overnight).

vieux *n.m.* **1** 'Dad', father. *Mon vieux est en froid avec ses voisins*: My old man's fallen out with the neighbours. **2** *(pl.) Mes vieux*: 'The old folk', my parents. **3** *Mon vieux* (term of familiarity): 'Old bean', old chap. *Alors, mon vieux, ça boume?* Well, mate, how are things? **4** *Un vieux de la vieille*: An 'old hand', 'one of the old brigade', the kind of diehard who has stuck through it all. **5** *Prendre un coup de vieux*: To age noticeably in a short period of time. *Depuis son deuil il a pris un coup de vieux!* Since his missus died he seems to have aged overnight!

vigne *n.f.* *Etre dans les vignes du Seigneur*: To be well and truly tiddly, in a state of beatific stupor.

vilain *n.m.* **1** *Il va y avoir du vilain!* I can see aggro ahead! – There's going to be trouble! **2** *Jeu de mains, jeu de vilains!* (Stern reproof to naughty child): Now then, don't fight! (When used in a different context, the expression is often ironic and jocular, as in the 'keep your hands to yourself' maidenly retort.)

village *n.m. Il est bien de son village (iron.)*: He's as green as they come – He's pretty simple. (The country bumpkin image is opposed here to the wily city-dweller's awareness.)

villégiature *n.f. Etre en villégiature (iron.)*: To be 'in the nick', to be in prison. (The 'nudge-nudge, wink-wink' irony stems from the standard meaning of the expression. *Etre en villégiature* cannot be equated with the explanation given to children and neighbours as to the whereabouts of a father/husband. See *voyage*.)

vinaigre *n.m.* **1** *Faire vinaigre*: To 'get one's skates on', to 'move sharpish', to hurry up. **2** *Ça tourne au vinaigre!* (of happening, events): Things are taking an ugly turn! (literally the situation is in the process of souring up).

vinasse *n.f. (pej.)*: 'Lousy plonk', really third-rate wine.

vingt-deux *num.adj.* **1** *Vingt-deux!* Look out! – Run for it! (This interjection is often, in a humorous context, followed by *v'là les flics!* without there being any police presence to fear. The plethora of would-be origins offered for the expression confirms its nebulous etymology.) **2** *Vingt-deux que . . .* : I bet you I can . . . (This expression, most often uttered by children and juveniles, is very much equatable with 'I bet you don't think I'll dare do this!' *Vingt-deux que je lui mets ma main sur la gueule!* O.K., I bet you I'll push his face in!)

violette *n.f.* **1** 'Tip', gratuity. (With this meaning, the word smacks of underworld transactions or favours where the tip is anything but modest. An alternative is *bouquet*.) **2** *Avoir les doigts de pied en bouquet de violettes (joc.)*: To be experiencing an orgasm. (This very picturesque expression reflects the intensity of the moment.)

violon *n.m.* **1** *(pol.) Le violon*: The cells at a police station. *Son haleine sentait le pastaga, il avait passé la nuit au violon*: His breath was heavy with Pernod and he had spent the night down at the station. **2** *C'est comme si je pissais dans un violon!* It's a total waste of time! (The potency of the expression lies in the imagery, an alternative being *c'est comme si je pissais dans un chapeau de paille troué!*) **3** *Boîte à violon*: 'Wooden overcoat', coffin.

vioque *n.m. & f.* (also: *vioc n.m.*): Old person (with a slightly pejorative connotation). *On dirait qu'elle a un penchant pour les vioques!* You have a feeling she fancies all those sugardaddies!

vioque *adj. (pej.)*: 'Past its prime', very old.

vioquerie *n.f. (pej.)*: **1** Item long due for the waste-bin, not worth keeping. **2** 'Would-be antique', knick-knack of little value worthy of a down-market jumble sale.

vioquir *v.intrans.* To be 'getting on' (in years), to be ageing.

vipère *n.f. Vipère de broussaille*: 'Prick', 'cock', penis.

virage *n.m.* **1** *Prendre le virage*: To make an adroit U-turn, to totally change one's line of action in a diplomatic and logical way. (The image of the motorist carefully 'negotiating a bend' is present in this expression.) **2** *Attendre quelqu'un au virage (fig.)*: To bide one's time in order to get even. *Il m'a chopé au virage!* In the end he got his own back!

virée *n.f.* Pleasurable outing. *On est allés faire une virée à la cambrousse*: We went out for a spin in the country.

virer *v.trans.* **1** To 'turf out', to 'chuck out', to dismiss. *Il s'est fait virer de son école*: He got expelled. **2** *Virer sa cuti* (of man or woman): To turn homosexual. (The *cuti-réaction* is the T.B. skin-test indicating that the human body has identified the tubercle bacillus. In the context of homosexuality, the expression relates to the discovery of 'new pleasures'.)

virer *v.intrans. (fig.)*: To 'make a U-turn', to have a complete change of mind about something.

virginité *n.f. Se refaire une virginité*: To 'turn over a new leaf', to make a fresh start hoping that the 'clean sheet' remains unblotted by the past. (This expression, which has no sexual connotation, can be equated with the remark made about a famous Hollywood actress of whom a critic said 'I knew her before she was a virgin!')

viron *n.m.* Short trip. *On a fait un viron dans sa nouvelle bagnole*: We went for a quick spin in his new motor.

vis *n.f. Serrer la vis à quelqu'un*: **a** To 'put the screws on someone', to put someone under quite a bit of pressure. **b** To throttle, to strangle someone.

vise-au-trou *n.f. Madame vise-au-trou (joc.)*: Midwife (also: *Madame guette-au-trou*).

viser *v.trans. Vise un peu cette nana!* Take a butchers at that smashing bird! (With its colloquial meaning, this verb is used only in the imperative.)

visible *adj. Ne pas être visible*: This expression relates to a personage who, for reasons of health or otherwise, does not wish to receive visitors.

visser *v.trans.* **1** To 'screw down', to force someone into submission. **2** *Etre mal vissé*: To be in a foul mood (also: *être mal luné*).

vite *adv. Vite fait (sur le gaz)*: 'Quick-quick' and often in a slapdash manner. *On s'est tapé un vite-fait*: We had ourselves a quick drink.

vitesse *n.f. Faire quelque chose en quatrième vitesse*: To do something at near breakneck speed (also: *faire quelque chose à la vitesse grand V*).

vitre *n.f. Casser les vitres*: To 'kick up a fuss', to make a scene.

vitreux *n.m.pl.* 'Oglers', 'peepers', eyes.

vitrier *n.m. Ton père n'était pas vitrier! (joc. & iron.)*: Move out of the light, I can't see! (The would-be wittiness of the expression, also extant in colloquial German, is evident as no-one is translucent.)

vitrine *n.f.* **1** *Faire du lèche-vitrines*: To go window-shopping. **2** *Si c'est pas dans la vitrine, voyez dans le magasin! (joc. & iron.)*: Don't just stand there, look closer! (This expression is often used in a sexual context where a partner issues a tongue-in-cheek taunt.)

vitriol *n.m. (joc.)*: 'Hooch', strong and dubious alcohol (usually the 'moonshine' variety. The 'rotgut' image derives from the standard meaning of *vitriol* which is the popular term for sulphuric acid).

vivoter *v.intrans.* To 'scrape along', to live a 'hand-to-mouth' existence, to live on meagre means.

vivre *v.intrans.* **1** *Etre difficile à vivre*: To be hard to get on with, to be difficult to live with. **2** *Vivre à la colle* (of couple): To 'live under the brush', to cohabit. **3** *Apprendre à vivre à quelqu'un*: To 'teach someone a lesson', to forcefully put someone in their place.

voile *n.f.* **1** *Etre à voile et à vapeur*: To be 'AC/DC', to be bisexual. **2** *Mettre les voiles*: To 'skedaddle', to 'scarper', to move away in haste. *Quand il a appris l'histoire on a dû mettre les voiles*: When he heard about it we had to get our skates on.

voir *v.trans. & intrans.* **1** *Va te faire voir chez les Grecs!* Get stuffed! – Get knotted! – Go to hell! **2** *Va-t'en voir (là-bas) si j'y suis! (iron.):* Why don't you just go away! – Can't you leave me alone?!

voiture *n.f.* **1** *Voiture pie:* Squad car, police car (see *pie).* **2** *Etre rangé des voitures* (Underworld slang): To be 'out of the game', to have retired from active involvement.

volaille *n.f.* **1** *Une volaille:* A 'prozzy', a prostitute. **2** *La volaille:* 'The fuzz', the police.

volante *n.f. (abbr. la Brigade Volante):* The 'flying squad'. (This term is used both by the police and outsiders.)

voler *v.trans. Ne l'avoir pas volé:* To have 'asked for it', to deserve the punishment meted out. *Ecoute, mon vieux, tu ne l'as pas volé, ta femme a bien fait de filer!* You deserve all you got; your wife was right to leave!

voler *v.intrans.* **1** *Voler dans les plumes à quelqu'un:* **a** To 'go for someone with fists flying', to attack someone physically with ferocity. **b** *(fig.):* To 'pitch into someone', to launch a ferocious verbal assault on someone. **2** *Voler bas* (of person): To be 'more than a trifle dim', to be pretty thick and stupid. **3** *Les mouches volent bas!* There's trouble brewing! (The imagery derives from the fact that many insects take to flying at a low altitude when a storm is imminent.)

volet *n.m. Mettre les volets:* To 'pop one's clogs', to 'snuff it', to die. (The image here is of a shop closing . . . permanently.)

voleur *n.m. Rouspéter comme un voleur:* To 'kick up a fuss' about something, to recriminate bitterly and loudly.

volière *n.f.* 'Cat-house', brothel (literally where the 'birds' hang out!).

volo *n.f. (abbr. volonté) A volo (adv.exp.):* At will, to one's heart's content.

volume *n.m. Faire du volume:* **a** (of salesman): To notch up some big orders. **b** To 'throw one's weight about', to swagger.

vôtre *poss.pron. A la bonne vôtre!* (Drinkers' toast): Here's mud in your eye! – To your good health!

voui *adv.* Yeah! – Yes! (This popular spoken corruption of *oui* is either uttered in a would-be humorous context or when the answer is not a straightforward acknowledgement. Also: *mouais.*)

vouloir *v.trans. & intrans.* **1** *En vouloir* (of eager young person): To be full of 'get-up-and-go', to be raring to achieve something. **2** *Je veux!* (Retort to a question): You bet! – And how! – Certainly! *Partir en vacances avec une bagnole, un peu que je veux!* What? Have my own car to go on holiday? You're on! **3** *Je m'en voudrais!* *(iron.):* Not bloody likely! – Certainly not!

voyage *n.m.* **1** *Etre (parti) en voyage:* To 'be doing time', to be in prison. (Whereas *être en villégiature* decidedly has a built-in ironic connotation, *être en voyage* is more equatable with a plausible excuse as to why 'Daddy isn't here'.) **2** *Les gens du voyage:* Circus folk (because their life is an itinerant one). **3** *Le grand voyage:* Death. *Faire le grand voyage:* To go to kingdom come. **4** *Emmener en voyage:* To 'have it off', to have intercourse. (The trip here relates to reaching the orgasmic heights of 'cloud nine'. *Elle y est allée de son voyage!* She was gone, real gone!)

voyageur *n.m.* Small glass of white wine. (The kind of quick drink that helps you on your way.)

voyeur *n.m.* Salacious ogler. (The translation 'Peeping Tom' offered by some dictionaries is inaccurate in that the *voyeur* delights in observing sexy goings-on that are not necessarily screened from public gaze.)

vozigues *pers.pron.* You, yourselves. *C'est pas pour vozigues, la bonne bouffe!* This good nosh isn't for the likes of you!

vrai *n.m.* **1** *Un vrai de vrai* (Underworld slang): A 'tough nut', a hard and hardy character *qui n'a pas froid aux yeux.* **2** *Pour de vrai:* **a** 'For real', in earnest. **b** 'For good', 'once and for all', permanently.

vrai *adv. (abbr. vraiment) Vrai?!* No kidding?! –Really?! **2** *Eh bien, vrai!* Well I never! – Would you believe it?!

vrille *n.f.* 'Les', 'dyke', lesbian.

vu *past part.* **1** *On aura tout vu!* Well, would you ever (believe that)?! **2** *C'est tout vu!* That's the way it is! – It's all settled! – It's a fact! (that needs no more arguing about). **3** *Ni vu ni connu, je t'embrouille!* Stock jocular phrase uttered when faced with an inexplicable state of muddle, the nearest colloquial equivalent being: 'Now you see it, now you don't!' **4** *Vu?* Agreed? (The elliptical answer to this elliptical question is an affirmative *vu!* equatable with O.K.!)

vue *n.f.* **1** *En mettre plein la vue à quelqu'un:* To 'pull out all the stops' in order to impress someone. *Côté technique, il essaie toujours de nous en mettre plein la vue!* He's always trying to blind us with science! **2** *S'en mettre plein la vue:* To 'get a salacious eyeful', to relish the contemplation of sexy goings-on. **3** *Avoir des vues sur quelqu'un* (of envisaged marital situation): To have one's sights on someone. **4** *A vue de nez:* At a rough guess. *A vue de nez, je dirais qu'il est boche!* If you ask me, I'd say he's a Kraut!

vurdon *n.m.* Gypsy caravan. (The kind of rickety trailer that would fail any police inspection. Also: *verdine.)*

W

wagon *n.m.* **1** 'Prozzy', prostitute. **2** *Accrocher les wagons*: To 'throw up', to 'puke', to vomit.

wagonnet *n.m. Recharger les wagonnets* (of glasses): To 'set 'em up again', to fill them up again. *Allez, on recharge les wagonnets, et on se casse!* O.K., let's have a refill and then we'll head for home!

Wagram *Proper name. (abbr. Salle Wagram)*: This vast hall, a popular venue for boxing and wrestling matches, pop concerts and political rallies is, as the name suggests, situated on the *Avenue Wagram* in Paris.

walk-over *n.m.* 'Push-over', easy task. (The word stems from the language of horse-racing, a walk-over being a race where for one reason or another only one contender is left, who to win must complete the course unopposed.)

wallace *n.f. (abbr. fontaine Wallace)*: Paris drinking fountain. (Sir Richard Wallace, the English philanthropist, 1818–90, gained everlasting eponymous fame by donating fifty small push-button water-dispensing fountains to the French capital.)

waterloo *n.m.* **1** Crushing and unexpected set-back. **2** Patch of bad luck. *On était en plein waterloo!* It was just one thing after another! (Obviously the heavy military defeat inflicted on Napoleon on 18 June 1815 is reflected in the colloquial meanings of the word. The same can be said of *Trafalgar*.)

waters *n.m.pl. Les waters*: 'The bog', the W.C. (The word is a truncation of water-closet and has a number of near-miss phonetic representations: *ouatères*, *vatères*, indicative of the speaker's literacy.)

X

X *Proper name. L'X*: The *Ecole Polytechnique*.

Y

y *adv.* **1** *Y aller de* . . . : To do something. (Colloquial expressions using this spoken format can usually be found under the heading of their complement, e.g. *Y aller de cinq*: To shake hands. *Y aller de sa goualante*: **a** To sing a song. **b** To voice a complaint. *Y aller de la sienne*: To tell a funny joke, etc.) **2** *Y passer* (of sexual partner): To succumb to advances. **3** *Y tâter*: To be quite good at something, to be more than proficient. *Le golf, il y tâte depuis longtemps*: He's no mean golfer these days.

y *pers.pron. (corr. il) Y faut pas faire ça!* You mustn't do that! *Y m'a bien dit que t'étais un salaud!* He sure as hell told me you were a swine! (Only lax pronunciation can explain this surprising deviation from the norm which is sadly filtering into the written language.)

ya *n.m. (abbr. yatagan)*: 'Chiv', blade, knife.

yaouled *n.m.* Young Arab. (This highly derogatory word coined during the years of North African colonization by the French is equatable with the English 'coon', 'wog'.)

yaourt *n.m.* **1** *Pot de yaourt (joc.)*: Bubble-car. (In the 50s, the most popular bubble-car in France was manufactured by Isetta. These vehicles with their large glass area and striking white colour quickly earned this nickname.) **2** *Stylo à yaourt (joc.)*: 'Prick', 'cock', penis.

yearling *n.m.* Teenage girl. (This appellation, an obvious borrowing from the language of horse-racing has, like the word *pouliche*, the connotation of 'pretty filly'.)

yeux *n.m.pl.* **1** *Faire les petits yeux*: To be dog-tired (literally to display the contracted pupils of one who has had a sleepless night). **2** *Ne pas avoir les yeux en face des trous*: To have a cock-eyed view of things (through excessive drink or other distractions). *Reparle-m'en demain, je n'ai pas les yeux en face des trous!* Tell me about it tomorrow, I can't think straight! **3** *Ne pas avoir les yeux dans sa poche*: To be 'on the ball', to have one's wits about one. **4** *Entre quat'z-yeux*: Between you, me and the gatepost; in confidence. *S'expliquer entre quat'z-yeux*: To have a punch-up or a row away from onlookers. (The expression can sometimes relate to a non-belligerent confrontation of views.) **5** *Coûter les yeux de la tête*: To 'cost the earth', to be very expensive.

yéyé *n.m. (slightly pej.)*: 'Beatnik'. (The origin of the word lies in the rock-and-roll dominated years when lowbrow refrain lyrics were mostly of the 'yeah-yeah-yeah' variety.)

yéyé *adj.inv.* (of music, clothes, and fashion in general): 'Beatnikish', likely to appeal to the youth of the late 50s and 60s.

youpin *n.m. (pej.)*: 'Yid', Jew.

youpin *adj. (pej.)*: 'Yid', Jewish.

youvoy *n.m.* (Underworld slang): 'Lout', hoodlum. (This *verlen* appellation is in fact quite derogatory in that it labels an outlaw seen as such amongst his own.)

yoyo *n.m.* **1** Character who spends his time running back and forth. **2** (Prostitute's slang): Busy evening's work (because she spends her time going up and down the staircase of the *hôtel de passe*).

yoyoter *v.intrans. Yoyoter de la mansarde*: To 'have bats in the belfry', to be bonkers, to be mad.

Yvans *n.m.pl. Les Yvans*: 'The Ruskies', 'the Reds', the Russians.

Z

zan *n.m.* **1** Liquorice pastille. (Another case of a brand-name, *Zan*, becoming generic.) **2** *Un (petit) bout de zan*: A 'nipper', a mite, a small child. (This appellation is sometimes used when referring to a woman whose child-like proportions tend to bring the 'daddy' out in men.)

zanzi *n.m. (abbr. zanzibar)*: Dice game.

zazou *n.m.* 'Teddy-boy'. (Strictly speaking, this derogatory appellation is historically separated from its English equivalent by some fifteen years. The *zazous* flourished in the 40s, teddy-boys in the 50s. In common, their flaunting of conventions, strange hairstyles and modes of dressing set them apart from the rest of society.)

zeb *n.m.* **1** 'Prick', 'cock', penis. **2** *Peau de zeb*: 'Fuck-all', 'bugger-all', nothing (also: *zébie*, *zob*).

zèbre *n.m. (slightly pej.)*: 'Geezer', 'bloke', fellow. *Et qui c'est ce zèbre?!* And who the hell's that nurk?!

zef *n.m.* Wind. (In direct contrast to its etymology, *zef* is no breeze or zephyr but the kind of wind that makes itself noticed.)

zèle *n.m. Faire du zèle*: To 'act the busy bee', to be officious and over-zealous. *Ne fais pas de zèle!* Just let things be, will you!

zéro *n.m.* **1** (of person): 'Nonentity', character of no importance whatsoever. *C'est un vrai zéro!* He's a real nobody! **2** *Le zéro*: 'The arse-hole', the anus, the anal sphincter. **3** *Les avoir à zéro*: To 'have the shits', to be in a blue funk, to be petrified. (Alain Rey and Jacques Cellard in their DICTIONNAIRE DU FRANÇAIS NON-CONVENTIONNEL associate semantically *le zéro* and fear, in spite of the fact that the accepted alternative to the above expression is *avoir le trouillomètre à zéro*.) **4** *Etre à zéro*: **a** To be 'back to square-one', to have lost all. **b** To be 'knackered', 'buggered', to be exhausted. **5** *Bander à zéro*: **a** *(lit.)*: To have 'a hard', to have 'the big stick', to have an erection. **b** *(fig.)*: To be 'over the moon' about something, to feel elated. *Il bandait à zéro de nous savoir dans la chtouille*: He was dead chuffed knowing that we were going through a tough patch. **6** *Zéro!* (also: *zéro pour la question!*): No way! – Nothing doing! – Certainly not! **7** *Avoir la boule à zéro*: To be as bald as a coot. (The origin of the expression lies not in the zero-shape of a bald head, but in the head-shears used by army and prison barbers, known as *zéro* or *double-zéro*.) **8** *A zéro (adv.exp.)*: Totally, completely. *On était affranchis à zéro*: We were fully genned-up. *On s'est fait avoir à zéro!* We were well and truly trounced!

zézette *n.f.* **1** *(pej.)*: 'Willy', 'cock', penis. (The word is derogatory in a would-be witty way and refers either to a limp penis or one of very modest proportions.) **2** Small glass of *pastis*. (Originally the word referred to a tot of absinth, but this lethal drink has long since been made illegal.)

zibar *n.m.* 'Prick', 'cock', penis. (Unlike *zézette*, this word refers to what some dictionaries politely term *le membre viril*.)

ziber *v.trans.* **1** To 'screw', to fuck, to have coition with. **2** To 'put one over', to 'con', to fool someone. *On s'est fait ziber comme des gosses!* We got done and never even realized it!

zieuter *v.trans.* To take a 'butcher's' at, to eye, to look at. (This is a compounded transcription of *les yeux*, with the *liaison*.)

zig *n.m.* (also: *zigue*): 'Geezer', 'bloke', fellow. *Un drôle de zig*: A queer cove. *Dans le fond, c'est un bon zig!* All in all, he's a good sort! (The cartoon strip *Zig et Puce* which survived into the 1960s gave this colloquial word an extended lease of life.)

zigoto *n.m. (slightly pej.)*: **1** 'Geezer', 'bloke', odd character. *Qui m'a fichu un zigoto pareil?* Where do you find nurks like that? **2** *Faire le zigoto*: **a** To show off (in a silly way). **b** To 'act the giddy goat', to play the fool (also: *zigomard*).

zigouigoui *n.m. (joc.):* 'Joystick', 'cock', penis. (San-Antonio illustrated the humorous connotation of the word in the expression *beau comme un zigouigoui de marié*.)

zigouiller *v.trans.* To 'bump off', to kill.

zig-zig *n.m. Faire zig-zig:* To 'have it off', to have intercourse.

zinc *n.m.* **1** 'Bar', bar counter. *On s'est tapé un demi au zinc:* We propped up the bar and had a couple of beers. **2** Plane, aeroplane. (Both meanings obviously derive from the metal of which the items were originally made.)

zinzin *n.m.* **1** 'Thingummy', 'doodah', indeterminate object. *Il y a un zinzin de cassé dans la machine!* I'm told something's stopped working in this contraption! **2** Irritating noise (the kind that drones on and on). **3** Fiddle, violin.

zinzin *adj.* 'Loony', 'bonkers', slightly mad. *Il est plutôt zinzin sur les bords!* You could say he's a bit of a fruitcake!

zizi *n.m.* **1** 'Thingummy', 'doodah', indeterminate object. **2** 'Willy', 'cock', penis. (The word really belongs to the register associated with children, but in adult colloquial speech is used within a humorous context.) **3** *Faire zizi pan-pan:* To 'have it off', to have intercourse.

zizique *n.f. (joc.):* Music (not the highbrow variety). *Allez, donne-nous un peu de zizique sur le poste!* Go on, turn your tranny on and see if you can find us a tune!

zob *n.m.* **1** 'Prick', 'cock', penis. **2** *Mon zob!* My arse! – Not bloody likely! **3** *Peau de zob!* Fuck all! – Bugger all! – Nothing!

zonard *n.m.* 'Down-and-outer', hobo-cumdrifter. (When the fortifications round Paris were demolished, the wasteland left, known as *la Zone*, became for a time a habitat for the homeless.)

zoner *v.trans.reflex.* To 'hit the sack', to go to bed. *J'ai mon taf, si on va pas se zoner, demain on sera raplapla!* It's way past my bedtime; if we don't get between the sheets we won't be up to much tomorrow!

zouave *n.m. Faire le zouave:* To 'act the giddy goat', to play the fool. *Fais pas le zouave!* Stop muckin' about!

zozo *n.m.* 'Dimwit', 'nincompoop', gullible fool.

zozores *n.f.pl.* 'Flappers', ears. (Like *zyeuter*, *zozores* is the product of an over-stressed *liaison* as in *les oreilles*.)

zut *interj.* **1** Drat! – Darn! – Blast! *Zut alors!* Damn and blast! (This mildest of French interjections likely to be encountered in colloquial speech lives on happily because of its innocuous nature.) **2** *Avoir un œil qui dit zut à l'autre (joc.):* To have a pronounced squint (also: *avoir un œil qui dit merde à l'autre*).

zyeuter *v.trans.* To take a 'butcher's' at, to eye, to look at. (This is a compounded transcription of *les yeux* with the *liaison*.)

zygue *n.m.* 'Geezer', 'bloke', fellow.